MARKETING IN A DIGITAL WORLD

SOLVING AN ETHICAL CONTROVERSY

CONTEMPORARY MARKETING

THIRD CANADIAN EDITION

DAVID L. KURTZ
University of Arkansas

H.F. (HERB) MACKENZIE
Brock University

KIM SNOW
York University

NELSON EDUCATION

NELSON / EDUCATION

Contemporary Marketing, Third Canadian Edition
by Louis E. Boone, David E. Kurtz, H.F. (Herb) Mackenzie, and Kim Snow

Vice President, Editorial Higher Education:
Anne Williams

Senior Acquisitions Editor:
Amie Plourde

Marketing Manager:
Dave Stratton

Developmental Editor:
Tammy Scherer

Photo Researcher:
Julie Pratt

Permissions Coordinator:
Julie Pratt

Content Production Manager:
Claire Horsnell

Production Service:
MPS Limited, a Macmillan Company

Copy Editor:
Wendy Thomas

Proofreader:
Jennifer A. McIntyre

Indexer:
Edwin Durbin

Senior Manufacturing Coordinator:
Joanne McNeil

Design Director:
Ken Phipps

Managing Designer:
Franca Amore

Interior Design:
Liz Harasymczuk Design

Cover Design:
Peter Papayanakis

Compositor:
MPS Limited, a Macmillan Company

Printer:
R.R. Donnelley

Library and Archives Canada Cataloguing in Publication

Kurtz, David L.

  Contemporary marketing / David L. Kurtz, H.F. MacKenzie, Kim Snow. —3rd Canadian ed.

Includes bibliographical references and indexes.

ISBN 978-0-17-650393-2

  1. Marketing—Textbooks.
I. MacKenzie, H. F. II. Snow, Kim, 1956- III. Title.

HF5415.K88 2011   658.8
C2011-905432-9

PKG ISBN-13: 978-0-17-664882-4
PKG ISBN-10: 0-17-664882-8

Dear Principles of Marketing Student:

Contemporary Marketing, Third Canadian Edition, was written for you. Our goal is to provide you with a truly "contemporary" resource containing the most current and relevant marketing information available.

An important theme of this book is connecting with the customer. We've done this by writing with you in mind. From student focus groups we learned what features work and what needed improvement. New **Marketing in a Digital World** and **Marketing and the SME** boxes have been added to each chapter. The **Marketing in a Digital World** boxes demonstrate how companies are embracing social media and other new technologies in their marketing strategies. The **Marketing and the SME** boxes examine how small and medium-sized companies market their products and services. The popular **Go Green** boxes in every chapter reflect your concern for environmental awareness in marketing. Chapter-opening features examine a successful product or organization and conclude with a short **connecting with customers** summary that helps you evaluate how this success was achieved. We've even made it easier for you to connect with what you've studied by providing answers to each chapter's **assessment check** questions—a perfect way to verify you've understood all the key concepts.

Career Readiness tip boxes in each chapter equip you with a winning playbook for business and social settings. Topics include "Culture Tips for Marketing," "Giving Helpful Feedback," and many more.

Solving an Ethical Controversy features integrated into each chapter provide you with a thorough treatment of many of the ethical issues affecting marketing. They list the pros and cons of real-world ethics quandaries such as "Putting the Lid on Bottled Water" and "Shelf-Space Wars: A Continuing Saga." The end-of-chapter **Ethics Exercises** give you additional hands-on experience with ethical decisions.

Contemporary Marketing, Third Canadian Edition, is truly student focused. Why are we so certain that you will find the text easy to understand, lively, and engaging? Because a dedicated group of marketing students at York University worked with us on the text to help achieve this goal. They generously donated their time to conduct research and contribute many of the examples in the text. We're convinced that this book truly connects with our customers. We hope you agree.

H. F. (Herb) MacKenzie

Kim Snow

CONNECTING

Because the business world moves at an unprecedented pace today, the Principles of Marketing course must race to keep up. Trends, strategies, and practices are constantly changing, though a few things remain the same—the need for excellence and the necessity to evolve and innovate.

You've come to trust *Contemporary Marketing* to cover every aspect of marketing with a critical but fair eye. A hallmark of the book is its focus on how marketing concepts apply to today's business issues. But *Contemporary Marketing*, Third Canadian Edition, goes far beyond ensuring overall accuracy and quality. Instructors have come to expect additional qualities from an introductory marketing text: complete, easy-to-understand coverage of all relevant topics in a lively, engaging writing style that makes students forget that they are reading a postsecondary-level textbook. You'll find this and so much more in *Contemporary Marketing*.

FEATURES OF THE THIRD CANADIAN EDITION

Here are just a few of the important themes, trends, and practices we've focused on for this edition:

- *Connecting with Customers*: Every opening vignette in the text concludes with a short summary entitled "Connecting with Customers." This enhances the discussion of whatever organization or product was discussed in that opening scenario and asks students to think critically about what they have done and continue to do to remain at the top of their markets. Understanding this connection can be a student's best help in understanding how marketing is conducted every day.

- *Concise Coverage*: A common complaint among both instructors and students is that Principles of Marketing texts are much too long to be covered in a single term. At the same time, they quickly state that they do not want a watered-down version of a text in the form of an "essentials" edition. The authors have worked diligently to streamline the Third Canadian Edition. By combining chapters on price concepts and pricing strategies, as well as condensing the material on relationship marketing and moving it to an appendix, the overall length of the book has been reduced from 18 to 16 chapters. At the same time, wording and examples in the chapters have been tightened to reduce the overall chapter length. The result is a text that provides the rigour and comprehensiveness instructors expect but is still short enough to cover.

- *Strategic Focus*: In response to instructors who dislike the overly descriptive nature of the typical Principles of Marketing text, the Third Canadian Edition of *Contemporary Marketing* continues to place the marketing planning chapter near the beginning of the text so that it can be assigned much earlier in the term, helping to equip students with a solid foundation of strategic thinking. The appendix "Creating an Effective Marketing Plan" immediately follows the discussion of strategic marketing planning in Chapter 2. It continues to provide detailed, real-life planning material and includes a planning case that illustrates the strategic marketing planning concepts discussed in the chapter. Each chapter closes with a special section assessing strategic implications of chapter concepts on marketing. Finally, the end-of-book appendix "Financial Analysis in Marketing" provides additional strategic and analytic tools for the reader.

- *Contemporary Topics*: The ethical focus of the earlier editions is maintained through the "Go Green" boxes, which appear in each chapter. Unique to the Canadian edition, these boxes describe issues in environmentally aware marketing today. Two new types of boxed features have been added to each chapter. "Marketing and the SME" boxes explore the unique opportunities and challenges small and medium-sized businesses face in today's rapidly changing environment. "Marketing in a Digital World" boxes identify how businesses are taking advantage of social media and the ever-expanding technologies available to marketers. These boxed features are sure to appeal to students by providing real-life examples related to the theoretical concept they are learning. Our reviewers recognized these boxes as a major strength of the text.

- *Updated Content*: In addition to new boxed features, 90 percent of the existing boxes have been revised. The "Etiquette Tips for Marketing Professionals" boxes have been renamed "Career Readiness" boxes, to address the importance of knowing key business behaviours and skills *before* entering the workplace, as well as using them within. All the chapter-opening vignettes are new or revised. References have been thoroughly updated; 75 percent are dated 2010 or later. A number of new, relevant advertisements and company screenshots appear throughout the chapters, providing real-life context for concepts discussed. Canadian companies and brands are featured throughout.

- *Marketoids*: Also unique to the Canadian edition are Marketoids, a trivia element in chapter margins. This feature introduces Canadian content in a fun yet informative way. All Marketoids have been updated in this edition; because this has been such a popular feature with students, those who wish can follow **www.twitter/mktgtoid** to receive a new Marketoid most working days of the academic year.

- *Case Studies*: Many instructors requested alternative cases to provide more flexibility for different assignments from one academic term to the next. In the Third Canadian Edition, there are still two cases in every chapter, one shorter and one longer and more comprehensive. This provides the instructor with flexibility to adjust to time constraints and multiple sections or to use different case assignments for different terms. The end-of-case questions have been fine-tuned to require more critical thinking. Overall, 75 percent of the cases are new, while 95 percent of the remaining cases have been updated.

KEY CHAPTER CHANGES

Here is an outline of the key changes and new features of the Third Canadian Edition. A list of all boxed feature and chapter-opening vignette titles can be found on the inside front cover of this textbook.

PART 1 DESIGNING CUSTOMER-ORIENTED MARKETING STRATEGIES

Chapter 1 Marketing: The Art and Science of Satisfying Customers

The opening vignette describes how Walmart has been focused on sustainability, an increasingly important issue in today's marketing environment. The chapter concludes with a case that describes sustainability initiatives at Hewlett-Packard (HP), and how it reduces, reuses, and recycles. The chapter has been condensed considerably, but the necessary topics for an introduction to marketing have been retained: how marketing is defined, the history of marketing, nontraditional marketing applications and its application to not-for-profit organizations, and how marketing has evolved from transaction-based to relationship marketing.

Chapter 2 Strategic Planning in Contemporary Marketing

Chapter 2 provides an important foundation for analyzing all aspects of marketing by demonstrating the importance of gathering reliable information to create an effective marketing plan. Marketing planning identifies the markets a company can best serve, as well as the most appropriate mix of approaches to satisfy the customers in those markets. An important addition to Chapter 2 is Ansoff's strategic growth opportunity matrix.

Chapter 3 The Marketing Environment, Ethics, and Social Responsibility

This chapter begins by describing five forces in marketing's external environment—competitive, political–legal, economic, technological, and social–cultural. They are the foundation for making decisions that involve the four marketing mix elements and the target market. A new section has been added on the global economic crisis. The second focus of this chapter is marketing ethics and social responsibility. This section describes the nature of marketers' responsibilities both to business and to society at large.

PART 2 UNDERSTANDING BUYERS AND MARKETS

Chapter 4 Consumer Behaviour

Several significant trends within the Canadian population and how these changes are affecting consumer behaviour are included in this chapter. Some of these trends are the retirement of baby boomers, the ever-increasing diversity of the Canadian population, the prevalence of social media, and the economic downturn. New research about Canadian core values, the changing Quebec market, and elastic consumers is also presented.

Chapter 5 Business-to-Business (B2B) Marketing

Chapter 5 discusses buying behaviour in organizational, or B2B, markets: how businesses, government, and marketing intermediaries purchase products that are used in their daily operations, are combined with other products to create finished goods, or are resold to other businesses or to consumers. Important topics include segmenting B2B markets, characteristics of B2B markets, business market demand, outsourcing and offshoring, the buying process, and roles within the buying centre.

Chapter 6 Serving Global Markets

The discussion of strategies, challenges, and opportunities for Canadian companies entering global markets has been retained in this chapter. The statistics throughout the chapter have been updated, and new examples such as Adidas's strategy for international expansion have been added.

PART 3 TARGET MARKET SELECTION

Chapter 7 Marketing Research, Decision Support Systems, and Sales Forecasting

Topics relating to online research, such as polling through social networks and online focus groups, have been added to this chapter. In addition, the topic of ethnographic research has been expanded. New examples, like the research performed for Boston Pizza when it sought to update its menu, have also been added.

Chapter 8 Market Segmentation, Targeting, and Positioning

Recent research relating to the increasing importance of women as consumers, and examples of how companies like Home Depot and Harley-Davidson are adjusting their marketing strategies accordingly, has been added to this chapter. Updated research on the cultural needs of Chinese, South Asian, and Black Canadian consumers has also been added. The topic of the cohort effect and the video-game generation has been expanded.

PART 4 PRODUCT DECISIONS

Chapter 9 Product and Service Strategies

The results of recent research showing that, for the first time, a low price is more important than product quality has been included in this chapter. New examples, such as Canadian Tire's expansion of its sporting goods and apparel line through the acquisition of the Forzani Group of stores, have also been included. Other new examples include Geox, the Italian shoe manufacturer, and how Nike developed Flywire, its new soccer shoe.

Chapter 10 Developing and Managing Brand and Product Strategies

New topics in Chapter 10 include laser coding for fruit and vegetables and more cost-effective packaging such as that introduced by StarKist—tuna in a pouch—or wine in plastic bags. Energizer Canada's and Pepsi's repositioning strategies are discussed, along with how Mattel extended its Barbie brand to include an interactive website and fashion-tainment.

PART 5 DISTRIBUTION DECISIONS

Chapter 11 Marketing Channels and Supply Chain Management

The opening vignette describes an extreme makeover for the Panama Canal, a change in the international environment that will have a tremendous impact on Canadian marketing channels and supply chain management. Chapter 11 discusses the role and types of marketing channels in marketing strategy, the channel decisions that marketers must make, channel conflict and cooperation, and logistics and supply chain management.

Chapter 12 Retailers, Wholesalers, and Direct Marketers

Chapter 12 discusses retailers, wholesalers, and direct marketers, and how they deliver products to their customers in a dynamic environment. Many of the changes are captured in this chapter, including the introduction of Joe Fresh Stand Alone, the growth of Kia Canada, the increasing opportunity for nonstore retailers, and the introduction of new business models such as Groupon, a company that facilitates how businesses connect with their customers.

PART 6 PROMOTIONAL DECISIONS

Chapter 13 Integrated Marketing Communications

The topic of public relations and publicity has been moved into this chapter. The importance of the Vancouver Olympic Games as a catalyst for multi-platform media used in promotional strategies is discussed. Up-to-date examples such as Air Canada's promotion aimed at young Toronto professionals have been included.

Chapter 14 Advertising and Digital Communications

Significant changes have been made to this chapter. Digital communication and social media strategies have been included. Updated examples have been used throughout, including Old Navy's "Old Navy's Original Hits, Original Styles" advertising campaign, the effect of Tiger Woods's personal problems on the products he endorsed, and the expansion of satellite radio.

Chapter 15 Personal Selling and Sales Promotion

The opening vignette describes how Salesforce.com is using technology to improve both the efficiency and the effectiveness of the sales forces of its customers. The chapter explores personal selling strategies, giving special attention to the relationship-building opportunities that the selling situation presents. Sales promotion, and how it can enhance promotional effectiveness, is also discussed.

PART 7 PRICING DECISIONS

Chapter 16 Price Concepts

Chapter 16 combines two chapters from the previous edition so that price concepts and pricing decisions now appear in a single chapter. All the important topics have been retained: pricing objectives and the marketing mix, methods for determining prices, pricing policies and strategies, global considerations and pricing, and pricing and the law. Examples throughout the chapter have been updated.

PEDAGOGY

As with the previous editions of *Contemporary Marketing*, the Third Canadian Edition is packed with pedagogical features to keep students interested and bring the text topics to life:

- *Assessment, Assessment, Assessment*: In every marketing department in the country, assessment and assurance of learning among students has become increasingly important. As a result, we've provided students with assessment checks after every main head in every chapter. Answers at the back of the chapter help students self-review to ensure they've understood the chapter's contents.

- *Critical Thinking*: In response to our reviewers, and reflecting the importance of analysis and independent thought in today's classrooms, Critical Thinking Exercises are included at the end of each chapter.

- *Business Etiquette*: Schools realize that it has become increasingly important to understand proper business etiquette when entering the business world, so more and more schools are adding business etiquette to their curriculums. Every chapter of *Contemporary Marketing* contains a Career Readiness box, addressing all aspects of proper behaviour, including communications etiquette, the importance of body language, and even the most effective way to create customer relationships. Student focus groups for the Third Canadian Edition revealed that this box is, perhaps surprisingly, one of the most-read and popular features of *Contemporary Marketing*!

- *Ethical Awareness*: Every chapter includes a special experiential feature called Solving an Ethical Controversy. This feature is designed to facilitate class debates of current ethical issues. Each begins with a brief background and is followed by a series of pro and con points designed to elicit class discussion of the issues. In addition, an Ethics Exercises section appears at the end of each chapter. These are short case scenarios that can be used as homework assignments or as a basis for classroom discussion.

- *Additional Pedagogical Features*: The authors conducted a thorough review of *Contemporary Marketing*'s instructional elements. In addition to the pedagogy described above, the Third Canadian Edition continues to offer these user-friendly features.

  1. *Review of Chapter Objectives*. In addition to a review of each chapter learning objective, a series of review questions is included as part of the chapter review.
  2. *Marketing Terms You Need to Know*. Page numbers are included.
  3. *Projects and Teamwork Exercises*. This section includes discussion questions.
  4. *Internet Exercises*. Several content-related Internet exercises are included for each chapter.

The repetitive Assurance of Learning Review feature has been removed from this edition, at the request of our reviewers.

THE CONTEMPORARY MARKETING RESOURCE PACKAGE

With its precedent-setting learning materials, *Contemporary Marketing* has continued to improve on its signature package features—equipping students and instructors with the most comprehensive collection of learning tools, teaching materials, and innovative resources available. As expected, the Third Canadian Edition continues to serve as the industry benchmark by delivering the most extensive, technologically advanced, user-friendly package on the market.

FOR THE INSTRUCTOR

The **Nelson Education Teaching Advantage (NETA)** program delivers research-based instructor resources that promote student engagement and higher-order thinking to enable the success of Canadian students and educators.

Instructors today face many challenges. Resources are limited, time is scarce, and a new kind of student has emerged: one who is juggling school with work, has gaps in his or her basic knowledge, and is immersed in technology in a way that has led to a completely new style of learning. In response, Nelson Education has gathered a group of dedicated instructors to advise us on the creation of richer and more flexible ancillaries that respond to the needs of today's teaching environments.

In consultation with our editorial advisory board, Nelson Education has completely rethought the structure, approaches, and formats of our key textbook ancillaries. We've also increased our investment in editorial support for our ancillary authors. The result is the Nelson Education Teaching Advantage and its key components. Each component includes one or more ancillaries prepared according to our best practices, and a document explaining the theory behind the practices.

The first NETA component for *Contemporary Marketing* is *NETA Assessment*. *NETA Assessment* relates to testing materials: not just Nelson's Test Banks and Computerized Test Banks, but also in-text self-tests, Study Guides and web quizzes, and homework programs like CNOW. Under *NETA Assessment*, Nelson's authors create multiple-choice questions that reflect research-based best practices for constructing effective questions and testing not just recall but also higher-order thinking. Our guidelines were developed by David DiBattista, a 3M National Teaching Fellow whose recent research as a professor of psychology at Brock University has focused on multiple-choice testing. All Test Bank authors receive training at workshops conducted by Professor DiBattista, as do the copy editors assigned to each Test Bank. A copy of *Multiple Choice Tests: Getting Beyond Remembering,* Professor DiBattista's guide to writing effective tests, is included with every Nelson Test Bank/Computerized Test Bank package. (Information about the NETA Test Bank prepared for *Contemporary Marketing* is included in the description of the IRCD below.)

The second NETA component for *Contemporary Marketing* is *NETA Presentation*. *NETA Presentation* has been developed to help instructors make the best use of PowerPoint in their classrooms. Featuring a clean and uncluttered design, *NETA Presentation* features slides with improved readability, more multimedia and graphic materials, activities to use in class, and tips for instructors on the Notes page. A copy of *NETA Guidelines for Classroom Presentations,* by Maureen Stone of StoneSoup Consulting, is included with each set of PowerPoint slides. (Information about the NETA PowerPoint prepared for *Contemporary Marketing* is included in the description of the IRCD below.)

Instructor's Resource CD (ISBN 0-17-663346-4)

Key instructor ancillaries are provided on the Instructor's Resource CD, giving instructors the ultimate tool for customizing lectures and presentations. (Downloadable Web versions are also available at **www.contemporarymarketing3e.nelson.com**.) The IRCD includes the following:

- ***NETA Assessment:*** The Test Bank was revised by Carolyn Capretta of McMaster University. It includes approximately 1800 multiple-choice questions written according to NETA guidelines for effective construction and development of higher-order questions. Also included are approximately 1400 true/false, 300 essay, and 300 matching questions. Each chapter of the Test Bank is organized by chapter objective, and each question categorized by difficulty level, type of question, and text page reference. Test Bank files are provided in Word format for easy editing and in PDF format for convenient printing whatever your system.

    The Computerized Test Bank by ExamView includes all the questions from the Test Bank. The easy-to-use ExamView software is compatible with both PC and Macintosh platforms. Create tests by selecting questions from the question bank, modifying these questions as desired, and adding new questions you write yourself. You can administer quizzes online and export tests to WebCT, Blackboard, and other formats.

- ***NETA Presentation:*** Microsoft PowerPoint lecture slides for every chapter have been adapted for the Third Canadian Edition by H. F. (Herb) MacKenzie and Kim Snow, the Canadian textbook authors, ensuring consistency with the content of the book. We offer two separate collections. The Basic PowerPoint collection contains 10 to 20 slides per chapter. This collection is a basic outline of the chapter. The Expanded PowerPoint collection includes 25 to 45 slides per chapter and provides a more complete overview of the chapter. The Expanded collection includes figures and tables from the chapter, Marketing Success boxes (which provide an informative glimpse into the stories behind triumphs in the world of marketing), Web links, and video links. PowerPoints are easily printed to create customized transparency masters. NETA principles of clear design and engaging content have been incorporated throughout.

- *Instructor's Manual with Collaborative Learning Exercises, Media Guide, and NETA Support.* Adapted by H. F. (Herb) MacKenzie and Kim Snow, the Canadian text authors, the *Instructor's Manual* contains both chapter-related and book-related materials. The chapter-related content includes chapter overviews, a summary of changes in the third edition, and lecture outlines (organized by learning objective and correlated to PowerPoint slides). You'll also find answers to all of the end-of-chapter materials and various critical-thinking exercises. Collaborative learning exercises are included for each chapter, which give students a completely different way to apply chapter concepts to their own lives. Book-related materials include support for the Nelson Education Testing Advantage (NETA) Test Bank (see details above) and a Media Guide. NETA support consists of a guide to creating effective tests, "Multiple Choice Tests: Getting Beyond Remembering," by David DiBattista of Brock University. The Media Guide offers complete video synopses for the end-of-chapter videos, the Second City continuing video case, the Marketing Minute videos, and the part-ending CBC videos.

- *Image Library.* Many of the figures and illustrations from the book are provided in jpeg format so that you can incorporate them into PowerPoint presentations you create yourself. (Note: Some graphics may not be available due to copyright restrictions.)

- *Resource Integration Guide (RIG).* The RIG is written to provide the instructor with a clear and concise guide to all of the ancillaries that accompany the text as well as how best to use these items in teaching a Principles of Marketing course. Not only are all of the book's ancillaries organized clearly for you, but we also provide planning suggestions, lecture ideas, and help in creating assignments. This guide will help instructors prepare for teaching the course, execute teaching plans, and evaluate student performance.

- *The Second City Theater, Inc., Continuing Case Video Appendix.* The written case sections and discussion questions that accompany these videos (described below) are divided into seven parts intended to complement the text.

- *End-of-Chapter Video Case Appendix.* A complete set of written cases accompanies these chapter videos (described below). The written segments contain discussion questions. As with the Second City cases, answers to the questions can be found in the *Instructor's Manual,* as can a complete video synopsis, a list of text concepts covered in the videos, and even more critical-thinking exercises.

- *CBC End-of-Part Video Cases.* Teaching notes for these current, dynamic videos are included in the Instructor's Manual & Media Guide.

- *Marketer's Minute Highlights.* Video segments for these end-of-part interviews are described below. Previews can be found in these highlight transcripts, and teaching notes are included in the Instructor's Manual & Media Guide.

- *Planning a Career in Marketing.* Career planning and awareness begin with the "Planning a Career in Marketing" feature, adapted by Stéfan Danis, CEO and Chief Talent Officer, and his team of experts at Mandrake Executive Search. (Mandrake is Canada's largest executive search firm with a specialty in the marketing field.) This popular feature ensures that students in Principles of Marketing courses keep up with the newest trends and shifts in career fields and offers practical insights to help students prepare for a successful business career.

- *Day One.* Day One—Prof InClass is a PowerPoint presentation that you can customize to orient your students to the class and their text at the beginning of the course.

- *TurningPoint.* Another valuable resource for instructors is TurningPoint classroom response software customized for *Contemporary Marketing.* Now you can author, deliver, show, access, and grade, all in PowerPoint . . . with no toggling back and forth between screens! JoinIn on

Turning Point is the only classroom response software tool that gives you true PowerPoint integration. With JoinIn, you are no longer tied to your computer. You can walk about your classroom as you lecture, showing slides and collecting and displaying responses with ease. There is simply no easier or more effective way to turn your lecture hall into a personal, fully interactive experience for your students. If you can use PowerPoint, you can use JoinIn on TurningPoint!

CourseMate

Nelson Education's Marketing CourseMate for *Contemporary Marketing* brings course concepts to life with interactive learning and exam preparation tools that integrate with the printed textbook. Students activate their knowledge through quizzes, games, and flashcards, among many other tools.

CourseMate provides immediate feedback that enables students to connect results to the work they have just produced, increasing their learning efficiency. It encourages contact between students and faculty: you can select to monitor your students' level of engagement with CourseMate, correlating their efforts to their outcomes. You can even use CourseMate's quizzes to practise "Just in Time" teaching by tracking results in the Engagement Tracker and customizing your lesson plans to address their learning needs.

The *Contemporary Marketing* CourseMate includes the following:

- an interactive eBook that includes note-taking and highlighting functionality
- interactive teaching and learning tools including:
  - quizzes (revised by Marina Jaffey of Camosun College)
  - flashcards
  - videos
  - concept maps (authored by Nishan Perera, of Kwantlen Polytechnic University)
  - "Beat the Clock" and crossword games
  - e-lectures
  - and more
- Engagement Tracker, a first-of-its-kind tool that monitors student engagement in the course.

Watch student comprehension and engagement soar as your class engages with CourseMate—you can find the access code in the bound-in card. Ask your Nelson representative for a demo today.

Video Resources (ISBN 0-17-664851-8)

Enhance your classroom experience with the exciting and relevant videos of the DVD prepared to accompany **Contemporary Marketing.** Designed to enrich and support chapter concepts, it includes the following:

- *The Second City Theater, Inc., End-of-Part Continuing Video Case.* No other company combines Second City Theater's unique brand of social and political satire with successful and proven business and marketing practices. These unique practices have helped The Second City grow from a small but successful comedy troupe into a large international business. With several theatres in two countries, troupes performing every day all over the world, and performances on international cruise lines, The Second City has found a way to turn comedy into business— and in the process they've had fun! Students and instructors alike know and love many of the famous faces that started performing at Second City—Dan Aykroyd, John Candy, Martin Short, Eugene Levy, Tina Fey, Gilda Radner, John Belushi, and the list goes on and on. But how many students realize just how important good business and marketing strategies are in keeping a comedy business that started in 1959 thriving and growing all the way into 2012 and beyond? We've focused on all the aspects of The Second City Theater's marketing strategy so that students can learn—in a way that's interesting and fun. So sit back, get some popcorn, and enjoy the show! Written case segments created for each part of the text contain critical-thinking questions designed to provoke discussion and interaction in the classroom setting. Answers to the questions can be found in the *Instructor's Manual,* as can a complete video synopsis, a list of text concepts covered in the videos, and even more critical-thinking exercises.

- *CBC End-of-Part Video Cases.* These videos will add visual impact and current, real-world examples to your lectures. Teaching notes for these current, dynamic clips are included in the Instructor's Manual & Media Guide.

- *Marketer's Minute Interviews.* Students often have an amazing ability to grasp chapter concepts and intellectually understand marketing and what a marketing career entails. However, they often do not understand how careers are created and maintained and fail to understand in a real-life sense what a career in marketing may involve on a day-to-day basis. Every part in the text ends with an interview of an actual marketing professional and includes information about his or her education, career path, and day-to-day responsibilities. Participants include global marketing manager for IBM Deborah McKenzie, Grace Mistry of BMO Bank of Montreal, Amanda Herold of Bell Canada, and Domenic Vivolo of Astral Media. The traits all of them have in common are their hard work, dedication, professionalism, and success. This feature gives students a true understanding of how to make the most of their marketing courses and launch a real marketing career for themselves. Teaching notes and transcripts for these interviews are included in the Instructor's Manual & Media Guide.

- *End-of-Chapter Video Cases.* To provide a third case option in our end-of-chapter cases, we've included a video case for each and every chapter, designed to exceed your every expectation. These cases focus on successful real companies' processes, strategies, and procedures. Real employees explain real marketing situations with which they have been faced, bringing key concepts from the chapter to life.

Students need to know the basics about life in the real world of marketing and how businesses succeed and grow—but they don't need a bunch of talking heads putting them to sleep. So although we admit that you will indeed see a few talking heads, they're just there because they really do know what they're talking about, and they have something important for students to hear. But do trust us . . . the videos we've created for *Contemporary Marketing* contain so much more! A complete set of written cases accompanies these chapter videos and can be found in the video case appendix on the IRCD. The written segments contain discussion questions. As with the Second City cases, answers to the questions can be found in the *Instructor's Manual,* as can a complete video synopsis, a list of text concepts covered in the videos, and even more critical-thinking exercises.

FOR THE STUDENT

CourseMate

The more you study, the better the results. Make the most of your study time by accessing everything you need to succeed in one place. The *Contemporary Marketing* CourseMate includes the following:

- An interactive eBook, which allows you to take notes, highlight, bookmark, search the text, and use in-context glossary definitions
- Interactive learning tools, including:
  - quizzes
  - flashcards
  - CBC and Marketer's Minute interview videos
  - "Beat the Clock" and Crossword games
  - e-lectures

. . . and more! Visit **http://www.contemporarymarketing3e.nelson.com** or **http://www.NelsonBrain .com** for more information and to access these resources for your text.

ACKNOWLEDGMENTS TO THE THIRD CANADIAN EDITION

Your authors have benefited immensely from the comments and suggestions of many reviewers and colleagues. This input has come via focus groups, publisher reviews, contributions to supplementary text materials, e-mailed suggestions, conference networking, classroom visits, and coffee shop chats. Regardless of the format, all these ideas have helped shape the Third Canadian Edition of *Contemporary Marketing* into a text that serves as the benchmark for other texts.

We'd like to thank the outstanding reviewers whose diligent and thoughtful comments were instrumental in our revisions:

Nelida Carryer, Kwantlen Polytechnic University
Theresa Champion, Niagara College
Jacqueline Cook, George Brown College
Rita Cossa, McMaster University
Glenn Davis, Red River College
Paul Dunne, College of the North Atlantic
Denyse Lafrance Horning, Nipissing University
Melanie Lang, University of Guelph
Jooseop Lim, Concordia University
Susan Myrden, Memorial University of Newfoundland
Richard Patterson, York University
Nishan Perera, Kwantlen Polytechnic University
G. Elizabeth Pett, Niagara College
Chun (Martin) Qiu, McGill University
Charles Royce, McGill University
Frances Steciuk, George Brown College
Keith Wallace, Kwantlen Polytechnic University

Every project of this nature involves many hours of work, but this project was made easier because of the assistance of many dedicated students from York University, who juggled their lecture, personal and work schedules to help out. We are grateful for their many hours of research and suggestions on how to make the book student friendly. Our sincere thanks go to the following:

Riaz Backer
Josha Chakkalakal
Stephanie Critelli
Elisa Damaso
Tracy Gibbons
Hekmat Kaadan

Varun Kalia
Inna Khvedantsevich
Rachel Lichtman
Nehal Mehra
Jovan Milosevic
Meisham Molou

Khanh Nguyen
Tiago Nunes
Nimesh Shah
Natalie Vacianna
Alexandra Vinichenko

York University marketing students

A special thank you to Sarah Van Vliet, a student at Brock University who helped research and draft some of the boxed features.

Thanks are also extended to all the students at Kwantlen Polytechnic University who participated in our marketing focus group. We learned a lot from you! Our sincere thanks go to:

Alina Monica Dobre
Chris Kozminski
Carolyn Molzahn

Penny Purvis
Ivjoat Kyle Rosode
Quyen Tu

Jerrica Velo
Bria Yelland

Student involvement resulted in a significant impact on the development of this book—helping the authors and Nelson Education produce the most student-focused introductory marketing book in Canada.

We appreciate the help of the marketing professionals who contributed to the Marketer's Minutes—Stéfan Danis, Deborah McKenzie, Charles Hendriks, Grace Mistry, Amanda Herold, Domenic Vivolo, and Victoria McManus. We also thank Stéfan Danis and his colleagues at Mandrake Executive Search for their contributions to the Prologue. Finally, this new edition would never have become a reality without our highly competent editorial, production, and marketing teams at Nelson Education. Sincere thanks go to Anne Williams, Vice President Editorial, Higher Education; Amie Plourde, Executive Editor; Tammy Scherer, Developmental Editor; Claire Horsnell, Content Production Manager; Peter Papayanakis, Designer; Dave Stratton, Marketing Manager; and Joanne McNeil, Manufacturing Buyer. Special thanks also go to freelancers for their dedicated and diligent work: Julie Pratt, Photo Researcher and Permissions Editor; and Wendy Thomas, Copy Editor.

We are grateful for the many suggestions and contributions of dozens of people who teach the introductory marketing course on a regular basis and are in the best position to comment on what works best—and what doesn't work at all. Every recommendation made a difference in the creation of the Third Canadian Edition. We welcome any comments, suggestions, or constructive criticisms you wish to provide.

H. F. (Herb) MacKenzie & Kim Snow

H. F. (HERB) MACKENZIE

Dr. H. F. (Herb) MacKenzie is Chair, Marketing, International Business, and Strategy, and an associate professor of marketing at Brock University, St. Catharines, Ontario. He has taught in the undergraduate, graduate, and executive education programs at universities in Canada, Europe, and the Middle East, and has been consulting to both private- and public-sector businesses since 1985. He has over 15 years of industrial sales and sales management experience and has published many cases, conference proceedings, and articles in the areas of sales management, buyer–seller relationships, and distribution channel management. He has co-authored Canadian editions of textbooks on selling, sales management, and marketing, and has edited four Canadian marketing casebooks. He has received numerous awards from his students, including Professor of the Year, Marketing Professor of the Year, and Faculty of Business Faculty Award of Excellence (twice).

Dr. Kim Snow is an associate professor of marketing at York University in Toronto. Dr. Snow received her MBA and PhD from the University of Bradford, U.K., and her Diploma in Business Administration from Wilfrid Laurier University. She has been a member of the faculty at York University since 1992. She has published numerous articles in the area of service marketing, service quality, customer satisfaction, and marketing research. She is faculty advisor for the American Marketing Association Student Chapter at York University and has been a judge on several student chapter competitions. She has been a member of the Editorial Advisory Board and Internet Editor for the Managing Service Quality Journal. Prior to joining York University, Kim spent 17 years working in the financial services industry.

KIM SNOW

During **Dave Kurtz's** high school days, no one in Salisbury, Maryland, would have mistaken him for a scholar. In fact, he was a mediocre student, so bad that his father steered him toward higher education by finding him a succession of back-breaking summer jobs. Thankfully, most of them have been erased from his memory, but a few linger, including picking peaches, loading watermelons on trucks headed for market, and working as a pipefitter's helper. Unfortunately, these jobs had zero impact on his academic standing. Worse yet for Dave's ego, he was no better than average as a high school athlete in football and track.

But four years at Davis & Elkins College in Elkins, West Virginia, turned him around. Excellent teachers helped get Dave on a sound academic footing. His grade point average soared—enough to get him accepted by the graduate business school at the University of Arkansas, where he met Gene Boone. Gene and Dave became longtime co-authors; together, they produced more than 50 books. Dave and Gene were involved in several entrepreneurial ventures.

Today, Dave is back teaching at the University of Arkansas, after tours of duty in Ypsilanti, Michigan; Seattle, Washington; and Melbourne, Australia. He is the proud grandfather of six "perfect" kids and a sportsman with a golf handicap too high to mention. Dave, his wife, Diane, and four demanding canine companions (Daisy, Lucy, Molly, and Sally) live in Rogers, Arkansas. Dave holds a distinguished professorship at the Sam M. Walton College of Business in nearby Fayetteville, home of the Arkansas Razorbacks.

contents in brief

contents

appendix
CREATING AN EFFECTIVE MARKETING PLAN   57

chapter 3
THE MARKETING ENVIRONMENT, ETHICS, AND SOCIAL RESPONSIBILITY   70

part 2

UNDERSTANDING BUYERS AND MARKETS 105

chapter 4

CONSUMER BEHAVIOUR 106

chapter 5

BUSINESS-TO-BUSINESS (B2B) MARKETING 136

chapter 10

DEVELOPING AND MANAGING BRAND AND PRODUCT STRATEGIES   294

part 5

DISTRIBUTION DECISIONS   323

chapter 11

MARKETING CHANNELS AND SUPPLY CHAIN MANAGEMENT   324

chapter 12
RETAILERS, WHOLESALERS, AND DIRECT MARKETERS   358

part 6
PROMOTIONAL DECISIONS   389

chapter 13
INTEGRATED MARKETING COMMUNICATIONS   390

chapter 14

ADVERTISING AND DIGITAL COMMUNICATIONS   428

part 7
PRICING DECISIONS   499

chapter 16
PRICING CONCEPTS AND STRATEGIES   500

part 1

DESIGNING CUSTOMER-ORIENTED MARKETING STRATEGIES

chapter 1

Marketing: The Art and Science of Satisfying Customers

CHAPTER OBJECTIVES

1. Define *marketing*, explain how it creates utility, and describe its role in the global marketplace.

2. Contrast marketing activities during the four eras in the history of marketing.

3. Explain the importance of avoiding marketing myopia.

4. Describe the characteristics of not-for-profit marketing.

5. Identify and briefly explain each of the five types of nontraditional marketing.

6. Explain the shift from transaction-based marketing to relationship and social marketing.

7. Identify the universal functions of marketing.

8. Demonstrate the relationship among ethical business practices, social responsibility, sustainability, and marketplace success.

WALMART HELPS SAVE THE WORLD WITH SUSTAINABILITY

The actions of Walmart, the world's largest retailer whose $400-billion-plus revenues surpass the GDPs of 40 countries, have drawn criticism in the past. Now the low-price giant hopes to lead in a positive direction with its Sustainability Index.

By leveraging Walmart's enormous buying power, the Index, which will ultimately provide millions of shoppers with a way to measure the environmental impact of each of the thousands of items it sells, could virtually remake the practice of retailing. To implement it—probably in the form of a scannable product label or packaging—the company will require its 60 000 consumer-products suppliers to reach back into their own supply chains and total the social and environmental impact of their offerings, whether it's trampolines or flat-screen TVs, orange juice or greeting cards. For measuring up, suppliers can expect preferential treatment on the shelves of Walmart's 8000 stores in 15 countries around the world.

"We're on the cusp of a major transition in the marketplace of what consumers demand to know and producers have to tell," says the CEO of an independent consumer products sustainability guide. Walmart's senior vice president of sustainability adds that the Index is also about "creating a new level of competition in ways that, historically, manufacturers have not competed. . . . It's going to be an algorithm that creates a score, and it will reward some suppliers better than others." That score will count

four criteria: energy and greenhouse gas emissions, materials, natural resources, and social impact.

In addition to the pressure of competition, however, Walmart is planning its own eventual departure from the Index project as an incentive to get suppliers, academics, government agencies, not-for-profit organizations, and even competitors to join the effort and pool sustainability data and ideas. It has created the independent Sustainability Consortium, intended to carry out what Walmart has begun. "This has to be more than Walmart or it won't achieve standardization," says the Consortium's co-director. Says another observer, "They are willing to get the ball rolling, but they want to hand it off to someone else." Already on board, and making "green" improvements, are Frito-Lay, Monsanto, Unilever, Seventh Generation, Disney, and General Mills. The latter has reduced yogurt packaging 20 percent to save 1200 tons of plastic a year.

The first step in the three-part process of creating the Index was to administer a 15-question survey to more than 1000 of the firm's top suppliers, asking about their current sustainability efforts. Responses revealed big differences in how deeply invested firms are in community development and how carefully they monitor use of natural resources. Next steps now under discussion include tests and feedback on the Index's labelling system in three product categories: electronics, food, and chemical-based products such as household cleaning fluids.

"Imagine one day when every product on the shelf has behind it enough information from a life-cycle-thinking perspective that [it] allows us to be much, much more intelligent about how we're buying," says Walmart's business strategy director. The company intends the Index also to weed out companies that engage in "greenwashing," making false or inflated claims of sustainability. "Can you have trackable, traceable supply chains that give you full visibility?" asks a manager at the Environmental Defense Fund, a Walmart partner. "It is extraordinarily difficult at this moment. But it can be done."[1]

connecting with customers

Low prices and innovation have been at the heart of Walmart's marketing philosophy since it opened its first store in 1962. In the 1980s, Walmart added its "greeters," opened the first one-hour photo lab, installed bar code-scanning equipment, and linked its operating units with two-way voice and data communication via satellite. In 1994, Walmart opened the first of its newly designed environmentally friendly buildings and expanded into Canada. A program to conserve wildlife habitats was launched in 2005, and a $4 generic prescription drug program was introduced the following year. Meanwhile, Walmart stepped up efforts to design its stores to conserve energy and natural resources and reduce pollution. In late 2010, the company opened a new 400 000-sq.-ft. fresh and frozen food distribution centre in Balzac, Alberta, which has been described as Canada's most innovative and sustainable facility.

Chapter Overview

- "I only drink Tim Hortons coffee."
- "I buy all my electronics at Future Shop."
- "My next car will be a Nissan Leaf."
- "I go to all the Vancouver Canucks games at General Motors Place."

THESE words are music to a marketer's ears. They may echo the click of an online purchase, the *ping* of a cash register, the cheers of fans at a stadium. Customer loyalty is the watchword of 21st-century marketing. Individual consumers and business purchasers have so many goods and services from which to choose—and so many different ways to purchase them—that marketers must continually seek out new and better ways to attract and keep customers. It took a while, but Skype finally introduced a voice over Internet protocol (VoIP) application for iPhone subscribers in Canada. The app—available free from Apple's Inc.'s App Store—has been downloaded more than six million times. Users can now call other Skype users around the world for free, and can place calls to landlines and other cell phones at rates much below those for wireless long-distance service.[2]

The technology revolution continues to change the rules of marketing during this first decade of the 21st century and will continue to do so in years beyond. The combined power of telecommunications and computer technology creates inexpensive global networks that transfer voice messages, text, graphics, and data within seconds. These sophisticated technologies create new types of products and demand new approaches to marketing existing products. Newspapers are learning this lesson the hard way, as circulation continues to decline around the country, due in large part to the rising popularity of blogs and auction and job-posting sites. Electronic reading devices such as the Amazon Kindle, on the other hand, have been picking up speed and enthusiastic fans.[3]

Communications technology also contributes to the globalization of today's marketplace, where businesses manufacture, buy, and sell across national borders. You can bid at eBay on a potential bargain or eat a Big Mac or drink Coca-Cola almost anywhere in the world, and your MP3 player was probably manufactured in China or South Korea. Both Honda and Toyota manufacture cars in Canada, while some Volkswagens are imported from Mexico. Finished products and components routinely cross international borders, but successful global marketing also requires knowledge to tailor products to regional tastes. Restaurants in Newfoundland and Labrador, for example, often have cod tongues on their menu. This delicacy is seldom found elsewhere in Canada.

Rapidly changing business landscapes create new challenges for companies, whether they are giant multinational firms or small boutiques, profit-oriented or not-for-profit. Organizations must react quickly to shifts in consumer tastes, competitive offerings, and other market dynamics. Fortunately, information technologies give organizations fast new ways to interact and develop long-term relationships with their customers and suppliers. Such links have become a core element of marketing today.

Every company must serve customer needs—create customer satisfaction—to succeed. We call customer satisfaction an art because it requires imagination and creativity, and a science because it requires technical knowledge, skill, and experience. Marketing strategies are the tools that marketers use to identify and analyze customers' needs, then show that their company's goods and services can meet those needs. Tomorrow's market leaders will be companies that can make the most of these strategies to create satisfied customers.

This Canadian edition of *Contemporary Marketing* focuses on the strategies that allow companies to succeed in today's interactive marketplace. This chapter sets the stage for the entire text, examining the importance of creating satisfaction through customer relationships. Initial sections describe the historical development of marketing and its contributions to society. Later sections introduce the universal functions of marketing and the relationship between ethical business practices and marketplace success. Throughout the chapter—and the entire book—we discuss customer loyalty and the lifetime value of a customer. ◆◆◆

WHAT IS MARKETING?

Production and marketing of goods and services—whether it's a new crop of organically grown vegetables or digital cable service—are the essence of economic life in any society. Like most business disciplines, marketing had its origins in economics. Later, marketing borrowed concepts from areas such as psychology and sociology to explain how people made purchase decisions. Mathematics, anthropology, and other disciplines also contributed to the evolution of marketing. These will be discussed in later chapters.

Economists contributed the concept of **utility**—the want-satisfying power of a good or service. Table 1.1 describes the four basic kinds of utility: form, time, place, and ownership.

Form utility is created when the firm converts raw materials and component inputs into finished goods and services. Because of its appearance, gold can serve as a beautiful piece of jewellery, but because it also conducts electricity well and does not corrode, it has many applications in the manufacture of electronic devices like cell phones and global positioning satellite units. By combining glass, plastic, metals, circuit boards, and other components, Nikon makes a digital camera and Samsung produces an LED television. With fabric and leather, Prada manufactures its high-fashion line of handbags. With a ship and the ocean, a captain and staff, and food and entertainment, Holland America Line creates a cruise. Although the marketing function focuses on influencing consumer and audience preferences, the organization's production function creates form utility.

Marketing creates time, place, and ownership utilities. *Time and place utility* occur when consumers find goods and services available when and where they want to purchase them. Vending machines and convenience stores focus on providing place utility for people buying newspapers, snacks, and soft drinks. The owners of Golf Without Limits created time and place utility when they opened their indoor golf centres in Waterloo and London, Ontario. Customers can play a round of simulated golf at any of 30 world-class courses, regardless of season, weather, or time of day.[4]

The transfer of title to goods or services at the time of purchase creates *ownership utility*. Purchasing a new smartphone, signing up for a Holland America cruise, or visiting Golf Without Limits creates ownership utility. All organizations must create utility to survive. Designing and marketing want-satisfying goods, services, and ideas are the foundation for the creation of utility. But where does the process start? In the toy industry, manufacturers try to come up with items that children will want to play with—creating utility. But that's not as simple as it sounds. At the Toy Fair held each February in New York, Canadian and U.S. retailers pore over the products displayed at booths of manufacturers and suppliers, looking for the next Webkinz toys or Lego building blocks—trends that turn into classics and generate millions of dollars in revenues over the years. Marketers also look for ways to revive flagging brands. The classic yo-yo might be making a high-tech comeback, as an aerospace engineer, working in his spare time, has begun releasing a line of precision-engineered models with price tags that can run to $100 or more. The limited-edition yo-yos have been selling out in a matter of days—and they have competitors.[5]

But how does an organization create a customer? Most take a three-step approach: identifying needs in the marketplace, finding out which needs the organization can profitably serve, and

① Define *marketing*, explain how it creates utility, and describe its role in the global marketplace.

utility Want-satisfying power of a good or service.

Marketoid

The game of golf accounts for approximately $11.3 billion of Canada's GDP and supports 341 794 jobs.

table 1.1   *Four Types of Utility*

TYPE	DESCRIPTION	EXAMPLES	ORGANIZATIONAL FUNCTION RESPONSIBLE
Form	Conversion of raw materials and components into finished goods and services	Dinner at Swiss Chalet; iPod; shirt from Mark's Work Wearhouse	Production*
Time	Availability of goods and services when consumers want them	Dental appointment; digital photographs; LensCrafters eyeglass guarantee; Canada Post Xpresspost	Marketing
Place	Availability of goods and services at convenient locations	Soft-drink machines outside gas stations; on-site day care; banks in grocery stores	Marketing
Ownership (possession)	Ability to transfer title to goods or services from marketer to buyer	Retail sales (in exchange for currency or credit-card payment)	Marketing

*Marketing provides inputs related to consumer preferences, but the actual creation of form utility is the responsibility of the production function.

Holland America uses the components of ship, ocean, captain, staff, food, and entertainment to create its finished service—a cruise.

developing goods and services to convert potential buyers into customers. Marketing specialists are responsible for most of the activities necessary to create the customers the organization wants. These activities include the following:

- identifying customer needs
- designing products that meet those needs
- communicating information about those goods and services to prospective buyers
- making the items available at times and places that meet customers' needs
- pricing the merchandise and services to reflect costs, competition, and customers' ability to buy
- providing the necessary service and follow-up to ensure customer satisfaction after the purchase[6]

A DEFINITION OF MARKETING

The word *marketing* encompasses such a broad scope of activities and ideas that settling on one definition is often difficult. Ask three people to define marketing, and three different definitions are likely to follow. We are exposed to so much advertising and personal selling that most people link marketing only to those activities. But marketing begins long before a product hits the shelf. It involves analyzing customer needs, obtaining the information necessary to design and produce goods or services that match buyer expectations, satisfying customer preferences, and creating and maintaining relationships with customers and suppliers. Marketing activities apply to profit-oriented businesses such as Canadian Tire and Amazon.ca as well as not-for-profit organizations such as Mothers Against Drunk Driving and the Canadian Red Cross. Even towns, cities, and provinces of Canada engage in marketing activities. Today's definition takes all these factors into account. **Marketing** is an organizational function and a set of processes for creating, communicating, and delivering value to customers and for managing customer relationships in ways that benefit the organization and its stakeholders.[7]

The expanded concept of marketing activities permeates all organizational functions in businesses and not-for-profit organizations. It assumes that organizations conduct their marketing efforts ethically

marketing
Organizational function and a set of processes for creating, communicating, and delivering value to customers and for managing customer relationships in ways that benefit the organization and its stakeholders.

and that these efforts serve the best interests of both society and the organization. The concept also identifies the marketing variables—product, price, promotion, and distribution—that combine to provide customer satisfaction. In addition, it assumes that the organization begins by identifying and analyzing who its potential customers are and what they need. At all points, the concept emphasizes creating and maintaining long-term relationships with customers and suppliers.

TODAY'S GLOBAL MARKETPLACE

Several factors have forced marketers—and entire nations—to extend their economic views to events outside their own national borders. First, international agreements are being negotiated in attempts to expand trade among nations. Second, the growth of electronic commerce and related computer technologies is bringing previously isolated countries into the marketplace for buyers and sellers around the globe. Third, the interdependence of the world's economies is a reality because no nation produces all the raw materials and finished goods its citizens need or consumes all its output without exporting some to other countries. Evidence of this interdependence is illustrated by the introduction of the euro as a common currency to facilitate trade among the nations of the European Union and the creation of trade agreements such as the North American Free Trade Agreement (NAFTA) and the World Trade Organization (WTO). As a result of NAFTA, Canada enjoys access to a market totalling more than 450 million people.

Rising oil prices affect the price that Canadian consumers pay for just about everything—not just gasoline at the pump. Dow Chemical raised the prices of its products up to 20 percent to adjust to its rising cost for energy. Dow supplies companies in industries such as agriculture and health care, all of which will be affected by the price hike. Airlines, too, are trying to respond to a near-doubling of the cost of jet fuel. Many have started charging customers for redeeming their reward miles, and Air Canada now charges $20 (per direction) for a second checked bag on domestic flights, $30 on flights to the United States, and $50 on flights to Europe.[8]

To remain competitive, companies must continually search for the most efficient manufacturing sites and most lucrative markets for their products. Canadian marketers now find tremendous opportunities serving customers not only in traditional industrialized nations but also in Latin America and emerging economies in central Europe, the Middle East, Asia, and Africa, where rising standards of living create increased customer demand for the latest products. Expanding operations beyond the Canadian market gives domestic companies access to more than 6.5 billion international customers. China is now the second-largest market in the world—only the United States is larger. But, with regard to new automobile sales, China is the world's largest market. In 1993, there were only 37 000 private cars in China but, today, Chinese consumers buy more than 12 million new cars each year.[9] So, automakers worldwide are extending their operations to China. In addition, China is beginning to compete in the global market, exporting cars that it manufactures to more than 170 countries.[10] Chinese-manufactured cars will, most likely, eventually be available in Canada. Interestingly, however, signs are mounting that China's increasing prosperity may be reducing its attractiveness as a low-cost labour source. Rising costs already are driving some foreign manufacturers out of the country. Mexico has taken the lead as the lowest-cost country for outsourced production, with India and Vietnam second and third, respectively; China stands in sixth place.[11]

Service firms also play a major role in today's global marketplace. Telecommunications firms like South Africa's MTN, Luxembourg's Millicom International, and Egypt's Orascom Telecom Holding have carved out new global markets for their products by following the lead of Finnish firm Nokia, among the first high-tech firms to create durable and affordable cell phones specifically designed for emerging markets. The opportunities for such telecom innovators will continue to grow as long as electricity-reliant personal computers remain out of reach for millions in the developing world. "Like a lot of people who made their first call on a mobile [phone], they will have their first experience with the Internet on a mobile," says one industry analyst.[12]

Canada is also an attractive market for foreign competitors because of its size, proximity to the United States, and the high standard of living that Canadian consumers enjoy. The United States has made more investment in Canada than in any other country. Companies such as Avon, Walmart, Home Depot, Lowe's, 3M, General Electric, and Dell are actively targeting Canadian consumers. Among them, they perform such activities as production, assembly, distribution, service, and selling in Canada. In fact, several of them use their Canadian operations as major global suppliers for some of their

assessment check 1

1.1 Define *marketing* and explain how it creates utility.

1.2 What three factors have forced marketers to embrace a global marketplace?

product lines, frequently exporting their goods and services to the United States as well as to other countries. Approximately 75 percent of all Canadian exports go to the United States, while about 50 percent of Canadian imports come from there. Nearly $1.4 billion in trade crosses the Canada–U.S. border every day.[13]

Although many global marketing strategies are almost identical to those used in domestic markets, more and more companies are tailoring their marketing efforts to the needs and preferences of consumers in foreign markets. It is often difficult to standardize a brand name on a global basis. The Japanese, for example, like the names of flowers or girls for their automobiles, names such as Bluebird, Bluebonnet, Violet, and Gloria. Canadians, on the other hand, prefer rugged outdoorsy names such as Challenger, Mustang, and Cherokee.

② **Contrast marketing activities during the four eras in the history of marketing.**

FOUR ERAS IN THE HISTORY OF MARKETING

exchange process
Activity in which two or more parties give something of value to each other to satisfy perceived needs.

The essence of marketing is the **exchange process**, in which two or more parties give something of value to each other to satisfy perceived needs. Often people exchange money for tangible goods, such as video games, clothes, or groceries. In other situations, they exchange money for intangible services, such as a haircut or an education. Many exchanges involve a combination of goods and services, such as dinner in a restaurant where dinner represents the good and the wait staff represents the service. People also make exchanges when they donate money or time to a charitable cause, such as Habitat for Humanity.

Although marketing has always been a part of business, its importance has varied greatly. Figure 1.1 identifies four eras in the history of marketing: (1) the production era, (2) the sales era, (3) the marketing era, and (4) the relationship era.

production orientation
Business philosophy stressing efficiency in producing a quality product, with the attitude toward marketing that "a good product will sell itself."

THE PRODUCTION ERA

Before 1925, most firms—even those operating in highly developed economies in Western Europe and North America—focused narrowly on production. Manufacturers stressed production of quality products and then looked for people to purchase them. The prevailing attitude of this era held that a high-quality product would sell itself. This **production orientation** dominated business philosophy for decades; business success often was defined solely in terms of production successes.

figure 1.1

Four Eras of Marketing History

ERA	Production	Sales	Marketing	Relationship
PREVAILING ATTITUDE	"A good product will sell itself."	"Creative advertising and selling will overcome consumers' resistance and persuade them to buy."	"The consumer rules! Find a need and fill it."	"Long-term relationships with customers and other partners lead to success."
APPROXIMATE TIME PERIOD*	Prior to 1920s	Prior to 1950s	Since 1950s	Since 1990s

*In Canada and other highly industrialized economies.

The production era reached its peak during the early part of the 20th century. Henry Ford's mass-production line exemplifies this orientation. Ford's slogan, "They [customers] can have any colour they want, as long as it's black," reflected the prevalent attitude toward marketing. Production shortages and intense consumer demand ruled the day. It is easy to understand how production activities took precedence.

However, building a new product is no guarantee of success, and marketing history is cluttered with the bones of miserable product failures despite major innovations—more than 80 percent of new products fail. Inventing an outstanding new product is not enough because it must also fill a perceived marketplace need. Otherwise, even the best-engineered, highest-quality product will fail. Even Henry Ford's horseless carriage took a while to catch on. People were afraid of motor vehicles; they spat out exhaust, stirred up dust on dirt roads, got stuck in mud, and tied up horse traffic. Besides, at the speed of seven miles per hour, they caused all kinds of accidents and disruption. It took savvy marketing by some early salespeople—and eventually a widespread perceived need—to change people's minds about the product. Today, most of us could not imagine life without a car and have refined that need to preferences for certain types of vehicles, including SUVs, convertibles, trucks, and hybrids.

THE SALES ERA

As production techniques in North America and Europe became more sophisticated, output grew during the period from the 1920s into the early 1950s. As a result, manufacturers began to increase their emphasis on effective sales forces to find customers for their output. In this era, firms attempted to match their output to the potential number of customers who would want it. Companies with a **sales orientation** assume that customers will resist purchasing nonessential goods and services and that the task of personal selling and advertising is to persuade them to buy.

Although marketing departments began to emerge from the shadows of production and engineering during the sales era, they tended to remain in subordinate positions. Many chief marketing executives held the title of sales manager. But selling is only one component of marketing. As marketing scholar Theodore Levitt once pointed out, "Marketing is as different from selling as chemistry is from alchemy, astronomy from astrology, chess from checkers."

THE MARKETING ERA AND THE EMERGENCE OF THE MARKETING CONCEPT

Personal incomes and consumer demand for goods and services dropped rapidly during the Great Depression of the 1930s, thrusting marketing into a more important role. Organizational survival dictated that managers pay close attention to the markets for their goods and services. This trend ended with the outbreak of World War II, when rationing and shortages of consumer goods became commonplace. The war years, however, created only a pause in an emerging trend in business: a shift in the focus from products and sales to satisfying customer needs.

The marketing concept, a crucial change in management philosophy, can be linked to the shift from a **seller's market**—one in which there were more buyers for fewer goods and services—to a **buyer's market**—one in which there were more goods and services than people willing to buy them. When World War II ended, factories stopped manufacturing war supplies and started turning out consumer products again, an activity that had, for all practical purposes, stopped during the war.

The advent of a strong buyer's market created the need for **consumer orientation** by businesses. Companies had to market goods and services, not just produce and sell them. This realization has been identified as the emergence of the marketing concept. Marketing would no longer be regarded as a supplemental activity performed after completion of the production process. Instead, the marketer would play a leading role in product planning. *Marketing* and *selling* would no longer be synonymous terms.

Today's fully developed **marketing concept** is a *company-wide consumer orientation* with the objective of achieving long-run success. All facets—and all levels, from top to bottom—of the organization must contribute first to assessing and then to satisfying customer wants and needs. Whether marketing manager, accountant, or product designer, every employee plays a role in reaching potential customers. Even during tough economic times, when companies tend to emphasize cutting costs and boosting revenues, the marketing concept focuses on the objective of achieving long-run success instead of short-term profits. Because the firm's survival and growth are built into

sales orientation
Belief that consumers will resist purchasing nonessential goods and services, with the attitude toward marketing that only creative advertising and personal selling can overcome consumers' resistance and persuade them to buy.

seller's market
Market in which there are more buyers for fewer goods and services.

buyer's market
Market in which there are more goods and services than people willing to buy them.

consumer orientation
Business philosophy incorporating the marketing concept that emphasizes first determining unmet consumer needs and then designing a system for satisfying them.

marketing concept
Company-wide consumer orientation with the objective of achieving long-run success.

H. F. (HERB) MACKENZIE

Apple exemplifies the marketing concept, creating consistently stylish and cutting-edge products. The iPad is a recent innovation.

the marketing concept, company-wide consumer orientation should lead to greater long-run profits.

Apple exemplifies the marketing concept in every aspect of its business. Its products are consistently stylish and cutting edge but without overwhelming users with every possible feature. "A defining quality of Apple has been design restraint," says one industry consultant. That hallmark restraint is a characteristic of Apple's founder, Steve Jobs, and is reflected in the work of Apple's designers, managers, and engineers, whose contributions to the company's new products Jobs credits for the company's ability to constantly surprise the marketplace. Apple's 2010 release, the iPad, was called a product that "may change the world." Says one business professor, "Real innovation in technology involves a leap ahead, anticipating needs that no one really knew they had and then delivering capabilities that redefine product categories. That's what Steve Jobs has done."[14] A strong market orientation—the extent to which a company adopts the marketing concept—generally improves market success and overall performance. It also has a positive effect on new-product development and the introduction of innovative products. Companies that implement market-driven strategies are better able to understand their customers' experiences, buying habits, and needs. Like Apple, these companies can, therefore, design products with advantages and levels of quality compatible with customer requirements.

THE RELATIONSHIP ERA

The fourth era in the history of marketing emerged during the final decade of the 20th century and continues to grow in importance. Organizations now build on the marketing era's customer orientation by focusing on establishing and maintaining relationships with both customers and

CAREER READINESS Network to Success

YOU may think only extroverts and social butterflies can build the personal networks that lead to business and career success. Not so! Networking is a skill anyone can learn. Here are some tips to get you started:

- Think of building your personal connections as making an investment in your future. It requires time and effort to become fruitful.
- Work on your network a little at a time. Start by attending one or two promising events a month or joining a professional networking service like LinkedIn or one or two professional groups you can find there, and stick with them.
- Be sure your online profile won't embarrass you with party photos or objectionable language.
- If you join a group or network that doesn't look immediately promising but you really enjoy it, keep going.
- Talk to new people everywhere, including social events like weddings and everyday places like checkout lines in stores.
- Don't hesitate to invite people to join you for coffee or a quick meal after work. Some of the most interesting contacts might just be shy.

- Carry information about yourself or your company to give out, such as an up-to-date brochure or business card.
- Remember, it's not all about you. Talk about relevant activities you've done, but be ready to ask questions that help others talk about themselves and their company or organization.
- Look for a few people who know a lot of other people, rather than many people in specific positions or types of businesses.
- Keep a record of people you want to stay in touch with, and don't wait for an occasion to get together. Follow-up and reciprocating are the keys to being remembered.
- Evaluate your results periodically. Which networking strategies are working best for you, and which can you improve?

Sources: Kristen Porter, "How to Grow Your Professional Networking," eHow, http://www.ehow.com, February 4, 2010; Rob May, "How to Network: For Introverts," Business Pundit, http://www.businesspundit.com, April 16, 2009; "How to Network Effectively," eHow, http://www.ehow.com, April 16, 2009; C. J. Hayden, "Network Your Way to a New Job or Career," About.com, http://humanresources.about.com, April 16, 2009.

MARKETING AND THE SME | QR Codes: A New Dimension in Customer Connection

TONIGHT you are hosting a dinner party for an important business associate who has just arrived from France. You are quite nervous as you know he has high expectations and is not easily impressed. The dinner menu you have prepared includes lobster bisque, filet mignon, asparagus, and mushrooms, and it will be followed by crème brûlée for dessert. The only decision left is the wine choice. You drive to your local wine store, hoping that someone there can give you advice.

As you wind through the wine racks, an unfamiliar black and white square on the side of a bottle catches your eye. It is a QR, or "quick response," code. The sales clerk shows you how to scan the code with your smartphone, and you are immediately brought to the wine maker's website where you view information specifically about the wine you are considering. The beauty of this is that the wine may have been put on the store shelf months before, but the website you view may have been updated only hours before you view it. Château des Charmes was one of the first Canadian wineries to take advantage of QR codes on its products and in its advertisements. With this technology, the winery can easily communicate important and up-to-date information to interested people.

QR codes are becoming popular on many products: on food items enabling you to check the nutritional value or ingredients, on medicine bottles so you can see dosage instructions and side effects, and even in advertisements and on billboards. You might, for example, see an ad or a billboard promoting a new perfume. By scanning the QR code, you can get additional information, possibly even a coupon for a special promotional trial offer, which you can then download to your smartphone. Through your phone, you might then check the location of the nearest retailer where you can use your coupon.

QR codes are the most popular two-dimensional codes in Japan, and they are quickly gaining popularity among the 4 billion or so mobile phone users around the world. QR codes are creating convergence between the many information media and are encouraging interactive consumer behaviour. They offer potential for many small businesses to improve the efficiency—and effectiveness—of their communications programs.

Sources: "QR Code Primer," Château des Charmes website, http://www.chateaudescharmes.com/QRCode_Primer.pdf, July 10, 2011; "7 Things You Should Know about QR Codes," Educause website, http://net.educause.edu/ir/library/pdf/ELI7046.pdf, July 10, 2011; Jeremy Lloyd, "Niagara Wine Gets New Look and QR Code," Marketing News, December 9, 2009; http://www.marketingmag.ca/news/marketer-news/niagara-wine-gets-new-look-and-qr-code-12439, July 11, 2011.

---

suppliers. **Relationship marketing** involves long-term, value-added relationships developed over time with customers and suppliers. Strategic alliances and partnerships among manufacturers, retailers, and suppliers often benefit everyone. The Boeing 787 Dreamliner, which has been under development and construction since 2004, is the result of an international team of companies working on the technology, design, and construction of the planes. Boeing and 43 global suppliers are working together to complete the planes. With orders for 876 planes, Boeing is proving that its long-term relationships are worth the effort.[15] The concept of relationship marketing, which is the current state of customer-driven marketing, is discussed in detail later in this chapter and informs much of the content of this book. On a personal level, see the "Career Readiness" feature for suggestions on creating your own personal network, a key to success in marketing and in business generally.

relationship marketing Development and maintenance of long-term, cost-effective relationships with individual customers, suppliers, employees, and other partners for mutual benefit.

CONVERTING NEEDS TO WANTS

Every consumer must acquire goods and services on a continuing basis to fill certain needs. Everyone must satisfy the fundamental needs for food, clothing, shelter, and transportation by purchasing things or, in some instances, temporarily using rented property and hired or leased transportation. By focusing on the benefits resulting from these products, effective marketing converts needs to wants. A need for a pair of pants may be converted to a desire for jeans—and further, a desire for jeans from Abercrombie & Fitch or Mark's Work Wearhouse. The need for food may be converted to a desire for a taco from Taco Bell or groceries from Sobeys or Real Canadian Superstore. But if the need for transportation isn't converted to a desire for a Honda Odyssey or a Ford Mustang, extra vehicles may sit unsold on a dealer's lot.

Consumers need to communicate. But converting that need to the desire for certain types of communication requires skill. It also requires listening to what consumers want. Consumers' demand for more cell

assessment check 2

2.1 What is the major distinction between the production era and the sales era?

2.2 What is the marketing concept?

2.3 Describe the relationship era of marketing.

phone and wireless services seems nearly unlimited, particularly with the surge in social networking sites—providing tremendous opportunities for companies. New products appear continually to feed that demand, such as increasingly popular broadband wireless services now offered by all cell phone carriers in a market currently dominated by Bell Canada, Rogers, and Telus. Though many consumers who use Internet-friendly phones and other devices tend to be business travellers, the wireless broadband industry is intent on improving its appeal to the social networking mass market, perhaps with flexible service plans, new features, and lower fees. One industry analysis group predicts that very soon "for most consumers, the smartphone will be the norm and not the exception."[16]

AVOIDING MARKETING MYOPIA

(3) Explain the importance of avoiding marketing myopia.

marketing myopia
Management's failure to recognize the scope of its business.

The emergence of the marketing concept has not been devoid of setbacks. One troublesome problem led marketing scholar Theodore Levitt to coin the term **marketing myopia**. According to Levitt, marketing myopia is management's failure to recognize the scope of its business. Product-oriented rather than customer-oriented management endangers future growth. Levitt cites many service industries—such as dry cleaning and electric utilities—as examples of marketing myopia. But many firms have found innovative ways to reach new markets and develop long-term relationships.

Apple, for instance, has been working for a while on developing solar-powered devices, and in response to customer demand for longer battery life for its devices, the firm has restarted work on ways to use solar power for battery recharging. Such innovations also hold out the promise of greener and more sustainable manufacturing processes that might eliminate the use of some toxic or nonrecyclable parts in its products that have drawn criticism of Apple from such groups as Greenpeace.[17] Table 1.2 illustrates how firms in a number of industries have overcome myopic thinking by developing broader marketing-oriented business ideas that focus on consumer need satisfaction.

assessment check 3

3.1 What is marketing myopia?

3.2 Give an example of how a firm can avoid marketing myopia.

EXTENDING THE TRADITIONAL BOUNDARIES OF MARKETING

Today's organizations—both profit-oriented and not-for-profit—recognize universal needs for marketing and its importance to their success. During a television commercial break, viewers might be exposed to an advertisement for a Kia Spectra, an appeal to help feed children in foreign countries, a message by a political candidate, and a commercial for Tim Hortons—all in the space of about two minutes. Two of these ads are paid for by firms attempting to achieve profitability and other objectives. The appeal for funds to feed children and the political ad are examples of communications by not-for-profit organizations and individuals.

table 1.2 *Avoiding Marketing Myopia*

COMPANY	MYOPIC DESCRIPTION	COMPANY MOTTO—AVOIDING MYOPIA
Nokia	A cell phone manufacturer	Connecting People
Visa	A credit card company	Life Takes Visa
Purolator	A courier company	Where Business Is Going
Corporate Express Canada	An office supplies company	Productivity in Your Hands
Michelin	A tire manufacturer	A Better Way Forward
Xerox	A photocopier manufacturer	The Document Company
La-Z-Boy	A furniture manufacturer	Comfort. It's What We Do.

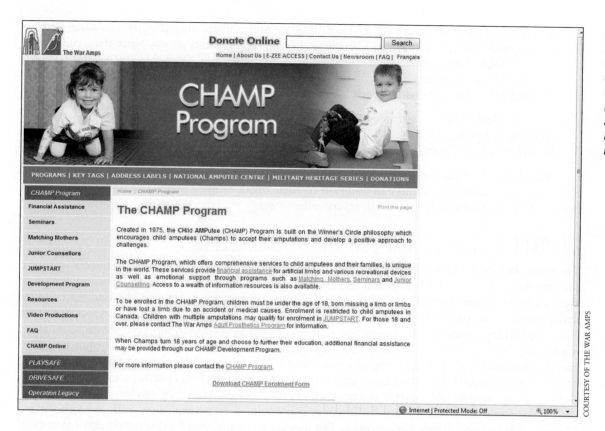

COURTESY OF THE WAR AMPS

Marketing helps raise money to support social causes. The War Amps is a not-for-profit organization that offers comprehensive services to child amputees and their families. Its CHAMP Program is unique in the world.

MARKETING IN NOT-FOR-PROFIT ORGANIZATIONS

There are approximately 161 000 not-for-profit and charity organizations in Canada, representing nearly $80 billion–or 7.8 percent–of GDP, making this sector larger than the manufacturing sector. It employs more than 2 million Canadians and is the second largest not-for-profit and voluntary sector in the world.[18] That makes not-for-profit organizations big business.

Not-for-profit organizations operate in both public and private sectors. Federal, provincial, and municipal government units and agencies pursue service objectives that are not keyed to profitability targets. The Canada Border Services Agency is a federal government agency that provides border security services and helps facilitate the flow of people and goods across the Canadian border; individual provincial government departments regulate labour safety, environmental conservation and natural resources, and alcohol control; municipal school boards are responsible for overseeing educational and curriculum standards for their district. The private sector contains an even greater array of not-for-profit organizations, including zoos, hospitals, universities and colleges, ethnic and religious associations, and charities, such as the Make-a-Wish Foundation of Canada. Regardless of their size or location, all these organizations need funds to operate. Adopting the marketing concept can make a great difference in their ability to meet their service objectives.

Some not-for-profits form partnerships with business firms that promote the organization's cause or message. The Hospital for Sick Children (SickKids) has been supported by Walmart since it came to Canada in 1994. In 2010, 75 Walmart Canada associates gathered at SickKids to celebrate $10 million in donations, raised through employee-led initiatives, the sale of Miracle Balloons, and a corporate donation-matching program.[19] Generally, the alliances formed between not-for-profit organizations and commercial firms benefit both. The reality of operating with multimillion-dollar budgets requires not-for-profit organizations to maintain a focused business approach. Consider some current examples:

- Food Banks Canada (FBC) represents community food banks across Canada. Approximately 870 000 different people access food banks monthly in Canada, nearly 40 percent of them children. FBC moves about 10 million pounds of food industry donations annually to its members, almost exclusively with donated transportation. Some of the many participating companies are Nestle Canada, Danone Canada, Loblaw, Kellogg Canada, ConAgra Foods Canada, and H. J. Heinz Co. of Canada.[20]

- Barely a week after the March 11, 2011, earthquake and tsunami hit Japan, the Canadian Red Cross sent $5 million, donated by Canadians, to help support relief efforts. Since then, millions of more dollars have been donated by individuals, companies, and charitable organizations across Canada. Many companies donated goods and services as well as money. Telus, for example, donated $100 000, but also provided free long-distance and wireless services to Japan.[21]

- M & M Meat Shops encourages its franchisees across Canada to support community-based charities and programs. Since 1989, at the corporate level, it has raised more than $16 million in support of the Crohn's and Colitis Foundation of Canada.[22]

The diversity of not-for-profit organizations suggests the presence of numerous organizational objectives other than profitability. In addition to their organizational goals, not-for-profit organizations differ from profit-seeking firms in several other ways.

CHARACTERISTICS OF NOT-FOR-PROFIT MARKETING

4 Describe the characteristics of not-for-profit marketing.

bottom line
Reference to overall company profitability.

The most obvious distinction between not-for-profit organizations and for-profit—commercial—firms is the financial **bottom line**, business jargon that refers to the overall profitability of an organization. For-profit organizations measure profitability, and their goal is to generate revenues above and beyond their costs to make money for all stakeholders involved, including employees, shareholders, and the organization itself. Not-for-profit organizations hope to generate as much revenue as possible to support their causes, whether it is feeding children, preserving wilderness, or helping single mothers find work. Historically, not-for-profits have had less exact goals and marketing objectives than for-profit firms, but in recent years, many of these groups have recognized that, to succeed, they must develop more cost-effective ways to provide services, and they must compete with other organizations for donors' dollars. Marketing can help them accomplish these tasks. Some groups are finding, for instance, that online social network sites, such as Facebook and MySpace, can bring them increased attention. But they are also using specialized networks devoted to social causes like YourCause.com and easy payment systems like Piryx to generate funds.[23]

Marketoid

Eighty-four percent of Canadians aged 15 and older donated money to a charitable donation in one recent year; 46 percent reported volunteering for an organization.

Other distinctions exist between for-profit and not-for-profit organizations as well, each of which influences marketing activities. Like profit-seeking firms, not-for-profit organizations may market tangible goods and/or intangible services. Pink products have long been important in raising both funds for and recognition of National Breast Cancer Awareness month in October every year. "Promotional items have been extremely important to the breast cancer awareness push," says the corporate relationship manager of the Susan G. Komen fund, a breast cancer fundraising group. "Not only are they essential for fundraising to find a cure, they are also key to spreading life-saving messages to audiences we might never reach without them. With the help of promotional items, it has finally become okay to talk about breast cancer."[24] But profit-seeking businesses tend to focus their marketing on just one public—their customers. Not-for-profit organizations, however, must often market to multiple publics, which complicates decision making about the correct markets to target. Many deal with at least two major publics—their clients and their sponsors—and often many other publics as well. A college or university targets prospective students as recipients of its marketing program, but it also markets to current students, parents of students, major donors, alumni, faculty, staff, local businesses, and local government agencies.

A service user of a not-for-profit organization may have less control over the organization's destiny than would be true for customers of a profit-seeking firm. Not-for-profit organizations also often possess some degree of monopoly power in a given geographic area. An individual contributor might object to United Way's inclusion of a particular local agency, but that agency will still receive a portion of that donor's contribution.

assessment check 4 ✓

4.1 What is the most obvious distinction between a not-for-profit organization and a commercial organization?

4.2 Why do for-profit and not-for-profit organizations sometimes form alliances?

NONTRADITIONAL MARKETING

5 Identify and briefly explain each of the five types of nontraditional marketing.

As marketing evolved into an organization-wide activity, its application has broadened far beyond its traditional boundaries of for-profit organizations engaged in the creation and distribution of tangible goods and intangible services. In many cases, broader appeals focus on causes, events, individuals,

table 1.3   *Categories of Nontraditional Marketing*

TYPE	BRIEF DESCRIPTION	EXAMPLES
Person marketing	Marketing efforts designed to cultivate the attention and preference of a target market toward a person	Athlete Steve Nash Political leader Stephen Harper Celebrity Nelly Furtado
Place marketing	Marketing efforts designed to attract visitors to a particular area; improve consumer images of a city, province, or country; and/or attract new business	Saskatchewan: Land of Living Skies Nova Scotia: Canada's Ocean Playground Manitoba: Friendly Manitoba
Cause marketing	Identification and marketing of a social issue, cause, or idea to selected target markets	"Reading is fundamental." "Friends don't let friends drive drunk." "Be a mentor."
Event marketing	Marketing of sporting, cultural, and charitable activities to selected target markets	Grey Cup 2010 Vancouver Winter Olympics Calgary Stampede
Organization marketing	Marketing efforts of mutual-benefit organizations, service organizations, and government organizations that seek to influence others to accept their goals, receive their services, or contribute to them in some way.	United Way: Without you, there would be no way. Canadian Red Cross: Anywhere. Anytime. Sierra Club: Explore, enjoy, and protect the planet.

organizations, and places. Table 1.3 lists and describes five major categories of nontraditional marketing: person marketing, place marketing, cause marketing, event marketing, and organization marketing. These categories can overlap—promotion for an organization may also encompass a cause; a promotional campaign may focus on both an event and a place.

PERSON MARKETING

Person marketing involves efforts designed to cultivate the attention, interest, and preferences of a target market toward a celebrity or authority figure. Celebrities can be real people or fictional characters. Political candidates engage in person marketing as they promote their candidacy for office. However, results of exit polls following the 2011 federal election suggest that the party leader—not the local candidate—sways the majority of voters. This may help explain why, in one Quebec riding, a candidate who barely spoke French, spent little time in her riding, and vacationed in Las Vegas during the campaign, won.[25] Authors such as Suze Orman of *The Road to Wealth* use person marketing to promote their books. Rachael Ray uses person marketing to promote her *Every Day with Rachael Ray* magazine, where she appears on every cover.

An extension of person marketing involves *celebrity endorsements*, in which well-known athletes, entertainers, and experts or authority figures promote products for companies or social causes for not-for-profit organizations. Proactiv Solution spends up to $15 million annually on celebrity endorsements to promote its acne treatment. Promotions have included stars such as Katy Perry, Avril Lavigne, Sean "Diddy" Combs, and Justin Bieber—reportedly paid $3 million for a two-year deal.[26] Actor William Shatner was seen in ads for Priceline.com, while his former *Star Trek* co-star Leonard Nimoy promoted the pain reliever Aleve. Athletes are the big winners in the celebrity endorsement arena—NBA star LeBron James has multimillion-dollar endorsement deals with Nike, Upper Deck, and the Coca-Cola Company. New York Giants quarterback Eli Manning has endorsement deals with Citizen Watch, Reebok, and Nabisco's Oreo brand, and with his brother, Indianapolis Colts' quarterback Peyton, faces off against Donald Trump in ads for Oreo cookies.[27]

PLACE MARKETING

Another category of nontraditional marketing is **place marketing**, which attempts to attract customers to particular areas. Cities, provinces, regions, and countries publicize their tourist attractions to lure vacation travellers. They also promote themselves as good locations for businesses. Place marketing has

person marketing
Marketing efforts designed to cultivate the attention, interest, and preference of a target market toward a person (typically a political candidate or celebrity).

place marketing
Marketing efforts to attract people and organizations to a particular geographic area.

become more important in the world economy—not only for tourism but also to recruit business and workers. Casino operator MGM is betting the house on its latest venture, the $8.5-billion CityCenter complex in Las Vegas, which is complete with four 61-storey hotel towers, high-end stores, and dozens of bars and restaurants—and, of course, a casino. Like other hospitality businesses in the city, MGM is hoping to reverse Las Vegas's recently flagging status as a tourist draw, offering pricing deals to push the number of visitors up to nearly 40 million a year.[28]

Although tourism is not the only aspect of place marketing, tourism has a major economic impact. Canada was the most popular destination for U.S. travellers in 2010; Americans charged $3.5 billion to their credit cards during trips to Canada.[29] However, the Canadian Tourism Commission is warning of increasing international competition and notes that Canada has dropped to fifteenth place from sixth place in the last decade. Austria, Germany, Hong Kong, Turkey, Malaysia, and Ukraine have surpassed Canada as sites for international tourist arrivals.[30]

China is expected to become the world's largest market for tourism, with an estimated 100 million outbound travellers annually by 2020. Canada currently receives about 200 000 travellers each year from China and expects double-digit growth in future years. Interest in Canada has increased greatly since Canada received approved destination status from China. As a result, in 2011, Canada launched its first major consumer-focused advertising campaign in China, with the tagline "Say Hello to Canada," aiming to attract Chinese tourists to Niagara Falls, Ottawa, Whistler, Banff, and other popular sites.[31]

CAUSE MARKETING

cause marketing
Identification and marketing of a social issue, cause, or idea to selected target markets.

A third category of nontraditional marketing, **cause marketing**, refers to the identification and marketing of a social issue, cause, or idea to selected target markets. Cause marketing covers a wide range of issues, including literacy, physical fitness, awareness of childhood obesity, environmental protection, elimination of birth defects, child-abuse prevention, and preventing drunk driving.

As mentioned earlier, an increasingly common marketing practice is for profit-seeking firms to link their products to social causes. Staples Canada, through its annual School Supply Drive, reached its 2010 goal of raising $1 million, which was distributed through local community-based charities to children in need. Since the inception of its Recycle for Education program, Staples has contributed $2.7 million to schools across Canada. In addition, in 2011, Staples implemented the Recycle for Education Contest and awarded a $50 000 computer lab makeover to first-place winner Dover Bay Secondary School in Nanaimo, B.C.[32]

Surveys show strong support for cause-related marketing by both consumers and company employees. In one recent survey, 92 percent of consumers had a more positive image of companies that support important social causes, and four of five respondents said that they would change brands to support a cause if the price and quality of the two brands remained equal.

EVENT MARKETING

event marketing
Marketing of sporting, cultural, and charitable activities to selected target markets.

Event marketing refers to the marketing of sporting, cultural, and charitable activities to selected target markets. It also includes the sponsorship of such events by firms seeking to increase public awareness and bolster their images by linking themselves and their products to the events. Sports sponsorships have gained effectiveness in increasing brand recognition, enhancing image, boosting purchase volume, and increasing popularity with sports fans in demographic segments corresponding to the sponsors' business goals.

Some people might say that the premier sporting event is baseball's World Series. Others claim it's the Olympics or the World Cup. Still others might argue that it's the Super Bowl, which many consumers claim they watch only to see the debut of commercials. Those commercials are expensive and can run as much as $3 million (U.S.) for 30 seconds of airtime, or $100 000 a second. But they reach an estimated 90 million viewers. Companies now also feed their commercials to websites and make them available for downloading to personal computers and video iPods. Experienced marketers caution that firms planning such a big expenditure should make it part of a larger marketing plan, not just a single shot at fame.

For those who prefer the international pageantry of the Olympics, marketers have plenty of plans. The promotion of upcoming Olympics—both summer and winter—begins years in advance. Before the end of each Olympics, hosts of the next games unveil their logo and the marketing

Marketoid

Twenty-three percent of Canadians aged 25 to 34 were born outside of Canada; they account for 40 percent of master's degrees and 49 percent of Ph.Ds.

takes off from there. Corporate sponsors such as Adidas and Nike try to target the next Olympic gold-medal winners, draping them in clothing and gear with company logos. The 2010 Vancouver Winter Olympics afforded opportunities for hundreds of firms to provide wine and beer for hospitality events, frames and tents, jewellery, team uniforms, energy generation and temperature control systems, beds for the athletes' village, natural gas, cold and flu remedies, organic groceries, hand sanitizers, and computer and accounting services.[33]

ORGANIZATION MARKETING

Organization marketing attempts to influence others to accept the goals of, receive the services of, or contribute in some way to an organization. Organization marketing includes mutual-benefit organizations (conservation groups, labour unions, and political parties), service and cultural organizations (colleges and universities, hospitals, and museums), and government organizations. Many organizations use organizational marketing to help raise funds. In 2011, Davorka Cvitkovic was appointed CEO of the fundraising arm of Manitoba's $310-million Canadian Museum for Human Rights, scheduled for completion in 2012. The organization had already raised about $125 million of its $150 million capital campaign goal, but it wanted to change focus to raise money outside of Manitoba. Cvitkovic has held senior fundraising positions with Simon Fraser University and the Canadian Arthritis Society.[34]

organization marketing
Marketing by mutual-benefit organizations, service organizations, and government organizations intended to influence others to accept their goals, receive their services, or contribute to them in some way.

assessment check 5

5.1 Identify the five major categories of nontraditional marketing.

5.2 Give an example of a way in which two or more of these categories might overlap.

GO GREEN | ## Tired of Blue, White, and Pink Jobs? Think Green

TRADITIONALLY, the colour green was described as dark, light, or bright. Today, we are more likely to describe green as army, asparagus, emerald, forest, hunter, jade, jungle, lime, moss, olive, pine, or sea green. Traditionally, "green" jobs were largely science-based positions: contaminant and waste management, environmental engineering, water conservation and quality management, soil testing, forest conservation, agronomy, etc. Today, green jobs are more likely to be cross-functional or cross-disciplinary, and many require only a marginal understanding of science. That's great news for many people, including want-to-be marketers. Green job opportunities are hot.

Todd Latham, publisher of two Toronto-based environmental magazines, sees opportunities for people who are simply passionate about the environment. This could include—among others—lawyers, accountants, builders, economists, journalists, and marketers. This may help explain why enrolments are declining in the majority of university-level degree programs that are focused on environmental careers, but green jobs are growing much faster than jobs in the overall economy. In Canada, more than a half-million people are employed in environmental jobs—more than 3 percent of working-age Canadians.

There are increasing opportunities for green entrepreneurs, people who want to start green businesses. As green products become more popular, there will be opportunities for green manufacturers, and they will employ green salespeople and green

marketers. There will be opportunities for new green service firms, such as Carbonzero, a Toronto-based firm that uses recognized international carbon accounting standards to measure greenhouse gas emissions for clients and then helps them reduce or neutralize their impact on the environment.

Many green jobs will continue to require technical or scientific backgrounds, and entry standards for some jobs are very high—either a master's degree or a Ph.D. However, a major task for many organizations within the environmental industry will be their ability to "sell" green science and gain popular acceptance. There will be key positions for those who can work with teams of people from various stakeholder groups—company technical people and senior-level management, government agencies, public interest groups—and communicate effectively with them. Many people in the industry—such as Michael Gerbis, president of Ottawa-based Delphi Group, an environmental consulting firm that has worked with many of Canada's Fortune 100 companies—see education and technical expertise as necessary but not sufficient qualities for new employees. Enthusiasm and communications skills are what differentiates the best green job applicants from the rest.

Sources: Derek Sankey, "Staffing the Green Machine," *Ottawa Citizen*, March 17, 2007, p. D10; Diana McLaren, "Green Jobs Take Root and Proliferate," *The Globe and Mail*, February 14, 2008, http://www.theglobeandmail.com, February 14, 2008; Delphi Group website, http://www.delphi.ca, April 14, 2008; Carbonzero website, http://www.carbonzero.ca, April 14, 2008.

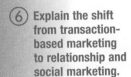

⑥ Explain the shift from transaction-based marketing to relationship and social marketing.

transaction-based marketing
Buyer and seller exchanges characterized by limited communications and little or no ongoing relationships between the parties.

figure 1.2

Converting New Customers to Advocates

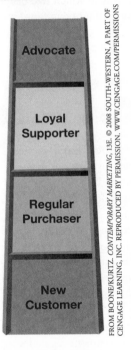

FROM BOONE/KURTZ. *CONTEMPORARY MARKETING*, 13E. © 2008 SOUTH-WESTERN, A PART OF CENGAGE LEARNING, INC. REPRODUCED BY PERMISSION. WWW.CENGAGE.COM/PERMISSIONS

mobile marketing
Marketing messages transmitted via wireless technology.

interactive marketing
Buyer–seller communications in which the customer controls the amount and type of information received from a marketer through such channels as the Internet and virtual reality kiosks.

FROM TRANSACTION-BASED MARKETING TO RELATIONSHIP MARKETING

As marketing progresses through the 21st century, a significant change is taking place in the way companies interact with customers. The traditional view of marketing as a simple exchange process, or **transaction-based marketing**, is being replaced by a different, longer-term approach that emphasizes building relationships one customer at a time. Traditional marketing strategies focused on attracting customers and closing deals. Today's marketers realize that, although it's important to attract new customers, it's even more important to establish and maintain a relationship with them so they become loyal repeat customers. These efforts must expand to include suppliers and employees as well. Over the long term, this relationship may be translated to the lifetime value of a customer—the revenues and intangible benefits that a customer brings to an organization over an average lifetime, minus the investment the firm has made to attract and keep the customer.

Marketers realize that consumers are getting more and more sophisticated. They quickly recognize marketing messages and may turn away from them if the messages don't contain information that consumers want and need. So marketers need to develop new techniques to establish and build trusting relationships between companies and their customers. As defined earlier in this chapter, relationship marketing refers to the development, growth, and maintenance of long-term, cost-effective exchange relationships with individual customers, suppliers, employees, and other partners for mutual benefit. It broadens the scope of external marketing relationships to include suppliers, customers, and referral sources. In relationship marketing, the term *customer* takes on a new meaning. Employees serve customers within an organization as well as outside it; individual employees and their departments are customers of and suppliers to one another. They must apply the same high standards of customer satisfaction to intradepartmental relationships as they do to external customer relationships. Relationship marketing recognizes the critical importance of internal marketing to the success of external marketing plans. Programs that improve customer service inside a company also raise productivity and staff morale, resulting in better customer relationships outside the firm.

Relationship marketing gives a company new opportunities to gain a competitive edge by moving customers up a loyalty ladder—from new customers to regular purchasers, then to loyal supporters of the firm and its goods and services, and finally to advocates who not only buy its products but recommend them to others, as shown in Figure 1.2.

Relationship building begins early in marketing. It starts with determining what customers need and want, then developing high-quality products to meet those needs. It continues with excellent customer service during and after purchase. It also includes programs that encourage repeat purchases and foster customer loyalty. Marketers may try to rebuild damaged relationships or rejuvenate unprofitable customers with these practices as well. Sometimes modifying a product or tailoring customer service to meet the needs of these customers can go a long way toward rebuilding a relationship.

USING INTERACTIVE AND SOCIAL MARKETING TO BUILD RELATIONSHIPS

Today's technology allows people to transmit memos, reports, and drawings quickly and inexpensively over phone lines, cables, or wireless devices. People can subscribe to personalized news services that deliver article summaries on specified topics directly to their computers or cell phones. They can communicate via email, voice mail, text messages, fax, videoconferencing, and computer networks; pay bills using online banking services; and use online resources to get information about things such as theatre events or a local Ford dealer's special sale. As an increasing number of Internet users use wireless devices such as smartphones or notebook computers to access the Web and check their email; the stage is set for **mobile marketing**—marketing messages transmitted via wireless technology.

Interactive media technologies combine computers and telecommunications resources to create software that users can control. Putting power into the hands of customers allows better communication, which can build relationships. **Interactive marketing** refers to buyer–seller communications in which the customer controls the amount and type of information received from a marketer. This technique provides immediate access to key product information when the consumer wants it, and it is increasingly taking place on social media sites such as Facebook,

Twitter, and blogs. **Social marketing** is the use of online social media as a communications channel for marketing messages. Social media is now the top online activity, and it's estimated that if Facebook were a country, it would be the fourth most populous in the world.[35] In one recent year, 50 million users posted 8 billion tweets on Twitter.[36] Following the death of Osama bin Laden, messaging hit 5106 tweets per second at times during the surge that lasted more than four hours. Tweets during Britain's royal wedding peaked at 3966 tweets per second, but reached 6939 tweets per second when New Year's 2011 arrived in Japan, and a record 7196 game-related messages per second during the 2011 Women's World Cup soccer final between the United States and Japan.[37] More than half the Fortune 100 companies have joined Twitter, and almost a third use Facebook and blogs. One Nielsen executive called social media "a catalyst for fresh thinking on how companies can improve customer service."[38]

Interactive marketing allows marketers and consumers to customize their communication. Customers may come to companies for information, creating opportunities for one-to-one marketing. They also can tell the company what they like or dislike about a product, and they can just as easily click the exit button and move on to another area. As interactive promotions grow in number and popularity, the challenge is to attract and hold consumer attention. "We can be more intimate with our marketplace customers and peers," says the president of the International Social Media Association. "Consumers are developing the expectation that companies are going to be more available and respond more quickly, that people are listening."[39]

One small business making good use of social media is Lou Dawg's Southern Sandwiches in Toronto. Co-owner Daryl D'Souza tried a print campaign, food drops to radio stations, begging for reviews, and handing out sample smoked chicken wings, but sales flatlined soon after his business opened. He recently started twittering on his iPhone, announcing new menu items and providing secret words that followers could use in the restaurant for free food. Sales jumped 22 percent in only a few months.[40] Kodak uses social media to accomplish what it calls "the 4 E's": engage, educate, excite, and evangelize. Says a company executive, "You have to create communication that engages the customer. Everyone talks about traditional ROIs [return on investment], but I talk about the new one, 'Return on Ignoring.' If you are ignoring this stuff, I can guarantee you are losing a fantastic business opportunity."[41]

Social media also allow larger exchanges in which consumers communicate with one another using email or social networking sites. These electronic conversations can establish innovative relationships between users and the business, providing customized information based on users' interests and levels of understanding.

By converting indifferent customers into loyal ones, companies generate repeat sales. The cost of maintaining existing customers is far below the cost of finding new ones, and these loyal customers are profitable. Some of the best repeat customers are those who are also willing to spread the word—create a buzz—about a product. **Buzz marketing** can be very effective in attracting new customers by bridging

social marketing
The use of online social media as a communications channel for marketing messages.

buzz marketing
Word-of-mouth messages that bridge the gap between a company and its products.

MARKETING IN A DIGITAL WORLD   Canada Goos Up Google Maps

HAVE you ever wanted to egg somebody's house—or even your school? Well, Kraft Canada and Google Maps have partnered to allow you to do that, virtually. You can smother homes, buildings, parks, and monuments with egg goo. But don't use real eggs; they are expensive and can get you in trouble. Go online and smother your chosen target with virtual goo from Cadbury Creme Eggs.

In a marketing campaign for their Easter Creme Eggs, Kraft Canada created a website where visitors could catapult an egg to hit a target of their choice. Visitors first select a destination on Google Maps as a target, pull back the catapult, launch an egg through the sky, and watch as it plummets to earth, smothering their chosen target in egg goo. Visitors are then encouraged to share their experience with others through email, Facebook, and Twitter.

The online campaign received about 140 000 visits between its launch in late February and the following Halloween, a clear marketing success. The application was also shared 3000 times on Facebook, tweeted about 300 times, and was mentioned on approximately 100 blogs. Mackenzie Davison, director of marketing, shares why he believes the online campaign has been a success: "It's very consistent with the brand itself. Creme Eggs are all about fun and the gooey filling. . . ."

So next time you want to egg something, visit www .returnofthegoo.ca.

Sources: Matt Semansky, "Cadbury Goos Up Google Maps," *Marketing*, March 24, 2011; Kraft Canada website, http://www.returnofthegoo.ca/en/#/launch, July 11, 2011.

TASTE THE EXPERIENCE

CHÂTEAU DES CHARMES

"MAKING WINE IS NOT WHAT WE DO. IT'S WHO WE ARE."

the Bosc Family

SCAN THIS CODE TO LEARN HOW YOU CAN VISIT US FOR FREE.
To download a free QR reader go to optiscan.com

VISIT OUR NEW WEBSITE CHATEAUDESCHARMES.COM

FOLLOW US @MBOSC

COURTESY OF CHÂTEAU DES CHARMES

QR codes, such as the one shown in this advertisement, are becoming increasingly popular as Canadian companies seek to market in a digitally-connected world.

the gap between a company and its products. Companies as diverse as Microsoft and KFC have tapped customers to create a buzz about their products. Firms that make the most efficient use of buzz marketing warn that it is not a "one-way" approach to building customer relationships. Buzz can be purely visual, too. "Visual buzz," according to one marketing strategist, is "not only about telling, but more and more about showing. You see a Nike poster in a friend's dorm room; perhaps you don't even talk about it, but you noticed it." A prime example, the strategist says, is Lance Armstrong's Live Strong bracelet.

Effective relationship marketing often relies heavily on information technologies such as computer databases that record customers' tastes, price preferences, and lifestyles. This technology helps companies become one-to-one marketers who gather customer-specific information and provide individually customized goods and services. The firms target their marketing programs to appropriate groups rather than relying on mass-marketing campaigns. Companies that study customer preferences and react accordingly gain distinct competitive advantages.

DEVELOPING PARTNERSHIPS AND STRATEGIC ALLIANCES

Relationship marketing does not apply just to individual consumers and employees. It also affects a wide range of other markets, including business-to-business relationships with the firm's suppliers and distributors as well as other types of corporate partnerships. In the past, companies have often viewed their suppliers as adversaries against whom they must fiercely negotiate prices, playing one off against the other. But this attitude has changed radically, as both marketers and their suppliers discover the benefits of collaborative relationships.

strategic alliances
Partnerships in which two or more companies combine resources and capital to create competitive advantages in a new market.

The formation of **strategic alliances** is also on the rise. A recent PriceWaterhouseCoopers survey of 1200 executives in 69 countries reported that half of them expected to enter into a joint venture or strategic alliance within a year.[42] Alliances take many forms, including product-development partnerships that involve shared costs for research and development and marketing, and vertical alliances in which one company provides a product or component to another firm, which then distributes or sells it under its own brand. Many alliances are formed simply to exploit competitive advantage. TransForce and DHL Express Canada announced a 10-year strategic alliance to provide a fully integrated shipping and logistics service. Transforce—through its subsidiary Loomis Express—would take over DHL Express Canada's domestic business, providing efficiencies through increased scale. The partnership also would allow it to provide better international services for its Canadian customers. DHL Express Canada would be able to focus on its core competency—international express—and to provide better service within Canada for its global customers. The two companies launched an integrated advertising campaign entitled "The Power of 2" to communicate how the alliance would "bring Canadian businesses the most powerful delivery service in Canada, and the world."[43]

Not-for-profit organizations often make use of strategic alliances to raise awareness and funds for their causes or to achieve their goals. Thrifty Foods, with its Food for Families campaign, raised $200 000 for Vancouver food banks. Sobeys' Ontario's Annual Charity Golf Tournament raised $50 000 to support the Boys and Girls Club of Canada. IGA stores in Quebec partnered with suppliers to raise $350 000 to support the Montreal Heart Institute Foundation. Sobeys, Price Chopper, and Foodland raised $68 000 to support child nutrition programs throughout Atlantic Canada.[44] These are just some examples of how the Sobeys group of companies partnered with more than 800 communities they serve across Canada.

assessment check 6

6.1 How does relationship marketing give companies a competitive edge?

6.2 Why are interactive and social marketing important tools for marketers?

6.3 What is a strategic alliance?

COSTS AND FUNCTIONS OF MARKETING

⑦ **Identify the universal functions of marketing.**

Firms must spend money to create time, place, and ownership utilities. Numerous attempts have been made to measure marketing costs in relation to overall product costs, and most estimates have ranged between 40 and 60 percent of total costs. On average, one-half of the costs involved in a product, such as a Subway sandwich, a Toyota Prius, or a financial planning lecture, can be traced directly to marketing. These costs are not associated with wheat, metal, or other raw materials. Nor are they associated with baking, welding, or any of the other production functions necessary for creating form utility. What functions does marketing perform, and why are they important in creating customer satisfaction?

As Figure 1.3 reveals, marketing is responsible for the performance of eight universal functions: buying, selling, transporting, storing, standardizing and grading, financing, risk taking, and securing marketing information. Some functions are performed by manufacturers, others by marketing intermediaries such as retailers or wholesalers (described in Chapter 12).

Buying and selling represent **exchange functions**. Buying is important to marketing on several levels. Marketers must determine how and why consumers buy certain goods and services. To be successful, they must try to understand consumer behaviour. In addition, retailers and other intermediaries must seek out products that will appeal to their customers. Marketers must also anticipate consumer preferences for purchases to be made several months later. Selling is the second half of the exchange process. It involves advertising, personal selling, and sales promotion in an attempt to match the firm's goods and services to consumer needs.

exchange functions
Buying and selling.

Transporting and storing are physical distribution functions. Transporting involves physically moving goods from the seller to the purchaser. Storing involves warehousing goods until they are needed for sale. Manufacturers, wholesalers, and retailers all typically perform these functions.

The final four marketing functions—standardizing and grading, financing, risk taking, and securing marketing information—are often called facilitating functions because they help the marketer perform the exchange and physical distribution functions. Quality and quantity control standards and grades, frequently established by government, reduce the need for purchasers to inspect each item. For example, if you request a certain size tire for your automobile, you expect to get it.

Financing is another marketing function because buyers often need access to funds to finance inventories prior to sales. Manufacturers often provide financing for their wholesale and retail customers. Some types of wholesalers perform similar functions for their markets. Finally, retailers frequently allow their customers to buy on credit, with either store charge cards or major credit cards.

The seventh function, risk taking, is part of most ventures. Manufacturers create goods and services based on research and their belief that consumers need them. Wholesalers and retailers acquire inventory

figure 1.3

Eight Universal Marketing Functions

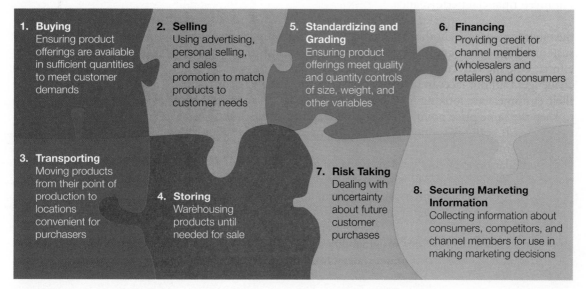

1. **Buying**
Ensuring product offerings are available in sufficient quantities to meet customer demands

2. **Selling**
Using advertising, personal selling, and sales promotion to match products to customer needs

5. **Standardizing and Grading**
Ensuring product offerings meet quality and quantity controls of size, weight, and other variables

6. **Financing**
Providing credit for channel members (wholesalers and retailers) and consumers

3. **Transporting**
Moving products from their point of production to locations convenient for purchasers

4. **Storing**
Warehousing products until needed for sale

7. **Risk Taking**
Dealing with uncertainty about future customer purchases

8. **Securing Marketing Information**
Collecting information about consumers, competitors, and channel members for use in making marketing decisions

based on similar expectations of future consumer demand. Entrepreneurial risk takers accommodate these uncertainties about future consumer behaviour when they market goods and services.

The final marketing function involves securing marketing information. Marketers gather information about potential customers—who they are, what they buy, where they buy, and how they buy. By collecting and analyzing marketing information, marketers can understand why consumers purchase some products while passing others by. This information also helps determine what consumers want and need—and how to offer goods and services to satisfy them. So marketing is the direct connection between a firm and its customers, the link that helps build and maintain lasting relationships.

assessment check 7

7.1 Which two marketing functions represent exchange functions?

7.2 Which two functions represent physical distribution functions?

7.3 Which four functions are facilitating functions?

---

⑧ Demonstrate the relationship among ethical business practices, social responsibility, sustainability, and marketplace success.

ETHICS AND SOCIAL RESPONSIBILITY: DOING WELL BY DOING GOOD

ethics
Moral standards of behaviour expected by a society.

Ethics are moral standards of behaviour expected by a society. Most companies do their best to abide by an ethical code of conduct, but sometimes organizations and their leaders fall short. Several years ago, energy giant Enron collapsed, taking with it the retirement savings of its employees and investors. In another scandal, executives from Tyco were convicted of using millions of company dollars for their personal benefit. And chemical manufacturer Monsanto was convicted not only of polluting a rural area's water sources and soil for decades but also of ignoring evidence its own scientists had gathered indicating the extent and severity of the pollution. Ethics matters in the public sector, too. Some see ethical concerns in the government's use of full-body scans at Canadian airports; see the "Solving an Ethical Controversy" feature for a discussion of the issues.

Most businesspeople do follow ethical practices. Over half of all major corporations now offer ethics training to employees, and most corporate mission statements include pledges to protect the environment, contribute to communities, and improve workers' lives. This book encourages you to follow the highest ethical standards throughout your business and marketing career.

social responsibility
Marketing philosophies, policies, procedures, and actions that have the enhancement of society's welfare as a primary objective.

Social responsibility includes marketing philosophies, policies, procedures, and actions whose primary objective is to enhance society and protect the environment through sustainable products and practices. As the chapter opener pointed out, Walmart, for instance, has made great strides in reducing its use of energy in its stores. Social responsibility often takes the form of philanthropy, making gifts of money or time to humanitarian causes. Many firms, both large and small, include social responsibility programs as part of their overall mission. These programs often produce such benefits as improved customer relationships, increased employee loyalty, marketplace success, and improved financial performance.

sustainable products
Products that can be produced, used, and disposed of with minimal impact on the environment.

Sustainable products, which can be produced, used, and disposed of with minimal impact on the environment, are another goal of socially responsible firms. Many such firms have added annual sustainability reports and a top-level executive position to develop and promote their sustainability efforts. One such executive is DuPont's chief sustainability officer, Linda Fisher, who says about the challenges DuPont faces in furthering its environmentally friendly efforts, "What our customers and their customers are looking for are products that are greener, more energy-efficient, but they'd like to keep the same price point. So they're demanding more. . . . Those are real cost issues and market issues. . . . It really is trying to balance the needs of industry and the economy with the needs of the environment. The two objectives tug at each other." But, says Fisher, given such basic factors as world population growth, "the fact is, we're going to have to become much more productive, and we need to do that in a sustainable way."[45]

Marketoid

Ninety-one percent of Canada's 2010 Best Employers report that the environment is one of their top drivers of social corporate responsibility.

What is the role of marketing in sustainability efforts? According to Fisher, "The folks we hire in marketing have a real interest in marketing around sustainability. Our public affairs and communications people are very involved. . . . No matter where you want to work, you can find an opportunity around sustainability."[46] Other sustainability and social responsibility officers agree that sustainability must permeate the firm's corporate strategy from the top down, so all areas in the firm can align their

SOLVING AN ETHICAL CONTROVERSY — Airport Scanners Show All Your Bumps and Curves

FULL-body scanners, fairly common in European and U.S. airports and train stations, have now come into wide use at security checkpoints in many Canadian airports. At a cost of about $250 000 each, the machines blur facial images and project chalk-like outlines of the body to reveal plastic or chemical explosives and weapons hidden in clothing or on the body that would elude a metal detector.

There are 41 full-body scanners in use in Canadian airports, mostly for secondary screening when a passenger sets off a metal detector. No one argues that airline travel should not be as safe as airlines and governments can possibly make it. How to do so, however, is a question that brings security and privacy needs into apparent conflict for some.

Can governments encourage public support of full-body scans without endangering privacy rights?

PRO

1. Scanning requires only that passengers stand in the screening room, fully clothed, for about five seconds, and the machines can neither store images nor print them.
2. Because of the way tasks are assigned at screening locations, no security officer is able to both view the image and interact with the passenger.

CON

1. Full-body scans are revealing, invasive, and undignified.
2. In addition to privacy concerns, scanning is a reactive move terrorists will quickly find their way around, and one that wastes millions of dollars better spent on preventive measures like better intelligence.

Where do you stand: pro or con?

Source: Transport Canada, "Full Body Scanners at Major Canadian Airports," http://www.tc.gc.ca/eng/mediaroom/backgrounders-menu-6248.htm, May 14, 2011.

---

environmental goals in the same direction for the greatest effectiveness. As Apple's sustainability report acknowledges, "switching off lights and recycling office waste aren't enough."[47]

Firms stand to gain needed credibility from their efforts to protect the environment by reducing waste and pollution. Not only has the recent economic downturn made it important for them to cut waste and cost as never before, including the costs of damage to the environment, but consumers now are more aware of the real need for such drives—and ready to support them. According to a Canadian group called Network for Business Sustainability, "customers are typically willing to pay 10 percent [premium] for sustainable products."[48] Some firms that have recently won praise for their efforts to eliminate dangerous or polluting ingredients in their products include Nokia and Sony Ericsson. Nokia, for instance, offers a recycling program with "takeback service" in 85 countries. "As we take our environmental responsibilities very seriously, it is of course rewarding to see our environmental efforts acknowledged in various rankings," said Nokia's head of sustainability. The environmental advocacy group Greenpeace recently gave high marks to Apple, which it has criticized in the past. "Apple beat all the other brands in removing polyvinyl chloride (PVC) and brominated flame retardants (BFRs) from all its products almost two years ahead of HP and the rest of the PC sector," the organization's report said. "Apple has demonstrated that there are no technical barriers to substituting PVC and BFRs with safer alternatives in smartphones, iPods, PCs, and TVs."[49]

assessment check 8

8.1 Define *ethics*.

8.2 What is *social responsibility*?

8.3 What are *sustainable products*?

Strategic Implications

Unprecedented opportunities have emerged from electronic commerce and computer technologies in business today. These advances and innovations have allowed organizations to reach new markets, reduce selling and marketing costs, and enhance their relationships with customers and suppliers. Thanks to the Internet and social media tools, business has grown into a global market.

Both profit-seeking and not-for-profit organizations must broaden the scope of their activities to prevent myopic results in their enterprises. If they fail to do so, they lose out on promising opportunities.

Marketers must constantly look for ways to create loyal customers and build long-term relationships with those customers, often on a one-to-one basis. They must be able to anticipate customer needs and satisfy them with innovative goods and services. They must be able to do this faster and better than the competition. And they must conduct their business according to the highest ethical and sustainability standards.   ◆◆◆

REVIEW OF CHAPTER OBJECTIVES

① **Define *marketing*, explain how it creates utility, and describe its role in the global marketplace.**

Marketing is an organizational function and a set of processes for creating, communicating, and delivering value to customers and for managing customer relationships in ways that benefit the organization and its stakeholders. Utility is the want-satisfying power of a good or service. Four basic kinds of utility exist: form, time, place, and ownership. Marketing creates time, place, and ownership utilities. Three factors have forced marketers to embrace a global marketplace: expanded international trade agreements; new technologies that have brought previously isolated nations to the marketplace; and greater interdependence of the world's economies.

② **Contrast marketing activities during the four eras in the history of marketing.**

During the production era, businesspeople believed that quality products would sell themselves. The sales era emphasized convincing people to buy. The marketing concept emerged during the marketing era, in which there was a company-wide focus on consumer orientation with the objective of achieving long-term success. The relationship era focuses on establishing and maintaining relationships between customers and suppliers. Relationship marketing involves long-term, value-added relationships.

③ **Explain the importance of avoiding marketing myopia.**

Marketing myopia is management's failure to recognize a company's scope of business. It focuses marketers too narrowly on products and thus misses potential opportunities to satisfy customers. To avoid it, companies must broadly define their goals so they focus on fulfilling consumer needs.

④ **Describe the characteristics of not-for-profit marketing.**

Not-for-profit organizations operate in both public and private sectors. The biggest distinction between not-for-profits and commercial firms is the bottom line—whether the firm is judged by its profitability levels. Not-for-profit organizations may market to multiple publics. A customer or service user of a not-for-profit organization may have less control over the organization's destiny than do customers of a profit-seeking firm. In addition, resource contributors to not-for-profits may try to exert influence over the organization's activities. Not-for-profits and for-profits may form alliances that effectively promote each other's causes and services.

⑤ Identify and briefly explain each of the five types of nontraditional marketing.

Person marketing focuses on efforts to cultivate the attention, interest, and preferences of a target market toward a celebrity or noted figure. Place marketing attempts to attract visitors, potential residents, and businesses to a particular destination. Cause marketing identifies and markets a social issue, cause, or idea. Event marketing promotes sporting, cultural, charitable, or political activities. Organization marketing attempts to influence others to accept the organization's goals or services and contribute to it in some way.

⑥ Explain the shift from transaction-based marketing to relationship and social marketing.

Relationship marketing represents a dramatic change in the way companies interact with customers. The focus on relationships gives a firm new opportunities to gain a competitive edge by moving customers up a loyalty ladder from new customers to regular purchasers and then to loyal supporters and advocates. Over the long term, this relationship may be translated to the lifetime value of a customer. Interactive technologies and social marketing (via Facebook, Twitter, and the like) allow marketers direct communication with customers, permit more meaningful exchanges, and put the customer in control. Organizations may form partnerships—called *strategic alliances*—to create a competitive advantage. These alliances may involve product development, raising awareness, and other activities.

⑦ Identify the universal functions of marketing.

Marketing is responsible for eight universal functions, divided into three categories: (1) exchange functions (buying and selling); (2) physical distribution (transporting and storing); and (3) facilitating functions (standardization and grading, financing, risk taking, and securing market information).

⑧ Demonstrate the relationship among ethical business practices, social responsibility, sustainability, and marketplace success.

Ethics are moral standards of behaviour expected by a society. Companies that promote ethical behaviour and social responsibility usually produce increased employee loyalty and a better public image. This image often pays off in customer growth, since many buyers want to associate themselves with—and be customers of—such firms. Social responsibility involves marketing philosophies, policies, procedures, and actions whose primary objective is the enhancement of society and the protection of the environment through sustainable products and practices. These actions also generally promote a firm's public image.

 assessment check answers

1.1 Define *marketing* and explain how it creates utility.
Marketing is an organizational function and a set of processes for creating, communicating, and delivering value to customers and for managing customer relationships in ways that benefit the organization and its stakeholders. It creates time, place, and ownership utilities.

1.2 What three factors have forced marketers to embrace a global marketplace?
International agreements are being negotiated in attempts to expand trade among nations. The growth of technology is bringing previously isolated countries into the marketplace. The interdependence of the world's economies is now a reality.

2.1 What is the major distinction between the production era and the sales era?
During the production era, businesspeople believed that quality products would sell themselves. But during the sales era, emphasis was placed on selling—persuading people to buy.

2.2 What is the marketing concept?
The marketing concept is a company-wide consumer orientation with the objective of achieving long-term success.

2.3 Describe the relationship era of marketing.
The relationship era focuses on building long-term, value-added relationships over time with customers and suppliers.

3.1 What is marketing myopia?
Marketing myopia is management's failure to recognize the scope of a company's business.

3.2 Give an example of how a firm can avoid marketing myopia.
A firm can find innovative ways to reach new markets with existing goods and services.

4.1 What is the most obvious distinction between a not-for-profit organization and a commercial organization?
The biggest distinction between for-profit and not-for-profit organizations is the bottom line—whether an organization is judged by its profitability.

4.2 Why do for-profit and not-for-profit organizations sometimes form alliances?

For-profits and not-for-profits may form alliances to promote each other's causes and services. For-profits may do so as part of their social responsibility programs.

5.1 Identify the five major categories of nontraditional marketing.

The five categories of nontraditional marketing are person, place, cause, event, and organization marketing.

5.2 Give an example of a way in which two or more of these categories might overlap.

Overlap can occur in many ways. An organization might use a person to promote its cause or event. Two organizations might use one marketing effort to promote an event and a place—for example, NBC Sports and the National Thoroughbred Racing Association combining to promote the Kentucky Derby at Churchill Downs.

6.1 How does relationship marketing give companies a competitive edge?

Relationship marketing can move customers up a loyalty ladder, generating repeat sales and long-term relationships.

6.2 Why are interactive and social marketing important tools for marketers?

Interactive marketing technologies create direct communication with customers, allow larger exchanges, and put the customer in control.

Social marketing media (Facebook, Twitter, for example) let companies show customers they are listening and will respond quickly.

6.3 What is a strategic alliance?

A strategic alliance is a partnership formed between two organizations to create a competitive advantage.

7.1 Which two marketing functions represent exchange functions?

Buying and selling are exchange functions.

7.2 Which two functions represent physical distribution functions?

Transporting and storing are physical distribution functions.

7.3 Which four functions are facilitating functions?

The facilitating functions are standardization and grading, financing, risk taking, and securing market information.

8.1 Define *ethics*.

Ethics are moral standards of behaviour expected by a society.

8.2 What is *social responsibility*?

Social responsibility involves marketing philosophies, policies, procedures, and actions whose primary objective is the enhancement of society.

8.3 What are *sustainable products*?

Sustainable products are those that can be produced, used, and disposed of with minimal impact on the environment.

MARKETING TERMS YOU NEED TO KNOW

These terms are printed in red in the text. They are defined in the margins of the chapter and in the Glossary that begins on p. G-1.

utility 5	relationship marketing 11	mobile marketing 18
marketing 6	marketing myopia 12	interactive marketing 18
exchange process 8	bottom line 14	social marketing 19
production orientation 8	person marketing 15	buzz marketing 19
sales orientation 9	place marketing 15	strategic alliances 20
seller's market 9	cause marketing 16	exchange functions 21
buyer's market 9	event marketing 16	ethics 22
consumer orientation 9	organization marketing 17	social responsibility 22
marketing concept 9	transaction-based marketing 18	sustainable products 22

PROJECT AND TEAMWORK EXERCISES

1. Consider each of the following firms and describe how the firm's goods and/or services can create different types of utility. If necessary, go online to the company's website to learn more about it. You can do this alone or in a team.
   a. Visa, MasterCard, or American Express; Swiss Chalet, Wendy's, Red Lobster, or another restaurant chain
   b. Flickr or another online digital photo service
   c. Calgary Stampede
   d. Amazon.ca
   e. Sobeys, Real Canadian Superstore, Overwaitea, or another grocery store chain

2. With a classmate, choose a Canadian-based company whose products you think will do well in certain markets overseas. The company can be anything from a music group to a clothing retailer—anything that interests you. Suggestions include Domino's Pizza, Arcade Fire, Molly Maid, or Lululemon Athletica. Then write a plan for how you would target and communicate with overseas markets.

3. Choose a company that interests you from the following list, or select one of your own. Research the company online, through business magazines, or through other sources to learn what seems to be the scope of its business. Write a brief description

of the company's current scope of business. Then describe strategies for avoiding marketing myopia and expanding the company's scope of business over the next 10 years.
   a. General Electric
   b. TD Canada Trust
   c. Delta Hotels and Resorts
   d. Research in Motion (RIM)
   e. Canadian Tire

4. With a classmate, choose one of the following not-for-profit organizations. Then come up with a for-profit firm with which you think your organization could form a strategic alliance. Create a presentation—an ad, a poster, or the like—illustrating and promoting the partnership.
   a. Canadian Cancer Society
   b. Make-A-Wish Foundation of Canada
   c. Habitat for Humanity Canada
   d. Save the Children Canada
   e. Humane Society of Canada

5. Research one of the following electronics companies, or another of your choosing, and study its efforts to improve the sustainability of its products, particularly their safe disposal. What does the company do well in this area? What could it do better?
   a. Toshiba
   b. Nintendo
   c. Microsoft
   d. Fujitsu
   e. Samsung

CRITICAL-THINKING EXERCISES

1. How does an organization create a customer?
2. How can marketers use interactive and social marketing to convert needs to wants and ultimately build long-term relationships with customers?
3. Why is utility such an important feature of marketing?
4. What benefits—monetary and nonmonetary—do social responsibility programs bring to a business?
5. Why is determining the lifetime value of a customer an important analysis for a company to make?
6. Why is it important for a firm to establish high ethical standards for sustainability? What role do you think marketers play in implementing these standards?

ETHICS EXERCISE

You are having lunch with a friend who works for an advertising agency that competes with yours. Suddenly he remembers an errand he has to run before returning to work, and he rushes off with a hasty goodbye after giving you some money to cover his lunch. As you gather your things to leave a few minutes later, you realize your friend left his notebook computer on the table, open to a report about a client. Your company is very interested in doing some work for this client in the future.

1. Would you take a quick look at the report before you return it to your friend? Why or why not?
2. Would you share any information in the report with anyone in your office? Why or why not?
3. When you return the notebook to your friend, would you mention the contents and offer your own commentary on them? Why or why not?

INTERNET EXERCISES

1. **Exploring the CMA's website.** The Canadian Marketing Association's website contains lots of useful and interesting information for students and others. One section is devoted to careers. Visit the CMA's website (www.the-cma.org). Answer the following questions:
   a. Describe the Canadian Marketing Association. What is its purpose?
   b. Click on "Find a Job" to visit *marketing-jobs.ca.* Find three marketing jobs you think you would like. What makes these jobs attractive to you?
   c. Click on "Student Membership." (See Membership Information on right side of page.) What are the benefits of having a student membership?

2. **Event marketing.** The Westminster Kennel Club runs one of the largest and most famous dog shows in the world. Review its website (www.westminsterkennelclub.org) and prepare a brief report relating what you learned to the material on event marketing in the chapter. Make sure to describe sponsor tie-ins and other joint marketing efforts.

3. **Sustainability.** Johnson & Johnson engages in a major effort to incorporate sustainability into its wide-ranging business activities. Visit the website listed here (www.jnj.com/connect/caring/environment-protection) and read about the firm's recent activities. How does Johnson & Johnson promote sustainability? What are some specific examples?

Note: Internet web addresses change frequently. If you don't find the exact sites listed, you may need to access the organization's or company's home page and search from there or use a search engine such as Google.

CASE 1.1

Reinventing IBM

IBM's successful management of globalization and technological change amounts to a reinvention of the company known as "Big Blue." A firm whose original name was International Business Machines and that relied nearly exclusively on computer manufacturing is now turning to software and services to provide it with a competitive edge in today's marketplace. To increase its margins, IBM first reduced its costs, in part by hiring lower-cost labour in India to run its data centres and to help its customers maintain their IBM software products. Big Blue also addressed flattening profits in its service businesses by automating as many tasks as possible. Its senior vice-president for global business services says, "The goal is to replace a lot of labour but to do it with software, not . . . with lower-cost labour."

The firm is also looking for profits in the higher-margin software sphere. "Software had to play a bigger role," says CEO Samuel Palmisano. "Then we could offset the transition in services." To achieve its goals, IBM bought more than 50 smaller software and service companies that specialized in security, data management, and e-commerce. IBM Canada employs the largest team of software developers outside the United States. Offices in Victoria, Vancouver, Edmonton, London, Markham, Ottawa, and Montreal are collectively known as the IBM Canada Lab, where software solutions are developed for customers around the world. "Software is now the largest provider of IBM profit, and our most stable source of growth," says the company's chief financial officer.

Higher-end services are proving profitable for IBM in new fields like energy management and conservation, fraud detection, traffic management using variable-pricing models, personalized medicine based on genetics, and Internet-based supercomputing known as *cloud computing*, which many believe is the next step in information technology. Blue Cloud, as IBM's supercomputing initiative is known, relies on open-source programming but will ultimately help sell more IBM software, hardware, and services that assist corporate clients to become more efficient, reduce power usage, and save costs. IBM Canada's manufacturing plant

in Bromont, Quebec, is the company's largest semiconductor packaging and test facility. Besides IBM products, this plant also performs custom assembly and testing for many original equipment manufacturers (OEMs). In total, IBM Canada exports nearly $2 billion annually in hardware, software, and services, making it one of Canada's largest exporters.

IBM is also tackling social media, testing in-house versions of networking and blogging tools like Facebook and Twitter. It currently uses them to connect and strengthen links among its 400 000 far-flung employees and work teams, but it also hopes they will attract bright new hires. And farther down the line, IBM hopes products like its new Atlas Connections, which digests email and chat content to help users build networks of contacts, will become industry-leading innovations that also become profitable. The company maintains that Atlas Connections is already "the fastest-growing software product in IBM history."

And Big Blue still hopes to challenge Microsoft in the office software arena. It's joined forces with Google and Sun Microsystems to offer free alternatives to Microsoft's popular Word, Excel, and PowerPoint programs.

Questions for Critical Thinking

1. How do IBM's plans for its goods and services meet the definition of marketing? How do you think they help create utility?
2. IBM has linked partnerships with Google and Sun Microsystems. What other partnerships do you think might be useful to its future plans? Why?

Sources: Company website, "IBM: Helping Canada and the World Work Better," http://www.ibm.com/ibm/ca/en/, May 13, 2011; "IBM Social Computing Guidelines," http://www.ibm.com, April 16, 2009; Stephen Baker, "Big Blue Embraces Social Media," *Business Week*, http://www.businessweek.com, May 22, 2008; Steve Lohr, "IBM to Push 'Cloud Computing,' Using Data from Afar," *The New York Times*, http://www.nytimes.com, November 15, 2007; Steve Lohr, "IBM to Offer Office Software Free in Challenge to Microsoft's Line," *The New York Times*, http://www.nytimes.com, September 18, 2007; Steve Lohr, "IBM Showing That Giants Can Be Nimble," *The New York Times*, http://www.nytimes.com, July 18, 2007.

CASE 1.2

Hewlett-Packard Reduces, Reuses, Recycles

Hewlett-Packard (HP), the world's largest information technology (IT) company, was founded in 1939 and ranks among the top 10 of the Fortune 500. HP operates in more than 170 countries and earned revenues of more than $126 billion in 2010. Its products range from small, hand-held devices to giant supercomputers and fall into three main business

groups: Personal Systems, which includes PCs, workstations, and mobile computing devices; Enterprise Business, including storage devices, servers, and business software; and Imaging and Printing, encompassing inkjet and laser printers, commercial printing services, and printing supplies.

For its leadership role in reporting and reducing its greenhouse-gas emissions, HP was recently named the "Greenest Big Company in America" by *Newsweek* magazine. In 2010, Mediacorp placed HP Canada on its list of Canada's Greenest Employers; this was the second consecutive year HP Canada made the list. HP has long been focused on contributing to each country and community in which it operates by reducing waste, raising standards among its global suppliers, and easing access to information technology around the world. Seeing itself as a "global steward," the firm recycles HP ink cartridges for free and accepts any brand of computer hardware and rechargeable batteries for recycling in the United States and Canada. In partnership with the National Cristina Foundation in the United States, HP also accepts used computer equipment for donation, as well as equipment for trade-in and resale, to reduce electronic waste.

"Recycling technology equipment is a win–win situation for everybody," HP believes. "It is good for the planet and good for business." In one recent year, the firm recycled more than 67 000 tonnes of hardware and print cartridges around the world, and it hopes soon to have recycled more than 800 000 tonnes of electronic products and supplies. The company estimates that in 2010, it has used more than 4.7 million kilograms of recycled plastic in the manufacture of its consumer printers. HP Canada has engaged retailers and provincial governments across the country to implement end-of-life electronics programs to divert waste electronics from landfill sites. As a result, more than 100 000 tonnes of waste electronics have been diverted from Canadian landfill sites.

HP's scientists estimate that businesses' use of technology consumes more than 350 million tonnes of coal each year, emitting more than twice that amount in the form of carbon dioxide waste. "We cannot continue to consume energy at our current rates," the company's website says. As part of its Design for the Environment strategy, HP's corporate phones and laptops use less energy thanks to displays that use ambient light, and soon the firm hopes to reduce the energy consumption and greenhouse-gas emissions of all its operations and products to 40 percent below their 2005 levels. It has already met its 2010 goal to reduce them to 25 percent below 2005 levels, and it is moving forward with plans to invest in renewable energy sources and to make it even easier to recycle every one of its products. The company opened a new data centre in Wynyard, U.K., in 2010 that is expected to reduce energy consumption by 40 percent, cut greenhouse gas emissions, and

save upwards of $15 million annually. Leading-edge energy savings devices are also incorporated in its Canadian head office in Mississauga, Ontario. A building automation system monitors conditions inside the building and adjusts the heating and cooling systems to best conserve energy. In most offices, sensor-controlled lights turn off automatically when there is no motion detected after about 20 minutes. Outside, a "smart" lawn irrigation system detects weather conditions and will not operate if rain is detected.

But HP isn't only cleaning up its own act; it's helping its customers too. It recently announced that its newest ProBook laptop models include a dedicated hardware circuit and "Power Assistant" software that can estimate and display the computers' energy use over time. With this feature, users can check bar charts or pie charts of energy use and reduce it, by customizing their power settings to reduce screen brightness, turn off certain networking features, run the processor at a lower speed, or squeeze out longer battery life. IT administrators can even manage a whole network of computers with Power Assistant, customizing the machines to go into energy-saving hibernate mode sooner, for instance. Future laptops and desktops from HP will boast the same innovative feature. "The way we see it," says HP, "environmental responsibility and business success go hand in hand.

Questions for Critical Thinking

1. What kind(s) of marketing utility do you think Hewlett-Packard's sustainability efforts provide for its customers? Are there any downsides to these programs?

2. HP has entered a partnership with the National Cristina Foundation in the United States to accept used computer equipment for donation. What other partners, or types of partners, might help the company achieve its sustainability goals in the future?

Sources: Company websites, "Changing the Equation" and "HP Environmental Citizenship Milestones," http://www.hp.com/canada/corporate/hp_info/environment/index.html, May 13, 2011; "Canadian Companion to the Global Citizenship Report," http://www.hp.com/canada/corporate/hp_info/environment/news/awards.html, May 13, 2011; http://www.hp.com, February 23, 2010; "HP and the Environment," DestinationGreenIt, http://www.destinationgreenit.com, November 16, 2009; Agam Shah, "HP Green Laptops to Cut Power Usage," TechWorld, http://news.techworld.com, October 13, 2009; "Hewlett-Packard Sets New GHG Emission Reduction Target," EcoSeed, http://www.ecoseed.org, September 22, 2009; Daniel McGinn, "The Greenest Big Companies in America," *Newsweek*, http://www.newsweek.com, September 21, 2009.

chapter 2

Strategic Planning in Contemporary Marketing

COURTESY OF APEXA LIFE SCIENCES INC.

CHAPTER OBJECTIVES

1. Distinguish between strategic planning and tactical planning.

2. Explain how marketing plans differ at various levels in an organization.

3. Identify the steps in the marketing planning process.

4. Describe successful planning tools and techniques, including Porter's Five Forces model, first and second mover strategies, SWOT analysis, and the strategic window.

5. Identify the basic elements of a marketing strategy.

6. Describe the environmental characteristics that influence strategic decisions.

7. Describe the methods for marketing planning, including business portfolio analysis, the BCG market share/market growth matrix, and the strategic growth opportunity matrix.

AFEXA LIFE SCIENCES: ITS DOWNS AND UPS

In 1996, CV Technologies (CVT) had a virtually unknown product: COLD-FX, a ginseng-derived remedy for the common cold and flu. It was sold in only a few health food stores until the Edmonton Oilers, who were using it, agreed to take part in a research study of the product's effectiveness. Unfortunately, by 2003 CVT was almost bankrupt—revenue was a mere $1.5 million, with a loss of $1.8 million—and had to cut back operations severely.

Although things looked bleak, CVT hired a public relations professional. As a result, publicity about the product proliferated. Sales grew rapidly, and the company outsourced some manufacturing to meet demand. In 2004, Don Cherry of *Hockey Night in Canada* became a celebrity spokesperson, and comedian Rick Mercer plugged the product on the *Rick Mercer Report*. Participating retail merchants increased from 1000 to 4000, and sales grew to $6.4 million. Marketing expenses were $1.3 million. The company made a small profit and described 2004 as its "breakout year."

Favourable publicity continued throughout 2005. CVT won an entrepreneur of the year award and was chosen as one of the 50 fastest-growing companies in Canada. CVT opened a Toronto sales and marketing office and entered the Quebec market, where it benefited from an association with the Montreal Canadiens. Distribution grew and sales quintupled.

In 2006, CVT started to focus on the U.S. market, as customers prepared for the 2006 cold and flu season. But U.S. sales were very disappointing, and many U.S. retailers returned inventory. Sales increased to $41.4 million, but marketing costs were

$8.3 million. Profit was a mere $639 thousand. In 2007, U.S. sales were disappointing. Many U.S. retailers returned inventory. Marketing expenses were $16.4 million, including $10.5 million to support the U.S. launch. CVT lost $9.8 million. In 2008, the company refocused on Canada, creating a national sales organization and developing stronger retailer relationships. Revenue increased, partly thanks to a 6 percent price hike, but this was offset somewhat by new promotional sales programs. Sales in the United States nearly doubled to $2.1 million despite decreased marketing effort there. Return of inventory from the United States was repackaged for sale in Canada, but profit was still reasonable: $4.6 million.

In 2009, CVT changed its name to Afexa Life Sciences Inc., expanded sales to Hong Kong and Macau, and introduced a new product: IMMUNITY-FX, a year-round daily immune booster. Afexa announced a sponsorship agreement with the Vancouver Organizing Committee for the 2010 Winter Olympics. Revenue was marginally down as retailers reduced inventory in the face of economic uncertainty. Profits, however, decreased to only $1.3 million, due to increased sales, administration, and R&D costs.

Sales grew in 2010 to $34.4 million, $8.5 million higher than the same period

in 2009 (based on only six months of sales data as the company moved its year end from September to March). Management attributed the increase to public concern about a pending flu pandemic. Earnings improved to $2.8 million for the six-month period. Revenue for 2011 showed a sharp decline to $39.6 million, and Afexa had a loss of nearly a million dollars. Retailers were over-stocked from the previous year and there was less concern about a flu pandemic.

Where does Afexa go from here? There is room for considerable growth. First, while COLD-FX is the market share leader in natural cold remedies, household penetration in Canada is still low. Clinical trials are underway on a special formulation of COLD-FX for pediatric use, as well as products related to cancer, diabetes, cholesterol management, and other conditions. In the United States, Afexa is considering seeking approval for COLD-FX as a botanical drug, a new category defined by the U.S. Food and Drug Administration. If successful, Afexa would be able to make expanded therapeutic health claims and better position itself in that market. Afexa is exploring regulatory approval for COLD-FX in China and is assessing market opportunities in Japan and Europe.[1]

---

connecting with customers

Afexa Life Sciences connects with customers by effectively combining traditional marketing media—radio and television ads, and point-of-purchase displays—with newer promotion techniques: public relations, celebrity endorsements, and word-of-mouth promotion. Its attention to quality and the strong endorsements it gets from athletes, doctors, and pharmacists have created awareness and credibility in all markets where its products are sold.

Chapter Overview

- "We have many products at various stages of development. How should we prioritize them for research and development? We also have potential to enter many markets around the world. Where are we likely to be most successful?"

- "We have fewer customers eating at our restaurant on weekends. Should we revamp our menu? Lower our prices? Use special promotions? Update the dining room decor?"

- "Recent marketing research shows we are not reaching our customer target—consumers in their early to mid-20s. Should we consider another advertising agency?"

MARKETERS face strategic questions every day—planning strategy is a critical part of the job. The marketplace changes continually in response to changes in consumer tastes and expectations, technological developments, competitors' actions, economic trends, and political and legal events, as well as product innovations and pressures from suppliers and distributors. Although the causes of these changes often lie outside a marketer's control, effective planning can anticipate many of the changes.

When the price of gas and jet fuel soared recently, travellers opted to stay closer to home—taking "staycations" instead of booking vacations to exotic, faraway places. This represents an opportunity for places such as Cavendish Beach, Prince Edward Island, and Banff, Alberta. Local water parks and amusement parks, nearby lakes, indoor playgrounds or gyms, and restaurants can market themselves as potential alternatives. Any destination that promotes itself to potential vacationers within a short drive could find itself adding up the profits.

This chapter provides an important foundation for analyzing all aspects of marketing by demonstrating the importance of gathering reliable information to create an effective plan. These activities provide a structure for a firm to use its unique strengths. Marketing planning identifies the markets a company can best serve as well as the most appropriate mix of approaches to satisfy the customers in those markets. While this chapter focuses on planning, we will examine in greater detail the task of marketing research and decision making in Chapter 7.   ◆◆◆

MARKETING PLANNING: THE BASIS FOR STRATEGY AND TACTICS

planning Process of anticipating future events and conditions and of determining the best way to achieve organizational goals.

Everyone plans. We plan which courses we want to take, which movie we want to see, and which outfit to wear to a party. We plan where we want to live and what career we want to pursue. Marketers engage in planning as well. **Planning** is the process of anticipating future events and conditions and of determining the best way to achieve organizational objectives. Of course, before marketing planning can even begin, an organization must define its objectives. Planning is a continuous process that includes identifying objectives and then determining the actions through which a firm can attain those objectives. The planning process creates a blueprint for marketers, executives, production staff, and everyone else in the organization to follow for achieving organizational objectives. It also defines checkpoints so that people within the organization can compare actual performance with expectations to indicate whether current activities are moving the organization toward its objectives.

Planning is important for both large and small companies. For years, Sir Richard Branson—founder of the airline Virgin Galactic—dreamed of launching a spaceship designed for commercial travel. The dream required complex design and engineering plans, including the launch of prototypes and rigorous rounds of safety testing. After one of the prototypes became the first privately owned, manned craft to reach space, the company's engineers went to work on a similar craft designed for commercial use, called SpaceShipTwo. Meanwhile, the idea of space travel has been marketed to wealthy clients, 430 of whom have either made a deposit or paid the full $200 000 price to be among

Galactic founder Sir Richard Branson has been looking toward commercial space travel for years. His planning has begun to pay off. After the successful launch of a prototype, the company is now working on a craft designed for commercial use.

the first in line for the historic trip. If the idea catches on, Branson and Virgin Galactic will have positioned themselves strategically to become the first—and possibly the only—firm to offer commercial space travel for the near future.[2] Here on earth—and at the other end of the size spectrum—Shuttleworth, a small firm that manufactures conveyors, had to re-evaluate its planning as its core business in electronics began to shrink. The company refocused its efforts on designing and building solar panel conveyors. Its new products have won acclaim, new customers, and a revitalized business.[3]

Marketing planning—implementing planning activities devoted to achieving marketing objectives—establishes the basis for any marketing strategy. Product lines, pricing decisions, selection of appropriate distribution channels, and decisions relating to promotional campaigns all depend on plans formulated within the marketing organization. In today's boundaryless organizations, many planning activities take place over the Internet with *virtual conferences*—teleconferences with computer interfaces. These conferences represent a new way to build relationships among people who are in different geographic locations. The "Career Readiness" feature describes how effectively these meetings can work.

An important trend in marketing planning centres on relationship marketing, which is a firm's effort at developing long-term, cost-effective links with individual customers and suppliers for mutual benefit. Good relationships with customers can arm a firm with vital strategic weapons, and that's as true in business-to-business industries as anywhere else.

Many companies now include relationship-building goals and strategies in their plans. Relationship marketers frequently maintain databases to track customer preferences. These marketers may also manipulate product spreadsheets to answer what-if questions related to prices and marketing performance. At Procter & Gamble, the inspiration for new or better products often comes from customers themselves. The company operates in more than 150 countries with 138 000 employees, many of whom serve as the eyes and ears of the firm. Some P&G executives and marketers actually spend time in the homes of consumers, observing how they cook and eat meals, when they play, and where they shop. Other employees are trained simply to have conversations with friends and family about their lifestyles and the goods or services they use. All of this interaction helps build relationships, and the information helps develop products.[4]

Marketoid

Among the first to-be-passengers on Virgin Galactic will be physicist Stephen Hawking and actor-comedian Russell Brand, who received a trip as a birthday present from his wife, Katie Perry.

marketing planning
Implementing planning activities devoted to achieving marketing objectives.

Going Across the Country or Around the World through Virtual Meetings

MANY companies now encourage virtual meetings to save time and travel costs. The recent economic downturn made virtual meetings not just popular but essential. Virtual meetings offer the opportunity for people to gather from across the country or around the world, any time of day or night. While this may seem like the ideal way to bring people together, there can be some pitfalls. Holding a conference by phone or Internet can be most effective if you follow these guidelines:

- Schedule the meeting in advance, and be sure everyone is available to sign on at the appointed time and remind participants of the time and duration of the meeting ahead of time.
- Prepare for the conference just as you would for an in-person meeting. Set goals for the meeting. Circulate an agenda, including your contact information. Have all your facts and figures in front of you.
- Begin the meeting with a quick introduction or reintroduction of all participants and identify the goals. Request that

anyone who needs to leave the conversation because of prior commitments announce when she or he is doing so.
- If your meeting doesn't involve video, state your name, such as "This is Emma," at the beginning of each time you speak. Speak clearly and slowly. Ask for agreement or disagreement from others, one by one.
- Do not engage in other tasks during the conference, regardless of whether other participants can see you. For example, don't read a memo or check your email during the meeting. Keep your full attention on the conference at hand.
- At the conclusion of the conference, designate someone to prepare minutes highlighting discussion points of the meeting and any conclusions, and email them to all participants.

Sources: Kate Harper, "Virtual Meetings That Work," *Kate Harper Coaching*, http://www.kateharper.com, February 4, 2010; "Virtual Meeting Etiquette," *HR.com*, http://www.hr.com, February 4, 2010; Cheryl Waters Likins, "The Best Practices for Facilitation of Virtual Meetings," eHow, http://www.ehow.com; "Virtual Meeting: Effective Meetings Enabled by Technology," *Persuasive Speeches Now*, http://www.persuasive-speechesnow.com, January 12, 2010.

STRATEGIC PLANNING VERSUS TACTICAL PLANNING

(1) Distinguish between strategic planning and tactical planning.

strategic planning
Process of determining an organization's primary objectives and adopting courses of action that will achieve these objectives.

tactical planning
Planning that guides the implementation of activities specified in the strategic plan.

Planning is often classified on the basis of its scope or breadth. Some extremely broad plans focus on long-range organizational objectives that will significantly affect the firm for five or more years. Other more targeted plans cover the objectives of individual business units over shorter periods.

Strategic planning can be defined as the process of determining an organization's primary objectives and then adopting courses of action that will eventually achieve these objectives. This process includes, of course, allocation of necessary resources. The word *strategy* dates back to a Greek term meaning "the general's art." Strategic planning has a critical impact on a firm's destiny because it provides long-term direction for its decision makers.

Strategic planning is complemented by **tactical planning**, which guides the implementation of activities specified in the strategic plan. Unlike strategic plans, tactical plans typically address shorter-term actions that focus on current and near-future activities that a firm must complete to implement its larger strategies. Sometimes tactical planning requires swift decision making and actions. Although Toyota's long-range strategic planning involves maintaining its status as the number-one automaker in the world, when the firm was faced with growing reports of stuck accelerators, its officials had to devise and implement quick tactics. Toyota recalled more than 12 million vehicles worldwide and offered a free repair on each vehicle.[5] Then Toyota had to work to regain the trust of its customers and restore its reputation for quality.

assessment check 1

1.1 Define *planning*.

1.2 Give an example of strategic planning and tactical planning.

PLANNING AT DIFFERENT ORGANIZATIONAL LEVELS

(2) Explain how marketing plans differ at various levels in an organization.

Planning is a major responsibility for every manager, so managers at all organizational levels devote portions of their workdays to planning. Top management—boards of directors, chief executive officers (CEOs), chief operating officers (COOs), and functional vice presidents, such as chief marketing officers—spend greater proportions of their time engaged in planning than do middle-level and supervisory-level managers. Also, top managers usually focus their planning on long-range strategic issues. In contrast, middle-level managers—such as advertising executives, regional sales managers, and marketing research directors—tend to focus on operational planning, which includes creating and implementing tactical plans for their own units. Supervisors often develop specific programs to meet goals in their areas of responsibility. Table 2.1 summarizes the types of planning undertaken at various organizational levels.

When it is most effective, the planning process includes input from a wide range of sources: employees, suppliers, and customers. Some marketing experts advocate developing a network of "influencers"—people who have influence over other people's opinions through authority, visibility, or expertise—to provide input and spread the word about company plans and products. According to a recent survey, 66 percent of responding marketers said that they plan to invest more heavily in social media marketing in the coming year, indicating that this method of communicating with potential customers is gaining rapidly in popularity.[6]

TOYOTA
moving forward

A temporary pause. To put you first.

Why we've temporarily stopped some of our plants:

As you may have heard, in rare cases, sticking accelerator pedals have occurred in some of our vehicles. We believe we are close to announcing an effective remedy. And we've temporarily halted production at some of our North American plants to focus on the vehicles we've recalled. Why have we taken this unprecedented action? Because it's the right thing to do for our customers.

To find out if your Toyota is affected and to get the very latest information about the recall, please visit:

toyota.com

©2010 Toyota Motor Sales, U.S.A., Inc.

Toyota Customer Experience Center
1-800-331-4331

Tactical planning can require swift decision making and actions. When Toyota was faced with growing reports of stuck accelerators, officials had to act quickly, recalling more than 2.3 million vehicles.

assessment check 2

2.1 How do marketing plans differ at different levels of the organization?

2.2 Why is it important to get input from others when planning?

table 2.1   **Planning at Different Managerial Levels**

	MANAGEMENT LEVEL	TYPES OF PLANNING EMPHASIZED AT THIS LEVEL	EXAMPLES
Top Management	Board of directors Chief executive officer (CEO) Chief operating officer (COO) Divisional vice presidents	Strategic planning	Organization-wide objectives; fundamental strategies; long-term plans; total budget
Middle Management	General sales manager Business unit manager Director of marketing research	Tactical planning	Quarterly and semi-annual plans; divisional budgets; divisional policies and procedures
Supervisory Management	District sales manager Supervisor—telemarketing office	Operational planning	Daily and weekly plans; unit budgets; departmental rules and procedures

Green Bags Outnumber Canadians

CANADIANS are among the world's most environmentally conscious consumers. While this might not have been readily apparent at the cash register during the recent recession, there is mounting evidence that environmentally responsible businesses will become increasingly favoured. Loblaw—Canada's largest grocery retailer—already claims to have sold more than 35 million reusable bags, more than the population of Canada. Millions of similar bags have been sold by other Canadian retailers, including grocery competitor Sobeys and Canadian Tire. These bags are a visible manifestation of Canadians' environmental stewardship. As a result of reusable bags—and a small fee for the plastic alternative—Loblaw claims to have diverted 2.5 billion plastic bags from Canadian landfills.

By surveying its own customers, Walmart found that 57 percent had environmental concerns. Walmart has become a business leader in environmental sustainability and has even developed its Packaging Scorecard, which it uses to help focus its suppliers on sustainability. Procter & Gamble (P&G), a major supplier to Walmart and the world's best-known consumer packaged goods company, is continuing to make improvements to the products it manufactures. P&G began introducing concentrated liquid detergents in the 1990s, and, subsequently, Walmart decided to sell only concentrated liquid detergents in its stores. In 2011, P&G began introducing compacted powder laundry detergents in a number of its main brands such as Tide and Cheer. Improvements to the granules' efficiency—with improved formulation to ensure similar or better performance—has allowed powder volume to be reduced by 33 percent—following earlier improvements that have already reduced volumes by 74 percent. Compaction improvements reduce packaging needs; save freight, handling, and storage costs; and also require less water and energy during manufacturing.

As consumers continue to focus retailers and manufacturers on environmental sustainability, retailers and manufacturers will continue to create awareness of its importance among consumers. Eventually, there will be a tipping point, and those marketers who are best prepared will have a competitive advantage.

Sources: Carly Weeks, "Bag Woes," *The Globe and Mail,* January 10, 2011, p. L1; Rebecca Coons, "P&G to Compact Powder Detergents Sold in North America," *Chemical Week,* September 13, 2010, p. 11; Erica Orange, "From Eco-Friendly to Eco-Intelligent," *The Futurist,* September–October 2010, pp. 28–32; Loblaw Companies 2010 Annual Report, http://www.loblaw.com, March 23, 2011.

---

③ **Identify the steps in the marketing planning process.**

STEPS IN THE MARKETING PLANNING PROCESS

The marketing planning process begins at the corporate level with the definition of a firm's mission. It then determines its objectives, assesses its resources, and evaluates environmental risks and opportunities. Guided by this information, marketers within each business unit then formulate a marketing strategy, implement the strategy through operating plans, and gather feedback to monitor and adapt strategies when necessary. Figure 2.1 shows the basic steps in the process.

figure 2.1

The Marketing Planning Process

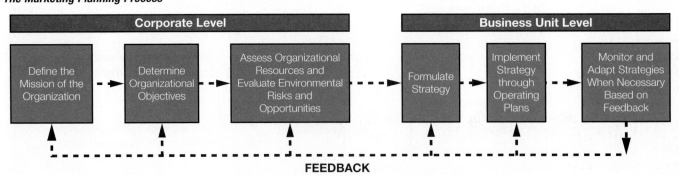

DEFINING THE ORGANIZATION'S MISSION AND OBJECTIVES

The planning process begins with activities to define the firm's **mission**, the essential purpose that differentiates the company from others. The mission statement specifies the organization's overall goals and operational scope and provides general guidelines for future management actions. Adjustments in this statement reflect changing business environments and management philosophies.

Although business writer Peter Drucker cautioned that an effective mission statement should be brief enough "to fit on a T-shirt," organizations typically define themselves with slightly longer statements. A statement may be lengthy and formal or brief and informal. Here are several examples:

- Sephora: "The beauty authority."
- Microsoft Office: "Real life tools."
- Infiniti: "Inspired performance."
- IBM: "Welcome to the decade of smart."
- Tim Hortons: "Always fresh. Always."

An organization lays out its basic objectives, or goals, in its complete mission statement. These objectives in turn guide development of supporting marketing objectives and plans. Soundly conceived objectives should state specific intentions such as the following:

- Generate a 15 percent profit over the next 24 months.
- Reduce waste by 20 percent.
- Add 25 new outlets within the next year.
- Improve 5 products within the next 6 months.
- Enter the Chinese market by 2015.
- Cut manufacturing costs by 10 percent.

ASSESSING ORGANIZATIONAL RESOURCES AND EVALUATING ENVIRONMENTAL RISKS AND OPPORTUNITIES

The third step of the marketing planning process involves an assessment of an organization's strengths, weaknesses, and available opportunities. Organizational resources include the capabilities of the firm's production, marketing, finance, technology, and employees. An organization's planners pinpoint its strengths and weaknesses. Strengths help them to set objectives, develop plans for meeting those objectives, and take advantage of marketing opportunities.

Chapter 3 will discuss environmental factors that affect marketing opportunities. Environmental effects can emerge both from within the organization and from the external environment. For example, social media have transformed interpersonal communications as well as communications between companies and their customers.

FORMULATING, IMPLEMENTING, AND MONITORING A MARKETING STRATEGY

Once a firm's marketers figure out their company's best opportunities, they can develop a marketing plan designed to meet the overall objectives. A good marketing plan revolves around an efficient, flexible, and adaptable marketing strategy.

A **marketing strategy** is an overall, company-wide program for selecting a particular target market and then satisfying consumers in that market through a careful blending of the elements of the marketing mix—product, distribution, promotion, and price—each of which is a subset of the overall marketing strategy.

In the two final steps of the planning process, marketers put the marketing strategy into action; then they monitor performance to ensure that objectives are being achieved. Sometimes strategies need to be modified if the product's or company's actual performance is not in line with expected results. Frito-Lay introduced a new biodegradable bag for several of its Sun Chips brand flavours. The company boasted

mission Essential purpose that differentiates one company from others.

Marketoid

The first Tim Hortons opened in Hamilton, Ontario, in 1964. The menu had two items: coffee and doughnuts. The selection of doughnuts highlighted two original creations: the Apple Fritter and the Dutchie, both still popular today.

marketing strategy Overall company-wide program for selecting a particular target market and then satisfying consumers in that market through the marketing mix.

SOLVING AN ETHICAL CONTROVERSY

Tiger Woods Drives His Career into the Rough

HIRING celebrities to endorse a line of products is common practice among marketers. When the celebrity is a popular entertainer or successful athlete, marketers are betting their products will enjoy the same popularity and success. But when the celebrity falls from grace—as Tiger Woods did when the scandal about his personal life made the news—the product sales can land in the weeds. Woods, who hid from the press as soon as the story broke, was accustomed to earning nearly $110 million in endorsements from companies including Nike, Gillette, AT&T, Accenture, and PepsiCo. Most of these sponsors subsequently scratched Woods from their roster.

The Tiger Woods story created enough turmoil that marketers are now re-evaluating their relationships with celebrities. "I don't think there's any question, at least in the short term, that advertisers will be more careful" about hiring athletes and other stars to endorse their products, observes Irving Rein, a professor at Northwestern University. In addition, marketers will likely insist on contract clauses or written statements prohibiting certain behaviours on the part of celebrity endorsers. "There might [even be] private investigators," notes one advertising executive. "These companies have the resources to do it." Meanwhile, you'll see a lot less of Tiger Woods—at least for the foreseeable future.

Should companies hold the celebrities who endorse their products accountable for their personal actions?

PRO

1. A celebrity who endorses a product is using his or her personal brand image to create a bond with consumers and boost sales. If a celebrity's image becomes tarnished, then consumers might abandon the product, costing the firm lost sales and—by association—a tarnished brand as well.
2. The high fees paid to a celebrity like Tiger Woods are marketing costs that are ultimately passed along to the consumer in the form of product price. So if the celebrity causes damage to the marketing campaign, the advertiser loses credibility and sales, and consumers don't get what they paid for.

CON

1. An endorsement is a marketing agreement dealing with a firm's goods and services and does not apply to the celebrity's personal life. Woods's personal crisis is not related to how well he represents the game of golf or the products he endorses. Consumers are savvy enough to discriminate between the two.
2. One celebrity's mistakes are not powerful enough to cause an entire marketing campaign—or sport— to crumble. If a firm's products are high quality, customers will continue to buy them anyway.

Where do you stand: pro or con?

Sources: Rhea Drysdale, "How Tiger Woods Can Rebuild His Image Online," *CNN*, March 1, 2010, http://www.cnn.com/2010/TECH/03/01/tiger.woods .online.image/index.html?section=cnn_latest; James Surowiecki, "Branded a Cheat," *The New Yorker*, December 21, 2009, http://www.lexisnexis.com .library.uark.edu; Nancy Dillon, "Shocked Advertisers Will Be on the Prowl for a 'Boy Scout,'" *Daily News*, December 15, 2009, http://www.dailynews.com; Dan Shingler, "Feeling Cheated as a Tiger Customer," *Crain's Cleveland Business*, December 14, 2009, http://www.lexisnexis.com.library.uark.edu; Ed Smith, "Is This the Time to Buy into the Woods Brand?" *The Times*, December 11, 2009, http://www.lexisnexis.com.library.uark.edu; "Advertisers Put Tiger Woods on Hold," *Bloomberg News*, December 10, 2009, http://www.fptradingdesk.com.

---

assessment check 3

3.1 Distinguish between an organization's mission and its objectives.

3.2 What is the importance of the final step in the marketing planning process?

the bags would be fully composted in 14 weeks, but one year later, the company pulled the bags in the United States as consumers were complaining that the bags were too noisy. Sales had dropped by 11 percent. In Canada, however, where composting rates are about 29 percent—versus 2 percent in the United States—the decision was made to keep the biodegradable bags.[7]

Sometimes a marketing strategy backfires. This can happen rapidly in the case of celebrity endorsements, as described in the "Solving an Ethical Controversy" feature.

④ Describe successful planning tools and techniques, including Porter's Five Forces model, first and second mover strategies, SWOT analysis, and the strategic window.

SUCCESSFUL STRATEGIES: TOOLS AND TECHNIQUES

We can identify a number of successful marketing planning tools and techniques. This section discusses four of them: Porter's Five Forces model, first and second mover strategies, SWOT analysis, and the strategic window. All planning strategies have the goal of creating a sustainable competitive advantage for a firm, in which other companies simply cannot provide the same value to their customers that the firm does—no matter how hard they try.

PORTER'S FIVE FORCES MODEL

A number of years ago, the renowned business strategist Michael E. Porter identified five competitive forces that influence planning strategies in a model called **Porter's Five Forces**. Porter later updated his model to include the impact of the Internet on the strategies that businesses use. As illustrated by Figure 2.2, the five forces are potential new entrants; bargaining power of buyers; bargaining power of suppliers; threat of substitute products; and rivalry among competitors.

Potential new entrants are sometimes blocked by the cost or difficulty of entering a market. It is a lot more costly and complicated to begin building aircraft than it is to start a home-based marketing consulting business. The Internet has reduced the barriers to market entry in many industries. In fact, most businesses now view an Internet presence as a requirement for success. If customers have considerable bargaining power, they can greatly influence a firm's strategy. The Internet can increase a customer's buying power by providing information that might not otherwise be easily accessible, such as supplier alternatives and price comparisons. Firms continue to compete to develop the most effective Internet marketing, because they know that customers are savvy users of technology. Microsoft recently announced the launch of its AdECN online advertising exchange, to compete with Google's already successful venture, which allows ad sellers and buyers to negotiate in real time.[8]

The number of available suppliers to a manufacturer or retailer affects their bargaining power. If a seafood restaurant in Manitoba has only one supplier of Nova Scotia lobsters, that supplier has significant bargaining power. But seafood restaurants located throughout Nova Scotia have many lobster suppliers available, which gives their suppliers less bargaining power.

If customers have the opportunity to replace a company's products with the goods or services from a competing firm or industry, the company's marketers may have to take steps to find a new market, change prices, or compete in other ways to maintain an advantage. McDonald's made what some considered a bold move when the firm announced that it would be offering lattes, cappuccinos, espressos,

Porter's Five Forces
Model developed by strategy expert Michael Porter, which identifies five competitive forces that influence planning strategies: the threat of new entrants, the threat of substitute products, rivalry among competitors, the bargaining power of buyers, and the bargaining power of suppliers.

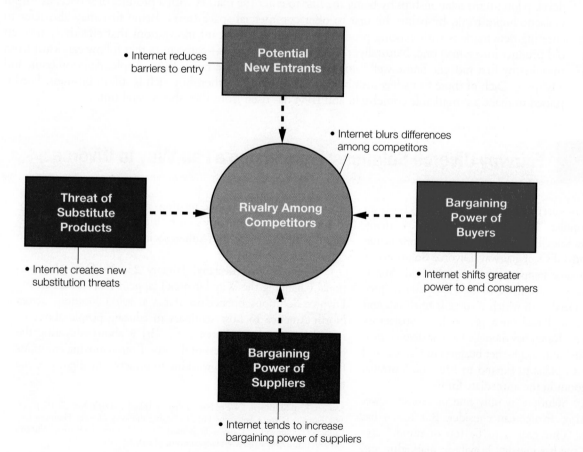

figure 2.2

Porter's Five Forces Model

When McDonald's started offering high-end coffee drinks, it entered into direct competition with Tim Hortons and Starbucks. The threat of a substitute product can create a need for a company's marketers to find new ways to compete.

© MATTHIAS SCHRADER/DPA/LANDOV

and other coffee drinks—in direct competition with Starbucks and Dunkin' Donuts. If McDonald's can serve premium beverages at a competitive price, it may become a major player in the coffee game. As McDonald's president Don Thompson says, "We want to be a beverage destination. For us, growing markets with great margins is the place to be."[9]

The four previous forces influence the rivalry among competitors. In addition, issues such as cost and differentiation or lack of differentiation of products—along with the Internet—influence the strategies that companies use to stand out from their competitors. With increased availability of information, which tends to level the playing field, rivalry heats up among competitors, who try to differentiate themselves from the crowd.

FIRST MOVER AND SECOND MOVER STRATEGIES

first mover strategy
Theory advocating that the company that is first to offer a product in a marketplace will be the long-term market winner.

Some firms like to adopt a **first mover strategy**—attempting to capture the greatest market share and develop long-term relationships by being the first to enter the market with a product or service, as Virgin Galactic hopes to do by being the first to offer commercial space travel. Being first may also refer to entering new markets with existing products or creating significant innovations that effectively turn an old product into a new one. Naturally, this strategy has its risks—companies that follow can learn from mistakes by first movers. Some well-known first movers include Ford, IBM, Apple, Amazon.com, and MySpace. Each of these firms has stumbled at one time or another, but each is still in business. Ford is poised to make a remarkable comeback, and IBM has risen from the ashes several times.

MARKETING AND THE SME	Fairway Divorce Solutions: Franchising a Fair Way to Divorce

FRANCHISING—discussed more in Chapter 11—is an increasingly popular "go-to-market" strategy as many small businesses search for growth opportunities. Karen Stewart, president and CEO of Fairway Divorce Solutions, is changing the way divorce happens around the world. She is turning divorce from a confrontational to a cooperative process—improving the speed with which divorce is finalized, and reducing stress and cost. Based on a personal, unsatisfactory experience with divorce, Karen has modelled a new divorce process and has now started to franchise her business in Canada and the United States, with plans to expand to Mexico, Australia, and the United Kingdom in the immediate future.

Fairway Divorce Solutions is only one of several newer options couples seeking divorce can consider. But Karen has one major objective. "Our goal is to be top of mind," says Stewart. To do that, she has invested heavily in marketing and advertising. She uses public relations and a branding company to coordinate the company's entry into new markets. She also uses Twitter, a blog, and other social media to increase the company's visibility.

Karen Stewart declared January 25, 2011, as "International Changing the Way Divorce Happens Day," and Fairway Divorce Solutions opened its doors at select locations across North America to host seminars to educate people about its new divorce process. Karen says, "[It] is about educating the public on the entire process of divorce, from removing emotions from decision making, to working to preserve the dignity of the family."

Sources: Kim Shiffman, "We're Not Going to Take It," *Profit*, May 2010, p. 12, 14; "Fairway Divorce Solutions Ltd.: Changing the Way Divorce Happens Day Launches Nationwide," *Marketwire*, January 24, 2011; Fairway Divorce Solutions website, http://www.fairwaydivorce.com, March 12, 2011.

Businesses often thrive on a **second mover strategy**, observing closely the innovations of first movers and then improving on them to gain advantage in the marketplace. Facebook appeared after MySpace. Target has followed in the footsteps of Walmart. Sometimes first movers are completely replaced by second movers and disappear from the marketplace altogether such as Books.com, which preceded Amazon.com.

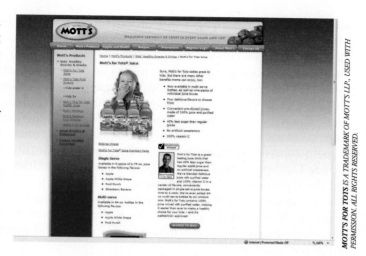

SWOT ANALYSIS

An important strategic planning tool, **SWOT analysis**, helps planners compare internal organizational strengths and weaknesses with external opportunities and threats. (SWOT is an acronym for *strengths, weaknesses, opportunities,* and *threats*.) This form of analysis provides managers with a critical view of the organization's internal and external environments and helps them evaluate the firm's fulfillment of its basic mission.

A company's strengths reflect its **core competencies**—what it does well. Core competencies are capabilities that customers value and competitors find difficult to duplicate. As Figure 2.3 shows,

When marketing research revealed that parents were adding water to their children's juice drinks to reduce sugar content, Dr Pepper Snapple Group leveraged these consumer insights to develop Mott's for Tots, a separate product line providing kids the Mott's juice they already love but with 40 percent less sugar.

second mover strategy Theory that advocates observing closely the innovations of first movers and then introducing new products that improve on the original offering to gain advantage in the marketplace.

SWOT analysis Analysis that helps planners compare internal organizational strengths and weaknesses with external opportunities and threats.

figure 2.3 **SWOT Analysis**

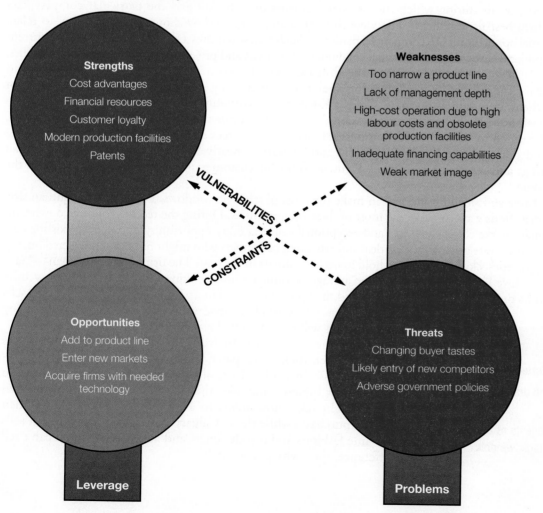

matching an internal strength with an external opportunity produces a situation known as *leverage*. Marketers face a problem when environmental threats attack their organization's weaknesses. Planners anticipate constraints when internal weaknesses or limitations prevent their organization from taking advantage of opportunities. These internal weaknesses can create vulnerabilities for a company—environmental threats to its organizational strength. While beverage maker Dr Pepper Snapple Group (DPSG) was under the umbrella of Britain's Cadbury, sales of its once popular drinks fizzled as distribution networks were neglected and marketers sometimes waited for weeks or months for decisions from Cadbury headquarters. But once DPSG successfully achieved a spin-off, it could concentrate on what it does best: making, distributing, and selling its 58 brands, which include Dr Pepper, Snapple, 7Up, and Canada Dry. Although soft-drink consumption in Canada and the United States has dropped, sales of Dr Pepper actually increased recently—and the firm's stock along with it. And DPSG is now putting considerable marketing effort into 7-Eleven, because no matter how good the products are, if they don't reach consumers they won't sell. "Strategy is fantastic," observes Tony English, a DPSG director of supermarket sales. "But execution is what brings the results in."[10]

Even if a company focuses on its core competencies, sometimes it needs to broaden its offerings to maintain a competitive edge. When marketing research revealed that parents were actually adding water to their children's juice drinks in order to reduce calories, DPSG came up with a new version of its Mott's apple juice, containing 40 percent less sugar but a full serving of juice. It's called Mott's for Tots. Another success has been Canada Dry Green Tea Ginger Ale, for consumers who are looking for the health benefits of green tea.[11]

THE STRATEGIC WINDOW

strategic window
Limited periods during which the key requirements of a market and the particular competencies of a firm best fit together.

The success of products is also influenced by conditions in the market. **Strategic windows** are the limited periods during which the key requirements of a market and the particular competencies of a firm best fit together.[12] The view through a strategic window shows planners a way to relate potential opportunities to company capabilities. Such a view requires a thorough analysis of (1) current and projected external environmental conditions, (2) current and projected internal company capabilities, and (3) how, whether, and when the firm can feasibly reconcile environmental conditions and company capabilities by implementing one or more marketing strategies. Fred Pritchard, owner of a kitchenware products business, Golda's Kitchen in Mississauga, Ontario, for example, saw a strategic window during the recent recession. While many competitors were focused on cutting costs, Fred decided to strengthen his business. He had the resources to invest for long-term growth. He expanded his product line by 20 percent and his staff by nearly 50 percent, improving his product offerings and service to customers. Demand from his customers remained strong throughout the recession.[13]

Large and small businesses can make the most of strategic windows. Despite its gargantuan size, Walmart finds ways to make the most of these opportunities. During the recent economic downturn, Walmart marketed its low prices and exceptional values at every opportunity—reassuring existing customers they were getting the best deal and attracting consumers who might not have considered buying their groceries, clothing, or household items at Walmart in the past. The firm's updated slogan—"Save money. Live better."—champions the average consumer who is looking for value. Walmart's website provides tips for money-saving meals and the opportunity to sign up for email alerts to price rollbacks and special offers. Marketers hope that when the economy rebounds, many of these shoppers will have become loyal Walmart customers.[14]

Small businesses can benefit from the same strategic window. As consumers tighten their belts, pawn shops and thrift stores often experience an increase in traffic. Instead of donating designer clothing to a not-for-profit organization like the Salvation Army, a well-dressed consumer might take those items to a local consignment shop—then make a few purchases while there. Calgary-based Sass Consignment sells brand-name fashions and top designers and advertises, "If you can't tell the difference, then why pay for it!"[15]

assessment check 4

4.1 Briefly explain each of Porter's Five Forces.

4.2 What are the benefits and drawbacks of a first mover strategy?

4.3 What are the four components of the SWOT analysis? What is a strategic window?

ELEMENTS OF A MARKETING STRATEGY

⑤ Identify the basic elements of a marketing strategy.

Success for a product in the marketplace—whether it is a tangible good, a service, a cause, a person, a place, or an organization—depends on an effective marketing strategy. It's one thing to develop a great product, but if customers don't get the message about it, the product will die. An effective marketing strategy reaches the right buyers at the right time, persuades them to try the product, and develops a strong relationship with them over time. The basic elements of a marketing strategy consist of (1) the target market and (2) the marketing mix variables of product, distribution, promotion, and price that combine to satisfy the needs of the target market. The outer circle in Figure 2.4 lists environmental characteristics that provide the framework within which marketing strategies are planned.

THE TARGET MARKET

A customer-driven organization begins its overall strategy with a detailed description of its **target market**: the group of people toward whom the firm decides to direct its marketing efforts and ultimately its merchandise. Sears Canada stores serve a target market consisting of consumers purchasing for themselves and their families. Other companies, such as Bombardier, market most of their products to business buyers such as Air Canada and government purchasers. Still other firms provide goods and services to retail and wholesale buyers. In every instance, however, marketers pinpoint their target markets as accurately as possible. Although the concept of dividing markets into specific segments is discussed in more detail in Chapter 8, it's important to understand the idea of targeting a market from the outset. Although it may be hard to imagine the classic Oreo cookie as anything other than two discs of chocolate with a white cream filling, Kraft Foods has reformulated the favourite to market it in China. The Chinese version is four layers of long, thin biscuits coated in chocolate, which is more appealing to consumers there. The move reflects Kraft Foods CEO Irene Rosenfeld's strategy of placing more authority in the hands of local business units around the world, trusting that people who live and work there know better what consumers want than the top Kraft Foods executives located at the firm's headquarters.[16] In addition to the Oreo reformulation, Kraft Foods has recently opened a new cookie factory in Russia named Bolshevik Biscuits.[17]

figure 2.4

Elements of a Marketing Strategy and Its Environmental Framework

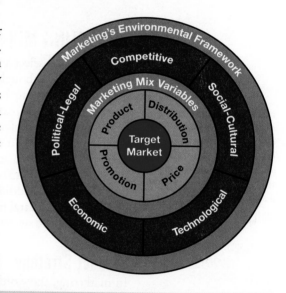

MARKETING IN A DIGITAL WORLD — Adding Social Media to Your Marketing Strategy

ARE you connected? Chances are you are—even if you're over thirty. And you've likely moved beyond simply searching websites to opting in for alerts from your favourite companies. You may be a regular user of one or several social media sites: Facebook, Foursquare, LinkedIn, MySpace, Squidoo, Twitter, YouTube, and more. Perhaps you are thinking about using social media as part of your marketing strategy. Good idea. Social media can help you increase your visibility, stay in touch with your target audience, and find prospective customers. But first: some advice.

Don't forget your marketing strategy. Remember your key questions: What is your mission? What are your objectives? Who is your target market? How much is your budget? Regardless of which sites you decide to use, you should always refer back to these important questions. Does the social media site you have chosen help you achieve your mission by advancing

one or more of your objectives? Does the social media site you have chosen reach your desired target market? Users of Facebook differ from users of MySpace, and both reach a different audience than LinkedIn. Are your social media plans within your budget? You might think social media is free. But there are many costs to consider. If you hire someone to manage your social media strategy, you have real costs. If you do it yourself, there are very real opportunity costs. Social media can quickly sap your time and prevent you from doing more important things. And social media can do more damage to your firm if you use it to attract people to a poorly designed website, or if you have an otherwise poor marketing strategy.

Think of social media as simply another marketing tool—like billboards, television advertisements, flyers, websites, promotional events, etc.—and then decide how you wish to use it to build your business.

target market
Group of people to whom a firm decides to direct its marketing efforts and ultimately its goods and services.

Diversity plays an ever-increasing role in targeting markets. By 2017, Canada is expected to have 1.8 million Chinese and another 1.8 million South Asian people—combined, they will make up approximately half of all visible minorities. Canada's banks are certainly paying attention. The Royal Bank of Canada already advertises in Punjabi, Hindi, Mandarin, and Cantonese. Scotiabank advertises during festivals such as Eid, Diwali, and Chinese New Year. TD Canada Trust employs ethnic, bi- or multi-lingual staff and makes sure there is promotional material at its branches in languages that ethnic Canadians prefer. Targeting consumers in specific global markets also represents a challenge—and an opportunity. India is an enormous market that is culturally diverse within itself, containing 27 geographical states, numerous languages and religious practices, and a variety of lifestyles. Traditional Indian culture is infused with Western influences. And while nearly half of all Indian citizens earn less than $1 per day, a growing middle class means increasing opportunities for brands such as Baskin-Robbins, Tropicana, and even Louis Vuitton. Marketers make mistakes, however. Kellogg's failed in its introduction of crispy breakfast cereals because the company didn't realize that Indian consumers don't like cold milk. But marketers can be successful if they tailor their practices to Indian preferences. Using traditional Indian kirana-style markets (small shops), Walmart has made a successful entry into retailing with smaller shops in urban areas and low prices.[18]

MARKETING MIX VARIABLES

After marketers select a target market, they direct their company's activities toward profitably satisfying that segment. Although they must manipulate thousands of variables to reach this goal, marketing decision making can be divided into four strategies: product, distribution, promotion, and pricing strategies. The total package forms the **marketing mix**—the blending of the four strategic elements to fit the needs and preferences of a specific target market. While the fourfold classification is useful to study and analyze, remember that the marketing mix can—and should—be an ever-changing combination of variables to achieve success.

marketing mix Blending of the four strategy elements—product, distribution, promotion, and pricing—to fit the needs and preferences of a specific target market.

Figure 2.4 (p. 43) illustrates the focus of the marketing mix variables on the central choice of the target market. In addition, decisions about product, distribution, promotion, and price are affected by the environmental factors in the outer circle of the figure. The environmental variables may play a major role in the success of a marketing program, and marketers must consider their probable effects.

Product Strategy

In marketing, the word *product* means more than a good, service, or idea. Product is a broad concept that also encompasses the satisfaction of all consumer needs in relation to a good, service, or idea. So **product strategy** involves more than just deciding what goods or services the firm should offer to a group of consumers. It also includes decisions about customer service, package design, brand names, trademarks, patents, warranties, the life cycle of a product, positioning the product in the marketplace, and new product development.

product strategy
Decisions about what goods or services a firm will offer its customers; also includes decisions about customer service, packaging, brand names, and the like.

Distribution Strategy

Marketers develop **distribution strategies** to ensure that consumers find their products in the proper quantities at the right times and places. Distribution decisions involve modes of transportation, warehousing, inventory control, order processing, and selection of marketing channels. Marketing channels are made up of institutions such as retailers and wholesalers—intermediaries that may be involved in a product's movement from producer to final consumer.

distribution strategy
Planning that ensures that consumers find their products in the proper quantities at the right times and places.

Technology is opening new channels of distribution in many industries. The Internet has caused the biggest revolution in distribution since the mail-order catalogue. Computer software and digital music files are obvious candidates, but a wide variety that includes DVDs, contact lenses, and even motorcycles can be found on the Web. Amazon announced in 2011 that its sales of electronic books surpassed sales of its printed books, less than four years after it introduced them.[19] Some publications, such as *Canadian Business* (www.canadianbusiness.com) and *The Globe and Mail* (www.theglobeandmail.com), offer both online and print content; the online content is free. But other publications have abandoned print altogether or were established entirely online in the first place.

Promotional Strategy

Promotion is the communications link between sellers and buyers. Organizations use varied ways to send messages about their goods, services, and ideas. They may communicate messages directly through salespeople or indirectly through advertisements and promotions. A favourite promotion among Canadians is the Tim Hortons Roll up the Rim to Win promotion, expanded in 2011—its 25th year—to include 47 million food prizes, plus gift cards, propane grills, mountain bikes, 3D home theatre packages, and 40 Toyota Matrix cars.[20]

In developing a promotional strategy, marketers blend the various elements of promotion to communicate most effectively with their target market. Many companies use an approach called integrated marketing communications (IMC) to coordinate all promotional activities so that the consumer receives a unified and consistent message. Consumers might receive newsletters, email updates, discount coupons, catalogues, invitations to company-sponsored events, and any number of other types of marketing communications about a product. Honda dealers mail maintenance and service reminders to their customers. A political candidate may send volunteer workers through a neighbourhood to invite voters to a local reception.

promotion
Communications link between buyers and sellers. Function of informing, persuading, and influencing a consumer's purchase decision.

Pricing Strategy

Pricing strategy deals with the methods of setting profitable and justifiable prices. It is closely regulated and subject to considerable public scrutiny. One of the many factors that influence a marketer's pricing strategy is competition. The computer industry has become all too familiar with price cuts by both current competitors and new market entrants. After years of steady growth, the market has become saturated with low-cost computers, driving down profit margins even farther. But sometimes conditions in the external marketing environment cause difficulties in pricing strategies. Political unrest overseas, the soaring price of fuel, or a freeze that destroys crops could all affect the price of goods and services. If the economy is booming, consumers generally have more confidence and are willing to shop more often and pay more for discretionary goods. But when the economy takes a downturn, consumers look for bargains—they want high quality at low prices. It is a challenge for marketers to strike the right balance in order to make enough profits to survive and grow. The Canadian economy suffered through the recent global recession, but sales here have been rebounding faster than in many markets around the world, helping make Canada an attractive place for foreign retail investment.[21]

pricing strategy
Methods of setting profitable and justifiable prices.

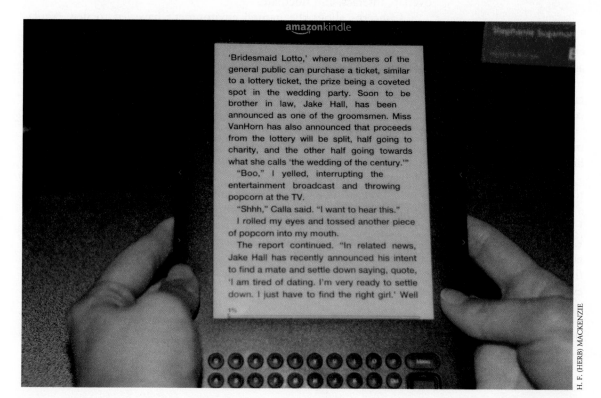

H. F. (HERB) MACKENZIE

Technology continually opens new channels of distribution. Amazon.com's Kindle allows consumers to download and read periodicals that were once available only in print, such as The Globe and Mail.

Automobile engineers have turned public concern and legal issues concerning the natural environment into opportunities by developing hybrid cars, biodiesel cars, and electric cars, such as this Nissan Leaf.

© JIM WEST/ALAMY

assessment check 5

5.1 What are the two components of every marketing strategy?

5.2 Identify the four strategic elements of the marketing mix.

⑥ Describe the environmental characteristics that influence strategic decisions.

Marketoid

An estimated 5 to 7 percent of global trade—or about $500 billion—involves counterfeit goods. The figure is expected to reach $2 trillion by 2025.

Marketoid

In the first fiscal quarter 2011, Canada's Research In Motion shipped 13.9 million BlackBerrys.

THE MARKETING ENVIRONMENT

Marketers do not make decisions about target markets and marketing mix variables in a vacuum. They must take into account the dynamic nature of the five dimensions of the marketing environment shown back in Figure 2.4 (p. 43): competitive, political-legal, economic, technological, and social-cultural factors. It's important to note that these five dimensions overlap, interact, and fluctuate.

Concerns about the natural environment have led to new regulations concerning air and water pollution, which affect the political-legal environment in which marketers operate. Efforts toward sustainability are now social-cultural factors as well because consumer awareness is turning into consumer preference. Automobile engineers, for instance, have turned public concerns and legal issues into opportunities by developing hybrid cars. In fact, the race to bring to market the most fuel-efficient vehicles for the future has become extremely competitive.

Businesses are increasingly looking to foreign shores for new growth markets. General Motors now sells more cars in China than it does in the United States.[22] Volkswagen, when it first decided to export its gasoline-electric hybrid, chose to enter China as well, rather than other European countries or North America.[23]

Technology continually changes the marketing environment. Marketers are now increasing efforts to get their messages to consumers via smartphones. Although smartphone advertising still represents a small percentage of most firm's advertising budgets, the medium is receiving a lot of attention. Pizza Hut has launched an iPhone ordering app, and Victoria's Secret recently posted its Fashion Show app. During one campaign, Volkswagen offered a free iPhone racing app called Real Racing GTI, giving its target market (young customers) the first opportunity to test drive its newest model GTI. "Launching the all-new GTI via [iPhone app] allows us to connect with this savvy GTI consumer within his or her everyday life in a way that no 30-second spot ever could," said VW's marketing vice president Tim Ellis.[24]

In the competitive environment, some experts have coined the phrase *rule of three*, meaning that in any industry, the three strongest, most efficient companies dominate between 70 and 90 percent of the market. Here are a few examples—all of which are household names:

- *Supermarkets:* Loblaws, Sobeys, Walmart
- *Cereal manufacturers:* General Mills, Kellogg's, Post

Marketers are increasing efforts to get their messages to consumers via smartphones. Pizza Hut, for example, has launched an iPhone ordering app.

© J E BEAM PHOTOGRAPHY

- *Running shoes:* Nike, Adidas, Reebok
- *Airlines:* Air Canada, WestJet, Porter Airlines
- *Pharmaceuticals:* Merck, Pfizer, Bristol-Myers Squibb[25]

While it may seem like an uphill battle for the remaining hundreds of companies in any given industry, each of these firms can find a strategy for gaining competitive ground.

The social-cultural environment includes a variety of factors, including prevailing cultural norms. As the novelty of bidding for auction items on eBay has worn off for consumers who don't necessarily have the time or desire to wait several days or a week for auction results, eBay has begun to reshape itself. Fixed-price purchase items are becoming the new norm. The "Buy It Now" option on many auctions now accounts for more than 40 percent of all purchases made on eBay.[25] This new trend also reflects economic factors, including how much consumers are willing and able to spend. The entire marketing environment provides a framework for all marketing activity. Marketers consider environmental dimensions when they develop strategies for segmenting and targeting markets and when they study consumer and organizational buying behaviour.

assessment check 6

6.1 What are the five dimensions of the marketing environment?

6.2 How is concern over the natural environment affecting the other dimensions?

METHODS FOR MARKETING PLANNING

⑦ Describe the methods for marketing planning, including business portfolio analysis, the BCG matrix, and the strategic growth opportunity matrix.

As growing numbers of companies have discovered the benefits of effective marketing planning, they have developed planning methods to assist in this important function. This section discusses business portfolio analysis and the strategic business unit concept, the market share/market growth matrix, and the strategic growth opportunity matrix.

BUSINESS PORTFOLIO ANALYSIS

Although a small company may offer only a few items to its customers, a larger organization frequently offers and markets many products to widely diverse markets. CIBC and BMO offer a wide range of financial products to businesses and consumers; Kraft Foods stocks supermarket shelves with

IBM, once known as a manufacturer of high-quality clocks, now markets computer systems and global IT services and solutions.

Building a Smarter Planet: 1 in a Series

Welcome to the decade of smart.

A year ago, we began a global conversation about how our planet is becoming smarter.

We talked about intelligence being infused into the systems and processes that make the world work—into things no one would recognize as computers: cars, appliances, roadways, power grids, clothes, even natural systems such as agriculture and waterways.

We said that trillions of digital devices, connected through the Internet, were producing a vast ocean of data. And all of that information—from the flow of markets to the pulse of societies—could be turned into knowledge because we had the computational power and advanced analytics to make sense of it all.

A year into this new era, the signs of a smarter planet are all around us. Smarter systems are being implemented and are creating value in every major industry and across every region of both the developed and developing worlds.

This idea isn't a metaphor, or a vision, or a proposal—it's a rapidly emerging reality.

In a study of 439 cities, those with transportation congestion systems showed an average reduction in travel delays of more than 700,000 hours annually.

A yearlong study by the U.S. Department of Energy's Pacific Northwest National Laboratory found that consumers within smart meter systems saved 10% on their power bills and cut their power usage by 15% during peak hours.

Eight hospitals and 470 primary care clinics were able to improve clinical results and operational efficiency by up to 10% through information access at the point of care.

Leading retailers have reduced supply chain costs by up to 30% and increased sales by up to 10%—through analyzing buying behaviors, aligning merchandising with demand and building end-to-end visibility from manufacture to sale.

Everywhere, forward-thinking leaders are achieving near-term ROI. But they are also discovering something deeper. They are finding the hidden treasures buried in their *data*.

Data is being captured today as never before. It's revealing everything from large and systemic patterns—of global markets, workflows, national infrastructures and natural systems—to the location, temperature, security and condition of every item in a global supply chain.

Then there's the growing torrent of information from billions of individuals using social media. They are customers, citizens, students and patients. They are telling us what they think, what they like and want, and what they're witnessing. In real time.

That's a lot of data, but data by itself isn't useful. In fact, it can be overwhelming—unless you can extract value from it. And now we can. With the right tools, we are beginning to see patterns, correlations and outliers.

With sophisticated mathematical models, we can take the measure of the world's information and actually begin to predict and react to changes in our systems. New York has smart crime fighting. Paris has smart healthcare. Galway has smart water. A smart grid in Copenhagen keeps energy flowing.

We've learned a lot over the past year about what it takes to build a smarter planet—and about the issues it raises. Issues like protecting personal information and securing critical infrastructures. We've learned that we will need global standards across all dimensions of these complex systems. New skills and fields of expertise. New ways of working and thinking. A smarter planet also requires a profound shift in management and governance.

Business leaders, policymakers and government officials around the world understand these challenges, and are stepping up to them. Above all, they realize that we cannot wait, cannot let this moment pass. The time to act is now. And the way to act is together. The decade of smart is under way.

Let's build a smarter planet. Join us and see what others are doing at **ibm.com/smarterplanet**

products such as macaroni and cheese and mayonnaise. Top managers at these larger firms need a method for spotting product lines that deserve more investment as well as lines that aren't living up to expectations. So they conduct a portfolio analysis, in which they evaluate their company's products and divisions to determine which are strongest and which are weakest. Much like securities analysts review their portfolios of stocks and bonds, deciding which to retain and which to discard, marketing planners must perform the same assessment of their products, the regions in which they operate, and other marketing mix variables. This is where the concept of an SBU comes in.

strategic business units (SBUs) Key business units within diversified firms.

Strategic business units (SBUs) are key business units within diversified firms. Each SBU has its own managers, resources, objectives, and competitors. A division, product line, or single product may define the boundaries of an SBU. Each SBU pursues its own distinct mission, and each develops its own plans independently of other units in the organization. A manufacturer that sells many different brands of laundry detergent may consider each a separate strategic business unit. PartSource is a strategic business unit of Canadian Tire.

Strategic business units focus the attention of company managers so that they can respond effectively to changing consumer demand within limited markets. Companies may have to redefine their SBUs as market conditions dictate. International Business Machines Corp. (IBM) was once known as a manufacturer of high-quality clocks. Today, the firm markets everything related to computers—computer servers and systems, software, Internet security, and printing paper and toner. Its slogan, "Welcome to the Decade of Smart," conveys the firm's forward-thinking philosophy. People now compete for the old IBM clocks, which have become valuable collectibles.[26]

THE BCG MARKET SHARE/MARKET GROWTH MATRIX

To evaluate each of their organization's strategic business units, marketers need some type of portfolio performance framework. A widely used framework was developed by the Boston Consulting Group. This market share/market growth matrix places SBUs in a four-quadrant chart that plots market share—the percentage of a market that a firm controls—against market growth potential. The position of an SBU along the horizontal axis indicates its market share relative to those of competitors in the industry. Its position along the vertical axis indicates the annual growth rate of the market. After plotting all of a firm's business units, planners divide them according to the matrix's four quadrants. Figure 2.5 illustrates this matrix by labelling the four quadrants stars, cash cows, question marks, and dogs. Firms in each quadrant require a unique marketing strategy.

Stars represent units with high market shares in high-growth markets. These products or businesses are high-growth market leaders. Although they generate considerable income, they need considerable inflows of cash to finance further growth. Research In Motion's BlackBerry was the number-one selling smartphone in North America in 2010—and third in the world—but it has been losing market share. In the first quarter of 2011, BlackBerry remained on top in the United States with 27.1 percent, Apple was second with 25.5 percent, but the combined phones using Google's Android operating system held 34.0 percent market share. During that period, Apple had doubled its smartphone sales, HTC tripled its sales, Samsung quadrupled its sales, and BlackBerry sales increased by 30 percent. While losing market share quickly in the United States, BlackBerry was still a strong market leader in Canada: 42 percent versus Apple's 31 percent.[27] *Cash cows* command high market shares in low-growth markets. Marketers for such an SBU want to maintain this status for as long as possible. The business produces strong cash flows, but instead of investing heavily in the unit's own promotions and production capacity, the firm can use this cash to finance the growth of other SBUs with higher growth potentials. For instance, Microsoft might use the profits from sales of its Windows operating system to finance research and development for new Internet-based technologies.[28]

figure 2.5

BCG Market Share/Market Growth Matrix

Industry Growth Rate / Relative Market Share	High	Low
High	**Stars** Generate considerable income **Strategy:** Invest more funds for future growth	**Question Marks** Have potential to become stars or cash cows **Strategy:** Either invest more funds for growth or consider disinvesting
Low	**Cash Cows** Generate strong cash flow **Strategy:** Milk profits to finance growth of stars and question marks	**Dogs** Generate little profits **Strategy:** Consider withdrawing

Question marks achieve low market shares in high-growth markets. Marketers must decide whether to continue supporting these products or businesses since question marks typically require considerably more cash than they generate. If a question mark cannot become a star, the firm should pull out of the market and target other markets with greater potential. Ford recently sold off its luxury brands Jaguar and Aston-Martin in order to concentrate on its more economical, fuel-efficient vehicles. *Dogs* manage only low market shares in low-growth markets. SBUs in this category promise poor future prospects, and marketers should seriously consider withdrawing from these businesses or product lines. In some cases, these products can be sold to other firms, where they are a better fit. IBM sold its PC business to Chinese manufacturer Lenovo so that it could concentrate on its business services.

STRATEGIC GROWTH OPPORTUNITY MATRIX

As part of its strategy planning, a company needs to consider potential growth opportunities. Once it has performed a portfolio analysis, a logical step for a company is to consider which among its strategic business units it will focus its attention upon for growth. Ansoff's strategic growth opportunity matrix is illustrated in Figure 2.6, showing the four growth options.

Market penetration is a strategy that a company uses when it attempts to build market share by selling existing products to existing customers. It is the least risky of growth strategies as the company is familiar with both its customers and its products. However, it is often difficult to increase market share in mature markets as any increase must come at the expense of competitors. It is sometimes easier in fast-growing markets. Even if a number of competitors are aiming at growth, they are not all aware of how well others are doing. A company that is happy with its 20 percent growth may not realize that a competitor is

figure 2.6 ***Ansoff's Strategic Growth Opportunity Matrix***

	Present Product	New Product
Present Market	**Market Penetration** When Tim Hortons promotes its Roll up the Rim to Win contest, it is following a market penetration strategy.	**Product Development** When KFC Canada introduced the Double Down, it was following a product development strategy.
New Market	**Market Development** When McCain Foods entered the African market to sell its frozen french fries, it was following a market development strategy.	**Diversification** When Zippo Manufacturing introduced a new cologne, it was following a diversification strategy.

growing at 40 percent. When Tim Hortons implements its Roll up the Rim to Win promotion each year, its intention is to further penetrate its market—that is, increase market share.

Market development occurs when a company tries to attract new customers for its existing products, sometimes by geographic expansion, but often by simply targeting new segments of customers. New Brunswick-based McCain Foods, the company that produces about a third of the world's frozen French fries, has been following a market development strategy for some time. McCain now sells its fries in eight or more African countries from Angola to Zambia. It employs 2000 people in South Africa, where it targets all segments from the affluent families to the working poor.[29]

Product development occurs when a company develops new products that it hopes to sell to existing customers. KFC Canada introduced the Double Down—two deep-fried chicken breasts, combined with two strips of bacon, two slices of processed cheese, and sauce—in summer 2010 and described it as its best new product introduction ever. Canadians bought more than 1 million of them in the few months they were offered, prompting KFC Canada to bring it back in summer 2011.[30] A product development strategy could also include introducing modified products, such as the introduction of iPad 2.

Diversification is the most risky of growth strategies as companies that follow this strategy attempt to sell new products to new markets—that is, they have little experience with either. Zippo Manufacturing Company, maker of the famous Zippo lighter, is being forced to consider diversification options as the worldwide tobacco industry becomes an increasingly "dying" industry—sorry for the pun. Zippo launched a new cologne in Italy in 2010 and expects to bring it to Canada in 2012.[31]

assessment check 7

7.1 What are SBUs?

7.2 Identify the four quadrants in the BCG matrix.

7.3 Identify the four strategic growth opportunities.

Strategic Implications of Marketing

Never before has planning been as important to marketers as the 21st century speeds ahead with technological advances. Marketers need to plan carefully, accurately, and quickly if their companies are to gain a competitive advantage in today's global marketplace. They need to define their organization's mission and understand the different methods for formulating a successful marketing strategy. They must consider a changing, diverse population and the boundaryless business environment created by the Internet. They must be able to evaluate when it's best to be first to get into a market and when it's best to wait. They need to recognize when they've got a star and when they've got a dog—when to hang on and when to let go. As daunting as this seems, planning can reduce the risk and worry of bringing new goods and services to the marketplace. ◆◆◆

REVIEW OF CHAPTER OBJECTIVES

① Distinguish between strategic planning and tactical planning.

Strategic planning is the process of identifying an organization's primary objectives and adopting courses of action toward these objectives. In other words, strategic planning focuses on the big picture of which industries are central to a firm's business. Tactical planning guides the implementation of the activities specified in the strategic plan. Once a strategy is set, operational managers devise methods (tactics) to achieve the larger goals.

② Explain how marketing plans differ at various levels in an organization.

Top management spends more time engaged in strategic planning than do middle- and supervisory-level managers, who tend to focus on narrower, tactical plans for their units. Supervisory managers are more likely to engage in developing specific plans designed to meet the goals assigned to them—for example, streamlining production processes so that they operate more efficiently.

③ **Identify the steps in the marketing planning process.**

The basic steps in the marketing planning process are defining the organization's mission and objectives; assessing organizational resources and evaluating environmental risk and opportunities; and formulating, implementing, and monitoring the marketing strategy.

④ **Describe successful planning tools and techniques, including Porter's Five Forces model, first and second mover strategies, SWOT analysis, and the strategic window.**

Porter's Five Forces are identified as the five competitive factors that influence planning strategies: potential new entrants, bargaining power of buyers, bargaining power of suppliers, threat of substitute products, and rivalry among competitors. With a first mover strategy, a firm attempts to capture the greatest market share by being first to enter the market; with a second mover strategy, a firm observes the innovations of first movers and then improves on them to gain advantage. SWOT analysis (strengths, weaknesses, opportunities, and threats) helps planners compare internal organizational strengths and weaknesses with external opportunities and threats. The strategic window identifies the limited periods during which the key requirements of a market and the competencies of a firm best fit together.

⑤ **Identify the basic elements of a marketing strategy.**

Development of a marketing strategy is a two-step process: (1) selecting a target market and (2) designing an effective marketing mix to satisfy the chosen target. The target market is the group of people toward whom a company decides to direct its marketing efforts. The marketing mix blends four strategy elements to fit the needs and preferences of a specific target market. These elements are product strategy, distribution strategy, promotional strategy, and pricing strategy.

⑥ **Describe the environmental characteristics that influence strategic decisions.**

The five dimensions of the marketing environment are competitive, political-legal, economic, technological, and social-cultural. Marketers must also address growing concern about the natural environment—including new regulations—and increasing cultural diversity in the global marketplace.

⑦ **Describe the methods for marketing planning, including business portfolio analysis, the BCG market share/market growth matrix, and the strategic growth opportunity matrix.**

The business portfolio analysis evaluates a company's products and divisions, including strategic business units (SBUs). The SBU focuses the attention of company managers so they can respond effectively to changing consumer demand within certain markets. The BCG matrix places SBUs in a four-quadrant chart that plots market share against market growth potential. The four quadrants are stars, cash cows, question marks, and dogs. The strategic growth opportunity matrix identifies four growth alternatives: penetration (same products, same markets), market development (same products, new markets), product development (new products, same markets), and diversification (new products, new markets).

assessment check answers

1.1 Define *planning*.

Planning is the process of anticipating future events and conditions and of determining the best way to achieve organizational objectives.

1.2 Give an example of strategic planning and tactical planning.

To survive in a challenging environment that includes soaring fuel costs, several airlines have decided to combine as part of their strategic planning. Tactical plans include cutting the

number of flights and charging passengers extra for checked baggage.

2.1 How do marketing plans differ at different levels of the organization?

Top managers usually focus their planning activities on long-range strategic issues. In contrast, middle-level managers focus on operational planning, which includes creating and implementing tactical plans for their own units. Supervisors develop specific programs to meet the goals in their areas of responsibility.

2.2 Why is it important to get input from others when planning?

Input from a variety of sources—other employees, suppliers, or customers—helps ensure that many ideas are considered. Involving those people in planning can also turn them into advocates for the plan.

3.1 Distinguish between an organization's mission and its objectives.

The firm's mission is the essential purpose that differentiates the company from others. Its objectives guide development of supporting marketing objectives and plans. Avon's mission is to be "the company for women." One of its objectives might be to convert all its packaging to recycled materials.

3.2 What is the importance of the final step in the marketing planning process?

In the final step of the marketing planning process, managers monitor performance to ensure that objectives are being achieved.

4.1 Briefly explain each of Porter's Five Forces.

Porter's Five Forces are the threats of potential new entrants, which increases competition in a market; bargaining power of buyers, which can depress prices; bargaining power of suppliers, which can increase cost or reduce selection; threat of substitute products, which can lure customers to other products; and rivalry among competitors, which can bring about price wars or divert companies from their main goals.

4.2 What are the benefits and drawbacks of a first mover strategy?

The benefits of a first mover strategy include being able to capture the greatest market share and develop long-term relationships with customers. Disadvantages include the possibility that companies that follow can learn from mistakes by first movers. Apple has been a first mover with its iPod and iPad products.

4.3 What are the four components of the SWOT analysis? What is a strategic window?

SWOT analysis helps planners compare internal organizational strengths and weaknesses with external opportunities and threats. SWOT is an acronym for *strengths, weaknesses, opportunities,* and *threats*. A strategic window defines the limited periods during which the key requirements of a market and the particular competencies of a firm best fit together.

5.1 What are the two components of every marketing strategy?

The basic elements of a marketing strategy are (1) the target market and (2) the marketing mix variables.

5.2 Identify the four strategic elements of the marketing mix.

The marketing mix consists of product, distribution, promotion, and price strategies.

6.1 What are the five dimensions of the marketing environment?

The five dimensions of the marketing environment are competitive, political-legal, economic, technological, and social-cultural factors.

6.2 How is concern over the natural environment affecting the other dimensions?

Concerns over the natural environment have led to new and tighter regulations on pollution, which affect the political-legal environment in which marketers operate. Efforts toward sustainability are now social-cultural factors as well because consumer awareness is turning into consumer preference.

7.1 What are SBUs?

Strategic business units (SBUs) are key business units within diversified firms. Each SBU has its own managers, resources, objectives, and competitors.

7.2 Identify the four quadrants in the BCG matrix.

The BCG matrix labels SBUs stars, cash cows, question marks, and dogs. Stars are the products with high market shares in high-growth markets; cash cows command high market shares in low-growth markets; question marks achieve low market shares in high-growth markets; and dogs manage only low market shares in low-growth markets.

7.3 Identify the four strategic growth opportunities.

The four strategic growth opportunities are penetration (same products, same markets), market development (same products, new markets), product development (new products, same markets), and diversification (new products, new markets).

MARKETING TERMS YOU NEED TO KNOW

These terms are printed in red in the text. They are defined in the margins of the chapter and Marketing Plan appendix and in the Glossary that begins on p. G-1.

planning 32
marketing planning 33
strategic planning 34
tactical planning 34
mission 37
marketing strategy 37
Porter's Five Forces 39

first mover strategy 40
second mover strategy 41
SWOT analysis 41
strategic window 42
target market 43
marketing mix 44
product strategy 44

distribution strategy 44
promotion 45
pricing strategy 45
strategic business units (SBUs) 48

PROJECTS AND TEAMWORK EXERCISES

1. Choose one of the following companies, or select another one whose goods and services are familiar to you. On your own or with a classmate, formulate a mission statement for that company. Then create a list of objectives that reflect your company's mission.
   a. Mark's Work Wearhouse
   b. Petro-Canada
   c. Tim Hortons
   d. Bell Canada

2. Using a first mover strategy, Apple's iPod, iPhone, and iPad have clearly established the lead in their markets. Research the products of another firm that produces either a digital music player or a smartphone to learn about its strategy. How has a second mover strategy benefited the firm? Has the second mover firm been able to catch Apple in sales?

3. Create a SWOT analysis for yourself, listing your own personal strengths, weaknesses, opportunities, and threats.

4. When rivals Samsung and Sony each unveiled their new 3D TVs at a major electronics store, some consumers couldn't tell the difference between the two. But the firm's strategies were very different. Sony now hires outside manufacturing firms to build its TVs, stating that the move will help cut costs and keep the company strong. In addition, Sony plans to add "Sony-unique applications," including Internet content and streaming Sony films before their DVD release. But Samsung insists on manufacturing its own TVs, including its own computer chips.[32] With a classmate, research these new offerings by both firms and evaluate their marketing strategy. Who is the target market for both of these TVs? How does product, distribution, promotion, and pricing fit into each firm's overall marketing strategy?

5. Use your library resources or an Internet search engine to collect information on one of the following companies (or select one of your own). Identify the firm's target market(s). Note that a large company might have more than one target market. Write a brief proposal for a marketing strategy to reach that market.
   a. MasterCard
   b. Costco
   c. Kia
   d. lululemon athletica

6. With a classmate, choose a company whose products you have purchased in the past. Create two ads for one of the company's products (or product lines). One ad should focus on the product itself—its features, packaging, or brand name. The second ad should focus on pricing. Present your ads to the class for discussion. Which ad is more effective for the product and why?

7. On your own or with a classmate, research a firm that has been around for a long time, such as Ford, General Electric, or DuPont. Use your research to determine the ways that technology has changed the marketing environment for your firm. Present your findings in class.

8. Suppose you are a marketer for Canadian toy manufacturer MEGA Brands. Top executives at the company have announced their ambition "to be the choice of every family around the world." They want you to look at the market potential in India in the next five years. Write a memo to your manager explaining how you think the social-cultural environment may affect your firm's marketing strategy in India.

9. Select one of the following industries and research which firms might fall into the top three in the industry, creating a rule of three:
   a. fast-food restaurants
   b. upscale hotels
   c. electronics retailing
   d. auto manufacturing

10. On your own or with a classmate, research one of the following large corporations. Select several product lines and classify each in the BCG matrix.
    a. Sears Canada
    b. Johnson & Johnson
    c. Conde Nast Publications
    d. General Electric (GE)

CRITICAL-THINKING EXERCISES

1. Suppose you are a marketer for a Canadian manufacturer of pet supplies. Two top executives have proposed expanding the company by opening retail stores and marketing pets on-site—puppies, kittens, rabbits, birds, fish, and the like. What are the potential benefits and drawbacks of making a move like this? How would you advise your company to proceed?

2. Netflix has made thousands of streaming videos available to its subscribers. How does this strategy demonstrate a strategic window for the company?

3. Choose one of the following products and describe how it may (or already has) become vulnerable to substitution. Then describe an overall strategy—with two or three tactics—for reducing this vulnerability.
   a. printed copies of periodicals or books
   b. television
   c. telephone landlines
   d. travel agencies

4. Research the website of one of the following retail firms to identify its target market. Then outline a strategy for expanding that target market.
   a. Tim Hortons
   b. Aritzia
   c. Roots Canada
   d. Dollarama

5. Research a company such as Molson Breweries or Kraft Foods that has a number of different successful SBUs. What factors do you think make these units—and this company— successful from a marketing standpoint?

ETHICS EXERCISE

Recent tests by the Canadian Food Inspection Agency found 4.3 grams of fat in a McDonald's chicken fajita, advertised as having 2.5 grams of fat; 19.4 grams of fat in KFC chicken strips, advertised as having 12 grams of fat; and 0.7 grams of trans fat—a fat that many consumers try to avoid—in a Fresco soft taco, advertised as having 0.2 grams of trans fat.[33] Frozen diet meals made by Lean Cuisine, Weight Watchers, and Healthy Choice, among others, averaged 8 percent higher in calories than listed on the package labels.[34] Imagine that you are a marketer for a food manufacturer that competes with these firms.

1. Create an advertisement for your firm's food. Decide on a strategy and tactics. Would you follow in the footsteps of some of your competition, or use accurate fat and calorie counts? Would you refer to the study that found discrepancies in your competitors' numbers?
2. Would you price your own firm's food higher or lower than the competition's? Why?

INTERNET EXERCISES

1. **Business portfolio analysis.** Occasionally, companies sell parts of themselves to other firms. One stated motive for such divestitures is that the sold assets are a poor strategic fit for the rest of their business portfolios. One recent example is the sale of a controlling interest in NBC Universal by General Electric to cable giant Comcast. Using a major search engine, research the sale of NBC Universal. In the context of business portfolio analysis, why did GE decide to sell, and why did Comcast decide to buy, NBC Universal?

2. **Mission and objectives.** Visit the website of the Sara Lee Corporation (www.saralee.com), whose slogan is "the joy of eating." Define the firm's mission and objectives, and discuss how its brands and activities support both.

3. **SWOT analysis.** Visit the website of an organization whose goods and services interest you—such as lululemon athletica, National Hockey League, Travelocity, Apple, or Amazon.ca. Based on your research, create a SWOT analysis for your firm. Outline your own ideas for increasing the firm's strengths and reducing its weaknesses.

Note: Internet web addresses change frequently. If you don't find the exact sites listed, you may need to access the organization's home page and search from there or use a search engine such as Google or Bing.

CASE 2.1

Food Fight

When east goes west and west goes east, there's bound to be problems. Today, Canada may be at the early stage of a pizza war, if you haven't already noticed. Let's back up and look at the foundations for this war.

No one was thinking about a pizza war in 1967 when Pizza Pizza was founded, but the company quickly became a favourite among Canadians, at least in Ontario. In 1979, Pizza Pizza introduced "the slice." It became the first pizzeria to sell individual slices of pizza to hungry Canadians—and the popularity of the chain quickly grew. High school, college, and university students, in particular, found an inexpensive but tasty lunch alternative, and one that was both convenient and filling. Over the years, Pizza Pizza expanded its food offerings to include a number of additional items. Chicken wings were added in the 1990s. Flavours included Honey Garlic—still the favourite today—Hot Sauce, and Sweet Chilli. In the fall of 2010, Pizza Pizza experimented with four additional flavours: Caribbean Jerk, Chipotle Amarillo, Sesame Ginger Teriyaki Thai, and Forty Creek Whisky BBQ, the last one developed in partnership with Ontario's only privately owned whisky distillery, Forty Creek Whisky. The new flavours were test-marketed at 24 Hamilton-area locations, and Pizza Pizza solicited customer feedback through its Facebook page and through Twitter. All four flavours were launched chain-wide in 2011. At approximately the same time, Pizza Pizza added Saint Cinnamon's "cinfully delicious" cinnamon poppers to its menu items for those customers wishing a tasty dessert following their meal.

No one was thinking about a pizza war in 1986 when Panago Pizza was founded, but the company quickly became a favourite among Canadians, at least in British Columbia. From its inception, Panago offered quality ingredients, adding or rotating its upscale toppings. Customers today can choose such interesting toppings as smoked oysters, wild pink shrimp, kalamata olives, sweet corn, chorizo sausage, meat-free pepperoni, grilled veggies (zucchini, eggplant, peppers), and more. Even the pizza sauce comes in a number of varieties: pesto, sweet and smoky tropical, passata tomato, chipotle cilantro, and more. Finally, crusts and cheeses are also offered in a variety of choices. In short, adventuresome customers can "engineer" their own pizza. Wayne Maillet, president of Franchise Specialists, says, "Panago positions itself as very lifestyle-oriented, with adventurous cuisine and a focus on changing the flavour profile."

By early 2011, both companies were busy invading "foreign" territory. Pizza Pizza had already opened eight locations across western Canada and had entered the Alberta market by acquiring Edmonton-based Pizza 73, an established brand name that it continues to maintain. Its expansion plans for most of western Canada were not announced, but it did state that it hoped to increase its presence in Manitoba from two locations to 14 locations within three years. Panago Pizza had 13 locations in eastern Canada and planned to open ten new locations by the end of 2011. The company knew it would face a strong entrenched competitor in eastern Canada. Pizza Pizza was the "slice" leader in Canada, selling nearly 14 million slices of pizza per year. Not willing to sell its pizza by the slice, Panago introduced its personal-sized pizzas in Ontario, betting that consumers would prefer to wait four minutes for them to be cooked in the company's patented ovens rather than settle for reheated slices that may have been sitting for an extended period under a heat lamp.

Both companies have a strong franchise base upon which to build. Pizza Pizza began 2011 with more than 600 franchisees; Panago Pizza was closing in on 200. The fight for good franchisees will be heating up as the two competitors continue their invasion plans.

Questions for Critical Thinking

1. Identify one goal for Pizza Pizza and one goal for Panago Pizza.
2. Describe Pizza Pizza's corporate strategy for growth. Does it differ from Panago Pizza's corporate growth strategy? Explain.
3. If you were interested in owning a fast-food franchise today, would you prefer to own a franchise of the entrenched brand or of the invading brand? What factors would you consider when making your choice?

Sources: Panago website, http://www.panago.com, March 16, 2011; Pizza Pizza website, http://www.pizzapizza.ca, March 16, 2011; Annette Boudreau, "Who'll Win the Pizza War?" *Profit*, December 2010–January 2011, pp. 17–18; Anonymous, "Pizza Pizza Launches New Chicken Wings Chain-Wide," *Marketwire*, January 24, 2011; Anonymous, "Saint Cinnamon Rolls Out at Pizza Pizza Locations in Canada," *Marketwire*, December 2, 2010; Anonymous, "Pizza Pizza Tempts Taste Buds in Hamilton with Pilot Program," *Marketwire*, November 25, 2010.

CASE 2.2

Starbucks' Strategy: It's a Small World After All

If your strategy is growth, you might as well go for the whole cuppa joe. That's what Starbucks is doing—expanding into international markets as if it were the most natural thing to do. To some experts, it is the best plan for a company that has been called by Wall Street analysts "the last great growth story." Starbucks has certainly been showing the way. As of January 2011, the company had 17,009 stores operating in more than 50 countries, just over half of them company owned. Some analysts, however, were skeptical. Why, for instance, would an American coffee maker try to pitch its brew against world-famous French dark espresso? "American coffee, it's only water. We call it *jus des chausettes*," sniffs Bertrand Abadie, a documentary filmmaker. (In case you don't speak fluent French, he called your favourite Starbucks flavour "sock juice.") But Starbucks now has more than 50 locations in France. Then there's China—a nation of about 1 billion tea drinkers. How does Starbucks intend to convert a nation whose favourite drink for the past 4500 years has been tea? "Quickly" is the answer. With about 400 current locations in China and 70 percent of the country's coffee-shop market, Starbucks plans to have 1500 locations by 2015. Profit per store is also higher in China than in the United States. Other countries are in the picture for growth as well, such as Japan and Spain. "We're taking the long view that opportunities are so large and that these are the early days," explains Starbucks CEO Howard Schultz.

According to Schultz, in the next few years, Starbucks intends to increase its global presence and continues to expand its opportunities to sell its coffees and coffee-related products through specialty operations outside its company-operated retail stores. "We're building a brand, not a fad," he explains. The Starbucks brand includes everything from its special flavours to its logo—a mermaid on a green background—which is already one of the most famous product images in North America.

Part of the company's strategy is to target younger consumers around the world. Austria's 20-something coffee drinkers already view Starbucks as something new and tasty. "The coffeehouses in Vienna are nice, but they are old. Starbucks is hip," says one newspaper editor. In Spain, the new Starbucks stores are teeming with teens, young adults, and tourists. "We're not going to capture everybody, but I see a younger generation of Spaniards and people of all sorts," observes CEO Schultz. The company is also selling a little bit of luxury in many of these countries, where the average income is lower than in the United States and Canada. A medium-size latte sells for 20 yuan, or about $2.65 in Shanghai, China—a luxury for a household whose monthly income might be around $143 (U.S.). But Chinese consumers view it as an affordable treat.

Scouting the right locations for international shops is also part of Starbucks' planning. In China, local marketers literally stand outside potential locations with hand-held clickers, tallying every possible customer who walks by. Young fashionable couples get enthusiastic clicks. These consumers represent the emerging middle class in China—people with a bit of extra cash to spend and a desire for consumer goods. Starbucks analyzes pedestrian traffic through a location and researches where the newer, trendy areas will be in the next few years. Then marketers figure out where consumers live, work, and play. Finally, they put together a plan for a new store.

Strategic alliances may be a vital factor in Starbucks' ultimate success around the world. In Japan, the firm has partnered with a local handbag manufacturer, Sazaby Inc. In Spain, Starbucks has joined forces with Grupo Vips, the second-largest family-owned restaurant operator in the country. And in France, Starbucks executives have talked with several companies, although Schultz denies he is looking for an outright partner. "Many of those conversations were not so much about partnering but learning about doing business in France and sharing information about their experience," he insists.

Growth is not easy or simple, and Starbucks will have to persevere in an uncertain marketing environment around the world. Some experts accuse Starbucks and other companies of trying to "sell American culture" to international consumers and predict that the novelty will wear off soon. The company has been caught in political turmoil as well. Consumers boycotted a Starbucks store in Lebanon in protest against the war in Iraq, and Starbucks was forced to close its stores in Tel Aviv because of the violent conflict between Israelis and Palestinians. Then there are the skeptics in France. "The first café was founded in Paris over 300 years ago," claims one French scholar. "Starbucks is not going to compete with the French café. The café isn't just somewhere to drink coffee, it's a place where people go for social contact. In a big place with hundreds of customers, that's difficult." But Schultz remains optimistic. "Perhaps we can be a great example of something that is American, that is very respectful of the French culture, and we want to bridge that gap."

On March 8, 2011, Starbucks marked its 40th anniversary. Plans for its next 40 years begin with the rollout of a new Starbucks logo: a simple uncluttered design that shows the familiar Starbucks icon, without the company name or the word "coffee." Perhaps Starbucks can get the whole world to sit down and drink a cup of American coffee. Or perhaps Starbucks is preparing the world for a host of new products besides its signature coffees.

Questions for Critical Thinking

1. Create a brief SWOT analysis of Starbucks focusing on its plans for international growth. Do you think this strategy is a good one for the company? Why or why not?
2. Identify the dimensions of the marketing environment that are mostly likely to affect Starbucks' strategy for global growth and explain why.

Sources: Starbucks website, http://www.starbucks.com, March 12, 2011; Anonymous, "ETC.: Thirsty China to Fuel Arabica Coffee Demand," *Calgary Herald*, January 28, 2011, p. C2; Andy Serwer, "Hot Starbucks to Go," *Fortune*, January 26, 2004, pp. 61–74; Noelle Knox, "Paris Starbucks Hopes to Prove U.S. Coffee Isn't Sock Juice," *USA Today*, January 16, 2004, p. B3; Laurent Rebours, "Starbucks Opens First French Shop to American Joe," *USA Today*, January 15, 2004, http://www.usatoday.com; Geoffrey A. Fowler, "Starbucks' Road to China," *Wall Street Journal*, July 14, 2003, pp. B1, B3; Jason Singer and Martin Fackler, "In Japan, Adding Beer, Wine to Latté List," *Wall Street Journal*, July 14, 2003, pp. B1, B3; Amy Wu, "Starbucks' World Won't Be Built in a Day," *Forbes.com*, June 27, 2003, http://www.forbes.com; Gavin Edwards, "The Logo," *Rolling Stone*, May 15, 2003, p. 110; Helen Jung, "Lattés for All: Starbucks Plans Global Expansion," *News Tribune*, April 20, 2003, http://www.globalexchange.org.

appendix

Creating an Effective Marketing Plan

Overview

"What are our mission and goals?"

"Who are our customers?"

"What types of products do we offer?"

"How can we provide superior customer service?"

THESE are some of the questions addressed by a **marketing plan**—a detailed description of the resources and actions needed to achieve stated marketing objectives. Chapter 2 discussed **strategic planning**—the process of anticipating events and market conditions and deciding how a firm can best achieve its organizational objectives. Marketing planning encompasses all the activities devoted to achieving marketing objectives, establishing a basis for designing a marketing strategy. This appendix deals in depth with the formal marketing plan, which is part of an organization's overall business plan. At the end of this appendix, you'll see what an actual marketing plan looks like. Each plan component for a hypothetical firm called Wild Canada Clothing is presented. ◆◆◆

COMPONENTS OF A BUSINESS PLAN

A company's **business plan** is one of its most important documents. The business plan puts in writing all the company's objectives, how they will be achieved, how the business will obtain financing, and how much money the company expects to earn over a specified time period. Although business plans vary in length and format, most contain at least some form of the following components:

- An *executive summary* briefly answers the who, what, when, where, how, and why questions for the plan. Although the summary appears early in the plan, it is typically written last, after the firm's executives have worked out the details of all the other sections.

- A *competitive analysis* section focuses on the environment in which the marketing plan is to be implemented. Although this section is more closely associated with the comprehensive business plan, factors specifically influencing marketing are likely to be included here.

- The *mission statement* summarizes the organization's purpose, vision, and overall goals. This statement provides the foundation upon which further planning is based.

- The overall business plan includes a series of *component* plans that present goals and strategies for each functional area of the enterprise. They typically include the following:

  The *marketing* plan, which describes strategies for informing potential customers about the goods and services offered by the firm as well as strategies for developing long-term relationships. At the end of this appendix, a sample marketing plan for Wild Canada Clothing is presented.

  The *financing plan*, which presents a realistic approach for securing needed funds and managing debt and cash flows.

marketing plan
Detailed description of the resources and actions needed to achieve stated marketing objectives.

strategic planning
Process of determining an organization's primary objectives and adopting courses of action that will achieve these objectives.

business plan Formal document that outlines a company's objectives, how they will be met, how the business will achieve financing, and how much money the firm expects to earn.

The *production plan*, which describes how the organization will develop its products in the most efficient, cost-effective manner possible.

The *facilities plan*, which describes the physical environment and equipment required to implement the production plan.

The *human resources plan*, which estimates the firm's employment needs and the skills necessary to achieve organizational goals, including a comparison of current employees with the needs of the firm, and which establishes processes for securing adequately trained personnel if a gap exists between current employee skills and future needs.

This basic format encompasses the planning process used by nearly every successful organization. Whether a company operates in the manufacturing, wholesaling, retailing, or service sector (or a combination), the components described here are likely to appear in its overall business plan. Regardless of the size or longevity of a company, a business plan is an essential tool for a firm's owners because it helps them focus on the key elements of their business. Even small firms that are just starting out need a business plan to obtain financing. Figure 1 shows the outline of a business plan for Wild Canada Clothing.

figure 1

Outline of a Business Plan

The Wild Canada Clothing Business Plan

I. Executive Summary
- Who, What, When, Where, How, and Why

II. Table of Contents

III. Introduction
- Mission Statement
- Concept and Company
- Management Team
- Product

IV. Marketing Strategy
- Demographics
- Trends
- Market Penetration
- Potential Sales Revenue

V. Financing the Business
- Cash Flow Analysis
- Pro Forma Balance Sheet
- Income Statement

VI. Facilities Plan
- Physical Environment
- Equipment

VII. Human Resource Plan
- Employment Needs and Skills
- Current Employees

VIII. Résumés of Principals

CREATING A MARKETING PLAN

Keep in mind that a marketing plan should be created in conjunction with the other elements of a firm's business plan. In addition, a marketing plan often draws from the business plan, restating the executive summary, competitive analysis, and mission statement to give its readers an overall view of the firm. The marketing plan is needed for a variety of reasons:

- To obtain financing because banks and most private investors require a detailed business plan—including a marketing plan component—before they will even consider a loan application or a venture capital investment.

- To provide direction for the firm's overall business and marketing strategies.

- To support the development of long-term and short-term organizational objectives.

- To guide employees in achieving these objectives.

- To serve as a standard against which the firm's progress can be measured and evaluated.

In addition, the marketing plan is where a firm puts into writing its commitment to its customers and to building long-lasting relationships. After creating and implementing the plan, marketers must re-evaluate it periodically to gauge its success in moving the organization toward its goals. If changes are needed, they should be made as soon as possible.

FORMULATING AN OVERALL MARKETING STRATEGY

Before creating a marketing plan, a firm's marketers formulate an overall marketing strategy. A firm may use a number of tools in marketing planning, including business portfolio analysis and the BCG matrix. Its executives may conduct a SWOT analysis, take advantage of a strategic window, study Porter's Five Forces model as it relates to their business, or consider adopting a first mover or second mover strategy, all of which are described in Chapter 2.

In addition to the planning strategies discussed in Chapter 2, marketers are likely to use **spreadsheet analysis,** which lays out a grid of columns and rows that organize numerical information in a standardized, easily understood format. Spreadsheet analysis helps planners answer various "what if" questions related to the firm's financing and operations. The most popular spreadsheet software is Microsoft Excel. A spreadsheet analysis helps planners anticipate marketing performance given specified sets of circumstances. For example, a spreadsheet might project the outcomes of different pricing decisions for a new product, as shown in Figure 2.

Once general planning strategies are determined, marketers begin to flesh out the details of the marketing strategy. The elements of a marketing strategy include identifying the target market, studying the marketing environment, and creating a marketing mix. When marketers have identified the target market, they can develop the optimal marketing mix to reach their potential customers:

- *Product strategy.* Which goods and services should the company offer to meet its customers' needs?

- *Distribution strategy.* Through which channel(s) and physical facilities will the firm distribute its products?

- *Promotional strategy.* What mix of advertising, sales promotion, and personal selling activities will the firm use to reach its customers initially and then develop long-term relationships?

- *Pricing strategy.* At what level should the company set its prices?

THE EXECUTIVE SUMMARY, COMPETITIVE ANALYSIS, AND MISSION STATEMENT

Because these three elements of the business plan often reappear in the marketing plan, it is useful to describe them here. Recall that the executive summary answers the who, what, when, where, how, and why questions for the business. The executive summary for Google would include references to its current strategic planning process for its search services, which relies on developing new "ways in which

spreadsheet analysis Grid that organizes information in a standardized, easily understood format.

figure 2

**How Spreadsheet
Analysis Works**

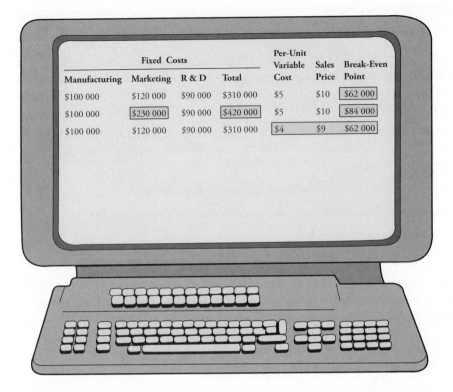

Fixed Costs				Per-Unit Variable Cost	Sales Price	Break-Even Point
Manufacturing	Marketing	R & D	Total			
$100 000	$120 000	$90 000	$310 000	$5	$10	$62 000
$100 000	$230 000	$90 000	$420 000	$5	$10	$84 000
$100 000	$120 000	$90 000	$310 000	$4	$9	$62 000

technology can improve upon existing ways of doing business."[1] It would go on to answer questions such as who is involved (key people and organizations), what length of time the plan represents, and how the goals will be met.

The competitive analysis focuses on the environment in which the marketing plan is to be implemented. For Travel Alberta, the strengthening of the Canadian dollar creates a major challenge. It becomes more difficult to convince international tourists that Alberta still provides value, at the same time that Albertans see that their own dollar goes farther when they decide to take foreign vacations.[2] Alberta does have one advantage over other Canadian provinces: it does not charge provincial sales tax. This helps make Alberta an attractive vacation destination for Canadians from other provinces.

The mission statement puts into words an organization's overall purpose and reason for being: what it does, whom it serves, and how it will be successful. The mission statement of Quebec-based Uniboard Canada is "to be the leading integrated supplier of engineered wood products in the furniture, store fixtures, millwork, kitchen cabinets, and flooring industries in North America." Uniboard differentiates itself by developing, expanding, and promoting value-added branded products more quickly and efficiently than its competitors. Its products are manufactured in 10 plants in Quebec, Ontario, and Ohio.[3]

DESCRIPTION OF THE COMPANY

Near the beginning of the marketing plan—typically following the executive summary and before the mission statement—a description of the company is included. The company description may include a brief history or background of the firm, the types of products it offers or plans to introduce, recent successes or achievements—in short, it consists of a few paragraphs containing the kind of information often found on the home page of a company's website.

STATEMENT OF GOALS AND CORE COMPETENCIES

The plan then includes a statement of the firm's goals and its core competencies—those things it does extremely well or better than anyone else. The goals should be specific and measurable and may be divided into financial and nonfinancial aims. A financial goal might be to add 75 new franchises in the next 12 months or to reach $10 million in revenues. A nonfinancial goal might be to enter the

European market or to add a new product line every other year. Travel Alberta, mentioned previously, has a stated financial objective of achieving $6.5 billion in tourism revenue by 2011. A nonfinancial objective is to achieve 80 percent satisfaction among industry users who seek information and marketing knowledge from the Travel Alberta website.[4]

Core competencies are what make a firm stand out from everyone else in the marketplace. Costco's core competency is offering a wide variety of consumer goods at low prices, including some luxury-brand items such as Lilaque crystal vases, Mont Blanc pens, and Royal Doulton figurines. Jim Sinegal, co-founder and CEO, is known for keeping costs low, but not wages and benefits. He believes strongly in the value of his company's nearly 119 000 employees and rewards them well. "Our attitude," he says, "is that if you hire good people and pay them a fair wage, then good things will happen for the company."[5]

Small businesses often begin with a single core competency and build their business and reputation on it. It is important for a new firm to identify its core competency in the marketing plan so that investors or banks understand why they should lend the firm money to get started or to grow to the next stage. Leslie Blesius successfully fended off competitors such as Pottery Barn and Restoration Hardware when she was establishing her upscale home furnishings shop. She focused on what she did better than the chains, offering personalized services such as in-home consultations and installations, more selection, and more custom options. "It's all about how much we can help," Blesius says. Her strategy was so successful that she was able to survive and even expand, offering new furniture lines and opening a bed and bath section.[6]

OUTLINE OF THE MARKETING ENVIRONMENT (SITUATION ANALYSIS)

Every successful marketing plan takes into consideration the marketing environment—the competitive, economic, political-legal, technological, and social-cultural factors that affect the way a firm formulates and implements its marketing strategy. Marketing plans may address these issues in different ways, but the goal is to present information that describes the company's position or situation within the marketing environment. J. Crew, for instance, has a well-known brand name and a CEO with an impressive track record: Mickey Drexler, who previously headed The Gap. The retail environment for stores like J. Crew is highly competitive. Merchandise that doesn't appeal to enough customers ends up on a clearance rack and hurts the bottom line. According to Drexler, the key to J. Crew's success is that it sells merchandise that "cannot be sold anywhere else." Drexler pushes his buyers to "outproduct" their competitors.[7] A marketing plan for J. Crew would include an evaluation of competing stores such as The Gap and Urban Outfitters, any technological advances that would affect such factors as merchandise distribution or inventory, social-cultural issues such as fashion preferences and spending habits of customers, and economic issues affecting a pricing strategy.

One such method for outlining the marketing environment in the marketing plan is to include a SWOT analysis, described in Chapter 2. A SWOT analysis identifies the firm's strengths, weaknesses, opportunities, and threats within the marketing environment. A SWOT analysis for J. Crew might include strengths such as its corporate leadership, brand name, and upscale target market. Weaknesses might include the risks inherent in the business of correctly spotting fashion trends. A major opportunity lies in the fact that J. Crew can expand almost anywhere—in fact, it plans to add between 25 and 35 new stores every year—and it will also expand its offerings to include a line of children's wear, a lower-priced casual line, and wedding attire. Threats include competition from other trendy stores, sudden changes in customer preferences, and economic dips that affect spending.[8] A SWOT analysis can be presented in chart format so it is easy to read as part of the marketing plan. The sample marketing plan in this appendix includes a SWOT analysis for Wild Canada Clothing.

THE TARGET MARKET AND MARKETING MIX

The marketing plan identifies the target market for the firm's products. In marketing its new Head & Shoulders Hair Endurance for Men, Procter & Gamble targeted males with thinning hair. The reason? The company's research revealed that more than 44 percent of males who experience hair loss also report dandruff in the months prior to the hair loss. The new shampoo reportedly reduces hair breakage by eliminating dandruff.[9] In another example of targeting, the Cute Overload website (www .cuteoverload.com) contains photos and videos of animals that visitors can share and about which they can post comments. But the site also offers a page-a-day desk calendar of the same name featuring images of puppies, kittens, birds, and chipmunks with humorous captions. Cute Overload targets women ages 18 to 34 who need a laugh and a brief escape from the real world. The calendars are also offered for sale on Amazon.com, and the retailer's inventory sold out in one day, which astonished the developer.[10]

The marketing plan also discusses the marketing mix the firm has selected for its products. Hollywood studios are known for implementing lavish strategies for promoting their films. Not only did Columbia Pictures use all the traditional means for launching *The Karate Kid*, a remake of the 1984 hit, it also partnered with other organizations and products to promote the movie. Little Caesars Pizza and PepsiCo co-sponsored a scratch-off game promotion featuring the film. Before the film's debut, Six Flags amusement parks held on-site competitions to identify the most talented karate students. And Apple's recently launched iPad included a free mobile game that promoted the film's opening. *The Karate Kid* raked in $56 million in revenues in its first weekend.[11]

BUDGET, SCHEDULE, AND MONITORING

Every marketing plan requires a budget, a time schedule for implementation, and a system for monitoring the plan's success or failure. Typically, a budget includes a breakdown of the costs incurred as the marketing program is implemented, offset by projected sales, profits, and losses over the time period of the program.

Most long-range marketing plans encompass a two- to five-year period, although companies that do business in industries such as auto manufacturing, pharmaceuticals, or lumber may extend their marketing plans further into the future because it typically takes longer to develop these products. However, marketers in most industries will have difficulty making estimates and predictions beyond five years because of the many uncertainties in the marketplace. Firms also may opt to develop short-term plans to cover marketing activities for a single year.

The marketing plan, whether it is long term or short term, predicts how long it will take to achieve the goals set out by the plan. A goal may be opening a certain number of new stores, market share growth, or achieving an expansion of the product line. Finally, the marketing program is monitored and evaluated for its performance. Monthly, quarterly, and annual sales targets are usually tracked; the efficiency with which certain tasks are completed is determined; customer satisfaction is measured and so forth. All of these factors contribute to the overall review of the program.

At some point, a firm may opt to implement an *exit strategy*, a contingency plan for the firm leaving the market. A common way for a large company to do this is to sell off a business unit. A number of these strategies have been implemented recently: for example, GMAC Financial Services exited the European mortgage market by selling its U.K. financial unit, GMAC-RFC, to Fortress Investment Group. The move is expected to help improve GMAC's financial performance.[12]

An exit strategy is equally important for a small business. There are 2.5 million small business owners in Canada. About 90 percent have sales under $1 million. A common growth strategy among such businesses is to open a second location. Deloitte partner Richard Carson says, "Many people don't think about the degree to which that second location will have synergy or cannibalization with the first."[13] Not having a good exit strategy when a second location is failing could result in bankruptcy.

SAMPLE MARKETING PLAN

The following pages contain an annotated sample marketing plan for Wild Canada Clothing. At some point in your career, you will likely be involved in writing—or at least contributing to—a marketing plan. And you'll certainly read many marketing plans throughout your business career. Keep in mind that the plan for Wild Canada is a single example; no one format is used by all companies. Also, the Wild Canada plan has been somewhat condensed to make it easier to annotate and illustrate the most vital features. The important point to remember is that the marketing plan is a document designed to present concise, cohesive information about a company's marketing objectives to managers, lending institutions, and others who are involved in creating and carrying out the firm's overall business strategy.

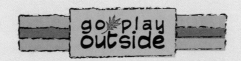

FIVE-YEAR MARKETING PLAN
WILD CANADA CLOTHING, INC.

TABLE OF CONTENTS

EXECUTIVE SUMMARY

This five-year marketing plan for Wild Canada Clothing has been created by its two founders to secure additional funding for growth and to inform employees of the company's current status and direction. Although Wild Canada was launched only three years ago, the firm has experienced greater-than-anticipated demand for its products, and research has shown that the target market of sports-minded consumers and sports retailers would like to buy more casual clothing than Wild Canada currently offers. The company is also interested in extending its product line as well as adding new product lines. In addition, Wild Canada plans to explore opportunities for online sales. The marketing environment has been very receptive to the firm's high-quality goods—casual clothing in trendy colours with logos and slogans that reflect the interests of outdoor enthusiasts around the country. Over the next five years, Wild Canada can increase its distribution, offer new products, and win new customers.

> The executive summary outlines the who, what, where, when, how, and why of the marketing plan. Wild Canada is only three years old and is successful enough that it now needs a formal marketing plan to obtain additional financing from a bank or private investors for expansion and the launch of new products.

COMPANY DESCRIPTION

Wild Canada Clothing was founded three years ago by entrepreneurs Lucy Neuman and Nick Russell. Neuman has an undergraduate degree in marketing and worked for several years in the retail clothing industry. Russell operated an adventure business called Go West!, which arranges group trips to locations in Manitoba, Saskatchewan, Alberta, and British Columbia, before selling the enterprise to a partner. Neuman and Russell, who have been friends since college, decided to develop and market a line of clothing with a unique—yet universal—appeal to outdoor enthusiasts.

> The company description summarizes the history of Wild Canada—how it was founded and by whom, what its products are, and why they are unique. It begins to "sell" the reader on the growth possibilities for Wild Canada.

Wild Canada Clothing reflects Neuman's and Russell's passion for the outdoors. The company's original cotton T-shirts, baseball caps, and fleece jackets and vests bear logos of different sports—such as kayaking, mountain climbing, bicycling, skating, surfing, and horseback riding. But every item shows off the company's slogan "Go Play Outside." Wild Canada sells clothing for both men and women, in the hottest colours with the coolest names—such as sunrise pink, sunset red, twilight purple, desert rose, cactus green, ocean blue, mountaintop white, and river rock grey.

Wild Canada attire is currently carried by small retail stores that specialize in outdoor clothing and gear. Most of these stores are concentrated in British Columbia, Alberta, Ontario, and Quebec. The high quality, trendy colours, and unique message of the clothing have gained Wild Canada a following among consumers between the ages of 25 and 45. Sales have tripled in the last year alone, and Wild Canada is currently working to expand its manufacturing capabilities.

Wild Canada is also committed to giving back to the community by contributing to local conservation programs. Ultimately, the company would like to develop and fund its own environmental programs. This plan will outline how Wild Canada intends to introduce new products, expand its distribution, enter new markets, and give back to the community.

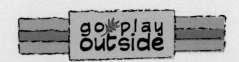

WILD CANADA'S MISSION AND GOALS

Wild Canada's mission is to be the leading producer and marketer of personalized, casual clothing for consumers who love the outdoors. Wild Canada wants to inspire people to get outdoors more often and enjoy family and friends while doing so. In addition, Wild Canada strives to design programs for preserving the natural environment.

During the next five years, Wild Canada seeks to achieve the following financial and nonfinancial goals:

- *Financial goals*

  1. Obtain financing to expand manufacturing capabilities, increase distribution, and introduce two new product lines.

  2. Increase revenues by at least 50 percent each year.

  3. Donate at least $25 000 a year to conservation organizations.

- *Nonfinancial goals*

  1. Introduce two new product lines—customized logo clothing and lightweight luggage.

  2. Enter new geographic markets, including the Atlantic Provinces.

  3. Develop a successful Internet site, while maintaining strong relationships with retailers.

  4. Develop its own conservation program aimed at helping communities raise money to purchase open space.

CORE COMPETENCIES

Wild Canada seeks to use its core competencies to achieve a sustainable competitive advantage, in which competitors cannot provide the same value to consumers that Wild Canada does. Already, Wild Canada has developed core competencies in (1) offering a high-quality, branded product whose image is recognizable among consumers; (2) creating a sense of community among consumers who purchase the products; and (3) developing a reputation among retailers as a reliable manufacturer and delivering the requested number of products on schedule. The firm intends to build on these competencies through marketing efforts that increase the number of products offered as well as distribution outlets.

By forming strong relationships with consumers, retailers, and suppliers of fabric and other goods and services, Wild Canada believes it can create a sustainable competitive advantage over its rivals. No other clothing company can say to its customers with as much conviction "Go Play Outside"!

SITUATION ANALYSIS

The marketing environment for Wild Canada represents overwhelming opportunities. It also contains some challenges that the firm believes it can meet successfully. Figure A illustrates a SWOT analysis of the company conducted by marketers to highlight Wild Canada's strengths, weaknesses, opportunities, and threats.

The SWOT analysis presents a thumbnail sketch of the company's position in the marketplace. In just three years, Wild Canada has built some impressive strengths while looking forward to new opportunities. Its dedicated founders, the growing number of brand-loyal customers, and sound financial management place the company in a good position to grow. However, as Wild Canada considers expansion of its product line and entrance into new markets, the firm will have to guard against marketing myopia (the failure to recognize the scope of its business) and quality slippages. As the company finalizes plans for new

It is important to state a firm's mission and goals, including financial and nonfinancial goals. Wild Canada's goals include growth and profits for the company as well as the ability to contribute to society through conservation programs.

This section reminds employees as well as those outside the company (such as potential lenders) exactly what Wild Canada does so well and how it plans to achieve a sustainable competitive advantage over rivals. Note that here and throughout the plan, Wild Canada focuses on relationships.

The situation analysis provides an outline of the marketing environment. A SWOT analysis helps marketers and others identify clearly a firm's strengths, weaknesses, opportunities, and threats. Again, relationships are a focus. Wild Canada has also conducted research on the outdoor clothing market, competitors, and consumers to determine how best to attract and keep customers.

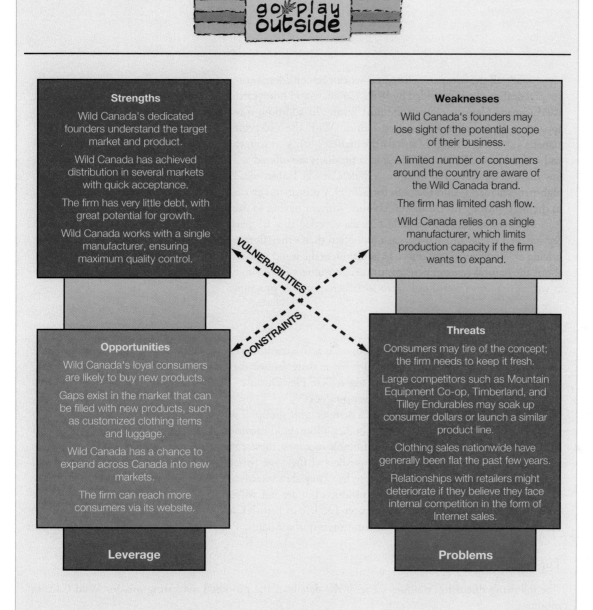

products and expanded Internet sales, its management will also have to guard against competitors who attempt to duplicate the products. However, building strong relationships with consumers, retailers, and suppliers should help thwart competitors.

COMPETITORS IN THE OUTDOOR CLOTHING MARKET

The outdoor retail sales industry sells more than $500 million worth of goods annually, ranging from clothing to equipment. The outdoor apparel market has many entries. L.L. Bean, Timberland, Bass Pro Shops, Patagonia, Tilley Endurables, and Mountain Equipment Co-op are among the most recognizable companies that offer these products. Smaller competitors such as Title IX, which offers athletic clothing for women, and Ragged Mountain, which sells fleece clothing for skiers and hikers, also grab some of the market. The outlook for the industry in general—and Wild Canada in particular—is positive for several reasons. First, consumers are participating in and investing in recreational activities that are near their homes. Second, consumers are looking for ways to enjoy their leisure time with friends and family without overspending. Third, consumers are gaining more confidence in the economy and are willing and able to spend more.

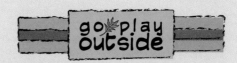

While all the companies listed earlier can be considered competitors, none offers the kind of trendy, yet practical products provided by Wild Canada—and none carries the customized logos and slogans that Wild Canada plans to offer in the near future. In addition, most of these competitors sell performance apparel in high-tech manufactured fabrics. With the exception of the fleece vests and jackets, Wild Canada's clothing is made of strictly the highest quality cotton, so it may be worn both on the hiking trail and around town. Finally, Wild Canada products are offered at moderate prices, making it affordable to buy them in quantity. For instance, a Wild Canada T-shirt sells for $15.99, compared with a competing high-performance T-shirt that sells for $29.99. Consumers can easily replace a set of shirts from one season to the next, picking up the newest colours, without having to think about the purchase.

A survey conducted by Wild Canada revealed that 67 percent of responding consumers prefer to replace their casual and active wear more often than other clothing, so they are attracted by the moderate pricing of Wild Canada products. In addition, as the trend toward health-conscious activities and concerns about the natural environment continues, consumers increasingly relate to the Wild Canada philosophy as well as the firm's contributions to socially responsible programs.

THE TARGET MARKET

The target market for Wild Canada products is active consumers between the ages of 25 and 45—people who like to hike, rock climb, bicycle, surf, figure skate, in-line skate, ride horses, snowboard or ski, kayak, and other such activities. In short, they like to "Go Play Outside." They might not be experts at the sports they engage in, but they enjoy themselves outdoors.

These active consumers represent a demographic group of well-educated and successful individuals; they are single or married and raising families. Household incomes generally range between $60 000 and $120 000 annually. Despite their comfortable incomes, these consumers are price conscious and consistently seek value in their purchases. Regardless of their age (whether they fall at the upper or lower end of the target range), they lead active lifestyles. They are somewhat status oriented but not overly so. They like to be associated with high-quality products but are not willing to pay a premium price for a certain brand. Current Wild Canada customers tend to live in British Columbia, Alberta, Ontario, and Quebec. However, one future goal is to target consumers in the Atlantic Provinces, Manitoba, and Saskatchewan.

> Wild Canada has identified its customers as active people between the ages of 25 and 45. However, that doesn't mean someone who is older or prefers to read about the outdoors isn't a potential customer as well. By pinpointing where existing customers live, Wild Canada can make plans for growth into new outlets.

THE MARKETING MIX

The following discussion outlines some of the details of the proposed marketing mix for Wild Canada products.

PRODUCT STRATEGY. Wild Canada currently offers a line of high-quality outdoor apparel items including cotton T-shirts, baseball caps, and fleece vests and jackets. All bear the company logo and slogan "Go Play Outside." The firm has researched the most popular colours for its items and given them names that consumers enjoy—sunset red, sunrise pink, cactus green, desert rose, and river rock grey, among others. Over the next five years, Wild Canada plans to expand the product line to include customized clothing items. Customers may select a logo that represents their sport—say, rock climbing. Then they can add a slogan to match the logo, such as "Get Over It." A baseball cap with a bicyclist might bear the slogan "Take a Spin." At the beginning, there would be 10 new logos and five new slogans; more would be added later. Eventually, some slogans and logos would be retired, and new ones introduced. This strategy will keep the concept fresh and prevent it from becoming diluted with too many variations.

The second way in which Wild Canada plans to expand its product line is to offer items of lightweight luggage—two sizes of duffel bags, two sizes of tote bags, and a daypack. These items would also

> The strongest part of the marketing mix for Wild Canada involves sales promotions, public relations, and nontraditional marketing strategies such as attending outdoor events and organizing activities like day hikes and bike rides.

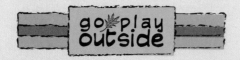

come in trendy and basic colours, with a choice of logos and slogans. In addition, every product would bear the Wild Canada logo.

DISTRIBUTION STRATEGY. Currently, Wild Canada is marketed through regional and local specialty shops scattered throughout British Columbia, Alberta, Ontario, and Quebec. So far, Wild Canada has not been distributed through national sporting goods and apparel chains. Climate and season tend to dictate the sales at specialty shops, which sell more T-shirts and baseball caps during warm weather and more fleece vests and jackets during colder months. Wild Canada obtains much of its information about overall industry trends in different geographic areas and at different types of retail outlets from its trade organization, the Canadian Outdoor Industry Association.

Over the next three years, Wild Canada seeks to expand distribution to retail specialty shops throughout the nation, focusing next on the Atlantic Provinces. The firm has not yet determined whether it would be beneficial to sell through a major national chain such as Bass Pro Shops, Mountain Equipment Co-op, or Sports Experts as these outlets could be considered competitors.

In addition, Wild Canada plans to expand online sales by offering the customized product line via Internet only, thus distinguishing between Internet offerings and specialty shop offerings. Eventually, the company may be able to place Internet kiosks at some of the more profitable store outlets so consumers could order customized products from the stores. Regardless of its expansion plans, Wild Canada fully intends to monitor and maintain strong relationships with distribution channel members.

PROMOTIONAL STRATEGY. Wild Canada communicates with consumers and retailers about its products in a variety of ways. Information about Wild Canada—the company as well as its products—is available via the Internet, direct mailings, and in person. The firm's promotional efforts also seek to differentiate its products from those of its competitors.

The company relies on personal contact with retailers to establish the products in their stores. This contact, whether in person or by phone, helps convey the Wild Canada message, demonstrate the products' unique qualities, and build relationships. Wild Canada sales representatives visit each store two or three times a year and offer in-store training on the features of the products for new retailers or for those who want a refresher. As distribution expands, Wild Canada will adjust to meet greater demand by increasing sales staff to make sure its stores are visited more frequently.

Sales promotions and public relations currently make up the bulk of Wild Canada's promotional strategy. Wild Canada staff works with retailers to offer short-term sales promotions tied to events and contests. In addition, Nick Russell is currently working with several trip outfitters to offer Wild Canada items on a promotional basis. Because Wild Canada also engages in cause marketing through its contribution to environmental programs, good public relations have followed.

Nontraditional marketing methods that require little cash and a lot of creativity also lend themselves perfectly to Wild Canada. Because Wild Canada is a small, flexible organization, the firm can easily implement ideas such as distributing free water, stickers, and discount coupons at outdoor sporting events. During the next year, the company plans to engage in the following marketing efforts:

- Create a Wild Canada Tour, in which several employees take turns driving around the country to campgrounds to distribute promotional items such as Wild Canada stickers and discount coupons.

- Attend canoe and kayak races, bicycling events, and rock climbing competitions with the Wild Canada truck to distribute free water, stickers, and discount coupons for Wild Canada shirts or hats.

- Organize Wild Canada hikes departing from participating retailers.

- Hold a Wild Canada design contest, selecting a winning slogan and logo to be added to the customized line.

An actual plan will include more specific financial details, which will be folded into the overall business plan. For more information, see the "Financial Analysis in Marketing" appendix on page A-1 of this book. In addition, Wild Canada states that, at this stage, it does not have plans to make a public stock offering or exit the market by merging with another firm.

PRICING STRATEGY. As discussed earlier in this plan, Wild Canada products are priced with the competition in mind. The firm is not concerned with setting high prices to signal luxury or prestige, nor is it attempting to achieve the goals of offsetting low prices by selling high quantities of products. Instead, value pricing is practised so that customers feel comfortable purchasing new clothing to replace the old, even if it is just because they like the new colours. The pricing strategy also makes Wild Canada products good gifts—for birthdays, graduations, or "just because." The customized clothing will sell for $2 to $4 more than the regular Wild Canada logo clothing. The luggage will be priced competitively, offering good value against its competition.

BUDGET, SCHEDULE, AND MONITORING

Though its history is short, Wild Canada has enjoyed a steady increase in sales since its introduction three years ago. Figure B shows these three years, plus projected sales for the next three years, including the introduction of the two new product lines. Additional financial data are included in the overall business plan for the company.

figure B

Annual Sales for Wild Canada Clothing: 2011–2016

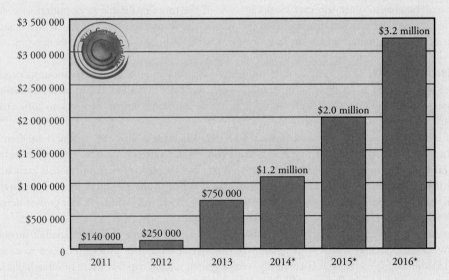

*Projected sales

The timeline for expansion of outlets and introduction of the two new product lines is shown in Figure C. The implementation of each of these tasks will be monitored closely and evaluated for its performance.

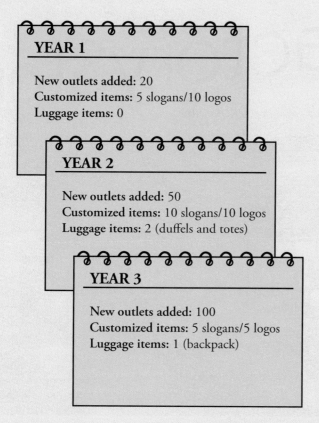

figure C

Timeline for First Three Years of Marketing Plan

Wild Canada anticipates continuing operations into the foreseeable future, with no plans to exit this market. Instead, as discussed throughout this plan, the firm plans to increase its presence in the market. At present, there are no plans to merge with another company or to make a public stock offering.

The Marketing Environment, Ethics, and Social Responsibility

CHAPTER OBJECTIVES

(1) Identify the five components of the marketing environment.

(2) Explain the types of competition marketers face and the steps necessary for developing a competitive strategy.

(3) Describe how marketing activities are regulated and how marketers can influence the political-legal environment.

(4) Outline the economic factors that affect marketing decisions and consumer buying power.

(5) Discuss the impact of the technological environment on a firm's marketing activities.

(6) Explain how the social-cultural environment influences marketing.

(7) Describe the ethical issues in marketing.

(8) Identify the four levels of the social responsibility pyramid.

CORPORATE RESPONSIBILITY AT NIKE: JUST DO IT!

Flash back to the late 1990s: Nike was the Big Name in everything athletic—shoes, apparel, equipment. Nike was also the subject of penetrating global scrutiny and criticism for sweatshop conditions in Asian factories where its products were made—this at a time when company revenues were soaring off the charts.

The sweatshop scandal may have been the catalyst that propelled Nike into a comprehensive transformation of its corporate persona. Every facet of the global business—workplace processes, business practices, supply chain, transparency—was put under the microscope. The result: a continuously evolving journey that, the company says, has positioned it to drive toward sustainability in all aspects of its operations.

Nike began its quest for greater corporate responsibility by establishing a global compliance team charged with building a corporate function that would be capable of constant reinvention as it also set standards, identified them, "put out fires," and charted Nike's course for the long term.

By 2001, the work of the Nike compliance team had evolved into what the company called its "second generation."

During the ensuing five-year period, the team worked to articulate work processes that address environmental, health, and workplace safety concerns; create tools and methods for measuring their progress; and enforce the processes across the global firm. The Nike team also gathered and consolidated industry data and shared the information widely, in an effort to create greater transparency not only inside the firm but also throughout the industry.

In 2006, Nike's efforts to create transparency helped move the compliance team into its next generation, which it regards as its "transformation" stage. Since that time, the team has channelled its energy into creating a sustainability strategy for sourcing, building excellence in factory remediation, and forming industry coalitions based on best practices. During this phase, Nike has pushed what it calls "responsible competitiveness," taking a more holistic look at its supply chain and seeking to identify problems and find ways to drive systemic change.

According to a recently issued corporate responsibility report, Nike succeeded in cutting its 2009 greenhouse gas emissions

across its global supply chain to 2007 levels. In addition, a program begun in 2008 to improve energy efficiency at its plants showed a 6 percent reduction in carbon emissions while production increased 9 percent. With heavy investments in teleconference technology, Nike has significantly reduced corporate air travel—a move that keeps more executives off planes and, presumably, enhances productivity. Nike has also joined with other organizations to lobby for legislation that would reward businesses for significant investments in carbon reduction.

The corporate responsibility report helps Nike communicate its vision of a "closed loop" business model, in which a supply chain would generate zero waste and all products and materials would be continuously reused—in other words, no pre- or post-consumer waste. As an example of this model, Nike points to its Air Jordan XX3, designed so that all the shoe's pieces fit together like a jigsaw puzzle, with no waste. Today, Nike senior leadership calls sustainability the "key to Nike's growth and innovation" and continues to grow as a responsible corporate citizen.[1]

---

connecting with customers

Nike co-founder Bill Bowerman may have said it best when he claimed, "If you have a body, you are an athlete." This statement—intended to encourage and motivate Nike employees—has also inspired athletes of all abilities to aim for their personal best. Today, Nike believes it can achieve its own personal best in a sustainable global economy by identifying ways for the company, its employees, consumers, and the planet to mutually thrive.

Chapter Overview

CHANGE is a fact of life for all people, including marketers. Adapting to change in an environment as complex and unpredictable as the world's energy usage is perhaps the supreme challenge. In response to the rising cost of fuel, many airlines are taking their less fuel-efficient aircraft out of service and eliminating flights.[2]

Although some change may be the result of crises, more often it is the result of a gradual trend in lifestyle, income, population, and other factors. Consumers are increasingly interested in buying "green" products—goods that minimize their impact on the environment. Technology can trigger a sudden change in the marketplace: in one fell swoop, it appeared that Internet music downloads had replaced traditional CDs. And within mere months of offering its iPhone, Apple introduced the iPod touch MP3 player, which borrowed touch-screen technology from the iPhone.

Marketers must anticipate and plan for change. They must set goals to meet the concerns of customers, employees, shareholders, and members of the general public. Industry competition, legal constraints, the impact of technology on product designs, and social concerns are some of the many important factors that shape the business environment. All potentially have an impact on a firm's goods and services. Although external forces frequently are outside the marketer's control, decision makers must still consider those influences together with the variables of the marketing mix in developing—and occasionally modifying—marketing plans and strategies that take these environmental factors into consideration.

This chapter begins by describing five forces in marketing's external environment—competitive, political-legal, economic, technological, and social-cultural. Figure 3.1 identifies them as the foundation for making decisions that involve the four marketing mix elements and the target market. These forces provide the frame of reference within which all marketing decisions are made. The second focus of this chapter is marketing ethics and social responsibility. This section describes the nature of marketers' responsibilities both to business and to society at large. ◆◆◆

1. Identify the five components of the marketing environment.

figure 3.1

Elements of the Marketing Mix Within an Environmental Framework

ENVIRONMENTAL SCANNING AND ENVIRONMENTAL MANAGEMENT

Marketers constantly monitor crucial trends and developments in the business environment. **Environmental scanning** is the process of collecting information about the external marketing environment to identify and interpret potential trends. The goal of this process is to analyze the information and decide whether these trends represent significant opportunities or pose major threats to the company. The firm can then determine the best response to a particular environmental change.

We are currently seeing unprecedented rising fuel and energy costs in Canada and an increasing concern about greenhouse gas emissions. Toronto-based Pollution Probe and Calgary-based Canadian Association for Wind Power see alternative sources of energy and technologies to reduce energy costs providing attractive opportunities for Canadian businesses, and *Profit* magazine says "green power" provides some of the best business opportunities for Canadian entrepreneurs.[3] RenewABILITY Energy Inc., based in Waterloo, Ontario, has developed a Power-Pipe, which reclaims and recycles hot water that would otherwise go down the drain. This provides users with considerable cost savings as reduced energy is needed to reheat the water and, along with reduced energy needs, there is a decrease in greenhouse gas emissions. This new product has applications in university residences, health clubs, apartment buildings, food processing plants, and pulp and paper mills, as well as in private homes.[4]

Environmental scanning is a vital component of effective **environmental management**. Environmental management involves marketers' efforts to achieve organizational objectives by predicting and influencing the competitive, political-legal, economic, technological, and social-cultural environments. In the political-legal environment, managers who are seeking modifications of regulations, laws, or tariff restrictions may lobby legislators or contribute to the campaigns of sympathetic politicians. In an about-face, global tobacco giant Altria, which recently changed its corporate name from Philip Morris, is gathering support among tobacco growers to lobby in favour of a bill to bring the tobacco industry under government regulatory power in the United States. Company management now favours the move because of the need to create uniform manufacturing and marketing standards that would apply for all tobacco companies.[5]

For many domestic and international firms, competing with established industry leaders frequently involves **strategic alliances**—partnerships with other firms in which the partners combine resources and capital to create competitive advantages in a new market. Strategic alliances are especially common in international marketing, where partnerships with local firms provide regional expertise for a company expanding its operations abroad. Members of such alliances share risks and profits. Alliances are considered essential in a country such as China, where laws require foreign firms doing business there to work with local companies. Through successful research and development efforts, firms may influence changes in their own technological environments. A research breakthrough may lead to reduced production costs or a technologically superior new product. While changes in the marketing environment may be beyond the control of individual marketers, managers continually seek to predict their impact on marketing decisions and to modify operations to meet changing market needs. Even modest environmental shifts can alter the results of those decisions.

assessment check 1

1.1 Define environmental scanning.

1.2 How does environmental scanning contribute to environmental management?

environmental scanning
Process of collecting information about the external marketing environment to identify and interpret potential trends.

Marketoid

In the last two decades, household energy use has increased about 25 percent in Canada, while the country's population increased by about 20 percent.

environmental management
Attainment of organizational objectives by predicting and influencing the competitive, political-legal, economic, technological, and social-cultural environments.

strategic alliance
Partnership in which two or more companies combine resources and capital to create competitive advantages in a new market.

THE COMPETITIVE ENVIRONMENT

As organizations vie to satisfy customers, the interactive exchange creates the **competitive environment**. Marketing decisions by individual firms influence consumer responses in the marketplace. They also affect the marketing strategies of competitors. As a consequence, decision makers must continually monitor competitors' marketing activities—their products, distribution channels, prices, and promotional efforts.

Few organizations have **monopoly** positions as the sole supplier of a good or service in the marketplace. Utilities, such as natural gas, electricity, water, and cable TV service, have traditionally accepted considerable regulation from local authorities who controlled such marketing-related factors as rates, service levels, and geographic coverage. In exchange, the utilities gained exclusive rights to serve a particular group of consumers. But the deregulation movement of the past three decades has ended total monopoly protection for most utilities. Many shoppers can choose from alternative cable TV and Internet providers, cell phone and traditional telephone carriers, and even gas and electric utilities. Some firms, such as pharmaceutical giants Merck and Pfizer, have *temporary* monopolies from patents on new drugs. When Health Canada approves a new drug for lowering cholesterol or improving sleep, its manufacturer is typically granted exclusive rights to produce and market the product during the life of the patent. This gives the manufacturer a chance to recoup the millions spent on developing and launching the drug. Once the patent expires, all bets are off—and competitors can flood the market with generic versions of the drug.

competitive environment Interactive process that occurs in the marketplace among marketers of directly competitive products, marketers of products that can be substituted for one another, and marketers competing for the consumer's purchasing power.

monopoly
Market structure in which a single seller dominates trade in a good or service for which buyers can find no close substitutes.

oligopoly Market structure in which relatively few sellers compete and where high start-up costs form barriers to keep out new competitors.

Rather than seeking sole dominance of a market, corporations increasingly prefer to share the pie with just a few rivals. Referred to by economists as an **oligopoly**, this structure of a limited number of sellers in an industry where high start-up costs form barriers to keep out new competitors deters newcomers from breaking into markets, while ensuring that corporations remain innovative. Commercial airplane manufacturers operate within an oligopolostic industry, currently dominated by Europe-based Airbus Industrie and U.S.-based Boeing. After earlier failures at building and marketing commercial airplanes, the Chinese government once again is attempting to enter this exclusive club. With the increasing numbers of Chinese air travellers, the government founded the Commercial Aircraft Corporation of China to build fuel-efficient jets domestically, in the hope that China can "buy local" and reduce its dependence on aircraft made in the West. China's "Big Plane" project, the C919, is scheduled to debut its first flight in 2014.[6]

TYPES OF COMPETITION

(2) **Explain the types of competition marketers face and the steps necessary for developing a competitive strategy.**

Marketers face three types of competition. The most *direct* form occurs among marketers of similar products, such as when a Petro-Canada station opens across the street from an Esso retail outlet. The cell phone market provides consumers with such alternative suppliers as Bell, Rogers, Fido, and Telus.

Costco—which sells a wide variety of goods, such as home generators and birthday cakes—also takes direct aim at luxury retailers. Costco offers diamond jewellery, cashmere sweaters, Fendi handbags, and even Suzuki grand pianos.[7]

A second type of competition is *indirect* and involves products that are easily substituted. In the fast-food industry, pizza competes with chicken, hamburgers, and tacos. In entertainment, a movie could be substituted for a concert or a night at the bowling alley. Canada's Wonderland, Six Flags La Ronde, and Vancouver's Playland—traditional hot spots for family vacations—now compete with outdoor adventure trips. Approximately one-half of Canadian adults will decide not to make this year's vacation a tranquil week at the beach or a trip to an amusement park. Instead, they'll choose to do something more adventurous—thrill-filled experiences such as skydiving, whitewater rafting, participating in an archaeological dig, or rock climbing. So marketers have to find ways to attract consumers to their specific brand as well as to their type of product.

Marketoid

Over 14 million Canadians shop at a Loblaw store every week.

Did you know that children's car seats have an expiry date?

If yours is past its date, you should replace it. The same is true if you've had a collision, if your child has outgrown the seat or if it's damaged.

For Government of Canada health and safety guidelines that you need to know as a parent, visit
HealthyCanadians.gc.ca/kids

HealthCanada_3794_Car Seat_250-E.indd 1   10-11-30

Health Canada helps inform Canadians about issues that are important to their health and safety.

A change such as a price increase or an improvement in a product's attributes can also affect demand for substitute products. As the prices for one type of energy soar, consumers look for cheaper, and more environmentally friendly, alternatives. Growing consumer interest in energy efficiency has led shoppers to look for products that have earned the Energy Star. In Canada, Energy Star is a program created through a voluntary arrangement between Natural Resources Canada's Office of Energy Efficiency and manufacturers and resellers of appliances, building materials, computers, new homes, tools, and other products that Energy Star levels of energy performance.[8] Advances in technology can give rise to other substitute products. Wireless fidelity, or Wi-Fi, makes the Internet available via radio waves and can be accessed at any number of public "hot spots" in a variety of locations, including airports, coffee shops, hotels, and libraries. The number of registered hot spots continues to grow worldwide, with more than 245 000 in existence.[9] While some hosts charge a fee, Wi-Fi increasingly is offered at no charge. And as technology continues to advance, industry observers expect Wi-Fi eventually will be replaced as the wireless standard. Two possible "next-generation" successors, WiMax and LTE (an acronym for long-term evolution), offer enhanced capabilities for numerous applications. Both boast a stronger, more secure signal and significantly greater range than does Wi-Fi.

The final type of competition occurs among all organizations that compete for consumers' purchases. Traditional economic analysis views competition as a battle among companies in the same industry (direct competition) or among substitutable goods and services (indirect competition). But marketers know that *all* firms compete for a limited number of dollars that consumers can or will spend. In this broader sense, competition means that purchase of a Honda Accord might compete with a vacation in Europe.

Because the competitive environment often determines the success or failure of a product, marketers must continually assess competitors' marketing strategies. New products, updated features or technology, increased service, and lower prices are all variations that marketers look for. When changes occur in the competition, marketers must decide how to respond.

DEVELOPING A COMPETITIVE STRATEGY

Marketers at every successful firm must develop an effective strategy for dealing with the competitive environment. One company may compete in a broad range of markets in many areas of the world. Another may specialize in particular market segments, such as those determined by customers' geographic location, age, or income characteristics. Determining a **competitive strategy** involves answering the following three questions:

1. Should we compete?

2. If so, in what markets should we compete?

3. How should we compete?

The answer to the first question depends on the firm's resources, objectives, and expected profit potential. A firm may decide not to pursue or continue operating a potentially successful venture that does not mesh with its resources, objectives, or profit expectations. The board of directors at Accor SA voted to "demerge" the company's two divisions—prepaid services and hotels—saying each could grow more quickly as separate businesses. Cable & Wireless, a telecom carrier operating in the United Kingdom, split its two divisions, a global communication services business and another enterprise operating fixed-line and mobile services in Panama, Macau, and several Caribbean countries.[10] Answering the second question requires marketers to acknowledge their firm's limited resources—sales personnel, advertising budgets, product development capability, and the like. They must allocate these resources to the areas of greatest opportunity. Some companies gain access to new technologies or markets through acquisitions and mergers. Johnson & Johnson's $1-billion purchase of Cougar Biotechnology, a developer of cancer drugs, was the latest in a string of leading biotech firms the company has acquired in recent years to broaden its in-house research capability.[11]

Answering the third question requires marketers to make product, distribution, promotion, and pricing decisions that give the firm a competitive advantage in the marketplace. Firms can compete on a variety of bases, including product quality, price, and customer service. Stonyfield Farm, the world's largest maker of organic yogurt, competes on an environmental basis by using organic ingredients. And although it's higher priced, the Stonyfield Farm brand has risen to number three—behind Yoplait and Dannon—partially because customers support the company's commitment to organic foods.[12] The company also invites Canadians to submit ideas for green initiatives that will benefit their communities, and it donates 10 percent of its annual profits to these projects.[13]

TIME-BASED COMPETITION

With increased international competition and rapid changes in technology, a steadily growing number of firms are using time as a strategic competitive weapon. **Time-based competition** is the strategy of developing and distributing goods and services more quickly than competitors. Although a video

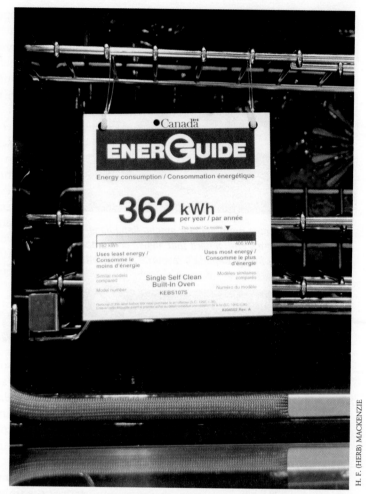

H. F. (HERB) MACKENZIE

An improvement in a product's attributes can affect indirect competition, increasing demand for that product over substitutes. For example, growing consumer interest in energy efficiency has led shoppers to consider Canada's EnerGuide energy consumption ratings.

competitive strategy
Methods through which a firm deals with its competitive environment.

time-based competition
Strategy of developing and distributing goods and services more quickly than competitors.

As gift cards become more popular among Canadians, bonappétit competes with a card that allows consumers to choose among five of Canada's favourite restaurants.

option on cell phones came late to the Canadian market, the new feature was a big hit, attracting new customers to cell phone providers. The flexibility and responsiveness of time-based competitors enable them to improve product quality, reduce costs, and expand product offerings to satisfy new market segments and enhance customer satisfaction.

In rapidly changing markets—particularly those that involve technology—time-based competition is critical to a firm's success. Research In Motion (RIM) launched its BlackBerry PlayBook in 2011—under pressure from Apple's iPad and iPad 2, and the threat of other competing products about to debut—to mixed reviews. While reviewers were quick to point out many good features of the product, some viewed the product as having been launched too soon to market. One reviewer commented, "RIM would have been better waiting at least until the basics were ready. After all, nobody remembers that you showed up late to the party. They only remember if you brought a half-baked cake."[14]

assessment check 2

2.1 Distinguish between direct and indirect competition and give an example of each.

2.2 What is time-based competition?

③ Describe how marketing activities are regulated and how marketers can influence the political-legal environment.

political-legal environment Component of the marketing environment consisting of laws and interpretations of laws that require firms to operate under competitive conditions and to protect consumer rights.

Competition Act The most comprehensive legislation in Canada, designed to help both consumers and businesses by promoting a healthy competitive environment.

THE POLITICAL-LEGAL ENVIRONMENT

Before you play the game, learn the rules! It is a bad idea to start playing a new game without first understanding the rules, yet some business-people exhibit a lack of knowledge about marketing's **political-legal environment**—the laws and their interpretations that require firms to operate under certain competitive conditions and to protect consumer rights. Ignorance of laws, ordinances, and regulations, or noncompliance with them, can result in fines, negative publicity, and expensive civil damage suits.

The existing Canadian legal framework was constructed on a piecemeal basis, often in response to issues that were important at the time individual laws were enacted. Businesspeople need considerable diligence to understand its relationship to their marketing decisions. Numerous laws and regulations affect those decisions, many of them vaguely stated and inconsistently enforced by a multitude of different authorities.

Regulations enacted at the federal, provincial, and municipal levels affect marketing practices, as do the actions of independent regulatory agencies. These requirements and prohibitions touch on all aspects of marketing decision making: designing, labelling, packaging, distributing, advertising, and promoting goods and services. To cope with the vast, complex, and changing political-legal environment, many large firms maintain in-house legal departments; small firms often seek professional advice from outside lawyers. All marketers, however, should be aware of the major regulations that affect their activities.

GOVERNMENT REGULATION

Marketing decisions are influenced by many laws and regulations—federal, provincial and territorial, and municipal. Table 3.1 lists many of the most important federal laws that affect marketing decisions in Canada. These laws have been enacted to ensure fair and competitive trade practices and to protect Canadian consumers.

The **Competition Act** is the most comprehensive legislation in Canada, and you will continue to see references to it in several later chapters. It replaced earlier pro-competition legislation, the 1923 Combines Investigation Act, which proved to be largely ineffective, partly because all violations under the Act had to be treated as criminal acts and guilt was almost impossible to prove, and partly because competition had to be virtually eliminated before legal action would be taken. Dissatisfaction with this Act eventually led to the passing of the Competition Act in 1975, later amended in 1986 when additional changes dealing primarily with mergers and acquisitions were made. The Competition Act is administered by Industry Canada, whose mission is to "foster a growing competitive, knowledge-based

Canadian economy." Among the areas Industry Canada is responsible for is "setting rules and services that support the effective operation of the marketplace." The Competition Act assists in this effort by fostering competition and by protecting consumers, both of which are necessary to have a healthy marketplace. Many of the laws and regulations within the Competition Act can be roughly categorized within three specific marketing areas: pricing, promotion, or distribution.

Among the pricing practices that are covered by the Competition Act are price fixing, bid rigging, price discrimination, predatory pricing, double ticketing, and resale price maintenance. Promotion issues include misleading advertising (or even verbal product misrepresentation), referral selling, and bait-and-switch selling. Distribution issues include refusal to deal, exclusive dealing, and pyramid selling. Table 3.2 summarizes these practices. Many of these topics are discussed in greater detail in later chapters that deal with these specific marketing areas.

Many of these practices, such as price fixing, bid rigging, price discrimination, predatory pricing, and misleading advertising, are criminal offences. Others such as tied selling, refusal to deal, and exclusive dealing are noncriminal offences where actions are taken based on how each particular situation reduces or interferes with competition or otherwise affects consumers in the marketplace.

Provincial and territorial consumer protection legislation in Canada is generally focused on the rights of buyers and sellers with respect to direct sales contracts. These sales include direct mail or telemarketing sales, door-to-door sales, or seminar sales where customers are enticed to a hotel, convention centre, or some other venue where the intention is to sell a product or service to them. This legislation is commonly referred to as the Consumer Protection Act or the Direct Seller's Act in most provinces or territories. These laws are also called "cooling-off" laws because an important aspect they have in common is the right of the buyer to reconsider a buying decision that was made under the persuasive influence of a salesperson. The cooling-off period may vary depending on the provincial or territorial legislation. A notice that informs the customer of the cooling-off period must be part of the contract. If a buyer demands that a contract be cancelled, the seller must return the purchase price and any trade-in that was taken (or a sum of money equal to the value of the trade-in) within a specified period of time. Companies should know what legislation covers each territory where they sell.

As you can see with federal legislation and with varied provincial and territorial legislation, there is a need to harmonize laws, regulations, and practices in order to raise awareness and to improve the marketplace for Canadian consumers. The Consumer Measures Committee, created under the Agreement on Internal Trade, is a joint federal, provincial, and territorial committee that focuses attention on common issues. In the areas of direct selling, cost of credit disclosure, the manufacture and selling of upholstered and stuffed articles, Internet sales contracts, and prohibited debt collection practices, harmonization is now complete.[15]

table 3.1   *Selected Federal Legislation of Interest to Canadian Marketers*
Agreement on Internal Trade Implementation Act
Bills of Exchange Act
Boards of Trade Act
Broadcasting Act
Canadian Tourism Commission Act
Competition Act
Competition Tribunal Act
Consumer Packaging and Labelling Act
Copyright Act
Food and Drugs Act
Hazardous Products Act
Industrial Design Act
Interest Act
Official Languages Act
Patent Act
Personal Information Protection and Electronic Documents Act
Precious Metals Marking Act
Radiocommunication Act
Standards Council of Canada Act
Telecommunications Act
Textile Labelling Act
Timber Marking Act
Trade-marks Act
Weights and Measures Act

GOVERNMENT REGULATORY AGENCIES

Governments at all levels have established regulatory agencies that influence marketing decisions and practices, including those related to product development and commercialization, packaging, pricing, advertising, personal selling, and distribution. Federal agencies may provide advice and assistance to Canadian businesses or may have responsibility to regulate specific industries. Those that regulate industries usually have well-defined responsibilities. The National Energy Board, for example, regulates

table 3.2   *Some Marketing Practices Covered by the Competition Act*

Price Issues:

Price fixing	Sellers collude to set prices higher than they would be in a free market
Bid rigging	Sellers collude to set prices with respect to one or more bids or quotations
Price discrimination	A seller charges different prices for the same quantity and quality of products to two customers who are in competition with each other
Predatory pricing	Sellers set prices so low they deter competition from entering a market, or with the intention to drive competition from the market
Double ticketing	An item has been ticketed with two prices (the lowest price must prevail although there are now limits to protect sellers)
Resale price maintenance	Manufacturers or other channel members try to influence the price at which products are sold to subsequent buyers

Promotion Issues:

Misleading advertising	Representations, in print or made orally, concerning a product are false or misleading
Referral selling	Price reductions or other inducements are offered to a customer for the names of other potential customers
Bait-and-switch selling	Sellers attract customers with low prices but then offer another product at a higher price because they are unable to provide the originally promoted item
Tied selling	A seller requires a buyer to purchase another product or to refrain from purchasing a product from a specific manufacturer as a condition to getting the product they want

Distribution Issues:

Refusal to deal	Sellers refuse to sell to legitimate buyers
Exclusive dealing	A seller refuses to sell to another channel member unless that customer agrees to buy only from that seller
Pyramid selling	Salespeople are paid to recruit additional salespeople, and each new salesperson pays to "invest" in the scheme, with some of that investment going to earlier participants in the scheme—not to be confused with genuine multi-level marketing plans

the construction and operation of interprovincial and international pipelines and power lines; pipeline traffic, tolls, and tariffs; the export and import of natural gas; and the export of oil and electricity, among other things. It also conducts studies into specific energy matters, holds public inquiries, monitors Canada's energy supplies, and provides energy advice to the Minister of Natural Resources in areas where it has expertise derived from its regulatory functions.[16]

One agency that is particularly important to marketers is the Canadian Radio-television and Telecommunications Commission (CRTC), which has the authority to regulate and supervise all aspects of the Canadian broadcasting system. The CRTC works closely with the broadcasting and telecommunications industry to establish standards relating to television violence, gender portrayal, ethnic and minority representation, advertising to children, quality and accessibility of service, and customer billing practices. The CRTC also regulates the companies that supply industry-related technology, including cable television, mobile telephones, satellite television and radio, and direct-to-home television. Some examples of other Canadian federal regulatory agencies and their major areas of responsibility are provided in Table 3.3.

OTHER REGULATORY FORCES

Public and private consumer interest groups and self-regulatory organizations are also part of the legal environment. Consumer interest organizations have mushroomed since the late 1970s, and today, hundreds of groups operate at national, provincial and territorial, and municipal levels. These

Marketoid

One-third of Canadians listen to the radio over the Internet; one-quarter of Canadians download or watch television over the Internet.

table 3.3   **Some Examples of Canadian Federal Regulatory Agencies**

FEDERAL AGENCY	MAJOR AREAS OF RESPONSIBILITY
Canada Border Services Agency	To ensure the security and prosperity of Canada by managing the access of people and goods to and from Canada.
Canadian Environmental Assessment Agency	To provide Canadians with high-quality environmental assessments that contribute to informed decision making in support of sustainable development.
Canadian Intellectual Property Office	To accelerate Canada's economic development by fostering the use of intellectual property systems and the exploitation of intellectual property information; encouraging invention, innovation, and creativity in Canada; administering the intellectual property systems in Canada (patents, trademarks, copyrights, industrial designs, and integrated circuit topographies); promoting Canada's international intellectual property interests.
Canadian Space Agency	To promote the peaceful use and development of space, to advance the knowledge of space through science, and to ensure that space science and technology provide social and economic benefits for Canadians.
Communications Research Centre Canada	To be the federal government's centre of excellence for communications R&D, ensuring an independent source of advice for public policy purposes. To help identify and close the innovation gaps in Canada's communications sector by engaging in industry partnerships, building technical intelligence, and supporting small and medium-sized high-technology enterprises.
Measurement Canada	To ensure equity and accuracy where goods and services are bought and sold on the basis of measurement, in order to contribute to a fair and competitive marketplace for Canadians.
Technology Partnerships Canada	To provide funding support for strategic research and development, and demonstration projects that will produce economic, social, and environmental benefits to Canadians.

organizations seek to protect consumers in as many areas as possible. People for the Ethical Treatment of Animals (PETA), which operates in Canada, the United States, India, Germany, and many other countries, opposes the use of animals for product testing. The Humane Society of Canada tries to "protect animals and the earth." Other groups attempt to advance the rights of minorities, Canadian seniors, the homeless, and other special-interest causes. The power of these groups has also grown. Pressure from anti-alcohol groups such as Mothers Against Drunk Driving has had an impact on criminal laws and offender sentencing in Canada.

Self-regulatory groups represent industries' attempts to set guidelines for responsible business conduct. Advertising Standards Canada (ASC) is the advertising industry's self-regulatory body. Its mission is to ensure the integrity and viability of advertising in Canada. ASC administers the Canadian Code of Advertising Standards, the principal instrument of self-regulation. ASC tries to promote truth and accuracy in advertising and to ensure that advertising is not offensive to viewers, listeners, or readers. It provides consumers with a mechanism to complain about any particular advertisement. It reviews and advocates voluntary resolution of advertising-related complaints between consumers and businesses. ASC also provides industry with a mechanism to resolve competitive disputes about advertising, and with a clearance service that is a fee-based review of advertising copy to help ensure that advertising complies with current laws and regulations.[17] In addition to ASC, many individual trade associations set business guidelines and codes of conduct and encourage members' voluntary compliance.

The Canadian Marketing Association (CMA) has over 800 corporate members who include the country's largest financial institutions, insurance companies, retailers, publishers, charitable organizations, relationship marketers, and others. It is the Canadian marketing industry's leading advocate on legislative matters and has participated in a variety of government-led initiatives on such issues as

Marketoid

In 2010, Advertising Standards Canada received 1200 complaints about 743 advertisements. Retail advertising accounted for 256 complaints.

privacy, electronic commerce, consumer protection, and the prevention of telemarketing fraud. The CMA has a number of internal task forces that develop self-regulatory standards and policies on ethics, privacy, and marketing to children and teenagers and has developed the Code of Ethics and Standards of Practice to which its members must adhere. In an effort to protect consumer privacy and curb unwanted mail or phone solicitation, the CMA provides a Do Not Contact service, which its members honour.

CONTROLLING THE POLITICAL-LEGAL ENVIRONMENT

Most marketers comply with laws and regulations. Doing so not only serves their customers but also avoids legal problems that could ultimately damage a firm's image and hurt profits. But smart marketers get ahead of the curve by providing products that will meet customers' future needs while also addressing government goals. Showing remarkable forward thinking, Toyota was one of the first automakers to commit to building hybrid cars. Its efforts were supported by a government tax break for purchasers of the first hybrids. Consumer groups and political action committees within industries may try to influence the outcome of proposed legislation or change existing laws by engaging in political lobbying or boycotts. Lobbying groups frequently enlist the support of customers, employees, and suppliers to assist their efforts.

④ Outline the economic factors that affect marketing decisions and consumer buying power.

gross domestic product (GDP) Sum of all goods and services produced by a nation in a year.

economic environment Factors that influence consumer buying power and marketing strategies, including stage of the business cycle, inflation, unemployment, income, and resource availability.

business cycle Pattern of stages in the level of economic activity: prosperity, recession, depression, and recovery.

THE ECONOMIC ENVIRONMENT

The overall health of the economy influences how much consumers spend and what they buy. This relationship also works the other way. Consumer buying plays an important role in the economy's health; in fact, consumer spending accounts for nearly 70 percent of the nation's total **gross domestic product (GDP)**, the sum of all goods and services produced by a nation in a year.[18] Because marketing activities are directed toward satisfying consumer wants and needs, marketers must first understand how economic conditions influence the purchasing decisions consumers make.

Marketing's **economic environment** consists of forces that influence consumer buying power and marketing strategies. They include the stage of the business cycle, inflation and deflation, unemployment, income, and resource availability.

STAGES IN THE BUSINESS CYCLE

Historically, the economy has tended to follow a cyclical pattern consisting of four stages: prosperity, recession, depression, and recovery. Consumer buying differs in each stage of the **business cycle**, and marketers must adjust their strategies accordingly. In times of prosperity, consumer spending maintains a brisk pace, and buyers are willing to spend more for premium versions of well-known brands. Growth in services such as banking and restaurants usually indicates a strong economy. When economists predict such conditions as low inflation and low unemployment, marketers respond by offering new products, increasing their promotional efforts, and expanding distribution. They might even raise prices to widen profit margins. But high prices for some items—such as energy—can affect businesses and consumers alike. Skyrocketing gasoline prices have led many consumers to seek other forms of transportation, including the electric bicycle which, in less than a decade, has grown to an $11-billion industry. Especially in China, India, and Europe, an electric bike enables many to postpone the more costly purchase of a car.[19]

During economic slowdowns, consumers focus on more basic, functional products that carry lower price tags. They limit travel, restaurant meals, and entertainment. They skip expensive vacations and cook their own meals. During a recession, marketers consider lowering prices and increasing promotions that include special offers to stimulate demand. They may also launch value-priced products likely to appeal to cost-conscious buyers.

Consumer spending sinks to its lowest level during a depression. The last true depression in Canada occurred during the 1930s. Although a severe depression could occur again, most experts see it as a slim possibility. Through its monetary and fiscal policies, the federal government attempts to control extreme fluctuations in the business cycle that lead to depression.

In the recovery stage, the economy emerges from recession and consumer purchasing power increases. But while consumers have money to spend, caution often restrains their willingness to buy. A family might buy a new car if no-interest financing is available. A couple might decide to book a trip through a discount travel firm such as Expedia.ca or Travelocity.ca. Companies like these can make the most of an opportunity and develop loyal customers by offering superior service at lower prices. Recovery still remains a difficult stage for businesses just climbing out of a recession because they must earn profits while trying to gauge uncertain consumer demand. Many cope by holding down costs. Some trim payrolls and close branch offices. Others cut back on business travel budgets, substituting teleconferencing and videoconferencing.

Business cycles, like other aspects of the economy, are complex phenomena that, despite the efforts of government, businesspeople, and others to control them, sometimes have a life of their own. Unforeseen natural disasters such as the 2011 floods in Manitoba and Quebec, the earthquake in Haiti, the tsunami in Japan, and the effects of war or peace all have an impact on business and the economy as a whole. The most effective marketers know how to recognize ways to serve their customers during the best of times—and the worst of times.

THE GLOBAL ECONOMIC CRISIS

Sometimes business cycles take a severe turn and affect consumers and businesses across the globe. That is the case with the recent recession, called the worst economic downturn since the Great Depression of the 1930s. Typically, nations' GDP rates grow—some modestly at 2 to 4 percentage points a year and some, such as rapidly expanding India and China, at or near double digits. With the crisis, economists predicted that the world economy might shrink for the first time in 60 years.

A struggling economy generates its own downward spiral: fearing worse days ahead, consumers and businesses become cautious about spending money and as they spend less, demand for many products also drops. Lessened demand forces employers to take extraordinary steps just to stay in business: institute a shortened workweek with reduced salaries or even slash the workforce. Canada was certainly not immune to the effects of the global recession, but it weathered the recession better than most nations.

Especially during a recession, marketers look to emphasize value in their offerings. Some slash prices or offer sales to help customers stretch their budget dollars. Automakers Ford and Hyundai recently assured new-car buyers that they would assist them with payments for a period of time if they lost their jobs or would take the cars back to avoid damaging consumers' credit. Retailers that emphasized affordable products, such as Walmart and McDonald's, saw their sales increase. With the severity of the recession, all marketers needed to reevaluate their strategies and concentrate on their most promising products. But it remains to be seen whether or how much consumers, now used to price reductions and special offers, will change their habits once they regain their economic footing in a recovery.

INFLATION AND DEFLATION

A major constraint on consumer spending, which can occur during any stage of the business cycle, is **inflation**—rising prices caused by some combination of excess demand and increases in the costs of raw materials, component parts, human resources, or other factors of production. Inflation devalues money by reducing the products it can buy through persistent price increases. These rising prices increase marketers' costs, such as expenditures for wages and raw materials, and the resulting higher prices may therefore negatively affect sales. Canadian inflation hit a heart-stopping high in 1981 of 12.6 percent and a low in 2008 of 1.4 percent, well below the 3.4 percent average inflation rate among industrial countries where there has been pressure from rising energy and food prices.[20]

inflation Rising prices caused by some combination of excess consumer demand and increases in the costs of one or more factors of production.

If inflation is so bad, is its opposite, *deflation*, better? At first, it might seem so. Falling prices mean that products are more affordable. But deflation can be a long and damaging downward spiral, causing a freefall in business profits, lower returns on most investments, and widespread job layoffs. The last time that Canada experienced significant deflation was in the Great Depression of the 1930s.

UNEMPLOYMENT

Unemployment is defined as the proportion of people in the economy who are actively seeking work but do not have jobs. Unemployment rises during recessions and declines in the recovery and prosperity stages of the business cycle. Like inflation, unemployment affects the ways consumers behave. Unless unemployment insurance, personal savings, and union benefits effectively offset lost earnings, unemployed people have relatively little income to spend—they buy food, pay the rent or mortgage, and try to keep up with utility bills. Canada's unemployment rate has been hovering near 8 percent in recent years, but has been gradually declining. Not surprisingly, when jobs are created, consumer confidence rises, and consumer spending increases.

INCOME

Income is another important determinant of marketing's economic environment because it influences consumer buying power. By studying income statistics and trends, marketers can estimate market potential and develop plans for targeting specific market segments. A rise in income represents a potential for increasing overall sales. Many marketers are particularly interested in **discretionary income**, the amount of money people have to spend after buying necessities such as food, clothing, and housing. Those whose industry involves the necessities seek to turn those needs into preferences for their goods and services. With slowdowns in the Canadian economy, consumers experienced a drop in their net worth because their homes and stock investments lost value. At the same time, Canadians are spending less on nonessential items, and a greater proportion of their income goes toward food and other necessities.[21]

Changes in average earnings powerfully affect discretionary income. Historically, periods of major innovation have been accompanied by dramatic increases in living standards and rising incomes. Automobiles, televisions, telephones, and computers are just a few of the innovations that have changed consumers' lives—and standards of living. Statistics Canada tracks personal income and discretionary income, then determines how much of that income is spent on personal consumption. Marketers can use these figures to plan their approaches to everything from product development to the promotion of their goods and services.

Not only does income affect how much money individuals donate to not-for-profit organizations, but it can also affect the amount of time they're willing to spend on charitable efforts. The "Career Readiness" feature discusses how the most successful organizations structure their workplace greening programs.

RESOURCE AVAILABILITY

Resources are not unlimited. Shortages—temporary or permanent—can result from several causes, including lack of raw materials, component parts, energy, or labour. The global financial crisis, coupled with extreme weather conditions such as drought and typhoons, signals the possibility of worldwide food shortages.[22]

One reaction to a shortage is **demarketing,** the process of reducing consumer demand for a product to a level that the firm can reasonably supply. Oil companies publicize tips on how to cut gasoline consumption, and utility companies encourage homeowners to install more insulation to reduce heating costs. Many cities promote mass transit and carpooling for consumers. A shortage presents marketers with a unique set of challenges. They may have to allocate limited supplies, a sharply different activity from marketing's traditional objective of expanding sales volume. Shortages may require marketers to decide whether to spread limited supplies over all customers or limit purchases by some customers so that the firm can completely satisfy others.

Marketers today have also devised ways to deal with increased demand for fixed amounts of resources. In its annual *Green Book,* the American Council for an Energy Efficient Economy (ACEEE) gives cars a "green score," rating vehicles on their manufacturers' use of scarce resources and attention to the environment in the production process. The recent winner? The ACEEE rated the Honda Civic GX, powered by emission-friendly compressed natural gas, at the top.[23]

CAREER READINESS   Turn Your Employees Green

AS a marketing professional, you might expect to work long days or travel for the company on short notice. But you may be surprised if your employer asks you to think first before printing emails, or reminds you to turn off the lights when you leave for the night. When it comes to the environment, employers are paying increasing attention to becoming responsible citizens—and they're asking employees to help.

If you've been asked to develop or manage a "green" initiative, try these tips:

- *Identify champions.* Look for colleagues in your office who show an interest in environmental causes, then enlist their help. People who already care about the environment are often glad to help get the word out.
- *Communicate briefly, but often.* Employees are bombarded with information; if you want your messages to be read, keep them short and to the point. For example, a sign at the copier station can say "Do you really need colour copies?" or "Save a tree; print duplex." Install recycling wastebaskets in workspaces. If your organization sponsors a "lunch-and-learn" program, invite engaging speakers to talk about recycling and related topics.

- *Grease the wheel.* Encourage employees to practise resource-saving behaviours, such as commuting via public transit or minimizing the use of paper and plastic. Include such gifts as a company-branded water bottle or coffee mug in the company's orientation of new hires. Hold random drawings for prizes like bus or train passes, pedometers, or thermal lunch bags.
- *Spread the fun.* Sponsor competitions to determine which department or work group is the greenest. Prizes can be small or substantial: green T-shirts for the winning team along with the privilege of wearing jeans on designated days all year, or an all-expenses-paid bus or bike tour—in a location of the winner's choice.

Sources: Kelly Spors, "How to Engage Employees in Workplace Greening," *Small Business Trends*, January 28, 2010, http://smallbiztrends.com; "Fairfield Companies Challenged to Go Green in 2010," *Acorn-Online*, January 11, 2010, http://www.acorn-online.com; "3,000 House Employees Learning to Go Green; Saving Energy and Money Takes Hold of Hill Culture," U.S. House of Representatives, January 8, 2010, http://cao.house.gov; Mary Tripsas, "Everybody in the Pool of Green Innovation," *The New York Times*, November 1, 2009, http://www.nytimes.com.

THE INTERNATIONAL ECONOMIC ENVIRONMENT

In today's global economy, marketers must also monitor the economic environment of other nations. Just as in Canada, a recession in the United States, Europe, or Japan changes buying habits. Changes in foreign currency rates compared with the Canadian dollar also affect marketing decisions. The high value of the Canadian dollar has made it more expensive to ship Canadian goods to the United States and has made it less attractive for U.S. companies to operate manufacturing plants here. Houston-based Men's Wearhouse owns 116 Moores retail stores in Canada, but it decided to close its manufacturing plant—Golden Brand Clothing (Canada)—in Montreal, due to intense foreign competition and the Canadian dollar's value. Labour costs and other factors affect Canadian firms' decisions to shift manufacturing operations overseas, decisions that have resulted in the loss of thousands of manufacturing jobs across the country, but most particularly in Ontario and Quebec.[24]

As China exports more and more goods to the world, including Canada, some people voice concern over the widening trade gap. Only recently have broad economic reforms allowed China to play in the global marketplace. Some wonder if China's entry into world markets might help the West economically. However, with its gross domestic product still relatively small, economists say China cannot rescue the world economy—yet. But they point to China's rapidly expanding economy, fuelled in part by a growing middle class with vast, untapped marketing potential.[25]

Politics in other countries affect the international economic environment, as well. Elections in countries such as Russia could result in a shift away from free-market policies. Turmoil in Venezuela could affect the oil industry.

In 2011, the International Monetary Fund in conjunction with the euro-area countries approved a loan worth approximately $150 billion over three years to help solve a major economic crisis in Greece. Under its bail-out plan, Greece must raise the retirement age, which for some groups begins around age 50; raise taxes on the wealthy and implement tax-evasion measures; increase taxes on luxury goods, alcohol, and tobacco; and reduce

assessment check 4

4.1 Identify and describe briefly the four stages of the business cycle.

4.2 Explain how inflation and income affect consumer buying decisions.

salary payments in the public sector. The level of fiscal adjustment is unprecedented and the measures tough, but the alternative would be much worse for Greece, already caught in a high-unemployment, low-growth cycle.[26]

THE TECHNOLOGICAL ENVIRONMENT

⑤ Discuss the impact
of the technological
environment on a
firm's marketing
activities.

**technological
environment**
Applications to
marketing of knowledge
based on discoveries in
science, inventions, and
innovations.

The **technological environment** represents the application to marketing of knowledge based on discoveries in science, inventions, and innovations. Technology leads to new goods and services for consumers; it also improves existing products, offers better customer service, and often reduces prices through new, cost-efficient production and distribution methods. Technology can quickly make products obsolete—email, for example, quickly eroded both letter writing and the market for fax machines—but it can just as quickly open new marketing opportunities, in entirely new industries.

Pets have been wearing RFID—radio-frequency identification—transmitters for years, in case they got lost. Now RFID tags are used in many industries to locate everything from library books to laundry detergent. An RFID tag contains a computer chip with an antenna. A reader scans the tag and transmits the data from the tag to a computer. This innovation means that retailers, manufacturers, and others can locate and track inventory without opening packages. Dow AgroSciences, a division of Dow Chemical, uses RFID technology in its electronic system that detects and eliminates termites. When the system detects termite activity, it activates the RFID tag to send a signal to the exterminator. But the use of RFID to track the movement of humans is controversial because of the privacy implications.[27] Technology can sometimes address social concerns. In response to societal pressure for fuel savings and environmental improvements, automakers used technology to develop more fuel-efficient vehicles and reduce dangerous emissions. Increased use of ethanol made from corn was another solution, but researchers have stepped up efforts to develop biofuels to replace gasoline. One such fuel, cellulosic ethanol, comes from cellulose—grass clippings, wood chips, yard waste—anything organic, even old tires. The biofuel emits significantly fewer greenhouse gases than gasoline and, if spilled, is less damaging to the environment. Scientists believe advances in technology eventually will make the fuel cost-effective to produce. Meanwhile, several start-up companies are working to create fuel from another organic source: algae. Low-cost, fast-growing, and carbon neutral, algae shows promise as a source of alternative energy.[28] See this chapter's "Solving an Ethical Controversy" feature for a debate concerning the use of phosphates.

Industry and government—as well as educational and other not-for-profit institutions—all play roles in the development of new technology. But improvements often come at a price. Research and development efforts by private industry represent a major source of technological innovation. The cost of bringing a new drug to market can run as high as $1.7 billion (U.S.).[29] Canadian companies may have a competitive advantage in the future as they continue to recruit visible minorities and immigrants from around the world. Beng Ong, a Singapore native and scientist at the Xerox Research Centre in Mississauga, has obtained more than 100 patents. Beng Ong says, "Typically, in research, you do not want someone from the same school or background. You want diversity in training."[30] Beng Ong and his multinational team have recently developed an inexpensive synthetic compound that may provide an easy-to-make alternative to the silicon chip.

Another major source of technology is the government, including the military. Air bags originated from airplane ejection seats, digital computers were first designed to calculate artillery trajectories, and the microwave oven is a derivative of military radar systems. Even the Internet was first developed by the U.S. Department of Defense as a secure military communications system. Although the United States has long been the world leader in research, competition from rivals in Europe, Japan, and other Asian countries is intense.

APPLYING TECHNOLOGY

Marketers monitor the technological environment for a number of reasons. Creative applications of new technologies not only give a firm a definite competitive edge but can also benefit society. Vancouver-based Angiotech Pharmaceuticals developed a drug-coated medical device called Taxus. Simply, it is a stent that is implanted in heart patients to keep blood vessels open and enhance blood flow, but it is coated with drugs that inhibit the growth of scar tissue, previously a common problem. Marketers who monitor new technology and successfully apply it may also enhance customer service.

VoIP—Voice over Internet Protocol—is an alternative to traditional telecommunications services provided by companies such as Rogers Communications. The telephone is not connected to a traditional phone jack but instead is connected to a personal computer with any type of broadband Internet connection. Special software transmits phone conversations over the Internet, rather than through telephone lines. A VoIP user dials the phone as usual. Recipients can receive calls made using VoIP through regular telephone connections—land or wireless. Moreover, you can call another person who has VoIP using a regular landline or cell phone. A growing number of consumers and businesses have embraced VoIP, mainly because of the cost savings. The VoIP business is also growing worldwide. One of the largest, Skype, has more than 500 million customers.[31]

As convenient as the Internet, cell phones, and Wi-Fi are for businesspeople and consumers, the networks that facilitate these connections aren't yet compatible with each other. So engineers are working on a new standard that would enable these networks to connect with each other—paving the way for melded services such as video exchanges between a cell phone and a computer. Called the Internet Protocol Multimedia Subsystem (IPMS), the new standard will attempt to create a common interface so that data can be carried across networks between different

VoIP—Voice over Internet Protocol
A phone connection through a personal computer with any type of broadband Internet connection.

assessment check 5

5.1 What are some of the consumer benefits of technology?

5.2 Why must marketers monitor the technological environment?

SOLVING AN ETHICAL CONTROVERSY

Sparkling Glassware May Kill Your Fish

DO you use a dishwasher? If so, chances are your detergent contains phosphates, a compound that breaks down the grease and removes food.

But phosphates are bad for the environment. Phosphorus, an element in phosphates, pollutes the water supply, nourishing algae and ultimately killing fish. Washington was the first U.S. state to ban the sale of dishwasher detergents containing phosphates; many states soon followed. In Canada, the federal government banned phosphates in July 2010. Rather than sell different formulas in Canada and different U.S. states, some detergent marketers now distribute zero- or low-phosphate brands throughout both countries.

Consumers are unhappy; many say the eco-friendly alternatives don't get their dishes clean. *Consumer Reports* has offered some tips for dishwasher users that will at least maximize the effectiveness of their dishwasher. Still, consumers miss the power of phosphates. However, most consumers at least acknowledge that keeping lakes and rivers phosphate-free is an important goal. We need to find ways to reduce the phosphorus that comes from phosphates in other products as well.

Should phosphates be banned from dishwasher detergent?

PRO

1. Water treatment plants are ineffective at breaking down phosphates. When phosphates enter the water supply, they serve as food for algae. Dying algae consumes the oxygen in a lake or stream, destroying the ecosystem.

2. Consumers have a choice of several eco-friendly alternatives to the traditional detergent formula. Companies like Procter & Gamble continue to improve their products to assure sparkling-clean dishes.

CON

1. Banning dishwasher detergents containing phosphates is overkill. The amount of phosphorus in the water supply estimated to come from dishwashing is tiny compared to the amount that comes from farms and lawns, where fertilizers are used.

2. Automatic dishwashers are a time- and water-saver and get dishes cleaner because they use hotter water. Phosphate-free detergents leave glassware cloudy and silverware spotty. Having to wash those items by hand defeats the purpose.

Where do you stand: pro or con?

Sources: Maggie Galehouse, "Don't Blame Your Dishwasher; Low-Phosphate Detergents Leave Dishes Less Clean," *Edmonton Journal*, February 12, 2011, p. I8; Wallace Kenyon, "The Dish on Phosphates," *National Post*, January 6, 2011, p. A2; Holly Martin, "Phosphate Ban May Make Cleaning Dishes More Difficult in Va., Md. and D.C.," *Manassas Environmental News Examiner*, January 27, 2010, http://www.examiner.com; Teresa F. Lindeman, "Phosphate Phaseout Has Dishwasher Soap Makers Scrambling for an Alternative," *Pittsburgh Post-Gazette*, November 29, 2009, http://www.post-gazette.com; Tom Avril, "The Dish on Phosphates," *Philadelphia Inquirer*, October 5, 2009, http://www.philly.com; Nicholas K. Geranios, "Spokane Residents Rebel over Dirty Dishes," TheEagle.com, March 28, 2009, http://www.theeagle.com.

Fujitsu and its resellers across Canada can help you look sharp and work smart with its latest ScanSnap technology.

THERE'S A LOT TO LIKE
ABOUT SCANSNAP.

BLAKE LIKES
S1100

SANDRA LIKES
S1300

JENNA LIKES
S1500

Likes

Likes

Likes

- The most portable ScanSnap
- Under 1 lb. and less than 2 in. tall
- Scan to PDF
- Scan to the cloud

ScanSnap it on the road!

- Compact & portable
- The smallest double-sided scanner with an automatic document feeder

ScanSnap it from home!

- The high speed, high performance ScanSnap
- Best value package, including full Adobe Acrobat®

ScanSnap it at your desk!

S1100   S1300   S1500

THE CHOICE IS YOURS.
ScanSnap enhances your profile in business by helping you look sharp and work smart!
With three members in the ScanSnap family, there's one **you'll** like to work with.
www.fujitsu.ca/scanners

ScanSnap

shaping tomorrow with you

FUJITSU

COURTESY OF FUJITSU CANADA

devices. The implications for various communications providers are enormous—not only will they find new ways to cooperate but they will also find new ways to compete. Subsequent chapters discuss in more detail how companies apply technologies—such as databases, blogs, and interactive promotional techniques—to create a competitive advantage.

(6) Explain how the social-cultural environment influences marketing.

social-cultural environment
Component of the marketing environment consisting of the relationship between among the marketer and society and its culture.

THE SOCIAL-CULTURAL ENVIRONMENT

As a nation, Canada is becoming older, more affluent, and more culturally diverse. The birthrate is falling, and *microculture* populations are rising. People express concerns about the environment, buying ecologically friendly products that reduce pollution. They value the time at home with family and friends, cooking meals at home and exchanging vacation photos over the Internet. Marketers need to track these trends to be sure they are in tune with consumers' needs and desires. These aspects of consumer lifestyles help shape marketing's **social-cultural environment**—the relationship among marketing, society, and culture.

To remain competitive, marketers must be sensitive to society's demographic shifts and changing values. These variables affect consumers' reactions to different products and marketing practices. As the baby boom generation—those born between 1946 and 1965—reaches middle age and retirement, marketers are scrambling to identify this generation's needs and wants. Fuelled by hopes of a long life with plenty of time and money to spend, the baby boom generation views retirement much differently than their predecessors did. Marketers already know that boomers feel young at heart and enjoy their leisure time, but they aren't playing canasta and shuffleboard—they're becoming "social media mavens" who spend a significant portion of their free time surfing the Web and connecting with friends and family on social networking sites like Facebook.[32] Some even launch a second career, starting their own small business. And boomers have a whole new take on the concept of grandparenting. More than past generations, boomer grandparents get actively involved in their grandchildren's daily lives and are more inclined to

| GO GREEN | **When You Have To Go, Go Green** |

JOEL Makower, founder of Greenbiz.com, says, "Green has gone from a movement to a market." Canadian businesses are beginning to recognize that there is a market for green products. A survey of 1000 Canadians by *Marketing* and Ipsos Reid found that 57 percent of respondents were willing to spend more for environmentally friendly products. Still, Canadians are slow to accept the idea of going green when it's finally time to go. The concept of going green—natural burial—started in the United Kingdom in 1993, and there are now approximately two dozen natural burial sites there.

In Canada, Royal Oak Burial Park in Victoria, British Columbia, has a natural/green burial site called Woodlands. Every internment zone will be protected in perpetuity and cannot be converted to a more conventional internment zone at some later date. There are some rules for those who wish to have a natural burial here:

- Remains may not be embalmed.
- Remains must be in a biodegradable shroud, container, or casket.
- Families may plant indigenous plants and trees on the gravesite.
- Individual markers will be replaced by a common memorial cairn—with the names inscribed on it—at the entrance to the site.

A Funeral Professional Council of Canada survey found that 55 percent of 1655 respondents over the age of 35 indicated they would like to learn more about green funerals. If there is a societal shift to natural burials, it won't be because of price, however. Sixty-five percent of respondents indicated they would be unlikely to pay more for a green funeral. Among the new products on the market are eco-friendly urns and caskets. Imperial Evergreen Casket of Burnaby, British Columbia, manufactures biodegradable caskets made of virgin wool and eco urns manufactured from a natural corn-based plastic. Northern Caskets of Ontario manufactures its EnviroCasket, made from sustainably harvested poplar wood and containing no dyes, chemicals, varnishes or stains, or metal hinges in its construction. Both products are competitively priced with more traditional caskets.

Sources: Shannon Proudfoot, "Eco-Friendly Caskets and Urns the Latest in Green Funerals," *Postmedia News,* October 10, 2010; Rebecca Harris, "Turning Green," *Marketing,* June 11, 2007, pp. 18–20, 24, 29–31; Barbara Righton, "Going Most Gently into the Night," *Maclean's,* February 18, 2008, p. 73; "Natural Burial at Royal Oak Burial Park," http://www.robp.ca/burial.shtml, June 22, 2008; Graeme Stemp-Morlock, "Green Burial Options Are Here," *Green Living Magazine,* http://www.naturalburial.coop/2008/05/29/green-burial-options-are-here/#more-487, June 22, 2008.

spend money on them. An estimated 20 percent of all travel involves grandchildren with grandparents, with or without their parents along. As they age, boomers will need health care goods and services and, should they live longer, they may need everything from physical therapy for a repaired knee to a motorized scooter to get around. Another social-cultural consideration is the increasing importance of cultural diversity. Canada is a mixed society composed of various micromarkets, each with its unique values, cultural characteristics, consumer preferences, and purchasing behaviours. Rogers Communications has been actively targeting these important micromarkets and now offers more than 109 multicultural channels, broadcasting in 24 languages.[33] Vice chairman Phil Lind says, "The multicultural market is relatively untapped compared to where it's going to be in the next five or 10 years. This thing is going to be really big."[34] Marketers also need to learn about cultural and societal differences among countries abroad, particularly as business becomes more and more global. Marketing strategies that work in Canada often fail when directly applied in other countries and vice versa. In many cases, marketers must redesign packages and modify products and advertising messages to suit the tastes and preferences of different cultures. Chapter 6 explores the social-cultural aspects of international marketing.

CONSUMERISM

Changing societal values have led to **consumerism,** defined as a social force within the environment that aids and protects the buyer by exerting legal, moral, and economic pressures on business. Today, everyone—marketers, industry, government, and the public—is acutely aware of the impact of consumerism on the nation's economy and general well-being.

In recent years, marketers have witnessed increasing consumer activism. There have been calls to ban Canadian seal product imports in the United Kingdom. Nestlé was targeted in Italy following the launch of its Partners' Blend fair-trade coffee. Adidas was focused on for using kangaroo leather in its sports shoes. Ryanair was criticized for its policy of having a quota on the number of disabled people

consumerism Social force within the environment designed to aid and protect the consumer by exerting legal, moral, and economic pressures on business and government.

H. F. (HERB) MACKENZIE

A rise in consumer activism has led many Canadian retailers to abandon plastic shopping bags in favour of reasonably priced, reusable cloth alternatives.

it will allow on each flight. In India, Coca-Cola was blamed for creating water shortages and pollution. Pepsi was targeted for using a performing chimpanzee in its advertising.[35] No organization, industry, or country is immune.

But firms cannot always adjust to meet the demands of consumer groups. The choice between pleasing all consumers and remaining profitable—thus surviving—defines one of the most difficult dilemmas facing business. Given these constraints, what do consumers have the right to expect from the companies from which they buy goods and services? The most frequently quoted answer came from a speech made by U.S. president John F. Kennedy more than four decades ago. Although this list does not amount to a definitive statement, it offers good rules of thumb that explain basic **consumer rights**:

1. *The right to choose freely.* Consumers should be able to choose from among a range of goods and services.

consumer rights In their most basic form, these rights include a person's right to choose goods and services freely, to be informed about these products and services, to be heard, and to be safe.

2. *The right to be informed.* Consumers should be provided with enough education and product information to enable them to be responsible buyers.

3. *The right to be heard.* Consumers should be able to express their legitimate displeasure to appropriate parties—that is, sellers, consumer assistance groups, and consumer affairs offices.

4. *The right to be safe.* Consumers should be assured that the goods and services they purchase are not injurious with normal use. Goods and services should be designed in such a way that the average consumer can use them safely.

These rights have formed the conceptual framework of much of the legislation enacted in Canada and the United States during the first 40 years of the consumer rights movement. However, the question of how best to guarantee them remains unanswered. In Canada, different classes of consumer products fall under the jurisdiction of different government agencies. Regulations concerning food are administered by the Canadian Food Inspection Agency. Food labelling regulations force disclosure of such details as expiration date, ingredients, and nutritional values on packaged foods. Vehicles fall under the jurisdiction of Transport Canada. Provincial governments may regulate the marketing of farm products, such as eggs and milk, and of service providers, such as homeopathic and chiropractic practitioners and insurance agents and brokers. They, and sometimes municipal governments, may regulate pesticide use.

Consumers' right to safety encompasses a vast range of products, such as automobiles and children's toys. Sometimes it seems as though safety recalls are reported in the media too regularly. You might even receive a letter in the mail from a manufacturer informing you of a recall for a part on your refrigerator or car. Health Canada makes it convenient for consumers to learn about product recalls. Its website, www.hc-sc.gc.ca, consolidates information on safety-related issues and includes a link on consumer product safety. There, consumers can find another link that provides advisories, warnings, and recall information. The user-friendly site organizes information into broad categories: children's products, personal care products, household products, recreational products, pesticides, and more.

Consumerism, along with the rest of the social-cultural environment for marketing decisions at home and abroad, is expanding in scope and importance. Today, no marketer can initiate a strategic decision without considering the society's norms, values, culture, and demographics. Understanding how these variables affect decisions is so important that some firms have created a new position—typically, manager of public policy research—to study the future impact on their organizations of a changing societal environment.

assessment check 6 ✓

6.1 Define consumerism.

6.2 Identify the four consumer rights.

| MARKETING IN A DIGITAL WORLD | **Digital Crime: Caveat Emptor** |

THE phrase *caveat emptor* ("let the buyer beware") should guide your response to unsolicited emails. Canadians lose millions of dollars every year to the army of digital criminals that is growing around the world. The Canadian Anti-Fraud Centre (CAFC) was formed in 1993 as a joint response by the Royal Canadian Mounted Police, the Ontario Provincial Police, and the Competition Bureau of Canada to coordinate education strategies and practices to thwart identity theft and mass marketing fraud scams involving Canadians. While criminals may solicit you by telephone, mail, fax, or in person, it is solicitation through email, the Internet, and text messaging that accounts for the largest percentage of dollar loss by Canadians: 33 percent. What are today's tech-savvy criminals doing?

Foreign money offers—sometimes referred to as Nigerian, 419, or West African fraud—are common. Offers frequently come by email or over the Internet (about 80 percent), usually asking for assistance to transfer money from an international country to Canada, in exchange for a percentage of the money once the transfer is completed. You must, of course, pay certain advance fees before the money can be released. Those who fall victim can expect to see the fees requests continue, and often increase, but they never see any money. In the first quarter of 2011, more than 1000 Canadians complained, reporting losses totalling $39 million, or an average of about $39 000 each.

Anti-virus scams are becoming more popular. Although some criminals solicit by telephone pretending to be from the person's Internet service provider, many come through pop-up ads while the person is searching on the Internet. These pop-ups—referred to as scareware—tell the viewer that their computer is infected and must be repaired quickly to avoid damage or loss of personal files. Of course, the fix can be downloaded from the Internet after the victim provides credit card information. The CAFC receives nearly 200 complaints per month from Canadians. Credit card charges range from $35 to $469 and are debited by banks in Russia, Germany, Latvia, Ukraine, and other countries.

Phishing, SMiShing, and vishing are all digital crimes. Phishing is a high-tech scam that uses authentic-looking email or pop-up messages to get unsuspecting victims to reveal personal information. SMiShing—also known as SMS phishing—uses text messages that sometimes contain a URL to mobile phones. When selected, victims may unknowingly download a Trojan horse to their mobile phone. Now that consumers are getting wise to phishing, some digital criminals are turning to vishing. Instead of directing victims to an Internet address, they are now directed to a phone number. These telephone numbers are manipulated so that they show a false caller ID, and, when the victim phones one, the technology used by the scammers recognizes telephone key strokes as the victim inputs personal information to "prove" their identity.

Sources: Canadian Anti-Fraud Centre website, "Mass Marketing Fraud & ID Theft Activities," *Quarterly Statistical Report* (January—March 2011), http://www.antifraudcentre-centreantifraude.ca/english/documents/QuarterlyStatisticalReport_Jan-Mar2011.pdf; Canadian Anti-Fraud Centre website, "Mass Marketing Fraud Trend Bulletin: Foreign Money Offers 2011-05-12," http://www.antifraudcentre-centreantifraude.ca/english/bulletins/2011/Foreign_Money_Offer%202011-05-12.pdf; Canadian Anti-Fraud Centre website, "Mass Marketing Fraud Trend Bulletin: Anti-Virus Bulletin 2011-04-15," http://www.antifraudcentre-centreantifraude.ca/english/bulletins/2011/Antivirus_1%202011-04-15.pdf; Royal Canadian Mounted Police website, "Scams Protection—A Student Practical Guide," http://www.rcmp-grc.gc.ca/scams-fraudes/student-etudiant-guide-eng.htm#smishing. All files accessed July 10, 2011.

ETHICAL ISSUES IN MARKETING

⑦ Describe the ethical issues in marketing.

The five environments described so far in this chapter do not completely capture the role that marketing plays in society and the consequent effects and responsibilities of marketing activities. Because marketing is closely connected with various public issues, it invites constant scrutiny. Moreover, since marketing acts as an interface between an organization and the society in which it operates, marketers often carry much of the responsibility for dealing with social issues that affect their firms.

Marketing operates outside the firm. It responds to that outside environment and in turn is acted on by environmental influences. Relationships with employees, suppliers, the government, consumers, and society as a whole frame the social issues that marketers must address. The way that marketers deal with these social issues has a significant effect on their firm's eventual success. The diverse social issues that marketers face can be divided into two major categories: marketing ethics and social responsibility. While these two categories certainly overlap, this simple classification system provides a method for studying these issues.

The wave of corporate fraud and conflicts of interest in big business during the past decade is still being addressed in the form of court trials and guilty pleas by wrongdoers. Cases against senior executives at Enron and Tyco International brought jail sentences for those who were convicted. Other companies have responded proactively, by tightening their own ethical codes and even hiring managers whose

figure 3.2   *Ethical Questions in Marketing*

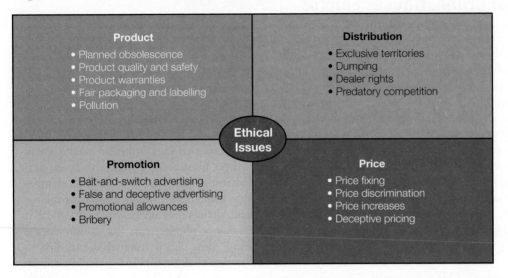

marketing ethics
Marketers' standards
of conduct and moral
values.

figure 3.3

Ten Steps for Corporations to Improve Standards of Business Ethics

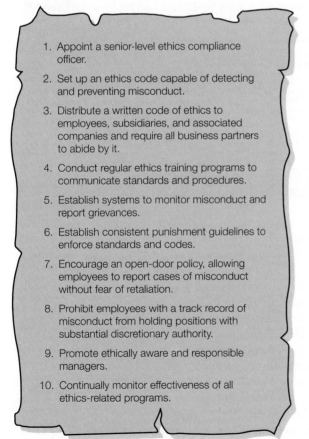

1. Appoint a senior-level ethics compliance officer.

2. Set up an ethics code capable of detecting and preventing misconduct.

3. Distribute a written code of ethics to employees, subsidiaries, and associated companies and require all business partners to abide by it.

4. Conduct regular ethics training programs to communicate standards and procedures.

5. Establish systems to monitor misconduct and report grievances.

6. Establish consistent punishment guidelines to enforce standards and codes.

7. Encourage an open-door policy, allowing employees to report cases of misconduct without fear of retaliation.

8. Prohibit employees with a track record of misconduct from holding positions with substantial discretionary authority.

9. Promote ethically aware and responsible managers.

10. Continually monitor effectiveness of all ethics-related programs.

Source: Adapted from FERRELL. *Business Ethics*, 6E. © 2005 South-Western, a part of Cengage Learning, Inc. Reproduced by permission. www.cengage.com/permissions.

role is specifically to enforce them. Hundreds of Canadian and U.S. companies now have such managers, including Dun & Bradstreet, Dow Corning, Nortel Networks, Walmart, and even the Government of Canada, which now has an ethics commission for the House of Commons and a Senate ethics officer.

Environmental influences have directed increased attention toward **marketing ethics,** defined as the marketer's standards of conduct and moral values. Ethics concern matters of right and wrong: the responsibility of individuals and firms to do what is morally right. As Figure 3.2 shows, each element of the marketing mix raises its own set of ethical questions. Before any improvements to a firm's marketing program can be made, each of them must be evaluated.

Creating an ethics program may be complicated and time consuming, but it is worthwhile. A code of ethics may mitigate some responsibility and help reduce some fines and sentences, but responsibility for its implementation ultimately rests with senior executives. If management doesn't openly support it, communicate its value internally, reward ethical behaviour, and punish unethical behaviour, its value becomes questionable. A step-by-step framework for building an effective program is shown in Figure 3.3. Cynics, of course, can always question the value of an ethics officer and a code of ethics. While Nortel Networks has an ethics officer and a 44-page *Code of Business Conduct,* it also had a senior ethics advisor and a code of ethics when it was involved in its most unethical business practices.[36]

Ensuring ethical practices means promising customers and business partners not to sacrifice quality and fairness for profit. In exchange, organizations hope for increased customer loyalty toward their brands. Yet issues involving marketing ethics are not always clear-cut. The issue of cigarette advertising, for example, has divided the ranks of advertising executives. Is it right for advertisers to promote a product that, while legal, has known health hazards?

For years, charges of unethical conduct have plagued the tobacco industry. In the largest civil settlement in history, tobacco manufacturers agreed to pay $206 billion (U.S.) to 46 U.S. states. Four other states—Florida, Minnesota, Mississippi, and Texas—had separate settlements totalling another $40 billion (U.S.). The settlement frees tobacco companies from claims for the cost of treating sick smokers. In Canada, British Columbia passed the Tobacco Damages and Health Care Cost Recovery Act and sued for $10 billion to recover past health care costs from tobacco companies. The tobacco companies filed an appeal, but it was rejected by the Supreme Court of Canada, paving the way for the province's lawsuit to proceed. New Brunswick filed a similar suit in 2008; Ontario filed a suit for $50 billion in 2009. The British Columbia case will be pivotal as it will be the first to come to trial, scheduled for September 2011.[37] Speculation is that the payoff in Canada will be higher per capita than in the United States because of Canada's public health care system,

figure 3.4

Test Your Workplace Ethics

Workplace Ethics Quiz

The spread of technology into the workplace has raised a variety of new ethical questions, and many old ones still linger. Compare your answers with those of others surveyed on page 119.

Office Technology

1. Is it wrong to use company email for personal reasons?
   ❑ Yes   ❑ No

2. Is it wrong to use office equipment to help your children or spouse do schoolwork?
   ❑ Yes   ❑ No

3. Is it wrong to play computer games on office equipment during the workday?
   ❑ Yes   ❑ No

4. Is it wrong to use office equipment to do Internet shopping?
   ❑ Yes   ❑ No

5. Is it unethical to blame an error you made on a technological glitch?
   ❑ Yes   ❑ No

6. Is it unethical to visit pornographic websites using office equipment?
   ❑ Yes   ❑ No

Gifts and Entertainment

7. What's the value at which a gift from a supplier or client becomes troubling?
   ❑ $25   ❑ $50   ❑ $100

8. Is a $50 gift to a boss unacceptable?
   ❑ Yes   ❑ No

9. Is a $50 gift from the boss unacceptable?
   ❑ Yes   ❑ No

10. Of gifts from suppliers: Is it okay to take a $200 pair of football tickets?
    ❑ Yes   ❑ No

11. Is it okay to take a $120 pair of theatre tickets?
    ❑ Yes   ❑ No

12. Is it okay to take a $100 holiday food basket?
    ❑ Yes   ❑ No

13. Is it okay to take a $25 gift certificate?
    ❑ Yes   ❑ No

14. Can you accept a $75 prize won at a raffle at a supplier's conference?
    ❑ Yes   ❑ No

Truth and Lies

15. Due to on-the-job pressure, have you ever abused or lied about sick days?
    ❑ Yes   ❑ No

16. Due to on-the-job pressure, have you ever taken credit for someone else's work or idea?
    ❑ Yes   ❑ No

Source: Ethics Officer Association, Belmont, MA; Leadership Group, Wilmette, IL; surveys sampled a cross-section of workers at large companies and nationwide; used with permission from Ethics Officer Association.

where health care costs are borne entirely by government. In the United States, most health care costs are borne by private insurers.[38]

People develop standards of ethical behaviour based on their own systems of values, which help them deal with ethical questions in their personal lives. However, the workplace may generate serious conflicts when individuals discover that their ethical beliefs are not necessarily in line with those of their employer. For example, employees may think that shopping online during a lunch break using a work computer is fine, but the company may decide otherwise. The quiz in Figure 3.4 highlights other everyday ethical dilemmas.

How can these conflicts be resolved? In addition to individual and organizational ethics, individuals may be influenced by a third basis of ethical authority—a professional code of ethics that transcends both organizational and individual value systems. A professional peer association can exercise collective oversight to limit a marketer's individual behaviour. Any code of ethics must anticipate the variety of problems that marketers are likely to encounter. Promotional matters tend to receive the greatest attention, but ethical considerations also influence marketing research, product strategy, distribution strategy, and pricing.

ETHICS IN MARKETING RESEARCH

Invasion of personal privacy has become a critical issue in marketing research. The proliferation of databases, the selling of address lists, and the ease with which consumer information can be gathered through Internet technology have all increased public concern. One marketing research tool particularly problematic is the promise of cash or gifts in return for marketing information that can then be sold to direct marketers. Consumers commonly disclose their demographic information in return for an email newsletter or a favourite magazine.

Privacy issues have mushroomed with the growth of the Internet, with huge consequences for both consumers and marketers. In June 2011, three hackers suspected of being members of Anonymous, a group of activists involved in coordinated attacks on governments, banks, and businesses, were

Marketoid

In 2010, Xentel DM Inc. was fined $500 000 for unauthorized telemarketing practices; Bell Canada was fined $1.3 million for abusing the do-not-call list that it is in charge of managing; Vancouver telemarketer Dillon Sherif was ordered to repay $925 000 to people he defrauded and was sentenced to 14 years in prison.

BusinessEthics.ca is a Canadian resource for business ethics. Concern with business ethics has led to the growth of ethics institutes across Canada.

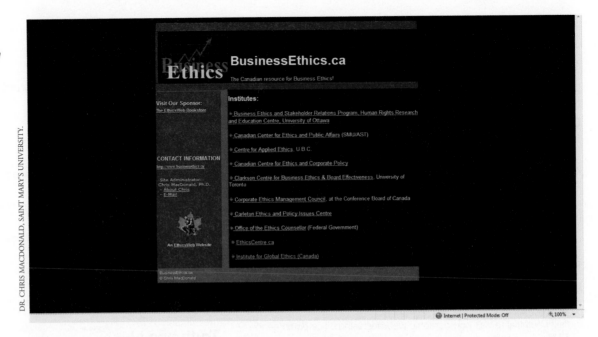

DR. CHRIS MACDONALD, SAINT MARY'S UNIVERSITY.

arrested in Spain. Police allege these hackers were involved in the cyber-attack on Sony, resulting in the theft of personal information from more than 100 million customer accounts and the subsequent shutting down of the PlayStation Network. The expected cost to Sony is approximately $173 million, including damages, IT spending, legal fees, lost sales, and expenses related to customer win-back programs.[39] Canadians concerned about Internet privacy can get a lot of information from the Electronic Commerce Branch of Industry Canada at www.ic.gc.ca/epic/site/ecic-ceac.nsf/en/home and by exploring its various programs and services. The Canadian Marketing Association also provides valuable services for Canadian consumers at www.the-cma.org. There are tips for protecting your privacy, dealing with spam, identifying fraudulent offers, and resolving complaints. You may also register online for its Do Not Contact service. This will reduce the number of contacts you receive because members of the Canadian Marketing Association agree to not contact registered users. Canadians can also visit the Canadian Radio-television and Telecommunications Commission website and register on Canada's National Do-Not-Call List, hoping to reduce the number of unwanted calls they receive.

ETHICS IN PRODUCT STRATEGY

Product quality, planned obsolescence, brand similarity, and packaging questions all raise ethical issues. Feeling the competition, some marketers have tried packaging practices that might be considered misleading, deceptive, or unethical. Larger packages take up more shelf space, and consumers notice them. An odd-sized package makes price comparisons difficult. Bottles with concave bottoms give the impression that they contain more liquid than they actually do. Are these packaging practices justified in the name of competition, or are they deceptive? Growing regulatory mandates appear to be narrowing the range of discretion in this area.

How do you evaluate the quality of a product like a beverage? By flavour or by ingredients? Citing several studies, some consumer advocates say that the ingredients in soft drinks—mainly the high sugar content—can be linked to obesity in consumers, particularly children. Not surprisingly, the beverage industry disagrees, arguing that lack of exercise and a poor diet in general are greater contributors to weight gain than regular consumption of soft drinks.

ETHICS IN DISTRIBUTION

Two ethical issues influence a firm's decisions regarding distribution strategy:

1. What is the appropriate degree of control over the distribution channel?

2. Should a company distribute its products in marginally profitable outlets that have no alternative source of supply?

The question of channel control typically arises in relationships between manufacturers and franchise dealers. For example, should an automobile dealership, a gas station, or a fast-food outlet be forced to purchase parts, materials, and supplementary services from the parent organization?

The second question concerns marketers' responsibility to serve unsatisfied market segments even if the profit potential is slight. Should marketers serve retail stores in low-income areas, serve users of limited amounts of the firm's product, or serve a declining rural market? These problems are difficult to resolve because they often involve individuals rather than broad segments of the general public. An important first step is to ensure that the firm consistently enforces its channel policies.

ETHICS IN PROMOTION

Promotion raises many ethical questions, because it is the most direct link between a firm and its customers. Personal selling has always been a target of criticism—and jokes about untrustworthiness. Used-car dealers, horse traders, and purveyors of quick remedies have been the targets of such barbs. But promotion covers many areas, ranging from advertising to direct marketing—and it is vital for marketers to monitor their ethics in all marketing communications. Truth in advertising—representing accurately a product's benefits and drawbacks, warranties, price, and availability—is the bedrock of ethics in promotion.

Marketing to children has been under close scrutiny for many years because children have not yet developed the skills to receive marketing messages critically. They simply believe everything they see and hear. With childhood obesity a serious concern in Canada, Kellogg Company announced it would change how it advertises its breakfast cereals to children worldwide, focusing solely on products that meet nutrition guidelines.[40] Other organizations such as General Mills, Kraft Foods, McDonald's, and Quaker Oats pledged to also emphasize healthy choices. Yet recent studies by Yale University and Children Now, a child advocacy group, found that the food industry continues to target children in promoting the least nutritious products.[41]

Promoting certain products to post-secondary students can raise ethical questions as well. These students are a prime market for firms that sell such products as electronics and beer. And it's the beer that has people worried, particularly because laws prohibit the sale of alcohol to students who are under the legal drinking age. Even if they don't drink illegally, students can collect and wear promotional hats, shirts, duffle bags, and other items that display popular alcohol names and logos. According to researcher Dr. James D. Sargent, "Promotional items are related to early onset drinking, and I think the responsible thing to do would be for these industries to quit distributing them."[42]

ETHICS IN PRICING

Pricing is probably the most regulated aspect of a firm's marketing strategy. As a result, most unethical price behaviour is also illegal. Some aspects of pricing, however, are still open to ethics abuses. For example, should some customers pay more for merchandise if distribution costs are higher in their areas? Do marketers have an obligation to warn vendors and customers of impending price, discount, or return policy changes?

Credit card companies often walk a fine line between ethical and unethical pricing practices. While consumers are almost always informed of credit card terms on their agreements, the print is usually tiny and the language hard to understand. For instance, a credit card issuer might advertise the benefits of its premium card. But the fine print explains that the firm is allowed to substitute a different plan—with a

Many organizations have modified how they advertise their products, pledging to emphasize the healthy benefits of snacks.

assessment check 7

7.1 Define marketing ethics.

7.2 Identify the five areas in which ethics can be a problem.

higher interest rate—if the applicant doesn't qualify for the premium card. In addition, certain laws allow companies to levy charges that consumers might not be aware of. For example, under a provision called universal default, a company can legally raise its interest rate on a card if the customer is late paying other bills—even if that credit card is paid on time.[43]

All these concerns must be dealt with in developing a professional ethic for pricing products. The ethical issues involved in pricing for today's highly competitive and increasingly computerized markets are discussed in greater detail in Chapter 16.

SOCIAL RESPONSIBILITY IN MARKETING

⑧ Identify the four levels of the social responsibility pyramid.

social responsibility
Marketing philosophies, policies, procedures, and actions that have the enhancement of society's welfare as a primary objective.

Companies can do business in such a way that everyone benefits—customers, the companies themselves, and society as a whole. While ethical business practices are vital to a firm's long-term survival and growth, **social responsibility** raises the bar even higher. In marketing, social responsibility involves accepting an obligation to give equal weight to profits, consumer satisfaction, and social well-being in evaluating a firm's performance. In addition to measuring sales, revenues, and profits, a firm must also consider ways in which it has contributed to the overall well-being of its customers and society.

Social responsibility allows a wide range of opportunities for companies to shine. If they are reluctant at first, government legislation can mandate socially responsible actions. Government may require firms to take socially responsible actions in matters of environmental policy, deceptive product claims, and other areas. Also, consumers, through their power to repeat or withhold purchases, may force marketers to provide honest and relevant information and fair prices. The four dimensions of social responsibility—economic, legal, ethical, and philanthropic—are shown in Figure 3.5. The first two dimensions have long been recognized, but ethical obligations and the need for marketers to be good corporate citizens have increased in importance in recent years.

figure 3.5

The Four-Step Pyramid of Corporate Social Responsibility

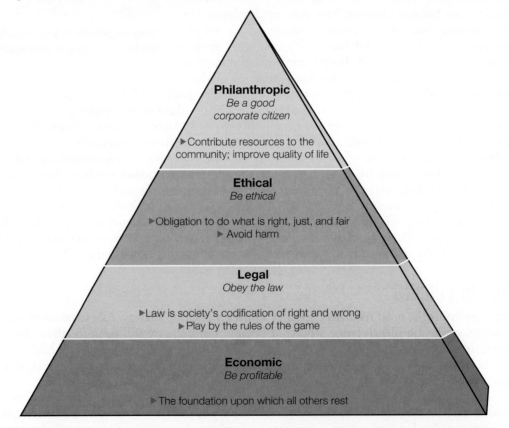

Source: Reprinted from Archie B. Carroll, "The Pyramid of Corporate Social Responsibility: Toward the Moral Management of Organizational Stakeholders," *Business Horizons* 34, July-August, 1991, with permission from Elsevier.

The locus for socially responsible decisions in organizations has always been an important issue. But who should accept specific accountability for the social effects of marketing decisions? Responses include the district sales manager, the marketing vice president, the firm's CEO, and even the board of directors. Probably the most valid assessment holds that all marketers, regardless of their stations in the organization, remain accountable for the social aspects of their decisions.

MARKETING'S RESPONSIBILITIES

The concept of business's social responsibility traditionally has concerned managers' relationships with customers, employees, and shareholders. In general, managers traditionally have felt responsible for providing quality products at reasonable prices for customers, adequate wages and decent working environments for employees, and acceptable profits for shareholders. Only occasionally did the concept extend to relations with the government and rarely with the general public.

Today, corporate responsibility has expanded to cover the entire societal framework. A decision to temporarily delay the installation of a pollution-control device may satisfy the traditional sense of responsibility. Customers would continue to receive an uninterrupted supply of the plant's products, employees would not face layoffs, and shareholders would still receive reasonable returns on their investments. Contemporary business ethics, however, would not accept this choice as socially responsible.

Contemporary marketing decisions must consider their global effect. Some clothing manufacturers and retailers have come under fire for buying from foreign suppliers who force employees to work in dangerous conditions or pay less than a living wage. In some cases, workers who attempted to form a union have been threatened, fired, and even beaten.[44] Marketers must also consider the long-term effects of their decisions and the well-being of future generations. Manufacturing processes that damage the environment or that use up natural energy resources are easy targets for criticism.

Marketers can use several methods to help their companies behave in socially responsible ways. Chapter 1 discussed cause marketing as one channel through which companies can promote social causes—and at the same time benefit by linking their people and products to worthy undertakings. Socially responsible marketing involves campaigns that encourage people to adopt socially beneficial behaviours, whether they be safe driving, eating more nutritious food, or improving the working conditions of people half a world away. And organizations that sponsor socially responsible programs not only help society but also develop goodwill for an organization, which could help the bottom line in the long run.

MARKETING AND ECOLOGY

Ecology—the relationship between organisms and their natural environments—has become a driving force in influencing the ways in which businesses operate. Many industry and government leaders rank the protection of the environment as the biggest challenge facing today's corporations. Environmental issues such as water pollution, waste disposal, acid rain, depletion of the ozone layer, and global warming affect everyone. They influence all areas of marketing decision making, including product planning and public relations, spanning such topics as planned obsolescence, pollution control, recycling waste materials, and resource conservation.

In creating new-product offerings that respond to consumer demands for convenience by offering extremely short-lived products, such as disposable diapers, ballpoint pens, razors, and cameras, marketers occasionally find themselves accused of intentionally offering products with limited durability—in other words, of practising planned obsolescence. In addition to convenience-oriented items, other products become obsolete when rapid changes in technology create superior alternatives. In the computer industry, upgrades that make products obsolete are the name of the game. The Saskatchewan Waste Electronic Equipment Program (SWEEP) was launched in 2007 in response to the province's mounting piles of obsolete electronic equipment. It was established by Electronic Products Stewardship Canada (EPSC), a not-for-profit organization founded by 16 leading electronics manufacturers. On June 15, 2011, SWEEP celebrated its recycling of the 20 millionth pound of end-of-life electronics products.[45]

Public concern about pollution of such natural resources as water and air affects some industries, such as pharmaceuticals or heavy-goods manufacturing, more than others. Still, the marketing system annually generates billions of tons of packaging materials such as glass, metal, paper, and plastics that

Saskatchewan Waste Electronic Equipment Program (SWEEP) was established by manufacturers, retailers, and other stakeholders for the purpose of coordinating the collection and recycling of obsolete electronic equipment.

add to the world's growing piles of trash and waste. Recycling such materials is another important aspect of ecology. HP uses recycled plastic from HP inkjet cartridges to make new inkjet cartridges. Since it patented the technology to recycle LaserJet and inkjet cartridges, it has recycled millions of pounds of used cartridges.[46] Recycling can benefit society by saving natural resources and energy as well as by alleviating a major factor in environmental pollution—waste disposal.

MARKETING AND THE SME

More Than Half of Small Businesses Spend Less Than $500 on Green Initiatives

DO you bring your green reusable bag to the grocery store? Do you separate your recycling and compost from the garbage? Do you drive a hybrid? Do you leave your grass clippings on the lawn? If you have answered yes to any of these questions or know family members or neighbours who do, it becomes obvious more consumers are going green. Whether it is a fad or a permanent change, it is clear that many people are becoming aware of and helping care for the environment. Businesses are picking up on consumers' demands to be green and are changing their practices.

Small businesses tend to have smaller budgets, but they are still finding room to include a line item for environmental initiatives. According to an Ipsos Reid poll conducted on behalf of RBC, approximately half of Canadian small businesses already have a green plan or are considering implementing one. Jim Hart, a national manager at RBC, states: "Going green helps companies build goodwill with customers, employees, shareholders, and the general public." Small businesses do not need to spend millions of dollars to be seen as environmentally friendly; in fact, 59 percent of businesses with a green plan have spent less than $500 on green initiatives in the past two years. But they are still having a positive effect. RBC helps small businesses striving to be greener by offering advice for engaging stakeholders and creating a green plan.

The following are selected highlights from the regional polls:

- Atlantic Canada: more likely to include energy reduction strategies (75 percent)
- Quebec: most likely to reduce or plan to reduce water use or water pollution (36 percent)
- Ontario: more likely to produce or plan to produce and sell green products and services (26 percent)
- Manitoba and Saskatchewan: more likely to include pollution prevention practices (36 percent)
- Alberta: more likely to include recycling as part of green strategy (94 percent); less likely to say plans will involve pollution prevention (15 percent)
- British Columbia: commitment to recycling (82 percent) and reducing energy use (60 percent)

Source: Ipsos website, "One Half of Small Business Owners Are Going Green," http://www.ipsos-na.com/news-polls/pressrelease.aspx?id=4823, July 11, 2011; Royal Bank of Canada (RBC) website, "Small Businesses Are 'Going Green': RBC Survey. News release, http://www.rbc.com/newsroom/2010/0618-green.html, July 11, 2011.

Many companies respond to consumers' growing concern about ecological issues through **green marketing**—the production, promotion, and reclamation of environmentally sensitive products. In the green marketing revolution of the early 1990s, marketers were quick to tie their companies and products to ecological themes. Consumers have responded by purchasing more and more of these goods, providing profits and opportunities for growth to the companies that make and sell them. Auto manufacturers such as Toyota and Honda are already making second-generation hybrid autos. Starbucks offers its own Ethos bottled water, along with a pledge to donate five cents from every bottle toward a $10-million program that will help improve drinking-water conditions around the world. General Electric has announced a corporate initiative called Ecomagination, backed by a $1.5-billion yearly investment in research on cleaner technologies. GE has also launched an ad campaign that highlights the environmental benefits of specific products and services.[47]

COURTESY OF STEAM WHISTLE BREWING

The good beer folks at Steam Whistle Brewing proudly strive to minimize their environmental footprint.

green marketing
Production, promotion, and reclamation of environmentally sensitive products.

assessment check 8

8.1 Identify the four levels of the social responsibility pyramid.

8.2 What are the benefits of green marketing?

Strategic Implications

Marketing decisions that businesses make are influenced by changes in the competitive, political-legal, economic, technological, and social-cultural environments. Marketing ethics and social responsibility will continue to play important roles in business transactions in your hometown and around the globe.

As the Internet and the rapid changes in technology that it represents are fully absorbed into the competitive environment, competition is even more intense than before. Much of the competition will result from innovations in technology and scientific discoveries. Business in the 21st century is propelled by information technologies, but sustained by creative thinking and the willingness of marketers to meet challenges. Marketers will face new regulations as the political and legal environment responds to changes in Canada and abroad. As the population ages and the social-cultural environment evolves, marketers will seek to meet the demands for new goods and services for consumers, such as increased health-related merchandise. As always, they will try to anticipate and make the most of every opportunity afforded by the business cycle.

Ethics and social responsibility must underlie everything that marketers do in the 21st century—those who find ways to "do well by doing good" will succeed. ◆◆◆

REVIEW OF CHAPTER OBJECTIVES

① Identify the five components of the marketing environment.

The five components of the marketing environment are (1) *the competitive environment*—the interactive process that occurs in the marketplace as competing organizations seek to satisfy markets; (2) *the political-legal environment*—the laws and interpretations of laws that require firms to operate under competitive conditions and to protect consumer rights; (3) *the economic environment*—environmental factors resulting from business fluctuations and resulting variations in inflation rates and employment levels; (4) *the technological environment*—applications to marketing of knowledge based on discoveries in science, inventions, and innovations; and (5) *the social-cultural environment*—the component of the marketing environment consisting of the relationship between the marketer and society and its culture.

② Explain the types of competition marketers face and the steps necessary for developing a competitive strategy.

Three types of competition exist: (1) direct competition among marketers of similar products; (2) competition among goods or services that can be substituted for one another; and (3) competition among all organizations that vie for the consumer's purchasing power. To develop a competitive strategy, marketers must answer the following questions: (1) Should we compete? The answer depends on the firm's available resources and objectives as well as its expected profit potential. (2) If so, in what markets should we compete? This question requires marketers to make product, pricing, distribution, and promotional decisions that give their firm a competitive advantage. (3) How should we compete? This question requires marketers to make the technical decisions involved in setting a comprehensive marketing strategy.

③ Describe how marketing activities are regulated and how marketers can influence the political-legal environment.

Marketing activities are influenced by federal, provincial and territorial, and municipal laws that require firms to operate under competitive conditions and to protect consumer rights. The Competition Act, administered by Industry Canada, is the most comprehensive legislation in Canada. Government regulatory agencies can provide advice and assistance to Canadian businesses or, like the National Energy Board, can have responsibility to regulate specific industries. Public and private consumer interest groups and industry self-regulatory groups also affect marketing activities. Marketers can seek to influence public opinion and legislative actions through advertising, political action committees, and political lobbying.

④ Outline the economic factors that affect marketing decisions and consumer buying power.

The primary economic factors are (1) the stage in the business cycle, (2) inflation and deflation, (3) unemployment, (4) income, and (5) resource availability. All are vitally important to marketers because of their effects on consumers' willingness to buy and consumers' perceptions regarding changes in the marketing mix variables.

⑤ Discuss the impact of the technological environment on a firm's marketing activities.

The technological environment consists of applications to marketing of knowledge based on discoveries in science, inventions, and innovations. This knowledge can provide marketing opportunities. It results in new products and improves existing ones, and it is a frequent source of price reductions through new production methods or materials. Technological applications also pose a threat because they can make existing products obsolete overnight. The technological environment demands that marketers continually adapt to change, since its scope of influence reaches into consumers' lifestyles, competitors' products, and industrial users' demands.

⑥ **Explain how the social-cultural environment influences marketing.**

The social-cultural environment is the relationship between marketing, society, and culture. To remain competitive, marketers must be sensitive to society's demographic shifts and changing values, which affect consumers' reactions to different products and marketing practices. Marketers must consider the increasing importance of cultural diversity, both in Canada and abroad. Changing societal values have led to consumerism. Consumerism is the social force within the environment designed to aid and protect the consumer by exerting legal, moral, and economic pressures on business. Consumer rights include the following: (1) the right to choose freely, (2) the right to be informed, (3) the right to be heard, and (4) the right to be safe.

⑦ **Describe the ethical issues in marketing.**

Marketing ethics encompass the marketer's standards of conduct and moral values. Each element of the marketing mix raises its own set of ethical questions. Ethics in product strategy may involve quality and safety, packaging and labelling, and pollution. Ethics in distribution may involve territorial decisions. In promotion, ethical issues include honesty in advertising and promotion to children. Pricing may raise questions about price fixing and discrimination, price increases, and deceptive pricing.

⑧ **Identify the four levels of the social responsibility pyramid.**

The four dimensions of social responsibility are (1) *economic*—to be profitable, the foundation upon which the other three levels of the pyramid rest; (2) *legal*—to obey the law, society's codification of right and wrong; (3) *ethical*—to do what is right, just, and fair and to avoid wrongdoing; (4) *philanthropic*—to be a good corporate citizen, contributing to the community and improving quality of life.

assessment check answers

1.1 Define environmental scanning.
Environmental scanning is the process of collecting information about the external marketing environment to identify and interpret potential trends.

1.2 How does environmental scanning contribute to environmental management?
Environmental scanning contributes to environmental management by providing current information about the five different environments so marketers can predict and influence changes.

2.1 Distinguish between direct and indirect competition and give an example of each.
Direct competition occurs among marketers of similar products, such as supermarkets or gas stations. Indirect competition involves products that are easily substituted. Pizza could compete with chicken wings or tacos. A trip to Canada's Wonderland could compete with a trip to a Toronto Blue Jays game.

2.2 What is time-based competition?
Time-based competition is the strategy of developing and distributing goods and services more quickly than competitors.

3.1 What are the purposes of the Competition Act?
The purposes of the Competition Act are to foster competition and protect consumers, both of which are necessary to have a healthy marketplace.

3.2 Name a self-regulatory group and describe its mission.
Advertising Standards Canada is the advertising industry's self-regulatory body. Its mission is to ensure the integrity and viability of advertising in Canada.

4.1 Identify and describe briefly the four stages of the business cycle.
The four stages of the business cycle are prosperity, recession, depression, and recovery.

4.2 Explain how inflation and income affect consumer buying decisions.
Inflation devalues money and therefore may restrict some purchasing, particularly goods and services that are not considered necessary. Income also influences consumer buying power—the more discretionary income a household has, the more goods and services can be purchased.

5.1 What are some of the consumer benefits of technology?
Technology can lead to new or improved goods and services, offer better customer service, and reduce prices. It can also address social concerns.

5.2 Why must marketers monitor the technological environment?
Marketers need to monitor the technological environment in order to stay current with—and possibly ahead of—competitors. If they don't, they may wind up with obsolete offerings.

6.1 Define consumerism.
Consumerism is a social force within the environment that aids and protects the buyer by exerting legal, moral, and economic pressures on business.

6.2 Identify the four consumer rights.
The four consumer rights are as follows: the right to choose freely, the right to be informed, the right to be heard, and the right to be safe.

7.1 Define *marketing ethics*.

Marketing ethics refers to the marketer's standards of conduct and moral values.

7.2 Identify the five areas in which ethics can be a problem.

The five areas of ethical concern for marketers are marketing research, product strategy, distribution, promotion, and pricing.

8.1 Identify the four levels of the social responsibility pyramid.

The four levels of social responsibility are economic, legal, ethical, and philanthropic.

8.2 What are the benefits of green marketing?

Green marketing, which responds to consumers' growing concerns about ecological issues, offers consumers high-quality products without health risks or damage to the environment. Many industries, including appliances, consumer electronics, construction, hospitality, and more, are finding that incorporating green practices rejuvenates their business.

MARKETING TERMS YOU NEED TO KNOW

These terms are printed in red in the text. They are defined in the margins of the chapter and in the Glossary that begins on p. G-1.

environmental scanning 72	Competition Act 76	VoIP—(Voice over Internet Protocol) 85
environmental management 73	gross domestic product (GDP) 80	social-cultural environment 86
strategic alliance 73	economic environment 80	consumerism 87
competitive environment 73	business cycle 80	consumer rights 88
monopoly 73	inflation 81	marketing ethics 90
oligopoly 74	unemployment 82	social responsibility 94
competitive strategy 75	discretionary income 82	green marketing 97
time-based competition 75	demarketing 82	
political-legal environment 76	technological environment 84	

PROJECTS AND TEAMWORK EXERCISE

1. With a classmate, choose two firms that compete directly with each other. Select two of the following or choose your own. Then develop a competitive strategy for your firm while your partner develops a strategy for his or hers. Present the two strategies to the class. How are they similar? How are they different?
   a. Home Depot and Rona or Lowe's
   b. Apple and Research In Motion (BlackBerry)
   c. Paramount Canada's Wonderland and Six Flags La Ronde or Vancouver's Playland
   d. Visa and MasterCard
   e. Bell Canada and Rogers Communications or Telus
   f. Tim Hortons and Starbucks
2. Track your own consumer purchasing decisions as they relate to your income. Compare your decisions during the academic year and the summer. Do you have a summer job that increases your income? How does that affect your decisions?
3. Canada Post essentially enjoys a monopoly on the delivery of most mail. With a classmate, develop a strategy for a business that would compete with Canada Post in areas that firms such as Purolator, UPS, FedEx, and DHL do not already address.
4. Choose one of the following products. Working in pairs or small groups, present arguments for and against having Canada impose certain regulations on the advertising of your product. (Note that some products already do have regulations—you can argue for or against them.)
   a. alcoholic beverages
   b. smokeless tobacco
   c. casinos
   d. prescription medications
5. With a classmate, research one of the recent large cases involving unethical and illegal activities by executives for companies such as Enron, Tyco, MCI, Nortel Networks, Martha Stewart Living Omnimedia, and Hollinger International. Describe the charges made against these executives and the outcome. Do you think they were fairly charged and punished? Why or why not?

CRITICAL-THINKING EXERCISES

1. Environmental scanning is important for any business wanting to identify important trends that may affect its future marketing actions. Identify five current trends that are predicted to have a major influence on Canadian businesses in the next decade. Explain how or whether each of these trends will affect you personally as a consumer.

2. Suppose you and a friend want to start a company that markets frozen fish dinners. What are some of the questions about the competitive environment that you would like to have answered before you begin production? How will you determine whom your customers are likely to be? How will you reach them?

3. The social-cultural environment can have a strong influence on the decisions marketers must make. In recent years, animal rights groups have targeted the manufacture and sale of foie gras, a European food delicacy made from goose and duck liver. Activists cite the cruel treatment of these birds, while chefs and restaurant owners claim otherwise. Animal rights groups are pressuring restaurants to stop serving foie gras. Others argue that consumers should be allowed a choice. What aspects of the social-cultural environment are affecting the marketing of foie gras? Which of the other components of the marketing environment may come into play, and how?

4. Approximately 400 million rebates—worth about $6 billion—are offered to Canadian and U.S. consumers by marketers every year. But do consumers like them? Often rebates require more effort than a consumer is willing to make to receive the cash back. Critics of the promotional effort say that marketers know this—and are banking on consumers' not redeeming them, resulting in extra income for retailers and manufacturers. Do you think rebate programs are ethical? Why or why not?

5. The disposal of nuclear waste has been an ongoing public safety issue, one with which marketers who work for nuclear power companies must deal. Most of Canada's nuclear waste is stored in Ontario, but smaller amounts exist in Quebec and New Brunswick. The Ontario government has been trying to negotiate nuclear storage at several Ontario towns but has met considerable resistance. Supporters argue that this is important to building Ontario's nuclear power capacity, while critics are skeptical of its safety and usefulness. As a marketer, how would you approach this issue?

ETHICS EXERCISE

Some retail firms protect their inventory against theft by locking their premises after hours even though maintenance and other workers are inside the stores working all night. Employees have charged that they are forbidden to leave the premises during work hours and that during an emergency, such as illness or injury, precious time is lost waiting for a manager to arrive who is authorized to unlock the doors. Although workers could open an emergency exit, in some cases they claim that they will be fired for doing so.

Employers assert that managers with keys are on the premises (or minutes away) and that locking employees in ensures their own safety as well as cutting down on costly "shrinkage."

1. Under what circumstances, if any, do you think locking employees in at night is appropriate?

2. If you feel this practice is appropriate, what safeguards do you think should be put into effect? What responsibilities do employers and employees have in such circumstances?

INTERNET EXERCISES

1. **Economic environment.** Statistics Canada projects changes in the Canadian population. Visit its website (www .statcan.gc.ca) and compare its projections to the current Canadian population figures. What will the Canadian population look like in the future? How will it be different from the current population? List two or three products or industries you feel will benefit from future population trends.

2. **Fair trade coffee.** Visit www.globalexchange.org/ campaigns/fairtrade/coffee to learn about fair-trade coffee. Prepare a brief report on the subject. How could a coffee manufacturer or retailer integrate fair trade products into its social responsibility efforts?

3. **Building a brand.** Visit the website for footwear manufacturer Ugg (www.uggaustralia.com) to learn about its efforts at building its brand. How has Ugg answered each of the five questions listed in the chapter concerning the development of a competitive strategy?

Note: Internet web addresses change frequently. If you don't find the exact sites listed, you may need to access the organization's home page and search from there or use a search engine such as Google or Bing.

ETHICS QUIZ ANSWERS

Here is how others have responded to the quiz on page 91.

1. 34 percent said personal email on company computers is wrong.
2. 37 percent said using office equipment for schoolwork is wrong.
3. 49 percent said playing computer games at work is wrong.
4. 54 percent said Internet shopping at work is wrong.
5. 61 percent said it is unethical to blame your error on technology.
6. 87 percent said it's unethical to visit pornographic sites at work.
7. 33 percent said $25 is the amount at which a gift from a supplier or client becomes troubling, while 33 percent said $50, and 33 percent said $100.
8. 35 percent said a $50 gift to the boss is unacceptable.
9. 12 percent said a $50 gift from the boss is unacceptable.
10. 70 percent said it's unacceptable to take the $200 football tickets.
11. 70 percent said it's unacceptable to take the $120 theatre tickets.
12. 35 percent said it's unacceptable to take the $100 food basket.
13. 45 percent said it's unacceptable to take the $25 gift certificate.
14. 40 percent said it's unacceptable to take the $75 raffle prize.
15. 11 percent reported they lied about sick days.
16. 4 percent reported they have taken credit for the work or ideas of others.

CASE 3.1

Dolores Labs Takes the Guesswork Out of Grunt Work

Software developer Lukas Biewald had a problem at the office. He needed an army of temporary workers to tackle a simple but huge task that couldn't be automated. However, he had neither the time nor the budget to work with a conventional temp agency to engage the workers. Instead, Biewald turned to Mechanical Turk, the online labour force operated by Amazon, for his temp workers. At Mechanical Turk, for about $2 an hour, employers can hire large numbers of freelancers (called "turkers") for a variety of menial tasks.

There was just one drawback, though: Biewald needed the work to be accurate, and he didn't have time to monitor the quality of the output he would receive.

Biewald's unmet need—for someone to assure an accurate, efficient labour force for his assignment—sparked the idea that eventually led him to found Dolores Labs: a business that, you could say, was born out of necessity.

Dolores Labs serves as a middleman between the emerging cadre of "cloud labour"—the thousands of online moonlighters available to do simple tasks at bargain-basement hourly rates—and the organizations that want to hire them. The company fills the need by ensuring accountability and quality output from the cloud labour.

How is Dolores Labs able to deliver on its claim? Through its product, CrowdFlower, which consists of a set of statistical quality control algorithms devised to evaluate the accuracy and speed of cloud workers for a given task. The company emphasizes scalability: using CrowdFlower, clients can design a job to custom specifications. CrowdFlower provides the labour to deliver the work accurately and efficiently.

CrowdFlower screens candidates by giving them a dummy assignment and comparing their performance to that of veteran workers whose performance level is known. With increasing demand for inexpensive yet reliable labour to perform low-budget tasks where accuracy is important—such as medical transcription, content monitoring, marketing research, piracy policing, and others—the future looks bright for Dolores Labs. Already, the company has signed nearly two dozen clients since its founding. It received $5 million in venture capital in 2010.

Meanwhile, CrowdFlower's capabilities are being applied in other interesting ways. Leadership at Dolores Labs provided CrowdFlower's help following the earthquake in Haiti, where it was used to deploy volunteers to appropriate tasks throughout the devastated nation.

Questions for Critical Thinking

1. How does each of the five components of the marketing environment come into play for Dolores Labs?
2. Dolores Labs' involvement in helping to create a system for delivering humanitarian aid to the people of Haiti after the 2010 earthquake illustrates how a high-tech business can benefit society in a "high-touch" way. What other kinds of projects could a company like Dolores Labs undertake that would create similar impact?

Sources: Company website, http://www.doloreslabs.com, February 23, 2010; Dave Foster, "Crowdsourcing the Haiti Relief," Ashoka.org, February 4, 2010, http://tech.ashoka.org; Leena Rao, "CrowdFlower Raises $5M for Cloud Sourced Labor," *TechCrunch.com*, January 20, 2010, http://techcrunch.com; Victoria Barret, "Dolores Labs Vets Web Sites on the Cheap," *Forbes*, March 30, 2009, http://www.forbes.com.

CASE 3.2

Steam Whistle Brewing: Golden Beer, Green Company

Why would a company wish to be "green"? For the very cynical, the answer is simply that it would not; that is, unless it is forced due to government regulation—enforced to protect the environment. Those who are less cynical might suggest that it would do so to get a competitive advantage, leading to future rewards. Maybe it would like to be first among competitors to promote its "greenness." This, of course, assumes that stakeholders value green companies, and there is increasing evidence that investors, customers, and employees all value companies that are socially responsible. There is a third reason: altruism. It might be difficult to prove altruism as the motive for greening a company, but surely there are companies owned or managed by people who simply want to "do the right thing."

One company that has been doing the right thing is Toronto-based Steam Whistle Brewing, not only leading its industry in green initiatives but arguably North America's greenest brewery. What makes Steam Whistle Brewing so green?

The company prides itself on "doing one thing, really, really well." Since its first beer came off the production line in 2000, Steam Whistle Brewing has made a single product: a Pilsner of exceptional quality. While beers can have upwards of 100 or more ingredients, Steam Whistle's Pilsner has only four: pure spring water, malted barley, hops, and yeast, all GMO-free—that is, free of genetically modified organisms. Although listing beer ingredients is not required in Canada, Steam Whistle Brewing proudly lists its ingredients on every bottle.

Of course, green beer needs to be in a green bottle. Steam Whistle's Pilsner is shipped in unique green glass bottles. These bottles contain 30 percent more glass than regular beer bottles, so they can be recycled up to 45 times, about three times more than other bottles. The company's logo is painted on each bottle, replacing the need for paper labels. This saves trees but also reduces the contaminants from glue and ink that would result from washing paper labels from used bottles. Steam Whistle Brewing proudly recycles every element it can from its packaging line, including broken glass, old bottle caps, cardboard cartons, and even shrink wrap, resulting in 94 percent of waste from operations being diverted from landfill. It was the first Canadian brewery to use 100-percent biodegradable cups for outdoor events. Made from cornstarch resin, these cups are completely compostable within 50 days. Leftover edibles at the company's several hundred on-site hosted events held each year are donated to a local street mission or a women's shelter. Organic waste unfit for consumption is composted. Even the "spent grain" from the brewing process is recycled. It is shipped to farmers to use for animal feed.

Since 2006, Canada Clean Fuels has been supplying Biodiesel B20 fuel so that the Steam Whistle truck fleet has an environmentally friendly fuel alternative. This B20 Biofuel is a mixture of soya and recycled cooking oils from restaurants. In 2011, the company added a new truck to its vintage fleet: a 1958 Chevy Apache, which it dubbed "Retro Electro." The custom-built truck was rescued from a metal scrap heap and was retrofitted with a high-efficiency electric motor. Steam Whistle Brewing gets its electricity from Bullfrog Power, a provider of green power, sourced from wind and hydro facilities that have been certified by Environment Canada as low impact and currently available in six of Canada's provinces.

To provide a comfortable working environment, Steam Whistle Brewing uses a unique green alternative to air conditioning, provided through Enwave Energy Corporation. Enwave draws cold water from Lake Ontario and passes it through pipes at Steam Whistle Brewing, where it chills the surrounding environment. The water then continues along to become part of Toronto's potable water supply. Using this system to chill the brewery work environment reduces the amount of carbon dioxide that would have been generated by conventional air conditioning by about 71 tonnes—or the equivalent of 16 fewer cars on the highway per annum. It also reduces electricity consumption by about what would be consumed by seven homes. Steam Whistle Brewing uses steam exclusively to heat water for brewing, for bottle washing, and for climate control, again supplied by Enwave Energy. This allows the company to use steam only as needed, rather than having to operate its own on-site gas-burning boiler that would need to be continually operating. To further conserve energy, Steam Whistle Brewing installed a state-of-the-art brew house that reduces the energy needed for brewing by recirculating the steam-heated water back into the system. It also reduces water consumption by nearly 70 percent compared to the older brew house it had been using. The company has been leaving lights off whenever possible, taking advantage of the natural light that is abundant throughout their heritage building. Motion sensors also help reduce electricity use, and energy-efficient bulbs and fixtures are installed as older ones need to be replaced. By keeping the older fixtures and bulbs in place as long as possible, the company helps reduce what it would otherwise have to send to landfill.

Steam Whistle Brewing has an active management plan to be as environmentally responsible as possible. But it goes beyond its manufacturing and administrative operations. The company encourages employees to use bike paths and mass transit where possible. It provides showers, a towel service, and a covered bike rack for employees. The employees have a strong sense of social responsibility and of being part of a culture where sustainability is important. Steam Whistle Brewing sponsors hundreds of charitable, cultural, and community events each year. Among the many rewards it has received: Canada's Top Employers for Young People 2010, Canada's Greenest Employers 2010, Greater Toronto's Top Employers 2010, Environmental Award of Excellence in the Energy Conservation category at the Green Toronto Awards 2009.

Creating a strong identity for a brand is always important, but particularly for those that are considered "badge" products, such as beer. Badge products through association say something about the user's personality or character and speak to others about the user; for example, "By having invested in this premium, socially conscious product, it demonstrates my beliefs." Sybil Taylor, the company's communications director, says, "That's why we think it's important that we share our environmental story. It's just one part of our personality, but it's an important part."

Questions for Critical Thinking

1. What is meant by Steam Whistle's "personality"? Describe it and explain why it is important.

2. Explain how each of the five forces in marketing's external environment—competitive, political-legal, economic, technological, and social-cultural—can affect Steam Whistle's green strategy.

3. How does Steam Whistle Brewing rate on the four-step pyramid of corporate social responsibility? Does it meet all the criteria for a socially responsible company? Explain.

Sources: Personal correspondence, Sybil Taylor, communications director, Steam Whistle Brewing, August 18, 2011; Company website, http://www.steamwhistle .ca, August 18, 2011; Company website, http://www.bullfrogpower.com, August 18, 2011; Company website, http://www.enwave.com, August 18, 2011; Simon Houpt, "How Green Is Your Beer?" *The Globe and Mail,* August 12, 2011, p. 5.

part 2

UNDERSTANDING BUYERS AND MARKETS

Consumer Behaviour

CHAPTER OBJECTIVES

① Define *consumer behaviour* and describe the role it plays in marketing decisions.

② Describe the interpersonal determinants of consumer behaviour: cultural, social, and family influences.

③ Explain each of the personal determinants of consumer behaviour: needs and motives, perceptions, attitudes, learning, and self-concept theory.

④ Distinguish between high-involvement and low-involvement purchase decisions.

⑤ Outline the steps in the consumer decision process.

⑥ Differentiate among routinized response behaviour, limited problem solving, and extended problem solving by consumers.

ARE OUR SHOPPING HABITS CHANGING?

Consumers are a mysterious bunch. Why do we walk into one store and not another? What makes us buy some products and walk past others? How is social media changing how we shop? Do we take longer to make purchase decisions when we have less money to spend? Do we respond more positively to certain words, images, and signs than others?

Several companies and individuals have set out to answer questions such as these for retailers across the globe. Paco Underhill and his team of researchers at Envirosell is one of the groups that digs up all kinds of helpful information about the way consumers behave. TNS, a global research company, and Toronto-based Delvinia have investigated how social media has affected how we shop.

In an economy where every sale and every customer counts, the insights provided by this type of research are important to both large and small retailers. The results of Envirosell's research help companies such as Walmart, Best Buy, and the Gap. Paco Underhill has also published several books providing the results of his research, including *What Women Want* and the *Call of the Mall*.

Envirosell conducts research in three major ways: by observing consumers in real time as they shop, by interviewing shoppers about their attitudes toward buying, and by making qualitative assessments about consumer behaviour using a variety of techniques.

One trend that Underhill and his group have noticed is that consumers generally make more decisions to purchase a product when they are actually in a store than beforehand—even if they come armed with a shopping list. As a result, stores can take advantage of an opportunity to market products with signs and displays that are attractive and convey the right marketing messages. Another trend is that shoppers are spending more time reading labels, comparing prices, and thinking about what they are buying. In grocery stores, consumers are removing items from their carts as they move along the checkout line. "They are experiencing buyer's remorse," notes Underhill. In general, consumers are doing more with less. They are spending less money on nonessentials like entertainment and replacing these purchases with free or inexpensive activities such as gardening, cooking, and watching television.

Delvinia found that the majority of shoppers went online to find out about prices, product features, and reviews from other consumers. They also found that consumers preferred the Internet for all aspects of the shopping experience except for actually making the purchase.

The research conducted by TNS showed that consumers were connecting with brands through Facebook and Twitter and that Canadians were more connected than other nations. Other factors like gender and age also affected how many brands consumers related to online. Most consumers said they connected with brands via the Internet so they could access special promotions.

If retailers observe and understand these trends, they can tailor their marketing to influence shoppers to make purchases. For example, if a retailer realizes that more than 60 percent of a shopper's time in the store may actually be spent waiting in line for a cashier, the retailer might put more effort into making attractive products available within reach from the line. If retailers understand which customers use social media as part of their shopping experience, they can develop social media campaigns as part of their marketing programs.[1]

connecting with customers

Customer shopping habits vary depending on their characteristics and on influences like social media. Companies selling products are better at connecting with their customers when they understand the changes in their customers' shopping behaviour. Research companies like Envirosell, TNS, and Delvinia offer marketing research to help these companies better understand consumer behaviour.

Chapter Overview

WHY does your best friend drive five kilometres out of the way for Tim Hortons coffee when the local coffee shop is much closer? Why do people prefer one brand of pop over another? The answers to these questions aren't obvious but they directly affect every aspect of the marketing strategy, from product development to pricing, distribution, and promotion. Developing a marketing strategy requires an understanding of the process by which consumers buy goods and services for their own use and organizational buyers purchase business products.

A variety of influences affect both individuals buying items for themselves and personnel purchasing products for their firms. This chapter fcuses on individual purchasing behaviour, which applies to all of us. **Consumer behaviour** is the process through which the ultimate buyer makes purchase decisions for everything from toothbrushes to autos to vacations. Chapter 5 will shift the focus to business buying decisions.

The study of consumer behaviour builds on an understanding of human behaviour in general. In their efforts to understand why and how consumers make buying decisions, marketers borrow extensively from the sciences of psychology and sociology. The work of psychologist Kurt Lewin, for example, provides a useful classification scheme for influences on buying behaviour. Lewin's work determined that behaviour is a function of the interactions of personal influences and pressures exerted by outside environmental forces.

Consumer behaviour is influenced by the interactions of interpersonal influences—such as culture, friends, classmates, co-workers, and relatives—and personal factors—such as attitudes, learning, and perception. In other words, inputs from others and an individual's psychological makeup affect his or her purchasing behaviour. Before looking at how consumers make purchase decisions, we first consider how both interpersonal and personal factors affect consumers. ◆◆◆

---

① **Define** *consumer behaviour* **and describe the role it plays in marketing decisions.**

consumer behaviour
Process through which buyers make purchase decisions.

Marketoid

As of April 1, 2011, the estimated population of Canada was 34 349 200; therefore there are 34 349 200 consumers in Canada or individuals who influence consumer purchases.

culture
Values, beliefs, preferences, and tastes handed down from one generation to the next.

INTERPERSONAL DETERMINANTS OF CONSUMER BEHAVIOUR

You don't make purchase decisions in a vacuum. You might not be aware of it, but every buying decision you make is influenced by a variety of external and internal factors. Consumers often decide to buy goods and services based on what they believe others expect of them. They may want to project positive images to peers or to satisfy the unspoken desires of family members. Marketers recognize three broad categories of interpersonal influences on consumer behaviour: cultural, social, and family influences. Figure 4.1 shows how these interpersonal determinants as well as personal determinants influence the consumer decision-making process. Personal determinants and the decision-making process are discussed later in the chapter.

CULTURAL INFLUENCES

Culture can be defined as the values, beliefs, preferences, and tastes handed down from one generation to the next. Culture is the broadest environmental determinant of consumer behaviour. Marketers need to understand its role in consumer decision making, both in Canada and abroad. They must also monitor trends in cultural values as well as recognize changes in these values.

Marketing strategies and business practices that work in one country may be offensive or ineffective in another. Strategies may even have to be varied from one area of a country to another. Nowhere is that more true than in Canada, where the population continues to diversify at a rapid pace. When you insert your bank card into an ATM, the first option on the screen often is what language you prefer for the transaction. As a result, companies like Home Depot are tailoring their marketing campaigns to different cultural groups. Home Depot's marketing strategy included having a campaign aimed at Cantonese-speaking customers with a focus on assisting them to prepare for the Chinese New Year.[2] The Canadian population is also moving rapidly away from the two original cultural groups; fewer Canadians identify themselves as of British or French ethnic origin.

figure 4.1

Integrated Model of the Consumer Decision Process

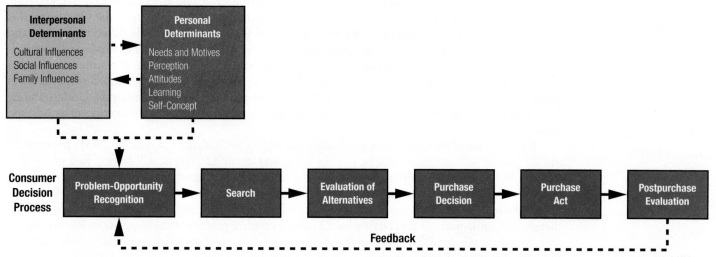

Source: Roger Blackwell, Paul W. Minard, and James F. Engel, *Consumer Behavior*, 10th Edition (Mason, OH: South-Western, 2004).

Core Values in Canadian Culture

Some cultural values change over time, but basic core values do not. Core values are underlying motivations that move society forward and are shaped by the people one grows up with. The Canadian Marketing Association has identified four core Canadian values, which are these: a unique balance between individualism and collectivism, an attitude of tolerance and acceptance, a heightened appreciation for a quality of life, and an essentially peaceful predisposition.[3] Michael Adams, president of the research company Environics, has studied the social values of the Canadian population for over 20 years. His extensive work in studying changing social values has covered not only the Canadian population but how we compare to our U.S. neighbours.[4]

Values that change over time also have their effects. As technology rapidly changes the way people exchange information, consumers adopt values that include communicating with anyone, anytime, anywhere in the world. The generation that includes older teens and young twenty-somethings is adept at learning and using rapidly changing communications technology, including smartphones. They regularly communicate via Facebook, Twitter, and other social media. Marketers are recognizing this, and in anticipation of more consumers adopting new communications technology, they are increasing their allocation of resources to reach consumers in this way.

Microcultures

Cultures are not homogeneous entities with universal values, even though core values tend to dominate. Each culture includes numerous **microcultures**—groups with their own distinct modes of behaviour. Understanding the differences among microcultures can help marketers develop more effective marketing strategies.

② Describe the interpersonal determinants of consumer behaviour: cultural, social, and family influence.

assessment check 1

1.1 Why is the study of consumer behaviour important to marketers?

1.2 Describe the work of Kurt Lewin.

COURTESY OF PILLER'S

The importance of family is a core value in Canadian culture. This ad promotes family life with special family moments.

Microcultures Smaller groups within a society that have their own distinct characteristics and modes of behaviour.

Canada, like many nations, is composed of a significant number of microcultures that differ by ethnicity, nationality, age, social class, location, religion, and geographic distribution. Canada's wealthy, who tend to live in established urban neighbourhoods, could be considered a microculture, but within that microculture could be found further microcultures. For example, the Quebec market has 15 different lifestyle types that have been identified as having significantly different product and activity preferences compared with the populations in other provinces. Another example of a microculture is Orthodox Jews, who purchase and consume only kosher foods. Younger consumers are quicker to use new technology than older consumers. New Canadians from various nations often seek out spices, vegetables, and meats that are considered tasty or popular in their homelands. Understanding these and other differences among microcultures contributes to successful marketing of goods and services.

Canada's racial mix continues to change. According to Statistics Canada, by 2031, between 25 and 28 percent of Canadians will be foreign-born, and 29 to 32 percent will belong to a group that classifies itself as a visible minority. This would be the highest proportion of the population ever and represents a remarkable increase from the 2006 census when only 20 percent of the population classified themselves in this group. Marketers need to be sensitive to these changes and to the differences in shopping patterns and buying habits among ethnic segments of the population. Businesses can no longer succeed by selling one-size-fits-all products; they must consider consumer needs, interests, and concerns when developing their marketing strategies.[5]

Other changes predicted for these microculture segments of the population will affect what products companies market and how they market them. For example, the composition of microculture segments is likely to change. By 2031, it is expected that the group identifying themselves as South Asian is likely to be larger than the Chinese group, making these the two largest ethnic groups in Canada. Blacks and Filipinos are predicted to remain as the third and fourth largest groups but the fastest-growing groups will be made up of those who are of West Asian and Arab heritage. These cultural groups tend to be younger than the rest of the population and are predicted to remain so. Toronto, Vancouver, and Montreal will be home to most of these cultural groups—71 percent—as is the case today, but they will represent an increasing percentage of the populations in these provinces.[6]

Marketing concepts may not always cross cultural boundaries without changes. For example, new immigrants may not be familiar with cents-off coupons and contests. Marketers may need to provide specific instructions when targeting such promotions to these groups.

Figure 4.2 shows the proportion of the Canadian population made up of minority groups. One group, the Quebecois or French Canadians, is more often viewed as one of Canada's two main cultural groups. Although no cultural or ethnic microculture is entirely homogeneous, researchers have found that each of these ethnic segments has identifiable consumer behaviour profiles.

Quebecois

From a marketing point of view, it doesn't make a difference whether you treat the Quebecois as a microculture or one of Canada's two main cultural groups. What does matter is that this group is very large and significantly different from the rest of Canada in many ways. However, like other cultural groups, the 7.7 million French-speaking inhabitants of Quebec and the pockets of French-speaking communities across

Source: Adapted from the Statistics Canada website article "Visible minority groups, 2006 counts, for Canada, provinces and territories—20% sample data" at http://www12.statcan.ca, June 30, 2008.

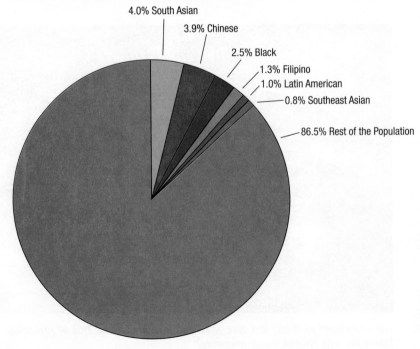

figure 4.2

Cultural Groups as a Percentage of the Total Population

- 4.0% South Asian
- 3.9% Chinese
- 2.5% Black
- 1.3% Filipino
- 1.0% Latin American
- 0.8% Southeast Asian
- 86.5% Rest of the Population

the rest of Canada are not a homogeneous group. Quebec is the largest French-speaking area in North America but there are also about 740 000 English-speaking residents in the province and as many other nationalities in the province as there are in the rest of Canada. Almost half of the population of Quebec lives in Montreal, and 65 percent of those are French speaking. Quebecois are more likely to live in cities than in rural areas.[7]

The population of Quebec, like many areas of Canada, is getting older. Currently, Quebec ranks as one of the youngest populations, but a variety of factors, such as a drastic decrease in birth rates and increasing life expectancy, will give Quebec one of the oldest populations by the year 2031. There are currently 1.1 million Quebecers over the age of 65 and this number is expected to double by 2031.[8]

Consumer behaviour depends on psychological and social factors. Jacques Bouchard, founder of a Quebec advertising agency and the father of made-in-Quebec advertising, studied the psychological and social factors that were important to Quebecois. The results of his work indicate that while the Quebecois are looking more and more like the rest of Canada, strong differences still exist in many areas, and there are lasting influences from the days when the differences were much greater. More recent research still supports the findings of Bouchard. For example, the Quebecois still prefer local entertainers. For marketers, this means that using international celebrities in their advertising to this market won't be as effective. In order for marketers to reach this market, using Quebec entertainment icons works best whether they are filmmakers, television personalities, or musicians. The tone used in promotional material also needs to reflect a different sense of humour; over-the-top absurdity or slapstick works better in ads than dry observational sarcasm. Advertising in Quebec is less likely to be multicultural, although this is changing slowly. There are also differences in how the Quebecois shop. The Quebecois are planners, which is why they are more likely to prepare a shopping list than other Canadians. They are also heavier users of perfumes, bath products, and other beauty products. They have a high consumption rate for beer and wine. Some marketing consulting firms specialize in the Quebec market, as discussed in the "Marketing and the SME" feature.[9]

Marketing to the Quebec population has moved through several distinct phases and seems to be on the brink of moving into yet another. Up to the 1970s, marketers used the same marketing strategies for Quebec as they used for the rest of Canada and merely translated advertising copy into French. Then along came Jacques Bouchard. He put forward the "twin beds" theory: where advertising was

MARKETING AND THE SME   Adopt, Adapt, or Create

"SUCCESSFUL brand building in Quebec is knowing when to adopt, adapt, or create for Quebec" is the statement that Eric Blais and his team at Headspace marketing see every time they walk into their boardroom. He advises his clients, "There are an awful lot of similarities between Quebec and ROC (rest of Canada), and they certainly often don't require a different approach. But sometimes, the differences can be a competitive advantage that you can leverage." Eric was born in Quebec and grew up there, but the offices of Headspace are in Toronto to be closer to its clients. Eric is quick to provide examples of each strategy.

When Weston Bakeries wanted to improve the brand image of its white Italian bread in the Quebec market, it turned to Eric Blais and his team. Moving away from Weston's traditional promotional approach of in-store advertising, Headspace teamed up with other marketing companies to produce a multimedia ad campaign. Television commercials were produced that featured two well-known Quebec actors, Anne Casabonne and Pierre-Francois Legende. The promotional material directs readers to a website where they can view the two actors preparing recipes. The print and television material was supported with online banners and YouTube videos.

An example of how Blais adapts an English promotion for the Quebec market is the work he did with Sleep Country Canada. The English television commercial for Sleep Country Canada featured the company's president, Christine Magee. The French version of the commercial was the same except for the spokesperson—Christine Magee was replaced with Sleep Country's vice president of operations. The reason for the switch, according to Blais, was that Magee did not speak French but the VP of operations was bilingual. Blais pointed out that the Quebecois shop for mattresses the same way as the rest of Canada so a slight change in the promotional material would work.

Sources: Matt Semansky, "Plus ça Change...," *Marketing*, http://www .marketingmag.ca, October 27, 2008; Headspace website, http:// headspacemarketing.com, March 31, 2011; Kristin Laird, "Weston Gadoua Taps into Passion for Cooking in D'Italiano Campaign," *Marketing*, http:// marketingmag.ca, April 12, 2010.

concerned, Quebec and the rest of Canada shared the same bedroom but slept in different beds. He demonstrated that marketing campaigns would be more successful if they were designed specifically for the Quebec market. Today, with the distinctions that have made Quebec unique disappearing and the move toward global markets, the "twin beds" theory is being challenged. Some feel that the Quebec identity has become so strong and established that the Quebecois are feeling less threatened by marketing that is more Canadian or global rather than specific to their market.[10]

Chinese Canadians

Chinese immigrants have been coming to Canada since 1788 when they first landed on Vancouver Island. This group didn't represent a significant number until the 1980s, a decade that saw a large insurgence of Hong Kong Chinese before the colony was repatriated by China in 1997. Along with the Hong Kong group came their wealth, talents, education, and an entrepreneurial spirit to invest in Canada. They established themselves in four major centres across the country: Vancouver, Toronto, Calgary, and Edmonton. These relatively large clusters mean that their cultural influence will be maintained for some time. The influx of people from Asian countries is expected to slow in the coming years but this group will maintain a large influence on Canadian society.[11]

The impact of this cultural group on marketing strategies is significant. Chinese-Canadian consumers spend $30 billion annually. The average Chinese household spends $63 500 a year, $5000 above the country's average. This group is generally young, is made up of early adopters, and likes high-end brands, particularly if they perceive they are getting the products at a good price. They relate best to advertising and packaging in their own language, feeling that it shows respect. They like to shop in Chinese malls and supermarkets such as T&T Supermarkets that carry imported products. This group also responds more favourably to advertising than the average Canadian.[12]

South-Asian Canadians

Like the Chinese Canadians, the South-Asian Canadian group comes from several cultures, including Punjabi, Urdu, and Tamil. This is the second-largest cultural group in Canada but is expected to surpass the Chinese by 2031. A large number of this group was born in Canada. The largest number lives in Toronto and surrounding communities, but significant numbers can be found in all the larger centres across the country. A smaller number of this group is elderly, suggesting that parents and grandparents did not accompany the family when they moved to Canada. South Asians tend to associate more with their own sub-ethnic group rather than the South-Asian community as a whole, a feature that fragments the segment into even smaller groups who maintain strong links with the communities they left.[13]

Some companies, Home Depot being a notable example, have started to develop marketing campaigns aimed at the South-Asian market. Their marketing program included in-store workshops demonstrating home repair projects in Punjabi and Hindi as well as in-store signage and bag stuffers. Home Depot also placed ads in Hindi and Punjabi newspapers. One marketing trend for this group is to take advantage of the South Asians' love for pop culture by sponsoring music festivals and getting the stars of Bollywood movies to promote products and brands.[14]

Other Cultural Groups

More than 80 ethnic groups live in Canada. Many of these groups live in clusters or pockets across the country. For example, Winnipeg has a large Filipino population.

People from different cultures are often used in ads to enhance the effect of the message.

Communities where these population clusters live have developed cultural infrastructures that include newspapers, social clubs, and even radio stations. In order to effectively market to specific cultural groups, both an understanding of these infrastructures and access to them are helpful. In Canada, as in most multicultural nations, marketing too is becoming more multicultural so it is important to understand which aspects of a marketing strategy will be affected by cultural influences and which won't.[15]

SOCIAL INFLUENCES

Every consumer belongs to a number of social groups. A child's earliest group experience comes from membership in a family. As children grow older, they join other groups such as friendship groups, neighbourhood groups, school groups, organizations, and sports teams. Adults are also members of various groups at work and in the community.

Group membership influences an individual's purchase decisions and behaviour in both overt and subtle ways. Every group establishes certain norms of behaviour. Norms are the values, attitudes, and behaviours that a group deems appropriate for its members. Group members are expected to comply with these norms. Members of such diverse groups as the Harley Owners Group (H.O.G.), the Canadian Medical Association, and any local social or cultural club tend to adopt their organization's norms of behaviour. Norms can even affect nonmembers. Individuals who aspire to membership in a group may adopt its standards of behaviour and values.

Differences in group status and roles can also affect buying behaviour. Status is the relative position of any individual member in a group; roles define behaviour that members of a group expect of individuals who hold specific positions within that group. Some groups (such as Rotary Club or Lions Club) define formal roles, and others (such as a book club among friends) impose informal expectations. Both types of groups supply each member with both status and roles; in doing so, they influence that person's activities—including his or her purchase behaviour.

Social media provides an opportunity for individuals to form and be influenced by new types of groups. Mailing lists and chat rooms allow groups to form around common interests. Some of these online virtual communities can develop norms and membership roles similar to those found in real-world groups. For example, to avoid criticism, members must observe rules for proper protocol in posting messages and participating in chats.

Groups influence an individual's purchase decisions more than is realized. Most people tend to adhere in varying degrees to the general expectations of any group that they consider important, often without conscious awareness of this motivation. The surprising impact of groups and group norms on individual behaviour has been called the Asch phenomenon, named after social psychologist S. E. Asch, who through his research first documented characteristics of individual behaviour.

Asch found that individuals would conform to majority rule, even if that majority rule went against their beliefs. The Asch phenomenon can be a big factor in many purchase decisions, from major choices such as buying a house or car to deciding whether to buy a pair of shoes on sale.

Reference Groups

Discussion of the Asch phenomenon raises the subject of **reference groups**—groups whose value structures and standards influence a person's behaviour. Consumers usually try to coordinate their purchase behaviour with their perceptions of the values of their reference groups. The extent of reference-group influence varies widely among individuals. Strong influence by a group on a member's purchase requires two conditions:

1. The purchased product must be one that others can see and identify.

2. The purchased item must be conspicuous; it must stand out as something unusual, a brand or product that not everyone owns.

Reference-group influence would significantly affect the decision to buy a Jaguar, for example, but it would have little or no impact on the decision to purchase a loaf of bread. Reference group influence can create what some marketers call "elastic customers"—consumers who make decisions to save or splurge in the same economy. During a slow economy, a customer might purchase generic brands at the supermarket but, because of reference group influence, spend those savings on designer jeans or a flat-screen TV. Banking on the fact that grandparents like to show off their grandchildren to

reference groups
People or institutions whose opinions are valued and to whom a person looks for guidance in his or her own behaviour, values, and conduct, such as family, friends, or celebrities.

GO GREEN   One Earth—One Chance...

that is the motto of the Sierra Club of Canada. The organization started in 1963 as a Canadian chapter of the U.S. organization and now has chapters across the country, including youth groups. The Sierra Club's mission is to "empower people to protect, restore and enjoy a healthy and safe planet."

The organization encourages its members to be as environmentally aware in their day-to-day lives as their educational and advocacy campaigns promote. Not only does the organization influence the consumer behaviour of its members but also the people of the many partner foundations, corporations, other organizations, and the general public. The organization's partners are as diverse as the projects the Sierra Club takes on, including the RBC Foundation and Frito Lay Canada.

Internal programs in place to reduce the Sierra Club's environmental footprint include encouraging their staff to use public transit, reducing the amount of paper used by the organization, and using only recycled paper. The group encourages the use of fair-trade organic coffee, tea, and chocolate. Even the organization's office equipment is second-hand and when no longer needed is recycled.

The external causes the Sierra Club is involved in include promoting a nuclear-free Canada, supporting the expansion of wind power, and slowing globalization by speaking out against free trade. Another project involves water conservation, ActionH2O, whereby the club is working with cities and towns to find ways to better manage the country's water supply. Club members support projects in areas where wild life is threatened through bad management, or where a species is threatened by logging or oil production.

The Sierra Club has been successful at getting their environmental message out and is an important part of the environmental movement in Canada. Members are often asked to give their advice on any new environmental issue affecting any region of the country.

Sources: Sierra Club Canada website, http://www.sierraclub.ca, June 25, 2011; "The Real Truth About Wind Energy: A Literature Review on Wind Turbines in Ontario," http://www.sierraclub.ca, June 10, 2011; Joe Castaldo, "Environment: Nuclear Options," http://canadianbusiness.com, April 11, 2011; Matthew McClearn, "Food: Something's Fishy," http://canadianbusiness.com, April 8, 2011.

---

friends—and are willing to spend money to do so, even if they skimp themselves—BabyGap recently launched a premium denim line for infants and toddlers.[16] A reference group that tries to change consumer consumption patterns is described in the "Go Green" feature.

Children are especially vulnerable to the influence of reference groups. They often base their buying decisions on outside forces such as what they see on television and the Internet (including social network sites) or the opinions of friends. Understanding this phenomenon, marketers sometimes take a step back so that older children, preteens, and teens can shop—even if they don't have their own money to spend. More retailers now welcome teens who browse but don't buy. These retailers know they are still developing loyal customers—the teens will return when they have their own or their parents' money.

In addition, marketers are recognizing the power of the Internet, including smartphones and social networking sites, as a tool for reaching children and teens—not just to market new or existing products, but to learn more about reference groups and upcoming trends. More than 90 percent of consumers ages 12 to 17 are online, and at least 60 percent are making purchases. They visit social networking sites on a regular basis, get information, and form opinions from these interactions. The "Marketing in a Digital World" feature describes an example of one of these sites that can influence purchase behaviour for teens and adults.[17]

Marketoid

By 2031, 29 to 32 percent of Canadians could be members of a visible minority group.

Social Classes

Research has identified six classes within the social structures of both small and large North American cities: the upper-upper, lower-upper, upper-middle, and lower-middle classes, followed by the working class and lower class. Class rankings are determined by occupation, income, education, family background, and residence location. Note that income is not always a primary determinant; pipe fitters paid at union scale earn more than many university professors, but their purchase behaviour may be quite different. Still, the ability to make certain purchases such as a private jet or an ocean-view home is an important factor in determining class.

Family characteristics, such as the occupations and incomes of one or both parents, have been the primary influences on social class. As women's careers and earning power have increased over the past few decades, marketers have begun to pay more attention to their position as influential buyers.

People in one social class may aspire to a higher class and therefore exhibit buying behaviour common to that class rather than to their own. For example, middle-class consumers often buy items they associate with the upper classes. Marketers of certain luxury goods appeal to these consumers. Tiffany—traditionally associated with high-end luxury goods—now offers its items in price ranges and locations attractive to middle-class consumers.

opinion leaders
Trendsetters who purchase new products before others in a group and then influence others in their purchases.

Opinion Leaders

In nearly every reference group, a few members act as **opinion leaders**. These trendsetters are likely to purchase new products before others in the group and then share their experiences and opinions via word of mouth. As others in the group decide whether to try the same products, they are influenced by the reports of opinion leaders. Generalized opinion leaders are rare; instead, individuals tend to act as opinion leaders for specific goods or services based on their knowledge of and interest in those products. Their interest motivates them to seek out information from mass media, manufacturers, and other sources and, in turn, transmit this information to associates through interpersonal communications. Opinion leaders are found within all segments of the population.

Information about goods and services may flow from the Internet, television, or other mass media to opinion leaders and then from opinion leaders to others. In other instances, information flows directly from media sources to all consumers. In still

A product for those aspiring to a higher social class.

other instances, a multi-step flow carries information from mass media to opinion leaders and then on to other opinion leaders before dissemination to the general public.

Some opinion leaders influence purchases by others merely through their own actions. Oprah Winfrey is one such individual. Through her on-air book clubs, she encouraged millions of viewers to read. And through many on-air wellness programs, she motivated viewers to commit to a more healthful lifestyle through diet and exercise. Recently, Winfrey launched her "No Phone Zone" campaign, urging viewers to sign an online pledge to refrain from texting or talking on their phones while driving. And although Winfrey is no longer doing her TV talk show, her production studio and other pursuits will continue. Her opinions are so well respected she is likely to continue influencing purchase decisions through her other activities.[18]

FAMILY INFLUENCES

Most people are members of at least two families during their lifetimes—the ones they are born into and those they eventually form later in life. The family group is perhaps the most important determinant of consumer behaviour because of the close, continuing interactions among family members. Like other groups, each family typically has norms of expected behaviour, different roles, and status relationships for its members.

The traditional family structure consists of a husband, wife, and children. However, according to Statistics Canada, this structure has been steadily changing over the last century. A number of demographic factors have contributed to this change. The birth rate has declined to less than two children per woman in Canada. An increase in the number of childless couples and higher divorce and separation rates have all contributed to smaller households and an increase in single-person households. There has also been a trend for young adults aged 20 to 29 to remain at home longer.[19] These statistics have important implications for marketers because they indicate a change in who makes buying decisions. Still, marketers describe the role of each spouse using these four categories:

1. *Autonomic role* is seen when the partners independently make equal numbers of decisions. Personal-care items would fall into the category of purchase decisions each would make for him- or herself.

2. *Husband-dominant role* occurs when the husband usually makes certain purchase decisions. Buying a wood stove or generator is a typical example.

3. *Wife-dominant role* has the wife making most of the buying decisions. Children's clothing is a typical wife-dominant purchase.

4. *Syncratic role* refers to joint decisions. The purchase of a house follows a syncratic pattern.

Numbers 2 and 3 on this list have changed dramatically over the years. The increasing occurrence of the two-income family means that women have a greater role in making large family purchases, such as homes, vacations, and automobiles. And studies show that women take the lead in choosing entertainment, such as movies and restaurants. Women now outspend men in the purchase of electronics. Conversely, as more highly educated women begin to out-earn their spouses, men are appearing more frequently at the grocery store because their wives are still at the office.[20] In addition,

The purchase of a new car is often influenced by family structure.

men are taking a more active role in child care. Both of these shifts in family life mean that marketers must consider both genders as potential customers when creating their marketing messages.

Studies of family decision making have also shown that households with two wage earners are more likely than others to make joint purchasing decisions. Members of two-income households often do their shopping in the evening and on weekends because of the number of hours spent at the workplace. Shifting family roles have created new markets for a variety of products. Goods and services that save time, promote family togetherness, emphasize safety, or encourage health and fitness appeal to the family values and influences of today.

Children and Teenagers in Family Purchases

Children and teenagers represent a huge market, and they influence what their parents buy, from cereal to cars. These consumers are bombarded with messages from a variety of media. They are presented with a wide array of choices. Preteens and teens now have their own spending money. They also have significant influence over the goods and services their families purchase. As teens obtain their driver's licences, they put pressure on their families to purchase more vehicles. While parents tend to focus on safety features and cost, teens lean toward style and performance. But teens don't necessarily shy away from practicality—in fact, marketing research shows that they want fuel-efficient cars that are environmentally friendly and cheaper to fill with gas.[21]

Children and teens are wired. Most teens and even some preteens make their own purchases online. Girls tend to make more online purchases than boys. Both genders download music, play games, and participate in interactive marketing online.[22] Firms like Apple and Toyota—both of which have Facebook pages—demonstrate that they understand how teens receive information and communicate.

> **assessment check 2**
>
> **2.1** List the interpersonal determinants of consumer behaviour.
>
> **2.2** What is a microculture?
>
> **2.3** Describe the Asch phenomenon.

Marketoid

Projections show that by 2031, 36 percent of the population under 15 years of age will belong to a visible minority.

PERSONAL DETERMINANTS OF CONSUMER BEHAVIOUR

Consumer behaviour is affected by a number of internal, personal factors in addition to interpersonal ones. Each individual brings unique needs, motives, perceptions, attitudes, learned responses, and self-concepts to buying decisions. This section looks at how these factors influence consumer behaviour.

(3) Explain each of the personal determinants of consumer behaviour: needs and motives, perceptions, attitudes, learning, and self-concept theory.

NEEDS AND MOTIVES

Individual purchase behaviour is driven by the motivation to fill a perceived need. A **need** is an imbalance between the consumer's actual and desired states. A person who recognizes or feels a significant or urgent need will then seek to correct the imbalance. Marketers attempt to arouse this sense of urgency by making a need "felt" and then influencing consumers' motivation to satisfy their needs by purchasing specific products.

Motives are inner states that direct a person toward the goal of satisfying a felt need. The individual takes action to reduce the state of tension and return to a condition of equilibrium.

need
Imbalance between a consumer's actual and desired states.

motive
Inner state that directs a person toward the goal of satisfying a need.

Maslow's Hierarchy of Needs

Psychologist Abraham H. Maslow developed a theory that characterized needs and arranged them into a hierarchy. Maslow identified five levels of needs, beginning with physiological needs and progressing to the need for self-actualization. A person must at least partially satisfy lower-level needs, according to Maslow, before higher needs can affect behaviour. In developed countries, where relatively large per-capita incomes allow most people to satisfy the basic needs on the hierarchy, higher-order needs may be more important to consumer behaviour. Table 4.1 illustrates products and marketing themes designed to satisfy needs at each level.

table 4.1 *Marketing Strategies Based on Maslow's Hierarchy of Needs*

PHYSIOLOGICAL NEEDS	Products	Vitamins, medicines, food, exercise equipment, bottled water
	Marketing Themes	Bayer—"Science for a better life"; Puffs facial tissues—"A nose in need deserves Puffs indeed"; Ocean Spray cranberry juice—"Crave the wave"
SAFETY NEEDS	Products	Car air bags, burglar alarm systems, retirement investments, insurance, smoke and carbon-monoxide detectors, medicines
	Marketing Themes	Volvo—"Protect the body. Ignite the soul"; Blue Cross—"Enjoy the Benefits of Good Health"
BELONGINGNESS NEEDS	Products	Beauty aids, entertainment, clothing, cars
	Marketing Themes	Old Navy clothing—"Spring Break from Coast to Coast"; Ford – "Built for Life in Canada"
ESTEEM NEEDS	Products	Clothing, cars, jewellery, hobbies, beauty spa services
	Marketing Themes	Lexus automobiles—"The Pursuit of Perfection"; Jenn-Air kitchen appliances—"For the Love of Cooking"
SELF-ACTUALIZATION NEEDS	Products	Education, cultural events, sports, hobbies, luxury goods, technology, travel
	Marketing Themes	Gatorade—"Is It in You?"; Dodge cars and truck—"Grab Life by the Horns"

Physiological Needs

Needs at the most basic level concern essential requirements for survival, such as food, water, shelter, and clothing. Nestlé promotes its Pure Life bottled water with the slogan "Healthy Hydration and Great Taste," emphasizing that it satisfies physiological needs.

I LIKE THAT IT MAKES BRUSHING SAFE.

THEY LIKE THAT IT MAKES BRUSHING FUN.

THANKS, ORAJEL.

Baby Orajel
4 Months – 18 Months

Orajel toddler
18 Months – 4 Years

Good brushing habits start with Orajel.
Plus, it's fluoride-free, so it's safe if swallowed. Thanks, Orajel.

COURTESY OF CHURCH & DWIGHT CO. INC.

Children often influence what their parents buy.

Safety Needs

Second-level needs include financial or lifestyle security, protection from physical harm, and avoidance of the unexpected. To gratify these needs, consumers may buy insurance, retirement plans, or security devices. The Co-operators Insurance appeals to these needs by saying, "A Better Place for You."

Social/Belongingness Needs

Satisfaction of physiological and safety needs leads a person to attend to third-level needs—the desire to be accepted by people and groups important to that individual. To satisfy this need, people may join organizations and buy goods or services that make them feel part of a group. Air Canada's Top Tier program is an example. Members have access to an exclusive club at the airport along with other benefits.

Esteem Needs

People have a universal desire for a sense of accomplishment and achievement. They also wish to gain the respect of others and even to exceed others' performance once lower-order needs are satisfied. Lexus automobiles reinforce their drivers' esteem needs with their advertising, which touts the company's "pursuit of perfection."

Self-Actualization Needs

At the top rung of Maslow's ladder of human needs is people's desire to realize their full potential and to find fulfillment by expressing their unique talents and capabilities. Companies that run exotic adventure trips aim to satisfy consumers' needs for self-actualization. Not-for-profit organizations that invite paying volunteers to assist in such projects as archaeological digs or building homes for the needy appeal to these needs as well.

Maslow noted that a satisfied need no longer has to be met. Once the physiological needs are met, the individual moves on to pursue satisfaction of higher-order needs. Consumers are periodically motivated by the need to relieve thirst and hunger, but their interests soon return to focus on satisfaction of safety, social, and other needs in the hierarchy. People may not always progress through the hierarchy; they may fixate on a certain level. For example, consumers who lived through an economic downturn may always be motivated to save money in order to avoid financial insecurity—a second-level need. Marketers who understand this can create opportunities for their firms by offering money-saving goods and services.

Critics have pointed out a variety of flaws in Maslow's reasoning. For example, some needs can be related to on more than one level, and not every individual progresses through the needs hierarchy in the same order; some bypass social and esteem needs and are motivated by self-actualization needs. However, the hierarchy of needs can offer an effective guideline for marketers who want to study consumer behaviour.

PERCEPTIONS

Perception is the meaning that a person attributes to incoming stimuli gathered through the five senses—sight, hearing, touch, taste, and smell. Certainly, a buyer's behaviour is influenced by his or her perceptions of a good or service. Researchers now recognize that people's perceptions depend as much on what they want to perceive as on the actual stimuli. It is for this reason that Holt Renfrew and Godiva chocolates are perceived differently from Walmart and Hershey, respectively.

A person's perception of an object or event results from the interaction of two types of factors:

1. Stimulus factors—characteristics of the physical object such as size, colour, weight, and shape

2. Individual factors—unique characteristics of the individual, including not only sensory processes but also experiences with similar inputs and basic motivations and expectations

Perceptual Screens

The average North American consumer is constantly bombarded by marketing messages. A typical supermarket now carries 30 000 different packages, each serving as a miniature billboard vying to attract consumers' attention. Over 6000 commercials a week are aired on network TV. As marketers compete for attention—and dollars—they get more creative about where they place their messages. Consumers might find a carton of eggs stamped with the name of a television show or takeout cartons emblazoned with the name of a major airline. Old-fashioned billboards—once thought to be obsolete—have made a comeback as large digital advertising screens.

The problem with all these messages is they create clutter in the minds of the consumer, causing them to ignore many promotional messages. People respond selectively to messages that break through their **perceptual screens**—the mental filtering processes through which all inputs must pass. Doubling the size of an ad, using certain colours or graphics, or developing unique packaging are some techniques that marketers use to get a positive response from consumers.

Word of mouth is probably the oldest marketing technique in existence. It is also one of the most effective. If one satisfied customer tells a friend, relative, neighbour, or

perception
Meaning that a person attributes to incoming stimuli gathered through the five senses.

Perceptual screens
Mental filter or block through which all inputs must pass to be noticed.

COURTESY OF CACTUS DESIGN WORKSHOP INC. AND THE DRAMBUIE LIQUEUR COMPANY.

Drambuie: Appealing to self-actualization needs.

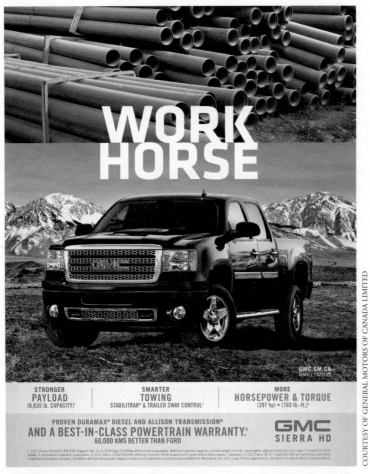

WORK HORSE

STRONGER
PAYLOAD
(6,635 lb. CAPACITY)¹

SMARTER
TOWING
STABILITRAK® & TRAILER SWAY CONTROL²

MORE
HORSEPOWER & TORQUE
(397 hp) ● (765 lb.-ft.)²

PROVEN DURAMAX® DIESEL AND ALLISON TRANSMISSION®
AND A BEST-IN-CLASS POWERTRAIN WARRANTY:²
60,000 KMS BETTER THAN FORD

GMC
SIERRA HD

GMC.GM.CA

Consumers' perceptions that one truck is stronger and more powerful than a competitor's truck could influence a consumer's purchase decision.

COURTESY OF GENERAL MOTORS OF CANADA LIMITED

co-worker about a positive experience with a product, that message quite often breaks through the listener's perceptual screen because trust between the two already exists.

On the other end of the scale lie newer, technology-based marketing tools. These include virtual reality (in which a consumer can test drive a car or tour a resort) and social media such as Facebook, Twitter, and LinkedIn. While investment in these new tools is increasing rapidly, it is interesting to note that the old methods remain strong.

With selective perception at work screening competing messages, it is easy to see the importance of marketers' efforts in developing brand loyalty. Satisfied customers are less likely to seek information about competing products. Even when competitive advertising is forced on them, they are less apt than others to look beyond their perceptual filters at those appeals. Loyal customers simply tune out information that does not agree with their existing beliefs and expectations.

ATTITUDES

Perception of incoming stimuli is greatly affected by our attitudes. In fact, a consumer's decision to purchase an item is strongly based on his or her attitudes about the product, store, or salesperson. **Attitudes** are a person's enduring favourable or unfavourable evaluations, emotions, or action tendencies toward some object or idea. As they form over time through individual experiences and group contacts, attitudes become highly resistant to change. Sometimes it takes a possible threat, such as global warming, to change consumers' attitudes. For example, many people have discovered the benefits of owning a hybrid car. Because favourable attitudes likely affect brand preferences, marketers are interested in determining consumer attitudes toward their offerings. Numerous attitude-scaling devices have been developed for this purpose.

attitudes
A person's enduring favourable or unfavourable evaluations, emotions, or action tendencies toward some object or idea.

Attitude Components

An attitude has cognitive, affective, and behavioural components. The *cognitive* component refers to the individual's information and knowledge about an object or concept. The *affective* component deals with feelings or emotional reactions. The *behavioural* component involves tendencies to act in a certain manner. For example, in deciding whether to shop at a specific retailer for a laptop computer, a consumer might obtain information about what the store offers from advertising, visits to the store, and input from family, friends, and co-workers—the cognitive component. The consumer might also receive affective input by listening to others about their shopping experiences at this store. Affective input might lead the person to make a judgment about the people who shop there and whether those people represent a group with which he or she would like to be associated. The consumer might decide to buy his or her new laptop at that store—the behavioural component. All three components maintain a relatively stable and balanced relationship to one another. Together, they form an overall attitude about an object or idea.

Changing Consumer Attitudes

A favourable consumer attitude is vital to the success of a marketing effort. Marketers can approach this in one of two ways:

1. by attempting to produce consumer attitudes that will lead to a purchase of an existing product, or

2. by evaluating existing consumer attitudes and creating or modifying products to appeal to these attitudes.

It's always easier to create and maintain a positive attitude toward a product than it is to change an unfavourable to a favourable. But if consumers view a product unfavourably, all is not lost. The seller may redesign it, offer new or desired options, or enhance service. Sometimes an attitude isn't unfavourable but consumers just don't feel a need for the product—they aren't motivated to make the purchase. So marketers must find a way to change shoppers' attitude to include the desire to buy. For example, although most consumers don't necessarily have a negative attitude toward sweet potatoes, they might not have a strong enough positive attitude to cause them to add sweet potatoes to their grocery list. In order to boost sales, marketers recently began to provide more information about sweet potatoes, including their high content of vitamins, antioxidants, and dietary fibre. This information addressed the cognitive component of consumers' attitude toward sweet potatoes, pushing it enough toward the positive that shoppers began to buy them more often.[23]

Modifying the Components of Attitude

Attitudes frequently change in response to inconsistencies among the three components. The most common inconsistencies result when new information changes the cognitive or affective components of an attitude. Marketers can modify attitudes by providing evidence of product benefits and by correcting misconceptions. Marketers may also change attitudes by engaging buyers

I believe in .CA

.CA is the only domain name reserved just for Canadians. So when you work in .CA, it works for you. It's like a Canadian flag that says you believe in a safe, secure and trustworthy Internet experience.

COURTESY OF THE CANADIAN INTERNET REGISTRATION AUTHORITY

Find your domain at getmyown.ca

.ca | Canadians Connected

Consumer attitudes toward the benefits of buying Canadian products and services may affect their purchase decisions.

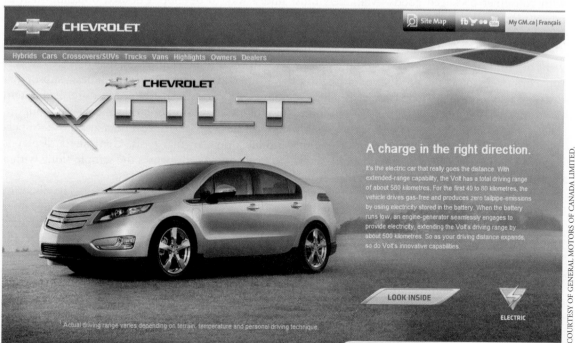

COURTESY OF GENERAL MOTORS OF CANADA LIMITED.

Companies often introduce new products in response to changing attitudes, as with the Chevrolet Volt, an electric vehicle with extended range capability.

in new behaviour. Free samples, for instance, can change attitudes by getting consumers to try a product.

Sometimes new technologies can encourage consumers to modify their attitudes. Consumers who sign up to receive Internet coupons for goods and services might be more likely to try these products without knowing a lot about them. Personalized shopping alerts from firms such as Amazon.com might encourage consumers to purchase a new book or CD by making shoppers feel as though the retailer cares about their individual reading or listening preferences.

LEARNING

learning
Knowledge or skill that is acquired as a result of experience, which changes consumer behaviour.

Marketers are concerned with how the process by which consumer decisions change over time and with the current status of those decisions. **Learning**, in a marketing context, refers to immediate or expected changes in consumer behaviour as a result of experience. The learning process includes the component of drive, which is any strong stimulus that impels action. Fear, pride, greed, thirst, pain avoidance, and rivalry are examples of drives. Learning also relies on a cue—any object or signal in the environment that determines the nature of the consumer's response to a drive. Examples of cues are a newspaper advertisement for a new Thai restaurant—a cue for a hungry person—and a Shell sign near a highway—a cue for a motorist who needs gasoline. A response is an individual's reaction to a set of cues and drives. The hungry person might go to the restaurant or the driver stop at the Shell station for gas.

Reinforcement is the reduction in drive that results from a proper response. As a response becomes more rewarding, it creates a stronger bond between the drive and the purchase of the product, likely increasing future purchases by the consumer. Reinforcement is the rationale that underlies frequent-buyer programs, which reward repeat purchasers for their loyalty. These programs may offer points for premiums, frequent-flyer miles, and the like. WestJet, like many airlines, offers incentives for booking online and for frequent fliers. However, so many companies now offer these programs that marketers must find ways to differentiate them. And firms that don't offer the programs quickly learn that consumers will bypass their products and move on to those of competitors.

Marketoid

By 2031, the South Asian population in Canada is expected to be between 3.2 million and 4.1 million.

Applying Learning Theory to Marketing Decisions

Shaping Process of applying a series of rewards and reinforcements to permit more complex behaviour to evolve over time.

Learning theory has some important implications for marketing strategists, particularly those involved with consumer packaged goods. Marketers must find a way to develop a desired outcome such as repeat purchase behaviour gradually over time. **Shaping** is the process of applying a series of rewards and reinforcements to permit more complex behaviour to evolve.

Both promotional strategy and the product itself play a role in the shaping process. Marketers want to motivate consumers to become regular buyers of certain merchandise. Their first step in getting consumers to try the product might be to offer a free sample package that includes a substantial discount coupon for the next purchase. This example uses a cue as a shaping procedure. If the item performs well, the purchase response is reinforced and followed by another inducement—the coupon. The reason a sample works so well is that it allows the consumer to try the product at no risk. Supermarket shoppers have the opportunity to sample products on a regular basis. Generally a display is set up near the aisle where the item is sold, staffed by a person who dispenses the sample along with a coupon for a future purchase.

The second step is to entice the consumer to buy the item with little financial risk. The discount coupon enclosed with the free sample prompts this action. Suppose the package that the consumer purchases has still another, smaller discount coupon enclosed. Again, satisfactory product performance and the second coupon provide reinforcement.

The third step is to motivate the person to buy the item again at a moderate cost. A discount coupon accomplishes this objective, but this time the purchased package includes no additional coupon. The only reinforcement comes from satisfactory product performance.

The final test comes when the consumer decides whether to buy the item at its true price without a discount coupon. Satisfaction with product performance provides the only continuing reinforcement.

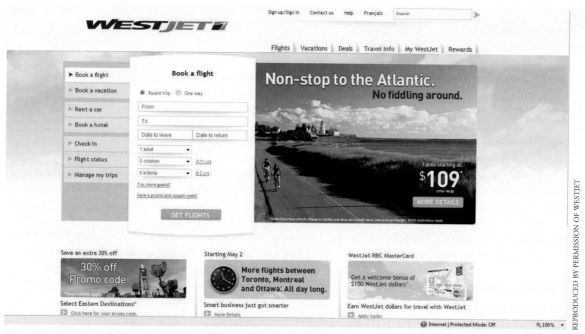

WestJet: Providing reinforcement for customer loyalty.

Repeat purchase behaviour is shaped by effective application of learning theory within a marketing strategy context.

SELF-CONCEPT THEORY

Our **self-concept**—our multifaceted picture of ourselves—plays an important role in our consumer behaviour. Perhaps you see yourself as a creative person, someone who thinks outside the box. You pride yourself on keeping up with the latest trends—in fact, you like to think of yourself as a trendsetter, ahead of the wave. You might express this self-concept by wearing certain clothes.

The concept of self emerges from an interaction of many of the influences—both personal and interpersonal—that affect buying behaviour. The individual's needs, motives, perceptions, attitudes, and learning lie at the core of his or her conception of self. In addition, family, social, and cultural influences affect self-concept.

A person's self-concept has four components: real self, self-image, looking-glass self, and ideal self. The *real self* is an objective view of the total person. The *self-image*—the way an individual views himself or herself—may distort the objective view. The *looking-glass self*—the way an individual thinks others see him or her—may also differ substantially from self-image because people often choose to project different images to others than their perceptions of their real selves. The *ideal self* serves as a personal set of objectives, since it is the image to which the individual aspires.

In purchasing goods and services, people are likely to choose products that move them closer to their ideal self-images. For example, suppose your ideal self-image is one of a trendsetter, but you generally have a hard time wearing anything other than conventional clothes. You might buy a designer purse or jacket in an effort to break out of the box and bring you closer to your ideal self-image. Social network media such as Facebook appeal to people's ideal self-image—users are often likely to post pictures and entries that paint themselves in a flattering light. But Facebook itself has come under fire recently in the way it saves and stores its members' information, as described in the "Solving an Ethical Controversy" feature.

self-concept
A person's multifaceted picture of himself or herself.

SOLVING AN ETHICAL CONTROVERSY

Facebook: Forced to Look in the Mirror

FACEBOOK now boasts more than 350 million users worldwide. That's approximately the entire population of Canada and the United States. The social networking site, first popular among university and college students, is now the virtual meeting place of high school students, adults, and even businesspeople. And although Facebook was once touted as a much more secure site for users than its predecessor, MySpace, recently the site has come under fire for instituting new privacy settings that aren't so private at all. Whereas the new settings have been marketed as designed to make it easier and simpler for users to control the flow of information about themselves, critics charge that the changes may not be as secure as users think they are.

Should social networking sites like Facebook do a better job of explaining changes in privacy settings, give users more options, and disclose the true intention of the changes?

PRO

1. Under the Facebook changes, users no longer have the option of hiding their profile picture, which has angered users as well as digital rights groups. This gives third parties—including businesses and individuals—open access to users' identity, including age and ethnicity. "These new privacy changes are clearly intended to push Facebook users to publicly share even more information than before. Even worse, the changes will actually reduce the amount of control that users have over some of their personal data," warns the one privacy expert.

2. "Facebook is nudging the settings toward the 'disclose everything' position. That's not fair from the privacy perspective," states another privacy expert. Ironically, that is exactly the opposite of Facebook's original stance.

CON

1. Facebook has done nothing unusual. "When you look at what's really visible, it's not a whole lot. Assuming one isn't a digital hermit, most of this information can be easily found in a Google search anyway," notes a business analyst for a marketing firm.

2. Facebook argues that its new settings, along with its process of instituting them, are "consistent with user expectations, and within the law."

Where do you stand: pro or con?

Sources: "Canada Privacy Office Launches New Facebook Probe," SFgate.com, http://www.sfgate.com, January 27, 2010; Ian Paul, "Facebook's Privacy Settings: 5 Things You Should Know," *ABC News*, http://abcnews.go.com, December 12, 2009; Joyce Hool, "Where Everybody Knows Your Name," *The Business Times Singapore*, http://0-www.lexisnexis.com.library.uark.edu, December 12, 2009; Edward C. Baig, "Users: Facebook Getting Grabby With Our Data," *USA Today*, http://www.usatoday.com, February 18, 2009.

---

(4) **Distinguish between high-involvement and low-involvement purchase decisions.**

High-involvement purchase decision
Buying decisions that evokes high levels of potential social or economic consequences.

THE CONSUMER DECISION PROCESS

Although we might not be aware of it, as consumers we complete a step-by-step process in making purchasing decisions. The time and effort devoted to a particular purchasing decision depend on how important it is.

Purchases with high levels of potential social or economic consequences are said to be **high-involvement purchase decisions.** Buying a car or deciding where to go to university or college are examples of high-involvement decisions. Routine purchases that pose little risk to the consumer are **low-involvement decisions.** Purchasing a candy bar from a vending machine is a good example.

Consumers generally invest more time and effort in buying decisions for high-involvement products than in those for low-involvement products. A home buyer will visit a number of listings, compare asking prices, apply for a mortgage, have the selected house inspected, and even have friends or family members visit the home before signing the final papers. Few buyers invest that much effort in choosing between Nestlé's and Cadbury's candy bars. Believe it or not, though, they will still go through the steps of the consumer decision process—but on a more compressed scale.

Figure 4.1, on page 109, shows the six steps in the consumer decision process. First, the consumer recognizes a problem or unmet need, searches for goods or services, and evaluates the alternatives before making a purchase decision. The next step is the actual purchase act. After buying the item, the consumer evaluates whether he or she made the right choice.

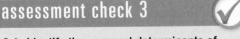

assessment check 3

3.1 Identify the personal determinants of consumer behaviour.

3.2 What are the human needs categorized by Abraham Maslow?

3.3 How do perception and learning differ?

Much of marketing involves steering consumers through the decision process in the direction of a specific product.

Consumers apply the decision process in solving problems and taking advantage of opportunities. Such decisions permit them to correct differences between their actual and desired states. Feedback from each decision serves as additional experience in helping guide subsequent decisions.

PROBLEM OR OPPORTUNITY RECOGNITION

During the first stage in the decision process, the consumer becomes aware of a gap between the existing situation and a desired situation. You have experienced this yourself. Perhaps you realize there is little food in the refrigerator. You are really hungry for a sandwich. By identifying the problem—an empty refrigerator—you can resolve it with a trip to the grocery store. Sometimes the problem is more specific. You might have a full refrigerator but no mustard or mayonnaise for sandwiches. This problem requires a solution as well.

Suppose you are unhappy with a particular purchase—say, a brand of cereal. Or maybe you just want a change from the same old cereal every morning. This is the recognition of another type of problem or opportunity—the desire for change.

What if you just got a raise at work? You might want to try some of the prepared gourmet take-home dinners offered by the local supermarket. These dinners are more expensive than the groceries you have purchased in the past, but now they are within financial reach. The marketer's main task during this phase of the decision-making process is to help prospective buyers identify and recognize potential problems or needs. This task may take the form of advertising, promotions, or personal sales assistance. A supermarket employee might suggest appetizers or desserts to accompany your gourmet take-home dinner.

⑤ **Outline the steps in the consumer decision process.**

Low-involvement purchase decision Routine purchase that poses little risk to the consumer, either socially or economically

evoked set Number of alternatives that a consumer actually considers in making a purchase decision.

SEARCH

During the second step in the decision process, the consumer gathers information about the attainment of a desired state. This search identifies different ways to solve the problem. A high-involvement purchase might mean conducting an extensive information search, whereas low-involvement purchases require much less research.

The search may cover internal or external sources of information. An internal search is simply a mental review: Is there past experience with the product? Was it good or bad? An external search involves gathering information from all kinds of outside sources—for instance, family, friends, co-workers or classmates, advertisements or salespeople, online reviews, and consumer magazines. Because conducting an external search requires time and effort, it is usually done for high-involvement purchases.

The search identifies alternative brands or models for consideration and possible purchase. The number of alternatives that a consumer actually considers in making a purchase decision is known in marketing as the **evoked set**. In some searches, consumers already know of the brands that merit further consideration; in others, their external searches develop such information. The number of brands included in the evoked set vary depending on both the situation and the person. For example, an immediate need might limit the evoked set, while someone who has more time to make a decision might expand the evoked set to choose from a broader range of options.

"The strong, silent type."

MAYTAG

MAYTAG HEATING & COOLING

Maytag® furnaces deliver dependable energy efficiency without making a lot of noise. Backed with a 12-year Worry-Free Limited Warranty, every furnace offers quality construction for more quiet and more comfort.

Visit **B&R HEARTH AND GEOTHERMAL** and choose the right dependable Maytag furnace for your home's total comfort all season long.

B&R HEARTH & GEOTHERMAL

3827 County Road 124
Nottawa, Ontario L0M 1P0
T: 705.445.0077 | TF: 1.888.805.4301
www.bandr.ca

Purchasing a new furnace would be a high-involvement purchase decision.

Consumers can now choose among more alternative products than ever before. This variety can confuse and complicate the analysis necessary to narrow the range of choices. Instead of comparing one or two brands, a consumer often faces a dizzying array of brands and sub-brands. Products that once included only one or two categories—regular coffee versus decaffeinated—are now available in many different forms—cappuccino, latte, tall skinny latte, flavoured coffee, espresso, and iced coffee, just to name a few possibilities. Researchers have conducted studies showing that too many choices—and resulting decisions—can cause anxiety and stress.[24] Recognizing this, and wanting to help consumers find their way through the maze of choices, some firms have set up online sites where shoppers can compare products.

Marketers try to influence buying decisions during the search process by providing persuasive information about their offerings in a format useful to consumers. The marketer must find creative ways to penetrate a consumer's evoked set of alternatives.

EVALUATION OF ALTERNATIVES

The third step in the consumer decision process is to evaluate the evoked set of options. Actually, it is difficult to completely separate the second and third steps because some evaluation takes place as the search progresses; consumers accept, discount, distort, or reject information as they receive it. For example, knowing that you are looking for a new pair of boots, your roommate might tell you about this great online site for shoes she visited recently. But you don't particularly like her taste in shoes or boots, so you reject the information, even though the site might have a pair of boots that you would have bought.

The outcome of the evaluation stage is the choice of a brand or product in the evoked set or possibly a decision to keep looking for alternatives. To complete this analysis, the consumer must develop a set of evaluative criteria to guide the selection. **Evaluative criteria** are the features that a consumer considers in choosing among alternatives. These criteria can either be objective facts (government tests of an automobile's mileage) or subjective impressions (a favourable view of a brand of clothing). Common criteria include price, brand name, and country of origin. Evaluative criteria can vary with the consumer's age, income level, social class, and culture; what's important to a senior citizen might not matter at all to a student. When it comes to dining out, an affluent senior might look for a restaurant with an upscale atmosphere and high-quality food; a budget-conscious student might choose a place that's inexpensive and fast to accommodate study hours or classes.

Marketers attempt to influence the outcome of this stage in three ways. First, they try to educate consumers about attributes that they view as important in evaluating a particular class of goods. They also identify which evaluative criteria are important to an individual and attempt to show why a specific brand fulfills those criteria. Finally, they try to induce a customer to expand the evoked set to include the product being marketed.

evaluative criteria
Features that a consumer considers in choosing among alternatives.

PURCHASE DECISION AND PURCHASE ACT

The search and alternative evaluation stages of the decision process result in the purchase decision and the actual purchase. At this stage, the consumer has evaluated each alternative in the evoked set based on his or her personal set of evaluative criteria and narrowed the alternatives down to one.

The consumer then decides where—or from whom—to make the purchase. Sometimes this decision is part of the evaluation; perhaps one seller is offering a better price or better warranty than another. The purchase may be made online or in person at a retail store. The delivery options might also influence the decision of where to purchase an item. For example, a local electronics store might deliver your HDTV for free, whereas an online retailer might charge $50 for delivery.

POST-PURCHASE EVALUATION

The purchase act produces one of two results. The buyer feels either satisfaction at the removal of the discrepancy between the existing and desired states or dissatisfaction with the purchase. Consumers are generally satisfied if purchases meet their expectations.

Sometimes, however, consumers experience some post-purchase anxieties called **cognitive dissonance.** This anxiety results from an imbalance among a person's knowledge, beliefs, and

cognitive dissonance
Imbalance among knowledge, beliefs, and attitudes that occurs after an action or decision is taken, such as a purchase.

attitudes. A consumer may experience dissonance after choosing a particular automobile over several other models when some of the rejected models have desired features that the chosen one does not provide.

Dissonance is likely to increase (1) as the dollar values of purchases increase, (2) when the rejected alternatives have desirable features that the chosen alternatives do not provide, and (3) when the purchase decision has a major effect on the buyer. In other words, dissonance is more likely with high-involvement purchases than with those that require low involvement. If you buy a soft drink and you don't like the flavour, you can toss it and buy a different one. But if you have spent more than $1000 on a TV and you aren't satisfied with it, you will most likely experience dissonance. You might try to reduce the dissonance by focusing on good reviews about your choice. Or you might show a friend all the neat features on your TV—without pointing out anything you find dissatisfactory.

Marketers can help buyers reduce cognitive dissonance by providing information that supports the chosen alternative. Automobile dealers recognize the possibility of buyer's remorse and often follow up purchases with letters or telephone calls from dealership personnel offering personal attention to any customer problems. Advertisements that stress customer satisfaction also help reduce cognitive dissonance.

A final method of dealing with cognitive dissonance is to change products. The consumer may ultimately decide that one of the rejected alternatives would have been the best choice and vows to purchase that item in the future. Marketers may capitalize on this with advertising campaigns that focus on the benefits of their products or with tag lines that say something like "If you're unhappy with them, try us." Sometimes cognitive dissonance results in an angry customer. The "Career Readiness" feature gives some hints on how to deal with this situation.

> ## assessment check 5 ✓
>
> **5.1** List the steps in the consumer decision process.
>
> **5.2** What is meant by the term *evoked set*?
>
> **5.3** What are evaluative criteria?

CAREER READINESS Handling Angry Customers

PART of building healthy, long-lasting relationships with customers is learning how to deal with them when they are dissatisfied or downright irate about the quality of goods and services they have received. Regardless of what kind of business you are in, at some point you will probably encounter someone who is upset. If you take a deep breath and follow these tips, you may find that you can handle the situation better than you thought you could. If all goes well, you may even strengthen your firm's relationship with that particular customer.

1. *Remain calm.* This is the most important rule for handling just about any interaction. Keep in mind that the customer isn't upset at you, personally—just frustrated with a product or your company. If you respond to someone's anger by getting angry yourself, the situation will only get worse. So keep cool, and the other person may cool down more quickly as well.

2. *Be respectful.* Be polite and respectful of the other person's feelings and state of mind. If you remain calm and considerate, you can help the customer focus specifically on the problem at hand.

3. *Listen carefully.* Everyone wants to be heard. Ask the customer to describe the problem to you. Listen carefully, and take notes if possible. As the person talks, he or she may begin to calm down.

4. *Confirm the problem.* When you think the customer has finished describing the complaint, repeat it back so you are sure you understand completely. Simply say, "Let me make sure I have understood you correctly," and restate the problem.

5. *Take responsibility for the next step.* If you have the authority to solve the problem, tell the customer exactly what you are going to do and when. If you do not have the authority, say so—and then explain what the next step will be. If at all possible, promise to follow the problem through to its solution, even if you are not able to make the correction yourself. A follow-up call to make sure the problem is resolved—and the customer is satisfied—is one more step toward building a lifelong relationship.

Sources: "Telephone Etiquette Guide," California State University–Fullerton, http://www.fullerton.edu, March 14, 2006; Gene Mage, "How to Deal with an Enraged Customer," Making It Work, http://www.makingitwork.com, March 14, 2006; Nancy Friedman, "Strategies for Handling Irate Callers," Networking Today, http://www.networkingtoday.ca, March 14, 2006.

⑥ Differentiate among routinized response behaviour, limited problem solving, and extended problem solving by consumers.

CLASSIFYING CONSUMER PROBLEM-SOLVING PROCESSES

As mentioned earlier, the consumer decision processes for different products require varying amounts of problem-solving efforts. Marketers recognize three categories of problem-solving behaviour: routinized response, limited problem solving, and extended problem solving. Some marketers base this problem-solving behaviour on the following: price, the level of involvement of the purchaser, the number of brands to choose from, frequency of purchases, and the customer's perceived risk.[25] Table 4.2 provides a summary. The classification of a particular purchase within this framework clearly influences the consumer decision process.

Routinized Response Behaviour

routinized response behaviour
Rapid consumer problem solving in which no new information is considered; the consumer has already set evaluative criteria and identified available options.

Consumers make many purchases routinely by choosing a preferred brand or one of a limited group of acceptable brands. This type of rapid consumer problem solving is referred to as **routinized response behaviour**. A routine purchase of a regular brand of soft drink is an example. The consumer has already set evaluative criteria and identified available options. External search is limited in such cases, which characterize extremely low-involvement products.

Limited Problem Solving

limited problem solving
Situation in which the consumer invests some small amount of time and energy in searching for and evaluating alternatives.

Consider the situation in which the consumer has previously set evaluative criteria for a particular kind of purchase but then encounters a new, unknown brand. The introduction of a new shampoo is an example of a **limited problem solving** situation. The consumer knows the evaluative criteria for the product but has not applied these criteria to assess the new brand. Such situations demand moderate amounts of time and effort for external searches. Limited problem solving is affected by the number of evaluative criteria and brands, the extent of external search, and the process for determining preferences. Consumers making purchase decisions in this product category are likely to feel involvement in the middle of the range.

Extended Problem Solving

extended problem solving
Situation that involves lengthy external searches and long deliberation; results when brands are difficult to categorize or evaluate.

Extended problem solving results when brands are difficult to categorize or evaluate. The first step is to compare one item with similar ones. The consumer needs to understand the product features before evaluating alternatives. Most extended problem-solving efforts involve lengthy external searches. High-involvement purchase decisions usually require extended problem solving.

assessment check 6

6.1 What is routinized response behaviour?

6.2 What does limited problem solving require?

6.3 Give an example of an extended problem-solving situation.

table 4.2 *Consumer Problem Solving*

	ROUTINIZED RESPONSE BEHAVIOUR	LIMITED PROBLEM SOLVING	EXTENSIVE PROBLEM SOLVING
Price	Low	Moderate	High
Level of involvement of the purchaser	Low	Moderate	High
The number of brands considered	Few	Moderate	Several
Frequency of purchases	High	Moderate	Low
Customer's perceived risk	Low	Moderate	High
Sometimes called	Habitual Buying Behaviour	Variety-Seeking or Dissonance-Reducing Buying Behaviour	Complex Buying Behaviour

Strategic Implications

Marketers who plan to succeed with today's consumers will understand how their potential market behaves. Cultural influences will play a big role in marketers' relationships with consumers, particularly as firms conduct business on a global scale but also as they try to reach diverse populations in Canada. In addition, family characteristics are changing—more seniors are living alone—which forecasts a change in the way families make purchasing decisions. One of the biggest shifts in family spending is the amount of power children and teenagers now wield in the marketplace. These young consumers are more and more involved and in some cases know more about certain products, such as electronics, than their parents do and very often influence purchase decisions. This holds true even with high-involvement purchases like the family car.

Marketers constantly work toward changing or modifying components of consumers' attitudes about their products to gain a favourable attitude and purchase decision. Finally, they will refine their understanding of the consumer decision process and use their knowledge to design effective marketing strategies. ◆◆◆

REVIEW OF CHAPTER OBJECTIVES

① **Define *consumer behaviour* and describe the role it plays in marketing decisions.**

Consumer behaviour refers to the buyer behaviour of individual consumers. Consumer behaviour plays a huge role in marketing decisions, including what goods and services to offer, to whom, and where. If marketers can understand the factors that influence consumers, they can develop and offer the right products to those consumers.

② **Describe the interpersonal determinants of consumer behaviour: cultural, social, and family influences.**

Cultural influences, such as the general work ethic or the desire to accumulate wealth, come from society. Core values may vary from culture to culture. Social or group influences include social class, opinion leaders, and reference groups with which consumers may want to be affiliated. Family influences may come from spouses, parents, grandparents, or children.

③ **Explain each of the personal determinants of consumer behaviour: needs and motives, perceptions, attitudes, learning, and self-concept theory.**

A need is an imbalance between a consumer's actual and desired states. A motive is the inner state that directs a person toward the goal of satisfying a need. Perception is the meaning that a person attributes to incoming stimuli gathered through the five senses. Attitudes are a person's enduring favourable or unfavourable evaluations, emotions, or action tendencies toward something. Learning refers to the immediate or expected changes in consumer behaviour as a result of experience. In self-concept theory, a person's view of himself or herself plays a role in purchasing behaviour. In purchasing goods and services, people are likely to choose products that move them closer to their ideal self-images.

④ **Distinguish between high-involvement and low-involvement purchase decisions.**

Purchases with high levels of potential social or economic consequences are called high-involvement purchase decisions. Examples include buying a new car or home. Routine purchases that pose little risk to the consumer are called low-involvement purchase decisions. Choosing a candy bar or a newspaper are examples.

(5) **Outline the steps in the consumer decision process.**

The consumer decision process consists of six steps: problem or opportunity recognition, search, alternative evaluation, purchase decision, purchase act, and post-purchase evaluation. The time involved in each stage of the decision process is determined by the nature of the individual purchases.

(6) **Differentiate among routinized response behaviour, limited problem solving, and extended problem solving by consumers.**

Routinized response behaviour refers to repeat purchases made of the same brand or limited group of items. Limited problem solving occurs when a consumer has previously set criteria for a purchase but then encounters a new brand or model. Extended problem solving results when brands are difficult to categorize or evaluate. High-involvement purchase decisions usually require extended problem solving.

assessment check answers

1.1 Why is the study of consumer behaviour important to marketers?
If marketers can understand the behaviour of consumers, they can offer the right products to consumers who want them.

1.2 Describe the work of Kurt Lewin.
Kurt Lewin proposed that behaviour is the function of the interactions of personal influences and pressures exerted by outside environmental forces. This research sheds light on how consumers make decisions.

2.1 List the interpersonal determinants of consumer behaviour.
The interpersonal determinants of consumer behaviour are cultural, social, and family influences.

2.2 What is a microculture?
A microculture is a group within a culture that has its own distinct mode of behaviour.

2.3 Describe the Asch phenomenon.
The Asch phenomenon is the impact of groups and group norms on individual behaviour.

3.1 Identify the personal determinants of consumer behaviour.
The personal determinants of consumer behaviour are needs and motives, perceptions, attitudes, learning, and self-concept theory.

3.2 What are the human needs categorized by Abraham Maslow?
The human needs categorized by Abraham Maslow are physiological, safety, social/belongingness, esteem, and self-actualization.

3.3 How do perception and learning differ?
Perception is the meaning that a person attributes to incoming stimuli. Learning refers to immediate or expected changes in behaviour as a result of experience.

4.1 Differentiate between high-involvement decisions and low-involvement decisions.
High-involvement decisions have high levels of potential social or economic consequences, such as selecting an Internet service provider. Low-involvement decisions pose little financial, social, or emotional risk to the buyer, such as a magazine or litre of milk.

4.2 Categorize each of the following as a high- or low-involvement product: shampoo, computer, popcorn, apartment, cell phone service.
High-involvement products are the computer, apartment, and cell phone service. Low-involvement products are the shampoo and popcorn.

5.1 List the steps in the consumer decision process.
The steps in the consumer decision process are problem or opportunity recognition, search, alternative evaluation, purchase decision, purchase act, and post-purchase evaluation.

5.2 What is meant by the term *evoked set*?
The evoked set is the number of alternatives that a consumer actually considers in making a purchase decision.

5.3 What are evaluative criteria?
Evaluative criteria are the features that a consumer considers in choosing among alternatives.

6.1 What is routinized response behaviour?
Routinized response behaviour is the repeated purchase of the same brand or limited group of products.

6.2 What does limited problem solving require?
Limited problem solving requires a moderate amount of a consumer's time and effort.

6.3 Give an example of an extended problem-solving situation.
An extended problem-solving situation might involve the purchase of a car or a postsecondary education.

MARKETING TERMS YOU NEED TO KNOW

These terms are printed in red in the text. They are defined in the margins of the chapter and in the Glossary that begins on p. G-1.

consumer behaviour 108
culture 108
microcultures 110
reference groups 113
opinion leaders 115
need 117
motive 117
perception 119

perceptual screens 119
attitudes 120
learning 122
Shaping 122
self-concept 123
high-involvement purchase decisions 124
low-involvement decisions 124

evoked set 125
evaluative criteria 126
cognitive dissonance 126
routinized response behaviour 128
limited problem solving 128
extended problem solving 128

PROJECT AND TEAMWORK EXERCISES

1. Choose a person whom you believe to be a true opinion leader. It might be a media celebrity, a political leader, a sports figure, or someone in another category entirely. Research ways in which the person has possibly shaped consumer attitudes toward various goods and services. Present your findings in class.

2. Consider your own participation in family purchases. How much influence did you have on your family's decisions as a child? As a teenager? Over what types of products did you have an influence—or not? Has this influence changed over time? Why or why not? Compare your answers with those of classmates.

3. One major trend in consumer spending that is likely to last for the next several years is a focus on value. "The Dollar Stores of the world are winning," notes Envirosell's Paco Underhill.[26] While consumers search for bargains, manufacturers and retailers of luxury goods are struggling to change consumer attitudes toward their products. On your own or with a classmate, choose one of the following luxury brands (or select one of your own) and create an advertisement for

the product that seeks to change consumer attitudes about your product.
   a. Mercedes-Benz car
   b. Louis Vuitton leather goods
   c. Tiffany jewellery
   d. Four Seasons Hotels and Resorts

4. Consider a purchase decision involving one of the following types of products: a tablet computer, a smartphone, or a vacation. Develop an evoked set of three alternatives for your purchase decision. Then create a list of evaluative criteria that you would use to choose among the alternatives. Research your alternatives in more detail—online, at a store, at a friend's apartment, and the like. Finally, make your purchase decision. Describe to the class how you made your decision—and why.

5. Choose a partner and select a low-involvement, routinized consumer product such as toothpaste or detergent. Create an ad that you think could stimulate consumers to change their preferred brand to yours.

CRITICAL-THINKING EXERCISES

1. Describe a group to which you belong—it might be a team or a club. Outline the norms of the group, the major roles that different members play, and your own status within the group. Have you ever sought to change your status? Why or why not?

2. What are the two conditions that must exist for a consumer to be influenced by a reference group? Have you ever made a purchase based on reference group influence? If so, what was the purchase and how did you come to the decision to make it? If not, why not?

3. Marketers point out that the five levels in Maslow's hierarchy of needs are sometimes combined or even bypassed by consumers making purchase decisions. Explain how each of the following could fulfill more than one need:

   a. A download of "We Are the World"
   b. A retirement investment account
   c. Body wash
   d. Dinner at a restaurant

4. What are some ways marketers can break through consumers' perceptual screens? If you were a marketer for a line of pet food for cats and dogs, what method might you use?

5. Suppose you are employed by a large electronics retailer, and a customer comes to you with cognitive dissonance over the purchase of an expensive computer system from your store the previous week. How would you work with the customer to help dispel that dissonance?

ETHICS EXERCISE

Marketers of online news content are struggling to change consumer attitudes about whether it is fair to charge for this content. While consumers are already willing to pay for movies, music, and games, they don't want to pay for news—whether it is from online versions of newspapers and magazines or online feeds of radio and talk shows. "Much of their content has basically become a commodity, readily available elsewhere for free," notes a Nielsen study. Yet these news formats are created by professionals, and can be expensive to produce.[27]

1. Express your own view. Is it ethical for marketers of online news content to begin charging consumers for their services? If so, under what circumstances? If not, why not?

2. Go online to research different news sources—those that are free (such as the headlines offered on Yahoo!) and those for which there is a charge (such as online magazine or newspaper subscriptions). Is there a difference in features or the extent of services offered?

3. Based on your research and your knowledge of consumer behaviour, what steps do you think news marketers might take to change consumer attitudes about whether news should be offered for free?

INTERNET EXERCISES

1. **Marketing to children.** Advertising and other marketing efforts directed toward children have long been controversial. Visit the website of Concerned Children's Advertisers (www.cca-kids.ca), an organization created by companies that have products aimed at children to address issues associated with marketing to children. What is the purpose of CCA? What are the major issues regarding marketing to children? What are some recent actions? Why have some prominent marketers, such as the Coca-Cola Company, decided to end advertising aimed at children? What are some of the issues related to marketing to children through the Internet? In your opinion, can industry self-regulation ever be an effective substitute for government regulation?

2. **Consumer decision making.** Assume you're in the market for both a new cell phone and cell phone provider. Follow the first three steps in the consumer decision process model shown in the text (problem-opportunity recognition, search, and evaluation of alternatives). Use the Internet to aid in your

consumer decision process. Prepare a report summarizing your experience. Compare and contrast your experience with an actual consumer purchase you recently made.

3. **Marketing strategies and Maslow's Hierarchy of Needs.** Visit the websites listed here. Review the marketing strategies shown on each site. Which level of Maslow's Hierarchy of Needs does each site emphasize? Be prepared to defend your answers.
   a. **www.michelin.ca**
   b. **www.starbucks.com**
   c. **www.holtrenfrew.com**
   d. **www.carnival.com**
   e. **www.unilever.com**

Note: Internet Web addresses change frequently. If you don't find the exact sites listed, you may need to access the organization's or company's home page and search from there or use a search engine such as Google.

CASE 4.1

How Colour Is Used in Marketing

Everyone has a favourite colour. When someone asks us what it is, we usually answer without hesitation. As consumers, we gravitate toward that colour in just about everything—clothing, room decor, cars, and the like. (Do you have a friend who always wears black? Or a roommate who insists on decorating entirely in purple?) We're also drawn to our favourite colour when we see it in packaging. Marketers know this. They do a great deal of research to determine

greater complexities in the perception of colour, as well as cultural determinants of colour preferences. To break through consumers' perceptual screens so they are attracted to the products being offered, marketers need to understand how colour is perceived in order to use it effectively.

Scientists know that colour literally affects the body and mind. Colours stimulate the nervous system and create emotional states. For example, red increases the heart and breathing rate. It also represents danger and caution. Advertisements that display words or product details—such as tooth decay prevention—against a red background may cause consumers to respond with a purchase in order to avoid getting cavities. McDonald's use of red in its colour scheme subliminally encourages consumers to order and eat their food quickly—the whole idea of fast food.

On the other hand, blue has a calming influence on the nervous system and evokes peace, freedom, optimism, trustworthiness, and creativity. If marketers want to emphasize the teeth-whitening properties of the toothpaste described earlier, using advertisements or packaging with a blue background would likely be most effective. The colour blue also suggests intelligence. IBM has always been known as "Big Blue." For a firm that develops and promotes high-tech products, the link to trustworthiness, creativity, and intelligence helps create a positive attitude among consumers. Green is another positive marketing colour, commonly representing nature, freshness, health, abundance, and money. General Mills has a green "G" as part of its logo. Freshness, health, nature, and abundance are all qualities that consumers would like to find in the food they buy.

Colour has certain meanings in different cultures—in Canada white signifies cleanliness and purity, but in China, white is associated with funerals and mourning. So a Canadian manufacturer of bedding or tablecloths would not want to try to market its crisp white linens to Chinese consumers. And whereas yellow signifies happiness in Canada, the colour symbolizes sadness in Greece and jealousy in France. This presents a difficulty for global marketers such as McDonald's, whose signature brand colours are red and yellow. Although the golden arches remain their true colour at the restaurants themselves, visitors to the McDonald's France site will find that pale blue and pale yellow are the predominant colours that appear on the site.

Understanding the psychology of colour—the way it can be used to affect perception and shape consumer attitudes toward goods and services—is an important tool for marketers. The next time you find yourself reaching for the green bottle of vitamins or asking to test drive the blue car, at least you'll know why.

Questions for Critical Thinking

1. Choose one of the following companies. What colour does it use predominantly in its logo or packaging? How do these colours affect the perception of its product?
   a. Boston Pizza
   b. Microsoft
   c. Mountain Equipment Co-op
   d. Starbucks
   e. Lick's Homeburgers & Ice Cream
2. Should a global firm like McDonald's or General Mills change the colours of its logo or packaging depending on the country in which it is marketing? Why or why not? How might this affect consumer attitudes toward the company and its products?

Sources: "Strategic Use of Color in Marketing Materials," Keysteps Internet Marketing, http://www.keysteps.com, February 23, 2010; Darrell Zahorsky, "What Color Is Your Business?" Small Business Information, About.com, http://sbinformation.about.com, February 23, 2010; Elaine Love, "Psychology of Colors Marketing," *Golden Nuggets for Entrepreneurs*, http://leloveforlife.blogspot.com, February 4, 2010; "Internet Marketing and the Psychology of Color," *Money Easy Tips*, http://moneyeasytips.com, January 30, 2010; "Marketing and the Psychology of Color," ArticleBase.com, http://www.articlesbase.com, November 20, 2009; Nancy Pekala, "Color Me Creative: New Study Analyzes the Psychology of Color," MarketingPower.com, http://www.marketingpower.com, February 27, 2009.

CASE 4.2

McDonald's—Adapting to Changing Consumer Behaviour

What influences a consumer's decision to have a hamburger for lunch or an Egg McMuffin for breakfast? Harvey's, Wendy's, Burger King, and McDonald's all sell hamburgers so what makes a customers go to one for lunch and not another? Why go to McDonald's for breakfast rather than Tim Hortons? These companies use many techniques to get customers in the door—having the product the customer wants, at the price they want, and using promotional techniques to get their message out. In order to keep customers coming back, these companies identify and respond to changes in their customers' behaviour.

McDonald's is one company that has figured it out. From its humble beginnings in the 1950s, McDonald's has grown to more than 33 000 locations in 118 countries serving more than 64 million customers each day. The company's first store outside the United States was built in 1967 in Richmond, British Columbia. Today there are more than 1400 restaurants in Canada employing more than 77 000 Canadians. McDonald's is successful because it understands its customers—what they want to eat, when they want to eat, what they want the restaurants to look like, and the level of service they expect. But even with all their successes, McDonald's does not always get it right.

The two original owners, brothers Dick and Mac McDonald, understood their customers and how they made the decision to purchase hamburgers. They designed their restaurant to produce wholesome classic American food and produce it quickly. Customers on their lunch break did not have time to wait for long food preparation processes. The original menu was limited to nine items to allow their kitchen process to work. The added benefit of this process was it allowed them to keep the prices well below that of their competition. Virtually the same concept is behind the success of McDonald's today—good food, good prices, and clean and efficient restaurants. What the company did change is the number of items on the menu and the look of the restaurants.

When McDonald's customers moved out of their teens, got married, and started having a family, the company saw an opportunity to increase its menu to accommodate these changing lifestyles. It added Happy Meals to the menu. A Happy Meal contains smaller-sized portions for children and a toy. Around the same time, the company started to include play areas for children. These elaborate rooms contained colourful playground-type equipment, like slides, to keep the children occupied while Mom and Dad finished their meals. Young families loved these changes. After a long day at the office, the parents did not have to make dinner for the children and the kids were tired after playing on the slides. The play areas were separate rooms with glass walls so the parents could keep an eye on the youngsters but the rest of the customers could eat their meals in peace.

The Happy Meal concept worked well until studies started to show that Canada had one of the highest rates of childhood obesity in the world. Similar studies in the United States showed the same the problem. McDonald's was targeted as contributing to this problem. Critics identified Happy Meals as contributing to the problem because hamburgers and french fries contained high amounts of fat and few nutrients. Other critics of the company found that the toys that came with Happy Meals encouraged children to eat these meals. McDonald's and several other companies were also criticized for their advertising. Studies have shown that advertising directed at children, particularly young children, significantly affects what they want to eat. Children seeing these ads put pressure on their parents to provide the food shown in the ads. McDonalds's responded to the criticism by providing healthy choices for their Happy Meals.

The problem of childhood obesity has not been solved. McDonald's is not the only company that is being targeted for its part in the problem; however the solutions being proposed will affect them. One area of California has asked for legislation preventing all fast-food restaurants from including toys in children's meals unless the meals have fewer than 485 calories and 600 mg of sodium. Other critics are calling for total bans on advertising to children. One study indicated that a total advertising ban by restaurants like McDonald's would reduce obesity in young children by 18 percent and obesity in older children by 14 percent. The more moderate critics have suggested that a total ban on advertising may not be necessary. They have suggested that if advertising to children was so effective, then advertising could be used to solve the problem—promote healthy eating habits.

Families with children are not the only customers to eat at McDonald's. In the mid-1970s, the company identified another change in consumer behaviour: busy people were no longer sitting down with the family for breakfast. The company responded to this change by introducing its breakfast menu, including the famous Egg McMuffin. Today several of the fast-food restaurant chains serve breakfast, and it is a segment of the fast-food market that continues to grow. In the last five years, breakfast sales represented 60 percent of the growth in this market in Canada. McDonald's is in direct competition with Tim Hortons for this market, with each company introducing new types of sandwiches in order to attract more customers.

McDonald's has also been changing its promotional techniques in an attempt to meet changing consumer behaviour. As part of one promotional campaign to promote the company's traditional products—the Big Mac and the Quarter Pounder with cheese—McDonald's used Facebook. The company invited its over 72 000 Facebook fans to vote for their favourite sandwich. In order to monitor the progress of the votes, the company had two large balloons floating over LandMark, Manitoba—the longitudinal centre of the country. The balloons were shaped like the sandwiches and were moved up and down depending on how many votes each sandwich received. The Facebook campaign was only one part of a larger campaign that also included television, radio, and outdoor methods.

McDonald's has used other social media in its promotions. The company used Twitter's suite of Promoted Products to geographically target customers to local promotions. The campaigns enabled McDonald's to connect with its customers in real time about promotions at the nearest store. Two of the promotions that used the Twitter geo-targeting capabilities were the Canadian fundraising event McHappy Day and the free coffee promotion. For the McHappy days promotion, the company used its @McD_Canada account to inform customers about upcoming events to support local children's charities. The Twitter messages were combined with a Facebook campaign for the free coffee promotion. Customers could upload a picture of themselves onto their Facebook sites and change the picture depending on how many free coffees they drank in a day.

One of the reasons McDonald's continues to be so successful is its ability to hold on to what made it successful in the first place—consistency, service, cleanliness, and value—while at the same time being able to identify and adapt to changes in consumer behaviour. The company has not been afraid to try new products or new promotional techniques in order to satisfy the ever-changing fast-food market.

Questions for Critical Thinking

1. What factors are involved in your own decisions about where and what to eat? Is this usually a high-involvement or low-involvement decision? Where do you eat most often? Why?
2. Do you think McDonald's is making a good marketing decision to adapt its products and promotional techniques to changing consumer behaviour? Why or why not?

3. Do you think McDonald's has done enough to deal with obesity in children? Why or why not?

Sources: McDonald's Canada website, http://www.mcdonalds.ca, August 29, 2010; Emily Bryson York, "Facebook and McDonald's to Partner on Location-Based App," *Marketing*, http//www.marketingmag.ca, May 7, 2010; Alicia Androich, "McDonald's Canada Is Lovin' Geo-Targeting," *Marketing*, http//www.marketingmag.ca, April 5, 2011; Jeff Beer, "McDonald's Burger Debate on Facebook and Up in the Air," *Marketing*, http://www.marketingmag.ca, July 20, 2010; Kristin Laird, "Tim Hortons Serves Up New Challenge to McDonalds's in the Morning," *Marketing*, http://www.marketingmag.ca, January 29, 2010; Eve Lazarus, "McDonald's Serves Biscuits for Breakfast," *Marketing*, http://www.marketingmag.ca, February 4, 2011; "Group Plans to Sue McDonald's Over 'Deceptive' Marketing to Kids," *Marketing*, http://www.marketingmag.ca, June 23, 2010; Lesley Young, "A Hard Lesson," *Marketing*, http://www.marketingmag.ca, July 8, 2008; Joanna Pachner and Alicia Androich, "Kids in Play," *Marketing*, http://www.marketingmag.ca, March 25, 2011; Chris Powell, "Canadian Dietitians Want Better Controls on Food Advertising to Kids," *Marketing*, http//www.marketingmag.ca, December 7, 2010; "Fast-Food Ad Ban Could Reduce Childhood Obesity by 18%: Study," *Marketing*, http//www.marketingmag.ca, November 20, 2008; Emily Bryson York, "Court Seeks to Break Bond Between Toys and Unhealthy Fast Food," *Marketing*, http://www.marketingmag.ca, April 29, 2010.

chapter 5

Business-to-Business (B2B) Marketing

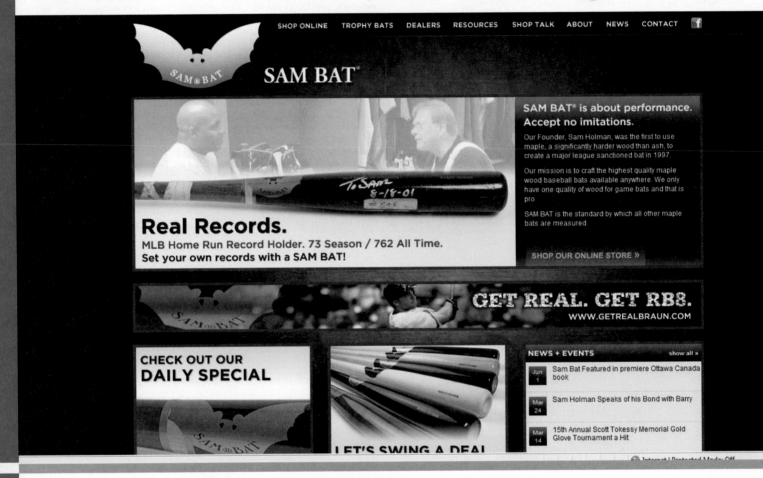

CHAPTER OBJECTIVES

1. Explain each of the components of the business-to-business (B2B) market.

2. Describe the major approaches to segmenting business-to-business (B2B) markets.

3. Identify the major characteristics of the business market and its demand.

4. Discuss the decision to make, buy, or lease.

5. Describe the major influences on business buying behaviour.

6. Outline the steps in the organizational buying process.

7. Classify organizational buying situations.

8. Explain the buying centre concept.

9. Discuss the challenges of and strategies for marketing to government, institutional, and international buyers.

SAM BATS SCORES A HOMER WITH MAJOR LEAGUE BASEBALL

Most Canadians, when they think of Major League Baseball (MLB), think of the Toronto Blue Jays. But there is much more to Canadian baseball. In the 2011 Major League Baseball amateur draft, 35 Canadians were selected. Twenty Canadians have made appearances in MLB in 2011, and more than 70 played in the minor leagues. Another 600 were playing American college baseball. True baseball enthusiasts may remember former Canadian baseball players such as Hall of Fame pitcher Ferguson Jenkins and former National League MVP Larry Walker (five all-star game appearances, seven Gold Glove awards, 367 home runs, and lifetime batting average of .314). But there is another Major League Baseball story that Canadians should know—the story of Sam Holman and the Sam Bat.

Sam Holman is the founder of Ottawa-based The Original Maple Bat Corp., a major supplier of bats to Major League teams. It all started when Bill MacKenzie, a scout for the Colorado Rockies and drinking buddy of Sam's, complained to him in a bar one night that baseball teams were regularly

breaking baseball bats and were spending lots of money for replacement ones. Sam immediately began to research baseball bats and soon built his first "Rideau Crusher" prototype. The bat was tested by members of the Ottawa Lynx Triple A team with positive reviews, but it was a trip to a Toronto Blue Jays batting practice in 1997 that was the real beginning for Sam's bats, now called Sam Bats. Centre fielder Joe Carter tried the bat and hit a homer on his first try. Since then, hundreds of Major League players have adopted Sam Bats. Barry Bonds set the single-season Major League home run record in 2001 (73) and holds the all-time home-run record (762). Following his 2001 season, he was quoted in the *Ottawa Record*: "Sam wants to give me the credit. But it took both of us to do it. I give thanks to God for my ability, and I give thanks to Sam for producing something that gives me a lot of confidence." *Sports Illustrated* called the Sam Bat a "21st-century Excalibur." What makes the Sam Bat different? It's made of maple instead of ash, the traditional wood used for baseball bats. The maple bats

are stronger and lighter than other wooden bats, making their swing speed faster and increasing their durability.

Sam Bats are expensive when you look at the initial price, and Sam Holman knew that he could not afford to heavily discount the price when he had only one major product and 80 percent of his business was done with one group of customers. He built his business based on product superiority. Sam's bats improve the performance of individual players, and the durability of the bat means that overall cost savings can result due to the reduced need for replacement bats.

As you will see in this chapter, in business-to-business marketing, sellers must frequently appeal to more than one person. The success of Sam Bats is because both the Major League teams and the players who use the bats see them as superior to competitors' bats. Price is one purchase criterion but seldom the deciding one; it is more often performance or the value that arises over the life of the product. Many business-to-business customers realize that "the lowest price is not always the lowest price."[1]

connecting with customers

The company describes its bat as "one of the prettiest and yet meanest bats in the world." It welcomes current professional players to provide a current bat—even if cracked—and it will produce a Sam Bat to demonstrate its superiority. Each bat has the distinctive Sam Bat logo, which can be seen from the furthest bleachers, and as batters improve their batting performance, their teams increase their win-loss records, and fan satisfaction increases. This is often an important advantage for business-to-business marketers—to be able to increase a customer's satisfaction, which often means increasing the customers' satisfaction.

Chapter Overview

WE are all aware of the consumer marketplace. As consumers, we're involved in purchasing needed items almost every day. In addition, we can't help noticing the barrage of marketing messages aimed at us through a variety of media. But the business-to-business marketplace is, in fact, significantly larger. The Government of Canada purchases goods and services worth more than $20 billion annually.[2] For example, it spends an estimated $2 million just for remanufactured toner cartridges.[3] Worldwide business-to-business commerce conducted over the Internet totals more than $2 trillion (U.S.).[4] Whether through face-to-face transactions, via telephone, or over the Internet, business marketers each day deal with complex purchasing decisions involving many decision makers. They range from simple reorders of previously purchased items to complex buys for which materials are sourced from all over the world. As illustrated by the opening vignette, they involve the steady building of relationships between organizations such as The Original Maple Bat Co. and Major League Baseball teams and players, as well as the ability to respond to changing circumstances in existing markets. Customer satisfaction and customer loyalty are major factors in the development of these long-term relationships and are often determined by factors other than price.

This chapter discusses buying behaviour in the business or organizational market. **Business-to-business, or B2B marketing** deals with organizational purchases of goods and services to support production of other products, to facilitate daily company operations, or for resale.

business-to-business (B2B) marketing Organizational sales and purchases of goods and services to support production of other products, for daily company operations, or for resale.

But you ask, "How do I go about distinguishing between consumer purchases and B2B transactions?" Actually, it's pretty simple. Just ask yourself two questions:

1. Who is buying the good or service?
2. Why is the purchase being made?

Consumer buying involves purchases made by people like you and me. We purchase items for our own use and enjoyment—and not for resale. By contrast, B2B purchases are made by businesses, government, and marketing intermediaries to be resold, combined with other items to create a finished product for resale, or used up in the day-to-day operations of the organization. So answer the two questions—"Who is buying?" and "Why?"—and you have the answer. ◆◆◆

NATURE OF THE BUSINESS MARKET

Firms usually sell fewer standardized products to organizational buyers than to ultimate consumers. Whereas you might purchase a cell phone for your personal use, a company generally has to purchase an entire communications system from a supplier such as Bell, whose Unified Communications service provides processes and tools to seamlessly enable real-time collaboration for a business customer's suppliers, customers, and employees.[5] Purchases such as this require greater customization, more decision making, and usually more decision makers. So the buying and selling process becomes more complex, often involving teams of decision makers and taking an average of 6 to 36 months to make decisions. Because of the complexity of the purchases, customer service is extremely important to B2B buyers. Advertising plays a much smaller role in the business market than in the consumer market, although advertisements placed in business magazines or trade publications are common. Business marketers advertise primarily to announce new products, to enhance their company image and presence, and to attract potential customers who would then deal directly with a salesperson. Personal selling plays a much bigger role in business markets than in consumer markets, distribution channels are shorter, customer relationships tend to last longer, and purchase decisions can involve many decision makers. Table 5.1 compares the marketing practices commonly used in both B2B and consumer marketing.

table 5.1 *Comparing Business-to-Business Marketing and Consumer Marketing*

	BUSINESS-TO-BUSINESS MARKETING	CONSUMER MARKETING
Product	Relatively technical in nature, exact form often variable, accompanying services very important	Standardized form, service important but less than for business products
Promotion	Emphasis on personal selling	Emphasis on advertising
Distribution	Relatively short, direct channels to market	Product passes through a number of intermediate links en route to consumer
Customer relations	Relatively enduring and complex	Comparatively infrequent contact, relationship of relatively short duration
Decision-making process	Diverse group of organization members makes decision	Individual or household unit makes decision
Price	Competitive bidding for unique items, list prices for standard items	List prices

Like final consumers, an organization purchases products to fill needs. However, its primary need—meeting the demands of its own customers—is similar from firm to firm. A manufacturer buys raw materials such as wood pulp, fabric, or grain to create the company's product. A wholesaler or retailer buys the manufactured products—paper, clothing, or cereal—to resell. Mattel buys products such as plastic and paints to produce its toys, Canadian Tire buys finished toys to sell to the public, and passenger airlines buy and lease aircraft from manufacturers such as Bombardier and Boeing. Institutional purchasers such as government agencies and nonprofit organizations also buy products to meet the needs of their constituents, whether it is global positioning system (GPS) mapping devices or meals ready to eat (MRE) for troops in the field.

Companies also buy services from other businesses. A firm may purchase legal and accounting services, an office cleaning service, a call centre service, or a recruiting service. Jan-Pro is a commercial cleaning service company in business since 1991. The chain has more than 75 master franchise offices throughout Canada and the United States, and more than 10 000 individual franchise operations.[6]

Environmental, organizational, and interpersonal factors are among the many influences in B2B markets. Budget, cost, and profit considerations all play parts in business buying decisions. In addition, the business buying process typically involves complex interactions among many people. An organization's goals must also be considered in the B2B buying process. Later sections of the chapter will explore these topics in greater detail.

Some firms focus entirely on business markets. For instance, DuPont sells materials such as polymers, coatings, and colour technologies to manufacturers that use them in a variety of products. Caterpillar makes construction and mining equipment, diesel and natural gas engines, and industrial gas turbines. SAP provides collaborative business software that lets companies work with customers and business partners using databases and other applications from every major software vendor. Other firms sell to both consumer and business markets. Intel's digital and wireless computer technology is found in business computing systems and personal computers. Bell, Rogers Communications, and Telus sell Internet and phone service to both consumers and businesses. Note also that marketing strategies developed in consumer marketing are often appropriate for the business sector. Final consumers are often the end users of products sold into the business market and, as explained later in the chapter, can influence the buying decision.

The B2B market is diverse. Transactions can range from orders as small as a box of paper clips or copy-machine toner for a home-based business to transactions as large as thousands of parts for an automobile manufacturer or massive turbine generators for an electric power plant. As mentioned earlier, businesses are also big purchasers of services, such as telecommunications, computer consulting, and transportation services. Four major categories define the business market: (1) the commercial market, (2) trade industries, (3) government organizations, and (4) institutions.

Many companies that are well-known consumer marketers also provide specialized goods and services for business customers.

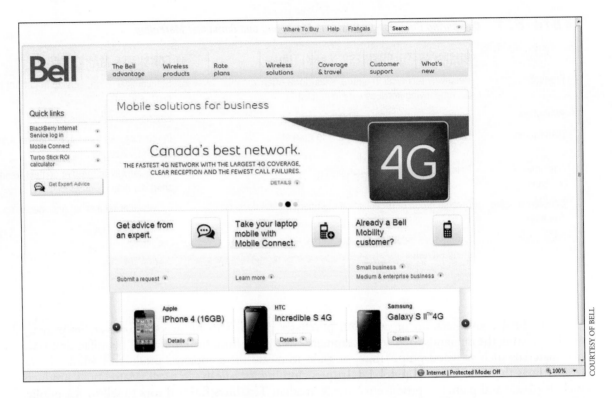

COURTESY OF BELL

COMPONENTS OF THE BUSINESS MARKET

① **Explain each of the components of the business-to-business (B2B) market.**

commercial market
Individuals and firms that acquire products to support, directly or indirectly, production of other goods and services.

trade industries
Retailers or wholesalers that purchase products for resale to others.

resellers
Marketing intermediaries that operate in the trade sector.

The **commercial market** is the largest segment of the business market. It includes all individuals and firms that acquire products to support, directly or indirectly, the production of other goods and services. When Dell buys computer chips from Intel, when Sobeys buys flour for an ingredient in its on-site baked breads, and when your business school buys pens for your instructor, these transactions all take place in the commercial market. Some products aid in the production of other items (the computer chips). Others are physically used up in the production of a good or service (the flour). Still others contribute to the firm's day-to-day operations (the pens). The commercial market includes manufacturers, farmers, and other members of resource-producing industries; construction contractors; and providers of such services as transportation, public utilities, financing, insurance, and real estate.

The second segment of the organizational market, **trade industries**, includes retailers and wholesalers, known as **resellers**, who operate in this sector. Most resale products, such as clothing, appliances, sports equipment, and automobile parts, are finished goods that the buyers sell to final consumers. Acco supplies paper clips, ring binders, vinyl envelopes, sheet protectors, and fasteners to Office Depot.[7] In other cases, the buyers may complete some processing or repackaging before reselling the products. A retail meat market may purchase a side of beef and then cut individual pieces for its customers. Lumber dealers and carpet retailers may purchase in bulk and then provide quantities and sizes to meet customers' specifications. In addition to resale products, trade industries buy computers, display shelves, and other products needed to operate their businesses. All of these goods—as well as maintenance items and specialized services, such as scanner installation, newspaper inserts, and radio advertising—represent organizational purchases.

The government category of the business market includes domestic units of government—federal, provincial or territorial, and municipal—as well as foreign governments. This important market segment makes a wide variety of purchases, such as highways and Internet services. The primary motivation of government purchasing is to provide some form of public benefit, such as national defence or pollution control. But government agencies have also become creative when it comes to selling—local police departments and federal and provincial agencies sell unclaimed shipments, seized assets, and surplus goods through public sales, public tenders, and auctions. Public Works and Government Services Canada operates eight Crown Assets Distribution Centres across Canada where it disposes of vehicles, boats, household appliances, jewellery, tools and agricultural equipment, and many other items.

Tenaquip: Connected in a Connected World

MANTA, the world's largest online community for connecting small businesses, lists 2981 industrial supplies companies in Canada. Many of these businesses are connecting with their customers online.

Tenaquip, a large Canadian industrial distributor with 16 locations in five provinces, offers more than 400 000 items. Visitors to its website can quickly check the products it sells and the hundreds of suppliers it represents, as well as the many services it offers. At one time, visitors could view a complete online catalogue. However, they can still request a catalogue online for one of several product categories or a complete 1944-page buyer's guide. Visitors can also visit the CEO's blog section and read about the latest news and events affecting the company and its industry. Registered customers can log in through the company's extranet to place orders or check product and order information.

In today's competitive business-to-business environment, communicating online with customers is critical. Companies such as Tenaquip understand this and are devoting increasing attention to their Web presence.

Sources: Manta website, http://www.manta.com/world/North+America/ Canada/industrial_supplies—E6055, July 11, 2011; Tenaquip website, http:// www.tenaquip.com, July 11, 2011.

Institutions, both public and private, are the fourth component of the business market. This category includes a wide range of organizations, such as hospitals, churches, skilled care and rehabilitation centres, colleges and universities, museums, and not-for-profit agencies. Some institutions—such as in higher education—must rigidly follow standardized purchasing procedures, but others have less formal buying practices. Business-to-business marketers often benefit by setting up separate divisions to sell to institutional buyers.

Marketoid

The Crown Assets Distribution website, http://crownassets.pwgsc. gc.ca, receives 50 000 visitors per month.

B2B MARKETS: THE INTERNET CONNECTION

Although consumers' use of Internet markets receives the bulk of public attention, about 93 percent of all Internet sales are B2B transactions.[8] Many business-to-business marketers have set up private portals that allow their customers to buy needed items. Service and customized pages are accessed through passwords provided by B2B marketers. Online auctions and virtual marketplaces offer other ways for buyers and vendors to connect with each other over the Internet.

During the early Internet boom, start-up companies rushed to connect buyers and sellers without considering basic marketing principles such as targeting their customers and making sure to fulfill their needs. As a result, many of these companies failed. But the companies that survived—and new firms that have learned lessons from others' mistakes—have established a much stronger marketing presence. For instance, they recognize that their business customers have a lot at stake and expect greater value and utility from the goods and services they purchase as well as streamlined marketing communications such as e-mail, blogs, and podcasts.[9] Another way for marketers to connect with each other online is through affiliate marketing. See the "Solving an Ethical Controversy" feature for some of the rewards and pitfalls of this strategy for driving Web traffic and sales.

The Internet also opens up foreign markets to sellers. One such firm, a cotton exchange called The Seam, survived the Internet boom and bust and is now bringing together global buyers of commodities like cotton, peanuts, and grain.[10]

© THE SEAM, LLC

The Seam survived the Internet boom and bust and now brings together global buyers of commodities like cotton, peanuts, and grain.

DIFFERENCES IN FOREIGN BUSINESS MARKETS

When The Seam first moved into other countries, its marketers had to consider the fact that foreign business markets may differ due to variations in government regulations and cultural practices. Some business products need modifications to succeed in foreign markets. In Australia, Japan, and Great

SOLVING AN ETHICAL CONTROVERSY

Cookies: To Stuff or Not to Stuff? That Is the Question

MANY people want to make quick money online. One legitimate B2B method of doing so is affiliate marketing. This strategy relies on the use of cookies (a small piece of text stored on a user's computer) to allow a website owner, the "affiliate," to earn commissions by helping drive traffic to a marketer's website when certain ads are clicked or products sold. Some describe affiliate marketing as an easy way for marketers to "hire" a commissioned sales force. However, unethical affiliates can collect extra commissions by "stuffing" site visitors' computers with cookies for sites and products they aren't promoting. When these cookies result in site visits or sales, the affiliates get commissions they haven't earned.

One enterprising white-collar crook was recently charged with selling cookie-stuffing software to defraud eBay. It's believed some of those who bought the software and participated in the scheme may have received as much as $10 000 a month in referral fees "despite the fact that no eBay advertising or link on the affiliate website or webpage had actually been clicked." While not illegal, cookie stuffing and other questionable methods of driving Internet traffic do risk the ire of powerful Internet companies like eBay and Google. Legitimate online networks and marketers may be less willing to work with a marketer who has earned a reputation for using these tools.

Should cookie stuffing be illegal?

PRO

1. Website owners who unethically stuff cookies on the computers of those who visit their site are in effect stealing commissions from the merchants they charge.
2. Cookie stuffing loads Internet users' computers with hidden tags that many consider an invasion of their privacy.

CON

1. It is up to Internet merchants to do business with honest affiliates and monitor their behaviour.
2. Cookie stuffing allows affiliate marketers to increase profits without hurting anyone.

Where do you stand: pro or con?

Sources: Jeff D. McQueen, "Black and White Affiliate Marketing Methods: What You Need to Know," ArticleSnatch.com, http://www.articlesnatch.com, March 11, 2010; Kundan Pandey, "Free Affiliate Marketing," Buzzle.com, http://www.buzzle.com, February 18, 2010; "Unethical? Or Just Smart Marketing?" FreeAffiliateMarketingInfo.com, http://www.freeaffiliatemarketinginfo.com, February 13, 2010; David Kravets, "Feds Bust Cookie-Stuffing Code Seller," Wired.com, http://www.wired.com, February 9, 2010.

GO GREEN

How to Mow Your Lawn Once a Month

PAUL Jenkins and Miriam Goldberger started Wildflower Farm (www.wildflowerfarm.com) nearly 25 years ago as a wholesale dried flower business. It quickly expanded to become a pick-your-own flower farm. Eventually, Paul and Miriam noticed clumps of rich green grass growing in shaded areas around trees near their farm and decided to see if this grass could provide natural grass pathways through their wildflower meadows. Some experimentation eventually led to the development of a drought-tolerant, low-maintenance turf grass, which they named Eco-Lawn.

Eco-Lawn is a blend of seven fine fescue grasses. It creates a deep root system so it can naturally find the nutrients it needs from the soil, eliminating the need for water, fertilizers, and chemicals. Slow-growing, Eco-Lawn needs mowing about once per month, although some people prefer to simply leave it to grow. The reduced need for water provides another benefit: Eco-Lawn is grub resistant.

Eco-Lawn grass seeds are grown in Oregon, where many of the world's best grass seed is grown. The seeds are shipped to

Wisconsin, where they are cleaned and packaged for Wildflower Farm, and are then shipped to a warehouse in Buffalo, New York, where the packages are stored. From this warehouse, Wildflower Farm ships to customers throughout the United States. Large shipments are brought to the company's location in Coldwater, Ontario, where they are sold from the company-owned retail location or shipped to retailers or consumers across Canada. Wildflower Farm now sells over 100 000 kilograms of grass seed annually, much of it for orders of one or two 2.25-kilogram bags. The company has started to focus on business markets, where order sizes are much larger. Miriam Goldberger has been travelling to cities such as San Francisco and Toronto, making "lunch and learn" presentations to landscape architects who are increasingly designing "green buildings," and to municipalities who want to reduce their lawn watering and maintenance costs. Wildflower Farm—and Eco-Lawn—is changing "lawnscaping" for homeowners and businesses across North America.

Sources: Wildflower Farm website, http://www.wildflowerfarm.com, May 23, 2011; personal interviews with Paul Jenkins and Miriam Goldberger, October 3–4, 2008.

Britain, for instance, motorists drive on the left side of the road. Automobiles must be modified to accommodate such differences.

Business marketers must be willing to adapt to local customs and business practices when operating abroad. They should also research cultural preferences. Factors as deceptively simple as the time of a meeting and methods of address for associates can make a difference. When Toronto-based Samco Machinery got a $3-million contract to supply roll-forming machinery to a subsidiary of India's car manufacturer Tata, it discovered doing business in India involves considerable red tape and a need to accommodate a more casual Indian attitude about the meaning of a signed contract.[11]

assessment check 1

1.1 Define B2B marketing.

1.2 What is the commercial market?

SEGMENTING B2B MARKETS

2 Describe the major approaches to segmenting business-to-business (B2B) markets.

Business-to-business markets include wide varieties of customers, so marketers must identify the different market segments they serve. By applying market segmentation concepts to groups of business customers, a firm's marketers can develop a strategy that best suits a particular segment's needs. The overall process of segmenting business markets divides markets based on different criteria, usually organizational characteristics and product applications. Among the major ways to segment business markets are demographics (size), customer type, end-use application, and purchasing situation.

SEGMENTATION BY DEMOGRAPHIC CHARACTERISTICS

As with consumer markets, demographic characteristics define useful segmentation criteria for business markets. For example, firms can be grouped by size or based on sales revenues or number of employees. Marketers may develop one strategy to reach Fortune 500 corporations with complex purchasing procedures and another strategy for small firms where decisions are made by one or two people. According to one study, many firms are actually increasing their outreach to small and midsize businesses. Microsoft, for instance, targets small-business customers online but also recently partnered with a user-contributed website called Kirtsy.com that focuses on female small-business owners.

Together Microsoft and Kirtsy offered free, informal hands-on instruction to groups around Canada and the United States in using social media as marketing tools. Said a senior marketing manager for Microsoft Office Live, "Today, there are lots of options for small business owners looking to leverage the Web to bring down marketing costs and connect with customers. . . . By holding these sessions, we hope to help entrepreneurs gain some valuable insights they can take back and immediately use to grow their businesses."[12]

SEGMENTATION BY CUSTOMER TYPE

Another useful segmentation approach groups prospects according to type of customer. Marketers can apply this concept in several ways. They can group customers by broad categories—manufacturer, service provider, government agency, not-for-profit organization, wholesaler, or retailer—and also by industry. These groups may be further divided using other segmentation approaches discussed in this section.

Customer-based segmentation is a related approach often used in the business-to-business marketplace. Organizational buyers tend to have much more precise—and complex—requirements for goods and services than ultimate consumers do. As a result, business products often fit narrower market segments than consumer products, which leads some firms to design business goods and services to meet detailed buyer specifications. Tetra Tech provides a variety of environmental services, including technology development, design, engineering, and remediation for organizations around the world. Because the company's customers include government agencies as well as private firms—and because customers' needs are different—Tetra Tech FW has 280 offices worldwide that offer a range of programs to suit each type of customer. For instance, the firm provides consulting services for utilities, helps communities clean up polluted water sources, and even conducts missions to clear public and private sites of unexploded military supplies.[13]

customer-based segmentation
Dividing a business-to-business market into homogeneous groups based on buyers' product specifications.

North American Industry Classification System (NAICS)

For many decades, the Canadian and U.S. governments used a system for subdividing the business marketplace into detailed segments. The Standard Industrial Classification (SIC) system standardized efforts to collect and report information on industrial activity, but the systems varied between the two countries.

SIC codes divided firms into broad industry categories: agriculture, forestry, and fishing; mining and construction; manufacturing; transportation, communication, electric, gas, and sanitary services; wholesale trade; retail trade; finance, insurance, and real-estate services; public administration; and nonclassifiable establishments. The system assigned each major category within these classifications its own two-digit number. Three-digit and four-digit numbers further subdivided each industry into smaller segments.

For roughly 70 years, B2B marketers used SIC codes as a tool for segmenting markets and identifying new customers. The system, however, became outdated with implementation of the North American Free Trade Agreement. Each NAFTA member—the United States, Canada, and Mexico—had its own system for measuring business activity. NAFTA required a joint classification system that would allow marketers to compare business sectors among the member nations. In effect, marketers required a segmentation tool they could use across borders. **The North American Industry Classification System (NAICS)** replaced the SIC and provides more detail than previously available. The NAICS created new service sectors to better reflect the economy of the 21st century. They include information on health care and social assistance and professional, scientific, and technical services.

Table 5.2 demonstrates the NAICS system for wine manufacturers. The NAICS uses six digits, compared with the four digits used in the SIC. The first five digits are fixed among the members of NAFTA. The sixth digit can vary among U.S., Canadian, and Mexican data. In short, the sixth digit accounts for specific data needs of each nation.[14] Knowing that Canadian wine manufacturers are classified under NAICS code 312130 allows suppliers to the wine industry to quickly identify and get valuable information on potential customers.

SEGMENTATION BY END-USE APPLICATION

A third basis for segmentation, **end-use application segmentation**, focuses on the precise way in which a business purchaser will use a product. For example, a printing equipment manufacturer may serve markets as varied as a local utility, a bicycle manufacturer, and the Department of National Defence. Each end use of the equipment may dictate unique specifications for performance, design, and price. Praxair, a supplier of industrial gases, for example, might segment its markets according to user. Steel and glass manufacturers might buy hydrogen and oxygen, while food and beverage manufacturers need carbon dioxide. Praxair also sells krypton, a rare gas, to companies that produce lasers, lighting, and thermal windows. Many small- and medium-sized companies also segment markets according to end-use application. Instead of competing in markets dominated by large firms, they concentrate on specific end-use market segments. The approximately two dozen companies that manufacture wooden baseball bats for Major League Baseball focus on specific end users who are very different from the youth and high-school players using aluminum bats.

North American Industry Classification System (NAICS) Classification used by NAFTA countries to categorize the business marketplace into detailed market segments.

Marketoid

NAICS Canada 2007 consists of 20 sectors, 102 subsectors, 324 industry groups, 718 industries, and 928 national industries.

end-use application segmentation Segmenting a business-to-business market based on how industrial purchasers will use the product.

table 5.2 *NAICS Classifications for Wine Manufacturers*

31	Manufacturing
312	Beverage and Tobacco Product Manufacturing
3121	Beverage Manufacturing
31213	Wineries
312130	Canadian Wineries

Source: NAICS, U.S. Census Bureau, http://www.census.gov/epcd/www/naics.html.

SEGMENTATION BY PURCHASE CATEGORIES

Firms have different structures for their purchasing functions, and B2B marketers must adapt their strategies according to those organizational buyer characteristics. Some companies designate centralized purchasing departments to serve the entire firm, and others allow each unit to handle its own buying. A supplier may deal with one purchasing agent or several decision makers at various levels. Each of these structures results in different buying behaviour.

When the buying situation is important to marketers, they typically consider whether the customer has made previous purchases or if this is the customer's first order, offering special rates or programs for valued clients. Toronto-based Akuni Adventures, for instance, offers a 10 percent discount to repeat customers, and discounts of between 10 and 30 percent for camps and organizations.[15]

Increasingly, businesses that have developed **customer relationship management (CRM)** systems—strategies and tools that reorient an entire organization to focus on satisfying customers—can segment customers by the stage of the relationship between the business and the customer. A B2B company, for example, might develop different strategies for newly acquired customers than it would for existing customers to which it hopes to cross-sell new products. Similarly, building loyalty among satisfied customers requires a different approach than developing programs to "save" at-risk customer relationships. An example of a very popular CRM software program is discussed in the opening vignette for Chapter 15.

customer relationship management (CRM) Combination of strategies and tools that drives relationship programs, reorienting the entire organization to a concentrated focus on satisfying customers.

assessment check 2

2.1 What are the four major ways marketers segment business markets?

2.2 What is the NAICS?

CHARACTERISTICS OF THE B2B MARKET

 (3) Identify the major characteristics of the business market and its demand.

Businesses that serve both B2B and consumer markets must understand the needs of their customers. However, several characteristics distinguish the business market from the consumer market: (1) geographic market concentration, (2) the sizes and numbers of buyers, (3) the purchase decision process, and (4) buyer–seller relationships. The next sections consider how these traits influence business-to-business marketing.

GEOGRAPHIC MARKET CONCENTRATION

The Canadian business market is more geographically concentrated than the consumer market. Manufacturers converge in certain regions of the country, making these areas prime targets for business marketers. For example, the Canadian chemical industry is largely concentrated in Alberta, Ontario, and Quebec. The oil and gas industry is largely concentrated in Newfoundland and Labrador and Alberta.

Certain industries locate in particular areas to be close to customers. Firms may choose to locate sales offices and distribution centres in these areas to provide more attentive service. It makes sense that the Ottawa area is favoured by companies that sell to the federal government. Satyam Computer Services Ltd., an India-based company with offices in 45 countries, recently opened a new office in Mississauga, Ontario. Sanjay Tugnait, the Canadian manager, says, "Many of our clients in the banking, pharmaceuticals, and manufacturing verticals [industries] have their offices in Mississauga."[16]

The Canadian automobile assembly industry is concentrated in southwestern Ontario. There is no surprise that so many automobile parts manufacturers are located in this area as well. As the suppliers to the industry concentrate near their customers, they then make the area more attractive for industry expansion. As Internet-based technology continues to improve, allowing companies to transact business even with distant suppliers, business markets may become less geographically concentrated. Much of government spending, for example, is now directed through the Internet.

SIZES AND NUMBERS OF BUYERS

In addition to geographic concentration, the business market features a limited number of buyers. Marketers can draw on a wealth of statistical information to estimate the sizes and characteristics of business markets. The federal government is the largest single source of such statistics. Information

The international market for jet engines, a limited-buyer market, is dominated by three manufacturers—United Technology's Pratt & Whitney unit, General Electric, and Rolls-Royce.

can be accessed from several important sources: Statistics Canada (www.statcan.gc.ca), Industry Canada (www.ic.gc.ca), and Strategis (www.strategis.ic.gc.ca). Many government units and trade organizations also operate websites that contain helpful information.

Many buyers in limited-buyer markets are large organizations. The international market for jet engines is dominated by three manufacturers: United Technology's Pratt & Whitney unit, General Electric, and Rolls-Royce. These firms sell engines to Boeing, Bombardier, and the European consortium Airbus Industrie. These aircraft manufacturers compete for business from passenger carriers such as Air Canada, Northwest Airlines, British Airways, KLM, and Singapore Airlines, along with cargo carriers such as Purolator, DHL, Federal Express, and UPS.

Trade associations and business publications provide additional information on the business market. Private firms such as Dun & Bradstreet publish detailed reports on individual companies. These data serve as a useful starting point for analyzing a business market. Finding data in such a source requires an understanding of the NAICS, which identifies much of the available statistical information.

THE PURCHASE DECISION PROCESS

To market effectively to other organizations, businesses must understand the dynamics of the organizational purchase process. Suppliers who serve business-to-business markets must work with many buyers, especially when selling to larger customers. Decision makers at several levels may influence final orders, and the overall process is more formal and professional than the consumer purchasing process. Purchasers typically require a longer time frame because B2B involves more complex decisions. Suppliers must evaluate customer needs and develop proposals that meet technical requirements and specifications. Also, buyers need time to analyze competing proposals. Often, decisions require more than one round of bidding and negotiation, especially for complicated purchases.

BUYER–SELLER RELATIONSHIPS

An especially important characteristic of B2B marketing is the relationship between buyers and sellers. These relationships are often more complex than consumer relationships, and they require superior communications among the organizations' personnel. Satisfying one major customer may mean the difference of millions of dollars to a firm.

Relationship marketing involves developing long-term, value-added customer relationships. A primary goal of business-to-business relationships is to provide advantages that no other vendor can provide—for instance, lower price, quicker delivery, better quality and reliability, customized product features, or more favourable financing terms. For the business marketer, providing these advantages means expanding the company's external relationships to include suppliers, distributors, and other organizational partners. CDW, for instance, relies on a variety of vendors to meet its own business, government, and education customers' technology needs with hardware, software, networking, and data storage. It has developed the CDW Supplier Diversity Program to increase and improve relationships with small-business suppliers owned by minorities, women, and veterans and thus must manage its supplier as well as its customer relationships successfully.[17]

MARKETING AND THE SME	**Small Businesses Need to Diversify Their Customer Base for Survival**

BUSINESS-to-business marketers—large and small—are increasingly focused on long-term customer relationships, critical to achieving their goals. When a customer severs its buying relationship with a large supplier, the results can be devastating. When Walmart announced the termination of its decade-long agreement with Toronto-based Cott Corporation, it put more than a third of Cott's business at risk. Almost immediately, Cott's stock price declined by 29 percent. Cott was fortunate that it also had a number of other large customers; however, the relationship never actually came to an end. Cott remained as Walmart's sole supplier in 2011.

But what happens when a small supplier loses a major customer? In 2011, Loblaws announced that after 20 years of selling Lisa's salad dressing, it would discontinue offering the brand. Vince Forgione, owner of Lisa's salad dressing, is still shipping to his smaller customers, but when Loblaws stopped buying, gone was more than 90 percent of his business: roughly $3.5 million. The small manufacturer, located in Concord, Ontario, is now at risk. Forgione says, "I've tried with some other places. . . . [But] you just can't replace something so big."

Why did the relationship end? Speculation is that listing fees were involved. These are fees that suppliers pay to large retailers to ensure that their products get shelf space in the retailer's stores. It is a common industry practice that favours larger suppliers who can afford these fees over smaller suppliers, many of whom cannot. However, Loblaws spokesperson Julija Hunter indicated that the decision had nothing to do with listing fees. Rather, she stated, it was a decision based on changing consumer tastes. She said, "Consumers are asking for different things. . . . We've tried to address this with the company as a partner for three or four years. . . . [Some] of these issues haven't been addressed by the supplier."

What is the lesson here for small businesses? You must diversify your customer base. Putting too much dependence on a single customer can jeopardize your business if the relationship with that customer ends.

Sources: Josh Rubin, "No More Room in the Fridge: Lisa's Salad Dressing Loses More than 90 Per Cent of Its Sales after Loblaw's Drops Brand," *Toronto Star*, June 2, 2011, p. 1; Jamie Sturgeon, "Cott Loses Exclusive Deal with Wal-Mart; Stock Plunges 29%," *National Post*, January 28, 2009, p. 2; David Pett, "Cott Shares Bubble Up on 'Buy' Rating; Deutsche Upgrade; 'Not for the Faint of Heart, but Cott Offers Value'," *National Post*, September 22, 2010, p. 8.

Close cooperation, whether through informal contacts or under terms specified in contractual partnerships and strategic alliances, enables companies to meet buyers' needs for quality products and customer service. This holds true both during and after the purchase process. Tetra Tech FW, mentioned earlier, has formal Client Service Quality and Shared Vision programs, which are designed to engage customers in continuous communication leading to customer satisfaction. For some tips on developing good relationships with potential customers at trade shows, see the "Career Readiness" feature.

Relationships between for-profit and not-for-profit organizations are just as important as those between two commercial organizations. Walmart is a long-time corporate sponsor of Children's Miracle Network, an international organization that helps improve children's health and welfare by raising funds for state-of-the-art care, cutting-edge research, and education. In 2010, Walmart Canada raised and donated $8.6 million to support children's hospitals across Canada.[18]

EVALUATING INTERNATIONAL BUSINESS MARKETS

Business purchasing patterns differ from one country to the next. Researching these markets poses a particular problem for B2B marketers. Of course, as explained earlier, NAICS is correcting this problem in the NAFTA countries.

In addition to quantitative data such as the size of the potential market, companies must also carefully weigh its qualitative features. This process involves considering cultural values, work styles, and the best ways to enter overseas markets in general. Nokia is supporting its push into cell phone markets in emerging economies by establishing nine satellite studios in China, India, and Brazil. There its designers can customize products and approaches to each market. The firm also has a chief

Trade Shows: Getting Your Foot in the Booth

REPRESENTING your company at a trade show is a challenging but rewarding experience. It takes some planning to put your best foot forward when meeting prospective clients.

Here are some tips for avoiding common mistakes in the booth:

- Make sure there is always one person in the booth with expertise in your company's offerings and who can answer questions from the most casual to the most interested.
- Prepare a script for everyone in the booth to ensure they all greet visitors quickly and pleasantly, with a competent one-minute introduction to the company and the benefits your goods or services offer.
- Show respect for your company, its mission, and its offerings.
- Remain standing to greet visitors. If you need a seat, get a tall stool so that you can stay at eye level with attendees.
- Keep the booth neat, clean, and well stocked at all times. Always leave the booth to eat or use your cell phone.

- Invite current customers to visit the booth and thank them for their loyalty. These customers are worth five to seven times the value of new ones.
- Don't use the trade show as an opportunity to catch up or gossip with your co-workers or the folks in the next booth. Nothing turns off potential visitors faster than the appearance that they are not the reason you're there.
- Remember that every impression you make during a show or convention is important, and first impressions count. Spend time listening to your visitors.
- Ask whether you can help answer any particular questions, and if you can, follow up by ensuring you've satisfied the potential customers and given them any appropriate literature or contact information.
- Always thank your visitors for stopping by.

Sources: Rob Hard, "Trade Show Booth Etiquette Can Attract or Repel Attendees," About.com, Event Planning, http://eventplanning.about.com, January 23, 2010; "Trade Show Staffing Strategies," Trade-Show-Advisor.com, http://www.tradeshowadvisor.com, January 23, 2010; "Boothmanship: The Etiquette to Man a Trade Show Booth," Catalyst Exhibits, http://www.catalystexhibit.com, January 23, 2010; Susan Friedmann, "Good News on the (Trade Show) Marketing Budget: Trends 2010," http://thetradeshowcoach.com, January 7, 2010.

global sourcing
Purchasing goods and services from suppliers worldwide.

anthropologist who travels around the world with a team to study how people in different countries use mobile phones. In the last few years, Nokia has sold more than 750 million basic mobile phones in emerging markets.[19] In today's international marketplace, companies often practise **global sourcing**, which involves contracting to purchase goods and services from suppliers worldwide. This practice can result in substantial cost savings, although product quality must be carefully monitored. India, China, and Malaysia are the world's top destinations for global IT sourcing, while Egypt, Jordan, and Vietnam recently moved up to make the top ten list.[20]

Global sourcing requires companies to adopt a new mind-set; some must even reorganize their operations. Among other considerations, businesses sourcing from several multinational locations should streamline the purchase process and minimize price differences due to labour costs, tariffs, taxes, and currency fluctuations.

assessment check 3a

3.1 Why is geographic segmentation important in the B2B market?

3.2 In what ways is the buyer–seller relationship important in B2B marketing?

3.3 What is global sourcing?

Marketoid

Chinese demand for wine is driving world wine market growth. Chinese consumers are expected to drink approximately 1.26 billion bottles of wine in 2013.

BUSINESS MARKET DEMAND

The previous section's discussion of business market characteristics demonstrated considerable differences between marketing techniques for consumer and business products. Demand characteristics also differ in these markets. In business markets, the major categories of demand include derived demand, joint demand, inelastic demand, volatile demand, and inventory adjustments. Figure 5.1 summarizes these different categories of business market demand.

DERIVED DEMAND

The term **derived demand** refers to the linkage between demand for a company's output and its purchases of resources such as machinery, components, supplies, and raw materials. The demand for computer microprocessor chips is *derived* from the demand for personal computers. If more businesses and individuals buy new computers, the demand for chips increases; if fewer computers are sold, the demand for chips decreases. Lear Corporation, for instance, supplied auto seats and other interior parts to companies like Ford and General Motors. In the wake of the car makers' recent plant closings and reduced production plans, demand for Lear products declined.[21]

Organizational buyers purchase two general categories of business products: capital items and expense items. Derived demand ultimately affects both. Capital items are long-lived business assets that must be depreciated over time. *Depreciation* is an accounting term that refers to charging a portion of a capital item's cost as a deduction against the company's annual revenue for purposes of determining its net income. Examples of capital items include major installations such as new manufacturing plants, office buildings, and computer systems.

Expense items, in contrast, are items consumed within short time periods. Accountants charge the cost of such products against income in the year of purchase. Examples of expense items include the supplies necessary to operate the business, such as paper clips or machine lubricants.

figure 5.1
Categories of Business Market Demand

derived demand
Demand for a resource that results from demand for the goods and services that are produced by that resource.

VOLATILE DEMAND

Derived demand creates volatility in business market demand. Assume that the sales volume for a gasoline retailer is increasing at an annual rate of 5 percent. Now suppose that the demand for this gasoline brand slows to a 3 percent annual increase. This slowdown might convince the firm to keep its current gasoline pumps and replace them only when market conditions improve. In this way, even modest shifts in consumer demand for a gasoline brand would greatly affect the pump manufacturer.

JOINT DEMAND

Another important influence on business market demand is **joint demand**, which results when the demand for one business product is related to the demand for another business product used in combination with the first item. Both lumber and concrete are required to build most homes. If the lumber supply falls, the drop in housing construction will most likely affect the demand for concrete. Another example is the joint demand for electrical power and large turbine engines. If consumers decide to conserve power, demand for new power plants drops, as does the demand for components and replacement parts for turbines.

joint demand
Demand for a product that depends on the demand for another product used in combination with it.

INELASTIC DEMAND

Inelastic demand means that demand throughout an industry will not change significantly due to a price change. If the price of lumber drops, a construction firm will not necessarily buy more lumber from its suppliers unless another factor—such as lowered mortgage interest rates—causes more consumers to purchase new homes.

inelastic demand
Demand that, throughout an industry, will not change significantly due to a price change.

INVENTORY ADJUSTMENTS

Adjustments in inventory and inventory policies can also affect business demand. Assume that manufacturers in a particular industry consider a 60-day supply of raw materials the optimal inventory level. Now suppose that economic conditions or other factors induce these firms to increase their inventories to a 90-day supply. The change will bombard the raw-materials supplier with new orders.

Marketoid

JIT was first perfected at Toyota by Taiichi Ohno, now frequently referred to as the father of JIT.

just-in-time (JIT) / JIT II
Inventory practices that seek to boost efficiency by cutting inventories to absolute minimum levels. With JIT II, suppliers' representatives work at the customer's facility.

sole sourcing
Purchasing a firm's entire stock of an item from just one vendor.

Further, **just-in-time (JIT)** inventory policies seek to boost efficiency by cutting inventories to absolute minimum levels and by requiring vendors to deliver inputs as the production process needs them. JIT allows companies to better predict which supplies they will require and the timing for when they will need them, markedly reducing their costs for production and storage. Widespread implementation of JIT has had a substantial impact on organizations' purchasing behaviour. Firms that practise JIT tend to order from relatively few suppliers. In some cases, JIT may lead to **sole sourcing** for some items—in other words, buying a firm's entire stock of a product from just one supplier. Electronic data interchange (EDI) and quick-response inventory policies have produced similar results in the trade industries. The latest inventory trend, **JIT II**, leads suppliers to place representatives at the customer's facility to work as part of an integrated, on-site customer–supplier team. Suppliers plan and order in consultation with the customer. This streamlining of the inventory process improves control of the flow of goods.

Although inventory adjustments are critical in manufacturing processes, they are equally vital to wholesalers and retailers. Perhaps nowhere is inventory management more complex than at Walmart, the largest retailer in the world, with sales of about $400 billion (U.S.). With no signs of slowing down, suppliers such as Procter & Gamble and Unilever—giants themselves—work closely with Walmart to monitor and adjust inventory as necessary. Other suppliers, such as Mega Toys, Parkway Imaging and Graphics, and Ruiz Foods generate a large portion of their total income from Walmart, so inventory management is critical for those companies as well.[22]

assessment check 3b

3.4 How does derived demand create volatile demand?

3.5 Give an example of joint demand.

3.6 How might JIT II strengthen marketing relationships?

H. F. (HERB) MACKENZIE

Derived demand also applies to expense items. When demand for a manufacturer's product declines, its production decreases, and its demand for operating supplies such as drill bits and other cutting tools also declines.

THE MAKE, BUY, OR LEASE DECISION

④ Discuss the decision to make, buy, or lease.

Before a company can decide what to buy, it should decide whether to buy at all. Organizational buyers must figure out the best way to acquire needed products. In fact, a firm considering the acquisition of a finished good, component part, or service has three basic options:

1. Make the good or provide the service in-house.

2. Purchase it from another organization.

3. Lease it from another organization.

Manufacturing the product itself, if the company has the capability to do so, may be the best route. It may save a great deal of money if its own manufacturing division does not incur costs for overhead that an outside vendor would otherwise charge.

On the other hand, most firms cannot make all the business goods they need. Often, it would be too costly to maintain the necessary equipment, staff, and supplies. Therefore, purchasing from an outside vendor is the most common choice. Xerox manufactures more than 50 different types of colour printers to meet nearly any business need—from affordable colour laser printers to high-performance ink-jet printers. Its wide array of products, coupled with its track record of a century of supplying businesses, has made it a leader in the B2B printer market.[23] Companies can also look outside their own plants for goods and services that they formerly produced in-house, a practice called *outsourcing* that the next section will describe in more detail.

In some cases, however, a company may choose to lease inputs. This option spreads out costs compared with lump-sum costs for upfront purchases. The company pays for the use of equipment for a certain period. A small business may lease a copier for a few years and make monthly payments. At the end of the lease term, the firm can buy the machine at a prearranged price or replace it with a

Xerox offers a portfolio of superior office products and outsourcing services that help customers reduce cost and improve efficiency.

COURTESY OF XEROX CANADA

different model under a new lease. This option can provide useful flexibility for a growing business, allowing it to easily upgrade as its needs change.

Companies can also lease sophisticated computer systems and heavy equipment. For example, some airlines prefer to lease airplanes rather than buy them outright because short-term leases allow them to adapt quickly to changes in passenger demand.

THE RISE OF OUTSOURCING AND OFFSHORING

offshoring
Movement of high-wage jobs from Canada to lower-cost overseas locations.

nearshoring
Moving jobs to vendors in countries close to the business's home country.

outsourcing
Using outside vendors to produce goods and services formerly produced in-house.

Chances are, if you dial a call centre for a firm such as Dell, GE, or Bell, your call will be answered by someone in India. In recent years, there has been a growing concern related to the movement of jobs to lower-cost overseas locations, a business practice referred to as **offshoring**. This relocation of business processes to a lower-cost location can involve production offshoring or services offshoring. China has emerged as the preferred destination for production offshoring, while India has emerged as the dominant player in services offshoring.

Some firms want to remain closer to home but take advantage of the benefits of locating some of their operations outside their home country, a practice known as **nearshoring**. In today's highly competitive marketplace, firms look to improve efficiency and cut costs on just about everything, including customer service, human resources, accounting, information technology, manufacturing, and distribution. **Outsourcing**—using outside vendors to produce goods and services formerly produced in-house—is a trend that continues to rise, but a recent report by the Boston Consulting Group predicts renewed manufacturing in the United States by 2015. The report further suggests that as more U.S. manufacturers reduce their overseas outsourcing, more Canadian manufacturers will benefit from their nearshoring activities.[24] Businesses outsource for several reasons: (1) they need to reduce costs to remain competitive, (2) they need to improve the quality and speed of software maintenance and development, and (3) outsourcing has begun to offer greater value than ever before.

Outsourcing allows firms to concentrate their resources on their core business. It also allows access to specialized talent or expertise that does not exist within the firm. The most frequently outsourced business functions include information technology (IT) and human resources, with other white-collar service jobs such as accounting, drug research, technical R&D, and film animation. Although most outsourcing is done by North American–based companies, the practice is rapidly becoming commonplace in Asia, Europe, and Central America.

China still leads the way in offshore manufacturing, making two-thirds of the world's copiers, microwaves, DVD players, and shoes, and virtually all of the world's toys. In recent years, however, China's very success and the resulting rise of an increasingly wealthy middle class have pushed up its labour and management costs and may have helped shift many companies to suppliers in Vietnam and India, where such costs are still low.[25]

Outsourcing can be a smart strategy if a company chooses a vendor that can provide high-quality products and perhaps at a lower cost than could be achieved by the company itself. This priority allows the outsourcer to focus on its core competencies. Successful outsourcing requires companies to carefully oversee contracts and manage relationships. Some vendors now provide performance guarantees to assure their customers that they will receive high-quality services that meet their needs.

PROBLEMS WITH OUTSOURCING AND OFFSHORING

Outsourcing and offshoring are not without their downsides. Many companies discover that their cost savings are less than vendors sometimes promise. Also, companies that sign multiyear contracts may find that their savings drop after a year or two. When proprietary technology is an issue, outsourcing raises security concerns. Similarly, companies that are protective of customer data and relationships may think twice about entrusting functions like customer service to outside sources.

In some cases, outsourcing and offshoring can reduce a company's ability to respond quickly to the marketplace, or they can slow efforts in bringing new products to market. Suppliers who fail to deliver goods promptly or provide required services can adversely affect a company's reputation with its customers.

Outsourcing and offshoring are controversial topics with unions, especially in the auto industry, as the percentage of component parts made in-house has steadily dropped. These practices can create conflicts between nonunion outside workers and in-house union employees, who fear job loss. Management initiatives to outsource jobs can lead to strikes and plant shutdowns. Even if they do not lead to disruption in the workplace, outsourcing and offshoring can have a negative impact on employee morale and loyalty.

assessment check 4

4.1 Identify two potential benefits of outsourcing.

4.2 Identify two potential problems with outsourcing.

THE BUSINESS BUYING PROCESS

⑤ **Describe the major influences on business buying behaviour.**

Suppose that CanMap, Inc., a hypothetical manufacturer of GPS devices for automakers, decides to upgrade its manufacturing facility with $5 million in new automated assembly equipment. Before approaching equipment suppliers, the company must analyze its needs, determine goals that the project should accomplish, develop technical specifications for the equipment, and set a budget. Once it receives vendors' proposals, it must evaluate them and select the best one. But what does *best* mean in this context? The lowest price or the best warranty and service contract? Who in the company is responsible for such decisions?

The business buying process is more complex than the consumer decision process. Business buying takes place within a formal organization's budget, cost, and profit considerations. Furthermore, B2B and institutional buying decisions usually involve many people with complex interactions among individuals and organizational goals. To understand organizational buying behaviour, business marketers require knowledge of influences on the purchase decision process, the stages in the organizational buying model, types of business buying situations, and techniques for purchase decision analysis.

INFLUENCES ON PURCHASE DECISIONS

B2B buying decisions react to various influences, some external to the firm and others related to internal structure and personnel. In addition to product-specific factors such as purchase price, installation, operating and maintenance costs, and vendor service, companies must consider broader environmental, organizational, and interpersonal influences.

Environmental Factors

Environmental conditions such as economic, political, regulatory, competitive, and technological considerations influence business buying decisions. CanMap may wish to defer purchases of the new equipment in times of slowing economic activity. During a recession, sales to automakers might drop because households hesitate to spend money on a new car. The company would look at the derived demand for its products, possible changes in its sources of materials, employment trends, and similar factors before committing to such a large capital expenditure.

Political, regulatory, and competitive factors also come into play in influencing purchase decisions. Passage of a privacy law that restricted GPS tracking would affect demand, as would competition from smartphones and other devices containing map features. Finally, technology plays a role in purchase decisions. When GPS systems were first introduced, many customers bought separate units to install in their cars. But as more new cars come factory-equipped with the units, the market for standalone boxes naturally decreases.

Organizational Factors

Successful business-to-business marketers understand their customers' organizational structures, policies, and purchasing systems. A company with a centralized procurement function operates differently from one that delegates purchasing decisions to divisional or geographic units. Trying to sell to the local store when head office merchandisers make all the decisions would clearly waste salespeople's time. Buying behaviour also differs among firms. For example, centralized buying tends to emphasize long-term relationships, whereas decentralized buying focuses more on short-term results. Personal selling skills and user preferences carry more weight in decentralized purchasing situations than in centralized buying.

How many suppliers should a company patronize? Because purchasing operations spend over half of each dollar their companies earn, consolidating vendor relationships can lead to large cost savings. However, a fine line separates maximizing buying power from relying too heavily on a few suppliers. Many companies engage in **multiple sourcing**—purchasing from several vendors. Spreading orders ensures against shortages if one vendor cannot deliver on schedule. However, dealing with many sellers can be counterproductive and take too much time. Each company must set its own criteria for this decision.

multiple sourcing
Purchasing from several vendors.

Interpersonal Influences

Many people may influence B2B purchases, and considerable time may be spent obtaining the input and approval of various organization members. Both group and individual forces are at work here. When committees handle buying, they must spend time to gain majority or unanimous approval. Also, each individual buyer brings to the decision process individual preferences, experiences, and biases.

Business marketers should know who will influence buying decisions in an organization for their products and should know each of their priorities. To choose a supplier for an industrial press, for example, a purchasing manager and representatives of the company's production, engineering, and quality control departments may jointly decide on a supplier. Each of these principals may have a different point of view that the vendor's marketers must understand.

To effectively address the concerns of all people involved in the buying decision, sales personnel must be well versed in the technical features of their products. They must also interact well with employees of the various departments involved in the purchase decision. Sales representatives for medical products—traditionally called detailers—frequently visit hospitals and doctors' offices to discuss the advantages of their new products and leave samples with clinical staff.

The Role of Merchandisers and Category Advisors

merchandisers
Trade sector buyers who secure needed products at the best possible prices.

systems integration
Centralization of the procurement function within an internal division or as a service of an external supplier.

category advisor (category captain)
Trade industry vendor who develops a comprehensive procurement plan for a retail buyer.

Many large organizations attempt to make their purchases through systematic procedures employing professional buyers. In the trade industries, these buyers, often referred to as **merchandisers**, are responsible for securing needed products at the best possible prices. Canadian Tire has buyers for hardware items and sporting goods that will ultimately be sold to consumers. Ford has buyers for components that will be incorporated into its cars and trucks. A firm's purchasing or merchandising unit devotes all its time and effort in determining needs, locating and evaluating alternative suppliers, and making purchase decisions.

Purchase decisions for capital items vary significantly from those for expense items. Firms often buy expense items routinely with little delay. Capital items, however, involve major fund commitments and usually undergo considerable review.

One way in which a firm may attempt to streamline the buying process is through **systems integration**, or centralization of the procurement function. One company may designate a lead division to handle all purchasing. Another firm may choose to designate a major supplier as the systems integrator. This vendor then assumes responsibility for dealing with all the suppliers for a project and for presenting the entire package to the buyer. In trade industries, this vendor is sometimes called a **category advisor** or **category captain**.

A business marketer may set up a sales organization to serve national accounts that deals solely with buyers at geographically concentrated corporate headquarters. A separate field sales organization may serve buyers at regional production facilities.

Corporate buyers often use the Internet to identify sources of supply. They view online catalogues and websites to compare vendors' offerings and to obtain product information. Some use Internet exchanges to extend their supplier networks.

assessment check 5

5.1 Identify the three major factors that influence purchase decisions.

5.2 What are the advantages and disadvantages of multiple sourcing?

MODEL OF THE ORGANIZATIONAL BUYING PROCESS

⑥ Outline the steps in the organizational buying process.

An organizational buying situation takes place through a sequence of activities. Figure 5.2 illustrates an eight-stage model of an organizational buying process. Although not every buying situation will require all these steps, this figure provides a good overview of the whole process.

Stage 1: Anticipate or Recognize a Problem/Need/Opportunity and a General Solution

Both consumer and business purchase decisions begin when the recognition of problems, needs, or opportunities triggers the buying process. Perhaps a firm's computer system has become outdated or an account representative demonstrates a new service that could improve the company's performance. Companies may decide to hire an outside marketing specialist when their sales stagnate.

The problem may be as simple as needing to provide a good cup of coffee to a firm's employees. The founders of Keurig Incorporated, which supplies about 2.5 million individually brewed cups of coffee to homes and offices each day, started by asking themselves, "Why do we brew coffee a pot at a time when we drink it a cup at a time?"[26]

Stage 2: Determine the Characteristics and Quantity of a Needed Good or Service

The coffee problem described in stage 1 translated into a service opportunity for Keurig. The small firm was able to offer a coffee system that would brew one perfect cup of coffee at a time, according to the preferences of

figure 5.2

Stages in the B2B Buying Process

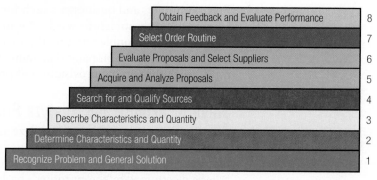

Obtain Feedback and Evaluate Performance	8
Select Order Routine	7
Evaluate Proposals and Select Suppliers	6
Acquire and Analyze Proposals	5
Search for and Qualify Sources	4
Describe Characteristics and Quantity	3
Determine Characteristics and Quantity	2
Recognize Problem and General Solution	1

Source: Based on Michael D. Hutt and Thomas W. Speh, *Business Marketing Management: A Strategic View of Industrial and Organizational Markets*, 8th Edition (Mason, OH: South-Western, 2004).

H. F. (HERB) MACKENZIE

The founders of Keurig Incorporated asked themselves, "Why do we brew coffee a pot at a time when we drink it a cup at a time?"

each employee. After finding success in the offices of many accounting, law, and medical practices, the company developed a single-cup brewer for home use and has most recently introduced a unique full-colour touch screen that allows coffee lovers to readily customize each cup's temperature and strength.[27]

Stage 3: Describe Characteristics and the Quantity of a Needed Good or Service

After determining the characteristics and quantity of needed products, B2B buyers must translate these ideas into detailed specifications. Customers told Keurig they wanted a foolproof, individual coffee maker. The Keurig system supplies a plastic K-Cup portion pack, containing ground coffee that the individual simply places in the coffee maker—no measuring of water or coffee is required. Out comes the perfect cup of coffee. Firms can easily base the quantity requirements of the Keurig system on the number of coffee-drinking employees they have or the amount of space they occupy.

Stage 4: Search for and Qualify Potential Sources

Both consumers and businesses search for good suppliers of desired products. The choice of a supplier may be relatively straightforward—for instance, because there was no other machine like it, its early adopters had no trouble selecting the Keurig coffee system. Other searches may involve more complex decision making. A company that wants to buy a group life or health insurance policy, for example, must weigh the varying provisions and programs of many different vendors.

Stage 5: Acquire and Analyze Proposals

The next step is to acquire and analyze suppliers' proposals, which are often submitted in writing. If the buyer is a government or public agency, this stage of the purchase process may involve competitive bidding. During this process, each marketer must develop its bid, including a price that will satisfy the criteria determined by the customer's problem, need, or opportunity. While competitive bidding is less common in the business sector, a company may follow the practice to purchase nonstandard materials, complex products, or products that are made to its own specifications.

Stage 6: Evaluate Proposals and Select Suppliers

Next in the buying process, buyers must compare vendors' proposals and choose the one that seems best suited to their needs. Proposals for sophisticated equipment, such as a large computer networking system, can include considerable differences among product offerings, and the final choice may involve trade-offs.

Price is not the only criterion for the selection of a vendor. Relationship factors such as communications and trust may also be important to the buyer. Other issues include reliability, delivery record, time from order to delivery, quality, and order accuracy. These are particularly important in the package delivery business. FedEx recently concluded a unique deal with a florist that allowed the package company to deliver Valentine's Day flowers on a Sunday for the first time in its history. FedEx was able to leverage its existing supply chain expertise and extensive flexible network—and the customer's distribution facility locations—to create a cost-effective solution that would satisfy this special need.[28]

Stage 7: Select an Order Routine

Once a supplier has been chosen, buyer and vendor must work out the best way to process future purchases. Ordering routines can vary considerably. Most orders will, however, include product descriptions, quantities, prices, delivery terms, and payment terms. Today, companies have a variety of options for submitting orders: written documents, phone calls, faxes, or electronic data interchange (EDI).

Stage 8: Obtain Feedback and Evaluate Performance

At the final stage, buyers measure vendors' performances. Sometimes this judgment will involve a formal evaluation of each supplier's product quality, delivery performance, prices, technical knowledge, and overall responsiveness to customer needs. At other times, vendors are measured according to

In business-to-business markets, price is often much less important than quality. Product failure for an inexpensive item can have tremendous financial consequences for a company.

whether they have lowered the customer's costs or reduced its employees' workloads. In general, bigger firms are more likely to use formal evaluation procedures, while smaller companies lean toward informal evaluations. Regardless of the method used, buyers should tell vendors how they will be evaluated.

Sometimes firms rely on independent organizations to gather quality feedback and summarize results. J. D. Power and Associates conducts research and provides information to a variety of firms so that they can improve the quality of their goods and services.

> **assessment check 6**
>
> **6.1** Why does the organizational buying process contain more steps than the consumer buying process?
>
> **6.2** List the steps in the organizational buying process.

CLASSIFYING BUSINESS BUYING SITUATIONS

⑦ **Classify organizational buying situations.**

As discussed earlier, business buying behaviour responds to many purchasing influences, such as environmental, organizational, and interpersonal factors. This buying behaviour also involves the degree of effort that the purchase decision demands and the levels within the organization where it is made. Like consumer behaviour, marketers can classify B2B buying situations into three general categories, ranging from least to most complex: (1) straight rebuying, (2) modified rebuying, and (3) new-task buying. Business buying situations may also involve reciprocity. The following sections look at each type of purchase.

Straight Rebuying

straight rebuy
Recurring purchase decision in which a customer repurchases a good or service that has performed satisfactorily in the past.

The simplest buying situation is a **straight rebuy**, a recurring purchase decision in which a customer reorders a product that has satisfied needs in the past. The buyer already likes the product and terms of sale, so the purchase requires no new information. The buyer sees little reason to assess competing options and so follows a routine repurchase format. A straight rebuy is the business market equivalent of routinized response behaviour in the consumer market. Purchases of low-cost items such as paper clips and pencils for an office are typical examples of straight rebuys. Marketers who maintain good relationships with customers by providing high-quality products, superior service, and prompt delivery can go a long way toward ensuring straight rebuys.

Modified Rebuying

modified rebuy
Situation in which a purchaser is willing to reevaluate available options for repurchasing a good or service.

In a **modified rebuy**, a purchaser is willing to reevaluate available options. Buyers may see some advantage in looking at alternative offerings within their established purchasing guidelines. They might take this step if their current supplier has let a rebuy situation deteriorate because of poor service or delivery performance. Price, quality, and innovation differences can also provoke modified rebuys. Modified rebuys resemble limited problem solving in consumer markets.

B2B marketers want to induce current customers to make straight rebuys by responding to all their needs. Competitors, on the other hand, try to lure those buyers away by raising issues that will convince them to reconsider their decisions.

new-task buy
First-time or unique purchase situation that requires considerable effort by decision makers.

New-Task Buying

The most complex category of business buying is the **new-task buy**—a first-time or unique purchase situation that requires considerable effort by the decision makers. The consumer market equivalent of new-task buying is extended problem solving. Many companies decide, for instance, that they want to buy a customized data centre rather than try to build their own. Companies such as Procter & Gamble, Nokia, Ericsson, Unilever, and Pfizer and organizations have contracted with Hewlett-Packard (HP) to outsource their data centre or information technology functions.[29] These one-time purchases require customers and HP to work closely together to determine which functions to outsource, which to keep in house (if any), and which hardware and software configurations best meet their needs. The consumer market equivalent of new-task buying is extended problem solving.

reciprocity
Buying from suppliers who are also customers.

A new-task buy often requires a purchaser to carefully consider alternative offerings and vendors. A company entering a new field must seek suppliers of component parts that it has never before purchased. This new-task buying would require several stages, each yielding a decision of some sort. These decisions would include developing product requirements, searching out potential suppliers, and evaluating proposals. Information requirements and decision makers can complete the entire buying process, or they may change from stage to stage.

The most complex category of business buying is new-task buying. It is common for a number of people to be involved in this type of buying decision.

H. F. (HERB) MACKENZIE

Reciprocity

Reciprocity—a practice of buying from suppliers that are also customers—is a controversial practice in a number of procurement situations. An office equipment manufacturer may favour a particular supplier of component parts if the supplier has recently made a major purchase of the manufacturer's products. Reciprocal arrangements traditionally have been common in industries featuring homogeneous products with similar prices, such as the chemical, paint, petroleum, rubber, and steel industries.

Reciprocity suggests close links among participants in the organizational marketplace. It can add to the complexity of B2B buying behaviour for new suppliers who are trying to compete with preferred vendors. Business-to-business buyers in Canada see it as a positive, widespread practice. In Japan, close ties between suppliers and customers are common. In the United States, reciprocal agreements are viewed as attempts to reduce competition.

ANALYSIS TOOLS

Two tools that help professional buyers improve purchase decisions are value analysis and vendor analysis. **Value analysis** examines each component of a purchase in an attempt to either delete the item or replace it with a more cost-effective substitute. Airplane designers have long recognized the need to make planes as light as possible. Value analysis supports using DuPont's synthetic material Kevlar in airplane construction because it weighs less than the metals it replaces. The resulting fuel savings are significant for the buyers in this marketplace.

Vendor analysis carries out an ongoing evaluation of a supplier's performance in categories such as price, EDI capability, back orders, delivery times, liability insurance, and attention to special requests. In some cases, vendor analysis is a formal process. Some buyers use a checklist to assess a vendor's performance. A checklist quickly highlights vendors and potential vendors that do not satisfy the purchaser's buying requirements.

value analysis
Systematic study of the components of a purchase to determine the most cost-effective approach.

vendor analysis
Assessment of supplier performance in areas such as price, back orders, timely delivery, and attention to special requests.

assessment check 7

7.1 What are the four classifications of business buying situations?

7.2 Differentiate between value analysis and vendor analysis.

THE BUYING CENTRE CONCEPT

(8) **Explain the buying centre concept.**

The buying centre concept provides a vital model for understanding B2B buying behaviour. A company's **buying centre** encompasses everyone who is involved in any aspect of its buying activity. A buying centre may include the architect who designs a new research laboratory, the scientist who works in the facility, the purchasing manager who screens contractor proposals, the chief executive officer who makes the final decision, and the vice president for research who signs the formal contracts for the project. Buying centre participants in any purchase seek to satisfy personal needs, such as participation or status, as well as organizational needs. A buying centre is not part of a firm's formal organizational structure. It is an informal group whose composition and size vary among purchase situations and firms.

buying centre
Participants in an organizational buying decision.

BUYING CENTRE ROLES

Buying centre participants play different roles in the purchasing decision process. **Users** are the people who will actually use the good or service. Their influence on the purchase decision may range from negligible to extremely important. Users sometimes initiate purchase actions by requesting products, and they may also help develop product specifications. Users often influence the purchase of office equipment.

Gatekeepers control the information that all buying centre members will review. They may exert this control by distributing printed product data or advertisements or by deciding which salespeople will speak to which individuals in the buying centre. A purchasing agent might allow some salespeople to see the engineers responsible for developing specifications but deny others the same privilege. The office manager for a medical group may decide whether to accept and pass along sales literature from a pharmaceutical detailer or sales representative.

Influencers affect the buying decision by supplying information to guide evaluation of alternatives or by setting buying specifications. Influencers are typically technical staff such as engineers or quality control specialists. Sometimes a buying organization hires outside consultants, such as architects, who influence its buying decisions.

The **decider** chooses a good or service, although another person may have the formal authority to do so. The identity of the decider is the most difficult role for salespeople to pinpoint. A firm's buyer may have the formal authority to buy, but the firm's chief executive officer may actually make the buying decision. Alternatively, a decider might be a design engineer who develops specifications that only one vendor can meet.

user
Individual or group that actually uses a business good or service.

gatekeeper
Person who controls the information that all buying centre members will review.

influencers
Typically, technical staff such as engineers who affect the buying decision by supplying information to guide evaluation of alternatives or by setting buying specifications.

decider
Person who chooses a good or service, although another person may have the formal authority to complete the sale.

buyer
Person who has the formal authority to select a supplier and to implement the procedures for securing a good or service.

The **buyer** has the formal authority to select a supplier and to implement the procedures for securing the good or service. The buyer often surrenders this power to more influential members of the organization, though. The purchasing manager often fills the buyer's role and executes the details associated with a purchase order.

B2B marketers face the task of determining the specific role and the relative decision-making influence of each buying centre participant. Salespeople can then tailor their presentations and information to the precise role that an individual plays at each step of the purchase process. Business marketers have found that their initial—and in many cases, most extensive—contacts with a firm's purchasing department often fail to reach the buying centre participants who have the greatest influence, since these people may not work in that department at all.

Consider the selection of meeting and convention sites for trade or professional associations. The primary decision maker could be an association board or an executive committee, usually with input from the executive director or a meeting planner; the meeting planner or association executive might choose meeting locations, sometimes with input from members; finally, the association's annual-meeting committee or program committee might make the meeting location selection. Because officers change periodically, centres of control may change frequently. As a result, destination marketers and hotel operators must constantly assess how an association makes its decisions on conference locations.

INTERNATIONAL BUYING CENTRES

Two distinct characteristics differentiate international buying centres from domestic ones. First, marketers may have trouble identifying members of foreign buying centres because of cultural differences in decision-making methods. Second, a buying centre in a foreign company often includes more participants than Canadian companies involve. International buying centres employ from 1 to 50 people, with 15 to 20 participants being commonplace. Global B2B marketers must recognize and accommodate this greater diversity of decision makers.

International buying centres can change in response to political and economic trends. Many European firms once maintained separate facilities in each European nation to avoid tariffs and customs delays. When the European Union lowered trade barriers between member nations, however, many companies closed distant branches and consolidated their buying centres. The Netherlands has been one of the beneficiaries of this trend.

assessment check 8

8.1 Identify the five roles of people in a buying centre decision.

8.2 What are some of the problems that Canadian marketers face in dealing with international buying centres?

⑨ Discuss the challenges of and strategies for marketing to government, institutional, and international buyers.

Marketoid

In one recent year, over $20 million worth of vehicles were sold by Crown Assets Distribution. Surplus aircraft sales accounted for about $6 million. Office furniture and equipment and computer equipment each accounted for less than $1 million.

DEVELOPING EFFECTIVE BUSINESS-TO-BUSINESS MARKETING STRATEGIES

A business marketer must develop a marketing strategy based on a particular organization's buying behaviour and on the buying situation. Clearly, many variables affect organizational purchasing decisions. This section examines three market segments whose decisions present unique challenges to B2B marketers: units of government, institutions, and international markets. Finally, it summarizes key differences between consumer and business marketing strategies.

CHALLENGES OF GOVERNMENT MARKETS

Government markets include the federal government, provincial and territorial governments, and municipal governments. These markets are large and are extremely important to many business marketers in Canada. Purchasing authorities for the various levels and units involved in these markets purchase a wide variety of products, including computers and office supplies; aircraft and component parts; vehicles and automotive supplies; safety clothing and equipment; concrete and lumber; and many other items. To compete effectively, business marketers must understand the unique challenges of selling to government units. One challenge results because government purchases typically involve dozens of interested parties who specify, evaluate, or use the purchased goods and services. These parties may or may not work within the government agency that officially handles a purchase. For example, much of the purchasing for the federal government is done through Public Works and Government Services Canada (PWGSC). This department, headquartered in Gatineau, Quebec, spends about $4.5 billion annually and employs about 12 000 people.[30]

Contractual guidelines create another important influence in selling to government markets. The government buys products under two basic types of contracts: fixed-price contracts, in which seller and buyer agree to a set price before finalizing the contract, and cost-reimbursement contracts, in which the government pays the vendor for allowable costs, including profits, incurred during performance of the contract. Each type of contract has advantages and disadvantages for B2B marketers. Although the fixed-price contract offers more profit potential than the alternative, it also carries greater risks from unforeseen expenses, price hikes, and changing political and economic conditions.

While there is some variability between departments, purchasing procedures are largely determined by the size of the individual purchase. For purchases below $5000, most departments use acquisition cards (credit cards), local purchase orders, or releases against standing offers. A standing offer is not a

Buyandsell.gc.ca is a procurement website and is the main location for suppliers to find information about doing business with the Government of Canada.

SOURCE: BUYANDSELL.GC.CA WEBSITE, OFFICE OF SMALL AND MEDIUM ENTERPRISES AND CLIENT ENGAGEMENT SECTOR, PWGSC, 2001. REPRODUCED WITH THE PERMISSION OF THE MINISTER OF PUBLIC WORKS AND GOVERNMENT SERVICES CANADA, 2011.

formal contract. PWGSC issues standing offers for a variety of regularly purchased goods and services that are often needed by several government units. Business marketers agree to provide these goods and services at specific prices for a particular period of time and under a predetermined set of terms and conditions. Once a standing offer has been issued by PWGSC, government units must generally use the standing offer for any purchases of items that are included in the standing offer and that meet the buying unit's requirements. The government saves money by increasing the volume it purchases from holders of standing offers, and the business marketers who hold the standing offers benefit from increased sales.

For purchases over $5000, most federal government units use the services of PWGSC, which then asks for proposals from qualified suppliers. Business marketers may register online with the federal government so that they are considered when the need for their products or services arises. More commonly, business marketers access MERX, a privately owned e-tendering service used by more than 2500 organizations, including the federal government; many provincial, territorial, and municipal governments; and other public sector purchasing authorities. Since public sector purchasing authorities have different thresholds at which purchasing procedures come into effect, business marketers need to know the particular policies used by each of the units to which they wish to sell.

While provincial and territorial governments individually purchase much less than the federal government, collectively they are more important. Purchasing procedures for provincial and territorial government purchasing units are generally similar to those used by the federal government; however, there is even more variability between them. Alberta, for example, uses the Alberta Purchasing Connection for its e-tendering requirements, while most provinces use MERX. The Province of Nova Scotia has been using the reverse trade show concept for several years. These shows are held at various locations around the province. Public sector units manage display booths, and representatives from private sector businesses visit them to access information on their purchasing needs and to explore whether these units might benefit from the products and services that these private businesses sell. Business marketers need to be aware of any unique conditions that exist in each province or territory where they sell.

Buying practices can differ among institutions of the same type. In a small school cafeteria, the chief dietitian may approve food purchases, while in a larger facility, food purchases may go through a committee.

CHALLENGES OF INSTITUTIONAL MARKETS

Institutions constitute another important market. Institutional buyers include a wide variety of organizations, such as schools, colleges, universities, hospitals, libraries, churches, and not-for-profit agencies.

Institutional markets are characterized by widely diverse buying practices. Some institutional purchasers behave like government purchasers because laws and political considerations determine their buying procedures. Many of these institutions, such as hospitals and prisons, may even be managed by government units.

Buying practices can differ between institutions of the same type. In a small hospital, the chief dietitian may approve all food purchases, while in a larger medical facility, food purchases may go through a committee consisting of the dietitian and a business manager, purchasing agent, and cook. Other hospitals may belong to buying groups, perhaps health maintenance organizations or local hospital cooperatives. Still others may contract with outside firms to prepare and serve all meals.

Within a single institution, a variety of buying influences may affect decisions. Many institutions, staffed by professionals, such as physicians, nurses, researchers, and instructors, may also employ purchasing managers or even entire purchasing departments. Conflicts may arise among these decision makers. Professional employees may prefer to make their own purchase decisions and resent giving up control to the purchasing staff. This conflict can force a business marketer to cultivate both professionals and purchasers. A salesperson for a pharmaceutical firm must convince physicians of the value to patients of a certain drug while simultaneously convincing the hospital's purchasing department that the firm offers competitive prices, good delivery schedules, and prompt service. Group purchasing is an important factor in institutional markets because many organizations join cooperative associations to pool purchases for quantity discounts. For example, the Niagara Public Purchasing Committee purchases for 52 participating agencies—including health care and educational institutions and government agencies—in the regional municipality of Niagara. Each purchasing authority can decide when and if it would like to participate in the tendering for any particular product or service. Responsibility for calling tenders and negotiating prices is shared among them, but control of ordering, scheduling, receiving, and payment remains with individual purchasing authorities.[31]

Diverse practices in institutional markets pose special challenges for B2B marketers. They must maintain flexibility in developing strategies for dealing with a range of customers, from large cooperative associations and chains to midsized purchasing departments and institutions to individuals. Buying centres can work with varying members, priorities, and levels of expertise. Discounts and effective distribution functions play important roles in obtaining—and keeping—institutions as customers.

CHALLENGES OF INTERNATIONAL MARKETS

To sell successfully in international markets, business marketers must consider buyers' attitudes and cultural patterns within areas where they operate. In Asian markets, a firm must maintain a local presence to sell products. Personal relationships are also important to business deals in Asia. Companies that want to expand globally often need to establish joint ventures with local partners. International marketers must also be poised to respond to shifts in cultural values.

Local industries, economic conditions, geographic characteristics, and legal restrictions must also be considered in international marketing. Many local industries in Spain specialize in food and wine; therefore, a maker of forklift trucks might market smaller vehicles to Spanish companies than to German firms, which require bigger, heavier trucks to serve the needs of that nation's large automobile industry.

Remanufacturing—production to restore worn-out products to like-new condition—can be an important marketing strategy in a nation that cannot afford to buy new products. Developing countries often purchase remanufactured factory machinery, which costs 35 to 60 percent less than new equipment.

remanufacturing
Efforts to restore older products to like-new condition.

Foreign governments represent another important business market. In many countries, the government or state-owned companies dominate certain industries, such as construction and other infrastructure sales. Additional examples include airport and highway construction, telephone system equipment, and computer networking equipment. Sales to a foreign government can involve an array of regulations. Many governments, like that of Canada, limit foreign participation in their defence programs. Joint ventures and countertrade are common, as are local content laws, which mandate domestic production of a certain percentage of a business product's components.

assessment check 9

9.1 What are some influences on government purchases?

9.2 Why is group purchasing important in institutional purchases?

9.3 What special factors influence international buying decisions?

Strategic Implications

To develop marketing strategies for the B2B sector, marketers must first understand the buying practices that govern the segment they are targeting, whether it is the commercial market, trade industries, government, or institutions. Similarly, when selling to a specific organization, strategies must take into account the many factors that influence purchasing. B2B marketers must identify people who play the various roles in the buying decision. They must also understand how these members interact with one another, other members of their own organizations, and outside vendors. Marketers must be careful to direct their marketing efforts to their organization, to broader environmental influences, and to individuals who operate within the constraints of the firm's buying centre. ◆◆◆

REVIEW OF CHAPTER OBJECTIVES

① **Explain each of the components of the business-to-business (B2B) market.**

The B2B market is divided into four segments: the commercial market, trade industries, governments, and institutions. The commercial market consists of individuals and firms that acquire products to be used, directly or indirectly, to produce other goods and services. Trade industries are organizations, such as retailers and wholesalers, that purchase for resale to others. The primary purpose of government purchasing, at all levels, is to provide some form of public benefit. The fourth segment, institutions, includes a diverse array of organizations, such as hospitals, schools, museums, and not-for-profit agencies.

② **Describe the major approaches to segmenting business-to-business (B2B) markets.**

Business markets can be segmented by (1) demographics, (2) customer type, (3) end-use application, and (4) purchasing situation. The North American Industry Classification System (NAICS), instituted after the passage of NAFTA, helps further classify types of customers by the use of six digits.

③ **Identify the major characteristics of the business market and its demand.**

The major characteristics of the business market are geographic concentration, size and number of buyers, purchase decision procedures, and buyer–seller relationships. The major categories of demand are derived demand, volatile demand, joint demand, inelastic demand, and inventory adjustments.

④ **Discuss the decision to make, buy, or lease.**

Before a company can decide what to buy, it must decide whether to buy at all. A firm has three options: (1) make the good or service in-house; (2) purchase it from another organization; or (3) lease it from another organization. Companies may outsource goods or services formerly produced in-house to other companies either within their own home country or to firms in other countries. The shift of high-wage jobs from the home country to lower-wage locations is known as *offshoring.* If a company moves production to a country close to its own borders, it uses a *nearshoring* strategy. Each option has its benefits and drawbacks, including cost and quality control.

⑤ **Describe the major influences on business buying behaviour.**

B2B buying behaviour tends to be more complex than individual consumer behaviour. More people and time are involved, and buyers often seek several alternative supply sources. The systematic nature of organizational buying is reflected in the use of purchasing managers to direct such efforts. Major organizational purchases may require elaborate and lengthy decision-making processes involving many people. Purchase decisions typically depend on combinations of such factors as price, service, certainty of supply, and product efficiency.

⑥ **Outline the steps in the organizational buying process.**

The organizational buying process consists of eight general stages: (1) anticipate or recognize a problem/need/opportunity and a general solution; (2) determine characteristics and quantity of needed good or service; (3) describe characteristics and quantity of needed good or service; (4) search for and qualify potential sources; (5) acquire and analyze proposals; (6) evaluate proposals and select supplier(s); (7) select an order routine; and (8) obtain feedback and evaluate performance.

⑦ **Classify organizational buying situations.**

Organizational buying situations differ. A straight rebuy is a recurring purchase decision in which a customer stays with an item that has performed satisfactorily. In a modified rebuy, a purchaser is willing to re-evaluate available options. New-task buying refers to first-time or unique purchase situations that require considerable effort on the part of the decision makers. Reciprocity involves buying from suppliers that are also customers.

⑧ **Explain the buying centre concept.**

The buying centre includes everyone who is involved in some fashion in an organizational buying action. There are five buying centre roles: users, gatekeepers, influencers, deciders, and buyers.

⑨ **Discuss the challenges of and strategies for marketing to government, institutional, and international buyers.**

A government purchase typically involves dozens of interested parties. Social goals and programs influence government purchases. Many Canadian government purchases involve complex contractual guidelines and often require detailed specifications and a bidding process. Institutional markets are challenging because of their diverse buying influences and practices. Group purchasing is an important factor, since many institutions join cooperative associations to get quantity discounts. An institutional marketer must be flexible enough to develop strategies for dealing with a range of customers. Discounts and effective distribution play an important role. An effective international business marketer must be aware of foreign attitudes and cultural patterns. Other important factors include economic conditions, geographic characteristics, legal restrictions, and local industries.

assessment check answers

1.1 Define B2B marketing.
Business-to-business, or B2B, marketing deals with organizational purchases of goods and services to support production of other products, to facilitate daily company operations, or for resale.

1.2 What is the commercial market?
The commercial market consists of individuals and firms that acquire products to be used, directly or indirectly, to produce other goods and services.

2.1 What are the four major ways marketers segment business markets?
Business markets can be segmented by (1) demographics, (2) customer type, (3) end-use application, and (4) purchasing situation.

2.2 What is the NAICS?
The North American Industry Classification System (NAICS) is a unified system for Canada, Mexico, and the United States to classify B2B market segments.

3.1 Why is geographic segmentation important in the B2B market?
Certain industries locate in particular areas to be close to customers. Firms may choose to locate sales offices and distribution centres in these areas to provide more attentive service. For example, the Ottawa area is favoured by companies that sell to the federal government.

3.2 In what ways is the buyer–seller relationship important in B2B marketing?
Buyer–seller relationships are often more complex than consumer relationships, and they require superior communication among the organizations' personnel. Satisfying one major customer may mean the difference of millions of dollars to a firm.

3.3 What is global sourcing?
Global sourcing involves contracting to purchase goods and services from suppliers worldwide.

3.4 How does derived demand create volatile demand?
Business demand often is derived from consumer demand. Even modest shifts in consumer demand can produce disproportionate—and volatile—shifts in business demand.

3.5 Give an example of joint demand.
Both lumber and concrete are required to build most homes. If the lumber supply falls, the drop in housing construction will most likely affect the demand for concrete.

3.6 How might JIT II strengthen marketing relationships?
JIT II leads suppliers to place representatives at the customer's facility to work as part of an integrated, on-site customer–supplier team. Suppliers plan and order in consultation with the customer. This streamlining of the inventory process improves control of the flow of goods.

4.1 Identify two potential benefits of outsourcing.
Outsourcing allows firms to concentrate their resources on their core business. It also allows access to specialized talent or expertise that does not exist within the firm.

4.2 Identify two potential problems with outsourcing.
Many companies discover that their cost savings are less than vendors sometimes promise. Also, companies that sign multiyear contracts may find that their savings drop after a year or two.

5.1 Identify the three major factors that influence purchase decisions.
In addition to product-specific factors such as purchase price, installation, operating and maintenance costs, and vendor service, companies must consider broader environmental, organizational, and interpersonal influences.

5.2 What are the advantages and disadvantages of multiple sourcing?
Spreading orders ensures against shortages if one vendor cannot deliver on schedule. However, dealing with many sellers can be counterproductive and take too much time.

6.1 Why does the organizational buying process contain more steps than the consumer buying process?
The additional steps arise because business purchasing introduces new complexities that do not affect consumers.

6.2 List the steps in the organizational buying process.
The steps in organizational buying are (1) anticipate or recognize a problem/need/opportunity and a general solution; (2) determine characteristics and quantity of needed good or service; (3) describe characteristics and quantity of needed good or service; (4) search for and qualify potential sources; (5) acquire and analyze proposals; (6) evaluate proposals and select supplier(s); (7) select an order routine; and (8) obtain feedback and evaluate performance.

7.1 What are the four classifications of business buying situations?
The four classifications of business buying are (1) straight rebuying, (2) modified rebuying, (3) new-task buying, and (4) reciprocity.

7.2 Differentiate between value analysis and vendor analysis.
Value analysis examines each component of a purchase in an attempt to either delete the item or replace it with a more cost-effective substitute. Vendor analysis carries out an ongoing evaluation of a supplier's performance in categories such as price, EDI capability, back orders, delivery times, liability insurance, and attention to special requests.

8.1 Identify the five roles of people in a buying centre decision.
There are five buying centre roles: users (those who use the product), gatekeepers (those who control the flow of information), influencers (those who provide technical information or specifications), deciders (those who actually choose the product), and buyers (those who have the formal authority to purchase).

8.2 What are some of the problems that Canadian marketers face in dealing with international buying centres?

International buying centres pose several problems. First, there may be cultural differences in decision-making methods. Second, a buying centre in a foreign company typically includes more participants than is common in Canada. Third, international buying centres can change in response to political and economic trends.

9.1 What are some influences on government purchases?

Social goals and programs often influence government purchases.

9.2 Why is group purchasing important in institutional purchases?

Group purchasing is an important factor because many institutions join cooperative associations to get quantity discounts.

9.3 What special factors influence international buying decisions?

An effective international business marketer must be aware of foreign attitudes and cultural patterns. Other important factors include economic conditions, geographic characteristics, legal restrictions, and local industries.

MARKETING TERMS YOU NEED TO KNOW

These terms are printed in red in the text. They are defined in the margins of the chapter and in the Glossary that begins on p. G-1.

business-to-business (B2B) marketing 138

commercial market 140

trade industries 140

resellers 140

customer-based segmentation 143

North American Industry Classification System (NAICS) 144

end-use application segmentation 144

customer relationship management (CRM) 145

global sourcing 148

derived demand 149

joint demand 149

inelastic demand 149

just-in-time (JIT) / just-in-time II 150

sole sourcing 150

offshoring 152

nearshoring 152

outsourcing 152

multiple sourcing 154

merchandisers 154

systems integration 154

category advisor (category captain) 154

straight rebuy 157

modified rebuy 158

new-task buy 158

reciprocity 158

value analysis 159

vendor analysis 159

buying centre 159

user 159

gatekeeper 159

influencers 159

decider 159

buyer 160

remanufacturing 163

PROJECT AND TEAMWORK EXERCISES

1. In small teams, research the buying process through which your school purchases the following products:
   a. computers for your school's computer lab
   b. computers for your campus bookstore
   c. garbage bags used by your campus custodial staff
   d. vehicles for your campus security and maintenance staff

   Be prepared to discuss how the buying process differs for these products.

2. As a team or individually, choose a commercial product, such as computer chips, flour for baking, paint, or equipment, and research and analyze its foreign market potential. Report your findings to the class.

3. In pairs or individually, select a firm in your area and ask to interview the person who is in charge of purchasing. In particular, ask the person about the importance of buyer–seller relationships in his or her industry. Report your findings to the class.

4. In pairs, select a business product in one of two categories—capital or expense—and determine how derived demand will affect the sales of the product. Create a chart showing your findings.

5. As a team, research a firm such as Nortel, Bombardier, or General Motors to learn how it is using outsourcing and/or offshoring. Then report on what you think the benefits and drawbacks to the firm might be.

6. Imagine that you and your teammates are buyers for a firm such as Tim Hortons, Canadian Tire, Delta Hotels & Resorts, or another firm you like. Map out a logical buying process for a new-task purchase for your organization.

7. Form a team to conduct a hypothetical team selling effort for the packaging of products manufactured by a food or beverage company such as Kraft or Labatt Breweries. Have each team member cover a certain concern, such as package design, delivery, or payment schedules. Present your marketing effort to the class.

8. Conduct further research into provincial or territorial government purchasing. Which provinces use MERX Canadian Public Tenders? What are the advantages of using MERX? Why might a provincial or territorial government decide to not use MERX?

9. Find an advertisement with marketing messages targeted for an institutional market. Analyze the ad to determine how the marketer has segmented the market, who in the buying centre might be the target of the ad, and what other marketing strategies might be apparent.

10. In teams, research the practice of remanufacturing of business products such as factory machinery for foreign markets. What challenges do marketers of such products face?

CRITICAL-THINKING EXERCISES

1. Imagine that you are a wholesaler for dairy products such as yogurt and cheese, which are produced by a cooperative of small farmers. Describe what steps you would take to build relationships with both the producers—farmers—and retailers, such as supermarkets.

2. Describe an industry that might be segmented by geographic concentration. Then identify some of the types of firms that might be involved in that industry. Keep in mind that these companies could be involved in other industries as well.

3. Imagine that you are in charge of making the decision to lease or buy a fleet of automobiles for the limousine service for which you work. What factors would influence your decision and why?

4. Do you think online selling to the federal government benefits marketers? What might be some of the drawbacks to this type of selling?

ETHICS EXERCISE

Suppose you work for a well-known local restaurant, and a friend of yours is an account representative for a supplier of restaurant equipment. You know that the restaurant owner is considering upgrading some of the kitchen equipment. Although you have no purchasing authority, your friend has asked you to arrange a meeting with the restaurant owner. You have heard unflattering rumours about this supplier's customer service.

1. Would you arrange the meeting between your friend and your boss?

2. Would you mention the customer-service rumours either to your friend or your boss?

3. Would you try to influence the purchase decision in either direction?

INTERNET EXERCISES

1. **Bombardier Inc.** Bombardier is a global company headquartered in Canada and is a world-class supplier of transportation machinery and equipment, such as aircraft and rail systems. Visit the Bombardier website. What are Bombardier's core businesses? Search this website to find information on Bombardier's suppliers and its customers. How does Bombardier use its website to manage its business relationships with them? **www.bombardier.com**

2. **Selling to national retailers.** A high percentage of B2B marketing consists of manufacturers selling products to national retailers. Each retailer establishes standards for vendors. Visit each of the following websites to learn more about what it takes to sell products to that retailer. Prepare a report on your findings.

   a. Canadian Tire: **www.canadiantire.ca** (click on Company Information, then on Join Our Team, and then on Canadian Tire Product Supplier Opportunities)
   b. Home Depot: **http://corporate.homedepot.com/wps/portal** (click on For Suppliers)
   c. Walmart: **www.walmartstores.com** (click on Suppliers)

Note: Internet Web addresses change frequently. If you don't find the exact sites listed, you may need to access the organization's or company's home page and search from there or use a search engine such as Google.

CASE 5.1

WFS Ltd.

WFS Ltd.—formerly Windsor Factory Supply—is a 100-percent employee-owned, full-line industrial distributor and, as such, all of its sales are B2B sales. It represents more than 3500 suppliers and sells to more than 4000 customers—mainly manufacturers, but also many government and institutional accounts. (It does for many business customers what Walmart and Canadian Tire do for consumers.) The company started in Windsor, Ontario, in 1955 as a two-man operation. Sales the first year were approximately $50 000.

The company was fortunate in many ways. First, it was strategically located close to the centre of automotive manufacturing in Canada, and the three large North American automobile manufacturers all became important customers. Second, it was close to the Canada–United States border. Many U.S. manufacturers who sold through Canadian distributors selected ones located in or near Toronto. That meant customers in Windsor who wanted to buy these products would have to place orders with a distributor located some distance away, wait for the distributor to order the material from the United States, and then wait for delivery of the material from the U.S. manufacturer—sometimes physically routed through their Canadian distributor. Deliveries could take days or even weeks. WFS would send two trucks across the border into Detroit each morning, one to each end of the city. When Canadian customers wanted important material from the United States, WFS would find a Detroit-area distributor, negotiate a discount as it would act as a sub-distributor, and bring the material into Canada, often the same day that the customer requested it.

Such willingness to provide outstanding service for its major customers helped WFS quickly grow. By the 1990s, the company had five additional locations: Leamington, Sarnia, Wallaceburg, London, and Mississauga. In early 2008, WFS acquired another industrial distributor, adding three more locations. Today, WFS has ten sales branches and warehouses in Ontario, a warehouse in Detroit, Michigan, and a sales branch and warehouse in South Carolina, which it built to serve one of its major customers there. WFS has always been willing to negotiate supply contracts with important customers. It operates what is referred to as commodity management programs, whereby it will carry inventory and manage the supply of a large number of specific items, guaranteeing their availability when and where the customer needs them. Sometimes, these programs result in on-site inventory agreements.

WFS has a strong internal culture and a healthy business philosophy. Sales are approaching $100 million. The company's foundation is built on quality, satisfaction, and dependability. President Rick Thurston describes the company philosophy: "Our business is built on relationships. Of course, we are always looking for opportunities, but we know that sometimes it is important to curb growth so that quality service to existing accounts is not compromised."

Questions for Critical Thinking

1. Describe how environmental factors, organizational factors, and interpersonal influences will affect sales for WFS.
2. How important is the buying centre concept to WFS? Explain.
3. How can commodity management programs and other special inventory management programs be used to add value for WFS's customers? How can such programs contribute to the company's long-term success?

Sources: WFS website, http://www.wfsltd.com, May 23, 2011; Rick Thurston, personal interview and correspondence, August 5, 2008.

CASE 5.2

Peerless Pump Puts Customers First

Pumps are the world's second most commonly used machines. They supply almost a quarter of global demand for electric motor energy. Peerless Pump Co. has been providing reliable pumps for high-value applications in the industrial, municipal, agriculture, and fire protection segments since 1923. By focusing on safety, quality, schedule, and cost—in that order—the firm has enjoyed steady growth and even increased its revenue expectations for the future. "Continued enthusiasm and management commitment make our future growth ambitions very attainable," says Fred Bock, Peerless vice president of marketing and business planning.

A company initiative called "One Peerless" focused the attention of the company's 430 employees, who work in many different global locations, on improving teamwork, communication, leadership, and continuous improvement (growth). "It is very easy to focus on needs. One Peerless takes a proactive approach to focusing on what our customers—both internal and external—truly want," Bock says. "One Peerless is a well-rounded operations, sales, and marketing plan that involves everyone associated with our company, from suppliers to employees to distributors to end users."

The company, with $120 million in annual sales, was acquired in 2007 from a private equity firm by Danish pump giant Grundfos, which has been expanding rapidly in eastern Europe and Asia, as well as a significant commitment to North America, where they see "significant growth potential."

"The synergies and similarities in corporate culture are significant and will allow for the acceleration of the growth that Peerless Grundfos have enjoyed over the past five years," added Bock, who also holds the position of North American marketing director for Grundfos.

Originally founded to supply agricultural irrigation pumps for orange growers, the company now counts water treatment facilities, stadiums, airports, and many of the world's tallest skyscrapers among its many clients. With energy costs increasing, such customers continue to increase their focus on saving money on operations wherever possible. Peerless assists its partners by applying a "life cycle cost" approach to its design and sales strategies by examining costs—in both time and resources—of repair rather than replacement of less efficient equipment.

Looking at the costs associated with installation, maintenance, and especially energy consumption over the long term— some pumps are in service for more than 50 years—allows Peerless to compare all possible solutions, from which the customer can evaluate the best one. The company identifies the particular pump features and specifications in each option that will best improve reliability and minimize energy consumption, even in pump systems that move large volumes of water 24 hours a day. Market growth for new equipment far exceeds repairs as a source of revenue; however, in order to minimize downtime from potential breakdowns and help customers make the right repair/replace decision, Peerless advocates and offers ongoing training of its engineers and customers in preventive maintenance and repair as well as recommends spare parts inventories. This strategic approach makes the continuous and open line of communication between the company and end user a necessity.

Questions for Critical Thinking

1. Do you think Peerless focuses on safety, quality, schedule, and cost in the right order to meet its customers' and distributors' needs? Why or why not? How do you think a B2B company can most accurately determine what its business customers need and want?

2. What benefits does Peerless gain from helping its customers evaluate system repair as a potential alternative to costly replacement of a pump system? What strategies and business tools do you think the company must have in place to fulfill this customer need? Why is it important for Peerless to address it, if it is not as profitable for the firm as selling a new system?

Sources: Personal communication with Fred Bock, Peerless Pump, April 2010; company website, http://www.peerlesspump.com, April 15, 2010; "Grundfos Pumps Opens New Facility in Houston," *The Air Conditioning/Heating/Refrigeration News,* March 16, 2010; "Andrew Warrington Named Peerless Pump Company's New President," http://contractormag.com, November 16, 2009.

Serving Global Markets

CHAPTER OBJECTIVES

① Describe the importance of global marketing from the perspectives of the individual firm and the nation.

② Identify the major components of the environment for global marketing.

③ Outline the basic functions of GATT, WTO, NAFTA, FTAA, and the European Union.

④ Identify the alternative strategies for entering international markets.

⑤ Differentiate between a global marketing strategy and a multi-domestic marketing strategy.

⑥ Describe the alternative marketing mix strategies used in global marketing and explain the attractiveness of Canada as a target market for international marketers.

"GLOBAL" FOCUS DRIVES McDONALD'S

McDonald's Corporation provides a classic example of the challenges facing organizations that seek to grow their business by offering their products to customers worldwide. When the company first opened restaurants internationally, it operated on the belief that customers should have the same dining experience whether they were in Kansas or Kuwait City. In those days, McDonald's relied almost exclusively on North Americans living abroad to manage the overseas business. Over time, McDonald's has achieved success with local talent in the countries where it operates and it has discovered it can maintain brand consistency even when catering to local taste preferences.

Today, McDonald's restaurants can be found in more than 100 countries worldwide. The company grew through franchising— 70 percent of the more than 30 000 McDonald's restaurants are privately owned and operated.

But McDonald's success has an appeal that transcends culture, and company sales are growing faster in its overseas markets. One recent monthly sales report showed sales growth in the United States at less than 3 percent while Europe showed sales growth for the same period at over 5 percent. Even sales in the Asia, Pacific, Middle East, and Africa regions showed sales growth at 4 percent.

As it extended its global reach, McDonald's has had to weather many storms. The company faced a beef scare connected to mad cow disease, and environmentalists accused McDonald's of using soybeans grown in an illegally deforested area of the Amazon rain forest. As a successful American company expanding into developing nations, McDonald's periodically ends up as the poster child for numerous anti-American and globalization protests. The company learns something from each experience and continues to move forward. For example, the company continues to incorporate environmentally friendly programs such as green technologies for its restaurants and product packaging. The company also works with its supply chain to minimize environmental impacts, sponsoring local anti-littering and community beautification programs. Although McDonald's operates on a global scale, the Big Mac does not reign supreme from Amsterdam to Mumbai. The operating formula behind the company's global growth has become "freedom within the framework." Under this decentralized model, the business units are "glocal"—not managed by North American expatriates, as in the early years, but by local talent. Country managers also have latitude to develop their own ad campaigns and cater to local tastes.

The French enjoy a McDonald's concoction known as a "Croque McDo," a sandwich made from ham and melted Swiss cheese on toasted bread. In India, where religious dietary laws forbid the consumption of beef, the Maharaja Mac is a popular sandwich made of two chicken patties and smoky-flavoured mayonnaise. Where the culture consumes more rice than potatoes, McDonald's restaurants may leave French fries off the menu in favour of rice-based dishes like the rice burger in Taiwan. The rice burger consists of shredded beef between two rice patties. Sweden recently introduced the Big Tasty—a 155-gram beef patty with barbecue sauce sharing a bun with three slices of cheese, lettuce, and tomatoes. The sandwich was such a hit that it now sells all over Europe, Latin America, and Australia. The company has no plans to introduce the Big Tasty in North America because of the high percentage of sales from drive-throughs—it is too messy to eat in the car.

Not all the company's overseas endeavours have been successful. The three restaurants in Iceland closed shortly after the global financial crisis hit. McDonald's in Iceland had to purchase its supplies from Germany, and the foreign exchange differences meant the Big Macs in Iceland would have been the most expensive in the world.[1]

---

connecting with customers

McDonald's connects with its customers by providing family restaurants in over 100 countries around the world. The company understands and caters to different cultural food choices by adapting the menu to local preferences.

Chapter Overview

CANADIAN and foreign companies are crossing national boundaries in unprecedented numbers in search of new markets and profits.

Global trade can be divided into two categories: **exporting**, marketing domestically produced goods and services abroad, and **importing**, purchasing foreign goods and services. Figure 6.1 shows the nations with which Canada trades. The United States accounts for 62.8 percent of our imported products and 73.2 percent of our exported products. Japan, the United Kingdom, and the European Union countries account for another 11.3 percent of exports.[2] Global trade is vital to a nation and its marketers for several reasons. It expands markets, makes production and distribution economies of scale possible, allows companies to explore growth opportunities in other nations, and makes them less dependent on economic conditions in their home nations. Many also find that global marketing and trade can help

them meet customer demand, reduce costs, and provide valuable information on potential markets around the world.

For North American marketers, global trade is especially important because the Canadian and U.S. economies represent a mature market for many products. Outside North America, however, it is a different story. Economies in many parts of sub-Saharan Africa, Asia, Latin America, central Europe, and the Middle East are growing rapidly. This opens up new markets for Canadian products as consumers in these areas have more money to spend and as the need for goods and services by foreign companies expands.

Global trade also builds employment. The United Nations estimates that 82 000 transnational corporations are operating today, employing more than 77 million workers directly and through subsidiaries.[3]

Global marketers carefully evaluate the marketing concepts described in other chapters. However, transactions that cross national borders involve additional considerations. For example, different laws, varying levels of technological capability, eco-

nomic conditions, cultural and business norms, and consumer preferences often require new strategies. Companies that want to market their products worldwide must reconsider each of the marketing variables (product, distribution, promotion, and price) in terms of the global marketplace. To succeed in global marketing, today's marketers answer questions such as these:

- How do our products fit into a foreign market?
- How can we turn potential threats into opportunities?
- Which strategic alternatives will work in global markets?

Many of the answers to these questions can be found by studying techniques used by successful global marketers. This chapter first considers the importance and characteristics of foreign markets. It then examines the international marketing environment, the trend toward multinational economic integration, and the steps that most firms take to enter the global marketplace. Next, the importance of developing a global marketing mix is discussed. The chapter closes with a look at Canada as a target market for foreign marketers. ◆◆◆

exporting Marketing domestically produced goods and services in foreign countries.

importing Purchasing foreign goods, services, and raw materials.

---

① **Describe the importance of global marketing from the perspectives of the individual firm and the nation.**

THE IMPORTANCE OF GLOBAL MARKETING

As the list of Canada's and the world's largest companies shown in Table 6.1 reveals, most if not all are in global markets. For most companies—large and small—global marketing is rapidly becoming a necessity. The demand for foreign products in the fast-growing economies of Pacific Rim and other Asian nations offers one example of the benefits of thinking globally. Canada is often viewed as an exporter of natural resources such as lumber, wheat, and energy products, but other products such as

table 6.1   *Largest Companies in the World and in Canada*

WORLD'S LARGEST COMPANIES			CANADA'S LARGEST COMPANIES
RANK	COMPANY	COUNTRY OF ORIGIN	BY PROFIT
1	JPMorgan Chase	United States	Royal Bank of Canada
2	General Electric	United States	Bank of Nova Scotia
3	Bank of America	United States	Toronto-Dominion Bank
4	ExxonMobil	United States	Research In Motion
5	ICBC	China	EnCana Corp.
6	Bank Santander	Spain	Canadian National Railway
7	Wells Fargo	United States	Teck Resources
8	HSBC Holdings	United Kingdom	Bank of Montreal
9	Royal Dutch Shell	Netherlands	Great-West Life Assurance
10	BP	United Kingdom	BCE Inc.

Sources: Data from Scott DeCarlo, "The Forbes Global 2000," http://www.forbes.com, April 30, 2011; "Rankings of Canada's Top 1000 Public Companies by Profit," *The Globe and Mail*, http://www.theglobeandmail.com, April 30, 2011.

machinery and industrial products are equally important to our economy. In a recent year, Canada exported $90.7 billion of energy products, $76 billion in equipment, and another $56.8 billion in automotive products. These amounts are lower than just before the financial crisis.[4]

The United States is by far our largest trading partner, as shown in Figure 6.1. The North American Free Trade Agreement and the improved pipeline infrastructure that allows more natural gas and crude oil to move across the border are contributing factors to the success of this relationship. Our next largest trading partner is the European Union, which has purchased over $19 billion worth of goods from us in one year. Japan and the United Kingdom also play an important role in our international trade, purchasing $9 and $16 billion a year respectively.[5]

Walmart currently ranks as the world's largest private employer with 2.1 million

figure 6.1

Top Canadian Trading Partners

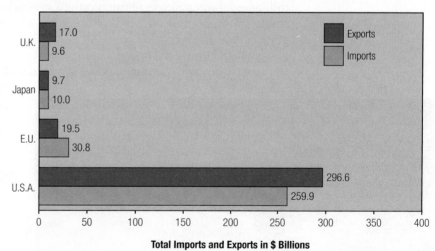

Total Imports and Exports in $ Billions

Source: Adapted from Statistics Canada's Summary Table, Imports, exports and trade balance of goods on a balance-of-payments basis, by country or country grouping; http://www40.statcan.gc.ca/l01/cst01/gblec02a-eng.htm?sdi=imports%20exports%20trade%20balance%20goods (accessed April 29, 2011).

employees and largest retailer. If Walmart were a country, industry observers estimate, it would rank seventh among China's trading partners, spending upwards of $18 billion per year in goods. The retail giant also allocates billions of dollars in expansion efforts abroad in China, Central America, India, Japan, South America, and the United Kingdom.[6]

The rapid globalization of business and the boundless nature of the Internet have made it possible for every marketer to become an international marketer. However, becoming an Internet global marketer is not necessarily easy. While larger firms have the advantage of more resources and wider distribution systems, smaller companies can build websites for as little as a few hundred dollars and can bring products to market quickly. The Internet allows companies like Gorilla Nation, which develops digital content and produces videos for marketing programs, to be based in Los Angeles, but have clients anywhere in the world. It has distribution and sales offices throughout the world, including Toronto and Montreal, which allow their sales team to interface with their customers.[7]

Just as some firms depend on foreign and Internet sales, others rely on purchasing raw materials abroad as input for their domestic manufacturing operations. A furniture manufacturer may depend on purchases of South American mahogany, while furniture retailers are taking advantage of Chinese-made styling and quality and that country's traditionally low prices.

SERVICE EXPORTS

Manufacturing no longer accounts for the lion's share of annual production output in Canada. Today, more than 7 of every 10 dollars included in the nation's gross domestic product (GDP) comes from services—banking, entertainment, business and technical services, retailing, and communications. Services also account for more than 75 percent of all employment in Canada. This profound shift from a largely manufacturing to a largely service economy is also reflected in the nation's exports.[8]

The importance of service exports to all nations and the difficulty in measuring service transactions has prompted the International Monetary Fund (IMF) to classify and define service categories and transactions, assisting government statistical agencies to collect and compare data. Service categories include travel, transportation, government services, and other (such as business services). A service transaction is included in a country's export numbers when a client, the service, or the supplier crosses a border or a commerce presence is set up abroad. A major contributing factor in services being exported and measured is technology. Information technology has allowed services that once were considered nontransferable or storable to travel long distances quickly and easily from where they are produced through sophisticated telecommunications networks. This trend is likely to continue as technological advancements reach developing countries, allowing services such as health, education, and banking to grow in these markets.[9]

Canada measures imports and exports of services under three major categories, travel, transportation, and commercial services. Each of these categories has several subcategories—for example, travel is further divided into business and personal travel. Under the transportation category, information is collected about water, air, and land transportation. The largest category, both in number of subgroups and the dollar amount of imports and exports, is commercial services. Included in this category are communication services, financial services, management services, and thirteen other subgroups.[10]

One important area of service exports is tourism. Tourism in Canada represents 2 percent of the Gross National Product, accounting for approximately $29 billion annually. In recent years, the number of visitors to Canada has been decreasing. The increasing value of the Canadian dollar and the worldwide economic slowdown are two reasons cited for the decline in the number of tourists. Even with the decline in the number of tourists visiting Canada, there are still about 650 000 Canadians working in jobs relating to tourism.[11]

JTB PHOTO/JAPAN TRAVEL BUREAU/PHOTOLIBRARY

The global coverage and international reputation of the Hilton name combine to generate additional sales revenues around the world as both business and vacation travellers select accommodations for their stays.

BENEFITS OF GOING GLOBAL

Besides generating additional revenue, firms expand their operations outside their home country to gain other benefits, including new insights into consumer behaviour, alternative distribution strategies, and advance notice of new products. By setting up foreign offices and production facilities, marketers may encounter new products, new approaches to distribution, or clever new promotions that they may be able to apply successfully in their domestic market or in other international markets.

Global marketers are typically well positioned to compete effectively with foreign competitors. A major key to achieving success in foreign markets is a firm's ability to adapt its products to local preferences and culture. As discussed earlier, McDonald's succeeded in other countries by paying attention to local tastes and modifying its menus. Similarly, Yum! Brands, parent of KFC and Pizza Hut, successfully launched KFC in China in 1987 by catering to Chinese tastes. China's first fast-food chain, KFC, augmented its familiar chicken-based menu with such Chinese staples as fish, porridge, fried dough, beef rice, bean curd, and egg tarts. Today, the company looks to repeat its success in the Indian market.[12]

A product as seemingly universal as pizza must be localized as well. Papa John's has more than 3400 pizza shops in 30 countries. Expansion plans continue in Asia, where the company intends to open 50 restaurants across China and South Korea, as well as additional stores in India, Ireland, Mexico, and Russia. But buying behaviours differ around the globe. While North Americans tend to prefer take-out or home delivery, customers in China and Russia like to eat pizza in a restaurant, so Papa John's built attractive seating areas and added soups and salads to the menu in those countries. In addition, as local tastes differ, so does Papa John's menu. In Egypt, the menu includes pasta and soups containing lentils, and the pizzas have exotic names: "Fisherman's Catch" includes shrimp and alfredo sauce; "Indian Splendor" features a topping of tandoori chicken.[13]

Since companies must perform the marketing functions of buying, selling, transporting, storing, standardizing and grading, financing, risk taking, and obtaining market information in both domestic and global markets, some may question the wisdom of treating global marketing as a distinct subject. But as this chapter will explain, there are similarities and differences that influence strategies for both domestic and global marketing.

The Canadian Tourism Commission provides international travellers with easy access to information about Canadian companies and events.

Papa John's has more than 3400 pizza shops worldwide. As local tastes differ, so do pizza toppings.

assessment check 1

1.1 Define importing and exporting.

1.2 What must global marketers be able to do effectively to reach international markets?

THE INTERNATIONAL MARKETING ENVIRONMENT

 ② Identify the major components of the environment for global marketing.

As in domestic markets, the environmental factors discussed in Chapter 3 have a powerful influence on the development of a firm's global marketing strategies. Marketers must pay close attention to changing demand patterns as well as competitive, economic, social-cultural, political-legal, and technological influences when they venture abroad.

INTERNATIONAL ECONOMIC ENVIRONMENT

A nation's size, per-capita income, and stage of economic development determine its prospects as a host for international business expansion. Nations with low per-capita incomes may be poor markets for expensive industrial machinery but good ones for agricultural hand tools. These nations cannot afford the technical equipment that powers an industrialized society. Wealthier countries may offer prime markets for many industries, particularly those producing consumer goods and services and advanced industrial products.

But some less-industrialized countries are growing fast. India and China, for example, may rival the United States in world economic importance in a generation or two. Although the U.S. per-capita GDP of $46 400 ranks way above China's $6500 and India's $2900, these nations have far larger populations and thus more potential human capital to develop in the future.[14] Their ability to import technology and foreign capital, as well as to train scientists and engineers and invest in research and development, ensures that their growth will be rapid and their income gaps with the developed countries will close quickly. Most recently, India's GDP rose 6.6 percent and China's rose 10.1 percent, but the United States' GDP grew only 2.1 percent.[15]

Infrastructure, the underlying foundation for modern life and efficient marketing that includes transportation, communications, banking, utilities, and public services, is another important economic factor to consider when planning to enter a foreign market. An inadequate infrastructure may constrain marketers' plans to manufacture, promote, and distribute goods and services in a particular country. People living in countries blessed with navigable waters often rely on them as inexpensive, relatively efficient alternatives to highways, rail lines, and air transportation. Thai farmers use their nation's rivers to transport their crops. Their boats even become retail outlets in so-called floating markets such as the one located outside the capital city of Bangkok. Often the population in rural areas begins to shift to where the infrastructure is more developed. This change is happening in both China and India. In 15 years, China's cities are projected to have an additional 350 million people. And in India, which claims one-sixth of the world's population, 42 cities have a population of 1 million or more, up from 32 such cities just two years ago.[16] Marketers expect developing economies to have substandard utility and communications networks. China encountered numerous problems in establishing a modern communications industry infrastructure. The Chinese government's answer was to bypass the need for landline telephone connections by leapfrogging technologies and moving directly to cell phones.

Changes in exchange rates can also complicate international marketing. An **exchange rate** is the price of one nation's currency in terms of another country's currency. Fluctuations in exchange rates can make a nation's currency more valuable or less valuable compared with those of other nations. In today's global economy, imbalances in trade, dependence on fossil fuels, and other conditions affect the currencies of many countries, not just one or two.

exchange rate Price of one nation's currency in terms of another country's currency.

Most members of the European Union have switched to the euro as the replacement to their traditional francs and liras. The long-range idea behind this common currency is that switching to a single currency would strengthen Europe's competitiveness in the global marketplace. Russian and many Eastern European currencies are considered *soft currencies* that cannot be readily converted into such hard currencies as the dollar, euro, or Japanese yen.

INTERNATIONAL SOCIAL-CULTURAL ENVIRONMENT

Before entering a foreign market, marketers should study all aspects of that nation's culture, including language, education, religious attitudes, and social values. The French love to debate and are comfortable with frequent eye contact. In China, humility is a prized virtue, colours have special significance, and it is insulting to be late. Swedes value consensus and do not use humour in negotiations. Navigating these rules that are commonly understood among the citizens of a country takes time, patience, and a willingness to learn about other cultures. The "Career Readiness" feature offers a few tips on doing business globally.

Language plays an important role in international marketing. Table 6.2 lists the world's 10 most frequently spoken languages. Marketers must make sure not only to use the appropriate language or languages for a country but also ensure that the message is correctly translated and conveys the intended meaning.

CAREER READINESS | Culture Tips for Marketing

WHEN working with people in other countries, remember: one size does not fit all. Study up on a country's culture in advance. Though the differences can be subtle, you ignore them at your own peril.

- **Greetings vary by culture.** North Americans shake hands, gripping firmly and pumping twice while looking the other person in the eye. In France and Germany, expect to pump once. In the Middle East, the handshake may continue during introductions. The traditional Japanese greeting was a bow, not a handshake, but these days, you're likely to get a handshake with a lighter grip and possibly a bow. Muslim women in traditional attire don't shake hands with men.

- **Be careful with humour.** North Americans regard a smile and a joke as appropriate icebreakers, but not so in Russia, where lightheartedness is reserved for social settings. The mood is also serious in Germany. Expect to engage in small talk in China before getting down to business, but keep it impersonal.

- **Here's my card.** Most cultures regard the business card as a representation of the person himself, so exchanging cards is not only practical but symbolic. Generally, present your card only after introductions have been made, and make sure it's face-up so the recipient can read it. To people from China, Hong Kong, Japan, or Singapore, present your card with both hands. Show respect by taking time to look at a business card offered to you, and place it carefully in front of you during a meeting. Put cards away deliberately and respectfully; never jam them into your pocket, particularly a back pocket.

- **Watch your hands.** The "OK" sign conveys different, sometimes obscene, meanings in other countries. In France, Germany, Sweden, and Switzerland, keep your hands out of your pockets unless you're reaching for your wallet. Belgians consider it rude to crack one's knuckles. Pointing is impolite in any country.

Sources: Edward Chalmers, "Business Etiquette in Europe," AskMen.com, http://www.askmen.com, February 19, 2010; Armando Gomez, "Business Travel Etiquette," AskMen.com, http://www.askmen.com, February 19, 2010; Lydia Ramsey, "International Business Etiquette Tips," *The Sideroad*, http://www.sideroad.com, February 19, 2010; Emily Maltby, "Expanding Abroad? Avoid Cultural Gaffes," *The Wall Street Journal*, http://online.wsj.com, January 19, 2010.

table 6.2   **The World's Most Frequently Spoken Languages**

RANK	LANGUAGE	NUMBER OF SPEAKERS
1	Mandarin (Chinese)	1.2 billion
2	Spanish	329 million
3	English	328 million
4	Arabic	221 million
5	Hindi	182 million
6	Bengali	181 million
7	Portuguese	178 million
8	Russian	144 million
9	Japanese	122 million
10	German	90 million

Source: Used by permission, © SIL International, *Ethnologue: Languages of the World*, Sixteenth edition, http://www.ethnologue.com/ethno_docs/distribution.asp?by=size, 2009.

Firms that rely on call centres located in India and staffed by Indian nationals have discovered an occasional language gap. But these employees do speak English, the worldwide language of commerce. Despite some glitches, the call centres, along with other outsourced operations, are booming, creating jobs and a new middle class in India. The country's economy has benefitted hugely from the influx of foreign direct investment that came after the country loosened restrictions of foreign ownership. India now boasts the fastest-growing market for wireless services: mobile phone sales tripled in a two-year period. IBM plans to recruit an additional 5000 employees in India in an effort to expand its business process outsourcing (BPO) operations there.[17]

Worldwide
card
replacement
when you're far
from home.

Whether your card's been
lost or stolen, we're here to help.
So you'll always land on your feet.

americanexpress.ca/potential

Realize
the
potential™

COURTESY OF AMEX BANK OF CANADA

American Express promotes credit card features for international travellers.

---

political risk assessment (PRA)
Units within a firm that evaluate the political risks of the marketplaces in which they operate as well as proposed new marketplaces.

INTERNATIONAL TECHNOLOGICAL ENVIRONMENT

More than any innovation since the telephone, Internet technology has made it possible for both large and small firms to be connected to the entire world. The Internet transcends political, economic, and cultural barriers, reaching to every corner of the globe. It has made it possible for traditional marketers to add new business channels. It also helps developing nations in becoming competitive with industrialized nations. However, a huge gap still exists between the regions with the greatest Internet usage and those with the least. Asia, Europe, and North America together account for nearly 80 percent of the world's total Internet usage, Latin America and the Caribbean follow with 10 percent, while Africa accounts for less than 6 percent, Oceania/Australia just over 1 percent, and the Middle East just over 3 percent. Despite those numbers, Africa and the Middle East have seen the greatest growth in Internet users.[18]

Technology presents challenges for global marketers that extend beyond the Internet and other telecommunications innovations. A major issue involving food marketers is genetic re-engineering. Although Canadian grocery shelves are filled with foods grown with genetically modified organisms (GMOs), most Canadians are unaware they are eating GMO foods because no labelling disclosures are required. In Europe, a number of countries—including Austria, Bulgaria, France, Germany, and Hungary—have banned the cultivation of GMO crops, but the European Court of Justice has yet to issue a ruling that would ban GMOs throughout the European Union. With soaring food costs and global grain shortages, governments the world over are rethinking their position on foods made from crops that are engineered to resist pests and drought.[19] This complex issue affects almost every marketer in the global food industry.

One Swedish company, Hyper Island, as described in the "Marketing in a Digital World" feature, trains executives around the world in how to take advantage new technology.

INTERNATIONAL POLITICAL-LEGAL ENVIRONMENT

Global marketers must continually stay abreast of laws and trade regulations in each country in which they compete. Political conditions often influence international marketing as well. Political unrest in places such as the Middle East, Afghanistan, Africa, Eastern Europe, Spain, and South America sometimes results in acts of violence, such as destruction of a firm's property or even deaths from bombings or other terrorist acts. As a result, many Western firms have set up internal **political risk assessment (PRA)** units or turned to outside consulting services to evaluate the political risks of the marketplaces in which they operate.

The political environment also involves labour conditions in different countries. For decades, Chinese labourers have suffered workplace abuses including forced labour, withholding of pay, and other unfair practices. But that may be changing with the recent passage of a labour law that gives workers more rights.[20]

The legal environment for firms operating abroad results from three forces: (1) international law, (2) Canadian law, and (3) legal requirements of host nations. International law emerges from the treaties, conventions, and agreements that exist among nations. Canada has several agreements or treaties with other governments. These agreements set terms for various aspects of commercial relations with other countries, such as the right to conduct business in the treaty partner's domestic market. Other international business agreements concern worldwide standards for various products, patents, trademarks, reciprocal tax treaties, export control, international air travel, and international communications. Since the 1990s, Europe has pushed for mandatory **ISO (International Organization for Standardization) certification**—internationally recognized standards that ensure a company's goods, services, and operations meet established quality levels. The organization has two sets of standards: the ISO 9000 series of standards sets requirements for quality in goods and

MARKETING IN A DIGITAL WORLD	**Hyper Island's Master Class**

WITH all the new social media and digital platforms for marketers to use, Hyper Island aims to tap into the knowledge marketers already have in order to take full advantage of these new opportunities. Hyper Island does this with an intensive three-day program.

Hyper Island is a Swedish firm started by Lars Lundh, David Erixon, and Jonathan Briggs. Hyper Island's main offices are located in an old prison on an island in the Swedish town of Karlskrona, but they also have offices in England and New York. The company started by offering longer-term training programs for those wanting a career in the ever-changing world of interactive media. These longer programs include mobile applications, interactive art director, and motion graphics among others. The company responded to another need in this new world of social media by offering three-day programs for those who couldn't take one of the company's 40-week programs.

The three-day sessions are called master classes and have three stages: disruption/setting the scene, possibilities/opportunities, and strategy/implementation.

All of the programs are designed around self-learning or exploring what you already know. One participant in the master class program shared some of his insight:

- A project is never over—you can always adapt it.
- You don't need to understand what is happening you just need to be able to respond to what is happening.
- Don't just copy what others are doing—get out there and try something new.
- Find the problem, solve it, and tell everyone about it.
- Focus on engaging the consumer.
- Brands are no longer owned by marketers—they are owned by your customers.
- Create movements instead promotions.

Social media is changing how marketers think, and Hyper Island is helping marketers change their way of thinking in order to take full advantage of the changes.

Sources: Mark Biernacki, "What I Learned on Hyper Island," *Marketing*, http://www.marketingmag.ca, May 24, 2011; Hyper Island website, http://www.hyperisland.se, May 28, 2011.

services; and the ISO 14000 series sets standards for operations that minimize harm to the environment. Today, many companies follow these certification standards as well. Currently, 160 countries participate in both series.[21] The Go Green box discusses further the ISO 14000 series of standards. The International Monetary Fund, another major player in the international legal environment, lends foreign exchange to nations that require it to conduct international trade. These agreements facilitate the entire process of world marketing.

The second dimension of the international legal environment, Canadian law, includes various trade regulations, tax laws, and import/export requirements that affect international marketing. The laws regarding international trade are administered by several different government agencies. For example, Agriculture and Agri-Food Canada has the responsibility for the agri-food (agriculture and food) trade policy. Other regulations such as the Export and Import Permit Act (EIPA) fall under the Department of Foreign Affairs and International Trade. The EIPA controls the flow of certain types of goods, including textiles, clothing, steel, and military items. Several government agencies, including International Trade Canada and canadabusiness.ca, a federal government website, are set up to assist companies to work through the various legal requirements. Canadabusiness.ca (http://canadabusiness.ca) is a comprehensive site covering customs requirements, standards and permits, requirements under international trade agreements, international law sources, and intellectual property. The federal government provides individual assistance to large and small companies wanting to enter foreign markets through its Trade Commissioner Service. The Canadian Trade Commissioner Service can also connect you to business contacts in more than 150 cities throughout the world with its Linkedin network.[22]

Finally, legal requirements of host nations affect foreign marketers. Despite China's many advances in recent years—and even as it attempts to build a modern economy—the Chinese government continues to censor the Internet. More than 338 million Chinese currently use the Internet, and an active cadre of Chinese "hacktivists" works to outwit the government's firewall and help fellow citizens gain unfettered access.[23]

ISO (International Organization for Standardization) certification
Internationally recognized standards that ensure a company's goods and services meet established quality levels and that ensure its operations minimize harm to the environment.

Thanks to a WTO ruling on banana importation, European shoppers are likely to see more bananas from Latin America in their supermarkets—along with a more affordable price.

TRADE BARRIERS

Assorted trade barriers also affect global marketing. These barriers fall into two major categories: **tariffs**—taxes levied on imported products—and administrative, or non-tariff, barriers. Some tariffs impose set taxes per kilogram, litre, or unit; others are calculated according to the value of the imported item. Administrative barriers are more subtle than tariffs and take a variety of forms such as customs barriers, quotas on imports, unnecessarily restrictive standards for imports, and export subsidies. Because the GATT and WTO agreements (discussed later in the chapter) eliminated tariffs on many products, countries frequently use non-tariff barriers to boost exports and control the flows of imported products.

Canada and other nations are constantly negotiating tariffs and other trade agreements. Two significant agreements are the North American Free Trade Agreement (NAFTA) and the Free Trade Area of the Americas (FTAA). NAFTA involves Canada, the United States, and Mexico. The FTAA involves Canada and 34 other countries within North, South, and Central America, including large countries like the United States, Argentina, and Brazil, and smaller ones like Bahamas and Haiti.[24]

Tariffs

Tariffs can be classified as either revenue or protective tariffs. **Revenue tariffs** are designed to raise funds for the importing government. Most early government revenue came from this source. **Protective tariffs**, which are usually higher than revenue tariffs, are designed to raise the retail price of an imported product to match or exceed that of a similar domestic product. Some countries use tariffs in a selective manner to encourage or discourage certain consumption practices and thereby reduce access to their local markets. For example, Canada has a policy called General Preferential Tariff (GPT) in which we give preferential treatment to imports from developing countries. Introduced in 1974, this policy was intended to stimulate growth in areas of the world that are less economically advanced. The policy was initially implemented for a 10-year period but has been extended several times and currently applies to more than 180 countries. The policy is constantly monitored, and changes have been implemented from time to time. Some products are not covered under this agreement such as some farm and clothing products.[25]

Other Trade Barriers

In addition to direct taxes on imported products, governments may erect a number of other barriers ranging from special permits and detailed inspection requirements to quotas on foreign-made items in an effort to stem the flow of imported goods—or halt them altogether. In one of the longest-running trade disputes, European shoppers paid about twice as much for bananas as did North Americans. Through a series of import licence controls, Europe had limited the importation of bananas from Latin American countries in an effort to protect producers from former European colonies in Africa and the Caribbean, who pay no tariff. The World Trade Organization ruled that the European tariffs on imported bananas unfairly discriminated against Latin American banana growers. After 16 years of wrangling, the European Union reached an agreement with Latin American growers, which will make them subject to lower tariffs—and likely lower cost bananas in Europe.[26]

Other forms of trade restrictions include import quotas and embargoes. **Import quotas** limit the number of units of products in certain categories that can cross a country's border for resale. The

tariff
Tax levied against imported goods.

revenue tariffs
Taxes designed to raise funds for the importing government.

protective tariffs
Taxes designed to raise the retail price of an imported product to match or exceed that of a similar domestic tariff.

import quotas
Trade restrictions that limit the number of units of certain goods that can enter a country for resale.

BENIS ARAPOVIC/SHUTTERSTOCK.COM

GO GREEN

ISO 14000

ISO stands for International Organization for Standardization, a non-governmental body that establishes management systems standards and certification processes used throughout the world. In fact, hundreds of thousands of organizations, both private and public, in 160 countries have implemented ISO best practices. The ISO has two families of standards: the 9000 series, which addresses "quality management," was first established in 1992, and in 1994 the 14000 series was developed to address "environmental management." Companies adhering to these two sets of standards can be recognized through a certification process. Two newer sets of standards have been developed to provide companies with guidelines in the areas of risk management and social responsibility.

The 14000 series of standards has two goals: to help organizations "minimize harmful effects on the environment caused by their activities, and to achieve continual improvement of its environmental performance." This set of standards was developed to apply to any organization, anywhere in the world regardless of size, culture, or social conditions. As with all such standards, there are advantages and disadvantages.

One of the major advantages for companies using the ISO 14000 series of standards is cost savings. The costs of implementing the program can often be more than recovered by savings from increased operational efficiencies. Being ISO certified may provide companies access to markets that would not be open to them otherwise. The certification process directs the entire company's attention toward how they deal with environmental issues throughout every process in the company. A review of corporate processes on an ongoing basis is one way for companies to constantly improve their environmental impact.

Some disadvantages include the time and cost involved in the certification process. Smaller companies may not have the expertise to go through the certification process. The certification process is just the first step for companies; they need to comply with the standards continuously.

Sources: International Organization for Standardization, http://www.iso.org, May 14, 2011; Frederic Marimon Viadiu, Marti Casadesus Fa, and Inaki Heras Saizarbitoria, "ISO 9000 and ISO 14000 Standards: An International Diffusion Model," *International Journal of Operations and Production Management*, Vol. 26, Nos. 1/2, 2006, pp. 141–66; Nicole Darnell, "Why Firms Mandate ISO 14001 Certification," *Business and Society*, Vol. 45, No. 3, 2006, pp. 354–82; Susan L. K. Biggs, "ISO 14001 Hits 10-Year Mark," *Quality Progress*, Vol. 40, No. 8 (August 2007), pp. 67–69; "ISO 9000 and ISO 14000—in Brief," International Organization for Standardization, http://www.iso.org, March 27, 2006; Leo Stander and Louis Theodore, *Environmental Regulatory Calculations Handbook*, John Wiley and Sons Inc., 2008.

---

quota is supposed to protect domestic industry and employment and to preserve foreign exchange, but it doesn't always work that way.

The ultimate quota is the **embargo**—a complete ban on the import of a product. Since 1960, the United States has maintained an embargo against Cuba in protest against Fidel Castro's dictatorship and policies such as expropriation of property and disregard for human rights. Not only do the sanctions prohibit Cuban exports—cigars and sugar are the island's best-known products—to enter the country, but they also apply to companies that profit from property that Cuba's communist government expropriated from Americans following the Cuban revolution. Several years ago, the discovery of mad cow disease and the potential for contaminated beef resulted in a number of embargoes. After working with the World Organisation for Animal Health, Canada was able to argue that mad cow disease was under control. Since that time Canada has been working with its trading partners to resume full trade in beef and related products.[27]

Other trade barriers include **subsidies**. China has long subsidized the cost of many products, to boost consumption. When Chinese wireless carriers recently subsidized the cost of 3G (third generation) handsets, they projected a six-fold increase in sales.[28] Some nations also limit foreign ownership in the business sector. And still another way to block international trade is to create so many regulatory barriers that it is almost impossible to reach target markets. China presents a maze of regulations controlling trade, and while the government continues to lift barriers, experienced businesspeople agree that it's important to have personal connections, or guanxi, to help navigate the bureaucratic challenges.[29]

Foreign trade can also be regulated by exchange control through a central bank or government agency. **Exchange control** means that firms that gain foreign exchange by exporting must sell foreign currencies to the central bank or other foreign agency, and importers must buy foreign currencies from the same organization. The exchange control authority can then allocate, expand, or restrict foreign exchange according to existing national policy.

embargo
A complete ban on the import of a product.

subsidy
Government financial support of a private industry.

exchange control
Method used to regulate the privilege of international trade among importing organizations by controlling access to foreign currencies.

Prepare
for landing.

The Emirates A380. A sky full of choices.

You could unwind with a hot shower, or close the doors to your First Class Private Suite. You could mingle in the onboard Lounge*, or just sleep under the stars in a Business Class lie-flat bed. With so many choices, you may find yourself wishing for a longer flight. Discover more at emirates.com/ca

Fly Emirates. Keep discovering.

emirates.com/ca

*Shower Spa and Private Suite available in First Class. Onboard Lounge available in First and Business Class.
Over 400 international awards including Air Transport World 2011 Airline of the Year. Discover frequent flyer benefits at skywards.com

COURTESY OF EMIRATES

Some industries, such as airlines, need special approvals from government agencies in order to do business in Canada.

DUMPING

The practice of selling a product in a foreign market at a price lower than it commands in the producer's domestic market is called **dumping**. Critics of free trade often argue that foreign governments give substantial support to their own exporting companies. Government support may permit these firms to extend their export markets by offering lower prices abroad. In retaliation for this kind of interference with free trade, some governments add import tariffs to products that foreign firms are dumping on their markets to bring prices in line with their domestically produced goods. In Canada, the Special Import Measures Act covers anti-dumping regulations.[30]

China recently fined the United States for dumping chicken feet into the Chinese market. Poultry processors in the United States see China as an attractive destination for the item, considered worthless in North America but regarded as a delicacy in southern China.[31]

assessment check 2

2.1 What are the three criteria that determine a nation's prospects as a host for international business expansion?

2.2 What are the two major categories of trade barriers?

---

③ Outline the basic functions of GATT, WTO, NAFTA, FTAA, and the European Union.

dumping
Practice of selling a product in a foreign market at a price lower than what it receives in the producer's domestic market.

free trade area
Region in which participating nations agree to the free trade of goods among themselves, abolishing tariffs and trade restrictions.

MULTINATIONAL ECONOMIC INTEGRATION

A noticeable trend toward multinational economic integration has developed since the end of World War II. Multinational economic integration can be set up in several ways. The simplest approach is to establish a **free trade area** in which participating nations agree to the free trade of goods among themselves, abolishing all tariffs and trade restrictions. Table 6.3 shows a sample of free trade agreements. A **customs union** establishes a free trade area plus a uniform tariff for trade with non-member nations. A **common market** extends a customs union by seeking to reconcile all government regulations affecting trade. Despite the many factors in its favour, not everyone is enthusiastic about free trade. Canadians and Americans have lost jobs when employers outsourced their work to countries like Mexico where wages are lower. Now, workers in Mexico face the same outsourcing threat as their employers begin outsourcing work to China, where wages are even lower. Although productivity and innovation are said to grow quickly with free trade, workers often find themselves working longer and for reduced pay as operations move overseas. But many firms view the change as a way to offer superior service. The "Solving an Ethical Controversy" feature debates another issue related to trade: the pros and cons of banning the sale of bottled water in a community.

table 6.3 *Examples of Other Trade Agreements*

TRADE AGREEMENT	COUNTRIES INVOLVED
ASEAN Free Trade Area (AFTA)	Brunei, Darussalam, Cambodia, Indonesia, Laos, Malaysia, Myanmar, Philippines, Singapore, Thailand, Viet Nam
Central America Integration System (SICA)	Belize, Costa Rica, El Salvador, Guatemala, Honduras, Nicaragua, Panama
Central Europe Free Trade Agreement (CEFTA)	Republic of Albania, Bosnia and Herzegovina, Republic of Croatia, Republic of Macedonia, Republic of Moldova, Montenegro, Republic of Serbia
Common Market for Eastern and Southern Africa (COMESA)	Burundi, Comoros, D.R. Congo, Djibouti, Egypt, Eritrea, Ethiopia, Kenya, Libya, Madagascar, Malawi, Mauritius, Rwanda, Seychelles, Sudan, Swaziland, Uganda, Zambia, Zimbabwe
G-3 Free Trade Agreement	Colombia, Mexico, Venezuela
Greater Arab Free Trade Area	Jordan, United Arab Emirates, Bahrain, Saudi Arabia, Oman, Qatar, Morocco, Syria, Lebanon, Iraq, Egypt, Palestine, Kuwait, Tunis, Libya, Sudan, Yemen
South Asian Free Trade Area	India, Pakistan, Nepal, Bangladesh, Sri Lanka, Maldives, Bhutan

Note: The countries involved in these agreements change from time to time.

Sources: Association of Southeast Asia website, http://www.aseansec.org, May 8, 2011; Central America Integrated System website, http://www.sica.int, May 8, 2011; Central Europe Free Trade Agreement website, http://www.cefta2006.com, May 8, 2011; Common Market for Eastern and Southern Africa website, http://www.comesa.int, May 8, 2011; "Group of 3-G#," http://www.investopedia.com, May 8, 2011; Greater Arab Free Trade Area website, http://www.mit.gov.jo, May 8, 2011; Agreement on South Asian Free Trade Area (SAFTA) website, http://www.cfr.org, May 8, 2011.

SOLVING AN ETHICAL CONTROVERSY | Putting the Lid on Bottled Water

BOTTLED water is big business. North Americans drink billions of litres of the stuff. But many people believe bottled water is also an environmental nuisance. Environmentalists say it takes millions of barrels of oil to produce the plastic bottles for just one year's consumption.

The bottles are also an environmental hazard. According to a recent estimate, less than one-fifth of them are properly recycled, with the rest ending up as litter or in landfills. Many municipalities—including Toronto—are limiting the sale of bottled water in some areas. Though Vancouver officials voted to phase out the sale of bottled water in government buildings, the city was obliged to honour earlier contracts that permitted sales of bottled water at the 2010 Winter Olympics. Little Bundanoon, Australia—population 2000—is believed to be the first city to ban the sale of bottled water altogether.

Should the sale of bottled water be banned?

PRO

1. Bottled water is too expensive. In most cases, it's merely tap water sold at highly inflated prices.
2. Plastic bottles are bad for the environment and manufacturing them requires oil, a scarce resource.
3. Scientists have discovered health hazards connected with the plastic in bottles.

CON

1. Bottled water is more convenient.
2. In underdeveloped countries and in areas hit by natural disaster (such as earthquakes in Haiti and Chile), the absence of potable water can be life-threatening. Bottled water becomes a necessity.
3. Bottled-water marketers are redesigning bottles to use less plastic, and many sponsor recycling programs.

Where do you stand: pro or con?

Sources: Jeromy Lloyd, "Brita Wades Through Bottled Water Debate," *Marketing*, http://www.marketingmag.ca, April 20, 2010; "Households and the Environment Survey," Statistics Canada, http://www.statcan.gc.ca, May 22, 2011; Tiffany Crawford, "Vancouver's Push to Ban Plastic Bottles Won't Hold During Olympics," *The Vancouver Sun*, http://www.vancouversun.com, January 29, 2010; Isobel Drake, "Asia Boosts Global Bottled Water Market," *Australian Food News*, http://ausfoodnews.com, January 15, 2010; "Bottle Ban," *Sunday Herald Sun*, http://www.heraldsun.com.au, October 11, 2009; Kathy Marks, "The Australian Town That Kicked the Bottle; Drinking Fountains Replace Shop-Bought Mineral Water in Environmental Initiative," *The Independent*, http://www.independent.co.uk, September 28, 2009; Nadia Jamal, "Bottler of Idea as Town Doesn't Go With the Flow," *Sunday Herald Sun*, http://www.heraldsun.com.au, September 27, 2009; "Australian Town in 'World-First' Bottled Water Ban," Space & Earth, http://www.physorg.com, September 26, 2009; "Aussie Town Votes to Ban Bottled Water," *Toronto Star*, http://www.thestar.com, September 8, 2009; Ylan Q. Mui, "Bottled Water Boom Appears Tapped Out," *The Washington Post*, http://www.washingtonpost.com, August 13, 2009.

customs union
Establishment of a free trade area plus a uniform tariff for trade with non-member unions.

common market
Extension of a customs union by seeking to reconcile all government regulations affecting trade.

General Agreement on Tariffs and Trade (GATT) International trade accord that has helped reduce world tariffs.

World Trade Organization (WTO) Organization that replaces GATT, overseeing GATT agreements, making binding decisions in mediating disputes, and reducing trade barriers.

North American Free Trade Agreement (NAFTA) Accord removing trade barriers among Canada, Mexico, and the United States.

Free Trade Area of the Americas (FTAA) Proposed free trade area stretching the length of the entire Western Hemisphere and designed to extend free trade benefits to additional nations in North, Central, and South America.

GATT AND THE WORLD TRADE ORGANIZATION

The **General Agreement on Tariffs and Trade (GATT)**, a trade accord that has sponsored several rounds of major tariff negotiations, substantially reducing worldwide tariff levels, has existed for six decades. In 1994, a seven-year series of GATT conferences, called the Uruguay Round, culminated in one of the biggest victories for free trade in decades.

The Uruguay Round reduced average tariffs by one-third, or more than $700 billion. Among its major victories were these:

• Reduced farm subsidies, which opened vast new markets for exports

• Increased protection for patents, copyrights, and trademarks

• Included services under international trading rules, creating opportunities for financial, legal, and accounting firms

• Phased out import quotas on textiles and clothing from developing nations, a move that cost textile workers thousands of jobs when their employers moved many of these domestic jobs to lower-wage countries, but benefitted retailers and consumers

A key outcome of the GATT talks was establishment of the **World Trade Organization (WTO)**, a 153-member organization that succeeds GATT. The WTO oversees GATT agreements, serves as a forum for trade negotiations, and mediates disputes. It also monitors national trade policy and works to reduce trade barriers throughout the world. Unlike GATT, WTO decisions are binding. Countries that seek to become members of the WTO must participate in rigorous rounds of negotiations that can last several years. Russia holds the record: having applied for membership in 1993, its application is still in negotiations.[32]

To date, the WTO has made only slow progress toward its major policy initiatives—liberalizing world financial services, telecommunications, and maritime markets. Trade officials have not agreed on the direction for the WTO. Big differences between developed and developing nations create a major roadblock to WTO progress, and its activities so far have focused more on dispute resolution through its Dispute Settlement Body than on reducing trade barriers. But the WTO also provides important technical assistance and training for the governments of developing countries.[33]

NAFTA

More than a decade after the passage of the **North American Free Trade Agreement (NAFTA)**, an agreement between Canada, the United States, and Mexico that removes trade restrictions among the three nations, negotiations among the nations continue. The three nations insist that they will not create a trade bloc similar to the European Union—that is, they will not focus on political integration but instead on economic cooperation. NAFTA is particularly important to Canadian marketers because the United States is this country's largest trading partner.

But NAFTA is a complex issue, and from time to time groups in one or more of the three countries chafe under the agreement. In Mexico, farm workers have charged that NAFTA puts their industry at a disadvantage. In the United States, critics argue that U.S. workers lose jobs to cheap labour south of the border. In Canada, some observers claim NAFTA has compromised the country's oil reserves. Yet since NAFTA's passage, these three countries daily conduct more than $2 billion in trade with each other and have experienced GDP growth as a result.[34]

THE FREE TRADE AREA OF THE AMERICAS

NAFTA was the first step toward creating a **Free Trade Area of the Americas (FTAA)**, stretching the length of the entire Western Hemisphere, from Alaska's Bering Strait to Cape Horn at South America's southern tip, encompassing 34 countries, a population of 800 million, and a combined gross domestic product of more than $11 trillion. The FTAA would be the largest free trade zone on earth and would offer low or nonexistent tariffs, streamlined customs, and no quotas, subsidies, or other barriers to trade. In addition to Canada, the United States, and Mexico, countries expected to be members of the proposed FTAA include Argentina, Brazil, Chile, Colombia, Ecuador, Guatemala, Jamaica, Peru, Trinidad and Tobago, Uruguay, and Venezuela. The FTAA still has many hurdles to overcome as countries wrangle for conditions that are most favourable to them.

THE EUROPEAN UNION

The best-known example of a multinational economic community is the **European Union (EU)**. As Figure 6.2 shows, 27 countries make up the EU: Finland, Sweden, Denmark, the United Kingdom, Ireland, the Netherlands, Belgium, Germany, Luxembourg, France, Austria, Italy, Greece, Spain, Portugal, Hungary, Poland, the Czech Republic, Slovakia, Slovenia, Estonia, Latvia, Lithuania, Malta, Bulgaria, Romania, and Cyprus. Three countries—Croatia, Macedonia, and Turkey—are candidates for membership. With a total population of more than 500 million people, the EU forms a huge market.[35]

The goal of the EU is to eventually remove all barriers to free trade among its members, making it as simple and painless to ship products between England and Spain as it is between Newfoundland and British Columbia. Also involved is the standardization of regulations and currencies that

figure 6.2

The 27 Members of the European Union

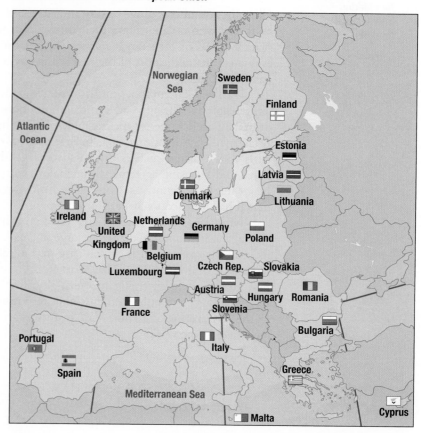

businesses must meet. Introduced in 1999, the EU's euro is the common currency in 16 member countries, with eight other EU countries planning to phase it in over time. Only Denmark, Sweden, and the United Kingdom have declined to use the euro.

In addition to simplifying transactions among members, the EU looks to strengthen its position in the world as a political and economic power. Its recently ratified Treaty of Lisbon is designed to further streamline operations and enables the EU to enter into international agreements as a political entity.[36] Mexico negotiated a trade agreement with the EU that makes it easier for European companies to set up operations in Mexico. The agreement gives EU companies the same privileges enjoyed by Canada and the United States and brings new investors to Mexico.

In some ways, the EU is making definite progress toward its economic goals. It is drafting standardized eco-labels to certify that products are manufactured according to certain environmental standards as well as creating guidelines governing marketers' uses of customer information. Marketers can also protect some trademarks throughout the entire EU with a single application and registration process through the Community Trade Mark (CTM), which simplifies doing business and eliminates having to register with each member country. Yet marketers still face challenges when selling their products in the EU. Customs taxes differ, and no uniform postal system exists. Using one toll-free number for several countries will not work, either, because each country has its own telephone system for codes and numbers.

European Union (EU)
Customs union that is moving in the direction of an economic union by adopting a common currency, removing trade restrictions, and permitting free flow of goods and workers throughout the member nations.

Marketoid

Canada's imports from China totalled $44.5 billion in 2010.

assessment check 3 ✓

3.1 What is the World Trade Organization (WTO)?

3.2 What countries are parties to NAFTA?

3.3 What is the goal of the European Union (EU)?

④ Identify the alternative strategies for entering international markets.

GOING GLOBAL

Globalization affects almost every industry and every individual throughout the world. Traditional marketers who decide to take their firms global may do so because they already have strong domestic market shares or their target market is too saturated to offer any substantial growth. Sometimes, by evaluating key indicators of the marketing environment, marketers can move toward globalization at an optimal time.

The German footwear firm Adidas made a big jump into the global market after its successful "Impossible Is Nothing" ad campaign, announcing it would purchase rival Reebok in an effort to overtake number one competitor Nike. Using the benefits of the EU while also making a play for the Asian market, Adidas marketers believe they have a good chance at winning the global game. Making deals with athletes, such as British soccer legend David Beckham and Italian tennis star Flavia Pennetta, and licensing agreements for major sports leagues have helped Adidas strengthen its brand in major markets around the world. The firm scored one of its biggest coups by introducing the official match ball for soccer's 2010 World Cup.[37]

Most large firms—and many smaller businesses—already participate in global commerce, and virtually every domestic marketer, large or small, recognizes the need to investigate whether to market its products overseas. It is not an easy step to take, requiring careful evaluation and preparation of a strategy. Common reasons that marketers cite for going global include globalization of customers, new customers in emerging markets, globalization of competitors, reduced trade barriers, advances in technology, and enhanced customer responsiveness. Some companies like Hapi Foods, described in the "Marketing and the SME" feature, start out by taking orders online and shipping products anywhere in the world.

MARKETING AND THE SME | Holy Crap

"THAT's good!"—that is what Jim Treliving, one of the Dragons on the popular television series *Dragons' Den*, said after just a couple bites of the breakfast cereal called Holy Crap.

Holy Crap is made by HapiFoods, a company started in 2009 by husband-wife team Brian and Corin Mullins of Sechelt, British Columbia. Corin is a retired flight attendant and Brian has a background in marketing and communications.

Holy Crap was originally launched on the market with the name HapiFoods but customers kept saying "Holy crap, that's good" and the couple decided to change the name to Holy Crap as a promotion for a couple of months. The name was never changed back to HapiFoods.

The cereal itself is a unique blend of seeds and fruits with the key ingredient being chia, or *Salvia hispanica L.*, an ancient super-food of the Aztecs. The product is gluten free, lactose free, high in fibre and iron, and contains omega three and six as well as antioxidants. All ingredients are grown organically.

Customers mix four tablespoons of milk or yogurt with two tablespoons of the cereal for a complete serving.

The couple distributed their product locally and through the Internet until the *Dragons' Den* experience changed their business. Before the television episode, the company processed about ten orders a day. Since the *Dragons' Den* program aired, the business has been processing ten orders every minute and the online orders are in the thousands. The product is also now available through health food stores across the country.

The company has been so successful that it has hired 15 new employees to keep up with the demand. They turned down an appearance on the *Today Show* for fear the increased demand it would generate would be more than the company could handle.

Sources: "Holy Crap Sales Soar with *Dragons' Den* Appearance," *Marketing*, http://www.marketingmag.ca, November 25, 2010; HapiFoods website; http://www.holycrap.ca, May 24, 2011.

STRATEGIES FOR ENTERING INTERNATIONAL MARKETS

Successful global marketing starts at the top. Without the enthusiasm and support of senior managers, an initiative is likely to fail. Once marketers have researched and identified markets for expansion, they may choose from among three basic strategies for entering international markets: importing and exporting; contractual agreements such as franchising, licensing, and subcontracting; and international direct investment. As Figure 6.3 shows, the level of risk and the firm's degree of control over global marketing increase with greater involvement. Firms often use more than one of these entry strategies.

IMPORTING AND EXPORTING

An importer is a firm that brings in goods produced abroad to sell domestically or to be used as components in its products. In making import decisions, the marketer must assess local demand for the product, taking into consideration factors such as the following:

- Ability of the supplier to maintain agreed-to quality levels

- Flexibility in filling orders that might vary considerably from one order to the next

- Response time in filling orders; and

- Total costs—including import fees, packaging, and transportation—in comparison with costs of domestic suppliers

Exporting, another basic form of global marketing, involves a continuous effort in marketing a firm's merchandise to customers in other countries. Many firms export their products as the first step in reaching international markets. Furniture retailer Ikea has built an entire exporting strategy around its modular furniture. Because Ikea's furniture is lightweight, packs flat, and comes in components that customers can assemble, the firm can ship its goods almost anywhere in the world at a low cost, unlike traditional furniture.[38]

First-time exporters can reach foreign customers through one or more of three alternatives: export-trading companies, export-management companies, or offset agreements. An export-trading company (ETC) buys products from domestic producers and resells them abroad. While manufacturers lose control over marketing and distribution to the ETC, it helps them export through a relatively simple and inexpensive channel, in the process providing feedback about the overseas market potential of their products.

The second option, an export-management company (EMC), provides the first-time exporter with expertise in locating international buyers, handling necessary paperwork, and ensuring that its goods meet local labelling and testing laws. However, the manufacturer retains more control over the export process when it deals with an EMC than if it were to sell the goods outright to an export-trading company. Smaller firms can get assistance with administrative needs such as financing and preparation of proposals and contracts from large EMC contractors.

The final option, entering a foreign market under an offset agreement, teams a small firm with a major international company. The smaller firm essentially serves as a subcontractor on a large foreign project. This entry strategy provides new exporters with international experience, supported by the assistance of the primary contractor in such areas as international transaction documentation and financing.

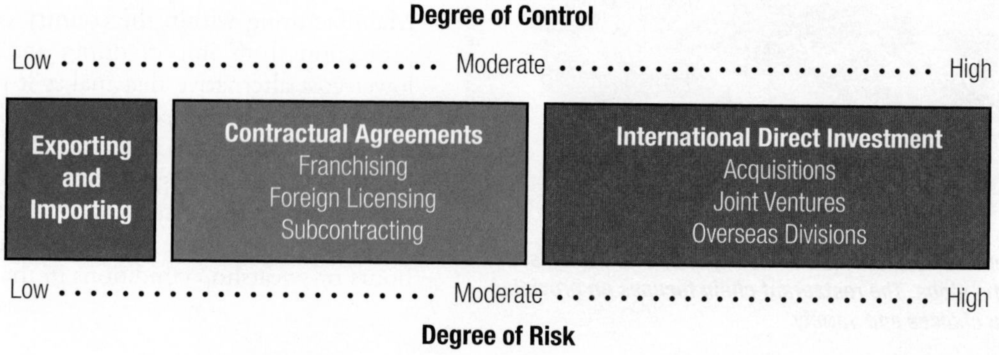

Degree of Control

Low ······················· Moderate ························ High

Exporting and Importing	Contractual Agreements Franchising Foreign Licensing Subcontracting	International Direct Investment Acquisitions Joint Ventures Overseas Divisions

Low ······················· Moderate ························ High

Degree of Risk

figure 6.3

Levels of Involvement in International Marketing

CONTRACTUAL AGREEMENTS

As a firm gains sophistication in global marketing, it may enter contractual agreements that provide several flexible alternatives to exporting. Both large and small firms can benefit from these methods. Franchising and foreign licensing, for example, are good ways to take services abroad. Subcontracting agreements may involve either production facilities or services.

Franchising

franchise
Contractual arrangement in which a wholesaler or retailer agrees to meet the operating requirements of a manufacturer or other franchiser.

A **franchise** is a contractual arrangement in which a wholesaler or retailer (the franchisee) agrees to meet the operating requirements of a manufacturer or other franchiser. The franchisee receives the right to sell the products and use the franchiser's name as well as a variety of marketing, management, and other services. Fast-food companies such as McDonald's have been active franchisers around the world.

One advantage of franchising is risk reduction by offering a proven concept. Standardized operations typically reduce costs, increase operating efficiencies, and provide greater international recognition. However, the success of an international franchise depends on its willingness to balance standard practices with local customer preferences. McDonald's and Pizza Hut are expanding into India with special menus that feature lamb, chicken, and vegetarian items, in deference to Hindu and Muslim customers who do not eat beef or pork.

Foreign Licensing

foreign licensing
Agreement that grants foreign marketers the right to distribute a firm's merchandise or to use its trademark, patent, or process in a specified geographic area.

subcontracting
Contractual agreements that assign the production of goods or services to local or smaller firms.

A second method of going global through the use of contractual agreements is **foreign licensing**. Such an agreement grants foreign marketers the right to distribute a firm's merchandise or use its trademark, patent, or process in a specified geographic area. These arrangements usually set certain time limits, after which agreements are revised or renewed.

Licensing offers several advantages over exporting, including access to local partners' marketing information and distribution channels and protection from various legal barriers. Because licensing does not require capital outlays, many firms, both small and large, regard it as an attractive entry strategy. Like franchising, licensing allows a firm to quickly enter a foreign market with a known product. The arrangement also may provide entry into a market that government restrictions close to imports or international direct investment. Entertainment software producer Electronic Arts entered into licensing agreements with consumer electronics accessory manufacturers to create and distribute accessories for iPod, Nintendo DS, and Wii under its EA SPORTS brand.[39]

Subcontracting

A third strategy for going global through contractual agreements is **subcontracting**, in which the production of goods or services is assigned to local companies. Using local subcontractors can prevent mistakes involving local culture and regulations. Manufacturers might subcontract with a local company to produce their goods or use a foreign distributor to handle their products abroad or provide customer service. Manufacturing within the country can provide protection from import duties and may be a lower-cost alternative that makes it possible for the product to compete with local offerings. But it can also have a downside if local suppliers don't make the grade or if a manufacturer imposes an unrealistically tight timeframe on a supplier to deliver the product, leading to long hours or sweatshop conditions in the factory.[40]

USED WITH PERMISSION FROM MCDONALD'S CORPORATION

As every international traveller knows, McDonald's has expanded its franchised fast-food operations around the globe. The restaurant chain focuses on providing all of its customers with menu choices and variety.

INTERNATIONAL DIRECT INVESTMENT

Another strategy for entering global markets is international direct investment in foreign firms, production, and marketing facilities. With so many Canadians coming from different parts of the world, it is not surprising that foreign direct investment inflows and outflows—the total of Canadian investments abroad and foreign investments in Canada—are important to our economic growth. Canadian firms invested over $600 billion in other countries in 2010. The two areas to which most of this investment went are the United States at $249 billion and the European Union at $157 billion. Total foreign investment into Canada for the same period amounted to $561 billion. The areas with the largest foreign investment in Canada were the United States at $306 billion and the European Union at $171 billion.[41]

Although high levels of involvement and high-risk potential are characteristics of investments in foreign countries, firms choosing this method often have a competitive advantage. Direct investment can take several forms. A company can acquire an existing firm in a country where it wants to do business, or it can set up an independent division outside its own borders with responsibility for production and marketing in a country or geographic region. Chinese firms have been seeking to purchase businesses in other countries, mostly in industries involving natural resources such as oil, natural gas, metals, and coal. However, they have been making inroads in industrial, technology, and finance companies as well. China is now the seventh-largest investor in Canada.[42]

Companies may also engage in international marketing by forming joint ventures, in which they share the risks, costs, and management of the foreign operation with one or more partners. These partnerships join the investing companies with nationals of the host countries. While some companies choose to open their own facilities overseas, others share with their partners. Because India puts limits on foreign direct investment, Walmart formed a partnership with Indian conglomerate Bharti Enterprises to open wholesale cash-and-carry stores in India. The stores do business under the name BestPrice Modern Wholesale.[43]

Although joint ventures offer many advantages, foreign investors have encountered problems in several areas throughout the world, especially in developing economies. Lower trade barriers, new technologies, lower transport costs, and vastly improved access to information mean that many more partnerships will be involved in international trade.

assessment check 4

4.1 What are the three basic strategies for entering international markets?

4.2 What is a franchise?

4.3 What is international direct investment?

FROM MULTINATIONAL CORPORATION TO GLOBAL MARKETER

(5) Differentiate between a global marketing strategy and a multi-domestic marketing strategy.

multinational corporation Firm with significant operations and marketing activities outside its home country.

A **multinational corporation** is a firm with significant operations and marketing activities outside its home country. Examples of multinationals are General Electric, Siemens, and Mitsubishi in heavy electrical equipment, and Timex, Seiko, and Citizen in watches. Since they first became a force in international business in the 1960s, multinationals have evolved in some important ways. First, these companies are no longer exclusively North American–based. Today, it is as likely for a multinational to be based in Japan, Germany, or Great Britain as in North America. Second, multinationals no longer think of their foreign operations as mere outsourcing appendages that carry out the design, production, and engineering ideas conceived at home. Instead, they encourage constant exchanges of ideas, capital, and technologies among all the multinational operations.

Multinationals often employ huge foreign workforces relative to their North American staffs. A large percentage of all Ford and IBM personnel are located outside North America. These workforces are no longer seen merely as sources of cheap labour. On the contrary, many multinationals centre technically complex activities in locations throughout the world. Texas Instruments does much of its research, development, design, and manufacturing in East Asia. In fact, it is increasingly common for multinationals to bring product innovations from their foreign facilities back to North America.

Multinationals have become global corporations that reflect the interdependence of world economies, the growth of international competition, and the globalization of world markets. For example, 60 percent of households in Hong Kong get their television services through ultra-high-speed broadband connections that turn their TVs into computers, a concept that has been slower to catch on in

North America. European and Asian consumers were using smart cards with embedded memory chips for retail purchases first. Chile has emerged as a highly attractive destination for multinational firms seeking to expand their "global footprint" by outsourcing some functions, particularly if the firms serve both English- and Spanish-speaking customers. Swiss engineering and technology giant ABB chose Chile as the site of its first remote service centre. The centre provides real-time monitoring, diagnostic, and technical assistance for a number of ABB's businesses.[44]

DEVELOPING AN INTERNATIONAL MARKETING STRATEGY

global marketing strategy
Standardized marketing mix with minimal modifications that a firm uses in all of its domestic and foreign markets.

In developing a marketing mix, international marketers may choose between two alternative approaches: a global marketing strategy or a multi-domestic marketing strategy. A **global marketing strategy** defines a standard marketing mix and implements it with minimal modifications in all foreign markets. This approach brings the advantage of economies of scale to production and marketing activities. Procter & Gamble (P&G) marketers follow a global marketing strategy for Pringles potato chips, its leading export brand. P&G sells one product with a consistent formulation in every country and meets 80 percent of worldwide demand with only six flavours of Pringles and one package design. This standardized approach saves money since it allows large-scale production runs and reinforces the brand's image. In addition, a global strategy can foster collaborative innovation, as with the development of Pringles Stixx, an extension of the popular product line.[45]

A global marketing perspective can effectively market some goods and services to segments in many nations that share cultures and languages. This approach works especially well for products with strong, universal appeal such as McDonald's, luxury items like Rolex watches, and high-tech brands like Microsoft. Global advertising outlets, such as international editions of popular consumer and business magazines and international transmissions of TV channels such as CNN, MTV, and the CNBC financial network, help marketers deliver a single message to millions of global viewers.

A global marketing strategy can be highly effective for luxury products that target upscale consumers everywhere. Marketers of diamonds and luxury watches, for instance, typically use advertising with little or no copy—just a picture of a beautiful diamond or watch with the name discreetly displayed on the page.

But a global strategy doesn't always work, as Domino's Pizza discovered after it opened stores in Asia. With its "30 minutes or it's free" policy, the company has been known for the fastest pizzas rather than the best-tasting ones. Apparently for Asians, the 30-minute guarantee wasn't attractive enough to offset how the food tasted, and Domino's ended up closing more than 50 stores in Hong Kong, Indonesia, Singapore, and Thailand. Domino's learned from its mistakes. It developed a new recipe for its pizzas and re-entered the Singapore market.[46]

Source raw materials in Canada.
Research development in UK.
Ship packages to China.

With over 8000 experts worldwide, HSBC has the capability to provide you with on-the-ground connections to help you grow your business internationally. Working with your relationship manager, you will gain insights and discover how to navigate and understand the international marketplace.

Visit an HSBC branch today and speak to a Business Banking relationship manager.

Find out more at hsbc.ca/worldwide

HSBC Business

The world's local bank

Issued by HSBC Bank Canada

COURTESY OF HSBC BANK CANADA

HSBC promotes its worldwide strategy.

A major benefit of a global marketing strategy is its low cost to implement. Most firms, however, find it necessary to practise market segmentation outside their home markets and tailor their marketing mixes to fit the unique needs of customers in specific countries. This **multi-domestic marketing strategy** assumes that differences between market characteristics and competitive situations in certain nations require firms to customize their marketing decisions to effectively reach individual marketplaces. Many marketing experts believe that most products demand multi-domestic marketing strategies to give them realistic global marketing appeal. Cultural, geographic, language, and other differences simply make it difficult to send one message to many countries. Specific situations may allow marketers to standardise some parts of the marketing process but customize others.

multi-domestic marketing strategy
Application of market segmentation to foreign markets by tailoring the firm's marketing mix to match specific target markets in each nation.

INTERNATIONAL PRODUCT AND PROMOTIONAL STRATEGIES

Global marketers can choose from among five strategies for selecting the most appropriate product and promotion strategy for a specific foreign market: straight extension, promotion adaptation, product adaptation, dual adaptation, and product invention. As Figure 6.4 indicates, the strategies centre on whether to extend a domestic product and promotional strategy into international markets or adapt one or both to meet the target market's unique requirements.

A firm may follow a one-product, one-message straight extension strategy as part of a global marketing strategy. This strategy permits economies of scale in production and marketing. Also, successful implementation creates universal recognition of a product for consumers from country to country. FedEx's global advertising campaign, "FedEx Delivers to a Changing World," has run in Brazil, China, Germany, India, Mexico, South Korea, and the United Kingdom. The campaign highlights how FedEx helps businesses reach new markets and connect in sustainable ways.[47]

Other strategies call for product adaptation, promotion adaptation, or both. Marketers in the greeting card industry adapt their product and messaging to cultural differences. For example, Russians are unlikely to send a card to a man on his 40th birthday. Reason: a common superstition in Russia that says big parties for a man celebrating that milestone attract "the Death." In Japan, where the parent–child relationship is formal, cards intended for a parent are also formal and express less sentimentality. And most cultures outside North America don't respond to images of Santa Claus and the Easter Bunny.[48]

Finally, a firm may select product invention to take advantage of unique foreign market opportunities. To match user needs in developing nations, an appliance manufacturer might introduce a hand-powered washing machine even though such products became obsolete in industrialized countries years ago. Although Chapter 10 discusses the idea of branding in greater detail, it is important to note here the importance of a company's recognizable name, image, product, or even slogan around the world.

assessment check 5

5.1 What is a multinational corporation?

5.2 What is the difference between a global marketing strategy and a multi-domestic marketing strategy?

6 Describe the alternative marketing mix strategies used in global marketing and explain the attractiveness of Canada as a target for international marketers.

Marketoid

United States and Mexico accounted for over 76 percent of Canada's exports in 2010.

Product Strategy

Promotion Strategy		Same Product	Product Adaptation	New Product
	Same Promotion	**Straight Extension** General Mills Cheerios Coca-Cola Mars Snickers candy bar	**Product Adaptation** Campbell's soup	**Product Invention** Nonelectric sewing machines Manually operated washing machines
	Different Promotion	**Promotion Adaptation** Bicycles/motorcycles Outboard motors	**Dual Adaptation** Coffee Some clothing	

figure 6.4

Alternative International Product and Promotional Strategies

INTERNATIONAL DISTRIBUTION STRATEGY

Distribution is a vital aspect of overseas marketing. Marketers must set up proper channels and anticipate extensive physical distribution problems. Foreign markets may offer poor transportation systems and warehousing facilities—or none at all. Global marketers must adapt promptly and efficiently to these situations to profit from overseas sales.

A distribution decision involves two steps. First, the firm must decide on a method of entering the foreign market. Second, it must determine how to distribute the product within the foreign market through that entry channel. Daimler AG had been marketing its subcompact car, the smart fortwo, through its Mercedes-Benz division in Canada and Europe. Seeing Americans' growing interest in fuel-efficient cars, Daimler decided to enter the U.S. market, establishing smart USA, with headquarters in a Detroit suburb.

PRICING STRATEGY

Pricing can critically affect the success of an overall marketing strategy for foreign markets. Considerable competitive, economic, political, and legal constraints often limit pricing decisions. Global marketers can succeed if they thoroughly understand these requirements.

Companies must adapt their pricing strategies to local markets and change them when conditions change. In India, Unilever's partner Hindustan Lever offers "penny packets" of shampoo to lower-income consumers, who typically cannot afford to buy an entire bottle of shampoo. Although local firms follow the same practice, Hindustan Lever wants to develop loyalty among these consumers so that if they move up the income scale, they will be more apt to buy the firm's higher-priced products as well.

An important development in pricing strategy for international marketing has been the emergence of commodity marketing organizations that seek to control prices through collective action. The Organization of Petroleum Exporting Countries (OPEC) is a good example of this kind of collective export organization.

COUNTERTRADE

countertrade
Form of exporting whereby goods and services are bartered rather than sold for cash.

In a growing number of nations, the only way a marketer can gain access to foreign markets is through **countertrade**—a form of exporting in which a firm barters products rather than selling them for cash. Less-developed nations sometimes impose countertrade requirements when they lack sufficient foreign currency to attain goods and services they want or need from exporting countries. These countries allow sellers to exchange their products only for domestic products as a way to control their balance-of-trade problems.

Countertrade became popular two decades ago, when companies wanted to conduct business in eastern European countries and the former Soviet Union. Those governments did not allow exchanges of hard currency, so this form of barter facilitated trade. PepsiCo made one of the largest countertrades ever when it exchanged $3 billion worth of Pepsi Cola for Russian Stolichnaya vodka, a cargo ship, and tankers from the former Soviet Union.

CANADA AS A TARGET FOR INTERNATIONAL MARKETERS

Foreign marketers regard Canada as an inviting target. It offers access to the North American markets, high levels of discretionary income, political stability, a generally favourable attitude toward foreign investment, and a relatively well-controlled economy.

Among the best-known industries in which foreign manufacturers have established Canadian production facilities is automobiles. Most of the world's leading auto companies have built assembly plants here. America's big three automakers (Ford, General Motors, and Chrysler) and Japan's (Honda and Toyota) all have manufacturing plants in Canada. In a recent year just under 2 million cars were produced in Canada, employing roughly 400 000 people in jobs either directly or indirectly related to the industry. In fact, Canada's automotive industry is ranked eighth in the world.[49]

Foreign car manufacturers have taken advantage of Canadian consumers' desire for foreign cars by locating many new assembly plants in Canada. This assembly-line worker is employed in Toyota's plant in Cambridge, Ontario.

Canada is a country rich in natural resources that are in demand worldwide as manufacturing increases in many areas of the world. This makes companies in the natural resource sector attractive for foreign investment. It is also one area of foreign investment that is meeting with some resistance and calls for caution from Canadian business leaders. Business leaders have been warning for years that foreign ownership of resources, telecommunications, and infrastructure-related companies could cause problems for Canada in the future.[50]

All the concern over foreign ownership and foreign companies investing in Canada may be academic, however. Foreign investors continue to purchase Canadian companies, invest in Canadian stocks, and purchase Canadian bonds.

assessment check 6

6.1 What are the five strategies for selecting the most appropriate product and promotion strategy for a specific international market?

6.2 What is countertrade?

6.3 What characteristics of Canada make it an inviting target for international marketers?

Strategic Implications

The first decade of the new century has marked a new era of truly global marketing, in which the world's marketplaces are accessible to nearly every firm. Marketers in both small, localized firms and giant businesses need to re-evaluate the strengths and weaknesses of their current marketing practices and realign their plans to meet the new demands of this era.

Marketers are the pioneers in bringing new technologies to developing nations. Their successes and failures will determine the direction global marketing will take and the speed with which it will be embraced. Actions of international marketers will influence every component of the marketing environments: competitive, economic, social-cultural, political-legal, and technological.

The greatest competitive advantages will belong to those marketers who capitalize on the similarities of their target markets and adapt to the differences. In some instances, the actions of marketers today help determine the rules and regulations of tomorrow.

Marketers need flexible and broad views of an increasingly complex customer. Goods and services will likely become more customized as they are introduced in foreign markets—yet some recognizable brands seem to remain universally popular just as they are. New and better products in developing markets will create and maintain relationships for the future. ◆◆◆

REVIEW OF CHAPTER OBJECTIVES

① **Describe the importance of global marketing from the perspectives of the individual firm and the nation.**

Global marketing expands a company's market, allows firms to grow, and makes them less dependent on their own country's economy for success. For the nation, global trade provides a source of needed raw materials and other products not available domestically in sufficient amounts, opens up new markets to serve with domestic output, and converts countries and their citizens into partners in the search for high-quality products at the lowest possible prices. Companies find that global marketing and international trade can help them meet customer demand, reduce certain costs, provide information on markets around the world, and increase employment.

② **Identify the major components of the environment for global marketing.**

The major components of the international environment are competitive, economic, social-cultural, political-legal, and technological. A country's infrastructure also plays an important role in determining how effective marketers will be in manufacturing, promoting, and distributing their goods and services.

③ **Outline the basic functions of GATT, WTO, NAFTA, FTAA, and the European Union.**

The General Agreement on Tariffs and Trade is an accord that has substantially reduced tariffs. The World Trade Organization oversees GATT agreements, mediates disputes, and tries to reduce trade barriers throughout the world. The North American Free Trade Agreement removes trade restrictions among Canada, Mexico, and the United States. The Free Trade Area of the Americas seeks to create a free trade area covering the entire Western Hemisphere. The European Union is a customs union whose goal is to remove all barriers to free trade among its members.

④ **Identify the alternative strategies for entering international markets.**

Several strategies are available to marketers, including exporting, importing, franchising, foreign licensing, subcontracting, and direct investment. This progression moves from the least to the most involvement by a firm.

⑤ **Differentiate between a global marketing strategy and a multi-domestic marketing strategy.**

A global marketing strategy defines a standard marketing mix and implements it with minimal modifications in all foreign markets. A multi-domestic marketing strategy requires firms to customize their marketing decisions to reach individual marketplaces.

⑥ **Describe the alternative marketing mix strategies used in global marketing and explain the attractiveness of Canada as a target market for international marketers.**

Product and promotional strategies include the following: straight extension, promotion adaptation, product adaptation, dual adaptation, and product invention. Marketers may also choose among distribution, pricing, and countertrade strategies.

Canada is attractive as a target market for marketers because it is close to the United States and has high levels of discretionary income, political stability, a relatively favourable attitude toward foreign investment, and a relatively well controlled economy.

assessment check answers

1.1 Define importing and exporting.

Importing involves purchasing foreign goods and services. Exporting refers to marketing domestically produced goods and services abroad.

1.2 What must global marketers be able to do effectively to reach international markets?

Global marketers must be able to adapt their goods and services to local preferences.

2.1 What are the three criteria that determine a nation's prospects as a host for international business expansion?

A nation's size, per-capita income, and stage of economic development determine its prospects as a host for international business expansion.

2.2 What are the two major categories of trade barriers?

The two categories of trade barriers are tariffs and nontariffs.

3.1 What is the World Trade Organization (WTO)?

The World Trade Organization (WTO) oversees GATT agreements and mediates disputes. It also continues efforts to reduce trade barriers around the world.

3.2 What countries are parties to NAFTA?

The United States, Canada, and Mexico are parties to NAFTA.

3.3 What is the goal of the European Union (EU)?

The European Union seeks to remove all barriers to free trade among its members and strengthen its position in the world as an economic and political power.

4.1 What are the three basic strategies for entering international markets?

The three basic strategies are importing and exporting, contractual agreements, and international direct investment.

4.2 What is a franchise?

A franchise is a contractual agreement in which a wholesaler or retailer (the franchisee) agrees to meet the operating requirements of a manufacturer or other franchiser.

4.3 What is international direct investment?

International direct investment is direct investment in foreign firms, production, and marketing facilities.

5.1 What is a multinational corporation?

A multinational corporation is a firm with significant operations and marketing activities outside the home country.

5.2 What is the difference between a global marketing strategy and a multi-domestic marketing strategy?

A global marketing strategy defines a marketing mix and implements it with minimal modifications in all foreign markets. A multi-domestic marketing strategy requires that firms customize their marketing decisions to reach individual marketplaces.

6.1 What are the five strategies for selecting the most appropriate product and promotion strategy for a specific international market?

The five strategies are the following: straight extension, promotion adaptation, product adaptation, dual adaptation, and product invention.

6.2 What is countertrade?

Countertrade is a form of exporting in which a firm barters products rather than selling them for cash.

6.3 What characteristics of Canada make it an inviting target for international marketers?

Canada is an inviting target because it offers access to the North American markets, has high levels of discretionary income, has political stability, has a generally favourable attitude toward foreign investment, and has a relatively well-controlled economy.

MARKETING TERMS YOU NEED TO KNOW

These terms are printed in red in the text. They are defined in the margins of the chapter and in the Glossary that begins on p. G-1.

exporting 172
importing 172
exchange rate 176
political risk assessment (PRA) 178
ISO (International Organization for Standardization) certification 178
tariff 180
Revenue tariffs 180
Protective tariffs 180
import quotas 180
embargo 181

subsidy 181
Exchange control 181
dumping 182
free trade area 182
customs union 182
common market 182
General Agreement on Tariffs and Trade (GATT) 184
World Trade Organization (WTO) 184
North American Free Trade Agreement (NAFTA) 184

Free Trade Area of the Americas (FTAA) 184
European Union (EU) 185
franchise 188
foreign licensing 188
subcontracting 188
multinational corporation 189
global marketing strategy 190
multi-domestic marketing strategy 191
countertrade 192

PROJECT AND TEAM WORK EXERCISES

1. Imagine that you and a classmate are marketers for one of the following companies: Apple Inc., Burger King, General Mills, or Mattel Toys. Choose one of the following markets into which your company could expand: Mexico, India, or China. Research the country's infrastructure, social-cultural environment, technological environment, and any trade barriers your firm might encounter. Then present your findings to the class, with a conclusion on whether you think the expansion would be beneficial.

2. Assume that you work for KFC, which already has outlets around the world. With a classmate, identify a country that KFC has not yet reached and write a brief plan for entering that country's market. Then create a print ad for that market (you can write the ad copy in English). It may be helpful to visit KFC's website for some ideas.

3. Rio de Janeiro, Brazil, is hosting the 2016 Summer Olympics. By yourself or with a classmate, identify a company that might benefit from promoting its goods or services at the Rio de Janeiro Olympics. In a presentation, describe which strategy you would use: straight extension, product or promotion adaptation, dual adaptation, or product invention.

4. Suppose you work for a firm that is getting ready to introduce a tablet computer to the Chinese marketplace. With a classmate, decide which strategies your firm could use most effectively for entering this market. Present your ideas either in writing or to the class.

5. Chinese automaker Geely (pronounced *jeely*) announced plans to enter the North American market. With a classmate, research Geely to find out more about the cars, then create an ad for the firm, targeting Canadian consumers.

CRITICAL-THINKING EXERCISES

1. Few elements in the global marketing environment are more difficult to overcome than the unexpected, such as natural disasters or outbreaks of disease such as the avian flu. Travel may be curtailed or halted by law, by a breakdown in infrastructure, or simply by fear on the part of consumers. Suppose you work for a firm that has resorts on several continents. As a marketer, what kinds of contingency plans might you recommend for your firm in the event of an unexpected disaster?

2. Zippo lighters have been around for decades. But as the number of smokers in Canada continues to decline, Zippo has spent the last half century scouting the world for new markets. Today, Zippo is a status symbol among Chinese consumers, who prefer North American products. To reduce the sale of made-in-China knockoffs, Zippo's ads show Chinese consumers how to identify a real Zippo. In addition, Zippo has worked with government officials to find a safe way to package its lighters for air travel. Both of these examples demonstrate a firm adapting to requirements of a new marketplace. Do you think a global marketing strategy or a multi-domestic strategy would work best if Zippo decided to enter other markets? Explain the reasons for your choice.

3. Do you agree with the goals and ideas of the proposed FTAA? Why or why not?

4. Do you agree with countertrade as a legitimate form of conducting business? Why or why not? Describe a countertrade agreement that Microsoft might make in another country.

5. Foreign investment continues to grow in Canada. Do you think this is a positive trend for Canadian businesses and consumers? Why or why not?

ETHICS EXERCISE

Cheap—and illegal—copies of pirated popular movies, video games, and music are often available for sale in Asia within days of their worldwide release. The entertainment industry has so far had little success in stopping the flow of these copies into consumers' hands. Do you think multinational economic communities should be more effective at combating piracy? Why or why not? What actions could they take?

INTERNET EXERCISES

1. **Chinese currency policy.** Critics contend that the Chinese government pursues policies that keep the value of the Chinese currency artificially low relative to other currencies such as the Canadian and U.S. dollars and the euro. Using Google News and other online news sources, research the current state of Chinese currency policy. Why would the Chinese government engage in such efforts? What impact do these efforts have on global trade? Assume you work for a Canadian-based firm that engages in extensive trading operations with China. What impact would a major revaluation of the Chinese currency have on your firm? Would the impact be the same if you were a U.S.-based firm? http://news.google.com

2. **Global marketing strategies.** Samsung—the Korean-based electronics company—has been quite successful over the past ten years at marketing its products worldwide. Visit the Samsung website and note two or three elements of the firm's global marketing strategy. Next, visit the websites of two other global electronics companies, such as Sony or Philips. Compare and contrast the marketing strategies used by all three companies.

   www.samsung.com
   www.philips.com
   www.sony.com

3. **World statistics.** The *CIA World Factbook* contains a wide range of information and statistics on individual countries. Go to the website listed below. Click on "Guide to Country Comparisons." Then click on the relevant section to obtain the top five countries in each of the following:
   a. per-capita GDP
   b. real growth in GDP
   c. inflation rate
   d. exports
   e. population growth rate
      https://www.cia.gov/library/publications/the-world-factbook/

Note: Internet Web addresses change frequently. If you don't find the exact site listed, you may need to access the organization's home page and search from there or use a search engine such as Google.

CASE 6.1

General Motors: Revved Up in China

For General Motors, the financial crisis will be a time to remember. A global recession—triggering massive layoffs, widespread unemployment, and faltering consumer confidence—sent cars sales plummeting. Recognizing that GM's demise would create a catastrophic ripple effect in the North American economy, the U.S. and Canadian federal governments and the government of Ontario pledged billions in bailout money to keep the giant automaker afloat.

During this time of financial hardship, GM had one bright spot: its performance in China. The world's largest and mostly untapped market for automobiles, China saw continued economic growth despite a worldwide recession, a claim few other nations could make.

GM has had operations in China for decades. Over time, the business grew to comprise nine joint ventures, two wholly owned firms, and over 30 000 employees making cars, trucks, and vans for a burgeoning Chinese middle class.

In addition to its Chinese brands Wuling and Jiefang, GM markets some names familiar to North American consumers: Buick, Cadillac, and Chevrolet. But a number of its best-selling models are made and sold only in Asia, including a group of fuel-efficient Chevys: the Spark and the Epica, a midsized sedan. Two other models—the Cruze, a small sedan, and the Aveo, hatchback—were first introduced in Asia but have since made it onto the North American market.

In one year China saw overall car-sales increases of 32 percent to over 18 million units. These record sales made China the largest vehicle market in the world and General Motors is benefiting. GM has been selling over 200 000 vehicles a month in this market. Experts predict car sales may slow over the short term as China removes some of its incentives. China had been supporting new car sales with a reduced tax incentive on small cars and a subsidiary on vehicle trade-ins for those Chinese living in rural areas.

General Motors currently estimates that it has just less than 15 percent market share in the Chinese vehicle market. The company plans to increase this market share figure by introducing 60 new or improved car models in this market over the next five years. Production of these new models has been made possible by GM's heavy investment in China. General Motors invests about $1 billion annually in this market. Recently the company entered into a $300-million joint venture with state-owned FAW Group to build light-duty trucks and vans. An estimated 200 000 vehicles are expected to roll off the assembly line after the first year of production, with future plans to export from the Chinese assembly plants.

In some respects, GM's success in China helped blunt the pain of the near collapse of the automaker. However, with the cars GM sells in China priced considerably less—pickups and vans range from $4000 to $7000—revenues from North American sales remain higher.

Some of General Motors' financial problems are the same issues faced by vehicle manufacturers around the world. The industry is manufacturing too many vehicles for the worldwide demand. The supply and demand problem has been made worse by the high levels of personal debt North American consumers are experiencing. Approximately two-thirds of all new car sales are financed, and with the recession many North American consumers are having difficulty obtaining the financing required to purchase new vehicles. High oil prices are prompting many consumers to purchase smaller cars, and although General Motors produces some smaller cars it also produces many larger car models. Another problem for General Motors is the fact that Honda and Toyota, once viewed as imports, are now manufactured in North America, and consumers now consider them domestic manufacturers.

General Motors has been working hard to overcome its problems but some experts feel it will be many years before the company is truly out of the woods; however, its strategy for the Chinese market is definitely helping the company.

Questions for Critical Thinking

1. Through overseas expansion, General Motors takes advantage of untapped markets. But that strategy came under criticism after the company received bailout money from the Canadian and U.S. governments. Do you think the criticism was warranted? Why or why not?
2. GM plans to introduce some of the car models made in China into the North American market. How do you think the

cars will be received? What advice would you give management about this strategy?

Sources: "General Motors China April Vehicle Sales Fall After Incentive Removed," Bloomberg News website, http://www.bloomberg.com, May 5, 2011; Matthew McClearn, "The Good, the Bad and the Ugly: General Motors of Canada Ltd.," Canadian Business website, http://www.canadianbusiness.com, May 24, 2011; General Motors website, "General Motors Sets February Sales Record in China," press release, http://media.gm.com, March 4, 2010; GM China website, http://www.gmchina.com, March 4, 2010; Joseph Szczesny, "Buick Drives Up Sales in China," *Morning Sun*, http://themorningsun.com, February 7, 2010; Elaine Kurtenbach, "GM's China Sales Nearly Double in January," *The Globe and Mail*, http://www.theglobeandmail.com, February 4, 2010; Peter Whoriskey, "GM Sales in China Surge 67 Percent in 2009," *The Washington Post*, http://www.washingtonpost.com, January 5, 2010; Alison Leung, "GM Sees Sales Growth Slowing in 2010," Reuters, http://reuters.com, November 22, 2009; Norihiko Shirouzu and Patricia Jiayi Ho, "GM Launches Trust Venture in China," *The Wall Street Journal*, http://online.wsj.com, August 31, 2009; Norihiko Shirouzu, "GM China Set to Expand Reach," pbs.org, http://www.pbs.org, August 14, 2009; Peter Whoriskey, "GM Emerges from Bankruptcy after Landmark Government Bailout," *The Washington Post*, http://www.washingtonpost.com, July 10, 2009.

CASE 6.2

Research In Motion

Research In Motion (RIM) is one company that understands how challenging international marketing can be but also how important it is to the success of the company.

In 1984 two friends, Mike Lazaridis and Mike Fregin, started a new business—RIM. Starting out with a $15 000 loan from Mike's parents and an equal amount from a Government of Ontario program to help young entrepreneurs get started, the two rented a two-room office and began inventing technology-related products.

Some of the company's early products involved electronic signs that could have the messages changed remotely. These early products provided the much-needed capital for the company to continue developing new products. Other early products include an electronic film counter for the National Film Board of Canada and controllers for manufacturing companies.

It wasn't until the early nineties that RIM started working on its wireless network technology. One of its first major sales involving wireless technology was modems for pager networks. The sale was to Ericsson. In contrast to RIM, Ericsson has been in the telecommunications business since 1876. Ericsson is still a major player in international telecommunications with more than 40 percent of the world's mobile telecommunications traffic passing through its networks. Ericsson is a Swedish company with some impressive numbers—customers in more than 180 countries, 27 000 patents registered—and through their many networks they manage more than 700 million subscribers.

RIM's first hand-held device was the RIM900. This device was built with Intel parts, ran on batteries, but did have a keyboard. The device was large and heavy compared to today's smartphone technology but the launch of the RIM900 brought some new opportunities and challenges for RIM. Orders for the

device started to roll in, some in the millions of dollars. However, production of the RIM900, along with the production of its other products, began to put pressure on its finances. The pressure was compounded when some of its international customers were slow in paying RIM for the products they ordered.

At the same time, success from the innovative products RIM was producing drew the attention of its competitors. RIM had several options at this point. It could have sold out to one of its major competitors, increased its loans from the banks, or investigated the possibilities of issuing shares for the first time. Up to this point, the company ownership had been in the hands of Lazaridis, Fregin, and a new addition to the senior management team, Jim Balsillie. Balsillie had been hired by the company as vice president of finance and business but quickly stepped into the role of co-CEO. Balsillie's investment of $125 000 gave him 33 percent ownership, leaving Lazaridis with 40 percent. The remainder of the company was owned by Fregin and another employee. In order to solve its money concerns, the company decided to increase its bank loans and issue shares for the first time.

By 1997 the company had entered into another major stage of its development. The second generation of the pager, the RIM 950, was developed and launched onto the market. Sales were in the millions of dollars. The company opened its first manufacturing plant and now had 100 employees. The new pager was being bought by American companies, and in Canada Rogers started to carry the new product. The launch of the RIM 950 also brought the first of a long list of awards for the company when the pager was named one the hottest new gadgets of the year.

Just two years later, in 1999, the first BlackBerry was launched. The main customers for the first BlackBerrys were business executives. Executives loved the idea of being able to communicate with their offices with a product that was so easy to use and convenient. The success of the Blackberry also meant the company needed more money to keep expanding its production facilities. It was around this time that the company listed its stocks on the Nasdaq, the American stock market dedicated to technology companies.

The company continued to expand. New versions of the BlackBerry hit the market, subscribers were in the thousands, production and office facilities continued to expand, and the company easily survived the dotcom meltdown.

Not everything was going the way the company wanted, however. The company was faced with a patent lawsuit from NTP, an American company. The case dragged on, and at one point a U.S. judge ruled that no more Blackberrys could be sold in the United States. This patent lawsuit and another were eventually settled by the company but cost them hundreds of millions of dollars.

An even greater threat to the company came when United Arab Emirates (UAE) declared a total ban on BlackBerry usage. Their concern was security—the Blackberry has such effective data security that communication over them could not be monitored by the UAE government. The policy only applies to corporate BlackBerry customers that use the ultra-secure BlackBerry Enterprise Server system. Data travelling over this system are encrypted, making it difficult for governments, or anyone else, to monitor. BlackBerry consumers using the less secure Internet Service would not be affected by the UAE regulations. RIM was able to persuade the UAE government not to enact such sweeping regulations but new regulations being considered could affect not only RIM's product but all smartphone devices.

It is important that RIM sort out international problems like the one it experienced with UAE because the majority of the company's income comes from international sales. According to the company's annual report in 2011, Canada accounted for 7 percent of the company's revenue, the U.S. another 39 percent, the United Kingdom about 11 percent, and over 40 percent came from other countries around the world.

RIM is not resting on its success with the BlackBerry. In order to capture some of the growing tablet market, RIM developed the BlackBerry Playbook.

Some say that RIM may not be able to sustain its brilliant performance of the past. Critics cite the fact that the iPhone and other smartphone products are outselling the BlackBerry. One of the reasons some cite for the move to the iPhone is that there are more applications available for it. Others critics say that RIM has a habit of over-promising on what its new technology can do and then the new devices do not live up to the customer's expectations.

RIM has a large number of supporters in the marketplace who say the company is doing everything right. They point to the company's balance sheet. RIM has cash in its bank accounts and no debt. The company also spends heavily on research and development, more than most companies in the technology business. One of the most important reasons given for why RIM will succeed in the future is that it has a better product. Given all the problems companies have had in the past with their computer systems being hacked, RIM's high-security encryption system seems a better bet for companies.

With the company's incredible successes in the past, it would seem a little early to be writing the company off just yet. The company has had sound business practices in the past and is likely to continue.

Questions for Critical Thinking

1. How should RIM market its products internationally? Do you think it is important for RIM to have different marketing strategies for different countries? Why or why not?
2. What challenges will RIM face in the future when selling its products overseas?

Sources: RIM company website, http://www.rim.com, May 30, 2011; Ericsson company website, http://www.ericsson.com, May 30, 2011; RIM Annual Report 2011; Adam Schreck, "RIM Says Any New Smartphone Curbs in UAE Would Apply to Others Too," *Canadian Business*, http://www.canadianbusiness.com, April 17, 2011; Henry Blodget, "RIM Is Dead," *Canadian Business*, June 13, 2011, pp. 30–32; Nick Waddell, "Long Live RIM," *Canadian Business*, June 13, 2011, pp. 31–33; Trevor Melanson, "Interactive: 25 Years of RIM," *Canadian Business*, http://www.canadianbusiness.com, May 18, 2011.

TARGET MARKET SELECTION

chapter 7

Marketing Research, Decision Support Systems, and Sales Forecasting

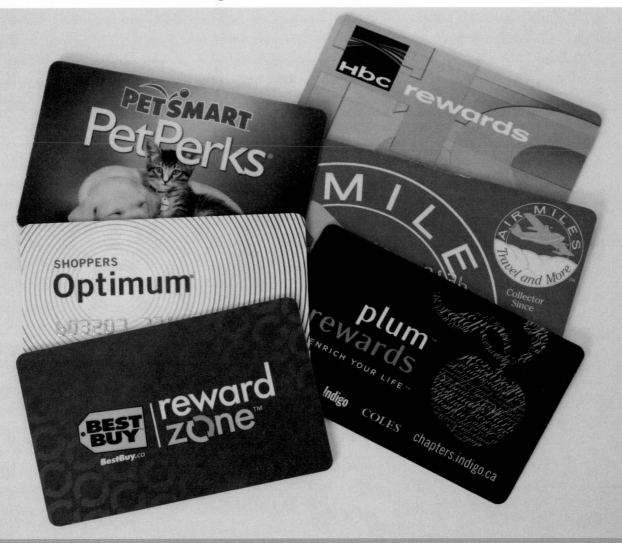

© JULIE PRATT

CHAPTER OBJECTIVES

(1) Describe the development of the marketing research function and its major activities.

(2) Explain the steps in the marketing research process.

(3) Distinguish between primary and secondary data and identify the sources of each type.

(4) Explain the different sampling techniques used by marketing researchers and identify the methods by which marketing researchers collect primary data.

(5) Explain the challenges of conducting marketing research in global markets and outline the most important uses of computer technology in marketing research.

(6) Identify the major types of forecasting methods.

POINTS CARDS OR MARKET RESEARCH

Air Miles, Petro-Points, and Canadian Tire Options are all examples of loyalty programs in which customers collect points that they later redeem for a product or service. Are these programs put in place to build customer loyalty or to collect information about customers? The simple answer is both. A properly designed loyalty program should be a tool for collecting and analyzing data on the customers who use them.

Loyalty programs have been around since the early 1980s but in Canada one of the oldest is Air Mile Rewards. Air Mile Rewards was started in the early 1990s by a Toronto-based company, Loyalty Group, with 13 organizations signing on. When companies join together for loyalty programs, as with Air Miles, they share the operations and marketing costs but they also share in the ongoing market research.

Canadians like loyalty programs so there is lots of information to share. Canada has one of the highest participation rates of all countries, second only to Britain, where these programs are offered. Roughly 94 percent of Canadians collect points in at least one scheme, and on average each Canadian home participates in over nine loyalty points programs.

Many companies that have loyalty programs collect information on each transaction or sale made by the card holder. Matching the transaction information to each customer's demographic information that customers provide when they sign on to the loyalty program allows companies to build profiles of individual consumer spending patterns. This information can then be used to group customers into segments. Researchers look for several characteristics when analyzing the transactions customers make. They are interested in when a customer last used his or her loyalty card and how often the card was used. The amount of each transaction is another important piece of information that allows companies to better understand their customers. This information helps companies determine who their best customers are, helps them develop marketing strategies to reach different customer groups, and allows them to determine what future purchasing patterns may look like.

Some companies match the transactional data available from loyalty card transactions with other research such as what customers' attitudes are toward the products and services offered by the company. One company that performs research to match customer spending patterns on their loyalty cards with their attitudes is Air Canada's Aeroplan program. The Aeroplan program goes even further with its research. The researchers look at what partner companies the customers interact with as well as the type of rewards each consumer gets with the points he or she has accumulated.

Loyalty programs can influence customer behaviour. The outcome most companies want from their loyalty programs would be a long-term relationship with the customer, but not all loyalty programs achieve this goal. Research shows that 36 percent of customers will change the brands they buy in order to achieve a higher number of points, and 42 percent will alter the time and place where they make a purchase in order to gain more points. Even more important to companies is the fact that 61 percent of customers are more likely to continue doing business with companies in whose loyalty programs they participate.

Companies participating in these loyalty programs reap benefits in addition to the valuable research on their customers' spending patterns. The information provided assists companies in designing communications programs that can build better relationships with their customers. Collecting loyalty points provides everyone involved with advantages: companies get loyal customers and valuable research and consumers get rewarded for purchases they make.[1]

---

connecting with customers

At first glance a loyalty program is a method for rewarding and encouraging repeat purchases. These programs have other benefits for the customers. As they amass more and more points, customers are building an emotional attachment to the companies and the brands the companies sell.

Chapter Overview

COLLECTING and managing information about what customers need and want is a challenging task for any marketer. **Marketing research** is the process of collecting and using information for marketing decision making. Data come from a variety of sources. Some results come from well-planned studies designed to elicit specific information. Other valuable information comes from sales force reports, accounting records, and published reports. Still other data emerge from controlled experiments and computer simulations.

marketing research
Process of collecting and using information for marketing decision making.

Thanks to new database technologies, some data that companies collect are compiled for them through their loyalty programs. Marketing research, by presenting pertinent information in a useful format, aids decision makers in analyzing data and in suggesting possible actions.

This chapter discusses the marketing research function. Marketers use research to understand their customers, target customer segments, and develop long-term customer relationships—all keys to profitability. Information

Marketoid

The annual Survey of Household Spending was introduced in Canada in 1997.

collected through marketing research underlies much of the material on market segmentation discussed in the following chapter. Clearly, the marketing research function is the primary source of the information needed to make effective marketing decisions. The use of technology to mine data and gather business and competitive intelligence is also discussed, as is technology's vast impact on marketing research decision making and planning. This chapter also explains how marketing research techniques are used to make accurate sales forecasts, a critical component of marketing planning. ◆◆◆

---

① Describe the development of the marketing research function and its major activities.

THE MARKETING RESEARCH FUNCTION

Before looking at how marketing research is conducted, we must first examine its historical development, the people and organizations it involves, and the activities it entails. Because an underlying purpose of research is to find out more about consumers, research is clearly central to effective customer satisfaction and customer relationship programs. Media technologies such as the Internet and virtual reality are opening up new channels through which researchers can tap into consumer information.

DEVELOPMENT OF THE MARKETING RESEARCH FUNCTION

More than 130 years have passed since the first organized marketing research project was undertaken in 1879. A second important milestone in the development of marketing research occurred 32 years later, when the first commercial research department was organized at Curtis Publishing, publishers of *The Saturday Evening Post.*

Most early research gathered little more than written testimonials from purchasers of firms' products. Research methods became more sophisticated during the 1930s as the development of statistical techniques led to refinements in sampling procedures and greater accuracy in research findings.

In recent years, advances in computer technology have significantly changed the complexion of marketing research. Besides accelerating the pace and broadening the base of data collection, computers have aided marketers in making informed decisions about problems and opportunities. Simulations, for example, allow marketers to evaluate alternatives by posing "what-if" questions. Marketing researchers at many consumer goods firms simulate product introductions through computer programs to determine whether to risk real-world product launches or even to subject products to test marketing.

WHO CONDUCTS MARKETING RESEARCH?

The size and organizational form of the marketing research function are usually tied to the structure of the company. Some firms organize research units to support different product lines, brands, or geographic areas. Others organize their research functions according to the types of research they need performed, such as sales analysis, new-product development, advertising evaluation, or sales forecasting.

Many firms outsource their research needs and thus depend on independent marketing research firms. These independent organizations might specialize in handling just part of a larger study, such as conducting consumer interviews. Firms can also contract out entire research studies.

Marketers usually decide whether to conduct a study internally or through an outside organization based on cost. Another major consideration is the reliability and accuracy of the information collected by an outside organization. Because collecting marketing data is what these outside organizations do full time, the information they gather is often more thorough and accurate than that collected by less experienced in-house staff. Often, an outside marketing research firm can provide technical assistance and expertise not available within the company's marketing department. Interaction with outside suppliers also helps to ensure that a researcher does not conduct a study only to validate a favourite viewpoint or preferred option.

Many people who perform marketing research, whether they work for a specialized marketing research company or within the marketing area of a company, belong to the Marketing Research and Intelligence Association (MRIA). The Marketing Research and Intelligence Association is a Canadian not-for-profit association representing all aspects of the market intelligence and survey research industry, including social research, competitive intelligence, data mining, insight, and knowledge management. Members include over 1800 practitioners, small to large research houses, and the many buyers of research services, such as financial institutions, major retailers, insurance companies, and manufacturers. The industry accounts for almost three-quarters of a billion dollars in market research activities annually.

Some companies combine their market research with environmental issues as described in the "Go Green" feature.

GO GREEN | Loyalty Cards Go Green

THE Air Miles Reward Program, owned by LoyaltyOne Inc., has been providing millions of Canadians with loyalty points every time they purchase a product or service at one of their partner companies since 1994. The program boasts that almost 66 percent of Canadian households collect Air Mile points.

In reviewing research that involved over 2000 participants across the country, the company determined that over 90 percent of Canadians felt it was important to purchase green products in order to help the environment. Another study revealed that 54 percent of respondents would purchase green products if there was a strong enough incentive to do so, such as bonus points on their Air Miles account. To satisfy these customers, LoyaltyOne Inc. launched the "My Planet" program.

The aim of the My Planet program was to reduce carbon dioxide emissions and harmful chemicals and to conserve natural resources. The company turned to TerraChoice, the green marketing firm, to help them determine the criteria for products to be included. Members of the My Planet program also have access to a Web-based learning centre that provides information on how to make better environmental choices in every part of their lives.

LoyaltyOne Inc. not only has programs to encourage others to be environmentally friendly but the company was named as one of Canada's Greenest Employers. The company has several programs in place that show they are serious about the environment, including a new state-of-the-art building with one of the largest rooftop solar installations. The company also has several other programs such as work from home, subsidized transit, and zero-waste initiatives.

LoyaltyOne Inc. is one company that not only promotes environmental awareness but also puts their commitment into action.

Sources: Company website, http://loyalty.com, June 18, 2011; Kristina Leung and Richard Yerema, "LoyaltyOne Inc.: Chosen as One of Canada's Greenest Employers for 2011," http://www.eluta.ca, April 20, 2011; Jeromy Lloyd, "Air Miles Takes My Planet In-Store," *Marketing*, http://www.marketingmag.ca, September 22, 2009.

MARKETING RESEARCH AND INTELLIGENCE ASSOCIATION

Marketing research companies range in size from sole proprietorships to national and international firms such as ACNielsen. They can be classified as syndicated services, full-service suppliers, or limited-service suppliers, depending on the types of services they offer to clients. Some full-service organizations are also willing to take on limited-service activities.

The Marketing Research and Intelligence Association is a not-for-profit association with chapters across Canada representing all aspects of the research industry.

syndicated service
Organization that provides standardized data to all customers.

Syndicated Services

An organization that regularly provides a standardised set of data to all customers is called a **syndicated service**. Companies providing syndicated product research may base their reports on personal interviews, exposure to advertising, or point-of-sale scanner data captured from a retail store. Clients include advertisers, advertising agencies, magazines, newspapers, broadcasters, and cable TV networks.

One syndicated service provider is J. D. Power and Associates, a global marketing information firm that specializes in surveying customer satisfaction, product quality, and buyer behaviour. Among its customers are companies in the telecommunications, travel and hotel, marine, utilities, health care, building, consumer electronics, automotive, and financial services industries.[2]

COURTESY ENVIRONICS

Environics is a full-service marketing research firm.

Full-Service Research Suppliers

An organization that contracts with clients to conduct complete marketing research projects is called a **full-service research supplier**. Environics Research Group, which has offices across Canada and the United States, is an example of a full-service company.[3] A full-service supplier becomes the client's marketing research arm, performing all the steps in the marketing research process (discussed later in this chapter).

full-service research supplier Marketing research organization that contracts with clients to conduct complete marketing research projects.

limited-service research supplier Marketing research firm that specializes in a limited number of research activities, such as conducting field interviews or performing data processing.

Limited-Service Research Suppliers

A marketing research firm that specializes in a limited number of activities, such as conducting field interviews or performing data processing, is called a **limited-service research supplier**. Nielsen Media Research specializes in tracking what people watch on TV, and who watches what, in more than 30 countries.[4] The firm also prepares studies to help clients develop advertising strategies and to track awareness and interest. Syndicated services can also be considered a type of limited-service research supplier.

Customer Satisfaction Measurement Programs

In their marketing research, firms often focus on tracking the satisfaction levels of current customers. For example, one research firm charges a monthly fee and provides services such as designing and managing a firm's customer feedback area on its website to moderating online discussion groups and analyzing comments.[5] Some marketers have gained valuable insights by tracking the dissatisfaction that led customers to abandon certain products for those of competitors. Some customer defections are only partial; customers may remain somewhat satisfied with a business but not completely satisfied. Such attitudes could lead them to take their business elsewhere. Studying the underlying causes of customer defections, even partial defections, can be useful for identifying problem areas that need attention.

Some organizations conduct their own measurement programs through online polls and surveys. Some fast-food restaurants and retailers have their employees point out special codes printed on their receipts. Entering the code on the company website brings up a customer satisfaction survey that offers respondents a chance to win prizes.

assessment check 1

1.1 Identify the different classifications of marketing research suppliers and explain how they differ from one another.

1.2 What research methods can be used to measure customer satisfaction?

THE MARKETING RESEARCH PROCESS

As discussed earlier, business executives rely on marketing research to provide the information they need to make effective decisions regarding their firm's current and future activities. The chances of making good decisions improve when the right information is provided at the right time during decision making. To achieve this goal, marketing researchers often follow the six-step process shown in Figure 7.1. In the initial stages, researchers define the problem, conduct exploratory research, and formulate a hypothesis to be tested. Next, they create a design for the research study and collect needed data. Finally, researchers interpret and present the research information. The following sections take a closer look at each step of the marketing research process.

DEFINE THE PROBLEM

A popular anecdote advises that well-defined problems or research questions are half-solved. A well-defined problem permits the researcher to focus on securing the exact information needed for the solution. Defining a question that is concise increases the speed and accuracy of the research process.

Researchers must carefully avoid confusing symptoms of a problem with the problem itself. A symptom merely alerts marketers that a problem exists. For example, suppose that a maker of frozen pizzas sees its market share drop from 8 to 5 percent in six months. The loss of market share is a symptom of a problem the company must solve. To define the problem, the firm must look for the underlying causes of its market share loss.

A logical starting point in identifying the problem might be to evaluate the firm's target market and marketing mix elements. Suppose, for example, a firm has recently changed its promotional strategies. Research might then seek to answer the question "What must we do to improve the effectiveness of our marketing mix?" The firm's marketers might also look at possible environmental changes. Perhaps a new competitor entered the firm's market. Decision makers will need information to help answer the question "What must we do to distinguish our company from the new competitor?"

When Boston Pizza was reviewing its menu with the aim of making some changes, the company went to the research firm Ipsos Reid for help. Ipsos Reid conducted a study in which it asked more than 1000 adults about their eating habits. The study took place between December 23 and December 28. The research determined that 46 percent of participants were happy to eat anything except turkey and 54 percent stated they had eaten too much turkey over the holidays. The results of the study not only enabled Boston Pizza to make the menu changes it wanted but also gave it the idea for promoting the changes. Promotional material for the new menus showed people with turkey brain, a condition caused by having a turkey drumstick in their heads, the cure for which was to sample Boston Pizza's new dishes.[6]

② Explain the steps in the marketing research process.

Marketoid

In 2009, average household spending declined in Newfoundland and Labrador, Prince Edward Island, Quebec, Ontario, and Alberta.

figure 7.1

The Marketing Research Process

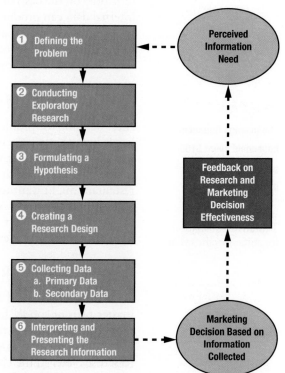

CONDUCT EXPLORATORY RESEARCH

exploratory research
Process of discussing a marketing problem with informed sources both within and outside the firm and examining information from secondary sources.

Once a firm has defined the question it wants to answer, researchers can begin exploratory research. **Exploratory research** seeks to discover the cause of a specific problem by discussing the problem with informed sources both within and outside the firm and by examining data from other information sources. Marketers might talk with their wholesalers, retailers, and customers. They might also ask for input from the sales force or look for overall market clues. In addition, exploratory research can include evaluation of company records, such as sales and profit analyses, and available competitive data. Marketing researchers often refer to internal data collection as a situation analysis. The term *informal investigation* is often used for exploratory interviews with informed persons outside the researchers' firms.

Using Internal Data

sales analysis
In-depth evaluation of a firm's sales.

Marketers can find valuable data in their firm's own internal records. Typical sources of internal data are sales records, financial statements, and marketing cost analyses. Marketers analyze sales performance records to gain an overall view of company efficiency and to find clues to potential problems. Easily prepared from company invoices or a computer database system, this **sales analysis** can provide important details to management. The study typically compares actual and expected sales based on a detailed sales forecast by territory, product, customer, and salesperson. Once the sales quota—the level of expected sales to which actual results are compared—has been established, it is a simple process to compare actual results with expected performance.

Other possible breakdowns for sales analysis separate transactions by customer type, product, sales method (Internet, mail, telephone, or personal contact), type of order (cash, debit, or credit), and order size. Sales analysis is one of the least expensive and most important sources of marketing information available to a firm.

Accounting data, as summarized in the firm's financial statements, can be another good tool for identifying financial issues that influence marketing. Using ratio analysis, researchers can compare performance in current and previous years against industry benchmarks. These exercises may hint at possible problems, but only more detailed analysis would reveal specific causes of indicated variations.

Marketoid

The average Canadian household spent $3840 on recreation in 2009.

A third source of internal information is *marketing cost analysis*—evaluation of expenses for tasks such as selling, warehousing, advertising, and delivery to determine the profitability of particular customers, territories, or product lines. Firms often examine the allocation of costs to products, customers, and territories. Marketing decision makers then evaluate the profitability of particular customers and territories on the basis of the sales produced and the costs incurred in generating those sales. Sometimes internal data can produce remarkably detailed customer profiles.

Like sales analysis and financial research, marketing cost analysis is most useful when it provides information linked to other forms of marketing research. A later section of this chapter will address how computer technologies can accomplish these linkages and move information among a firm's units.

Marketoid

The average Canadian household spent $100 going to the movies in 2009.

FORMULATE A HYPOTHESIS

After defining the problem and conducting an exploratory investigation, the marketer needs to formulate a **hypothesis**—a tentative explanation for some specific event. A hypothesis is a statement about the relationship among variables that carries clear implications for testing this relationship. It sets the stage for more in-depth research by further clarifying what researchers need to test. For example, a restaurant might want to see whether good customer service is related to its increased sales, so its marketers would conduct a survey of customers to test this hypothesis.

hypothesis
Tentative explanation for some specific event.

Not all studies test specific hypotheses, however, a carefully designed study can benefit from the rigour introduced by developing a hypothesis before beginning data collection and analysis.

CREATE A RESEARCH DESIGN

To test hypotheses and find solutions to marketing problems, a marketer creates a research design, a master plan or model for conducting marketing research. In planning a research project, marketers must be sure that the study will measure what they intend to measure. A second important research design consideration is the selection of respondents. Marketing researchers use sampling techniques (discussed later in the chapter) to determine which consumers to include in their studies.

Test kitchens and willing research participants are indispensable in the fast-food business. At McDonald's test kitchen, the company reviews 1800 new menu ideas each year. After input from the business research and marketing teams about where the firm is looking to pick up business, the company's and suppliers' chefs get together for brainstorming. About 30 ideas each year get a closer look, and about half of those are presented to the fast-food chain's management team. Between three and five are actually launched in a given year.[7]

COLLECT DATA

3 Distinguish between primary and secondary data and identify the sources of each type.

Marketing researchers gather two kinds of data: secondary data and primary data. **Secondary data** are information from previously published or compiled sources. Data Statistics Canada collects when it does a census are secondary data when used by companies. **Primary data** refer to information collected for the first time specifically for a marketing research study. An example of primary data is statistics collected by a company from a survey that asks current customers about their preferences for product improvements. The type of data that companies collect can be controversial, as described in the "Solving an Ethical Controversy" feature.

Secondary data offer two important advantages: (1) it is almost always less expensive to gather secondary than primary data, and (2) researchers usually spend less time to locate and use secondary data. A research study that requires primary data may take three to four months to complete, while a researcher can often gather secondary data in a matter of days.

Secondary data do have limitations that primary data do not. First, published information can quickly become obsolete. A marketer analyzing the population of various areas may discover that even the most recent census figures are already out of date because of rapid growth and changing demographics. Second, published data collected for an unrelated purpose may not be completely relevant to the marketer's specific needs. For example, census data do not reveal the brand preferences of consumers.

secondary data
Previously published information.

primary data
Information collected for a specific investigation.

SOLVING AN ETHICAL CONTROVERSY
What Kind of Information Should Marketers Collect?

A critical part of a marketer's job is to collect information about existing and potential customers. But at what point does this information gathering cross the line to become an invasion of people's privacy? The debate over whether universities and colleges, governments, and other organizations should be allowed to collect certain information continues. For example, is it all right to collect information about ethnic backgrounds, or should we be collecting information regarding children's online activities?

In Canada, there are laws regulating the type of information that can be collected about individuals and how this information is used. However, some researchers argue that this information can also benefit these individuals if used properly.

Is the collection of sensitive information an invasion of an individual's privacy?

PRO

1. Collecting sensitive information serves no positive purpose in most cases and may lead to stereotyping or prejudiced behaviour.
2. Collecting sensitive information, such as ethnic background, does not necessarily provide an

accurate picture of a person. There are so many different factors affecting how people behave that one piece of data alone does not provide enough information.

CON

1. People can always opt not to offer sensitive information to organizations.
2. Sensitive information can help not-for-profit and for-profit organizations serve their customers better. For example, if a firm knows that a customer speaks a certain language, the organization can provide customer service representatives who can communicate with him or her or products that better meet their needs. Knowing where children are spending their online time could provide information for Web designers to develop sites that are better suited to their needs.

Where do you stand: pro or con?

Sources: Marketing Research and Intelligence Association (MRIA) website, http://www.mria-arim.ca, June 18, 2011; "Stampede Accused of Sexist, Homophobic Market Research," *Marketing*, January 6, 2010, http://www.marketingmag.ca, Joanna Pachner and Alicia Androich, "Kids in Play," *Marketing*, March 25, 2011, http://www.marketingmag.ca.

Although research to gather primary data can cost more and take longer, the results can provide richer, more detailed information than secondary data offer. The choice between secondary and primary data is tied to cost, applicability, and effectiveness. Many marketing research projects combine secondary and primary data to fully answer marketing questions. This chapter examines specific methods for collecting both secondary and primary data in later sections.

Marketoid

The average Canadian household spent $1900 on equipment and furniture in 2009.

INTERPRET AND PRESENT RESEARCH INFORMATION

The final step in the marketing research process is to interpret the findings and present them to decision makers in a format that allows managers to make effective judgments. Possible differences in interpretations of research results may occur between marketing researchers and their audiences due to differing backgrounds, levels of knowledge, and experience. Both oral and written reports should be presented in a manner designed to minimize such misinterpretations.

Marketing researchers and research users must cooperate at every stage in the research process. Too many studies go unused because management considers the results are of little use, once they hear lengthy discussions of research limitations or unfamiliar terminology. Marketing researchers must remember to direct their reports toward management and not to other researchers. They should spell out their conclusions in clear and concise terms that can be put into action. Reports should confine technical details of the research methods to an appendix, if they are included at all. By presenting research results to all key executives at a single sitting, researchers can ensure that everyone will understand the findings. Decision makers can then quickly reach consensus on what the results mean and what actions are to be taken.

MARKETING RESEARCH METHODS

Clearly, data collection is an integral part of the marketing research process. One of the most time-consuming parts of collecting data is determining what method the marketer should use to obtain the data. This section discusses the most commonly used methods by which marketing researchers find both secondary and primary data.

SECONDARY DATA COLLECTION

Secondary data come from many sources. The overwhelming quantity of secondary data available at little or no cost challenges researchers to select only data that are relevant to the problem or issue being studied.

Secondary data consist of two types: internal and external data. Internal data, as discussed earlier, include sales records, product performance reviews, sales force activity reports, and marketing cost reports. External data come from a variety of sources, including government records, syndicated research services, and industry publications. Computerized databases provide access to vast amounts of data from both inside and outside an organization. The following sections on government data, private data, and online sources focus on databases and other external data sources available to marketing researchers.

Government Data

All levels of government—federal, provincial, and municipal—provide information, much of it free. The two largest sources of information are provided by two federal government agencies, Statistics Canada (www.statcan.gc.ca) and Industry Canada (www.ic.gc.ca).

Statistics Canada collects, organizes, and publishes information gained from a census taken every five years, several hundred other annual surveys, and internal government sources of data. The first census was taken in Canada in 1666 when the 3215 residents of New France were asked their age, sex, marital status, and occupation. The first census as a country was completed in 1871, and the basic format has changed little since that time, although the type and number of questions has evolved. In

1971, Statistics Canada became a separate department of the government, devoted entirely to information management.

In early May every five years, surveys are mailed to every home in Canada. In 2011, the census consisted of eight questions that had been used on the previous survey and two added questions on language. Another change that occurred in 2011 was the elimination of the longer version of the survey. For the first time, the questions that were in included in the second version of the questionnaire became part of the National Household Survey. The National Household Survey is conducted within a month of the census and includes approximately 4.5 million households.[8]

Industry Canada's mission is to "foster a growing, competitive, knowledge-based Canadian economy." In order to achieve this mission, Industry Canada provides business and consumer information on its website. The site includes millions of electronic documents, thousands of links to related websites, and statistical data relating to Canada and other countries. People visiting the site can obtain information about consumer trends, laws, exporting, investing, and financing, as well as economic statistics.[9]

Industry Canada's website contains a wealth of data, including company directories, guides on business and the environment, and Industry Canada services. Marketers can use such secondary data to learn about markets and their customers.

Provincial and municipal governments also provide information about their areas. Some of the information on their websites comes from Statistics Canada but other information is collected locally. The aim of these government-sponsored websites is to provide relevant information quickly.

Private Data

Many private organizations provide information for marketing decision makers. A trade association may be an excellent source of data on activities in a particular industry. A listing of trade associations is available in many libraries or online and can help marketers track down associations that may have data pertinent to their industry or company. Also, the advertising industry continuously collects data on audiences reached by various media.

Business and trade magazines also publish a wide range of valuable data. Most libraries offer listings of international periodicals that can point researchers in the direction of trade publications that publish industry-specific research. General business magazines can also be good sources. Magazines such as *Marketing, Strategy,* and *Canadian Business* publish information about specific markets, consumer behaviour, environmental trends, retail sales, and new products, along with other topics.

Because few libraries carry specialized trade journals, the best way to gather data from them is either directly from the publishers or through online periodical databases like ProQuest Direct's *ABI/Inform,* available at many libraries. Increasingly, trade publications maintain Web home pages that allow archival searches. Larger libraries can often provide directories and other publications that can help researchers find secondary data. For instance, directories are available that list market research reports, studies, and surveys that are available either free or for a fee.

Several firms offer information to businesses by subscription. These companies provide global database services with continuing data on consumer attitudes, lifestyles, and buying behaviour in many countries.

Electronic systems that scan UPC (Universal Product Code) bar codes speed purchase transactions, and they also provide data used for inventory control, ordering, and delivery. Scanning technology is widely used by grocers and other retailers and by marketing research companies, such as ACNielsen. These scanner-based information services track consumer purchases of a wide variety of UPC-coded products. Retailers can use this information to target customers with the right merchandise at the right time.

Newer techniques that rely on radio-frequency identification (RFID) technology are in growing use. Walmart is one of the companies that has been testing the technology. Radio frequency chips placed on the tags of clothing allow the company to track individual items of clothing. The technology makes it easier for salespeople to find the right size and colour for customers and allows for much faster inventory checks.[10]

Nielsen SalesNet uses the Internet to deliver scanner data quickly to clients. Data are processed as soon as they are received from supermarkets and are then forwarded to marketing researchers so they can perform more in-depth analysis. At the same time, Nielsen representatives summarize the data in both graphic and spreadsheet form and post it on the Internet for immediate access by clients.

Online Sources of Secondary Data

The tools of cyberspace sometimes simplify the hunt for secondary data. Hundreds of databases and other sources of information are available online. A well-designed, Internet-based marketing research project can cost less yet yield faster results than offline research.

The Internet has spurred the growth of research aggregators—companies that acquire, catalogue, reformat, segment, and then resell premium research reports that have already been published. Aggregators put valuable data within reach of marketers who lack the time or the budget to commission custom research. Because Web technology makes their databases easy to search, aggregators are able to compile detailed, specialized reports quickly and cost-effectively.[11] Social networking sites also yield valuable marketing information. Social networks may also provide secondary private data. Google Analytics is a business tool for measuring online sales, tracking email and ad campaigns, and benchmarking key measures against competitors. Marketers are beginning to use it to collect information from sites mentioned on Twitter, while Facebook has partnered with Nielsen Co. to poll users about their reactions to ads on the site in an effort to demonstrate the ads' effectiveness.[12] YouTube now offers a service called YouTube Insight that gives its video-uploading account holders an array of statistics, graphs, and maps about the audiences they attract, far more specific than just the number of views it used to collect.[13]

Researchers must, however, carefully evaluate the validity of information they find on the Internet. People without in-depth knowledge of the subject matter may post information in a newsgroup. Similarly, Web pages might contain information that has been gathered using questionable research methods. The phrase *caveat emptor* (let the buyer beware) should guide evaluation of secondary data on the Internet.

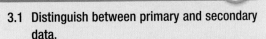

assessment check 3

3.1 Distinguish between primary and secondary data.

3.2 What are the major methods of collecting secondary data?

SAMPLING TECHNIQUES

Before undertaking a study to gather primary data, researchers must first identify which participants to include in the study. **Sampling** is the process of selecting survey respondents or research participants. It is important because, if a study fails to involve consumers who accurately reflect the target market, the research is likely to yield misleading conclusions.

The total group of people that the researcher wants to study is called the **population** or universe. For a political campaign study, the population would be all eligible voters. For research about a new lipstick line, it might be all women in a certain age bracket. The sample is a representative group chosen from this population. Researchers rarely gather information from a study's total population, resulting in a census. Unless the total population is small, the costs of a census are simply too high. Sometimes limitations can reduce the size of the sample. Online surveys often draw large self-selected, rather than random, groups of respondents who don't usually represent the total population. Vague questions and surveys that are too long further reduce the number of respondents and can skew the results even further.[14]

Samples can be classified as either probability samples or nonprobability samples. A **probability sample** is one that gives every member of the population a chance of being selected. Types of probability samples include simple random samples, stratified samples, and cluster samples.

In a simple random sample, every member of the relevant universe has an equal opportunity of selection. The weekly lotteries sponsored by provincial lottery organizations, such as British Columbia Lottery Corporation, where every numbered ball has an equal chance of dropping out of the machine, are an example of a simple random sample. In a stratified sample, randomly selected subsamples of different groups are represented in the total sample. Stratified samples provide efficient, representative groups that are relatively homogeneous for a certain characteristic for such studies as opinion polls, in which groups of individuals share various divergent viewpoints. In a cluster sample, researchers select a

sampling
Process of selecting survey respondents or research participants.

population (universe)
Total group that researchers want to study.

probability sample
Sample that gives every member of the population a chance of being selected.

sample of subgroups (or clusters) from which they draw respondents. Each cluster reflects the diversity of the whole population being sampled. This cost-efficient type of probability sample is widely used when the entire population cannot be listed or enumerated.

In contrast, a **nonprobability sample** relies on personal judgment somewhere in the selection process. In other words, researchers decide which particular groups to study. Types of nonprobability samples are convenience samples and quota samples. A convenience sample is a nonprobability sample selected from among readily available respondents; this sample is often called an *accidental sample* because those included just happen to be in the place where the study is being conducted. Mall intercept surveys and TV call-in opinion polls are good examples. Marketing researchers sometimes use convenience samples in exploratory research but not in definitive studies. A quota sample is a nonprobability sample that is divided to maintain the proportion of certain characteristics among different segments or groups as is seen in the population as a whole. In other words, each field worker is assigned a quota that specifies the number and characteristics of the people to contact. It differs from a stratified sample, in which researchers select subsamples by some random process; in a quota sample, they hand-pick participants.

nonprobability sample
Sample that involves personal judgment somewhere in the selection process.

PRIMARY RESEARCH METHODS

Marketers use a variety of methods for conducting primary research, as Figure 7.2 shows. The principal methods for collecting primary data are observation, surveys and interviews, and controlled experiments. The choice among these methods depends on the issues under study and the decisions that marketers need to make. In some cases, researchers may decide to combine techniques during the research process.

Observation Method

In observational studies, researchers view the overt actions of subjects being studied. Marketers trying to understand how consumers behave in certain situations find observation to be a useful technique. Observation tactics may be as simple as counting the number of cars passing by a potential site for a fast-food restaurant or checking the licence plates at a shopping centre near a provincial border or near the Canada–U.S. border to determine where shoppers live.

Technological advances provide increasingly sophisticated ways for observing consumer behaviour. The television industry relies on data from people meters, which are electronic remote-control devices that record the TV-viewing habits of individual household members to measure the popularity of TV shows. Traditional people meters require each viewer to press a button each time he or she turns on the TV, changes channels, or leaves the room.

Some observers expect that communications technology will also change the way consumers respond to advertising. Internet users are more willing than ever to use real money for purchases that arise during social gaming and social networking sessions. Technology is also yielding new ways to observe people such as software that maps consumers' movements around cities through smartphones. Some of these new observational technologies are controversial and often require the consumer to opt in, a feature that may skew the research results.

figure 7.2

Types of Primary Research

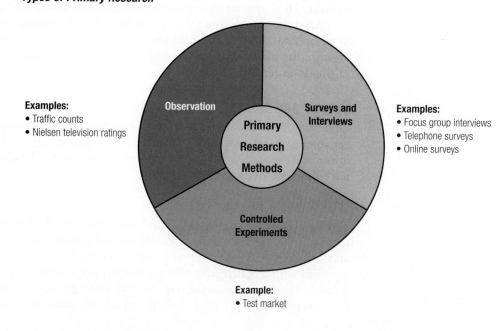

Examples:
- Traffic counts
- Nielsen television ratings

Observation

Surveys and Interviews

Primary Research Methods

Controlled Experiments

Examples:
- Focus group interviews
- Telephone surveys
- Online surveys

Example:
- Test market

Videotaping consumers in action is also gaining acceptance as a research technique. Cookware manufacturers may videotape consumers cooking in their own kitchens to evaluate how they use their pots and pans. A toothbrush manufacturer asked a marketing research firm to videotape consumers brushing their teeth and using mouthwash in its quest to develop products that would leave behind the sensation of cleanliness and freshness.

In an effort to understand what makes younger consumers tick, a trend-forecasting firm auditioned and hired a panel of more than 300 "diverse, trend-setting, savvy teens" for its Trendwatch Panel. The teens participate in focus group discussions and respond to research queries on the company's online bulletin board.[15]

Interpretative Research—Ethnographic Studies

interpretative research
Observational research method developed by social anthropologists in which customers are observed in their natural setting and their behaviour is interpreted based on an understanding of social and cultural characteristics; also known as *ethnography*, or going native.

Another type of primary research is **interpretative research**, a method in which a researcher observes a customer or group of customers in their natural setting and interprets their behaviour based on an understanding of the social and cultural characteristics of that setting.

Interpretative research has attracted considerable interest in recent years. Developed by social anthropologists as a method for explaining behaviour that operates below the level of conscious thought, interpretative research can provide insights into consumer behaviour and ways in which consumers interact with brands.

In interpretive research, the researcher first spends an extensive amount of time studying the culture, and for that reason, the studies often are called *ethnographic* studies. The word *ethnographic* means that a researcher takes a cultural perspective of the population being studied. For that reason, interpretive research often is used to interpret consumer behaviour within a culture where language, ideals, values, and expectations are subject to different cultural influences. After experiencing a number of product failures in low-income markets in Latin America, Procter & Gamble (P&G) began an "immersion research" program called "Living It," in which P&G managers and executives spent time with low-income families around the world, living in their homes to develop a better understanding of their needs and desires. P&G's subsequent sales suggest that the effort was worthwhile. Among the mistakes the firm corrected was a low-sudsing detergent it introduced in Mexico, unaware that most of its customers there were manual labourers who associated suds with cleaning power.[16]

Interpretative research focuses on understanding the meaning of a product or the consumption experience in a consumer's life. Its methods capture consumers interacting with products in their environment—in other words, capturing what they actually do, not what they say they do. Typically, subjects are filmed in specific situations, such as socializing with friends in a bar for research into beverage consumption, or for extended periods of time for paid participants. Paid participants may be followed by a videographer who records their day-to-day movements and interactions, or they may film themselves. Some companies even pay consumers to wear mini-video cameras attached to visors and linked to a sound recorder. These systems record consumer behaviour while participants are shopping or doing chores.

An iPhone application developed by a British research agency allows ethnographic researchers to take photos, notes, and audio and video clips of subjects while conducting their studies. Users can organize the material by theme and send it to their email account to review it later. A BlackBerry version is under development.[17]

Survey and Interview Methods

Observation alone cannot supply all the desired information. Researchers must ask questions to get information on attitudes, motives, and opinions. It is also difficult to get exact demographic information—such as income levels—from observation. To discover this information, researchers can use either interviews or questionnaires.

Telephone Interviews

Telephone interviews are a quick and inexpensive method for obtaining a small quantity of relatively impersonal information. Simple, clearly worded questions are easy for interviewers to pose over the phone and are effective at drawing appropriate responses. Telephone surveys have relatively high response rates, especially with repeated calls; calling a number once yields a response rate of 50 to 60 percent, but calling a number five times raises the response rate to 85 percent. To maximize responses and save costs, some researchers use computerized dialling and digitally synthesized voices that interview respondents.

However, phone surveys have several drawbacks. Most important, many people refuse to take part in them. Their reasons include lack of time, the nuisance factor, negative associations of phone surveys with telemarketing, and poorly designed surveys or questions that are difficult to understand. The Telecommunications Act excludes marketing research from the national Do Not Call Registry.[18]

Many respondents are hesitant to give personal information about themselves over the telephone. Results may be biased by the omission of typical households where adults are off working during the day. Other households, particularly market segments such as single women and physicians, are likely to have unlisted numbers. While computerized random dialling can give access to unlisted numbers, it may be restricted in some areas.

The popularity of caller-ID systems to screen unwanted calls is another obstacle for telephone researchers. The Personal Information Protection and Electronic Documents Act outlines the rights and responsibilities of both the market researcher and the respondents. The importance of proper identification of the purpose of the research may reduce the importance of issues like caller-ID.[19]

Other obstacles restrict the usefulness of telephone surveys abroad. In areas where telephone ownership is rare, survey results will be highly biased. Telephone interviewing is also difficult in countries that lack directories or charge landline telephone customers on a per-minute basis, or where call volumes congest limited phone line capacity.

Personal Interviews

The best means for obtaining detailed information about consumers is usually the personal interview because the interviewer can establish rapport with respondents and explain confusing or vague questions. In addition to contacting respondents at their homes or workplaces, marketing research firms can conduct interviews in rented space in shopping centres, where they gain wide access to potential buyers of the merchandise they are studying. These locations sometimes feature private interviewing space, videotape equipment, and food-preparation facilities for taste tests. As mentioned earlier, interviews conducted in shopping centres are typically called **mall intercepts**. Downtown retail districts and airports provide other valuable locations for marketing researchers. Sometimes personal interviews are combined with other techniques to get a better understanding of the issue being researched as described in the "Marketing and the SME" feature.

Marketoid

Over 77 percent of households in Canada have at least one cell phone.

mall intercepts
Interviews conducted inside retail shopping centres.

MARKETING AND THE SME	**FACESofCHANGE: Multimedia Research**

CONDUCTING a research study online is a great way to reach certain demographics, particularly the 18- to 24-year-olds. Maura Hanley is president of Big*Reach* Learning, a small company that provides training and consulting services. Maura wanted to see if the results of an online survey could be enhanced by combining an online study with other media. She describes it as "a research project designed to reach an even deeper understanding of the relationships between media, people and brands." She called this research project FACESofCHANGE.

In order to test her FACESofCHANGE theory, Maura needed to combine online research with other media in a study that would reach university students. Another company, studentawards inc., operated a website that was designed to provide students with information about scholarships funds. Students visiting the student-awards website to find scholarship and bursary information could agree to participate in research projects. Studentawards inc. seemed the perfect partner for Maura's FACESofCHANGE research project.

The two companies asked 1255 members of the studenta-wards inc. panel to complete an online survey. After the survey results were analyzed, 23 of the participants were asked to take part in further research using videotaped interviews. Questions in both research projects covered the same topics. Topics included

the students' attitudes toward online privacy, online advertising, social media activities, and smartphone ownership and usage.

Some interesting differences occurred when the students were asked more in-depth questions in the video interview. For example, in the online survey, 76 percent of the students stated that they were concerned about their privacy when online. When asked to explain further in the video interviews, students' main concerns were about safety and reputation. Students also revealed that although they did not like receiving spam, they really did not mind getting advertising about products and services they were interested in.

Social media is changing how companies promote their products and services and how we conduct marketing research, with different websites sharing their members' information and various media involved in a single research project.

Sources: Chris Powell, "BIGREACH Explores Gap Between Survey and 'Real World' Responses," *Marketing*, June 10, 2011, http://www.marketingmag.ca; BigReach Learning Company website, http://bigreachlearning.com, June 13, 2011; "BigReach Learning Inc. Launches FACESofCHANGE, a Multimedia Approach to Market Research," BigReach Learning press release, May 31, 2011, http://faceofchange.tv/press; "Studentawards and BigReach Learning Understand Youth" BigReach Learning press release, June 8, 2011, http://facesofchange.tv.press; studentawards inc website, http://www.studentawardsinc.com, June 13, 2011.

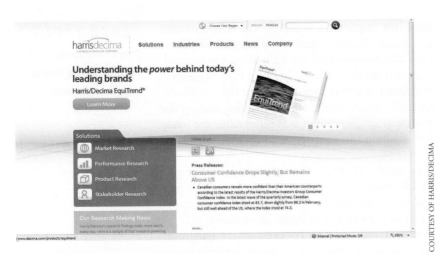

Harris/Decima conducts online surveys.

Focus Groups

Marketers also gather research information through the popular technique of focus group interviews. A **focus group** brings together 8 to 12 individuals in one location to discuss a subject of interest. Unlike other interview techniques that elicit information through a question-and-answer format, focus groups usually encourage a general discussion of a predetermined topic. Focus groups can provide quick and relatively inexpensive insight into consumer attitudes and motivations.

In a focus group, the leader, or moderator, typically begins by explaining the purpose of the meeting and suggesting an opening topic. The moderator's main purpose, however, is to stimulate interaction among group members to encourage their discussion of numerous points. The moderator may occasionally interject questions as catalysts to direct the group's discussion. The moderator's job is difficult, requiring preparation and group facilitation skills.

Focus group sessions often last one or two hours. Researchers usually record the discussion on tape, and observers frequently watch through a one-way mirror. Some research firms also allow clients to view focus groups in action through videoconferencing systems.

Focus groups are a particularly valuable tool for exploratory research, developing new-product ideas and preliminary testing of alternative marketing strategies. They can also aid in the development of well-structured questionnaires for larger scale research.

Focus groups do have a few drawbacks. For instance, one argumentative participant can intimidate everyone else in the group, just as one person who won't open up in the discussion can hold others back. In addition, some group members may say what they think researchers want to hear, offer ideas and opinions for which they have no supporting evidence or experience, or assume everyone feels the same way they do.[20]

Researchers are finding ways to re-create the focus group environment over the Internet. With experienced moderators who have the technical skills to function fluently online, it is possible to gain valuable qualitative information at a fraction of the cost it takes to run a traditional focus group session. Online focus groups can be both cost and time efficient, with immediate results in the form of chat transcripts. The convenience of online conversations tends to improve attendance as well, particularly among those who are otherwise difficult to include, such as professionals and people who travel frequently, and the problem of peer pressure is virtually eliminated. Some drawbacks include the lack of ability to see body language and nonverbal cues, the difficulty of testing any products in which taste or smell are relevant, and the potential for samples to be non-representative because they are limited to those who have Internet access and a certain comfort level with technology.

Mail Surveys

Although personal interviews can provide very detailed information, cost considerations usually prevent an organization from using personal interviews in a large-scale study. A mail survey can be a cost-effective alternative. Mail surveys can provide anonymity that may encourage respondents to give candid answers. They can also help marketers track consumer attitudes through ongoing research and sometimes provide demographic data that may be helpful in market segmentation.

Mail questionnaires do, however, have several limitations. First, response rates are typically much lower than for personal interviews. Second, because researchers must wait for respondents to complete and return questionnaires, mail surveys usually take a considerably longer time to conduct. A third limitation is that questionnaires cannot answer unanticipated questions that occur to respondents as they complete the forms. In addition, complex questions may not be suitable for a mail questionnaire. Finally, unless they gather additional information from non-respondents through other means, researchers must worry about possible bias in the results stemming from differences between respondents and non-respondents.

focus group
Simultaneous personal interview of a small group of individuals, which relies on group discussion about a certain topic.

Researchers try to minimize these limitations by carefully developing and pretesting questionnaires. Researchers can boost response rates by keeping questionnaires short and by offering incentives—typically discount coupons or money.

Online Surveys and Other Internet-Based Methods

The growing population of Internet users has spurred researchers to conduct online surveys. Using the Web, they are able to speed the survey process, increase sample sizes, ignore geographic boundaries, and dramatically reduce costs. While a standard research project can take up to eight weeks to complete, a thorough online project may take two weeks or less. Less intrusive than telephone surveys, online research allows participants to respond at their leisure. The ease of answering online may even encourage higher response rates. For some tips on creating online surveys, see the "Career Readiness" feature.

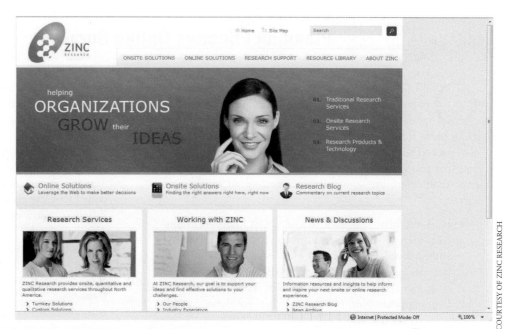

In an increasingly competitive business climate, companies turn to organizations like Zinc that provide assistance with research projects.

COURTESY OF ZINC RESEARCH

Businesses and other organizations are increasingly including questionnaires on their Web pages to solicit information about consumer demographics, attitudes, and comments and suggestions for improving goods and services or improving marketing messages. Online polling is also increasingly popular. Social networking sites, on which consumers around the world now spend an average of five and a half hours a month (up from just three hours the year before), show no signs of slowing down. Facebook has the highest on-site time (nearly six hours a month), and the largest number of unique users—nearly 210 million worldwide.[21] While companies have struggled for ways to measure the impact of social media, more tools than ever exist for tracking which ones drive traffic to any particular site or sites and thus would be the best sites on which to post polls and questionnaires.

At present, no industry-wide standards define techniques for measuring Web use. Some sites ask users to register before accessing the pages; others merely keep track of the number of "hits," or number of times a visitor accesses a page. Marketers have tried to place a value on a site's "stickiness"—longer-lasting site visits—as a means of measuring effectiveness. Others use "cookies," which are electronic identifiers deposited on viewers' computers, to track click-through behaviour—the paths users take as they move through the site. However, because some consumers change their Internet service providers frequently and special software is available to detect and remove them, cookies have lost some of their effectiveness.

Research suggests that about 50 percent of marketing executives are unsure of the return they are getting for their online marketing efforts. Meanwhile, some observers believe the traditional measure of ROI, or return on investment, must evolve into one or more other results that are easier for online marketers to actually measure, such as the sales success rate, the ability to build self-moderating customer service programs within social networks, or the creation of brand advocates, perhaps tracked with click-through sales or promotional codes. Others look to turn the often intangible effects of

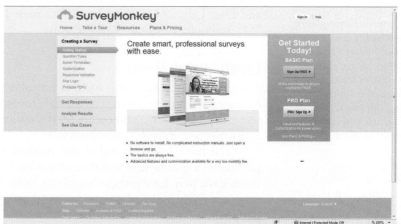

SurveyMonkey.com provides assistance with all aspects of online surveys.

COURTESY OF SURVEYMONKEY.COM

CAREER READINESS | Planning Effective Online Surveys

ONLINE surveys are significantly less expensive than paper questionnaires and telephone interviews. They offer respondents anonymity, which helps most people speak more freely, and the chance to answer questions at their own pace. They do require a bit of planning, however, to make sure that you get the results you want and don't waste respondents' time. Here are some tips for creating successful online surveys.

- Find out what you want to know. List items you want customers to tell you, and prioritize them. Then create and rank a list of your own questions about your business, its goals, or its products. Write a third list of recent customer complaints or suggestions. Compare the lists. Issues appearing on two or more lists are those you'll want to ask about.

- Decide how to organize the results. This will help you determine whether to ask about category breakdowns like age, gender, income bracket, geographic location, and educational attainment.

- Determine how much effort you want to spend analyzing write-in comments, as opposed to easy-to-tabulate multiple-choice and yes/no responses.

- Recognize that people won't spend a long time answering questions. Keep the survey and its instructions short and to the point.

- Word questions carefully. Avoid complex constructions like double negatives, keep questions neutral (don't lead respondents to the answer), and weed out acronyms and abbreviations.

- Make sure the survey is professional looking, and have at least two people proofread it carefully.

- Test the survey on people in different departments of your firm. You may get valuable insights from their different points of view.

- Tabulate the test surveys to make sure there won't be any technical glitches in the live survey.

- Edit once more to make sure each question will provide you with information that's really useful to your business.

- Motivate your sample to respond by explaining the purpose of your survey and how the information you gather can benefit them. Consider email reminders, or even an incentive like a gift certificate or raffle, to boost your response rate.

Sources: "Guidelines for Conducting an Online Survey," Survey-Hosting.com, http://www.survey-hosting.com, March 31, 2010; Sharon Long, "5 Survey Tips to Decrease Survey Abandonment and Non-Response," Survey.Cvent.com, http://survey.cvent.com, February 4, 2010; "How to Conduct an Online Survey and Engage Customers in a Dialogue," SurveyPro, http://www.surveypro.com, May 5, 2009; "How to Conduct an Online Customer Survey," EHow, http://www.ehow.com, May 5, 2009.

---

social media into new measures like user time spent interacting with others, degree of user involvement, and level of user attention.[22]

Certainly, observing consumers online, where users spend more time than with any other medium including TV, offers marketers the opportunity to monitor the buying decision process, understand what turns a browser into a buyer, see how shoppers compare product features, and grasp the relative impacts on purchase decisions of marketing and price. Details like these help advertisers grow increasingly accurate about where they place their messages. Companies like Optimum Public Relations and Dare Labs have teamed up to determine how effective online research can be as described in the "Marketing in a Digital World" feature.

controlled experiment
Scientific investigation in which a researcher manipulates a test group (or groups) and compares the results with those of a control group that did not receive the experimental controls or manipulations.

test-marketing
Marketing research technique that involves introducing a new product in a specific area and then measuring its degree of success.

Experimental Method

The third—and least-used—method for collecting primary data is the **controlled experiment.** A marketing research experiment is a scientific investigation in which a researcher controls or manipulates a test group (or groups) and compares the results with those of a control group that did not receive the experimental controls or manipulations.

The most common use of this method by marketers is **test-marketing,** or introducing a new product in a specific area and then observing its degree of success. Up to this point, a product development team may have gathered feedback from focus groups. Other information may have come from shoppers' evaluations of competing products. Test-marketing is the first stage at which the product performs in a real-life environment.

The Coca-Cola Company and Procter & Gamble have used streaming ads in a section of MySpace to invite users to try free samples of new products or incentives. (The soft drink giant

MARKETING IN A DIGITAL WORLD	Can Facebook Likes Predict Election?

THAT is what a team from Optimum Public Relations, a division of the Cossette Communication Group, and Dare Labs wanted to find out when they set up their Facebook experiment. The team referred to the research as "The Social Election Experiment." The idea came from a team at Facebook who compared the results of the House and Senate elections in the United States to see whether Facebook support for a candidate translated into an election win. The U.S. results proved that 74 percent of House candidates and 80 percent of Senate races compared to the candidates' Facebook "likes."

Although the team from Optimum Public Relations and Dare Labs started with the U.S. idea, the Canadian experiment was designed to track the candidates as they campaigned. Every candidate across the country was identified and their Facebook pages were monitored. Ridings were included in the experiment if there were at least two candidates in the riding who had a Facebook page. The number of Facebook "likes" for each candidate were tabulated and reported on a daily basis. In addition to individual results for each candidate, results were reported for the most liked candidate and least liked candidate of all the candidates, the most active of all ridings, and the closest race.

Did the more than 16 million Canadian Facebook users accurately predict the election results? Facebook "likes" showed a 57 percent accuracy on a national level but increased to 76 percent for major urban centres like Toronto, Ottawa, and Montreal. The larger urban centres had more candidates with Facebook pages, which could have accounted for the higher accuracy level.

Using Facebook to try to predict election results was only one reason for conducting the experiment. The Optimum Public Relations and Dare Lab team also wanted to determine whether they could use a similar type of experiment to predict the value of Facebook marketing and promotional campaigns.

Sources: Chris Powell, "How Facebook 'Likes' and Election Results Match Up," *Marketing*, June 17, 2011, http://www.marketingmag.ca; Canadian Council of Public Relation Firms website, http://ccprf.ca, June 18, 2011; The Social Election Experiment website, http://socialelection.ca, June 18, 2011; Optimum West company website, http://www.opimumwest.com, June 18, 2011.

offered a free music download.)[23] Some firms omit test-marketing and move directly from product development to full-scale production. These companies cite three problems with test-marketing:

1. Test-marketing is expensive. A firm can spend more than $1 million depending on the size of the test-market city and the cost of buying media to advertise the product.

2. Competitors quickly learn about the new product. By studying the test market, competitors can develop alternative strategies.

3. Some products are not well suited to test-marketing. Few firms test-market long-lived, durable goods such as cars because of the major financial investments required for their development, the need to establish networks of dealers to distribute the products, and requirements for parts and servicing.

Companies that decide to skip the test-marketing process can choose several other options. A firm may simulate a test-marketing campaign through computer-modelling software. By plugging in data on similar products, it can develop a sales projection for a new product. Another firm may offer an item in just one region or in another country, adjusting promotions and advertising based on local results before going to other geographic regions. Another option may be to limit a product's introduction to only one retail chain to carefully control and evaluate promotions and results.

> ### assessment check 4
>
> 4.1 What is sampling?
>
> 4.2 What are the different types of probability and nonprobability samples?
>
> 4.3 What are the major methods of collecting primary data?
>
> 4.4 Identify the different types of survey methods.
>
> 4.5 How is interpretative research typically conducted and when should ethnographic research be used?

 Explain the challenges of conducting marketing research in global markets and outline the most important uses of computer technology in marketing research.

CONDUCTING INTERNATIONAL MARKETING RESEARCH

As corporations expand globally, they need to gather correspondingly more knowledge about consumers in other countries. Although marketing researchers follow the same basic steps for international studies as for domestic ones, they often face some very different challenges.

Nielsen is a global information and media company.

Organizations can tap into many secondary sources as they research global markets. One major information source is the government, particularly Industry Canada. Another useful source for Canadian companies is the U.S. government. Both Industry Canada and the U.S. Department of Commerce publish reports that discuss marketing activities in many other countries. Commercial guides for almost every country in the world are compiled by local embassies. Industry Canada provides information on competition, international agreements, and directories of local contacts through its online database or its international trade offices located across the country.[24]

When conducting international research, companies must be prepared to deal with both language issues—communicating their message in the most effective way—and cultural issues, or capturing local citizens' interests while avoiding missteps that could unintentionally offend them. Companies also need to take a good look at a country's business environment, including political and economic conditions, trade regulations affecting research studies and data collection, and the potential for short- and long-term growth. Many marketers recommend using local researchers to investigate foreign markets.

Businesses may need to adjust their data collection methods for primary research in other countries because some methods do not easily transfer across national frontiers. Face-to-face interviewing, for instance, remains the most common method for conducting primary research outside North America.

COMPUTER TECHNOLOGY IN MARKETING RESEARCH

The ability to quickly gather and analyze business intelligence can create a substantial strategic advantage. Computer databases provide a wealth of data for marketing research, whether they are maintained outside the company or designed specifically to gather important facts about its customers. This section addresses important uses of computer technology related to marketing research: marketing information systems (MISs), marketing decision support systems (MDSSs), data mining, business intelligence, and competitive intelligence.

MARKETING INFORMATION SYSTEMS (MIS)

marketing information system (MIS)
Planned, computer-based system designed to provide managers with a continuous flow of information relevant to their specific decisions and areas of responsibility.

In the past, many marketing managers complained that their information problems resulted from too much rather than too little information. Reams of data were difficult to use and not always relevant. At times, information was almost impossible to find. Modern technological advances have made constraints like these obsolete.

A **marketing information system (MIS)** is a planned, computer-based system designed to provide decision makers with a continuous flow of information relevant to their areas of responsibility. A component of the organization's overall management information system, a marketing information system deals specifically with marketing data and issues.

A well-constructed MIS serves as a company's nerve centre, continually monitoring the market environment—both inside and outside the organization—and providing instantaneous information. Marketers can store data for later use, classify and analyze that data, and retrieve it easily when needed.

MARKETING DECISION SUPPORT SYSTEMS (MDSS)

marketing decision support system (MDSS)
Marketing information system component that links a decision maker with relevant databases and analysis tools.

A **marketing decision support system (MDSS)** consists of software that helps users quickly obtain and apply information in a way that supports marketing decisions. Taking MIS one step further, it allows managers to explore and connect such varying information as the state of the market, consumer behaviour, sales forecasts, competitors' actions, and environmental changes. MDSSs consist of four main characteristics: they are interactive, investigative, flexible, and accessible. An MDSS can create simulations or models to illustrate the likely results of changes in marketing strategies or market conditions.

While an MIS provides raw data, an MDSS develops this data into information useful for decision making. For example, an MIS might provide a list of product sales from the previous day. A manager could use an MDSS to transform this raw data into graphs illustrating sales trends or reports estimating the impacts of specific decisions, such as raising prices or expanding into new regions.

DATA MINING

Data mining is the process of searching through computerized data files to detect patterns. It focuses on identifying relationships that are not obvious to marketers—in a sense, answering questions that marketing researchers may not even have thought to ask. The data are stored in a huge database called a *data warehouse*. Software for the marketing decision support system is often associated with the data warehouse and is used to mine data. Once marketers identify patterns and connections, they use this intelligence to check the effectiveness of different strategy options.

Data mining is an efficient way to sort through huge amounts of data and to make sense of that data. It helps marketers create customer profiles, pinpoint reasons for customer loyalty or the lack thereof, analyze the potential returns on changes in pricing or promotion, and forecast sales. Data mining also offers considerable advantages in retailing, the hotel industry, banking, utilities, and many other areas and holds the promise of providing answers to many specific strategic questions.

One research firm conducted a data-mining study of car sales to link motivation to purchase. It found that all vehicles segments, including luxury buyers, were affected by a carmaker's longstanding reputation for the reliability and durability of its vehicles.[25]

data mining
Process of searching through customer databases to detect patterns that guide marketing decision making.

Marketoid

The percentage of Canadian households with landline phone services declined to 89 percent in 2009.

BUSINESS INTELLIGENCE

Business intelligence is the process of gathering information and analyzing it to improve business strategy, tactics, and daily operations. Using advanced software tools, marketers gather information from both within and outside the organization. Business intelligence can thus tell the firm how its own sales operation is doing or what its top competitors are up to.

The key is not only gathering the information but also getting it into a form that employees can make sense of and use for decision making and strategizing. Software can help users collect, aggregate, and create reports with outside information available on the Web from such databases as Dun & Bradstreet. As with other types of research, there are some research companies who specialize in collecting business intelligence information.

COMPETITIVE INTELLIGENCE

Competitive intelligence is a form of business intelligence that focuses on finding information about competitors using published sources, interviews, observations by salespeople and suppliers in the industry, government agencies, public filings such as patent applications, and other secondary sources, including the Internet. Its aim is to uncover the specific advantages a competitor has, such as new-product launches, new features in existing goods or services, or new marketing or promotional strategies. Even a competitor's advertising can provide clues. Marketers use competitive intelligence to make better decisions that strengthen their own competitive strategy in turn.

assessment check 5

5.1 What are some organizations that can serve as sources of international secondary marketing data?

5.2 Distinguish between an MIS and an MDSS.

5.3 What is data mining?

5.4 Describe the process of collecting business and competitive intelligence.

⑥ Identify the major types of forecasting methods.

SALES FORECASTING

A basic building block of any marketing plan is a **sales forecast,** an estimate of a firm's revenue for a specified future period. Sales forecasts play major roles in new-product decisions, production scheduling, financial planning, inventory planning and procurement, distribution, and human-resource

sales forecast
An estimate of a firm's revenue for a specified future period.

table 7.1   *Benefits and Limitations of Various Forecasting Techniques*

TECHNIQUES	BENEFITS	LIMITATIONS
Qualitative Methods		
Jury of executive opinion	Opinions come from executives in many different departments; quick; inexpensive	Managers may lack background knowledge and experience to make meaningful predictions
Delphi technique	Group of experts can accurately predict long-term events such as technological breakthroughs	Time-consuming; expensive
Sales force composite	Salespeople have expert customer, product, and competitor knowledge; quick; inexpensive	Inaccurate forecasts may result from low estimates of salespeople concerned about their influence on quotas
Survey of buyer intentions	Useful in predicting short-term and intermediate sales for firms that serve only selected customers	Intentions to buy may not result in actual purchases; time-consuming; expensive
Quantitative Methods		
Market test	Provides realistic information on actual purchases rather than on intent to buy	Alerts competition to new-product plans; time-consuming; expensive
Trend analysis	Quick; inexpensive; effective with stable customer demand and environment	Assumes the future will continue the past; ignores environmental changes
Exponential smoothing	Same benefits as trend analysis, but emphasizes more recent data	Same limitations as trend analysis, but not as severe due to emphasis on recent data

qualitative forecasting
Use of subjective techniques to forecast sales, such as the jury of executive opinion, Delphi technique, sales force composite, and surveys of buyer intentions.

Marketoid

Food, shelter, and clothing represented 34 percent of the average Canadian household budget in 2009.

quantitative forecasting
Use of statistical forecasting techniques such as trend analysis and exponential smoothing.

jury of executive opinion
Qualitative sales forecasting method that assesses the sales expectations of various executives.

planning. An inaccurate forecast may lead to incorrect decisions in each of these areas. A number of software programs, such as Forecast Pro or SAS, offer companies sales forecasting applications to help automate the forecasting process.

Marketing research techniques are used to deliver effective sales forecasts. A sales forecast is also an important tool for marketing control because it sets standards against which to measure actual performance. Without such standards, no comparisons can be made.

Planners rely on short-run, intermediate, and long-run sales forecasts. A short-run forecast usually covers a period of up to one year, an intermediate forecast covers one to five years, and a long-run forecast extends beyond five years. Although sales forecasters use an array of techniques to predict the future—ranging from computer simulations to studying trends identified by futurists—their methods fall into two broad categories: qualitative and quantitative forecasting.

Qualitative forecasting techniques rely on subjective data that report opinions rather than exact historical data. **Quantitative forecasting** methods, by contrast, use statistical computations such as trend extensions based on past data, computer simulations, and econometric models. As Table 7.1 shows, each method has benefits and limitations. Consequently, most organizations use a combination of both techniques.

QUALITATIVE FORECASTING TECHNIQUES

Planners apply qualitative forecasting methods when they want judgmental or subjective indicators. Qualitative forecasting techniques include the jury of executive opinion, Delphi technique, sales force composite, and survey of buyer intentions.

Jury of Executive Opinion

The technique called the **jury of executive opinion** combines and averages the outlooks of top executives from such areas as marketing, finance, production, and purchasing. Top managers bring the following capabilities to the process: experience and knowledge about situations that influence sales, open-minded attitudes toward the future, and awareness of the bases for their judgments. This quick and inexpensive method generates good forecasts for sales and new-product development. It works best for short-run forecasting.

Delphi Technique

Like the jury of executive opinion, the **Delphi technique** solicits opinions from several people, but it also gathers input from experts outside the firm, such as academic researchers, rather than relying completely on company executives. It is most appropriately used to predict long-run issues, such as technological breakthroughs, that could affect future sales and the market potential for new products.

The Delphi technique works as follows: a firm selects a panel of experts and sends each a questionnaire relating to a future event. After combining and averaging the answers, the firm develops another questionnaire based on these results and sends it back to the same people. The process continues until it identifies a consensus. Although firms have successfully used Delphi to predict future technological breakthroughs, the method is both expensive and time consuming.

Sales Force Composite

The **sales force composite** technique develops forecasts based on the belief that organization members closest to the marketplace—those with specialized product, customer, and competitive knowledge—offer the best insights concerning short-term future sales. It typically works from the bottom up. Management consolidates salespeople's estimates first at the district level, then at the regional level, and finally countrywide to obtain an aggregate forecast of sales that reflects all three levels.

The sales force composite approach has some weaknesses, however. Because salespeople recognize the role of their sales forecasts in determining sales quotas for their territories, they are likely to make conservative estimates. Moreover, their narrow perspectives from within their limited geographic territories may prevent them from considering the impact on sales of trends developing in other territories, forthcoming technological innovations, or the major changes in marketing strategies. Consequently, the sales force composite gives the best forecasts in combination with other techniques.

Survey of Buyer Intentions

A **survey of buyer intentions** gathers input through mail-in questionnaires, online feedback, telephone polls, and personal interviews to determine the purchasing intentions of a representative group of present and potential customers. This method suits firms that serve limited numbers of customers but often proves impractical for those with millions of customers. Also, buyer surveys gather useful information only when customers willingly reveal their buying intentions. Moreover, customer intentions do not necessarily translate into actual purchases. These surveys may help a firm to predict short-run or intermediate sales, but they employ time-consuming and expensive methods.

QUANTITATIVE FORECASTING TECHNIQUES

Quantitative techniques attempt to eliminate the subjectiveness of the qualitative methods. They include such methods as market tests, trend analysis, and exponential smoothing.

Test Markets

One quantitative technique, the test market, frequently helps planners in assessing consumer responses to new-product offerings. The procedure typically begins by establishing one or more test markets to gauge consumer responses to a new product under actual marketplace conditions. Market tests also permit experimenters to evaluate the effects of different prices, alternative promotional strategies, and other marketing mix variations by comparing results among different test markets.

The primary advantage of market tests is the realism that they provide for the marketer. However, these expensive and time-consuming experiments may also communicate marketing plans to competitors before a firm introduces a product to the total market.

Trend Analysis

Trend analysis develops forecasts for future sales by analyzing the historical relationship between sales and time. It implicitly assumes that the collective causes of past sales will continue to exert similar influences in the future. When historical data are available, planners can quickly and inexpensively complete trend analysis. Software programs can calculate the average annual increment of change for

Delphi technique
Qualitative sales forecasting method that gathers and redistributes several rounds of anonymous forecasts until the participants reach a consensus.

sales force composite
Qualitative sales forecasting method based on the combined sales estimates of the firm's salespeople.

Marketoid

The average Canadian household spent 14 percent of its budget on transportation in 2009.

survey of buyer intentions
Qualitative sales forecasting method that samples opinions among groups of present and potential customers concerning their purchase intentions.

trend analysis
Quantitative sales forecasting method that estimates future sales through statistical analyses of historical sales patterns.

exponential smoothing Quantitative forecasting technique that assigns weights to historical sales data, giving the greatest weight to the most recent data.

the available sales data. This average increment of change is then projected into the future to come up with the sales forecast. So, if the sales of a firm have been growing $15.3 million on average per year, this amount of sales could be added to last year's sales total to arrive at next year's forecast.

Of course, trend analysis cannot be used if historical data are not available, as in new-product forecasting. Also, trend analysis makes the dangerous assumption that future events will continue in the same manner as the past. Any variations in the determinants of future sales will cause deviations from the forecast. In other words, this method gives reliable forecasts during periods of steady growth and stable demand. If conditions change, predictions based on trend analysis may become worthless. For this reason, forecasters have applied more sophisticated techniques and complex, new forecasting models to anticipate the effects of various possible changes in the future.

Exponential Smoothing

A more sophisticated method of trend analysis, the **exponential smoothing** technique, weighs each year's sales data, giving greater weight to results from the most recent years. Otherwise, the statistical approach used in trend analysis is applied here. For example, last year's sales might receive a 1.5 weight, while sales data from two years ago could get a 1.4 weighting. Exponential smoothing is considered the most commonly used quantitative forecasting technique.

assessment check 6

6.1 Describe the jury of executive opinion.

6.2 What is the Delphi technique?

6.3 How does the exponential smoothing technique forecast sales?

Strategic Implications

Marketing research can help an organization develop effective marketing strategies. Most new products eventually fail to attract enough buyers to remain viable. Why? A major reason is the seller's failure to understand market needs.

Consider, for example, the hundreds of dot-com companies that went under. A characteristic shared by all those failing businesses is that virtually none of them was founded on sound marketing research. Very few used marketing research techniques to evaluate sales potential, and even fewer studied consumer responses after the ventures were initiated. While research might not have prevented every dot-com meltdown, it might have helped a few of those businesses survive.

Marketing research ideally matches new products to potential customers. Marketers also conduct research to analyze sales of their own and competitors' products, to gauge the performance of existing products, to guide the development of promotional campaigns, and to develop and refine products. All these activities enable marketers to fine-tune their marketing strategies and reach customers more effectively and efficiently.

Marketing researchers have at their disposal a broad range of techniques with which to collect both quantitative and qualitative data on customers, their lifestyles, behaviours, attitudes, and perceptions. Vast amounts of data can be rapidly collected, accessed, interpreted, and applied to improve all aspects of business operations. Because of customer relationship management technology, that information is no longer generalized to profile groups of customers—it can be analyzed to help marketers understand every customer.   ◆◆◆

REVIEW OF CHAPTER OBJECTIVES

① **Describe the development of the marketing research function and its major activities.**

Marketing research, or the collection and use of information in marketing decision making, is changing faster than ever before. Today, the most common marketing research activities are (1) determining market potential, market share, and market characteristics and (2) conducting sales analyses and competitive product studies. Most large companies now have internal marketing research departments. However, outside suppliers still remain vital to the research function. Some perform the complete research task, while others specialize in a limited area or provide specific data services.

② **Explain the steps in the marketing research process.**

The marketing research process can be divided into six specific steps: (1) defining the problem, (2) conducting exploratory research, (3) formulating hypotheses, (4) creating a research design, (5) collecting data, and (6) interpreting and presenting the research information. A clearly defined problem focuses on the researcher's search for relevant decision-oriented information. Exploratory research refers to information gained both within and outside the firm. Hypotheses, tentative explanations of specific events, allow researchers to set out specific research designs—that is, the series of decisions that, taken together, make up master plans or models in order to conduct the investigations. The data collection phase of the marketing research process can involve either or both primary (original) and secondary (previously published) data. After the data are collected, researchers must interpret and present the results in a way that will be meaningful to management.

③ **Distinguish between primary and secondary data and identify the sources of each type.**

Primary data can be collected by the firm's own researchers or by independent marketing research companies. Three principal methods of primary data collection are observation, survey and interview, or experiment. Secondary data can be classified as either internal or external. Sources of internal data include sales records, product evaluation, sales force reports, and records of marketing costs. Sources of external data include the government and private sources, such as business magazines. Both external and internal data can also be obtained from computer databases.

④ **Explain the different sampling techniques used by marketing researchers and identify the methods by which marketing researchers collect primary data.**

Samples can be categorized as either probability samples or nonprobability samples. A probability sample is one in which every member of the population has a known chance of being selected. Probability samples include simple random samples, in which every item in the relevant universe has an equal opportunity to be selected; stratified samples, which are constructed such that randomly selected subsamples of different groups are represented in the total sample; and cluster samples, in which geographic areas are selected from which respondents are drawn. A nonprobability sample is arbitrary and does not allow application of standard statistical tests. Nonprobability sampling techniques include convenience samples, in which readily available respondents are picked, and quota samples, which are divided so that different segments or groups are represented in the total sample.

The methods marketing researchers use to collect primary data include observation, survey and interviews, and experiments. Observation data are gathered by observing consumers via devices such as people meters or videotape. Survey and interview data can be collected through telephone interviews, mail surveys, personal interviews, focus groups, or a variety of online methods. Telephone interviews provide over half of all primary marketing research data. They give the researcher a fast and inexpensive way to get small amounts of information but generally not detailed or personal information. Personal interviews are costly but allow researchers to get detailed information from respondents. Mail surveys are a means of conducting national studies at a reasonable cost; their main disadvantage is potentially inadequate response rates. Focus groups elicit detailed, qualitative information that provides insight not only into behaviour but also into consumer attitudes and perceptions. Online surveys can yield fast responses but face obstacles such as the adequacy of the probability sample. The experimental method creates verifiable statistical data through the use of test and control groups to reveal actual benefits from perceived benefits.

⑤ **Explain the challenges of conducting marketing research in global markets and outline the most important uses of computer technology in marketing research.**

The major challenge of conducting marketing research in global markets is finding information. Many resources are available to help organizations research global markets. Government resources include Statistics Canada, Industry Canada, small-business development centres, and foreign embassies. Private companies, such as marketing research firms and companies that distribute research from other sources, are another resource. Electronic networks offer online international trade forums, in which marketers can establish global contacts.

Important uses of computer technology in marketing research include (1) a marketing information system (MIS)—a planned, computer-based system designed to provide managers with a continuous flow of information relevant to their specific decision-making needs and areas of responsibility; (2) a marketing decision support system (MDSS)—a marketing information system component that links a decision maker with relevant databases and analysis tools; (3) data mining—the process of searching through consumer information files or data warehouses to detect patterns that guide marketing decision making; (4) business intelligence—the process of gathering information and analyzing it to improve business strategy, tactics, and daily operations; and (5) competitive intelligence—the form of business intelligence that focuses on finding information about competitors using published sources, interviews, observations by salespeople and suppliers in the industry, government agencies, public filings such as patent applications, and other secondary methods, including the Internet.

⑥ Identify the major types of forecasting methods.

There are two categories of forecasting methods. Qualitative methods are more subjective since they are based on opinions rather than exact historical data. They include the jury of executive opinion, the Delphi technique, the sales force composite, and the survey of buyer intentions. Quantitative methods are more factual and numerical measures such as test markets, trend analysis, and exponential smoothing.

assessment check answers

1.1 Identify the different classifications of marketing research suppliers and explain how they differ from one another.

Marketing research suppliers can be classified as syndicated services, which regularly send standardized data sets to all customers; full-service suppliers, which contract to conduct complete marketing research projects; or limited-service suppliers, which specialize in selected activities.

1.2 What research methods can be used to measure customer satisfaction?

Some companies look at feedback from existing customers—for instance, hiring marketing research firms to collect and analyze customer feedback at their websites. Other firms collect feedback about customer defections—why a customer no longer uses a product. Other organizations conduct research through online polls and surveys.

2.1 What are the six steps in the marketing research process?

The marketing research process can be divided into six specific steps: (1) defining the problem, (2) conducting exploratory research, (3) formulating hypotheses, (4) creating a research design, (5) collecting data, and (6) interpreting and presenting the research information.

2.2 What is the goal of exploratory research?

Exploratory research seeks to discover the cause of a specific problem by discussing the problem with informed sources within and outside the firm and examining data from other information sources.

3.1 Distinguish between primary and secondary data.

Primary data are original; secondary data have been previously published.

3.2 What are the major methods of collecting secondary data?

Sources of internal data include sales records, product evaluations, sales force reports, and records of marketing costs.

4.1 What is sampling?

Sampling is the process of selecting representative survey respondents or research participants from the total universe of possible participants.

4.2 What are the different types of probability and nonprobability samples?

Types of probability samples include simple random samples, stratified samples, and cluster samples. Nonprobability samples are convenience samples and quota samples.

4.3 What are the major methods of collecting primary data?

Three principal methods of primary data collection are observation, survey and interview, and experiment.

4.4 Identify the different types of survey methods.

Different survey methods may include telephone interviews, personal interviews, focus groups, mail surveys, and online or other Internet-based methods.

4.5 How is interpretative research typically conducted and when should ethnographic research be used?

Interpretative research observes a customer or group of customers in their natural setting and interprets their behaviour based on social and cultural characteristics of that setting. Ethnographic research is used to look at the consumer behaviour of different groups of people.

5.1 What are some organizations that can serve as sources of international secondary marketing data?

Industry Canada and the U.S. Department of Commerce offer reports and guides for many countries.

5.2 Distinguish between an MIS and an MDSS.

A marketing information system (MIS) is a planned, computer-based system designed to provide managers with a continuous flow of information relevant to their specific decision-making needs and areas of responsibility. A marketing decision support system (MDSS) is a marketing information system component that links a decision maker with relevant databases and analysis tools to help answer "what-if" questions.

5.3 What is data mining?

Data mining is the process of searching through huge consumer information files or data warehouses to detect patterns that can help marketers ask the right questions and guide marketing decision making.

5.4 Describe the process of collecting business and competitive intelligence.

Business intelligence is the process of gathering information and analyzing it to improve business strategy, tactics, and daily operations. Competitive intelligence focuses on finding information about competitors using published sources, interviews, observations by salespeople and suppliers in the industry, government agencies, public filings such as patent applications, and other secondary methods including the Internet.

6.1 Describe the jury of executive opinion.

The jury of executive opinion combines and averages the outlooks of top executives from areas such as marketing, finance, production, and purchasing.

6.2 What is the Delphi technique?

The Delphi technique solicits opinions from several people within the firm but also includes input from experts outside the firm such as academic researchers.

6.3 How does the exponential smoothing technique forecast sales?

Exponential smoothing weighs each year's sales data, giving greater weight to results from the most recent years.

MARKETING TERMS YOU NEED TO KNOW

These terms are printed in red in the text. They are defined in the margins of the chapter and in the Glossary that begins on p. G-1.

marketing research 204	population 212	data mining 221
syndicated service 206	probability sample 212	Qualitative forecasting 222
full-service research supplier 206	nonprobability sample 213	Quantitative forecasting 222
limited-service research supplier 206	interpretative research 214	jury of executive opinion 222
exploratory research 208	mall intercepts 215	Delphi technique 223
sales analysis 208	controlled experiment 218	survey of buyer intentions 223
hypothesis 208	test-marketing 218	trend analysis 223
secondary data 209	marketing information system (MIS) 220	sales force composite 223
primary data 209	marketing decision support system (MDSS) 220	exponential smoothing 224
sampling 212		focus group 216
		sales forecast 221

PROJECT AND TEAMWORK EXERCISES

1. Nielsen offers data collected by optical scanners from the United Kingdom, France, Germany, Belgium, the Netherlands, Austria, Italy, and Finland. This scanner data tracks sales of UPC-coded products in those nations. In small teams, imagine that you are one of Nielsen's clients. One team might be a retail chain, another an Internet company, and still another a toy manufacturer. Discuss the types of marketing questions these data might help you answer. Share your list with other teams.

2. Discuss some of the challenges Pizza Hut might face in conducting marketing research in potential new international markets. What types of research would you recommend the company use in choosing new countries for expansion?

3. Working alone or with a partner, choose a new product idea, or a variation on an existing product, that you think would appeal to your classmates, such as yogurt or an energy drink in a new flavour, and devise a test-marketing plan for it. Determine where you will test your product and which variables you will assess, such as price and promotional activities. Be prepared to present your plan to the class and include a description of the information you hope your test market will provide.

4. Interpretative research offers marketing researchers many possibilities, including the opportunity to improve product features such as packaging for food or over-the-counter medication that is difficult for seniors or people with disabilities to open. List some other ways in which you think this observation method can help make existing product offerings more appealing or more useful to specific kinds of users. What kind of products would you choose, and how would you test them?

5. McDonald's conducts extensive marketing research for all its new products, including new menu items for its overseas stores. Due to cultural and other differences and preferences, the company cannot always extrapolate its results from one country to another. For instance, Croque McDo fried ham-and-cheese sandwiches are unlikely to be as popular in North America as they are in France, which invented the *croque monsieur* sandwich on which McDonald's product is based. Can you think of any other kinds of firms that share this limitation on global applications of their research? In contrast, what sorts of questions *could* multinational firms answer on a global basis? Why?

CRITICAL THINKING EXERCISES

1. Some companies are broadening their markets by updating classic products to appeal to younger people's tastes and preferences. What primary and secondary market information would you want to have if you were planning to reinvigorate an established brand in each of the following categories? Where and how would you obtain the information?
   a. Household cleaner
   b. Moist packaged cat food
   c. Spray starch
   d. Electrical appliances
2. Marketers sometimes collect primary information by using so-called *mystery shoppers* who visit stores anonymously (as if they were customers) and note such critical factors as store appearance and ambiance, items in stock, and quality of service, including waiting time and courtesy of employees. (The CEO of Staples has gone on mystery shopper trips and sometimes asked his mother to make similar trips.) Prepare a list of data that you would want to obtain from a mystery shopper surveying a chain of gas stations in your area. Devise a format for gathering the information that combines your need to compile the data electronically and the researcher's need to remain undetected while visiting the stores.
3. Select a sales forecasting method (or combination of methods) for each of the following information needs and explain why you chose it.
   a. Prediction of next year's sales based on last year's figures
   b. Prediction of next year's sales based on weighted data from the last five years
   c. Expected sales categorized by district and by region
   d. Estimated product usage for the next year by typical consumers
   e. Probable consumer response to a new product
4. The Internet provides ready access to secondary information but is also a portal to an almost limitless store of primary information via social networking sites, message boards, chat rooms, e-mail questionnaires, newsgroups, and website registration forms. What are some specific drawbacks of each of these methods for obtaining primary information from customers?

ETHICS EXERCISE

Consumer groups sometimes raise objections to marketers' methods of collecting primary data from customers. They object to such means as product registration forms; certain types of games, contests, or product offers; and "cookies" and demographic questionnaires on company websites. Marketers believe that such tools offer them an easy way to collect market data. Most strictly control the use of such data and never link identifying information with consumers' financial or demographic profiles. However, the possibility of abuse or error always exists.

Research the code of ethics of the Canadian Marketing Association (CMA), American Marketing Association (AMA), and the Marketing Research and Intelligence Association (MRIA). Note especially the guidelines for use of the Internet in marketing research.

1. Check the websites of a few large consumer-products companies. How effective do you think these sites are at informing visitors about the use of "cookies" on the sites? Do you think marketers could or should improve their protection of site visitors' privacy? If so how?
2. Do you think the code of ethics of these organizations would be violated if marketers compile a mailing list based on information provided on warranty and product registration cards and then use the list to send customers new-product information? Why or why not? Does your opinion change if the company also sends list members special discount offers and private sale notices?

INTERNET EXERCISES

1. **Focus groups.** Visit some websites that discuss the proper way to organize and conduct a focus group; one site is listed below. After reviewing the material, prepare a brief report on this subject.
   http://managementhelp.org, www.ehow.com
2. **Marketing research firm services.** Nielsen is one of the world's largest marketing research firms. Go to the firm's website (http://ca.nielsen.com). Assume you run a small online retailer. What types of marketing research services could a firm like Nielsen provide to your company? What are some of the benefits?
3. **Data analysis.** Statistics Canada publishes data on the Canadian population. Visit its website (www.statcan.gc.ca). Review the types of information that is available. How up to date is it? Is there information that you don't find that could be helpful for marketers?

Note: Internet Web addresses change frequently. If you don't find the exact sites listed, you may need to access the organization's home page and search from there or use a search engine such as Google.

CASE 7.1

Market Research Companies Scan the Globe for Marketing Data

Almost every day we hear something on the news about the eating habits of adults and children or the effect of rising gas prices on our spending habits. For instance, you may hear a piece saying that Canadians prefer salty snacks to sweet ones or rising gas prices are cutting into other spending. But how do we know this? Where does this information come from? A great deal of this information comes from global marketing research companies like the NPD Group or Nielsen.

The NPD Group was founded in 1966 and now provides information and expertise in more industries, national and global, than any other research firm. Using tools such as customer panels, retail sales tracking, and customized research projects, the company works with clients in the automotive, beauty, technology, entertainment, fashion, office supplies, software, toys, and wireless industries. The NPD Group helps more than 1600 clients identify new markets, develop new products and marketing strategies, find out what's selling and where across the retail network, and understand consumer buying decisions and satisfaction. The result for clients is a deeper, broader view of the market, and often an increased share of the market as well.

Another major player in the global marketing research industry, Nielsen, has been collecting information about consumers for more than 50 years. The data Nielsen collects come from over 100 countries around the world. Nielsen groups their research into two categories: what consumers watch, and what consumers buy. Nielsen collects information on what people are watching on their television or mobile screens and their online viewing habits, mainly for advertising and media companies. The company collects information from retailers on what consumers are purchasing and consumer behaviour information for companies in such industries as packaged goods. In most cases these companies release the full results of their studies only to companies who pay for the reports. Both companies do provide part of the results on their websites and through press releases. Even the partial results of studies conducted by companies like NPD and Nielsen can assist in making marketing decisions.

One study looked at how consumer behaviour had changed after the international economic downturn. As countries around the world slowly recovered from the global recession, Canadian shoppers showed a renewed confidence but their shopping habits had changed. Although Canadians felt more comfortable that their jobs were secure and even thought that the increased value in the Canadian dollar was good for the economy, the increase in the price of gas and food were causing enough concern to alter spending patterns.

The increase in gas prices alone had caused 86 percent of Canadians to change their shopping and driving habits. More than half of all Canadians would focus more on activities closer to home and approximately a third of Canadians would investigate

having their groceries delivered rather than going to the store. Other changes in shopping behaviour caused by higher gas prices included eating out less often, changing the stores where they shopped to ones closer to home, and shopping around for the gas station with the lowest price. The increase in gas prices also caused consumers to buy less expensive brands, shop at the large warehouse-type stores that had lower prices, purchase products in larger packages, and purchase more products that were on sale.

Another study looked at how consumers were changing their eating habits. This study used forecasting techniques along with cohort aging analysis to predict what Canadians would be eating ten years in the future. The study answered questions like these: Do our habits change as we get older and are eating habits different from one generation to another? As part of this study the eating habits of Canadians and Americans were compared. This study determined that Canadians prefer salty snacks, like potato chips or cheese and crackers, to sweet ones. Americans have more of a sweet tooth and their consumption of sweet snacks and desserts is expected to continue to increase. The results of this study also indicated that Canadians and Americans have different eating habits when it comes to breakfast. Americans preferred breakfast choices they could take out of their freezers and heat but Canadians' consumption of these products was declining. Consumers in both countries liked easy meals such as frozen pizza or canned soups. Having results from studies like this allows food companies to develop products for the different markets.

Another study looked at where people were buying toys in five different countries: France, Germany, Italy, Spain, and the United Kingdom. The study looked at how much people were spending on toys for children 14 years and younger in each of these countries. In France, Germany, and Spain over 40 percent of toys were purchased in toy stores. In Italy only 34 percent were purchased in toy stores while 39 percent were purchased at the supermarket. The lowest category for each country was in a department store; all countries saw less than 10 percent of toys purchased there, except Spain, which was just over the 10 percent level.

With all the information collected from these studies, the companies can forecast future trends and adjust their marketing strategies. Some trends that could cause companies to adjust their marketing strategies could include (1) both Canadians and Americans are paying down debt with their extra cash, resulting in fewer large-ticket items being purchased, (2) consumers are spending less on household items, clothes, entertainment, and packaged goods, and (3) consumers continue to identify concerns about health care and the economy.

What advice can the research companies give to retailers and manufacturers in order to best deal with new consumer attitudes and behaviours? Businesses need to understand the new fragmented multimedia environment. Social media and smartphones are growing in popularity at record paces. Current smartphone ownership is at 18 percent but almost 30 percent said they intended to purchase one within the next 12 months. Canadians are also using social media in record numbers—60 percent said they regularly visit social media sites and more than 25 percent say they spend six hours or more a week visiting these sites. Companies need to reevaluate their media mix in order to include social media sites. The good news for companies is that promoting products and services through social media sites is one of the most efficient ways of reaching consumers. Other advice for companies is to ensure a balance between social media and traditional media, take a long-term view, and connect with consumers.

The other area of the marketing plan that is important for the changing consumer is price. According to the research companies, determining the right price for products will not be as easy as determining new media choices. Lower promoted prices are not generating the increase in sales they did at one time but the new value-conscious consumer is still concerned about price.

Global research companies like the NPD Group and Nielsen provide a great deal of information both in the reports they sell to companies and what they make available free through press releases and on their websites.

Questions for Critical Thinking

1. Eating habits tend to be long-term trends. What implications do you think the findings of these studies will have on food manufacturers and grocery stores? Will these findings affect farmers, schools, employers, and government agencies? If so, what do you think the effect will be?

2. What trends that have been identified by the research companies do you think will continue and which ones will change? How should companies adjust their marketing plans according to these trends?

Sources: The NDP Group company website, http://ndp.com, June 6, 2011; Nielsen company website, http://www.nielsen.com, June 12, 2011; Carmen Alliston, "Value Is Defining Canada's Consumer Future," Nielsen company website, http://blog.nielsen.com, June 12, 2011; Carmen Alliston, "Connecting with the Canadian Consumer," Nielsen company website, http://blog.nielsen.com, June 12, 2011; "NPD Insights," Newsletter from the NDP Group, April 2011; Matt Semansky, "Topline: Nielsen Tells Marketers to Focus on Promotions," *Marketing*, May 13, 2011, http://marketingmag.ca; Kim McLynn, "Canadians Like Salty Snacks, American Like Sweet Snacks but Both Like Convenience," NDP website, May 25, 2011, http://ndp.com; Carmen Allison, "Rising Gas Prices Continue to Take a Toll," Nielsen website, May 19, 2011, http://blog.nielsen.com.

CASE 7.2

Mapping the Market—Location-Based Marketing

Just as Internet marketers can track the number of visitors to their websites, so do marketers in the physical world want to be able to understand where consumers go, when, how often, and who else is there. Discovering what similarly located people have in common can help them target advertising with pinpoint accuracy.

Collecting highly detailed mapping information is easier than ever thanks to Wi-Fi and smartphones like the iPhone and BlackBerry, used by millions of consumers. Hundreds of applications for these mobile devices already tap the user's physical location to offer walking or driving directions, locate friends, and recommend nearby stores and restaurants. "The phone in your hands is the bridge between the virtual and real world," said a web executive at Nokia. Remaining marketing challenges are overcoming consumers' resistance to unsolicited ads on their cell phones and working out privacy issues inherent in the highly specific mapping capabilities that now are possible.

A recent study involving 43 000 Canadians and Americans asked how participants were using location-based social networks (LBSNs). The results indicated that these applications were still in the introduction stage because 84 percent said they had never even heard of LBSNs and only 4 percent had actually used them. The demographics of the early users are very specific—70 percent are 19 to 35 years old, 80 percent are male, and 70 percent are college or university educated. Experts indicate this is the typical demographic for early adopters of new technology.

Two companies that were early to market with geolocation platforms are Foursquare and Gowalla. Both companies provide similar features, and along with these features comes new terms to describe them. One of the most commonly used features is "check in." "Check in" allows owners of phones with an enabled GPS feature to send their location back to Foursquare or Gowalla, allowing the phone to be tracked in real time. Marketers can send promotional material—ads or coupons—when the phone enters a retail store. Marketers could also send a customer satisfaction survey when the customers leave the store. When the check-in feature is used with a social network such as Facebook or Twitter, the phone owner can notify all his or her friends of his or her location.

Some companies have set up reward systems for customers who "check in" at their locations. For example, if you eat at your favourite restaurant five times and your phone has checked in, you could receive a free meal. Other companies have identified customers who shop or eat at their business and give them special discounts.

Another feature allows users to "shout" or leave a virtual message for others in the area to find. Customers could "shout" that a certain item on the menu is really delicious and restaurant owners could "shout" about the specials they are offering on a particular day.

What has marketers so excited about location-based social networks is the information it can provide. Marketers can determine where customers are at any given moment. If a customer takes a certain route to work each day, marketers could ensure their promotional material is located along that route.

Location-based social networks do have some issues to work out. The biggest issues concern privacy. The companies providing location information to marketers have had difficulty keeping this information from being hacked. Another issue is personal and property security. If your location can be determined at any time, then thieves would also know when you are not at home.

Experts predict the problems associated with location-based social networks will be worked out and that the use of this technology will grow at record speeds.

Questions for Critical Thinking

1. What are some ways marketers could make use of location-based social networks? What are the advantages and disadvantages of these uses?
2. What are the advantages and disadvantages of location-based social networks from a customer's point of view? Do the advantages outweigh the disadvantages?

Sources: Kunur Patel, "Location-Based Marketing to Swell by 2015," *Marketing*, March 22, 2010, http://www.marketingmag.ca; Jeromy Llloyd, "Checking Out Check-ins," *Marketing*, August 24, 2010, http://www.marketingmag.ca; Jeff Beer, "Location Based Marketing Association Launching in Toronto," *Marketing*, October 4, 2010, http://www.marketingmag.ca; Company website, Sense Networks Inc, http://www.sensenetworks.com, March 2, 2010; Matt Marshall, "Sense Networks Gets $6M in Hotly Contested Deal for 'Tribe' Advertising," *DigitalBeat*, http://digital.venturebeat.com, June 26, 2009; Kate Greene, "Mapping a City's Rhythm," *Technology Review*, http://www.technologyreview.com, March 13, 2009; Stephen Baker, "The Next Net," *Businessweek*, March 9, 2009, pp. 42–45.

chapter 8

Market Segmentation, Targeting, and Positioning

TISCHENKO IRINA/SHUTTERSTOCK.COM

CHAPTER OBJECTIVES

1. Identify the essential components of a market, outline the role of market segmentation in developing a marketing strategy, and describe the criteria necessary for effective segmentation.

2. Explain the geographic, demographic, and psychographic approaches to segmenting consumer markets.

3. Describe product-related segmentation.

4. Identify the steps in the market segmentation process and discuss four basic strategies for reaching target markets.

5. Summarize the types of positioning strategies, and explain the reasons for positioning and repositioning products.

NEL

MOOOO-RE MILK PLEASE

A recent study found that the highest milk consumers were children four to nine years old, but even at this age only 63 percent of them were getting the recommended amount of milk products daily to be healthy. Other findings from this study found that females in all other age groups were less likely to consume the recommended amount of milk than men in the same age groups. In fact, only 17 percent of females aged 10 to 16 were getting the recommended amount of dairy products daily.

These statistics were startling enough to the health care community but they were a call to action for the various organizations that promote dairy products across the country. The challenge was to decide what types of promotional material would get the message out to the different regions of the country and across so many different customer groups.

The Dairy Farmers of Canada have used a calendar featuring recipes that include dairy products to promote dairy products. The calendar is distributed across the country by including it in regional newspapers. The organization hopes that families will display the calendar in their kitchens to remind them every day to consume dairy products. For the 35th anniversary edition of the calendar Canadians were asked to vote on their favourite recipes from past calendars. But while a kitchen calendar might get the message out to families, it did not seem to be as effective for other customer groups.

The BC Dairy Foundation took a more innovative approach aimed directly at the teen market with its "weak" campaign. A spokesperson for the ad agency developing the campaign said, "Our goal is to make milk a more socially relevant beverage of choice. When we are speaking about the health benefits of milk to teens in their own language, they tend to listen more." The campaign is a take-off on infomercials. The organization designed ten wacky products, including towel clothes—for those too tired to dry themselves after a shower—and the food lifter—for those who needed help getting food to their mouths. They opened the Weak Shop in Vancouver where customers could purchase the products. The chair pants—a device that attaches to your pants and turns into a chair whenever you need to sit—sell for around $70. Along with each purchase, the customer receives a two-litre carton of milk and everyone visiting the store gets a free sample of milk. The campaign was supported with print, outdoor posters, online advertising, and social media sites. All profits from the sale of the products go to a local children's charity.

Another innovative promotional campaign aimed at a broader market was developed by the Quebec Milk Bureau and its ad agencies. The bureau called its promotion "*reconfort*," and it was based on grandma's hand-knit hats and scarves. Launched in the winter, the campaign included topping bus shelters with knitted hats and wrapping street columns with knitted scarves. To support the knitted garments showing up in unusual locations around Montreal and Quebec City, the organization had knitted puppets on its website. Three knitted puppet characters showed up in the bus shelters; commuters could plug their earphones in to listen to the puppets providing advice or telling folk tales. Evening events were also organized where the puppets could entertain the audience with their folk tales and grandmothers could provide knitting lessons. The campaign is credited with an increase in milk sales during the months it ran.

Calendars in kitchens across the country aimed at families, wacky products sold in a downtown Vancouver shop aimed at teens, or knitted puppets entertaining the commuters of Quebec might seem unusual themes to get Canadians consuming more dairy products but these promotions and others like them across the country seem to be working.[1]

---

connecting with customers

Milk marketing associations across the country are using innovative techniques to make different customer groups aware of the health benefits of drinking milk. By using social media to reach teens, providing recipes for the cook in the family, and catching attention with knitted scarves to reach a broader market, these organizations are connecting with their customers.

Chapter Overview

EACH of us is unique. We come from different backgrounds, live in different households, and have different interests and goals. You and your best friend may shop at different stores, listen to different music, play different sports, and take different courses in college or university. Suppose you like country music, but your best friend prefers oldies hits. Marketers for all kinds of music-related products, whether it's digital songs or live concerts, want to capture your interest as well as that of your friends. Do you play an instrument or sing, or are you a fan who goes to clubs and downloads music? Marketers look at current customers and potential customers to figure out what their characteristics are, whether they can identify certain subgroups, and how they can best offer products to meet their needs. Your interests and needs, your lifestyle and income, the city where you live, and your age all contribute to the likelihood

market Group of people with sufficient purchasing power, authority, and willingness to buy.

that you will listen to and buy certain types of music. All these factors make up a market. A **market** is composed of people with sufficient purchasing power, authority, and willingness to buy. And marketers must use their expertise to understand the market for a good or service, whether it's a download by your favourite artist, a new radio station, or a 12-string guitar.

Many markets include consumers with different lifestyles, backgrounds, and income levels. Nearly everyone buys toothpaste, but that does not mean every consumer has the same lifestyle, background, or income. So it is unusual for a single marketing mix strategy to attract all sectors of a market. By identifying, evaluating, and selecting a target market to pursue, such as consumers who prefer toothpaste made with all-natural ingredients or those who want an extra-whitening formula, marketers are able to develop more

target market Group of people to whom a firm decides to direct its marketing efforts and ultimately its goods and services.

efficient and effective marketing strategies. On the other hand, some products—such as luxury sports cars or fly fishing supplies—are intended for a more specific market. In either case, the **target market** for a product is the specific segment of consumers most likely to purchase a particular product.

Marketing now takes place on a global basis more than ever, incorporating many target markets. To identify those markets, marketers must determine useful ways for segmenting different populations and communicating with them successfully. This chapter discusses useful ways to accomplish this objective, explaining the steps of the market segmentation process and strategies for reaching target markets. Finally, it looks at the role of positioning in developing a marketing strategy. ◆◆◆

Marketoid

In 2009, the per capita consumption of skim milk was 8.6 litres.

---

① Identify the essential components of a market, outline the role of market segmentation in developing a marketing strategy, and describe the criteria necessary for effective segmentation.

consumer products Products bought by ultimate consumers for personal use.

TYPES OF MARKETS

Products are usually classified as either consumer products or business products. **Consumer products** are bought by ultimate consumers for personal use, such as cell phones or fashion magazines. **Business products** are goods and services purchased for use either directly or indirectly in the production of other goods and services for resale. Most goods and services purchased by individual consumers, such as DVDs or restaurant meals, are considered consumer products. Rubber and raw cotton are examples of items generally purchased by manufacturers and are, therefore, classified as business products. B. F. Goodyear buys rubber to manufacture tires; textile manufacturers convert raw cotton into cloth.

However, in many cases, a single product can serve different uses. Tires purchased for the family car constitute consumer products, but tires purchased by the Ford Motor Company to be mounted on its Ford Focus are business products because they become part of another product destined for resale. Or a product that was once a business product might be modified for consumer use, and vice versa. A line of professional cookware sold to restaurants—a business product—could be adapted by its manufacturer to become a line of cookware for home use—a consumer product. If you want to determine the classification of an item, just think about who is going to buy the product, who will use it, and how or why the product will be used. The bottle of mouthwash you buy at the supermarket is a consumer product, but if a large hotel chain purchases large quantities of the same mouthwash from a wholesaler, it becomes a business product.

business products Goods and services purchased for use either directly or indirectly in the production of other goods and services for resale.

THE ROLE OF MARKET SEGMENTATION

There are 6.8 billion people in the world today, roughly 34 million of whom live in Canada.[2] In today's business world, there are too many variables in consumer needs, preferences, and purchasing power to attract all consumers with a single marketing mix. That's not to say that firms must actually change products to meet the needs of different market segments—although they often do—but they must attempt to identify the factors that affect purchase decisions and then group consumers according to the presence or absence of these factors. Finally, they adjust marketing strategies to meet the needs of each group.

Consider motor vehicles. Unlike a century ago, when Henry Ford pronounced that customers could order any colour of car they liked—as long as it was black—today there is a make, model, and colour for every taste and budget. But auto manufacturers need to adjust their messages for different markets. And savvy marketers are looking toward markets that show growth, such as the South Asian population, which is the fastest-growing ethnic group in the country, and the aging baby boomers, whose needs for goods and services are changing.[3]

The division of the total market into smaller, relatively homogeneous groups is called **market segmentation**. Both profit-oriented and not-for-profit organizations practise market segmentation.

market segmentation Division of the total market into smaller, relatively homogeneous groups.

CRITERIA FOR EFFECTIVE SEGMENTATION

Segmentation doesn't automatically guarantee success in the marketing arena; instead, it is a tool for marketers to use. Its effectiveness depends on four basic requirements.

1. The market segment must present measurable purchasing power and size.

   With jobs, incomes, and decision-making power, female consumers represent a hefty amount of purchasing power. Globally women control $12 trillion of the world's $18.4 trillion in consumer spending in a year. Canadian women purchase 68 percent of new cars, 56 percent of home computers, and just over half of consumer electronics.[4] Companies such as Home Hardware and Home Depot recognize the importance of women to their success. Home Depot runs "Do-it-Herself" workshops for home renovation projects such as installing floor tiles or replacing light fixtures.[5]

2. Marketers must find a way to promote effectively and to serve the market segment.

   Because women now wield such purchasing power in the technology market, marketers need to find different ways to appeal to them. Some companies have taken this advice to heart. Research In Motion, which manufactures the BlackBerry, has created ads featuring working moms.

3. Marketers must then identify segments that are sufficiently large to give them good profit potential.

   Since women—who make up about half of the Canadian population—are influencing more than 50 percent of all electronic purchases, there is plenty of profit potential for the electronics industry. But marketers need to understand the customer.

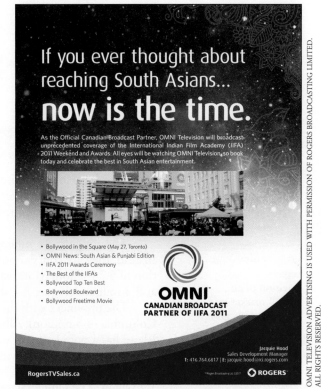

Rogers OMNI Television—promoting opportunities to buy media around the International Indian Film Academy Awards.

When Dell computers tried to market its computers to women using a website that emphasized counting calories and finding recipes instead of talking about the computers themselves, women were outraged. Dell changed the site within weeks of the launch.[6]

4. The firm must aim for segments that match its marketing capabilities.

Targeting a large number of small markets can be an expensive, complex, and inefficient strategy, so smaller firms may decide to stick with a particular niche, or target market. But Harley-Davidson, once thought to be the exclusive domain of men, has experienced a surge in purchases by women, who represent the fastest-growing segment of the motorcycle business and currently account for nearly one in four motorcyclists. So Harley-Davidson runs targeted ads in women's magazines and hosts events geared specifically for women, featuring demonstrations and social gatherings where women riders can meet and network.[7]

SEGMENTING CONSUMER MARKETS

Market segmentation attempts to isolate the traits that distinguish a certain group of consumers from the overall market. An understanding of the group's characteristics—such as age, gender, geographic location, income, and buying patterns—plays a vital role in developing a successful marketing strategy. In most cases, marketers seek to pinpoint a number of factors affecting buying behaviour in the target segment. Marketers in the travel industry consider employment trends, changes in income levels and buying patterns, age, lifestyle, and other factors when promoting their goods and services. To boost flagging attendance at its theme parks, Disney World advertises to adults who are empty nesters and groups of friends instead of focusing entirely on families with young children. Marketers rarely identify totally homogeneous segments, in which all potential customers are alike; they always encounter some differences among members of a target group, but they must be careful to ensure that their segments accurately reflect consumers.

In the next sections, we discuss the four common bases for segmenting consumer markets: geographic segmentation, demographic segmentation, psychographic segmentation, and product-related segmentation. These segmentation approaches can give important guidance for marketing strategies, provided they identify significant differences in buying behaviour.

assessment check 1

1.1 Define target market.

1.2 Distinguish between a consumer product and a business product.

1.3 Define market segmentation and describe the role of market segmentation.

1.4 Identify the four criteria for effective segmentation.

(2) Explain the geographic, demographic, and psychographic approaches to segmenting consumer markets.

geographic segmentation
Division of an overall market into homogeneous groups based on their locations.

GEOGRAPHIC SEGMENTATION

Marketers have long practised geographic segmentation—dividing an overall market into homogeneous groups on the basis of their locations. Geographic location does not ensure that all consumers in a location will make the same buying decisions, but this segmentation approach does help identify some general patterns.

The roughly 34 million people living in Canada are not scattered evenly across the country. Instead, they are concentrated in major metropolitan areas. Toronto is the largest city, with a population of 5.7 million. Montreal is the second largest with 3.8 million, and third place goes to Vancouver at 2.3 million.[8] Figure 8.1 shows populations of the 10 largest cities in Canada.

The provinces with the most residents are Ontario (13.2 million), Quebec (7.9 million), British Columbia (4.5 million), Alberta (3.7 million), and Manitoba (1.2 million). In contrast, Prince Edward Island has a population of only 143 000, 32 000 of whom live in Charlottetown.[9]

A look at the worldwide population distribution illustrates why so many firms are pursuing customers around the globe. China has the most citizens, with 1.3 billion people, and India is second with 1.2 billion. The United States is third with about 308 million, and Indonesia is fourth with 240 million. Japan is a distant tenth with 127 million.[10] As in Canada, much of the world's population lives in urban environments. The two largest cities in the world are Shanghai, China, with 16.3 million, and Bombay,

TRADE MARK OF CANADIAN TIRE CORPORATION LIMITED. USED UNDER LICENCE.

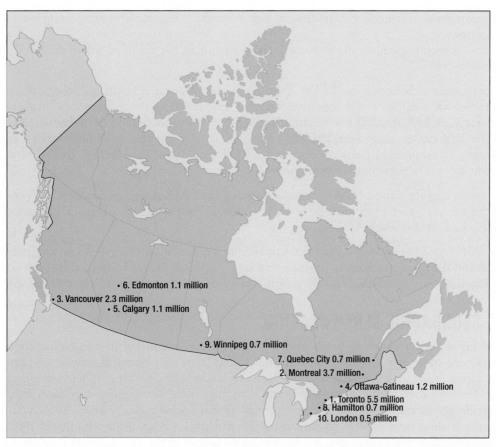

figure 8.1

Canada's 10 Largest Cities

Source: Adapted from the Statistics Canada article "Population of census metropolitan areas (2001 Census boundaries)," available at http://www40.statcan.gc.ca/l01/cst01/demo05a.htm, accessed June 24, 2008.

India, with 13.8 million. The two largest metropolitan areas are Tokyo, Japan, with more than 37.7 million and Mexico City, with 23.6 million.[11]

Population size alone, however, may not be reason enough for a business to expand into a specific country. Businesses also need to look at a wide variety of economic variables. Some businesses may decide to combine their marketing efforts for countries that share similar population and product-use patterns instead of treating each country as an independent segment. This grouping is taking place with greater frequency throughout the European Union as the currency and trade laws of the member nations are becoming more unified.

While population numbers indicate the overall size of a market, other geographic indicators such as job growth give useful guidance to marketers depending on the type of products they sell. Automobile manufacturers might segment geographic regions by household income because it is an important factor in the purchase of a new car.

Geographic areas also vary in population migration patterns. The most recent Canadian census data indicate that 68 percent of the population lives in 33 metropolitan areas across the country. These 33 metropolitan areas accounted for 90 percent of the population growth. The largest growth was in Alberta at 10.6 percent and Ontario at 6.6 percent. The fastest-growing cities in Canada are Barrie, Ontario, and Calgary, Alberta, which in one year showed growth rates of 19.2 percent and 13.4 percent respectively.[12]

The move from urban to suburban areas after World War II created a need to redefine the urban marketplace. This trend radically changed cities' traditional patterns of retailing and led to the decline in many downtown shopping areas—although recent trends have been toward the revitalization

Canadian Tire provides products in every area of the country.

of downtown areas. Subsequently, traditional city boundaries became almost meaningless for marketing purposes.

In an effort to respond to these changes, the government has classified urban data into the following categories:

census metropolitan area (CMA) Geographic area surrounding an urban core with a population of at least 100 000.

1. **A census metropolitan area (CMA)** is the largest classification. A CMA is a geographic area surrounding an urban core with a population of at least 100 000. Once Statistics Canada classifies an area as a CMA, it will always count as a CMA even if the population drops below 100 000. As of the 2006 census, there were 33 CMAs across the country, including six new ones—Brantford, Guelph, Peterborough, Barrie, Moncton, and Kelowna. CMAs are further divided into census subdivisions if certain conditions are present.

census agglomeration (CA) Geographic area with a population over 10 000.

2. **A census agglomeration (CA)** is virtually the same as a CMA except it is smaller. The population of the urban core of a CA must be at least 10 000. If the population of the urban core of a CA falls below 10 000, the CA is retired.

In defining CMAs and CAs, Statistics Canada has kept in mind that many companies use both Canadian and American statistics to compare markets. Although the methods used by both countries are not identical, they are similar enough that markets from both countries can be compared.[13]

USING GEOGRAPHIC SEGMENTATION

Demand for some categories of goods and services can vary according to geographic region, and marketers need to be aware of how these regions differ. Marketers of major brands are particularly interested in defining their **core regions**, the locations where they get 40 to 80 percent of their sales.

core region Region from which most major brands get 40 to 80 percent of their sales.

Residence location within a geographic area is an important segmentation variable. City dwellers often rely on public transportation and may get along fine without cars, whereas those who live in the suburbs or rural areas depend on their own cars and trucks. Also, those who live in the suburbs spend more on lawn and garden-care products than do people in the city. Climate is another important segmentation factor. Consumers who live in chilly areas, for example, eat more soup than people who live in warmer southern climates. But here's a surprise—they also eat a great deal of ice cream!

Geographic segmentation provides useful distinctions when regional preferences or needs exist. A consumer might not want to invest in a snow blower or flood insurance but may have to because of the location of his or her home. But it's important for marketers not to stop at geographic location as a segmentation method because distinctions among consumers also exist within a geographic location. Consider those who relocate from one region to another for work or family reasons. They may bring with them their preferences from other parts of the country. Using several segmentation variables is probably a much better strategy for targeting a specific market.

GEOGRAPHIC INFORMATION SYSTEMS (GISs)

Super Bowl Sunday is more than a sporting event—it is also the single biggest sales day of the year for pizza. On that day alone hundreds of thousands of pizzas are delivered across North America. For companies in the pizza business, it is important that they have a delivery system that is as streamlined and efficient as possible. Delivery companies traditionally plan their routes by using statistical databases, maps, and reports. These sources provide valuable information but not in a format that is quick and easy to use. So most delivery companies have

Geographic segmentation is illustrated by the buying habits of suburban homeowners.

invested in geographic information systems. Once used mainly by the military, geographic information systems (GISs) are computer systems that assemble, store, manipulate, and display data by their location. GISs simplify the job of analyzing marketing information by relating data to their locations. The result is a geographic map overlaid with digital data about consumers in a particular area. A growing number of companies benefit from using a GIS to locate new outlets, assign sales territories, plan distribution centres—and map out the most efficient delivery routes. Google Earth is a recent application of GIS technology that allows computer users to view different parts of the world close up. Users simply type in an address and zoom into it, whether it's a house, a theme park, a school, or a store.

DEMOGRAPHIC SEGMENTATION

The most common method of market segmentation—**demographic segmentation**—defines consumer groups according to demographic variables such as gender, age, income, occupation, education, household size, and stage in the family life cycle. This approach is also called *socioeconomic segmentation*. Marketers review vast quantities of available data to complete a plan for demographic segmentation. One of the primary sources for demographic data in Canada is Statistics Canada. Marketers can obtain many of the census statistics online at **www.statcan.gc.ca**.

The following discussion considers the most commonly used demographic variables. Keep in mind, however, that while demographic segmentation is helpful, it can also lead to stereotyping—a preconception about a group of people—which can alienate a potential market or cause marketers to miss a potential market altogether. The idea is to use segmentation as a starting point, not as an end point. Demographic segmentation can help marketers communicate effectively with their target markets, as described in the "Career Readiness" feature.

demographic segmentation
Division of an overall market into homogeneous groups based on variables such as gender, age, income, occupation, education, sexual orientation, household size, and stage in the family life cycle; also called *socioeconomic segmentation*.

SEGMENTING BY GENDER

Gender is an obvious variable that helps define the markets for certain products, but segmenting by gender can be tricky. In some cases, the segmenting is obvious—lipstick for women, facial shaving products for men. But in recent years, the lines have increasingly blurred. Men wear earrings and use skin-care products, once both the province of women. Women purchase power tools and

---

CAREER READINESS   **Communicating with Your Target Market**

AS a marketer you learn to create and communicate messages for the people you want to purchase your firm's goods and services. The messages you send can have a major impact on potential customers' decisions to buy your products or those offered by a competitor. Understanding the needs and preferences of your target market will help you communicate effectively with the right people. The following suggestions will help you succeed:

- Develop an understanding of your target market before attempting to market products to them. This way, you will gain credibility among your consumers.
- Tailor your message directly to the group of consumers you want to reach. Don't try to sell your products to everyone.
- Use appropriate language for the recipients of your message. Become familiar with the conventional sayings, wording, and tone suitable for your audience.

- Use images that illustrate to your market segment that you understand their culture, beliefs, and lifestyle. This will also communicate that you understand their needs and preferences.
- Create messages that provide clear solutions to specific problems or needs consumers may have.
- Always be respectful of the consumers you intend to serve. Address their needs and preferences seriously.

Sources: Laura Lake, "In Marketing You Must Know Your Target," About.com Marketing, http://www.marketing.about.com, April 18, 2010; Greg Beverly, "12 Great Reasons to Know Your Target Market," Info Central Online, February 21, 2010, http://www.infocentralonline.com; Chelsea Nicole, "The Best Ways to Communicate With Your Target Market," QViews.com, January 28, 2010, http://www.qviews.com.

He chooses his sweaters.
You choose his soy beverage.

So Nice   So Nice   So Nice

Market segmentation often falls along gender lines. This ad features a man but is directed toward the female in the household.

pickup trucks, once considered traditionally male purchases. So marketers of cars and trucks, power tools, jewellery, and skin-care products have had to change the way they segment their markets. Nivea, well known for its skin-care products for women and babies, created an entire line of men's skin-care products called Nivea for Men. Some companies successfully market the same—or similar—products to both men and women. Visa markets its small-business credit card services to firms owned by both men and women.

As purchasing power in many households has shifted toward women, marketers have learned that female consumers who regularly use the Internet make most of the decisions about retail items. Companies like Frito-Lay understand this trend. One of the company's online promotional campaigns featured the adventures of four cartoon women. The portal allowed women to interact with the cartoon women, submit stories, or view short webisodes featuring the cartoon women and Frito-Lay baked snack-food products.[14]

SEGMENTING BY AGE

Age is another variable that marketers use to segment their markets. As with gender, age seems to be an easy distinction to make—baby food for babies, retirement communities for seniors. But the distinctions become blurred as consumers' roles and needs change and as age distribution shifts and changes in each group take place. Baby aspirin is no longer marketed just to parents for their infants; now it is also marketed to adults to help prevent heart disease.

School-Age Children

School-age children—and those who are even younger—exert considerable influence over family purchases, as marketers are keenly aware, particularly in the area of food. Marketing and advertising to children, particularly online promotions, is an area of concern to many. Recent research shows that 20 percent of children aged two to five can play with a smartphone. Some food and broadcast companies have formed organizations like Concerned Children's Advertisers in order to promote responsible advertising toward children but very little regulation in this area exists.[15]

Tweens and Teens

Tweens—also called *preteens*—and teens are a rapidly growing market. According to recent research, this group is very influential when it comes to purchases of food, clothing, and technology. This group influences their breakfast and lunch menus up to 97 percent of the time and they influence the choice of the restaurant for the family's dinner out 98 percent of the time. The numbers are the same for their clothing—they influence their clothing purchases 95 percent of the time. Members of this group don't fall into a single category, but they reflect the diversity of the population in general. If marketers could describe this group with one characteristic, it would likely be interactive. They grew up with the Internet, and they expect to be actively involved in their entertainment. They would rather determine the outcome of a video game than watch to see who won a football game on television. Even the television shows they watch—like *American Idol*— provide opportunities for input. They are completely comfortable in the digital world, and many cannot imagine life without their cell phones and iPods. When they want to communicate with friends—or parents—they send text messages. They expect a vast array of choices when it comes to programming, media alternatives, and interactive experiences. The big challenge for marketers is keeping up with them, let alone staying a step ahead. Phone companies and car companies have increased their spending on advertising to older teens, while snacks, clothing, and video games claim the attention of the younger set.[16]

Meet Mona

FOR more 70 years Agropur, a cooperative of dairy farmers that was started in Quebec, has been processing billions of litres of milk annually. In an attempt to make milk cool for teens, they developed Mona, a black and white magical Holstein cow. Mona appears on milk cartons, point-of-purchase display material, and on Facebook, and she even has her own website.

Mona is a pretty smart cow according to her website. She spends her grazing time ruminating about life. Visitors to her website can ask Mona questions like "Which of my friends is the cutest? I mean, really!" or "Which of my friends has the best Moo technique?" but first they need to log in with Facebook Connect. Mona answers the visitors' questions based on their friends from the Facebook site.

Visitors can also meet Mona. Mona tells visitors that if they think cows are boring they are super wrong. Visitors can then learn some amazing facts about cows like Mona. For example, did you know that Mona can fill up 82 glasses of milk a day or that Mona drinks a bathtub full of water every day?

Mona also likes to kiss people's Facebook profile picture but Mona, being a cow, is a pretty sloppy kisser—she leaves lots of drool on the picture.

Mona likes to give away money too. Visitors can enter a code from their milk carton to win an instant prize or—"Holy Cow!"—they could win up to $10 000. The dollar amount of the grand prize increases by two dollars for every visitor to Mona's Facebook page.

A spokesperson for the ad agency that created Mona said, "Our objective is not to focus so much on the grand prize, but rather to get young people to talk about this funny promotion."

Sources: Agropur website, http://www.agropur.com, April 16, 2011; Mona Mania website, http://http://monamania.ca, April 16, 2011; Caroline Fortin, "Agropur Launches Mona Mania to Make Milk Cool," *Marketing*, http://www.marketingmag.ca, March 14, 2011.

Marketing to this group can be challenging but also lucrative. This is one of the largest groups of consumers in Canada and they know what they want. Using social media to get information to this group can be effective, as described in the "Marketing in a Digital World" feature.

Generation X

The group born between 1966 and 1981, now generally in their early 30s to early 40s, are often referred to as **Generation X**. This group faced some economic and career challenges as they began their adult lives and started families: housing costs were high and debt associated with postsecondary education loans and credit cards was soaring. But their financial squeeze should ease as they enter their prime earning years. This group is very family oriented—not defining themselves by their careers as much as previous generations—well educated, and optimistic. Like their younger counterparts, Gen Xers are comfortable with the Internet. Even if they make a purchase at a retail store, they are likely to have researched their choices online. But like their elders, they were raised on television—so the TV is still an important marketing tool.[17]

As this generation matures, they are growing more concerned about social issues and protecting the natural environment, both of which they view as affecting the well-being of their children.

Generation X
The group born between 1966 and 1981—who are now between ages 31 and 46.

Baby Boomers

Baby boomers—people born between 1947 and 1965—are a popular segment to target because of their numbers and income levels. Almost one in every three Canadians was born in this period. This group has been described as rebellious and spoiled, when in fact only about 25 percent of the boomers fit that description. They came of age with early television and with TV commercials serving as a backdrop to most of their lives.[18]

Not surprisingly, baby boomers are a lucrative segment for many marketers. Baby boomers account for 60 percent of consumer spending in Canada and they like to shop online, spending $1.5 billion online annually.[19] Different subgroups within this generation complicate segmentation and targeting strategies. Some boomers put off having children until their 40s, while others their age have already become grandparents. Boomers tend to value health and quality of life—a fact not lost on marketers for products like organic food, financial investments, travel, and fitness. But boomers are also quick to embrace new technology, even as they age. They spend up to 15 hours a week online and nearly half of all boomers maintain a Facebook page.[20]

baby boomers
People born between the years of 1947 and 1965.

"Living in Elliot Lake has allowed us to fulfill our retirement dreams. What will you do with the money you save?"

Elliot Lake Retirement Living

Where Life Affords More...

Choose from a variety of living options to suit your lifestyle and budget.

- Apartments from $475/month
- Townhomes from $587/month
- Homes from $615/month

Call now for a package or to book a Discovery Tour of Elliot Lake that includes **2 FREE NIGHTS** at the new Hampton Inn.

1.800.461.4663
www.retireelliotlake.com

ELLIOT LAKE
retirement living

COURTESY OF ELLIOT LAKE RETIREMENT LIVING

This Elliot Lake ad is aimed at those who are retired or thinking of retiring.

The motorcycle industry has boomers clearly in its sights. As a group, baby boomers are significantly more physically active than their counterparts in previous generations. However, boomers are beginning to experience the wide range of health problems that typically come with age—back pain and muscle aches—making it difficult for them to continue to ride their two-wheel motorcycles. With baby boomers comprising more than 40 percent of the motorcycling population, several manufacturers have introduced trikes—that is, three-wheeled motorcycles. The trikes even include luxury features like GPS navigation, cruise control, and stereo speakers.[21]

Seniors

Marketers also recognize a trend dubbed the greying of the population. By 2031, 23 percent of the Canadian population will be over 65. As Canadians have continued to live longer, the median age of the Canadian population has dramatically increased.

The current median age is now 39.5 years, up from 25.4 years in 1996. The average life expectancy in Canada has increased for both genders to age 78 for men and to age 83 for women. Explanations for these increases in life spans include better medicines and healthier lifestyles.[22] With discretionary income and rates of home ownership higher than those of other age groups, they also account for a high proportion of new car sales and travel dollars spent. Many marketers have found that seniors are a group worth targeting. Although many seniors live on modest, fixed incomes, those who are well off have both time and money to spend on leisure activities and luxury goods. Knowing this, some unethical marketers try to take advantage of seniors, as discussed in the "Solving an Ethical Controversy" feature.

Other important characteristics of the group include the following:

- Families experienced economic hardship during this group's childhood.

- They built the suburbs.

- They value hard work.

- They like to associate with people who have similar views and backgrounds.

- They are concerned with personal safety.

- They spend money conservatively, but have reached a level of financial comfort where they like to indulge in some luxury.

- They are not likely to be the first to try new products.[23]

Understanding just a few of these characteristics helps marketers develop goods and services and create marketing messages that will reach this group.

cohort effect
Tendency of members of a generation to be influenced and bound together by events occurring during their key formative years—roughly 17 to 22 years of age.

The Cohort Effect: The Video Game Generation

Marketers can learn from a sociological concept called the **cohort effect**, the tendency of members of a generation with common characteristics—like an interest in sustainability—to be influenced and bound together by significant events occurring during their key formative years, roughly ages 17 to 22. These events help define the core values of the age group that eventually shapes consumer preferences and behaviour. For elderly seniors, the events would be the Great Depression and World War II

SOLVING AN ETHICAL CONTROVERSY

Taking Advantage of Seniors

AS baby boomers age, industry observers predict the number of financial scams targeting this group will increase dramatically. Seniors are vulnerable to unethical, sometimes illegal practices, particularly involving insurance, mortgages, and investments. The recent economic downturn has intensified seniors' need to preserve their assets, making them prime targets for financial scams. Consumer and elder advocacy groups are working to stop such practices.

Should special laws be enacted to protect seniors from marketing abuses?

PRO

1. Investing events that target seniors with "no obligation" lunch or dinner seminars are nothing more than a high-pressure sales pitch masquerading as an educational workshop. Seniors are coerced into making investments immediately, without full disclosure of the risks involved.

2. Preying on fear or taking advantage of their lack of understanding, some companies induce seniors to buy products they don't need or can't afford, such as reverse mortgages, prepaid funerals, or annuities. Some products are outright scams, and others are legitimate products wholly unsuitable for the buyer.

CON

1. Seniors are consumers. Marketers should be allowed to gather information on them and target them for purchase just like any other group of consumers.
2. All consumers can be targets of fraud. Seniors do not need special protection.

Where do you stand: pro or con?

Sources: Teri Cettina, "Fraud: 5 Scams Aimed at the Elderly," Bankrate.com, http://www.bankrate.com, March 23, 2010; Ken and Daria Dolan, "Top Scams That Target Seniors," WalletPop.com, December 11, 2009, http://www.walletpop.com; Jennifer Levitz, "Laws Take on Financial Scams against Seniors," *The Wall Street Journal*, May 19, 2009, http://online.wsj.com.

---

because many were in this age bracket at that time. For older baby boomers, it would be the Vietnam War and the women's rights movement.

The current cohort—generally consisting of those born during the late 1970s to the early 1990s—may be the most cohesive to date. Marketers have called this group by several names: Generation Y, the Millennial Generation, Generation Next, and the Echo Boomers (an echo of baby boomers). Others called it the 9/11 Generation because its members were in their formative years during the terrorist attacks of September 11, 2001.

But something else happened during this group's formative years to shape its preferences and behaviours: while they were coming of age, so too were video games. For this reason, we call this cohort the **Video Game Generation**.

The early versions of video games were developed during the 1950s and 1960s and were displayed on oscilloscopes, mainframe computers, and television screens. Atari and Magnavox were the first commercial entrants on the scene, with Atari introducing its Pong game and Magnavox launching the Odyssey home video game system. During the late 1970s and 1980s, other competitors entered the market: Activision, Commodore, Nintendo, Sega, and more. As the technology improved, the games and systems became more sophisticated, with 3-D, realistic graphics, laser disks, and hand-held consoles. The industry has continued to evolve, with the introduction of PlayStation, the Nintendo DS, Microsoft's Xbox, and the Wii. Today, more consumers regularly play video games—at home, on their mobile phone, on the beach, anywhere—than go to the movies.

Members of the Video Game Generation are highly visual and are generally comfortable with all forms of technology. They gravitate to activities that provide constant entertainment and immediate gratification. They get their information from social media like Facebook as opposed to traditional media, and they prefer instant messaging and texting to email.

The significance of the cohort effect for marketers lies in understanding the general characteristics of the Video Game Generation as it responds to its life-defining events. The social and economic influences it experiences help form members' long-term beliefs and goals in life—and can have a lasting effect on their buying habits and the product choices they make.[24]

Video Game Generation
A group called by several names: Generation Y, the Millennial Generation, Generation Next, the 9-11 generation, and the Echo Boomers (an echo of baby boomers).

SEGMENTING BY ETHNIC GROUP

According to Statistics Canada, the ethnic makeup of our population is changing. Other than the two largest ethnic groups, English and French, between 29 and 32 percent of the people in Canada will be from different ethnic backgrounds by 2031. By 2006, 66 percent of Canada's population growth was the result of immigration.[25]

The three largest groups, Chinese, South Asians, and Blacks, account for 75 percent of those indicating an ethnic category on the Statistics Canada census; however, the South Asian group may catch up to the Chinese in numbers by 2017. From a marketer's perspective, it is important to understand the spending patterns of these groups.[26]

French and English

Many companies today realize there are major differences between the French- and English-speaking markets in Canada besides language, but these markets have not always been treated differently. Marketers from various organizations have attempted to reach the Quebecois market but for many years, companies ran their English ads in Quebec in direct translations.[27]

The father of made-in-Quebec marketing, Jacques Bouchard, spent 30 years studying the Quebecois consumer. He explains the differences between the French and English consumers using a six-element model based on roots.

- Root number one, Rural Root, refers to Quebecois who feel the need to be closer to nature. There is a high number of fishermen and hunters, and they crave a simple life but describe their lives as hectic. They like to keep their traditions alive.

- The Minority Root describes Quebecois in relation to other parts of the world. They live for the moment, generally are tolerant and understanding, and have a matriarchal family structure.

- The North American Root explains how they enjoy an American lifestyle—they love to shop and describe their homes as "lived in."

- The Catholic Root looks at the influence of religion.

- The Latin Root is reflected in the importance of enjoying life.

- The French Root is evident in their feeling of connection with a region.[28]

One tradition that has not changed is the love for hockey in Quebec. During the playoffs one season, Boston Pizza capitalized on the strong feelings for the Montreal Canadiens by changing its name to Montreal Pizza. It is the type of promotion the Quebecois love.[29]

Chinese Canadians

One of the largest ethnic groups in Canada, the Chinese, is not a homogeneous segment. While it is true that most Chinese Canadians live in Toronto, Vancouver, and Montreal, they did not all come from the same areas of the world, nor are their shopping habits similar.

When Hong Kong was repatriated, a large number of fairly wealthy immigrants arrived in Canada; since then, arrivals from Hong Kong have slowed while those arriving from mainland China, Taiwan, and Southeast Asia are on the increase. People from each of these environments bring

Marketoid

In 2009 Canadians drank over five litres of chocolate milk per person.

figure 8.2

Canadian Visible Minority Populations

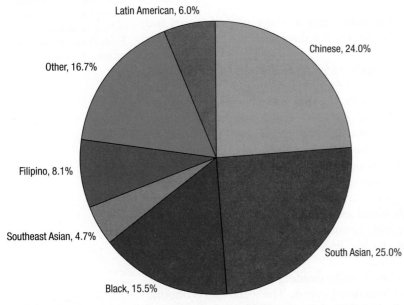

Adapted from the Statistics Canada website article "Visible minority groups, 2006 counts, for Canada, provinces and territories—20% sample data," available at http://www12.statcan.gc.ca, accessed June 30, 2008.

different values with them based on their home country and, in some cases, a different language. Hong Kong, for example, is heavily influenced by its past connection to Britain, and people from Hong Kong place higher importance on recognition and status. Physical comforts and luxuries are important to consumers from mainland China. The only democratic Chinese country is Taiwan, where national identity plays an important role. The values that all Chinese cultures share include a trust in family, hard work, thrift, and a tendency to save and invest in both tangible and liquid assets.[30]

Chinese consumers tend to be superstitious—colours and numbers are important. They like red and gold but not white because it is the colour of mourning. When pricing products and services, the numbers two, three, eight, and nine are good but four is considered unlucky. It is important for the Chinese to look respected or important to their friends and family. Status is important to this market so they are purchasers of luxury products. Advertising in their language is important to older Chinese consumers but there is more than one language, depending on where they came from. Younger Chinese customers generally speak English. Chinese consumers read their ethnic newspapers and spend more time on the Internet than other Canadians. Marketers who understand these characteristics will be more successful when marketing to this group.[31]

South Asian Canadians

South Asians are another large group in Canada but they are the largest ethnic group in Ontario. Their countries of origin include India, Pakistan, and Bangladesh. This group is value and brand conscious. They have a greater tendency to be conspicuous consumers as a way of demonstrating success. The female head of the household is often the major decision maker for most items, including food, appliances, cars, and homes. Purchase decisions in this group are often influenced by the attitudes of family and friends. This group watches cricket, Bollywood movies, and television programming from their country of origin. This is not a homogeneous group. While many are well educated, just as many come from small villages and have blue-collar jobs. Family is important to this group. It is not unusual for more than one generation to be living together.[32]

Black Canadians

The Black Canadian group represents an $11-billion market annually. This group has not received the same amount of attention from marketers as the Chinese or South Asian Canadians. Members of this community originate in Africa or the Caribbean. Canadian marketers are often criticized about the type of marketing that is directed at Black Canadians. Within this community there are many microcultures, and a strategy that works for one may not work for another. This group is also compared to the Black community in the United States, and while some within this group are not offended by this, others are. Members of this group are heavy purchasers of skin- and hair-care products but often have difficulty finding products that will work with their skin and hair colours and textures.[33]

Other Ethnic Groups

Ethnic backgrounds in Canada are more diverse than just those mentioned, and the number of ethnic groups represented is growing. So is their spending. The Hispanic/Latino group in Canada comes from Spanish-speaking countries such as Mexico, Italy, and Portugal and is not nearly as large as in the United States. Whatever ethnic influences motivate the shopping habits of Canadians, one thing is for sure: the ethnic consumer will become more important in the future if projected immigration rates are realized. Some marketing companies specialize in meeting the needs of Canada's different ethnic communities as discussed in the "Marketing and the SME" feature.

SEGMENTING BY FAMILY LIFE CYCLE STAGES

Still another form of demographic segmentation employs the stages of the **family life cycle**—the process of family formation and dissolution. The underlying theme of this segmentation approach is that life stage, not age per se, is the primary determinant of many consumer purchases. As people move from one life stage to another, they become potential consumers for different types of goods and services.

family life cycle
Process of family formation and dissolution.

MARKETING AND THE SME   Multicultural Moguls

"IMMIGRANT Entrepreneurs: Multicultural Moguls" is how a *Financial Post* article about AV Communications starts off. Marvi Yap and Anna Maramba both came to Canada from the Philippines. Marvi, who ran an advertising agency in the Philippines, was surprised to see that Canadian advertisers were trying to connect with ethnic markets by using mainstream advertising.

The women pulled together a team as multicultural as the markets they wanted to serve. Their seven-member team can speak 20 different languages and brings together cultural experience from around the world.

As part of a panel discussing the state of multicultural marketing in Canada during a conference, the art director for the team pointed out, "Many marketers still fall into the trap of stereotypes—for example trying to address an audience of Mexicans just by putting a sombrero on a particular ad."

AV Communications has used some unique promotion strategies to reach their clients' customers. One of the company's clients, Western Union, wanted to promote its money-wiring services. Yap and Maramba realized that the Canadian Philippine community

regularly sent money home. Understanding the importance of celebrity endorsements to this group, Yap and Maramba organized a concert featuring celebrities from the Philippines, promoting the celebrities as Western Union ambassadors. Tickets were available through Western Union agents.

Another of their promotions was directed at Mexican workers in Canada who were here on short-term contracts to work on farms. Western Union sponsored a cinema that would visit the farms, and AV Communications created a survival handbook for the workers. The handbook included information on topics such as biking regulations in Canada and information on how to send money home.

The company's unique promotional style worked. It took only a year for the Filipino market segment to become Western Union's third-largest ethnic customer segment in Canada.

Sources: Ijeoma Ross, "Polished Pitch Will Help Little Ad Firm Catch Big Fish," *The Globe and Mail*, http://theglobeandmail.com, October 6, 2008; AV Communications website, http://avcommunications.ca, April 20, 2011; Rebecca Harris, "Marketing's Multicultural Marketing Conference Breaks Down Barriers to Creativity," *Marketing*, http://www.marketingmag.ca, March 26, 2010.

Marketoid

The per capita consumption of all milk products in 2009 was only 81 litres.

An unmarried person setting up an apartment for the first time is likely to be a good prospect for inexpensive furniture and small home appliances. This consumer probably budgets carefully, ruling out expenditures on luxury items. On the other hand, a young single person who is still living at home will probably have more money to spend on products such as a car, entertainment, and clothing. As couples marry, their consumer profiles change. Couples without children are frequent buyers of personalized gifts, power tools, furniture, and homes. Eating out and travel may also be part of their lifestyles.

The birth of a first child changes any couple's consumer profile considerably; parents must buy cribs, changing tables, baby clothes, baby food, car seats, and similar products. Parents usually spend less on the children who follow the first because they have already bought many essential items for the first child. Today, the average woman gives birth to fewer children than she did a century ago and usually waits until she is older to have them. The most recent statistics indicate that 11 percent of women had their first child when they were 35 or older.[34] This means that, if they work outside the home, older women are likely to be more established financially, with more money to spend. However, if a woman chooses to stay at home after the birth of a child, income can drop dramatically.

Families typically spend the most during the years their children are growing—on basics such as housing, food, and clothing and more specialized items such as braces and college. Thus, they often look to obtain value wherever they can. Marketers can create satisfied and loyal customers among this group by giving them the best value possible.

Once the children are grown and on their own—or at least off to university or college—married couples enter the empty-nest stage. Empty nesters may have the disposable incomes necessary to purchase premium products once university or college tuitions and mortgages are paid off. They may travel more, eat out more often, redecorate the house, or go back to school themselves. They may

COURTESY OF INDIGO BOOKS & MUSIC INC.

Many firms have websites designed specifically for the Quebec market.

treat themselves to a new and more luxurious car or buy a vacation home. In later years, empty nesters may decide to sell their homes and become customers for retirement or assisted living communities. They may require home-care services or more health care products. However, many older adults will continue to work a couple of days a week. A recent study found that one-third of Canadians expect to retire at age 65 but 20 percent expect to still be working at seventy.[35]

One trend noted by researchers in the past decade is an increase in the number of grown children who have returned home to live with their parents. Called boomerangs, some of these grown children bring along families of their own. Another trend is the growing number of grandparents who care for grandchildren on a regular basis—making them customers all over again for baby and child products such as toys, food, and safety devices.

This ad targets families with young children—an example of segmenting by family life-cycle stage.

SEGMENTING BY HOUSEHOLD TYPE

According to Statistics Canada, from 1981 to 2006, the average size of households in Canada declined from 2.9 to 2.5 people.[36] There are several reasons for the trend toward smaller households: lower fertility rates (including the decision to have fewer children or no children at all), young people's tendency to postpone marriage, the frequency of divorce, and the ability and desire of many people to live alone.

Today's households represent a wide range of diversity. They include households with a married couple and their children; households that are blended through divorce or loss of a spouse and remarriage; those headed by a single parent, same-sex parents, or grandparents; couples without children; groups of friends; and single-person households.

Couples without children may be young or old. If they are seniors, their children may have already grown and are living on their own. The percentage of couples with no children under the age 25 living at home has increased steadily for the last 10 years. Couples living common-law (living together but not married) has also seen a significant increase, reaching 15.5 percent by 2006. This trend is strongest in Quebec, where common-law relationships represent 25 percent of all common-law families in Canada.[37] Couples who are younger and do not have children are considered attractive to marketers because they often have high levels of income allowing them to spend more freely. These couples typically eat out often, take expensive vacations, and buy luxury cars.

The 2001 census was the first time data on same-sex partnerships was collected. In the 2006 census, same-sex couples represented only 0.6 percent of all couples, with 54 percent of these being male; however, female same-sex couples were more likely to have children living with them.[38] Since same-sex marriage was legalized in Canada in 2005, same-sex couples in Canada have the same legal, social, and financial benefits as opposite-sex couples.

People live alone for a variety of reasons—sometimes by choice and sometimes by necessity such as divorce or widowhood. In response, marketers have modified their messages and their products to meet the needs of single-person households. Food industry manufacturers are downsizing products and offering more single-serving foods such as soup and macaroni and cheese.

Regardless of the type of household, households are often used to collect information about trends in society as can be seen by the ongoing study of households and the environment discussed in the Go Green box.

SEGMENTING BY INCOME AND EXPENDITURE PATTERNS

Part of the earlier definition of *market* described people with purchasing power. Not surprisingly, then, a common basis for segmenting the consumer market is income. Marketers often target geographic areas known for the high incomes of their residents. Or they might consider age or household type when determining potential buying power.

Households and the Environment

ENVIRONMENTAL trends are so important in today's society that Statistics Canada, Environment Canada, and Health Canada have joined forces to collect information about how Canadian households are adapting to environmentally friendly products and practices. The results of the studies are available on the Statistics Canada website under EnviroStats.

As part of this initiative, Statistics Canada performed the Households and the Environment Survey (HES). Over 20 000 households across Canada were asked questions relating to household activities that would have both positive and negative impacts on the environment. Topics covered included water (its quality, consumption, and conservation), energy use, indoor environments, household hazardous waste, and purchasing decisions. The results were compared to similar studies conducted since the 1990s.

With regard to water, the survey found almost 66 percent of households drank tap water. Canadian households that primarily drank bottled water dropped 6 percent in the two-year period from the previous survey. The survey also found that 63 percent of Canadian households had water-saving shower-heads, up from 42 percent in 1994, and 42 percent had a water-saving toilet, up from 15 percent in 1994.

The energy-use part of the survey found that Canadians are purchasing more environmentally friendly devices. The number of households using at least one compact fluorescent light increased from 19 percent in 1994 to 75 percent. Households with programmable thermostats increased from 16 percent in 1994 to 49 percent and about 60 percent of households with programmable thermostats lowered the temperature overnight. Canadian households are moving back to clotheslines with 64 percent of respondents stating they had used a clothesline during the year.

The study also highlighted how Canadians were dealing with household hazardous waste. Just under 60 percent of households with leftover or unwanted medications disposed of them correctly. Just over 60 percent of households with unwanted paint or solvents dropped them off at disposal centres.

Sources: "Households and the Environment: 2009," Statistics Canada, Catalogue no. 11-526-X; "Household and the Environment Survey," http://www.statcan.gc.ca, July 11, 2007, December 12, 2007; EnviroStats, Winter 2007, http://www.statcan.gc.ca, December 30, 2007.

Engel's Laws

How do expenditure patterns vary with income? Over a century ago, Ernst Engel, a German statistician, published what became known as Engel's laws—three general statements based on his studies of the impact of household income changes on consumer spending behaviour. According to Engel, as household income increases, the following will take place:

1. A smaller percentage of expenditures go for food.

2. The percentage spent on housing, household operations, and clothing remains constant.

3. The percentage spent on other items (such as recreation and education) increases.

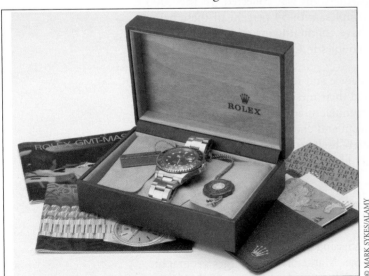

An ad targeting people with significant disposable income.

Are Engel's laws still valid? Recent studies say yes, with a few exceptions. Researchers note a steady decline in the percentage of total income spent on food and beverages as income increases. Although high-income families spend greater absolute amounts on food items, their purchases represent declining percentages of their total expenditures compared with low-income families.[39] In addition, that percentage has declined over the last century.[40] But as food prices become inflated, consumers change how they shop—they may spend the same to buy fewer items, spend more to buy the same items, or try to spend less and buy as many items as possible within the new budget. Marketers note that consumers are more selective, on the alert for bargains at the supermarket.

The second law remains partly accurate. However, the percentage of fixed expenditures for housing and household operations has increased over the past 30 years, and the percentage spent on clothing rises with increased income. The third law remains true, with the exception of personal-care costs, which appear to decline as a percentage of increased income.

Engel's laws can help marketers target markets at all income levels. Regardless of the economic environment, consumers still buy luxury goods and services. One reason is that some companies now offer their luxury products at different price levels. Mercedes-Benz has its lower-priced C-class models, while the jewellery store Birks sells a $100 sterling silver heart pendant with chain. Both of these firms continue to offer their higher-priced items as well but have chosen to broaden their market by serving other consumers.

DEMOGRAPHIC SEGMENTATION ABROAD

Marketers often face a difficult task in obtaining the data necessary for demographic segmentation abroad. Many countries do not have scheduled census programs. Germany skipped counting from 1970 to 1987, and France conducts a census about every seven years. In contrast, Japan conducts a census every five years; however, the mid-decade assessments are not as complete as the end-of-decade counts.

Also, some foreign data include demographic divisions not found in the Canadian census. Not all countries collect information on religious affiliation, for instance. On the other hand, some of the standard segmentation data for Canadian markets are not available abroad. Many nations do not collect income data. Great Britain, Japan, Spain, France, and Italy are examples. Similarly, family life-cycle data are difficult to apply in global demographic segmentation efforts. Ireland acknowledges only three marital statuses—single, married, and widowed—while Latin American nations and Sweden count their unmarried cohabitants.

One source of global demographic information is the Industry Canada website. Industry Canada provides a searchable online database of population statistics for many countries. Another source is the United Nations, which sponsors national statistical offices that collect demographic data on a variety of countries.

PSYCHOGRAPHIC SEGMENTATION

psychographic segmentation Division of a population into groups that have similar psychological characteristics, attitudes, values, and lifestyles.

AIO statements Items on lifestyle surveys that describe various activities, interests, and opinions of respondents.

Marketers have traditionally referred to geographic and demographic characteristics as the primary bases for dividing consumers into homogeneous market segments. Still, they have long recognized the need for fuller, more lifelike portraits of consumers in developing their marketing programs. As a result, psychographic segmentation can be a useful tool for gaining sharper insight into consumer purchasing behaviour.

WHAT IS PSYCHOGRAPHIC SEGMENTATION?

Psychographic segmentation divides a population into groups that have similar psychological characteristics, attitudes, values, and lifestyles. Lifestyle refers to a person's mode of living; it describes how an individual operates on a daily basis. Consumers' lifestyles are composites of their individual psychological profiles, including their needs, motives, perceptions, and attitudes. A lifestyle also bears the mark of many other influences, such as family, job, social activities, and culture.

The most common method for developing psychographic profiles of a population is to conduct a large-scale survey that asks consumers to agree or disagree with a collection of several hundred AIO statements. These **AIO statements** describe various activities, interests, and opinions. The resulting data allow researchers to develop lifestyle profiles. Marketers can then develop a separate marketing strategy that closely fits the psychographic makeup for each lifestyle segment.

Marketing researchers have conducted psychographic studies on hundreds of goods and services such as beer and air travel. Many businesses turn to psychographic research in an effort to learn what consumers in various demographic and geographic segments want and need.

Psychographic segmentation.

figure 8.3

The VALS™ Framework

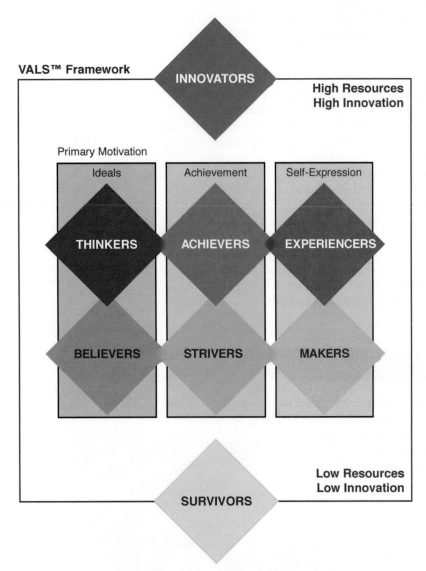

Source: SRI Consulting Business Intelligence, http://www.sric-bi.com/VALS/

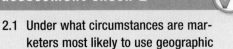

2.1 Under what circumstances are marketers most likely to use geographic segmentation?

2.2 What is demographic segmentation and what are the major categories of demographic segmentation?

2.3 What is psychographic segmentation?

2.4 Name the eight categories of VALS.

VALS™

A quarter century ago, the research and consulting firm SRI International developed a psychographic segmentation system called VALS, an acronym for *VALues and Lifestyles.* Initially VALS categorized consumers by their social values—how they felt about issues such as legalization of marijuana or abortion. Today VALS is owned and managed by SRI Consulting Business Intelligence (SRIC-BI), an SRI spin-off that has revised the system to link it more closely with consumer buying behaviour. The revised VALS system categorizes consumers by characteristics that correlate with purchase behaviour. It is based on two key concepts: resources and self-motivation. VALS divides consumers into eight psychographic categories: innovators, thinkers, achievers, experiencers, believers, strivers, makers, and survivors. Figure 8.3 details the profiles for these categories and their relationships.

The VALS framework in the figure displays differences in resources as vertical distances, and primary motivation is represented horizontally. The resource dimension measures income, education, self-confidence, health, eagerness to buy, and energy level. Primary motivations divide consumers into three groups: principle-motivated consumers, who have a set of ideas and morals—principles—that they live by; achievement-motivated consumers, who are influenced by symbols of success; and action-motivated consumers, who seek physical activity, variety, and adventure.

SRIC-BI has created several specialized segmentation systems based on this approach. Japan-VALS segments the Japanese marketplace with an emphasis on early adopters of new ideas and products. With a questionnaire of 49 items, marketers using JapanVALS zero in on consumer needs, differentiate their brands, and develop more targeted tools and strategies. GeoVALS estimates the percentage of each VALS type by U.S. zip code. Marketers can identify zip codes with the highest concentration of the segment they want to reach, they can use the information to choose locations for retail outlets, and they can tailor marketing messages for a local audience.[41]

Other tools available include Canada's Social Value Tribes, developed by Michael Adams and Environics Research Group Ltd. Environics crunches the numbers on hundreds of personal variables that include political views, religious affiliations, and social attitudes and comes up with 12 psychographic categories within three tribes that reflect Canadian social values. Depending on your own variables, you might be a "thrill-seeking materialist" or an "aimless dependent," both fitting into the Gen X Tribe. Information about each group's fundamental motivation and key values is available.[42]

PSYCHOGRAPHIC SEGMENTATION OF GLOBAL MARKETS

As JapanVALS suggests, psychographic profiles can cross national boundaries. An international marketing research firm surveyed 7000 people in 35 countries. From the resulting data, the company identified six psychographic consumer segments that exist in all 35 nations, although to varying degrees:

- *Strivers*, the largest segment, value professional and material goals more than the other groups. One-third of the Asian population and one-fourth of Russians are strivers. They are slightly more likely to be men than women.

- *Devouts* value duty and tradition. While this segment comprises 22 percent of all adults, they are most common in Africa, the Middle East, and developing Asia. They are least common in Western Europe and developed Asian countries. Worldwide, they are more likely to be female.

- *Altruists* emphasize social issues and societal well-being. Comprising 18 percent of all adults, this group shows a median age of 44 and a slightly higher percentage of women.

- *Intimates* value family and personal relationships. They are divided almost equally between males and females. One American or European in four would be categorized as intimates, but only 7 percent of consumers in developing Asia fall into this category.

- *Fun seekers*, as you might guess from their name, focus on personal enjoyment and pleasurable experiences. They make up 12 percent of the world's population, with a male–female ratio of 54 to 46. Many live in developed Asia.

- *Creatives*, the smallest segment, account for just 10 percent of the global population. This group seeks education, technology, and knowledge, and their male–female ratio is roughly equal.

Researchers note that some principles and core beliefs—such as protecting the family—apply to more than one psychographic segment.

VALS™
Segmentation system that divides consumers into eight psychographic categories: actualizers, fulfilleds, believers, achievers, strivers, experiencers, makers, and strugglers.

USING PSYCHOGRAPHIC SEGMENTATION

No one suggests that psychographic segmentation is an exact science, but it does help marketers quantify aspects of consumers' personalities and lifestyles to create goods and services for a target market. Psychographic profile systems like VALS can paint useful pictures of the overall psychological motivations of consumers. These profiles produce much richer descriptions of potential target markets than other techniques can achieve. The enhanced detail aids in matching a company's image and product offerings with the types of consumers who use its products.

Identifying which psychographic segments are most prevalent in certain markets helps marketers plan and promote more effectively. Often, segments overlap. In a recent study of mobile phone users, researchers discovered five distinct segments, which they named basic planners, mobile professionals, pragmatic adopters, social connectors, and mobitati. Mobile phones have become so prevalent that the user population is large enough to be studied and segmented.[43]

Psychographic segmentation is a good supplement to segmentation by demographic or geographic variables. For example, marketers may have access to each consumer type's media preferences in network television, cable television, Internet use, radio format, magazines, and newspapers. Psychographic studies may then refine the picture of segment characteristics to give a more elaborate lifestyle profile of the consumers in the firm's target market. A psychographic study could help marketers of goods and services across the country predict what kinds of products consumers in particular cities would be drawn to and eliminate those that are not attractive.

The cookie you love for the ones you love.

Because you want what's best for your loved ones.
Praeventia products are made from carefully selected high quality ingredients. They also contain polyphenols (antioxidants), inulin (a prebiotic dietary fibre) that promotes digestive health or ß-glucans (Wellmune WGP®) that activate key immune cells.

All these great benefits in a delicious snack!
Available in individual packs.

Good for your little **sweethearts!**

Leclerc

praeventia.ca

COURTESY OF BISCUITS LECLERC LTD.

With its focus on family relationships, this ad appeals to intimates.

③ Describe
product-related
segmentation.

**product-related
segmentation**
Division of a population
into homogeneous
groups based on their
relationships to the
product.

PRODUCT-RELATED SEGMENTATION

Product-related segmentation involves dividing a consumer population into homogeneous groups based on their relationships to the product. This segmentation approach can take several forms:

1. Segmenting based on the benefits that people seek when they buy a product

2. Segmenting based on usage rates for a product

3. Segmenting according to consumers' brand loyalty toward a product

SEGMENTING BY BENEFITS SOUGHT

This approach focuses on the attributes that people seek and the benefits they expect to receive from a good or service. It groups consumers into segments based on what they want a product to do for them. Consumers who drink Starbucks premium coffees are not just looking for a dose of caffeine. They are willing to pay extra to savour a pleasant experience, one that makes them feel pampered and appreciated. Women who work out at Curves want to look their best and feel healthy. Pet owners who feed their cats and dogs Science Diet believe that they are giving their animals a great-tasting, healthy pet food.

Even if a business offers only one product line, however, marketers must remember to consider product benefits. Two people may buy the same product for very different reasons. A box of baking soda could end up serving as a refrigerator freshener, a toothpaste substitute, an antacid, or a deodorizer for a cat's litter box.

SEGMENTING BY USAGE RATES

Marketers may also segment a total market by grouping people according to the amounts of a product that they buy and use. Markets can be divided into heavy-user, moderate-user, and light-user segments. The **80/20 principle** holds that a big percentage of a product's revenues—maybe 80 percent—comes from a relatively small, loyal percentage of total customers—perhaps 20 percent. The 80/20 principle is sometimes referred to as Pareto's Principle. Although the percentages need not exactly equal these figures, the general principle often holds true: relatively few heavy users of a product can account for much of its consumption.

80/20 principle
Generally accepted rule
that 80 percent of a
product's revenues come
from 20 percent of its
total customers.

Depending on their goals, marketers may target heavy, moderate, or light users as well as non-users. A company may attempt to lure heavy users of another product away from their regular brands to try a new brand. Non-users and light users may be attractive prospects because other companies are ignoring them. Usage rates can also be linked to other segmentation methods such as demographic and psychographic segmentation.

SEGMENTING BY BRAND LOYALTY

A third product-related segmentation method groups consumers according to the strength of the brand loyalty they feel toward a product. A classic example of brand loyalty segmentation is a frequent-purchase program—it might be frequent flyer, frequent stay, or frequent purchase of shoes or gasoline. Other companies attempt to segment their market by developing brand loyalty over a period of time, through consumers' stages of life. Children whose parents dress them in Baby Gap clothes may grow up to wear Gap Kids and Gap clothing.

Companies fight for loyalty on just about every front. After McDonald's rolled out its McCafe line of coffee drinks, Burger King announced it would begin serving Seattle's Best Coffee in its restaurants. Adding Seattle's Best to its menu—a brand that Starbucks acquired—enables Burger King to take direct aim at McDonald's on yet another front.[44]

USING MULTIPLE SEGMENTATION BASES

Segmentation is a tool that can help marketers increase their accuracy in reaching the right markets. Like other marketing tools, segmentation is probably best used in a flexible manner—for instance, combining geographic and demographic segmentation techniques or dovetailing product-related segmentation with segmentation by income and expenditure patterns. The important point to keep in mind is that segmentation is a tool to help marketers get to know their potential customers better and ultimately satisfy their needs with the appropriate goods and services.

assessment check 3

3.1 List the three approaches to product-related segmentation.

3.2 What is the 80/20 principle?

THE MARKET SEGMENTATION PROCESS

④ Identify the steps in the market segmentation process and discuss four basic strategies for reaching target markets.

To this point, the chapter has discussed various bases on which companies segment markets. But how do marketers decide which segmentation base—or bases—to use? Firms may use a management-driven method, in which segments are predefined by managers based on their observation of the behavioural and demographic characteristics of likely users. Or they may use a market-driven method, in which segments are defined by asking customers which attributes are important. Then marketers follow a four-stage process.

1. DEVELOP A RELEVANT PROFILE FOR EACH SEGMENT

After identifying promising segments, marketers should understand the customers in each one. This in-depth analysis of customers helps managers accurately match buyers' needs with the firm's marketing offers. The process must identify characteristics that both explain the similarities among customers within each segment and account for differences among segments.

The task at this stage is to develop a profile of the typical customer in each segment. Such a profile might include information about lifestyle patterns, attitudes toward product attributes and brands, product-use habits, geographic locations, and demographic characteristics.

2. FORECAST MARKET POTENTIAL

In the second stage, market segmentation and market opportunity analysis combine to produce a forecast of market potential within each segment. Market potential sets the upper limit on the demand that competing firms can expect from a segment. Multiplying by market share determines a single firm's maximum sales potential. This step should define a preliminary go or no-go decision from management because the total sales potential in each segment must justify resources devoted to further analysis. For example, in deciding whether to market a new product to teens, electronics firms need to determine the demand for it and the disposable income of that group.

3. FORECAST PROBABLE MARKET SHARE

Once market potential has been estimated, a firm must forecast its probable market share. Competitors' positions in targeted segments must be analyzed, and a specific marketing strategy must be designed to reach these segments. These two activities may be performed simultaneously. Moreover, by settling on a marketing strategy and tactics, a firm determines the expected level of resources it must commit—that is, the costs it will incur to tap the potential demand in each segment.

Apple's iPod took the marketplace by storm, followed by the iPhone, and analysts believe these two products helped boost sales of the iMac computers as well. Apple's introduction of the iPad was met with a flood of orders: an estimated 75 million were sold on the first day alone.[45]

4. SELECT SPECIFIC MARKET SEGMENTS

The information, analysis, and forecasts accumulated throughout the entire market segmentation decision process allow management to assess the potential for achieving company goals and to justify committing resources in developing one or more segments. Demand forecasts, together with cost projections, determine the profits and the return on investment (ROI) that the company can expect from each segment. Marketing strategy and tactics must be designed to reinforce the firm's image, yet keep within its unique organizational capabilities.

At this point in the analysis, marketers weigh more than monetary costs and benefits; they also consider many difficult-to-measure but critical organizational and environmental factors. The firm may lack experienced personnel to launch a successful attack on an attractive market segment. Similarly, a firm with a dominant market position may face possible legal problems with the Competition Bureau if it increases its market concentration or is seen to be engaging in anti-competitive acts.[46] This assessment of both financial and nonfinancial factors is a difficult but vital step in the decision process.

STRATEGIES FOR REACHING TARGET MARKETS

Marketers spend a lot of time and effort developing strategies that will best match their firm's product offerings to the needs of particular target markets. An appropriate match is vital to the firm's marketing success. Marketers have identified four basic strategies for achieving consumer satisfaction: undifferentiated marketing, differentiated marketing, concentrated marketing, and micromarketing.

UNDIFFERENTIATED MARKETING

undifferentiated marketing
Strategy that focuses on producing a single product and marketing it to all customers; also called *mass marketing.*

A firm may produce only one product or product line and promote it to all customers with a single marketing mix; such a firm is said to practise **undifferentiated marketing**, sometimes called *mass marketing*. Undifferentiated marketing was much more common in the past than it is today.

While undifferentiated marketing is efficient from a production viewpoint, the strategy also brings inherent dangers. A firm that attempts to satisfy everyone in the market with one standard product may suffer if competitors offer specialized alternatives to smaller segments of the total market and better satisfy individual segments. In fact, firms that implement strategies of differentiated marketing, concentrated marketing, or micromarketing may capture enough small segments of the market to defeat another competitor's strategy of undifferentiated marketing. The golden arches of McDonald's have always stood for quick, inexpensive meals. Consumers could count on the same food and same dining experience at every McDonald's they visited. But McDonald's marketers are changing the firm's strategy somewhat in response to a trend that says consumers want a little luxury with their burger and fries and a more varied dining experience from restaurant to restaurant. Some stores feature wall-mounted televisions, a colour scheme featuring earth tones, wood fixtures, pendant lighting, and video game stations for children.[47]

DIFFERENTIATED MARKETING

differentiated marketing
Strategy that focuses on producing several products and pricing, promoting, and distributing them with different marketing mixes designed to satisfy smaller segments.

Firms that promote numerous products with differing marketing mixes designed to satisfy smaller segments are said to practise **differentiated marketing**. By providing increased satisfaction for each of many target markets, a company can produce more sales by following a differentiated marketing strategy than undifferentiated marketing would generate. A marketer of a variety of meat products might practise a differentiated strategy. In order to increase sales, it might introduce a new snack food for children to take to school for lunch. In general, however, differentiated marketing also raises costs. Production costs usually rise because additional products and variations require shorter production runs and increased setup times. Inventory costs rise because more products require added storage space and increased efforts for record keeping. Promotional costs also rise because each segment demands a unique promotional mix.

Despite higher marketing costs, however, an organization may be forced to practise differentiated marketing to diversify and reach new customers. The travel industry now recognises the need to target smaller groups of travellers with specialized interests. One company, for instance, may target seniors with trips that focus on history, hiking, golfing, cooking, or other special interests.

CONCENTRATED MARKETING

concentrated marketing
Focusing marketing efforts on satisfying a single market segment; also called *niche marketing.*

Rather than trying to market its products separately to several segments, a firm may opt for a concentrated marketing strategy. With **concentrated marketing** (also known as **niche marketing**), a firm focuses its efforts on profitably satisfying only one market segment. This approach can appeal to a small firm that lacks the financial resources of its competitors and to a company that offers highly specialised goods and services. American Express, a large firm with many financial products, introduced two new credit cards designed for very specific markets: The Knot, for engaged couples, and The Nest, for newlyweds.

Several stores sell skateboards, but West 49 is aimed straight at tweens and teens. This chain of skateboard shops is located in malls, because tweens don't drive. They make the stores cool places for kids to hang out. The stores have Nintendo games available for free to encourage kids to visit the stores even if they aren't going to buy a new board that day. They employ salespeople who are aged 16 to 19 and who really enjoy skateboarding, so the tweens feel comfortable asking questions. The salespeople are kept up to date on the latest changes through training and websites, which really isn't required because of their passion for the sport.[48]

MICROMARKETING

The fourth targeting strategy, still more narrowly focused than concentrated marketing, is **micromarketing**, which involves targeting potential customers at a very basic level, such as by postal code, specific occupation, or lifestyle. Ultimately, micromarketing can target even individuals themselves. The salesperson at your favourite clothing boutique may contact you when certain merchandise that she thinks you will like arrives at the store. The Internet allows marketers to make micromarketing even more effective. By tracking specific demographic and personal information, marketers can send email directly to individual consumers who are most likely to buy their products. If you purchase a book via Chapters.Indigo.ca, the company will offer to send you email notices about other books that may be of interest.

But micromarketing, like niche marketing, can become too much of a good thing if companies spend too much time, effort, and marketing dollars to unearth a market that is too small and specialised to be profitable. In addition, micromarketing may cause a company to lose sight of other larger markets. So it's important for marketers to assess the situation and pursue the most profitable markets.

micromarketing
Targeting potential customers at very narrow, basic levels, such as by postal code, specific occupation, or lifestyle—possibly even individuals themselves.

Marketoid

In 2009 the per capita consumption of cheese in Canada was over 12 kg.

SELECTING AND EXECUTING A STRATEGY

Although most organizations adopt some form of differentiated marketing, no single best choice suits all firms. Any of the alternatives may prove most effective in a particular situation. The basic determinants of a market-specific strategy are (1) company resources, (2) product homogeneity, (3) stage in the product life cycle, and (4) competitors' strategies.

A firm with limited resources may have to choose a concentrated marketing strategy. Small firms may be forced to select small target markets because of limitations in their sales force and advertising budgets. On the other hand, an undifferentiated marketing strategy suits a firm selling items perceived by consumers as relatively homogeneous. Marketers of grain, for example, sell standardized grades of generic products rather than individual brand names. Some petroleum companies implement undifferentiated marketing to distribute their gasoline to the mass market.

The firm's strategy may also change as its product progresses through the stages of the life cycle. During the early stages, undifferentiated marketing might effectively support the firm's effort to build initial demand for the item. In the later stages, however, competitive pressures may force modifications in products and in the development of marketing strategies aimed at segments of the total market.

The strategies of competitors also affect the choice of a segmentation approach. A firm may encounter obstacles to undifferentiated marketing if its competitors actively cultivate smaller segments. In such instances, competition usually forces each firm to adopt a differentiated marketing strategy.

Having chosen a strategy for reaching their firm's target market, marketers must then decide how best to position the product. The concept of **positioning** seeks to put a product in a certain

(5) **Summarize the types of positioning strategies, and explain the reasons for positioning and repositioning products.**

positioning Placing a product at a certain point or location within a market in the minds of prospective buyers.

Our coffee's creating quite a stir.

The delicious taste of our Canadian Blend is rivaled only by its incredible value. Made with a premium blend of perfectly roasted 100% Arabica beans, you might say it's making other brands wake up and smell the coffee.

Compliments
Canadian Blend Coffee 326 g
$5⁹⁹

Compliments

COURTESY OF SOBEYS INC.

Sobeys Inc. positions its Compliments *private label products against the competition by promoting quality and value.*

position, or place, in the minds of prospective buyers. Marketers use a positioning strategy to distinguish their firm's offerings from those of competitors and to create promotions that communicate the desired position.

To achieve this goal of positioning, marketers follow a number of positioning strategies. Possible approaches include positioning a product according to the following categories:

1. *Attributes*—Kashi, "7 whole grains on a mission"

2. *Price/quality*—Omega watches, "We measure the 100th of a second that separates winning from taking part"

3. *Competitors*—Walmart, "Save Money, Live Better"

4. *Application*—Blue Cross, "Enjoy the Benefits of Good Health"

5. *Product user*—Fisher-Price, "Play, Laugh, Grow"

6. *Product class*—BMW, the "ultimate driving machine"

Whatever strategy they choose, marketers want to emphasize a product's unique advantages and to differentiate it from competitors' options. A **positioning map** provides a valuable tool in helping managers position products by graphically illustrating consumers' perceptions of competing products within an industry. Marketers can create a competitive positioning map from information solicited from consumers or from their accumulated knowledge about a market. A positioning map might present two different characteristics—price and perceived quality—and show how consumers view a product and its major competitors based on these traits. The hypothetical positioning map in Figure 8.4 compares selected retailers based on possible perceptions of the prices and quality of their offerings.

Sometimes changes in the competitive environment force marketers to **reposition** a product—changing the position it holds in the minds of prospective buyers relative to the positions of competing products. Repositioning may even be necessary for already successful products or firms in order to gain greater market share. After General Motors sold its Saab division to Netherlands-based automaker Spyker, the new owner announced it would reposition the brand as "a performance-oriented niche car with an industry-leading environmental strategy."[49]

figure 8.4

Hypothetical Positioning Map for Selected Retailers

positioning map
A tool that helps marketers place products in a market by graphically illustrating consumers' perceptions of competing products within an industry.

repositioning
Changing the position of a product within the minds of prospective buyers relative to the positions of competing products.

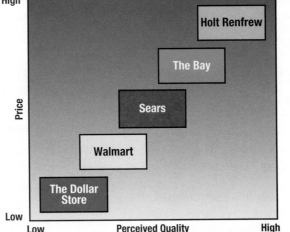

High

Holt Renfrew

The Bay

Sears

Walmart

The Dollar Store

Low

Price

Low   Perceived Quality   High

assessment check 5 ✓

5.1 What are the four determinants of a market-specific strategy?

5.2 What is the role of positioning in a marketing strategy?

Strategic Implications

To remain competitive, today's marketers must accurately identify potential customers. They can use a variety of methods to accomplish this, including segmenting markets by gender and geographic location. The trick is to figure out the best combination of methods for segmentation to identify the most lucrative, long-lasting potential markets. Marketers must also remain flexible, responding to markets as they change—for instance, following a generation as it ages or reaching out to new generations by revamping or repositioning products.

The greatest competitive advantage will belong to firms that can pinpoint and serve markets without segmenting them to the point where they are too small or specialized to garner profits. Marketers who can reach and communicate with the right customers have a greater chance of attracting and keeping those customers than marketers who are searching for the wrong customers in the wrong place. ◆◆◆

REVIEW OF CHAPTER OBJECTIVES

① **Identify the essential components of a market, outline the role of market segmentation in developing a marketing strategy, and describe the criteria necessary for effective segmentation.**

A market consists of people and organizations with the necessary purchasing power, willingness, and authority to buy. Consumer products are purchased by the ultimate consumer for personal use. Business products are purchased for use directly or indirectly in the production of other goods and services. Certain products may fall into both categories.

Market segmentation is the process of dividing a total market into several homogeneous groups. It is used in identifying a target market for a good or service. Segmentation is the key to deciding a marketing strategy.

Effective segmentation depends on these four basic requirements: (1) The segment must have measurable purchasing power and size; (2) marketers can find a way to promote to and serve the market; (3) marketers must identify segments large enough for profit potential; and (4) the firm can target a number of segments that match its marketing capabilities.

② **Explain the geographic, demographic, and psychographic approaches to segmenting consumer markets.**

Geographic segmentation divides the overall market into homogeneous groups according to population locations. Demographic segmentation classifies the market into groups based on characteristics such as age, gender, and income level. Psychographic segmentation uses behavioural profiles developed from analyses of consumers' activities, opinions, interests, and lifestyles to identify market segments.

③ **Describe product-related segmentation.**

Product-related segmentation can take three basic forms: segmenting based on the benefits that people seek when they buy a product; segmenting based on usage rates for a product; and segmenting according to consumers' brand loyalty toward a product.

④ **Identify the steps in the market segmentation process and discuss four basic strategies for reaching target markets.**

Market segmentation is the division of markets into relatively homogeneous groups. Segmentation follows a four-step sequence: (1) developing user profiles; (2) forecasting the overall market potential; (3) estimating market share; and (4) selecting specific market segments.

Four strategies are (1) undifferentiated marketing, which uses a single marketing mix; (2) differentiated marketing, which produces numerous products, each with its own mix; (3) concentrated marketing, which directs all the firm's marketing resources toward a small segment; and (4) micromarketing, which targets potential customers at basic levels, such as postal code or occupation.

⑤   **Summarize the types of positioning strategies, and explain the reasons for positioning and repositioning products.**

Positioning strategies include positioning a good or service according to attributes, price/quality, competitors, application, product user, and product class. Positioning helps distinguish a firm's products from those of competitors and provides a basis for marketing communications. Changes in the competitive environment may require repositioning to maintain or even grab more of the market share.

assessment check answers

1.1 Define target market.
A target market is the specific segment of consumers most likely to purchase a particular product.

1.2 Distinguish between a consumer product and a business product.
A consumer product is purchased by the ultimate buyer for personal use. A business product is purchased for use directly or indirectly in the production of other goods and services.

1.3 Define market segmentation and describe the role of market segmentation.
Market segmentation is the process of dividing a total market into several homogeneous groups.

The role of market segmentation is to identify the factors that affect purchase decisions and then group consumers according to the presence or absence of these factors.

1.4 Identify the four criteria for effective segmentation.
The four criteria for effective segmentation are these: (1) the market segment must present measurable purchasing power and size, (2) marketers must find a way to promote effectively and to serve the market segment, (3) marketers must identify segments that are sufficiently large to give them good profit potential, and (4) the firm must aim for segments that match its marketing capabilities.

2.1 Under what circumstances are marketers most likely to use geographic segmentation?
Marketers usually use geographic segmentation when regional preferences exist and when demand for categories of goods and services varies according to geographic region.

2.2 What is demographic segmentation and what are the major categories of demographic segmentation?
Demographic segmentation defines consumer groups according to demographic variables. The major categories of demographic segmentation are gender, age, ethnic group, family life cycle, household type, income, and expenditure patterns.

2.3 What is psychographic segmentation?
Psychographic segmentation divides a population into groups that have similar psychological characteristics, values, and lifestyles.

2.4 Name the eight categories of VALS.
The eight categories are innovators, thinkers, achievers, experiencers, believers, strivers, makers, and survivors.

3.1 List the three approaches to product-related segmentation.
The three approaches are segmenting by benefits sought, segmenting by usage rates, and segmenting by brand loyalty.

3.2 What is the 80/20 principle?
The 80/20 principle states that a big percentage (80 percent) of a product's revenues comes from a relatively small number (20 percent) of loyal customers.

4.1 Identify the four stages of the process of market segmentation.
The four stages are developing user profiles, forecasting the overall market potential, estimating market share, and selecting specific market segments.

4.2 Why is forecasting important to market segmentation?
Forecasting is important because it can define a preliminary go or no-go decision based on sales potential. It can help a firm avoid a disastrous move or point out opportunities.

4.3 Explain the difference between undifferentiated and differentiated marketing strategies and the benefits of concentrated marketing.
Undifferentiated marketing promotes a single product line to all customers with a single marketing mix. Differentiated marketing promotes numerous products with different marketing mixes designed to satisfy smaller segments. Concentrated marketing can allow a firm to focus on a single market segment, which is especially appealing to smaller firms and those that offer highly specialized goods and services.

5.1 What are the four determinants of a market-specific strategy?
The four determinants are company resources, product homogeneity, stage in the product life cycle, and competitors' strategies.

5.2 What is the role of positioning in a marketing strategy?
Positioning places a product in a certain position in the minds of prospective buyers so that marketers can create messages that distinguish their offerings from those of competitors.

MARKETING TERMS YOU NEED TO KNOW

These terms are printed in red in the text. They are defined in the margins of the chapter and in the Glossary that begins on p. G-1.

market 234
target market 234
consumer products 234
business products 235
market segmentation 235
geographic segmentation 236
census metropolitan area (CMA) 238
census agglomeration (CA) 238
core region 238

demographic segmentation 239
Generation X 241
baby boomers 241
cohort effect 242
Video Game Generation 243
family life cycle 245
psychographic segmentation 249
AIO statements 249
VALTM 250

product-related segmentation 252
80/20 principle 252
undifferentiated marketing 254
differentiated marketing 254
concentrated marketing 254
micromarketing 255
positioning 255
positioning map 256
repositioning 256

PROJECTS AND TEAMWORK EXERCISES

1. On your own or with a partner, choose one of the following consumer products and think about how it could be used as a business product. Then create a business advertisement for your product
   a. Lawn care products
   b. Microwave oven
   c. Tennis balls
   d. Bottled water
   e. Smartphone
   f. Vacuum cleaner

2. With a classmate, choose one of the following products you believe is generally targeted for either men or women and create an advertisement for the product aimed at the opposite gender.
   a. Barbecue grill and accessories
   b. Hunting or fishing supplies
   c. Nail salon
   d. Minivan
   e. Large-screen TV

3. Create a chart showing how your family's income and expenditure patterns have changed over the years as the family life cycle changes. You don't need exact figures, just the general picture. If possible, interview other family members for additional information.

4. With a classmate, choose a product and come up with a slogan representing each of the six positioning approaches for the product.

5. On your own or with a classmate, select one of the following products. Visit the firm's website to see how the product is positioned, then create an advertisement showing how you think marketers could reposition the product to gain greater market share.
   a. Gatorade
   b. Dove soap
   c. Barilla pasta
   d. Fiskars scissors
   e. Hallmark cards

CRITICAL-THINKING EXERCISES

1. Create a profile of yourself as part of a market segment. Include the following:
   a. Geographic location
   b. Gender and age
   c. Household type
   d. Income and spending habits.

2. Select one of the following products and explain how you would use segmentation by income and expenditure patterns to determine your targeted market.
   a. Disney theme parks
   b. Sony Cyber-shot camera
   c. Stouffer's Lean Cuisine
   d. Smart fortwo car

3. How do you think the Internet has affected differentiated marketing techniques?

4. Choose one of the following products and describe a marketing approach that segments the target market by benefits sought:
   a. Kryptonite bicycle lock
   b. College or university
   c. Pella windows and doors
   d. Water park
   e. Dairy Queen Ice Cream

5. Visit the website for a large company such as Kraft Foods, Sony, or Campbell Soups. Look for ways the firm practises differentiated marketing. How do you think this approach benefits the firm?

ETHICS EXERCISE

Marketers are making a new pitch to men—at the risk of political incorrectness. Marketers for firms such as Unilever and Wendy's have been frustrated at not being able to reach young male consumers with their messages. After searching for clues about what this crowd likes, these firms have created marketing campaigns designed to grab their attention—perhaps at the expense of other consumers. Some advertising is designed to appeal to "bad boy" attitudes, lowbrow humour, and sex.

1. What are some of the pitfalls of this kind of segmentation?
2. Do you think these ads will be successful in the long run? Why or why not?
3. Should marketers be concerned about offending one market segment when trying to reach another? Why or why not?

INTERNET EXERCISES

1. **Psychographic segmentation.** Visit the websites of Caterpillar, Hilton Hotels, and PepsiCo. How does each firm employ psychographic segmentation (such as VALS approach) to the marketing of its product? Is there a relationship between the use of psychographic segmentation and the types of products sold by each firm?
   a. www.cat.com
   b. www.hilton.com
   c. www.pepsico.com
2. **Market segmentation.** Go to the website of Siemens (http://siemens.com). How does Siemens segment its market, such as geographic, product related, demographic,

or brand loyalty? Does the firm use more than one method of product segmentation? Why or why not?
3. **Target market.** Visit the website of Philips (www.philips.com). What strategy or strategies does the firm employ for reaching its target market? Does it rely more on undifferentiated or differentiated marketing?

Note: Internet Web addresses change frequently. If you don't find the exact sites listed, you may need to access the organization's or company's home page and search from there or use a search engine such as Google.

CASE 8.1

Molson Coors Adapts to a Changing Market

The Canadian market for alcoholic beverages is roughly $20 billion a year. Statistics Canada keeps track of sales in this market with three categories: beer, wine, and spirits. The spirits category includes drinks like vodka, rum, and brandy.

Canadians are beer drinkers. Beer sales represented 46 percent of the total alcoholic beverage market for the year ending March 2010. However, beer sales have been declining in relation to the other categories, down from 52 percent ten years earlier. The per capita consumption of beer is over 83 litres per person. Ontario, Quebec, and British Columbia saw the highest beer sales. The highest per capita beer sales were in the Yukon and Newfoundland.

In contrast to the beer market, wines sales have been increasing. Wine sales accounted for 29 percent of the total market. Red wine accounted for 63 percent of all wines sales. Imported products, both red and white wines, increased with 75 percent of red wines and 61 percent of white wines sold in Canada coming from other countries. The highest total wine sales were in Quebec, Ontario, and British Columbia. On a per capita basis, the Quebecers were the highest wine drinkers and British Columbia came in second.

Sales of spirits have been declining. Sale of whisky-type products were the highest in market share, accounting for 27 percent of spirit sales. Vodka sales have been increasing, amounting to 23 percent of the category. The provinces with the highest sale of spirits are Ontario, British Columbia, and Alberta. On a per capita basis the highest consumers of spirits could be found in the Yukon and Newfoundland.

So how do companies like Molson Coors' brewery, which contains the name of one of Canada's oldest brands, deal with declining overall sales in their market and the threat of imported beer brands? Molson had been experiencing declining sales since the late 1990s when it was using the popular "I am Canadian" promotion, so a new approach to its marketing strategy was needed. Its new marketing strategy included Olympic sponsorship, new products, and a new segmentation strategy.

Molson Coors was an official Olympic sponsor and the company's marketing campaign was effective. The company's promotional campaign for the Olympics was called "Made in Canada." The company launched its new television commercial during the opening ceremonies. To support the television ads, the company launched its "Gear Up For Gold" Facebook application.

Visitors to their Facebook site could create a picture of themselves wearing a Team Canada hockey jersey. Molson Coors also invited Canadians to submit photos to be incorporated in a photo mosaic on the side of its Vancouver brewery—more than 13 000 pictures were sent in.

Molson Coors also realized there were certain segments of the market it was not reaching, namely women and health-conscious men. The company developed a low-calorie beer it named Molson Canadian 67 because of the 67 calories in each bottle. In order to get the message out, ads were run in magazines like *Food & Drink*, *Chatelaine*, and *Flare*. Other advertising to launch the new product included television ads and online and print ads. Another new product was developed for the Quebec market.

The company also changed its segmentation strategy. Instead of trying to make its beer brands seem more hip and cool in order to reach the 18- to 24-year-old markets, it decided to move away from segmenting the market on demographics. Its new segmentation strategy would focus on values profiles. For example, the value profile for the Molson Export product was courage, determination, and effort.

Molson Coors was rewarded for the changes in its marketing strategy by an increase in sales and the Marketer of the Year award.

Questions for Critical Thinking

1. If Molson Coors wanted to expand its target markets further, what segment or segments of the market might the firm include? Can you think of value profiles for those segments?
2. What promotions—social media, mobile, etc.—could Molson Coors use to reach its target markets?

Sources: Jeff Beer, "Canadians Don't Tippy-Toe, Says New Molson Ad," *Marketing*, http://www.marketingmag.ca, February 12, 2010; "Molson Credits Olympics for Rising Sales of Flagship Canadian Brand," *Marketing*, http://www.marketingmag.ca, May 4, 2010; Matt Semansky, "Molson Targets the Calorie-Conscious With New Beer," *Marketing*, http://www.marketingmag.ca, October 5, 2009; Kristin Laird and David Brown, "Molson M Goes on Sale in Quebec," *Marketing*, http://www.marketingmag.ca, November 19, 2009; "After a Tough Quarter, Molson to Launch Two More Brands," *Marketing*, http://www.marketingmag.ca, November 4, 2009; Caroline Forth, "Molson Export Focuses on Action," *Marketing*, http://www.marketingmag.ca, January 12, 2011; Jeromy Lloyd, Matt Semansky, Kristin Laird, Lesley Young, Nicolas Ritoux, Eve Lazarus, and Jeff Beer, "The Top Marketers of 2010," *Marketing*, http://www.marketingmag.ca, November 22, 2010; "Control and Sale of Alcoholic Beverages," Statistics Canada, *The Daily*, April 20, 2011, http://www.statcan.gc.ca.

CASE 8.2

Household CFO

Marketers used to call the household CFO (household chief financial officer) the female head of the household—so why the name change? Research shows that women are responsible for the majority of household buying decisions. Women control and spend most of the disposable income in Canadian households. The challenge for marketers is to understand this consumer. Research shows that the characteristics of this group are very diverse and constantly evolving, and their purchase decision making is different from men.

Canadian women make up slightly more than half of the population. The percentage of women in the older age groups is higher than men because they have a higher life expectancy—roughly five years longer. In fact, 69 percent of the over 85 age group is female. Nineteen percent of the female population was born in a country other than Canada and of this group 62 percent live in Toronto or Vancouver.

Although about 50 percent of women are living in a husband-and-wife relationship, this percent has been steadily decreasing. This means that more women are living alone—over one and a half million. The number of women living alone has more than doubled in the last 30 years. More senior women are living alone, but 20 percent of households headed by single women also include children. Canadian women are also having fewer children.

Women are slightly less likely to have a university degree than men; however, this is likely to change in the future as more women are now attending university. Women are still underrepresented at the doctorate level, representing slightly over a quarter of this group. Women are still less likely to pursue a higher education in the areas of math, science, or engineering.

Women in Canada have an average annual income of around $30 000 but this was roughly $17 000 a year less than men. Women in Newfoundland and New Brunswick earned the least, while women in Ontario and Alberta earned the most. Women aged 45 to 54 had the largest average annual income at just below $41 000 while women aged 16 to 19 had the lowest, at $7100. Female single-parent families had the lowest average annual income of any family group at just over $42 000 compared to male single-parent families at over $60 000. The highest income by family group was for two-parent families with children at over $100 000.

Indicators of financial security include saving for retirement and home ownership. Women are less likely to save for retirement than men. Not only did fewer women contribute to a retirement savings plan, those that did contribute tended to contribute less. Women, however, are more likely to be home owners. Women who lived alone have a slightly higher level of home ownership than their male counterparts at 49 percent compared to 47 percent respectively. More than half of the single-parent families owned their homes as opposed to renting accommodation.

Research shows that there is a difference between men and women on what is important to them and what influences their purchase decisions. This could be why so many marketers are not engaging their female customers with their current marketing programs. Women want to build a relationship with a brand they trust. Women feel good about their increasing importance as consumers but they view the world differently than men do. They want to make a difference in the world, particularly as it relates to world peace and prosperity. Women, especially those with children, want to give back to their communities. Women want marketers to answer the question "How will this product or service make my life better?"

Women are early adopters of technology. They use social media, the Internet, smartphones, and texting. Technology keeps women connected to their families, helps them organize their busy lives, and when they have time entertains them. Marketers need to have a multi-platform campaign in order to reach this group because their use of technology changes depending on the time of day. In the morning, women are online for approximately two hours but the majority of that time is spent on work-related issues. Over lunch, their online activity drops and changes to mostly shopping or entertainment sites. During the afternoon, their online activity changes back to work-related issues but they visit sites that will provide information on what to make for dinner. The evening's online activities consist of games and social networks. When women were asked how they spend their time online, 99 percent said they check their email and 78 percent are on Facebook. The next highest online activities, measured by time, were doing their banking (70 percent), research (68 percent), food-related sites (63 percent), and coupon sites (56 percent).

Some industries and companies have found ways to engage women, but others are missing their targets totally. For example, the banking industry is not doing a good job of connecting with women. Research shows that 60 percent of women trust a used car salesperson more than their financial institution. Thirty-four percent of Canadian women have a financial plan. What is important to them is paying down their debts and being able to pay their bills each month. Financial experts believe that women should also be concerned about their financial futures given the higher divorce rates and the fact they live longer than their male counterparts.

Two companies that are engaging women are Avon and Unilever's Dove campaigns. Both of these companies developed cause-related marketing campaigns.

Avon sponsors events related to breast cancer. The company doesn't just hand out information or put pink ribbons on its packages, it finds ways to really get involved. At one event, the company provided product samples for those taking part. The event involved women walking or running over a two-day period to raise money for research. Participants were supplied with Avon products throughout the event. At the end of the event, participants were asked which of the sponsoring companies they remembered and why. Avon was a standout in the minds of the women taking part in the event. Avon provided sunscreen and hand sanitizer at each rest stop and stocked the showers with soap at the overnight camping area. One women who did not use Avon products before the event commented, "I could not make it through the day without these little items I found along the way." She went on to blog about Avon's effort to connect with those involved in the event.

Dove's self-esteem campaign was first launched in 2004 but it is still successful. Based on research that found that women and girls do not feel they are beautiful, the company developed a campaign to change these attitudes. Using several different platforms to engage different customers groups, the "Campaign for Real Beauty" has been an award winner. Whether it's the television commercials, You Tube videos, or workshops for teens, the company keeps the theme in mind. The company supports the Dove Self-Esteem Fund, which provides resources for teachers, moms, and mentors to build esteem in young girls and women.

It is clear that companies like Avon and Unilever understand the difference in the way men and women make purchase decisions and what is important to women.

Questions for Critical Thinking

1. If you were a marketer of products like Avon or Unilever aimed at women, what are some ways you could segment this market?

2. What are some ways that Canadian financial institutions could improve their image with women?

3. How can companies use technology such as social media, the Internet, or smartphones to better engage women?

Sources: "Advertorial: "How Will It Make My Life Better? Asks Mom" *Marketing*, http://www.marketingmag.ca, April 19, 2011; "Marketing to Women Panelists Pick Their Faves," *Marketing*, http://www.marketingmag.ca, April 19, 2011; Kristin Laird, "Dove's Tips on Keeping Campaigns Fresh," *Marketing*, http://www.marketingmag.ca, April 19, 2011; Kristin Laird, "Dove's New Dish on Beauty," *Marketing*, http://www.marketingmag.ca, April 19, 2011; Kristin Laird, "Beyond the Ribbon," *Marketing*, http://www.marketingmag.ca, April 19, 2011; Alicia Androich and Kristin Laird, "Lessons for Reaching Households CFOs at Marketing to Women Conference," *Marketing*, http://www.marketingmag.ca, April 19, 2010; Alicia Androich, "A Look Inside Canadian Women's Online Habits," *Marketing*, http://www.marketingmag.ca, April 19, 2011; Cara Williams, "Economic Well-Being," Statistics Canada, Component of Statistics Canada Catalogue no. 89-503-X, Women in Canada: A Gender-based Statistical Report, December 2010; "Women in Canada: Edition: A Gender-based Statistical Report," Fifth Edition, Statistics Canada, Catalogue no. 89-503-XIE.

part 4

PRODUCT DECISIONS

chapter 9 **Product and Service Strategies**

chapter 10 **Developing and Managing Brand and Product Strategies**

Product and Service Strategies

CHAPTER OBJECTIVES

① Define product, distinguish between goods and services, and how they relate to the goods–services continuum, and explain the importance of the service sector in today's marketplace.

② Describe the classifications of consumer and business goods and services.

③ Explain how quality is used by marketers as a product strategy and why firms develop lines of related products.

④ Describe the way marketers typically measure product mixes and make product mix decisions.

⑤ Explain the concept of the product life cycle and identify the different stages.

⑥ Describe how a firm can extend a product's life cycle, and explain why certain products may be deleted.

GREEN WORKS: CLOROX AIMS TO CLEAN UP THE ENVIRONMENT

When you do laundry, you want your clothes to come out clean. Add a little bleach, and those athletic socks emerge a crisp white. Clorox has been whitening socks, T-shirts, towels, and sheets—anything needing a dose of bleach—for more than a century. While consumers are loyal to the brand, until now no one would have pointed to Clorox products as good for the environment. In fact, detergents in general, along with household cleaners, have come under fire from environmental groups for the chemicals they contain and for the residues they leave in groundwater and the soil. So why are people suddenly using *Clorox* and *green* in the same sentence?

The Clorox Co. has developed a line of natural, biodegradable household cleaners—including an all-purpose cleaner, window cleaner, and bathroom cleaner—called Green Works. The new products are available at traditional supermarkets, Walmart, and Canadian Tire, so people don't have to travel to specialty stores to find them. Best of all, they work. In the past, Clorox has been reluctant to join the league of green products because of the products' negative reputation among mainstream consumers. "There are four reasons this [green] category has been held

back," explains the brand manager for Green Works. "There's a perception that natural products don't work. They've been very expensive. People often have to go to special stores to get them. And there's not a brand that consumers know and trust." But the only growing niche of the market for household cleaners is the green one. So Clorox decided to take the plunge with a new group of products—its first new branded line in 20 years. Company scientists came up with a line of cleaners that are at least 90 percent natural and made from plant- or mineral-based ingredients instead of petroleum. In addition, they are not tested on animals.

Although getting these products on store shelves wasn't easy, the company has another hurdle: to get skeptical consumers to buy them. Some might continue to believe the products won't work. Others might dismiss the line as an opportunistic attempt to cash in on an eco-friendly trend. Clorox, which had built a solid reputation for traditional cleaning products, didn't have expertise when it came to environmental issues. So the firm's marketers made a bold move: they approached the Sierra Club for help. If people were wary that Clorox could produce an environmentally friendly cleaner, maybe the Sierra Club could provide some

credibility. "The only way to [be successful with this] is to combine a very well-known cleaning brand with a very green brand. And we are the green brand," explains the executive director of the Sierra Club. After extensive testing, the Sierra Club agreed to endorse the Green Works line.

Within one year of launching the product line, Clorox was market leader in the category with 42 percent market share. Clorox attributed the success of the line to having a good product, an established distribution network, and a lower price than the competition. The product line also won a Best New Product Award in the packaging category. Contest judges stated, "It has everything an environmentally friendly cleaner should have right down to the recyclable packaging." Another sign that the product category was not going away was the fact that competitors developed similar products but while the competitor's product were more environmentally friendly than their current products, they were not as good as the Green Works line.

The success of the Green Works line also prompted the company to change its approach to other products. Clorox committed to disclosing all ingredients in all its products.[1]

connecting with customers

Clorox responds to the growing concerns consumers have about the environment by developing a new line of cleaning products, Green Works. The cleaners have ingredients like coconut oil, corn, and lemon and recyclable packaging.

Chapter Overview

We've discussed how marketers conduct research to determine unfilled needs in their markets, how customers behave during the purchasing process, and how firms expand their horizons overseas. Now our attention shifts to a company's marketing mix, the blend of four elements of a marketing strategy—product, distribution, promotion, and price—to satisfy the target market. This chapter focuses on how firms select and develop the goods and services they offer, starting with planning which products to offer. The other variables of the marketing mix—distribution channels, promotional plans, and pricing decisions—must accommodate the product strategy selected.

Marketers develop strategies to promote both tangible goods and intangible services. Any such strategy begins with investigation, analysis, and selection of a particular target market, and it continues with the creation of a marketing mix designed to satisfy that segment. Both tangible goods and intangible services intend to satisfy consumer wants and needs, but the marketing efforts supporting them may be vastly different.

Many firms sell both types of products, offering innovative goods and ongoing service to attract and retain customers for the long term. Doing so can be profitable, as you'll see in this chapter.

This chapter examines both the similarities and the differences in marketing goods and services. It then presents basic concepts—product classifications, development of product lines, and the product life cycle—that marketers apply in developing successful products. Finally, the chapter discusses product deletion and product mix decisions. ◆◆◆

① **Define product, distinguish between goods and services and how they relate to the goods–services continuum, and explain the importance of the service sector in today's marketplace.**

Marketoid

In 2009, more than 75 percent of Canadians were employed in jobs in the service sector.

product Bundle of physical, service, and symbolic attributes designed to satisfy a customer's wants and needs.

service Intangible task that satisfies the needs of consumer and business users.

good Tangible products that customers can see, hear, smell, taste, or touch.

WHAT IS A PRODUCT?

At first, you might think of a product as an object you hold in your hand, such as a baseball or a toothbrush. You might also think of the car you drive as a product. But this doesn't take into account the idea of a service as a product. Nor does it consider the idea of what the product is used for. So a television is more than a box with a screen and a remote control. It's really a means of providing entertainment—your favourite movies, news programs, or reality shows. Marketers acknowledge this broader conception of product; they realize that people buy *want satisfaction* rather than objects.

You might feel a need for a television to satisfy a want for entertainment. You might not know a lot about how the device itself works, but you understand the results. If you are entertained by watching TV, then your wants are satisfied. If, however, the television is working just fine but you don't like the programming offered, you may need to satisfy your desire for entertainment by changing your service package to include premium channels. The service and its offerings is a product.

Marketers think of a product as a compilation of package design and labelling, brand name, price, availability, warranty, reputation, image, and customer-service activities that add value for the customer. Consequently, a **product** is a bundle of physical, service, and symbolic attributes designed to satisfy a customer's wants and needs.

WHAT ARE GOODS AND SERVICES?

Services are intangible products. A general definition identifies **services** as intangible tasks that satisfy the needs of consumer and business users. But you can't hold a service in your hand the way you can **goods**, which are tangible products that customers can see, hear, smell, taste, or touch. Most service providers cannot transport or store their products; customers simultaneously buy and consume these products, like haircuts, car repairs, and visits to the dentist. One way to distinguish services from goods is the **goods–services continuum**, as shown in Figure 9.1.

This spectrum helps marketers visualize the differences and similarities between goods and services. A car is a pure good, but the dealer may also offer repair and maintenance services or include the services in the price of a lease. The car falls at the pure good extreme of the continuum because

Pure Good

Car

Dinner in an
Exclusive
Restaurant

Pure Service

Hair Salon

figure 9.1

**The Goods–Services
Continuum**

the repair and maintenance services are an adjunct to the purchase. A dinner at an exclusive restaurant is a mix of goods and services. It combines the physical goods of gourmet food with the intangible services of attentive wait staff, elegant surroundings, and perhaps a visit to your table by the chef or restaurant owner to make sure your meal is perfect. At the other extreme, a dentist provides pure service—cleaning teeth, filling cavities, taking X-rays. The dentist's office may also sell items such as electric toothbrushes or night guards, but it's the service that is primary in patients' minds.

You can begin to see the diversity of services. Services can be distinguished from goods in several ways:

goods–services continuum Spectrum along which goods and services fall according to their attributes, from pure good to pure service.

1. *Services are intangible.* Services do not have physical features that buyers can see, hear, smell, taste, or touch prior to purchase. Service firms essentially ask their customers to buy a promise—that the haircut be stylish, that the insurance will cover injuries, that the lawn will be mowed.

2. *Services are inseparable from the service providers.* Consumer perceptions of a service provider become their perceptions of the service itself. The name of a doctor, lawyer, or hair stylist is synonymous with the service they provide. A bad haircut can deter customers, while a good one will attract more to the salon. A house-cleaning service such as Merry Maids depends on its workers to leave each house spotless, because its reputation is built on this service.

3. *Services are perishable.* Providers cannot maintain inventories of their services. A day spa can't stockpile facials or pedicures. A travel agent can't keep quantities of vacations on a shelf. For this reason, some service providers, such as airlines and hotels, may raise their prices during times of peak demand—such as during spring break from school—and reduce them when demand declines.

4. *Companies cannot easily standardize services.* However, many firms are trying to change this. Most fast-food chains promise that you'll get your meal within a certain number of minutes and that it will taste the way you expect it to. A hotel chain may have the same amenities at each location—a pool, fitness room, free breakfast, or movies.

5. *Buyers often play important roles in the creation and distribution of services.* Service transactions frequently require interaction between buyer and seller at the production and distribution stages. While some restaurant chains are attempting to standardize to meet customers' expectations, others are striving to customize, involving consumers in decisions about how food is prepared or presented—which is a service in itself.

6. *Service standards show wide variations.* An upscale steakhouse and your school cafeteria are both restaurants. Their customers, however, experience considerably different cuisine, physical surroundings, service standards, and prices.

Keep in mind that a product often blurs the distinction between services and goods. Avis is a service that provides rental cars, which are goods. Lenscrafters provides eye examinations—services from optometrists—while also selling eyeglasses and contact lenses (goods). An example of how a service can use online marketing is described in the "Marketing in a Digital World" feature.

Insurance companies provide services to protect your possessions.

Join the Burger Backlash Revolution

TACO Bell, the Mexican food alternative to traditional fast food, has declared war on burgers. Taco Bell's founder, Glen Bell, opened a hot dog and burger drive-in restaurant in the same town as the first McDonald's restaurant in the early 1950s. Bell decided to change the focus of his chain to Mexican food in order to provide customers with an alternative to burgers.

Bell sold the Taco Bell chain to PepsiCo in the 1970s but Taco Bell's battle with burgers is still going on. The burger backlash campaign is symbolized by an arm holding a burrito with a Taco Bell tattoo and a banner with the burger backlash Web address—burgerbacklash.ca.

The burger backlash campaign is Taco Bell's first social media campaign. Aimed at their target market of 18- to 24-year-old males, the burger backlash website invites visitors to join the burger revolution. Visitors are enticed to find out more with a headline type announcement proclaiming "Big Burger is watching—watch back." The burger conspiracy is exposed in a short video clip where the burger barons are seen plotting their

next move. The burger barons are retro black and white photos of men in business suits. At the end of the video clip, visitors are invited to "connect with Facebook to create the ultimate burger backlash experience."

The burger backlash headquarters website also encourages fans to "join—expose—pledge—speak out—and eat."

The campaign is supported with two 15-second television spots and signage in the Taco Bell restaurants. Video is included on other websites such as MSN.ca and TSN.ca and transit shelter ads. All promotional material directs viewers to the Burgerbacklash.ca website.

Whether the burger backlash campaign gets more people to eat Mexican food or not, Taco Bell did "make a stand against boring."

Sources: Burgerbacklash website, http://www.burgerbacklash.ca, July 4, 2011; Taco Bell company website, http://www.tacobell.ca, July 4, 2011; Chris Powell, "Taco Bell Takes On 'Big Burger' in New Campaign," *Marketing*, http://www.marketingmag.ca, June 28, 2011.

IMPORTANCE OF THE SERVICE SECTOR

You would live a very different life without service firms to fill many needs. You could not place a phone call, log on to the Internet, flip a switch for electricity, or even take a college or university course if organizations did not provide such services. During an average day, you probably use many services without much thought, but these products play an integral role in your life.

The service sector makes a crucial contribution to the Canadian economy by providing both products and jobs. Several of Canada's largest companies are pure services, such as the Royal Bank of Canada and the Bank of Nova Scotia. Other large companies, Research In Motion Ltd., for example, while not entirely a service firm, provide services in conjunction with the goods they sell.[2]

The Canadian service sector now makes up more than 70 percent of the economy and is growing faster than the goods-producing sector. The service sector employs about 75 percent of Canadians and continues to increase. Many service sector jobs are knowledge intensive and therefore employ a high number of university- and college-educated employees. Some of Canada's highest-paying jobs are also in services.[3]

Services also play a crucial role in the international competitiveness of Canadian firms. Canadian service exports represent more than 12 percent of products exported by Canadian firms. The United States is Canada's largest trading partner in services as it is in manufactured goods. The European Union, Japan, Brazil, and China are also important trade partners for service companies. International trade of services is less dependent on the U.S. market for service exports than companies in the goods-producing sector. Canada is one of the world's largest service exporters.[4]

Observers cite several reasons for the growing importance of services, including consumers' desire for speed and convenience and the technological advances that allow firms to fulfill this demand. Services that involve wireless communications, data

Professional services: An important part of the service sector.

backup and storage, and even meal preparation for busy families are on the rise. Consumers are also looking to advisors to help plan for a financially secure future and for insurance to protect their homes and families.

Most service firms emphasize marketing as a significant activity for two reasons. First, the growth potential of service transactions represents a vast marketing opportunity. Second, the environment for services is changing. For instance, increased competition is forcing traditional service industries to differentiate themselves from their competitors. Providing superior service is one way to develop long-term customer relationships and compete more effectively. Relationship marketing is just one of the ways service firms can develop and solidify their customer relationships.

CLASSIFYING GOODS AND SERVICES FOR CONSUMER AND BUSINESS MARKETS

A firm's choices for marketing a good or service depend largely on the offering itself and on the nature of the target market. Product strategies differ for consumer and business markets. Consumer products (sometimes called B2C products) are those destined for use by ultimate consumers. **Business products** or **B2B products** (also called *industrial* or *organizational products*), as discussed in Chapter 5, contribute directly or indirectly to the output of other products for resale. Marketers further subdivide these two major categories into more specific categories, as discussed in this section.

Some products fall into both categories. A case in point is prescription drugs. Traditionally, pharmaceutical companies marketed prescription drugs to doctors, who then made the purchase decision for their patients by writing the prescription. Thus the medications could be classified as a business product. However, many drug companies now advertise their products in consumer-oriented media, including magazines and television. Even though it is not legal to show these ads on Canadian television, Canadian cable and satellite television services provide access to American channels so Canadian consumers see these ads.

TYPES OF CONSUMER PRODUCTS

The most widely used product classification system focuses on the buyer's perception of a need for the product and his or her buying behaviour. However, **unsought products** are marketed to consumers who may not yet recognize any need for them. Examples of unsought products are long-term-care insurance and funeral services.

However, relatively few products fall into the unsought category. Most consumers recognize their own needs for various types of consumer purchases and actively seek them, so customer buying behaviour variations are the key to distinguishing the various categories. The most common classification scheme for sought products divides consumer goods and services into three groups based on customers' buying behaviour: convenience, shopping, and specialty. Figure 9.2 illustrates samples of these three categories, together with the unsought classification.

② Describe the classifications of consumer and business goods and services.

business-to-business (B2B) product Product that contributes directly or indirectly to the output of other products for resale; also called industrial or organizational product.

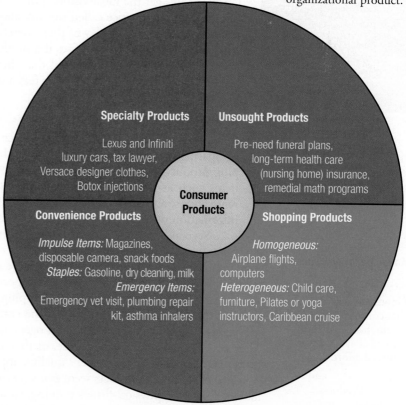

figure 9.2

Classification of Consumer Products

unsought products
Products marketed to consumers who may not yet recognize a need for them.

An unsought product.

convenience products
Goods and services that consumers want to purchase frequently, immediately, and with minimal effort.

impulse goods and services Products purchased on the spur of the moment.

Convenience Products

Convenience products refer to goods and services that consumers want to purchase frequently, immediately, and with minimal effort. Milk, bread, and soft drinks are convenience products. Convenience services include 24-hour quick-stop stores, walk-in hair salons, copy shops, and dry cleaners.

Marketers further subdivide the convenience category into impulse items, staples, or emergency items. **Impulse goods and services** are purchased on the spur of the moment, such as a visit to a car wash or a pack of gum tossed in at the register. Some marketers have even come up with ways to make impulse shopping on the Internet attractive. Canada Flowers, a site that provides flowers, gift baskets, and plants, promotes same-day delivery on its website. Consumers can order such items as roses for a birthday or a "get well soon" arrangement and it will be delivered the same day anywhere in Canada.[5]

Staples are convenience goods and services that consumers constantly replenish to maintain a ready inventory; gasoline, toothpaste, and dry cleaning are good examples. Marketers spend many hours and dollars creating messages for consumers about these products, partly because there are so many competitors.

Emergency goods and services are bought in response to unexpected and urgent needs. A snow shovel purchased during a snowstorm and an emergency visit to a vet with a sick pet are examples. Depending on your viewpoint, the products offered by Canada Flowers as last-minute gifts could also fall into this category!

Since consumers devote little effort to purchase decisions about convenience products, marketers must strive to make these exchanges as simple as possible. Store location can boost a convenience product's visibility. Marketers compete vigorously for prime locations, which can make all the difference between a consumer choosing one gas station, vending machine, or dry cleaner over another.

In addition, location *within* a store can make the difference between success and failure of a product, which is why manufacturers fight so hard for the right spot on supermarket shelves. Typically, the larger and more powerful grocery manufacturers such as Sara Lee, Kellogg, and General Mills get the most visible spots. But visibility to consumers sometimes comes at a price, often through a practice called slotting allowances, or slotting fees, money paid by producers to retailers to guarantee display of their merchandise. According to retailers, the purpose of slotting allowances is to cover their losses if a product doesn't sell. The practice of slotting fees has been investigated and it was discovered that these fees are far from uniform; they vary greatly across product categories, in both whether fees are charged and, if they are, how large the fees will be.

Shopping Products

In contrast to the purchase of convenience items, consumers buy **shopping products** only after comparing competing offerings on such characteristics as price, quality, style, and colour. Shopping products typically cost more than convenience purchases. This category includes tangible items such as clothing, furniture, and appliances as well as services such as child care, home renovations, auto repairs, and insurance. The purchaser of a shopping product lacks complete information prior to the buying trip and gathers information during the buying process.

Several important features distinguish shopping products: physical attributes, service attributes such as warranties and after-sale service terms, prices, styling, and places of purchase. A store's name and reputation have considerable influence on people's buying behaviour. The personal selling efforts of salespeople also provide important promotional support.

Buyers and marketers treat some shopping products, such as refrigerators and washing machines, as relatively *homogeneous* products. To the consumer, one brand seems largely the same as another. Marketers may try to differentiate homogeneous products from competing products in several ways. They may emphasize price and value, or they may attempt to educate buyers about less obvious features that contribute to a product's quality, appeal, and uniqueness.

Other shopping products seem *heterogeneous* because of basic differences among them. Examples include furniture, physical-fitness training, vacations, and clothing. Differences in features often separate competing heterogeneous shopping products in the minds of consumers. Perceptions of style, colour, and fit can all affect consumer choices.

All have clear bins.

Clear bins let you see dirt and dust collect as you clean your home. But how much is captured is not always so clear.

But Dyson cyclone technology captures more dirt than any other.

When James Dyson developed the world's first cyclonic vacuum cleaner, everyone advised against having a clear bin. But inside you could watch cyclonic forces separate the dirt and dust from the airflow.

Generating 136,000G, Dyson cyclone technology captures more dirt than any other. It is protected by 190 patents.

dyson
The vacuum cleaner that doesn't lose suction.
www.dyson.com

Examples of a convenience product and a shopping product.

Specialty Products

Specialty products offer unique characteristics that cause buyers to prize those particular brands. They typically carry high prices, and many represent well-known brands. Examples of specialty goods include Hermès scarves, Gucci leather goods, Ritz-Carlton resorts, Tiffany jewellery, and Lexus automobiles. Specialty services include professional services such as financial, legal, and medical services.

Purchasers of specialty goods and services know exactly what they want—and they are willing to pay accordingly. These buyers begin shopping with complete information, and they refuse to accept substitutes. Because consumers are willing to exert considerable effort to obtain specialty products, producers can distribute them through relatively few retail locations. In fact, some firms intentionally limit the range of retailers that carry their products to add to their cachet. Both highly personalized service by sales associates and image advertising help marketers promote specialty items. Because these products are available in so few retail outlets, advertisements frequently list their locations or give toll-free telephone numbers that provide customers with this information.

In recent years some makers of specialty products have broadened their market by selling some of their goods through company-owned discount outlets. But these stores nearly always carry items from previous years' inventory. The stores attract consumers who want to own specialty items but who cannot or do not wish to pay their high prices.

CLASSIFYING CONSUMER SERVICES

Like tangible goods, services are also classified based on the convenience, shopping, and specialty products categories. But added insights can be gained by examining several factors that are unique to classifying services. Service firms may serve consumer markets, business markets, or both. A firm offering architectural services may design either residential or commercial buildings or both. A cleaning service may clean houses, offices, or both. In addition, services can be classified as equipment-based or people-based. A car wash is an equipment-based service, whereas a law office is people-based. Marketers may ask themselves any of these five questions to help classify certain services:

1. What is the nature of the service?
2. What type of relationship does the service organization have with its customers?
3. How much flexibility is there for customization and judgment on the part of the service provider?
4. Do demand and supply for the service fluctuate?
5. How is the service delivered?[6]

staples Convenience goods and services that consumers constantly replenish to maintain a ready inventory.

emergency goods and services Products bought in response to unexpected and urgent needs.

shopping products Products that consumers purchase after comparing competing offerings.

specialty products Products that offer unique characteristics that cause buyers to prize those particular brands.

table 9.1   *Marketing Impact of the Consumer Products Classification System*

	CONVENIENCE PRODUCTS	SHOPPING PRODUCTS	SPECIALTY PRODUCTS
Consumer Factors			
Planning time involved in purchase	Very little	Considerable	Extensive
Purchase frequency	Frequent	Less frequent	Infrequent
Importance of convenient location	Critical	Important	Unimportant
Comparison of price and quality	Very little	Considerable	Very little
Marketing Mix Factors			
Price	Low	Relatively high	High
Importance of seller's image	Unimportant	Very important	Important
Distribution channel length	Long	Relatively short	Very short
Number of sales outlets	Many	Few	Very few; often one per market area
Promotion	Advertising and promotion by producer	Personal selling and advertising by both producer and retailer	Personal selling and advertising by both producer and retailer

A marketer attempting to classify the activities of a boarding kennel would answer these questions in one way; a marketer evaluating a lawn care service would come up with different answers. For example, customers would bring their pets to the kennel to receive service, while the lawn care staff would travel to customers' homes to provide service. Workers at the kennel are likely to have closer interpersonal relationships with pet owners—and their pets—than lawn care workers, who might not meet their customers at all. A marketer assessing demand for the services of a ski resort or a food concession at the beach is likely to find fluctuations by season. And a dentist has flexibility in making decisions about a patient's care, whereas a delivery service must arrive with a package at the correct destination, on time.

APPLYING THE CONSUMER PRODUCTS CLASSIFICATION SYSTEM

The three-way classification system of convenience, shopping, and specialty goods and services helps to guide marketers in developing a successful marketing strategy. Buyer behaviour patterns differ for the three types of purchases. For example, classifying a new food item as a convenience product leads to insights about marketing needs in branding, promotion, pricing, and distribution decisions. Table 9.1 summarizes the impact of this classification system on the development of an effective marketing mix.

The classification system, however, also poses a few problems. The major obstacle in implementing this system results from the suggestion that all goods and services must fit within one of the three categories. Some fit neatly into one category, but others share characteristics of more than one category. For example, how would you classify the purchase of a new automobile? Before classifying the expensive good, which is handled by a few exclusive dealers in the area as a specialty product, consider other characteristics. New car buyers often shop extensively among competing models and dealers before deciding on the best deal. And there is a wide range of models, features, and prices to consider. At one end of the spectrum is a basic Ford that could be purchased for less than $20 000. At the other end is what people are calling European super cars such as the Lamborghini Murcielago, at $450 000, or the Aston Martin One-77, priced at more than $1 million. These cars are fast, powerful, and hard to find—which boosts their value.[7]

So it's a good idea to think of the categorization process as a continuum representing degrees of effort expended by consumers. At one end of the continuum, they casually pick up convenience items; at the other end, they search extensively for specialty products. Shopping products fall between these extremes. In addition, car dealers may offer services, both during and after the sale, that play a big role in the purchase decision. On this continuum, the new car purchase might

INGVALD KALDHUSSATER/SHUTTERSTOCK.COM

Jewellery: A specialty product.

appear between the categories of shopping and specialty products but closer to specialty products.

A second problem with the classification system emerges because consumers differ in their buying patterns. One person may walk into a hair salon and request a haircut without an appointment, while another may check references and compare prices before selecting a stylist. But the first consumer's impulse purchase of a haircut does not make hair styling services a convenience item. Marketers classify goods and services by considering the purchase patterns of the majority of buyers.

TYPES OF BUSINESS PRODUCTS

Business buyers are professional customers. Their job duties require rational, cost-effective purchase decisions. For instance, General Mills applies much of the same purchase decision process to buying flour that Kellogg's does.

The classification system for business products emphasizes product uses rather than customer buying behaviour. B2B products generally fall into one of six categories for product uses: installations, accessory equipment, component parts and materials, raw materials, supplies, and business services. Figure 9.3 illustrates the six types of business products.

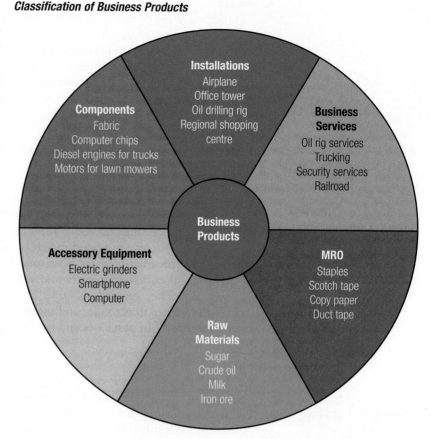

figure 9.3

Classification of Business Products

Installations

The specialty products of the business market are called **installations**. This classification includes major capital investments for new factories and heavy machinery and for telecommunications systems. Purchases of new airplanes by Air Canada or Air Inuit are considered installations.

Since installations last for long periods of time and their purchases involve large sums of money, they represent major decisions for organizations. Negotiations often extend over several months and involve numerous decision makers. Vendors often provide technical expertise along with tangible goods. Representatives who sell custom-made equipment work closely with buying firms' engineers and production personnel to design the most satisfactory products possible.

Price typically does not dominate purchase decisions for installations. A purchasing firm buys such a product for its efficiency and performance over its useful life. The firm also wants to minimize breakdowns. Downtime is expensive because the firm must pay employees while they wait for repairs on the machine. In addition, customers may be lost during downtime. Installations are major investments often designed specifically for the purchasers. Training of the buyer's workforce to operate the equipment correctly, along with significant after-sale service, is usually involved. As a result, marketers of these systems typically focus their promotional efforts on employing highly trained sales representatives, often with technical backgrounds. Advertising, if the firm uses it at all, emphasizes company reputation and directs potential buyers to contact local sales representatives.

Most installations are marketed directly from manufacturers to users. Even a one-time sale may require continuing contacts for regular product servicing. Some manufacturers prefer to lease extremely expensive installations to customers rather than sell the items outright, and they assign personnel directly to the lessees' sites to operate or maintain the equipment.

Accessory Equipment

Only a few decision makers may participate in a purchase of **accessory equipment**—capital items that typically cost less and last for shorter periods than installations. Although quality and service exert important influences on purchases of accessory equipment, price may significantly affect these decisions. Accessory equipment includes products such as power tools, computers, and smartphones.

installations Business products like factories, assembly lines, and huge machinery that are major capital investments.

accessory equipment Capital items like desktop computers and printers that typically cost less and last for shorter periods of time than installations.

Although these products are considered capital investments and buyers depreciate their costs over several years, their useful lives generally are much shorter than those of installations.

Marketing these products requires continuous representation and dealing with the widespread geographic dispersion of purchasers. To cope with these market characteristics, a wholesaler—often called an industrial distributor—might be used to contact potential customers in its own geographic area. Customers usually do not require technical assistance, and a manufacturer of accessory equipment often can distribute its products effectively through wholesalers. Advertising is an important component in the marketing mix for accessory equipment.

Component Parts and Materials

component parts and materials Finished business products of one producer that become part of the final products of another producer.

Whereas business buyers use installations and accessory equipment in the process of producing their own final products, **component parts and materials** represent finished business products of one producer that become part of the final products of another producer. Some materials, such as flour, undergo further processing before becoming part of the finished product. Textiles, paper pulp, and chemicals are also examples of component parts and materials. Bose supplies its luxury sound systems to auto manufacturers such as Audi, Infiniti, and Cadillac. Marketers for the auto manufacturers believe that Bose systems are a good match between premium sound and their luxury vehicles, comparing the high performance of the Bose sound systems to the high performance of their cars.[8]

Purchasers of component parts and materials need regular, continuous supplies of uniform-quality products. They generally contract to purchase these items for set periods of time. Marketers commonly emphasize direct sales, and satisfied customers often become regular buyers. Wholesalers sometimes supply fill-in purchases and handle sales to smaller purchasers.

Raw Materials

raw materials Natural resources such as farm products, coal, copper, or lumber, which become part of a final product.

Farm products, such as beef, cotton, eggs, milk, poultry, and soybeans, and natural resources, such as coal, copper, iron ore, and lumber, constitute **raw materials**. These products resemble component parts and materials in that they become part of the buyers' final products. Cargill supplies many of the raw materials for finished food products—dry corn ingredients, flour, food starch, oils and shortenings, soy protein and sweeteners, and beef and pork. Food manufacturers then take and turn these materials into finished products, including cake and barbecued ribs.[9]

Most raw materials carry grades determined according to set criteria, assuring purchasers of the receipt of standardized products of uniform quality. As with component parts and materials, vendors

Installation product.

ANSON HUNG/GETSTOCK.COM

commonly market raw materials directly to buying organizations. Wholesalers are increasingly involved in purchasing raw materials from foreign suppliers.

Price is seldom a deciding factor in a raw materials purchase since the costs are often set at central markets, determining virtually identical transactions among competing sellers. Purchasers buy raw materials from the firms they consider best able to deliver the required quantities and qualities.

Supplies

If installations represent the specialty products of the business market, operating supplies are its convenience products. **Supplies** constitute the regular expenses that a firm incurs in its daily operations. These expenses do not become part of the buyer's final products.

Supplies are also called **MRO items** because they fall into three categories: (1) maintenance items, such as brooms, filters, and light bulbs; (2) repair items, such as nuts and bolts used in repairing equipment; and (3) operating supplies, such as printer ink cartridges, mouse batteries, and pens. Staples sells all kinds of supplies to small, medium, and large businesses. Companies can purchase everything in the way of office necessities: paper, labels, and file folders. The firm also offers services such as printing and binding; companies can digitally submit the material to be printed.[10]

A purchasing manager regularly buys operating supplies as a routine job duty. Wholesalers often facilitate sales of supplies due to the low unit prices, the small order size, and the large number of potential buyers. Since supplies are relatively standardized, heavy price competition frequently keeps costs under control. However, a business buyer spends little time making decisions about these products. Exchanges of products frequently demand simple telephone, Web, or EDI (electronic data interchange) orders or regular purchases from a sales representative of a local wholesaler.

Accessory equipment.

supplies Regular expenses that a firm incurs in its daily operations.

MRO items Business supplies that include maintenance items, repair items, and operating supplies.

business services Intangible products that firms buy to facilitate their production and operating processes.

Business Services

The **business services** category includes the intangible products that firms buy to facilitate their production and operating processes. Examples of business services are financial services, leasing and rental services that supply equipment and vehicles, insurance, security, legal advice, and consulting. As mentioned earlier, many service providers sell the same services to both consumers and organizational buyers—telephone, gas, and electric, for example—although service firms may maintain separate marketing groups for the two customer segments.

Organizations also purchase many adjunct services that assist their operations but are not essentially a part of the final product. Companies like Chapters/Indigo that receive orders by phone or over the Internet count on Canada Post to deliver their books, music, and gifts. Although Canada Post's services are not part of Chapters' products, they are essential to the firm's operations.

Price may strongly influence purchase decisions for business services. The buying firm must decide whether to purchase a service or provide that service internally. This decision may depend on how frequently the firm needs the service and the specialized knowledge required to provide it. In the case of Chapters/Indigo, it would not be cost effective for the company to do its own delivering.

Purchase decision processes vary considerably for different types of business services. A firm may purchase window-cleaning services through a routine and straightforward process similar to that for buying operating supplies. In contrast, a purchase decision for highly specialized environmental engineering advice requires complex analysis and perhaps lengthy negotiations similar to those for

table 9.2   *Marketing Impact of the Business Products Classification System*

FACTOR	INSTALLATIONS	ACCESSORY EQUIPMENT	COMPONENT PARTS AND MATERIALS	RAW MATERIALS	SUPPLIES	BUSINESS SERVICES
Organizational Factors						
Planning time	Extensive	Less extensive	Less extensive	Varies	Very little	Varies
Purchase frequency	Infrequent	More frequent	Frequent	Infrequent	Frequent	Varies
Comparison of price and quality	Quality very important	Quality and price important	Quality important	Quality important	Price important	Varies
Marketing Mix Factors						
Price	High	Relatively high	Low to high	Low to high	Low	Varies
Distribution channel length	Very short	Relatively short	Short	Short	Long	Varies
Promotion method	Personal selling by producer	Advertising	Personal selling	Personal selling	Advertising by producer	Varies

total quality management (TQM) Continuous effort to improve products and work processes with the goal of achieving customer satisfaction and world-class performance.

purchases of installations. This variability of the marketing mix for business services and other business products is outlined in Table 9.2.

The purchase of the right business services can make a difference in a firm's competitiveness. The Regus Group provides businesses with facilities for meetings and conferences in 500 cities in more than 80 countries. These facilities are fully furnished and equipped with every electronic medium and amenity a business could possibly need. They are staffed with trained support personnel. Regus serves large and small companies, including those relying on mobile and home-based workers. The firm's services allow businesses to customize their office and meeting needs while saving money during periods when office space is not necessary on a full-time basis.[11] One example of a business service is discussed in the "Marketing and the SME" feature.

MARKETING AND THE SME   **Fresh Baked Produces Branded Entertainment**

EXPANDING digital options for marketers are changing the way companies promote their products and services. Expanding digital capabilities is also changing how marketers view the best way to engage customers in brands.

A company called Fresh Baked, a small firm that embraces the new digital options, produces branded entertainment. According to Robert Tait, president of Fresh Baked, "To be true brand entertainment . . . the show, the concept itself has to emanate from the brand." Branded entertainment is not a commercial or product placement in a television show or movie. Branded entertainment needs to catch viewers' attention—they need to want to watch. In order to produce good branded entertainment, you need to start with the brand and the values the brand is trying to portray.

According to Robert Tait, the best venue for branded entertainment is the Web. A company wanting to create branded entertainment would create a plot with characters that the target market for the product can relate to, shoot the "webisode" using known actors, and promote it through social media. If the

webisode catches the attention of the target market, the company produces a series of webisodes by continuing the plot. Marketers can use the webisode to engage customers further by having special deals for products that interest them or have customers sign on to receive further information from the company.

One company that is using branded entertainment is VH Sauces. Its webisodes, called "Life Unjarred," are about Randy Matthews and his family. You can view the episodes, get recipes and product information, or find out about the company. There are links to Randy's blog, Twitter account, Facebook page, and YouTube videos.

While not all industry experts agree with Tait's vision for branded entertainment, the webisodes that have been produced have certainly caught the attention of the audiences they were directed at.

Sources: Jeromy Lloyd, "Going Hollywood," *Marketing*, http://www.marketingmag.ca, February 1, 2010; Jeromy Lloyd, "Media vs. Agencies," *Marketing*, http://www.marketingmag.ca, February 17, 2011; Life Unjarred website, http://lifeunjarred.com, July 4, 2011; Fresh Baked website, http://www.freshbakedent.com, July 4, 2011.

QUALITY AS A PRODUCT STRATEGY

③ Explain how quality is used by marketers as a product strategy and why firms develop lines of related products.

No matter how a product is classified, nothing is more frustrating to a customer than having a new item break after just a few uses or having it not live up to expectations. The cell phone that hisses static at you unless you stand still or the seam that rips out of your new jacket aren't life-altering experiences, but they do leave an impression of poor quality that likely will lead you to make different purchases in the future. Then there's the issue of service quality—the department store that seems to have no salespeople or the computer help line that leaves you on hold for 20 minutes.

Quality is a key component to a firm's success in a competitive marketplace. The efforts to create and market high-quality goods and services have been referred to as **total quality management (TQM)**. TQM expects all of a firm's employees to continually improve products and work processes with the goal of achieving customer satisfaction and world-class performance. This means that engineers design products that work, marketers develop products that people want, and salespeople deliver on their promises. Managers are responsible for communicating the goals of total quality management to all staff members and for encouraging workers to improve themselves and take pride in their work. Of course, achieving maximum quality is easier said than done, and the process is never complete. Many companies solicit reviews or feedback from customers to improve goods and services. As a customer, you can provide valuable insight to marketers by providing honest feedback, as described in the "Career Readiness" feature.

WORLDWIDE QUALITY PROGRAMS

Although the movement began in the 1920s as an attempt to improve product quality by improving the manufacturing process, it was during the 1980s that the quality revolution picked up speed in corporations. The campaign to improve quality found leadership in large manufacturing firms such as Ford, Xerox, and Motorola that had lost market share to

Farm Credit Canada supplies businesses with services designed for them.

ALL consumers have positive and negative experiences with the goods and services they purchase. When companies ask for feedback, they are looking for information that will help them improve the products they offer, either by enhancing the items themselves or the services that support them. You can use your training as a marketer to provide valuable feedback to companies. When doing so, keep in mind the following tips:

- *Be honest.* Describe clearly and accurately your experience with the company and its products, including salespeople, tech support, and anyone else with whom you have contact. If you were dissatisfied, avoid engaging in an angry tirade; instead, calmly outline the facts.
- *Be concise.* Include only the details most relevant to the product's performance. In that way, the company can concentrate on exactly what needs improvement. Don't go into a long description unless you are asked for more information.
- *Be polite.* Avoid rude language or comments. The point is to find a solution to a problem, if one exists, not to offend those asking for your views.

- *Be positive.* Don't forget to tell the firm what *does* work and what you like about its products. Positive feedback lets a company know what it is doing right. Try to give specific examples—features of the product, results you've had, and so on.
- *Offer suggestions.* You might not be able to give a design engineer the specs to improve your car's interior, but you could say, "It would be great if I had a place to store my iPod" or "I wish the cup holder was easier to reach."
- *Thank the company for listening.* Even if you are taking an online survey, offer a thank-you to the firm if there is a space for additional comments. The company's marketers will know you appreciate the opportunity to give feedback, and they might contact you for further insights.

Sources: eBay, "Feedback Etiquette," http://reviews.ebay.com, April 30, 2010; IBM, "Forum Use and Etiquette," http://www.ibm.com, April 30, 2010; Amy Gallo, "How to Give Your Boss Feedback," *Harvard Business Review*, http://blogs.hbr.org, March 24, 2010.

Japanese competitors. Smaller companies that supplied parts to large firms then began to recognize quality as a requirement for success. Some companies today are using a process called Sigma Six, in which cross-functional teams work at improving the quality of their products and services by eliminating virtually all defects. Today, commitment to quality has spread to service industries, not-for-profit organizations, government agencies, and educational institutions.

In order to assist Canadian companies improve quality and to advance the quality movement in Canada, an independent, not-for-profit organization was developed to work in partnership with the Canadian government. The National Quality Institute (NQI) provides advice on change management, facilitates organizational assessments, organizes events to promote quality, offers educational certification programs, and presents the annual Canada Awards for Excellence.[12] In the United States, the Malcolm Baldrige National Quality Award was established in 1987 to recognize excellence in management.

ISO 9001:2000 Standards that define international, generic criteria for quality management and quality assurance.

The quality movement is also strong in European countries. The European Union's **ISO 9001:2000** standards define international, generic criteria for quality management and quality assurance. These standards were originally developed by the International Organization for Standardization in Switzerland to ensure consistent quality among products manufactured and sold throughout the nations of the European Union (EU). The standards now include criteria for systems of management as well. Although most other ISO standards are specific to particular products or processes, ISO 9001 applies to any organization, regardless of the goods or services it produces. Many European companies require suppliers to complete ISO certification, which is a rigorous process that takes several months to complete, as a condition of doing business with them. The Canadian member body of ISO is the Standards Council of Canada.[13]

assessment check 2

2.1. What are the three major classifications of consumer products?

2.2 Identify five factors marketers should consider in classifying consumer services.

2.3 What are the six main classifications of business products?

2.4 What are the three categories of supplies?

BENCHMARKING

benchmarking Method of measuring quality by comparing performance against industry leaders.

Firms often rely on an important tool called **benchmarking** to set performance standards. The purpose of benchmarking is to achieve superior performance that results in a competitive advantage in the marketplace. A typical benchmarking process involves three main activities: identifying manufacturing or business processes that need improvement, comparing internal processes to those of industry leaders, and implementing changes for quality improvement.

Benchmarking requires two types of analyses: internal and external. Before a company can compare itself with another, it must first analyze its own activities to determine strengths and weaknesses. This assessment establishes a baseline for comparison. External analysis involves gathering information about the benchmark partner to find out why the partner is perceived as the industry's best. A comparison of the results of the analysis provides an objective basis for making improvements. Some large firms that have engaged in benchmarking are 3M, DuPont, General Mills, and Kraft Foods. These firms conduct formal, complex programs, but smaller firms may decide to use benchmarking as well.[14] Sometimes companies use benchmarking to determine how they are doing to reduce waste, as described in the "Go Green" feature.

QUALITY OF SERVICES

service encounter Point at which the customer and service provider interact.

As a consumer, your perception of the quality of the service you have purchased is usually determined during the **service encounter**—the point at which the customer and service provider interact. Employees such as cashiers and customer service representatives have a powerful impact on their customers' decision to return or not. You might pass the word to your friends about the friendly staff at a local breakfast eatery, the slow cashiers at a local supermarket, or the huge scoops of ice cream you got at the nearby ice cream stand. Those words form powerful marketing messages about the services you received.

service quality Expected and perceived quality of a service offering.

Service quality refers to the expected and perceived quality of a service offering, and it has a huge effect on the competitiveness of a company. The findings of a survey conducted by the firm Colloquy reinforce the importance of service quality. Its latest survey results show that, for the first

GO GREEN   **Fast Food Goes Green**

COMPANIES like McDonald's and Tim Hortons have often been criticized for the amount of trash they produce. Much of it can be found littering the roadsides and city streets. Even small differences in the amount of garbage these companies produce can make a big impact on the environment. Both companies and others in the fast-food industry are trying to make an environmental difference through internal programs and by sponsoring environmental events.

The challenge for companies in this industry is not only the fact that they need to have packaging that enables their food to reach the customer at the right temperature but the fact that different regions of the country have different laws pertaining to recycling.

Tim Hortons makes public the results of its environmental efforts annually in its "Sustainability and Responsibility Report." The report contains such information as how their paper hot-drink cups have been redesigned, including the paper, ink, and lids, in order improve recycling and composting. Not only does the report identify the corporate environment goals but it also provides a summary of the company's performance for each goal and what the next steps are for the company.

McDonald's approach to the problem does not provide the same level of detailed information as Tim Hortons. The McDonald's website does describe its efforts to reduce, reuse, and recycle and in some cases provides examples. After conducting a waste audit, the company determined that a large amount of the waste produced by the company came from behind-the-counter activities. In order to bring the level of waste down, the company uses shipping containers for its hamburger buns and milk products that can be returned to the supplier for reuse.

Redesigned hot-drink cups and sending shipping containers back to the supplier may seem like small efforts, but because these companies are so large and produce so much waste even small moves make big differences.

Sources: McDonald's Canada company website, http://www.mcdonalds.ca, July 3, 2011; Tim Hortons company website, http://www.timhortons.com, July 3, 2011; Kristin Laird, "Tim Hortons Is Turning Green," *Marketing*, http://www.marketingmag.ca, May 29, 2009.

---

time ever, low price was more important than customer service. The company has attributed this change to the tougher economic times prevailing since its previous study. However, customer service was listed as the second most important factor.[15]

Service quality is determined by five variables:

1. *Tangibles*, or physical evidence. A tidy office and clean uniform are examples.

2. *Reliability*, or consistency of performance and dependability.

3. *Responsiveness*, or the willingness and readiness of employees to provide service. A salesperson who asks, "How may I help you?" is an example.

4. *Assurances*, or the confidence communicated by the service provider.

5. *Empathy*, or the service provider's efforts to understand the customer's needs and then individualize the service.

If a gap exists between the level of service that customers expect and the level they think they have received, it can be favourable or unfavourable. If you get a larger steak than you expected or your plane arrives ahead of schedule, the gap is favourable, and you are likely to try that service again. But if your steak is tiny, cold, and overcooked or your plane is two hours late, the gap is unfavourable, and you will probably find another restaurant or mode of transportation next time.

Bank of Montreal understands the needs of families with younger children.

67 calories
of Molson Canadian 67

67 calories
of a Mojito

CANADIAN
67

You can have a little.   Or you can have it all.

Molson Canadian 67 is a premium light beer with a clean, crisp, fresh taste, specially brewed to
67 calories per 341ml bottle. That's about half the calories of wines or mixed drinks.

Calculations based on an average serving (6 oz glass of wine and single serving of mixed drinks. Details at molsoncanadian67.ca

67

MOLSON COORS CANADA

Molson expands its beer line with a product aimed at those counting calories.

DEVELOPMENT OF PRODUCT LINES

Few firms today market only one product. A typical firm offers its customers a **product line**—that is, a series of related products. The motivations for marketing complete product lines rather than concentrating on a single product include the desire to grow, enhancing the company's position in the market, optimal use of company resources, and exploiting the product life cycle. The following subsections examine each of the first three reasons. The final reason, exploiting the stages of the product life cycle, is discussed in the section that focuses on strategic implications of the product life cycle concept.

DESIRE TO GROW

A company limits its growth potential when it concentrates on a single product, even though the company may have started that way, as retailer Roots did with its single negative-heel shoe. Now the company sells a complete line of casual wear for men and women, not to mention hats and watches along with bags and home furnishings. The company has grown to 120 stores in Canada and the United States, with 40 more in Asia, in addition to its online retailing. The company customizes its products for films, television shows, musical groups, and sports teams.[16]

ENHANCING THE COMPANY'S POSITION IN THE MARKET

product line Series of related products offered by one company.

A company with a line of products often makes itself more important to both consumers and marketing intermediaries than a firm with only one product. A shopper who purchases a hat for outdoor activities often buys related clothes. For instance, Tilley Endurables offers a wide range of products, allowing consumers to completely outfit themselves for outdoor activities or travel. They can purchase hats, pants, shorts, dresses, socks, and even towels. The company sells its products in company stores in Toronto, Montreal, and Vancouver, through its mail-order catalogue, and on the Internet. In addition, many other stores throughout Canada and around the world carry Tilley clothes. The company started making hats, advertising them in sailing magazines and selling them at boating shows. Few would know about Tilley products if the company had not expanded beyond its original hat.[17] Business buyers often expect a firm that manufactures a particular product to offer related items as well.

assessment check 3

3.1 What is TQM?

3.2 What are the five variables of service quality?

3.3 List the four reasons for developing a product line.

OPTIMAL USE OF COMPANY RESOURCES

product mix Assortment of product lines and individual product offerings that a company sells.

By spreading the costs of its operations over a series of products, a firm may reduce the average production and marketing costs of each product. The Calgary Stampede is a good example. Once the site of a single 10-day event, today the Stampede Development Park is the location of year-round events promoting tourism, economic development, education, and entertainment.[18]

4 Describe the way marketers typically measure product mixes and make product mix decisions.

THE PRODUCT MIX

A company's **product mix** is the assortment of product lines and individual product offerings that the company sells. The right blend of product lines and individual products allows a firm to maximize sales opportunities within the limitations of its resources. Marketers typically measure product mixes according to width, length, and depth.

table 9.3   *Johnson & Johnson's Mix of Health Care Products*

OVER-THE-COUNTER MEDICINES	NUTRITIONALS	SKIN AND HAIR CARE	ORAL CARE	MEDICAL DEVICES AND DIAGNOSTICS
Motrin pain reliever	Lactaid digestive aid	Aveeno lotions	REACH dental floss	Ethicon surgical instruments and systems
Tylenol pain reliever	Splenda sweetener	Clean & Clear facial cleansers and toners	REACH toothbrushes	Lifescan diabetes management products
Reactine Allergy		Johnson's baby shampoo	Steri/sol mouth rinse	Orthopedic joint replacement products
		Neutrogena soaps and shampoos	Listerine Pocketpaks	Veridex diagnostic tests

Source: Information from Johnson & Johnson website, http://www.jnjcanada.com, June 26, 2011.

PRODUCT MIX WIDTH

The *width* of a product mix refers to the number of product lines the firm offers. As Table 9.3 shows, Johnson & Johnson offers a broad line of retail consumer products in the Canadian market, as well as business-to-business products to the medical community. Consumers can purchase over-the-counter medications, nutritional products, dental care products, and first-aid products, among others. Health care professionals can obtain prescription drugs, medical and diagnostic devices, and wound treatments. LifeScan, one of Johnson & Johnson's subsidiaries, offers a range of products designed to help diabetes patients manage their condition. DePuy, another subsidiary, manufactures orthopaedic implants and joint replacement products. At the drugstore, consumers can pick up some of J&J's classic products, such as Motrin and Visine.[19]

PRODUCT MIX LENGTH

The *length* of a product mix refers to the number of different products a firm sells. Table 9.3 identifies some of the hundreds of health care products offered by Johnson & Johnson. Some of J&J's most recognizable brands are Band-Aid, Motrin, Tylenol, and Neutrogena.

PRODUCT MIX DEPTH

Depth refers to variations in each product that the firm markets in its mix. Johnson & Johnson's Band-Aid brand bandages come in a variety of shapes and sizes, including Perfect Fit, Flexible Fabric for Knuckle and Fingertip, and Advance Healing Blister Cushions.

PRODUCT MIX DECISIONS

Establishing and managing the product mix have become increasingly important marketing tasks. Adding depth, length, and width to the product mix requires careful thinking and planning—otherwise a firm can end up with too many products, including some that don't sell well. To evaluate a firm's product mix, marketers look at the effectiveness of its depth, length, and width. Has the firm ignored a viable consumer segment? It may improve performance by increasing product line depth to offer a product variation that will attract the new segment. Can the firm achieve economies in its sales and distribution efforts by adding complementary product lines to the mix? If so, a wider product mix may seem appropriate. Does the firm gain equal contributions from all products in its portfolio? If not, it may decide to lengthen or shorten the product mix to increase revenues. Geox is an Italian shoe manufacturer known for its patented breathable fabric that keeps feet cool and comfortable. With sales of more than $1 billion, Geox is expanding both ways: in width and length. The firm offers trendy shoe styles, including sandals and sneakers. In addition, Geox has launched apparel and shoe lines for men and children, made of similar breathable fabrics that help keep consumers cool and dry.[20]

Another way to add to the mix is to purchase product lines from other companies. Or a firm can acquire entire companies through mergers or acquisitions. Canadian Tire expanded its sporting goods

Febreze creates depth in its product mix with variations on scents.

line extension
Development of individual offerings that appeal to different market segments while remaining closely related to the existing product line.

and sporting apparel lines by purchasing the Forzani Group of stores, which includes Sport Chek, Sport Mart, Athletes World, and Nevada Bob's Golf retailers.[21]

A firm should assess its current product mix for another important reason: to determine the feasibility of a line extension. A **line extension** adds individual offerings that appeal to different market segments while remaining closely related to the existing product line. When Maple Leaf Foods wanted to appeal to consumers who were concerned about their health, it launched its Schneider's Country Naturals product line. The product line included hot dogs, hams, sliced meats, and bacon.[22]

The marketing environment also plays a role in a marketer's evaluation of a firm's product mix. In the case of Canadian Tire and Maple Leaf Foods, the social-cultural environment had shifted so that consumers were looking for more options in their sporting goods and natural food choices.

Careful evaluation of a firm's current product mix can also help marketers in making decisions about brand management and new-product introductions. Chapter 10 examines the importance of branding, brand management, and the development and introduction of new products.

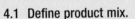

assessment check 4 ✓

4.1 Define product mix.

4.2 How do marketers typically measure product mixes?

---

⑤ Explain the concept of the product life cycle and identify the different stages.

THE PRODUCT LIFE CYCLE

product life cycle
Progression of a product through introduction, growth, maturity, and decline stages.

Products, like people, pass through stages as they age. Successful products progress through four basic stages: introduction, growth, maturity, and decline. This progression, known as the **product life cycle**, is shown in Figure 9.4.

The product life cycle concept applies to products or product categories within an industry, not to individual brands. For instance, smartphones and tablet computers moved rapidly from the introduction stage into the growth stage. Digital cameras are now in the maturity stage, while traditional film cameras are in decline. There is no set schedule or time frame for a particular stage of the life cycle. Some products pass through certain stages rapidly, while others move more slowly. CDs have been around for more than a quarter of a century but are declining, due in part to the increase in digital music download.[23] Additionally, retailers can shorten a product's life cycle for other reasons, as the "Solving an Ethical Controversy" feature explores.

INTRODUCTORY STAGE

During the **introductory stage** of the product life cycle, a firm works to stimulate demand for the new market entry. Products in this stage might bring new technology to a product category. Since the product is unknown to the public, promotional campaigns stress information about its features. Additional promotions try to induce distribution channel members to carry the product. In this phase, the public becomes acquainted with the item's merits and begins to accept it.

A product whose introductory stage has been successful is the GPS mapping device. Although global positioning systems have been around for a number of years, their introduction to the consumer market was more recent.

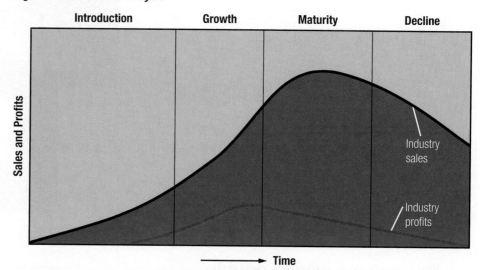

figure 9.4

Stages in the Product Life Cycle

By promoting its practical application and making the devices easy to use, marketers have seen GPS sales increase rapidly, moving the products quickly toward the growth stage.[24]

Technical problems and financial losses are common during the introductory stage as companies fine-tune product design and spend money on advertising. Many users remember early problems with the Internet—jammed portals, order-fulfilling glitches, dot-coms that went bust. Users of GPS devices

Marketoid

The total revenue for the food services industry for 2009 was $48 billion.

SOLVING AN ETHICAL CONTROVERSY

Shelf-Space Wars: A Continuing Saga

DURING the recent economic downturn, when large retailers like Walmart trimmed the number of product brands displayed on their shelves, they were focused on enhancing profits. Eliminating those brands that don't move as quickly gives retailers more than one benefit. They can provide shelf space to the best-selling, fastest-moving national brands and also increase space for their house brand, typically lower in cost. Shelf space represents an ongoing battle for consumer products companies, who spend millions of dollars in advertising and promotion to keep their brands present in the consumer's mind.

Is it ethical for retailers to drop national brands in order to provide more space for their house brand?

PRO

1. Merchants have the right to alter their product assortment as it suits them. Moreover, retailers are under no obligation to offer every brand (and every product) indefinitely.
2. To survive during an economic downturn, many businesses look for ways to offer goods that customers perceive as affordable.

CON

1. The prospect of eliminating shelf space may be a way for a large retailer to coerce companies into offering more attractive pricing agreements.
2. Cutting popular brands and increasing the amount of shelf space designated for a house brand is risky. Consumers want variety when they shop, and they may decide to shop elsewhere rather than switch brands, a habit that results in decreased sales and lost customers for the retailer.

Where do you stand: pro or con?

Sources: Jason Notte, "Retailers Get Push-Back as Brands Disappear," TheStreet.com, http://www.thestreet.com, March 17, 2010; Chris Burritt, "Wal-Mart Brings Back Goods as Shoppers Turn to Lowe's," Bloomberg.com, http://www.bloomberg.com, March 8, 2010; Parija Kavilanz, "Dumped Brand Names Fight to Stay in Stores," CNNMoney.com, http://www.money.cnn.com, February 16, 2010; "Wal-Mart Cuts Food Storage Bag Brands," *Store Brand Decisions*, http://www.storebranddecisions.com, February 9, 2010; Zoe Wood, "Brands Fighting for Shelf Space Now That Wal-Mart Believes Less Is More," *The Observer*, http://www.observer.guardian.co.uk, August 16, 2009.

Using promotion—and product extensions—to extend the maturity stage of the product life cycle.

Products in the maturity stage like Campbell's Soup increase sales by providing new uses for their products.

introductory stage First stage of the product life cycle, in which a firm works to stimulate demand for the new market entry.

Marketoid

In 2009, Canadian service companies generated $870 billion worth of output.

growth stage Second stage of the product life cycle, which begins when a firm starts to realize substantial profits from its investment in the product.

maturity stage Third stage of the product life cycle, in which industry sales level out.

reported some glitches but also conceded that some problems stem from learning how to operate the devices correctly.

GROWTH STAGE

Sales volume rises rapidly during the **growth stage** as new customers make initial purchases and early buyers repurchase the product, such as smartphones and GPS devices. The growth stage usually begins when a firm starts to realize substantial profits from its investment. Word-of-mouth reports, mass advertising, and lowered prices all encourage hesitant buyers to make trial purchases of new products. In the case of big-screen TVs, low prices generally have not been a factor—many cost several thousand dollars. "Big-screen" now refers to a TV that is about 60 inches. As sales volume rises, competitors enter the marketplace, creating new challenges for marketers. As plasma technology was gradually replaced by LCD and LED-LCD models, companies with competing technologies vied for dominance, the TVs themselves grew larger, and prices continued to vary considerably.[25]

MATURITY STAGE

Sales of a product category continue to grow during the early part of the **maturity stage**, but eventually, they reach a plateau as the backlog of potential customers dwindles. By this time, many competitors have entered the market, and the firm's profits begin to decline as competition intensifies.

At this stage in the product life cycle, differences between competing products diminish as competitors discover the product and promotional characteristics most desired by customers. Available supplies exceed industry demand for the first time. Companies can increase their sales and market shares only at the expense of competitors, so the competitive environment becomes increasingly important. In the maturity stage, heavy promotional outlays emphasize any differences that still separate competing products, and brand competition intensifies. Some firms try to differentiate their products by focusing on attributes such as quality, reliability, and service. Others focus on redesign or other ways of extending the product life cycle. Nike athletic shoes could be said to be in the maturity stage. With hundreds of athletic shoes on the market, it is difficult to differentiate competing products. But a Nike innovation has enabled the manufacture of shoes that weigh considerably less yet are able to take the pounding of a professional athlete. The innovation is Flywire, a lightweight thread made of Vectran fibres. Most recently, the company has applied Flywire technology to athletic shoes for professional soccer players. Flywire shoes are so simple and inexpensive to manufacture that Nike could be looking at a whole new life cycle for its time-honoured shoes.[26]

DECLINE STAGE

In the **decline stage** of a product's life, innovations or shifts in consumer preferences bring about an absolute decline in industry sales. Dial telephones became touch-tone phones, which evolved to portable phones, which are now being replaced by conventional cell phones, which in turn were replaced by camera phones, and now smartphones are on the market.

> **decline stage** Final stage of the product life cycle, in which a decline in total industry sales occurs.

Some manufacturers refuse to give up in the decline stage. Young consumers, accustomed to CDs and digital downloads, are beginning to turn their attention to vinyl records. They have discovered their parents' and grandparents' collection of LPs and have hauled old record turntables out of the attic. If curiosity led them to the discovery, the sound and graphics of a record seem to be holding their interest. Marketers in the music industry have taken notice, and some bands have begun to issue limited numbers of records along with CDs and MP3 formats. They don't expect vinyl to become the primary medium for music but are happy to resurrect a classic product for a new generation of listeners.[27]

The traditional product life cycle differs from fad cycles. Fashions and fads profoundly influence marketing strategies. Fashions are currently popular products that tend to follow recurring life cycles. For example, bell-bottom pants that were popular in the 1960s and 1970s have returned as flares or boot-cut pants. In contrast, fads are products with abbreviated life cycles. Most fads experience short-lived popularity and then quickly fade, although some maintain residual markets among certain segments. Webkinz (the stuffed animals that have their own online Webkinz World) are an example of a fad.

assessment check 5

5.1 Identify the four stages of the product life cycle.

5.2 During which stage or stages are products likely to attract the most new customers?

EXTENDING THE PRODUCT LIFE CYCLE

⑥ Describe how a firm can extend a product's life cycle, and explain why certain products may be deleted.

Marketers usually try to extend each stage of the life cycles for their products as long as possible. Product life cycles can stretch indefinitely as a result of decisions designed to increase the frequency of use by current customers, increase the number of users for the product, find new uses, or change package sizes, labels, or product quality.

INCREASING FREQUENCY OF USE

During the maturity stage, the sales curve for a product category reaches a maximum point if the competitors exhaust the supply of potential customers who previously had not made purchases. However, if current customers buy more frequently than they formerly did, the total amount of sales will rise even though no new buyers enter the market.

For instance, consumers buy some products during certain seasons of the year. Marketers can boost purchase frequency by persuading these people to try the product year round. For decades, most people used sunscreen only during warm and sunny seasons of the year. With greater warnings about the risks of sun damage and skin cancer, however, companies now advertise the benefits of using sunscreen year round.

INCREASING THE NUMBER OF USERS

A second strategy for extending the product life cycle seeks to increase the overall market size by attracting new customers who previously have not used the product. Marketers may find their products in

© JULIE PRATT

Jello increases the number of users by introducing variations of the product.

different stages of the life cycle in different countries. This difference can help firms extend product growth. Items that have reached the maturity stage in Canada may still be in the introductory stage somewhere else.

In recent years, the Walt Disney Company has spent time and money on advertising its theme parks to attract adults in addition to young families. Television commercials portray empty nesters taking off to Disney World for a second honeymoon once their children are grown.

FINDING NEW USES

Finding new uses for a product is an excellent strategy for extending a product's life cycle. New applications for mature products include oatmeal as a cholesterol reducer, antacids as a calcium supplement, and aspirin for promoting heart health.

Marketers sometimes conduct contests or surveys to identify new uses for their products. They may post the results or their own new ideas on their websites. Arm & Hammer's website lists a variety of alternative uses throughout the house for its baking soda. Consumers can use baking soda to clean crayon off walls, as an antacid to settle an upset stomach, and as an agent to balance the pH in swimming pool water. The firm has even developed packaging with special vents to control odours in freezers and refrigerators.[28]

CHANGING PACKAGE SIZES, LABELS, OR PRODUCT QUALITY

Many firms try to extend their product life cycles by introducing physical changes in their offerings. Alternatively, new packaging and labels with updated images and slogans can help revitalize a product. Kraft Foods Canada is rejuvenating the Cracker Barrel cheese line through the introduction of new packing. The new packages are a warmer dark brown colour in order to make them appear more approachable. The package change and promotional material focus on how wholesome the product is, emphasizing the fact Kraft does not use preservatives. Cracker Barrel cheese is a product that consumers have been buying for more than 50 years. The new packaging and promotion increased sales of the brand by 15 percent in a single year.[29]

assessment check 6

6.1 Describe the four strategies for extending a product's life cycle.

6.2 Under what circumstances do firms decide to delete a product from their line?

PRODUCT DELETION DECISIONS

To avoid wasting resources promoting unpromising products, marketers must sometimes prune product lines and eliminate marginal products. Marketers typically face this decision during the late maturity and early decline stages of the product life cycle. Periodic reviews of weak products should justify either eliminating or retaining them. After battling it out with Sony in the DVD player arena, Toshiba conceded defeat and announced it would stop making its HD DVD player. That left Sony the winner in the marketplace with its Blu-ray format.

A firm may continue to carry an unprofitable item to provide a complete line for its customers. For example, while most grocery stores lose money on bulky, low-unit-value items such as salt, they continue to carry these items to meet shopper demand.

Shortages of raw materials sometimes prompt companies to discontinue production and marketing of previously profitable items. A firm may even drop a profitable item that fails to fit into its existing product line or fails to fit the direction in which the firm wants to grow. Some of these products return to the market carrying the names of other firms that purchase these "orphan brands" from the original manufacturers. In the largest relaunch in hotel history, InterContinental Hotels Group undertook a $1-billion relaunch of its Holiday Inn chain. Over a three-year period, 3300 Holiday Inns will emerge with a redesigned logo, updated lobbies and guest bathrooms, and new signage, landscaping, lighting, and bedding. What's more, all employees will be retrained under the chain's new "Stay Real" program.[30]

Strategic Implications

Marketers who want their businesses to succeed will continue to develop new goods and services to attract and satisfy customers. They will engage in continuous improvement activities, focusing on quality and customer service. And they will continually evaluate their company's mix of products.

Marketers everywhere are constantly developing new and better products that fit their firm's overall strategy. Technological innovations are one area in which new products quickly replace old ones. Marketers are sometimes faced with the dilemma of lagging sales for formerly popular products. They must come up with ways to extend the lives of certain products to extend their firm's profitability and sometimes must recognize and delete those that no longer meet expectations.   ◆◆◆

REVIEW OF CHAPTER OBJECTIVES

① **Define product, distinguish between goods and services and how they relate to the goods–services continuum, and explain the importance of the service sector in today's marketplace.**

Marketers define a product as the bundle of physical, service, and symbolic attributes designed to satisfy customers' wants and needs. Goods are tangible products that customers can see, hear, smell, taste, or touch. Services are intangible tasks that satisfy the needs of customers. Goods represent one end of a continuum, and services represent the other. The service sector makes a crucial contribution to the Canadian economy by means of products and jobs. The service sector now makes up more than 70 percent of the economy. Services have grown because of consumers' desire for speed, convenience, and technological advances.

② **Describe the classifications of consumer and business goods and services.**

Consumer products—both goods and services—are classified as convenience products (frequently purchased items), shopping products (products purchased after comparison), and specialty products (those that offer unique characteristics that consumers prize).

Business products are classified as installations (major capital investments), accessory equipment (capital items that cost less and last for shorter periods than installations), component parts and materials (finished business products of one producer that become part of the final products of another producer), raw materials (natural resources such as lumber, beef, or cotton), supplies (the regular expenses that a firm incurs in daily operations), and business services (the intangible products that firms buy to facilitate their production and operating processes).

③ **Explain how quality is used by marketers as a product strategy and why firms develop lines of related products.**

Many companies use total quality management (TQM) in an effort to encourage all employees to participate in producing the best goods and services possible. Companies may also participate in ISO 9001:2000 certification or benchmarking to evaluate and improve quality. Consumers often evaluate service quality on the basis of tangibles, reliability, responsiveness, assurance, and empathy, so marketers of service firms strive to excel in all these areas.

Companies usually produce several related products rather than individual ones to achieve the objectives of growth, optimal use of company resources, and increased company importance in the market, and to make optimal use of the product life cycle.

④ **Describe the way marketers typically measure product mixes and make product mix decisions.**

Marketers must decide the right width, length, and depth of product lines. Width is the number of product lines. Length is the number of products a company sells. Depth refers to the number of variations of a product available in a product line. Marketers evaluate the effectiveness of all three elements of the product mix. They may purchase product lines from other companies or extend the product line if necessary. Firms may also acquire entire companies and their product lines through mergers and acquisitions.

⑤ **Explain the concept of the product life cycle and identify the different stages.**

The product life cycle outlines the stages that a product goes through, including introduction, growth, maturity, and decline. During the introductory stage, marketers work to stimulate demand for the new product. New customers make initial purchases and repurchases of the product in the growth stage. Sales continue to grow during the maturity stage but eventually level off. In the decline stage, sales are reduced due to innovations or a shift in consumer preferences.

⑥ **Describe how a firm can extend a product's life cycle, and explain why certain products may be deleted.**

Marketers can extend the product life cycle by increasing frequency of use or number of users, finding new uses for the product, or changing package size, label, or quality. If none of these is successful, or if the product no longer fits a firm's line, the firm may decide to delete a product from its line.

assessment check answers

1.1 Define the term *product*.
A product is a bundle of physical, service, and symbolic attributes designed to satisfy a customer's wants and needs.

1.2 Why is the understanding of want satisfaction so important to marketers?
The understanding of want satisfaction is important to marketers because it helps them understand why people purchase certain goods and services.

1.3 Describe the goods–services continuum and list the six characteristics that distinguish services from goods.
The goods–services continuum is a spectrum that helps marketers visualize the differences and similarities between goods and services.
The six characteristics distinguishing services from goods are the following: (1) services are intangible, (2) services are inseparable from the service providers, (3) services are perishable, (4) companies cannot easily standardize services, (5) buyers often play important roles in the creation and distribution of services, (6) service standards show wide variations.

1.4 Identify two reasons that services are important to the Canadian economy and business environment.
The service sector makes an important contribution to the economy with products and jobs. Services also play a vital role in the international competitiveness of Canadian firms.

1.5 Why do service firms emphasize marketing?
The growth of potential service transactions represents a vast marketing opportunity, and the environment for services is changing—so marketers need to find new ways to reach customers.

2.1 What are the three major classifications of consumer products?
The three major classifications are convenience products, shopping products, and specialty products.

2.2 Identify five factors marketers should consider in classifying consumer services.

The five factors are the following: (1) the nature of the service, (2) the relationship between the service organization and its customers, (3) flexibility for customization, (4) fluctuation of supply and demand, and (5) the way the service is delivered.

2.3 What are the six main classifications of business products?

The six main classifications of business products are the following: (1) installations, (2) accessory equipment, (3) component parts and materials, (4) raw materials, (5) supplies, and (6) business services.

2.4 What are the three categories of supplies?

The three categories of supplies are maintenance items, repair items, and operating supplies.

3.1 What is TQM?

TQM stands for total quality management, a process that expects all of a firm's employees to continually improve its products and work processes.

3.2 What are the five variables of service quality?

The five variables of service quality are tangibles, reliability, responsiveness, assurances, and empathy.

3.3 List the four reasons for developing a product line.

The four reasons firms want to develop product lines are the following: (1) a desire to grow, (2) enhancing the company's position in the market, (3) optimal use of company resources, and (4) exploiting the stages of the product life cycle.

4.1 Define product mix.

The product mix is a company's assortment of product lines and individual product offerings.

4.2 How do marketers typically measure product mixes?

The product mix is measured by width, length, and depth.

5.1 Identify the four stages of the product life cycle.

The four stages of the product life cycle are introduction, growth, maturity, and decline.

5.2 During which stage or stages are products likely to attract the most new customers?

Products usually attract the most new customers during the introductory and growth stages.

6.1 Describe the four strategies for extending a product's life cycle.

The four strategies are increasing frequency of use, increasing the number of users, finding new users, and changing packaging or quality.

6.2 Under what circumstances do firms decide to delete a product from their line?

Firms may decide to delete a product if none of the strategies for extending a product's life work, if raw materials become unavailable, or if the product no longer fits the existing or future product line.

MARKETING TERMS YOU NEED TO KNOW

These terms are printed in red in the text. They are defined in the margins of the chapter and in the Glossary that begins on p. G-1.

product 266	specialty products 271	benchmarking 278
service 266	installations 273	service encounter 278
good 266	accessory equipment 273	service quality 278
goods–services continuum 267	component parts and materials 274	product line 280
business-to-business (B2B) product 269	raw materials 274	product mix 280
unsought products 269	supplies 275	line extension 282
convenience products 270	MRO items 275	product life cycle 282
impulse goods and services 270	business services 275	introductory stage 283
staples 270	total quality management 276	growth stage 284
emergency goods and services 270	total quality management (TQM) 277	maturity stage 284
shopping products 270	ISO 9001:2000 278	decline stage 285

PROJECTS AND TEAMWORK EXERCISES

1. On your own or with a classmate, choose one of the following goods (or choose one of your own). Visit the company's website to learn as much as you can about your product and the way it is marketed. Then create a marketing strategy for developing the services to support your product and make it stand out from others.
   a. BlackBerry smartphone
   b. Mini Cooper car
   c. Ikea furniture
   d. Apple iPad
2. On your own or with a classmate, create an advertisement for an unsought product such as a remedial reading or math course, a warranty for a big-screen TV, a first-aid kit, or the like. How can your ad turn an unsought product into one actually desired by consumers?
3. Consider a customer service experience you have had in the last month or so. Was it positive or negative? Describe your experience to the class and then discuss how the firm might improve the quality of its customer service—even if it is already positive.
4. With a classmate, choose one of the following firms or another that interests you. Visit the firm's website and measure its product mix. Then create a chart like the one for Johnson & Johnson in Table 9.3, identifying the company's major product lines, along with a few specific examples.
   a. Champion athletic clothing
   b. Conde Nast magazines
   c. Wyndham Hotels
   d. Panasonic
   e. Audi
5. With the same classmate, create a plan for further extending one of the firm's product lines. Describe the strategy you would recommend for extending the line as well as new products that might be included.

CRITICAL-THINKING EXERCISES

1. Draw a line representing the goods–services continuum. Then place each of the following along the continuum. Briefly explain your decision.
   a. Skype
   b. Teleflora.com
   c. Walmart
   d. Kia dealership
   e. Netflix
2. Make a list of all the convenience products you buy in a week. Does the list change from week to week based on need or your budget? What would it take to make you switch from one product to another?
3. Imagine your favourite restaurant. List as many installations, raw materials, and supplies as you think the restaurant owner or manager must be responsible for purchasing.
4. Why is it important for even a small company to develop a line of products?
5. Choose one of the following goods and services and describe your strategy for taking it to the next stage in its product life cycle. For products in the maturity or decline stage, describe a strategy for extending their life cycle.
   a. smartphone (growth)
   b. MP3 players (maturity)
   c. Text messaging (growth)
   d. Pressure cooker (decline)
   e. Duct tape (maturity)
6. Describe a fad that has come and gone during your lifetime, such as Beanie Babies. Did you take part in the fad? Why or why not? How long did it last? Why do you think it faded?

ETHICS EXERCISE

The airline industry has suffered recent setbacks, such as the high cost of fuel, that have forced the major carriers to cut back on many of their services. Some airlines have started charging passengers for checked luggage and others have announced they are going to even charge for carry-on bags. Most airlines charge for in-flight snacks or don't serve any at all. Airlines have reduced the number of flights they operate to certain destinations, packing planes full to overflowing; some restrict the use of frequent flyer miles, making it difficult to cash them in. Then there are the record-setting delays and lost luggage claims. All of these factors add up to less than enjoyable flying experiences for most travellers, many of whom are going to find other modes of transportation or just stay home.[31] Suppose you are a marketer for one of the major airlines. Your company is facing difficulty providing acceptable service to the passengers on its flights, but you need to find a way to emphasize the positive features of your airline's service.

1. Using the five variables of service quality as your guideline, what steps would you take—within your realm of control—to close the gap between the level of service passengers expect and the level they have been receiving?
2. How might you attract business customers? Would you give them a level of service that is different from families and other consumers who are flying for pleasure?

INTERNET EXERCISES

1. **Product classifications.** Visit the website of each of the following companies. Review their product offerings and classify some of their products as being a convenience, shopping, or specialty product.
   a. Gillette (www.gillette.com)
   b. Procter & Gamble (www.pg.com)
   c. Unilever (www.unilever.com)

2. **ISO certification.** The International Organization for Standardization (ISO) is responsible for the development and implementation of product standards. Go to the ISO's website (www.iso.org) and answer the following questions:
   a. Who belongs to ISO and how is it administered?
   b. How are ISO standards developed?
   c. What are some of the advantages of ISO certification?

3. **Product life cycle.** Arm & Hammer baking soda was first sold more than 100 years ago. Visit the Arm & Hammer site (www.armhammer.com). Review the history of the product and then prepare a brief report outlining how the makers of Arm & Hammer baking soda have been able to extend the product's life cycle.

Note: Internet Web addresses change frequently. If you don't find the exact sites listed, you may need to access the organization's home page and search from there or use a search engine such as Google.

CASE 9.1

The Canadian Word for Coffee—Tims

What could be more Canadian than hockey? How about a coffee and doughnut? Even more Canadian would be a coffee and doughnut shop started by and named after a hockey player. Tim Hortons is so Canadian that terms like "double, double" (coffee with double cream and double sugar) and Tims (coffee) are part of everyday language across the country. If that wasn't enough of a sign that Tim Hortons is doing it right, it has even been named Marketer of the Year by *Marketing* magazine. The reasons it is so successful are easy—quality products and an efficient operation.

In 1964, an NHL player, Tim Horton, opened a coffee shop in Hamilton, Ontario. The original store sold only beverages and doughnuts but it was a place for the average person to meet friends. In 1965, Ron Joyce left the Hamilton police department to run the store, and in 1967, he became a full partner in the company. Tragedy struck in 1974, when Tim Horton, then playing for the Buffalo Sabres, was killed in a car accident returning home after a game in Toronto. Shortly after the accident, Joyce bought Horton's share of the business to become sole owner of the 40-store chain. It was at this time that the company decided to focus all its efforts on providing an always-fresh product and outstanding service. Another important milestone in the company's history occurred in 1995, when it merged with Wendy's International Inc., a company based in the United States. As of 2006, Tim Hortons operates as a standalone public company with its stocks trading on both the Toronto and New York exchanges. There are more than 3000 stores in Canada and more than 600 in the United States.

The company has grown in several ways. The number of menu items has expanded significantly. The number of locations across Canada and in different countries has grown. While product development was important to the success of the company, two things were kept in mind: the ever-changing tastes of its customers and the stores' ability to deliver a quality product and service.

When the first Tim Hortons opened only two items were on the menu—coffee and doughnuts. There were a large number of varieties of doughnuts. It took 14 years before the menu saw any significant changes. It was at this time that the Timbit was introduced. While some could argue that a Timbit is still a doughnut, its introduction was the start of many new menu items. The 1980s were a decade of expansion for the menu with new items appearing almost annually. First to appear on the menu was the muffin, followed closely by cakes, pies, croissants, and cookies. The first lunch menu item appeared in 1985 when soup and chili were added. The lunch menu continued to expand in to the 1990s with sandwiches. Around this time the company also started to move away from its traditional menu aimed at the average Canadian by adding flavoured and iced cappuccinos and café mochas to the menu.

In 2005, the company made its first move into the breakfast market by introducing yogurt and fruit to its lineup. A year later the company was ready to take on McDonald's for the breakfast market. Research conducted at the time indicated that Tim Hortons was the most popular place for Canadians to stop for their morning coffee but McDonald's Egg McMuffin was the most popular breakfast sandwich. Tim Hortons was in the right position in the market to take advantage of the fast-growing segment. It introduced its egg breakfast sandwich, which is available on a fresh baked biscuit, English muffin, or bagel with sausage or bacon and cheese. The product introduction was accompanied by a promotional campaign to get the word out. The promotional campaign included billboards, in-store material, and television and radio ads along with online promotions. The product launch also included an introductory price for the first month. The move into the breakfast market was so successful for the company that within four years of moving into the market, the company held 51 percent market share.

Once the breakfast menu was developed and launched, the company has started selling ice cream and related products in some of its locations.

During this time the company also expanded the types of merchandise offered in the restaurants and online. When customers asked for Tims coffee to enjoy at home, the company responded by producing cans and pouches of its famous coffee for home brewing. The company has expanded this product line to include several different varieties of teas, cappuccinos, and hot chocolate. Also available are travel mugs in a various sizes and styles, gift baskets, coffee makers, and even toque and hat sets.

Expanding the menu was not the only expansion that Tim Hortons was going through. The number of outlets had expanded continuously from the beginning. In Canada roughly 95 percent of the stores are owned by franchisees. Not only are the stores found on many street corners in communities large and small, they are in shopping malls, universities, hospitals, and gas stations. It took the company more than 20 years to get the first 300 stores open but expansion has been rapid since. After the merger with Wendy's, expansion into the U.S. market began, mostly in northern states. While not all U.S. locations have been successful—the company closed more than 30 stores in the New England area—company officials say expansion into the U.S. market will continue.

Tim Hortons has announced that it intends to take the brand global. Almost 300 self-serve kiosks are already located in convenience stores in England and Ireland. There was the famous outlet on the military base in Kandahar serving Canadian soldiers and military personnel from the other countries serving in Afghanistan. When NATO did a review of the fast-food outlets in Kandahar, most were asked to close but the Tim Hortons outlet was asked to remain. NATO felt the other fast-food companies were a distraction for the soldiers. The company plans on expanding on the success of Kandahar by opening outlets in other Persian Gulf countries, including the United Arab Emirates, Qatar, Bahrain, Kuwait, and Oman. The Persian Gulf expansion is taking place through a partnership with the Dubai based company the Apparel Group.

Throughout all the expansion, new stores, and additional menu items, the company has stayed true to its customer. The marketing team describes the company as "unpretentious, friendly, honest, caring and dependable," which is also how it describes its customers. The team reinforces this image in everything it does—in its commercials, community involvement, sponsorship programs, and its Children's Foundation. It advertises on TV, radio, billboards, and in newspapers but is best known for its TV ads and children's sport programs. The Timbit sports program sponsors children's sports teams. In addition, it supports several programs connected with professional teams. The promotional material in the company's global and U.S. markets moves away from emphasizing the company as traditionally Canadian to a focus on the stores being cafés and bake shops.

What's next for Tim Hortons? If the company stays true to its past strategic plans, it will continue expanding its menus and its global locations.

Questions for Critical Thinking

1. At what stage of the product life cycle is Tim Hortons? What steps can be taken to manage the product portfolio?
2. How important do you think product and service quality are as a product strategy for Tim Hortons?

Sources: "Tim Hortons Moving to Persian Gulf," *Marketing*, http://marketingmag.ca, February 7, 2011; "Tim Hortons Makes Smoothie Move," *Marketing*, March 3, 2011; "Tim Hortons Charts Course for Global Expansion," *Marketing*, http://www.marketingmag.ca, May 14, 2010; "Tim Hortons Closing Poorly Performing U.S. Stores, Kiosks," *Marketing*, http://www.marketingmag.ca, November 11, 2010; Kristin Laird, "Tim Hortons Serves Up New Challenge to McDonald's in the Morning," *Marketing*, http://www.marketingmag.ca, January 29, 2010; Rebecca Harris, "Down-Home Smarts," *Marketing*, February 7, 2005, pp. 15–19; Tim Hortons website, http://www.timhortons.com, July 3, 2011; "Tim Hortons Is Marketing's Marketer of the Year," *Marketing Daily*, February 4, 2005; Rebecca Harris, "A Cup of Canadiana: Tim Hortons, Oakville, Ont.," *Marketing*, December 13, 2004.

CASE 9.2

New Balance "Experiences" China

New Balance has invaded China. The company is over 100 years old. It got its start manufacturing and selling arch supports to people like police officers and waiters, whose work kept them on their feet all day. During the 1970s, the company switched its focus to designing and marketing athletic shoes for "the everyday athlete," with proper fit being its key selling point. Over time, New Balance added an apparel line and has become a leading name in the industry. The company's family of brands includes Dunham and Aravon.

The first New Balance retail stores in China, called "Experience Stores," opened in Beijing and Shanghai in 2010, with hundreds more planned for the near future. The store's decor emphasizes the company's century-long heritage and accomplishments. Walk in the front door and you'll swear you've just entered a shoe store from the 1950s. The space evokes all five senses: comfortable, well-worn leather couches; framed archival photographs, advertisements, and other paraphernalia from the company's early days; an oak scent in the air, reminiscent of the smell of an old-time shoe store; and piped-in sounds from the "be-bop" era, including such artists as the Everly Brothers, Little Richard, Fats Domino, Jerry Lee Lewis, and Bill Haley and the Comets. Each Experience Store has a time line that extends from the first to the second floor, tracing the company's history and accomplishments and hinting at the future. Programmed in-store messaging promotes the company's products and draws shoppers to the second floor, where the merchandise is displayed in a decidedly 21st-century setting. (Recent consumer research suggests that up to 40 percent of consumers are influenced by such in-store messaging.)

To plan for its entry into China, New Balance engaged leading Asian branding consultants Equal Strategy to create a "total sensory experience." The Experience Stores exemplify the concept of "sensory branding": that is, the process of creating a brand experience that calls upon all the senses in reflecting a company's brand.

Consistent with the company's Total Fit campaign, the store openings include healthy running tips, pointers on foot care, and inspirational stories from China's most well-known runners. The Beijing launch included a street carnival reminiscent of the 1960s. To further celebrate the openings, New Balance sponsored an international marathon in Hong Kong, featuring 88 Chinese entrants and six-kilometre runs in the cities of Nanjin and Hangzhou.

In order to celebrate the company's classic 576 range of sneakers and to promote its new Chinese stores, it launched a new series of products—the China Mask series. The four shoes in the collection were designed based on the face-changing tradition of the Sichuanese Opera. Performers in the Sichuanese Opera use masks with different facial expressions that the actors switch in seconds to tell the opera's story. Three of the shoes in the 576 China Mask series, the Jing, Mo, and Chou models were available in selected New Balance retail stores. The shoes are constructed of mesh, suede, and patent leather and come in three colours—red, green, and orange. The fourth shoe in the collection, the Wu Shuang model (one of a kind), is a limited-edition release and available only in China. In order to authenticate the limited release, shoes each had a serial number stitched onto the tongue of the shoe.

At the same time as the China Mask Collection of shoes was released, the company introduced a new line of matching clothing. The clothing line was available in more stores around the world.

Questions for Critical Thinking

1. Do you think opening retail stores in China is a good move for New Balance? Why or why not?
2. New Balance calls its new retail stores "Experience Stores." In your opinion, what does the company mean by "experience," and how does the experience translate to sales?

Sources: "New Balance to Launch Chinese Opera-Themed Footwear Line," *Sports Business Daily*, http://www.sportsbusinessdaily.com, August 5, 2008; "New Balance Unveils China Mask Collection—Traditional Chinese Opera Fused Into Iconic 576 Design," press release, http://www.newbalance.com, http://newbalance.com, April 6, 2010; George Kiel III, "New Balance Experience Store in Shanghai," *NiceKicks*, http://www.nicekicks.com, February 11, 2010; "The World's First New Balance Experience Store Brought to Life Through a Sensory Approach," *Newswire*, http://www.i-newswire.com, August 23, 2009; Rosemary Feitelberg, "New Balance to Open Experience Unit in Beijing," *Women's Wear Daily*, http://www.wwd.com, August 14, 2009.

chapter 10

Developing and Managing Brand and Product Strategies

CHAPTER OBJECTIVES

① Determine how to define a brand and identify the different types of brands.

② Explain the strategic value of brand equity and the benefits of category and brand management.

③ Discuss how companies develop a strong identity for their products and brands.

④ Identify and briefly describe each of the new-product development strategies.

⑤ Describe the consumer adoption process.

⑥ List the stages in the new-product development process and explain the relationship between product safety and product liability.

LOBLAWS LEADS THE WAY IN BRANDING GROCERIES

Since Theodore Pringle Loblaw and J. Milton Cork first opened Loblaw Groceterias in 1919, the company has been at the forefront of innovation. The company has changed how people shop for groceries, the products they buy, and how the grocery industry brands its products. Some of these innovations came about because it was the right idea for the time and other changes came about in order to save the company.

The very first store changed the way people shopped for groceries. The store layout allowed customers to pick their own groceries from shelves rather than the traditional type of grocery store where a clerk selected items from behind a counter.

During the 1970s, a time when family budgets were stretched due to major economic changes such as increasing oil prices and interest rates, many companies introduced generic products. Loblaws introduced its No Name series of products at this time. No Name products were priced significantly lower than other brands and could be identified on the store shelves by their distinctive labels. Some grocery stores used white labels with black lettering, but Loblaws labels were yellow with black lettering to better match the company's colours. Customers often found the No Name products to be of equal quality to other branded products.

The company may not have been the first to introduce generic brands but it took the concept one step further: it opened its first No Frills store. The No Frills stores were originally designed to feature the No Name line of products.

The 1970s brought other changes to the company. A new management team was hired, which included Don Watt and Dave Nichol. Don Watt's background was design and Dave Nicol had marketing experience. Watt redesigned the stores, from layout to lighting. The redesign included bringing the high-margin produce to the front of the store.

Watt and Nicol also introduced another new concept in the grocery industry, a premium line of store-branded products. Most grocery stores had a line of store-branded products that were less expensive versions of the branded products they carried. Watt and Nicol decided to develop a range of premium branded products, and the President's Choice line of products was introduced. To promote new products to the Canadian market, a full-colour newsletter was introduced. "Dave Nichol's Insider Report" featured Dave Nichol, his dog, and all the President's Choice products that had been developed since the last report. It also included cheeky stories and recipes that contained President's Choice products as ingredients. President's Choice products are developed by a team of Loblaws employees and company suppliers. Team members travel the world in search of new food ideas and develop a version that will be enjoyed by Canadian consumers. Today the company offers more than 3500 President's Choice products, including food, gardening supplies, and beauty products. Spill-off lines have been developed such as the President's Choice Blue Menu products, which offer a healthier alternative, President's Choice Organics, and President's Choice Green products.

How successful is the President's Choice brand? It is the second-strongest brand in the grocery industry in Canada; only Kraft Foods has a stronger brand. Loblaws is also the market leader in the Canadian grocery industry with over $30 billion in sales annually. Loblaws annual sales are more than twice as high as its nearest competitor. It seems consumers agree with the President's Choice slogan: "Worth switching supermarkets for." That is not all customers agree with. Research shows that Canadians like store-brand products; 60 percent believe store brands are as good quality as their brand-name counterparts, and 68 percent believe that store brands offer extremely good quality for the price.[1]

connecting with customers

Loblaws has successfully connected with its customers by providing them with President's Choice branded products that make their lives easier. This is evident in the fact that Loblaws holds the largest market share in the Canadian grocery market.

Chapter Overview

BRANDS play a huge role in our lives. We try certain brands for all kinds of reasons: on recommendations from friends, because we want to associate ourselves with the images certain brands possess, or because we remember colourful advertisements. We develop loyalty to certain brands and product lines for varying reasons as well—the quality of a product, price, and habit are a few examples. This chapter examines the way companies make decisions about developing and managing the products and product lines that they hope will become consumer necessities. Developing and marketing a product and product line and building a desired brand image are costly propositions. To protect its investment and maximize the return on it, a specialized marketer called a *category manager* must carefully nurture both existing and new products. The category manager is responsible for an entire product line.

This chapter focuses on two critical elements of product planning and strategy. First, it looks at how firms build and maintain identity and competitive advantage for their products through branding. Second, it focuses on the new-product planning and development process. Effective new-product planning and meeting the profit responsibility that a category manager has for a product line require careful preparation. The wants and desires of consumers change constantly, and successful marketers manage to keep up with—or stay just ahead of—those changes. ◆◆◆

① **Determine how to define a brand and identify the different types of brands.**

brand Name, term, sign, symbol, design, or some combination that identifies the products of one firm while differentiating them from the competition's.

MANAGING BRANDS FOR COMPETITIVE ADVANTAGE

Think of the last time you went shopping for groceries. As you moved through the store, chances are your recognition of various brand names influenced many of your purchasing decisions. Perhaps you chose Colgate toothpaste over competitive offerings or loaded Heinz ketchup into your cart instead of the store brand. Walking through the snack food aisle, you might have reached for Doritos or Lay's potato chips without much thought.

Marketers recognize the powerful influence that products and product lines have on customer behaviour, and they work to create strong identities for their products and protect them. Branding is the process of creating that identity. A **brand** is a name, term, sign, symbol, design, or some combination that identifies the products of one firm while differentiating these products from competitors' offerings. Canada's best managed brands as determined by Interbrand are illustrated in Table 10.1.

table 10.1   *Canada's Best Managed Brands*

CANADA	VALUE (MILLIONS)
1 Thomson Reuters	9,413
2 Toronto Dominion Bank	6,668
3 Royal Bank of Canada	6,171
4 BlackBerry	6,000
5 Shoppers Drug Mart	3,425
6 Tim Hortons	2,654
7 Bell	2,452
8 Rogers	2,276
9 Scotiabank	2,159
10 Bank of Montreal	1,972
11 Canadian Tire	1,906

Source: Interbrand, "Best Canadian Brands 2010," Interbrand Corporation website, http://www.interbrand.com/en/Interbrand-offices/Interbrand-Toronto/Best-Canadian-Brands-2010.aspx (accessed July 5, 2011).

table 10.2 *Selected Brands, Brand Names, and Brand Marks*

BRAND TYPE	
Private brand	Sam's Choice (Walmart) or President's Choice (Loblaws)
Family brand	RAID insect sprays or Campbell soups
Individual brand	Purex or Clorox
Brand name	Kleenex or Cheetos
Brand mark	Colonel Sanders for KFC or Mr. Peanut for Planters

As you read this chapter, consider how many brands you are aware of—both those you are loyal to and those you have never tried or have tried and abandoned. Table 10.2 shows some selected brands, brand names, and brand marks. Satisfied buyers respond to branding by making repeat purchases of the same product because they identify the item with the name of its producer. One buyer might derive satisfaction from an ice cream cone with the brand name Chapman; another might derive the same satisfaction from one with the name Breyers or Neilson.

BRAND LOYALTY

Brands achieve widely varying consumer familiarity and acceptance. A snowboarder might insist on a Burton snowboard, but the same consumer might show little loyalty to particular brands in another product category such as soap. Marketers measure brand loyalty in three stages: brand recognition, brand preference, and brand insistence.

Brand recognition is a company's first objective for newly introduced products. Marketers begin the promotion of new items by trying to make them familiar to the public. Advertising offers one effective way for increasing consumer awareness of a brand. Glad is a familiar brand in Canada, and it drew on customers' recognition of its popular sandwich bags and plastic wraps when it introduced a new plastic food wrap that seals around items with just the press of a finger. Other tactics for creating brand recognition include offering free samples or discount coupons for purchases. Once consumers have used a product, seen it advertised, or noticed it in stores, it moves from the unknown to the known category, which increases the probability that some of those consumers will purchase it.

At the second level of brand loyalty, **brand preference**, buyers rely on previous experiences with the product when choosing it, if available, over competitors' products. You may prefer Nike shoes or Roots clothes to other brands and buy their new lines as soon as they are offered. If so, those products have established brand preference.

Brand insistence, the ultimate stage in brand loyalty, leads consumers to refuse alternatives and to search extensively for the desired merchandise. A product at this stage has achieved a monopoly position with its consumers. Although many firms try to establish brand insistence with all consumers, few achieve this ambitious goal. Companies that offer specialty or luxury goods and services, such as Rolex watches or Lexus automobiles, are more apt to achieve this status than those that offer mass-marketed goods and services.

One problem facing many brand names is the persistence of counterfeiting. See the accompanying "Solving an Ethical Controversy" feature for some questions about how far to carry the fight against fakes.

TYPES OF BRANDS

Brands are classified in many ways: private, manufacturer's or national, family, and individual brands. In making branding decisions, firms weigh the benefits and disadvantages of each type of brand. Some firms, however, sell their goods without any efforts at branding. These items are called **generic products**. They are characterized by plain labels, little or no advertising, and no

brand recognition
Consumer awareness and identification of a brand.

brand preference
Consumer reliance on previous experiences with a product to choose that product again.

brand insistence
Consumer refusal of alternatives and extensive search for desired merchandise.

generic products
Products characterized by plain labels, no advertising, and the absence of brand names.

SOLVING AN ETHICAL CONTROVERSY

Counterfeiters: Is It Worth the Fight to Stop Them?

MILLIONS of counterfeit goods are produced every year. Criminal organizations, which are behind many of the world's counterfeiting operations, are making billions on sales of phony branded products every year. Shoes, perfumes, watches, appliances, stereos, car parts, food, prescription drugs, alcohol, sportswear, designer clothing, toys, cosmetics, and even champagne are frequent targets of counterfeiters, as are music, electrical products, and MP3 players.

It has been estimated that the jobs, taxes, and sales lost to counterfeiters every year amount to billions, and most large companies are spending millions annually in the fight against fakes. But no one sees an end to counterfeiting. Not all countries have signed on to copyright protection treaties, and continuing attempts to get them to police illegal operations have met with limited success. Also, technologies of various kinds are making it easier all the time to produce and market bogus branded goods.

Should companies continue to invest more and more in trying to prevent counterfeiting of their brands?

PRO

1. Counterfeit drugs can be tainted and therefore dangerous. Other counterfeit goods are often shoddy and unreliable, such children's clothing or electrical devices that can catch fire easily.

2. These knock-offs carrying well-respected brand names are often poor imitations of the real item, and their presence in the marketplace is likely to cause irreparable harm to the overall image of the legitimate products carrying the brand.

CON

1. Counterfeiters will always find an easy market for bargain-priced goods and so will never give up.

2. The effort of fighting counterfeiters is very hard for foreign firms, unless they can secure the cooperation of local authorities in stamping out this problem.

Where do you stand: pro or con?

Sources: Royal Canadian Mounted Police website, http://www.rcmp-grc.gc.ca, July 11, 2011; Canadian Anti-Counterfeiting Network website, http://www.cacn .ca, July 11, 2011; Sarah McBride, "The Hunt for Movie Pirates," *The Wall Street Journal*, April 12, 2004, pp. B1, B3; Erwin Lemuel G. Oliva, "Canon Seeks Alliance with Vendors vs. Counterfeit Goods," *Inquirer News Service*, http://news.inq7.net/ index.index.php, April 20, 2004; "How Can I Protect Myself from Counterfeit Goods?" BBC News, http://www.bbc.co.uk, April 17, 2004; "Psst. Wanna Real Rolex?" *The Economist*, http://www.economist.com, January 22, 2004; Michael Wilson, "2 Chinatown Stores Raided in Counterfeit-Goods Sweep," *The New York Times*, http://www.nytimes.com, December 3, 2003; Timothy W. Maier, "Counterfeit Goods Pose Real Threat," Insight, http://www.insight mag.com, October 30, 2003; Matthew Benjamin, "A World of Fakes," *U.S. News & World Report*, July 14, 2003, pp. 46–47.

---

brand names. Common categories of generic products include food and household staples. These no-name products were first sold in Europe at prices as much as 30 percent below those of branded products. This product strategy was introduced in North America three decades ago. The market shares for generic products increase during economic downturns but subside when the economy improves. However, many consumers request generic substitutions for certain brand-name prescriptions at the pharmacy whenever they are available.

Manufacturers' Brands versus Private Brands

manufacturer's brand Brand name owned by a manufacturer or other producer.

private brand Brand offered by a wholesaler or retailer.

Manufacturers' brands, also called *national brands*, define the image that most people form when they think of a brand. A **manufacturer's brand** refers to a brand name owned by a manufacturer or other producer. Well-known manufacturers' brands include Hewlett-Packard, Sony, Pepsi-Cola, Dell, and Heinz. In contrast, many large wholesalers and retailers place their own brands on the merchandise they market. The brands offered by wholesalers and retailers are usually called **private brands** (or private labels). Although some manufacturers refuse to produce private label goods, most regard such production as a way to reach additional market segments. Walmart offers many private label products at its stores, including its Old Roy dog food.

The growth of private brands has paralleled that of chain stores. Manufacturers not only sell their well-known brands to stores but also put the store's own label on similar products. Such leading manufacturers as Westinghouse and Heinz generate ever-increasing percentages of their total incomes by producing goods for sale under retailers' private labels. Private brands are popular in the grocery business, where it is estimated that Canadians spend over $11 billion on private label consumer goods, about $850 per household. Worldwide private labels sales bring in more than $85 billion; private label goods are especially popular in western European countries such as Germany and the United Kingdom.[2]

Some retailers like Rona, the home hardware and renovation company, and Staples, the office supply company, are developing products for their private label lines that are also environmentally friendly.[3]

Captive Brands

The nation's major retailers—for example, Canadian Tire—have come up with a spin-off of the private label idea. So-called **captive brands** are national brands that are sold exclusively by a retail chain. Captive brands typically provide better profit margins than private labels. One of Canadian Tire's captive brands is the Debbie Travis line of home decor products. Canadian Tire is hoping to not only increase its decor business but also attract younger shoppers into its stores.[4]

Family and Individual Brands

A **family brand** is a single brand name that identifies several related products. For example, KitchenAid markets a complete line of appliances under the KitchenAid name, and Johnson & Johnson offers a line of baby powder, lotions, plastic pants, and baby shampoo under its name. All Heinz products, such as the company's tomato ketchup and its vegetable soup, carry the Heinz brand.

The great taste you love with 25% less sodium. Almost everyone's happy about it.

Family and individual brands.

Alternatively, a manufacturer may choose to market a product as an **individual brand**, which uniquely identifies the item itself, rather than promoting it under the name of the company or under an umbrella name covering similar items. Unilever, for example, markets Knorr, Bertolli, Lipton, and Slim-Fast food products, Pond's and Sunsilk beauty products, and Lifebuoy and Dove soaps. PepsiCo's Quaker Oats unit markets Aunt Jemima breakfast products and Gatorade beverages. Individual brands cost more than family brands to market because the firm must develop a new promotional campaign to introduce each new product to its target market. Distinctive brands are extremely effective aids in implementing market segmentation strategies.

On the other hand, a promotional outlay for a family brand can benefit all items in the line. Family brands also help marketers introduce new products to both customers and retailers. Since supermarkets stock thousands of items, they hesitate to add new products unless they are confident they will be in demand.

Family brands should identify products of similar quality, or the firm risks harming its overall product image. If Rolls-Royce marketers were to place the Rolls name on a low-end car or a line of discounted clothing, they would severely tarnish the image of the luxury car line. Conversely, Lexus, Infiniti, and Porsche put their names on luxury sport-utility vehicles to capitalize on their reputations and to enhance the acceptance of the new models in a competitive market.

Individual brand names should, however, distinguish dissimilar products. Kimberly-Clark markets two different types of diapers under its Huggies and Pull-Ups names. Procter & Gamble offers shaving products under its Gillette name; laundry detergent under Cheer, Tide, and other brands; and dishwasher detergent under Cascade.

captive brand
National brands that are sold exclusively by a retail chain.

Marketoid

Iceland has the highest Internet usage with 90 percent of the residents using the Internet each year.

assessment check 1

1.1 What is a brand?

1.2 Differentiate among brand recognition, brand preference, and brand insistence.

1.3 Identify the different types of brands.

1.4 How are generic products different from branded products?

family brand
Single brand name that identifies several related products.

individual brand
Single brand that uniquely identifies a product itself.

Products marketed by Honda using a family brand.

(2) **Explain the strategic value of brand equity and the benefits of category and brand management.**

brand equity
Added value that a respected, well-known brand name gives to a product in the marketplace.

Marketoid

In 2007, Canada's Internet usage was 77 percent.

BRAND EQUITY

As individuals, we often like to say that our strongest asset is our reputation. The same is true of organizations. A brand can go a long way toward making or breaking a company's reputation. A strong brand identity backed by superior quality offers important strategic advantages for a firm. First, it increases the likelihood that consumers will recognize the firm's product or product line when they make purchase decisions. Second, a strong brand identity can contribute to buyers' perceptions of product quality. Branding can also reinforce customer loyalty and repeat purchases. A consumer who tries a brand and likes it will probably look for that brand on future store visits. All these benefits contribute to a valuable form of competitive advantage called *brand equity.*

Brand equity refers to the added value that a certain brand name gives to a product in the marketplace. Brands with high equity confer financial advantages on a firm because they often command comparatively large market shares and consumers may pay little attention to differences in prices. Studies have also linked brand equity to high profits and stock returns. Service companies are also aware of the value of brand equity. Sometimes companies increase their brand equity by performing community improvement projects as discussed in the "Go Green" feature.

In global operations, high brand equity often facilitates expansion into new markets. Currently, Apple is the most valuable brand in the world according to a study by Millward and Brown but the Interbrand study shows Coca-Cola as number one. Similarly, Disney's brand equity allows it to market its goods and services in Europe and Japan—and now China. What makes a global brand powerful? According to Interbrand Corp., which measures brand equity in dollar values, a strong brand is one that has the power to increase a company's sales and earnings. A global brand is generally defined as one where at least 20 percent of total sales are generated outside its home country.[5]

The global advertising agency Young & Rubicam (Y&R) developed another brand equity system called the Brand Asset Valuator. Y&R's database of consumers' brand perceptions contains more than 400 000 consumer interviews and information on 20 000 brands across 44 countries. According to Y&R, a firm builds brand equity sequentially on four dimensions of brand personality. These four dimensions are differentiation, relevance, esteem, and knowledge:

- *Differentiation* refers to a brand's ability to stand apart from competitors. Brands such as Porsche and Victoria's Secrets stand out in consumers' minds as a symbol of unique product characteristics.

GO GREEN	**Molson Canadian Red Leaf Project**

ENVIRONMENTAL project or promotional campaign— a little of both, but for everyone involved it turned out to be a winning idea. In the summer of 2011, Molson Canadian teamed up with Evergreen for a summer promotion that worked for the environment as well.

From mid-June to the end of August, ten parks across the country benefitted from tree-planting events. Volunteers from each community spent a morning planting trees—100 000 trees in all. For an additional incentive for the volunteers, the first 100 volunteers for each event received a ticket to an outdoor concert in the same city.

Molson's financed the Red Leaf Project by donating a dollar from the sale of every six pack of Molson Canadian in Ontario to Evergreen. Evergreen is a national charity that works with organizations across the country to create green spaces in urban environments. Another partner in the Molson Canadian Red Leaf Project was TreeCanada. TreeCanada is also a not-for-profit, charitable organization that provides education, technical assistance, and resources to encourage Canadians across the country, in both urban and rural locations, to plant trees.

The Red Leaf Project is not the only environmental project or fund-raising event that Molson has been involved in. As part of Canada Day celebrations, 50 cents from the sale of Molson Canadian beer at participating Boston Pizza locations was donated to the Evergreen organization. Molson partnered with the World Wildlife Fund (WWF), the Loblaws group of companies, and the Vancouver Aquarium in the Great Canadian Shoreline Cleanup. The shoreline cleanup project has been taking place in communities across the country since 2003. The number of communities participating has grown from just below 500 the first year to over 1500 in some years.

So whether Molson's started its environmental projects as a promotional campaign or as a result of the company's commitment to the environment, all Canadians benefit from these events.

Sources: The Shoreline Cleanup website, http://shorelinecleanup.ca, July 10, 2011; The Red Leaf Project website, http://redleafproject.ca, July 10, 2011; TreeCanada website, http://www.treecanada.ca, July 10, 2011; Molson website, http://blog.molson.com, July 10, 2011; Evergreen website, http://www.evergreen.ca, July 10, 2011.

- *Relevance* refers to the real and perceived appropriateness of the brand to a big consumer segment. A large number of consumers must feel a need for the benefits offered by the brand. Brands with high relevance are Hallmark and Microsoft.

- *Esteem* is a combination of perceived quality and consumer perceptions about the growing or declining popularity of a brand. A rise in perceived quality or in public opinion about a brand enhances a brand's esteem. But negative impressions reduce esteem. Brands with high esteem are General Mills and Honda.

- *Knowledge* refers to the extent of customers' awareness of the brand and understanding of what a good or service stands for. Knowledge implies that customers feel an intimate relationship with a brand. Examples are Jell-O and Band-Aid.[6]

THE ROLE OF CATEGORY AND BRAND MANAGEMENT

Because of the tangible and intangible value associated with strong brand equity, marketing organizations invest considerable resources and effort in developing and maintaining these dimensions of brand personality. Traditionally, companies assigned the task of managing a brand's marketing strategies to a **brand manager**. Today, because they sell about 80 percent of their products to national retail chains, major consumer goods companies have adopted a strategy called **category management**. In this strategy a manufacturer's *category manager* maximizes sales for the retailer by overseeing an entire product line, often tracking sales history with data from the retail checkout point and aggregating it with sales data for the entire category (obtained from third-party vendors) and qualitative data such as customer surveys.[7] One of the duties of both brand and categories managers is promoting their brands as discussed in the "Marketing in a Digital World" feature.

Unlike traditional product managers, category managers have profit responsibility for their product group and also help the retailer's category buyer maximize sales for the whole category, not just the particular manufacturer's product. These managers are assisted by associates usually called *analysts*. Part of the shift to category management was initiated by large retailers, which realized they could benefit from the marketing muscle of large grocery and household goods producers such as

brand manager
Marketer within an organization who is responsible for a single brand.

category management
Product management system in which a category manager— with profit and loss responsibility—oversees a product line.

MARKETING IN A DIGITAL WORLD   Joe Fresh

JOE Fresh, the clothing line launched by Loblaws, is affordable and stylish. The creative director for the line is Joseph Mimran, no stranger to the fashion industry. Before coming to Loblaws to take the role of creative director of the Joe Fresh line and the PC Home collection of interior decor and accessories, Mimran spent more than 20 years in the fashion industry. Alfred Sung, Caban, and Club Monaco are labels Mimran has worked on.

When Joe Fresh teamed up with Mattel to produce a limited line of underwear and sleepwear for girls and women, they used an online contest to get the message out. The "Barbie loves Joe Fresh" line also included a tote bag. The prize for the online contest was a Barbie Ultimate Sleepover for ten.

The Barbie contest is not the only online promotion that Loblaws has used to promote the Joe Fresh line. When Facebook launched its Facebook Deals option, Joe Fresh was one of the first companies to sign on. Consumers with a smartphone can get discounts while shopping if they "check in" on the store's special Facebook page. Shoppers can claim the discount by showing the coupon that appears on their phone displays to the cashier when paying. An added benefit to the retail store is the market research information. Demographic information about shoppers will be shared by Facebook if there are enough shoppers using the feature.

For the Quebec market, a different approach was needed—or least that is what the digital branding agency Cloudraker felt. The folks at Cloudraker fell in love with the Joe Fresh brand but believed the brand could benefit from a made-in-Quebec-for-the-Quebec-market approach. The folks at Cloudraker wanted to generate the same word-of-mouth enthusiasm that worked for the rest of Canada through social media.

While the Joe Fresh brand is promoted using several different approaches, the digital promotions are a good fit with its target market.

Sources: Joe Fresh website, http://www.joefresh.com, July 16, 2011; Jeff Beer, "Cloudraker to Make Joe Fresh More Social in Quebec," *Marketing*, February 4, 2010, http://www.marketingmag.ca; Cloudraker website, http://www.cloudraker.com, July 16, 2011; "Facebook Deals Free for Canadian Marketers," *Marketing*, February 1, 2011, http://www.marketingmag.ca; Kristin Laird, "Joe Fresh Begins Relationship with Barbie," *Marketing*, November 3, 2010, http://www.marketingmag.ca.

Kraft and Procter & Gamble. As a result, producers began to focus their attention on in-store merchandising instead of mass-market advertising. Some manufacturers that are too small to dedicate a category manager to each retail chain assign a category manager to each major channel, such as grocery, convenience, drugstore, and so on.[8]

Some of the steps companies follow in the category management process are defining the category based on the target market's needs, scoping out a consumer's decision process when shopping in the category, identifying consumer groups and the store clusters with the greatest sales potential, creating a marketing strategy and performance goal for each cluster and using a scorecard to measure progress, defining and executing the tactics, and tracking progress.[9] Hershey's vending division offers category management services to its institutional customers, providing reduced inventory costs, improved warehouse efficiency, and increased sales.[10]

assessment check 2 ✓

2.1 What is brand equity?

2.2 What are the four dimensions of brand personality?

2.3 Define brand manager.

2.4 How does category management help retailers?

---

③ Discuss how companies develop a strong identity for their products and brands.

PRODUCT IDENTIFICATION

Organizations identify their products in the marketplace with brand names, symbols, and distinctive packaging. Almost every product that is distinguishable from another gives buyers some means of identifying it. Sunkist Growers, for instance, stamps its oranges with the name Sunkist. Iams stamps a pawprint on all of its pet food packages. For well over 100 years, Prudential Insurance Co. has used the Rock of Gibraltar as its symbol. Choosing how to identify the firm's output represents a major strategic decision for marketers. Produce growers have another option besides gummed paper stickers for identifying fruits and vegetables: laser coding. This technology marks fruits and vegetables with their name, identification number, and country of origin. The tattoos are visible and edible, good news for consumers who are tired of peeling tiny stickers from their apples and tomatoes. Although the stickers provide valuable information in the form of price look-up (PLU) codes that a supermarket cashier enters into the computer system to retrieve pricing information, the stickers must also be removed from the produce before it can be eaten. The laser codes include the PLU code and eliminate sticky labels.[11]

BRAND NAMES AND BRAND MARKS

A name plays a central role in establishing brand and product identity. The American Marketing Association defines a **brand name** as the part of the brand that can be spoken. It can consist of words, numbers, or letters that form a name that identifies and distinguishes the firm's offerings from those of its competitors. Firms can also identify their brands by brand marks. A **brand mark** is a symbol or pictorial design that distinguishes a product such as Mr. Peanut for Planters nuts.

Effective brand names are easy to pronounce, recognize, and remember. Short names, such as Nike, Ford, and Bounty, meet these requirements. Marketers try to overcome problems with easily mispronounced brand names by teaching consumers the correct pronunciations. For example, early advertisements for the Korean carmaker Hyundai explained that the name rhymes with *Sunday*. Sensitivity to clear communication doesn't end with the choice of brand name; marketers should also be aware of how well they get their point across in interpersonal communications. The "Career Readiness" feature provides some tips for avoiding jargon in marketing communication.

A brand name should also give buyers the correct connotation of the product's image. The name Lunchables for Kraft's prepackaged lunches suggests a convenient meal that can be eaten anywhere. Nissan's X-Terra connotes youth and extreme sports to promote the off-road SUV, and the iPod Nano uses a name that aptly suggests its tiny size. A brand name must also qualify for legal protection. The Trade-marks Act states that registered trademarks should not contain names or surnames unless the name is viewed in the mind of the consumer as that product, such as McDonald's. Clearly descriptive words such as sweet for baked goods cannot become registered trademarks.[12]

brand name
Part of a brand consisting of words, numbers, or letters that can be spoken and that identifies and distinguishes a firm's offerings from those of its competitors.

brand mark
Symbol or pictorial design that distinguishes a product.

CAREER READINESS **Using Jargon in Everyday Communication**

WIRELESS technology has supercharged the pace of everyday life and with it comes the temptation to use the shorthand common to text messaging in other everyday communications. But consider these facts:

- When you use abbreviations like "btw" and "p&c" in your communication, you're using jargon. And by its very definition, jargon can be confusing and misleading. For example, while it might be obvious to you that "btw" stands for "by the way," to another person it may mean "between." You may interpret "p&c" to mean "private and confidential," but to people in the insurance industry, it stands for "property and casualty." And think of the potential danger in using "jk" when you mean "just kidding": your reader may skip right past those two letters or mistake them for someone's initials.
- Jargon excludes. When you use jargon and people don't understand your message, they may peg you as someone

who's not open or friendly. In fact, recent studies reveal that jargon users are perceived as less likable. Would you really want a client or customer to feel that way about you?

- Using jargon in business communication could be a deal breaker. Although the jargon of text-messaging has become increasingly common, it's too casual for business correspondences and creates a poor impression as you search for—or try to succeed at—the new job. And if your manager is older than you—say, a member of the baby boom generation—he or she is unlikely to be impressed.

Sources: Tim Burres, "Abbreviations Used in E-Mail," Videojug.com, http://www.videojug.com, May 11, 2010; Todd Hicks, "Why Business Jargon and Acronyms Must Be Avoided in Communication," Associated Content.com, January 14, 2010; "How to Write and Effective Business Communication Email," eHow.com, July 10, 2009, http://www.ehow.com.

Disney and Baby Einstein brand marks on one product.

PR NEWSWIRE/THE BABY EINSTEIN COMPANY/ASSOCIATED PRESS

Marketers feel increasingly hard pressed to coin effective brand names, as multitudes of competitors rush to stake out brand names for their own products. Some companies register names before they have products to fit the names to prevent competitors from using them.

When a class of products becomes generally known by the original brand name of a specific offering, the brand name may become a descriptive generic name. If this occurs, the original owner may lose exclusive claim to the brand name. The generic names nylon, aspirin, escalator, kerosene, and zipper started as brand names. Other generic names that were once brand names are cola, yo-yo, linoleum, and shredded wheat.

Marketers must distinguish between brand names that have become legally generic terms and those that seem generic only in many consumers' eyes. Consumers often adopt legal brand names as descriptive names. Jell-O, for instance, is a brand name owned exclusively by Kraft Foods, but many consumers casually apply it as a descriptive name for gelatine desserts. Similarly, many people use the term Kleenex to refer to facial tissues. English and Australian consumers use the brand name Hoover as a verb for vacuuming. One popular way to look something up on the Internet is now to "Google it." Xerox is such a well-known brand name that people frequently—though incorrectly—use it as a verb to mean photocopying. To protect its valuable trademark, Xerox Corporation has created advertisements explaining that Xerox is a brand name and registered trademark and should not be used as a verb.

TRADEMARKS

Businesses invest considerable resources in developing and promoting brands and brand identities. The high value of brand equity encourages firms to take steps in protecting the expenditures they invest in their brands.

trademark
Brand for which the owner claims exclusive legal protection.

A **trademark** is a brand for which the owner claims exclusive legal protection. A trademark should not be confused with a trade name, which identifies a company. The Coca-Cola Company is a trade name, but Coke is a trademark of the company's product. Some trade names duplicate companies' brand names.

Protecting Trademarks

Marketoid

The United Kingdom and Germany have the same Internet usage rate as Canada.

Trademark protection confers the exclusive legal right to use a brand name, brand mark, and any slogan or product name abbreviation. It designates the origin or source of a good or service. Frequently, trademark protection is applied to words or phrases, such as *Bud* for Budweiser.

Firms can also receive trademark protection for packaging elements and product features such as shape, design, and typeface. In Canada, the Trade-marks Act allows companies to register "distinguishing guises," which identify the shape of the product, packaging, or wrapping. The act gives companies the right to take legal action for trademark infringement even if other products using its brand are not particularly similar or easily confused in the minds of consumers. The Trade-marks Office, the government agency responsible for registering trademarks, will not police or monitor a trademark to ensure no one else is infringing on it.[13]

The Internet may be the next battlefield for trademark infringement cases. Some companies are attempting to protect their trademarks by filing infringement cases against companies using similar Internet addresses or using unauthorized versions of the same name.

trade dress
Visual components that contribute to the overall look of a brand.

Trade Dress

Visual cues used in branding create an overall look sometimes referred to as **trade dress**. These visual components may be related to colour selections, sizes, package and label shapes, and similar factors.

For example, McDonald's golden arches, Merrill Lynch's bull, and the yellow of Shell's seashell are all part of these products' trade dress. A combination of visual cues may also constitute trade dress. Consider a Mexican food product that uses the colours of the Mexican flag: green, white, and red. Trade dress disputes have led to numerous courtroom battles.

DEVELOPING GLOBAL BRAND NAMES AND TRADEMARKS

Cultural and language variations make brand-name selection a difficult undertaking for international marketers; an excellent brand name or symbol in one country may prove disastrous in another. An advertising campaign for E-Z washing machines failed in the United Kingdom because the British pronounce z as "zed," unlike Americans. A firm marketing a product in several countries must also decide whether to use a single brand name for universal promotions or tailor names to individual countries. Most languages contain *o* and *k* sounds, so *okay* has become an international word. Most languages also have a short *a*, so Coca-Cola works as an effective brand abroad.

PACKAGING

A firm's product strategy must also address questions about packaging. Like its brand name, a product's package can powerfully influence buyers' purchase decisions.

Marketers are applying increasingly scientific methods to their packaging decisions. Rather than experimenting with physical models or drawings, more and more package designers work with special computer graphics programs that create three-dimensional images of packages in thousands of colours, shapes, and typefaces. Another software program helps marketers design effective packaging by simulating the displays shoppers see when they walk down supermarket aisles.

Companies conduct marketing research to evaluate current packages and to test alternative package designs. Marketers at Sara Lee identified convenience, value, and flavour as significant trends for convenience stores. For this reason, Sara Lee offers these retailers special programs that take advantage of those trends, including "on-the-go" packaging of several Sara Lee products, such as individually wrapped bakery items and sandwiches.[14]

A package serves three major objectives: (1) protection against damage, spoilage, and pilferage; (2) assistance in marketing the product; and (3) cost effectiveness. Let's briefly consider each of these objectives.

Protection against Damage, Spoilage, and Pilferage

The original objective of packaging was to offer physical protection for the merchandise. Products typically pass through several stages of handling between manufacturing and customer purchases, and a package must protect its contents from damage. Furthermore, packages of perishable products must protect the contents against spoilage in transit and in storage until purchased by the consumer. Fears of product tampering have forced many firms to improve package designs. Over-the-counter medicines are sold in tamper-resistant packages covered with warnings informing consumers not to purchase merchandise without protective seals intact. Many grocery items and light-sensitive products are packaged in tamper-resistant containers as well. Products such as spaghetti sauce and jams, packaged in glass jars, often come with vacuum-depressed buttons in the lids that pop up the first time the lids are opened.

Many packages offer important safeguards for retailers against pilferage. Shoplifting and employee theft cost retailers millions of dollars each year. To limit this activity, many packages feature oversized cardboard backings too large to fit into a shoplifter's pocket or purse. Efficient packaging that protects

Balderson: Trademark of cheese.

against damage, spoilage, and theft is especially important for international marketers, who must contend with varying climatic conditions and the added time and stress involved in overseas shipping.

Assistance in Marketing the Product

The proliferation of new products, changes in consumer lifestyles and buying habits, and marketers' emphasis on targeting smaller market segments have increased the importance of packaging as a promotional tool. Many firms are addressing consumers' concerns about protecting the environment by designing packages made of biodegradable and recyclable materials. To demonstrate serious concern regarding environmental protection, Procter & Gamble, Coors, McDonald's, and other firms have created ads that describe their efforts in developing environmentally sound packaging.

In a grocery store where thousands of different items compete for notice, a product must capture the shopper's attention. Marketers combine colours, sizes, shapes, graphics, and typefaces to establish distinctive trade dress that sets their products apart from the products of competitors. Packaging can help establish a common identity for a group of items sold under the same brand name. Like the brand name, a package should evoke the product's image and communicate its value.

Packages can also enhance convenience for the buyers. Pump dispensers, for example, facilitate the use of products as varied as mustard and insect repellent. Squeezable bottles of honey and ketchup make the products easier to use and store. Packaging provides key benefits for convenience foods such as meals and snacks packaged in microwavable containers, juice drinks in aseptic packages, and frozen entrees and vegetables packaged in single-serving portions.

Some firms increase consumer utility with packages designed for reuse. Empty peanut butter and jelly jars have long doubled as drinking glasses. Parents can buy bubble bath in animal-shaped plastic bottles suitable for bathtub play. Packaging is a major component in Avon's overall marketing strategy. The firm's decorative, reusable bottles have even become collectibles.

label
Branding component that carries an item's brand name or symbol, the name and address of the manufacturer or distributor, information about the product, and recommended uses.

Cost-Effective Packaging

Although packaging must perform a number of functions for the producer, marketers, and consumers, it must do so at a reasonable cost. Sometimes changes in the packaging can make packages both cheaper and better for the environment. When StarKist introduced tuna in pouches, along with its standard cans, sales of the product increased. Vineyards have moved toward packaging wine in plastic bags instead of bottles with corks. Wine in plastic bags within a box is not only less expensive but the wine is easier to ship, easier to display in the stores, and eliminates the possibility that the wine will become contaminated by the cork.[15]

Labelling

Labels were once a separate element that was applied to a package; today, they are an integral part of a typical package. Labels perform both promotional and informational functions. A **label** carries an item's brand name or symbol, the name and address of the manufacturer or distributor, information about the product's composition and size, and recommended uses. The right label can play an important role in attracting consumer attention and encouraging purchases.

A number of regulations control package labelling in Canada, some at the federal level and others at the provincial level. The federal government has enacted the Competition Act, the Hazardous Products Act, the Food and Drugs Act, the Consumer Packaging and Labelling Act, and the Textile Labelling Act. The Competition Act, which is administered by the Competition Bureau, regulates false or misleading information. The Hazardous Products Act is administered by Health Canada. This act protects consumers by regulating the sale, advertising, or importing of potentially dangerous materials. The Food and Drugs Act regulates the information required on the labels of food, drugs, cosmetics, and medical devices. Consumer textile articles are dealt with under the Textile Labelling Act. The Consumer Packaging and Labelling Act specifically relates to labels for food

Kraft Dinner introduces a new product but keeps the packaging close to the original product.

COURTESY OF KRAFT CANADA INC.

products, ensuring that accurate information describes ingredients and quantities in both French and English.[16]

The **Universal Product Code (UPC)** designation is another important aspect of a label or package. Introduced in 1974 as a method for cutting expenses in the supermarket industry, UPCs are numerical barcodes printed on packages. Optical scanner systems read these codes, and computer systems recognize items and print their prices on cash register receipts. Although UPC scanners are costly, they permit both considerable labour savings over manual pricing and improved inventory control. The Universal Product Code is also a major asset for marketing research. However, many consumers feel frustrated when only a UPC is placed on a package without an additional price tag because they do not always know how much an item costs if the price labels are missing from the shelf.

Radio-frequency identification (RFID) tags—electronic chips that carry encoded product identification—may replace some of the functions of UPC codes, such as price identification and inventory tracking. But consumer privacy concerns about the amount of information RFID tracking can accumulate may limit their use to aggregate packaging such as pallets, rather than units sized for individual sale.

Universal Product Code (UPC) Numerical bar code system used to record product and price information.

BRAND EXTENSIONS

Some brands become so popular that marketers may decide to use them on unrelated products in pursuit of instant recognition for the new offerings. The strategy of attaching a popular brand name to a new product in an unrelated product category is known as **brand extension**. This practice should not be confused with line extensions, which refers to new sizes, styles, or related products. A brand extension, in contrast, carries over from one product nothing but the brand name. In establishing brand extensions, marketers hope to gain access to new customers and markets by building on the equity already established in their existing brands. Nintendo extended its participative Wii video-game line with Wii Fit Plus, an extension on its popular Wii Fit fitness software.[17]

Targeting the seven- to twelve-year-old age group, Mattel extended its Barbie fashion doll brand in an effort to sustain the interest of older children. It launched the "Barbie Girl" experience, which includes a free interactive website and a subscription-based "VIP" version, both with opportunities for children to create a virtual world where they can design their own room, cruise a cybermall, and more. A Barbie-inspired hand-held MP3 device interacts with the sites. Mattel also offers a free website for parents, with tools and resources for cyberspace safety. The flagship Barbie Store in Shanghai offers a "fashion-tainment" experience complete with a playroom also available for parties, a kid-sized salon, and a café. Visitors to the Barbie Store can also buy Barbie-branded apparel—mostly in shades of pink.[18]

brand extension Strategy of attaching a popular brand name to a new product in an unrelated product category.

brand licensing Firm's authorization of other companies to use its brand names.

BRAND LICENSING

A growing number of firms have authorized other companies to use their brand names. Even colleges and police services have licensed their logos and trademarks. This practice, known as **brand licensing**, expands a firm's exposure in the marketplace, much as a brand extension does. The brand name's owner also receives an extra source of income in the form of royalties from licensees, typically 8 to 12 percent of wholesale revenues.[19]

Brand experts note several potential problems with licensing, however. Brand names do not transfer well to all products. The PetSmart PetsHotel was a winner, as was *American Idol* camp, but recent losers were Precious Moments coffins, Donald Trump steaks, and Girls Gone Wild apparel. If a licensee produces a poor-quality product or an item ethically is incompatible with the original brand, the arrangement could damage the reputation of the brand. Consider the failure of two odd brand extensions: Cheetos lip balm and Bic disposable underwear.[20]

Brand overextension is another risk. Starbucks extended its coffee brand to a "lifestyle" brand by marketing coffee beans in supermarkets and selling CDs, books, and

Advil introduces a new product.

3.1 Distinguish between a brand name and a trademark.

3.2 What are the three purposes of packaging?

3.3 Describe brand extension and brand licensing.

a broad food menu in its retail outlets. By moving away from the qualities that helped make it successful, the brand suffered and market share declined, resulting in the closing of nearly 1000 Starbucks stores. The company's latest brand extension—an instant coffee, sold in single-serving packets—seems to fly in the face of the traditional Starbucks image of a barista carefully brewing an individual cup of coffee for an appreciative customer who savours the experience.[21]

④ Identify and briefly describe each of the new-product development strategies.

NEW-PRODUCT PLANNING

As its offerings enter the maturity and decline stages of the product life cycle, a firm must add new items to continue to prosper. Regular additions of new products to the firm's line help protect it from product obsolescence.

New products are the lifeblood of any business, and survival depends on a steady flow of new entries. Some new products may implement major technological breakthroughs. Other new products simply extend existing product lines. In other words, a new product is one that either the company or the customer has not handled before.

market penetration strategy Strategy that seeks to increase sales of existing products in existing markets.

product positioning Consumers' perceptions of a product's attributes, uses, quality, and advantages and disadvantages relative to competing brands.

market development strategy Strategy that concentrates on finding new markets for existing products.

product development Introduction of new products into identifiable or established markets.

PRODUCT DEVELOPMENT STRATEGIES

A firm's strategy for new-product development varies according to its existing product mix and the match between current offerings and the firm's overall marketing objectives. The current market positions of products also affect product development strategy. Figure 10.1 identifies four alternative development strategies as market penetration, market development, product development, and product diversification.

A **market penetration strategy** seeks to increase sales of existing products in existing markets. Firms can attempt to extend their penetration of markets in several ways. They may modify products, improve product quality, or promote new and different ways to use products. Packaged goods marketers often pursue this strategy to boost market share for mature products in mature markets. Product positioning often plays a major role in such a strategy.

Product positioning refers to consumers' perceptions of a product's attributes, uses, quality, and advantages and disadvantages relative to competing brands. Marketers often conduct marketing research studies to analyze consumer preferences and to construct product positioning maps that plot their products' positions in relation to those of competitors' offerings.

Energizer Canada is repositioning its line of batteries to show not only the performance of the products but the social responsibility of the company. As part of the repositioning strategy, the company is even changing its slogan from "Keep Going" to "Now That's Positivenergy." The pink bunny will not be changed. As part of the repositioning campaign, Energizer Canada has partnered with the charity Evergreen in a program to develop and sustain green spaces across the country. The repositioning is supported with an online campaign and packaging promotion for some of the company's products.[22]

A **market development strategy** concentrates on finding new markets for existing products. Market segmentation, discussed in Chapter 8, provides useful support for such an effort. The banks have succeeded in developing a new market by targeting Chinese residents, particularly in Toronto and Vancouver, with special media promotions, including television, billboards, and newspaper ads, aimed at them.[23]

The strategy of **product development** refers to the introduction of new products into identifiable or established markets. Responding to moviegoers' recently revived interest in 3-D, Panasonic introduced a 3-D home entertainment system. The system includes a pair of special 3-D eyewear as well as a Blu-ray disk player for playing movies at home in 3-D format.[24]

figure 10.1

Alternative Product Development Strategies

	Old Product	New Product
Old Market	Market Penetration	Product Development
New Market	Market Development	Product Diversification

Firms may also choose to introduce new products into markets in which they have already established positions to try to increase overall market share. These new offerings are called *flanker brands*. The fragrance industry uses this strategy extensively when it develops scents that are related to their most popular products. The flanker scents are related in both their smell and their names. The food industry also uses this strategy. Coke, for example, routinely introduces new varieties such as Coke Zero.

Finally, a **product diversification strategy** focuses on developing entirely new products for new markets. Some firms look for new target markets that complement their existing markets; others look in completely new directions. PepsiCo's CEO regards obesity as one of the world's most significant health issues and wants her company to be part of the solution, not the problem. PepsiCo began diversifying its product line beyond items that are "fun for you" to items that are "good for

Established companies introduce new products.

you," including juices, nuts, and oatmeal. The company's growing family of "good for you" products accounts for nearly 20 percent of sales.[25]

In selecting a new-product strategy, marketers should keep in mind an additional potential problem: **cannibalization**. Any firm wants to avoid investing resources in a new-product introduction that will adversely affect sales of existing products. A product that takes sales from another offering in the same product line is said to cannibalize that line. A company can accept some loss of sales from existing products if the new offering will generate sufficient additional sales to warrant its investment in its development and market introduction.

THE CONSUMER ADOPTION PROCESS

In the **adoption process**, consumers go through a series of stages from first learning about the new product to trying it and deciding whether to purchase it regularly or to reject it. These stages in the consumer adoption process can be classified as follows:

1. *Awareness.* Individuals first learn of the new product, but they lack full information about it.

2. *Interest.* Potential buyers begin to seek information about it.

3. *Evaluation.* They consider the likely benefits of the product.

4. *Trial.* They make trial purchases to determine its usefulness.

5. *Adoption/Rejection.* If the trial purchase produces satisfactory results, they decide to use the product regularly.

Marketers must understand the adoption process to move potential consumers to the adoption stage. Once marketers recognize a large number of consumers at the interest stage, they can take steps to stimulate sales by moving these buyers through the evaluation and trial stages. Riceworks, for example, gave away samples of its new whole-grain gluten-free product, Gourmet Brown Rice Crisps, at outdoor events and high-traffic locations one summer as a way to introduce the product. Using a trailer with pictures of the product painted on the sides, "brand ambassadors" handed out product samples.[26]

ADOPTER CATEGORIES

First buyers of new products, the so-called **consumer innovators**, are people who purchase new products almost as soon as these products reach the market. Later adopters wait for additional information and rely on the experiences of initial buyers before making trial purchases. Consumer innovators welcome innovations in each product area. Some computer users, for instance, rush to install new software immediately after each update becomes available.

product diversification strategy Developing entirely new products for new markets.

cannibalization Loss of sales of an existing product due to competition from a new product in the same line.

adoption process Stages that consumers go through in learning about a new product, trying it, and deciding whether to purchase it again.

consumer innovators People who purchase new products almost as soon as the products reach the market.

 assessment check 4

4.1 Distinguish between market penetration and market development strategies.

4.2 What is product development?

4.3 What is product diversification?

(5) Describe the consumer adoption process.

figure 10.2

**Categories of Adopters
Based on Relative Times
of Adoption**

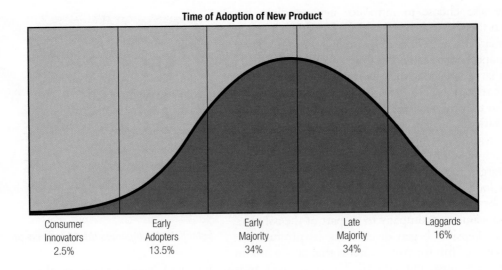

Time of Adoption of New Product

Consumer Innovators 2.5% | Early Adopters 13.5% | Early Majority 34% | Late Majority 34% | Laggards 16%

A number of studies about the adoption of new products have identified five categories of purchasers based on relative times of adoption. These categories, shown in Figure 10.2, are consumer innovators, early adopters, early majority, late majority, and laggards.

While the adoption process focuses on individuals and the steps they go through in making the ultimate decision about whether to become repeat purchasers of the new product or to reject it as a failure to satisfy their needs, the **diffusion process** focuses on all members of a community or social system. The focus here is on the speed at which an innovative product is accepted or rejected by all members of the community.

Figure 10.2 shows the diffusion process as following a normal distribution from a small group of early purchasers (called *innovators*) to the final group of consumers (called *laggards*) to make trial purchases of the new product. A few people adopt at first, and then the number of adopters increases rapidly as the value of the product becomes apparent. The adoption rate finally diminishes as the number of potential consumers who have not adopted, or purchased, the product diminishes. Typically, innovators make up the first 2.5 percent of buyers who adopt the new product; laggards are the last 16 percent to do so. Figure 10.2 excludes those who never adopt the product.

diffusion process
Process by which new goods or services are accepted in the marketplace.

IDENTIFYING EARLY ADOPTERS

It's no surprise that identifying consumers or organizations that are most likely to try a new product can be vital to a product's success. By reaching these buyers early in the product's development or introduction, marketers can treat these adopters as a test market, evaluating the product and discovering suggestions for modifications. Since early purchasers often act as opinion leaders from whom others seek advice, their attitudes toward new products quickly spread to others. Acceptance or rejection of the innovation by these purchasers can help forecast its expected success. New-car models are multiplying, for instance, and many are sporting a dizzying variety of options such as ports to accommodate—and integrate—the driver's iPod, wireless phone, and laptop. Improved stability controls, collision warnings, and "smart engines" that save fuel are also available.

A large number of studies have established the general characteristics of first adopters. These pioneers tend to be younger, are better educated, and enjoy higher incomes than other consumers. They are more mobile than later adopters and change both their jobs and addresses more often. They also rely more heavily than later adopters on impersonal information sources; more hesitant buyers depend primarily on company-generated promotional information and word-of-mouth communications.

Rate of Adoption Determinants

Frisbees progressed from the product introduction stage to the market maturity stage in a period of six months. In contrast, it took 13 years to convince corn farmers to use hybrid seed corn, an innovation capable of doubling crop yields. Five characteristics of a product innovation influence its adoption rate:

1. *Relative advantage.* An innovation that appears far superior to previous ideas offers a greater relative advantage—reflected in lower price, physical improvements, or ease of use—and increases the product's adoption rate.

2. *Compatibility.* An innovation consistent with the values and experiences of potential adopters attracts new buyers at a relatively rapid rate. Consumers already comfortable with the miniaturization of communications technology may be attracted to smartphones, for instance, and the iPhone's two- by three-inch screen.

3. *Complexity.* The relative difficulty of understanding the innovation influences the speed of acceptance. In most cases, consumers move slowly in adopting new products that they find difficult to understand or use. Farmers' cautious acceptance of hybrid seed corn illustrates how long an adoption can take.

4. *Possibility of trial use.* An initial free or discounted trial of a good or service means that adopters can reduce their risk of financial or social loss when they try the product. A coupon for a free item or a free night's stay at a hotel can accelerate the rate of adoption.

5. *Observability.* If potential buyers can observe an innovation's superiority in a tangible form, the adoption rate increases. In-store demonstrations or even advertisements that focus on the superiority of a product can encourage buyers to adopt a product.

Marketers who want to accelerate the rate of adoption can manipulate these five characteristics, at least to some extent. An informative promotional message about a new allergy drug could help consumers overcome their hesitation in adopting this complex product. Effective product design can emphasize an item's advantages over the competition. Everyone likes to receive something for free, so giving away small samples of a new product lets consumers try it at little or no risk. In-home demonstrations or trial home placements of items such as furniture or carpeting can achieve similar results. Marketers must also make positive attempts to ensure the innovation's compatibility with adopters' value systems.

ORGANIZING FOR NEW-PRODUCT DEVELOPMENT

A firm needs to be organized in such a way that its personnel can stimulate and coordinate new-product development. Some companies contract with independent design firms to develop new products. Many assign product-innovation functions to one or more of the following entities: new-product committees, new-product departments, product managers, and venture teams.

New-Product Committees

The most common organizational arrangement for activities in developing a new product is to centre these functions in a new-product committee. This group typically brings together experts in such areas as marketing, finance, manufacturing, engineering, research, and accounting. Committee members spend less time conceiving and developing their own new-product ideas than reviewing and approving new-product plans that arise elsewhere in the organization. The committee might review ideas from the engineering and design staff or perhaps from marketers and salespeople who are in constant contact with customers.

Since members of a new-product committee hold important jobs in the firm's functional areas, their support for any new-product plan likely foreshadows approval for further development. However, new-product committees in large companies tend to reach decisions slowly and maintain conservative views. Sometimes members compromise so they can return to their regular responsibilities.

New-Product Departments

Many companies establish separate, formally organized departments to generate and refine new-product ideas. The departmental structure overcomes the limitations of the new-product committee system and encourages innovation as a permanent full-time activity. The new-product department is responsible for all phases of a development project within the firm, including screening decisions, developing product specifications, and coordinating product testing. The head of the department wields substantial authority and typically reports to the chief executive officer, chief operating officer, or a top marketing executive.

Product Managers

product manager
Marketer within an organization who is responsible for an individual product or product line; also called a brand manager.

A **product manager** is another term for a brand manager, a function mentioned earlier in the chapter. This marketer supports the marketing strategies of an individual product or product line. Procter & Gamble, for instance, assigned its first product manager in 1927, when it made one person responsible for Camay soap.

Product managers set prices, develop advertising and sales promotion programs, and work with sales representatives in the field. In a company that markets many products, product managers fulfill key functions in the marketing department. They provide individual attention for each product and support and coordinate efforts of the firm's sales force, marketing research department, and advertising department. Product managers often lead new-product development programs, including creation of new-product ideas and recommendations for improving existing products.

However, most consumer goods companies such as Procter & Gamble and General Mills have either modified the product manager structure or done away with it altogether in favour of a category management structure. Category managers have profit and loss responsibility, which is not characteristic of the product management system. This change has largely come about because of customer preference, but it can also benefit a manufacturer by avoiding duplication of some jobs and competition among the company's own brands and its managers.

Venture Teams

venture team
Associates from different areas of an organization who work together in developing new products.

A **venture team** gathers a group of specialists from different areas of an organization to work together in developing new products. The venture team must meet criteria for return on investment, uniqueness of product, serving a well-defined need, compatibility of the product with existing technology, and strength of patent protection. Although the organization sets up the venture team as a temporary entity, its flexible life span may extend over a number of years. When purchases confirm the commercial potential of a new product, an existing division may take responsibility for that product, or it may serve as the nucleus of a new business unit or of an entirely new company. Some marketing organizations differentiate between venture teams and task forces. A new-product task force assembles an interdisciplinary group working on temporary assignment through their functional departments. Its basic activities centre on coordinating and integrating the work of the firm's functional departments on a specific project.

Unlike a new-product committee, a venture team does not disband after every project. Team members accept project assignments as major responsibilities, and the team exercises the authority it needs to both plan and implement a course of action. To stimulate product innovation, the venture team typically communicates directly with top management, but it functions as an entity separate from the basic organization.

assessment check 5

5.1 Who are consumer innovators?

5.2 What characteristics of a product innovation can influence its adoption rate?

⑥ **List the stages in the new-product development process and explain the relationship between product safety and product liability.**

THE NEW-PRODUCT DEVELOPMENT PROCESS

Once a firm is organized for new-product development, it can establish procedures for moving new-product ideas to the marketplace. Developing a new product is often time-consuming, risky, and expensive. Usually, firms must generate dozens of new-product ideas to produce even one successful product. In fact, the failure rate of new products averages 80 percent. Products fail for a number of reasons, including inadequate market assessments, lack of market orientation, poor screening and project evaluation, product defects, and inadequate launch efforts. And these blunders cost a bundle: firms invest nearly half of the total resources devoted to product innovation on products that

MARKETING AND THE SME

The Honibe–Honey Drop

THE Honibe story sounds like it could have been written by Lucy Maud Montgomery, who wrote the Anne of Green Gables story that takes place on Prince Edward Island, because that is where Island Abbey Foods Limited is located. John Rowe used his knowledge in engineering to develop and market an award-winning new product—the Honey Drop.

While Rowe was on a camping trip, his jar of honey broke and spilled all over his clothes and tent. When Rowe researched the market to find a honey-based product that was solid enough to take on camping trips, he found there wasn't one. He set out to change that and developed the Honey Drop. The Honey Drop is like a sugar cube, solid until placed in a hot liquid. The business was set up with his brother, Justin, as vice president of sales and his wife, Susan, company CFO.

The Honey Drop was originally available only through the company website, Nostickyfingers.com. The company gained international recognition early on by winning the Global SIAL d'Or, and the company's signature product—the Honey Drop—won best new product award. Rowe likens the win of the SIAL d'Or awards to winning the food Oscars. The company gained national exposure after appearing on the *Dragon's Den* program where several of the Dragons agreed to invest the money the company was looking for to expand its product line and to move into new markets.

The company now has several products in its line—all 100 percent dried honey. Their products include the Honey Drop, the alternative to the sugar cube; Honey Delights, a honey candy; Honey Lozenges, available in several flavours; and Honey Sprinkles, which are a sugar substitute.

With so much success so quickly, one can only imagine what kind of ending Lucy Maud Montgomery would write for this story.

Sources: Company website, http://www.honibe.com, July 11, 2011; "P.E.I. Company Wins Prestigious Food Award," Canadian Manufacturing website, http://www.canadianmanufacturing.com, July, 11, 2011; "Sweetening the Pot," Progressive Media, http://www.progressmedia.ca, July 11, 2011; "Global SIAL d'Or Awards Honors Honey Drop," The Gourmet Retailer, October 19, 2010, http://www.gourmetretailer.com.

become commercial failures. Sometimes new products are the beginning of entirely new companies as discussed in the "Marketing and the SME" feature.

A new product is more likely to become successful if the firm follows a six-step development process shown in Figure 10.3: (1) idea generation, (2) screening, (3) business analysis, (4) development, (5) test marketing, and (6) commercialization. Of course, each step requires decisions about whether to proceed further or abandon the project. And each step involves a greater financial investment.

Traditionally, most companies have developed new products through phased development, which follows the six-step process in an orderly sequence. Responsibility for each phase passes first from product planners to designers and engineers, to manufacturers, and finally to marketers. The phased-development method can work well for firms that dominate mature markets and can develop variations on existing products. But with rapid changes in technology and markets, many companies feel pressured to speed up the development process.

This time pressure has encouraged many firms to implement accelerated product development programs. These programs generally consist of teams with design, manufacturing, marketing, and sales personnel who carry out development projects from idea generation to commercialization. This method can reduce the time needed to develop products because team members work on the six steps concurrently rather than in sequence.

Whether a firm pursues phased development or parallel product development, all phases can benefit from planning tools and scheduling methods such as the program evaluation and review

figure 10.3

Steps in the New-Product Development Process

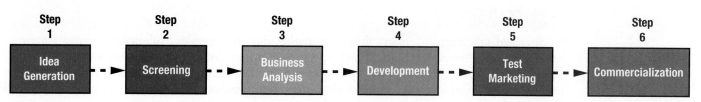

technique (PERT) and the critical path method (CPM). These techniques, originally developed by the U.S. Navy, map out the sequence of each step in a process and show the time allotments for each activity. Detailed PERT and CPM flowcharts help marketers to coordinate all activities entailed in the development and introduction of new products.

IDEA GENERATION

New-product development begins with ideas from many sources: suggestions from customers, the sales force, research and development specialists, competing products, suppliers, retailers, and independent inventors. Bose Corporation has built its brand by staying at the forefront of technology. Spending an estimated $100 million a year on research, the company leads the market for products using advanced technology; sound systems for businesses, cars, and consumer home use; and the award-winning Wave radio and Wave and Acoustic Wave music systems.[27] Hallmark, the world's largest producer of greeting cards, maintains a massive, world-class design studio at its headquarters, where a creative staff of 800 comes up with 19 000 new cards and other products each year.[28] Similarly, ongoing research by scientists at lawn-care industry leader ScottsMiracle-Gro helps the company fine-tune its understanding of consumer needs as it develops products and incorporates environmentally responsible behaviour throughout its operations.[29]

SCREENING

Screening separates ideas with commercial potential from those that cannot meet company objectives. Some organizations maintain checklists of development standards in determining whether a project should be abandoned or considered further. These checklists typically include factors such as product uniqueness, availability of raw materials, and the proposed product's compatibility with current product offerings, existing facilities, and present capabilities. The screening stage may also allow for open discussions of new-product ideas among different parts of the organization.

BUSINESS ANALYSIS

concept testing
Method for subjecting a product idea to additional study before actual development by involving consumers through focus groups, surveys, in-store polling, and the like.

A product idea that survives the initial screening must then pass a thorough business analysis. This stage consists of assessing the new product's potential market, growth rate, and likely competitive strengths. Marketers must evaluate the compatibility of the proposed product with organizational resources.

Concept testing subjects the product idea to additional study prior to its actual development. This important aspect of a new product's business analysis represents a marketing research project that attempts to measure consumer attitudes and perceptions about the new-product idea. Focus groups and in-store polling can contribute effectively to concept testing. The screening and business analysis stages generate extremely important information for new-product development because they (1) define the proposed product's target market and customers' needs and wants and (2) determine the product's financial and technical requirements. Firms that are willing to invest money and time during these stages tend to be more successful at generating viable ideas and creating successful products.

Marketoid

The highest individual Internet usage rate is in British Columbia and Alberta at 85 percent.

DEVELOPMENT

Financial outlays increase substantially as a firm converts an idea into a visible product. The conversion process is the joint responsibility of the firm's development engineers, who turn the original concept into a product, and of its marketers, who provide feedback on consumer reactions to the product design, package, colour, and other physical features. Many firms implement computer-aided design and manufacturing systems to streamline the development stage, and prototypes may go through numerous changes before the original mock-up becomes a final product.

TEST-MARKETING

As discussed in Chapter 7, many firms test-market their new-product offerings to gauge consumer reaction. After a company has developed a prototype, it may decide to test-market it to measure consumer reactions under normal competitive conditions. Test marketing's purpose is to verify that the product will perform well in a real-life environment. If the product does well, the company can proceed

Companies like Unilever are constantly developing new products.

REPRODUCED WITH PERMISSION OF UNILEVER PLC AND GROUP COMPANIES.

to commercialization. If it flops, the company has two options. It can fine-tune certain features and reintroduce it or pull the plug on the project altogether. Industries that rely heavily on test-marketing are snack foods and movies. Of course, even if a product tests well and reaches the commercialization stage, it may still take a while to catch on with the general public.

COMMERCIALIZATION

When a new-product idea reaches the commercialization stage, it is ready for full-scale marketing. Commercialization of a major new product can expose the firm to substantial expenses. It must establish marketing strategies, fund outlays for production facilities, and acquaint the sales force, marketing intermediaries, and potential customers with the new product.

PRODUCT SAFETY AND LIABILITY

A product can fulfill its mission of satisfying consumer needs only if it ensures safe operation. Manufacturers must design their products to protect users from harm. Products that lead to injuries, either directly or indirectly, can have disastrous consequences for their makers. **Product liability** refers to the responsibility of manufacturers and marketers for injuries and damages caused by their products. Chapter 3 discussed some of the major consumer protection laws that affect product safety. Product safety is controlled by laws that are administered by different government agencies as well as voluntary standards. The laws covering product safety include the Hazardous Products Act, the Motor Vehicle Safety Act, and many acts and regulations under the Canadian Food Inspection Agency. These laws cover many areas of product safety, such as regulating and even banning certain products, requiring packaging that is not injurious to children, and ensuring food safety. In addition to the laws relating to product safety, two standards organizations operate in Canada: the National Standards System and the Standards Council of Canada. Standards are technical specifications or other criteria that companies adhere to either voluntarily or because they are required to by law.

Regulatory activities and the increased number of liability claims have prompted companies to sponsor voluntary improvements in safety standards. Safety planning is now a vital element of product strategy, and many companies now publicize the safety planning and testing that go into the development of their products. Volvo, for example, is well known for the safety features it designs into its automobiles, and consumers recognize that fact when they decide to purchase a Volvo.

product liability
Responsibility of manufacturers and marketers for injuries and damages caused by their products.

assessment check 6

6.1 Where do ideas for new products come from?

6.2 What is concept testing and what happens in the commercialization stage?

6.3 What role do the various product safety acts play in protecting consumers?

6.4 What role do standards play in protecting the safety of consumers?

Strategic Implications

Marketers who want to see their products reach the marketplace successfully have a number of options for developing them, branding them, and developing a strong brand identity among consumers and business customers. The key is to integrate all the options so that they are compatible with a firm's overall business and marketing strategy and ultimately the firm's mission. As marketers consider ideas for new products, they need to be careful not to send their companies in so many different directions as to dilute the identities of their brands, making it nearly impossible to keep track of what their companies do well. Category management can help companies develop a consistent product mix with strong branding while at the same time meeting the needs of customers. Looking for ways to extend a brand without diluting it or compromising brand equity is also an important marketing strategy. Finally, marketers must continue to work to produce high-quality products that are also safe for all users. ◆◆◆

REVIEW OF CHAPTER OBJECTIVES

① Determine how to define a brand and identify the different types of brands.

Marketers recognize the powerful influence products and product lines have on customer behaviour, and they work to create strong identities for their products and protect them. Branding is the process of creating that identity. A brand is a name, term, sign, symbol, design, or some combination that identifies the products of one firm while differentiating these products from competitors' offerings.

A generic product is an item characterized by a plain label, no advertising, and no brand name. A manufacturer's brand is a brand name owned by a manufacturer or other producer. Private brands are brand names placed on products marketed by a wholesaler or retailer. A family brand is a brand name that identifies several related products. An individual brand is a unique brand name that identifies a specific offering within a firm's product line to avoid grouping it under a family brand.

② Explain the strategic value of brand equity and the benefits of category and brand management.

Brand equity provides a competitive advantage for a firm because consumers are more likely to buy a product that carries a respected, well-known brand name. Brand equity also smoothes the path for global expansion.

Category management is beneficial to a business because it gives direct responsibility for creating profitable product lines to category managers and their product group. Consumers respond to branding by making repeat purchases of favoured goods and services. Therefore, managing brands and categories of brands or product lines well can result in a direct response from consumers, increased profits and revenues for companies, and greater consumer satisfaction. Brand and category managers can also enhance relationships with business customers such as retailers.

③ Discuss how companies develop a strong identity for their products and brands.

Effective brands communicate to a buyer an idea of the product's image. Trademarks, brand names, slogans, and brand icons create an association that satisfies the customer's expectation of the benefits that using or having the product will yield.

④ Identify and briefly describe each of the new-product development strategies.

The success of a new product can result from four product development strategies: (1) market penetration, in which a company seeks to increase sales of an existing product in an existing market; (2) market development, which concentrates on finding new markets for existing products; (3) product development, which is the introduction of new products into identifiable or established markets; and (4) product diversification, which focuses on developing entirely new products for new markets.

⑤ **Describe the consumer adoption process.**

In the adoption process, consumers go through a series of stages from learning about the new product to trying it and deciding whether to purchase it again. The stages are called awareness, interest, evaluation, trial, and adoption/rejection.

⑥ **List the stages in the new-product development process and explain the relationship between product safety and product liability.**

The stages in the six-step new-product development process are (1) idea generation, (2) screening, (3) business analysis, (4) development, (5) test-marketing, and (6) commercialization. These steps may be performed sequentially or, in some cases, concurrently.

Product safety refers to the goal of manufacturers to create products that can be operated safely and will protect consumers from harm. Product liability is the responsibility of marketers and manufacturers for injuries and damages caused by their products. There are major consumer protection laws in place to protect consumers from faulty products.

 assessment check answers

1.1 What is a brand?
A brand is a name, term, sign, symbol, design, or some combination that identifies the products of one firm while differentiating these products from competitors' offerings.

1.2 Differentiate among brand recognition, brand preference, and brand insistence.
Brand recognition is a company's first objective for newly introduced products and aims to make these items familiar to the public. Brand preference means buyers rely on previous experiences with the product when choosing it over competitors' products. Brand insistence leads consumers to refuse alternatives and to search extensively for the desired merchandise.

1.3 Identify the different types of brands.
The different types of brands are manufacturer's (or national) brands, private brands, captive brands, family brands, and individual brands.

1.4 How are generic products different from branded products?
Generic products are characterized by plain labels, little or no advertising, and no brand names.

2.1 What is brand equity?
Brand equity refers to the added value that a certain brand name gives to a product in the marketplace.

2.2 What are the four dimensions of brand personality?
The four dimensions of brand personality are differentiation, relevance, esteem, and knowledge.

2.3 Define brand manager.
The person at a company with the task of managing a brand's marketing strategies.

2.4 How does category management help retailers?
Category management helps retailers by providing a person— a category manager—to oversee an entire product line and maximize sales for that retailer. It teams the consumer-goods producer's marketing expertise with the retailer's in-store merchandising efforts to track and identify new opportunities for growth.

3.1 Distinguish between a brand name and a trademark.
A brand name is the part of the brand consisting of letters or words that can be spoken and that forms a name distinguishing a firm's offerings from competitors. A trademark is a brand for which the owner claims exclusive legal protection.

3.2 What are the three purposes of packaging?
A package serves three major objectives: (1) protection against damage, spoilage, and pilferage; (2) assistance in marketing the product; and (3) cost effectiveness.

3.3 Describe brand extension and brand licensing.
Brand extension is the strategy of attaching a popular brand name to a new product in an unrelated product category. Brand licensing is the strategy of authorizing other companies to use a brand name.

4.1 Distinguish between market penetration and market development strategies.
In a market penetration strategy, a company seeks to increase sales of an existing product in an existing market. In a market development strategy, the company concentrates on finding new markets for existing products.

4.2 What is product development?
Product development refers to the introduction of new products into identifiable or established markets.

4.3 What is product diversification?

A product diversification strategy focuses on developing entirely new products for new markets.

5.1 Who are consumer innovators?

Consumer innovators are the first buyers of new products—people who purchase new products almost as soon as these products reach the market.

5.2 What characteristics of a product innovation can influence its adoption rate?

Five characteristics of a product innovation influence its adoption rate: relative advantage, compatibility, complexity, possibility of trial use, and observability.

6.1 Where do ideas for new products come from?

New-product development begins with ideas from many sources: suggestions from customers, the sales force, research and development specialists, assessments of competing products, suppliers, retailers, and independent inventors.

6.2 What is concept testing and what happens in the commercialization stage?

Concept testing subjects the product idea to additional study prior to its actual development. When a new-product idea reaches the commercialization stage, it is ready for full-scale marketing.

6.3 What role do the various product safety acts play in protecting consumers?

The various safety acts regulate the safety of consumer products such as food and automobiles.

6.4 What role do standards play in protecting the safety of consumers?

Standards are technical specifications or other criteria that companies adhere to either voluntarily or because they are required to by law.

MARKETING TERMS YOU NEED TO KNOW

These terms are printed in red in the text. They are defined in the margins of the chapter and in the Glossary that begins on p. G-1.

brand 296	category management 301	market development strategy 308
brand recognition 297	brand name 303	product development 308
brand preference 297	brand mark 303	product diversification
brand insistence 297	trademark 304	strategy 309
generic products 297	trade dress 304	cannibalization 309
manufacturer's brand 298	label 306	adoption process 309
private brand 298	Universal Product Code	consumer innovators 309
captive brand 299	(UPC) 307	diffusion process 310
family brand 299	brand extension 307	product manager 312
individual brand 299	brand licensing 307	venture team 312
brand equity 300	market penetration strategy 308	concept testing 314
brand manager 301	product positioning 308	product liability 315

PROJECTS AND TEAMWORK EXERCISES

1. Locate an advertisement for a product that illustrates an especially effective brand name, brand mark, packaging, and overall trade dress. Explain to the class why you think this product has a strong brand identity.

2. With a classmate, search a grocery store for a product that you think could benefit from updated or new package design. Then sketch out a new package design for the product, identifying and explaining your changes as well as your reasons for the changes. Bring the old package and your new package design to class to share with your classmates.

3. What category of consumer adopter best describes you? Do you follow the same adoption pattern for all products, or are you an early adopter for some and a laggard for others? Create a graph or chart showing your own consumer adoption patterns for different products.

4. Which product labels do you read? Over the next several days, keep a brief record of the labels you check while shopping. Do you read nutritional information when buying food products? Do you check care labels on clothes before you buy them? Do you read the directions or warnings on a product you haven't used before? Make notes about what influenced your decision to read or not read the product labels. Did you feel they provided enough information, too little, or too much?

5. Some brands achieve customer loyalty by retaining an air of exclusivity and privilege, even though that often comes along with high price tags. Louis Vuitton, the maker of luxury leather goods, is one such firm. What kind of brand loyalty is this, and how does Vuitton achieve it?

CRITICAL-THINKING EXERCISES

1. In this chapter, you learned that Mattel has launched a "Barbie Girls" experience in an attempt to sustain the interest of older girls in the Barbie brand. Do you think this strategy will work for Mattel? Why or why not? Identify another well-known product that appeals to a specific age group. Do you think a similar strategy would be successful? Why or why not?

2. General Mills and several other major food makers have begun producing organic foods. But they have deliberately kept their brand names off the packaging of these new products, thinking that the kind of customer who goes out of his or her way to buy organic products is unlikely to trust multinational brands. Other companies, however, such as Heinz and PepsiCo, are betting that their brand names will prove to be persuasive in the $11-billion organic foods market. Which strategy do you think is more likely to be successful? Why?

3. After the terrorist attacks of 9/11, an ad hoc task force of DDB Worldwide advertising professionals in 17 countries set out to discover what people abroad thought of the United States. In the course of their research, they developed the concept of "America as a Brand," urged U.S. corporations with overseas operations to help "restore" positive impressions of Brand America around the world, and urged the United States to launch Alhurra as an alternative to the popular Al Jazeera network. Do you think foreigners' perception of a country and its culture can be viewed in marketing terms? Why or why not?

4. Brand names contribute enormously to consumers' perception of a brand. One writer has argued that alphanumeric brand names, such as the Toyota RAV4, Jaguar's X-Type sedan, the Xbox game console, and the GTI from Volkswagen, can translate more easily overseas than "real" names like Golf, Jetta, Escalade, and Eclipse. What other advantages and disadvantages can you think of for each type of brand name? Do you think one type is preferable to the other? Why?

ETHICS EXERCISE

As mentioned in the chapter, some analysts predict that barcodes may soon be replaced by a wireless technology called *radio frequency identification (RFID)*. RFID is a system of installing tags containing tiny computer chips on, say, supermarket items. These chips automatically radio the location of the item to a computer network where inventory data are stored, letting store managers know not only where the item is at all times but also when and where it was made and its colour and size. Proponents of the idea believe RFID will cut costs and simplify inventory tracking and reordering. It may also allow marketers to respond quickly to shifts in demand, avoid under- and overstocking, and reduce spoilage by automatically removing outdated perishables from the shelves. Privacy advocates, however, think the chips provide too much product-preference information that might be identified with individual consumers. In the meantime, Walmart is requiring its major suppliers to begin using the new technology on products stocked by the giant retailer.

1. Do you think RFID poses a threat to consumer privacy? Why or why not?

2. Do you think the technology's possible benefits to marketers outweigh the potential privacy concerns? Are there also potential benefits to consumers, and if so, what are they?

3. How can marketers reassure consumers about privacy concerns if RFID comes into widespread use?

INTERNET EXERCISES

1. **Patents.** Visit the website of Industry Canada (www.ic.gc.ca). Review the patent application procedure. Note how much it costs to apply for a patent, how the patent application is evaluated, the benefits of a patent, and the length of time a patent is valid. Prepare a brief report to your class on the patent application process.

2. **Packaging.** Companies use packaging to help market their products. Visit each of the following websites and prepare a brief report on how each company has used packaging as part of its brand management strategy.
   a. H. J. Heinz: **www.heinz.com**
   b. Campbell Soup: **www.campbellsoup.com**
   c. General Mills (Yoplait Yogurt): **www.yoplait.com**

3. **Brands.** Several sources compile lists each year of the world's most valuable brands. Two are *BusinessWeek* magazine and a consulting firm called Brand Finance. Visit both websites (**www.businessweek.com** and **www. brandfinance.com**) and review the most recent lists of the world's most valuable brands. How many firms are presented on both lists? Where are these firms located? What criteria do *BusinessWeek* and Brand Finance use in determining brand equity? Which brands have improved their values the most over the past couple of years?

Note: Internet Web addresses change frequently. If you don't find the exact sites listed, you may need to access the organization's or company's home page and search from there or use a search engine such as Google.

CASE 10.1

Branding Canada

Tourism is big business. Tourism represents almost 2 percent of Canada's gross domestic product amounting to just below $30 billion annually. Visitors to Canada who stayed at least one night spent just under $12 billion in one year or an average of $750 for each trip. In one year about 16 million international visitors came into the country—half came for business reasons and half were here for a holiday. In order to look after all these visitors to the country, approximately 600 000 Canadians work in jobs related to the tourism sector.

The Canadian Tourism Commission (CTC), the federal government body responsible for tourism, groups visitors into three market segments according to the number of visitors. Most visitors to Canada come from the United States. The second group is considered to be Canada's core tourism market. Visitors from the United Kingdom, France, Germany, and Australia are part of this group. The third group of countries is considered to be Canada's emerging or transitional markets. Visitors from Japan, South Korea, Mexico, Brazil, China, and India are in this group.

Canada collects a large amount of data about visitors in order to assist companies in the tourism sector to satisfy their needs. Two major sources of information about Canadian visitors are Statistics Canada and the Canada Border Services Agency. For example, we know that most visitors stay for one week and that the average party size is two people. There is roughly the same numbers of men and women visitors. By far the largest number of visitors is in the over-55 age group. The destination for most visitors is Ontario, with British Columbia and Quebec coming in second and third.

Because tourism is so important to the Canadian economy, several organizations are responsible for promoting Canada. At the federal level the CTC) has this responsibility. Every province and many regions also have groups that develop promotional material. The CTC is a Crown corporation responsible to the Minister of Industry. Since 2007, the CTC has been through a process of reviewing everything it does in areas such as its management structure and its marketing plan. As part of that review process, the decision was made to "rebrand" Canada. The new branding involves a new theme—"Canada: keep exploring" The CTC decided to focus the promotional material for the "Canada: keep exploring" campaign on four main ideas. One part of the campaign was called the brand promise and the slogan used was "Create your own extra-ordinary experiences." The other three main ideas for the promotion were expression, emotion, and exploration. The CTC also developed five "selling propositions," which are vibrant cities on the edge of nature; personal journeys by land, water, and air; active adventure among awe-inspiring natural wonders; award-winning Canadian local cuisine; and connecting with Canadians.

One of the marketing programs developed by the CTC is called "Signature Experiences." The target market for this program is high-spending international visitors. Tourist companies across the country are invited to apply to become part of the collection that includes Edible British Columbia—a tour of Granville Island

Market—the Calgary Stampede, Alexander Keith's brewery in Halifax, and the Stratford Shakespeare Festival. The program is promoted in social media, in travel media public relations, and on the Internet. The CTC wants to have around 100 experiences in the collection. The "Signature Experiences" promotion is a move away from marketing different areas of the country to marketing experiences available to international travellers.

Not all marketing organizations across the country aim their promotions at foreign visitors. Newfoundland and Labrador's tourism agency has targeted people who live in Toronto with its "East Coast Beauty" campaign. Pictures of humpback whales, icebergs, and country clotheslines were projected onto the sides of buildings throughout the city of Toronto during the evening. Newfoundland and Labrador's tourism agency was trying to entice Toronto residents to escape the smoggy, humid summer days in the city and vacation in the eastern part of Canada.

Newfoundland and Labrador Tourism has used other innovative techniques to promote its area. As part of the promotional campaign that is based on the fact that Newfoundland and Labrador has a unique time zone that is 30 minutes ahead of the rest of the Atlantic Provinces, a joint promotion was undertaken with WestJet airlines. For one 24-hour period, the two organizations gave away a trip every half hour. The contest was presented on Facebook. Research undertaken by the organization showed that their core market was in the age group of 45 and older. This age group is also the fastest-growing segment of Facebook users.

Newfoundland and Labrador Tourism is not the only east-coast province to target the Toronto market. Nova Scotia's department of economic and rural development and tourism developed a 3D cinema spot to run in the Toronto market. The ad ran before 3D films like *Kung Fu Panda* and the *Pirates of the Caribbean*. The ad was called "Shaped by the Sea" and included aerial shots of the Nova Scotia coastline. This campaign also included television and print ads.

Tourism Toronto and Tourisme Montréal teamed up for a promotion they called the "Cheating Wall." Research by these organizations determined that residents of both Toronto and Montreal were more likely to visit American cities like New York than they were to visit each other. It seems that the hockey rivalry between the Montreal Canadiens and the Toronto Maple Leafs meant that a visit to the other city was perceived as a betrayal to their hockey teams. Video screens were mounted in both cities where viewers could participate in video chats during scheduled events or just view a special performance. Facebook and online versions were also available along with a chance to win an Air Canada flight between the two cities.

One region of Quebec, Outaouais, has a unique problem—no one knows about it. Research conducted on behalf of Outaouais Tourism determined that only 1 percent of the people surveyed had ever heard of the region and most could not find it on a map. The region gets about 3 million visitors a year but Outaouais Tourism decided it needed to improve its recognition with both the Ontario and Quebec markets. The organization developed a humorous campaign based on obvious falsehoods. The campaign included television commercials, magazine ads, posters, and online advertising in both French and English. The objective of the campaign was to increase the region's awareness factor to 10 percent by the year 2015.

Events like the Olympic Games and visits by members of the royal family provide the world with information about Canadian destinations through news coverage. The goodwill provided by such events can be just as easily destroyed by bad news coverage, such as was experienced by the 2010 G20 summit riots in Toronto or the Vancouver riots following the 2011 National Hockey League playoff game. The difference is how the two cities handled the bad news coverage. In Toronto, there was a great deal of promotional material before the riots, like ads in the *New Yorker* and a marketing pavilion that included a really expensive fake lake, but the tourism marketing organizations did very little after the riots to try to recover from the bad publicity. Vancouver learned from the Toronto experience. With the help of ad agency DDB Canada, images of Vancouver that included the plywood walls covered with apologies and pictures of Vancouver residents out the morning after the riots cleaning the streets went to news agencies. Everyone involved in the Vancouver campaign admitted that they could not undo the riot pictures but at least the aftermath shots gave a more balanced picture of the city.

Whether it is the CTC promoting unique experiences across the country or Outaouais Tourism letting Canadians know where they are, tourism organizations across the country spend a great deal of money branding Canada.

Questions for Critical Thinking

1. What are the main elements the different marketing organizations are using to build a brand identity for Canada? Discuss the effectiveness of each strategy.

2. Are there any other branding strategies these marketing organizations could use to brand the country? What are they? Why do you think these strategies would be more effective?

Sources: Chris Powell, "Toronto/Montreal Go to the Wall in New Tourism Campaign," *Marketing*, http://www.marketingmag.ca, June 10, 2011; Matt Semansky, "Nova Scotia Does Tourism in 3D," *Marketing*, http://www.marketingmag.ca, June 15, 2011; Matt Semansky, "Newfoundland Tourism and WestJet Holding Facebook Contest," *Marketing*, http://www.marketingmag.ca, June 20, 2011; Brandon Terry, "East Coast Beauty Projected in Downtown Toronto," *Marketing*, http://www.marketingmag.ca, July 7, 2011; Matt Semansky, "Canadian Tourism Sells 'Signature Experiences' to High-End Travelers," *Marketing*, http://www.marketingmag.ca, July 12, 2011; Caroline Fortin, "Outaouais Tourism Tells Tall Tales," *Marketing*, http://www.marketingmag.ca, June 2, 2011; Eve Lazarus, "DDB Canada Helps Vancouver's Sullied Image," *Marketing*, http://www.marketingmag.ca, June 21, 2011; "It's Not a Fake Lake, It's Marketing," *Marketing*, http://www.marketingmag.ca, June 8, 2010; "Canadian Ads Take Over *The New Yorker*," *Marketing*, http://www.marketingmag.ca, June 23, 2010; Norma Ramage, "Royal Visit Good for Alberta Tourism Business," *Marketing*, http://www.marketingmag.ca, July 5, 2011; "Travel and Tourism," Canada Yearbook 2010, Statistics Canada, Catalogue no. 11-402-X, pp. 403–12, http://www.statcan.gc.ca, July 14, 2011; "Government Revenue Attributable to Tourism," Statistics Canada, *The Daily,* November 10, 2010, http://www.statcan.gc.ca, July 14, 2011; Canadian Tourism Commission website, http://www.canadatourism.com, July 16, 2011; "New Directions to Reclaim Growth: 2011–2015 Corporate Plan Summary," Canadian Tourism Commission website, http://www.canadatourism.com, July 16, 2011; "U.S. and Overseas Travel to Canada: Short-Term Competitive Outlook First Quarter of 2011," Canadian Tourism Commission website, http://www.canadatourism.com, July 16, 2011; "Tourism Snapshot: 2010 Year-in-Review," Canadian Tourism Commission website, http://www.canadatourism.com, July 16, 2011.

CASE 10.2

Ferrari Runs on Brand Power

Who wouldn't want to own a Ferrari? Since its founding in 1947, Ferrari has worked to build a tradition of uncompromising quality. Its ultra-elegant motorcars, with their sleek lines, high-performance engines, and hand-tooled leather interiors, are almost unbelievably deluxe.

The Ferrari tradition is also built on exclusivity: the company limits its annual production. And with a robust menu of customizable features, literally every car it makes is unique. Discriminating buyers can select the Bose radio-navigator, which includes radio, audio DVD, Bluetooth, and satellite radio systems. Another optional feature is a satellite anti-theft system integrated with the car alarm and approved by all the major international insurance companies. The backlog of orders on some models is up to two years.

Despite this demand, with a starting price of just under $200 000, a Ferrari is out of the reach for most of us. Even so, the Ferrari Company has managed to capture the attention of wistful car owners the world over by carefully nurturing its brand and offering an array of extensions like die-cast kits, pocket-sized Hot Wheels cars, branded wristwatches, audio systems—even a $10 000 Segway transporter.

The company's ongoing sponsorship of Formula One Grand Prix racing has helped generate worldwide awareness of the brand. So, while owning one of these legendary vehicles or driving a Formula One racecar through the European countryside may not be possible for most people, they can still experience the Ferrari lifestyle by buying a piece of branded paraphernalia: a hat, jacket, T-shirt, key ring, or other collectible emblazoned with the distinctive Ferrari rearing stallion logo. The Ferrari store, a retail chain, has outlets in selected cities across Asia, Europe, and North America, including Toronto and Calgary. The stores have been a smash hit. During a recent Formula One racing event in Shanghai, the local Ferrari store sold over $100 000 in merchandise in a single day.

Ferrari also licenses its name to dozens of partner companies who put the Ferrari name on a wide variety of products such as hand-held games, fitness equipment, perfumes, and teddy bears. In a recent year, revenues from licensing royalties and the sale of Ferrari merchandise alone totaled $725 million.

Want more entertainment? The Ferrari theme park near Abu Dhabi in the United Arab Emirates offers an assortment of family rides, virtual simulations, and a racing school for wannabe speedsters, plus the usual array of Ferrari-branded merchandise.

There are four Ferrari dealerships in Canada: Montreal, Toronto, Calgary, and Vancouver. Each dealership uses different methods to promote the Ferrari brand within its community. The Montreal dealership, the newest of the four, held a gala grand opening event to let the community know it had arrived. Over 400 guests and media representatives sipped wine and ate hors d'oeuvres while Ferrari's North American president presented the dealership with the chrome-plated exhaust of the 2004 Ferrari Formula One car. The Vancouver dealership holds special events such as the Ferrari driving experience, a two-day precision driving school for Ferrari owners and their guests. The event is held at the local racetrack in order to control the environment. The Toronto and Calgary dealerships are owned by the same person, Remo Ferri, an Italian who started his career as a mechanic. He opened the Toronto Ferrari dealership in 1976. Ferri promotes the brand in Ontario by supporting local charities such as the Princess Margaret Hospital Foundation and SickKids Foundation. In order to raise money for the SickKids Foundation, the dealership holds an annual car rally for over 100 Ferrari and other performance car owners. The rally has raised almost $2 million since the event started.

From Ferrari corporate headquarters to the local Ferrari dealers, all those involved in the company promote the brand.

Questions for Critical Thinking

1. Through the years, Ferrari has been very successful at brand extension. Do these extensions hurt the brand? Why or why not? What else can the company do to extend the brand?

2. Even though most of the world's consumers can't afford its product, Ferrari has managed to build a strong brand with loyal followers who aspire to the Ferrari lifestyle. By opening a Ferrari theme park in Abu Dhabi, the company hopes to further extend its brand. But not all concepts are seamlessly transferable, as the Walt Disney Company discovered when it opened its Euro Disney theme park outside Paris. It was three years before Euro Disney had a profitable quarter. In your opinion, what should Ferrari do to ensure success at its theme park?

Sources: Ferrari Ontario website, http://www.ferrari-of-ontario.com, July 9, 2011; Ferrari Vancouver website, http://www.ferrarimaseratiofvancouver.com, July 9, 2011; Ferrari Quebec website, http://www.ferrariquebec.com, July 9, 2011; Company website, http://www.ferrari.com, May 19, 2009; David Menzies, "You Too Can Own a Ferrari," *National Post*, July 7, 2008, http://autos.canada.com; "Gameloft Licenses Ferrari: Fast Mobile Games Coming Soon!" Intomobile, http://www.intomobile.com, March 20, 2008; Robert Frank, "Gentlemen, Start Your Dishwashers," *The Wall Street Journal*, http://blogs.wsj.com, February 15, 2008; "Ferrari Revs into Retail, Announcing Plans for 40 Store Openings," Edmunds, http://www.edmunds.com, October 22, 2007; Tim Urquhart, "Leveraging the Legend," *World Motor Sport Marketplace*, October 2007, pp. 60–63; Noah B. Joseph, "At Park Opening in '09, It's All Ferrari, All the Time," *The New York Times*, http://www.nytimes.com, June 10, 2007; Frank Filipponio, "Ferrari Store—Los Angeles Opens in the Beverly Center," *Autoblog*, http://www.autoblog.com, March 27, 2007; "Ferrari at the Geneva Auto Show," *Easier Motoring*, http://www.easier.com, March 7, 2007.

part 5

DISTRIBUTION DECISIONS

chapter 11

Marketing Channels and Supply Chain Management

© AP IMAGES/JIM MONE

CHAPTER OBJECTIVES

① Describe the types of marketing channels and the roles they play in marketing strategy.

② Outline the major channel strategy decisions.

③ Describe the concepts of channel management, conflict, and cooperation.

④ Identify and describe the different vertical marketing systems.

⑤ Explain the roles of logistics and supply-chain management in an overall distribution strategy.

⑥ Identify the major components of a physical distribution system.

⑦ Compare the major modes of transportation.

⑧ Discuss the role of transportation intermediaries, combined transportation modes, and warehousing in improving physical distribution.

PANAMA CANAL UNDERGOES EXTREME MAKEOVER

The Panama Canal is one of the world's most famous examples of engineering know-how. Built in 1914—at a cost of $336 million and 22 000 workers' lives—this 77-kilometre-long "ditch" made it possible for ships to cross the Isthmus of Panama, a thin strip of land that separates the Atlantic and Pacific oceans. Over its ten decades of operation, the canal has served as a critical artery for global trade. In recent times, the canal welcomed 14 000 ships passing through each year, carrying about 5 percent of the world's ocean cargo—280 million tons.

Shipping companies once designed their ocean-going vessels to fit the Panama Canal's locks, and these vessels, which came to be known as "Panamax" ships, still carry much of the world's cargo. During the 1970s, however, ships began to be built longer and wider. These days, for example, some of the ships moving through the Panama Canal are three times longer than a football field. Even for some vessels that regularly make the journey, passage through the canal's narrow Miraflores Locks is a tense, nerve-wracking exercise, with barely a couple of feet to spare on either side. Today, the newest breed of ship, up to 366 metres long and 49 metres wide, and known as "post-Panamax," cannot navigate the canal at all.

With the canal now too narrow for more than one-third of the world's cargo ships, Panamanian government officials saw the writing on the wall: unless they took action to upgrade it, the canal would become obsolete. As a result, voters in Panama approved a $5.25-billion expansion project. The new locks will be 60 percent longer and 40 percent wider. When it reopens in 2014, the remodelled canal will be able to handle nearly triple its current shipping capacity, including tankers that hold as much as 1 million barrels of oil as well as container ships that carry up to 12 500 cargo containers.

Who aside from Panama will be the big winners? Currently, the United States is the biggest user of the canal, but China is closing the gap. The canal will give China better access to Brazil's iron ore and Venezuela's oil, and it will provide better access to the Atlantic Ocean for Chinese shippers. Ports such as Halifax, Nova Scotia, with its deep-water harbour that can accommodate larger ships, could see greatly increased activity. Of course, west-coast ports such as Vancouver, British Columbia, may see their activity reduced. Smaller countries such as Chile will also benefit. It will more easily move copper and wine to markets on the east coast of North America.

The 1999 transfer of the Panama Canal from the United States to Panama has proved to be a game-changer for the tiny tropical nation. Whereas the U.S. government had administered the canal as a federal agency—for example, maintaining a toll schedule just high enough to cover operating costs—the Panama Canal Authority operates the canal like a commercial enterprise. The canal authority introduced a tariff schedule scaled to different-sized cargoes and charges extra for certain services. Under Panamanian management, shipping traffic in the canal increased significantly, from 200 000 ships in 1995 to more than 4.6 million in a recent year. Today, the canal represents 14 percent of Panama's gross domestic product. The expansion plan, which is reportedly on time and on budget, is being financed chiefly through retained earnings from the canal; the rest is underwritten by global lenders. The Panama Canal Authority predicts that the expanded canal will double the country's economy, create jobs, and ease poverty.[1]

connecting with customers

When it opened in 1914, the Panama Canal quickly changed the face of trade between the East and West. Shortly, it will change the face of trade again—not only because of the increased number of ships passing through but also because of its implications for other businesses and other major modes of transportation. At a time when energy prices are rapidly increasing, the Panama Canal will help all shippers reduce transport costs. But it is also becoming more environmentally responsible. The expanded canal will hold about 65 percent more water, but will ultimately use less than the 2 billion gallons of water the old locks used daily. More than half of the water used will also be recycled.

Chapter Overview

DISTRIBUTION—moving goods and services from producers to customers—is the second marketing mix variable and an important marketing concern. Firms depend on waterways like the Panama Canal to be able to move their goods from one destination to another. A distribution strategy has two critical components: (1) marketing channels and (2) logistics and supply chain management.

A **marketing channel**—also called a **distribution channel**—is an organized system of marketing institutions and their interrelationships that enhances the physical flow and ownership of goods and services from producer to consumer or business user. The choice of marketing channels should support the firm's overall marketing strategy. In contrast, **logistics** refers to the process of coordinating the flow of information, goods, and services among members of the marketing channel. **Supply-chain management** is the control of activities of purchasing, processing, and delivery through which raw materials are transformed into products and made available to final consumers. Efficient logistical systems support customer service, enhancing customer relationships—an important goal of any marketing strategy.

A key aspect of logistics is physical distribution, which covers a broad range of activities aimed at efficient movement of finished goods from the end of the production line to the consumer. Although some marketers use the terms *transportation* and *physical distribution* interchangeably, these terms do not carry the same meaning.

Physical distribution extends beyond transportation to include such important decision areas as customer service, inventory control, materials handling, protective packaging, order processing, and warehousing.

Well-planned marketing channels and effective logistics and supply-chain management provide ultimate users with convenient ways for obtaining the goods and services they desire. This chapter discusses the activities, decisions, and marketing intermediaries involved in managing marketing channels and logistics. Chapter 12 looks at other players in the marketing channel: retailers, direct marketers, and wholesalers. ◆◆◆

---

① Describe the types of marketing channels and the roles they play in marketing strategy.

distribution Movement of goods and services from producers to customers.

marketing (distribution) channel System of marketing institutions that enhances the physical flow of goods and services, along with ownership title, from producer to consumer or business user.

THE ROLE OF MARKETING CHANNELS IN MARKETING STRATEGY

A firm's distribution channels play a key role in its overall marketing strategy because these channels provide the means by which the firm makes the goods and services available to ultimate users. Channels perform four important functions. First, they facilitate the exchange process by reducing the number of marketplace contacts necessary to make a sale. Suppose you want to buy a Blackberry PlayBook. You've heard a lot of hype about it since it was introduced, but you're not sure how it compares to the Apple iPad. You visit the manufacturer's website, where you read about its features and watch a demonstration. You decide to visit your nearest Staples store so you can actually "test drive" one. The dealer forms part of the channel that brings you, a potential buyer, and Research In Motion, the manufacturer, together to complete the exchange process. It's important to keep in mind that all channel members benefit when they work together; when they begin to disagree or—worse yet—compete directly with each other, everyone loses.

Distributors adjust for discrepancies in the market's assortment of goods and services via a process known as *sorting*, the second channel function. A single producer tends to maximize the quantity it makes of a limited line of goods, while a single buyer needs a limited quantity of a wide selection of merchandise. Sorting alleviates such discrepancies by channelling products to suit both the buyer's and the producer's needs.

The third function of marketing channels involves standardizing exchange transactions by setting expectations for products, and it involves the transfer process itself. Channel members tend to standardize payment terms, delivery schedules, prices, and purchase lots among other conditions. Standardization helps make the transactions efficient and fair. The final marketing channel function is to facilitate searches by both buyers and sellers. Buyers search for specific goods and services to fill their needs, while sellers attempt to learn what buyers want. Channels bring buyers and sellers together to complete the exchange process. Hundreds of distribution channels exist today, and no single channel best serves the needs of every company. Instead of searching for the best channel for all products, a marketing manager must analyze alternative channels in light of consumer needs to determine the most appropriate channel or channels for the firm's goods and services.

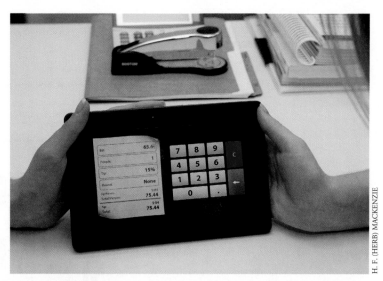

If you are interested in learning more about the PlayBook, you may want to try it at a local dealer.

Marketers must remain flexible because channels may change over time. Today's ideal channel may prove inappropriate in a few years. Or the way a company uses that channel may change. Two decades ago, Michael Dell came up with a revolutionary way to sell computers—by the telephone, directly to consumers. Later, Dell added Internet sales to its operations. Next, the firm added another channel for making its computers available to consumers: retail giant Best Buy. Today, Dell is exploiting another channel to sell computers: reaching its consumers through Twitter. By continuing to identify new channels for distribution, Dell stays engaged with current and prospective customers.[2] The following sections examine the diverse types of channels available to marketers and the decisions marketers must make to develop an effective distribution strategy that supports their firm's marketing objectives.

logistics Process of coordinating the flow of information, goods, and services among members of the distribution channel.

supply-chain management Control of the activities of purchasing, processing, and delivery through which raw materials are transformed into products and made available to final consumers.

physical distribution Broad range of activities aimed at efficient movement of finished goods from the end of the production line to the consumer.

marketing intermediary (middleman) Wholesaler or retailer that operates between producers and consumers or business users.

TYPES OF MARKETING CHANNELS

The first step in selecting a marketing channel is determining which type of channel will best meet both the seller's objectives and the distribution needs of customers. Figure 11.1 depicts the major channels available to marketers of consumer and business goods and services.

Most channel options involve at least one **marketing intermediary**. A marketing intermediary (or *middleman*) is an organization that operates between producers and consumers or business users. Retailers and wholesalers are both marketing intermediaries. A retail store owned and operated by someone other than the manufacturer of the products it sells is one type of marketing intermediary. A **wholesaler** is an intermediary that takes title to the goods it handles and then distributes these goods to retailers, other distributors, or B2B customers. Although some analysts believed that the Internet would ultimately render many intermediaries obsolete, that hasn't happened. Research In Motion provides on its website a list of all the dealers that resell its Blackberry products. But, like many manufacturers, it also uses its website to enhance customer service. When you visit Research In Motion's website, for example, you can see product information and demonstrations, download software and applications, get user guides and manuals, and find out how and where to get technical support for your products.

Marketers must remain flexible because channels change over time. Dell products, originally available only through direct-to-customer selling, are now sold at Best Buy and other select retailers, and Dell is exploring another channel to sell computers: reaching its consumers through Twitter.

figure 11.1
Alternative Marketing Channels

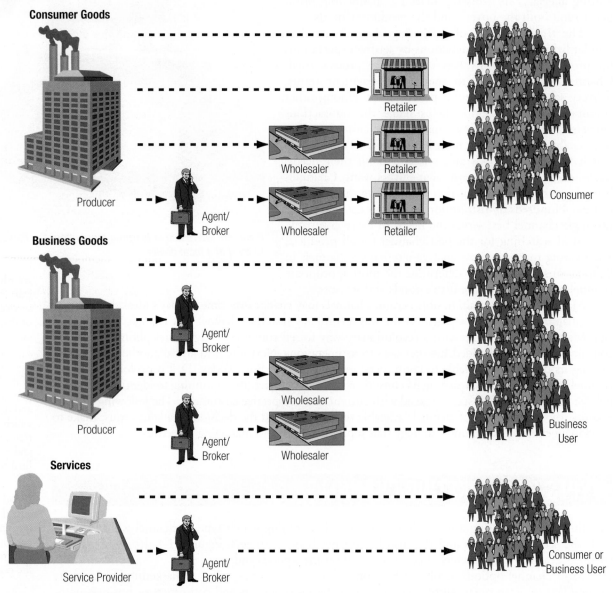

wholesaler Channel
intermediary that
takes title to the goods
it handles and then
distributes these goods to
retailers, other distributors,
or B2B customers.

A short marketing channel involves few intermediaries. In contrast, a long marketing channel involves many intermediaries working in succession to move goods from producers to consumers. Business products usually move through short channels due to geographic concentrations and comparatively fewer business purchasers. Service firms market primarily through short channels because they sell intangible products and need to maintain personal relationships within their channels. Haircuts, manicures, and dental cleanings are all provided through short channels. Not-for-profit organizations also tend to work with short, simple, and direct channels. Any marketing intermediaries in such channels usually act as agents, such as independent ticket agencies or fundraising specialists.

DIRECT SELLING

The simplest and shortest marketing channel is a direct channel. A **direct channel** carries goods directly from a producer to the business purchaser or ultimate user. Some customers prefer to purchase through a direct channel. However, as discussed in the "Marketing and the SME" feature, for some products, customers need to be equally careful, regardless of whether the seller is a producer or a marketing intermediary. This channel forms part of **direct selling**, a marketing strategy in which a

MARKETING AND THE SME

Direct Selling: It's Good for the Dogs, but Be Careful

WHAT is a puppy mill? Most people think of puppy mills as questionable operations that breed dogs and then sell them through pet retailers to consumers. The risk to pet owners is that they end up paying top dollar, and they get a pet that lives a life fraught with behavioural and/or health problems. But the reality is that many puppy mills do sell direct to pet owners.

One pet owner in British Columbia recently had her pet Bichon Frisé, Sailor, euthanized after more than six years of chronic health problems. The breeder she bought Sailor from was investigated in 2011, and 71 dogs were seized after they were found to be "in distress" and in need of veterinary care. This seizure sparked a debate about what a puppy mill is. There is little consensus. Puppy mill operators sell direct to consumers and through channel intermediaries, sometimes directly to retailers, but also through wholesalers who then sell to retail pet stores. However, they all have one common trait: profit is their main motivation, and the physical or psychological well-being of their dogs is secondary.

Cindy Berube is a reputable and responsible breeder of Portuguese water dogs (www.charbr.com). She maintains only three to four adult dogs and has a total of two or three litters per year. All her dogs live and interact daily with her family. Cindy's dogs participate in conformation events (dog shows), obedience trials, agility trials, and water-work trials. New puppies are handled daily and get desensitized to sights and sounds through planned activities. Prospective pet owners are interviewed and must complete a questionnaire before they are allowed to buy one of her dogs. Through her website, Cindy provides prospective owners with information on raising puppies and provides pictures and information on all her dogs and on previous litters.

How do you find a good breeder such as Cindy and avoid puppy mills? The best way is to visit the breeders, and don't be shy when investigating their operation. How many dogs do they have? How often do they breed? Look at the bitch and at the litter mates. See how the dogs react to you and to other people. Investigate the dogs' living conditions. Ask what health tests are done on the dogs, both parents and pups. Does the breeder show dogs, and what breed clubs does the breeder belong to? Be very suspicious of any breeder who is not cooperative. When you are looking for a puppy, remember that buying directly from a breeder is no guarantee that you are not buying from a puppy mill. Be suspicious and investigate carefully. Canadians love their dogs, all 6.4 million of them. The relationship between a dog and its owner is far too important to leave to chance.

Sources: Sandra McCulloch, "Seizure of Melville Dogs Prompts Debate Over Puppy Mills," *Times–Colonist* (Victoria, BC), July 28, 2011, p. 6; Lauryn Hayden, "Put Puppy Mills Out of Business: Do Research, Ask Questions of Breeder to Get Happy, Healthy Dog," *The Province* (Vancouver), July 31, 2011, p. 22; "Choosing a Breeder," http://www.qualitydogs.com, August 3, 2011; Charbr Portuguese Water Dogs website, http://www.charbr.com, August 3, 2011; Jean Wood, Canadian Animal Health Institute, email correspondence August 4, 2011.

---

producer establishes direct sales contact with its product's final users. Direct selling is an important option for goods that require extensive demonstrations in convincing customers to buy. The "Career Readiness" feature contains suggestions for making successful sales calls.

Direct selling plays a significant role in business-to-business marketing. Most major installations, accessory equipment, and even component parts and raw materials are sold through direct contacts between producing firms and final buyers. Many people in business enjoy successful sales careers. Think about the textbook you are now reading. Probably it was originally purchased by your campus bookstore. But it would be the publisher's salesperson who sold the book to the bookstore, most likely after the salesperson convinced your instructor to choose this text for his or her course. Direct selling is also important in consumer-goods markets. Direct sellers such as Avon Canada, Pampered Chef, and Tupperware Canada sidestep competition in store aisles by developing networks of independent representatives who sell their products directly to consumers. Many of these companies practise a direct selling strategy called the *party plan,* originally popularized by Tupperware. Jewellery boutique company Stella & Dot—recently new to Canada—is one such business. Launched by entrepreneur Jessica Herrin, Stella & Dot jewellery is sold at home-based parties, or "trunk shows," by independent sales representatives. The jewellery, which appeals to women of all ages, is accessible and affordable—and is often worn by TV celebrities. Stella & Dot recently topped $30 million in sales.[3] The Internet provides another direct selling channel for both B2B and B2C purchases. Consumers who want to sport designer handbags—but don't want to pay full price for them—can rent them from got2haveithandbags.com and receive them within three to five business days. For those who like to change bags often but can't or won't pay the hundreds or thousands of dollars for Prada's, Gucci's, or Louis Vuitton's latest, the site may be a real bargain.

Direct mail can be an important part of direct selling—or it can encourage a potential customer to contact an intermediary such as a retailer. Either way, it is a vital communication piece for many marketers.

direct channel Marketing channel that moves goods directly from a producer to the business purchaser or ultimate user.

direct selling Strategy designed to establish direct sales contact between producer and final user.

Successful Salespeople Make Positive First Impressions That Last

WHEN you make a sales call to a prospective or current customer, you represent the face and voice of your firm. The way people perceive you is the way they perceive your company, so you want to make a good first impression as well as a positive lasting impression. Most likely, you will receive training—either by your supervisor or someone else in your company—in the fine art of a successful sales call. Here are a few additional tips to help you:

- *Do your homework.* Be sure you know the correct spelling and pronunciation of the company you are visiting—and the person you are scheduled to meet. Familiarize yourself with the company's goods or services and past history with your company.
- *Assess the company's potential needs.* Don't launch into a "data dump" about your products before learning what the customer needs. If you have familiarized yourself with the customer's business, you should be able to ask a few intelligent questions and really listen to the answers. Then, you can offer a few ideas for solutions.
- *Dress appropriately and arrive on time.* Wear the proper business attire for your industry, whether it's a business suit or business casual clothing. Cover any tattoos or body piercings and wear conservative jewellery. In other words, play it safe. Always arrive a few minutes before the scheduled time. Doing so shows respect for your customer's time and indicates you are serious about doing business.

- *Be conservative in your behaviour.* Always stand to greet your customer. Smile, shake hands, and follow the customer to wherever the meeting will take place. Address him or her with the title "Mr." or "Ms.," and do not assume the person wishes to be called by first name until you are invited to do so.
- *Turn off your cell phone.* If possible, turn off your cell phone before entering the building for your meeting. At least, turn it off when you enter the meeting. Never take a call during a meeting, and make one only if it will help the progress of the meeting. For example, a customer might have a question only your supervisor can answer. A successful sales call requires your total attention on the customer.
- *Follow up the meeting with a thank-you.* After the sales call, be sure to follow up with a phone call, email, or note to thank the person—regardless of the outcome. Even if the call did not produce a sale or other immediate results, it could possibly have laid the groundwork for a future relationship.

Sources: Dan Seidman, "Practice What You Preach in Sales," Monster Career Advice, http://career-advice.monster.com, April 18, 2010; Robert Estupinian, "Three Successful Sales Call Strategies for Entrepreneurs," *Bay Area Mastermind*, April 1, 2010, http://www.bayareamastermind.com; Geoffrey James, "Sales Calls: Four Key Rules to Make Them More Effective," BNet.com, March 25, 2010, http://blogs.bnet.com.

CHANNELS USING MARKETING INTERMEDIARIES

Although direct channels allow simple and straightforward marketing, they are not practical in every case. Some products serve markets in different areas of the country or world, or have large numbers of potential end users. Other categories of goods rely heavily on repeat purchases. The producers of these goods may find more efficient, less expensive, and less time-consuming alternatives to direct channels by using marketing intermediaries. This section considers five channels that involve marketing intermediaries.

Producer to Wholesaler to Retailer to Consumer

The traditional channel for consumer goods proceeds from producer to wholesaler to retailer to user. This method carries goods between literally thousands of small producers with limited lines and local retailers. A firm with limited financial resources will rely on the services of a wholesaler that serves as an immediate source of funds and then markets to hundreds of retailers. On the other hand, a small retailer can draw on a wholesaler's specialized distribution skills. In addition, many manufacturers hire their own field sales representatives to service retail accounts with marketing information. Wholesalers may then handle the actual sales transactions.

Producer to Wholesaler to Business User

Similar characteristics in the organizational market often attract marketing intermediaries to operate between producers and business purchasers. The term *industrial distributor* commonly refers to intermediaries in the business market that take title to the goods.

Producer to Agent to Wholesaler to Retailer to Consumer

In markets served by many small companies, a unique intermediary—the agent—performs the basic function of bringing buyer and seller together. An agent may or may not take possession of the goods but never takes title. The agent merely represents a producer by seeking a market for its products or a wholesaler (which does take title to the goods) by locating a supply source.

Producer to Agent to Wholesaler to Business User

Like agents, brokers are independent intermediaries who may or may not take possession of goods but never take title to these goods. Agents and brokers also serve the business market when small producers attempt to market their offerings through large wholesalers. Such an intermediary, often called a **manufacturers' representative**, provides an independent sales force to contact wholesale buyers. A kitchen equipment manufacturer may have its own manufacturers' representatives to market its goods, for example.

Producer to Agent to Business User

For products sold in small units, only merchant wholesalers can economically cover the markets. A merchant wholesaler is an independently owned wholesaler that takes title to the goods. By maintaining regional inventories, this wholesaler achieves transportation economies, stockpiling goods and making small shipments over short distances. For a product with large unit sales, however, and for which transportation accounts for a small percentage of the total cost, the producer-agent-business user channel is usually employed. The agent in effect becomes the producer's sales force, but bulk shipments of the product reduce the intermediary's inventory management function.

DUAL DISTRIBUTION

Dual distribution refers to movement of products through more than one channel to reach the firm's target market. Sears Canada, for instance, has a three-pronged distribution system, selling through stores, catalogues, and the Internet. Marketers usually adopt a dual distribution strategy either to maximize their firm's coverage in the marketplace or to increase the cost effectiveness of the firm's marketing effort. Nintendo and Netflix recently partnered to offer entertainment through more than one channel. Traditionally, customers order their favourite movies online and have the DVDs delivered to their mailboxes. Under the new agreement, Netflix subscribers with a monthly subscription can stream movies and TV programs and view them on their Wii console at no extra cost.[4]

REVERSE CHANNELS

While the traditional concept of marketing channels involves the movement of goods and services from producer to consumer or business user, marketers should not ignore **reverse channels**—channels designed to return goods to their producers. Reverse channels have gained increased importance with rising prices for raw materials, increasing availability of recycling facilities, and passage of additional antipollution

manufacturers' representative Agent wholesaling intermediary that represents manufacturers of related but noncompeting products and receives a commission on each sale.

dual distribution Network that moves products to a firm's target market through more than one marketing channel.

reverse channel Channel designed to return goods to their producer.

Many manufacturers rely on industrial distributors such as Acklands-Grainger to get their products to final customers in business-to-business markets.

and conservation laws. Purchase a new set of tires, and you'll probably pay a recycling charge for disposing of the old tires. The intent is to halt the growing litter problem of illegal tire dumps. Automotive and marine batteries contain potentially toxic materials, including 11 kilograms of lead, plastic, and sulphuric acid. Despite this, 99 percent of the elements in a spent battery can be reclaimed, recycled, and reused in new batteries. Environmentally friendly consumers can turn in their old batteries at the time they purchase new ones. To help in this effort, the Canadian Automobile Association (CAA) holds an annual CAA Great Battery Roundup during which consumers can drop off their dead batteries.[5]

Some reverse channels move through the facilities of traditional marketing intermediaries. In provinces that require bottle deposits, retailers and local bottlers may perform these functions in the consumer beverage industry. For other products, manufacturers—or governments—establish redemption centres, develop systems for rechannelling products for recycling, and create specialized organizations to handle disposal and recycling. Staples collects empty ink and toner cartridges at its stores, rewarding customers who recycle rather than dispose of the items. Nike's Reuse-A-Shoe program collects people's cast-off athletic shoes and recycles virtually the entire shoe. These recycling efforts are likely to help build customer loyalty and enhance the brands' reputations.[6]

Reverse channels also handle product recalls and repairs. An appliance manufacturer might send recall notices to the buyers of a washing machine. An auto manufacturer might send notices to car owners advising them of a potential problem and offering to repair it at no cost through local dealerships.

assessment check 1

1.1 Distinguish between a marketing channel and logistics.

1.2 What are the different types of marketing channels?

1.3 What four functions do marketing channels perform?

---

② **Outline the major channel strategy decisions.**

CHANNEL STRATEGY DECISIONS

Marketers face several strategic decisions in choosing channels and marketing intermediaries for their products. Selecting a specific channel is the most basic of these decisions. Marketers must also resolve questions about the level of distribution intensity, assess the desirability of vertical marketing systems, and evaluate the performance of current intermediaries.

SELECTION OF A MARKETING CHANNEL

Consider the following questions: What characteristics of a franchised dealer network make it the best channel option for a company? Why do operating supplies often go through both agents and merchant wholesalers before reaching their actual users? Why would a firm market a single product through several channels? Marketers must answer many such questions in choosing marketing channels.

A variety of factors affect the selection of a marketing channel. Some channel decisions are dictated by the marketplace in which the company operates. In other cases, the product itself may be a key variable in picking a marketing channel. Finally, the marketing organization may base its selection of channels on its size and competitive factors. Individual firms in a single industry may choose different channels as part of their overall strategy to gain a competitive edge. Book publishers, for instance, may sell through bookstores, directly to consumers on their own websites, or through nontraditional outlets, including specialty retailers such as craft stores or home improvement stores.

Market Factors

Channel structure reflects a product's intended markets, either for consumers or business users. Business purchasers usually prefer to deal directly with manufacturers (except for routine supplies or small accessory items), but most consumers make their purchases from retailers. Marketers often sell products that serve both business users and consumers through more than one channel.

Other market factors also affect channel choice, including the market's needs, its geographic location, and its average order size. To serve a concentrated market with a small number of buyers, a direct channel offers a feasible alternative. But in serving a geographically dispersed potential trade area in which customers purchase small amounts in individual transactions—the conditions that characterize the consumer-goods market—distribution through marketing intermediaries makes sense.

Product Factors

Product characteristics also guide the choice of an optimal marketing channel strategy. Perishable goods, such as fresh fruit and vegetables, milk, and fruit juice, move through short channels. Trendy or seasonal fashions, such as swimsuits and ski wear, are also examples.

Vending machines represent another short channel. Typically, you can buy a bag of Skittles, Lay's potato chips, or a bottle of Dasani water from a vending machine. But how about underwear, dried squid, or a beer? If you're a guest at Tokyo's Shibuya Excel Hotel, you can do just that.[7] In Los Angeles, you can get a Quicksilver brand bikini or board shorts from a vending machine in the lobby of the Standard Hotel. In Shanghai, you can purchase live crab.[8] Complex products, such as custom-made installations and computer equipment, are often sold directly to ultimate buyers. In general, relatively standardized items that are also nonperishable pass through comparatively long channels. Products with low unit costs, such as cans of dog food, bars of soap, and packages of gum, typically travel through long channels. Perishable items such as fresh flowers, meat, and produce require much shorter channels.

Perishable goods—such as fresh fruit—move through short channels, sometimes directly from the grower to the consumer.

Organizational and Competitive Factors

Companies with strong financial, management, and marketing resources feel less need for help from intermediaries. A large, financially strong manufacturer can hire its own sales force, warehouse its own goods, and extend credit to retailers or consumers. But a small firm with fewer resources may do better with the aid of intermediaries. Lana Diaz describes her Vancouver-based company, StaplesOnline, as the "go to" silk company for the local movie and television production industry. Her silk products have been worn by many actors as a second skin; silk keeps them warm and healthy as they work long hours, often outdoors. Lana says, "Retailers were very important when we began to establish our brand, and they are still very important to our success today. Retailers fill an important role on our behalf for our national customers. They allow people who do not like to shop online an opportunity to feel and try on our silk in a store in their area. This is very powerful."[9]

A firm with a broad product line can usually market its products directly to retailers or business users because its own sales force can offer a variety of products. High sales volume spreads selling costs over a large number of items, generating adequate returns from direct sales. Single-product firms often view direct selling as unaffordable.

The manufacturer's desire for control over marketing its products also influences channel selection. Some manufacturers choose to sell their products only at their own stores. Manufacturers of specialty or luxury goods, such as scarves from Hermès and watches from Rolex, limit the number of retailers that can carry their products.

Businesses that explore new marketing channels must be careful to avoid upsetting their channel intermediaries. Conflicts frequently arose as companies began to establish an Internet presence in addition to traditional outlets. Today, firms look for new ways to handle both without damaging relationships. NBC and Apple struck a deal in which NBC would sell its television programs through the iTunes store, but the agreement turned sour over issues of price and piracy (the unauthorized use or reproduction of copyrighted material). However, the two resumed their alliance after figuring out a way to add antipiracy features (or countermeasures against copyright infringement) and rework the price agreement for NBC's programming.[10] Table 11.1 summarizes the factors that affect the selection of a marketing channel. The table also examines the effect of each factor on the channel's overall length.

table 11.1 *Factors Influencing Marketing Channel Strategies*

	CHARACTERISTICS OF SHORT CHANNELS	CHARACTERISTICS OF LONG CHANNELS
Market factors	Business users	Consumers
	Geographically concentrated	Geographically dispersed
	Extensive technical knowledge and regular servicing required	Little technical knowledge and regular servicing not required
	Large orders	Small orders
Product factors	Perishable	Durable
	Complex	Standardized
	Expensive	Inexpensive
Organizational factors	Manufacturer has adequate resources to perform channel functions	Manufacturer lacks adequate resources to perform channel functions
	Broad product line	Limited product line
	Channel control important	Channel control not important
Competitive factors	Manufacturer feels satisfied with marketing intermediaries' performance in promoting products	Manufacturer feels dissatisfied with marketing intermediaries' performance in promoting products

DETERMINING DISTRIBUTION INTENSITY

Another key channel strategy decision is the intensity of distribution. *Distribution intensity* refers to the number of intermediaries through which a manufacturer distributes its goods in a particular market. Optimal distribution intensity should ensure adequate market coverage for a product. Adequate market coverage varies depending on the goals of the individual firm, the type of product, and the consumer segments in its target market. In general, however, distribution intensity varies along a continuum with three general categories: intensive distribution, selective distribution, and exclusive distribution.

Intensive Distribution

intensive distribution
Distribution of a product through all available channels.

An **intensive distribution** strategy seeks to distribute a product through all available channels in a trade area. Because Campbell Soup practises intensive distribution for many of its products, you can pick up a package from its microwavable line just about anywhere—the supermarket, the drugstore, and even Staples. Usually, an intensive distribution strategy suits items with wide appeal across broad groups of consumers.

Selective Distribution

selective distribution
Distribution of a product through a limited number of channels.

In another market coverage strategy, **selective distribution**, a firm chooses only a limited number of retailers in a market area to handle its line. Italian design firm Gucci sells its merchandise only through a limited number of select boutiques worldwide. By limiting the number of retailers, marketers can reduce total marketing costs while establishing strong working relationships within the channel. Moreover, selected retailers often agree to comply with the company's strict rules for advertising, pricing, and displaying its products. *Cooperative advertising*—in which the manufacturer pays a percentage of the retailer's advertising expenditures and the retailer prominently displays the firm's products—can be used for mutual benefit, and marginal retailers can be avoided. Where service is important, the manufacturer usually provides training and assistance to the dealers it chooses.

Exclusive Distribution

exclusive distribution
Distribution of a product through a single wholesaler or retailer in a specific geographic region.

When a producer grants exclusive rights to a wholesaler or retailer to sell its products in a specific geographic region, it practises **exclusive distribution**. The automobile industry provides a good example of exclusive distribution. A city with a population of 40 000 may have a single Ford dealer. Exclusive distribution agreements also govern marketing for some major appliance and apparel brands.

Marketers may sacrifice some market coverage by implementing a policy of exclusive distribution. However, they often develop and maintain an image of quality and prestige for the product. If it's harder to find a Free People silk dress, the item seems more valuable. In addition, exclusive distribution limits marketing costs since the firm deals with a smaller number of accounts. In exclusive distribution, producers and retailers cooperate closely in decisions concerning advertising and promotion, inventory carried by the retailers, and prices.

Legal Problems of Exclusive Distribution

Exclusive distribution presents potential legal problems in three main areas: exclusive dealing, market restriction, and tied selling. Although none of these practices is illegal per se, all may break the law if they reduce competition or tend to create monopolies.

As part of an exclusive distribution strategy, marketers may try to enforce an exclusive dealing agreement, which prohibits a marketing intermediary (a wholesaler or, more typically, a retailer) from handling competing products. Producers of high-priced shopping goods, specialty goods, and accessory equipment often require such agreements to ensure total concentration on their own product lines. Such contracts violate the Competition Act only if the producer's or dealer's sales volumes represent a substantial percentage of total sales in the market area. While exclusive distribution is legal for companies first entering a market, such agreements violate the Competition Act if used by firms with a sizable market share seeking to bar competitors from the market.

Producers may also try to set up **closed sales territories** to restrict their distributors to certain geographic regions. This protects distributors from rival dealers in their exclusive territories. Some beverage distributors have closed territories, as do distributors of plumbing fixtures.[11] But the downside of this practice is that the distributors sacrifice opportunities to open new facilities or market the manufacturers' products outside their assigned territories. The legality of a system of closed sales territories depends on whether the restriction decreases competition. If so, it will violate the Competition Act.

The legality of closed sales territories also depends on whether the system imposes horizontal or vertical restrictions. Horizontal territorial restrictions result from agreements between retailers or wholesalers to avoid competition among sellers of products from the same producer. Such agreements consistently have been declared illegal. Vertical territorial restrictions—those between producers and wholesalers or retailers—are more likely to meet legal criteria. Such agreements likely satisfy the law in cases where manufacturers occupy relatively small market shares. In such instances, the restrictions may actually increase competition among competing brands; the wholesaler or retailer faces no competition from other dealers carrying the manufacturer's brand, so it can concentrate on effectively competing with other brands.

The third legal question of exclusive distribution involves **tying agreements**, which allow channel members to become exclusive dealers only if they also carry products other than those that they want to sell. In the apparel industry, for example, an agreement might require a dealer to carry a comparatively unpopular line of clothing to get desirable, fast-moving items. Tying agreements are reviewable under the Competition Act and not an offence. These practices are, therefore, not prohibited unless an order has been obtained after a review by the Competition Tribunal. Prohibiting such practices is more likely to happen when they reduce competition or create monopolies that keep competitors out of major markets.

StaplesOnline values its retailers across Canada. Retailers that sell the company's knit silk clothing can often add value beyond what consumers can get from online sites.

closed sales territory Exclusive geographic selling region of a distributor.

tying agreement An arrangement that requires a marketing intermediary to carry items other than those they want to sell.

Because Campbell Soup practises intensive distribution for many of its products, you can pick up a package of its microwavable line just about anywhere—the supermarket, the drugstore, or even Sears.

WHO SHOULD PERFORM CHANNEL FUNCTIONS?

A fundamental marketing principle governs channel decisions. A member of the channel must perform certain central marketing functions. Responsibilities of the different members may vary, however. Although independent wholesalers perform many functions for manufacturers, retailers, and other wholesaler clients, other channel members could fulfill these roles instead. A manufacturer might bypass its wholesalers by establishing regional warehouses, maintaining field sales forces, serving as sources of information for retail customers, or arranging details of financing. For years, auto manufacturers have operated credit units that offer new-car financing.

An independent intermediary earns a profit in exchange for providing services to manufacturers and retailers. This profit margin is low, however, ranging from 1 percent for food wholesalers to 5 percent for durable goods wholesalers. Manufacturers and retailers could retain these costs, or they could market directly and reduce retail prices—but only if they could perform the channel functions and match the efficiency of the independent intermediaries.

To grow profitably in a competitive environment, an intermediary must provide better service at lower costs than manufacturers or retailers can provide for themselves. In this case, consolidation of channel functions can represent a strategic opportunity for a company.

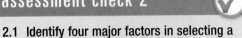

assessment check 2

2.1 Identify four major factors in selecting a marketing channel.

2.2 Describe the three general categories of distribution intensity.

③ Describe the concepts of channel management, conflict, and cooperation.

CHANNEL MANAGEMENT AND LEADERSHIP

Distribution strategy does not end with the choice of a channel. Manufacturers must also focus on channel management by developing and maintaining relationships with the intermediaries in their marketing channels. Positive channel relationships encourage channel members to remember their partners' goods and market them. Manufacturers also must carefully manage the incentives offered to induce channel members to promote their products. This effort includes weighing decisions about pricing, promotion, and other support efforts that the manufacturer performs.

Increasingly, marketers are managing channels in partnership with other channel members. Effective cooperation allows all channel members to achieve goals that they could not achieve on their own. Keys to successful management of channel relationships include the development of high levels of coordination, commitment, and trust between channel members.

Not all channel members wield equal power in the distribution chain, however. The dominant member of a marketing channel is called the **channel captain**. This firm's power to control a channel may result from its control over some type of reward or punishment to other channel members, such as granting an exclusive sales territory or taking away a dealership. Power might also result from contractual arrangements, specialized expert knowledge, or agreement among channel members about their mutual best interests.

channel captain
Dominant and controlling member of a marketing channel.

In the grocery industry, consumer goods manufacturers, such as Procter & Gamble and Kraft Foods, once were considered channel captains. Today, retail giants like Loblaws, Sobeys, Provigo, and Safeway face competition from all quarters: discounters like Giant Tiger, club stores like Costco, and even dollar stores like Dollarama. To survive in the competitive grocery industry, supermarket owners are diversifying their retail formats from traditional stores to include natural and organic and upscale items in their stores to satisfy a wider variety of customers, and to compete with chains such as Whole Foods Market and smaller specialty stores. But the pressure on traditional chains is coming from another strategy: supercentres like Walmart and Target. Walmart is continuing its expansion in the grocery market; in fact, its grocery receipts now account for more than half of its U.S. sales and continue to grow in Canada.[12]

CHANNEL CONFLICT

Marketing channels work smoothly only when members cooperate in well-organized efforts to achieve maximum operating efficiencies. Yet channel members often perform as separate, independent, and even competing forces. Two types of conflict—horizontal and vertical—may hinder the normal functioning of a marketing channel.

Horizontal Conflict

Horizontal conflict sometimes results from disagreements among channel members at the same level, such as two or more wholesalers or two or more retailers, or among marketing intermediaries of the same type, such as two competing discount stores or several retail florists. More often, horizontal conflict causes sparks between different types of marketing intermediaries that handle similar products. In an effort to resolve such a situation, many countries have initiated "open skies" agreements, lifting restrictions on air carriers and clearing the path for increased competition. Many airlines around the world are now permitted to choose routes based on demand within government limitations and will be able to set prices and capacity without interference. Negotiators on both sides predict more cooperative marketing arrangements among the carriers. Canada has not been a signatory to any of these agreements, but a recent report has called for Canada to adopt such a policy, allowing foreign airlines unfettered access to Canada in exchange for similar rights abroad for Canada's airlines.[13]

The resolution of vertical conflict between cable companies and electronics manufacturers paved the way for "tru2way," an initiative that will allow devices not only to receive but also to send digital information.

© AP IMAGES/PRNEWSFOTO/PANASONIC

Vertical Conflict

Vertical relationships may result in frequent and severe conflict. Channel members at different levels find many reasons for disputes, such as when retailers develop private brands to compete with producers' brands or when producers establish their own retail stores or create mail-order operations that compete with retailers. Producers may annoy wholesalers and retailers when they attempt to bypass these intermediaries and sell directly to consumers. After years of conflict, cable companies have reached an agreement with the electronics industry so that manufacturers can produce TVs and other electronic devices that will work—regardless of the cable provider. Comcast and Time Warner are participating in the initiative, called "tru2way," which will allow devices to receive *and send* digital information. The new standardization across the cable networks should foster the development of two-way communication from TVs to set-top boxes to PCs and other devices.[14]

THE GREY MARKET

Another type of channel conflict results from activities in the grey market. As Canadian manufacturers license their technology and brands abroad, they sometimes find themselves in competition in the Canadian market against versions of their own brands produced by overseas affiliates. These **grey goods**, goods produced for sale in one market and then diverted to another market, enter Canadian channels through the actions of unauthorized foreign distributors. While licensing agreements usually prohibit foreign licensees from selling in Canada, and exclusive distribution agreements prohibit manufacturers from selling to non-authorized Canadian resellers, no such rules inhibit their distributors. Other countries also have grey markets. For example, while Amazon is not licensed to sell its Kindle in China, the product is available on China's grey market.

Similarly, even before the iPad's official global release, enterprising individuals had bought them up for resale at an inflated price in Hong Kong.[15]

grey goods Goods produced for sale in one market and then diverted to another market.

ACHIEVING CHANNEL COOPERATION

The basic antidote to channel conflict is effective cooperation among channel members. Cooperation is best achieved when all channel members regard themselves as equal components of the same organization. The channel captain is primarily responsible for providing the leadership necessary to achieve this kind of cooperation.

assessment check 3

3.1 What is a channel captain? What is its role in channel cooperation?

3.2 Identify and describe the three types of channel conflict.

Imax, Sony, and Discovery Communications formed a joint venture to create a 3-D television channel. The new channel, to be distributed by Discovery, will include a programming mix that includes sports, entertainment, and some natural-history shows.[16]

VERTICAL MARKETING SYSTEMS

④ Identify and describe the different vertical marketing systems.

vertical marketing system (VMS) Planned channel system designed to improve distribution efficiency and cost effectiveness by integrating various functions throughout the distribution chain.

forward integration Process through which a firm attempts to control downstream distribution.

backward integration Process through which a firm attempts to gain greater control over inputs in its production process, such as raw materials.

corporate marketing system VMS in which a single owner operates the entire marketing channel.

administered marketing system VMS that achieves channel coordination when a dominant channel member exercises its power.

contractual marketing system VMS that coordinates channel activities through formal agreements among participants.

Efforts to reduce channel conflict and improve the effectiveness of distribution have led to the development of vertical marketing systems. A **vertical marketing system (VMS)** is a planned channel system designed to improve distribution efficiency and cost effectiveness by integrating various functions throughout the distribution chain.

A vertical marketing system can achieve this goal through either forward or backward integration. In **forward integration**, a firm attempts to control downstream distribution. For example, a manufacturer might set up a retail chain to sell its products. **Backward integration** occurs when a firm attempts to gain greater control over inputs in its production process. A manufacturer might acquire the supplier of a raw material the manufacturer uses in the production of its products. Backward integration can also extend the control of retailers and wholesalers over producers that supply them.

A VMS offers several benefits. First, it improves chances for controlling and coordinating the steps in the distribution or production process. It may lead to the development of economies of scale that ultimately saves money. A VMS may also let a manufacturer expand into profitable new businesses. However, a VMS also involves some costs. A manufacturer assumes increased risk when it takes control of an entire distribution chain. Manufacturers may also discover that they lose some flexibility in responding to market changes.

Marketers have developed three categories of VMSs: corporate systems, administered systems, and contractual systems. These categories are outlined in the sections that follow.

CORPORATE AND ADMINISTERED SYSTEMS

When a single owner runs organizations at each stage of the marketing channel, it operates a **corporate marketing system**. Roots, for example, sells its branded products through more than 120 retail locations in Canada and the United States, and more than 40 in Aisa.[17] An **administered marketing system** achieves channel coordination when a dominant channel member exercises its power. Even though Goodyear sells its tires through independently owned and operated dealerships, it controls the stock that these dealerships carry. Other examples of channel captains leading administered channels are McKesson Canada and Shoppers Drug Mart.

CONTRACTUAL SYSTEMS

Instead of common ownership of intermediaries within a corporate VMS or the exercising of power within an administered system, a **contractual marketing system** coordinates distribution through formal agreements among channel members. In practice, three types of agreements set up these systems: wholesaler-sponsored voluntary chains, retail cooperatives, and franchises.

Wholesaler-Sponsored Voluntary Chain

Sometimes an independent wholesaler will try to preserve a market by strengthening its retail customers through a wholesaler-sponsored voluntary chain. The wholesaler adopts a formal agreement with its retailers to use a common name and standardized facilities and to purchase the wholesaler's goods. The wholesaler may even develop a line of private brands to be stocked by the retailers. This practice often helps smaller retailers compete with rival chains—and strengthens the wholesaler's position as well.

True Value Company, with more than 5000 stores and 12 regional distribution centres serving 54 countries, is a good example of a voluntary chain.[18] Because a single advertisement will promote all the retailers in the trading area, a common store name and similar inventories allow it to save on advertising costs.

The first home cleaned by Molly Maid was in Mississauga, Ontario, in 1979. Now, there are franchise locations across Canada, in the United States, the United Kingdom, Japan, and Portugal.

Retail Cooperative

In a second type of contractual VMS, a group of retailers establishes a shared wholesaling operation to help them compete with chains. This is known as a **retail cooperative**. The retailers purchase ownership shares in the wholesaling operation and agree to buy a minimum percentage of their inventories from this operation. The members typically adopt a common store name and develop common private brands.

retail cooperative
Group of retailers that establish a shared wholesaling operation to help them compete with chains.

Franchise

A third type of contractual vertical marketing system is the **franchise**, in which a wholesaler or dealer (the franchisee) agrees to meet the operating requirements of a manufacturer or other franchiser. Franchising is a huge and growing industry. There are more than 85 000 franchise units (franchisees) in Canada, controlled by about 950 franchisors. Total annual sales exceed $70 billion. After the United States, Canada is the world's most developed franchise market.[19] Table 11.2 shows the 20 fastest-growing franchises in the United States. Most of these now operate in Canada as well. Other important franchise operations in Canada are Tim Hortons, Canadian Tire, M&M Meat Shops, and Rona Inc.

Franchise owners pay anywhere from several thousand to more than a million dollars to purchase and set up a franchise. Typically, they also pay a royalty on sales to the franchising company. In exchange for these initial and ongoing fees, the franchise owner receives the right to use the company's brand name as well as services such as training, marketing, advertising, and volume discounts. Major franchise chains justify the steep price of entry since it allows new businesses to sell winning brands. But if the brand enters a slump or the corporation behind the franchise makes poor strategic decisions, franchisees are often hurt.

franchise
Contractual arrangement in which a wholesaler or retailer agrees to meet the operating requirements of a manufacturer or other franchiser.

assessment check 4

4.1 What are vertical marketing systems (VMSs)? Identify the major types.

4.2 Identify the three types of contractual marketing systems.

table 11.2 *Entrepreneur.com's Top 20 Franchise 500 Rankings*

RANK	FRANCHISE NAME/DESCRIPTION	STARTUP COSTS
1	7-Eleven Inc.: Convenience store	Varies
2	Subway: Fast food—submarine sandwiches and salads	$80K–310K
3	Dunkin' Donuts: Fast food—coffee, doughnuts, baked goods	Varies
4	Pizza Hut: Fast-food—pizza	$1.1M–1.7M
5	McDonald's: Fast-food—hamburgers, chicken, salads	$950K–1.8M
6	Sonic Drive In Restaurants: Drive-in restaurant	$820K–2.3M
7	KFC Corp.: Fast food—chicken	$1.1M–1.7M
8	InterContinental Hotels Group: Hotels	Varies
9	Domino's Pizza LLC: Fast food—pizza, breadsticks, buffalo wings	$118.5K–460.3K
10	RE/MAX Int'l. Inc.: Real estate	$35K–200K
11	UPS Store, The/Mail Boxes Etc.: Postal, business and communications services	$170.8K–279.4K
12	Ace Hardware Corp.: Hardware and home improvement store	$400K–1.1M
13	Jani-King: Commercial cleaning	$11.3K–34.1K+
14	Jiffy Lube Int'l. Inc.: Fast oil change	$214K–273K
15	Arby's: Fast food—sandwiches, chicken, salads	$336.5K–2.4M
16	Baskin-Robbins USA Co.: Ice cream, frozen yogurt, frozen beverages	$156.9K–560.4K
17	Circle K: Convenience store	$648K
18	Kumon Math & Reading Centers: Supplemental education	$30.96K–129.4K
19	Great Clips Inc.: Hair salon	$110K–202K
20	Bonus Building Care: Commercial cleaning	$8.8K–14.7K

Source: http://www.entrepreneur.com/franchises/rankings/franchise500-115608/2008,-1.html with permission of Entrepreneur Media, Inc. © 2008 by Entrepreneur Media, Inc. www.entrepreneur.com. All rights reserved.

(5) Explain the roles of logistics and supply-chain management in an overall distribution strategy.

LOGISTICS AND SUPPLY-CHAIN MANAGEMENT

Pier 1 imports its eclectic mix of items from vendors in more than 50 countries, most representing small companies. If high-demand items or seasonal products are late into its six North American distribution centres or are shipped in insufficient quantities, the company may miss opportunities to deliver popular shopping choices to its more than 1000 retail stores and could lose ground to such competitors as Pottery Barn and Crate & Barrel. The situation facing Pier 1 illustrates the importance of logistics. Careful coordination of Pier 1's supplier network, shipping processes, and inventory control is the key to its continuing success. In addition, the store's buyers develop relationships with suppliers in all participating countries.[20] The boxed feature, "Marketing in a Digital World," describes the importance of good logistics to the success of the virtual store operation recently launched by Home Plus in South Korea.

Effective logistics requires proper supply-chain management, the control of activities of purchasing, processing, and delivery through which raw materials are transformed into products and made available to final consumers. The **supply chain**, also known as the *value chain,* is the complete sequence of suppliers and activities that contribute to the creation and delivery of goods and services. The supply chain begins with the raw-material inputs for the manufacturing process of a product and then proceeds to the actual production activities. The final link in the supply chain is the movement of finished products through the marketing channel to customers. Each link of the chain benefits the consumers as raw materials move through manufacturing to distribution. The chain encompasses all activities that enhance the value of the finished goods, including design, quality manufacturing, customer service, and delivery. Customer satisfaction results directly from the perceived value of a purchase to its buyer.

supply chain Complete sequence of suppliers and activities that contribute to the creation and delivery of merchandise.

MARKETING IN
A DIGITAL WORLD

Smart Phones: Smart Shopping

LOGISTICAL management plays a major role in ensuring that customers get what they want, where and when they need it. Companies can provide value-added service by offering an improved or supplemental service that customers do not normally receive or expect. UK-based Tesco is the second-largest grocery retailer in South Korea, where it renamed itself Home Plus. It recently faced the problem of how to grow without expanding the number of physical locations that it operated in the country. The solution: virtual stores, but not what North Americans would normally consider virtual stores. Home Plus added value through a unique service: let customers order by smartphone while waiting for their train.

Tesco plastered subway walls with pictures of grocery products laid out in much the same fashion as they would be in their physical stores. The pictures were backlit and each item contained a QR code. By scanning them with a smartphone, shoppers could add the items to their shopping basket, arrange payment electronically, and have the goods delivered directly to their home. Fortunately, Home Plus had already solved any logistical problems with home delivery.

Have these Home Plus virtual stores been successful? In their first three months of operation, sales increased by 130 percent and the number of consumers who registered for the company's online membership increased by 76 percent. Over 10 000 customers tried the stores. Home Plus has grown to be South Korea's largest online grocer and is a very close second to leader E-Mart in overall sales.

Why did it work? It might partly be explained by novelty, but there is certainly more to it than that. South Koreans are among the world's most hardworking people. Choosing subway walls was a smart move as people in subways often have time on their hands while they wait for their train and are frequently workers who have money but who are time constrained. South Korea, as well, has among the most electronically connected consumers in the world. South Koreans, numbering less than 50 million, own more than 10 million smartphones. Their subways have mobile connectivity. Considering all these factors, it is easy to see why its subway virtual stores have done so well.

Sources: "Tesco Builds Virtual Shops for Korean Commuters," *The Telegraph*, http://www.telegraph.co.uk/technology/mobile-phones/8601147/Tesco-builds-virtual-shops-for-Korean-commuters.html, August 3, 2011; "Grocery Shopping Via Smartphone on South Korean Subways," http://www.springwise.com/retail/homeplus, Food & Beverage, Retail, July 6, 2011; Willis Lee, "How Korea's Homeplus Brought a Smartphone Supermarket to the Subway," http://www.penn-olson.com, June 25, 2011.

To manage the supply chain, businesses must look for ways to maximize customer value in each activity they perform. Supply-chain management takes place in two directions: upstream and downstream, as illustrated in Figure 11.2. **Upstream management** involves managing raw materials, inbound logistics, and warehouse and storage facilities. **Downstream management** involves managing finished product storage, outbound logistics, marketing and sales, and customer service.

Companies choose a variety of methods for managing the supply chain. They can include high-tech systems such as radio-frequency identification (discussed in the next section) and regular person-to-person meetings. JDA Software Group helps other businesses track and manage their global supply chains. Using its proprietary software solutions, JDA helps its clients enhance customer service and improve inventory management.[21] Logistics plays a major role in giving customers what they need when they need it, and thus is central in the supply chain. Another important component of this chain, *value-added service*, adds some improved or supplemental service that customers do not normally receive or expect. The following sections examine methods for streamlining and managing logistics and the supply chain as part of an overall distribution strategy.

RADIO FREQUENCY IDENTIFICATION (RFID)

One tool that marketers are using to help manage logistics is **radio frequency identification (RFID)** technology. With RFID, a tiny chip with identification information that can be read from a distance by a radio-frequency scanner is placed on an item. These chips are already widely used in tollway pass transmitters, allowing drivers to zip through toll booths without stopping or rolling down their windows to toss change into baskets.

They are also embedded in employee ID cards that workers use to open office doors without keys. But businesses such as retail giant Walmart, manufacturer Procter & Gamble, credit card firms MasterCard and Visa, and German retailer Metro AG are eagerly putting the technology to wider use;

upstream management
Controlling part of the supply chain that involves raw materials, inbound logistics, and warehouse and storage facilities.

downstream management
Controlling part of the supply chain that involves finished product storage, outbound logistics, marketing and sales, and customer service.

radio frequency identification (RFID)
Technology that uses a tiny chip with identification information that can be read from a distance by a scanner using radio waves.

figure 11.2

The Supply Chain of a Manufacturing Company

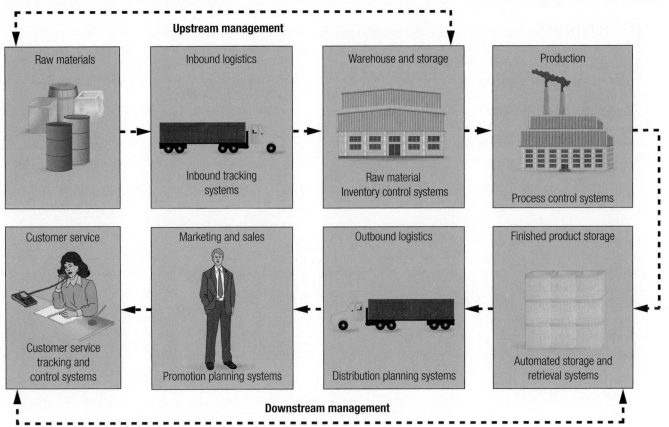

Source: From STAIR/REYNOLDS, *Principles of Information Systems*, 7E. © 2006 South-Western, a part of Cengage Learning, Inc. Reproduced by permission. www.cengage.com/permissions

they say it will speed deliveries, make consumer bar codes obsolete, and provide marketers with valuable information about consumer preferences. Walmart requires its biggest suppliers to attach RFID tags to pallets and cases of products such as Coca-Cola and Dove soap, saying that the technology will vastly improve its ability to track inventory and keep the right amount of products in stock.

Boeing Company manufactures airplanes at its plant in Everett, Washington—a 100-acre complex said to be the largest building in the world. A Boeing plane is made up of 2 to 3 million individual parts, and by using RFID tags and Wi-Fi technology to track and locate those parts throughout the supply chain process, Boeing saves time and paperwork.[22]

ENTERPRISE RESOURCE PLANNING

enterprise resource planning (ERP) system
Software system that consolidates data from among a firm's various business units.

Software is an important aspect of logistics management and the supply chain. An **enterprise resource planning (ERP) system** is an integrated software system that consolidates data from among the firm's units. Roughly two-thirds of ERP system users are manufacturers concerned with production issues such as sequencing and scheduling. German software giant SAP offers systems that allow businesses to manage their customer relations. And eBay uses an SAP system to interact with its top customers in Europe.[23]

As valuable as it is, ERP and its related software aren't always perfect. For example, ERP failures were blamed for Hershey's inability to fulfill all its candy orders during one Halloween period, when a fall-off in sales was blamed on a combination of shipping delays, inability to fill orders, and partial shipments while candy stockpiled in warehouses. Several major retailers were forced to shift their purchases to other candy vendors.

LOGISTICAL COST CONTROL

In addition to enhancing their products by providing value-added services to customers, many firms are focusing on logistics for another important reason: to cut costs. Distribution functions currently represent almost half of a typical firm's total marketing costs. To reduce logistical costs, businesses are re-examining each link of their supply chains to identify activities that do not add value for customers. By eliminating, reducing, or redesigning these activities, they can often cut costs and boost efficiency. As just described, new technologies such as RFID can save businesses millions—or even billions—of dollars.

Because of increased security requirements in recent years, businesses involved in importing and exporting have faced a major rise in logistical costs. U.S. Customs and Border Protection has initiated a voluntary program for transportation carriers that requires them to ensure the integrity of their own security practices. Canadian carriers that participate in the Customs-Trade Partnership Against Terrorism (C-TPAT) program are eligible to receive expedited service at major border crossings. They also help ensure their access to the United States in the event of another high-security alert, when only security-approved carriers will be allowed to cross the border.[24]

Third-Party Logistics

Some companies try to cut costs and offer value-added services by outsourcing some or all of their logistics functions to specialist firms. **Third-party (contract) logistics firms** (3PL firms) specialize in handling logistical activities for their clients. Third-party logistics is a huge industry, estimated to be about $130 billion in 2011 in North America alone.[25]

Through outsourcing alliances, producers and logistical service suppliers cooperate in developing innovative, customized systems that speed goods through carefully constructed manufacturing and distribution pipelines. Although many companies have long outsourced transportation and warehousing functions, today's alliance partners use similar methods to combine their operations.

third-party (contract) logistics firm
Company that specializes in handling logistics activities for other firms.

assessment check 5

5.1 What is upstream management? What is downstream management?

5.2 Identify three methods for managing logistics.

PHYSICAL DISTRIBUTION

⑥ Identify the major components of a physical distribution system.

A firm's physical distribution system is an organized group of components linked according to a plan for achieving specific distribution objectives. It contains the following elements:

1. *Customer service.* What level of customer service the distribution activities should support.

2. *Transportation.* How the firm should ship its products.

3. *Inventory control.* How much inventory the firm should maintain at each location.

4. *Protective packaging and materials handling.* How the firm can package and efficiently handle goods in the factory, warehouse, and transport terminals.

5. *Order processing.* How the firm should handle orders.

6. *Warehousing.* Where the distribution system will locate stocks of goods and the number of warehouses the firm should maintain.

All these components function in interrelated ways. Decisions made in one area affect efficiency in others. The physical distribution manager must balance each component so that the system avoids stressing any single aspect to the detriment of overall functioning. A firm might decide to reduce transportation costs by shipping its products by less costly—but slow—water transportation. But slow deliveries would likely force the firm to maintain higher inventory levels, raising those costs. This mismatch between system elements often leads to increased production costs. So balancing the components is crucial.

The general shift from a manufacturing economy to a service economy in Canada has affected physical distribution in two key ways. First, customers require more flexible—yet reliable—transportation service. Second, the number of smaller shipments is growing much faster than the number of large shipments. Although traditional, high-volume shipments will continue to grow, they will represent a lower percentage of the transportation industry's revenues and volume.

THE PROBLEM OF SUBOPTIMIZATION

Logistics managers seek to establish a specified level of customer service while minimizing the costs of physically moving and storing goods. Marketers must first decide on their priorities for customer service and then figure out how to fulfill those goals by moving goods at the best cost. Meshing together all the physical distribution elements is a huge challenge that firms don't always meet.

suboptimization
Condition that results when individual operations achieve their objectives but interfere with progress toward broader organizational goals.

Suboptimization results when the managers of individual physical distribution functions attempt to minimize costs, but the impact of one task on the others leads to less than optimal results. Imagine a hockey team composed of record-holding players. Unfortunately, despite the individual talents of the players, the team fails to win a game. This is an example of suboptimization. The same thing can happen at a company when each logistics activity is judged by its own accomplishments instead of the way it contributes to the overall goals of the firm. Suboptimization often happens when a firm introduces a new product that may not fit easily into its current physical distribution system.

Effective management of the physical distribution function requires some cost trade-offs. By accepting relatively high costs in some functional areas to cut costs in others, managers can minimize their firm's total physical distribution costs. Of course, any reduction in logistical costs should support progress toward the goal of maintaining customer-service standards.

CUSTOMER-SERVICE STANDARDS

Customer-service standards state the goals and define acceptable performance for the quality of service that a firm expects to deliver to its customers. Internet retailers such as 1-800-FLOWERS.ca thrive because of their ability to ship within hours of receiving an order. This company works with a network of florists across Canada, which allows it to guarantee same-day delivery, every day except Sunday—Mother's Day an exception.[26] A pizza shop might set a standard to deliver customers' pizzas hot and fresh to their homes within 30 minutes of their order. An auto repair shop might set a standard to complete all oil changes in a half hour. All are examples of customer service standards.

Designers of a physical distribution system begin by establishing acceptable levels of customer service. These designers then assemble physical distribution components in a way that will achieve this standard at the lowest possible total cost. This overall cost breaks down into five components: (1) transportation, (2) warehousing, (3) customer service/order processing, (4) administrative costs, and (5) inventory control.

TRANSPORTATION

The transportation industry has been largely deregulated. Deregulation has been particularly important for motor carriers, railroads, and air carriers. Many transporters are now free to develop unique solutions to shippers' needs. The trucking industry now operates far more efficiently than it did under government regulation; many carriers have reduced empty mileage by two-thirds. Railroads are enjoying a new boom: once hauling mostly commodities like corn and grain, they now transport cross-country the huge loads of goods coming from China through coastal ports. Railroads can move a greater amount of freight for less fuel than trucks. In North America, more than 1.5 million rail cars carry freight on 278 000 kilometres of track, with the industry generating $42 billion in annual revenues.[27]

Typically adding 10 percent to the cost of a product, transportation and delivery expenses represent the largest category of logistics-related costs for most firms. Also, for many items—particularly perishable ones such as fresh fish or produce—transportation makes a central contribution to satisfactory customer service.

Many logistics managers have found that the key to controlling their shipping costs is careful management of relationships with shipping firms. Freight carriers use two basic rates: class and commodity rates. A class rate is a standard rate for a specific commodity moving between any pair of destinations.

Trucking companies move about 90 percent of all consumer goods within Canada and about two-thirds, by value, of our trade with the United States.

A carrier may charge a lower commodity rate, sometimes called a *special rate,* to a favoured shipper as a reward for either regular business or a large-quantity shipment. Railroads and inland water carriers frequently reward customers in this way. In addition, the railroad and motor carrier industries sometimes supplement this rate structure with negotiated, or contract, rates. In other words, the two parties finalize terms of rates, services, and other variables in a contract.

Classes of Carriers

Freight carriers are classified as common, contract, and private carriers. **Common carriers**, often considered the backbone of the transportation industry, provide transportation services as for-hire carriers to the general public. The government still regulates their rates and services, and they cannot conduct their operations without permission from the appropriate regulatory authority. Common carriers move freight via all modes of transport. FedEx is a major common carrier serving businesses and consumers. One way the firm remains competitive is by developing new methods for enhancing customer service. FedEx has a service called InSight, a free online service that essentially reverses the package-tracking process—instead of following a package from shipment to delivery, customers can go online to find out what is going to be delivered to them that day. One FedEx customer that has benefited greatly from this new service is a greenhouse, which ships perishable goods—begonias, miniature poinsettias, and other plants—to florists and nursery departments of such big-box stores as Home Depot, Lowe's, and Walmart. With InSight, the company can easily track the status of its shipments.[28]

Contract carriers are for-hire transporters that do not offer their services to the general public. Instead, they establish contracts with individual customers and operate exclusively for particular industries, such as the motor freight industry. These carriers operate under much looser regulations than common carriers.

Private carriers do not offer services for hire. These carriers provide transportation services solely for internally generated freight. As a result, they observe no rate or service regulations. Many large retailers operate their own private fleets in Canada.

common carriers
Businesses that provide transportation services as for-hire carriers to the general public.

contract carriers
For-hire transporters that do not offer their services to the general public.

private carriers
Transporters that provide service solely for internally generated freight.

assessment check 6

6.1 What are the six major elements of physical distribution?

6.2 What is suboptimization?

⑦ Compare the major modes of transportation.

Major Transportation Modes

Logistics managers choose among five major transportation alternatives: railroads, motor carriers, water carriers, pipelines, and air freight. Each mode has its own unique characteristics. Logistics managers select the best options by matching these features to their specific transportation needs.

Railroads

Railroads continue to control the largest share of the freight business as measured by tonne-kilometres. The term *tonne-kilometre* indicates shipping activity required to move one tonne of freight one kilometre. Rail shipments quickly rack up tonne-kilometres because this mode provides the most efficient way to move bulky commodities over long distances. Rail carriers generally transport huge quantities of coal, chemicals, grain, nonmetallic minerals, lumber and wood products, and automobiles. The railroads have improved their service standards through a number of innovative concepts, such as unit trains, run-through trains, **intermodal operations**, and double-stack container trains. Unit trains carry much of the coal, grain, and other high-volume commodities shipped, running back and forth between single loading points (such as a mine) and single destinations (such as a power plant) to deliver a commodity. Run-through trains bypass intermediate terminals to speed up schedules. They work similarly to unit trains, but a run-through train may carry a variety of commodities.

In piggyback operations, one of the intermodal operations, highway trailers and containers ride on railroad flatcars, thus combining the long-haul capacity of the train with the door-to-door flexibility of the truck. A double-stack container train pulls special rail cars equipped with bathtub-shaped wells so they can carry two containers stacked on top of one another. By nearly doubling train capacity and slashing costs, this system offers enormous advantages to rail customers. Canada's two major railways, Canadian Pacific Railway (CP) and Canadian National Railway (CN), are both focused on lowering fuel consumption and smog-causing emissions. These environmental improvements are starting to be noticed by customers. Mike LoVecchio, senior manager, media relations for CP, says, "Double-stacked intermodal freight trains can replace more than 200 trucks on our highways."[29]

Motor Carriers

Trucks transport about 90 percent of all consumer goods products within Canada and about two-thirds, by value, of our trade with the United States. Canadian for-hire truckers haul more than 600 million tonnes of freight annually and, in one recent year, they transported more than 225 billion tonne-kilometres of freight.[30] Trucking offers some important advantages over the other transportation modes, including relatively fast shipments and consistent service for both large and small shipments. Motor carriers concentrate on shipping manufactured products, while railroads typically haul bulk shipments of raw materials. Motor carriers, therefore, receive greater revenue per tonne shipped, making road transportation one of the most expensive shipping methods.

Technology has also improved the efficiency of trucking. Many trucking firms now track their fleets via satellite communications systems, and in-truck computer systems allow drivers and dispatchers to make last-minute changes in scheduling and delivery. The Internet is also adding new features to motor carrier services.

Even so, the trucking industry must adjust to changes in the marketing environment. Trucking firms report a shortage of long-haul drivers, causing delays in some deliveries and higher costs, along with the rising cost of fuel, to customers. Some firms offer drivers regional runs and dedicated routes for more predictable work hours, as well as better pay. They also recruit husband-and-wife teams for the long-haul routes, which is becoming a popular practice.[31]

Water Carriers

Two basic types of transport methods move products over water: inland or barge lines and ocean-going, deepwater ships. Barge lines efficiently transport bulky, low unit value commodities such as grain, gravel, lumber, sand, and steel. Montreal-based Canada Steamship Lines operates a fleet of 11 self-unloaders and eight bulk carriers on the Great Lakes–St. Lawrence Waterway system.[32]

Ocean-going ships carry a growing stream of containerized freight between ports around the world. Vancouver, Canada's largest port, handled 118 million tonnes of cargo in 2010.[33] Approximately half of Canadian international trade, by value, is carried by marine transportation.[34] Supertankers from global companies such as Maersk Sealand are the size of three football fields, almost double the capacity of other vessels. At full capacity, the ships can cut the cost of shipping a container across the Pacific by

intermodal operations Combination of transport modes such as rail and highway carriers (piggyback), air and highway carriers (birdyback), and water and highway carriers (fishyback) to improve customer service and achieve cost advantages.

Marketoid

Share of transportation and warehousing GDP by transportation mode: truck (28.4 percent), air (9.2 percent), rail (8.6 percent), pipeline (8.2 percent), and water (1.8 percent).

a fifth. Shippers that transport goods via water carriers incur very low costs compared to the rates for other transportation modes. Standardized modular shipping containers maximize savings by limiting loading, unloading, and other handling.

Ships often carry large refrigerated containers, called reefers, for transporting everything from fresh produce to medical supplies. These containers, along with their non-refrigerated counterparts, improve shipping efficiency because they can easily be removed from a ship and attached to trucks or trains. Although shipping by water has traditionally been less expensive than other modes of transportation, costs for this mode have increased dramatically because of tightened security measures. Industry experts predict these costs will continue to climb over the next several years.[35]

The "Solving an Ethical Controversy" feature discusses a recent issue involving ocean-going vessels: the issue of piracy.

SOURCE: CANADIAN NATIONAL RAILWAY COMPANY ("CN"), REPRODUCED BY AUTHORIZATION OF CN.

CN's double-stack container trains serve the port of Vancouver as seen here, along with other Canadian and U.S. ports.

SOLVING AN ETHICAL CONTROVERSY   Guns on the High Seas?

IT was once the stuff of swashbuckling novels and adventure movies: piracy on the high seas. Lately, however, pirate attacks on ocean-going cargo vessels have become a reality. In the first three months of 2011, 142 attacks were reported that resulted in seven deaths, 18 ships captured, and 344 hostages being taken. The majority of these attacks have occurred in the Gulf of Aden—one of the world's most important shipping lanes—where Somali pirates have become increasingly active and have escalated their torture of hostages in an effort to pressure ship owners to pay higher ransoms. At the end of March 2011, Somali pirates were holding 28 ships and 596 crew members. A recent report set the cost of piracy at $12 billion (U.S.).

A Canadian company, Current Corporation, has developed a night vision system that can detect a small boat, such as the ones used by pirates, at a distance of 14 kilometres. At a price of $440 000, such a system would allow ships to consider a range of possible responses from increasing speed, calling for help, changing course, or preparing for attack. An international navy is trying to protect shipping, and the UN Security Council asked in April 2011 that an international court and prison system with new laws be established to deal with Somali pirates. However, one Norwegian shipping magnate expressed a view shared by other fleet owners: "Shoot on sight." He argued that it is the only way to police large ocean areas.

Should crews of ocean-going vessels be permitted to bear arms?

PRO

1. Pirates have become increasingly sophisticated in their tactics. By training and arming senior officers

or bringing aboard highly trained military veterans, civilian ships can defend themselves. The knowledge alone that ships are armed would serve as a deterrent to piracy.
2. A ship that travels unarmed into regions known to be dangerous is arguably an unsafe workplace and an unseaworthy vessel.

CON

1. Piracy is rare. In a recent year, approximately 33 000 ships travelled through the Gulf of Aden, so only a small number have sustained attacks, and fewer still were captured.
2. Knowing that a crew is armed would encourage pirates to resort to even more dangerous tactics, leading to an escalating situation merchant sailors aren't trained to handle.

Where do you stand: pro or con?

Sources: Colin Freeman, "Kidnapping and Torture On the High Seas: Somali Pirates Are More Sophisticated, While Employing the Brutality Associated with Their Medieval Predecessors," *Vancouver Sun*, April 19, 2011, p. 5; Steve Brearton, "Sailing Dangerous Waters," *The Globe and Mail*, April 16, 2011, p. 8; Anonymous, "Ship Attacks Hit Record," *The Province* (Vancouver), April 15, 2011, p. 35; Anonymous, "UN Council Backs New Measures for Pirates," *Edmonton Journal*, April 12, 2011; Brian Morton, "Port Moody Company Puts Pirates in Its Crosshairs; Current Corporation Provides Camera System to World's Ships, Including South Korean Coast Guard," *Vancouver Sun*, March 9, 2011, p. 2.

TransCanada Pipelines' natural gas pipeline construction in Stittsville, Ontario.

Pipelines

Although the pipeline industry ranks third after railroads and motor carriers in tonne-kilometres transported, many people scarcely recognize its existence. Oil pipelines carry two types of commodities: crude (unprocessed) oil and refined products, such as gasoline, jet fuel, and kerosene. In addition, one so-called *slurry pipeline* carries coal in suspension after it has been ground up into a powder and mixed with water. TransCanada Pipelines owns about 57 000 kilometres of pipeline and transports most of Western Canada's natural gas to markets in Canada and the United States.[36] Enbridge is Canada's largest transporter of crude oil and delivers more than 2.2 million barrels per day of crude oil and liquids through its 24 613-kilometre system, the world's longest system.[37]

Although pipelines offer low maintenance and dependable methods of transportation, a number of characteristics limit their applications. They have fewer locations than water carriers, and they can accommodate shipments of only a small number of products. Finally, pipelines represent a relatively slow method of transportation; liquids travel through this method at an average speed of only five to six kilometres per hour.

Air Freight

Although the air freight industry grew steadily for many years, recently that growth has levelled off—at least in certain market sectors, such as overnight delivery service. But firms are adapting. UPS recently revamped its services, now offering an expanded international express service called UPS Express Freight. The service provides guaranteed time-definite, overnight to three-day door-to-door delivery, including customs clearance, to large global metropolitan areas. UPS is also offering two less expensive, nonguaranteed services: UPS Air Freight Direct and UPS Air Freight Consolidated. Both are available worldwide and provide package pickup, delivery, and customs clearance.[38] Purolator Courier remains Canada's largest domestic air shipper, handling more than 1.1 million pieces for pickup and delivery each day. Purolator handles more than 180 000 kilograms of air freight each night.[39]

Comparing the Five Modes of Transport

Table 11.3 compares the five transportation modes on several operating characteristics. Although all shippers judge reliability, speed, and cost in choosing the most appropriate transportation methods, they assign varying importance to specific criteria when shipping different goods. For example, while motor carriers rank highest in availability in different locations, shippers of petroleum products frequently choose the lowest ranked alternative, pipelines, for their low cost. Examples of types of goods most often handled by the different transports follow:

table 11.3   *Comparison of Transport Modes*

MODE	SPEED	DEPENDABILITY IN MEETING SCHEDULES	FREQUENCY OF SHIPMENTS	AVAILABILITY IN DIFFERENT LOCATIONS	FLEXIBILITY IN HANDLING	COST
Rail	Average	Average	Low	Low	High	Average
Water	Very slow	Average	Very low	Limited	Very high	Very low
Truck	Fast	High	High	Very extensive	Average	High
Pipeline	Slow	High	High	Very limited	Very low	Low
Air	Very fast	High	Average	Average	Low	Very high

- *Railroads:* lumber, iron, steel, coal, automobiles, grain, chemicals;

- *Motor carriers:* clothing, furniture, fixtures, lumber, plastic, food, leather, machinery;

- *Water carriers:* fuel, oil, coal, chemicals, minerals, and petroleum products; automobiles, electronics, and many low-value products from foreign manufacturers;

- *Pipelines:* oil, diesel fuel, jet fuel, kerosene, natural gas; and

- *Air freight:* flowers, medical testing kits, and gourmet food products directly to consumers.

assessment check 7

7.1 Identify the five major modes of transport.

7.2 Which mode of transport is currently experiencing resurgence, and why?

Freight Forwarders and Supplemental Carriers

Freight forwarders act as transportation intermediaries, consolidating shipments to gain lower rates for their customers. The transport rates on less-than-truckload (LTL) and less-than-carload (LCL) shipments often double the per-unit rates on truckload (TL) and carload (CL) shipments. Freight forwarders charge less than the highest rates but more than the lowest rates. They profit by consolidating shipments from many customers until they can ship at TL and CL rates. The customers gain two advantages from these services: lower costs on small shipments and faster delivery service than they could achieve with their own LTL and LCL shipments.

In addition to the transportation options reviewed so far, a logistics manager can ship products via a number of auxiliary, or supplemental, carriers that specialize in small shipments. These carriers include Purolator, Canpar, UPS, FedEx, and Canada Post.

8 Discuss the role of transportation intermediaries, combined transportation modes, and warehousing in improving physical distribution.

GO GREEN   **Green Supply Chains Are Golden**

IMPROVING efficiency throughout the supply chain can result in truly significant improvements to the environment. Of course, the most necessary improvements are those that affect transportation. Over one-quarter of all greenhouse gas emissions in Canada come from transportation, and without improvements things will continue to get worse as the number of tractor-trailer registrations in Canada continues to increase, up nearly one-third in a recent five-year period. Recognizing the need for change, Transport Canada has implemented its eco-FREIGHT program, aimed at reducing the impact of transportation on the environment and health and, in collaboration with Supply Chain and Logistics Association Canada (SCL), sponsors the SCL Green Supply Chain Award. SCL provides a number of checklists on its website for companies that wish to "green" their supply chain. Visit www.sclcanada.org.

Among the methods of greening logistics are these: use less transportation and use better modes of transportation. One way to use less transportation is to optimize routing. Frito Lay Canada optimizes its routing with software that carefully sequences stops and picks the shortest routes among them. It has reduced the distance travelled by its fleet by nearly a million kilometres. Another way to reduce transportation is to maximize loads. Sobeys redesigned many of its stores to accommodate larger trucks, allowing vehicles to make more deliveries per trip. Loblaws started using multi-axle trucks for some primary freight routes, so more weight could be hauled using a single power source. Reducing packaging can also save transportation. Hewlett-Packard reduced the packaging per camera from 396 to

164 grams, allowing it to ship 720 units per pallet instead of the 200 units it previously shipped on each pallet. An improvement can also be made by reducing the number of empty back-hauls that occur when trucks take shipments in one direction and are then forced to return empty. Hudson's Bay Company has partnered with nearly 200 companies that need to ship goods in the opposite direction from where it ships.

Using the best mode of transportation may simply require alternative shipping methods. Mountain Equipment Co-op lowered its greenhouse gas emissions by over 30 percent, simply by changing from truck to rail for shipments from its west coast distribution centre to its east coast stores. As noted earlier in this chapter, a single double-stacked intermodal freight train can replace more than 200 trucks on the road. According to New Brunswick Southern Railway research, a 20-car freight train emits less than half of the CO_2 that would be emitted by 20 loaded transport trucks.

Whether they decide to go with less or better, companies that have started to implement actions to "green" their supply chain will have an advantage as government regulation and consumer concern continue to increase.

Sources: Supply Chain and Logistics Association Canada website, http://www.sclcanada.org, May 26, 2011; "What Impact Transportation Has on the Environment," *Truck News*, June 2007, p. 6; David Shipley, "The Resurgence of Rail Transportation; As CN Rail Prepares to Convene Its Shareholder Meeting in Moncton, the Company Says Rail Is Enjoying a Renaissance," *New Brunswick Telegraph Journal* (Saint John), April 21, 2007, pp. C1–2; Robert J. Bowman, "The Greening of the Supply Chain," SupplyChain-Brain.com, November 1, 2006, http://www.supplychainbrain.com.

Sobeys operates 22 distribution centres—such as this one in Stellarton, Nova Scotia—that serve more than 1300 stores owned or franchised across Canada.

Intermodal Coordination

Transportation companies emphasize specific modes and serve certain kinds of customers, but they sometimes combine their services to give shippers the service and cost advantages of each. *Piggyback* service, mentioned in the section on rail transport, is the most widely used form of intermodal coordination. *Birdyback* service, another form of intermodal coordination, sends motor carriers to pick up a shipment locally and deliver that shipment to local destinations; an air carrier takes it between airports near those locations. *Fishyback* service sets up a similar intermodal coordination system between motor carriers and water carriers.

Intermodal transportation generally gives shippers faster service and lower rates than either mode could match individually because each method carries freight in its most efficient way. However, intermodal arrangements require close coordination between all transportation providers.

Recognizing this need, multimodal transportation companies have formed to offer combined activities within single operations. Piggyback service generally joins two separate companies—a railroad and a trucking company. A multimodal firm provides intermodal service through its own internal transportation resources. Shippers benefit because the single service assumes responsibility from origin to destination. This unification prevents disputes over which carrier delayed or damaged a shipment.

WAREHOUSING

Products flow through two types of warehouses: storage and distribution warehouses. A storage warehouse holds goods for moderate to long periods in an attempt to balance supply and demand for producers and purchasers. For example, Conestoga Cold Storage operates five fully automated controlled-atmosphere—also called *cold storage*—warehouses in Canada. It has a total storage volume of 27 million cubic feet where it stores and consolidates shipments to serve all points in Canada and the United States.[40] In contrast, a distribution warehouse assembles and redistributes goods, keeping them moving as much as possible. Many distribution warehouses or centres physically store goods for less than 24 hours before shipping them to customers.

Logistics managers have attempted to save on transportation costs by developing central distribution centres. A manufacturer might send a single, large, consolidated shipment to a break-bulk centre—a central distribution centre that breaks down large shipments into several smaller ones and delivers them to individual customers in the area. Many Internet retailers use break-bulk distribution centres.

As part of a multi-year expansion program, Caterpillar Logistics Services is building a $65-million parts distribution centre near Dayton, Ohio. The new facility will cover more than 1 million square feet and employ 500 to 600 people. The facility will serve as a convenient inbound receiving centre close to suppliers and provide improved delivery of parts to Caterpillar dealers and customers in Canada and the United States.[41]

Automated Warehouse Technology

Logistics managers can cut distribution costs and improve customer service dramatically by automating their warehouse systems. Although automation technology represents an expensive investment, it can provide major labour savings for high-volume distributors such as grocery chains. A computerized system might store orders, choose the correct number of cases, and move those cases in the desired sequence to loading docks. This kind of warehouse system reduces labour costs, worker injuries, pilferage, fires, and breakage.

Warehouse Locations

Every company must make a major logistics decision when it determines the number and locations of its storage facilities. Two categories of costs influence this choice: (1) warehousing and materials handling costs and (2) delivery costs from warehouses to customers. Large facilities offer economies of scale in facilities and materials handling systems; per-unit costs for these systems decrease as volume increases. Delivery costs, on the other hand, rise as the distance from warehouse to customer increases.

Warehouse location also affects customer service. Businesses must place their storage and distribution facilities in locations from which they can meet customer demands for product availability and delivery times. They must also consider population and employment trends. For example, because of Moncton's central location in the Atlantic region, many firms have established distribution centres in the area. Pratt & Whitney Canada, a designer and manufacturer of aircraft engines, has a distribution centre in Amsterdam, Holland, to serve its customers in Europe, Africa, and the Middle East, and another in Singapore to serve its customers in the Pacific Rim Region.[42]

INVENTORY CONTROL SYSTEMS

Inventory control captures a large share of a logistics manager's attention because companies need to maintain enough inventory to meet customer demand without incurring unneeded costs for carrying excess inventory. Some firms attempt to keep inventory levels under control by implementing just-in-time (JIT) production. Others are beginning to use RFID technology, discussed earlier in this chapter.

Retailers often shift the responsibility—and costs—for inventory from themselves back to individual manufacturers. **Vendor-managed inventory (VMI)** systems like this are based on the assumption that suppliers are in the best position to spot understocks or surpluses, cutting costs along the supply chain that can be translated into lower prices at the checkout. Hubbell Inc., which manufactures electrical products for commercial and industrial customers, found that using a VMI system tightened the procurement cycle and generated cost savings. VMI also enables Hubbell to serve its distribution partners more efficiently, enhancing the supply chain relationship.[43]

vendor-managed inventory (VMI) Inventory management system in which the seller—based on an existing agreement with a buyer—determines how much of a product is needed.

ORDER PROCESSING

Like inventory control, order processing directly affects the firm's ability to meet its customer service standards. A company may have to compensate for inefficiencies in its order processing system by shipping products via costly transportation modes or by maintaining large inventories at many expensive field warehouses.

Order processing typically consists of four major activities: (1) conducting a credit check; (2) keeping a record of the sale, which involves tasks such as crediting a sales representative's commission account; (3) making appropriate accounting entries; and (4) locating orders, shipping them, and adjusting inventory records. A stockout occurs when an order for an item is not available for shipment. A firm's order-processing system must advise affected customers of a stockout and offer a choice of alternative actions.

As in other areas of physical distribution, technological innovations improve efficiency in order processing. Many firms are streamlining their order processing procedures by using email and the Internet, often their least costly fulfillment channel.

materials handling system Set of activities that move production inputs and other goods within plants, warehouses, and transportation terminals.

PROTECTIVE PACKAGING AND MATERIALS HANDLING

Logistics managers arrange and control activities for moving products within plants, warehouses, and transportation terminals, which together compose the **materials handling system**. Two important concepts influence many materials handling choices: unitizing and containerization.

Unitizing combines as many packages as possible into each load that moves within or outside a facility. Logistics managers prefer to handle materials on pallets (platforms, generally made of wood, on which goods are transported). Unitizing systems often lash materials in place with steel bands or shrink packaging. A shrink package surrounds a batch of materials with a sheet of plastic that shrinks after heating, securely holding individual pieces together. Unitizing promotes efficient materials handling because each package requires minimal labour to move. Securing the materials together also minimizes damage and pilferage. Imperial Sugar uses an efficient process in distributing its products as *unitized pallets*—that is, a pallet holding merchandise ready for in-store display. To create these pallets, the company invested in a unitizer, a machine that stacks 495 bags of sugar more quickly—and more exactly—than human hands can. Customers such as Costco receive the pallets and move them directly to the selling floor.[44]

Marketoid

Vancouver is Canada's largest port, handling more than $75 billion in goods annually with more than 160 trading economies. Its economic impact includes 129 500 jobs, $6.1 billion in wages, $10.5 billion in GDP, and $22 billion in economic output.

containerization
Process of combining several unitized loads into a single, well-protected load for shipment.

Logistics managers extend the same concept through **containerization**—combining several unitized loads. A container of oil rig parts, for example, can be loaded in Alberta and trucked or shipped by rail to Vancouver, and then loaded on a ship headed to Saudi Arabia.

In addition to the benefits outlined for unitizing, containerization also markedly reduces the time required to load and unload ships. Containers limit in-transit damage to freight because individual packages pass through few handling systems en route to purchasers.

assessment check 8

8.1 What are the benefits of intermodal transportation?

8.2 Identify the two types of warehouses and explain their function.

Strategic Implications

Several factors, including the burgeoning e-commerce environment, are driving changes in channel development, logistics, and supply-chain management. As the Internet continues to revolutionize the ways manufacturers deliver goods to ultimate consumers, marketers must find ways to promote cooperation among existing dealer, retailer, and distributor networks while harnessing the power of the Web as an alternative channel. This system demands not only delivery of goods and services faster and more efficiently than ever before but also superior service to Web-based customers.

In addition, increased product proliferation—grocery stores typically stock almost 50 000 different items—demands logistics systems that can manage many brands delivered through many channels worldwide. Those channels must be finely tuned to identify and rapidly rectify problems such as retail shortfalls or costly overstocks. The trend toward leaner retailing, in which the burden of merchandise tracking and inventory control is switching from retailers to manufacturers, means that to be effective, logistics and supply chain systems must result in cost savings. ◆◆◆

REVIEW OF CHAPTER OBJECTIVES

① **Describe the types of marketing channels and the roles they play in marketing strategy.**

Marketing (distribution) channels are the systems of marketing institutions that enhance the physical flow of goods and services, along with ownership title, from producer to consumer or business user. In other words, they help bridge the gap between producer or manufacturer and business customer or consumer. Types of channels include direct selling, selling through intermediaries, dual distribution, and reverse channels. Channels perform four functions: facilitating the exchange process, sorting, standardizing exchange processes, and facilitating searches by buyers and sellers.

② **Outline the major channel strategy decisions.**

Decisions include selecting a marketing channel and determining distribution intensity. Selection of a marketing channel may be based on market factors, product factors, organizational factors, or competitive factors. Distribution may be intensive, selective, or exclusive.

③ **Describe the concepts of channel management, conflict, and cooperation.**

Manufacturers must practise channel management by developing and maintaining relationships with the intermediaries in their marketing channels. The channel captain is the dominant member of the channel. Horizontal and vertical conflict can arise when there is disagreement among channel members. Cooperation is best achieved when all channel members regard themselves as equal components of the same organization.

④ **Identify and describe the different vertical marketing systems.**

A vertical marketing system (VMS) is a planned channel system designed to improve distribution efficiency and cost effectiveness by integrating various functions throughout the distribution chain. This coordination may be achieved by forward integration or backward integration. Options include a corporate marketing system, operated by a single owner; an administered marketing system, run by a dominant channel member; and a contractual marketing system, based on formal agreements among channel members.

⑤ Explain the roles of logistics and supply-chain management in an overall distribution strategy.

Effective logistics requires proper supply-chain management. The supply chain begins with raw materials, proceeds through actual production, and then continues with the movement of finished products through the marketing channel to customers. Supply-chain management takes place in two directions: upstream and downstream. Tools that marketers use to streamline and manage logistics include radio frequency identification (RFID), enterprise resource planning (ERP), and logistical cost control.

⑥ Identify the major components of a physical distribution system.

Physical distribution involves a broad range of activities concerned with efficient movement of finished goods from the end of the production line to the consumer. As a system, physical distribution consists of six elements: (1) customer service, (2) transportation, (3) inventory control, (4) materials handling and protective packaging, (5) order processing, and (6) warehousing. These elements are interrelated and must be balanced to create a smoothly functioning distribution system and to avoid suboptimization.

⑦ Compare the major modes of transportation.

The five major modes of transport are railroads, motor carriers, water freight, pipelines, and air freight. Railroads rank high on flexibility in handling products; average on speed, dependability in meeting schedules, and cost; and low on frequency of shipments. Motor carriers are relatively high in cost but rank high on speed, dependability, shipment frequency, and availability in different locations. Water carriers balance their slow speed, low shipment frequency, and limited availability with lower costs. The special nature of pipelines makes them rank relatively low on availability, flexibility, and speed, but they are also low in cost. Air transportation is high in cost but offers very fast and dependable delivery schedules.

⑧ Discuss the role of transportation intermediaries, combined transportation modes, and warehousing in improving physical distribution.

Transportation intermediaries facilitate movement of goods in a variety of ways, including piggyback, birdyback, and fishyback services—all forms of intermodal coordination. Methods such as unitization and containerization facilitate intermodal transfers.

assessment check answers

1.1 Distinguish between a marketing channel and logistics.
A marketing channel is an organized system of marketing institutions and their interrelationships designed to enhance the flow and ownership of goods and services from producer to user. Logistics is the actual process of coordinating the flow of information, goods, and services among members of the marketing channel.

1.2 What are the different types of marketing channels?
The different types of marketing channels are direct selling, selling through intermediaries, dual distribution, and reverse channels.

1.3 What four functions do marketing channels perform?
The four functions of marketing channels are (1) facilitating the exchange process by reducing the number of marketplace contacts necessary for a sale; (2) sorting; (3) standardizing exchange transactions; and (4) facilitating searches by buyers and sellers.

2.1 Identify four major factors in selecting a marketing channel.
The four major factors in selecting a marketing channel are market, product, organizational, and competitive.

2.2 Describe the three general categories of distribution intensity.
Intensive distribution seeks to distribute a product through all available channels in a trade area. Selective distribution chooses a limited number of retailers in a market area. Exclusive distribution grants exclusive rights to a wholesaler or retailer to sell a manufacturer's products.

3.1 What is a channel captain? What is its role in channel cooperation?
A channel captain is the dominant member of the marketing channel. Its role in channel cooperation is to provide the necessary leadership.

3.2 Identify and describe the three types of channel conflict.
Horizontal conflict results from disagreements among channel members at the same level. Vertical conflict occurs when channel members at different levels disagree. The grey market causes conflict because it involves competition in the Canadian market of brands produced by overseas affiliates.

4.1 What are vertical marketing systems (VMSs)? Identify the major types.

Vertical marketing systems are planned channel systems designed to improve the effectiveness of distribution, including efficiency and cost. The three major types are corporate, administered, and contractual.

4.2 Identify the three types of contractual marketing systems.

The three types of contractual systems are wholesale-sponsored voluntary chains, retail cooperatives, and franchises.

5.1 What is upstream management? What is downstream management?

Upstream management involves managing raw materials, inbound logistics, and warehouse and storage facilities. Downstream management involves managing finished product storage, outbound logistics, marketing and sales, and customer service.

5.2 Identify three methods for managing logistics.

Methods for managing logistics include RFID technology, enterprise resource planning (ERP) systems, and logistical cost control.

6.1 What are the six major elements of physical distribution?

The major elements of physical distribution are customer service, transportation, inventory control, materials handling and protective packaging, order processing, and warehousing.

6.2 What is suboptimization?

Suboptimization occurs when managers of individual functions try to reduce costs but create less than optimal results.

7.1 Identify the five major modes of transport.

The five major modes of transport are railroads, motor carriers, water carriers, pipelines, and air freight.

7.2 Which mode of transport is currently experiencing a resurgence, and why?

Railroad transport is currently experiencing a resurgence because of the cost of fuel and its efficiency in transporting large amounts of freight for less fuel.

8.1 What are the benefits of intermodal transportation?

Intermodal transportation usually provides shippers faster service and lower rates than a single mode could offer.

8.2 Identify the two types of warehouses and explain their function.

The two types of warehouses are storage and distribution. Storage warehouses hold goods for moderate to long periods of time in order to balance supply and demand. Distribution warehouses assemble and redistribute goods as quickly as possible.

MARKETING TERMS YOU NEED TO KNOW

These terms are printed in red in the text. They are defined in the margins of the chapter and in the Glossary that begins on p. G-1.

distribution 326
marketing (distribution) channel 326
logistics 326
supply-chain management 326
physical distribution 326
marketing intermediary (middleman) 327
wholesaler 327
direct channel 328
direct selling 328
manufacturers' representative 331
dual distribution 331
reverse channel 331
intensive distribution 334
selective distribution 334
exclusive distribution 334

closed sales territory 335
tying agreement 335
channel captain 336
grey goods 337
vertical marketing system (VMS) 338
forward integration 338
backward integration 338
corporate marketing system 338
administered marketing system 338
contractual marketing system 338
retail cooperative 339
franchise 339
supply chain 340
upstream management 341
downstream management 341

radio frequency identification (RFID) 341
enterprise resource planning (ERP) system 342
third-party (contract) logistics firm 343
suboptimization 344
common carriers 345
contract carriers 345
private carriers 345
intermodal operations 346
vendor-managed inventory 351
materials handling system 351
vendor-managed inventory 352
materials handling system 352
containerization 352

PROJECTS AND TEAMWORK EXERCISES

1. The traditional channel for consumer goods runs from producer to wholesaler to retailer to user. With a classmate, select a product from the following list (or choose one of your own) and create a chart that traces its distribution system. You may go online to the firm's website for additional information.
   a. a kayak from the Mountain Equipment Co-op website or catalogue
   b. a ticket to a Blue Jays baseball game
   c. automotive GPS systems

2. On your own or with a classmate, identify, draw, and explain a reverse channel with which you are familiar. What purpose does this reverse channel serve to businesses? To the community? To consumers?

3. With a classmate, choose a product you think would sell best through a direct channel. Then create a brief sales presentation for your product and present it to class. Ask for feedback.

4. With a classmate, choose one of the franchises listed in Table 13.2 (on page 406) or another franchise that interests

you. Visit the website of the company to learn more about how its goods and services are distributed. Create a chart outlining the firm's physical distribution system.

5. It takes a lot to move an elaborate stage performance like Cirque du Soleil, Big Apple Circus, or a rock band from one location to another while it is on tour. With a classmate, choose a touring performance that interests you—a music group, a circus, a theatre performance, a NASCAR race, or the like—and imagine you are in charge of logistics. Create a chart showing what modes of transportation you would select to move the performance, how you would warehouse certain items during downtime, and what methods you would use to control costs.

CRITICAL-THINKING EXERCISES

1. Imagine a vending machine that would charge more for hot drinks—coffee, tea, and cocoa—during cold weather. What is your opinion of a temperature-sensitive vending machine? Consumers who live in colder climates might pay more over a longer time period each year than consumers who live in warmer climates. Would your opinion change if alternatives were nearby, say, a convenience store or a vending machine that is not temperature sensitive? Do you think such a machine would be successful? Why or why not?

2. Auto dealerships often have exclusive distribution rights in their local markets. How might this affect the purchase choices consumers make? What problems might a dealership encounter with this type of distribution?

3. Choose one of the following firms and identify which marketing channel or channels you think would be best for its goods or services. Then explain the market factors, product factors, and organizational and competitive factors contributing to your selection.

a. Chapters
b. The Keg restaurant
c. *Canadian Business* magazine
d. Canada's Wonderland
e. lululemon

4. In their most basic form, RFID tags track the progress of products from warehouse to retail shelf to checkout counter. But they have great potential to provide marketers with more information about consumers' purchase patterns. In what ways might RFID technology be used to serve customers better? What problems might arise?

5. After a trip to India, where you were inspired by the craftsmanship of artisans who make jewellery and artifacts, you decide to establish an import business focusing on their work. How would you determine distribution intensity for your business? What mode (or modes) of transportation would you use to get the goods to Canada? How and where would you warehouse the goods? Explain your answers.

ETHICS EXERCISE

1. As more and more firms do business globally, transporting goods from one part of the world to another, there has been a surge in piracy—criminals making off with cargo shipments filled with everything from component parts to finished goods. A tractor-trailer loaded with electronics might be stolen from a truck stop; a warehouse stacked with pallets of new clothing, TVs, or just about anything else might be susceptible to theft. Large, sophisticated cargo theft gangs have been identified by law enforcement authorities in Halifax, Montreal, Toronto, and Vancouver. However, members of the supply chain can work together to close the net around would-be thieves, developing stronger relationships with each other and law enforcement.[45] What steps might manufacturers take to achieve the kind of channel cooperation that could reduce or prevent cargo theft?

2. How might transportation firms use security measures to build trust with customers and strengthen their position in the marketplace?

INTERNET EXERCISES

1. **Packaging.** Companies use packaging to assist in the marketing of their products. Visit each of the following websites and prepare a brief report on how each company has used packaging as part of its brand management strategy.
a. H.J. Heinz: **www.heinz.com**
b. Campbell Soup: **www.campbellsoup.ca**
c. Yoplait yogurt: **www.yoplait.ca**

2. **Vendor-managed inventory.** Visit the following website to learn more about vendor-managed inventory (**www.vendormanagedinventory.com**). Review the definition of vendor-managed inventory, how a vendor-managed inventory program should be set up, the benefits of vendor-managed inventory, and some of the problems with a vendor-managed inventory system. Prepare a brief oral report on the subject that you can present to your class.

3. **RFID developments.** Go to the website of *RFID Journal* (**www.rfidjournal.com**). Review the material and prepare a report outlining some of the more significant developments in RFID technology.

Note: Internet Web addresses change frequently. If you don't find the exact sites listed, you may need to access the organization's home page and search from there or use a search engine such as Google.

CASE 11.1

Heavy Metal at Hyundai

Shipping is a major mode of transportation in the physical distribution of many products, including oil, cars, electronics, and bathroom tiles. Shipping is a complex industry with few players willing to take on the risks associated with building expensive new ships, handling potential environmental disasters, and negotiating through a complicated array of international regulations. Despite these risks, shipbuilding itself is enjoying a recent boom. The upturn is due to the phase-out of single-hull ships (replaced by new, double-hull vessels), the upswing of China's economy that fuels more trade between Asia and North America, and the increasing demand for oil from developing countries.

The largest player in the global shipbuilding industry is Korea's Hyundai Heavy Industries, followed by Daewoo and Samsung. Not surprisingly, the world's largest shipyard also belongs to Hyundai. Built more than three decades ago, the yard now runs so efficiently that it can turn out a new $80-million vessel every four days of operation. Despite the firm's current prowess, Hyundai engineers continue to develop plans for even larger, more complex ships. On the drawing board is a supervessel that could carry as many as 10 000 steel containers—or 30 million pairs of sneakers.

Why doesn't the firm feel comfortable with its first-place position? China has been outspoken about its intent to become the leading shipbuilder in the world by 2015. China already puts pressure on leaders in other industries, including North American manufacturers of numerous products. With its large workforce and lower wages, China is poised to take on just about any industry it wants. So Hyundai executives continually develop new strategies for improving or enhancing their products as they develop new ones. As the old ore carriers and oil tankers are phased out of the shipping market in general, Hyundai looks for ways to build the enormous container ships. But—just like an auto manufacturer—marketers also seek ways to "load" them with expensive features. "We obviously want the more value-added-type vessel—[liquid natural gas] carriers, more complicated container vessels, ice-glass carriers," explains Han Dae Yoon, chief marketing officer of Hyundai's shipbuilding division. "Shipbuilders have to be selective." By focusing on the higher end of the market—letting Chinese shipbuilders take contracts for simple tankers and bulk carriers—Hyundai keeps itself out front. "Now the South Koreans are moving more toward the Lexus end in order to have an edge over the Chinese," notes Peter E. Bartholomew of Industrial Research and Consulting.

China's exploding economy has also created another potential challenge for Hyundai—a shortage of some building materials such as steel, which can make up 20 percent of the material on one ship. This shortage caused the price of steel plate to jump 70 percent in one year, contributing to a $30-million loss by the firm in one quarter. But Hyundai is still ahead of its competition, perhaps because its leaders take nothing for granted. Even with Hyundai's nine dry docks booked solidly with contracts for 102 ships worth a total of more than $8 billion, no one at Hyundai rests. "When you are being chased, you have to do something that the chaser cannot do," says Han Dae Yoon. That means building bigger, better ships—faster.

Questions for Critical Thinking

1. With what types of intermediaries do you think Hyundai must maintain relationships?
2. Describe ways in which Hyundai can manage its supply chain effectively.
3. What role does Hyundai play in the global marketplace?

Souces: James Brooke, "Korean Shipbuilders See China's Shadow," *Seoul Times*, May 20, 2006, http://theseoultimes.com; Moon Ihlwan, "Korea's Shipbuilding Industry Sails Ahead," *BusinessWeek*, May 12, 2006, http://www.businessweek.com; Hyundai Heavy Industries website, http://english.hhi.co.kr, May 8, 2006.

CASE 11.2

Walmart Canada: Managing a Complex Supply Chain

Walmart has developed one of the best supply chains in the world. It had no choice. With more than 8700 facilities in 15 countries, including China and India, and revenues that exceed $400 billion, supply-chain problems are experienced to a greater extent by Walmart than by most of its competitors. This provides motivation for Walmart to seek the best supply-chain management solutions it can find, and everyone else watches Walmart to see what innovative solutions it will develop. Indeed, Walmart has been leading the world in a number of supply-chain management initiatives: it was an early adopter of UPC bar codes, a driver of electronic data interchange (EDI) systems, and has, in recent years, been promoting the use of radio frequency identification (RFID) technology. One of its best known innovations is its development of cross-docking, a system where goods get trucked to Walmart distribution centres, get unloaded, and, literally, cross the dock, only to be loaded on trucks about to leave for retail stores across Canada. These goods are never held in storage.

While many supply-chain issues are important system-wide, Walmart must sometimes develop supply-chain management solutions that are unique to specific areas where it operates. In Canada, Walmart today faces some unique and urgent challenges. One of its greatest current threats is the impending entry of Target to the Canadian marketplace. Target intends to open up to 150 stores in Canada beginning in 2013. Research suggests that among all Canadian retailers, Walmart has the most to lose when Target enters Canada. In preparation for Target's entry, Walmart has aggressively expanded its supercentre concept across the country. Since its first supercentre in Canada opened in Ontario in 2006, Walmart has opened supercentres in British Columbia, Alberta, and Saskatchewan. By 2012, Walmart plans to expand from 124 to 164 supercentres, expanding the concept to Manitoba and Quebec, with projects that represent nearly a half-billion-dollar investment.

The supercentre format includes groceries in addition to the products sold in Walmart's more traditional store formats. But a major category that customers want when buying groceries is fresh produce. Walmart has been playing catch-up with its Canadian competitors but now is moving fresh produce from its warehouse to store locations in one day, instead of the two to three days that were required previously. The improved speed to shelf has reduced by 25 percent the amount of produce that Walmart has had to throw out as spoilage. To achieve the increased shipping efficiency, Walmart has dropped an entire step in its produce-handling process. Suppliers now ship directly to Walmart's warehouse on pallets that are ready to be redirected to retail locations without additional handling. The company's Ontario operations are expected to be a model for other Walmart operations across Canada.

To support its 104 company stores from Manitoba to British Columbia, Walmart recently opened a $115-million fresh-food distribution centre in Balzac, Alberta. The state-of-the-art, 400 000-square-foot building is one of Canada's largest refrigerated buildings. The distribution centre uses hydrogen fuel cells and solar, thermal, and wind power, and many additional sustainability features that are expected to save about $4.8 million in energy costs over five years. It will employ about 600 people and will be operated by Supply Chain Management, one of Canada's largest third-party logistics providers, based in Mississauga, Ontario.

While this distribution centre will service its stores in western Canada, Quebec will present its own problems for Walmart, not the least of which will be operating in an environment where more than half of the supermarket workers in the province are unionized, compared to less than 40 percent across Canada. At the same time that Walmart is introducing its supercentre format to Quebec, Sobeys Quebec, a major competitor, has begun construction of a 500 000-square-foot automated distribution centre to service its IGA stores there. Jean-Claude Dufour, a professor at Université Laval and an expert in food distribution, believes Walmart will have difficulty building a local supply network to compete in the province. In all provinces except Quebec, the grocery business is controlled by large retail chains; however, in Quebec, more than 60 percent of grocery sales go through independent retailers who are adept at managing relationships with local produce suppliers. For Walmart to meet its global sustainability pledge to source 30 percent of fresh produce locally will be challenging. Walmart has been studying Quebec consumers very carefully, however, and has already learned from some of its competitors' mistakes. Quebec consumers are not as price-sensitive for certain products as consumers in other provinces, and they expect a greater variety of cheeses and locally made brands of chocolate.

While Walmart continually tries to improve its supply chain, its supply-chain partners also contribute improvements, and Walmart Canada works very closely with them. Solutions 2 Go, for example, handles Canadian distribution for nearly every video-game publisher in North America. The company convinced Walmart Canada to implement a "value program" that involved better merchandising of budget games, installing new display cases and racks to better serve Walmart shoppers. Sales increased by 50 percent in the category and resulted in Walmart putting this third-party merchandiser in charge of merchandising game accessories at all Walmart Canada stores. Walmart also works closely with the many transport carriers that help move inventory to and from the various Walmart locations. In 2011, Walmart Canada held its second annual carrier awards dinner. Among the awards presented were Carrier of the Year and Inbound Carrier of the Year (Interstate Freight Systems of Brampton, Ontario), Store Delivery Carrier of the Year (Erb Transport of New Hamburg, Ontario), Strive for Excellence Award (H&R Transport of Lethbridge, Alberta), and Innovative Carrier of the Year (Bison Transport of Winnipeg, Manitoba). These awards help recognize the importance that transportation carriers play in establishing and maintaining a superior supply chain.

As it constantly strives to improve its supply chain to lower inventory and operating costs, and to provide better service and selection for its customers, Walmart Canada continues to be a dominant force in an increasingly competitive industry.

Questions for Critical Thinking

1. Identify some potential conflict issues that could arise within Walmart Canada's supply chain. How can Walmart Canada best manage these issues? Explain.
2. Identify two types of third-party logistics providers used by Walmart Canada. Why does Walmart Canada make use of third-party logistics providers?
3. What supply-chain management activities, aside from the ones mentioned, must Walmart Canada also manage?

Sources: Hollie Shaw, "Walmart, Canadian Tire Falling in Target's Crosshairs," *Star-Phoenix* (Saskatoon), July 9, 2011; "Walmart To Take Over Zellers Sites," *Gazette* (Montreal), June 25, 2011, p. C3; "Walmart Awards Top Canadian Carriers," *Truck News*, March 2011, p. 54; Mark Cardwell, "Le Supercentre," *Canadian Grocer*, March 2011, pp. 10–11; Hollie Shaw, "Walmart Counters Target With Supercentre Rollout; New Stores To Offer Food Along With Fashion," *Calgary Herald*, January 27, 2011, p. C6; Allison Lampert, "Walmart Targets Grocery Buyers: Expands Presence as Competitor Looms," *Gazette* (Montreal), January 27, 2011, p. 1; Marina Strauss, "Walmart Takes a Bite Out of Food Costs," *The Globe and Mail*, November 17, 2010, p. 5; Mario Toneguzzi, "Walmart Showcases Innovative Food Warehouse Near Balzac," *Calgary Herald*, November 11, 2010, p. C3; Eleanor Beaton, "Birth of a Giant," *Profit*, November 2010, pp. 48–49.

chapter 12

Retailers, Wholesalers, and Direct Marketers

CHAPTER OBJECTIVES

1. Explain the wheel of retailing.

2. Discuss how retailers select target markets.

3. Show how the elements of the marketing mix apply to retailing strategy.

4. Explain the concepts of retail convergence and scrambled merchandising.

5. Identify the functions performed by wholesaling intermediaries.

6. Outline the major types of independent wholesaling intermediaries and the appropriate situations for using each.

7. Compare the basic types of direct marketing and nonstore retailing.

8. Describe how the Internet has altered the wholesaling, retailing, and direct marketing environments.

TILLEY ENDURABLES: THE COMPANY A HAT BUILT

What is water-repellent, mildew-proof, machine-washable, guaranteed for life, insured against loss or theft (50 percent deductible), and comes with an owner's manual printed in seven languages, floats in water, blocks UV rays, and is made from preshrunk 10-ounce cotton duck? That's easy: it's the original Tilley hat, a simple product that helped launch a major Canadian retailer.

It all started in 1980 after Alex Tilley, an avid sailor, became frustrated with sailing hats that blew off his head when sailing and then either sank before they could be retrieved or shrank after getting wet. He decided to oversee the building of a better hat. He soon had some prototypes he was comfortable attaching his name to and began selling them from his home in suburban Toronto. To build sales, Alex tried advertising. His first ads appeared in *Gam*, a Canadian sailing magazine, and he paid for them with some Tilley hats. He sent a Tilley hat to the editor of *Yachting* and was fortunate to get a one-third-page editorial. Within a year, he was selling Tilley hats at boat shows across North America, sometimes in the hundreds.

Next Alex decided to add a second product: Tilley shorts. Again, the focus was on quality. Lockstitches were used, and all the stress points were bar-tacked. The seat was double-layered so that any friction would be between the two layers and not between the cloth and a boat deck. These too were guaranteed for life, but they were priced at a 50 percent premium over competitors' products. Sales were disappointing and Alex eventually decided that it was "time to drop [his] shorts." Fortunately, Canada had a team in the 1983 America's Cup races, and Alex decided to present the team with complimentary hats and shorts. Word spread quickly, and at the Annapolis Sailboat Show that fall people began to ask for the shorts. They also asked for pants, not for sailing but for travelling, again requesting the same quality.

What does Tilley Endurables sell today? The company's product line expansion has been phenomenal. From the original Tilley hat, Tilley Endurables now offers more than 50 models of hats—for summer and winter, in various colours and materials. There is a full range of travel and adventure clothing, including shorts, pants, shirts, jackets, dresses, and all types of travel accessories—all of superior quality. Nearly everything Tilley Endurables sells is made in Canada where, Alex says, "we can keep an eye on it." Exceptions include a water bottle made in Washington, and "the world's best socks," made to Alex's "unholey" specifications.

From its humble beginning through home sales and its expansion into a mail-order business in 1984, the company has now established an online store (www.tilley.ca) and six retail locations: two in Toronto—including the company's flagship store—and one each in Montreal, Brossard (Montreal), Mississauga, and Vancouver. Tilley products can be purchased through one of several hundred retailers across Canada. Outside Canada, Tilley products are available from more than 2600 retailers.

What has been responsible for Tilley's success? Referring to everything Tilley Endurables sells, Alex says, "We make the best in the world. Then we make it better!" How does Alex want to be remembered? He says, "I would like my epitaph to be 'A good man who built a better hat.'"[1]

connecting with customers

How does Tilley Endurables connect with its customers? Obviously, product quality is the foundation. But providing value-added information and services for travellers and adventurers on its website also helps: how to protect against pickpockets, how to pack "smart," tips for travelling by plane, how and where to research information on destinations, and much more. Visitors can view an online catalogue or request a printed version. Alex Tilley has travelled to more than a thousand cities in more than 50 countries wear-testing and researching potential products for Tilley Endurables. His favourite country: Guatemala. His favourite people to visit: the Balinese, the Bhutanese, and the people of Newfoundland and Labrador.

Chapter Overview

IN exploring how today's retailing sector operates, this chapter introduces many examples that explain the combination of activities involved in selling goods to ultimate consumers. Then the chapter discusses the role of wholesalers and other intermediaries who deliver goods from the manufacturers into the hands of retailers or other intermediaries. Finally, the chapter looks at nonstore retailing. Direct marketing, a channel consisting of direct communication to consumers or business users, is a major form of nonstore retailing. It includes not just direct mail and telemarketing but also direct-response advertising, infomercials, and Internet marketing. The chapter concludes by looking at a less pervasive but growing aspect of nonstore retailing—automatic merchandising. ◆◆◆

---

① **Explain the wheel of retailing.**

retailing
Activities involved in selling merchandise to ultimate consumers.

Marketoid

Canadian annual retail sales exceed $450 billion, but wholesale sales were $685 billion.

wheel of retailing
Hypothesis that each new type of retailer gains a competitive foothold by offering lower prices than current outlets charge; the result of reducing or eliminating services.

RETAILING

Retailers are the marketing intermediaries who are in direct contact with ultimate consumers. **Retailing** describes the activities involved in selling merchandise to these consumers. Retail outlets serve as contact points between channel members and ultimate consumers. In a very real sense, retailers represent the distribution channel to most consumers since a typical shopper has little contact with manufacturers and virtually no contact with wholesaling intermediaries. Retailers determine locations, store hours, number of sales personnel, store layouts, merchandise selections, and return policies— factors that often influence the consumers' images of the offerings more strongly than consumers' images of the products themselves. Both large and small retailers perform the major channel activities: creating time, place, and ownership utilities.

Retailers act as both customers and marketers in their channels. They sell products to ultimate consumers, and at the same time, they buy from wholesalers and manufacturers. Because of their critical location in the marketing channel, retailers often perform a vital feedback role. They obtain information from customers and transmit that information to manufacturers and other channel members.

EVOLUTION OF RETAILING

The development of retailing illustrates the marketing concept in operation. Early retailing in North America can be traced to the establishment of trading posts, such as the Hudson's Bay Company, and to pack peddlers who carried their wares to outlying settlements. The first type of retail institution, the general store, stocked a wide range of merchandise that met the needs of an isolated community or rural area. Supermarkets appeared in the early 1930s in response to consumers' desire for lower prices. In the 1950s, discount stores delivered lower prices in exchange for reduced services. The emergence of convenience food stores in the 1960s satisfied consumer demand for fast service, convenient locations, and expanded hours of operation. The development of off-price retailers in the 1980s and 1990s reflected consumer demand for brand-name merchandise at prices considerably lower than those of traditional retailers. In recent years, Internet-enabled retailing has increased in influence and importance.

A key concept, known as the **wheel of retailing**, attempts to explain the patterns of change in retailing. According to the wheel of retailing, a new type of retailer gains a competitive foothold by offering customers lower prices than current outlets charge and maintains profits by reducing or eliminating services. Once established, however, the innovator begins to add more services, and its prices gradually rise. It then becomes vulnerable to new low-price retailers that enter with minimum services—and so the wheel turns, as illustrated in Figure 12.1. The Canadian retail graveyard is littered with former giants such as Eaton's, Woolco, Kmart, and catalogue retailer Consumers Distributing.

Many major developments in the history of retailing appear to fit the wheel's pattern. Early department stores, chain stores, supermarkets, discount stores, hypermarkets, and catalogue retailers all emphasized limited service and low prices. Most of these retailers gradually increased prices as they added services.

Some exceptions disrupt this pattern, however. Suburban shopping centres, convenience food stores, and vending machines never built their appeals around low prices. Still, the wheel pattern has been a good indicator enough times in the past to make it an accurate indicator of future retailing developments.

The wheel of retailing suggests that retailing is always changing. From Walmart's beginnings in the 1960s, founder Sam Walton held mandatory weekly Saturday morning meetings for Walmart executives. It was at these legendary assemblies that managers planned strategy, debated business philosophy, and built competitive advantage—in short, where the company culture was formed. Today, those meetings convene monthly, not weekly. Why the change? Some observers speculate the meetings no longer served their purpose. Whatever the reason, Walmart's change from weekly to monthly Saturday morning meetings signals the end of an era.[2]

figure 12.1

Wheel of Retailing

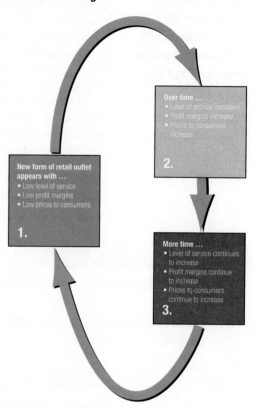

assessment check 1

1.1 What is retailing?

1.2 Explain the wheel-of-retailing concept.

RETAILING STRATEGY

Like manufacturers and wholesalers, a retailer develops a marketing strategy based on the firm's goals and strategic plans. The organization monitors environmental influences and assesses its own strengths and weaknesses in identifying marketing opportunities and constraints. A retailer bases its key decisions on two fundamental steps in the marketing strategy process: (1) selecting a target market and (2) developing a retailing mix to satisfy the chosen market. The retailing mix specifies merchandise strategy, customer-service standards, pricing guidelines, target market analysis, promotion goals, location/distribution decisions, and store atmosphere choices. The combination of these elements projects a desired retail image. Retail image communicates the store's identity to consumers. As Figure 12.2 points out, components of retailing strategy must work together to create a consistent image that appeals to the store's target market.

Kia Canada recently set new retail image standards for all of its 168 dealerships across Canada, hoping to reach aggressive new sales targets. President William Lee acknowledged the growing importance of dealers and that the company would be focusing on quality, sustainability, and consistency as criteria. The new retail strategy appears to be working as the company recently established a new best one-month sales record: nearly 7000 vehicles sold across Canada, a 34 percent increase over the same month from the previous year.[3]

SELECTING A TARGET MARKET

A retailer starts to define its strategy by selecting a target market. Factors that influence the retailer's selection are the size and profit potential of the market and the level of competition for its business. Retailers pore over demographic, geographic, and psychographic profiles to segment markets. In the end, most retailers identify their target markets by certain demographics.

(2) **Discuss how retailers select target markets.**

figure 12.2

Components of Retail Strategy

The importance of identifying and targeting the right market is dramatically illustrated by the erosion of department store retailing. While mall anchor stores struggle to attract customers, stand-alone store Target makes a memorable splash with edgy advertising that incorporates its signature red doughnut-shaped logo in imaginative ways. And although Target can be categorized as a discount retailer, it has differentiated itself from competitors such as Walmart by offering trendy, quality merchandise at low prices. Target has announced the locations for its first 105 Canadian stores, which will begin opening in 2013. More than 30 000 Canadians already have Target credit cards, testimony to its popularity among cross-border shoppers from Canada.[4]

Deep-discount retailers, such as Dollarama and Buck-or-Two, originally targeted lower-income bargain hunters. They had less glamorous, but high-traffic, locations. Low-price merchandise was crammed into narrow, cluttered aisles. Customers were attracted by many cents-off basics, such as shampoo, cereal, and laundry detergent, and sometimes picked up higher-margin goods as they approached the checkout. Increasingly, these retailers are appearing in more upscale locations, including shopping malls. They are improving the attractiveness of their stores and their product assortment to target more upper-middle-class consumers who are increasingly shopping for the bargains they offer.

By creating stores with wide aisles and clean presentation and offering friendly service and high-end product lines such as Laura Ashley paints, home improvement chain Lowe's competes with arch rivals Home Depot and Rona. Lowe's ambiance helps make the store more appealing to female shoppers, who account for half of all home improvement store customers.[5]

After identifying a target market, a retailer must then develop marketing strategies to attract these chosen customers to its stores or website. The following sections discuss tactics for implementing different strategies.

assessment check 2 ✓

2.1 How does a retailer develop a marketing strategy?

2.2 How do retailers select target markets?

③ Show how the elements of the marketing mix apply to retailing strategy.

MERCHANDISING STRATEGY

A retailer's merchandising strategy guides decisions regarding the items it will offer. A retailer must decide on general merchandise categories, product lines, specific items within lines, and the depth and width of its assortments. Joe Fresh, a brand of clothing introduced by Loblaws in 2006 and sold through Loblaws stores, has rapidly expanded its product line so that, by 2011, Loblaws launched Joe Fresh Stand Alone, opening stand-alone stores in Canada and the United States where it can show off its stylish, well-priced clothing and accessories.[6]

To develop a successful merchandise mix, a retailer must weigh several priorities. First, it must consider the preferences and needs of its previously defined target market, keeping in mind that the competitive environment influences these choices. The retailer must also consider the overall profitability of each product line and product category.

Category Management

As mentioned in Chapter 10, a popular merchandising strategy is *category management,* in which a category manager oversees an entire product line for both vendors and retailers and is responsible for the profitability of the product group. Category management seeks to improve the retailer's product category performance through more coordinated buying, merchandising, and pricing. Rather than focusing on the performance of individual brands, such as Flex shampoo or Kleenex tissue, category management

Stoney Creek Furniture—Canada's largest furniture showroom—has a very broad and a very deep product assortment: something for everyone.

evaluates performance according to each product category. Laundry detergent, skin-care products, and paper goods, for example, are each viewed as individual profit centres, and different category managers supervise each group. Those that underperform are at risk of being dropped from inventory, regardless of the strength of individual brands. To improve their profitability, for example, some department stores have narrowed their traditionally broad product categories to eliminate high-overhead, low-profit lines such as toys, appliances, and furniture.

The Battle for Shelf Space

As discussed in Chapter 11, large-scale retailers are increasingly taking on the role of channel captain within many distribution networks. Some have assumed traditional wholesaling functions, while others dictate product design and specifications to manufacturers. The result is a shift in power from the manufacturers of top-selling brands to the retailer that makes them available to customers.

Adding to the pressure is the increase in the number of new products and variations on existing products. To identify the varying items within a product line, retailers refer to a specific product offering as a **stockkeeping unit (SKU)**. Within the skin-care category, for example, each facial cream, body moisturizer, and sunscreen in each of a variety of sizes and formulations is a separate SKU. The proliferation of new SKUs has resulted in a fierce battle for space on store shelves.

H.F. (HERB) MACKENZIE

Shelf space is important if you want to be noticed: if you're not on the shelf, you can't be chosen when the consumer makes his or her choice.

stockkeeping unit (SKU) Offering within a product line such as a specific size of liquid detergent.

Help Save the Planet and Get Bamboozled

CANADIAN retailers are adding "green" products to their shelves and, not surprisingly, sales are beginning to increase. Two problems that many green products face, however, are price and persuading customers that they perform at least as well as their conventional alternatives.

Some of the latest green products are manufactured wholly or in part from bamboo, and while they may not always solve the first problem, price, they frequently outperform existing products. Bamboo is the fastest-growing plant in the world—some species as fast as 1.5 metres per day. Bamboo forests release 35 percent more oxygen into the atmosphere than equivalent forests. The "woody" plant combines strength with versatility, making it possible to manufacture flooring, tile, countertops, kitchen cabinets, bathroom vanities, and, once it is pulped and spun, one of the world's softest yarns. From this yarn, manufacturers are making goods as varied as diapers, panties, and boxer briefs; sweaters and T-shirts; and even suits, bath towels, and bedroom linens.

Bamboo products are beginning to appear at many Canadian retailers, large and small. You can find bamboo in OhSoSoft towels and linens at Beddazzle Bedroom and Bathroom Studio in Tecumseh, Ontario; sweaters at Laura Canada; the oqoqo line at lululemon; and at online retailer Bamboo Clothes.ca. Canadian designers Arnold Brandt (men's wear) and Linda Lundström (women's wear) are now using bamboo in some fabrics. Even babies—who have had a bum wrap for centuries—now have bamboo diapers. Bamboo is especially suited for diapers: it is 60 percent more absorbent than cotton and dries 20 percent more quickly. It is hypoallergenic and naturally antibacterial, and its tiny micro-holes promote ventilation, helping it prevent bad odour longer. Manufactured in Scotland and imported into Canada by Montreal-based Bummis, which holds North American distribution rights, Bamboozle diapers are now available from several Canadian retail stores. A diapering kit composed of diapers and covers retails for $160, considerably less than the estimated $2500 to $3000 it would cost to keep a baby in disposable diapers.

Sources: Stephanie Whittaker, "Women of the Cloth: The Bottom Line for Bummis Is More Than Just Dollars and Cents," *The Gazette* (Montreal), April 16, 2007, p. B.1; Karen Hall, "Bamboo Comfort; Strong as Steel, Soft as Cashmere," *Windsor Star*, August 18, 2007, p. H1; Shelley Boettcher, "Bamboo: The Latest Eco-Darling," *Calgary Herald*, March 16, 2007, p. C11; Donna Nebenzahl, "Bamboo Fashioned into Floors, Beds, and Clothes," *Edmonton Journal*, November 24, 2007, p. I10.

Increasingly, major retailers, such as Sears Canada and Loblaws, make demands in return for providing shelf space. They may, for example, seek pricing and promotional concessions from manufacturers as conditions for selling their products. Retailers such as Walmart also require that manufacturers participate in their electronic data interchange (EDI) and quick-response systems. Manufacturers unable to comply may find themselves unable to penetrate the marketplace.

Slotting allowances are just one of the range of nonrefundable fees grocery retailers receive from manufacturers to secure shelf space for new products. A manufacturer can pay a retailer as much as $40 000 per item just to get its new products displayed on store shelves.[7] Other fees include failure fees (imposed if a new product does not meet sales projections), annual renewal fees (a "pay to stay" inducement for retailers to continue carrying brands), trade allowances, discounts on high-volume purchases, survey fees for research done by the retailers, and even fees to allow salespeople to present new items.

Marketoid

A 2011 *Consumer Reports* survey found that 64 percent of respondents reported leaving a store in the previous 12 months due to poor customer service.

CUSTOMER-SERVICE STRATEGY

Some stores build their retailing strategy around heightened customer services for shoppers. Gift wrapping, alterations, return privileges, product demonstrations, bridal registries, consultants, interior design services, delivery and installation, and perhaps even electronic shopping via store websites are all examples of services that add value to the shopping experience. A retailer's customer-service strategy must specify which services the firm will offer and whether it will charge customers for these services. Those decisions depend on several conditions: store size, type, and location; merchandise assortment; services offered by competitors; customer expectations; and financial resources. The "Solving an Ethical Controversy" feature discusses what it's like to be a part-time employee.

SOLVING AN ETHICAL CONTROVERSY   The Permanent Temp Is Alive and Well

THE recent recession generated widespread layoffs and caused soaring unemployment. Traditionally, as the economy begins to improve, employers start hiring again, but this time, most hiring is for contingent, or temporary, workers. As organizations regroup, they're recasting many formerly full-time permanent jobs as part-time or temporary. A CareerBuilder survey found 34 percent of hiring managers planned to hire contingent workers in 2011, up from 30 percent in 2010, and 28 percent in 2009. Many employers believe hiring temps is a safer way to go because, in most cases, temps are ineligible for health insurance, the retirement plans, paid vacation, and other benefits. During a recession, hiring becomes a buyer's market: a disproportionate number of candidates—many of them overqualified—are vying for a handful of jobs. Reconfiguring the work into contract positions can be a risky strategy because it disrupts the organization's culture and creates feelings of mistrust among the regular workforce who survived the layoffs.

Is it ethical to replace full-time employees with contract workers?

PRO

1. Hiring contract workers may be the only way a business can stay afloat. If the business fails, not only does everyone lose their jobs, the business disappears from the economy.

2. Recent events show that having a full-time job on the company payroll is no guarantee of permanence. While most people prefer a job with benefits, many realize they're better off staying nimble in case of layoffs.

CON

1. Holding down a contract position when what you really need is full-time employment has a chilling effect on a household's disposable income and consumer confidence, which in turn affects how quickly an economy can lift itself out of recession.

2. The recession flooded the job market with experienced workers who applied for many temporary jobs typically filled by younger, less experienced candidates. Employers get an unfair advantage when they can slot a more experienced employee into a lower-paying job.

Where do you stand: pro or con?

Sources: Diane Stafford, "Hiring Takes 'ad hoc' Approach," *Vancouver Sun*, January 15, 2011, p. 10; "You're Hired. For Now," *Kiplinger's Personal Finance*, March 2010, pp. 13–14; Chris Zappone, "Full-Time Worries for Part-Time Workers," WAtoday.com, February 12, 2010, http://www.watoday.com; "Employment-Population Ratio, Part Time Workers, Temporary Workers," Calculated Risk.com, February 5, 2010, http://www.calculatedrisk.com; Phil Villareal, "Target Employee Says 8K Full Timers Will Be Part-Time," Consumerist .com, February 3, 2010, http://consumerist. com; Jessica Dickler, "Battle Brews over Hourly Jobs," CNNMoney.com, February 2, 2010, http://money.cnn.com.

The basic objective of all customer services focuses on attracting and retaining target customers, thus increasing sales and profits. Some services—such as convenient restrooms, lounges, and complimentary coffee—enhance shoppers' comfort. Other services are intended to attract customers by making shopping easier and faster than it would be without the services. Some retailers, for example, offer child-care services for customers.

Consumers can also get "virtual assistance" from companies like Virtuosity and CallWave, which manage phone calls by allowing users to switch among voice mail, email, and real-time cell and landline calls using voice commands. Virtuosity's Virtual Assistant software can answer, screen, and route calls much like a living, breathing administrative assistant. Similarly, CallWave's Voicemail-to-Text service screens mobile calls, converts voice mail to text, and helps users manage their time.[7]

A customer-service strategy can also support efforts in building demand for a line of merchandise. Despite the trend toward renovation, redecorating, and do-it-yourself home projects, Home Depot was experiencing slowing sales until its recent decision to revamp its own stores, improve customer service, and upgrade its marketing efforts. Home Depot experienced solid growth with the strategy, assuring its customers with its familiar slogan "More saving. More doing."

PRICING STRATEGY

Prices reflect a retailer's marketing objectives and policies. They also play a major role in consumer perceptions of a retailer. Consumers realize, for example, that when they enter a Hermès boutique, they will find such expensive merchandise as leather handbags priced at $2450 and up, along with belts at $400 and up. In contrast, customers of Giant Tiger or Winners expect totally different merchandise and prices. At a Gucci boutique in Milan, New York, or Tokyo, they will find such expensive products as $275 snakeskin belts and $900 handbags. Customers at any of Dollar Giant's locations across Canada expect a totally different type of merchandise; the company's motto is "Nothing over a dollar."

MARKETING AND THE SME	**Eat at Your Own Risk: Lanny Dares You**

EATING contests have always been exciting events around the world: blueberry pies, tacos, hot dogs, chicken wings, pizza, oysters, hot peppers, and even poutine. Whatever is your pleasure, you will likely find an eating contest for it somewhere.

The sixth annual Canada Day hot pepper eating contest was recently held in Beijing. Gabriel Monroe defended his title against eight challengers, eating 60 hot peppers. In New Brunswick, six media members participated in the Moose Challenge at Moose's Wild Pub. To win, each had to eat a one-pound burger, topped with four cheese slices, four strips of bacon, four slices of tomato, and two dill pickles, along with a one-pound serving of poutine and a 16-ounce beverage. Three succeeded.

Many small restaurants and family businesses offer contests that run continuously for patrons who wish to "take the challenge." Those who meet the challenge generally get a free meal and, frequently, a T-shirt or some other prize that promotes the business. But Lanny's Chili Hut on the shore of Gillies Lake in downtown Timmins, Ontario—a small town of less than 43 000 people that boasts of being the hometown of 21 current and former NHL players and singer Shania

Twain—offered a unique challenge in 2011 to all patrons who wished to accept it.

To enter the contest, patrons had to pay a $20 entry fee. Then they had to eat approximately six pounds of menu items, including Bubba Poutine, Hell Burgers, Chili Dogs, and Big Daddy Dogs, subject to change throughout the season. Winners got their entry fee refunded, along with a T-shirt that confirmed "I beat the Lanny's Chili Hut Challenge at Gillies Lake." To go one step further, if at least 10 people entered during a particular month, the top winner would receive a bonus $50 (and the top annual winner would receive $100). The top winner who accomplished the feat in less than 30 minutes would also receive $50. To protect the business, all contestants had to sign a waiver absolving Lanny's from any responsibility as a result of their participation.

Sources: "Canada Day Hot Pepper Eating Contest," *The Beijinger*, June 25, 2011, http://www.thebeijinger.com/gallery/Canada-Day-Hot-Pepper-Eating -Contest, August 3, 2011; "T&T Staffers Chow Down for Charity," *Times & Transcript*, July 8, 2011, available http://timestranscript.canadaeast.com/ news/article/1421919, August 3, 2011; Lanny's Chili Hut promotional flyer, handed out at Lanny's Chili Hut during the 2011 season.

Markups and Markdowns

markup
Amount that a retailer adds to the cost of a product to determine its selling price.

The amount that a retailer adds to a product's cost to set the final selling price is the **markup**. The amount of the markup typically results from two marketing decisions:

1. *Services performed by the retailer.* Other things being equal, stores that offer more services charge larger markups to cover their costs.

2. *Inventory turnover rate.* Other things being equal, stores with a higher turnover rate can cover their costs and earn a profit while charging a smaller markup.

A retailer's markup exerts an important influence on its image among present and potential customers. In addition, the markup affects the retailer's ability to attract shoppers. An excessive markup may drive away customers; an inadequate markup may not generate sufficient income to cover costs and return a profit. Retailers typically state markups as percentages of either the selling prices or the costs of the products.

markdown
Amount by which a retailer reduces the original selling price of a product.

Marketers determine markups based partly on their judgments of the amounts that consumers will pay for a given product. When buyers refuse to pay a product's stated price, however, or when improvements in other items or fashion changes reduce the appeal of current merchandise, a retailer must take a **markdown**. The amount by which a retailer reduces the original selling price—the discount typically advertised for a sale item—is the markdown. Markdowns are sometimes used to evaluate merchandisers. For example, a department store might base its evaluations of buyers partly on the average markdown percentages for the product lines for which they are responsible.

The formulas for calculating markups and markdowns are provided in the "Financial Analysis in Marketing" appendix at the end of the text.

LOCATION/DISTRIBUTION STRATEGY

Retail experts often cite location as a potential determining factor in the success or failure of a retail business. A retailer may choose to locate at an isolated site, in a central business district, or in a planned shopping centre. The location decision depends on many factors, including the type of merchandise, the retailer's financial resources, characteristics of the target market, and site availability.

In recent years, many localities have become saturated with stores. As a result, some retailers have re-evaluated their location strategies. A chain may close individual stores that do not meet sales and profit goals. Other retailers have experimented with nontraditional location strategies. GoodLife Fitness has approximately 50 of its 275 Canadian outlets in Real Canadian Superstore locations. These stores offer high traffic and ample parking, and attract women aged 35 to 50 with high household incomes. Real Canadian Superstore strengthened its position as a one-stop-shop for customers, and GoodLife Fitness benefited from increased visibility, credibility, and access to Canada's fastest-growing fitness segment.[8]

Locations in Planned Shopping Centres

planned shopping centre Group of retail stores planned, coordinated, and marketed as a unit.

Over the past several decades, retail trade has shifted away from traditional downtown retailing districts and toward suburban shopping centres. A **planned shopping centre** is a group of retail stores designed, coordinated, and marketed to shoppers in a geographic trade area. Together, the stores provide a single convenient location for shoppers as well as free parking. They facilitate shopping by maintaining uniform hours of operation, including evening and weekend hours.

There are five main types of planned shopping centres. The smallest, the *neighbourhood shopping centre,* is likely to consist of a group of smaller stores, such as a drugstore, a dry cleaner, a card and gift shop, and perhaps a hair-styling salon. This kind of centre provides convenient shopping for 5000 to 50 000 shoppers who live within a few minutes' commute. It contains 5 to 15 stores, and the product mix is usually confined to convenience items and some limited shopping goods.

A *community shopping centre* serves 20 000 to 100 000 people in a trade area extending a few kilometres from its location. It contains anywhere from 10 to 30 retail stores, with a branch of a local department store or some other large store as the primary tenant. In addition to the stores found in a neighbourhood centre, a community centre probably encompasses more stores featuring shopping goods, some professional offices, a branch bank, and perhaps a movie theatre or supermarket. Community shopping centres typically offer ample parking, and tenants often share some promotion costs. With the advent of stand-alone big-box retailers, some community shopping centres have declined in popularity. Some department stores are also moving away from the strategy of locating in shopping centres and opting for freestanding stores. A *regional shopping centre* is a large facility with at least 300 000 square feet of shopping space. Its marketing appeal usually emphasizes major department stores with the power to draw customers, supplemented by as many as 200 smaller stores. A successful regional centre needs a location within 30 minutes' driving time of at least 250 000 people. A regional centre—or a super-regional centre such as the West Edmonton Mall—provides a wide assortment of convenience, shopping, and specialty goods, plus many professional and personal service facilities. Some shopping centres are going green, working to reduce their carbon footprint with mandatory recycling programs, maximizing the use of natural light, and installing heat-reflecting roofing that reduces the need for air conditioning.[9]

A *power centre*, usually located near a regional or super-regional mall, brings together several huge specialty stores, such as Rona, Designer Depot, Costco, Canadian Tire, Michaels, or Pier 1 Imports, as stand-alone stores in a single trading area. Rising in popularity during the 1990s, power centres offered value because they underpriced department stores and provided a huge selection of specialty merchandise. Heated competition from cost-cutter Walmart and inroads from more upscale discounters such as Target are currently hurting the drawing power of these centres. A fifth type of planned centre has emerged, known as a *lifestyle centre.* This retailing format seeks to offer a combination of shopping, movie theatres, stages for concerts and live entertainment, decorative fountains and park benches in greenways, and restaurants and bistros in an attractive outdoor environment. At around 300 000 to 1 million square feet, the centres are large, but they seek to offer the intimacy and easy access of neighbourhood village retailing with a fashionable cachet. Convenience, safety, and pleasant ambiance are also part of the appeal. Canada's first lifestyle centre, The Village at Park Royal located in West Vancouver, has old-fashioned gas lamps and a lighthouse. Each store differs in design and colour, and the main street has many sculptures and plantings, along with a pond and stepping stones where children can play. There are no big anchor stores but rather a mix of just the right upscale tenants—lululemon athletica, Danier Leather, Urban Barn, and Kiss & Makeup, for instance. Restaurants are also much more prominent in lifestyle centres than in enclosed malls.[10]

To fill the empty spaces in malls and attract shoppers, malls are increasingly adding businesses that offer entertainment and experiences. Today, many shopping centres include movie theatre complexes, indoor playgrounds, arcade games, bowling alleys, and more. The West Edmonton Mall boasts the world's largest indoor amusement park, which includes the world's largest indoor triple-loop roller coaster; the world's largest indoor wave pool; and the world's tallest indoor bungee tower.[11]

PROMOTIONAL STRATEGY

To establish store images that entice more shoppers, retailers use a variety of promotional techniques. Through its promotional strategy, a retailer seeks to communicate to consumers information about its stores—locations, merchandise selections, hours of operation, and prices. If merchandise selection changes frequently to follow fashion trends, advertising is typically used to promote current styles effectively. In addition, promotions help retailers attract shoppers and build customer loyalty.

Innovative promotions can pay off in unexpected ways. IKEA China used the interiors of the elevators in 20 Beijing apartment buildings to demonstrate to residents how small apartments can be inexpensively transformed into comfortable living spaces. The elevators were covered with floor-to-ceiling posters picturing ingeniously styled and decorated apartments, and the elevator operators gave out IKEA catalogues to their passengers. "It's a strategic decision to go where the competition isn't," said IKEA's worldwide marketing communications manager.[12]

National retail chains often purchase advertising space in newspapers, on radio, and on television. Other retailers are experimenting with promoting over the Internet or using Bluetooth's wireless technology to send marketing messages to customers' cell phones. Consumers are increasingly using their smartphones to surf the Web. To promote its bands, Warner Music Group launched a Wireless Application Protocol (WAP)–based site designed specifically for mobile browsing. Special analysis software enables Warner to analyze the browsing data by the user's device, origin of the session, and other criteria.[13] Retailers also try to combine advertising with in-store merchandising techniques that influence decisions at the point of purchase. Spain-based Zara stores offer fast fashion—inexpensive but trendy apparel that changes frequently. Merchandise arrives directly from the factory on plastic shipping hangers and already tagged. Clerks move items immediately to the selling floor, later replacing the plastic hangers with Zara's traditional wooden ones. Items typically sell out before they need to be marked down, creating a sense of exclusivity. Zara shoppers tend to visit often, sometimes even daily, to check out the new arrivals on the plastic hangers. Meanwhile, store managers wielding hand-held computers pay close attention to what shoppers consider hot—or not—and alert Zara's designers, reordering best-selling merchandise in minutes instead of the hours it once required.[14]

A friendly, well-trained, and knowledgeable salesperson plays a vital role in conveying the store's image to consumers and in persuading shoppers to buy. To serve as a source of information, a salesperson must possess extensive knowledge regarding credit policies, discounts, special sales, delivery terms, layaways, and returns. To increase store sales, the salesperson must persuade customers that the store sells what those customers need. To this end, salespeople should receive training in selling up and suggestion selling.

By *selling up*, salespeople try to persuade customers to buy higher-priced items than originally intended. For example, an automobile salesperson might convince a customer to buy a more expensive model than the car that the buyer had initially considered. Of course, the practice of selling up must always respect the constraints of a customer's real needs. If a salesperson sells customers something that they really do not need, the potential for repeat sales dramatically diminishes.

Another technique, *suggestion selling*, seeks to broaden a customer's original purchase by adding related items, special promotional products, or holiday or seasonal merchandise. Here, too, the salesperson tries to help a customer recognize true needs rather than unwanted merchandise. Beauty advisers in upscale department stores are masters of suggestion selling. Beauty retail chain Sephora creates a spa mood by treating customers like royalty. Sephora employees, called "cast members," receive special training before they hit the sales floor. Customers are encouraged to take their time, sample the wares, and indulge their senses in a stress-free environment.[15]

Just as knowledgeable and helpful sales personnel can both boost sales and set retailers apart from competitors, poor service influences customers' attitudes toward a retailer. Increasing customer complaints about unfriendly, inattentive, and uninformed salespeople have prompted many retailers to intensify their attention to training and motivating salespeople. Older training methods are giving way to online learning in many firms.

STORE ATMOSPHERICS

atmospherics
Combination of physical characteristics and amenities that contribute to a store's image.

While store location, merchandise selection, customer service, pricing, and promotional activities all contribute to a store's consumer awareness, stores also project their personalities through **atmospherics**—physical characteristics and amenities that attract customers and satisfy their shopping needs. Atmospherics include both a store's exterior and interior decor.

A store's exterior appearance, including architectural design, window displays, signs, and entryways, helps to identify the retailer and attract its target market shoppers. The Canadian Tire red triangle and green maple leaf is an exterior element that readily identifies this retailer. Other retailers design eye-catching exterior elements aimed at getting customers' attention. Consumers readily recognize Tim Hortons, Chapters, and Future Shop locations by their building designs. Many of the more than 100 Canadian locations of East Side Mario's attract customers with their signature giant tomatoes on their buildings.

The interior decor of a store should also complement the retailer's image, respond to customers' interests, and, most important, induce shoppers to buy. Interior atmospheric elements include store layout, merchandise presentation, lighting, colour, sounds, scents, and cleanliness. At one time, Tim Hortons locations could be described as dark,

Atmospherics, which includes the store's exterior, vary from retailer to retailer and from country to country.

smoky, and male-dominated, attractive only to a small group of customers. The company improved its product offering, but more important, it consciously decided to improve its atmospherics to appeal particularly to women. Tim Hortons was among the first Canadian food outlets to isolate smoking and then to ban it outright. Much of the interior visual appearance was improved, and the bar stool counters, a common store feature, were replaced with family-friendly tables. As a result, Tim Hortons customers now cross all income groups and ages. You are as likely to see a Lexus in the parking lot as you are to see a pickup truck.

When designing the interior and exterior of a store, marketers must remember that many people shop for reasons other than just purchasing needed products. Other common reasons for shopping include escaping the routine of daily life, avoiding weather extremes, fulfilling fantasies, and socializing with family and friends. Retailers expand beyond interior design to create welcoming and entertaining environments that draw shoppers. The Canadian Tire Concept 20/20 stores' new atmospherics, including design, product displays, open plan layout, lighting, and other features, have resulted in customers spending an average of 40 percent more browsing time per shopping trip.[16]

assessment check 3

3.1 What is an SKU?

3.2 What are the two components of a markup?

3.3 What are store atmospherics?

TYPES OF RETAILERS

Because new types of retailers continue to evolve in response to changes in consumer demand, a universal classification system for retailers has yet to be devised. Certain differences do, however, define several categories of retailers: (1) forms of ownership, (2) shopping effort expended by customers, (3) services provided to customers, (4) product lines, and (5) location of retail transactions.

As Figure 12.3 points out, most retailing operations fit in different categories. A 7-Eleven outlet may be classified as a convenience store (category 2) with self-service (category 3) and a relatively broad product line (category 4). It is both a store-type retailer (category 5) and a member of a chain (category 1).

CLASSIFICATION OF RETAILERS BY FORM OF OWNERSHIP

Perhaps the easiest method for categorizing retailers is by ownership structure, distinguishing between chain stores and independent retailers. In addition, independent retailers may join wholesaler-sponsored voluntary chains, band together to form retail cooperatives, or enter into franchise agreements with manufacturers, wholesalers, or service-provider organizations. Each type of ownership has its own unique advantages and strategies.

Chain Stores

Chain stores are groups of retail outlets that operate under central ownership and management and handle the same product lines. Chains have a major advantage over independent retailers in economies of scale. Volume purchases allow chains to pay lower prices than their independent rivals must pay. Since a chain may encompass hundreds of retail stores, it can afford extensive advertising, sales training, and sophisticated computerized systems for merchandise ordering, inventory management, forecasting, and accounting. Also, the large sales volume and wide geographic reach of a chain may enable it to advertise in a variety of media.

Independent Retailers

The Canadian retailing structure supports a large number of small stores, many medium-size stores, and a small number of large stores. Approximately 70 percent of the more than 227 000 retail locations in Canada earn less than $500 000 in annual sales. Two-thirds of Canadian retailers employ four or fewer employees.[17] Most of these retail locations are independent retailers.

figure 12.3

Bases for Categorizing Retailers

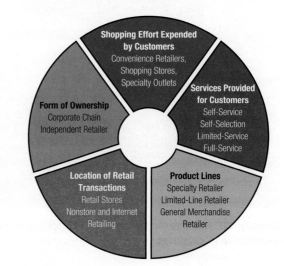

convenience retailer
Store that appeals to customers with accessible location, long hours, rapid checkout, and adequate parking.

specialty retailer
Store that combines carefully defined product lines, services, and reputation to persuade shoppers to spend considerable shopping effort there.

Independent retailers compete with chains in a number of ways. The traditional advantage of independent stores is friendly, personalized service. Cooperatives offer another strategy for independents. For instance, cooperatives such as Best Western Hotels and Pharmasave help independents compete with chains by providing volume buying power as well as advertising and marketing programs.

CLASSIFICATION BY SHOPPING EFFORT

Another classification system is based on the reasons consumers shop at particular retail outlets. This approach categorizes stores as convenience, shopping, or specialty retailers.

Convenience retailers focus their marketing appeals on accessible locations, long store hours, rapid checkout service, and adequate parking facilities. Local food stores, gasoline stations, and dry cleaners fit this category. GreenStop, Canada's new chain of alternative-fuel stations—offering biodiesel and other ethanol blends—features convenience stores that sell solar-roasted coffee and organic veggie wraps instead of candy bars and cigarettes.[18]

Shopping stores typically include furniture stores, appliance retailers, clothing outlets, and sporting goods stores. Consumers usually compare prices, assortments, and quality levels at competing outlets before making purchase decisions. Consequently, managers of shopping stores attempt to differentiate their outlets through advertising, in-store displays, well-trained and knowledgeable salespeople, and appropriate merchandise assortments.

Specialty retailers combine carefully defined product lines, services, and reputations in attempts to convince consumers to expend considerable effort to shop at their stores. Examples include Edie Hats (Vancouver), The Camera Store (Calgary), Woodlands Gallery (Winnipeg), and Aerobics First (Halifax). Many specialty retailers, such as Gap, La Senza, and Running Room, have locations across Canada.

CLASSIFICATION BY SERVICES PROVIDED

Another category differentiates retailers by the services they provide to customers. This classification system consists of three retail types: self-service, self-selection, or full-service retailers.

The 7-Eleven convenience stores are classified as self-service stores, while Safeway and Sobeys grocery stores are examples of self-selection stores. Both categories sell convenience products people can purchase frequently with little assistance. Full-service retailers such as Holt Renfrew focus on fashion-oriented merchandise, backed by a complete array of customer services.

Globally, 7-Eleven has more than 34 800 franchised or licensed convenience store locations in 17 countries.

CLASSIFICATION BY PRODUCT LINES

Product lines also define a set of retail categories and the marketing strategies appropriate for firms within those categories. Grouping retailers by product lines produces three major categories: specialty stores, limited-line retailers, and general merchandise retailers.

Specialty Stores

A *specialty store* typically handles only part of a single product line. However, it stocks this portion in considerable depth or variety. Specialty stores include a wide range of retail outlets: examples include fish markets, grocery stores, men's and women's shoe stores, and bakeries. Although some specialty stores are chain outlets, most are independent small-scale operations. They represent perhaps the greatest concentration of independent retailers who develop expertise in one product area and provide narrow lines of products for their local markets.

Specialty stores should not be confused with specialty products. Specialty stores typically carry convenience and shopping goods. The label *specialty* reflects the practice of handling a specific, narrow line of merchandise. For example, Lady Foot Locker is a specialty store that offers a wide selection of name-brand athletic footwear, apparel, and accessories made specifically for women.

Limited-Line Retailers

Customers find a large assortment of products within one product line or a few related lines in a **limited-line store**. This type of retail operation typically develops in areas with a large enough population to sufficiently support it. Examples of limited-line stores are Golf Town (golf clothing and equipment) and The Brick (furniture). These retailers cater to the needs of people who want to select from complete lines in purchasing particular products.

A unique type of limited-line retailer is known as a **category killer**. These stores offer huge selections and low prices in single product lines. Stores within this category—for example, Best Buy, Toys "R" Us, and Home Depot—are among the most successful retailers in the nation. Category killers at first took business away from general merchandise discounters, which were not able to compete in selection or price. Recently, however, expanded merchandise and aggressive cost cutting by warehouse clubs and by Walmart have turned the tables. Competition from Internet companies that are able to offer unlimited selection and speedy delivery have also taken customers away. While they still remain a powerful force in retailing, category killers are not invulnerable.

limited-line store Retailer that offers a large assortment within a single product line or within a few related product lines.

category killer Store offering huge selections and low prices in single product lines.

General Merchandise Retailers

General merchandise retailers, which carry a wide variety of product lines that are all stocked in some depth, distinguish themselves from limited-line and specialty retailers by the large number of product lines they carry. The general store described earlier in this chapter is a primitive form of a general merchandise retailer. This category includes variety stores, department stores, and mass merchandisers such as discount stores, off-price retailers, and hypermarkets.

general merchandise retailer Store that carries a wide variety of product lines, stocking all of them in some depth.

Variety Stores

A retail outlet that offers an extensive range and assortment of low-price merchandise is called a *variety store*. Less popular today than they once were, many of these stores have evolved into or given way to other types of retailers such as discount stores or hybrid combinations of drugstores and variety stores, such as Herbie's Drug & Food Warehouse. The country's variety stores now account for less than 1 percent of all retail sales. However, variety stores remain popular in other parts of the world. Many retail outlets in Spain and Mexico are family-owned variety stores.

Department Stores

In essence, a **department store** is a series of limited-line and specialty stores under one roof. By definition, this large retailer handles a variety of merchandise, including men's, women's, and children's clothing and accessories; household linens and dry goods; home furnishings; and furniture. It serves as a one-stop shopping destination for almost all personal and household products. The Bay and Sears Canada are classic examples.

Department stores built their reputations by offering wide varieties of services, such as charge accounts, delivery, gift wrapping, and liberal return privileges. As a result, they incur relatively high operating costs, averaging about 45 to 60 percent of sales.

Department stores have faced intense competition over the past several years. Relatively high operating costs have left them vulnerable to competition from specialty stores, discount stores, and Internet retailers. In addition, department stores' traditional locations in downtown business districts have suffered from problems associated with limited parking, traffic congestion, and population migration to the suburbs.

department store Large store that handles a variety of merchandise, including clothing, household goods, appliances, and furniture.

The Bay, however, is fighting back. Internal processes have been streamlined and decision making has become more decentralized. End-of-season inventory has been reduced. Store aisles are cleaner and more attractive. According to Ron Telpner, chair and CEO of the BrainStorm Group, the staff are easier to recognize and more communicative. There is a new boutique-style approach to merchandising, and a new in-house brand, Baia, is targeted at the up-market consumer. According to Telpner, the Bay's new strategy is to become everything that specialty stores represent with regard to core competencies and retail execution, but under a single roof.[19]

Mass Merchandisers

mass merchandiser
Store that stocks a wider line of goods than a department store, usually without the same depth of assortment within each line.

Mass merchandising has made major inroads into department store sales by emphasizing lower prices for well-known brand-name products, high product turnover, and limited services. A **mass merchandiser** often stocks a wider line of items than a department store but usually without the same depth of assortment within each line. Discount houses, off-price retailers, hypermarkets, and catalogue retailers are all examples of mass merchandisers.

Discount Houses

discount house
Store that charges low prices but may not offer services such as credit.

A **discount house** charges low prices and offers fewer services. Early discount stores sold mostly appliances. Today, they offer soft goods, drugs, food, gasoline, and furniture.

By eliminating many of the "free" services provided by traditional retailers, these operations can keep their markups 10 to 25 percent below those of their competitors. Some of the early discounters have since added services, stocked well-known name brands, and boosted their prices. In fact, many now resemble department stores.

A discount format that is gaining strength is the *warehouse club.* Costco is the largest warehouse club in Canada. These no-frills, cash-and-carry outlets offer consumers access to name-brand products at deeply discounted prices. Selection at warehouse clubs includes such varied items as gourmet popcorn, fax machines, peanut butter, luggage, and sunglasses sold in vast warehouse-like settings. Attracting business away from almost every retailing segment, warehouse clubs now even offer fresh food and gasoline. Customers must be members to shop at warehouse clubs.

Off-Price Retailers

Another version of a discount house is an *off-price retailer.* This kind of store stocks only designer labels or well-known brand-name clothing at prices equal to or below regular wholesale prices and then passes the cost savings along to buyers. While many off-price retailers are located in outlets in downtown areas or in freestanding buildings, a growing number are concentrating in *outlet malls*—shopping centres that house only off-price retailers.

Inventory at off-price stores changes frequently as buyers take advantage of special price offers from manufacturers selling excess merchandise. Off-price retailers such as Winners, Home Sense, and Home Outfitters also keep their prices below those of traditional retailers by offering fewer services. Off-price retailing has been well received by today's shoppers. France-based retailer Vente-privée.com sells high-fashion overstock merchandise through invitation-only clearance sales conducted solely on the Web.[20]

Hypermarkets and Supercentres

hypermarket
Giant one-stop shopping facility offering wide selections of grocery items and general merchandise at discount prices, typically filling up 200 000 or more square feet of selling space.

supercentre
Large store, usually smaller than a hypermarket, that combines groceries with discount store merchandise.

Another innovation in discount retailing is the creation of **hypermarkets**—giant one-stop shopping facilities that offer wide selections of grocery and general merchandise products at discount prices. Store size determines the major difference between hypermarkets and supercentres. Hypermarkets typically fill up 200 000 or more square feet of selling space, about a third larger than most **supercentres**. With regard to merchandise strategy, hypermarkets generally carry a larger proportion of food items than supercentres, including fresh meat, fish, and produce. Despite great success in Europe, hypermarkets have had limited success in the United States, and even less success in Canada, where they can be found only in Quebec.

Walmart is testing a new type of hypermarket in the United States. Online shoppers at Walmart.com can choose to have their order shipped free to a local Walmart store and then pick it up at a drive-through window. So far, management says shoppers seem to appreciate the convenience.[21]

CLASSIFICATION OF RETAIL TRANSACTIONS BY LOCATION

Although most retail transactions occur in stores, nonstore retailing serves as an important marketing channel for many products. In addition, both consumer and business-to-business marketers rely on nonstore retailing to generate orders or requests for more information that may result in future orders.

Direct marketing is a broad concept that includes direct mail, direct selling, direct response retailing, telemarketing, Internet retailing, and automatic merchandising. The last sections of this chapter will consider each type of nonstore retailing.

RETAIL CONVERGENCE AND SCRAMBLED MERCHANDISING

Many traditional differences no longer distinguish familiar types of retailers, rendering any set of classifications less useful. **Retail convergence**, whereby similar merchandise is available from many retail outlets distinguished by price more than any other factor, is blurring distinctions between types of retailers and the merchandise mix they offer. A few years ago, a customer looking for a fashionable coffeepot might have headed straight for Williams-Sonoma or Starbucks. Today, she's just as likely to pick one up at Canadian Tire or Walmart, where she can check out new spring fashions or stock up on paper goods. The Gap is no longer pitted only against American Eagle Outfitters or L.L. Bean but against designer-label brands at department stores and Joe Fresh at Real Canadian Superstore, too. Grocery stores compete with Walmart Supercenter and Costco. Walmart has beefed up its already robust product mix to include VUDU broadband streaming services for the consumer electronics products it sells alongside the apparel, housewares, fine jewellery, and more.[22]

Scrambled merchandising—in which a retailer combines dissimilar product lines in an attempt to boost sales volume—has also muddied the waters. Drugstores, such as the newly renovated Shoppers Drug Mart stores, not only fill prescriptions but offer cameras, cards, magazines, small appliances, home decor accessories, and even fresh and prepared foods. Speaking for Loblaw, spokesperson Geoff Wilson says, "We are still very much a food retailer first—that is our heritage. But we . . . see the opportunity in leveraging the food traffic to sell general merchandise, and the vehicle associated with selling general merchandise is the Real Canadian Superstores." The company is allocating as much as 75 percent of its new square footage to general merchandise such as clothing, housewares, and toys.[23]

④ Explain the concepts of retail convergence and scrambled merchandising.

retail convergence
A situation in which similar merchandise is available from many retail outlets, resulting in the blurring of distinctions between type of retailer and merchandise offered.
scrambled merchandising
Retailing practice of combining dissimilar product lines to boost sales volume.

assessment check 4 ✓

4.1 How do we classify retailers by form of ownership?

4.2 Categorize retailers by shopping effort and by services provided.

4.3 List several ways to classify retailers by product line.

Scrambled merchandising is practised by many retailers. Best Buy has recently added musical instruments to its stores.

H. F. (HERB) MACKENZIE

⑤ **Identify the functions performed by wholesaling intermediaries.**

wholesaler
Channel intermediary that takes title to goods it handles and then distributes these goods to retailers, other distributors, or B2B customers.

wholesaling intermediary
Comprehensive term that describes wholesalers as well as agents and brokers.

WHOLESALING INTERMEDIARIES

Recall from Chapter 11 that several distribution channels involve marketing intermediaries called **wholesalers**. These firms take title to the goods they handle and sell those products primarily to retailers or to other wholesalers or business users. They sell to ultimate consumers only in insignificant quantities if at all. **Wholesaling intermediaries**, a broader category, include not only wholesalers but also agents and brokers, who perform important wholesaling activities without taking title to the goods.

FUNCTIONS OF WHOLESALING INTERMEDIARIES

As specialists in certain marketing functions, as opposed to production or manufacturing functions, wholesaling intermediaries can perform these functions more efficiently than producers or consumers. The importance of these activities results from the utility they create, the services they provide, and the cost reductions they allow.

Creating Utility

Wholesaling intermediaries create three types of utility for consumers. They enhance time utility by making products available for sale when consumers want to purchase them. They create place utility by helping to deliver goods and services for purchase at convenient locations. They create ownership (or possession) utility when a smooth exchange of title to the products from producers or intermediaries to final purchasers is complete. Possession utility can also result from transactions in which actual title does not pass to purchasers, as in rental-car services.

Providing Services

Table 12.1 lists a number of services provided by wholesaling intermediaries. The list clearly indicates the marketing utilities—time, place, and possession utility—that wholesaling intermediaries create or

table 12.1 *Wholesaling Services for Customers and Producer-Suppliers*

SERVICE	BENEFICIARIES OF SERVICE	
	Customers	Producer-Suppliers
Buying Anticipates customer demands and applies knowledge of alternative sources of supply; acts as purchasing agent for customers.	Yes	No
Selling Provides a sales force to call on customers, creating a low-cost method for servicing smaller retailers and business users.	No	Yes
Storing Maintains warehouse facilities at lower costs than most individual producers or retailers could achieve. Reduces risk and cost of maintaining inventory for producers.	Yes	Yes
Transporting Customers receive prompt delivery in response to their demands, reducing their inventory investments. Wholesalers also break bulk by purchasing in economical carload or truckload lots, then reselling in smaller quantities, thereby reducing overall transportation costs.	Yes	Yes
Providing Marketing Information Offers important marketing research input for producers through regular contacts with retail and business buyers. Provides customers with information about new products, technical information about product lines, reports on competitors' activities and industry trends, and advisory information concerning pricing changes, legal changes, and so forth.	Yes	Yes
Financing Grants credit that might be unavailable for purchases directly from manufacturers. Provides financing assistance to producers by purchasing products in advance of sale and by promptly paying bills.	Yes	Yes
Risk Taking Evaluates credit risks of numerous, distant retail customers and small-business users. Extends credit to customers that qualify. By transporting and stocking products in inventory, the wholesaler assumes risk of spoilage, theft, or obsolescence.	Yes	Yes

Forward-Looking Retailers Must Also Look Backwards

TO be a successful retailer, you need good rapport with your customers. But did you know you also need to build a solid relationship with the vendors who supply your merchandise and other goods? How you identify and work with suppliers can make or break your business. Here are some tips:

- *Get acquainted.* You can't tell much about a business if you're dealing exclusively online or by phone. Try to meet for a cup of coffee: perhaps you'll be at the same trade show or in each other's city. Ask questions; you're trying to ascertain whether the supplier's business is legit and financially sound.
- *Visit the warehouse.* Ask to see the vendor's distribution centre. Is it clean and in good condition? Are goods housed properly and safely? Ask about your vendor's inventory system. How does it work?
- *Do a price check.* Are the vendor's prices competitive? If not, why? Is there some compelling reason to favour a more costly supplier? Those higher prices affect your bottom line.

- *Know the policies.* Is there a minimum order and if so, what is it? How are goods shipped and when will they arrive? What happens if they arrive damaged? Late? Not at all? What are the terms of payment: cash or credit? What will that credit cost you? Make sure you know about the policies upfront—and any guarantees offered.
- *Be a good customer.* It may sound like a no-brainer, but be the kind of customer you want your customers to be. Pay your bills on time and don't squeeze your supplier; you're not the only one with a payroll to meet and bills to pay.

Sources: Danny J. Vanguard, "How to Build a Good Business Relationship with Your Wholesale Supplier," Ezinearticles.com, http://ezinearticles.com, February 27, 2010; Trevor Marshall, "What to Look for in a Wholesale Distributor," http://articles.rsorange.com, February 27, 2010; Paris Burstyn, "Wholesale Doesn't Cannibalize Sales But Opens Up New Revenue," *Telecoms Europe,* September 21, 2009, http://www.telecomseurope.net; "The Best of the Fresh: This Wholesale Distributor Is a Dominant Force in Several Western Regions of the Country," *American Executive,* September 1, 2009, http://www.americanexecutive.com.

enhance. These services also reflect the basic marketing functions of buying, selling, storing, transporting, providing market information, financing, and risk taking.

Of course, many types of wholesaling intermediaries provide varying services, and not all of them perform every service listed in the table. Producer-suppliers rely on wholesaling intermediaries for distribution and selection of firms that offer the desired combinations of services. In general, however, the critical marketing functions listed in the table form the basis for any evaluation of a marketing intermediary's efficiency. The risk-taking function affects each service of the intermediary.

Dominion Citrus Limited, based in Etobicoke, Ontario, supplies fresh produce and various packaging and sorting services to retailers, food service companies, and other food distribution businesses. It procures, processes, packs, sorts, grades, warehouses, and distributes to over 400 customers, mainly in Ontario and Quebec, but also in the United States and Europe.[24]

The "Career Readiness" feature discusses how to identify and work with a wholesale distributor.

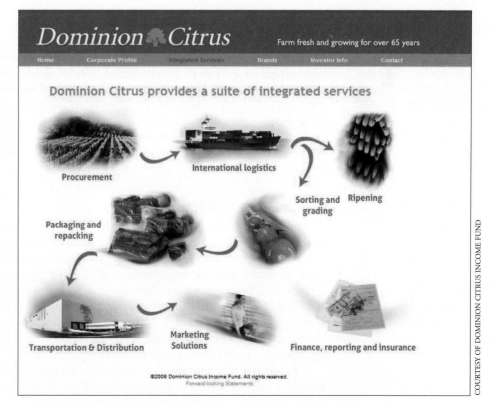

Dominion Citrus is a wholesaler that offers a suite of integrated services aimed at providing value-added solutions to its customers.

figure 12.4

Transaction Economies through Wholesaling Intermediaries

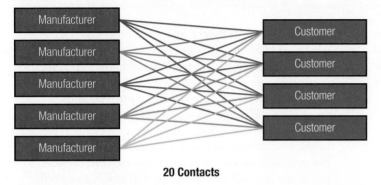

20 Contacts

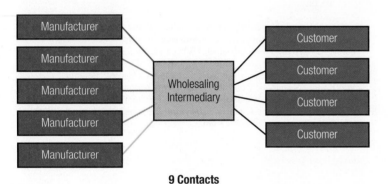

9 Contacts

Lowering Costs by Limiting Contacts

When an intermediary represents numerous producers, it often cuts the costs of buying and selling. The transaction economies are illustrated in Figure 12.4, which shows five manufacturers marketing their outputs to four different customers. Without an intermediary, these exchanges create a total of 20 transactions. Adding a wholesaling intermediary reduces the number of transactions to nine.

WFS Ltd.—formerly Windsor Factory Supply—represents more than 3500 suppliers and sells to more than 4000 customers. The company now has ten Canadian branches, a branch in South Carolina, and a warehouse near Detroit, Michigan. With sales approaching $100 million, WFS sells such things as maintenance, repair, and operating supplies; plumbing supplies; and health and safety equipment.[25]

assessment check 5

5.1 What is a wholesaler? How does it differ from a wholesaling intermediary?

5.2 How do wholesaling intermediaries help sellers lower costs?

⑥ Outline the major types of independent wholesaling intermediaries and the appropriate situations for using each.

TYPES OF WHOLESALING INTERMEDIARIES

Various types of wholesaling intermediaries operate in different distribution channels. Some provide wide ranges of services or handle broad lines of goods, while others specialize in individual services, goods, or industries. Figure 12.5 classifies wholesaling intermediaries by two characteristics: ownership and title flows (whether title passes from manufacturer to wholesaling intermediary). There are three basic ownership structures: (1) manufacturer-owned facilities, (2) independent wholesaling intermediaries, and (3) retailer-owned cooperatives and buying offices. The two types of independent wholesaling intermediaries are merchant wholesalers, which take title of the goods, and agents and brokers, which do not.

Manufacturer-Owned Facilities

Several reasons lead manufacturers to distribute their goods directly through company-owned facilities. Some perishable goods need rigid control of distribution to avoid spoilage; other goods require complex installation or servicing. Some goods need aggressive promotion. Goods with high-unit values allow profitable sales by manufacturers directly to ultimate purchasers. Manufacturer-owned facilities include sales branches, sales offices, trade fairs, and merchandise marts.

A *sales branch* carries inventory and processes orders for customers from available stock. Branches provide a storage function like independent wholesalers and serve as offices for sales representatives in their territories. They are prevalent in marketing channels for chemicals, commercial machinery and equipment, motor vehicles, and petroleum products.

A *sales office,* in contrast, does not carry inventory, but it does serve as a regional office for a manufacturer's sales personnel. Locations close to the firm's customers help limit selling costs and support active customer service. For example, many Ontario manufacturers have established sales offices in eastern and western Canada.

A *trade fair* (or trade exhibition) is a periodic show at which manufacturers in a particular industry display their wares for visiting retail and wholesale buyers. For example, the Canadian Giftware &

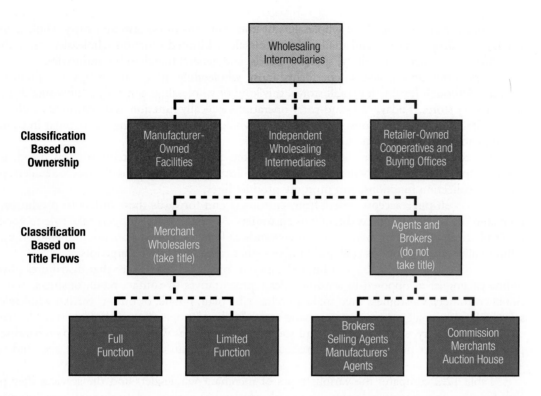

figure 12.5

**Major Types
of Wholesaling
Intermediaries**

Tableware Association holds a trade fair in January and August of each year in Toronto where exhibitors display their products to more than 25 000 retail buyers. Smaller gift fairs are held regularly in Halifax, Calgary, Vancouver, and many other Canadian cities.

A *merchandise mart* provides space for permanent showrooms and exhibits, which manufacturers rent to market their goods. One of the world's largest merchandise marts is Chicago's Merchandise Mart Center, a 7-million-square-foot complex that hosts more than 30 seasonal buying markets each year. Many large merchandise marts are located in the United States, but they attract exhibitors from Canada and around the world.

Independent Wholesaling Intermediaries

Many wholesaling intermediaries are independently owned. These firms fall into two major categories: merchant wholesalers and agents and brokers.

Merchant Wholesalers

A **merchant wholesaler** takes title to the goods it handles. Merchant wholesalers account for roughly 60 percent of all sales at the wholesale level. Further classifications divide these wholesalers into full-function or limited-function wholesalers, as indicated in Figure 12.5. WFS Ltd., mentioned in the previous section, is a merchant wholesaler.

A full-function merchant wholesaler provides a complete assortment of services for retailers and business purchasers. Such a wholesaler stores merchandise in a convenient location, allowing customers to make purchases on short notice and minimizing inventory requirements. The firm typically maintains a sales force that calls on retailers, makes deliveries, and extends credit to qualified buyers. Full-function wholesalers are common in the drug, grocery, and hardware industries. In the business-goods market, full-function merchant wholesalers (often called *industrial distributors*) sell machinery, inexpensive accessory equipment, and supplies.

A **rack jobber** is a full-function merchant wholesaler that markets specialized lines of merchandise to retailers. A rack jobber supplies the racks, stocks the merchandise, prices the goods, and makes regular visits to refill shelves. Sometimes rack jobbers are the exclusive supplier of a retailer—as in the case of Anderson Merchandisers, a rack jobber in the entertainment sector, which grew by being the supplier to Walmart stores' consumer electronics departments.[26]

merchant wholesaler
Independently owned wholesaling intermediary that takes title to the goods it handles; also known as an industrial distributor in the business goods market.

rack jobber Full-function merchant wholesaler that markets specialized lines of merchandise to retail stores.

Marketoid

Acklands-Grainger, Canada's largest merchant wholesaler with 170 branches and six distribution centres from coast to coast, has a 3040-page catalogue and stocks more than 120 000 products in its inventory.

truck wholesaler (or truck jobber) Limited-function merchant wholesaler that markets perishable food items.

drop shipper Limited-function merchant wholesaler that accepts orders from customers and forwards these orders to producers, which then ship directly to the customers who placed the orders.

mail-order wholesaler Limited-function merchant wholesaler that distributes catalogues instead of sending sales personnel to contact customers.

commission merchant Agent wholesaling intermediary who takes possession of goods shipped to a central market for sale, acts as the producer's agent, and collects an agreed-upon fee at the time of the sale.

Limited-function merchant wholesalers fit into four categories: cash-and-carry wholesalers, truck wholesalers, drop shippers, and mail-order wholesalers. Limited-function wholesalers serve the food, coal, lumber, cosmetics, jewellery, sporting goods, and general merchandise industries.

A *cash-and-carry wholesaler* performs most wholesaling functions except for financing and delivery. Although feasible for small stores, this kind of wholesaling generally is unworkable for large-scale grocery stores. Today, cash-and-carry operations typically function as departments within regular full-service wholesale operations. Cash-and-carry wholesalers are becoming less popular in Canada but are still commonplace in some European countries.

A **truck wholesaler**, or **truck jobber**, markets perishable food items such as bread, tobacco, potato chips, candy, and dairy products. Truck wholesalers make regular deliveries to retailers, perform sales and collection functions, and promote product lines.

A **drop shipper** accepts orders from customers and forwards these orders to producers, which then ship the desired products directly to customers. Although drop shippers take title to goods, they never physically handle or even see the merchandise. These intermediaries often operate in industries selling bulky goods—such as coal and lumber—that customers buy in large lots.

A **mail-order wholesaler** is a limited-function merchant wholesaler that distributes physical or online catalogues as opposed to sending sales representatives to contact retail, business, and institutional customers. Customers then make purchases by mail, phone, or online. Such a wholesaler often serves relatively small customers in outlying areas. Mail-order operations mainly exist in the hardware, cosmetics, jewellery, sporting goods, and specialty food lines as well as in general merchandise. Some popular mail-order products are pharmaceuticals, roasted bean coffee, Christmas trees and wreaths, and popcorn.

Table 12.2 compares the various types of merchant wholesalers and the services they provide. Full-function merchant wholesalers and truck wholesalers rank as relatively high-cost intermediaries due to the number of services they perform, while cash-and-carry wholesalers, drop shippers, and mail-order wholesalers provide fewer services and set lower prices since they incur lower operating costs.

Agents and Brokers

A second group of independent wholesaling intermediaries, agents and brokers, may or may not take possession of the goods they handle, but they never take title. They normally perform fewer services than merchant wholesalers, working mainly to bring together buyers and sellers. Agents and brokers fall into five categories: commission merchants, auction houses, brokers, selling agents, and manufacturers' representatives (reps).

Commission merchants, who predominate in the markets for agricultural products, take possession when producers ship goods such as grain, produce, and livestock to central markets for sale. Commission merchants act as producers' agents and receive agreed-upon fees when they make sales. Since customers inspect the products and prices fluctuate, commission merchants receive considerable

table 12.2   *Comparison of the Types of Merchant Wholesalers and Their Services*

SERVICE	Full-Function	LIMITED-FUNCTION WHOLESALER			
		Cash-and-Carry	Truck	Drop Shipper	Mail-Order
Anticipates customer needs	Yes	Yes	Yes	No	Yes
Carries inventory	Yes	Yes	Yes	No	Yes
Delivers	Yes	No	Yes	No	No
Provides market information	Yes	Rarely	Yes	Yes	No
Provides credit	Yes	No	No	Yes	Sometimes
Assumes ownership risk by taking title	Yes	Yes	Yes	Yes	Yes

latitude in marketing decisions. The owners of the goods may specify minimum prices, but the commission merchants sell these goods at the best possible prices. The commission merchants then deduct their fees from the sales proceeds.

An *auction house* gathers buyers and sellers in one location and allows potential buyers to inspect merchandise before submitting competing purchase offers. Auction house commissions typically reflect specified percentages of the sales prices of the auctioned items. Auctions are common in the distribution of tobacco, used cars, artwork, livestock, furs, and fruit. The Internet has led to a new type of auction house that connects customers and sellers in the online world. A well-known example is eBay, which auctions a wide variety of products in all price ranges.

Brokers work mainly to bring together buyers and sellers. A broker represents either the buyer or the seller, but not both, in a given transaction, and the broker receives a fee from the client when the transaction is completed. Intermediaries that specialize in arranging buying and selling transactions between domestic producers and foreign buyers are called *export brokers*. Brokers operate in industries characterized by large numbers of small suppliers and purchasers, such as real estate, frozen foods, and used machinery. Since they provide one-time services for sellers or buyers, they cannot serve as effective channels for manufacturers seeking regular, continuing service. A firm that seeks to develop a more permanent channel might choose instead to use a selling agent or manufacturers' agent.

A **selling agent** typically exerts full authority over pricing decisions and promotional outlays, and it often provides financial assistance for the manufacturer. Selling agents act as independent marketing departments because they can assume responsibility for the total marketing programs of client firms' product lines. Selling agents mainly operate in the coal, lumber, and textiles industries. For a small, poorly financed, production-oriented firm, such an intermediary might prove the ideal marketing channel.

While a manufacturer may deal with only one selling agent, a firm that hires **manufacturers' representatives** often delegates marketing tasks to many of these agents. Such an independent salesperson may work for a number of firms that produce related, noncompeting products. Manufacturers' reps are paid on a commission basis, such as 6 percent of sales. Unlike selling agents, who may contract for exclusive rights to market a product, manufacturers' agents operate in specific territories. They may develop new sales territories or represent relatively small firms and those firms with unrelated lines. Uponor Canada—with a head office and warehouse in Regina, Saskatchewan, and a manufacturing plant in Saint John, New Brunswick—sells radiant floor heating systems, polyethylene plumbing systems, and fire protection systems. It uses a national network of manufacturers' representatives to sell its products to wholesale distributors across Canada.[27]

The importance of selling agents in many markets has declined because manufacturers want better control of their marketing programs than these intermediaries allow. In contrast, the volume of sales by manufacturers' agents has more than doubled and now accounts for 37 percent of all sales by agents and brokers. Table 12.3 compares the major types of agents and brokers on the basis of the services they perform.

broker
Agent wholesaling intermediary who does not take title to or possession of goods in the course of its primary function, which is to bring together buyers and sellers.

selling agent
Agent wholesaling intermediary for the entire marketing program of a firm's product line.

manufacturers' representative
Agent wholesaling intermediary who represents manufacturers of related but noncompeting products and who receives a commission on each sale.

assessment check 6

6.1 What is the difference between a merchant wholesaler and a rack jobber?

6.2 Differentiate between agents and brokers.

---

table 12.3 *Services Provided by Agents and Brokers*

SERVICE	Commission Merchant	Auction House	Broker	Manufacturers' Agent	Selling Agent
Anticipates customer needs	Yes	Sometimes	Sometimes	Yes	Yes
Carries inventory	Yes	Yes	No	No	No
Delivers	Yes	No	No	Sometimes	No
Provides market information	Yes	Yes	Yes	Yes	Yes
Provides credit	Sometimes	No	No	No	Sometimes
Assumes ownership risk by taking title	No	No	No	No	No

RETAILER-OWNED COOPERATIVES AND BUYING OFFICES

Retailers may assume numerous wholesaling functions in an attempt to reduce costs or provide special services. Independent retailers sometimes band together to form buying groups that can achieve cost savings through quantity purchases. Other groups of retailers establish retailer-owned wholesale facilities by forming cooperative chains. Large chain retailers often establish centralized buying offices to negotiate large-scale purchases directly with manufacturers.

(7) Compare the basic types of direct marketing and nonstore retailing.

direct marketing Direct communications, other than personal sales contacts, between buyer and seller, designed to generate sales, information requests, or store or website visits.

DIRECT MARKETING AND OTHER NONSTORE RETAILING

Although most retail transactions occur in stores, nonstore retailing is an important marketing channel for many products. Both consumer and business-to-business marketers rely on nonstore retailing to generate leads or requests for more information that may result in future orders.

Direct marketing is a broad concept that includes direct mail, direct selling, direct-response retailing, telemarketing, Internet retailing, and automatic merchandising. Direct and interactive marketing expenditures amount to hundreds of billions of dollars in yearly purchases across North America. The last sections of this chapter consider each type of nonstore retailing.

DIRECT MAIL

Direct mail is a major component of direct marketing. It comes in many forms, such as sales letters, postcards, brochures, booklets, catalogues, house organs (periodicals published by organizations to cover internal issues), and DVDs. Both not-for-profit and profit-seeking organizations make extensive use of this distribution channel.

Direct mail offers several advantages such as the ability to select a narrow target market, achieve intensive coverage, send messages quickly, choose from various formats, provide complete information, and personalize each mailing piece. Response rates are measurable and higher than other types of advertising. In addition, direct mailings stand alone and do not compete for attention with magazine articles and television programs. On the other hand, the per-reader cost of direct mail is high, effectiveness depends on the quality of the mailing list, and some consumers object strongly to direct mail, considering it "junk mail."

Direct-mail marketing relies heavily on database technology in managing lists of names and in segmenting these lists according to the objectives of the campaign. Recipients get targeted materials, often personalized with their names within the ad's content.

Catalogues are a popular form of direct mail, with more than 10 000 different consumer specialty mail-order catalogues—and thousands more for business-to-business sales—finding their way to almost every home and business in Canada and the United States. In a typical year, mail-order catalogues generate billions of dollars in consumer and business markets. Catalogue marketing continues to grow at a faster rate than brick-and-mortar retailers. Catalogues can be a company's only or primary sales method. L.L. Bean and Spiegel are well-known examples. Brick-and-mortar retailers such as Canadian Tire, Tilley Endurables, and IKEA Canada also distribute catalogues. All these companies now accept orders over their websites or by telephone, making it virtually impossible to tell what impact catalogues have on sales. However, this does not cause concern for Cass Hall, marketing manager at IKEA Canada, who says, "We've always looked at it as a broader shopping tool. Traditionally it's been to drive people into the store and help plan their visit. More and more it's a branding tool for us."[28]

Environmental concerns and new technologies are changing catalogue marketing. Today's catalogues can be updated quickly, providing consumers with the latest information and prices. Online catalogues allow marketers to display products in three-dimensional views and can include video sequences of product demonstrations.

DIRECT SELLING

Through direct selling, manufacturers completely bypass retailers and wholesalers. Instead, they set up their own channels to sell their products directly to consumers. Avon, Amway, Pampered Chef, and Tupperware are all direct sellers. This channel was discussed in detail in Chapter 11.

DIRECT-RESPONSE RETAILING

Customers of a direct-response retailer can order merchandise by mail or telephone, by visiting a mail-order desk in a retail store, or by computer or fax machine. The retailer then ships the merchandise to the customer's home or to a local retail store for pickup.

Many direct-response retailers rely on direct mail, such as catalogues, to create telephone and mail-order sales and to promote in-store purchases of products featured in the catalogues. Some firms, such as Lillian Vernon, make almost all their sales through catalogue orders. Mail-order sales have grown at about twice the rate of retail store sales in recent years.

Direct-response retailers are increasingly reaching buyers through the Internet and through unique catalogues that serve special market niches. Many catalogues sell specialty products, such as kitchenware for the professional cook, art supplies, or supplies for the home renovator.

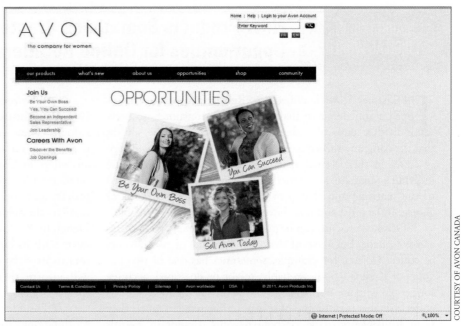

Avon is known and respected for direct selling through its many independent sales representatives across Canada and throughout the world.

Direct-response retailing also includes home shopping, which runs promotions on cable television networks to sell merchandise through telephone orders. One form of home shopping, the *infomercial,* has existed for years. Infomercials can be short—one to two minutes—or run up to 30 minutes. Both have demonstrated success at generating revenues. The "king of infomercials," the late Billy Mays, became famous for hawking such products as OxiClean, Orange Glo, and Mighty Putty. Mays created a "brand" that projected authority, no matter what he was selling. Industry observers say Mays was successful because he was likeable and managed to get consumers to buy products they didn't know they needed.[29]

TELEMARKETING

Telemarketing refers to direct marketing conducted entirely by telephone. It is the most frequently used form of direct marketing. It provides marketers with a high return on their expenditures, an immediate response, and the opportunity for personalized two-way conversations. Telemarketing is discussed in further detail in Chapter 15.

assessment check 7

7.1 What is direct marketing?

7.2 What is direct mail?

INTERNET RETAILING

Internet-based retailers sell directly to customers via virtual storefronts on the Web. They usually maintain little or no inventory, ordering directly from vendors to fill customer orders received via their websites. In recent years, conventional retailers have anxiously watched the rise—and then the demise—of many poorly planned, financed, and marketed Internet-based retailers. During the dot-com bust, 130 e-tailers failed. Even early successes like Ezshop, an online home furnishings retailer, eventually ran aground. Traditional retailers, using the Web to support brick-and-mortar stores—the so-called *brick-and-click retailers*—have had much better staying power. Sears Canada, Future Shop, and Canadian Tire, for example, have succeeded in extending their expertise to the Web. Costco offers thousands of products on its website, many of which are not available at store locations. Customers who wish can also request e-mail alerts or go online to read the *Costco Connection* magazine.

(8) **Describe how the Internet has altered the wholesaling, retailing, and direct marketing environments.**

New Products Sometimes Create New Products and New Opportunities for Online Retailers

IN Chapter 5, we described how Keurig Incorporated developed a coffee system that would allow consumers to brew individual cups of coffee of their choice, and the success that the company subsequently enjoyed. But to brew single cups of coffee in their Keurig machines, consumers must purchase individual-sized cups—referred to as K-cups—that are inserted in the machine and that provide each consumer's flavour of choice. In fact, tea and hot chocolate K-cups are also available.

Of course K-cups can be purchased from many retail stores across Canada, but most of them sell only one or two flavours of coffee. Costco, for example, sometimes has one or two flavours of K-cups—both, arguably, might be described as coffee for people who are not really serious about their coffee. Serious coffee drinkers turn to one of several online retailers when they want fruity, zesty, dark, or bold flavours. Brands of K-cups include Wolfgang Puck, Timothy's, Green Mountain, Caribou Coffee, Coffee People, Dolce Gusto, JavaOne, Starbucks, Newman's Own, Diedrich, and several dozen more. Many manufacturers are adding K-cups to their line of beverage products, and online retailers generally carry a wide selection of brands as their strategy to appeal to coffee drinkers.

Online retailers such as SingleCup.ca and Van Houtte (www.vanhoutte.com) offer hundreds of choices to consumers. These and other online retailers offer free shipping, depending on order size, and delivery is available almost anywhere in Canada within a few days. Many online coffee retailers offer volume discounts, sometimes on individual orders, and sometimes to preferred customers who become regular shoppers. SingleCup.ca offers customers "Hot & Delicious K-Cup Recipes" on its website. Van Houtte connects with its customers with an online coffee blog, and visitors to its website can sign up for a monthly newsletter that will inform them of upcoming contests, promotions, and special offers.

If Tim Hortons changed the way Canadians think of their morning Joe, Keurig is moving some Canadians forward by offering them the ability to select their favourite flavours to suit each occasion. All they need to do is select their favourite online K-cup source.

Sources: Company websites, http://www.shoffee.com, http://www.singlecup.ca, http://www.vanhoutte.com, August 3, 2011.

AUTOMATIC MERCHANDISING

The world's first vending machines dispensed holy water for five-drachma coins in Egyptian temples around 215 B.C. This retailing method has grown rapidly ever since; today, approximately 5000 North American vending machine operators sell more than $6 billion in convenience goods annually.[30]

Although vending machines have traditionally been limited to snacks and soft drinks, Japanese consumers use automatic merchandising for products as varied as fresh sushi and new underwear. Recently, Canadian marketers have begun to realize the potential of this underused marketing tool. The three major soft-drink companies recently agreed to remove sweetened drinks such as pop and iced tea from vending machines in elementary and high schools nationwide. The calorie-laden drinks will be replaced by bottled water, low-fat milk, and 100 percent fruit juice or sports drinks. The ability to accept credit cards has enabled vending machines to sell high-end items like iPods, headphones, and Sony PlayStation games. Technological advances such as touch screens, animation, and digital imagery make the buying experience fun—and even allow customers to read the back of the package before they buy.[31]

H. F. (HERB) MACKENZIE

Vending machines are common throughout Canada, but are an even more popular form of merchandising in Japan.

assessment check 8

8.1 Describe Internet-based retailers.

8.2 Explain how the Internet has enhanced retailers' functions.

Strategic Implications

As the Internet revolution steadily becomes a way of life—both for consumers and for the businesses marketing goods and services to them—technology will continue to transform the ways in which retailers, wholesalers, and direct marketers connect with customers.

In the retail sector, the unstoppable march toward lower and lower prices has forced retailers from Sears Canada to dollar stores to re-evaluate everything, including their logistics, supply networks, and profit margins. Many have used the power of the Internet to strengthen such factors as store image, the merchandising mix, customer service, and the development of long-term relationships with customers.

Though manufacturers first anticipated that Internet technology would enable them to bypass such intermediaries as wholesalers and agents, bringing them closer to the customer, the reality is quite different. Successful wholesalers have been able to establish themselves as essential links in the supply, distribution, and customer-service network. By leveraging technology, they have been able to carve out new roles, providing such expert services as warehousing or fulfillment to many retail clients.

The Internet has empowered direct marketers by facilitating ever more sophisticated database segmentation. Traditional catalogue and direct mail marketers have integrated Internet sites, Web advertising, and e-mailing programs into a cohesive targeting, distribution, and repeat-buying strategy. ◆◆◆

REVIEW OF CHAPTER OBJECTIVES

① **Explain the wheel of retailing.**

The wheel of retailing is the hypothesis that each new type of retailer gains a competitive foothold by offering lower prices than current suppliers and maintains profits by reducing or eliminating services. Once established, the innovator begins to add more services, and its prices gradually rise, making it vulnerable to new low-price retailers. This turns the wheel again.

② **Discuss how retailers select target markets.**

A retailer starts to define its strategy by selecting a target market. The target market dictates, among other things, the product mix, pricing strategy, and location strategy. Retailers deal with consumer behaviour at the most complicated level, and a clear understanding of the target market is critical. Strategies for selecting target markets include merchandising, customer services, pricing, location/distribution, and promotional strategies.

③ **Show how the elements of the marketing mix apply to retailing strategy.**

A retailer must first identify a target market and then develop a product strategy. Next, it must establish a customer-service strategy. Retail pricing strategy involves decisions on markups and markdowns. Location is often the determining factor in a retailer's success or failure. A retailer's promotional strategy and store atmosphere play important roles in establishing a store's image.

④ **Explain the concepts of retail convergence and scrambled merchandising.**

Retail convergence is the coming together of shoppers, goods, and prices, resulting in the blurring of distinctions between types of retailers and the merchandise mix they offer. Similar selections are available from many sources and are differentiated mainly by price. Scrambled merchandising refers to retailers' practice of carrying dissimilar product lines in an attempt to generate additional sales volume. Retail convergence and scrambled merchandising have made it increasingly difficult to classify retailers.

⑤ **Identify the functions performed by wholesaling intermediaries.**

The functions of wholesaling intermediaries include creating utility, providing services, and lowering costs by limiting contacts.

(6) **Outline the major types of independent wholesaling intermediaries and the appropriate situations for using each.**

Independent wholesaling intermediaries can be divided into two categories: merchant wholesalers and agents and brokers. The two major types of merchant wholesalers are full-function merchant wholesalers, such as rack jobbers, and limited-function merchant wholesalers, including cash-and-carry wholesalers, truck wholesalers, drop shippers, and mail-order wholesalers. Full-function wholesalers are common in the drug, grocery, and hardware industries.

Limited-function wholesalers are sometimes used in the food, coal, lumber, cosmetics, jewellery, sporting goods, and general merchandise industries. Agents and brokers do not take title to the products they sell; this category includes commission merchants, auction houses, brokers, selling agents, and manufacturers' reps. Companies seeking to develop new sales territories, firms with unrelated lines, and smaller firms use manufacturers' reps. Commission merchants are common in the marketing of agricultural products. Auction houses are used to sell tobacco, used cars, livestock, furs, and fruit. Brokers are prevalent in the real estate, frozen foods, and used machinery industries.

(7) **Compare the basic types of direct marketing and nonstore retailing.**

Direct marketing is a distribution channel consisting of direct communication to a consumer or business recipient. It generates orders and sales leads that may result in future orders. Because direct marketing responds to fragmented media markets and audiences, growth of customized products, and shrinking network broadcast audiences, marketers consider it an important part of their planning efforts. While most Canadian retail sales take place in stores, such nonstore retailing activities as direct mail, direct selling, direct-response retailing, telemarketing, Internet retailing, and automatic merchandising are important in marketing many types of goods and services.

(8) **Describe how the Internet has altered the wholesaling, retailing, and direct marketing environments.**

The Internet has affected everything from how supply networks operate to how relationships are formed with customers. Successful wholesalers have carved out a niche as a source of expertise offering faster, more efficient, Web-enabled distribution and fulfillment. The Internet has allowed retailers to enhance their merchandising mix and their customer service by, among other things, giving them access to much broader selections of goods. Direct marketers have merged their traditional catalogue or direct mail programs with an Internet interface that allows for faster, more efficient, and more frequent contact with customers and prospects.

assessment check answers

1.1 What is retailing?
Retailing describes the activities involved in selling merchandise to ultimate consumers.

1.2 Explain the wheel-of-retailing concept.
The wheel of retailing is the hypothesis that each new type of retailer gains a competitive foothold by offering lower prices than current suppliers and maintains profits by reducing or eliminating services.

2.1 How does a retailer develop a marketing strategy?
A retailer develops a marketing strategy based on its goals and strategic plans.

2.2 How do retailers select target markets?
Strategies for selecting target markets include merchandising, customer services, pricing, location/distribution, and promotional strategies.

3.1 What is an SKU?
An SKU or stock-keeping unit is a specific product offering within a product line.

3.2 What are the two components of a markup?
A markup consists of the product's cost and an amount added by the retailer to determine its selling price.

3.3 What are store atmospherics?
Store atmospherics are physical characteristics and amenities that attract customers and satisfy their shopping needs.

4.1 How do we classify retailers by form of ownership?
There are two types of retailers by form of ownership: chain stores and independent retailers.

4.2 Categorize retailers by shopping effort and by services provided.
Convenience retailers and specialty retailers are classified by shopping effort; self-service, self-selection, and full-service describe retailers in terms of services provided.

4.3 List several ways to classify retailers by product line.
Retailers classified by product line include specialty stores, limited-line retailers, and general-merchandise retailers.

General-merchandise retailers include variety stores, department stores, and mass merchandisers.

5.1 What is a wholesaler? How does it differ from a wholesaling intermediary?

A wholesaler is a channel intermediary that takes title to goods it handles and then distributes these goods to retailers, other distributors, or B2B customers. A wholesaling intermediary can be a wholesaler, an agent, or a broker and perform wholesaling activities without taking title to the goods.

5.2 How do wholesaling intermediaries help sellers lower costs?

Wholesaling intermediaries lower the number of transactions between manufacturers and retail outlets, thus lowering distribution costs.

6.1 What is the difference between a merchant wholesaler and a rack jobber?

A merchant wholesaler takes title to the goods it handles. A rack jobber is a full-function merchant wholesaler that markets specialized lines of merchandise to retailers.

6.2 Differentiate between agents and brokers.

Agents and brokers may or may not take possession of the goods they handle but they never take title. Brokers work mainly to bring together buyers and sellers. A selling agent typically exerts full authority over pricing decisions and promotional outlays and often provides financial assistance for the manufacturer.

7.1 What is direct marketing?

Direct marketing is a distribution channel consisting of direct communication to a consumer or business recipient. It generates orders and sales leads that may result in future orders.

7.2 What is direct mail?

Direct mail is a form of direct marketing that includes sales letters, postcards, brochures, booklets, catalogues, house organs, and DVDs.

8.1 Describe Internet-based retailers.

Internet-based retailers sell directly to customers via virtual storefronts on the Web. They usually maintain little or no inventory, ordering directly from vendors to fill customers' orders.

8.2 Explain how the Internet has enhanced retailers' functions.

The Internet has allowed retailers to enhance their merchandising mix and their customer service by, among other things, giving them access to much broader selections of goods. Direct marketers have merged their traditional catalogue or direct-mail programs with an Internet interface that allows for faster, more efficient, and more frequent contact with customers and prospects.

MARKETING TERMS YOU NEED TO KNOW

These terms are printed in red in the text. They are defined in the margins of the chapter and in the Glossary that begins on p. G-1.

retailing 360
wheel of retailing 360
stockkeeping unit (SKU) 363
markup 366
markdown 366
planned shopping centre 366
atmospherics 368
convenience retailer 370
specialty retailer 370
limited-line store 371
category killer 371

general merchandise retailer 371
department store 371
mass merchandiser 372
discount house 372
hypermarket 372
supercentre 372
scrambled merchandising 373
retail convergence 373
wholesaling intermediary 374
wholesaler 374
rack jobber 377

merchant wholesaler 377
commission merchant 378
truck wholesaler (truck jobber) 378
drop shipper 378
mail-order wholesaler 378
manufacturers' representative 379
broker 379
selling agent 379
direct marketing 380

PROJECTS AND TEAMWORK EXERCISES

1. Research and then classify each of the following retailers:
   a. Canadian Tire
   b. Bonnie Togs
   c. Danier Leather
   d. Stoney Creek Furniture
   e. Golf Town
2. Visit a local Walmart store and observe such aspects as product placement, shelf placement, inventory levels on shelves, traffic patterns, customer service, and checkout efficiency. Discuss what makes Walmart the world's most successful retailer.

3. Winners has become known for trendy clothes and stylish housewares, all readily available in spacious stores at reasonable prices. Visit a local Winners store or the company's website and compare its product selection to a hardware store and/or a department store. Make a list of each store's advantages and disadvantages, including convenience, location, selection, service, and general prices. Do any of its product lines overlap? How are they different from each other?

4. In pairs, match each industry with the most appropriate type of wholesaling intermediary.

  ___ hardware   a. drop shipper
  ___ perishable foods   b. truck wholesaler
  ___ lumber   c. auction house
  ___ wheat   d. full-function merchant wholesaler
  ___ used cars   e. commission merchant

5. In teams, develop a retailing strategy for an Internet retailer. Identify a target market and then suggest a mix of merchandise, promotion, service, and pricing strategies that would help a retailer to reach that market via the Internet. What issues must Internet retailers address that do not affect traditional store retailers?

6. With a classmate, visit two or three retail stores that compete with one another in your area and compare their customer-service strategies. (You might wish to visit each store more than once to avoid making a snap judgment.) Select at least five criteria and use them to assess each store. How do you think each store sees its customer-service strategy as fitting into its overall retailing strategy? Present your findings in detail to the class.

7. Visit a department store and compare at least two departments' pricing strategies based on the number of markdowns you find and the size of the discount. What, if anything, can you conclude about the success of each department's retailing strategy?

8. Think of a large purchase you make on a nonroutine basis, such as a new winter coat or expensive clothing for a special occasion. Where will you shop for such items? Will you travel out of your way? Will you go to the nearest shopping centre? Will you look on the Internet? Once you have made your decision, describe any strategies used by the retailer that led you to this decision. What would make you change your mind about where to shop for this item?

9. Outlet malls are a growing segment of the retail market. Visit a local outlet mall or research one on the Internet. What types of stores are located there? How do the product selection and price compare with typical stores?

10. Addition Elle is a national chain of stores that feature clothing for plus-size women. Recommend an appropriate retailing strategy for this type of retailer.

CRITICAL-THINKING EXERCISES

1. Retail chain Anthropologie sells a unique mix of women's clothing and home furnishings. Since its founding in 1992, Anthropologie has opened stores across the United States, in Canada, and in Great Britain. The retailer aims to create a shopping "experience" where its customers—independent-minded college-educated female professionals between ages 30 and 45—can find their own look. No two Anthropologie stores are exactly alike, and the chain does not use advertising. Visit the website at **www.anthropologie.com**. How does it differentiate itself from its competitors?

2. Several major retailers have begun to test the extreme mark-down strategy that lies behind popular "dollar" stores such as Great Canadian Dollar Store or Dollar Giant. Walmart and A&P, for example, are opening sections in selected stores that feature items such as snacks and beauty supplies priced at $1. Is this experiment simply a test of pricing strategy? What else might motivate these retailers to offer such deep discounts?

3. When A and B Sound, a company with 21 music stores that controlled 20 percent of recorded music sales in Western Canada, filed for court protection from its creditors, it was only one symptom of the general decline of the retail music store. Industry analysts blame such things as music downloading programs and changes in consumers' tastes. Most, however, feel that music stores will somehow remain viable. What are some changes that these retailers could make in their merchandising, customer service, pricing, location, and other strategies to try to reinvent their business?

4. McDonald's has traditionally relied on a cookie-cutter approach to its restaurant design. One store looked essentially like every other—until recently. The chain has decided to loosen its corporate design mandate to fit within special markets and to update its image with customers. Research McDonald's makeover efforts. What types of changes has the company made and where? How have changes in atmospherics helped the chain with customers? Have the changes you researched modified your perception of McDonald's at all? If so, how?

ETHICS EXERCISE

As the largest company in the world, with 2.1 million employees worldwide and $405 billion (U.S.) in sales in a recent year, many people would argue that Walmart has become too big and powerful. It has twice as many stores in Mexico as it does in Canada, and it is the largest private-sector employer in that country. It imports so much from China that, if it were a country, Walmart would be China's eighth-largest trading partner, ahead of Britain and Russia. Walmart is currently opening a new store approximately every 42 hours. Some observers believe Walmart is also responsible for the low inflation rates and high productivity gains of recent years in Canada and the United States, accounting for as much as 12 percent of total productivity gains since the late 1990s. However, its unbeatable buying power and efficiency have forced many local stores to close when Walmart opens a new store in their area.

1. Some economists fear what might happen to the economy if Walmart has a bad year (so far it has had more than four decades of nonstop growth). Should retailers have that much influence on the economy? Why or why not?

2. Walmart is selective about what it sells, refusing, for instance, to carry music or computer games with mature ratings, magazines with content that it considers too adult, or a popular morning-after pill. Because of its sheer size, these decisions can become influential in the culture. Do you think this is a positive or negative effect of the growth of this retailer? Why?

INTERNET EXERCISES

1. **Retailing strategy.** Visit the website of electronics retailer Best Buy (**www.bestbuy.ca**). The website is classified as a shopping site, or online store. Review the material in the chapter on retailing strategy and store atmospherics. Answer the following questions.
   a. How does the design and layout of the Best Buy Web store appeal to the company's target market(s)?
   b. How would you describe the atmospherics created by the online store? If you can visit a brick-and-mortar store, compare the store's atmospherics to the Web store.
   c. In what ways does Best Buy use its online store to enhance its brick-and-mortar stores?
2. **Shopping centre trends.** Visit the website listed here (**http://retailtrafficmag.com**). Click on "development" and then "trends." Review the material and then prepare a brief report on some of the major trends in shopping centre development.

3. **Retailing statistics.** Statistics Canada (**www.statscan .gc.ca**) reports regularly on Canadian retail sales and wholesale sales. Visit the website listed below and access the most recent retail sales and wholesale sales reports. Be prepared to consider and report on the following questions:
   a. What trends can you identify in Canadian retail sales and wholesale sales?
   b. By how much have retail sales and wholesale sales grown over the past month? Over the past year?
   c. Are retail sales or wholesale sales greater? Which is growing more quickly?
   d. Are you more likely to see seasonal patterns in retail sales or wholesale sales? Why?
   e. What have you found that is interesting and more recent than what is provided in your text?

Note: Internet Web addresses change frequently. If you don't find the exact sites listed, you may need to access the organization's or company's home page and search from there or use a search engine such as Google.

CASE 12.1

Groupon: Finding Strength in Numbers

Want a deep discount on a deep-dish pizza . . . a day at a health spa . . . Major League Baseball tickets? If you like a bargain, e-coupon site Groupon may be for you. Or suppose you're opening a gym: you need customers, and you need them fast. You can advertise your business and hope to reach people with the desire and the cash to join. Or using the power of social commerce offered by a site like Groupon, you gain exposure for your new business and attract interested shoppers through a discounted membership deal.

Groupon uses the Internet to help business owners connect with prospective customers. The rules are simple: Groupon works with the business to create a deal offering a discount on goods or services. Owners set the terms of the deal: the minimum and maximum number of takers and the discount amount (usually around 50 percent but sometimes more). Groupon features the deal for one day. If a prescribed number of shoppers—typically 50—take the deal, it's a go. If not, the deal expires and no money changes hands. Meanwhile, Groupon makes money by pocketing a finder's fee on successful deals.

Groupon helps businesses reach target audiences without costly advertising and lets them mine a segment that doesn't respond to conventional appeals: young professionals ages 20 to 30 who are typically online constantly.

Subscribing is easy, and the site is fun: there's a new deal each day in each of the cities in Canada and the United States where Groupon currently operates. The deals represent a broad array of products and services. Some of them are your everyday purchases, like a haircut, a Chinese dinner, or a supermarket trip. Other deals may come from a new business in your city or an experience you haven't tried, such as kayaking lessons, theatre tickets, or a museum membership. As Groupon knows, the fact that the experience comes with a discount may be the push you need to buy. Subscribers have just a day to grab the deal.

But nothing is entirely risk free. A successful Groupon deal creates a surge of business that brings the owner little or no profit. Where owners see profit is in follow-on business. Until then, a business can capsize under the surge if the owner hasn't taken care to set things up wisely, with minimum and maximum limits and the right discount amount.

Today, Groupon has more than 2 million subscribers and, in some regions, a waiting list of business owners ready to make a deal.

Questions for Critical Thinking

1. Coupons are a tried-and-true promotion method, and the Internet includes other couponing sites. How does Groupon differentiate itself?
2. Groupon's business strategy harnesses what it calls "collective buying power." What facets of the marketing environment have enabled a business like Groupon to emerge and become successful?

Sources: Jesse Hempel, "Social Media Meets Retailing," *Fortune*, March 22, 2010, p. 30; Wailin Wong, "Groupon Spawns Rivals on Social Media Bargain-Hunting Scene," *Chicago Tribune*, February 22, 2010, http://www.chicagotribune.com; Heather Green, "Coaxing Shoppers of a Feather to Flock Together," *BusinessWeek*, December 14, 2009, http://www.businessweek.com; Taylor Buley, "The Best Discounts on the Web," *Forbes*, November 25, 2009, http://www.forbes.com; John Sviokla, "Groupon's Four Keys to Customer Interaction," *Harvard Business Review*, September 14, 2009, http://blogs.hbr.org; Mary Pilon, "Finding Group Discounts Online," *The Wall Street Journal*, August 11, 2009, http://blogs.wsj.com; Gabriella Boston, "Site Leverages Power of Group Purchases," *Washington Times*, July 8, 2009, http://www.washingtontimes.com; Brad Tuttle, "Q&A with Groupon.com Founder Andrew Mason," *Time*, June 24, 2009, http://money.blogs.time.com.

CASE 12.2

Let's Have a Party—Bring Your Wallet

Direct selling is an important marketing channel (discussed in Chapter 11) and provides opportunity for people interested in exploring personal selling (to be discussed in Chapter 15). It is an important form of nonstore retailing; sales have been increasing between 10 and 20 percent per year over the past decade and are now nearly $2.2 billion annually in Canada, where there are more than 75 direct selling companies. They employ more than 600 000 independent salespeople—called representatives, distributors, dealers, or consultants.

One direct selling company that has been particularly successful in recent years is The Pampered Chef. It has been operating in the United States since 1980 and in Canada since 1996. Sales in Canada have now exceeded $50 million annually. Although the company accepts orders directly through its website, most products are sold through in-home cooking demonstrations, referred to as Cooking Shows. Basically, this is a "party plan"—a salesperson makes a demonstration of some of the more than 200 available products at the home of a "party host." Often, the party host has been a participant at a previous Cooking Show where the salesperson has asked for volunteers to host a future Cooking Show. Guests at the parties receive a small gift for their attendance, while hosts receive a larger gift for hosting the party. Salespeople take orders at the party and collect payment immediately or when the product is delivered to the purchaser. More than 1 million Cooking Shows are held annually in North America.

Pampered Chef consultants have a lot of personal freedom. In recent years, they have even been able to have their personal websites, but the company does have a number of restrictions to ensure its image in the marketplace is protected. As independent business owners, some work a few hours per week, or a few days per month. Others, such as Terri Newberry, work six hours per day, four or five days, and several evenings per week. Some sell to supplement their own or family income; some treat this as their primary source of income and achieve considerable success. When Terri Newberry, for example, started as a Pampered Chef consultant, she earned just over $500 her first month, $1000 her

fourth month, and progressed to just under $10 000 per month after about ten years. In Canada, there are seven levels of salespeople from consultant to senior executive director. Salespeople can earn more than just their commission. Depending on their sales level, they can earn free products, jewellery, and even vacation cruises. In one recent year, 3300 Pampered Chef salespeople stayed at the Four Seasons in Palm Beach, Florida, and then cruised aboard Royal Caribbean's *Navigator of the Seas* and *Enchantment of the Seas*.

Why is The Pampered Chef so successful? Certainly a lot of credit goes to its independent sales force, and the party plan method of retailing. But it could not do this without a selection of quality products and a company philosophy that promotes honesty and fairness for its salespeople and customers. The Pampered Chef is a member of the Direct Sellers Association (DSA), as are approximately 70 percent of all direct selling companies in Canada. All member companies must rededicate annually to abide by the DSA code of ethics, which provides appropriate business practices with respect to product sales, consumer care, and recruitment and sales force relations. Host a party—fill your wallet.

Questions for Critical Thinking

1. Why is the party plan such a successful method of nonstore retailing? How can companies such as The Pampered Chef continue to maintain their strong growth in the future?
2. Would you ever consider becoming a Pampered Chef consultant? Why or why not? What factors in the marketing environment would provide future opportunities for you as a Pampered Chef consultant? What factors do you see as potential future threats? Explain.

Sources: Direct Sellers Association website, http://www.dsa.ca; The Pampered Chef website, http://www.pamperedchef.com; The Pampered Chef–Canada website, http://www.pamperedchef.ca; The Pampered Chef blog, http://mlmblog.typepad.com/pampered_chef/2006/06/home_is_where_t.html; Paul Burnham Finney, "When Top Salespeople Get to Ride the Waves," *International Herald Tribune*, May 8, 2006, http://www.iht.com/articles/2006/05/08/business/cruise.php; all websites accessed December 10, 2007.

part 6

PROMOTIONAL DECISIONS

chapter 13

Integrated Marketing Communications

THE CANADIAN PRESS/DAVE CHIDLEY

CHAPTER OBJECTIVES

1. Explain how integrated marketing communications relates to the development of an optimal promotional mix and describe the communication process.

2. Explain how the promotional mix relates to the objectives of promotion.

3. Identify the different elements of the promotional mix and explain how marketers develop an optimal promotional mix.

4. Describe the role of public relations, publicity, sponsorships, and direct marketing in integrated marketing communications.

5. Discuss the factors that influence the effectiveness of a promotional mix and contrast pushing and pulling strategies.

6. Explain how marketers budget for and measure the effectiveness of promotion and discuss the value of marketing communications.

HOCKEYVILLE

"It's about pride. It's about passion for hockey. It's about unshakeable community spirit." This is how the Canadian Broadcasting Corporation website describes the Kraft Hockeyville campaign. But it is also about promotion.

The Kraft Hockeyville promotional campaign began in 2006 and has grown every year. Kraft Canada, in partnership with the Canadian Broadcasting Corporation, the National Hockey League, and the National Hockey League Players' Association, wants people to nominate their local hockey arena for the honour of being the Hockeyville arena of the year. The application process is easy: just explain in 500 words or less how your community demonstrates the hockey spirit and send along up to three photos to support your story. The competition is open to all Canadian communities, and you only have to be 13 years old or older to enter. The stakes are high. The winning community receives $100 000 to upgrade its local arena, gets to host an NHL pre-season hockey game, and is awarded a trophy. The applications are judged on three criteria—community spirit, a passion for hockey, and originality.

The Kraft Hockeyville promotion is not all about community spirit—it also promotes Kraft products. Products like Kraft Dinner, Cracker Barrel cheese, Maxwell House coffee, Ritz crackers, and Oreo cookies have all been featured in the promotion. These products have seen an increase in sales from 4 to 6 percent over the years of the campaign. Using promotional techniques like print material, television, a website, Facebook, Twitter, and YouTube, Kraft Canada gets the Hockeyville message out to Canadians across the country.

Some unique promotional techniques have been part of the campaign. The CBC's television program *Little Mosque on the Prairie* had an episode that included the Hockeyville competition. Mercy, the fictitious Saskatchewan town where the series takes place, submitted an application to be considered for the Hockeyville honour. The submission by the *Little Mosque on the Prairie* characters included pictures of themselves along with their story on why Mercy should win. This example of product integration was not a first for Kraft or for the CBC. The CBC used this approach with programs like *Being Erica* and *Heartland,* and an episode of CTV's *Corner Gas* included the Kraft product Cheez Whiz.

The Kraft Hockeyville Campaign has won several awards over the years. It has been honoured by the Sponsorship Marketing Council for Best in Show and gold awards in the Sustained Success and Sports Sponsorship categories. In its reasons for naming the Kraft Hockeyville Campaign the overall winner, the Sponsorship Marketing Council cited the fact that over 9.3 million Canadians voted for their favourite town, the campaign generated millions of visits to social media sites, and the Kraft products involved in the promotion outperformed other products in their category.

The National Hockey League has also benefited from the Kraft Hockeyville campaign. Although marketing budgets have been pinched due to the recession, and media fragmentation and the introduction of new technology have led to changes in marketing programs, sports sponsorship has held its value. For the 2009–10 season, the National Hockey League saw an increase in sponsorship revenue of over 20 percent from the previous year. Although this increase is not solely attributed to the Kraft Hockeyville campaign, it certainly was one of the company's most successful projects. For the Canadian market, forging promotional partnerships with the National Hockey League is a pretty sure bet, particularly when the target audience is men, but the Kraft campaign included a wider market.

The award-winning Kraft Hockeyville campaign was a win-win no matter how it is measured—communities across the country, Kraft, the National Hockey League, and the players' association all benefit from sponsorship deals like this one.[1]

---

connecting with customers

Kraft, the Canadian Broadcasting Corporation, the National Hockey League, and the National Hockey League Players' Association connect with customers by promoting community spirit through their award-winning promotional campaign. Using promotional media such as television, print, websites, and Facebook, these organizations produced a campaign that benefits them and the customer.

Chapter Overview

TWO of the four components of the marketing mix—product and distribution strategies— were discussed in previous chapters. The three chapters in Part 6 analyze the third marketing mix variable—promotion. **Promotion** is the function of informing, persuading, and influencing the consumer's purchase decision.

This chapter introduces the concept of integrated marketing communications, briefly describes the elements of a firm's promotional mix—personal and nonpersonal promotion—and explains the characteristics that determine the success of the mix. Next, we identify the objectives of promotion and describe the importance of developing promotional budgets and measuring the effectiveness of promotion. Finally, we discuss the importance of the business, economic, and social aspects of promotion. Chapter 14 covers advertising and other nonpersonal selling elements of the promotional mix, online and digital communications. Chapter 15 completes this part of the book by focusing on personal selling and sales promotion.

Throughout *Contemporary Marketing,* special emphasis has been given to new information that shows how technology is changing the way marketers approach *communication,* the transmission of a message from a sender to a receiver. Consumers receive **marketing communications**—messages that deal with buyer–seller relationships—from a variety of media, including television, radio, magazines, direct mail, the Internet, and cell phones. Marketers can broadcast an ad on the Web to mass markets or design a customized appeal targeted to a small market segment. Each message the customer receives from any source represents the brand, company, or organization. A company needs to coordinate all these messages for maximum total impact and to reduce the likelihood the consumer will completely tune them out.

To prevent this loss of attention, marketers are turning to **integrated marketing communications (IMC)**, which coordinates all promotional activities—media advertising, direct mail, personal selling, sales promotion, public relations, and sponsorships—to produce a unified, customer-focused promotional message (Figure 13.1). As you saw in the opening story, Kraft and its partner organizations used IMC to get the message out about the Hockeyville competition. IMC is a broader concept than marketing communications and promotional strategy. It uses database technology to refine the marketer's understanding of the target audience, segment this audience, and select the best type of media for each segment.

This chapter shows that IMC involves not only the marketer but

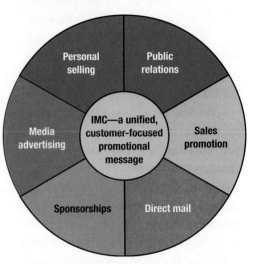

figure 13.1

Integrated Marketing Communications (IMC)

also all other organizational units that interact with the consumer. Marketing managers set the goals and objectives of the firm's promotional strategy in accordance with overall organizational objectives and marketing goals. Based on these objectives, the various elements of the promotional strategy are formulated into an integrated communications plan. This plan becomes a central part of the firm's total marketing strategy to reach its selected market segments. The feedback mechanism, including marketing research and field reports, completes the system by identifying any deviations from the plan and suggesting improvements. ◆◆◆

INTEGRATED MARKETING COMMUNICATIONS

Stop and think for a moment about all the marketing messages you receive in a single day. You click on the television for the morning news, and you see plenty of commercials. Listen to the car radio on the way to work or school, and you can sing along with the jingles. You get catalogues, coupons, and fliers in the mail. People even leave promotional fliers under your car's windshield wiper while it sits in the parking lot. When you go online, you're deluged with banner and pop-up ads and even marketing related email. Marketers know that you are receiving many types of communication. They know they need to compete for your attention. So they look for ways to reach you in a coordinated manner through integrated marketing communications.

Successful marketers use the marketing concept and relationship marketing to develop customer-oriented marketing programs. The customer is at the heart of integrated marketing communications. An IMC strategy begins not with the organization's goods and services but with consumer wants or needs and then works in reverse to the product, brand, or organization. It sends receiver-focused rather than product-focused messages.

Rather than separating the parts of the promotional mix and viewing them as isolated components, IMC looks at these elements from the consumer's viewpoint: as information about the brand, company, or organization. Even though the messages come from different sources—sales presentations, word of mouth, TV, radio, newspapers, and online services—consumers may perceive them as "advertising" or a "sales pitch." IMC broadens promotion to include all the ways a customer has contact with an organization, adding to traditional media and direct mail such sources as package design, store displays, sales literature, and online and interactive media. Unless the organization takes an integrated approach to present a unified, consistent message, it may send conflicting information that confuses consumers.

Conflicting messages that could confuse or mislead consumers came to light in a study conducted by TerraChoice described in the "Go Green" feature.

BRING THE WHOLE ROYAL FAMILY.

NOW OPEN!

Celebrate India's kings and the masterpieces they inspired. November 20 – April 3
MAHARAJA
THE SPLENDOUR OF INDIA'S ROYAL COURTS
25 AND UNDER GET IN FREE   Details: ago.net
AGO Art Gallery of Ontario

Organized in collaboration with the Victoria and Albert Museum, London   V&A

Patrons of the Exhibition and generous supporters of the "FREE for 25 and under" offer

Government Partners

FAIRFAX FINANCIAL HOLDINGS LIMITED   THE GLOBE AND MAIL   ROGERS   Scotiabank Group   Ontario Cultural Attractions Fund OCAF   Canada

COURTESY OF THE ART GALLERY OF ONTARIO

---

(1) Explain how integrated marketing communications relates to the development of an optimal promotional mix and describe the communication process.

Marketoid

National advertising and related services industries saw their operating revenues increase by 3 percent in 2008.

Marketoid

Firms in the advertising industry in Canada earned $6.7 billion in operating revenues in 2008.

Joint integrated marketing promotion.

promotion Communications link between buyers and sellers. Function of informing, persuading, and influencing a consumer's purchase decision.

marketing communications Messages that deal with buyer–seller relationships.

integrated marketing communications (IMC) Coordination of all promotional activities to produce a unified, customer-focused promotional message.

GO GREEN   "Greenwashing"

TERRACHOICE is a firm specializing in green marketing. The firm helps companies by advising on strategy development, communication programs, purchasing, training, education, ecolabelling, and more. Its environmental marketing recommendations are based on established criteria produced by such organizations as the International Organization for Standardization (ISO), U.S. Environmental Protection Agency, and the Competition Bureau of Canada.

As part of an ongoing research project into environmental claims companies were making about their products, TerraChoice brought fresh global visibility to the term "Greenwash"—the act of misleading consumers about the environmental practices of a company or the environmental benefits of a product. Their research looks at thousands of products and, in the 2010 study, they found that ninety five percent of these products were guilty of making false or misleading "green" claims. As part of this research, TerraChoice also identified seven categories or "Sins of Greenwashing":

- Sin of the Hidden Trade-off—This sin occurs when a product makes a claim based on a narrow set of attributes while ignoring other, possibly more important factors.
- Sin of No Proof—If there was no supporting information or reliable third-party certification, this sin was committed.
- Sin of Vagueness— A claim that is poorly defined or so broad as to be meaningless falls into this group.
- Sin of Irrelevance—A sin that falls under this heading is making a true statement, but it is unimportant or not helpful.
- Sin of Lesser of Two Evils—These claims, while true, would distract the purchaser from a greater environmental issue.
- Sin of Fibbing— This claim is totally false.
- Sin of Worshipping False Labels – This sin occurs when a product gives the impression of a fictitious third-party endorsement

Source: TerraChoice website, http://www.terrachoice.com, accessed January 5, 2011.

Today's business environment is characterized by many diverse markets and media, creating both opportunities and challenges. The success of any IMC program depends on identifying the members of an audience and understanding what they want. Without accurate, current information about existing and potential customers, their purchase histories, needs, and wants, marketers may send the wrong message. But they cannot succeed simply by improving the quality of the messages or by sending more of them. IMC must not only deliver messages to intended audiences but also gather responses from them. Databases and interactive marketing are important IMC tools that help marketers collect information from customers and segment markets according to demographics and preferences. Marketers can then design specialized communications programs to meet the needs of each segment.

The increase in media options provides more ways to give consumers product information; however, it can also create information overload. Marketers have to spread available

Some connections simply can't be made on the internet.

GIRLS NEED GUIDES. For more information or to enroll your daughter, call 1.800.565.8111 or visit us at girlguides.ca

Girl Guides of Canada promote the benefits of their organization to both girls and their moms.

COURTESY GIRL GUIDES OF CANADA

dollars across fragmented media markets and a wider range of promotional activities to achieve their communication goals. Mass media such as TV ads, while still useful, are no longer the mainstays of marketing campaigns. In fact, the Internet is the only medium that saw an increase in advertising spending in recent years. Internet ads are likely to be directed at a more focused target market.[2] Audiences are also more fragmented. So to reach desired groups, organizations are turning to niche marketing by advertising in special-interest magazines, by purchasing time on cable TV channels, by reaching out through telecommunications media such as cell phones or the Internet, and by sponsoring events and activities. Without an IMC program, marketers frequently encounter problems within their own organizations because separate departments have authority and responsibility for planning and implementing specific promotional mix elements.

The coordination of an IMC program often produces a competitive advantage based on synergy and interdependence among the various elements of the promotional mix. With an IMC strategy, marketers can create a unified personality for the product or brand by choosing the right elements from the promotional mix to send the message. At the same time, they can develop more narrowly focused plans to reach specific market segments and choose the best form of communication to send a particular message to a specific target audience. IMC provides a more effective way to reach and serve target markets than less coordinated strategies. Establishing an effective IMC program requires teamwork.

IMPORTANCE OF TEAMWORK

IMC requires a big-picture view of promotion planning, a total strategy that includes all marketing activities, not just promotion. Successful implementation of IMC requires that everyone involved in every aspect of promotion—public relations, advertising, personal selling, and sales promotion—functions as part of a team. The team members must present a consistent, coordinated promotional effort at every point of customer contact with the organization. This way, they save time, money, and effort. They avoid duplication of efforts, increasing marketing effectiveness and reducing costs. Ultimately, it means that the result—the IMC program—is greater than the sum of its parts.

Teamwork involves both in-house resources and outside vendors. It involves marketing personnel; members of the sales force who deal with wholesalers, retailers, and organizational buyers; and customer-service representatives. A firm gains nothing from a terrific advertisement featuring a great product, an informational website, and a toll-free number if unhelpful salespeople frustrate customers when they answer the phones. The company must train its representatives to send a single positive message to consumers and also to solicit information for the firm's customer database.

IMC also challenges the traditional role of the advertising agency. A single agency may no longer fulfill all a client's communications requirements, including traditional advertising and sales promotions, interactive marketing, database development, direct marketing, and public relations. To best serve client needs, an agency will often assemble a team with members from other companies.

ROLE OF DATABASES IN EFFECTIVE IMC PROGRAMS

With the explosive growth of the Internet, marketers have the power to gather more information faster and to organize it more easily than ever before. By sharing this detailed knowledge appropriately among all relevant parties, a company can lay the foundation for a successful IMC program.

The move from mass marketing to a customer-specific marketing strategy—a characteristic of online marketing—requires not only a means of identifying and communicating with the firm's target market but also information regarding important characteristics of each prospective customer. Organizations can compile different kinds of data into complete databases with customer information, including names and addresses, demographic data, lifestyle considerations, brand preferences, and buying behaviour. This information provides critical guidance in designing an effective IMC strategy that achieves organizational goals and finds new opportunities for increased sales and profits. This increased ability to acquire huge amounts of data poses a new challenge: how to sift through it

Indigo uses a website and a free shipping promotion as part of its IMC campaign.

efficiently so that it becomes useful information. Newer technology allows researchers to do exactly that—working with millions of sets of data to make very specific analyses.

Direct sampling is another method frequently used to quickly obtain customer opinions regarding a particular firm's goods and services. If you've ever received a free sample of bath soap, aspirin, or even a newspaper in your mailbox, you've been the recipient of direct sampling.

THE COMMUNICATION PROCESS

When you have a conversation with someone, do you wonder whether the person understood your message? Do you worry that you might not have heard the person correctly? Marketers have the same concerns—when they send a message to an intended audience or market, they want to make sure it gets through clearly and persuasively. That is why the communication process is so important to marketing. The top portion of Table 13.1 shows a general model of the communication process and its application to promotional strategy.

The **sender** acts as the source in the communication system as he or she seeks to convey a **message** (a communication of information, advice, or a request) to a receiver. An effective message accomplishes three tasks:

sender Source of the message communicated to the receiver.

message Communication of information, advice, or a request by the sender to the receiver.

1. It gains the receiver's attention.

2. It achieves understanding by both receiver and sender.

3. It stimulates the receiver's needs and suggests an appropriate method of satisfying them.

table 13.1 **Relating Promotion to the Communication Process**

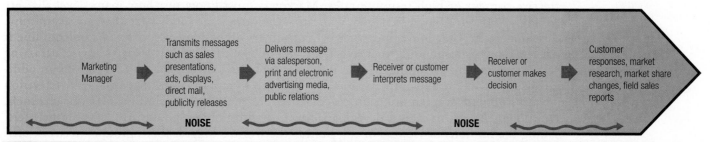

Type of Promotion	Sender	Encoding by Sender	Channel	Decoding by Receiver	Response	Feedback
Personal selling	IBM e-solutions networking system	Sales presentation on new applications of system	IBM sales representative	Office manager and employees discuss sales presentation and those of competing suppliers.	Order is placed for IBM e-solutions system installation.	Customer asks about a second system for subsidiary company.
Dollar-off coupon (sales promotion)	Kellogg's Special K cereal	Coupons prepared by Kellogg's marketing department and advertising agency	Coupon insert in weekend newspaper	Newspaper reader sees coupon for Special K cereal and saves it.	Special K is purchased by consumer using coupon.	Kellogg researchers see increase in market share.
Television advertising	Paramount Canada's Wonderland	Advertisement developed by Wonderland's advertising agency featuring the new park rides	Network television ads air during program with high percentages of viewers under 20 years old	Teens and young adults see ad and decide to try out the park.	Wonderland tickets are purchased.	Customers purchase season ticket packages for Wonderland.

Table 13.1 also provides several examples of promotional messages. Although the types of promotion may vary from a highly personalized sales presentation to such nonpersonal promotions as television advertising and dollar-off coupons, each goes through every stage in the communications process.

The three tasks just listed are related to the **AIDA concept** (attention-interest-desire-action), the steps consumers take in reaching a purchase decision. First, the promotional message must gain the potential consumer's attention. It then seeks to arouse interest in the good or service. At the next stage, it stimulates desire by convincing the would-be buyer of the product's ability to satisfy his or her needs. Finally, the sales presentation, advertisement, or sales promotion technique attempts to produce action in the form of a purchase or a more favourable attitude that may lead to future purchases.

The message must be **encoded**, or translated into understandable terms, and transmitted through a communications channel. **Decoding** is the receiver's interpretation of the message. The receiver's response, known as **feedback**, completes the system. Throughout the process, **noise** (in such forms as ineffective promotional appeals, inappropriate advertising media, or poor radio or television reception) can interfere with the transmission of the message and reduce its effectiveness.

The marketer is the message sender in Table 13.1. He or she encodes the message in the form of sales presentations, advertising, displays, or publicity releases. The **channel** for delivering the message may be a salesperson, a public relations announcement, a website, or one of the numerous advertising media. Decoding is often the most troublesome step in marketing communications because consumers do not always interpret promotional messages in the same way that senders do. Since receivers usually decode messages according to their own frames of reference or experiences, a sender must carefully encode a message in a way that matches the frame of reference of the target audience. Consumers today are bombarded daily by hundreds of sales messages through many media channels. This communications traffic can create confusion as noise in the channel as the number of messages increase. Since the typical shopper will choose to process only a few messages, ignored messages waste communications budgets.

AIDA concept Steps through which an individual reaches a purchase decision: attention, interest, desire, and action.

encoding Translating a message into understandable terms.

decoding Receiver's interpretation of a message.

feedback Receiver's response to a message.

noise Any stimulus that distracts a receiver from receiving a message.

channel Medium through which a message is delivered.

The AIDA concept is also vital to online marketers. It is not enough to say a website has effective content or high response rates. Marketers must know just how many "eyeballs" are looking at the site, how often they come to view a message, and what they are examining. Most important, they must find out what consumers do besides just look. The bottom line is that if nobody is responding to a website, it might as well not exist. Experts advise attracting users' attention by including people in advertisements and other communications in addition to new content and formats. For the Winter Olympic Games in Vancouver, television networks offered programming on several different platforms, including network channels, cable channels, websites, and downloadable clips and mobile updates for smartphone users. Calling the millions of viewers of the games "the world's biggest focus group," network officials planned to measure viewers' use of new and mobile media, and hired market research companies to help track viewership as well as Olympics-related word-of-mouth on social sites. One network gave 2000 viewers a Portable People Meter to measure television viewing and outfitted others with measuring devices for their BlackBerrys and iPhones. The networks saw the Olympics Games as a great opportunity to better understand how the new media environment works.[3]

Feedback, the receiver's response to the message, provides a way for marketers to evaluate the effectiveness of the message and tailor their responses accordingly. Feedback may take the form of attitude changes, purchases, or nonpurchases. In some instances, organizations use promotion to create favourable attitudes toward their goods or services in the hope of future purchases. Other promotional communications have the objective of directly stimulating consumer purchases. Marketers using infomercials that urge the viewer to call a toll-free number to place orders for music collections, the latest fitness fad, or other products can easily measure their success by counting the number of calls they receive that result in orders.

Even nonpurchases may serve as feedback to the sender. Failure to purchase may result from ineffective communication in which the receivers do not believe it, don't remember it, or even associate it with another firm's products. Alternatively, receivers may remember it correctly, but the message may have failed to persuade them that the firm's products are better than those of the competition. So marketers need to be keenly aware of the reasons that messages fail.

Noise represents interference at some stage in the communication process. It may result from disruptions such as transmissions of competing promotional messages over the same communications channel, misinterpretation of a sales presentation or advertising message, receipt of the promotional message by the wrong person, or random events such as people conversing or leaving the room during a television commercial. Noise can also result from distractions within an advertising message itself. Buzzwords and jargon can create a linguistic jungle for consumers who are just trying to find out more about a product. AARP— the U.S.–based, international nonprofit organization representing people aged 50 and older—surveyed 1200 adults and found more than half were confused by the language of the investment industry. This confusion often resulted in people in this age group saving too little or making costly mistakes because they didn't understand terms like *basis point* and *expense ratio*. "We learned that jargon is one of the key reasons for investor hesitation and missteps, and so off-putting for some, that it discourages investing altogether."[4]

Noise can be especially problematic in international communications. One problem is that there may be too many competing messages. Italian television channels, for instance, broadcast all advertisements during a single half-hour slot each night. Or technology may be poor, and language translations inaccurate. Nonverbal cues, such as body language and tone of voice, are important parts of the communication process, and cultural differences may lead to noise and misunderstandings. For example, in North America, the round o sign made with the thumb and first finger means "okay." However, in Mediterranean countries, it means "zero" or "the worst." A Tunisian interprets this same sign as "I'll kill you," and to a Japanese consumer it means "money." It's easy to see how misunderstanding could arise from this single gesture.

Perhaps the most misunderstood language for North American marketers is English. With 74 English-speaking nations, local terms can confuse anyone trying to communicate globally.

The following examples illustrate how easy it can be for marketers to make mistakes in English-language promotional messages:

- *Police:* bobby (Britain), garda (Ireland), police wallah (South Asia)

- *Porch:* stoep (South Africa), gallery (Caribbean)

- *Bar:* pub (Britain), hotel (Australia), boozer (Australia, Britain, New Zealand)

- *Bathroom:* loo (Britain), dunny (Australia)

- *Ghost or monster:* duppy (Caribbean), taniwha (New Zealand)

- *Barbecue:* braai (South Africa), barbie (Australia)

- *Truck:* lorry (Britain and Australia)

- *Soccer:* football (the rest of the world)

Faulty communications can be especially risky on a global level, where noise can lead to some interesting misinterpretations. Here are three international examples:

- *On a sign in a Bucharest hotel lobby:* The lift is being fixed for the next day. During that time, we regret that you will be unbearable.

- *From a Japanese information booklet about using a hotel air conditioner:* Cooles and Heates: If you want just condition of warm in your room, please control yourself.

- *In an Acapulco hotel:* The manager has personally passed all the water served here.

Marketers involved in IMC can benefit from some of the suggestions offered in the "Career Readiness" feature.

Marketoid

In 2008, Ontario generated the highest advertising industry revenues at $3788 million, representing 57 percent of the industry total.

assessment check 1

1.1 Define *promotion*.

1.2 What is the difference between marketing communications and integrated marketing communications (IMC)?

1.3 What are the three tasks accomplished by an effective message?

1.4 Identify the four steps of the AIDA concept and explain noise.

CAREER READINESS | Body Language: Watch What You "Say"

COMMUNICATING is much more than words. Gestures, posture, eye contact, facial expression, and distance from others all signal our thoughts and can allow us to gauge the thoughts of others. While nonverbal communications, often called body language, are not infallible guides to what people are feeling, some carry nearly universal meaning. In centuries past, for instance, a handshake indicated the absence of hidden weapons, and today it is still a signal of trust. Here are a few ideas about nonverbal communications and what they generally mean:

- "Open" body language signals a welcoming and attentive attitude. Posture is relaxed and easy, hands are visible, and eyes are making contact. The message is that the person is receptive to you and attentive to what you may say.

- Tensed shoulders, crossed arms and/or legs, and lack of eye contact can suggest the person feels threatened or hostile and is trying to protect himself or herself. Trust might be lacking, which will hamper open communication.

- Body language sometimes sends a different message than the speaker's words are sending. For instance, some

people laugh when they are embarrassed, and in some cultures it is common to smile when disappointed. Be cautious about taking the verbal message at face value when it conflicts with the nonverbal one.

- Standing too close to someone is often perceived as a threatening gesture, one that violates the individual's "personal space." Be aware that personal space varies among cultures.

- Angry people sometimes lean forward in conversation, but this posture can also indicate high interest. Look for other clues before you interpret.

Finally, consider your own body language, and notice how a change of posture or the addition of a smile can change your message, and your mood.

Sources: Phillip Khan-Panni, "20 Essential International Body Language Tips," ByteStart http://www.bytestart.co.uk, March 31, 2010; "How to Read Body Language," EHow, http://www.ehow.com, March 31, 2010; "Body Language—Top 10 Tips for Reading Client Posture and Gestures," LanguagesMblog, http://languagesmblog.co.uk, February 28, 2010; James Borg, "10 Minute Body Language Tips," *The Daily Telegraph*, http://www.telegraph.co.uk, February 8, 2010.

② Explain how the promotional mix relates to the objectives of promotion.

OBJECTIVES OF PROMOTION

What specific tasks should promotion accomplish? The answers to this question seem to vary as much as the sources consulted. Generally, however, marketers identify the following objectives of promotion:

1. Provide information to consumers and others.
2. Increase demand.
3. Differentiate a product.
4. Accentuate a product's value.
5. Stabilize sales.

PROVIDE INFORMATION

The traditional function of promotion was to inform the market about the availability of a particular good or service. In fact, marketers still direct much of their current promotional efforts at providing product information to potential customers. An advertisement for a musical performance typically provides information about the performer, time, and place. A commercial for a theme park offers information about rides, location, and admission price. Information can also help differentiate a product from its competitors by focusing on its features or benefits.

primary demand Desire for a general product category.

selective demand Desire for a specific brand within a product category.

In addition to traditional print and broadcast advertising, marketers often distribute a number of high-tech, low-cost tools to give consumers product information. Online videos are currently used to promote products such as cosmetics, automobiles, and exercise equipment, providing virtual demonstrations of the products. Consumers still regard these media as a novelty, so they are less likely to throw them out or click elsewhere. The "Solving an Ethical Controversy" feature discusses who controls customers' reviews and rankings of local businesses from online sources.

SOLVING AN ETHICAL CONTROVERSY   **Should Companies Filter Their Online Reviews?**

"GETTING Yelped," for business owners, is the experience of receiving negative reviews. Yelp.com allows users to review and rank local restaurants, hotels, and other businesses. It initially allowed advertisers to place a positive review at the top of the list, only subtly identified as a "sponsored result." But several firms complained, claiming it routinely highlighted negative reviews unless firms agreed to become advertisers when it would substitute positive reviews it had systematically removed.

Should advertisers be able to manipulate the reviews potential customers see?

PRO

1. Businesses have the right to control their own message, whether it's a marketing campaign they pay for, a promotion they plan and run, or a sponsored search result on a website.
2. Yelp runs a spam filter to eliminate reviews by obviously biased sources such as a firm's competitors

or friends and relatives. Letting the business owner make similar filtering choices is no different.

CON

1. One of the complaints was that "business listings on Yelp.com are in fact biased in favour of businesses that buy Yelp advertising."
2. Consumers' right to know is threatened when advertisers can literally buy reviews. Unlike impartial results, reviews and rankings can influence consumers' buying decisions and should not be for sale.

Where do you stand: pro or con?

Sources: Claire Cain Miller, "Yelp Makes Changes in Response to Small Business Owners," *The New York Times*, http://bits.glogs.nytimes.com, April 6, 2010; Jason Kincaid, "Yelp Hit with Second Extortion Lawsuit, CEO Calls It Meritless," TechCrunch.com, http://techcrunch.com, March 4, 2010; Peter Burrows and Joseph Galante, "Yelp: Advertise or Else?" *BusinessWeek*, http://www.businessweek.com, March 3, 2010; Caroline McCarty, "Yelp CEO: This Lawsuit Is Bunk," *CNet News*, http://news.cnet.com, February 26, 2010.

INCREASE DEMAND

Most promotions pursue the objective of increasing demand for a product. Some promotions are aimed at increasing **primary demand**, the desire for a general product category such as smartphones. Millions of dollars are spent each year to promote tourism across the country. Funded by different levels of government, tourism-related companies such as airlines, local hotels, restaurants, and tourist attractions, this type of promotion has the objective of increasing the number of visitors to an area. These visitors will spend their vacation money in more than one place.[5]

Primary-demand promotions are also typical for firms holding exclusive patents on significant product improvements and for marketers who decide to expand overseas, creating new markets for their products in other parts of the world. When Procter & Gamble first introduced its Pampers disposable diapers in Hungary, most parents were using overpants with paper inserts to diaper their babies. So early Pampers television ads focused on generating interest in the novel product.

More promotions, however, are aimed at increasing **selective demand**, the desire for a specific brand. When Frito-Lay Canada launched the world's first compostable chip bag, it was hoping to increase sales and create awareness. The award winning Frito-Lay promotion consisted of a "greenventers" contest where contestants could win a spot on the popular television program *Dragon's Den*. The promotion was supported with television ads and live auditions. Frito-Lay could not have been happier with the results—sales volume increased by 30 percent and brand awareness increased by 67 percent.[6]

Knorr: Offering product information and benefits to consumers.

Ford promotions highlight features of the car.

Gillette: Differentiating its product by the amount of protection.

DIFFERENTIATE THE PRODUCT

product differentiation
When consumers regard a firm's products as different in some way from those of competitors.

A frequent objective of the firm's promotional efforts is **product differentiation**. Homogeneous demand for many products results when consumers regard the firm's output as virtually identical to its competitors' products. In these cases, the individual firm has almost no control over marketing variables such as price. A differentiated demand schedule, in contrast, permits more flexibility in marketing strategy, such as price changes. It may seem difficult to differentiate among the many fashion retailers hoping to attract the cool, fashion-forward female market particularly when the brand is as old as the Hudson's Bay Company (HBC). The store that was thought to be the destination to buy bedding and appliances underwent a transform starting in 2008 when the retailing expert Bonnie Brooks was hired as president and CEO. The new look and feel of the stores was just right to introduce the newest trends and the latest styles and labels. In order for HBC to achieve this new position in the market, hundreds of underperforming brands were dropped and were replaced with 250 of the most up-to-date fashion labels. The new look of the stores and new designer labels were supported with radio ads featuring president and CEO Bonnie Brooks.[7]

ACCENTUATE THE PRODUCT'S VALUE

Promotion can explain the greater ownership utility of a product to buyers, thereby accentuating its value and justifying a higher price in the marketplace. This objective benefits both consumer and business products. A firm's promotional messages must build brand image and equity and at the same time deliver a call to action. Advertising typically offers reasons a good or service fits into the consumer's lifestyle. Today, consumers everywhere value their time; the challenge for marketers is to demonstrate how their products will make their lives better.

Marketers must choose their words wisely when creating messages that accentuate their product's value. One expert advises staying away from five words: *quality, value, service, caring,* and *integrity.* These overused words are vague and tend to fall on deaf ears.[8]

STABILIZE SALES

Sales of most goods and services fluctuate throughout the year. Sales fluctuations may result from cyclical, seasonal, or irregular demand. Ice cream, ski trips, and swimming pools have obvious fluctuations, as do snow shovels and lawn mowers. Sales of bottled water and flashlights might spike before a storm, while vacation rentals might be cancelled in the path of the same oncoming bad weather. Stabilizing these variations is often an objective of promotional strategy. Although it may seem less obvious than ice cream, coffee sales follow a seasonal pattern, rising during the colder months and dropping when the weather turns warm. To stimulate summer sales of coffee, Tim Hortons created the iced cappuccino, promoting it as a "deep down creamy cool" treat.[9]

assessment check 2

2.1 What are the objectives of promotion?

2.2 Why is product differentiation important to marketers?

(3) Identify the different elements of the promotional mix and explain how marketers develop an optimal promotional mix.

ELEMENTS OF THE PROMOTIONAL MIX

Like the marketing mix, the promotional mix requires a carefully designed blend of variables to satisfy the needs of a company's customers and achieve organizational objectives. The **promotional mix** works like a subset of the marketing mix. With the promotional mix, the marketers attempt to create an optimal blend of various elements to achieve promotional objectives. The components of the promotional mix are personal selling and nonpersonal selling, including advertising, sales promotion, direct marketing, public relations, and guerrilla marketing.

promotional mix Subset of the marketing mix in which marketers attempt to achieve the optimal blending of the elements of personal and nonpersonal selling to achieve promotional objectives.

Personal selling, advertising, and sales promotion usually account for the bulk of a firm's promotional expenditures. However, direct marketing, guerrilla marketing, sponsorships, and public relations also contribute to integrated marketing communications. Later sections of this chapter examine the use of public relations, sponsorships, and direct marketing, and Chapters 14 and 15 present detailed discussions of the other elements. This section defines the elements and reviews their advantages and disadvantages.

PERSONAL SELLING

Personal selling is the oldest form of promotion, dating back as far as the beginning of trading and commerce. Traders vastly expanded both market sizes and product varieties as they led horses and camels along the Silk Road from China to Europe roughly between 300 B.C.E. and A.D. 1600, conducting personal selling at both ends. Personal selling may be defined as a seller's promotional presentation conducted on a person-to-person basis with the buyer. This direct form of promotion may be conducted face to face, over the telephone, through videoconferencing, or through interactive computer links between the buyer and seller.

Careers in personal sales may include real estate, insurance, financial investment, or sales of tractors, cars, or vacuum cleaners; individuals may work in retail or wholesaling; they may be regional managers or in the field. In other words, the range of jobs, as well as the products they represent, is huge.

NONPERSONAL SELLING

Nonpersonal selling includes advertising, product placement, sales promotion, direct marketing, guerrilla marketing, publicity, and public relations. Advertising and sales promotion are usually regarded as the most important forms of nonpersonal selling. About one-third of marketing dollars spent on nonpersonal selling activities are allocated for media advertising; the other two-thirds fund trade and consumer sales promotions.

Advertising

Advertising is any paid, nonpersonal communication through various media about a business, not-for-profit organization, product, or idea by a sponsor identified in a message that is intended to inform, persuade, or remind members of a particular audience. It is a major promotional mix component for thousands of organizations. Mass consumption and geographically dispersed markets make advertising particularly appropriate for marketing goods and services aimed at large audiences likely to respond to the same promotional messages.

Advertising primarily involves mass media, such as newspapers, television, radio, magazines, movie screens, and billboards, but also includes electronic and computerized forms of promotion such as Web commercials, DVDs, and television monitors in supermarkets. The rich potential of the Internet as an advertising channel to reach millions of people one at a time has attracted the attention of companies large and small, local and international. As consumers become increasingly savvy—and tune out messages that don't interest them—marketers are finding new ways to grab their attention. Advertising is discussed in more detail in Chapter 14.

Product Placement

Product placement is a form of nonpersonal selling in which the marketer pays a motion picture or television program owner a fee to display his or her product prominently in the film or show. The practice gained attention more than two decades ago in the movie *E.T.: The Extra-Terrestrial* when Elliott, the boy who befriends E.T., lays out a trail of Reese's Pieces for the extraterrestrial to follow, to draw the alien from his hiding place. Product sales for Reese's Pieces candies went through the roof. (Interestingly, this was not the moviemaker's first choice of candy; Mars turned down the opportunity to have its M&Ms appear in the film.) Today, hundreds of products appear in movies and on television shows, and the fees charged to marketers for these placements have soared. Apple Computer had 12 exposures in a season-opener of the show *24*, while Pontiac's brand was seen seven times and mentioned once. Nissan's Altima was featured in the premiere episode of *Parenthood*, for which it was also the exclusive sponsor.[10]

Some firms have moved to the next generation of product placement, seeking new places for their merchandise. One popular venue for product placement is video games, and product placements are turning up on Twitter as well.[11]

Sales Promotion

Sales promotion consists of marketing activities other than personal selling, advertising, guerrilla marketing, and public relations that stimulate consumer purchasing and dealer effectiveness. This broad category includes displays, trade shows, coupons, contests, samples, premiums, product demonstrations,

personal selling Interpersonal influence process involving a seller's promotional presentation conducted on a person-to-person basis with the buyer.

nonpersonal selling Promotion that includes advertising, product placement, sales promotion, direct marketing, guerrilla marketing, and public relations—all conducted without being face to face with the buyer.

advertising Paid, nonpersonal communication through various media about a business, not-for-profit organization, product, or idea by a sponsor identified in a message that is intended to inform, persuade or remind members of a particular audience.

product placement Form of promotion in which a marketer pays a motion picture or television program owner a fee to display a product prominently in the film or show.

Marketoid

In 2008, twenty-two percent of Canadian advertising revenues were generated in Quebec, with another 9 percent coming from British Columbia.

sales promotion Marketing activities other than personal selling, advertising, guerrilla marketing, and public relations that stimulate consumer purchasing and dealer effectiveness.

If we're this careful when we prep, imagine how we paint.

Benjamin Moore Painters have mastered the art of the perfect paint job. They arrive on time, protect your belongings and leave everything the way they found it. From their expert craftsmanship to their respect for you and your home, a Benjamin Moore Painter's work is 100% guaranteed. **Come home to perfection. Call for** your free estimate.

Painting & Decorating Services

1-866-PAINT-A1
benjaminmoore.ca

COURTESY OF BENJAMIN MOORE

Benjamin Moore includes a toll-free phone number and website address in its ads.

and various nonrecurring, irregular selling efforts. Sales promotion provides a short-term incentive, usually in combination with other forms of promotion, to emphasize, assist, supplement, or otherwise support the objectives of the promotional program. Restaurants, including those that serve fast food, often place certain items on the menu at a lower price "for a limited time only." Advertisements may contain coupons for free or discounted items for a specified period of time. Or companies may conduct sweepstakes for prizes such as new cars or vacations, which may even be completely unrelated to the products the company is selling.

Movie promotional tie-ins are a classic example. Although this is still a popular—and profitable—type of promotion, some companies are discovering they aren't getting the return on their investment that they had hoped for. If the movie flops, it may be bad news for the product as well. And some fast-food and snack companies are growing wary of tie-ins with films bearing G and PG ratings, due to past criticism that such deals help promote junk food to children. Creative control and quick results keep television advertising attractive to marketers, while the rising cost of airing spots on such high-profile broadcasts as the Super Bowl and the Olympics grabs an ever-larger share of their advertising budgets.

Sales promotion geared to marketing intermediaries is called **trade promotion**. Companies spend about as much on trade promotion as on advertising and consumer-oriented sales promotion combined. Trade promotion strategies include offering free merchandise, buyback allow-

trade promotion
Sales promotion that appeals to marketing intermediaries rather than to consumers.

ances, and merchandise allowances along with sponsorship of sales contests to encourage wholesalers and retailers to sell more of certain products or product lines. Sales promotion is discussed in more detail in Chapter 15.

Direct Marketing

Another element in a firm's integrated promotional mix is direct marketing, the use of direct communication to a consumer or business recipient designed to generate a response in the form of an order, a request for further information (lead generation), or a visit to a place of business to purchase specific goods or services (traffic generation). While many people equate direct marketing with direct mail, this promotional category also includes telemarketing, direct-response advertising and infomercials, direct-response print advertising, and electronic media. Direct marketing is such an important element of the promotional mix that it is discussed in depth later in this chapter and the digital or online types of direct marketing are discussed in Chapter 14.

Public Relations and Publicity

public relations Firm's communications and relationships with its various publics.

Public relations refer to a firm's communications and relationships with its various publics. These publics include customers, suppliers, stockholders, employees, the government, and the general public. Public relations programs can conduct either formal or informal contacts. The critical point is that every organization, whether or not it has a formally organized program, must be concerned about its public relations.

Publicity is the marketing-oriented aspect of public relations. It can be defined as the non-paid-for communication about the company or product, generally in some media form. Compared with personal selling, advertising, and even sales promotion, expenditures for public relations are usually low in most firms. Since companies do not pay for publicity, they have less control over the publication by the press or electronic media of good or bad company news. But this often means that consumers find this type of news source more believable than if the information were disseminated directly by the company. Of course, bad publicity can damage a company's reputation and diminish brand equity. Public relations and publicity are discussed in greater detail later in the chapter.

publicity Non-paid-for communication about the company or products, generally in some media form.

Guerrilla Marketing

Guerrilla marketing uses unconventional, innovative, and low-cost techniques to attract consumers' attention. It is a relatively new approach used by marketers whose firms are underfunded for a full marketing program. Many of these firms can't afford the huge costs involved in the orthodox media of print and broadcasting, so they need to find an innovative, low-cost way to reach their market. But some large companies, such as PepsiCo and Toyota, engage in guerrilla marketing as well.

guerrilla marketing Unconventional, innovative, and low-cost marketing techniques designed to get consumers' attention in unusual ways.

Buzz marketing can be part of guerrilla marketing. This type of marketing works well to reach students and other young adults. Marketing firms may hire students to mingle among their own classmates and friends, creating buzz about a product. Often called *campus ambassadors,* they may wear logo-bearing T-shirts or caps, leave Post-it notes with marketing messages around campus, and chat about the good or service with friends during class breaks or over meals.

Viral marketing is another form of guerrilla marketing that has rapidly caught on with large and small firms. Evian used the paid placement on YouTube of the "roller babies" ad as the central part its overall campaign. In a ten-month period, the ad had 102 million views, 500 000 Facebook fans, and 130 000 comments. The viral campaign was so successful that Evian moved to ads on television.[12]

The results of guerrilla marketing can be funny and outrageous—even offensive to some people. But they almost always get consumers' attention. Some guerrilla marketers stencil their company and product names anywhere graffiti might appear. Street artists are hired to plaster company and product logos on blank walls or billboards. Ethical issues of cluttering public spaces aside, the messages do seem to draw interest.

ADVANTAGES AND DISADVANTAGES OF TYPES OF PROMOTION

As Table 13.2 indicates, each type of promotion has both advantages and shortcomings. Although personal selling entails a relatively high per-contact cost, it involves less wasted effort than do non-personal forms of promotion such as advertising. Personal selling often provides more flexible promotion than the other forms because the salesperson can tailor the sales message to meet the unique needs—or objections—of each potential customer.

The major advantages of advertising come from its ability to create instant awareness of a good, service, or idea; build brand equity; and deliver the marketer's message to mass audiences for a relatively low cost per contact. Major disadvantages include the difficulty in measuring advertising effectiveness and high media costs. Sales promotions, in contrast, can be more accurately monitored and measured than advertising, produce immediate consumer responses, and provide short-term sales increases. Direct marketing gives potential customers an action-oriented choice, permits narrow audience segmentation and customization of communications, and produces measurable results. Public relations efforts such as publicity frequently offer substantially higher credibility than other promotional techniques. Guerrilla marketing efforts can be innovative and highly effective at a low cost to marketers with limited funds, as long as the tactics are not too outrageous, but it is more difficult to reach people. The marketer must determine the appropriate blend of these promotional mix elements to effectively market the firm's goods and services.

assessment check 3

3.1 Differentiate between personal and nonpersonal selling.

3.2 What are the six major categories of nonpersonal selling?

table 13.2 *Comparison of the Six Promotional Mix Elements*

	PERSONAL SELLING	ADVERTISING	SALES PROMOTION	DIRECT MARKETING	PUBLIC RELATIONS	GUERRILLA MARKETING
Advantages	Permits measurement of effectiveness Elicits an immediate response Tailors the message to fit the customer	Reaches a large group of potential consumers for a relatively low price per exposure Allows strict control over the final message Can be adapted to either mass audiences or specific audience segments	Produces an immediate consumer response Attracts attention and creates product awareness Allows easy measurement of results Provides short-term sales increases	Generates an immediate response Covers a wide audience with targeted advertising Allows complete, customized, personal message Produces measurable results	Creates a positive attitude toward a product or company Enhances credibility of a product or company	Is low cost Attracts attention because it is innovative Is less cluttered with competitors trying the same thing
Disadvantages	Relies almost exclusively upon the ability of the salesperson Involves high cost per contact	Does not permit totally accurate measurement of results Usually cannot close sales	Is non-personal in nature Is difficult to differentiate from competitors' efforts	Suffers from image problem Involves a high cost per reader Depends on quality and accuracy of mailing lists May annoy consumers	May not permit accurate measurement of effect on sales Involves much effort directed toward non-marketing-oriented goals	May not reach as many people If the tactics are too outrageous, they may offend some people

④ Describe the role of public relations, publicity, sponsorships, and direct marketing in integrated marketing communications.

PUBLIC RELATIONS

Organizational public relations efforts date back to 1889, when George Westinghouse hired two people to publicize the advantages of alternating-current electricity and to refute arguments originally championed by Thomas Edison for direct-current systems.

Public relations is an efficient, indirect communications channel through which a firm can promote products, although it serves broader objectives than those of other components of promotional strategy. It is concerned with the prestige and image of all parts of the organization. Today, public relations plays a larger role than ever within the promotional mix, and it may emphasize more marketing-oriented information. In addition to its traditional activities, such as surveying public attitudes and creating a good corporate image, PR also supports advertising in promoting the organization's goods and services.

Public relations is in a period of major growth as a result of increased public pressure on industries regarding corporate ethical conduct and environmental and international issues. International expenditures on public relations are growing more rapidly than those for advertising and sales promotion. Many top executives are becoming more involved in public relations as well. The public expects top managers to take greater responsibility for company actions than they have accepted in the past. Those who refuse are widely criticized and censured.

The PR department is the link between the firm and the media. It provides press releases and holds news conferences to announce new products, the formation of strategic alliances, management changes, financial results, or similar developments. The PR department may issue its own publications as well, including newsletters, brochures, and reports.

The Internet has actually changed some PR planning, as PR representatives now have more direct access to the public instead of having their messages filtered through journalists and the news media. This direct access gives them greater control over their messages.

Many not-for-profit organizations use PR techniques to achieve their promotional objectives. The Salvation Army is one example with its annual Christmas "Fill the Kettle" campaign; PR programs were launched to publicize its fund-raising efforts after the Haiti earthquake. Supported by online, television, radio, and print ads, the Salvation Army showed situations in which donations helped people in need.[13]

MARKETING AND NONMARKETING PUBLIC RELATIONS

Nonmarketing public relations refers to a company's messages about general management issues. When a company makes a decision that affects any of its publics, input from public relations specialists can help smooth its dealings with those publics. A company that decides to close a plant would need advice on how to deal with the local community, while a firm during a long strike might try to achieve a favourable attitude from the public. Either of these situations might be considered a crisis, as would a massive product recall. Companies that have a plan of action and can effectively handle a crisis by generating positive public relations generally can survive these types of crisis.

nonmarketing public relations Organizational messages about general management issues.

In contrast, **marketing public relations (MPR)** refers to narrowly focused public relations activities that directly support marketing goals. MPR involves an organization's relationships with consumers or other groups about marketing concerns and can be either proactive or reactive.

With proactive MPR, the marketer takes the initiative and seeks out opportunities for promoting the firm's products, often including distribution of press releases and feature articles. For example, companies send press releases about new products to newspapers, television stations, and relevant consumer, business, and trade publications. It is a powerful marketing tool since it adds news coverage that reinforces direct promotion activities.

marketing public relations (MPR) Narrowly focused public relations activities that directly support marketing goals.

Reactive MPR responds to an external situation that has potential negative consequences for the organization. Two recent high-profile examples of companies using MPR to respond to a crisis are BP and Toyota. BP's efforts did not seem to have the desired effect mainly because the public felt the company's message was not genuine. Toyota, on the other hand, seems to have weathered its recall crisis. The company responded in the same simple, honest language used before the recall to explain what the brand stood for.[14]

PUBLICITY

The aspect of public relations that is most directly related to promoting a firm's products is publicity. It has been said that if advertising is the hammer, publicity is the nail. It creates credibility for the advertising to follow. Firms generate publicity by creating special events, holding press conferences, and preparing news releases and media kits. Lululemon has used this approach effectively. Although the company was aware that only official sponsors of the Olympics could use the event in promotional material, lululemon decided to try an offbeat approach. The company launched a new line of clothing just before the Olympics that it called "Cool Sporting Event That Takes Place in British Columbia Between 2009 & 2011 Edition." The Olympic Committee was not amused and took action to have the name changed.[15]

While publicity generates minimal costs compared with other forms of promotion, it does not deliver its message entirely for free. Publicity-related expenses include the costs of employing marketing personnel assigned to create and submit publicity releases, printing and mailing costs, and related expenses.

Firms often pursue publicity to promote their images or viewpoints. Other publicity efforts involve organizational activities such as plant expansions, mergers and acquisitions, management changes, and research breakthroughs. A significant amount of publicity, however, provides information about goods and services, particularly new products.

Because many consumers consider news stories to be more credible than advertisements as sources of information, publicity releases are often sent to media editors for possible inclusion in news stories. The media audiences perceive the news as coming from the communications media, not the sponsors. The information in a publicity release about a new good or service can provide valuable assistance for a television, newspaper, or magazine writer, leading to eventual broadcast or publication. Publicity releases sometimes fill voids in publications, and at other times, they become part of regular features. In either case, they offer firms valuable supplements to paid advertising messages. An example of a company that uses publicity effectively is discussed in the "Marketing and the SME" box.

MARKETING AND THE SME | TerraChoice: Using Public Relations and Publications

SCOTT McDougall is president and chief executive officer of TerraChoice, the firm that performs and publishes research concerned with the "sins of greenwashing," discussed in the Go Green feature. Scott, a biologist, has devoted his career to giving environmental issues a high profile. At TerraChoice Scott assists other companies with environmental strategies and ecolabelling.

So how does TerraChoice let the world know about its services? When the company completes a study, it publishes the results in its online magazine and sends out press releases. The press releases worked. Representatives from various media contacted the company to find more information. Scott appeared on *Canada AM*, in *Business Week*, and in interviews with the CBC, the BBC, and CNBC. The company's research has also been featured in the *New York Times*, *The Economist*, *Newsweek*, *Marketing Magazine*, *USA Today*, *Fast Company*, and the UK's *Guardian*. Another way Scott gets his environmental message out is going on speaking tours.

In addition to public relations appearances and speaking tours, Scott is the editor of two online publications, *eQ* and *ecomarkets*. These magazines are available on TerraChoice's website.

eQ publishes articles relating to company projects such as "A Greener, Cleaner Future: How to Market 'Green' in Consumer Cleaning Products," which discusses how to differentiate and communicate the benefits of a "green" cleaning product. The magazine also includes articles that would be of interest to anyone wanting to know more about environmental issues, such as an interview with Dr. David Suzuki, in which he discusses his current projects and his views about greenwashing.

The second publication, *ecomarkets*, presents statistical information in articles such as "Green Purchasing Behaviors" and "The Economy's Impact on Green Purchasing." Topics covered include how green products compare to conventional products in price and performance.

TerraChoice and Scott McDougall have been successful at using public relations and publications to let people know about the company and environmental issues.

Sources: Terrachoice website, http://www.terrachoice.com, January 22, 2011; Anita Lahey, "Get 'Em While They're Free," *Canadian Business*, April 30, 1999, pp. 70–73.

SPONSORSHIPS

One of the most significant trends in promotion offers marketers the ability to integrate several elements of the promotional mix. Commercial sponsorships of an event or activity apply personal selling, advertising, sales promotion, and public relations in achieving specific promotional goals. These sponsorships, which link events with sponsors and with media such as TV, radio, print, and the Internet, have become a multibillion-dollar business worldwide.

sponsorship Relationship in which an organization provides funds or in-kind resources to an event or activity in exchange for a direct association with that event or activity.

Sponsorship occurs when an organization provides money or in-kind resources to an event or activity in exchange for a direct association with that event or activity. The sponsor purchases two things: (1) access to the activity's audience and (2) the image associated with the activity. Sponsorships typically involve advertising, direct mail and sales promotion, publicity in the form of media coverage of the event, and personal selling at the event itself. They also involve relationship marketing, bringing together the event, its participants, the sponsoring firms, and their channel members and major customers. Marketers underwrite varying levels of sponsorships, depending on the amount their companies wish to spend and the types of events.

Commercial sponsorship is not a new phenomenon. Aristocrats in ancient Rome sponsored gladiator competitions and chariot races featuring teams that were often supported financially by competing businesses. More than 2000 years ago, wealthy Athenians underwrote drama, musical, and sporting festivals. Craft guilds in 14th-century England sponsored plays (occasionally insisting that the playwrights insert "plugs" for their lines of work in the scripts).

Although they include both commercial and not-for-profit events, today's sponsorships are most prevalent in sports—NASCAR races, the Olympics, and the World Cup, and thousands of smaller events as well. Local firms may sponsor hockey, baseball, and soccer teams.

Companies may also sponsor concerts or art exhibits, reading and child-care programs, programs that support small businesses and create new jobs, and humanitarian or cause-related programs such as the Make-A-Wish Foundation and Habitat for Humanity.

HOW SPONSORSHIP DIFFERS FROM ADVERTISING

Even though sponsorship spending and traditional advertising spending represent forms of nonpersonal selling, they are different in many ways. These differences include potential cost effectiveness, the sponsor's degree of control versus that of advertising, the nature of the message, and audience reaction.

Escalating costs of traditional advertising media have made commercial sponsorships a cost-effective alternative. Except for the really large events—which often have several sponsors—most are less expensive than an advertising campaign that relies on television, print, and other advertising. In addition, sponsors often gain the benefit of media coverage anyway, because associated events are covered by the news. And in the case of naming rights of such venues as sports arenas, the name serves as a perpetual advertisement. Examples include the Rogers Centre in Toronto, the Scotiabank Place in Ottawa, and the Bell Centre in Montreal.

Marketers have considerable control over the quantity and quality of market coverage when they advertise. Sponsors have little control of sponsored events beyond matching the audiences to profiles of their own target markets. Instead, event organizers control the coverage, which typically focuses on the event—not the sponsor. In contrast, a traditional advertisement allows the marketer to create an individual message containing an introduction, a theme, and a conclusion.

Audiences react differently to sponsorship as a communications medium than to other media. The sponsor's investment provides a recognizable benefit to the sponsored activity that the audience can appreciate. As a result, sponsorship is often viewed more positively than traditional advertising. Some

Several companies come together to sponsor Movies for Mommies.

marketers have tried to take advantage of this fact by practising **ambush marketing**, in which a firm that is not an official sponsor tries to link itself to a major international event, such as the Olympics or a concert tour by a musical group. While it might be tempting to assume that smaller firms with limited marketing budgets would be most likely to engage in ambush marketing, this is not always the case. Scotiabank's "Show Your Colours" campaign was one of many the Vancouver Olympic organizers were not happy with. In a promotional campaign that started shortly before the Olympic Games, Scotiabank took advantage of the fact that the colour of the Canadian flag matches its own corporate colours. Olympic organizers felt the campaign misled people into thinking Scotiabank was one of the official sponsors of the games.[16] While creating a vague advertisement is not illegal, some ambush practices clearly are. If a non-sponsor used the Olympic rings in an advertisement, the ad would be an illegal use of a trademark.

ambush marketing
Attempt by a firm that is not an official sponsor of an event or activity to link itself to the event or activity.

To assess the results of sponsorships, marketers use some of the same techniques by which they measure advertising effectiveness. However, the differences between the two promotional alternatives often necessitate some unique research techniques as well. A few corporate sponsors attempt to link expenditures to sales. Other sponsors measure improved brand awareness and image as effectiveness indicators; they conduct traditional surveys before and after the events to secure this information. Still other sponsors measure the impact of their event marketing in public relations terms.

DIRECT MARKETING

Few promotional mix elements are growing as fast as direct marketing. In fact, in 2009, Canadian companies spent an estimated $1479 million on catalogue and direct mail alone.[17] Both business-to-consumer and business-to-business marketers rely on this promotional mix element to generate orders

Marketoid

In 2008, Saskatchewan had the lowest advertising revenues at only 1 percent of the country's total.

or sales leads (requests for more information) that may result in future orders. Direct marketing also helps increase store traffic, improving the chances that consumers will evaluate and perhaps purchase the advertised goods or services.

Direct marketing opens new international markets of unprecedented size. Many different forms of digital marketing channels have become the focus of direct marketers, and Web marketing is international marketing. Consumers in Europe and Japan are proving to be responsive to direct marketing. But most global marketing systems remain undeveloped, and many are almost dormant.

Direct marketing communications pursue goals beyond creating product awareness. Marketers want direct marketing to persuade people to place an order, request more information, visit a store, call a toll-free number, or respond to an email message. In other words, successful direct marketing should prompt consumers to take action. Since direct marketing is interactive, marketers can tailor individual responses to meet consumers' needs. They can also measure the effectiveness of their efforts more easily than with advertising and other forms of promotion. Direct marketing is a very powerful tool that helps organizations win new customers and enhance relationships with existing ones.

The growth of direct marketing parallels the move toward integrated marketing communications in many ways. Both respond to fragmented media markets and audiences, growth in customized products, shrinking network broadcast audiences, and the increasing use of databases to target specific markets. Lifestyles also play a role because today's busy consumers want convenience and shopping options that save them time.

Databases are an important part of direct marketing. Using the latest technology to create sophisticated databases, a company can select a narrow market segment and find good prospects within that segment based on desired characteristics. Marketers can cut costs and improve returns on dollars spent by identifying customers who are most likely to respond to messages and by eliminating others from their lists who are not likely to respond. In fact, mining information about customers is a trend boosted by the growth of e-commerce.

DIRECT MARKETING COMMUNICATIONS CHANNELS

Direct marketing uses many different media forms: direct mailing, such as brochures and catalogues; telecommunications initiated by companies or customers; television and radio through special offers, infomercials, or shopping channels; the Internet via email and electronic messaging; print media such as newspapers and magazines; and specialized channels such as electronic kiosks. Each works best for certain purposes, although marketers often combine two or more media in one direct marketing program. As long as it complies with current "do not call" regulations, a company might start with telemarketing to screen potential customers and then follow up by sending more material by direct mail to those who are interested.

Direct Mail

direct mail
Communications in the form of sales letters, postcards, brochures, catalogues, and the like conveying messages directly from the marketer to the customer.

As the amount of information about consumer lifestyles, buying habits, and wants continues to mount, direct mail has become a viable channel for identifying a firm's best prospects. Marketers gather information from internal and external databases, surveys, personalized coupons, and rebates that require responses. **Direct mail** is a critical tool in creating effective direct-marketing campaigns. It comes in many forms, such as sales letters, postcards, brochures, booklets, catalogues, *house organs* (periodicals issued by organizations), and DVDs.

Direct mail offers advantages such as the ability to select a narrow target market, achieve intensive coverage, send messages quickly, choose from various formats, provide complete information, and personalize each mailing piece. Response rates are measurable and higher than other types of advertising. In addition, direct mailings stand alone and do not compete for attention with magazine ads or radio and TV commercials. On the other hand, the per-reader cost of direct mail is high, effectiveness depends on the quality of the mailing list, and some consumers object to what they consider junk mail.

Recently some firms have been trying a direct mail tactic that has sparked some debate—sending marketing messages that appear to be from the government, banks, or even a personal friend. The envelope might bear a logo that looks like a government department; inside is a solicitation for refinancing a loan. Another might have what looks like a handwritten note from a friend but actually contains an ad for a fitness centre. Some envelopes look like bank statements. All are intended to cut through the clutter that appears in consumer mailboxes.

Catalogues

Catalogues have been part of the Canadian marketing scene since as long ago as 1884, when Timothy Eaton used them to reach customers who could not shop at his Yonge Street store in Toronto. For many families, particularly those living in rural areas, the Eaton's catalogue was their only means of obtaining items they needed, whether it was dry goods or hardware. These early catalogues are even being reproduced today as memorabilia. Catalogues from stores such as Sears and Canadian Tire have been around so long that they have become a tradition in many households. References to children thumbing through the Sears Wish Book trying to decide what toys they wanted for Christmas or choosing their first bike from the Canadian Tire catalogue have been said to be as Canadian as references to the Mounties or maple syrup.[18]

From a customer's point of view, the advantages of catalogue shopping include convenience, time saving, availability, amount of information, special interest, and less sales pressure. Catalogue shopping can be done at any time without relying on store hours or needing to consider the time it takes to drive to the malls, parking, or dealing with crowds.

From a company's point of view, the advantages of catalogue selling include the ability to target niche markets and being able to display a large number of products. Companies may experience lower overheads, lower costs per sale, and better inventory control. However, catalogues are expensive and time-consuming to produce.

Telemarketing

Although its use has been limited by legislation, telemarketing remains a frequently used form of direct marketing. It provides marketers with a high return on their expenditures, an immediate response, and the opportunity for personalized two-way conversations. In addition to business-to-consumer direct marketing, business-to-business telemarketing is another form of direct customer contact.

Telemarketing refers to direct marketing conducted entirely by telephone, and it can be classified as either outbound or inbound contacts. Outbound telemarketing involves a sales force that uses only the telephone to contact customers, reducing the cost of making personal visits. The customer initiates inbound telemarketing, typically by dialling a toll-free number that firms provide for customers to use at their convenience to obtain information and/or make purchases.

New predictive dialler devices improve telemarketing's efficiency and reduce costs by automating the dialling process to skip busy signals and answering machines. When the dialler reaches a human voice, it instantaneously puts the call through to a salesperson. This technology is often combined with a print advertising campaign that features a toll-free number for inbound telemarketing.

Because recipients of both consumer and business-to-business telemarketing calls often find them annoying, the federal government has passed legislation relating to telemarketing activities. The legislation is administered by Bell Canada. Not all unwanted calls will be stopped by this legislation; survey research firms, registered charities, political parties, and companies that already have a relationship with the consumer will be exempt from these new rules. Companies conducting telemarketing activities will be required to update their call list every 30 days and those not complying could face fines. The largest fine handed out to a company for violating the legislation was $1.3 million imposed—ironically—on Bell Canada in December 2009.[19]

telemarketing
Promotional presentation involving the use of the telephone on an outbound basis by salespeople or on an inbound basis by customers who initiate calls to obtain information and place orders.

Direct Marketing via Broadcast Channels

Broadcast direct marketing can take three basic forms: brief direct-response ads on television or radio, home shopping channels, and infomercials. Direct-response spots typically run 30, 60, or 90 seconds and include product descriptions and toll-free telephone numbers for ordering. Often shown on cable television and independent stations and tied to special-interest programs, broadcast direct marketing usually encourages viewers to respond immediately by offering them a special price or a gift if they call within a few minutes of an ad's airing. Radio direct-response ads also provide product descriptions and addresses or phone numbers to contact the sellers. However, radio often proves

Marketoid

Advertising agencies generated the largest portion of operating revenue for the industry at 42 percent.

expensive compared with other direct marketing media, and listeners may not pay close enough attention to catch the number or may not be able to write it down because they are driving a car, which accounts for a major portion of radio listening time.

home shopping channel Television direct marketing in which a variety of products are offered and consumers can order them directly by phone or online.

Home shopping channels such as Shop TV Canada and The Shopping Channel represent another type of television direct marketing. Broadcasting around the clock, these channels offer consumers a variety of products, including jewellery, clothing, skin care products, home furnishings, computers, cameras, kitchen appliances, and toys. In essence, home shopping channels function like on-air catalogues. The channels also have websites that consumers can browse through to make purchases. In both cases, customers place orders via toll-free telephone numbers and pay for their purchases by credit card.

infomercial Paid 30-minute product commercial that resembles a regular television program.

Infomercials are 30-minute or longer product commercials that resemble regular television programs. Because of their length, infomercials do not get lost as easily as 30-second commercials can, and they permit marketers to present their products in more detail. But they are usually shown at odd hours, and people often watch only portions of them. Think of how many times you have channel-surfed past an infomercial for Bow-flex or Proactiv skin care. Infomercials provide toll-free telephone numbers so that viewers can order products or request more information. Although infomercials incur higher production costs than prime-time 30-second ads on national network TV, they generally air on less expensive cable channels and in late-night time slots on broadcast stations.

Electronic Direct Marketing Channels

Anyone who has ever visited the Web is abundantly aware of the growing number of commercial advertisements that now clutter their computer screen. Web advertising is a recurring theme throughout this text, corresponding to its importance as a component of the promotional mix. In 2009, Canadian companies spent $1746 million on Web advertising, a 9 percent increase over the previous year.[20]

Web advertising, however, is only one component of electronic direct marketing. E-mail direct marketers have found that traditional practices used in print and broadcast media are easily adapted to electronic messaging. You may be receiving periodic e-mail notices from retailers from whom you've

eBay was founded in September 1995. Today, the eBay community includes more than 100 million registered members worldwide. It is the most popular shopping destination on the Internet.

made past purchases, telling you about new products or special offers. Banner ads on your cell phone might offer "click to call" options for responding. You might see a billboard or commercial promoting a code you can text to enter a sweepstakes or get a discount coupon. Experts agree that the basic rules for online direct marketing mirror those of traditional practices. Any successful offline direct marketing campaign can be applied to e-mail promotions. Electronic media deliver data instantly to direct marketers and help them track customer buying cycles quickly. As a result, they can place customer acquisition programs online for less than the cost of traditional programs.

Other Direct Marketing Channels

Print media such as newspapers and magazines do not support direct marketing as effectively as do Web marketing and telemarketing. However, print media and other traditional direct marketing channels are still critical to the success of all electronic media channels. Magazine ads with toll-free telephone numbers enhance inbound telemarketing campaigns. Companies can place ads in magazines or newspapers, include reader-response cards, or place special inserts targeted for certain market segments within the publications. Newspapers are savvy about the Internet, producing online versions of their content—which naturally include online, interactive ads.

Kiosks provide another outlet for electronic sales. In its drive to transform its business, Kodak's in-store photo kiosks, the largest fleet of such retail kiosks in the world, now provide customers with access to their Facebook photos, as well as to pictures stored on Kodak's Gallery.[21]

assessment check 4

4.1 Distinguish between marketing public relations and nonmarketing public relations.

4.2 What is publicity?

4.3 Define sponsorship and explain how sponsorship is different from advertising.

4.4 Define direct mail.

4.5 What are the benefits of electronic direct marketing?

DEVELOPING AN OPTIMAL PROMOTIONAL MIX

(5) Discuss the factors that influence the effectiveness of a promotional mix and contrast pushing and pulling strategies.

By blending advertising, personal selling, sales promotion, and public relations to achieve marketing objectives, marketers create a promotional mix. Since quantitative measures are not available to determine the effectiveness of each mix component in a given market segment, the choice of an effective mix of promotional elements presents one of the marketer's most difficult tasks. Several factors influence the effectiveness of a promotional mix: (1) the nature of the market, (2) the nature of the product, (3) the stage in the product life cycle, (4) the price, and (5) the funds available for promotion.

NATURE OF THE MARKET

The marketer's target audience has a major impact on the choice of a promotion method. When a market includes a limited number of buyers, personal selling may prove a highly effective technique. However, markets characterized by large numbers of potential customers scattered over sizable geographic areas may make the cost of contact by personal salespeople prohibitive. In such instances, extensive use of advertising often makes sense. The type of customer also affects the promotional mix. Personal selling works better in high-priced, high-involvement purchases—for instance, a target market made up of industrial purchasers or retail and wholesale buyers—than in a target market consisting of ultimate consumers. Similarly, pharmaceutical firms use large sales forces to sell prescription drugs directly to physicians and hospitals, but they also advertise to promote over-the-counter medications for the consumer market. So the drug firm must switch its promotional strategy from personal selling to consumer advertising based on the market it is targeting.

Air Canada responded to changes in the market by using direct marketing. As travellers became increasingly frustrated at how uncomfortable air travel had become, Air Canada launched its "Go Far" campaign. It was aimed at the young, affluent professionals aged 25 to 40 who travelled for business or pleasure. The promotional campaign ran in the major cities across the country where these young professions worked, with emphasis on the downtown area of Toronto. One ad in the campaign showed a young woman sitting in an airline seat watching a screen embedded in the back of the seat in front—the tagline was "Count the movies, not the hours. Touch-screen TV at your seat."[22]

Promotion focusing on the nature of the product.

NATURE OF THE PRODUCT

A second important factor in determining an effective promotional mix is the product itself. Highly standardized products with minimal servicing requirements usually depend less on personal selling than do custom products with technically complex features or requirements for frequent maintenance. Marketers of consumer products are more likely to rely heavily on advertising than are business products. For example, soft drinks lend themselves more readily to advertising than do large pieces of business machinery.

Promotional mixes vary within each product category. In the B2B market, for example, installations typically rely more heavily on personal selling than does marketing of operating supplies. In contrast, the promotional mix for a convenience product is likely to involve more emphasis on manufacturer advertising and less on personal selling. However, personal selling plays an important role in the promotion of shopping products, and both personal and nonpersonal selling are important in the promotion of specialty items. A personal-selling emphasis is also likely to prove more effective than other alternatives in promotions for products involving trade-ins.

STAGE IN THE PRODUCT LIFE CYCLE

The promotional mix must also be tailored to the product's stage in the product life cycle. In the introductory stage, both nonpersonal and personal selling are used to acquaint marketing intermediaries and final consumers with the merits of the new product. Heavy emphasis on personal selling helps inform the marketplace of the merits of the new good or service. Salespeople contact marketing intermediaries to secure interest in and commitment to handling the newly introduced item. Trade shows are frequently used to inform and educate prospective dealers and ultimate consumers about its merits over current competitive offerings. Advertising and sales promotion are also used during this stage to create awareness, answer questions, and stimulate initial purchases.

Scotties: Promoting a mature product.

As the product moves into the growth and maturity stages, advertising gains relative importance in persuading consumers to make purchases. Marketers continue to direct personal-selling efforts at marketing intermediaries in an attempt to expand distribution. As more competitors enter the marketplace, advertising begins to stress product differences to persuade consumers to purchase the firm's brand. In the maturity and early decline stages, firms frequently reduce advertising and sales promotion expenditures as market saturation is reached and newer products with their own competitive strengths begin to enter the market.

PRICE

The price of an item is the fourth factor that affects the choice of a promotional mix. Advertising dominates the promotional mixes for low-unit-value products due to the high per-contact costs in personal selling. Advertising permits a low promotional expenditure per sales unit because it reaches mass audiences. For low-value consumer goods, such as chewing gum, soft drinks, and snack foods, advertising is the most feasible means of promotion. Even shopping products can be sold at least partly on the basis of price. On the other hand, consumers of high-priced items such as luxury cars expect lots of well-presented information from qualified salespeople. High-tech direct marketing promotions such as video presentations on a notebook computer or via cell phone, fancy brochures, and personal selling by informed, professional salespeople appeal to these potential customers.

FUNDS AVAILABLE FOR PROMOTION

A real barrier in implementing any promotional strategy is the size of the promotional budget. A single 30-second television commercial during the Super Bowl telecast costs an advertiser between $2.5 and $2.8 million. While millions of viewers may see the commercial, making the cost per contact relatively low, such an expenditure exceeds the entire promotional budgets of thousands of firms, a dilemma that at least partially explains how guerrilla marketing got its start. And if a company wants to hire a celebrity to advertise its goods and services, the fee can run into the millions of dollars a year. Table 13.3 summarizes the factors that influence the determination of an appropriate promotional mix.

table 13.3   *Factors Influencing Choice of Promotional Mix*

	EMPHASIS	
	PERSONAL SELLING	**ADVERTISING**
Nature of the market		
Number of buyers	Limited number	Large number
Geographic concentration	Concentrated	Dispersed
Type of customer	Business purchaser	Ultimate consumer
Nature of the product		
Complexity	Custom-made, complex	Standardized
Service requirements	Considerable	Minimal
Type of good or service	Business	Consumer
Use of trade-ins	Trade-ins common	Trade-ins uncommon
Stage in the product life cycle	Often emphasized at every stage; heavy emphasis in the introductory and early growth stages in acquainting marketing intermediaries and potential consumers with the new good or service	Often emphasized at every stage; heavy emphasis in the latter part of the growth stage, as well as the maturity and early decline stages, to persuade consumers to select specific brands
Price	High unit value	Low unit value

PULLING AND PUSHING PROMOTIONAL STRATEGIES

pulling strategy
Promotional effort by the seller to stimulate final-user demand, which then exerts pressure on the distribution channel.

pushing strategy
Promotional effort by the seller directed to members of the marketing channel rather than final users.

Marketers may implement essentially two promotional alternatives: a pulling strategy or a pushing strategy. A **pulling strategy** is a promotional effort by the seller to stimulate final-user demand, which then exerts pressure on the distribution channel. When marketing intermediaries stock a large number of competing products and exhibit little interest in any one of them, a firm may have to implement a pulling strategy to motivate them to handle its product. In such instances, this strategy is implemented with the objective of building consumer demand so that consumers will request the product from retail stores. Advertising and sales promotion often contribute to a company's pulling strategy.

In contrast, a **pushing strategy** relies more heavily on personal selling. Here the objective is promoting the product to the members of the marketing channel rather than to final users. To achieve this goal, marketers employ cooperative advertising allowances to channel members, trade discounts, personal selling efforts by salespeople, and other dealer supports. Such a strategy is designed to gain marketing success for the firm's products by motivating representatives of wholesalers and/or retailers to spend extra time and effort promoting the products to customers. About half of manufacturers' promotional budgets are allocated for cash incentives used to encourage retailers to stock their products.

Timing also affects the choice of promotional strategies. The relative importance of advertising and selling changes during the various phases of the purchase process. Prior to the actual sale, advertising usually is more important than personal selling. However, one of the primary advantages of a successful advertising program is the support it gives the salesperson who approaches the prospective buyer for the first time. Selling activities are more important than advertising at the time of purchase. Personal selling provides the actual mechanism for closing most sales. In the post-purchase period, advertising regains primacy in the promotional effort. It affirms the customer's decision to buy a particular good or service and reminds him or her of the product's favourable qualities by reducing any cognitive dissonance that might occur.

The promotional strategies used by auto marketers illustrate this timing factor. Car, truck, and SUV makers spend heavily on consumer advertising to create awareness before consumers begin the purchase process. At the time of their purchase decisions, however, the personal-selling skills of dealer salespeople provide the most important tools for closing sales. Finally, advertising is used frequently to maintain post-purchase satisfaction by citing awards such as *Motor Trend*'s Car of the Year and results of J. D. Power's customer-satisfaction surveys to affirm buyer decisions.

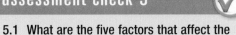

assessment check 5

5.1 What are the five factors that affect the choice of a promotional mix?

5.2 Why is the choice of a mix a difficult task for marketers?

5.3 Explain what a pulling strategy and a pushing strategy are.

⑥ Explain how marketers budget for and measure the effectiveness of promotion and discuss the value of marketing communications.

BUDGETING FOR PROMOTIONAL STRATEGY

Promotional budgets may differ not only in amount but also in composition. Business-to-business marketers generally invest larger proportions of their budgets in personal selling than in advertising, while the reverse is usually true of most producers of consumer goods.

Evidence suggests that sales initially lag behind promotional expenses for structural reasons—funds spent filling up retail shelves, boosting low initial production, and supplying buyer information. This fact produces a threshold effect in which few sales may result from substantial initial investments in promotion. A second phase might produce sales proportionate to promotional expenditures—the most predictable range. Finally, promotion reaches the area of diminishing returns where an increase in promotional spending fails to produce a corresponding increase in sales.

For example, an initial expenditure of $40 000 may result in sales of 100 000 units for a consumer goods manufacturer. See Figure 13.2 for a display of this example. An additional $10 000 expenditure during the second phase may generate sales of 40 000 more units, and another $10 000 may produce sales of an additional 30 000 units. The cumulative effect of the expenditures and repeat sales will have generated increasing returns from the promotional outlays. However, as the advertising budget moves from $60 000 to $70 000, the marginal productivity of the additional expenditure may fall to 25 000 units. At some later point, the return may actually become zero or negative as competition intensifies, markets become saturated, and marketers employ less expensive advertising media.

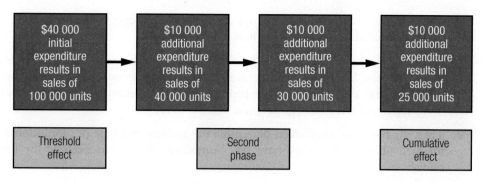

figure 13.2

Consumer-Goods Manufacturer Promotional Expenses

The ideal method of allocating promotional funds would increase the budget until the cost of each additional increment equals the additional incremental revenue received. In other words, the most effective allocation procedure increases promotional expenditures until each dollar of promotional expense is matched by an additional dollar of profit. This procedure, referred to as marginal analysis, maximizes the input's productivity. The difficulty arises in identifying the optimal point, which requires a precise balance between marginal expenses for promotion and the resulting marginal receipts. In addition, as marketing communications become more integrated, it becomes harder to identify exact amounts that companies spend on individual elements of promotion.

Traditional methods used for creating a promotional budget include the percentage-of-sales and fixed-sum-per-unit methods, along with techniques for meeting the competition and achieving task objectives. Each method is briefly examined in Table 13.4.

The **percentage-of-sales method** is perhaps the most common way of establishing promotional budgets. The percentage can be based on sales either from some past period (such as the previous year) or forecasted for a future period (the current year). While this plan is appealingly simple, it does not effectively support the achievement of basic promotional objectives. Arbitrary percentage allocations can't provide needed flexibility. In addition, sales should depend on promotional allocation rather than vice versa.

The **fixed-sum-per-unit method** allocates a predetermined amount to each sales or production unit. This amount can also reflect either historical or forecasted figures. Producers of high-value consumer durable goods, such as automobiles, often use this budgeting method.

Another traditional budgeting approach, the **meeting competition method**, simply matches competitors' outlays, either in absolute amounts or relative to the firms' market shares. But this method doesn't help a company gain a competitive edge. A budget that is appropriate for one company may not be appropriate for another.

percentage-of-sales method Method of promotional budgeting in which a dollar amount is based on a percentage of past or projected sales.

fixed-sum-per-unit method Method of promotional budgeting in which a predetermined amount is allocated to each sales or production unit.

meeting competition Method of promotional budgeting that simply matches competitors' outlays.

table 13.4 *Promotional Budget Determination*

METHOD	DESCRIPTION	EXAMPLE
Percentage-of-sales method	Promotional budget is set as a specified percentage of either past or forecasted sales.	"Last year we spent $10 500 on promotion and had sales of $420 000. Next year we expect sales to grow to $480 000, and we are allocating $12 000 for promotion."
Fixed-sum-per-unit method	Promotional budget is set as a predetermined dollar amount for each unit sold or produced.	"Our forecast calls for sales of 14 000 units, and we allocate promotion at the rate of $65 per unit."
Meeting competition method	Promotional budget is set to match competitor's promotional outlays on either an absolute or relative basis.	"Promotional outlays average 4 percent of sales in our industry."
Task-objective method	Once marketers determine their specific promotional objectives, the amount (and type) of promotional spending needed to achieve them is determined.	"By the end of next year, we want 75 percent of the area high school students to be aware of our new, highly automated fast-food prototype outlet. How many promotional dollars will it take, and how should they be spent?"

task-objective method
Development of a promotional budget based on evaluation of the firm's promotional objectives.

The **task-objective method** develops a promotional budget based on a sound evaluation of the firm's promotional objectives. The method has two steps:

1. The firm's marketers must define realistic communication goals that they want the promotional mix to achieve. Say that a firm wants to achieve a 25 percent increase in brand awareness. This step quantifies the objectives that promotion should attain. These objectives in turn become integral parts of the promotional plan.

2. Then the company's marketers determine the amount and type of promotional activity required for each objective that they have set. Combined, these units become the firm's promotional budget.

A crucial assumption underlies the task-objective approach: marketers can measure the productivity of each promotional dollar. That assumption explains why the objectives must be carefully chosen, quantified, and accomplished through promotional efforts. Budgeters should avoid general marketing objectives such as "We want to achieve a 5 percent increase in sales." A sale is a culmination of the effects of all elements of the marketing mix. A more appropriate promotional objective might be "We want to achieve an 8 percent response rate from a targeted direct mail advertisement."

Promotional budgeting always requires difficult decisions. Still, recent research studies and the spread of computer-based models have made it a more manageable problem than it used to be.

MEASURING THE EFFECTIVENESS OF PROMOTION

Marketers know that part of a firm's promotional effort is ineffective. Evaluating the effectiveness of a promotion today is a far different exercise in marketing research than it was even a few decades ago. For years, marketers depended on store audits conducted by large organizations like Nielsen. Other research groups conducted warehouse withdrawal surveys of shipments to retail customers. These studies were designed to determine whether sales had risen as a direct result of a particular promotional campaign. During the 1980s, the introduction of scanners and automated checkout lanes completely changed marketing research. For the first time, retailers and manufacturers had a tool to obtain sales data quickly and efficiently. The problem was that the collected data were used for little else other than determining how much of which product was bought at what price and at what time.

By the 1990s, marketing research entered another evolutionary period with the advent of the Internet. Now marketing researchers can delve into each customer's purchase behaviour, lifestyle, preferences, opinions, and buying habits. All this information can also be obtained in a matter of seconds. The next section explains the impact of electronic technologies on measuring promotional effectiveness. However, marketers today still depend on two basic measurement tools: direct sales results tests and indirect evaluations.

direct sales results test
Method for measuring promotional effectiveness based on the specific impact on sales revenues for each dollar of promotional spending.

Most marketers would prefer to use a **direct sales results test** to measure the effectiveness of promotion. Such an approach would reveal the specific impact on sales revenues for each dollar of promotional spending. This type of technique has always eluded marketers, however, due to their inability to control other variables operating in the marketplace. A firm may receive $20 million in additional sales orders following a new $1.5-million advertising campaign, but the market success may really have resulted from the products benefiting from more intensive distribution as more stores decide to carry them or price increases for competing products rather than from the advertising outlays.

indirect evaluation
Method for measuring promotional effectiveness by concentrating on quantifiable indicators of effectiveness such as recall and readership.

Marketers often encounter difficulty isolating the effects of promotion from those of other market elements and outside environmental variables. **Indirect evaluation** helps researchers concentrate on quantifiable indicators of effectiveness, such as recall (how much members of the target market remember about specific products or advertisements) and readership (size and composition of a message's audience). The basic problem with indirect measurement is the difficulty in relating these variables to sales. Will the fact that many people read an ad lead directly to increased sales?

Marketers need to ask the right questions and understand what they are measuring. Promotion to build sales volume produces measurable results in the form of short-term returns, but brand-building programs and efforts to generate or enhance consumers' perceptions of value in a product, brand, or organization cannot be measured over the short term.

MEASURING ONLINE PROMOTIONS

The latest challenge facing marketers is how to measure the effectiveness of electronic media. Early attempts at measuring online promotional effectiveness involved counting hits (user requests for a file) and visits, pages downloaded or read in one session. But it takes more than counting "eyeballs" to measure online promotional success. What matters is not how many times a website is visited but how many people actually buy something. Traditional numbers that work for other media forms are not necessarily relevant indicators of effectiveness for a website. For one thing, the Web combines both advertising and direct marketing. Web pages effectively integrate advertising and other content, such as product information, that may often prove to be the page's main—and most effective—feature. For another consideration, consumers generally choose the advertisements they want to see on the Internet, whereas traditional broadcast or print media automatically expose consumers to ads.

One way that marketers measure performance is by incorporating some form of direct response into their promotions. This technique also helps them to compare different promotions for effectiveness and rely on facts rather than opinions. Consumers may say they will try a product when responding to a survey question yet not actually buy it. A firm may send out three different direct mail offers in the same promotion and compare response rates from the groups of recipients receiving each alternative. An offer to send for a sample may generate a 75 percent response rate, coupons might show a 50 percent redemption rate, and rebates might appeal to only 10 percent of the targeted group.

The two major techniques for setting Internet advertising rates are cost per impression and cost per response. **Cost per impression** is a measurement technique that relates the cost of an ad to every thousand people who view it. In other words, anyone who sees the page containing the banner or other form of ad creates one impression. This measure assumes that the site's principal purpose is to display the advertising message. **Cost per response (click-throughs)** is a direct marketing technique that relates the cost of an ad to the number of people who click it. However, not everyone who clicks on an ad makes a purchase. So the **conversion rate** measurement was developed, which is the percentage of website visitors who actually make a purchase. All three rating techniques have merit. Site publishers point out that click-through rates are influenced by the creativity of the ad's message. Advertisers, on the other hand, point out that the Web ad has value to those who click it for additional information.

cost per impression Measurement technique that relates the cost of an ad to every thousand people who view it.

cost per response (also called *click-throughs*) Direct marketing technique that relates the cost of an ad to the number of people who click it.

conversion rate The percentage of visitors to a website who make a purchase.

Marketoid

In 2008, the Canadian ad industry's operating profit margins were 10 percent.

THE VALUE OF MARKETING COMMUNICATIONS

The nature of marketing communications is changing as new formats transform the traditional idea of an advertisement or sales promotion. Sales messages are now placed subtly, or not so subtly, in movies and television shows, blurring the lines between promotion and entertainment and changing the traditional definition of advertising. Messages show up at the beach in the form of skywriting, in restrooms, on stadium turnstiles, buses, and even police cars.

Despite new tactics by advertisers, promotion has often been the target of criticism. Some people complain that it offers nothing of value to society and simply wastes resources. Others criticize promotion's role in encouraging consumers to buy unnecessary products that they cannot afford. Many ads seem to insult people's intelligence or offend their sensibilities, and they criticize the ethics—or lack thereof—displayed by advertisers and salespeople.

New forms of promotion are considered even more insidious because marketers are designing promotions that bear little resemblance to paid advertisements. Many of these complaints cite issues that constitute real problems. Some salespeople use unethical sales tactics. Some product advertising hides its promotional nature or targets consumer groups that can least afford the advertised goods or services. Many television commercials contribute to the growing issue of cultural pollution. One area that has sparked both criticism and debate is promotion aimed at children.

While promotion can certainly be criticized on many counts, it also plays a crucial role in modern society. This point is best understood by examining the social, business, and economic importance of promotion.

Promotional message addressing a social concern.

SOCIAL IMPORTANCE

We live in a diverse society characterized by consumer segments with differing needs, wants, and aspirations. What one group finds tasteless may be quite appealing to another. But diversity is one of the benefits of living in our society because it offers us many choices and opportunities. Promotional strategy faces an averaging problem that escapes many of its critics. The one generally accepted standard in a market society is freedom of choice for the consumer. Consumer buying decisions eventually determine acceptable practices in the marketplace.

Promotion has also become an important factor in campaigns aimed at achieving social objectives. Advertising agencies often donate their time and expertise in creating public service announcements (PSAs) aimed at promoting such important causes as stopping drug abuse. TBWA Toronto, an advertising agency, created a series of PSAs for MADD (Mothers Against Drunk Drivers). The ads were designed to take a different approach to the message about not drinking and driving. No tearful family members for TBWA. The television ads were humorous skits based on myths about how to beat the Breathalyzers such as sucking on an penny with the tagline "Fighting a copper with a copper."[23]

Promotion performs an informative and educational task crucial to the functioning of modern society. As with everything else in life, what is important is how promotion is used rather than whether it is used. A good example of how promotion benefits society is described in the "Marketing in a Digital World" box.

MARKETING IN A DIGITAL WORLD | **Online Marketing? Guerrilla Marketing?**

THE First United Church of Vancouver is located in the heart of the city in an area known for high drug addiction and homelessness. The church describes it as "a community located at the margins of society—but a community without margins."

Rather than ignoring the problems in the area, the church took a proactive stance. The programs the church runs include a thrift shop to provide clothing, a meal program, serving four hot meals a day to anyone who shows up, a shelter where anyone is welcome to sleep, and subsidized housing in the form of three apartment buildings.

In order to provide these programs, the church needed help from the community. It needed to get the message out about its programs and the situation the homeless faced every day. It particularly wanted to let the world know that the homeless were people, not just individuals to be ignored as they were passed on the sidewalk.

In order to get its message out, the church has a website explaining its programs and how to make a contribution. The website also contains a link to a site called "street stories" that provides pictures and a brief biography of people living on the street. Church events can also be followed on Twitter, on Facebook, by an RSS feed, and on its YouTube channel.

The advertising agency DDB Canada teamed up with the church to mount an awareness campaign. On a cold, rainy December morning, three life-sized sculptures of human figures were placed in the area of the church. The sculptures were posed as homeless people, one as a panhandler, one pushing a shopping cart, and another lying in a sleeping bag. Each figure had handouts directing people to the Facebook profiles of three people the church helped and a sign asking people passing by to "Help get someone off the street."

Sources: Eve Lazarus, "First United Hits Vancouver Streets," *Marketing*, http://www.marketingmag.ca, January 13, 2011; First United Church of Vancouver website, http://www.firstunited.ca, January 15, 2011.

BUSINESS IMPORTANCE

Promotional strategy has become increasingly important to both large and small business enterprises. The well-documented, long-term increase in funds spent on promotion certainly attests to management's faith in the ability of promotional efforts to encourage attitude changes, brand loyalty, and additional sales. It is difficult to conceive of an enterprise that would not attempt to promote its good or service in some manner. Most modern institutions simply cannot survive in the long run without promotion. Business must communicate with its publics.

Nonbusiness enterprises also recognize the importance of promotional efforts. The Canadian government is the leading advertiser in Canada, promoting many concepts and programs. The Canadian Tourism Commission, which is funded by the federal government, has a budget of around $70 million annually.[24]

ECONOMIC IMPORTANCE

Promotion has assumed a degree of economic importance because it provides employment for millions of people. More important, however, effective promotion has allowed society to derive benefits not otherwise available. For example, the criticism that promotion costs too much isolates an individual expense item and fails to consider its possible beneficial effects on other categories of expenditures.

Promotional strategies increase the number of units sold and permit economies of scale in the production process, thereby lowering the production costs for each unit of output. Lower unit costs allow lower consumer prices, which in turn make products available to more people. Similarly, advertising subsidizes the information content of newspapers and the broadcast media. In short, promotion pays for many of the enjoyable entertainment and educational opportunities in contemporary life as it lowers product costs.

Marketoid

Operating expenses for companies in the advertising business totalled $6 billion in 2007.

assessment check 6

6.1 What is the most common way of establishing a promotional budget?

6.2 What is the task-objective budgeting method? Describe its two steps.

6.3 What is the direct sales results test and what is indirect evaluation?

6.4 Identify the three areas in which promotion exerts influence.

Strategic Implications

With the incredible proliferation of promotional messages in the media, today's marketers—consumers themselves—must find new ways to reach customers without overloading them with unnecessary or unwanted communications. Sponsorship and guerrilla marketing have emerged as effective strategies for large and small companies, but ambush marketing has raised ethical concerns. Product placement has gained in popularity, in movies, television shows, and video games.

In addition, it is difficult to overstate the impact of the Internet on the promotional mix of 21st-century marketers—for small and large companies alike. Even individual entrepreneurs find the Internet to be a lucrative launch pad for their enterprises. But even though cyberspace marketing has been effective in business-to-business transactions and, to a lesser extent, for some types of consumer purchases, a major source of Internet revenues is advertising.

Integrating marketing communications into an overall consumer-focused strategy that meets a company's promotional and business objectives has become more and more critical in the busy global marketplace. Chapter 14 will examine specific ways marketers can use advertising and online communications to convey their messages; then Chapter 15 will discuss personal selling, sales force management, and sales promotion in the same manner. ◆◆◆

REVIEW OF CHAPTER OBJECTIVES

① **Explain how integrated marketing communications relates to the development of an optimal promotional mix and describe the communication process.**

Integrated marketing communications (IMC) refers to the coordination of all promotional activities to produce a unified, customer-focused promotional message. Developing an optimal promotional mix involves selecting the personal and nonpersonal selling strategies that will work best to deliver the overall marketing message as defined by IMC.

In the communication process, a message is encoded and transmitted through a communications channel; then it is decoded, or interpreted by the receiver; finally, the receiver provides feedback, which completes the system. The AIDA concept (attention-interest-desire-action) explains the steps through which a person reaches a purchase decision after being exposed to a promotional message. The marketer sends the promotional message, and the consumer receives and responds to it via the communication process.

② **Explain how the promotional mix relates to the objectives of promotion.**

The objectives of promotion are to provide information, stimulate demand, differentiate a product, accentuate the value of a product, and stabilize sales. The promotional mix, which is the blend of numerous variables intended to satisfy the target market, must fulfill the overall objectives of promotion.

③ **Identify the different elements of the promotional mix and explain how marketers develop an optimal promotional mix.**

The different elements of the promotional mix are personal selling and nonpersonal selling (advertising, product placement, sales promotion, direct marketing, and public relations). Guerrilla marketing is frequently used by marketers with limited funds and firms attempting to attract attention for new-product offerings with innovative promotional approaches. Marketers develop the optimal mix by considering the nature of the market, the nature of the product, the stage in the product life cycle, price, and funds available for promotion.

④ **Describe the role of public relations, publicity, sponsorships, and direct marketing in integrated marketing communications.**

Public relations consists of the firm's communications and relationships with its various publics, including customers, employees, shareholders, suppliers, government, and the society in which it operates. Publicity is the dissemination of newsworthy information about a product or organization. This information activity is frequently used in new product introductions. Although publicity is welcomed by firms, negative publicity is easily created when a company enters a grey ethical area with the use of its promotional efforts. Sponsorship, which occurs when an organization provides money or in-kind resources to an event or activity in exchange for a direct association with the event or activity, has become a hot trend in promotion. The sponsor purchases access to an activity's audience and the image associated with the activity, both of which contribute to the overall promotional message being delivered by a firm. Direct marketing involves direct communication between a seller and a B2B or final customer. It includes such promotional methods as telemarketing, direct mail, direct-response advertising and infomercials on TV and radio, direct-response print advertising, and electronic media.

⑤ **Discuss the factors that influence the effectiveness of a promotional mix and contrast pushing and pulling strategies.**

Marketers face the challenge of determining the best mix of components for an overall promotional strategy. Several factors influence the effectiveness of the promotional mix: (1) the nature of the market; (2) the nature of the product; (3) the stage in the product life cycle; (4) price; and (5) the funds available for promotion.

In a pulling strategy, marketers attempt to stimulate final-user demand, which then exerts pressure on the distribution channel. In a pushing strategy, marketers attempt to promote the product to channel members rather than final users. To do this, they rely heavily on personal selling.

⑥ **Explain how marketers budget for and measure the effectiveness of promotion and discuss the value of marketing communications.**

Marketers may choose among several methods for determining promotional budgets, including percentage-of-sales, fixed-sum-per-unit, meeting competition, or task-objective, which is considered the most flexible and most effective. Today, marketers use either direct sales results tests or indirect evaluation to measure effectiveness. Both methods have their benefits and drawbacks because of the difficulty of controlling variables.

Despite a number of valid criticisms, marketing communications provide socially important messages, are important to businesses, and contain economic importance. As with every communication in society, it is important to consider how promotion is used rather than whether it is used at all.

assessment check answers

1.1 Define *promotion*.
Promotion is the function of informing, persuading, and influencing the consumer's purchase decision.

1.2 What is the difference between marketing communications and integrated marketing communications (IMC)?
Marketing communications are messages that deal with buyer-seller relationships, from a variety of media. IMC coordinates all promotional activities to produce a unified, customer-focused promotional message.

1.3 What are the three tasks accomplished by an effective message?
An effective message gains the receiver's attention; it achieves understanding by both receiver and sender; and it stimulates the receiver's needs and suggests an appropriate method of satisfying them.

1.4 Identify the four steps of the AIDA concept and explain noise.
The four steps of the AIDA concept are attention, interest, desire, and action. Noise represents interference at some stage in the communication process.

2.1 What are the objectives of promotion?
The objectives of promotion are to provide information to consumers and others, to increase demand, to differentiate a product, to accentuate a product's value, and to stabilize sales.

2.2 Why is product differentiation important to marketers?
Product differentiation, distinguishing a good or service from its competitors, is important to marketers because they need to create a distinct image in consumers' minds. If they can do so, they can then exert more control over variables such as price.

3.1 Differentiate between personal selling and nonpersonal selling.
Personal selling involves a promotional presentation conducted on a person-to-person basis with a buyer. Nonpersonal selling involves communication with a buyer in any way other than on a person-to-person basis.

3.2 What are the six major categories of nonpersonal selling?
The six major categories of nonpersonal selling are advertising, product placement, sales promotion, direct marketing, public relations, and guerrilla marketing.

4.1 Distinguish between marketing public relations and nonmarketing public relations.
Marketing public relations refers to narrowly focused public relations activities that directly support marketing goals. Nonmarketing public relations refers to a company's messages about general issues.

4.2 What is publicity?
Publicity is nonpersonal stimulation of demand for a good, service, place, idea, person, or organization by unpaid placement of significant news regarding the product in a print or broadcast medium.

4.3 Define sponsorship and explain how sponsorship is different from advertising.
Sponsorship occurs when an organization pays money or in-kind resources to an event or activity in exchange for a direct association with that event or activity. Although sponsorship generates brand awareness, the sponsor has little control over the message or even the coverage, unlike advertising.

4.4 Define direct mail.
Direct mail is communications in the form of letters, postcards, brochures, and catalogues containing marketing messages and sent directly to a customer or potential customer.

4.5 What are the benefits of electronic direct marketing?
Electronic media deliver data instantly to direct marketers and help them track customer buying cycles quickly.

5.1 What are the five factors that affect the choice of a promotional mix?
The five factors affecting the choice of a promotional mix are the nature of the market, the nature of the product, the stage in the product life cycle, price, and the funds available for promotion.

5.2 Why is the choice of a mix a difficult task for marketers?
The choice of a mix is difficult because no quantitative measures are available to determine the effectiveness of each component in a given market segment.

5.3 Explain what a pulling strategy and a pushing strategy are.
A pulling strategy is a promotional effort by the seller to stimulate final-user demand. A pushing strategy is an effort to promote a product to the members of the marketing channel.

6.1 What is the most common way of establishing a promotional budget?

The most common method of establishing a promotional budget is the percentage-of-sales method.

6.2 What is the task-objective budgeting method? Describe its two steps.

The task-objective method develops a promotional budget based on an evaluation of the firm's promotional objectives. Its two steps are defining realistic communication goals and determining the amount and type of promotional activity required for each objective set.

6.3 What is the direct sales results test and what is indirect evaluation?

The direct sales results test reveals the specific impact on sales revenues for each dollar of promotional spending. Indirect evaluation helps researchers concentrate on quantifiable indicators of effectiveness.

6.4 Identify the three areas in which promotion exerts influence.

The three areas in which promotion exerts influence are society, business, and the economy.

MARKETING TERMS YOU NEED TO KNOW

These terms are printed in red in the text. They are defined in the margins of the chapter and in the Glossary that begins on p. G-1.

promotion 392
marketing communications 392
integrated marketing communications (IMC) 392
sender 396
message 396
AIDA concept 397
encoding 397
decoding 397
feedback 397
noise 397
channel 397
primary demand 401
selective demand 401
promotional mix 402

product differentiation 402
personal selling 403
nonpersonal selling 403
advertising 403
product placement 403
sales promotion 403
public relations 404
trade promotion 404
publicity 405
guerrilla marketing 405
nonmarketing public relations 407
marketing public relations (MPR) 407
sponsorship 408
ambush marketing 409
direct mail 410

telemarketing 411
home shopping channel 412
infomercial 412
pulling strategy 416
pushing strategy 416
percentage-of-sales method 417
fixed-sum-per-unit method 417
meeting competition 417
task-objective method 418
direct sales results test 418
indirect evaluation 418
cost per impression 419
cost per response (also called *click-throughs*) 419
conversion rate 419

PROJECTS AND TEAMWORK EXERCISES

1. Not-for-profit organizations rely on IMC just as much as for-profit firms do. The Egyptian government, which owns the remains and artifacts of the boy pharaoh King Tutankhamun, has sent the King Tut collection on a worldwide tour of selected nations and museums. Many organizers, including *National Geographic*, are involved in a multimillion-dollar marketing campaign promoting the exhibit, titled Tutankamun and the Golden Age of the Pharaohs. On your own or with a classmate, conduct online research to learn how museums and other organizers have used IMC to promote this or other tours. Present your findings to the class.

2. On your own or with a friend, select a print advertisement that catches your attention and analyze it according to the AIDA concept (attention-interest-desire-action). Identify features of the ad that catch your attention, pique your interest,

make you desire the product, and spur you toward a purchase. Present your findings to the class.

3. Watch a television show and see how many products you can find placed within the show. Present your findings to the class.

4. With a classmate, choose a good or service that you feel could benefit from guerrilla marketing. Imagine that you have a limited promotional budget and come up with a plan for a guerrilla approach. Outline several ideas and explain how you plan to carry them out. Present your plan to the class.

5. Evaluate two or three pieces of direct mail that you have received lately. Which items caught your attention and at least made you save the mailing? Which items did you toss in the trash without even opening or considering beyond an initial glance? Why?

CRITICAL-THINKING EXERCISES

1. Choose one of the following products and discuss what you think the objective(s) of promotion should be for the product:
   a. beef
   b. Kraft Macaroni & Cheese
   c. Ford Focus
   d. cell phone service
2. Identify a corporate sponsorship for a cause or program in your area, or find a local company that sponsors a local charity or other organization. What do you think the sponsor is gaining from its actions? Be specific. What does the sponsored organization receive? Do you think this sponsorship is good for your community? Explain.
3. What are some of the advantages and disadvantages of using a celebrity spokesperson to promote a good or service? How might this affect a firm's public relations efforts?
4. Take a careful look at a direct mail catalogue that you have received recently. Who is the audience for the products? Did the firm target you correctly?
5. Describe a public service announcement that you have seen recently. Do you believe that the announcement will help the organization achieve its goals? Why or why not?

ETHICS EXERCISE

Pop-up ads, those unsolicited messages that sometimes pop onto your computer screen and block the site or information you're looking for until you close or respond to them, are inexpensive to produce and cost nearly nothing to send. But they are so annoying to some computer users that dozens of special programs have been written to block them from appearing on the screen during Internet use.

1. Do you think that because they are unsolicited, pop-up ads are also intrusive? Are they an invasion of privacy? Explain your reasoning.
2. Do you consider the use of pop-up ads to be unethical? Why or why not?

INTERNET EXERCISES

1. **Pulling versus pushing strategies.** Review the material in the chapter on pulling and pushing strategies and go to the websites of Honda Motors (www.honda.ca) and S. C. Johnson (www.scjohnson.ca). Based on the websites, which firm appears to follow more of a pulling promotion strategy? Which firm follows more of a pushing promotional strategy? Be prepared to defend your answers.
2. **Product placement.** Visit the website listed here (www.brandchannel.com/brandcameo_films.asp). It tracks product placements in movies. Review the material on the website and then answer the following questions.
   a. Which movies have had the largest number of product placements?
   b. Which brands have appeared most often?
   c. What are some of the benefits and risks to marketers of movie product placements?
3. **Public relations.** Visit the websites of at least three large multinational corporations. Examples are Siemens, DuPont, and BP Oil. Review the material on the websites and prepare a brief report outlining how each firm includes public relations as part of its promotional strategy.

Note: Internet Web addresses change frequently. If you don't find the exact sites listed, you may need to access the organization's or company's home page and search from there or use a search engine such as Google or Bing.

CASE 13.1

McCain Foods—It's All Good

McCain Foods is on a journey to transform its products, packaging, and promotional material. The tagline in a recent print advertisement sums it up: "Shouldn't food be the only ingredient in food?"

The trend in recent years is toward healthier lifestyles, including the food we eat. This trend was supported by recent research carried out by TNS, a global research firm. Its research found that 85 percent of Canadians wanted prepared food to be made with real ingredients they recognized and 86 percent wanted food companies to be more transparent about the ingredients in their prepared foods.

McCain Foods, based in Florenceville, New Brunswick, listened to the research. In fact, it prompted the company to carry out some research of its own. The company presented customer groups with lists of ingredients used in its food products. The customers were asked if they knew what the ingredient was and whether they wanted the ingredient in their food products. The results of all this research was that customers wanted the ingredients ending in "ates," "ites," and "ides" out of their food.

McCain's commitment to better food included partnering with nutrition and medical experts and its own health and wellness advisory groups to come up with some criteria. McCain's promise is that a minimum of 60 percent of its new products will meet the following criteria: low fat—30 percent or less of total calories; low salt—less than 230 milligrams; trans-fat free—under 0.5 grams; and low saturated fats—10 percent or less of total calories.

Starting with the frozen pizza, pizza pockets, and potato products, the company changed existing products and developed new products to meet the criteria. It started by eliminating all unnecessary ingredients. Next it changed the packaging. When an ingredient was not something one found in everyone's kitchen, the package carried an explanation about why it was in the product. All this research and product change cost the company more than $10 million.

The company was now ready to start promoting its new products. Two 30-second commercials were produced. Using a background showing farmers gathering fresh vegetables from their fields, a voice states, "Instead of asking 'What's for dinner?' consumers should be asking 'What's in dinner?'" The second commercial promotes one of the new products, McCain Purely Potatoes. This product has several versions: after the potatoes are washed and peeled, they are cut in either chunks, cubes, or slices before being frozen. The commercial shows customers how easy it is to make mashed potatoes using this product. The televi-

sion commercials were supported with print ads asking questions like "What's standing between you and mashed potatoes?" The print ads informed consumers they could go to the company website, McCain.ca, for more information. Social media and public relations campaigns were also included in the campaign.

Were the millions spent on research and development and promotion worth it? The company has seen increased sales of its Rising Crust and Thin Crust Pizzas of 9 percent from the previous year and 7.5 percent in its Superfries product. The company attributes this success to its promotional efforts, stating that 85 percent of Canadian mothers saw the ads and the public relations campaign had roughly 32 million media impressions. These numbers would indicate that McCain's has a winning strategy; however, the biggest winner might be its customers who have healthier food for themselves and their children.

Questions for Critical Thinking

1. What elements does McCain include in its marketing program? Is it effective? Would you change any part of it? Why?

2. What do you think McCain's should do next in order to build on its "It's all good" strategy?

Sources: Kristin Laird, "McCain Foods," *Marketing*, November 8, 2010, p. 12; Kristin Laird, "Real Food, Real Good," *Marketing*, March 1, 2010, p. 5; Kristin Laird, "McCain Foods Wants To Be All Natural," *Marketing*, http://www.marketingmag.ca; January 13, 2010; Kristin Laird, "McCain Asks What's In Your Food," *Marketing*, http://www.marketingmag.ca, January 25, 2010; McCain website, http://www.mccain.com, January 21, 2010; TNS website, http://www.tns.com, January 21, 2010.

CASE 13.2

Scotiabank—Show Your Colours

Scotiabank is one of Canada's oldest and largest companies. Scotiabank began business in 1832 in Halifax as the Bank of Nova Scotia and opened its first branch in 1837. By the 1880s, the company had begun opening branches across Canada and in the Unites States, mainly in the Midwest states. Today Scotiabank is a diversified financial services company operating in 50 countries around the world with around 14 million customers. The company has products to satisfy the needs of retail, corporate, and commercial customers.

For a company this large to put together an integrated marketing communications program is a daunting task. In Canada alone the company has more than 7 million customers, over 1000 retail branches, and almost 3000 ATMs. One of the challenges for Scotiabank with so many customers is that it also has many segments to reach, but it has been able to develop a very successful integrated marketing communications program. In fact, Scotiabank's marketing program is so successful that the bank was named as one of Canada's Top Ten Marketers of 2010 by *Marketing* magazine.

What is Scotiabank's secret to marketing success? Aside from the traditional methods of promotion, Scotiabank has used some innovative techniques that have worked well. It has even been accused of ambush marketing, usually thought to be used by smaller companies with less marketing money available. Scotiabank's "Show Your Colours" campaign was one of its most successful and the one that brought the accusation of ambush marketing. It launched this campaign just before the Winter Olympics, promoting the fact that Scotiabank's brand colours are the same as the country's flag. Canadians were encouraged to upload stories and photos to the Scotiabank's website to demonstrate their patriotism. The campaign was supported with in-branch point-of-sale material and cinema ads running at Cineplex theatres across the country. The campaign might not have caused so much controversy if it wasn't for the message "This is our moment, Canada," which every participant received when they added their story or picture to the website. Cries of "ambush" came from the Vancouver Olympic Committee and the Royal Bank of Canada, the official financial sponsor of the Olympic Games, who felt the campaign misled Canadians into thinking Scotiabank was an Olympics sponsor. In the end, Scotiabank was allowed to continue the campaign, claiming it wasn't about Olympics sponsorship but rather national spirit. The campaign was a success. More than 14 000 images were uploaded to the site and more than 42 000 people entered votes. A second phase of the campaign was launched shortly after the first, which included a smartphone application. The second campaign encouraged participants to take pictures of the "Show Your Colours" logo. This time, however, the bank changed the wording of the tagline in order to keep the Olympics organizers happy.

Another successful promotion for Scotiabank was "Let the Savings Begin." Research conducted by the financial services industry found that people felt banking services and products were too complex and they had difficulty understanding them. The "Let the Savings Begin" campaign tried to correct this. The campaign promoted the banks' savings and credit-card programs that allowed customers to save automatically. This campaign was part of an ongoing promotion aimed at changing people's savings habits. While the campaign used many traditional promotional techniques like television and transit and print ads, it also used some innovative tactics. The bank hired Valerie Pringle, the journalist and host of the television program *Canadian Antiques Roadshow*. Pringle was hired not to promote any products but rather just to talk to Canadians about their savings habits in what the bank called "kitchen table-type conversations." Another tactic employed by the bank was to send bank employees out to the streets with gift cards. The gift cards were given to people entering coffee shops and came with a message attached relating to the savings campaign. The lower-key approach worked. More than 150 000 Canadians, existing and new customers of Scotiabank, started using the automatic savings products the bank offered.

The real cornerstone of Scotiabank's promotion is its many and diverse sponsorship programs. The Scotiabank brand reaches out to many different customer segments through sports and cultural events. What could be more Canadian than hockey? Scotiabank refers to itself as "Canada's Hockey Bank." It is the official bank of the National Hockey League, National Hockey League Players' Association, National Hockey League Alumni, and the Canadian Women's Hockey League. It is the official sponsor of the Calgary Flames, the Ottawa Senators, and the London Knights. In both Calgary and Ottawa, Scotiabank has paid for the naming rights for the arenas these teams play in, the Scotiabank Saddledome and Scotiabank Place. Along with the CBC, Scotiabank sponsors Hockey Day. The 11th edition of Hockey Day was hosted by Whitehorse. Many events take place throughout the day, not the least of which are three hockey games in which the Canadian NHL teams play each other. Some of the other hockey events sponsored by Scotiabank include the Scotiabank Canadian Multicultural Hockey Championship, Girls' Hockey Fest, and the World Pond Hockey Championship.

Scotiabank has a similar sponsorship program with the Canadian Football League. It is the official bank for the league and the Grey Cup and supports the players' associations. It is also the official bank for the BC Lions, Edmonton Eskimos, Calgary Stampeders, Saskatchewan Roughriders, Winnipeg Blue Bombers, and Hamilton Tiger Cats.

Among the many cultural events that Scotiabank sponsors are Caribana (now called Scotiabank Toronto Caribbean Carnival), Buskerfest, Banque Scotia 21K de Montréal, AIDS Walk for Life, Scotiabank Toronto Waterfront Marathon, Scotiabank Nuit Blanche, and the Scotiabank Giller Prize. Caribana is a Toronto festival celebrating everything Caribbean, including a massive parade. Buskerfest brings together street performers from around the world. The Banque Scotia 21K de Montréal and the Toronto Waterfront Marathon are races attracting thousands of runners. Communities across the country organize events for the AIDS Walk for Life event, and the money raised supports community-based AIDS programs. For one night a year, the city of Toronto celebrates contemporary art at Nuit Blanche with hundreds of local and international artists taking part. The Giller Prize celebrates the best of Canadian writers.

Along with all of these corporate-level sponsorships, Scotiabank has a program to support employee-led initiatives in the area of education, health, social services, arts and culture, and community-based programs. Scotiabank branches around the world hosted local women's groups on International Women's Day as part of this program.

For all of these good works, Scotiabank has earned the designation of an Imagine Caring Company, given to companies that donate at least 1 percent of profits to support charities and nonprofit groups.

Questions for Critical Thinking

1. Identify the different customer groups that would be attracted to each of the sponsorship events. Suggest other types of promotion that would also attract these groups.
2. What are the benefits and drawbacks of each of the sponsored events?
3. If you were hired by Scotiabank to change its integrated marketing communications program, what changes would you make? Why?

Sources: Scotiabank website, http://www.scotiabank.com, January 20, 2011; Bank of Nova Scotia: Company Profile, Datamonitor, http://www.datamonitor.com, January 16, 2011; Kristin Laird, "Scotiabank," *Marketing*, November 8, 2010; Jeromy Lloyd, "Olympic Marketers Discuss Their War on 'Ambush Marketers,'" *Marketing*, http://www.marketingmag.ca, January 18, 2010; Jeff Beer, "Scotiabank Mobilizes for Caribana," *Marketing*, http://www.marketingmag.ca, January 16, 2010; Jeromy Lloyd, "Scotiabank Continues Showing Its Colours'" *Marketing*, http://www.marketingmag.ca, January 16, 2011; Jeromy Lloyd, "Scotiabank and Valerie Pringle Talk About Saving Money," *Marketing*, http://www.marketingmag.ca, January 19, 2011.

chapter 14

Advertising and Digital Communications

CHAPTER OBJECTIVES

① Identify the three major advertising objectives and the two basic categories of advertising.

② List the major advertising strategies and describe the process of creating an advertisement.

③ Identify the major types of advertising appeals and discuss their uses.

④ List and compare the major advertising media.

⑤ Outline the organization of the advertising function and the role of an advertising agency.

⑥ Explain the role of ethics in an organization's promotional strategy and how marketers assess promotional effectiveness.

SNICKERS: "YOU'RE NOT YOU WHEN YOU'RE HUNGRY"

Snickers, the iconic nougat, caramel, and nut-laden candy bar, has a great "life story." Despite being introduced during the Great Depression, it rose to become the world's best-selling chocolate candy bar. Today, it's a brand worth more than $2 billion.

Snickers owes it all to a young man named Frank Mars, who during his convalescence from polio learned the fine points of candy making from his mother. Mars began selling candy for a living and had commercial success in 1923 with a candy bar he named Milky Way. In 1929, Mars moved the family business to Chicago to take advantage of the more central location and the proximity to rail shipping. The following year, Mars introduced the Snickers bar, a treat named after the family's favourite horse, and priced it at five cents.

Perhaps because Snickers contained peanuts, advertising initially positioned it as more of a food item than candy bar: a nutritious, high-quality snack that satisfies your hunger. Snickers' sales soon outpaced Milky Way's and, in spite of desperate economic times, Snickers became a runaway hit. Throughout the 1930s and into the 1940s, Snickers advertising continued to emphasize the peanuts. From 1949 to 1952, as the sponsor of *The Howdy Dowdy Show*, one of early television's most popular children's programs, Snickers' popularity grew.

Mars concentrated on building market share for Snickers with advertising. Its most famous and longest-running campaign, "Packed with Peanuts, Snickers Satisfies," was created by the ad agency Ted Bates Worldwide and ran from 1979 to 1995.

As consumers became more health conscious and turned their focus to healthier food choices, such as granola and energy bars, Snickers faced some challenges. However, the brand countered by reaching back to the market segment that viewed its first television commercials: baby boomers. Another campaign, "Snacklish," featured the highly recognizable Snickers logo and packaging, but with a play on the word "Snickers"—for example, a sign with the image of a Snickers bar atop a taxicab with the word "Snaxi" where you would normally see the "taxi" sign.

But Snickers' most famous advertising to date aired during the Super Bowl XLIV. A spot titled "Game" showcased the talents of octogenarians Betty White and Abe Vigoda, two TV sitcom stars from the 1970s. Under the tagline "You're not you when you're hungry," White scrimmages with a group of 20-something men before being tackled and landing on her back in a mud puddle. After taking a quick break to wolf down a Snickers bar, White morphs into a young man, his energy restored, who's ready to get back into the game. With a score of 8.68, the commercial won the Super Bowl Ad Meter competition, one of the most influential gauges of an ad's popularity.

For advertisers, the Super Bowl represents an annual sink-or-swim opportunity to showcase creative talent before a global audience recently estimated at more than 106 million viewers. Although many of the American ads are not seen in Canada during the Super Bowl program itself, Canadians have access to these ads through other media. Not all companies believe investing in an ad airing during the Super Bowl is worth the money. A recent informal study conducted by *Marketing* magazine of top marketing and media professionals found that 35 percent felt Super Bowl ads were not a valuable asset while 25 percent had the opposite point of view.

The Snickers Super Bowl commercial did not disappoint. Within days of airing, the ad went viral and then became a global sensation. Fans subsequently launched a Facebook campaign to persuade the producer of *Saturday Night Live* to engage Betty White as a guest host—an episode that garnered the show's highest ratings since 2008.[1]

---

connecting with customers

From its introduction during an economic depression, the Snickers bar captured the hearts of consumers. Decades later, it endures as the world's most popular candy bar and a recognizable product around the globe. The company used advertising to promote Snickers, making it a fixture in the everyday life of consumers.

Chapter Overview

FROM the last chapter, you already know the nonpersonal elements of promotion include advertising. Thousands of organizations rely on nonpersonal selling to develop their promotional mixes and integrated marketing communications strategies. Advertising is the most visible form of nonpersonal promotion, as witnessed by the success of the Snickers bar, and marketers often use it together with sales promotion (discussed in the next chapter) to create effective promotional campaigns. Television is probably the most obvious medium for nonpersonal selling dollars. But marketers are becoming increasingly creative in identifying new or unusual media through which to deliver their messages. Some companies are delivering their promotional messages on beverage cups, cocktail napkins, and other consumables used aboard the flights of commercial airlines where the ads will be seen by millions of air travellers.[2]

Marketers seeking excitement for new-product launches—and the rejuvenation of older products—pay millions for celebrities to promote their products. Ford put *Mad Men* star John Slattery in its "Smarter Than Luxury" Campaign promoting the Lincoln MKX and MKZ hybrid cars. CoverGirl signed actress Drew Barrymore as its glamour spokesperson.[3]

This chapter begins with a discussion of the types of advertising and explains how advertising is used to achieve a firm's objectives. It then considers alternative advertising strategies and the process of creating an advertisement. Next we provide a detailed look at various advertising media channels: television, radio, print advertising, direct mail, and outdoor and interactive media. The chapter then focuses on the importance of digital communications and cross promotions. Alternative methods of measuring the effectiveness of both digital and offline nonpersonal selling are examined. We conclude the chapter by exploring current ethical issues relating to nonpersonal selling. ◆◆◆

① Identify the three major advertising objectives and the two basic categories of advertising.

ADVERTISING

Twenty-first-century advertising is closely related to integrated marketing communications (IMC) in many respects. While IMC involves a message dealing with buyer–seller relationships, advertising consists of paid nonpersonal communication through various media with the purpose of informing or persuading members of a particular audience. Advertising is used by marketers to reach target markets with messages designed to appeal to business firms, not-for-profit organizations, or ultimate consumers.

The world's leading advertisers are Procter & Gamble, Unilever, and L'Oreal, each spending more than $3 billion annually.[4] Advertising spending varies among industries as well as companies. The cosmetics industry is widely known for large amounts spent on advertising, as is the auto manufacturing industry. Advertising spending is expected to increase between 5 and 7 percent in the next few years, with the increases coming from the automotive, telecom, financial, travel, and retail sectors.[5]

As previous chapters have discussed, the emergence of the marketing concept, with its emphasis on a company-wide consumer orientation, boosted the importance of integrated marketing communications. This change in turn expanded the role of advertising. Today, a typical consumer is exposed to hundreds of advertising messages each day. Advertising can provide an efficient, inexpensive, and fast method of reaching the ever-elusive, increasingly segmented consumer market.

TYPES OF ADVERTISING

Advertisements fall into two broad categories: product advertising and institutional advertising. **Product advertising** is nonpersonal selling of a particular good or service. This is the type of advertising the average person usually thinks of when talking about most promotional activities.

Institutional advertising, in contrast, promotes a concept, an idea, a philosophy, or the goodwill of an industry, company, organization, person, geographic location, or government agency. This term has a broader meaning than *corporate advertising*, which is typically limited to advertising sponsored by a specific profit-seeking firm. Institutional advertising is often closely related to the public relations function.

OBJECTIVES OF ADVERTISING

Marketers use advertising messages to accomplish three primary objectives: to inform, to persuade, and to remind. These objectives may be used individually or, more typically, in conjunction with each other. For example, an ad for a not-for-profit agency may inform the public of the existence of the organization and at the same time persuade the audience to make a donation, join the organization, or attend a function.

Informative advertising seeks to develop initial demand for a good, service, organization, person, place, idea, or cause. The promotion of any new market entry tends to pursue this objective because marketing success at this stage often depends simply on announcing availability. Therefore, informative advertising is common in the introductory stage of the product life cycle.

Persuasive advertising attempts to increase demand for an existing good, service, organization, person, place, idea, or cause. Persuasive advertising is a competitive type of promotion suited to the growth stage and the early part of the maturity stage of the product life cycle. The candy-coated chocolate treat Smarties used this approach when a talking blue cat showed up in its commercial as a way to get 13- to 17-year-olds' attention.[6]

Reminder advertising strives to reinforce a previous promotional activity by keeping the name of a good, service, organization, person, place, idea, or cause before the public. It is common in the latter part of the maturity stage and throughout the decline stage of the product life cycle. Procter & Gamble, for instance, seeks to remind consumers, particularly women, about the stain-fighting qualities of its Tide detergent by focusing on the emotional commitment many people have to clothing.[7]

Figure 14.1 illustrates the relationship between advertising objectives and the stages of the product life cycle. Informative advertising tends to work best during the early stages, while reminder advertising is effective later on. Persuasive advertising, if done well, can be effective through the entire life cycle.

Traditionally, marketers stated their advertising objectives as direct sales goals. A more current and realistic standard, however, views advertising as a way to achieve communications objectives, including informing, persuading, and reminding potential customers of the product. Advertising attempts to condition consumers to adopt favourable views regarding a promotional message. The goal of an ad is to improve the likelihood that a customer will buy a particular good or service. In this sense, advertising illustrates the close relationship between marketing communications and promotional strategy.

To get the best value for a firm's advertising investment, marketers must first determine what that firm's advertising objectives are. Effective advertising can enhance consumer perceptions of quality in a good or service, leading to increased customer loyalty, repeat purchases, and protection against price wars. In addition, perceptions of superiority pay off in the firm's ability to raise prices without losing market share.

Trying to Make More Informed Food Choices?

The % Daily Value in the Nutrition Facts table can help.

Health Canada: institutional advertising.

SOURCE: A COLLABORATION OF FOOD & CONSUMER PRODUCTS OF CANADA AND HEALTH CANADA. HEALTH CANADA, 2011. REPRODUCED WITH THE PERMISSION OF THE MINISTER OF HEALTH, 2011.

product advertising
Nonpersonal selling of a particular good or service.

institutional advertising
Promotion of a concept, idea, philosophy, or goodwill of an industry, company, organization, person, geographic location, or government agency.

figure 14.1

Advertising Objectives in Relation to Stage in the Product Life Cycle

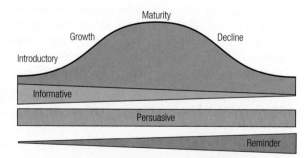

assessment check 1

1.1 What are the goals of institutional advertising?

1.2 At what stage in the product life cycle are informative ads used? Why?

1.3 What is reminder advertising?

② List the major advertising strategies and describe the process of creating an advertisement.

informative advertising
Promotion that seeks to develop initial demand for a good, service, organization, person, place, idea, or cause.

persuasive advertising
Promotion that attempts to increase demand for an existing good, service, organization, person, place, idea, or cause.

reminder advertising
Advertising that reinforces a previous promotional activity by keeping the name of a good, service, organization, person, place, idea, or cause before the public.

ADVERTISING STRATEGIES

If the primary function of marketing is to bring buyers and sellers together, then advertising is the means to an end. Effective advertising strategies accomplish at least one of three tasks: informing, persuading, or reminding consumers. The secret to choosing the best strategy is developing a message that best positions a firm's product in the audience's mind. Among the advertising strategies available for use by marketers are comparative advertising and celebrity advertising as well as plans about global and interactive ads. Channel-oriented decisions such as retail and cooperative advertising can also be devised.

Marketers often combine several of these advertising strategies to ensure that the advertisement accomplishes set objectives. As markets become more segmented, the need for personalized advertising increases. The next sections describe strategies that contemporary marketers may use to reach their target markets.

COMPARATIVE ADVERTISING

Firms whose products are not the leaders in their markets often favour **comparative advertising**, a promotional strategy that emphasizes advertising messages with direct or indirect comparisons to dominant brands in the industry. In contrast, advertising by market leaders seldom acknowledges competing products even exist, and when they do, they usually do not point out any benefits of the competing brand.

Wireless telecommunications carriers have been battling it out in media advertising, promoting their calling plans and inviting comparison to competitors. Some offer "in" calling, free text messaging, no roaming charges, or extended hours at reduced rates to compete against similar offers from other companies.

A generation ago, comparative advertising was not the norm; in fact, it was frowned on. But some industry experts now encourage comparative advertising, believing such ads keep marketers competitive and consumers better informed about their choices. Generally speaking, when there is competition through advertising, prices tend to go down because people can shop around. This benefit has proved increasingly true for online consumers, who now use shopping bots (described in Chapter 16) to help find the best prices on goods and services.

CAREER READINESS **How to Handle a Business Crisis**

ALL organizations face crises during their lifetime. While most crises are relatively small—missing a deadline, arriving late to a client meeting—some are genuinely massive in scale. Recalls of food and products or revelations of unethical investment practices create real public relations crises for individual firms as well as entire industries. But crises can be managed effectively. Here are a few tips for handling a business crisis:

- *Have a plan.* Establish a plan for dealing with crises before one ever arises. Appoint key people to communicate and lead.
- *Pay attention.* If a bad situation seems to be unfolding, don't ignore it. Get the facts and implement your plan.
- *Move promptly.* A crisis is not like a storm that will blow over if you wait. Letting too much time elapse causes the public to think you're stonewalling.
- *Communicate.* You will probably have to communicate several times during the crisis and afterward. Be direct and concise. Provide necessary information and show concern and empathy for those affected. Do not point fingers or speculate. Reassure listeners that communication will continue.

- *Apologize if appropriate.* If you or your firm has made a mistake, acknowledge it. Apologize and then focus on solutions.
- *Find solutions.* Work with colleagues, customers, or others in the industry, if necessary, to correct the problem. This may mean devising both an immediate and a long-term solution.
- *Follow through.* Any promises made during this time must be kept. If your firm says it will replace all defective products with new ones, for example, do so.
- *Learn from your mistakes.* A business crisis is costly. Once it's passed, it's important for your organization to reflect on what happened and take steps to ensure it doesn't recur.

Sources: "Business Crisis Management: Handling a Work-Place Crisis," MoneyInstructor.com, http://www.moneyinstructor.com, June 9, 2010; "Crisis Management," *Encyclopedia of Small Business*, http://www.enotes.com, June 9, 2010; William Neuman, "McDonald's Offers Cash in Recall of Shrek Glasses," *The New York Times*, June 8, 2010, http://www.nytimes.com; "Produce Co. Issues Voluntary Spinach Recall," KSBW.com, June 4, 2010, http://www.ksbw.com.

CELEBRITY TESTIMONIALS

A popular technique for increasing advertising readership in a cluttered promotional environment and improving overall effectiveness of a marketing message involves the use of celebrity spokespeople. This type of advertising is also popular in foreign countries. In Japan, a majority of ads use celebrities, both local and international stars. Since the Winter Olympics in Vancouver, ads using medal winners, such as freestyle skiing champion Alex Bilodeau, have become popular.[8] However, it is important for companies to be sure their brand's tie to a celebrity makes sense and is genuine.

Both the number of celebrity ads and the dollars spent on those ads have increased in recent years. Professional athletes such as LeBron James are among the highest-paid product endorsers, raking in millions each year. In a recent year, James reportedly had about $170 million in endorsement deals with such firms as the Coca-Cola Company, McDonald's, Nike, and State Farm. With the exception of Nike, none of the others has anything to do with basketball.[9] In the top six superstars—in recent annual earnings from endorsements—are golfer Phil Mickelson, $53 million; race car driver Dale Earnhardt Jr., $22 million; and NBA player Shaquille O'Neal, $15 million.[10]

One advantage of associations with big-name personalities is improved product recognition in a promotional environment filled with hundreds of competing 15- and 30-second commercials. Advertisers use the term *clutter* to describe this situation. As e-marketing continues to soar, one inevitable result has been the increase in advertising clutter as companies rush to market their goods and services online or with digital communications media. But marketers need to remember that an effective digital communication must have meaningful content and helpful service.

Another advantage to using celebrities occurs when marketers are trying to reach consumers of various ethnic groups. Advertisements shown in the Quebec market often use a local celebrity. Pepsi has used this approach successfully since 1985. Comedian Claude Meunier, who often writes his own material for the spots, has been referred to as the face of Pepsi. Research conducted by Pepsi throughout the years showed the importance of understanding the market. Ads in which Meunier was less involved in the creative aspect were less effective in communicating the Pepsi message.[11]

A celebrity testimonial generally succeeds when the celebrity is a credible source of information for the product being promoted. The most effective ads of this type establish relevant links between the celebrities and the advertised goods or services, such as the models and actresses who endorse cosmetics. Several studies of consumer responses show that celebrities improve the product's believability, recall of the product, and brand recognition. Celebrity endorsements also create positive attitudes, leading to greater brand equity.

However, a celebrity who endorses too many products may create marketplace confusion. Customers may remember the celebrity but not the product or brand; worse, they might connect the celebrity to a competing brand. Another problem arises if a celebrity is linked with a scandal or has legal problems, as marketers do not want their products associated with a negative image. After Tiger Woods's recent marital problems, several sponsors, including Gatorade, severed their ties with him.[12]

Some advertisers try to avoid problems with celebrities by using cartoon characters as endorsers. Some advertisers may actually prefer cartoon characters because the characters can never say anything negative about the product, they do exactly what the marketers want them to do, and they cannot get involved in scandals. The only drawback is high licensing fees; popular animated characters often cost more than live celebrities. Companies may create their own cartoon characters or "talking" animals, which eventually become celebrities in their own right as a result of many appearances in advertisements, as is the case with the Energizer bunny and the Geico gecko.

In recent years, marketers have begun to consider celebrities as marketing partners rather than pretty or famous faces who can sell goods and services. Hockey star Sidney Crosby has marketing deals with Reebok, Tim Hortons, and Verizon.[13]

comparative advertising Advertising strategy that emphasizes messages with direct or indirect promotional comparisons between competing brands.

Soap dries

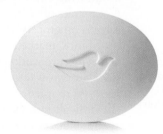

Dove isn't Soap

How do you want your skin to feel?

Dove Beauty Bar doesn't dry like soap can. It contains 1/4 pure moisturizing cream, richly blended with mild cleansers, so your skin can hold on to more moisture. Everyday moisture is the key to beautiful skin. And who knows moisture better than Dove?

dove.ca

Comparative advertising: Dove compared with traditional soap.

individualEYES!
exact eyelights mascara • liner • shadow in 4 customized collections
You've got one-of-a-kind eyes. Make them shine with a shade collection designed to
brighten your eyes. **Tell us what makes you a COVERGIRL @ facebook.com/covergirl**

Queen Latifah's eyes shine with the Exact Eyelights Collection for brown eyes.

COURTESY OF PROCTER & GAMBLE

Queen Latifah promoting CoverGirl.

retail advertising
Advertising by stores
that sell goods or
services directly to the
consuming public.

cooperative advertising
Strategy in which
a retailer shares
advertising costs with
a manufacturer or
wholesaler.

interactive advertising
Two-way promotional
messages transmitted
through communication
channels that induce
message recipients to
participate actively in the
promotional effort.

RETAIL ADVERTISING

Most consumers are confronted daily with **retail advertising**, which includes all advertising by retail stores that sell goods or services directly to the consuming public. While this activity accounts for a sizable portion of total annual advertising expenditures, retail advertising varies widely in its effectiveness. One study showed that consumers often respond with suspicion to retail price advertisements. Source, message, and shopping experience seem to affect consumer attitudes toward these advertisements.

An advertiser once quipped that the two most powerful words to use in an ad are "New" and "Free"—and these terms are often capitalized on in retail ads. Although "Free" may be featured only in discussions of customer services, the next best term—"Sale"—is often the centrepiece of retail promotions. And "New" typically describes new lines of products being offered. However, many retail stores continue to view advertising as a secondary activity, although that is changing. Local independent retailers rarely use advertising agencies, perhaps because of the expense. Instead, store managers may accept responsibility for advertising in addition to their other duties. Management can begin to correct this problem by assigning one individual the sole responsibility and authority for developing an effective retail advertising program.

A retailer often shares advertising costs with a manufacturer or wholesaler in a technique called **cooperative advertising**. For example, an apparel marketer may pay a percentage of the cost of a retail store's newspaper advertisement featuring its product lines. Cooperative advertising campaigns originated to take advantage of the media's practice of offering lower rates to local advertisers than to national ones. Later, cooperative advertising became part of programs to improve dealer relations. The retailer likes the chance to secure advertising that it might not be able to afford otherwise. Cooperative advertising can strengthen vertical links in the marketing channel, as when a manufacturer and retailer coordinate their resources. It can also involve firms at the same level of the supply chain. In a horizontal arrangement, a group of retailers—for example, all the Ford dealers in Edmonton—might pool their resources.

INTERACTIVE ADVERTISING

Millions of advertising messages float across idle—and active—computer screens in homes and offices around the country every day. Net surfers play games embedded with ads from the site sponsors. Companies offer free email service to people willing to receive ads with their personal messages. Video screens on grocery carts display ads for shoppers to see as they wheel down the aisles of grocery stores.

Since marketers realize that two-way communications provide more effective methods for achieving promotional objectives, they are interested in interactive media. **Interactive advertising** involves two-way promotional messages transmitted through communication channels that induce message recipients to participate actively in the promotional effort. Achieving this involvement is the difficult task facing contemporary marketers. Although interactive advertising has become nearly synonymous with e-commerce and the Web, it also includes other formats such as kiosks in shopping malls or text messages on cell phones. Multimedia technology, the Internet, and commercial digital services are changing the nature of advertising from a one-way, passive communication technique to more effective, two-way marketing communications. Interactive advertising creates dialogue between marketers and individual shoppers, providing more materials at the user's request. The advertiser's challenge is to gain and hold consumer interest in an environment where these individuals control what they want to see.

Interactive advertising changes the balance between marketers and consumers. Unlike the traditional role of advertising—providing brief, entertaining, attention-catching messages—interactive media provide information to help consumers throughout the purchase and consumption processes. In a sense, it becomes closer to personal selling as consumers receive immediate responses to questions or requests for more information about goods and services. Interactive advertising provides consumers with more information in less time to help them make necessary comparisons between available products.

Successful interactive advertising adds value by offering the viewer more than just product-related information. An ad on the Web can do more than promote a brand; it can create a company store, provide customer service, and offer additional content. Many marketers at companies both large and small are hoping that such ads will soon be so finely targeted that they can cut through increasing "advertising clutter" and reach only consumers who are ready to hear their message. In one survey, marketers learned that online video ads scored a 65 percent general recall with viewers, as compared with 46 percent for TV ads. Marketers theorize that the video ad scored better because there are fewer of them than TV ads—and viewers are more inclined to sit through online commercials.[14]

Most firms deliver their interactive advertising messages through proprietary online services and through the Web. In fact, online ad spending is expected to reach the $2.2-billion mark shortly, surpassing newspaper ad spending for the first time ever.[15]

CROSS PROMOTION

In recent years, marketers have begun to combine their promotional efforts for related products using a technique called **cross promotion**, in which marketing partners share the cost of a promotional campaign that meets their mutual needs—an important benefit in an environment of rising media costs. Relationship marketing strategies like co-marketing—cooperative arrangement in which two businesses jointly market each other's products—and co-branding—cooperative arrangement in which two or more business team up to closely link their names on a single product—are forms of cross promotion. Marketers realize that these joint efforts between established brands provide greater benefits for both organizations; investments of time and money on such promotions will become increasingly important to many partners' growth prospects. Recently, Coldplay's *Viva la Vida* album was cross-promoted with Apple's iTunes website.

CREATING AN ADVERTISEMENT

Marketers spend billions a year on advertising campaigns in Canada alone. With so much money at stake, they must create effective, memorable ads that increase sales and enhance their organizations' images. They cannot afford to waste resources on mediocre messages that fail to capture consumers' attention, communicate their sales message effectively, or lead to a purchase, donation, or other positive action for the organization.

Research helps marketers create better ads by pinpointing goals that an ad needs to accomplish, such as educating consumers about product features, enhancing brand loyalty, or improving consumer perception of the brand. These objectives should guide the design of the ad. Marketers can also discover what appeals to consumers and can test ads with potential buyers before committing funds for a campaign.

Marketers sometimes face specific challenges as they develop advertising objectives for services. They must find a creative way to fill out the intangible images of most services and successfully convey the benefits that consumers receive. The "Always Fresh" message of Tim Hortons, along with a picture of a steaming cup of coffee, is an example of how creative advertising can make the intangible nature of services tangible.

TRANSLATING ADVERTISING OBJECTIVES INTO ADVERTISING PLANS

Once a company defines its objectives for an advertising campaign, it can develop its advertising plan. Marketing research assists managers in making strategic decisions that guide choices in technical areas such as budgeting, copywriting, scheduling, and media selection. Post-tests, which are discussed in greater detail later in the chapter, measure the effectiveness of advertising and form the basis for feedback concerning possible adjustments. The elements of advertising planning are shown in Figure 14.2. Experienced marketers know

cross promotion
Promotional technique in which marketing partners share the cost of a promotional campaign that meets their mutual needs.

figure 14.2

Elements of the Advertising Planning Process

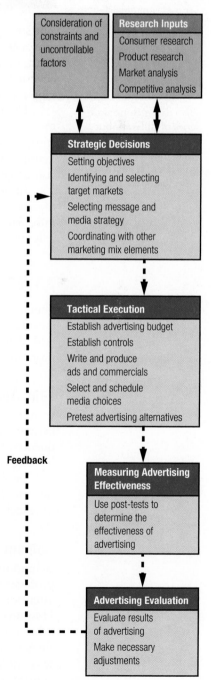

the importance of following even the most basic steps in the process, such as market analysis.

As Chapter 8 explained, positioning involves developing a marketing strategy that aims to achieve a desired position in a prospective buyer's mind. Marketers use a positioning strategy that distinguishes their good or service from those of competitors. Effective advertising then communicates the desired position by emphasizing certain product characteristics, such as performance attributes, price/quality, competitors' shortcomings, applications, user needs, and product classes.

(3) Identify the major types of advertising appeals and discuss their uses.

ADVERTISING MESSAGES

The strategy for creating a message starts with the benefits a product offers to potential customers and moves to the creative concept phase, in which marketers strive to bring an appropriate message to consumers using both visual and verbal components. Marketers work to create an ad with meaningful, believable, and distinctive appeals—one that stands out from the clutter and is more likely to escape zapping by the television remote control or clicking by a mouse.

Usually, ads are created not individually but as part of specific campaigns. An **advertising campaign** is a series of different but related ads that use a single theme and appear in different media within a specified time period. Old Navy's "Old Navy Records: Original Hits. Original Styles" is an example. Old Navy is using original music it produced for the campaign to reinforce the fact that it also designs the clothes it carries in its stores.[16]

In developing a creative strategy, advertisers must decide how to communicate their marketing message. They must balance message characteristics, such as the tone of the appeal, the extent of information provided and the conclusion to which it leads the consumer, the side of the story the ad tells, and its emphasis on verbal or visual primary elements.

advertising campaign Series of different but related ads that use a single theme and appear in different media within a specified time period.

ADVERTISING APPEALS

Should the tone of the advertisement focus on a practical appeal such as price or gas mileage, or should it evoke an emotional response by appealing to, say, fear, humour, sex, guilt, or fantasy? This is another critical decision in the creation of memorable ads that possess the strengths needed to accomplish promotional objectives.

Fear Appeals

In recent years, marketers have relied increasingly on fear appeals. Ads for insurance, autos, and even batteries imply that incorrect buying decisions could lead to property loss, injury, or other bad consequences. Even ads for business services imply that if a company doesn't purchase the advertised services, its competitors will move ahead or valuable information may be lost.[17]

Fear appeals can backfire, however. Viewers are likely to practise selective perception and tune out statements they perceive as too strong or not credible. Some consumer researchers believe that viewer or reader backlash will eventually occur due to the amount of advertising based on fear appeals.

Humour in Advertising Messages

A humorous ad seeks to create a positive mood related to a product or service, but advertising professionals differ in their opinions of the ads' effectiveness. Some believe that humour distracts attention from brand and product features; consumers remember the humour but not the product. Humorous ads, because they are so memorable, may lose their effectiveness sooner than ads with other kinds of appeals. In addition, humour can be tricky because what one group of consumers finds funny may not be funny at all to another group. Men and women sometimes have a different sense of humour, as do people of different ages. This distinction may become even greater across cultures.

Ads Based on Sex

Ads with sex-based appeals immediately attract the consumer's attention. Advertisements for Victoria's Secret lingerie and clothing are designed this way. While many people accept these and other ads, they do not appeal to everyone. And marketers using sex-based appeals know they walk a fine line between what is acceptable to the consumers they want to reach—and what is not. Sometimes, in fact, a firm's image can be hurt by its advertising approach. A recent ad campaign for Brazilian beer Debassa Bem Loura starring Paris Hilton has attracted the attention of the country's regulatory body, Conar, which is investigating reports that the ads are sexually provocative—even by Brazil's standards.[18]

Marketoid

In 2009 Canadian companies spent just under $15 million on radio advertising.

DEVELOPING AND PREPARING ADS

The final step in the advertising process—the development and preparation of an advertisement—should flow logically from the promotional theme selected. This process should create an ad that becomes a complementary part of the marketing mix with a carefully determined role in the total marketing strategy. Preparation of an advertisement should emphasize features like its creativity, its continuity with past advertisements, and possibly its association with other company products.

What immediate tasks should an advertisement accomplish? Regardless of the chosen target, an advertisement should (1) gain attention and interest, (2) inform or persuade, and (3) eventually lead to a purchase or other desired action. It should gain attention in a productive way; that is, it should instill some recall of the good or service. Otherwise, it will not lead to buying action.

Gaining attention and generating interest—cutting through the clutter—can be formidable tasks. Stimulating buying action is often difficult because an advertisement cannot actually close a sale. Nevertheless, if an ad gains attention and informs or persuades, it probably represents a worthwhile investment of marketing resources. Too many advertisers fail to suggest how audience members can purchase their products if they desire to do so. Creative design should eliminate this shortcoming.

The e-Harmony ad shows the four major elements of this print advertisement: headline, illustration, body copy, and signature. *Headlines* and *illustrations* (photographs, drawings, or other artwork) should work together to generate interest and attention. *Body copy* informs, persuades, and stimulates buying action. The *signature*, which may include the company name, address, phone number, Web address, slogan, trademark, or simply a product photo, names the sponsoring organization. An ad may also have one or more headings subordinate to the main headline that either link the main headline to the body copy or subdivide sections of the body copy.

After advertisers conceive an idea for an ad that gains attention, informs and persuades, and stimulates purchases, their next step involves refining the thought sketch into a rough layout. Continued refinements of the rough layout eventually produce the final version of the advertisement design that is ready to be executed, printed, or recorded.

The creation of each advertisement in a campaign requires an evolutionary process that begins with an idea and ultimately results in a finished ad that is ready for distribution through print or electronic media. The idea itself must first be converted into a thought sketch, which is a tangible summary of the intended message. Advances in technology allow advertisers to create novel, eye-catching advertisements. Innovative computer software packages now allow artists to merge several images to create a single image with a natural, seamless appearance.

CREATING INTERACTIVE ADS

Web surfers want engaging, lively content that takes advantage of the medium's capabilities and goes beyond what they find elsewhere. The Web's major advantages make it possible for advertisers to provide that, offering speed, information, two-way communications, self-directed entertainment, and personal

Elements of a typical ad.

choice. Web ads are also vibrant in their visual appeal and some believe they will not experience the swings in spending that traditional ad media do.

Web ads have grown from information-based home pages to innovative, interactive channels for transmitting messages to cyberaudiences, including advergames, banners, keyword ads, advertorials, interstitials, pop-ups, and adware. *Advergames* are either online games created by marketers to promote their products to targeted audiences in an interactive way or ads or product placements inserted into online video games. New technology provides more flexibility for online games, allowing product placements to be inserted and removed at any time rather than just during the game development. Promotions can now be targeted to much smaller audiences, making online games affordable to smaller companies. After the Canadian Armed Forces ran spots in several games, they experienced a roughly 200 percent increase in gamers who were likely to consider the military as a career.[19]

banners Advertisements on a Web page that link to an advertiser's site.

Banners, advertisements on a Web page that link to an advertiser's site, are the most common type of advertising on the Web. They can be free of charge or cost thousands of dollars per month depending on the amount of hits the site receives. Online advertisers often describe their Internet ads in terms of richness, referring to the degree to which new technologies—such as streaming video, 3-D animation, JavaScript, and interactive capabilities—are implemented in the banners.[20]

Banners have evolved into a more target-specific technique for Internet advertising with the advent of *missiles:* messages that appear on the screen at exactly the right moment. When a customer visits the site of Company A's competitor, a missile can be programmed to appear on the customer's monitor that allows the customer to click a direct link to Company A's site. However, many people feel the use of such missiles is a questionable practice.

Keyword ads are an outcropping of banner ads. Used in search engines, keyword ads appear on the results page of a search and are specific to the term being searched. Advertisers pay search engines to target their ads and display only the banners when users search for relevant keywords, allowing marketers to target specific audiences. For example, if a user searched the term *digital camera*, keyword ads might appear for electronic boutiques or camera shops that sell digital cameras.

Banner designs that have evolved into larger advertising squares that closely resemble advertisements in the telephone book's yellow Pages are called advertorials. Advertisers quickly expanded on these advertorials with *interstitials*—ads that appear between Web pages of related content. Interstitials appear in a separate browser window while the user waits for a Web page to download.

Then there are pop-ups, which are little advertising windows that appear in front of the top window of a user's computer screen, and pop-unders, which appear under the top window. Many users complain that interstitials, like pop-ups and missiles, are intrusive and unwanted. Interstitials are more likely to contain large graphics and streaming presentations than banner ads and therefore are more difficult to ignore than typical banner ads. But despite complaints, some studies show that users are more likely to click interstitials than banners.

Perhaps the most intrusive form of online advertising is *adware*, which allows ads to be shown on users' screens through the use of software downloaded to their computers without their consent or through trickery. Such software can be difficult to remove, and some industry experts believe that reputable marketers should avoid dealing with Internet marketing firms that promote the use of adware.

Revenues for *social network advertising* on sites such as Facebook and MySpace are skyrocketing. In a recent year, firms spent an estimated $2.2 billion worldwide on this type of advertising and the number is expected to grow. However, the very nature of the advertising makes it difficult to evaluate and measure its effectiveness. For example, if a virtual bottle of Coca-Cola appears on Facebook or in an online game, how likely is it that consumers will actually purchase Coke the next time they want something to drink?[21]

assessment check 3

3.1 What are some common emotional appeals used in advertising?

3.2 What are the main types of interactive ads?

MEDIA SELECTION

④ List and compare the major advertising media.

One of the most important decisions in developing an advertising strategy is the selection of appropriate media to carry a firm's message to its audience. The media selected must be capable of accomplishing the communications objectives of informing, persuading, and reminding potential customers of the good, service, person, or idea being advertised.

Research identifies the ad's target market to determine its size and characteristics. Advertisers then match the target characteristics with the media best able to reach that particular audience. The objective of media selection is to achieve adequate media coverage without advertising beyond the identifiable limits of the potential market. Finally, cost comparisons between alternatives should determine the best possible media purchase.

Table 14.1 compares the major advertising media advantages and disadvantages. *Broadcast media* include television (network and cable) and radio. Newspapers, magazines, outdoor (out of home) advertising, and direct mail represent the major types of print media. Electronic media include the Internet and kiosks. A recent study projected that many firms will shift away from traditional advertising and more toward direct marketing, especially Internet and mobile media, in the next few years. Broadcast and print media will be discussed in this section and electronic and digital communications will be discussed in the next section.

TELEVISION

Television, network and cable combined, still accounts for more than one of every three advertising dollars spent in the world.[22] The attractiveness of television advertising is that marketers can reach local and national markets. Whereas most newspaper advertising revenues come from local advertisers, the greatest share of television advertising revenues comes from organizations that advertise nationally. The newer trend in television advertising is virtual ads—banner-type logos and brief messages that are superimposed onto television coverage of sporting events so that they seem to be a part of the arena's signage but cannot be seen by anyone attending the game. Then there are streaming headlines run by

table 14.1   *Comparison of Advertising Media Alternatives*

MEDIA OUTLET	ADVANTAGES	DISADVANTAGES
Broadcast		
Network television	Extensive coverage; repetition; flexibility; prestige	High cost; brief message; limited segmentation
Cable television	Same strengths as network TV; less market coverage since not every viewer is a cable subscriber	Same disadvantages as network TV, although cable TV ads are considerably more targeted to specific viewer segments
Radio	Immediacy; low cost; flexibility; targeted audience; mobility; captive audience	Brief message; highly fragmented audience
Print		
Newspapers	Tailored to individual communities; ability to refer back to ads	Limited life
Direct mail	Selectivity; intense coverage; speed; flexibility; opportunity to convey complete information; personalization	High cost; consumer resistance; dependence on effective mailing list
Magazines	Selectivity; quality image reproduction; long life; prestige	Lack of flexibility
Outdoor	Quick, visual communication of simple ideas; link to local goods and services; repetition	Brief exposure; environmental concerns
Electronic		
Internet	Two-way communications; flexibility; link to self-directed entertainment	Poor image reproduction; limited scheduling options; difficult to measure effectiveness

Source: Reprinted with permission from the March 8 issue of Advertising Age Fact Pack 2008 Edition. Copyright © Crain Communications Inc. 2008.

some news stations, which are paid for by corporate sponsors whose names and logos appear within the news stream.

Other trends in television advertising include the abbreviated spot—a 15- or 30-second ad—that costs less to make and buy and is too quick for most viewers to zap with their remote control—and single-advertiser shows. These advertisements work well when viewers are watching live, but as more consumers record programs with DVRs, as many as 70 percent fast-forward through even the briefest commercials.[23]

Websites that aggregate TV programming, like Hula and Clicker, have become top video destinations on the Internet. There viewers can watch complete, high-resolution episodes of current TV programs on their computers. The sites are free and do not require any additional wires or boxes for access. Instead, viewers see brief ads they seem to tolerate in order to watch their favourite shows. Hulu has added a new feature called Hulu Plus that, for a monthly fee, allows viewers to watch a complete season of shows. In addition to episodes from more than 10 000 TV shows, Clicker's archive includes 20 000 movies and 80 000 music videos from 20 000 artists.[24]

In the past decade, ad spending for television has changed significantly mainly due to changes in the industry. The number of specialty channels has increased and the number of homes subscribing to cable, satellite, or the new digital services has also increased. Television ad spending still accounts for a large proportion of advertising, but other media are closing in and the growth of ad spending on specialty channels is outpacing convention television.[25]

Television advertising offers the advantages of mass coverage, powerful impact on viewers, repetition of messages, flexibility, and prestige. Its disadvantages include loss of control of the promotional message to the telecaster, which can influence its impact; high costs; and some public distrust. Compared with other media, television can suffer from lack of selectivity because specific TV programs may not reach consumers in a precisely defined target market without a significant degree of wasted coverage. However, the growing specialization of cable TV channels can help to resolve the problem. Finally, some types of products are actually banned from television advertising. Tobacco goods, such as cigarettes, cigars, and smokeless tobacco, fall into this category.

RADIO

Radio advertising has always been a popular media choice for up-to-the-minute newscasts and for targeting advertising messages to local audiences. But in recent years, radio has become one of the fastest-growing media alternatives. As more and more people find they have less and less time, radio provides immediate information and entertainment at work, at play, and in the car. In addition, as e-commerce continues to grow globally, more people are travelling abroad to seek out new markets. For these travellers, radio stations, including those airing over the Internet, are a means of staying in touch with home—wherever that may be. Marketers frequently use radio advertising to reach local audiences. But in recent years, it has been playing an increasingly important role as a national—and even global—listening favourite. Thousands of online listeners use the Internet to tune in on radio stations from almost every city— an easy-listening station in London, a top-40 Hong Kong broadcaster, or a chat show from Toronto. Other listeners equip their vehicles with satellite radio to maintain contact with their hometown or destination stations during long trips.

Satellite radio providers offer much higher-quality digital signals than regular radio stations, with many more available channels that are mostly free of government regulations and are generally commercial-free. XM Radio, the first such service to be licensed, began airing commercials on a few of its nearly 200 music, sports, and talk channels. XM and its competitor, Sirius Satellite Radio, both charge an annual subscription fee. As of May 2011, the Canadian arm of XM and Sirius merged, giving the new combined company more than 1.7 million subscribers. The U.S. counterparts merged two years earlier.[26]

Advertisers like radio for its ability to reach people while they drive because they are a captive audience. Other benefits include low cost, flexibility, and mobility. Stations can adapt to local preferences by changing formats, such as going from country and western to an all-news or sports station. The variety of stations allows advertisers to easily target audiences and tailor their messages to those listeners. Disadvantages to radio advertising include highly segmented audiences (reaching most people in a market may require ads placed on several stations), the temporary nature of messages (unlike print ads, radio and TV ads are instantaneous and must be rebroadcast to reach consumers a second time), and a minimum of research information compared with television.

While most radio listening is done in cars or with headset-equipped portables, technology has given birth to Internet radio. Web-cast radio allows customers to widen their listening times and choices through their computers.

NEWSPAPERS

Newspaper advertising continues to dominate local markets, accounting for 24 percent of annual advertising expenditures in Canada.[27] In addition to retail advertisements, classified advertising is an important part of newspaper revenues.

Newspapers' primary advantages start with flexibility because advertising can vary from one locality to the next. Newspapers also allow intensive coverage for ads. Readers control their exposure to the advertising message, unlike television or radio advertising messages, and can refer back to newspaper ads. Newspaper advertising does have some disadvantages: hasty reading and relatively poor reproduction quality, although that is changing as technology improves.

Newspapers have also begun to struggle to "get through the noise" of other advertisers. To retain big advertisers, some companies have launched annual, semiannual, or monthly magazines featuring a single topic such as fashion or business. These magazines provide advertisers with higher reproduction qualities for their ads and take advantage of the finely tuned distribution capabilities of the newspapers. Another way newspapers are moving ahead is through the Internet. After years of avoiding the Internet, most papers have an online version. The changing environment in the newspaper industry is discussed in the "Go Green" feature.

MAGAZINES

Advertisers divide magazines into two broad categories: consumer magazines and business magazines. These categories are also subdivided into monthly and weekly publications. Canadians like to read magazines: roughly 6.6 million subscriptions are sold in a year and Canadian companies spent around $590 million to advertise in them.[28] The primary advantages of magazine advertising include the following: the ability to reach precise target markets, quality reproduction, long life, the prestige

---

| GO GREEN | **Paperless Newspapers?** |

IF you listen to some of the industry experts, the newspaper as we know it today is in trouble and paperless newspapers will be what we see in the future. That makes sense—paperless newspapers are less expensive to produce and no trees are killed to print them. If you look at the statistics for the newspaper industry in the United States, the experts would be right—newspapers are in trouble—but the Canadian market is different.

Canadian companies are spending less to advertise in newspapers, a drop of 18 percent from 2008 to 2009. This statistic alone could cause the newspaper industry some problems because it needs those ad dollars to stay alive. As it turns out, Canadians want both digital newspapers, mobile or online, and the print version—90 percent of Canadians read a newspaper either in print or online.

Research shows that the Canadian newspaper industry is definitely changing but it has a strong base to build on. In 2009, spending on newspaper ads was the second largest of any media, representing 22 percent. Newspaper ads are also effective—75 percent of newspaper readers say they look at the ads—but

so are the ads on the online versions. Research shows that ads on newspaper websites outperform ads on other sites in every category studied.

It looks like the print version of the newspaper will be around awhile yet, but the transformation to different news options is happening at an unprecedented pace. Whether Canadians get their news by reading a newspaper, going to a website, subscribing to a newspaper through iTunes or Google or their smartphones, companies are taking advantage of all these platforms to advertise their products. In this ever-changing environment one thing is for sure: both the newspaper company and the advertiser are reaching the majority of Canadians.

Sources: Canadian Media Directors' Council Media Digest 10/11; Tom Gierasimczuk, "The Good News Is Mobile," *Marketing*, http://www.marketingmag.ca, February 8, 2011; "Yahoo Setting Up Digital Newsstand for Tablets in Attempt to Revive Ad Sales," *Marketing*, http://www.marketingmag.ca, February 11, 2011; Matt Semansky, "Paper Tigers," *Marketing*, http://www.marketingmag.ca, February 8, 2011; "Newspapers Unhappy With Apple's iTunes Rules," *Marketing*; http://www.marketingmag.ca, February 8, 2011; Chris Powell, "Newspaper Ad Revenue Down 14% in 2009: Statscan," *Marketing*, http://www.marketingmag.ca, February 14, 2011.

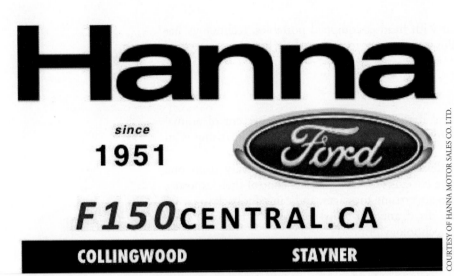

Signage is an example of outdoor advertising.

associated with some magazines, and the extra services that many publications offer. The primary disadvantage is that magazines lack the flexibility of newspapers, radio, and television.

Media buyers study circulation numbers and demographic information for various publications before choosing optimal placement opportunities and in negotiating rates. The same advertising categories have claimed the title for big spenders for several years running. Automotive, retail, and movies and media advertising have held their first, second, and third places, respectively, each year and have continued to show strong growth percentages. Advertisers seeking to promote their products to target markets can reach them by advertising in the appropriate magazines.

DIRECT MAIL

As discussed in Chapter 13, direct mail advertising consists of sales letters, postcards, leaflets, folders, booklets, catalogues, and house organs (periodicals published by organizations to cover internal issues). Its advantages come from direct mail's ability to segment large numbers of prospective customers into narrow market niches, speed, flexibility, detailed information, and personalization. Disadvantages of direct mail include high cost per reader, dependence on the quality of mailing lists, and some consumers' resistance to it.

The advantages of direct mail explain its widespread use. Data are available on previous purchase patterns and preferred payment methods, as well as household characteristics such as number of children or seniors. Direct mail accounts for an estimated $1479 million of advertising spending each year in Canada.[29] The downside to direct mail is clutter, otherwise known as *junk mail*. So much advertising material is stuffed into people's mailboxes every day that the task of grabbing consumers' attention and evoking some interest is daunting to direct mail advertisers. Also, some consumers find direct mail annoying.

OUTDOOR ADVERTISING

Outdoor advertising, sometimes called out-of-home, is perhaps the oldest and simplest media business around. It attracts $416 million in advertising spending, representing about 3 percent of the Canadian total.[30] Traditional outdoor advertising takes the form of billboards, painted displays such as those that appear on the walls of buildings, and electronic displays. Transit advertising includes ads placed both inside and outside buses, subway trains and stations, and commuter trains. Some firms place ads on the roofs of taxicabs, on bus stop shelters and benches, on entertainment and sporting event turnstiles, in public restrooms, and even on parking meters. A section of highway might be cleaned up by a local real estate company or restaurant, with a nearby sign indicating the firm's contributions. All these are forms of outdoor advertising.

This form of advertising has the advantages of immediate communication of quick and simple ideas, repeated exposure to a message, and strong promotion for locally available products. Outdoor advertising is particularly effective along metropolitan streets and in other high-traffic areas.

But outdoor advertising, just like every other type, is subject to clutter. It also suffers from the brevity of exposure to its messages by passing motorists. Driver concerns about rush-hour safety and limited time also combine to limit the length of exposure to outdoor messages. As a result, most of these ads use striking, simple illustrations, short selling points, and humour to attract people interested in products such as vacations, local entertainment, and lodging.

A third problem involves public concern over aesthetics. Many areas of the country, for example, regulate the placement of outdoor advertising near major highways. Critics have even labelled billboard advertising as "pollution on a stick."

New technologies are helping to revive outdoor advertising. Technology livens up the billboards themselves with animation, large sculptures, and laser images. Three organizations assist companies with outdoor advertising: the Canadian Out-of-Home Measurement Bureau, the Out-of-Home Marketing Association of Canada, and the Canadian Out-of-Home Digital Association.[31] New uses are also helping to revive outdoor advertising. Organizations are using billboards to promote social causes such as encouraging the public to get vaccinated.[32]

OTHER ADVERTISING MEDIA

As consumers filter out appeals from traditional and Internet ads, marketers need new ways to catch their attention. In addition to the major media, firms use a vast number of other vehicles to communicate their messages. One such device is a special kiosk with web cameras and software that can recognize, track, and render images on the screen. At the kiosk, customers can see themselves on a screen through the webcam while holding up a two-dimensional brochure of the advertiser's product. The system transforms the picture into a three-dimensional image of the consumer with the product. Marketers believe this type of system increases an advertiser's engagement with the consumer in a new way.[33]

The website for Marketing *magazine advertises upcoming events.*

Ads also appear on T-shirts, inlaid in store flooring, in printed programs of live theatre productions, and as previews on movie DVDs. Directory advertising includes the familiar Yellow Pages in telephone books, along with thousands of business directories. Some firms pay to have their advertising messages placed on hot-air balloons, blimps, banners behind airplanes, and scoreboards at sporting events. Individuals sometimes agree to paint their own vehicles with advertising messages or tattoo them onto their bodies for a fee. Hot Jobs.com, Yahoo!, and Nokia are just some of the advertisers who pay to have their logos and company messages placed on cars. The drivers are chosen based on their driving habits, routes, occupations, and living and working locations and are paid a monthly fee for the use of the outside of their vehicles as advertising space.[34]

DIGITAL COMMUNICATIONS

Electronic media and digital communications—especially the Internet—are growing up, and the options available to marketers is also expanding quickly. Keyword ads dominate online, accounting for more than 47 percent of annual online ad spending around the world.[35] Not surprisingly, digital and interactive advertising budgets are being beefed up at a growing number of companies. Digital advertising can include email, online communities and social networks, blogs and podcasts, and video. A look at how some companies are integrating their digital promotions with television advertising is highlighted in the "Marketing in a Digital World" feature.

EMAIL

The volume of email today exceeds that of regular mail. Contemporary marketers use this communication function of the Internet to advance their marketing objectives.

Companies have long used email to communicate with customers, suppliers, and other partners. Most companies have links on their websites that allow visitors to send email directly to the most appropriate person or division within the company. Many online

Magazine ad promoting the Toronto Star *newspaper.*

Social Media Part of Super Bowl Promotions

WEBSITES, video games, Twitter, and YouTube all played a part in Super Bowl ads even before the game started. At least one of these promotions was run only for the Canadian market. Unlike other years when Super Bowl ads were a closely guarded secret until game time, for Super Bowl XLV several companies tried to get more bang for the millions of dollars they spent on their Super Bowl promotions.

Frito-Lay Canada launched its new promotional contest during the Canadian edition of the Super Bowl. The company invited viewers to write the ending to the 60-second commercial that ran during the game. Contestants sent their endings to a website for a chance to win money prizes or a trip.

Mercedes-Benz started its promotion before the game. The four teams heading for the game were part of a road race. The cars advanced, depending on the number of tweets the company received supporting each team.

Twentieth Century Fox and Anheuser-Busch each had codes in their commercials. Twentieth Century Fox's ad promoting the movie *Rio* had a code that allowed players of the smartphone game Angry Birds to advance to the next game level. Anheuser-Busch's code was part of a Facebook game where contestants could guess the plot of its commercials. If the contestant guessed right, he or she could view an extra commercial that was available only online.

Other companies, like Volkswagen, released their ads early on YouTube. In the Volkswagen ad, a miniature Darth Vader tries using "the Force" on a Passat.

How successful were these social media promotions? Mercedes had more than 85 000 visitors to its Facebook page, and 1.8 million viewed the video on YouTube. Volkswagen was equally successful—13 million viewed the commercial on YouTube before the game even started.

Sources: Volkswagen company website, http://www.vw.ca, February 26, 2011; Mercedes-Benz Canada company website, http://www.mercedes-benz.ca, February 26, 2011; PepsiCo Canada company website, http://www.fritolay.ca, February 26, 2011; Anheuser-Busch company website, http://www.anheuser-busch.com, February 26, 2011; "Super Bowl Advertisers Kick Off Early with Social Media," *Marketing*, http://www.marketingmag.ca, February 4, 2011; "On Advertising's Biggest Night, Eminem Gets Animated, Rosanne Gets Clocked," *Marketing*, http://www.marketingmag.ca, February 7, 2011; Kristin Laird, "Doritos Begins New Campaign With No Ending," *Marketing*, http://www.marketingmag.ca, February 4, 2011.

retailers have gone even further by offering their customers live help. Using a form of instant messaging, live help provides a real-time communications channel between consumers and customer service representatives.

Firms also use email to inform customers about events such as new products and special promotions. While using email in this manner can be quite cost effective, companies have to be careful. A growing number of customers consider such emails to be spam, the popular name for junk email. A recent study found as much as 95 percent of all email is spam, up from 70 percent three years before and only 5 percent six years ago.[36] It is no wonder many Internet users employ spam filters that automatically eliminate junk email from their inboxes.

ONLINE COMMUNITIES AND SOCIAL NETWORKS

In addition to email, many firms use Internet forums, newsgroups, electronic bulletin boards, and social networks that appeal to people with common interests. Members congregate online and exchange views and information on topics of interest. These communities may be organized for commercial or noncommercial purposes. Old Navy used a video placed on Facebook and YouTube of the Supermodelquins trying out for a commercial when the company decided to switch to its "Original Hits. Original Styles" campaign.[37]

Online communities can take several forms, but all offer specific advantages to users and organizations. Online forums, for instance, are Internet discussion groups. Users log in and participate by sending comments and questions or receiving information from other forum members. Forums may operate as electronic bulletin boards, as libraries for storing information, or even as a type of classified ad directory. Firms often use forums to ask questions and exchange information with customers.

Newsgroups are noncommercial Internet versions of forums. Here, people post and read messages on specific topics. Tens of thousands of newsgroups are on the Internet, and the number continues to rise. Electronic bulletin boards are specialized online services that centre on a specific topic or area of interest. For instance, mountain bikers might check online bulletin boards to find out about the latest equipment or new places to ride. Whereas newsgroups resemble two-way conversations, electronic bulletin boards are more like announcements.

Social networking sites have grown dramatically. Facebook currently has in excess of 350 million members—10 million Canadians use the site daily—and is still growing fast around the world.[38] Twitter reportedly turned down an acquisition offer from Facebook and Google of between $8 and $10 billion and now boasts more than 200 million regular users, up from 58 million a year earlier.[39]

Many observers believe marketers have quickly caught up to their customers in the savvy use of social networking communities, and they will next become expert not only in exploiting their communication capabilities but also in tapping the huge and detailed databases they represent. Twitter, for instance, has been working on ways to let companies identify community members who might be interested in their products and to create profiles of those who follow these firms on the site. Twitter is also moving into advertising. One senior social media analyst, says, "Twitter is building an ad platform that encourages advertisers to do things that people will want to engage with and actively discourages treating it as just another platform, which is one of the reasons for optimism in thinking Twitter could succeed quite well."[40]

To get the most from social networking communities, marketers may want to consider their social marketing campaigns as if they were new products, complete with a launch phase, marketing support, and sales and customer services components.[41] Facebook already boasts hundreds of thousands of business pages, including those of large companies like the Coca-Cola Company, Starbucks, Adidas, Eastman Kodak, and Pizza Hut, all of which have millions of Facebook fans. Acknowledging the extra power of such sites when accessed from mobile devices, Pizza Hut's director of digital marketing says Facebook's presence "makes us very relevant to the audience, and lets us communicate with them where they are, in a way that our website can't do."[42]

Small companies, not to be outdone, make up a third of the business with Facebook pages. One nightclub asked its bartender to maintain its Facebook page as a way to offer discounts and specials and publicize special events. "It's one of the best ways we can reach a vast audience," the employee says. "After my shift, I can blast it to 650 friends in 30 seconds. I don't have to go around to each person, or call them up." A small bakery chain that specializes in cupcakes agrees. The company uses Facebook to run quizzes and contests and entice new customers and Facebook fans with offers of free cupcakes.[43]

Online communities are not limited to consumers. They also facilitate business-to-business marketing. Using the Internet to build communities helps companies find other organizations, including suppliers, distributors, and competitors, that may be interested in forming an alliance. Marketers wanting to expand internationally frequently seek advice from other members of their online community.

BLOGS AND PODCASTS

Another popular digital communication method is the blog. Short for web log, a blog is web page that serves as a publicly accessible journal for an individual or organization. Typically updated daily or even more frequently, these are hybrid diary-guide sites. Using *RSS* (Really Simple Syndication) software, readers continually are kept up to date on new material posted on their favourite blogs whenever they are online. Unlike email and instant messaging, blogs let readers post comments and ask questions aimed at the author. Some blogs also incorporate wikis. A wiki is a web page anyone can edit so a reader can, in addition to asking questions or posting comments, actually make changes to the web page. Podcasts are another technology where anyone from bloggers to traditional media sources can prepare an audio or video recording and then post it to a website from which it can be downloaded to any digital device that can play the file.

Given the growing interest in blogs and podcasts, it hasn't taken long for marketers to incorporate them into their e-business strategies. Of particular interest to marketers are blogs that focus on new-technology products, because they can prove effective at quickly forming public opinion. To try to reduce the damage from rumours and misinformation, some companies have decided to treat bloggers as members of the press and acknowledge their ability to spread news and influence. Other firms set up their own blogs. Many believe that corporate blogs, if done properly, can also help build brand trust.

Many companies allow, and even encourage, employees to start their own blogs, believing employee blogs can serve useful functions. FastLane is the blog of General Motors' top executives. It attracts about 7500 unique visitors every day with dozens of comments posted for each blog entry. The company's director of new media designed the blog. He commented, "I had been studying blogs for a few years and felt that a blog would have the potential to help humanize the company. And being able to hear customer feedback was important." Among other start-up issues, the blog had to educate it audience. "Our blog was a product blog, and we had to be clear that the blog was not going to respond to other issues such as policies or customer service issues." GM's blog is often mentioned as an outstanding company blog.[44]

OTHER DIGITAL COMMUNICATIONS

Other digital communication techniques used by marketers include mobile or cell marketing, video ads, search engine marketing, and digital coupons.

As video and broadcast capabilities expand, advertising comes to cell phones in interesting ways. Mobile advertising revenues in Canada recently hit an estimated $2.7 million and are expected to continue their explosive growth. Through emerging technology known as augmented reality, virtual imaging can be incorporated into real-time video on a mobile phone, creating an exciting new experience for cell phone users.[45]

Pre-roll video ads, marketing messages that play before an online video, are becoming more popular, although users have shown some resistance. YouTube is one of the few sites to let viewers opt out of watching. Widgets are tiny interactive applications Internet users can copy and add to their MySpace or Facebook pages or their personal websites to play music, video, or slide shows. Marketers are adopting the use of widgets at a rapid rate.[46]

Another type of digital advertising is search marketing. This is considered one of the most effective forms of Web-based advertising. Companies pay search engines fees to have their websites or ads pop up after a user enters certain words into the search engine, or to make sure their firm's listing appears toward the top of the search results. Google and other search engines now include "Sponsored Links" on the right side of the search results page. A user who clicks on one of the sites listed under the Sponsored Links is taken to that site, and the company pays the search engine a small fee. Google and Microsoft among others have made major investments in improving their search marketing services and capabilities.

Another way companies use the Web to promote their products is through digital coupons. For instance, customers can visit a company's website to learn about a new product and then print a discount coupon redeemable at participating retailers. Another coupon-like site is Groupon. Groupon emails discounts coupons to subscribers who then forward them to friends. If enough people sign up for the emailed offer, the company promoting the deal honours the coupons; otherwise the promotional deal is invalid. A large number of Groupon's customers are small businesses who see the service as a great way to promote their company to a wider audience.[47]

Marketoid

The online game *Call of Duty: Modern Warfare 2* made $550 million in the first week of sales.

MEDIA SCHEDULING

media scheduling
Setting the timing and sequence for a series of advertisements.

Once advertisers have selected the media that best match their advertising objectives and promotional budget, attention shifts to **media scheduling**—setting the timing and sequence for a series of advertisements. A variety of factors influences this decision as well. Sales patterns, repurchase cycles, and competitors' activities are the most important variables.

Seasonal sales patterns are common in many industries. An airline might reduce advertising during peak travel periods and boost its media schedule during low travel months. *Repurchase cycles* may also play a role in media scheduling—products with shorter repurchase cycles will more likely require consistent media schedules throughout the year. Competitors' activities may influence advertising in two ways: by avoiding scheduling media during periods of heavy advertising by competitors, and by matching competitors' advertising schedules.

Advertisers use the concept of reach, frequency, and gross rating points to measure the effectiveness of media scheduling plans. *Reach* refers to the number of different people or households exposed to an advertisement at least once during a certain period, typically four weeks. *Frequency* refers to the number of times an individual is exposed to an advertisement during a certain period. By multiplying reach times frequency, advertisers quantitatively describe the total weight of a media effort, which is called *gross rating point (GRP = frequent × reach).*

Recently, marketers have questioned the effectiveness of reach and frequency to measure the ad success of digital media. The theory behind frequency is that the average advertising viewer needs a minimum of three exposures to a message to understand it and connect it to a specific brand. Web surfers tend to perceptually screen out ads much more quickly—hence, the greater importance of building customer relationships through advertisements.

A media schedule is typically created in the following way. Say an auto manufacturer wants to advertise a new model designed primarily to appeal to professional consumers in their 30s. The model would be introduced in November with a direct mail piece offering test drives. Outdoor, newspaper, and magazine advertising would support the direct mail campaign but also follow through the winter and into the spring and summer. The newspaper ads might actually be cooperative, for both the manufacturer and local dealers. Early television commercials might air during a holiday television special in mid-December, and then one or more expensively produced, highly creative spots would be first aired during the Super Bowl in late January. Another television commercial—along with new print ads—might be scheduled for fall clearance sales as the manufacturer gets ready to introduce next year's models. This example illustrates how marketers might plan their advertising year for just one product. While this example illustrates a media schedule for a larger company with a significant advertising budget, smaller companies with smaller budgets are less likely to use television unless they decide to use a local channel.

assessment check 4

4.1 What types of products are banned from advertising on television?

4.2 What are some advantages radio offers to advertisers? What about newspapers?

4.3 What are online communities and social networks? Explain how online communities can help companies market their products and improve customer service.

4.4 Define *media scheduling* and identify the most important factors influencing the scheduling decision.

ORGANIZATION OF THE ADVERTISING FUNCTION

⑤ Outline the organization of the advertising function and the role of an advertising agency.

Although the ultimate responsibility for advertising decision making often rests with top marketing management, organizational arrangements for the advertising function vary among companies. A producer of a technical industrial product may operate with a one-person department within the company, who works primarily to write copy for submission to trade publications. A consumer goods company, on the other hand, may staff a large department with advertising specialists.

The advertising function is usually organized as a staff department reporting to the vice president (or director) of marketing. The director of advertising is an executive position with the responsibility for the functional activity of advertising. This position requires not only a skilled and experienced advertiser but also an individual who communicates effectively within the organization. The success of a firm's promotional strategy depends on the advertising director's willingness and ability to communicate both vertically and horizontally. The major tasks typically organized under advertising include advertising research, design, copywriting, media analysis, and in some cases, sales and trade promotion.

ADVERTISING AGENCIES

Most large companies in industries characterized by sizable advertising expenditures hire an independent **advertising agency**, a firm whose marketing specialists assist businesses in planning and preparing advertisements. Advertising is a huge global industry. Ranked by worldwide revenue, the top ad agencies are Dublin-based WPP, followed by Omnicom (New York), Publicis (Paris), Interpublic (New York), and Tokyo-based Dentsu.[48] Changes occurring in the ad agency industry, mainly brought on by digital media, are discussed in the "Marketing and the SME" feature.

Most large advertisers cite several reasons for relying on agencies for at least some aspects of their advertising. Agencies typically employ highly qualified specialists who provide a degree of creativity and objectivity that is difficult to sustain in a corporate advertising department. Some agencies also manage to reduce the cost of advertising by allowing the advertiser to avoid many of the fixed expenses associated with maintaining an internal advertising department.

Figure 14.3 shows a hypothetical organization chart for a large advertising agency. Although job titles may vary among agencies, the major functions may be classified as creative services; account services; marketing services, including media services, marketing research, and sales promotion; and

advertising agency
Firm whose marketing specialists assist advertisers in planning and preparing advertisements.

MARKETING AND THE SME

Who Does Digital Best?

THE decision to go with a small ad agency versus one of the international companies has troubled marketing executives forever. When you bring specialized talents needed for the new digital marketing into the question it becomes more complicated. How do you produce a truly integrated marketing strategy when you use several different specialized ad agencies for each part of your campaign? Even the seasoned marketing professionals can't agree on this question.

Natasha Koifman, president and founder of the public relations firm NKPR, not only believes that the smaller firms can do social marketing better but she also thinks the new digital media can be done best by public relations specialists. Natasha explained situation this way: "I think what's happening to the landscape right now is there's a separation between the PR agency, ad agency and social media agencies and the reality is . . . we're (PR agencies) actually the ones driving and creating the content."

The argument for companies to go with the specialized digital agencies is presented by David Jones, vice president, Social Strategy Proximity Canada, who says, "Our ability to inform, educate, entertain, engage and create human bonds with words, images and experiences through a combination of ones and zeros and across massive distances is unrivalled."

Some industry experts believe the answer is not in public relations versus digital but an entirely new model for agencies. The industry trend is definitely toward smaller, more flexible agencies that can provide their clients with faster and cheaper creative solutions. These smaller agencies have fewer full-time employees but have an army of freelance specialists at their disposal. This new industry model for the digital world has even developed its own vocabulary and techniques. Terms like "co-opetion" or "frenemy" came into being when agencies that worked together on one project were fighting against each other for the opportunity to do other projects. One of the new techniques is called "crowdsourcing"—the process of posing a question or problem to a large group of people to try to get the best answer quickly.

Maybe the question is not who does digital best but what other changes we will see in the ad agency world as companies try to make the most of the digital media options.

Sources: The American Marketing Association website, http://www.marketingpower .com, February 25, 2011; Jeromy Lloyd, "Media vs. Agencies," *Marketing*, http:// www.marketingmag.ca, February 17, 2011; Jeromy Lloyd, "New Agnecies vs. Old Agencies," *Marketing*, http://www.marketingmag.ca, February 17, 2011; Kristin Laird, "NKPR Is Now a Social Media Shop, Too," *Marketing*, http:// www.marketingmag.ca, February 8, 2011; Jeromy Lloyd, "Who Should Own a Client's Social Media Duties?" *Marketing*, http://www.marketingmag.ca, February 17, 2011.

finance and management. Whatever organization structure is selected, an agency often stands or falls on its relationships with its clients. The fast pace and pressure of ad agencies are legendary, but good communication remains paramount to maintaining that relationship.

assessment check 5

5.1 What is the role of an advertising agency?

5.2 What are some advantages of using an agency?

figure 14.3

Advertising Agency Organizational Chart

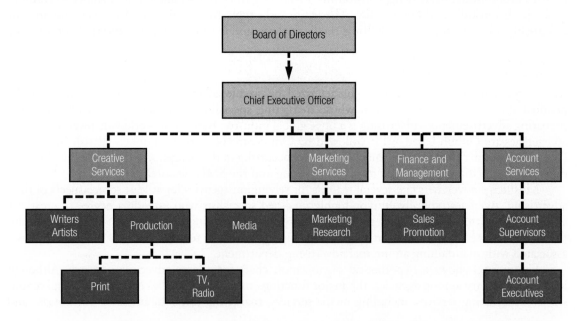

MEASURING PROMOTIONAL EFFECTIVENESS

Each element of the promotional mix represents a major expenditure for a firm. Although promotional prices vary widely, advertisers typically pay a fee based on the cost to deliver the message to viewers, listeners, or readers—the so-called *cost per thousand (CPM)*. Billboards are the cheapest way to spend advertising dollars, with television and some newspapers the most expensive. So while price is an important factor in media selection, it is by no means the only one—or all ads would appear on billboards!

Because promotion represents such a major expenditure for many firms, they need to determine whether their campaigns accomplish appropriate promotional objectives. Companies want their advertising agencies and in-house marketing personnel to demonstrate how promotional programs contribute to increased sales and profits. Marketers are well aware of the number of advertising messages and sales promotions that consumers encounter daily, and they know that these people practise selective perception and simply screen out many messages.

By measuring promotional effectiveness, organizations can evaluate different strategies, prevent mistakes before spending money on specific programs, and improve their promotional programs. As the earlier discussion of promotional planning explained, any evaluation program starts with objectives and goals; otherwise, marketers have no yardstick against which to measure effectiveness. However, determining whether an advertising message has achieved its intended objective is one of the most difficult undertakings in marketing. Sales promotions and direct marketing are somewhat easier to evaluate because they evoke measurable consumer responses. Like advertising, public relations is also difficult to assess on purely objective terms.

MEASURING ADVERTISING EFFECTIVENESS

Measures to evaluate the effectiveness of advertising, while difficult and costly, are essential parts of any marketing plan. Without an assessment strategy, marketers will not know whether their advertising achieves the objectives of the marketing plan or whether the dollars in the advertising budget are well spent. To answer these questions, marketers can conduct two types of research. **Media research** assesses how well a particular medium delivers the advertiser's message, where and when to place the advertisement, and the size of the audience. Buyers of broadcast time base their purchases on estimated Nielsen rating points, and the networks have to make good if ratings do not reach promised levels. Buyers of print advertising space pay fees based on circulation. Circulation figures are independently certified by specialized research firms.

The other major category, **message research**, tests consumer reactions to an advertisement's creative message. Pretesting and post-testing, the two methods for performing message research, are discussed in the following sections.

As the role of marketing expands in many organizations, marketers are employing increasingly sophisticated techniques to measure marketing effectiveness not only throughout the company but through the entire marketing channel. As more firms also conduct multichannel promotional efforts, keeping track of the data is a challenge. However, when they do so, they can better track which channels are most effective.[49]

Pretesting

To assess an advertisement's likely effectiveness before it actually appears in the chosen medium, marketers often conduct **pretesting**. The obvious advantage of this technique is the opportunity

6 Explain the role of ethics in an organization's promotional strategy and how marketers assess promotional effectiveness.

media research Advertising research that assesses how well a particular medium delivers an advertiser's message, where and when to place the advertisement, and the size of the audience.

pretesting Research that evaluates an ad during its development stage.

message research Advertising research that tests consumer reactions to an advertisement's creative message.

ARE **TAX CUTS FOR PENSIONERS** WORKING FOR YOU?

Pension Income Splitting is one of a wide range of tax cuts available to people all across Canada. By choosing this option each tax year, pensioners can split up to 50% of eligible pension income with their spouse or common law partner and reduce their overall tax paid.

Find out how to get Pension Income Splitting working for you. It makes sense to file electronically and on time.

For more information on these and other tax cuts, go to cra.gc.ca/taxcuts or call 1-877-959-1-CRA.

Government Gouvernement of Canada du Canada

Canada

CANADA REVENUE AGENCY. REPRODUCED WITH PERMISSION OF THE MINISTER OF PUBLIC WORKS AND GOVERNMENT SERVICES CANADA. 2011

Magazine ad promoting tax cuts by the Government of Canada.

COURTESY OF THE OLINGER GROUP, WWW.OLINGERGROUP.COM

Focus groups and personal interviews can be used to pretest ads.

to evaluate ads when they are being developed. Marketers can conduct a number of different pretests, beginning during the concept phase in the campaign's earliest stages, when they have only rough copy of the ad, and continuing until the ad layout and design are almost completed.

Pretesting employs a variety of evaluation methods. For example, focus groups can discuss their reactions to mock-ups of ads using different themes, headlines, or illustrations. To screen potential radio and television advertisements, marketers often recruit consumers to sit in a studio and indicate their preferences by pressing two buttons, one for a positive reaction to the commercial and the other for a negative reaction. Sometimes proposed ad copy is printed on a postcard that also offers a free product; the number of cards returned represents an indication of the copy's effectiveness. *Blind product tests* are also frequently used. In these tests, people are asked to select unidentified products on the basis of available advertising copy.

Mechanical and electronic devices offer yet another method of assessing how people read advertising copy. One mechanical test uses a hidden camera to photograph eye movements of readers. The results help advertisers determine headline placement and copy length. Another mechanical approach measures the galvanic skin response—changes in the electrical resistance of the skin produced by emotional reactions.

Marketoid

Canadians send 122 million text messages a day.

post-testing Research that assesses advertising effectiveness after it has appeared in a print or broadcast medium.

split runs Methods of testing alternative ads by dividing a cable TV audience or a publication's subscribers in two, using two different ads, and then evaluating the relative effectiveness of each.

Post-testing

Post-testing assesses advertising copy after it has appeared in the appropriate medium. Pretesting generally is a more desirable measurement method than post-testing because it can save the cost of placing ineffective ads. However, post-testing can help in planning future advertisements and in adjusting current advertising programs.

One of the most popular post-test methods is a readership test, also called a recognition test. In this test, people who have read selected magazines are interviewed to determine whether they observed various ads in them. A copy of the magazine is used as an interview aid, and each interviewer starts at a different point in the magazine and asks aided and unaided questions relating to the ads. For larger ads, respondents are asked about specifics, such as headlines and copy.

Unaided recall tests are another method of post-testing the effectiveness of advertisements. Respondents do not see copies of the magazine after their initial reading but are asked to recall the ads from memory.

Inquiry tests are another popular form of post-test. Advertisements sometimes offer gifts—generally product samples—to people who respond to them. The number of inquiries relative to the advertisement's cost forms a measure of its effectiveness.

Split runs allow advertisers to test two or more ads at the same time. Although advertisers traditionally place different versions in newspapers and magazines, split runs on cable television systems frequently test the effectiveness of TV ads. With this method, advertisers divide the cable TV audience or a publication's subscribers in two: half view advertisement A and the other half view advertisement B. The relative effectiveness of the alternatives is then determined through inquiries or recall and recognition tests.

Regardless of the exact method they choose, marketers must realize that pretesting and post-testing are expensive efforts. As a result, they must plan to use these techniques as effectively as possible.

MEASURING PUBLIC RELATIONS EFFECTIVENESS

As with other forms of marketing communications, organizations must measure PR results based on their objectives both for the PR program as a whole and for specific activities. In the next step, marketers must decide what they want to measure. This choice includes determining whether

"Noted %" indicates the percentage of readers interviewed who saw any part of the advertisement; 63% noted this ad.

"Read Some %" indicates the percentage of readers interviewed who read any amount of the body copy; 52% read some of the ad.

And you thought we only made cars.

Sure, Honda is best known for its automobiles. But we are, first and foremost, an engineering company. As well as the world's largest engine manufacturer. Today, we build some of the most dependable motorcycles, personal watercraft, lawnmowers, marine engines, generators, snowblowers, tillers and all-terrain vehicles out there. And, yes. We also manufacture those world-renowned cars.

From our low-emission automobiles to our clean and quiet marine engines, every Honda is designed to balance the thrill of fun and performance with society's need for fuel efficiency and cleaner air. Ultimately, it's the kind of thinking that improves the quality of life. And, certainly, the adventuresome quality of your weekends. Get things going at honda.com. **HONDA** The power of dreams.

"Associated %" indicates the percentage of readers interviewed who saw any part of the ad that indicates the brand or advertiser; 62% associated this ad with Honda.

"Read Most %" indicates the percentage of readers interviewed who read more than half of the body copy; 20% read most of the ad.

Magazine advertisement with Starch Scores—one method of measuring recall.

the message was heard by the target audience and whether it had the desired influence on public opinion.

The simplest and least costly level of assessment measures outputs of the PR program: whether the target audience received, paid attention to, understood, and retained the messages directed to them. To make this judgment, the staff could count the number of media placements and gauge the extent of media coverage. They could count attendees at any press conference, evaluate the quality of brochures and other materials, and pursue similar activities. Formal techniques include tracking publicity placements, analyzing how favourably their contents portrayed the company, and conducting public opinion polls.

To analyze PR effectiveness more deeply, a firm could conduct focus groups, interviews with opinion leaders, and more detailed and extensive opinion polls. The highest level of effectiveness measurement looks at outcomes: did the PR program change people's opinions, attitudes, and behaviour? PR professionals measure these outcomes through before-and-after polls (similar to pretesting and post-testing) and more advanced techniques like psychographic analysis (discussed in Chapter 8).

EVALUATING INTERACTIVE MEDIA

Marketers employ several methods to measure how many users view Web advertisements: *hits* (user requests for a file), *impressions* (the number of times a viewer sees an ad), and *click-throughs* (when the user clicks the ad to get more information). *View-through* rates measure responses over time. However, some of these measures can be misleading. Because each page, graphic, or multimedia file equals one hit, simple interactions can easily inflate the hit count, making it less accurate. To increase effectiveness, advertisers must give viewers who do click through their site something good to see. Successful Web campaigns use demonstrations, promotions, coupons, and interactive features.

Internet marketers price ad banners based on cost per thousand (CPM). Websites that sell advertising typically guarantee a certain number of impressions—the number of times an ad banner is downloaded and presumably seen by visitors. Marketers then set a rate based on that guarantee times the CPM rate.

assessment check 6

6.1 What is CPM, and how is it measured?

6.2 Distinguish between media research and message research.

6.3 Describe several research techniques used in post-testing.

ETHICS IN NON-PERSONAL SELLING

Marketoid

Seventy-five percent of
Canadian households have
access to a wireless phone.

Chapter 3 introduced the topic of marketing ethics and noted that promotion is the element in the marketing mix that raises the most ethical questions. People actively debate the question of whether marketing communications contribute to better lives. The final section of this chapter takes a closer look at ethical concerns in advertising and public relations.

ADVERTISING ETHICS

Even though advertising to children and beer ads are legal, these types of promotions continue to be debated as important ethical issues. One area of controversy is advertising aimed at children. When it comes to influencing parents' purchase decisions, nothing beats influencing kids. By promoting goods and services directly to children, firms can sell not only to them but to the rest of the household, too. However, as the feature "Solving an Ethical Controversy" points out, many parents and consumer advocates question the ethics of promoting directly to children. Their argument: at a time when kids need to learn how to consume thoughtfully, they are being inundated with promotional messages teaching the opposite.

Another issue is the insertion of product messages in media programs without full disclosure of the marketing relationship to audiences. To woo younger consumers, especially teens and those in their 20s, advertisers attempt to make these messages appear as different from advertisements as possible; they design ads that seem more like entertainment.

Alcoholic beverage advertising on television is another controversial area. Beer marketers advertise heavily on television and spend far more on advertising in print and outdoor media than do marketers of hard-liquor brands. While all areas of Canada have some restrictions on advertising of alcoholic beverages, some want much stricter regulation of all forms of such advertising on television and other media. Some areas of the country run ads promoting responsible drinking and the dangers of drinking and driving in an effort to show the other side of the drinking issue. Critics decry advertisements with

---

SOLVING AN ETHICAL CONTROVERSY

Should the Government Curb Advertising That Targets Children?

MARKETERS of goods and services designed for children have always targeted at least some of their advertising to the end users. However, once television programming began to be developed for children, the amount and intensity grew. In addition, over the years, the practice of using TV as a "babysitter" became increasingly common, with TV advertising to children even more pervasive. Child advocacy groups have prevailed on marketers and the advertising industry to be more responsible for their activities. In 2007, the Canadian Children's Food and Beverage Advertising Initiative was developed in order to shift the food products advertised to children under 12 to healthy options. This initiative is voluntary and, although some companies like Kellogg Canada and McDonald's support it, not all companies have agreed to take part.

Should the government curb advertising that targets children?

PRO

1. Because of their age, children are easily manipulated and unduly influenced by advertising and need to be protected.

2. Research on advertising to children reveals that children who watch TV ads consume more calories, particularly those of low-nutrient foods they see on TV. The link to childhood obesity is clear.

CON

1. Government regulation of TV advertising to children would be the first step to regulating other types of advertising.

2. Only parents can parent—and that includes monitoring their children's TV viewing.

Where do you stand: pro or con?

Sources: Jane E. Brody, "Risks for Youth Who Eat What They Watch," *The New York Times*, April 19, 2010, http://www.nytimes.com; Jon Eggerton, "FTC Asks for More Media Self-Regulation on Children's TV Protections," *Broadcasting & Cable*, April 12, 2010, http://www.broadcastingcable.com; Stephen Clifford, "A Fine Line When Ads and Children Mix," *The New York Times*, February 15, 2010, http://www.nytimes.com; Chris Powell, "ASC Says Children's Advertising 'Significantly Different' Thanks to Initiative," *Marketing*, http://www.marketingmag.ca, August 26, 2010.

messages implying that drinking the right beer will improve a person's social life or help to win a sports contest. The Northwest Territories and Nunavut have the tightest restrictions on alcohol ads.

In cyberspace ads, it is often difficult to separate advertising from editorial content since many sites resemble magazine and newspaper ads or television infomercials. Another ethical issue surrounding advertising online is the use of cookies, small text files that are automatically down-loaded to a user's computer whenever a site is visited. Each time the user returns to that site, the site's server accesses the cookie and gathers information: What site was visited last? How long did the user stay? What was the next site visited? Marketers claim that this device helps them determine consumer preferences and argue that cookies are stored in the user's PC, not the company's website. The problem is that cookies can and do collect personal information without the user's knowledge.

DECEPTIVE ADVERTISING

Deceptive advertising refers to exaggerated claims of a product's superiority or the use of subjective or vague statements that may not be literally true. Although there are a few laws in Canada dealing with deceptive advertising, the Competition Act does regulate deceptive ads relating to pricing.

Exaggeration in ads is not new. Consumers seem to accept advertisers' tendencies to stretch the truth in their efforts to distinguish their products and get consumers to buy. This inclination may provide one reason that advertising does not encourage purchase behaviour as successfully as sales promotions do. A tendency toward exaggeration does raise some ethical questions, though: Where is the line between claims that attract attention and those that provide implied guarantees? To what degree do advertisers deliberately make misleading statements?

Advertising Standards Canada (ASC) is the self-regulatory body for the advertising industry. The 160 members of this organization promote the integrity and viability of advertising, hoping that effective self-control will reduce the number of laws enacted to control abuse. To date they have been effective in doing so. They administer the Canadian Code of Advertising Standards, which includes those aspects covered in the Competition Act, as well as other issues such as those relating to advertising to children. This group also investigates any complaints relating to the industry but they have no authority to enforce their decisions.[50]

General boasts of product superiority are considered so self-praising or exaggerated that the average consumer would not rely on them to make a buying decision. A quantifiable statement, on the other hand, implies a certain level of performance. For example, tests can establish the validity of a claim that a brand of long-life light bulbs outlasts three regular light bulbs.

ETHICS IN PUBLIC RELATIONS

Several public relations issues open organizations to criticism. Various PR firms perform services for the tobacco industry; publicity campaigns defend unsafe products. Also, marketers must weigh ethics before they respond to negative publicity. For example, do firms admit to problems or product deficiencies, or do they try to cover them up?

Strategic Implications

As greater portions of corporate ad budgets continue to migrate to the Web, marketers must be increasingly aware of the benefits and pitfalls of Internet advertising. But they should not forget the benefits of other types of advertising as well.

Promotion industry experts agree that e-commerce broadens marketers' job tasks, though many promotional objectives still remain the same. Today, advertisers need 75 different ways to market their products in 75 countries in the world and innumerable market segments. Advertisers also agree that, in years to come, channels will become more homogeneous while markets become more fragmented. ◆◆◆

REVIEW OF CHAPTER OBJECTIVES

(1)   **Identify the three major advertising objectives and the two basic categories of advertising.**

The three major objectives of advertising are to inform, to persuade, and to remind. The two major categories of advertising are product advertising and institutional advertising. Product advertising involves the nonpersonal selling of a good or service. Institutional advertising is the nonpersonal promotion of a concept, idea, or philosophy of a company or organization.

(2)   **List the major advertising strategies and describe the process of creating an advertisement.**

The major strategies are comparative advertising, which makes extensive use of messages with direct comparisons between competing brands; celebrity, which uses famous spokespeople to boost an advertising message; retail, which includes all advertising by retail stores selling products directly to consumers; interactive, which encourages two-way communication either via the Internet or kiosks and cross promotion, where partners share the cost of promotions.

An advertisement evolves from pinpointing goals, such as educating consumers, enhancing brand loyalty, or improving a product's image. From those goals, marketers move to the next stages: creating a plan, developing a message, developing and preparing the ad, and selecting the appropriate medium (or media). Advertisements often appeal to consumers' emotions with messages focusing on fear, humour, or sex.

(3)   **Identify the major types of advertising appeals and discuss their uses.**

Sometimes, emotional appeals to fear, humour, sex, guilt, or fantasy can be effective. Marketers need to recognize that fear appeals can backfire; people's sense of humour can differ according to gender, age, and other factors; and use of sexual imagery must not overstep the bounds of taste.

(4)   **List and compare the major advertising media.**

The major media include broadcast (television and radio), newspapers and magazines, direct mail, outdoor, and interactive and digital communications. Each medium has benefits and drawbacks. Newspapers are flexible and dominate local markets. Magazines can target niche markets. Interactive media encourage two-way communication. Outdoor advertising in a high-traffic location reaches many people every day; television and radio reach even more. Direct mail allows effective segmentation. Digital communication can be flexible and cost effective.

(5)   **Outline the organization of the advertising function and the role of an advertising agency.**

Within a firm, the advertising department is usually a group that reports to a marketing executive. Advertising departments generally include research, art and design, copywriting, and media analysis. Outside advertising agencies assist and support firms. These specialists are usually organized by creative services, account services, marketing services, and finance.

(6)   **Explain the roles of ethics in an organization's promotional strategy and how marketers assess promotional effectiveness.**

Marketers should be careful to construct ethically sound promotional campaigns, avoiding such practices as exaggeration and deceit.

The effectiveness of advertising can be measured by both pretesting and post-testing. Pretesting is the assessment of an ad's effectiveness before it is actually used. It includes such methods as sales conviction tests and blind product tests. Post-testing is the assessment of the ad's effectiveness after it has been used. Commonly used post-tests include readership tests, unaided recall tests, inquiry tests, and split runs.

assessment check answers

1.1 What are the goals of institutional advertising?

Institutional advertising promotes a concept, an idea, a philosophy, or the goodwill of an industry, company, organization, person, geographic location, or government agency.

1.2 At what stage in the product life cycle are informative ads used? Why?

Informative ads are common in the introductory stage of the product life cycle because they develop initial demand for a good, service, organization, person, place, idea or cause.

1.3 What is reminder advertising?

Reminder advertising strives to reinforce previous promotional activity by keeping the name of a good, service, organization, person, place, idea, or cause before the public.

2.1 What is comparative advertising? What makes a successful celebrity testimonial?

Comparative advertising makes extensive use of messages with direct comparisons between competing brands. Successful celebrity ads feature figures who are credible sources of information for the product being promoted.

2.2 What is cooperative advertising?

In cooperative advertising a manufacturer or wholesaler shares advertising costs with a retailer.

2.3 What is an advertising campaign? What are an advertisement's three main goals?

An advertising campaign is a series of different but related ads that use a single theme and appear in different media within a specified time period. Advertising's three main goals are to educate consumers about product features, enhance brand loyalty, and improve consumer perception of the brand.

2.4 What are the advantages of cross promotion?

Cross promotion divides the cost of a promotional campaign that meets the mutual needs of marketing partners and provides greater benefits for both in return.

3.1 What are some common emotional appeals used in advertising?

Advertisers often focus on making emotional appeals to fear, humour, sex, guilt, or fantasy.

3.2 What are the main types of interactive ads?

Interactive ads include Internet banners, pop-ups, keyword ads, advertorials, advergames, and interstitials.

4.1 What types of products are banned from advertising on television?

Tobacco goods such as cigarettes, cigars, and smokeless tobacco are banned from television advertising.

4.2 What are some advantages radio offers to advertisers? What about newspapers?

Radio ads allow marketers to target a captive audience and offer low cost, flexibility, and mobility. Newspaper ads are flexible and provide intensive coverage of the market. Readers can also refer back to newspaper ads.

4.3 What are online communities and social networks? Explain how online communities can help companies market their products and improve customer service.

Online communities and social networks can take several forms and include Internet discussion groups and electronic bulletin boards, as well as networking sites like MySpace and Facebook. Users log in and participate by sending comments and questions or receiving information from other forum members. Companies use online communities to ask questions and exchange information with customers.

4.4 Define *media scheduling* and identify the most important factors influencing the scheduling decision.

Media scheduling sets the timing and sequence for a series of advertisements. Sales patterns, repurchase cycles, and competitors' activities are the most important variables in the scheduling decision.

5.1 What is the role of an advertising agency?

An advertising agency's role is to help businesses plan and prepare advertisements.

5.2 What are some advantages of using an agency?

Advantages of using an ad agency are the availability of highly qualified specialists who provide creativity and objectivity, and sometimes cost savings.

6.1 What is CPM and how is it measured?

CPM is cost per thousand, a fee based on cost to deliver the advertiser's message to viewers, listeners, or readers.

6.2 Distinguish between media research and message research.

Media research assesses how well a particular medium delivers the advertiser's message, where and when to place the ad, and the size of the audience. Message research tests consumer reactions to an advertisement's creative message.

6.3 Describe several research techniques used in post-testing.

Commonly used post-tests include readership tests, unaided recall tests, inquiry tests, and split runs.

MARKETING TERMS YOU NEED TO KNOW

These terms are printed in red in the text. They are defined in the margins of the chapter and in the Glossary that begins on p. G-1.

product advertising 431	comparative advertising 433	media scheduling 446
institutional advertising 431	cooperative advertising 434	advertising agency 447
informative advertising 432	retail advertising 434	media research 449
persuasive advertising 432	interactive advertising 434	message research 449
reminder advertising 432	cross promotion 435	pretesting 449
informative advertising 432	advertising campaign 436	post-testing 450
reminder 432	banners 438	split runs 450

PROJECTS AND TEAMWORK EXERCISES

1. Choose a print ad to cut out and place on a poster board. With a marker, identify all the elements of the ad. Then identify what you believe is the objective of the ad—to inform, persuade, or remind. Finally, identify the strategy used—comparative, celebrity, retail, or cross promotion. If there is an interactive component offered, note that too.

2. Choose a magazine that interests you and analyze the advertisements in one issue. Describe whom you think the magazine's readers are by reviewing the ads.

3. With a classmate, create your own plan for cross-promoting two products you think would be good candidates for cross promotion.

4. Access the Internet and surf around to some sites that interest you. How many banner ads or pop-ups do you see? Do you like to view these ads, or do you find them intrusive? Which are most appealing? Which are least?

5. With a classmate, choose a product you have purchased in the past and come up with a plan for using a nontraditional advertising medium, such as balloons, T-shirts, water bottles, anything you imagine will grab people's attention, and promote the product effectively. If possible, create a prototype for your ad. If not, create a sketch of your ad. Present your new ad to the class.

CRITICAL-THINKING EXERCISES

1. What are some of the benefits and drawbacks of using celebrity testimonials in advertising? Identify an ad you believe makes effective use of a celebrity's endorsement, and explain why.

2. Choose one of the following products and outline a possible media schedule for advertising.
   a. Toy
   b. Line of bathing suits
   c. Line of candles

3. Select two different advertisers' television or print ads for the same product category (cars or soft drinks, for instance) and decide what emotion each appeals to. Which ad is more effective and why?

4. Do outdoor ads and pop-up ads have any characteristics in common? What are they?

5. Imagine that a writer says that children exposed to deception in ads grow into teens who are healthily skeptical of advertising claims. Find several print ads aimed at children, and identify what you think might be deception in these ads. Select one ad you think children would be influenced by and rewrite the ad without the deception.

6. Some marketers believe that marketing in schools—through advertisements on book covers, product placement in lesson plans, and ads in educational videos—is acceptable only if the ads are designed to help schools financially by giving them supplies they cannot afford or helping them get money to buy these items. Others feel advertising has no place in schools at all, but the majority expect it to increase in the future. Find out about advertiser participation in the schools in your area. Do you agree that it has a benefit? Why or why not? Interview a few high school students you know and find out what they think. Prepare a brief report about your findings.

ETHICS EXERCISE

In an effort to target the youngest of consumers, some firms have begun to advertise tiny mobile phones sized to fit the hands of children. These phones are designed specifically for the younger set—it's a real phone, not a toy. In Europe, where the phone is marketed, some parents and consumer groups are objecting to the marketing of the product, noting the long-term health effects of cell phone use are unknown, and young children are quickly impressed by advertising. "The mobile telephone industry is acting like the tobacco industry by designing products that addict the very young," argues one environmental advocacy group for children.[51]

1. Do you believe that the companies manufacturing and promoting these phones are acting in an ethical manner? Why or why not? Be sure to use concepts from this chapter to build your argument.
2. What steps might these companies take to promote these phones in order to reduce the negative publicity?

INTERNET EXERCISES

1. **Future of newspaper advertising.** Using a news source, such as Google news (http://news.google.com) or Yahoo! News (http://news.yahoo.com), research the current status of newspaper advertising. How much has ad revenue changed in recent years? Do you agree or disagree that the future of newspaper advertising lies online?
2. **Super Bowl advertising.** Visit the website listed here (www.superbowl-commercials.org). How many different organizations ran ads during the most recent Super Bowl game? Which organizations have run the most ads in Super Bowl games? During the most recent Super Bowl game, which ads were rated the highest? The lowest rated? How much has the cost of a 30-second Super Bowl ad changed since the first game was played?

3. **Not-for-profit advertising.** Review the material in the chapter on creating an advertisement and then go to the website listed here (http://marketing.about.com/cs/nonprofitmrktg/a/8stepnonprofit.htm). It outlines the basic steps involved in creating an advertisement for a not-for-profit organization. Review the material and prepare a brief report comparing and contrasting the process of creating an advertisement for a for-profit and a not-for-profit organization.

Note: Internet Web addresses change frequently. If you don't find the exact sites listed, you may need to access the organization's or company's home page and search from there or use a search engine such as Google.

CASE 14.1

Lululemon

Lululemon founder Chip Wilson moved from businesses related to surfing and snowboards into yoga. His first idea was to open a store that could be a community hub for healthy living aimed at busy professional women juggling jobs and families. In November 2000 he opened a store in Kitsilano, in the beach area of Vancouver. He quickly found that his vision was too broad and that one store could not carry everything from diet to exercise.

After taking his first yoga class, he realized that the cotton clothing being worn was inappropriate and he set out to change it. His passion for the technical aspects of athletic fabrics came to the fore and he started experimenting. In order to pay the bills, his design studio was used as a yoga studio at night. This concept became the foundation for all future lululemon stores.

What makes lululemon different from all other athletic clothing stores out there? The major difference is the way it markets its stores and products. The company has a unique approach to research and promotion. Television, radio, newspaper, and outdoor advertising do not fit into the company's promotional strategy. As for traditional market research, the company feels the world is changing too quickly and if it waited for traditional research results it would be six months behind.

Instead of using traditional product development, market research, and promotional strategies, lululemon combines all these into a process that works for them. Their products include yoga clothing for both men and women, along with yoga accessories. The clothes are made with specially designed fabrics from either all-natural fibres or a blend of natural fibres. The fabrics are designed with unique features allowing users to feel more comfortable while working out. The yoga wear is quick drying and lightweight and retains its shape. Other features are built into the garments themselves in order to avoid irritation and to ensure the clothing stays in place while working out.

Lululemon has made its design process part of its promotional strategy. On a regular basis, groups of certified yoga instructors in the communities where a store is located meet with representatives of the company's design team. In exchange for their feedback on new designs, they receive a store discount. Individuals who embody the lululemon culture are designated as ambassadors. Ambassadors are provided products for a year in exchange for their input into the design of new clothing and are featured in communication material such as the website. An added bonus to these two programs is that people involved in the programs will promote lululemon products to others.

Another part of the lululemon promotional strategy is its stores. There are lululemon retail stores in Canada, the United States, Hong Kong, and Australia. Each store is designed specifically for its community and each runs its own promotions. Each store organizes local events in order to create brand awareness.

The company does do some print ads, mainly for strategic reasons. In an attempt to inform larger athletic apparel companies that lululemon owns the yoga market, ads are placed in magazines such as *Yoga Journal* and *Runner's World*. A large part of the company's promotional activities include publicity and events that support local communities. Although the company was not an official sponsor of the Vancouver Olympics, it had several promotional activities connected to the games. The company introduced a new clothing line called "A Cool Sporting Event That Takes Place in British Columbia Between 2009 & 2011" that the Olympic organizers were not happy about. A representative from the Olympic committee commented, "We expected better sportsmanship from a local Canadian company than to produce a clothing line that attempts to profit from the games but doesn't support the games or the success of the Canadian Olympic team." Other promotional events surrounding the Vancouver Olympics did not cause the company any problems. In a joint effort with a yoga studio, the company provided free yoga classes and teamed up with Labatt to sponsor an evening's entertainment in Club Bud during the games.

The unusual promotion, marketing research, and product development strategies seem to be working for the company and its founder Chip Wilson. Chip was honoured for his contributions to the marketing field by being inducted into the Marketing Hall of Legends as a Visionary.

Questions for Critical Thinking

1. Do you think lululemon's unique marketing program is as effective as television commercials? Why or why not?
2. Do you think lululemon's marketing program will work in the other countries where it has stores? Why or why not?

Sources: Lululemon website, http://www.lululemon.com, March 6, 2011; Eve Lazarus, "The Tao of Lululemon," *Marketing*, April 14, 2008, pp. 22–27; David Brown, "Labatt Opening Club Bud for the Olympics," *Marketing*, http://www.marketingmag.ca, January 19, 2010; Rebecca Harris, "Eight Industry Giants Join the Marketing Hall of Legends," *Marketing*, http://www.marketingmag.ca, February 26, 2010; "Visionary," *Marketing*, http://www.marketingmag.ca February 26, 2010; "Lululemon Offering Free Yoga During the Olympics," *Marketing*, http://www.marketingmag.ca, January 12, 2010.

CASE 14.2

Multiplatform Marketing—Transforming an Industry

Never before have consumers had so many choices on where to get their information about products and services nor have marketers had as many choices on how to spend their marketing dollars. Many of these new choices for both consumers and marketers involve digital or social media. The result of this explosion in promotional options is an advertising and media industry in total transformation. Many marketers are using more and different media than ever before but sometimes wonder whether all these choices are cost effective. The media companies, television, radio, mobile, and others are working through all the new options in order to provide marketers and consumer the best options.

The Vancouver Winter Olympic Games—A Pivotal Point

A pivotal point in this industry transformation was the Vancouver Olympic Games. Before the Vancouver Games, the Olympics marketing hype was all about sponsorship. Sponsorship was still important for the Vancouver Games but for the first time ever media platforms (cell phones, computers, television) were getting a lot of hype. Getting all the media organized was the responsibility of Canada's Olympic Broadcast Media Consortium.

This was no easy task, considering all the players involved—media companies, advertisers, and ad agencies—that had to pull together to make this happen. The first step was an almost unheard of joining of two industry rivals—CTV with an 80 percent ownership stake and Rogers Media with the other 20 percent. The motto of this union was "like never before" and that really summed up what happened next.

The consortium took a consumer-centric approach to delivering media content that required state-of-the-art technological skills not to mention getting such fierce enemies to work together. Canadians were able to watch the games when they wanted, how they wanted, and the events they wanted to see. Olympic coverage was available on regular television channels, on specialty television channels, on multicultural television channels, on websites, via mobile devices, and on radio and in newspapers. The list of media carrying Olympic games and special coverage was impressive: CTV, TSN, RDS, Sportnet, OLN, Omni, APTN, CTVOlmpics.ca, RDSolympics.ca, Fan 590, 680 News, and *The Globe and Mail*.

The consortium pulled technical experts from both media giants to develop a state-of-the-art news and information portal.

Every minute of the competition in every sport was available to viewers in real time. The high-definition-quality broadcasts used a streaming player allowing viewers to pause, replay, or rewind the programs as the action was occurring. Viewers were guided to key moments in the competition through an interactive and data-embedded video player on the websites. A free iPhone app linked to CTVOlympics.ca was made available two months before the games started. An enhanced iPhone app was available for a small fee just before the games started.

Once the consortium had its media plans in place, it needed to get companies to sign up for advertising spots. This was another daunting task. The world was in a recession and the price of advertising during the Olympics was high. Not to be slowed down, the consortium decided to do some market research before putting together the advertising packages it would offer. Consortium members went out to talk to perspective advertisers, asking them what business objectives their companies wanted to achieve if they bought advertising from the consortium. The research resulted in a set of targeted marketing approaches the consortium could take, one of which was partnering with perspective advertisers in order for companies to get the most value for their advertising dollars.

The coverage of the games was complemented by other programs shown before or during the 17-day event. McDonald's sponsored a series called "Difference Makers," telling the story of people who contributed to the athletes' careers. GE's series, called "Superbodies," showed in 3D how athletes' muscles performed during competition. The GE series won a Gemini award.

The statistics on how many people visited the websites and viewed live coverage of the games on television is impressive. Olympic Games coverage reached 99 percent of Canadians, who consumed 1.5 billion hours of the competitions. The average Canadian watched 38 hours of Olympic programming, and overall television viewing went up 22 percent during the time Vancouver hosted the world. The statistics for the online and interactive viewing on the websites are equally impressive. There were 12.3 million individual visits. In total, 215 million Web pages were viewed, amounting to 28.5 million videos watched. Canadians also watched roughly 260 000 videos on their mobile devices.

The consortium was not the only organization to launch new technology during the games. The Vancouver games were called the Twitter games, with social media newsroom available for those wanting to tweet. Sega even launched an official Olympic video game.

The Companies

Although companies were slow to start buying the expensive advertising available, the arrival of the Olympic torch in Canada was the catalyst that prompted companies to spend more than $700 million on Olympic promotional activities.

Months before the games began, the Royal Bank of Canada, an official sponsor of the games, organized a cross-country torch relay in which more than 2300 Canadians carried the flame. The event lasted for 106 days and was supported with a contest to determine who would carry the torch and other

advertising, including a television commercial. Canadians who wanted the opportunity to carry the torch submitted their story to a dedicated website.

Bell Canada, who became an Olympic sponsor after out-bidding Telus and the Western Canada Telecommunications company, invested heavily in Olympic activities. Bell not only contributed $200 million in cash but worked closely with the consortium described above. Bell Canada was also present onsite in Vancouver. Its large public pavilion showcased its products and was home to a large number of high-definition television sets broadcasting the competitions.

Another Olympic sponsor, Samsung, used its Vancouver exposure to launch its new Omnia II phone with the Wireless Olympic Works (WOW) application. Like the consortium's iPhone application, WOW provided real-time competition updates. Samsung supported these initiatives with television ads. The new phone was supplied to Olympic volunteers to use during the games but many could be seen using their own iPhones and BlackBerrys.

Other organizations, such as the Canadian Tourism Commission (CTC), also used the Olympics to launch massive digital promotional programs. The CTC is the organization responsible for marketing Canada throughout the world. As part of its marketing program for the Olympics, the organization produced more than 2300 hours of high-definition film footage and 500 photos for the social media portion of the campaign. For the 80 broadcasters carrying the promotional material, it produced an additional 50 video stories, 25 each of Olympic athletes and Canada-themed features. In order to make the most of this digital material, the CTC installed a new digital management system.

The Results

Introducing new technology is risky at the best of times but add the pressure of launching new technology when the world is watching and any problems would also have worldwide press. The consortium was ready, and if there were problems they were small enough that the damage was limited.

Advertisers working with the consortium were quick to praise them. A typical comment was "A very talented group of individuals came together and really understood the medium, the event and what their partners and sponsors were looking for." Other companies felt the unique approach really worked and that the consortium worked before, during, and after the games to provide the best opportunities for them.

Bell Canada was so impressed with its experience throughout the Olympics that the company purchased CTV the following September. For Bell, the purchase allowed it to continue to develop its mobile strategy. CTV had the content from the numerous television stations, including TSN, that Bell could repackage for its mobile customers. CTV also had strong relationships with advertisers that Bell could tap into. The new company could continue to build on what was started with their Olympic partnership.

However, giving customers so many options to view the Olympics did not change their viewing habits significantly. The majority of customers still watched Olympic coverage on television. Online viewing mirrored that of television in both content and time. Some viewers would watch the games on television and go to the websites to see replays.

All these viewing options had an impact on public relations, good and bad public relations. When things started to wrong early in the games—the death of a competitor, warm weather, and problems with the opening ceremonies—negative comments were everywhere, on Facebook, Twitter, and YouTube. The Olympic organizers were able to monitor these comments and took immediate action to try to correct problems as they occurred. Not all problems were corrected, but just the fact that Olympic organizers handled the press with such efficiency turned the situations from negatives to positives.

The Future

The success of all the new digital media at the Olympics is only the beginning, according to many experts. Companies are looking at finding ways to effectively deal with hyper-connectivity, consumer-controlled media, and the ways this is changing an entire industry.

Not all companies have been as successful with their moves into the digital world as those involved in the Olympic coverage. Experts agree that social media has exploded, but the way forward for companies is not quite so clear. What most experts do agree on is that digital marketing works best when it is well done and integrated with other marketing and promotional activities.

Another major change that has gained momentum since the Olympics is in the media industry itself. Newspapers are going paperless. Radio stations are moving into video. Telephone companies are expanding in order to provide more content. One trend for mobile communications is location-based marketing. In location-based marketing, companies are working on applications that will send promotional messages and even coupons to customers as they shop. Companies are also working on the technology to bring 3D to mobile media. Whatever new technology hits the market, digital marketing is changing how companies provide information to their customers and will continue to do so.

Questions for Critical Thinking

1. Advertising messages follow consumers as they work, shop, commute, vacation, and even visit public restrooms. Marketers are enthusiastic about innovative advertising, but does it work? Do you think wildly unusual advertising is effective? Why or why not?

2. What else can marketers do to break through advertising clutter? Are they merely creating even more clutter by advertising on everything? Do you think you think digital marketing will reduce advertising clutter? Why or why not?

3. Do you think digital advertising is more or less effective than other types of advertising? Why or why not? What do you think the advantages and disadvantages of digital advertising are?

Sources: Kunur Patel, "What iPad's Slick New Features Mean for Marketers," *Advertising Age*, http://adage.com, March 2, 2011; Jeff Beer, "After Online, 3D Will Change Sports Broadcasting: CMDC Conference Told," *Marketing*, http://www.marketingmag.ca, April 3, 2010; Emily Bryson York, "McDonald's to Use Facebook's Upcoming Location Feature," *Advertising Age*, http://adage.com, May 6, 2010; Kristin Laird, "Canada Post Helping Canadians Shop Online," *Marketing*, http://www.marketingmag.ca, March 3, 2011; Jeff Beer, "Own the (PR) Podium," *Marketing*, http://www.marketingmag.ca, April 16, 2010; Alicia Androich, "Astral Radio Puts Video on the Web," *Marketing*, http://www.marketingmag.ca, March 1, 2011; Chris Powell, "Social Climbers," *Marketing*, http://www.marketingmag.ca, March 19, 2010; Jeromy Lloyd, "Feeling Unsocial," *Marketing*, http://www.marketingmag.ca, June 10, 2010; Jeromy Lloyd, "Online Complements Olympic TV Viewing, Alon Marcovic Tells MESH," *Marketing*, http://www.marketingmag.ca, May 16, 2010; Chris Powell, "Gold Mettle," *Marketing*, http://www.marketingmag.ca, January 10, 2011; Jeff Beer, Matt Semansky, Jeromy Lloyd, and Chris Powell, "The Top Media Players of 2010," *Marketing*, http://www.marketingmag.ca, November 22, 2010; Charlene Rooke, "Brand Olympics: The Best *Marketing* Campaigns of the 2010 Vancouver Winter Games," http://sparksheet.com, February 1, 2010; Eve Lazarus, "CTC Hopes Media Outreach Will Bring Olympic Afterglow," *Marketing*, http://www.marketingmag.ca, February 5, 2010; Kristin Laird, "The A-List," *Marketing*, http://www.marketingmag.ca, May 31, 2010; Kristin Laird, "Gold Medal Marketing," *Marketing*, http://www.marketingmag.ca, March 1, 2010; Kristin Laird, "Broadcast Consortium Gets App'd for Games," *Marketing*, http://www.marketingmag.ca, January 5, 2010; Kristin Laird, "Broadcast Consortium Gets App'd for Games," *Marketing*, http://www.marketingmag.ca, January 5, 2010; Kristin Laird, "RBC Lights Up For Olympic Torch Relay," *Marketing*, http://www.marketingmag.ca, December 17, 2009; "The 25th Annual Gemini Special Awards Announced," http://www.Geminiawards.ca, March 3, 2011.

Personal Selling and Sales Promotion

CHAPTER OBJECTIVES

①　Describe the role of today's salesperson.

②　Describe the four sales channels.

③　Describe the major trends in personal selling.

④　Identify and briefly describe the three basic sales tasks.

⑤　Outline the seven steps in the sales process.

⑥　Identify the seven basic functions of a sales manager.

⑦　Explain the role of ethical behaviour in personal selling.

⑧　Describe the role of sales promotion in the promotional mix, and identify the different types of sales promotion.

SALESFORCE.COM: LIVING IT UP ON A CLOUD

In the digital age, successful salespeople have a system—that is, a software platform that helps them track customers and prospects, monitor their progress with key accounts, oversee their billing and collection activity—in short, to help them keep tabs on the myriad of details surrounding a job in sales.

However, few employers have the time or resources to develop a truly customized system for their sales force. Instead, firms typically license a software package from a company like SAP or Oracle, then pay to have the software customized and purchase monthly maintenance, tech support, and other services.

This costly arrangement puzzled Marc Benioff, an Oracle executive at the time. He pondered whether there was a way to develop a more affordable option. Benioff came up with the answer—Salesforce.com. In a modest apartment, he launched his fledgling company, and the "End of Software" era began.

Using Salesforce CRM, businesses can leverage the capabilities of the Internet to create their own customized customer relationship management (CRM) system. And they do it with a software product that's not a product at all.

That is, Salesforce CRM doesn't sit in a box on a shelf, waiting to be ordered, delivered, and installed on your computer. Rather, CRM resides on an Internet "cloud," available at an affordable price. Business customers access CRM from the cloud, then easily customize it to their individual requirements.

Salesforce CRM is an example of what is known as "on-demand software," which customers can access and use at their convenience. Salesforce.com is a pioneer in cloud computing and one of the most successful players in the SaaS ("software as a service") category in the rapidly growing technology marketplace. As Benioff discovered, using the Internet to develop, market, and distribute products makes it highly affordable and exceedingly efficient.

For large organizations, Salesforce.com developed an "enterprise edition" of CRM. Clients can begin using CRM even before it is fully integrated into the organization's existing systems. Once integration is complete, the transition to the new platform is swift and relatively uncomplicated. Salesforce.com's clientele continues to grow and currently includes such giants as Alltel, Dell, *The Wall Street Journal*, Sprint, and Time Warner Cable among its more than 78 000 customers.

Since the success of Salesforce.com, other on-demand software providers have emerged, automating a variety of corporate activities, such as travel-budget and personnel management. Meanwhile, the company has built a global presence and recently opened its third data centre, in Singapore, to take advantage of the burgeoning Asia-Pacific market for enterprise cloud computing.

One of Salesforce.com's latest innovations is Force.com, a hosting site for data centres and platform technologies. Force. com can even be used as a platform for launching new SaaS companies. FinancialForce.com, one of the programs, offers the systems and services needed by finance and accounting departments, such as ledgers, budgeting, spreadsheets, accounts payable and receivable, and more. Industry observers predict that FinancialForce.com will do for the finance and accounting world what Salesforce.com has done for customer relationship management.

Salesforce.com may have looked and operated like a typical dotcom of the 1990s. However, unlike thousands of those businesses, it succeeded because it saw—and satisfied—a valid need in the marketplace.[1]

---

connecting with customers

Salesforce.com connects with its customers by creating innovative products that add value to its customers' businesses. Salesforce.com CRM software helps customers' salespeople manage their sales. This on-demand software—available on an Internet "cloud"—is both affordable and efficient and has become an important tool used by salespeople around the world.

Chapter Overview

THE Salesforce.com story illustrates how important it is for marketers to not simply sell products but to understand their customers and connect with them through product innovations that make life easier. In exploring personal selling strategies, this chapter gives special attention to the relationship-building opportunities that the selling situation presents.

Personal selling is the process of a seller's person-to-person promotional presentation to a buyer. The sales process is essentially interpersonal, and it is basic to any enterprise. Accounting, engineering, human resource management, production, and other organizational activities produce no benefits unless a seller matches the needs of a client or customer. The fact that almost 10 percent of the Canadian labour force is employed in sales positions testifies to the importance of selling. While the average firm's advertising expenses may represent from 1 to 3 percent of total sales, personal selling expenses are likely to equal 10 to 15 percent. This makes personal selling the single largest marketing expense in many firms.

personal selling
Interpersonal influence process involving a seller's promotional presentation conducted on a person-to-person basis with the buyer.

Personal selling is a primary component of a firm's promotional mix when one or more of several well-defined factors are present:

1. Customers are geographically concentrated.
2. Individual orders account for large amounts of revenue.
3. The firm markets goods and services that are expensive, are technically complex, or require special handling.
4. Trade-ins are involved.
5. Products move through short channels.
6. The firm markets to relatively few potential customers.

For example, personal selling is an important component of the promotional mix for a car dealer, although both dealers and manufacturers also rely heavily on advertising. Because cars and trucks are expensive, customers usually like to go to a dealership to compare models, discuss a purchase, or obtain service, and trade-ins often are involved. So a dealer's salespeople provide valuable assistance to the customer.

Table 15.1 summarizes the factors that influence the importance of personal selling in the overall promotional mix based on four variables: consumer, product, price, and marketing channels. This chapter also explores *sales promotion*, which includes all marketing activities other than personal selling, advertising, and publicity that enhance promotional effectiveness. ◆◆◆

---

① Describe the role of today's salesperson.

THE EVOLUTION OF PERSONAL SELLING

Selling has been a standard business activity for thousands of years. As long ago as 2000 B.C., the Code of Hammurabi protected the rights of the Babylonian salesman, who was referred to as a *peddler*. Throughout Canadian history, selling has been a major factor in economic growth. Early peddlers travelled with their goods from town to town and farm to farm, helping expand trade among early settlers. Today, professional salespeople are problem solvers who focus on satisfying the needs of customers before, during, and after sales are made. Armed with knowledge about their firm's goods or services, those of competitors, and their customers' business needs, salespeople pursue a common goal of creating mutually beneficial long-term relationships with customers.

Personal selling is a vital, vibrant, dynamic process. As domestic and foreign competition increases emphasis on productivity, personal selling is taking on a more prominent role in the marketing mix. Salespeople must communicate the advantages of their firms' goods and services over those of competitors. They must be able to do the following:

• Focus on a customer's situation and needs and create solutions that meet those needs.

• Follow through and stay in touch before, during, and after the sale.

table 15.1 *Factors Affecting the Importance of Personal Selling in the Promotional Mix*

VARIABLE	CONDITIONS THAT FAVOUR PERSONAL SELLING	CONDITIONS THAT FAVOUR ADVERTISING
Customer	Geographically concentrated	Geographically dispersed
	Relatively low numbers	Relatively high numbers
Product	Expensive	Inexpensive
	Technically complex	Simple to understand
	Custom-made	Standardized
	Special handling requirements	No special handling requirements
	Transactions frequently involve trade-ins	Transactions seldom involve trade-ins
Price	Relatively high	Relatively low

- Know their own industry and their customers' industry, and have a firm grasp not only of their own firm's capabilities but also of their competitors' abilities.

- Work hard to exceed their customers' expectations, even if it means going above and beyond the call of duty.

Relationship marketing affects all aspects of an organization's marketing function, including personal selling. This means marketers in both internal and external relationships must develop different sales skills. Instead of working alone, many salespeople now unite their efforts in sales teams. The customer-focused firm wants its salespeople to form long-lasting relationships with buyers by providing high levels of customer service rather than going for quick sales. Even the way salespeople perform their jobs is constantly changing. Growing numbers of companies have integrated communications and computer technologies into the sales routine. These trends are covered in more detail later in the chapter.

Personal selling is an attractive career choice today. Good salespeople are always in demand as the number of sales positions continues to increase in most industrialized countries. Approximately 10 percent of the Canadian workforce is employed in sales positions.[2] Company executives usually recognize a good salesperson as a performance-oriented person who can solve problems, communicate clearly, and manage relationships. In fact, many corporations are headed by executives who began their careers in sales.

Marketoid

A 48 000-sq.-ft. house in Oakville, Ontario, sold for $45 million in 2006. In 2010, a 65 000-sq.-ft. home—believed to be Canada's largest—was offered for sale for $25 million, in Haileybury, Ontario.

assessment check 1

1.1 What is personal selling?

1.2 What is the main focus of today's salespeople?

THE FOUR SALES CHANNELS

(2) Describe the four sales channels.

Personal selling occurs through several types of communication channels: over-the-counter selling (including online selling), field selling, telemarketing, and inside selling. Each of these channels includes both business-to-business and direct-to-customer selling. Although telemarketing and online selling are lower-cost alternatives, their lack of personal interaction with existing or prospective customers often makes them less effective than personalized, one-to-one field selling and over-the-counter channels. In fact, many organizations use a number of different channels.

OVER-THE-COUNTER SELLING

The most frequently used sales channel, **over-the-counter selling**, typically describes selling in retail and some wholesale locations. Most over-the-counter sales are direct-to-customer, although business customers are frequently served by wholesalers with over-the-counter sales reps. Customers typically

over-the-counter selling Personal selling conducted in retail and some wholesale locations in which customers come to the seller's place of business.

Some Gap and Banana Republic stores added call buttons and delivery doors to their fitting rooms so that salespeople can offer more service.

visit the seller's location on their own initiative to purchase desired items. Some visit their favourite stores because they enjoy shopping. Others respond to many kinds of appeals, including direct mail, personal letters of invitation from store personnel, and advertisements for sales, special events, and new-product introductions.

Marketers are getting increasingly creative in their approach to over-the-counter selling. Sony of Canada holds an annual "Ladies Night"—a special event to engage and inform women on the latest consumer electronics technologies. National marketing manager J. D. Revilla says, "Women account for 70 percent of the buying decisions made about consumer electronics products, according to recent research. Women are also making up an increasingly larger percentage of early adopters of new technology."[3]

Electronics giant Best Buy continues to outsell its competitors; with more than 1000 stores, the firm's sales total more than $50 billion (U.S.).[4] Perhaps Best Buy's success is because of the training its salespeople receive. The training focuses on the firm's mantra: CARE Plus. *C* stands for contact with the customer. *A* means asking questions to learn what the customer needs. *R* represents making recommendations to the customer. *E* stands for encouragement, praising the customer for a wise purchase.

Local retailers often know their customers by name. They also know their customers' likes and dislikes. The owner of a bookstore in your hometown might call you when a new book by your favourite author arrives. Taking a page from this type of selling, Amazon.ca creates personalized messages for its customers as well—even though its salespeople have never met their customers in person. Amazon's software can send you reminders for gift purchases, recommend related purchases, or even stop you from making the same purchase twice. The site also welcomes you by name when you log on.

Regardless of a retailer's innovation, a few things remain the same in selling. For example, customers never like hearing salespeople say the following:

- "That's not my department."

- "If it's not on the rack [or shelf], we don't have it."

- "I don't know. I'm new here."

- "I'm closing" or "I'm on a break."

- "The computer is down."[5]

While these quotes may seem humorous, they also ring true. You've probably heard them, and you may have said them yourself if you've worked in a retail environment. But each statement conveys the message that the salesperson is not willing or able to serve the customer—exactly the opposite of what every marketer wants to convey.

FIELD SELLING

field selling
Sales presentations made at prospective customers' locations on a face-to-face basis.

Field selling involves making sales calls on prospective and existing customers at their businesses or homes. Some situations involve considerable creative effort, such as the sales of major computer installations. Often, the salesperson must convince customers first that they need the good or service and then that they need the particular brand the salesperson is selling. Field sales of large industrial installations such as Boeing's 787 Dreamliner also often require considerable technical expertise.

Largely because it involves travel, field selling is considerably more expensive than other selling options. Rising prices of fuel, air fares, car rentals, and hotel rates have forced up the cost of business trips. Needing to find ways to trim costs while increasing productivity, some firms have replaced

SOLVING AN ETHICAL CONTROVERSY

Hey, Mister? Wanna Buy a Ticket?

WHETHER you attended public or private elementary school, most likely at some time in your childhood you sold merchandise to help your school raise funds. Whether it's drumming up financial support for worthy causes or selling merchandise such as calendars, raffle tickets, or magazine subscriptions, most schools regard their student population as a ready-made sales force, expected to go door to door to sell. Although most schools claim fund-raising is voluntary, it's a fact of life that children feel some pressure to participate in it, if only not to appear "different" from their peers. Many schools are taking a closer look at the nature and number of fund-raisers they sponsor, and some are creating new parameters. For example, many institutions are making the fund-raising task voluntary. But one thing is certain: most people find it hard to say no to a pint-sized salesperson.

Should schools use children as salespersons?

PRO

1. Helping your school raise funds is a rite of passage for kids. And the money raised through such initiatives provides items that a school might not otherwise be able to afford, such as playground equipment, a public-address system, computers, sports equipment, and more.
2. The behaviours involved in selling are important skills for children to learn. Selling to friends and neighbours can help children build confidence and communication skills.

CON

1. Children are in school to learn, not to be mini-salespeople; they should not be responsible for filling their school's coffers. Schools—not their students—are wholly responsible for their financial management.
2. There are safety concerns involved in having children go door to door. If schools need to raise funds, let them hire a professional fund-raising firm.

Where do you stand: pro or con?

Sources: Monica Patrick, "Crafts for Kids to Sell," http://www.ehow.com, August 2, 2010; Daniel Austin, "Schools End Lucrative Casino Fundraisers; Catholic Ban," *National Post*, December 10, 2009, http://www.nationalpost .com; Innocent Madawo, "Why Are Our Schools Using Children As Fundraisers?" *Toronto Sun*, November 9, 2009, http://www.torontosun.com; Sharon Kennedy Wynne, "Run! School Fundraisers Are Coming," *St. Petersburg Times*, September 20, 2009, http://www.tampabay.com; Marilyn Sokol, "Boosters Make Huge Difference at Schools," *St. Petersburg Times*, September 11, 2009, http://www .tampabay.com.

---

certain travel with conference calls, while others require salespeople to stay in less expensive hotels and spend less on meals. Some firms have simply shortened the time allowed for trips.

In fairly routine field selling situations, such as calling on established customers in industries such as food, textiles, or wholesaling, the salesperson basically acts as an order taker who processes regular customers' orders. But more complex situations may involve weeks of preparation, formal presentations, and many hours of post-sales work. Field selling is a lifestyle that many people enjoy; they also cite some of the negatives, such as travel delays and impact on family life. The "Solving an Ethical Controversy" feature describes a controversial type of field selling: schools' and organizations' use of children as salespeople.

Some firms view field selling as a market in itself and have developed goods and services designed to help salespeople do their jobs. Panasonic manufactures the Toughbook series—a line of tablet computers loaded with Microsoft Office software and designed with field sales reps in mind. The computer has a magnesium alloy case—significantly stronger than the plastic cases of standard computers—and is built for rugged handling. The Toughbook can withstand a six-foot drop and is rain-, dust-, and vibration-resistant.[6]

Taking their cue from the successes of businesses such as Avon, Mary Kay Cosmetics, and Tupperware, thousands of smaller businesses now rely on field selling in customers' homes. Often called **network marketing**, this type of personal selling relies on lists of family members and friends of the salesperson or "party host" who organizes a gathering of potential customers for an in-home demonstration of products. Mary Kay Cosmetics, with more than 600 Canadian sales consultants and over 36 000 worldwide, enjoyed global sales of $2.6 billion (U.S.) in one recent year.[7]

Marketoid

Toronto-based Sun Life Financial, in a strategic alliance with Aditya V. Birla Group, has an insurance sales group of more than 148 000 advisors in 600 branches in India.

network marketing
Personal selling that relies on lists of family members and friends of the salesperson, who organizes a gathering of potential customers for a demonstration of products.

Panasonic manufactures the Toughbook series with field sales reps in mind, building a strong case for rugged handling.

The Girl Scouts have been successfully field-selling their cookies for decades, despite an inexperienced sales force and short selling season.

TELEMARKETING

telemarketing
Promotional presentation involving the use of the telephone on an outbound basis by salespeople or on an inbound basis by customers who initiate calls to obtain information and place orders.

outbound telemarketing
Sales method in which sales personnel place phone calls to prospects and try to conclude the sale over the phone.

Telemarketing, a channel in which the selling process is conducted by phone, serves two general purposes—sales and service—and two general markets—business-to-business and direct-to-customer. Both inbound and outbound telemarketing are forms of direct marketing.

Outbound telemarketing involves a sales force that relies on the telephone to contact customers, reducing the substantial costs of personal visits to customers' homes or businesses. Technologies such as predictive diallers, autodialling, and random-digit dialling increase chances that telemarketers will reach customers at home. *Predictive diallers* weed out busy signals and answering machines, nearly doubling the number of calls made per hour. *Autodialling* allows telemarketers to dial numbers continually; when a customer answers the phone, the call is automatically routed to a sales representative. *Random-digit dialling* allows telemarketers to reach unlisted numbers and block caller-ID.

A major drawback of telemarketing is that most consumers dislike the practice. The Canadian Radio-television and Telecommunications Commission implemented the Canadian Do Not Call List in late 2008, and, by the end of 2010, there were nearly 9 million listed numbers, 102 active investigations, and 25 fines. Political parties, registered charities, marketing researchers and pollsters, newspapers, and businesses that have had business dealings with the phone call recipient within the previous 18 months are exempted and can override the list.[8] Xentel DM Inc., however, paid a $500 000 "administrative monetary penalty" for calling consumers who were on the list to promote events both on its own behalf or on behalf of charities that were not registered with the Canada Revenue Agency.[9] Why do some firms still use telemarketing? The average call cost is low, and companies point to a significant rate of success.

Inbound telemarketing typically involves a toll-free number that customers can call to obtain information, make reservations, and purchase goods and services. When a customer calls a toll-free number, the caller can be identified and routed to the person with whom he or she has done business previously, creating a human touch not possible before. This form of selling provides maximum convenience for customers who initiate the sales process. Many large catalogue merchants such as Pottery Barn, L. L. Bean, and Lands' End keep their inbound telemarketing lines open 24 hours a day, 7 days a week.

Some firms are taking dramatic steps to incorporate inbound telemarketing into their overall marketing strategy. The majority of call-centre positions in Canada are inbound positions, and these are beginning to require greater technical knowledge and better sales process skills, resulting in higher salaries.[10] A growing number of inbound customer service jobs across Canada are available for people who wish to work from home.

Telemarketing positions in Canada require greater technical knowledge and better sales process skills, resulting in higher salaries.

INSIDE SELLING

The role of many of today's telemarketers is a combination of field selling techniques applied through inbound and outbound telemarketing channels with a strong customer orientation, called **inside selling**. Inside sales reps perform two primary jobs: they turn opportunities into actual sales, and they support technicians and purchasers with current solutions. Inside sales reps do far more than read a canned script to unwilling prospects. Their role goes beyond taking orders to solving problems, providing customer service, and selling. For this reason, some inside sales positions are paying salaries that approach those of field salespeople, and incentive plans can increase their compensation considerably. A successful inside sales force relies on close working relationships with field sales representatives to solidify customer relationships.

INTEGRATING THE VARIOUS SELLING CHANNELS

Figure 15.1 illustrates how firms are likely to blend alternative sales channels—over-the-counter selling, field selling, telemarketing, and inside selling—to create a successful cost-effective sales organization. Existing customers whose business problems require complex solutions are likely to be best served by the traditional field sales force. Other current customers who need answers but not the same attention as the first group can be served by inside sales reps who call on them as needed. Over-the-counter sales reps serve existing customers by supplying information and advice and completing sales transactions. Telemarketers may be used to strengthen communication with customers or to re-establish relationships with customers that may have lapsed over a few months.

inbound telemarketing
Sales method in which prospects call a seller to obtain information, make reservations, and purchase goods and services.

inside selling
Selling by phone, mail, and electronic commerce.

Marketoid

In December 2010, Bell Canada received a $1.3-million fine, the largest ever handed out by the Canadian Radio-television and Telecommunications Commission for violating Canada's telemarketing laws.

assessment check 2

2.1 What is over-the-counter selling?

2.2 What is field selling?

2.3 Distinguish between inbound and outbound telemarketing.

figure 15.1

Alternative Sales Channels for Serving Customers

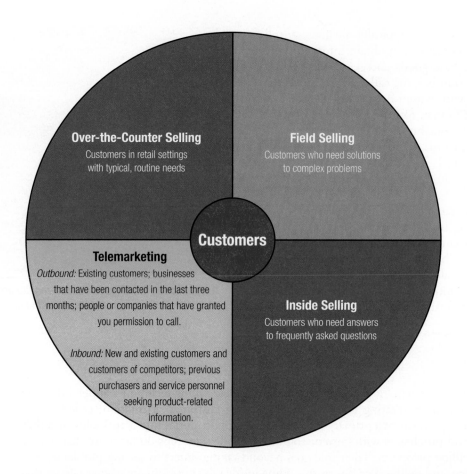

③ Describe the major trends in personal selling.

TRENDS IN PERSONAL SELLING

In today's complex marketing environment, effective personal selling requires different strategies from those used by salespeople in the past. As pointed out in the discussion of *buying centres* in Chapter 5, rather than selling one on one, in B2B settings it is now customary to sell to teams of corporate representatives who participate in the client firm's decision-making process. In business-to-business sales situations involving technical products, customers expect salespeople to answer technical questions—or bring along someone who can. They also want representatives who understand technical jargon and can communicate using sophisticated technological tools. Patience is also a requirement because the B2B sales cycle, from initial contact to closing, may take months or even years. To address all these concerns, companies rely on three major personal selling approaches: relationship selling, consultative selling, and team selling. Regardless of the approach, however, experts agree on a few basic guidelines for conducting successful personal selling.

RELATIONSHIP SELLING

relationship selling
Regular contacts between sales representatives and customers over an extended period to establish a sustained seller–buyer relationship.

Most firms now emphasize **relationship selling**, a technique for building a mutually beneficial partnership with a customer through regular contacts over an extended period. Such buyer–seller bonds become increasingly important as companies cut back on the number of suppliers and look for companies that provide high levels of customer service and satisfaction. Salespeople must also find ways to distinguish themselves and their products from competitors. To create strong, long-lasting relationships with customers, salespeople must meet buyers' expectations. Table 15.2 summarizes the results of several surveys that indicate what buyers expect of professional salespeople.

The success of tomorrow's marketers depends on the relationships they build today in both the business-to-consumer and business-to-business markets. Discount Car & Truck Rentals has been in business for more than 30 years and has a history of building strong customer relationships through

table 15.2 *What Buyers Expect from Salespeople*

Buyers prefer to do business with salespeople who

- Orchestrate events and bring to bear whatever resources are necessary to satisfy the customer
- Provide counselling to the customer based on in-depth knowledge of the product, the market, and the customer's needs
- Solve problems proficiently to ensure satisfactory customer service over extended time periods
- Demonstrate high ethical standards and communicate honestly at all times
- Willingly advocate the customer's cause within the selling organization
- Create imaginative arrangements to meet buyers' needs
- Arrive well prepared for sales calls

its innovative customer service. The company was the first in Canada to focus on the insurance replacement business, to offer customer pick-up and drop-off service, and to implement a customer loyalty program: its One, Two, Free program, providing customers with a free third-weekend rental.[11]

Relationship selling is equally important in business-to-business sales, if not more so. Discount Car & Truck Rentals has built strong relationships with its business customers by meeting their demand for commercial truck rentals when their resources are strained due to high-peak periods. Owner Herb Singer says, "We're their safety valve."[12]

CONSULTATIVE SELLING

Field representatives and inside sales reps require sales methods that satisfy today's cost-conscious, knowledgeable buyers. One such method, **consultative selling**, involves meeting customer needs by listening to customers, understanding—and caring about—their problems, paying attention to details, and following through after the sale. It works hand in hand with relationship selling in building customer loyalty. Xerox has turned itself around by employing consultative selling. Keith Stock, vice president of education and learning for North America, recalls, "We've become very focused on the customer[s] and helping them solve their business problems, rather than just placing another piece of equipment. We identify opportunities at the customer site and turn that into sales for Xerox."[13]

Online companies have instituted consultative selling models to create long-term customers. Particularly for complicated, high-priced products that require installation or specialized service, Web sellers must be able to quickly communicate the benefits and features of their products. They accomplish this through consultative selling.

Cross-selling—offering many goods or services to the same customer—is another technique that capitalizes on a firm's strengths. It costs a bank five times more to acquire a new customer than to cross-sell to an existing one. Moreover, research shows that the more a customer buys from an institution, the less likely that person is to leave. So a customer who opens a chequing account at a local bank may follow with a safety deposit box, a mortgage loan, and a guaranteed line of credit.

TEAM SELLING

Another development in the evolution of personal selling is **team selling**, in which the salesperson joins with specialists from other functional areas of the firm to complete the selling process. Teams can be formal and ongoing or created for a specific short-term selling situation. Although some salespeople have hesitated to embrace the idea of team selling, preferring to work alone, a growing number believe that team selling brings better results. Customers often prefer the team approach, which makes them feel well served. Consider a restaurant meal. If the host, servers, wine steward, chef, and kitchen crew are all working well together as a team, your experience at the restaurant is likely to be positive. But if the service stops and starts, your order is recorded wrong, the food is cold, the silverware is dirty, and the staff seems grouchy, you probably won't eat at that restaurant again. In fact, you may not even finish the meal.

consultative selling
Meeting customer needs by listening to customers, understanding their problems, paying attention to details, and following through after the sale.

cross-selling
Selling several, often unrelated, goods and services to the same customer based on knowledge of that customer's needs.

team selling
Selling situation in which several sales associates or other members of the organization are recruited to assist the lead sales representative in reaching all those who influence the purchase decision.

If It Walks, Talks, and Looks Like a Salesperson . . .

WHILE people say you can't tell a book by its cover, it's human nature to form impressions about others from their appearance. If you want a career in sales, pay attention to your appearance. Successful salespeople know the first hurdle is dressing in a way that makes others feel comfortable. In industries where it's important that customers feel confident about the service rendered, such as airlines and hospitals, employees often wear uniforms. Other employers may specify a general dress code so their employees are easily distinguishable.

Unfortunately, some firms don't give their employees much guidance on dressing for sales calls. But a prospective customer will notice your appearance and form an impression about you. Although great latitude exists in industries like entertainment, here's what's safe to wear in most other settings:

- Men: Two-piece suit and dress shirt. Shirt and tie can be plain or patterned, as long as they complement each other. Shoes may be oxfords or loafers, and remember to shine them.
- Women: Skirt suit or pantsuit, with a shirt or shell under the jacket, or a dress with a jacket. Low- to medium-heeled shoes with stockings. In some settings, women can wear contrasting jacket-skirt or jacket-pants combinations.
- For both genders: A blazer or sport coat and dress pants, or even a golf shirt and khakis, are acceptable in some industries. Just make sure everything is clean and pressed. Watch your personal hygiene and don't go overboard with fragrances.
- What's *never* appropriate on a sales call: denim, T-shirts, bare feet, athletic shoes, or flip-flops. Anything tight fitting, low cut, or midriff baring. Avoid visible tattoos and piercings, other than a couple in the earlobe.
- A rule of thumb: If in doubt, it's better to be a bit overdressed rather than underdressed. It shows respect for your customer.

Sources: Thad Peterson, "Dress Appropriately for Interviews," Monster.com, http://career-advice.monster.com, May 6, 2010; "Dress for Success No Matter What Your Job," *St. Petersburg Times*, March 13, 2010, http://www.tampabay.com; Walethia Aquil, "Dress for Success in 2010," SelfGrowth.com, January 14, 2010, http://www.selfgrowth.com.

Another advantage of team selling is the formation of relationships between companies rather than between individuals. In sales situations that call for detailed knowledge of new, complex, and ever-changing technologies, team selling offers a distinct competitive edge in meeting customers' needs. In most computer software B2B departments, a third of the sales force is made up of technically trained, nonmarketing experts such as engineers or programmers. A salesperson continues to play the lead role in most sales situations, but technical experts bring added value to the sales process. Some companies establish permanent sales-and-tech teams that conduct all sales presentations together; others have a pool of engineers or other professionals who are on call for different client visits.

virtual sales team
Network of strategic partners, suppliers, and others who recommend a firm's goods or services.

Some resourceful entrepreneurs have begun building a **virtual sales team**—a network of strategic partners, trade associations, suppliers, and others who are qualified and willing to recommend a firm's goods or services. Vancouver-based Indochino, with customers in 60 countries, bills itself "a global leader in online custom-made suits" and targets men who don't have access to traditional custom tailors. It has cut costs by selling directly to customers, without using expensive sales staff. Customers take their own measurements, then Indochino, through its office in Shanghai where its suits are assembled, produces the suits, which it sells for around $400.[14]

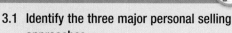

assessment check 3

3.1 Identify the three major personal selling approaches.

3.2 Distinguish between relationship selling and consultative selling.

④ Identify and briefly describe the three basic sales tasks.

SALES TASKS

Today's salesperson is more concerned with establishing long-term buyer–seller relationships and helping customers select the correct products for meeting their needs than with simply selling whatever is available. Where repeat purchases are common, the salesperson must be certain that the buyer's purchases are in his or her best interest; otherwise, no future relationship will be possible. The seller's interests are tied to the buyer's in a mutually beneficial relationship.

While all sales activities assist the customer in some manner, they are not all alike. Three basic sales tasks can be identified: (1) order processing, (2) creative selling, and (3) missionary sales. Most of today's salespeople are not limited to performing tasks in a single category. Instead, they often perform all three tasks to some extent. A sales engineer for a computer firm may be doing 50 percent missionary sales, 45 percent creative selling, and 5 percent order processing. Most sales positions are classified on the basis of the primary selling task performed.

Then there's the philosophy that *everyone* in the organization, regardless of what his or her job description is, should be engaged in selling. Calgary-based WestJet believes delivering great customer service is paramount for every employee, from the reservations agent to the baggage handler to the flight attendant. This strong service culture earned WestJet the 2010 Airline Staff Service Excellence Award North America at the World Airline Awards in Hamburg, Germany.[15]

ORDER PROCESSING

Order processing, which can involve both field selling and telemarketing, is most often typified by selling at the wholesale and retail levels. For instance, a Pepsi-Cola route salesperson who performs this task must take the following steps:

order processing
Selling, mostly at the wholesale and retail levels, that involves identifying customer needs, pointing them out to customers, and completing orders.

1. *Identify customer needs.* The route salesperson determines that a store has only seven cases left in stock when it normally carries an inventory of 40 cases.

2. *Point out the need to the customer.* The route salesperson informs the store manager of the inventory situation.

3. *Complete (write up) the order.* The store manager acknowledges the need for more of the product. The driver unloads 33 cases of Mountain Dew, and the manager signs the delivery slip.

Order processing is part of most selling positions. It becomes the primary task in situations where needs can be readily identified and are acknowledged by the customer. Even in such instances, however, salespeople whose primary responsibility involves order processing will devote some time persuading their wholesale or retail customers to carry more complete inventories of their firms' merchandise or to handle additional product lines. They also are likely to try to motivate purchasers to feature some of their firms' products, increase the amount of shelf space devoted to these items, and improve product location in the stores.

Technology now streamlines order-processing tasks. Some retailers now use interactive store kiosks, a recent innovation that provides a touch screen that lets customers browse a store's catalogue, compare brands and product features, and even place their order—all from a single user-friendly device, putting an end to endlessly cruising store aisles in search of sales staff.[16]

CREATIVE SELLING

When a considerable amount of decision making is involved in purchasing a good or service, an effective salesperson uses creative selling techniques to solicit an order. In contrast to the order-processing task, which deals mainly with maintaining existing business, creative selling generally is used to develop new business either by adding new customers or by introducing new goods and services. New products or upgrades to more expensive items often require creative selling. The salesperson must first identify the customer's problems and needs and then propose a solution in the form of the good or service being offered. When a company is attempting to expand an existing business relationship, creative selling techniques are used in over-the-counter selling, field selling, inside selling, and telemarketing.

creative selling
Personal selling that involves situations in which a considerable degree of analytical decision making on the buyer's part results in the need for skillful proposals of solutions for the customer's needs.

Creative selling can generate "buzz" for a product. When Ford wanted to create excitement about its new small car, the Fiesta, it launched an imaginative campaign that involved offering 100 consumers the opportunity to drive a Fiesta at no charge for six months. The only condition: each individual was to drive the car someplace different each month, then report the results on such social media as Facebook, Twitter, and YouTube. As a result, Fiesta garnered 6.5 million YouTube views, and Ford received 50 000 requests for more information about the Fiesta. In the first six days of the campaign, the company sold 10 000 cars.[17]

When Ford wanted to create excitement about its new Fiesta, it launched a campaign that involved offering 100 consumers the opportunity to drive a Fiesta at no charge for six months.

© TERRI MILLER/E-VISUAL COMMUNICATIONS, INC.

missionary selling
Indirect type of selling in which specialized salespeople promote the firm's goodwill among indirect customers, often by assisting customers in product use.

sales incentives
Programs that reward salespeople for superior performance.

⑤ Outline the seven steps in the sales process.

MISSIONARY SELLING

Missionary selling is an indirect approach to sales. Salespeople sell the firm's goodwill and provide their customers with information and technical or operational assistance. A cosmetics company salesperson may call on retailers to check on special promotions and overall product movement, even though a wholesaler takes orders and delivers merchandise. For years, large pharmaceutical companies operated the most aggressive missionary selling, courting doctors (the indirect customer) by providing lavish restaurant meals, educational seminars, and other incentives in the hope of persuading them to prescribe a particular brand to patients. While the doctor is clearly the decision maker, the transaction is not complete until the patient hands the prescription over to a pharmacist. But recent changes to the code of ethical practices established by Canada's Research-Based Pharmaceutical Companies (Rx&D) prohibit missionary salespeople from offering incentives of value to their customers. Salespeople must now focus on educating health care professionals.[18]

Some missionary salespeople, however, do offer **sales incentives** such as trips, gas cards, free product upgrades, and other inducements to their customers. Missionary sales may involve both field selling and telemarketing. Many aspects of team selling can also be seen as missionary sales, as when technical support salespeople help design, install, and maintain equipment; when they train customers' employees; and when they provide information or operational assistance.

assessment check 4

4.1 What are the three major tasks performed by salespeople?

4.2 What are the three steps of order processing?

THE SALES PROCESS

If you have worked in a retail store, or if you've sold magazine subscriptions or candy to raise money for your school or sports team, you will recognize many of the activities involved in the following list of steps in the sales process. Personal selling encompasses the following sequence of activities: (1) prospecting and qualifying, (2) approach, (3) presentation, (4) demonstration, (5) handling buyer concerns, (6) closing, and (7) follow-up.

As Figure 15.2 indicates, these steps follow the AIDA concept (attention-interest-desire-action). Once a sales prospect has been qualified, an attempt is made to secure his or her attention. The presentation and demonstration steps are designed to generate interest and desire. Successful handling of buyer resistance should arouse further desire. Action occurs at the close of the sale.

Salespeople modify the steps in this process to match their customers' buying processes. A neighbour who eagerly looks forward to the local symphony orchestra's new concert season each year needs no presentation except for details about scheduled performances and perhaps whether any famous musicians will be on the bill. But the same neighbour would expect a demonstration from an auto dealer when looking for a new car or might appreciate a presentation of dinner specials by the waiter prior to ordering a meal at a restaurant.

PROSPECTING AND QUALIFYING

Prospecting, the process of identifying potential customers, may involve hours, days, or weeks of effort, but it is a necessary step. Leads about prospects come from many sources: the Internet, computerized databases, trade show exhibits, previous customers, friends and neighbours, other vendors, non-sales employees in the firm, suppliers, and social and professional contacts. Although a firm may emphasize personal selling as the primary component of its overall promotional strategy, direct mail and advertising campaigns are also effective in identifying prospective customers.

Before salespeople begin their prospecting effort, they must be clear about what their firm is selling and create a "brand story," that is, define their product in terms of what it can do for a customer. Because customers are generally looking for solutions to problems or ways to make their lives better or businesses more successful, this focus on the customer is critical. Once they develop a brand story, the sales team must be consistent about telling it at every possible point of contact, whether in a face-to-face conversation with a prospect, in advertising, or in promoting the product to the media.[19]

figure 15.2

The AIDA Concept and the Personal Selling Process

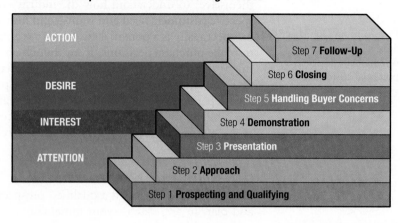

prospecting
Personal selling function of identifying potential customers.

MARKETING AND THE SME	**Master of the Double Sell**

IT has often been said that nothing happens until somebody sells something. In many small businesses, that somebody is often the president or owner. Dean Pelley, president and CEO of Mad Rock Marine Solutions Inc., certainly knows this. He is a master of the "double sell"—first to get regulatory approval, and then to actual customers.

As a graduate student at Memorial University, he and colleague Jason Dawe started their company in order to build a better lifeboat.

However, they soon narrowed their focus to just lifeboat hooks. They discovered that the industry standard was for "fail open" hooks, which meant that the hooks defaulted to the open position if there were problems during launch. Passengers were frequently injured or even killed as lifeboats then spilled occupants into the water. Dean and Jason, following eight prototypes and three years of R&D, finally received regulatory approval for their RocLoc, a lifeboat hook with a "fail closed" design. But the approval came after a lot of selling. Dean, through a graduate school connection, secured a spot as a Canadian delegate to the London-based International Maritime Organization (IMO) in 2004. He had to do a lot of lobbying to get approval, which he finally received in 2005. But his RocLoc, at $25 000 each, was considerably more expensive than fail-open hooks. With

two lifeboats on most typical ships, each of which would need a RocLoc, Pelley had a considerable job to sell his product to ship owners, who generally favoured the least expensive alternative that satisfied regulatory conditions.

The first RocLoc order came in 2006. Pelley made several sales trips to Norway, where he received help from Canadian trade commissioners, who identified prospects, set up appointments, and, in one instance, even chauffeured him between sales calls. Pelley says, "They gave us the credibility. The fact that a trade commissioner was setting up the meeting assured foreign clients that we weren't some fly-by-night operation." Sales now approach $4 million, mostly to customers in the United States and Singapore. Pelley continues his lobbying at the IMO, and in 2010 a technical subcommittee of the IMO recommended that the fail-closed design become the new minimum standard. If such approval is eventually received, Pelley will have a lot more selling to do. He estimates there are 40 000 ships worldwide that would need their hooks replaced. At $50 000 per ship, that is growth opportunity.

Sources: Anonymous, "If You Can't Beat 'Em, Then Change the Rules, *Profit*, December 2010–January 2011, p. 46; Annette Bourdeau, "New and Improved," *Profit*, May 2009, pp. 38–39, 41, 43; Anonymous, "Lots of Sympathy, a Little Advice," *Canadian Business*, April 11–24, 2005, pp. 76–77.

In addition, salespeople must be well informed about the goods and services of the industry in general. They need to find out how other goods are marketed and packaged. They can try out a service themselves to understand how the industry operates. In these ways, they will understand what prospective customers need and want—and how they can serve them. **Qualifying**—determining that the prospect really is a potential customer—is another important sales task. Not all prospects are qualified to make purchase decisions. Even though an employee in a firm might like your products, he or she might not be authorized to make the purchase. A consumer who test-drives a Porsche might fall in love with it—but not be able to afford the purchase price. Qualifying can be a two-way street. As a sales representative, you might determine that a certain prospect is qualified to make a purchase. But the prospect must agree in order for the process to go forward. If either you or the prospect determine at the outset that there's no chance for a purchase, then it's best to move on.

APPROACH

Once you have identified a qualified prospect, you need to collect all available, relevant information and plan an **approach**—your initial contact with the prospective customer. If your firm already has a relationship with the customer or has permission to contact the person, you may use telemarketing. But, before you do so, gather as much information as you can.

Information gathering makes **precall planning** possible. As mentioned earlier, educate yourself about the industry in general, as well as goods and services offered by competitors. Read any marketing research that is available. Go to trade shows—you can learn a lot about many companies and their products at one location, usually in one day. Also learn as much as you can about the firm you are planning to approach—browse the company's website, find online news articles and press releases about the company, talk with other people in the industry. Know its product offerings well. If possible, buy at least one of the firm's products and use it yourself. Identify ways you can help the firm do whatever it does better. Without invading an individual customer's privacy, see if there is anything you have in common—perhaps you grew up in the same town or you both like to play golf.[20] All of this planning will help you make an effective approach.

As you plan your approach, try to answer the following questions:

- Whom am I approaching and what are their jobs within the company?

- What is their level of knowledge? Are they already informed about the idea I am going to present?

- What do they want or need? Should I speak in technical terms or provide general information?

- What do they need to hear? Do they need to know more about specific products or how those products can serve them? Do they need to know how the product works? Do they need to know about cost and availability?

If you are a retail salesperson, you can ask a shopper questions to learn more about his or her needs and preferences. Say you work at a large sporting-goods store. You might ask a young male shopper whether he works out at home, what equipment he already has, what his fitness goals are. The answers to these questions should lead you in the direction of a sale.

PRESENTATION

In a **presentation**, you convey your marketing message to the potential customer. You will describe the product's major features, point out its strengths, and cite other customers' successes with the product. One popular form of presentation is a *features-benefits* framework wherein you talk about the good or service in terms that are meaningful to the buyer. If you work for a car dealership, you might point out safety features such as side airbags and built-in car seats to a young couple.

Your presentation should be well organized, clear, and concise. If appropriate, you might use visual sales support materials such as a chart, a brochure, a DVD, or a video streamed from your laptop. If this is your first presentation to a potential customer, it will likely be more detailed than a routine call to give an existing customer some updates. Regardless of the situation, though, be attuned to your audience's response so you can modify your presentation—even on the spur of the moment— to meet their needs.

qualifying
Determining a prospect's needs, income, and purchase authority as a potential customer.

approach
Salesperson's initial contact with a prospective customer.

precall planning
Use of information collected during the prospecting and qualifying stages of the sales process and during previous contacts with the prospect to tailor the approach and presentation to match the customer's needs.

presentation
Personal selling function of describing a product's major features and relating them to a customer's problems or needs.

Making effective presentations is an important skill when selling products, services, or ideas.

H. F. (HERB) MACKENZIE

Many presentations now use computer-based multimedia, which can offer everything from interactivity to current pricing information. Companies like SlideShare and BrainShark, which enable users to share their presentations online, are now offering video capabilities. Users can embed video into their presentations along with traditional PowerPoint slides and other images.[21] However, technology must be used efficiently to be effective. For example, a company's website can be an excellent selling tool if it is easy for salespeople to present and buyers to use. A salesperson can actually use the site during a presentation by showing a potential customer how to use it to learn about and purchase products.[22]

In a **cold calling** situation, the approach and presentation often take place at the same time. Cold calling means phoning or visiting the customer without a prior appointment—and making a sales pitch on the spot. Cold calling requires nerve, skill, and creativity—but salespeople who are successful at it still point to the importance of preparation. Steven J. Schwartz, a Canadian sales trainer and coach, says that with good call planning, strategic message scripting, and effective message delivery, telephone cold calls can be turned into hot calls.[23]

cold calling
Contacting a prospect without a prior appointment.

DEMONSTRATION

One of the most important advantages of personal selling is the opportunity to demonstrate a product. During a **demonstration**, the buyer gets a chance to try the product or at least see how it works. A demonstration might involve a test drive of the latest hybrid car or an in-store cooking class using pots and pans that are for sale.

Many firms use new technologies to make their demonstrations more outstanding than those of their competitors. Multimedia interactive demonstrations are now common. Visitors to the Black & Decker website can click on video demonstrations of such products as the Alligator Lopper (an electric branch clipper) and the Scumbuster Extreme power floor scrubber.[24] The key to an outstanding demonstration—one that gains the customer's attention, keeps his or her interest, is convincing, and stays in the customer's memory—is planning. But planning should also include time and space for improvisation. During your demonstration, you should be prepared to stop and answer questions, redemonstrate a certain feature, or even let the customer try the product firsthand.

demonstration
Stage in the personal selling process in which the customer has the opportunity to try out or otherwise see how a good or service works before purchase.

table 15.3   *Common Buyer Concerns*

CONCERN RELATED TO:	QUESTION	STATEMENT
Product	What makes this product unique?	I don't see why this product is better than the one I have.
Price	Is this the best price you can offer?	Your price is certainly not within my budget.
Source	Will you be with this company next year if I have a problem?	I am very satisfied with my current supplier.
Time	Why would I want to buy more hockey equipment in May?	May is a poor month to buy hockey equipment.
Need	Why do I need a new cell phone?	I already have a cell phone that meets my needs.

HANDLING BUYER CONCERNS

buyer concerns
Expressions of sales resistance by the prospect.

Buyer concerns—sometimes called *objections*—are expressions of sales resistance. Potential customers often have legitimate questions and concerns about a good or service they are considering, so it is reasonable for a salesperson to expect them. There are five types of concerns: product, price, source, time, and need. They may be expressed as questions or statements, as illustrated in Table 15.3. Concerns might appear in the form of stalling or indecisiveness. "Let me call you back," your customer might say, or "I need to talk to Ed about this."

You can answer concerns without being aggressive or rude. Use a buyer concern as an opportunity to reassure your buyer about price, features, durability, availability, and the like. If the objection involves price, you might be able to suggest a less expensive model or a payment plan. If the concern involves a comparison to competitive products, point out the obvious—and not so obvious—benefits of your own.

CLOSING

closing Stage of the personal selling process in which the salesperson asks the customer to make a purchase decision.

The moment of truth in selling is the **closing**—the point at which the salesperson asks the prospect for an order. If your presentation has been effective and you have handled all buyer concerns, a closing would be the natural conclusion to the meeting. But you may still find it difficult to close the sale. Closing does not have to be thought of as a hard sell. Instead, a salesperson can ask low-pressure questions such as "Would you like to give this a try?" "Can I answer any more questions for you?" or "May I have your approval to proceed?"

Other methods of closing include the following:

1. Addressing the prospect's major concern about a purchase and then offering a convincing argument. ("If I can show you how the new heating system will reduce your energy costs by 25 percent, would you be willing to let us install it?")

2. Posing choices for the prospect in which either alternative represents a sale. (Would you prefer the pink sweater or the green one?)

3. Advising the prospect that a product is about to be discontinued or will go up in price soon. (But be completely honest about this—you don't want a customer to learn later that this was not true.)

4. Remaining silent so the prospect can make a decision on his or her own.

5. Offering an extra inducement designed to motivate a favourable buyer response, such as a quantity discount, an extended service contract, or a low-interest payment plan.

Even if the meeting or phone call ends without a sale, the effort is not over. You can use a written note or an email to keep communication open, letting the buyer know that you are ready and waiting to be of service.

FOLLOW-UP

The word *close* can be misleading because the point at which the prospect accepts the seller's offer is where much of the real work of selling begins. In today's competitive environment, the most successful salespeople make sure that today's customers will also be tomorrow's.

| MARKETING IN A DIGITAL WORLD | **Managing Customer Relationships with Social Media** |

SUCCESSFUL salespeople are particularly good at establishing and maintaining strong personal and business relationships. Today, many are finding ways to do so through social media. Many customers—both individuals and businesses—are using social media, and they often post information that a salesperson should monitor, and possibly respond to, if relationship management is a priority. Your customers may be active on Facebook, LinkedIn, Twitter, and other similar sites. Most of these social media allow you to receive alerts—that is, be notified—when new postings relevant to you occur. You should monitor this activity, watching for important relationship information.

Some posters provide information on their personal interests and activities, including birthdays, celebrations, vacations, hobbies, and other notable life experiences. You can respond instantly, if appropriate, adding more information or simply acknowledging their posting. Or you might record the information in your personal database and use it during a subsequent sales call to point out common interests or friends, or simply to make some social contact with your customer during the early part of your sales call. You can sometimes also be forewarned about topics to avoid or things that you might not want to mention during a sales presentation.

If you are a frequent user of social media yourself, be sure your postings help build your professional image. Remember that once you hit "send," you no longer have control over what you said, how it will be used, or where, in the future, it might appear.

It is not enough to close the sale and move on. Relationship selling involves reinforcing the purchase decision and making sure the company delivers the highest-quality merchandise. As a salesperson, you must also ensure that customer service needs are met and that satisfaction results from all of a customer's dealings with your company. Otherwise, some other company may get the next order.

These post-sale activities, which often determine whether a person will become a repeat customer, constitute the sales **follow-up**. Sales experts believe in a wide array of follow-up techniques, ranging from expensive information folders to less expensive holiday cards and online greetings. Some suggest phone calls at regular intervals. Others prefer automatic email reminders when it is time to renew or reorder. At the very least, however, you should try to contact customers to find out whether they are satisfied with their purchases. This step allows you to psychologically reinforce the customer's original decision to buy. It also gives you an opportunity to correct any problems and ensure the next sale. Follow-up helps strengthen the bond you are trying to build with customers in relationship selling. You have probably experienced follow-up as a customer—if your auto dealership called to see if you were satisfied with recent service, or if your veterinarian phoned to find out if your pet was feeling better.

follow-up Post-sale activities that often determine whether an individual who has made a recent purchase will become a repeat customer.

assessment check 5

5.1 Identify the seven steps of the sales process.

5.2 Why is follow-up important to the sales effort?

MANAGING THE SALES EFFORT

 6 Identify the seven basic functions of a sales manager.

The overall direction and control of the personal selling effort are in the hands of sales managers. In a typical geographic sales structure, a district or divisional sales manager might report to a regional or zone manager. This manager in turn reports to a national sales manager or vice president of sales.

The sales manager's job requires a unique blend of administrative and sales skills depending on the specific level in the sales hierarchy. Sales skills are particularly important for first-level sales managers because they are involved daily in the continuing process of training and directly leading the sales force. But as people rise in the sales management hierarchy, they require more managerial skills and fewer sales skills to perform well. Ann Livermore, executive vice president of Hewlett-Packard, is passionate about her job. While her company has traditionally maintained an engineering focus, she has recently steered it toward a sales focus by hiring upper-level managers and executives with sales backgrounds. "There's a new energy about closing deals—about hating to lose," she says. "It's easier for an engineer to analytically describe why you lost a deal. But sales managers are much more emotional about it. There's a different hunger."[25]

Sales force management links individual salespeople to general management. The sales manager performs seven basic managerial functions: (1) recruitment and selection, (2) training, (3) organization, (4) supervision, (5) motivation, (6) compensation, and (7) evaluation and control. Sales managers perform these tasks in a demanding and complex environment. They must manage an increasingly diverse sales force that includes more women and minorities. Women account for almost half of Canadian professional salespeople, and their numbers are growing at a faster rate than that for men. As the workforce composition continues to change, an even more diverse blend of people will be needed to fill a growing number of sales positions.[26]

RECRUITMENT AND SELECTION

Recruiting and selecting successful salespeople are among the sales manager's greatest challenges. After all, these people will collectively determine just how successful the sales manager is. New salespeople—like you—might come from colleges and universities, trade and business schools, other companies, and even the firm's current non-sales staff. A successful sales career offers satisfaction in all the following five areas that a person generally considers when deciding on a profession:

1. *Opportunity for advancement.* Salespeople work in positions of high visibility, and good salespeople can demonstrate their ability to perform in a short period of time. This places them in an excellent position for advancement as opportunities arise.

2. *Potential for high earnings.* Salespeople have the opportunity to earn among the highest salaries in many organizations.

3. *Personal satisfaction.* A salesperson derives satisfaction from achieving success in a competitive environment and from helping customers satisfy their wants and needs.

4. *Job security.* Selling provides a high degree of job security because there is always a need for good salespeople. Selling skills are also frequently transferable from one sales job to another.

5. *Independence and variety.* Salespeople often work independently, calling on customers in their territory. They have the freedom to make important decisions about meeting their customers' needs and frequently report that no two workdays are the same.

Careful selection of salespeople is important for two reasons. First, a company invests a substantial amount of time and money in the selection process. Second, hiring mistakes can damage relationships with customers and overall performance and are also costly to correct. Most larger firms use a seven-step process in selecting sales personnel: application screening, initial interview, in-depth interview, testing, reference checks, physical examination, and hiring decision. An application screening is typically followed by an initial interview. If the applicant looks promising, an in-depth interview is conducted. During the interview, a sales manager looks for the person's enthusiasm, organizational skills, ambition, persuasiveness, ability to follow instructions, and sociability.

Next, the company may administer aptitude, interest, and knowledge tests. One testing approach gaining in popularity is the assessment centre. This technique, which uses situational exercises, group discussions, and various job simulations,

H. F. (HERB) MACKENZIE

During an interview, a sales manager looks for enthusiasm, organizational skills, sociability, and other traits.

allows the sales manager to measure a candidate's skills, knowledge, and ability. Assessment centres enable managers to see what potential salespeople can do rather than what they say they can do. Before hiring a candidate, firms should check references and review company policies. Once a job offer has been made, firms can request a physical examination; however, they are required by law in Canada to make reasonable accommodation for people with a disability, unless it will cause undue hardship for the company.

TRAINING

To shape new sales recruits into an efficient sales organization, managers must conduct an effective training program. The principal methods used in sales training are on-the-job training, individual instruction, in-house classes, and external seminars.

Popular training techniques include instructional videos or DVDs, lectures, role-playing exercises, and interactive computer programs. Simulations can help salespeople improve their selling techniques. Many firms supplement their training by enrolling salespeople in executive development programs at local colleges and by hiring specialists to teach customized training programs. In other instances, sales reps attend courses and workshops developed by outside companies. Salespeople can earn the Certified Sales Professional (CSP) designation after successfully completing training through the Canadian Professional Sales Association. This training program focuses on consultative selling, an approach discussed earlier in this chapter, which is particularly appropriate for business-to-business sales, but also for financial services sales, or anywhere that understanding customer needs is especially important.

Some companies incorporate training into their regular sales meetings. In such settings, colleagues share their experiences and are motivated to reassess their own skills and try new techniques. Ongoing sales training is important for both new and veteran salespeople. Sales managers often conduct training informally, travelling with field reps and then offering constructive criticism or suggestions. Mentoring programs can be especially effective for new salespeople.

ORGANIZATION

Sales managers are responsible for the organization of the field sales force. General organizational alignments, which are usually made by top marketing management, may be based on geography, products, types of customers, or some combination of these factors. Figure 15.3 presents a streamlined organizational chart illustrating each of these alignments.

A product sales organization is likely to have a specialized sales force for each major category of the firm's products. This approach is common among industrial product companies that market large numbers of highly technical, complex products that are sold through different marketing channels.

Firms that market similar products throughout large territories often use geographic specialization. Multinational corporations may have different sales divisions in different countries. A geographic organization may also be combined with one of the other organizational methods. However, many companies are moving away from using territorial sales reps as they adopt customer-focused sales forces. For example, a single territory that contains two major customers might be redefined so the same sales rep covers both customers. Customer-oriented organizations use different sales force strategies for each major type of customer served. Some firms assign separate sales forces for their consumer and organizational customers. Others have sales forces for specific industries,

figure 15.3

Basic Approaches to Organizing the Sales Force

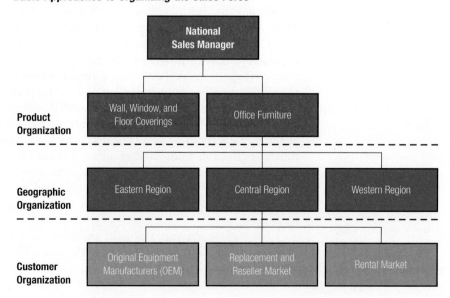

such as financial services, educational, and automotive. Sales forces can also be organized by customer size, with a separate sales force assigned to large, medium, and small accounts.

national accounts organization
Promotional effort in which a dedicated sales team is assigned to a firm's major customers to provide sales and service needs.

Many firms using a customer-oriented structure adopt a **national accounts organization**. This format strengthens a firm's relationship with its largest customers by assigning senior sales personnel or sales teams to major accounts. Organizing by national accounts helps sales representatives develop cooperation among departments to meet special needs of the firm's most important customers. An example of national account selling is the relationship between Walmart and its major vendors. Walmart Canada is such an important account that many of its suppliers, including Procter & Gamble, have dedicated several salespeople who are responsible solely for this one account. Other examples of companies that have national accounts programs in Canada are Bell Mobility, Johnson & Johnson, Elizabeth Arden, and McCain Foods.

As companies expand their market coverage across national borders, they may use a variant of national account sales teams. These global account teams may be staffed by local sales representatives in the countries in which a company is operating. In other instances, the firm selects highly trained sales executives from its domestic operations. In either case, specialized training is critical to the success of a company's global sales force.

The individual sales manager also has the task of organizing the sales territories within his or her area of responsibility. Factors such as sales potential, strengths and weaknesses of available personnel, and workloads are considered in territory allocation decisions.

SUPERVISION

span of control
Number of representatives who report to first-level sales managers.

Sales managers have differing opinions about the supervision of a sales force. Individuals and situations vary, so it is impossible to write a recipe for the exact amount of supervision needed in all cases. However, a concept known as **span of control** helps provide some general guidelines. Span of control refers to the number of sales representatives who report to first-level sales managers. The optimal span of control is affected by such factors as complexity of work activities, ability of the individual sales manager, degree of interdependence among individual salespeople, and the extent of training each salesperson receives. A 6-to-1 ratio has been suggested as the optimal span of control for first-level sales managers supervising technical or industrial salespeople. In contrast, a 10-to-1 ratio is recommended if sales representatives are calling on wholesale and retail accounts.

MOTIVATION

expectancy theory
Theory that motivation depends on an individual's expectations of his or her ability to perform a job and how that performance relates to attaining a desired reward.

What motivates salespeople to perform their best? The sales manager is responsible for finding the answer to this question. The sales process involves problem solving, which sometimes includes frustration—particularly when a sale is delayed or falls through. Information sharing, recognition, bonuses, incentives, and benefits can all be used to help defray frustration and motivate sales staff. Developing an enthusiastic sales staff who are happy at their jobs is the goal of the sales manager. Motivation is an important part of the company's success.

Creating a positive, motivating environment doesn't necessarily mean instituting complex or expensive incentive programs. Monetary reward—cash—is often considered king. But sometimes simple recognition—a thank-you, a dinner, a year-end award—can go a long way. It is important for the sales manager to figure out what types of incentives will be most effective with his or her particular group of employees. Some firms go all out, dangling luxury items such as computers, digital cameras, or trips in front of the sales force as rewards. A Caribbean cruise, a trip to Disney World, or a weekend at a luxury spa could be the carrot that works, particularly if family members are included. Some firms purchase gift cards from retailers such as Future Shop or Canadian Tire to distribute to sales staff who perform well. But not all incentive programs are effective at motivating employees. A program with targets that are set too high, that isn't publicized, or that allows only certain sales personnel to participate can backfire. So it is important for sales management to plan carefully for an incentive program to succeed.

Sales managers can also gain insight into the subject of motivation by studying the various theories of motivation developed over the years. One theory that has been applied effectively to sales force motivation is **expectancy theory**, which states that motivation depends on the expectations an individual has of his or her ability to perform the job and on how performance relates to attaining rewards that the individual values.

Sales managers can apply the expectancy theory of motivation by following a five-step process:

1. Let each salesperson know in detail what is expected with regard to selling goals, service standards, and other areas of performance. Rather than setting goals just once a year, many firms do so on a semi-annual, quarterly, or even monthly basis.

2. Make the work valuable by assessing the needs, values, and abilities of each salesperson and then assigning appropriate tasks.

3. Make the work achievable. As leaders, sales managers must inspire self-confidence in their salespeople and offer training and coaching to reassure them.

4. Provide immediate and specific feedback, guiding those who need improvement and giving positive feedback to those who do well.

5. Offer rewards that each salesperson values, whether it is an incentive as described previously, opportunity for advancement, or a bonus.

COMPENSATION

Money is an important part of any person's job, and the salesperson is no exception. So deciding how best to compensate the sales force can be a critical factor in motivation. Sales compensation can be based on a commission, a straight salary, or a combination of both. Bonuses based on end-of-year results are another popular form of compensation. The increasing popularity of team selling has also forced companies to set up reward programs to recognize performance of business units and teams. Today, about one in four firms rewards business-unit performance.

A **commission** is a payment tied directly to the sales or profits that a salesperson achieves. A salesperson might receive a 5 percent commission on all sales up to a specified quota, and a 7 percent commission on sales beyond that point. This approach to sales compensation is increasingly popular. But while commissions reinforce selling incentives, they may cause some sales force members to overlook non-selling activities, such as completing sales reports, delivering promotion materials, and servicing existing accounts. In addition, salespeople who operate entirely on commission may become too aggressive in their approach to potential customers, a practice that could backfire.

A **salary** is a fixed payment made periodically to an employee. A firm that bases compensation on salaries rather than commissions might pay a salesperson a set amount weekly, bi-monthly, or monthly. A company must balance benefits and disadvantages in paying predetermined salaries to compensate managers and sales personnel. A straight salary plan gives management more control over how sales personnel allocate their efforts, but it reduces the incentive to find new markets and land new accounts.

Many firms have found that it's best to develop compensation programs that combine features of both salary and commission plans. A new salesperson often receives a base salary while in training, even if he or she moves to full commission later on. If the salesperson does a lot of driving as part of the job, he or she may receive a vehicle. If the person works from home, there might be an allowance toward setting up an office there.

Total compensation packages vary according to industry, with the finance, insurance, and real estate industries coming out on top, followed closely by general services. Compensation also varies according to years of experience in sales. Table 15.4 provides information on base salaries and total cash for both inside and field salespeople with various levels of experience.

EVALUATION AND CONTROL

Perhaps the most difficult tasks required of sales managers are evaluation and control. Sales managers are responsible for setting standards and choosing the best methods for measuring sales performance. Sales volume, profitability, and changes in market share are the usual means of evaluating sales effectiveness. They typically involve the use of **sales quotas**—specified sales or profit targets that the firm expects salespeople to achieve. A particular sales representative might be expected to generate sales of

commission Incentive compensation directly related to the sales or profits achieved by a salesperson.

salary Fixed compensation payment made periodically to an employee.

sales quota Level of expected sales for a territory, product, customer, or salesperson against which actual results are compared.

table 15.4   *Sales Compensation, Canada*

	BASE SALARY, $000'S			TOTAL CASH, $000'S		
	25%ile	50%ile	75%ile	25%ile	50%ile	75%ile
Sales trainees	$43.3	$47.9	$56.9	$47.7	$55.1	$63.3
Sales representatives—intermediate	$50.0	$57.8	$66.8	$57.2	$66.8	$80.0
Sales representatives—senior	$64.7	$77.0	$87.3	$77.1	$92.4	$112.3
Inside sales—associate	$31.7	$40.7	$42.6	$33.7	$42.1	$51.9
Inside sales—intermediate	$38.2	$44.1	$50.9	$41.0	$49.7	$59.5
Inside sales—senior	$48.9	$53.3	$58.9	$52.9	$61.5	$77.7

NOTES
In addition to base salary, sales positions are generally eligible to earn an annual incentive or bonus. The median target incentive opportunity for these roles, as a percentage of base salary, is 13.5%, $15.0%, 23.0%, 10.0%, 10.0%, and 10.0% for each of the above roles, respectively. The median organization size (in terms of revenues) is about $500 million.
Source: Sales Compensation, Canada, from 2010 Mercer Benchmark Database. Reproduced by permission of Mercer (Canada) Limited.

$1.2 million in his or her territory during a given year. In many cases, the quota is tied to the compensation system. Technology has greatly improved the ability of sales managers to monitor the effectiveness of their sales staffs. Databases help sales managers to quickly divide revenues by salesperson, by account, and by geographic area.

In today's marketing environment, other measures such as customer satisfaction, profit contribution, share of product-category sales, and customer retention are also coming into play. This is the result of three factors:

1. A long-term orientation that results from emphasis on building customer relationships.

2. The fact that evaluations based on sales volume alone may lead to overselling and inventory problems that may damage customer relationships.

3. The need to encourage sales representatives to develop new accounts, provide customer service, and emphasize new products. Sales quotas tend to put focus on short-term selling goals rather than long-term relationships.

The sales manager must follow a formal system that includes a consistent series of decisions. This way, the manager can make fair and accurate evaluations. The system helps the sales manager answer three general questions:

1. *Where does each salesperson's performance rank relative to predetermined standards?* This comparison takes into consideration any uncontrollable variables on sales performance, such as a natural disaster or unforeseen change in the industry. Each adjusted rank is stated as a percentage of the standard.

2. *What are the salesperson's strong points?* The manager might list areas of the salesperson's performance in which he or she has performed above the standard. Or strong points could be placed in such categories as technical ability, processes, and end results.

3. *What are the salesperson's weak points?* No one likes to hear criticism, but when it is offered constructively, it can be motivation to improve performance. The manager and employee should establish specific objectives for improvement and set a timetable for judging the employee's improvement.

In completing the evaluation summary, the sales manager follows a set procedure so that all employees are treated equally:

• Each aspect of sales performance for which a standard exists should be measured separately. This helps prevent the so-called *halo effect,* in which the rating given on one factor influences those on other performance variables.

• Each salesperson should be judged on the basis of actual sales performance rather than potential ability. This is why rankings are important in the evaluation.

- Sales managers must judge each salesperson on the basis of sales performance for the entire period under consideration, rather than for a few particular incidents.

- The evaluation should be reviewed by a third party—such as the manager's boss or a human resources manager—for completeness and objectivity.

Once the evaluation is complete, both manager and salesperson should focus on positive action—whether it is a drive toward new goals or correcting a negative situation. An evaluation should be motivation for improved performance.

assessment check 6

6.1 What are the seven basic functions performed by a sales manager?

6.2 Define *span of control*.

6.3 What are the three main questions a sales manager must address as part of a salesperson's evaluation?

ETHICAL ISSUES IN SALES

(7) Explain the role of ethical behaviour in personal selling.

Promotional activities can raise ethical questions, and personal selling is no exception. A difficult economy or highly competitive environment may tempt some salespeople—particularly those new to the business—to behave in ways that they might later regret. They might use the company car for personal errands or pad an expense report. They might give expensive gifts to customers. But today's experienced, highly professional salespeople know that long-term success requires a strong code of ethics. They also know that a single breach of ethics could have a devastating effect on their careers.

Some people believe that ethical problems are inevitable because of the very nature of the sales function. And in the wake of corporate scandals in which top executives have benefited at the expense of customers, employees, and shareholders, ethical managers are working harder than ever to build trust. So they reinforce ethics codes that may already be in place and strengthen ethics training. Salespeople who earn the Certified Sales Professional (CSP) designation through the Canadian Professional Sales Association (CPSA) must agree to abide by the CPSA Sales Institute Code of Ethics (Figure 15.4).

figure 15.4

CPSA Sales Institute Code of Ethics

The CPSA Sales Institute Code of Ethics is the set of principles and standards that a certified sales professional will strive to adhere to with customers, organizations, competitors, communities, and colleagues.

The Certified Sales Professional pledges and commits to uphold these standards in all activities:

I will:

1. Maintain honesty and integrity in all relationships with customers, prospective customers, and colleagues and continually work to earn their trust and respect.

2. Accurately represent my products or services to the best of my ability in a manner that places my customer or prospective customer and my company in a position that benefits both.

3. Respect and protect the proprietary and confidential information entrusted to me by my company and my customers and not engage in activities that may conflict with the best interest of my customers or my company.

4. Continually upgrade my knowledge of my products/services, skills, and my industry.

5. Use the time and resources available to me only for legitimate business purposes. I will only participate in activities that are ethical and legal, and when in doubt, I will seek counsel.

6. Respect my competitors and their products and services by representing them in a manner which is honest, truthful, and based on accurate information that has been substantiated.

7. Endeavour to engage in business and selling practices which contribute to a positive relationship with the community.

8. Assist and counsel my fellow sales professionals where possible in the performance of their duties.

9. Abide by and encourage others to adhere to this Code of Ethics.

As a certified sales professional, I understand that the reputation and professionalism of all salespeople depends on me as well as others engaged in the sales profession, and I will adhere to these standards to strengthen the reputation and integrity for which we will strive. I understand that failure to consistently act according to this Code of Ethics may result in the loss of the privilege of using my professional sales designation.

Source: http://www.cpsa.com/SalesCertification/Gui/Html/CodeofEthics.asp. Reprinted by permission.

Sales managers and top executives can do a lot to foster a corporate culture that encourages honesty and ethical behaviour. Here are some characteristics of such a culture:

- *Employees understand what is expected of them.* A written code of ethics—which should be reviewed by all employees—in addition to ethics training helps educate employees in how to conduct ethical business.

- *Open communication.* Employees who feel comfortable talking with their supervisors are more apt to ask questions if they are uncertain about situations or decisions and to report any violations they come across.

- *Managers lead by example.* Workers naturally emulate the ethical behaviour of managers. A sales manager who is honest with customers, doesn't accept inappropriate gifts, and leaves the company car at home during a vacation is likely to be imitated by his or her sales staff.

- Regardless of corporate culture, every salesperson is responsible for his or her own behaviour and relationship with customers. If, as a new salesperson, you find yourself uncertain about a decision, ask yourself these questions. The answers should help you make an ethical decision.

1. Does my decision affect anyone other than myself and the bottom line?

2. Is my success based on making the sale or creating a loyal customer?

3. Are my dealings with my customers in their best interest and not exploiting their trust?

4. What price will I pay for this decision?[27]

assessment check 7

7.1 Why is it important for salespeople to maintain ethical behaviour?

7.2 What are the characteristics of companies that foster corporate cultures that encourage ethical behaviour?

---

8 Describe the role of sales promotion in the promotional mix, and identify the different types of sales promotions.

sales promotion Marketing activities other than personal selling, advertising, and publicity that enhance consumer purchasing and dealer effectiveness.

SALES PROMOTION

Sales promotion includes those marketing activities other than personal selling, advertising, and publicity designed to enhance consumer purchasing and dealer effectiveness. Sales promotion can be traced back as far as the ruins of Pompeii and Ephesus. In Canada, companies have been giving away trinkets and premiums for more than 100 years.

Sales promotion techniques were originally intended as short-term incentives aimed at producing an immediate response—a purchase. Today, however, marketers recognize sales promotion as an integral part of the overall marketing plan, and the focus has shifted from short-term goals to long-term objectives of building brand equity and maintaining continuing purchases. A frequent-flyer program enables an airline to build a base of loyal customers. A frequent-stay program allows a hotel chain to attract regular guests.

Both retailers and manufacturers use sales promotions to offer consumers extra incentives to buy. These promotions are likely to stress price advantages, giveaways, or special offerings. The general objectives of sales promotion are to speed up the sales process and increase sales volume. Promotions can also help build loyalty. Through a consumer promotion, a marketer encourages consumers to try the product, use more of it, and buy it again. The firm also hopes to foster sales of related items and increase impulse purchases. Back-to-school sales are one type of sales promotion. Retailers run them each fall to attract shoppers who need clothing and supplies for the new academic year. In recent campaigns, Office Max and Staples sold a different school item, like pencils or pocket folders, for a penny each week, as well as offering 50 percent off big-ticket items such as electronics and furniture.[28] Today, consumers have many more choices among products than in the past, and for this reason many marketers create special programs to build loyalty among their customers. However, with loyalty programs no longer unique, marketing and sales professionals work to build loyalty among their customers by managing customer relationships and regularly evaluating those relationships to determine how they can enhance them.[29]

Because sales promotion is so important to a marketing effort, an entire promotion industry exists to offer expert assistance in its use and to design unique promotions, just as an entire advertising industry offers similar services for advertisers. These companies, like advertising agencies, provide other firms with assistance in promoting their goods and services.

Sales promotions often produce their best results when combined with other marketing activities. Ads create awareness, while sales promotions lead to trial or purchase. After a presentation, a salesperson may offer a potential customer a discount coupon for the good or service. Promotions encourage immediate action because they impose limited time frames. Discount coupons and rebates usually have expiration dates. In addition, sales promotions produce measurable results, making it relatively easy for marketers to evaluate their effectiveness. If more people buy shoes during a buy-one-get-one-free promotion at a shoe store, its owners know the promotion was successful.

Retailers use sales promotions to offer consumers extra incentives to buy.

It is important to understand what sales promotions can and cannot do. They can encourage interest in both new and mature products, help introduce new products, encourage trial and repeat purchases, increase usage rates, neutralize competition, and reinforce advertising and personal selling efforts. On the other hand, sales promotions cannot overcome poor brand images, product deficiencies, or poor training for salespeople. While sales promotions increase volume in the short term, they may not lead to sales and profit growth in the long run.

Sales promotion techniques may serve all members of a marketing channel. In addition, manufacturers may use trade promotion methods to promote their products to resellers. Sales promotion techniques include the following consumer-oriented promotions: samples, bonus packs, premiums, coupons, refunds, contests, sweepstakes, and specialty advertising. Trade-oriented promotions include trade allowances, point-of-purchase advertising, trade shows, dealer incentives, contests, and training programs.

CONSUMER-ORIENTED SALES PROMOTIONS

In the promotion industry, marketers use all types of sales promotions, including games, contests, sweepstakes, and coupons to persuade new and existing customers to try their products. Consumer-oriented sales promotions encourage repurchases by rewarding current users, boosting sales of complementary products, and increasing impulse purchases. These promotions also attract consumer attention in the midst of advertising clutter. Figure 15.5 illustrates the objectives of popular sales promotion alternatives and identifies their strengths and weaknesses.

It's important for marketers to use sales promotions selectively because, if they are overused, consumers begin to expect price discounts at all times, which ultimately diminishes brand equity. The following sections describe the various forms of consumer-oriented sales promotions.

Coupons and Refunds

Coupons, the most widely used form of sales promotion, offer discounts on the purchase price of goods and services. Canadians receive about 3.6 billion coupons per year and redeem 100 million of them, saving about $134 million.[30] Consumers can redeem the coupons at retail outlets, which receive the face value of the coupon plus a handling fee from the manufacturer. The coupon industry has been somewhat "clipped" in recent years due to the growing clout of retailers and more complex accounting

Marketoid

Brian McPherson of Edmonton, Alberta, started saving Canadian Tire money when he bought a hockey stick at age 14. In 2011, he purchased a new riding lawn mower with $1053 worth of coupons, after saving them for 15 years.

coupon Sales promotion technique that offers a discount on the purchase price of goods or services.

figure 15.5

**Most Popular Sales
Promotion Alternatives**

KIND OF PROMOTION	OBJECTIVES	STRENGTHS	WEAKNESSES
Coupons	Stimulate trial or brand switching	Attract price-sensitive customers who might not otherwise buy Encourage retailer support	Not all retailers accept coupons Have often been counterfeited or redeemed by some retailers without consumer purchases
Refunds (or rebates)	Encourage customers to buy	Help halt sales declines or reduce inventories if new products are about to enter the market	May reduce perceived value of the product Easy for competition to match
Samples	Stimulate trial of new products	Low customer risk creates awareness and trial	May be very costly for the company
Bonus Packs	Encourage customers to buy and minimize brand switching	Reward loyal customers for continued purchase	Customers will not need to repurchase for a longer period
Premiums	Stimulate trial or create goodwill	Customers like free merchandise and may induce trial of complementary product	May be costly for the company
Contests	Encourage consumers to buy and channel members to increase inventories	A predetermined number of winners, hence cost is usually predictable May create excitement	Require careful thought to be creative and to avoid costly legal responsibilities
Sweepstakes	Encourage customers to buy and minimize brand switching	A predetermined number of winners, hence cost is usually predictable Consumers like them because little effort is required	Sales may decline following the promotion
Specialty Advertising	Encourage customer loyalty	Create awareness and help to reinforce previous and future advertising messages Good customer acceptance	May be very costly for company and may become less effective if competition offers a better promotional item

rules that make couponing less attractive to some marketers. In addition, consumers receive so many coupons that they cannot possibly redeem them all.

Mail, magazines, newspapers, package inserts, and, increasingly, the Internet are the standard methods of distributing coupons. But another distribution channel for coupons has emerged: cell phones. Thanks to advances in bar-code technology, retailers can distribute coupons digitally to cell phone users, who can also redeem the coupons digitally when they shop.

Coupons, which offer discounts on goods and services, can be redeemed at retail outlets.

Refunds, or rebates, offer cash back to consumers who send in proof of purchasing one or more products. Refunds help packaged goods companies to increase purchase rates, promote multiple purchases, and reward product users. Although many consumers find the refund forms too bothersome to complete, plenty still do. Refunds appear to be less popular for inexpensive consumer packaged goods today than they once were, but they are still used to promote more expensive electronic goods, such as smart phones.

refund
Cash given back to consumers who send a proof of purchase for one or more products.

SAMPLES, BONUS PACKS, AND PREMIUMS

Marketers are increasingly adopting the "try it, you'll like it" approach as an effective means of getting consumers to try and then purchase their goods and services. **Sampling** refers to the free distribution of a product in an attempt to obtain future sales. Samples may be distributed door to door, by mail, via demonstrations in stores or at events, or by including them in packages with other products. Sampling produces a much higher response rate than previously believed. A recent study demonstrated that households that participated in sampling events created a 475 percent sales increase on the day of the event, compared to non-sampled households. Those that sampled products were also 11 percent more likely to repurchase the product in the 20 weeks following the event and were 6 percent more likely to buy another product from the same brand franchise.[31]

sampling Free distribution of a product in an attempt to obtain future sales.

With sampling, marketers can target potential customers and be certain that the product reaches them. At the 2011 John Molson Undergraduate Case Competition held at Concordia University in Montreal, 24 business school teams of four students participated in the week-long event. One event involved a 24-hour research case, where many teams worked very long hours. Many team members welcomed the free samples of Red Bull that were sampled during the event.[32] Sampling provides an especially useful way to promote new or unusual products because it gives the consumer a direct product experience. A survey of 10 000 Canadians found sampling was very effective for creating awareness of new products in grocery stores (61 percent) and was the most effective method for introducing new products to the first of the new adopters (89 percent).[33]

A major disadvantage of sampling is the high cost involved. Not only must the marketer give away small quantities of a product that might otherwise have generated revenues through regular sales, but the market is also in effect closed for the time it takes consumers to use up the samples. In addition, the marketer may encounter problems in distributing the samples. Hellmann's marketers annoyed consumers instead of pleasing them when the firm distributed sample packets of Italian and French salad dressing in home-delivered newspapers. Many of the packets burst when the papers hit the driveways.

A **bonus pack** is a specially packaged item that gives the purchaser a larger quantity at the regular price. For instance, some companies make bonus offers such as "two for the price of one," "buy two and get one free," or "30 percent more for the same price." **Premiums** are items given free or at reduced cost with purchases of other products. For example, McDonald's frequently gives children's toys as a premium with its Happy Meals. Premiums have proven effective in motivating consumers to try new products or different brands. A premium should have some relationship with the product or brand it accompanies, though. A home improvement centre might offer free measuring tapes to its customers, for example.

Contests and Sweepstakes

Firms often sponsor contests and sweepstakes to introduce new goods and services, to attract additional customers, and to collect contact information from participants that can later be used for targeting customers. **Contests** require entrants to complete a task such as solving a puzzle or answering questions in a trivia quiz. **Sweepstakes**, on the other hand, choose winners by chance, so no product purchase is necessary. They are more popular with consumers than contests because they do not take as much effort for consumers to enter. Marketers like them, too, because they are inexpensive to run and the number of winners is predetermined. With some contests, the sponsors cannot predict the number of people who will correctly complete the puzzles or gather the right number of symbols from scratch-off cards.

Marketers are increasingly turning to the Internet for contests and sweepstakes, because of its relatively low cost and its ability to provide data immediately. Interactivity is also a key part of the online experience—as consumers become more engaged in the contest or sweepstakes event, they also build a relationship with the firm and its products. Doritos has run several contests where people were asked to name a new flavour of chip; in a recent contest, they were asked to "kill" one of two flavours of chip. Tony Matta, vice president of parent company PepsiCo Foods Canada, admitted that sales for the new flavours were not spectacular. However, sales may not be the most important objective of such promotions. New flavours keep the brand current among the target customers—primarily males aged 20 to 24—and at top-of-mind awareness.[34]

Specialty Advertising

The origin of specialty advertising has been traced to the Middle Ages, when artisans gave wooden pegs bearing their names to prospects, who drove them into the walls at home to serve as convenient hangers for armour. Corporations began putting their names on a variety of products in the late 1800s, as newspapers and print shops explored new methods to earn additional revenues from their expensive printing presses. Today, just about everyone owns a cap or T-shirt with the name or logo of a company, organization, or product displayed on it.

Specialty advertising is a sales promotion technique that places the advertiser's name, address, and advertising message on useful articles that are then distributed to target customers. In Canada, this industry employs more than 25 000 people and generates sales in excess of $2.1 billion.[35] Wearable products are the most popular, accounting for nearly a third of specialty advertising sales. Pens, mugs, glassware, and calendars are other popular forms.

Advertising specialties help to reinforce previous or future advertising and sales messages. Useful promotional items are retained 81 percent of the time, and 62 percent of recipients do business with the advertiser after receiving the specialty advertising item. Neilsen Media calculates that the cost per impression (CPI) is lowest for promotional specialties–$0.004–than for any other form of advertising.[36] Companies use this form of promotion to highlight store openings and new products, motivate salespeople, increase visits to trade show booths, and remind customers about their products.

TRADE-ORIENTED PROMOTIONS

Sales promotion techniques can also contribute effectively to campaigns aimed at retailers and wholesalers. **Trade promotion** is sales promotion that appeals to marketing intermediaries rather than to final consumers. Marketers use trade promotions in push strategies by encouraging resellers to stock

bonus pack Specially packaged item that gives the purchaser a larger quantity at the regular price.

premium Item given free or at a reduced cost with purchase of other products.

contest Sales promotion technique that requires entrants to complete a task, such as solving a puzzle or answering questions on a quiz, for the chance to win a prize.

sweepstakes Sales promotion technique in which prize winners are selected by chance.

Marketoid

The Promotional Product Professionals of Canada (PPPC) is a 1700-member not-for profit, Montreal-based organization. Members can search its database of 350 000 promotional products from PPPC suppliers.

specialty advertising Sales promotion technique that places the advertiser's name, address, and advertising message on useful articles that are then distributed to target consumers.

trade promotion Sales promotion that appeals to marketing intermediaries rather than to consumers.

new products, continue to carry existing ones, and promote both effectively to consumers. The typical firm actually spends half its promotional budget on trade promotion—as much money as it spends on advertising and consumer-oriented sales promotions combined. Successful trade promotions offer financial incentives. They require careful timing and attention to costs and are easy to implement by retailers. These promotions should bring quick results and improve retail sales.

Trade Allowances

Among the most common trade promotion methods are **trade allowances**—special financial incentives offered to wholesalers and retailers that purchase or promote specific products. These offers take various forms. A buying allowance gives retailers a discount on goods. They include off-invoice allowances through which retailers deduct specified amounts from their invoices or receive free goods, such as one free case for every 10 ordered, when they order certain quantities. When a manufacturer offers a promotional allowance, it agrees to pay the reseller a certain amount to cover the costs of special promotional displays or extensive advertising that features the manufacturer's product. The goal is to increase sales to consumers by encouraging resellers to promote their products effectively.

As mentioned in previous chapters, some retailers require vendors to pay a special slotting allowance before they agree to take on new products. These fees guarantee slots, or shelf space, for newly introduced items in the stores. This practice is common in large supermarket chains. Retailers defend these fees as essential to cover the added costs of carrying the products, such as redesigning display space and shelves, setting up and administering control systems, managing inventory, and taking the risks inherent in stocking new products. The fees can be sizable, from several hundred dollars per store to many thousands of dollars for a retail chain and millions of dollars for nationally distributed products.

trade allowance
Financial incentive offered to wholesalers and retailers that purchase or promote specific products.

Point-of-Purchase Advertising

A display or other promotion located near the site of the actual buying decision is known as **point-of-purchase (POP) advertising**. This method of sales promotion capitalizes on the fact that buyers make many purchase decisions within the store, so it encourages retailers to improve on-site merchandising.[37] Product suppliers assist the retailer by creating special displays designed to stimulate sales of the item being promoted.

Free-standing POP promotions often appear at the ends of shopping aisles. On a typical trip to the supermarket, you might see a POP display for Disney videos, Coppertone sunscreen, or Duracell batteries. Retailers such as Rona, Staples, and Canadian Tire all use POP advertising displays frequently. Electronic kiosks, which allow consumers to place orders for items not available in the store, have begun to transform the POP display industry, as creators of these displays look for ways to involve consumers more actively as well as entertain them.

point-of-purchase (POP) advertising
Display or other promotion located near the site of the actual buying decision.

Trade Shows

To influence resellers and other members of the distribution channel, many marketers participate in **trade shows**. These shows are often organized by industry trade associations; frequently, they are part of these associations' annual meetings or conventions. Vendors who serve the industries display and demonstrate their products for attendees. Every year, over 4300 different shows in Canada and the United States draw more than 1.3 million exhibitors and 85 million attendees. Industries that hold trade shows include manufacturers of sporting goods, medical equipment, electronics, automobiles, clothing, and home furnishings. Service industries include hair styling, health care, travel, and restaurant franchises. The Canadian Gift & Tableware Association holds Canada's largest trade show in Toronto each January and August, where 1100 exhibitors attract more than 25 000 retail buyers.[38]

Because of the expense involved in trade shows, a company must assess the value of these shows on several criteria, such as direct sales, any increase in product awareness, image building, and any contribution to the firm's marketing communications efforts. Trade shows give especially effective opportunities to introduce new products and to generate sales leads. Some types of shows reach ultimate consumers as well as channel members. Home, recreation, and automobile shows, for instance, allow businesses to display and demonstrate home improvement, recreation, and other consumer products to entire communities.

trade show
Product exhibition organized by industry trade associations to showcase goods and services.

Asian ECO Fair Attracts Buying Missions from 46 Countries

EACH fall, a major trade show is held in Hong Kong—Eco Expo Asia—dedicated to the environmental industry. In 2010, 266 exhibitors from 19 countries participated. The four-day event featured four main exhibit categories: air quality, energy efficiency and energy, waste management and recycling, and eco-friendly products. The popularity of the trade show is growing as world interest in environmental issues continues to build. This fifth annual trade show attracted a third more exhibitors than the previous year, and exhibition space increased by 70 percent to 9950 square metres.

Trade shows are great venues for sales and technical people to connect with important buyers and other influencers who are looking for solutions to their buying problems. Eco Expo Asia attracted over 40 buying missions representing more than 640 companies from 46 countries and regions around the world. Participating countries included Canada, India, Japan, Russia, Sweden, Thailand, and the United States. Fatima Lai, trade commissioner, Consulate General of Canada in Hong Kong, says, "Eco Expo Asia attracts professional industry buyers from all over the world, so we are here to help Canadian SMEs to showcase their technologies across international markets." Consistent with the trade fair theme, Eco Expo Asia made its own contributions to environmental improvement:

- Waste separation bins were extensively used.
- Exhibition booths used energy-saving light bulbs.
- Recycled paper and soy-based ink were used for printed materials.
- Plastic bags were prohibited.
- Carpeting costs saved by exhibitors who opted for carpet-free booths were donated to environmental causes.

The final day of the trade show was open to the general public. Visitors got to test drive the Volkswagen Touareg Hybrid and were offered a test ride on an electric bus developed by Great Dragon International.

Source: Hong Kong Trade Development Council website, http://www.hktdc .com/fair/ecoexpoasia-en, March 20, 2011.

Dealer Incentives, Contests, and Training Programs

push money
Cash reward paid to retail salespeople for every unit of a product they sell.

Manufacturers run dealer incentive programs and contests to reward retailers and their salespeople who increase sales and, more generally, to promote specific products. These channel members receive incentives for performing promotion-related tasks and can win contests by reaching sales goals. Manufacturers may offer major prizes to resellers such as trips to exotic places. **Push money** (which retailers commonly refer to as *spiffs*) is another incentive that gives retail salespeople cash rewards for every unit of a product they sell. This benefit increases the likelihood that the salesperson will try to convince a customer to buy the product rather than a competing brand.

For more expensive and highly complex products, manufacturers often provide specialized training for retail salespeople. This background helps sales personnel explain features, competitive advantages, and other information to consumers. Training can be provided in several ways: a manufacturer's sales representative can conduct training sessions during regular sales calls, or the firm can distribute sales literature and DVDs.

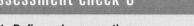

assessment check 8

8.1 Define sales promotion.

8.2 Identify at least four types of consumer-oriented sales promotions.

8.3 Identify at least three types of trade-oriented sales promotions.

Strategic Implications

Today's salespeople are a new breed. Richly nourished in a tradition of sales, their roles are strengthened even further through technology. However, as many companies are discovering, nothing can replace the power of personal selling in generating sales and in building strong, loyal customer relationships.

Salespeople today are a critical link in developing relationships between the customer and the company. They communicate customer needs and wants to co-workers in various units within an organization, enabling a cooperative, company-wide effort in improving product offerings and in better satisfying individuals within the target market. For salespeople, the greatest benefit of electronic technologies is the ability to share knowledge when it is needed with those who need to know, including customers, suppliers, and employees. Because buyers are now more sophisticated, demanding more rapid and lower-cost transactions, salespeople must be quick and creative as they find solutions to their customers' problems. Product life cycles are accelerating, and customers who demand more are apt to switch from one product to another. Recognizing the long-term impact of keeping satisfied buyers—those who make repeat and cross-purchases and provide referrals—versus dissatisfied buyers, organizations are increasingly training their sales forces to provide superior customer service and rewarding them for increasing satisfaction levels.

The traditional skills of a salesperson included persuasion, selling ability, and product knowledge. But today's sales professional is more likely to possess communication skills, problem-solving skills, and knowledge of products, customers, industries, and applications. Earlier generations of salesperson tended to be self-driven; today's sales professional is more likely to be a team player as well as a customer advocate who serves his or her buyers by solving problems.

The modern professional salesperson is greatly assisted by the judicious use of both consumer-and trade-oriented sales promotions. Often overlooked in promotional discussions of high-profile advertising, the typical firm allocates more promotional dollars for sales promotion than for advertising. The proven effectiveness of sales promotion makes it a widely used promotional mix component for most marketers. ◆◆◆

REVIEW OF CHAPTER OBJECTIVES

① **Describe the role of today's salesperson.**

Today's salesperson seeks to form long-lasting relationships with customers by providing high levels of customer service rather than going for the quick sale. Firms have begun to integrate their computer and communications technologies into the sales function, so people involved in personal selling have an expanded role.

② **Describe the four sales channels.**

Over-the-counter selling involves providing product information and arranging for completion of the sales transaction when customers come to the seller's location. Field selling involves making personal sales calls to customers. Under certain circumstances, telemarketing is used to provide product information and answer questions from customers who call. Inside selling relies on phone, mail, and e-commerce to provide sales and product services for customers on a continuing basis.

③ **Describe the major trends in personal selling.**

Companies are turning to relationship selling, consultative selling, and team selling. Relationship selling occurs when a salesperson builds a mutually beneficial relationship with a customer on a regular basis over an extended period. Consultative selling involves meeting customer needs by listening to customers, understanding and caring about their problems, paying attention to the details, and following through after the sale. Team selling occurs when the salesperson joins with specialists from other functional areas of the firm to complete the selling process.

④ **Identify and briefly describe the three basic sales tasks.**

Order processing is the routine handling of an order. It characterizes a sales setting in which the need is made known to and is acknowledged by the customer. Creative selling is persuasion aimed at making the prospect see the value of the good or service being presented. Missionary selling is indirect selling, such as making goodwill calls and providing technical or operational assistance.

⑤ **Outline the seven steps in the sales process.**

The basic steps in the sales process are prospecting and qualifying, approach, presentation, demonstration, handling objections, closing, and follow-up.

⑥ **Identify the seven basic functions of a sales manager.**

A sales manager links the sales force to other aspects of the internal and external environments. The manager's functions are recruitment and selection, training, organization, supervision, motivation, compensation, and evaluation and control.

⑦ **Explain the role of ethical behaviour in personal selling.**

Ethical behaviour is vital to building positive, long-term relationships with customers. Although some people believe that ethical problems are inevitable, employers can do much to foster a corporate culture that encourages honesty and ethical behaviour. In addition, each salesperson is responsible for his or her own behaviour and relationship with customers.

⑧ **Describe the role of sales promotion in the promotional mix, and identify the different types of sales promotions.**

Sales promotion includes activities other than personal selling, advertising, and publicity designed to enhance consumer purchasing and dealer effectiveness. Sales promotion is an integral part of the overall marketing plan, intended to increase sales and build brand equity. Promotions often produce their best results when combined with other marketing activities. Consumer-oriented sales promotions include coupons, refunds, samples, bonus packs, premiums, contests and sweepstakes, and specialty advertising. Trade-oriented promotions include trade allowances, point-of-purchase (POP) advertising, trade shows, and dealer incentives, contests, and training programs.

assessment check answers

1.1 What is personal selling?
Personal selling is the process of a seller's person-to-person promotional presentation to a buyer.

1.2 What is the main focus of today's salespeople?
The main focus of today's salespeople is to build long-lasting relationships with customers.

2.1 What is over-the-counter selling?
Over-the-counter selling describes selling in retail and some wholesale locations. Most of these transactions take place directly with customers.

2.2 What is field selling?
Field selling involves making sales calls on prospective and existing customers at their businesses or homes.

2.3 Distinguish between outbound and inbound telemarketing.
Outbound telemarketing takes place when a salesperson phones customers; inbound telemarketing takes place when customers call the firm.

3.1 Identify the three major personal selling approaches.
The three major personal selling approaches are relationship selling, consultative selling, and team selling.

3.2 Distinguish between relationship selling and consultative selling.
Relationship selling is a technique for building a mutually beneficial partnership with a customer. Consultative selling involves meeting customer needs by listening to, understanding, and paying attention to their problems, then following up after a sale.

4.1 What are the three major tasks performed by salespeople?
The three major tasks are order processing, creative selling, and team selling.

4.2 What are the three steps of order processing?
The three steps of order processing are identifying customer needs, pointing out the need to the customer, and completing the order.

5.1 Identify the seven steps of the sales process.
The seven steps of the sales process are prospecting and qualifying, approach, presentation, demonstration, handling objections, closing, and follow-up.

5.2 Why is follow-up important to the sales effort?
Follow-up allows the salesperson to reinforce the customer's purchase decision, strengthen the bond, and correct any problems.

6.1 What are the seven basic functions performed by a sales manager?
The seven basic functions of a sales manager are recruitment and selection, training, organization, supervision, motivation, compensation, and evaluation and control.

6.2 Define span of control.
Span of control refers to the number of sales representatives who report to first-level sales managers.

6.3 What are the three main questions a sales manager must address as part of a salesperson's evaluation?
The three main questions a sales manager must address are these: Where does each salesperson's performance rank relative

to predetermined standards? What are the salesperson's strong points? What are the salesperson's weak points?

7.1 Why is it important for salespeople to maintain ethical behaviour?

Salespeople need to maintain ethical behaviour because it is vital to their firm's relationships with customers and because they are representing their company. A breach of ethics could also be detrimental to an individual's career.

7.2 What are the characteristics of companies that foster corporate cultures that encourage ethical behaviour?

Characteristics of corporations fostering ethical behaviour include the following: employees who understand what is expected of them, open communication, and managers who lead by example.

8.1 Define sales promotion.

Sales promotion includes marketing activities other than personal selling, advertising, and publicity designed to enhance consumer purchasing and dealer effectiveness.

8.2 Identify at least four types of consumer-oriented sales promotions.

Consumer-oriented sales promotions include coupons, refunds, samples, bonus packs, premiums, contests, sweepstakes, and specialty advertising.

8.3 Identify at least three types of trade-oriented sales promotions.

Trade-oriented sales promotions include trade allowances, POP advertising, trade shows, dealer incentives, contests, and training programs.

MARKETING TERMS YOU NEED TO KNOW

These terms are printed in red in the text. They are defined in the margins of the chapter and in the Glossary that begins on p. G-1.

personal selling 464	sales incentives 474	sales quota 483
over-the-counter selling 465	prospecting 475	sales promotion 486
field selling 466	qualifying 476	coupon 487
network marketing 467	approach 476	refund 489
telemarketing 468	precall planning 476	sampling 489
outbound telemarketing 468	presentation 476	bonus pack 490
inbound telemarketing 469	cold calling 477	premium 490
inside selling 469	demonstration 477	contest 490
relationship selling 470	buyer concern 478	sweepstakes 490
consultative selling 471	closing 478	specialty advertising 490
cross-selling 471	follow-up 479	trade promotion 490
team selling 471	national accounts organization 482	trade allowance 491
virtual sales team 472	span of control 482	point-of-purchase (POP) advertising 491
order processing 473	expectancy theory 482	trade show 491
creative selling 473	commission 483	push money 492
missionary selling 474	salary 483	

PROJECTS AND TEAMWORK EXERCISES

1. Cross-selling can be an effective way for a firm to expand. On your own or with a classmate, locate an advertisement for a firm that you believe could benefit from cross-selling. List ways it could offer multiple goods or services to the same customer. Then create a new ad illustrating the multiple offerings.

2. With a partner, choose one of the following sales situations. Then take turns coming up with creative ways to close the deal—one of you plays the customer and the other plays the salesperson. Present your closing scenarios to the class.

   a. You are a new sales associate at a car dealership, and a potential customer has just test driven one of your newest models. You have handled all the customer's concerns and settled on a price. You don't want the customer to leave without agreeing to purchase the car.

   b. You operate a lawn care business and have visited several homeowners in a new development. Three of them have already agreed to give your service a try. You are meeting with the fourth and want to close that sale, too.

3. As sales representatives for a cooperative of organic farmers, you and a classmate are invited to make a sales presentation to a national supermarket chain. List the most important messages you wish to relate and then role-play the sales presentation.

4. On your own or with a classmate, go online and research a firm such as Kraft, General Mills, Ford, or Burger King to find out what kinds of consumer-oriented promotions the company is conducting for its various brands or individual products. Which promotions seem the most appealing to you as a consumer? Why? Present your findings to the class.

5. With a classmate, design a specialty advertising item for one of the following companies or its products, or choose one of your own. Present your design sketches to the class.
   a. Canada's Wonderland (Toronto), La Ronde (Montreal), Calaway Park (Calgary), or Playland (Vancouver)
   b. Tim Hortons
   c. Porsche
   d. Telus or Fido wireless
   e. The Green Beanery (www.greenbeanery.ca)
   f. Apple iPad

CRITICAL-THINKING EXERCISES

1. Since the implementation of Canada's Do Not Contact registry, some Canadians witnessed an increase in door-to-door selling as well as emails containing sales messages. As a marketer, do you think this type of selling is effective? Why or why not?

2. Montreal-based Van Houtte Inc. operates the largest coffee services network in North America and serves more than 74 000 workplaces. You will find their coffee served in car dealerships, doctors' offices, real estate offices, and in many other types of offices across Canada. Getting equipment and supplies into these offices requires personal selling to office managers, administrative support people, doctors, and even company owners. What role does relationship selling play in this situation? What kind of training should these salespeople receive?

3. Assume that a friend asks you to solicit donations for a local charity. (You pick the charity.) Outline your approach and presentation as a salesperson would.

4. Why is the recruitment and selection stage of the hiring process one of a sales manager's greatest challenges?

5. Food manufacturers often set up tables in supermarkets and offer free samples to shoppers, along with coupons for the promoted items. Sometimes restaurants offer free coffee or drink refills. What other products might lend themselves to sampling? Make a list. Pick one of the items and come up with a sampling plan for it. Where and when would you sample? To whom would you offer samples?

ETHICS EXERCISE

You have been hired by a discount sporting-goods retailer in an over-the-counter sales position. You have completed a training course that includes learning about the products, assisting customers, and cross-selling. You have made several good friends in the training course and sometimes get together after work to go running, play golf, or have dinner. You've noticed that one of your friends has really taken the training course to heart and has adopted a very aggressive attitude toward customers in the store, pushing them to buy just about anything, whether they need it or not.

1. Do you agree with your friend's actions? Why or why not?
2. Should you discuss the situation with your friend? Should you discuss it with your supervisor? Explain your response.

INTERNET EXERCISES

1. **Sales careers.** Visit the website for the Canadian Professional Sales Association (www.cpsa.com). The CPSA provides sales certification where salespeople who qualify can earn the designation of Certified Sales Professional, or CSP. What are the requirements to earn this designation? What are the benefits for salespeople who become CSPs? Visit www.cpsa.com/students and see how students could benefit from a student membership in the CPSA.

2. **Using the Internet.** The chapter discussed how many marketers are using the Internet to support personal selling and enhance sales promotion activities. Review the chapter material and then complete the following exercises.
   a. Many companies now use the Internet to demonstrate their products. Visit http://ca.blackberry.com/smartphones and view the product information. Make a list of your observations and bring your list to class to participate in a class discussion on the subject.
   b. An increasing number of Canadian websites feature information on contests and sweepstakes. Visit www.sweepstakes.ca, www.canadasweepstakes.com, and www.contestcanada.com. Evaluate each of these websites. What kinds of products or prizes are available? Which do you believe is the best? Why? What is your overall assessment of online sweepstakes and contests?

3. **CES.** The Consumer Electronics Show (CES) is one of the largest trade shows in the world. Visit the CES website (www.cesweb.org) and answer the following questions:
   a. When and where is the CES held?
   b. How many attended the most recent CES? How many firms and organizations had exhibits?
   c. What were the major new products introduced at the most recent CES?

Note: Internet Web addresses change frequently. If you don't find the exact sites listed, you may need to access the organization's home page and search from there or use a search engine such as Google.

CASE 15.1

Selling Food Equipment Solutions

TFI Food Equipment Solutions (TFI) is a Canadian industrial distributor that regularly exceeds $20 million in sales revenue—sometimes exceeding this by a considerable amount when several large sales are made during a particularly good year. Sales come mainly from two major product lines—Taylor and Henny Penny. These manufacturers produce equipment used in food service operations in institutions, stores, and restaurants and account for nearly 90 percent of TFI sales. The two product lines complement each other very well. Taylor is focused on ice cream and beverage equipment. Henny Penny produces fryers, rotisseries, blast chillers/freezers, heated food display units, etc.

To service its customers, TFI employs two types of salespeople. Nine salespeople service the single-outlet market. Single-outlet customers include many smaller, independent convenience, variety, and grocery stores. Salespeople each have a protected territory that is part of the five provinces where TFI has been appointed to represent Taylor and Henny Penny—Ontario, and the four Atlantic provinces (New Brunswick, Nova Scotia, Prince Edward Island, and Newfoundland and Labrador). The busiest period for sales to single-outlet customers is just prior to the summer, when demand for ice cream and beverages peaks. These salespeople get company vehicles, and their out-of-pocket expenses are reimbursed by TFI. They are not paid a salary but earn commissions of 12 to 18 percent of sales revenue, depending on what is sold and the final price that they negotiate for each sale. Salespeople are expected to sell $400 000 (usually between 35 and 50 sales) of equipment annually, although some sell considerably more.

TFI also employs three national account salespeople. Judi Saliba and Vico Singh sell to accounts such as Tim Hortons, Burger King, Esso, Harvey's, KFC, Mac's Convenience Stores, McDonald's, Milestone's Grill & Bar, Wendy's, and other large multi-outlet businesses. Bill Moyer specializes in servicing the supermarket chains: Loblaws, Sobeys, and Walmart, among others. Because the selling tasks are different—relationship management and providing service are even more important—these salespeople receive a high salary component, ranging between $50 000 and $70 000, and a smaller commission (1 to 4 percent) since the sales revenue from these accounts is so much greater. These accounts contribute approximately 43 percent of total company sales revenue, while the single-outlet customers contribute approximately 31 percent. The balance of sales revenue comes from parts and service sales.

Alex Pettes, president and co-owner of TFI, manages the selling function; that is, he fills the role as sales manager. Alex is highly motivated and his infectious enthusiasm has helped create a winning sales team at TFI. Over the last decade, Alex has developed his unique persona: Commander Alex Pettes, Sales Fighter Pilot Squadron Leader of the USS TFI. He begins each sales meeting—and the presentations he makes to salespeople and sales managers from other companies—as Commander Pettes.

Alex likes to talk about how he sees salespeople as "fighter pilots." He has developed a four-level pyramid to illustrate the similarities he sees between them. At the base, for a foundation, Alex sees good salespeople and fighter pilots as being calm and confident, yet slightly cocky. This is not arrogance, but rather the calm, controlled confidence of the well-trained and competent professional. At level two, Alex says that good salespeople and fighter pilots know their equipment, environment, competition, and mission. Neither simply fly around hoping to find opportunities; they plan for achievement. At the third level, Alex sees good salespeople and fighter pilots as "ever learning, ever improving." He recognizes the need of both to continue the learning process long after their formal education, and he likes to quote a favourite expression of McDonald's founder Ray Kroc: "Green and growing or ripe and rotting." Finally, at the top level, Alex sees both good salespeople and fighter pilots as having a whatever-it-takes winning attitude.

His personal philosophy informs how he sees and manages his salespeople. He believes that the responsibility for poor sales performance rests solely with the sales manager. He also believes that you cannot motivate other people, but that the sales manager must create an environment where salespeople can motivate themselves. Alex says, to create this environment, sales managers must provide three things: leadership, coaching, and training.

- *Leadership.* Sales managers must lead from the front, lead by example. They need to be "servant leaders," and they must remove barriers and obstacles that prevent salespeople from achieving their goals.
- *Coaching.* All the best performers—athletes, singers, actors, and even businesspeople—have a coach. It is a one-on-one, planned process of assistance, designed to help another person achieve their goals. Great sales managers are great coaches.
- *Training.* Sales managers must ensure that salespeople receive whatever product or sales training they need to succeed.

To help keep himself motivated and provide personal direction, Alex has developed his personal mission statement, which he recites three times each day:

I AM the Commander. I AM the Leader at the Front.

I AM the most positive, enthusiastic, vibrant person, who loves God and his family and continually contributes in the service to others.

I AM having everything in life I want as I help and serve enough other people get what they want.

The key to selling at TFI is to show customers how they can increase their business and make a profit; that is, TFI, and the TFI salespeople, succeed by helping their customers succeed.

Questions for Critical Thinking

1. Why does TFI employ two different types of salespeople?
2. What are the implications of having two different types of salespeople for sales management? Explain.

3. Do you agree with Alex Pettes that the responsibility for poor sales performance rests solely with the sales manager? Why or why not?

Sources: Interviews with Alex Pettes, president, TFI Food Equipment Solutions, 2007–2011; Alex Pettes, *From the Flight Deck* (Bloomington, IN: iUniverse, 2010).

CASE 15.2

Personal Selling and Sales Promotion at Scholfield Honda

"We want our customer to have a long-term relationship with us," explains Vinnie Koc, a sales consultant with Scholfield Honda, "by providing them [with] the service that Scholfield Honda has always provided." Scholfield Honda is one of Honda's larger dealerships, and for good reason. It was voted one of the best places to work in its local community. Roger Scholfield, owner and general manager of the dealership, attributes the company's success, both internally and with its customers, to the simple fact that "we can train anybody to do anything, but we can't train you to be a happy person." To ensure that those on the front line of every sale are the best in the business, Scholfield takes the new hire process very seriously. Every interview is vetted by at least three senior people, and Scholfield meets each potential hire before a final decision is made. The result is a staff of sales and service people who actually want to come to work every day and who believe in the product they are selling. In sales, where trust and attitude are everything, that's a pretty big deal. Scholfield's policy of "hiring good attitudes" is simple. Lose your good attitude, and the door is just a few feet away.

"I love my job," says Koc. "I love Hondas, and my whole family drives a Honda. I love the product, and I love to help people." He also loves his generous commissions and bonuses from Scholfield and extra incentives provided by Honda. As anyone who has bought a car knows, bargaining is just part of the game, and at Scholfield, they try to make it less of a contest and more of a conversation. Koc estimates that about 75 percent of his customers know what they want and know what they want to pay. They've done research, checked Blue Book values, and looked at prices in different parts of the country. They don't want to mess around. Koc understands this and treats each customer with the same respect he would want. The dealership gives its sales consultants a reasonable amount of freedom to work with customers on price. Koc keeps a spreadsheet of prices of the different models and features for customers to compare and make a reasonable offer. He takes every offer to his managers and negotiates with them to find a price each party can live with. Sometimes, that may mean less commission for him, but he's making an investment in repeat customers and referrals.

A close second to the personal sales experience customers receive at Scholfield Honda is advertising. The company advertises in print, on the radio, on television, and on local billboards. It has its own on-site advertising agency, Scholfield Creative, dedicated to keeping every man, woman, and child abreast of sales, rebates, and incentives available at the dealership.

As soon as he sits down with a client, Koc reviews all the sales that are currently available. A large part of his business is driven by ads, but for those who may not be up on the latest deals, taking the time can make all the difference because "it might trigger something in their mind and we can go ahead and do the deal that day," he says.

While most people come to Scholfield Honda because of its reputation, they come back because of the experience. From test drive to trade-in, every customer is treated like family, and Scholfield wouldn't have it any other way.

Questions for Critical Thinking

1. How important is sales force management in Scholfield Honda's overall success? Why?
2. Which steps in the sales process are most important in a consumer's decision to purchase a car?

part 7

PRICING DECISIONS

chapter 16   **Pricing Concepts and Strategies**

chapter 16

Pricing Concepts and Strategies

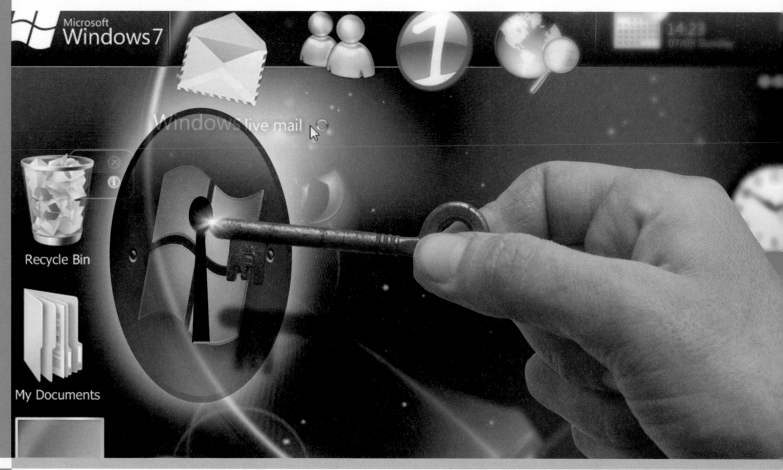

CHAPTER OBJECTIVES

① Identify the major categories of pricing objectives.

② Explain the methods of determining prices.

③ Compare the alternative pricing strategies and explain when each strategy is most appropriate.

④ Describe how prices are quoted.

⑤ Identify the various pricing policy decisions that marketers must make.

⑥ List and explain a number of special issues in pricing.

⑦ Outline the legal constraints on pricing.

MICROSOFT: SALES TAKE OFF AS PRICES TUMBLE

With its near-monopoly on PC software, especially its flagship Windows products, Microsoft has long been able to maintain premium prices for its products no matter how the economy or the computer industry has fared. Now, however, in what *BusinessWeek* calls "a risky experiment in price elasticity," the company is shifting to a new pricing strategy. Microsoft is reducing the prices of some of its most popular software products worldwide and even giving some away free, to try to grow market share in selected business and consumer market segments.

For instance, Windows customers upgrading to Windows 7 could purchase it retail for $40 less than Microsoft charged for its last new operating system, Vista. That's a bigger discount than the firm has offered on a new Windows version in a long time. Microsoft hopes customers will be persuaded to upgrade Windows 7 more often, especially those who opt for the cheaper Starter edition, which they can later enhance by adding premium features. Customers who bought a new PC during Windows 7's introduction got an even better deal. They were

offered either a 50 percent discount on the software or a free upgrade from the older Vista operating system. "We definitely saw the results of aggressive pricing," said one software industry analyst.

While sales of upgrades and new versions were relatively strong, helped by favourable reviews, Windows 7 didn't appear to be creating much new demand for PCs in its early months on the market, which could mean the company will have to support its predecessor operating systems Vista and Windows XP longer than it had planned. Many suppliers still had inventory of less expensive laptops and notebooks that were running on these systems. But home users and students buying the discounted Home Premium version of Windows 7 were expected to make up in volume for lower sales of the Ultimate version, which sells for more. The company also hopes to attract more corporate buyers with new prices for both software and Internet services. "We're focusing on gaining share in those areas that are most critical," says the head of Microsoft's business division.

Microsoft is also discounting its Office software package, with promotions that

amount to a 33 percent price reduction (even lower abroad), and to compete with Google and others, it offered free versions of two component Office programs, Word and Excel. Sales of Office were up 415 percent following the promotions.

In another price innovation, customers willing to install less powerful Office 2010 software were able to download it free (though with advertising) from the Internet. And in addition to selling its email program Exchange for download on CD, Microsoft will sell it online for a monthly fee, which is cheaper for the customer, though only about a third as profitable for the company. "I'm not saying it will be easy," said Microsoft's CEO Steven Ballmer. "But we have great opportunities to grow total profit dollars."

One further price cut was made to try to discourage piracy. In China, it cut the price of its software to $29 as a test and watched sales climb more than 800 percent. It was "like taking firewood from under [piracy's] cauldron," according to one Chinese software distributor's vice president. Microsoft agrees and plans to make the price cut permanent.[1]

---

connecting with customers

Few companies generate stronger reactions than Microsoft: some people hate it, some people love it, but many use its products. Why has it been so successful? Of course it has a portfolio of innovative products that it consistently updates and improves, but it also has been a masterful marketer. It has combined effective promotion with outstanding distribution that few companies in any industry are able to match. Now the company has turned its attention to developing an innovative pricing strategy designed to increase its market share and improve its profits.

Chapter Overview

ONE of the first questions customers ask is "How much does it cost?" Marketers understand the critical role that price plays in the customer's decision-making process. For products as varied as lipstick and business consulting services, marketers must develop strategies that price products to achieve their firms' objectives.

As a starting point for examining pricing strategies, consider the meaning of the term *price*. A **price** is the exchange value of a good or service—in other words, whatever that product can be exchanged for in the marketplace. Today, that usually denotes money required to purchase a product.

price Exchange value of a good or service.

Prices are both difficult to set and dynamic; they shift in response to a number of variables. Higher prices may convey the image of quality or even prestige; lower prices may connote value or, sometimes, poor quality. Setting prices is neither a one-time decision nor a standard routine. Some companies change prices once a year or less frequently; others change prices monthly or more frequently.

Companies translate pricing objectives into pricing decisions, considering costs, supply and demand, competition, channel needs, and the law. This chapter introduces the concept of price and its role in the economic system and marketing strategy. It discusses the process of determining

a profitable but justifiable (or fair) price. It examines various pricing strategies and price structures, such as reductions from list prices and geographical considerations. It then looks at the primary pricing policies, including psychological pricing, price flexibility, product-line pricing, and promotional pricing, as well as price-quality relationships. Competitive and negotiated prices are discussed, as is the transfer pricing dilemma. Finally, the chapter concludes by describing important factors in pricing goods and services for online and global markets, as well as legal considerations that affect pricing decisions. ◆◆◆

---

① Identify the major categories of pricing objectives.

PRICING OBJECTIVES AND THE MARKETING MIX

The extent to which any or all of the factors of production—natural resources, capital, human resources, and entrepreneurship—are employed depends on the prices those factors command. A firm's prices and the resulting purchases by its customers determine the company's revenue, influencing the profits it earns. Overall organizational objectives and more specific marketing objectives guide the development of pricing objectives, which in turn lead to the development and implementation of more specific pricing policies and procedures.

A firm might, for instance, set a major overall goal of becoming the dominant producer in its domestic market. It might then develop a marketing objective of achieving maximum sales penetration in each region, followed by a related pricing objective of setting prices at levels that maximize sales. These objectives might lead to the adoption of a low-price policy implemented by offering substantial price discounts to channel members.

Price affects and is affected by the other elements of the marketing mix. Product decisions, promotional plans, and distribution choices all affect the price of a good or service. For example, products distributed through complex channels involving several intermediaries must be priced high enough to cover the markups needed to compensate wholesalers and retailers for services they provide. Basic so-called *fighting brands* are intended to capture market share from higher-priced, options-laden competitors by offering relatively low prices to entice customers to give up some options in return for a cost savings.

Pricing objectives vary from firm to firm, and they can be classified into four major groups: (1) profitability objectives, (2) volume objectives, (3) meeting competition objectives, and (4) prestige objectives. Not-for-profit organizations, as well, must consider objectives of one kind or another when developing pricing strategies. Table 16.1 outlines the pricing objectives marketers rely on to meet their overall goals.

table 16.1 *Pricing Objectives*

OBJECTIVE	PURPOSE	EXAMPLE
Profitability objectives	Profit maximization Target return	Microsoft's initially high price for the Xbox 360
Volume objectives	Sales maximization Market share	Dell's low-priced PCs increase market share and sales of services
Meeting competition objectives	Value pricing	Walmart's lower prices on private house brands
Prestige objectives	Lifestyle Image	High-priced luxury autos such as Lexus and stereo equipment by Bose
Not-for-profit objectives	Profit maximization Cost recovery Market incentives Market suppression	Reduced or zero tolls for high-occupancy vehicles to encourage carpooling

PROFITABILITY OBJECTIVES

Marketers at for-profit firms must set prices with profits in mind. Even not-for-profit organizations realize the importance of setting prices high enough to cover expenses and provide a financial cushion to cover unforeseen needs and expenses. As the Russian proverb says, "There are two fools in every market: one asks too little, one asks too much." For consumers to pay prices that are either above or below what they consider to be the going rate, they must be convinced they are receiving fair value for their money. The "Marketing and the SME" feature describes how one consultant manages the careful balance between charging too much and charging too little.

MARKETING AND THE SME | If You Were for Sale, What Would You Charge?

WHAT are you worth? Most people don't have to seriously consider this, but if you are a consultant, and time is money, you must decide exactly how you will charge for your time.

When Laura Ricciuto was doing her MBA, she was hired by her university's MBA business consulting group and was involved in a number of marketing-related consulting projects. Pricing was not really an issue as clients paid $250 per day for consulting services, and only the time required to complete a consulting project had to be estimated. But when Laura graduated in 2008, she decided to start her own consultancy: Kaizen Marketing & Creative Design House. Under Laura's guidance, the company has evolved from projects focused on market research, business planning, and strategy development to include a number of additional marketing-related services focused more on tactical issues: brand development, graphic design, campaign advertisements, Web development, and more. When it comes to setting a price for her services, Laura says she uses one of three methods: project-based, value-based, or hourly-based pricing.

The following are some of the things that professionals such as Laura must consider when determining their worth and what they will charge:

- *Experience and expertise:* As consultants gain experience in a particular area, they become more knowledgeable and, hence, more valuable to their clients. They can charge a higher price.
- *Exclusivity:* Specialists are usually worth more than generalists. When consultants specialize in an area so that there are fewer qualified competitors, they can charge a higher price.
- *Target market:* Some customers are more price-sensitive than others. Larger corporations tend to be less price-sensitive than small business clients. Of course, a good portfolio of customers, large and small, would be a valuable asset for most consultants, and this usually requires some pricing flexibility.

Sources: Laura Ricciuto, personal interview, January 13, 2011; Kaizen Marketing & Creative Design House website, http://kaizenmarketing.ca/about, January 19, 2011.

H. F. (HERB) MACKENZIE

Computer technology allowed airlines to automate many services and put passengers in charge of other services, such as checking in at electronic kiosks.

Economic theory is based on two major assumptions. It assumes, first, that firms will behave rationally and, second, that this rational behaviour will result in an effort to maximize gains and minimize losses. Some marketers estimate profits by looking at historical sales data; others use elaborate calculations based on predicted future sales. It has been said that setting prices is an art, not a science. The talent lies in a marketer's ability to strike a balance between desired profits and the customer's perception of a product's value.

Marketers should evaluate and adjust prices continually to accommodate changes in the environment. The technological environment, for example, forces Internet marketers to respond quickly to competitors' pricing strategies. Search capabilities performed by shopping bots (described later in this chapter) allow customers to compare prices locally, nationally, and globally in a matter of seconds.

Intense price competition, sometimes conducted even when it means forgoing profits altogether or reducing services, often results when rivals battle for leadership positions in new-product categories. For some years, passenger airlines cut costs in order to compete on pricing. Computer technology allowed them to automate many services and put passengers in charge of other services, such as making reservations online and checking in at electronic kiosks. As a result, passengers now pay sharply higher fares and find amenities, such as in-flight meals, pillows and blankets, and audio headsets, all cost extra. Most airlines now also charge for a second checked bag, for reserved seating with extra legroom, and for booking tickets by telephone.[2]

Profits are a function of revenue and expenses:

$$\text{Profits} = \text{Revenue} - \text{Expenses}$$

Revenue is determined by the product's selling price and number of units sold:

$$\text{Total Revenue} = \text{Price} \times \text{Quantity Sold}$$

Therefore, a profit-maximizing price rises to the point at which further increases will cause disproportionate decreases in the number of units sold. A 10 percent price increase that results in only an 8 percent cut in volume will add to the firm's revenue. However, a 10 percent price hike that results in an 11 percent sales decline will reduce revenue.

marginal analysis
Method of analyzing the relationship among costs, sales price, and increased sales volume.

Economists refer to this approach as **marginal analysis**. They identify **profit maximization** as the point at which the addition to total revenue is just balanced by the increase in total cost. Marketers must resolve a basic problem of how to achieve this delicate balance when they set prices. Relatively few firms actually hit this elusive target. A significantly larger number prefer to direct their effort toward more realistic goals.

profit maximization
Point at which the additional revenue gained by increasing the price of a product equals the increase in total costs.

Consequently, marketers commonly set **target-return objectives**—short-run or long-run goals usually stated as percentages of sales or investment. The practice has become particularly popular among large firms in which other pressures interfere with profit-maximization objectives. In addition to resolving pricing questions, target-return objectives offer several benefits for marketers. For example, these objectives serve as tools for evaluating performance; they also satisfy desires to generate "fair" profits as judged by management, shareholders, and the public.

target-return objectives
Short-run or long-run pricing objectives of achieving a specified return on either sales or investment.

VOLUME OBJECTIVES

Some economists and business executives argue that pricing behaviour actually seeks to maximize sales within a given profit constraint. In other words, they set a minimum acceptable profit level and then seek to maximize sales (subject to this profit constraint) in the belief that the increased sales are more important in the long-run competitive picture than immediate high profits. As a result, companies should continue to expand sales as long as their total profits do not drop below the minimum return acceptable to management.

Sales maximization can also result from nonprice factors such as service and quality. Marketers succeeded in increasing sales for Dr. Scholl's new shoe insert, Dynastep, by advertising heavily in magazines. The ads explained how the Dynastep insert would help relieve leg and back pain. Priced around $14 for two inserts—twice as much as comparable offerings—Dynastep ran over its competitors to become number one in its category.

Another volume-related pricing objective is the **market-share objective**—the goal of controlling a specified minimum share of the market for a firm's good or service. Apple applied this strategy to its iPhone 3G (8Gb) price reduction. The company introduced annual updates for three years, dropping the price each time from the original $399 to $99, and eventually introduced a new model iPhone 4 (16Gb) for $159. Apple will undoubtedly be looking to continue price decreases as, according to one industry analyst, the cost of phones and service plans is the biggest barrier to incremental demand in both mature markets and in emerging markets such as China.[3]

market-share objective Volume-related pricing objective in which the goal is to achieve control of a portion of the market for a firm's good or service.

The PIMS Studies

Market-share objectives may prove critical to the achievement of other organizational objectives. High sales, for example, often mean more profits. The **Profit Impact of Market Strategies (PIMS) project**, an extensive study conducted by the Marketing Science Institute, analyzed more than 2000 firms and revealed that two of the most important factors influencing profitability were product quality and market share. Companies such as clothier Northern Reflections and Best Buy, the electronics giant, have introduced loyalty programs as a means of retaining customers and protecting their market share. When consumer spending slowed in the recent recession, "many chains . . . lost customers they wish they could have retained," said the global retail director of Accenture, the consultancy firm. "Retailers now feel the pressure to constantly work on creating additional services that will keep shoppers loyal."[4]

Profit Impact of Market Strategies (PIMS) project Research that discovered a strong positive relationship between a firm's market share and product quality and its return on investment.

The relationship between market share and profitability is evident in PIMS data that reveal an average 32 percent return on investment (ROI) for firms with market shares above 40 percent. In contrast, average ROI decreases to 24 percent for firms whose market shares are between 20 and 40 percent. Firms with a minor market share (less than 10 percent) generate average pre-tax investment returns of under 10 percent.[5]

The relationship also applies to a firm's individual brands. PIMS researchers compared the top four brands in each market segment they studied. Their data revealed that the leading brand typically generates after-tax ROI of 18 percent, considerably higher than the second-ranked brand. Weaker brands, on average, fail to earn adequate returns.

Marketers have developed an underlying explanation of the positive relationship between profitability and market share. Firms with large shares accumulate greater operating experience and lower overall costs relative to competitors with smaller market shares. Accordingly, effective segmentation strategies might focus on obtaining larger shares of smaller markets and on avoiding smaller shares of larger ones. A firm might achieve higher financial returns by becoming a major competitor in several smaller market segments than by remaining a relatively minor player in a larger market.

MEETING COMPETITION OBJECTIVES

A third set of pricing objectives seeks simply to meet competitors' prices. In many lines of business, firms set their own prices to match those of established industry price leaders. Price is a pivotal factor in the ongoing competition between long-distance telephone services and wireless carriers. In addition to unlimited calls within Canada for $6.99 a month, Skype, the Internet calling company owned by Microsoft, allows unlimited calls to

Canadian Tire regularly offers product discounts in its retail stores across Canada.

H. F. (HERB) MACKENZIE

Dollarama uses value pricing to sell many popular items at prices often far below those of its competition.

overseas landline phones in 40 other countries for $13.99 a month. The countries include most of Europe, as well as Australia, New Zealand, China, Japan, Korea, and Malaysia.[6]

Pricing objectives tied directly to meeting prices charged by major competitors deemphasize the price element of the marketing mix and focus more strongly on nonprice variables. Pricing is a highly visible component of a firm's marketing mix and an easy and effective tool for obtaining a differential advantage over competitors. It is, however, a tool that other firms can easily duplicate through price reductions of their own. Because price changes directly affect overall profitability in an industry, many firms attempt to promote stable prices by meeting competitors' prices and competing for market share by focusing on product strategies, promotional decisions, and distribution—the nonprice elements of the marketing mix.

Value Pricing

value pricing Pricing strategy emphasizing benefits derived from a product in comparison to the price and quality levels of competing offerings.

When discounts become normal elements of a competitive marketplace, other marketing mix elements gain importance in purchase decisions. In such instances, overall product value, not just price, determines product choice. In recent years, a new strategy—**value pricing**—has emerged that emphasizes the benefits a product provides in comparison to the price and quality levels of competing offerings. This strategy typically works best for relatively low-priced goods and services. Real Canadian Superstore periodically advertises "Every day, find over 2000 prices rounded down." Customers get value prices on many items throughout the store.

Value-priced products generally cost less than premium brands, but marketers point out that value does not necessarily mean *inexpensive*. The challenge for those who compete on value is to convince customers that low-priced brands offer quality comparable to that of a higher-priced product. An increasing number of alternative products and private-label brands has resulted in a more competitive marketplace in recent years. Palazzi Bros. Carpet and Tile, with three designer showrooms in Ontario, celebrated its 50th anniversary in 2010. Brothers Marco and Paul attribute their success to quality workmanship and materials. After 50 years in the industry, they are able to negotiate competitive prices with their suppliers, allowing their customers to benefit from value pricing and superior products. Even customers with very limited budgets can have breathtaking floors for as little as $1 per square foot.[7]

Value pricing is perhaps best seen in the personal computer industry. In the past few years, PC prices have collapsed, reducing the effectiveness of traditional pricing strategies intended to meet competition. Falling prices have helped sales grow as much as 15 percent worldwide in a recent quarter. Worldwide PC sales were expected to rise as economic recovery strengthened, but some observers think prices might begin to inch up as the cost of components rise.[8]

PRESTIGE OBJECTIVES

The final category of pricing objectives, unrelated to either profitability or sales volume, is prestige objectives. Prestige pricing establishes a relatively high price to develop and maintain an image of quality and exclusiveness that appeals to status-conscious consumers. Such objectives reflect marketers' recognition of the role of price in creating an overall image of the firm and its product offerings.

Prestige objectives affect the price tags of such products as Tilley hats, lululemon athletica sports clothing, and Tag Heuer watches. When a perfume marketer sets a price of $400 or more per ounce,

Marketoid

Big Splash (Hong Dong in Chinese), an 11-month-old red Tibetan mastiff, sold in 2011 in Qingdao, China, for 10 million yuan, about $1.5 million (U.S.).

this choice reflects an emphasis on image far more than the cost of ingredients. Analyses have shown that ingredients account for less than 5 percent of a perfume's cost. Thus advertisements for Joy that promote the fragrance as the "costliest perfume in the world" use price to promote product prestige.

In the business world, private jet ownership imparts an image of prestige, power, and high price tags—too high for most business travellers to consider. Recognizing that cost is the primary factor that makes jet ownership prohibitive, companies such as London, Ontario-based OurPLANE and Calgary-based AirSprint have created an alternative: fractional ownership. Corporate boards of directors pressed to cut costs in a weak economy are much more willing to pay for a share in a jet than to purchase a whole new aircraft.[9]

PRICING OBJECTIVES OF NOT-FOR-PROFIT ORGANIZATIONS

Pricing is also a key element of the marketing mix for not-for-profit organizations. Pricing strategy can help these groups achieve a variety of organizational goals:

1. *Profit maximization.* While not-for-profit organizations by definition do not cite profitability as a primary goal, there are numerous instances in which they do try to maximize their returns on single events or a series of events. A $1000-a-plate political fundraiser is a classic example.

2. *Cost recovery.* Some not-for-profit organizations attempt to recover only the actual cost of operating the unit. Mass transit and toll roads and bridges are common examples. The amount of recovered costs is often dictated by tradition, competition, or public opinion.

3. *Market incentives.* Other not-for-profit groups follow a lower-than-average pricing policy or offer a free service to encourage increased usage of the good or service. OC Transpo provides public transit services in Ottawa. It has offered free bus service after 9:00 p.m. on Canada Day to encourage use during a period when there would be street closures and when downtown traffic would be congested.

4. *Market suppression.* Price can also discourage consumption. High prices help to accomplish social objectives independent of the costs of providing goods or services. Illustrations include tobacco and alcohol taxes (the so-called sin taxes), parking fines, tolls, and gasoline excise taxes.

Prestige objectives help market exclusive products, such as Tag Heuer watches.

assessment check 1a

1.1 What are target-return objectives?

1.2 What is value pricing?

1.3 How do prestige objectives affect a seller's pricing strategy?

assessment check 1b

1.4. What goals does pricing strategy help a not-for-profit organization achieve?

METHODS FOR DETERMINING PRICES

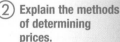
② Explain the methods of determining prices.

Marketers determine prices in two basic ways—by applying the theoretical concepts of supply and demand and by completing cost-oriented analyses. During the first part of the 20th century, most discussions of price determination emphasized the classical concepts of supply and demand. During the last half of the century, however, the emphasis began to shift to a cost-oriented approach. Hindsight reveals certain flaws in both concepts.

H. F. (HERB) MACKENZIE

The Coca-Cola Company has introduced size-reduced bottles and cans for prices that range from 50 percent more to double the per-millilitre price of regular-size bottles and cans.

customary prices
Traditional prices that customers expect to pay for certain goods and services.

demand Schedule of the amounts of a firm's product that consumers will purchase at different prices during a specified time period.

supply Schedule of the amounts of a good or service that firms will offer for sale at different prices during a specified time period.

pure competition
Market structure characterized by homogeneous products in which there are so many buyers and sellers that none has a significant influence on price.

Treatments of this subject often overlook another concept of price determination—one based on the impact of custom and tradition. **Customary prices** are retail prices that consumers expect as a result of tradition and social habit. Candy makers have attempted to maintain traditional price levels by greatly reducing overall product size. Similar practices have prevailed in the marketing of soft drinks as bottlers attempt to balance consumer expectations of customary prices with the realities of rising costs. Sometimes customary prices hide a real price increase, however, when the quantity of the product has been imperceptibly reduced. Georgia Pacific, one of North America's leading paper goods manufacturers, shrank the size of each sheet on its rolls of Northern brand toilet paper by a fraction of an inch and reduced the number of sheets per roll from 300 to 286. A customer service rep for the company confirmed the move was made to prevent a price increase. The Coca-Cola Company has introduced a "90-calorie portion-control mini-can" and offers eight-packs of the smaller-size cans for prices that range from 50 percent more to double the per-ounce price of regular size cans.[10]

Changes in the price of oil on world markets presents another example of supply and demand. Crude oil prices increase as demand increases and decrease as supply increases. The value of Canadian exports soared as the average price for crude oil peaked temporarily near $150 a barrel in mid-2008 as demand far exceeded supply. Canada has the second-largest volume of crude oil reserves in the world, and its supply far exceeds current aggregate Canadian demand. Approximately 99 percent of Canada's excess oil production—which is about two-thirds of the oil it produces—goes to the United States.[11]

Higher gas prices have effects on other consumer costs as well. With gas at record highs, hybrid cars are in greater demand than ever before, and some dealers have months-long waiting lists even at premium prices. The "Go Green" feature describes how the Toyota Prius may have commanded a premium price when it was first introduced to Canada and the search for new energy-saving alternatives. The newest fuel-efficient Toyota Prius models get 25 kilometres per litre (highway driving). The company's group vice president and general manager said, "Since Prius was first introduced, the company demographics has shifted from an early adopter to a mainstream shopper." The company hopes to keep Prius in the number-one spot among hybrids and unveiled a new "plug-in" version at the North American International Auto Show in 2011.[12]

PRICE DETERMINATION IN ECONOMIC THEORY

Microeconomics suggests a way of determining prices that assumes a profit-maximization objective. This technique attempts to derive correct equilibrium prices in the marketplace by comparing supply and demand. It also requires more complete analysis than actual business firms typically conduct.

Demand refers to a schedule of the amounts of a firm's product that consumers will purchase at different prices during a specified time period. **Supply** refers to a schedule of the amounts of a good or service that will be offered for sale at different prices during a specified period. These schedules may vary for different types of market structures. Businesses operate and set prices in four types of market structures: pure competition, monopolistic competition, oligopoly, and monopoly.

Pure competition is a market structure with so many buyers and sellers that no single participant can significantly influence price. Pure competition presupposes other market conditions as well: homogeneous products and ease of entry for sellers due to low start-up costs. The agricultural sector exhibits many characteristics of a purely competitive market, making it the closest actual example. But the Canadian Organic Livestock Association (COLA) is now marketing certified organic beef across North America, attempting to differentiate a higher-quality product.

| GO GREEN | **China Searching for Solutions Before It Chokes On Its Own Success** |

DAVID Suzuki, Canada's well-known science broadcaster and environmental activist, claims ownership of North America's first Prius, Toyota's initial hybrid car. Suzuki may have been happy contributing to a better environment but, as an early adopter, he undoubtedly paid an economic premium. Now the alternatives available to Canadians are many and, while prices for "green" cars remain high, they are certainly getting more affordable, and the number of alternative models continues to increase.

If North American car manufacturers do not quickly develop green alternatives, the Chinese may—within a few decades—do to North America what the Japanese did only a few decades ago. China has become a "car" culture. Less than two decades ago, there were only 37 000 private cars in China. In 2009, China overtook the United States as the world's largest car market, and the country now exports more cars than it imports. Chinese cars can be found in more than 170 countries, although not in Canada or the United States.

As the result of rapidly growing consumer demand for vehicles in China, Chinese society is paying the same price that other highly mobile societies pay: congestion and pollution. At the end of 2010, there were 4.7 million cars registered in Beijing alone. The city's Third Ring Road, where cars once travelled at 45 kilometres per hour, has slowed to between 7 and 20 kilometres per hour, depending on traffic conditions. Drivers may have to sit for an hour to get on a ramp leading to the elevated highway that will take them across the city. And pollution is a real problem. Cars must now drive in the city centre on alternate days only, depending on whether the car's licence plate number is odd or even. But Beijing is only the 13th-most polluted city in the world—behind six other Chinese cities—according to the World Health Organization.

What has this pollution done for China? Aside from the human cost, pollution has encouraged manufacturers, with the help of government regulation, to look for solutions. One solution is to improve the efficiency of cars, and China now has legislated fuel-efficiency standards that are more than 20 percent better than the United States hopes to impose in 2020. Second, China now sells domestically a Chinese-made, plug-in hybrid car. The government is considering a law that would require foreign car manufacturers to share technology related to electric vehicles or be prevented from selling cars in China. Don't be surprised if Chinese-manufactured electric cars appear within a few decades at a dealership near you, and at a very competitive price. However, some analysts believe it may be even longer before that happens. With demand so strong in China, there is little advantage to look for additional export markets. Chinese consumers are expected to purchase over 20 million cars in 2011, and that will still mean that only about 30 of every 1000 Chinese consumers will own a car, compared to about 700 of every 1000 consumers in North America.

Sources: "OK, Listen Up. Green Is Not the Colour of Nerds," *Calgary Herald*, January 26, 2011, p. F5; Dave Hall, "Predictions of Auto Invasion from China Overstate Reality; It May Be Decades Before They're Capable of Competing in North America, Analyst Says," *Gazette* (Montreal), January 25, 2011, p. B16; Karl Gerth, *As China Goes, So Goes the World* (New York, NY: Hill and Wang, 2010), pp. 19–41; Bill Schiller, "Tangled Up in Traffic: Love Affair with Cars Halts Chinese Capital," *Toronto Star*, December 21, 2010, p. B1.

Monopolistic competition typifies most retailing and features large numbers of buyers and sellers. These diverse parties exchange heterogeneous, relatively well-differentiated products, giving marketers some control over prices.

Relatively few sellers compete in an **oligopoly**. Pricing decisions by each seller are likely to affect the market, but no single seller controls it. High start-up costs form significant barriers to entry for new competitors. Each firm's demand curve in an oligopolistic market displays a unique kink at the current market price. Because of the impact of a single competitor on total industry sales, competitors usually quickly match any attempt by one firm to generate additional sales by reducing prices. Price cutting in such industry structures is likely to reduce total industry revenues. Oligopolies operate in the petroleum refining, automobile, airline, banking, and tobacco industries.

A **monopoly** is a market structure in which only one seller of a product exists and for which there are no close substitutes. Legislation has nearly eliminated all but temporary monopolies, such as those created through patent protection. Regulated industries, such as utility companies, constitute another form of monopoly. The government allows regulated monopolies in markets in which competition would lead to an uneconomical duplication of services. In return for such a licence, government reserves the right to regulate the monopoly's rate of return.

The four types of market structures are compared in Table 16.2 on the following bases: number of competitors, ease of entry into the industry by new firms, similarity of competing products, degree of control over price by individual firms, and the elasticity or inelasticity of the demand curve

monopolistic competition Market structure involving a heterogeneous product and product differentiation among competing suppliers, allowing the marketer some degree of control over prices.

oligopoly Market structure in which relatively few sellers compete and where high start-up costs form barriers to keep out new competitors.

monopoly Market structure in which a single seller dominates trade in a good or service for which buyers can find no close substitutes.

table 16.2   *Distinguishing Features of the Four Market Structures*

CHARACTERISTICS	PURE COMPETITION	MONOPOLISTIC COMPETITION	OLIGOPOLY	MONOPOLY
TYPE OF MARKETING STRUCTURE				
Number of competitors	Many	Few to many	Few	No direct competitors
Ease of entry into industry	Easy	Somewhat difficult	Difficult	Regulated by government by new firms
Similarity of goods or services offered by competing firms	Similar	Different	Can be either similar or different	No directly competing services
Control over prices by individual firms	None	Some	Some	Considerable
Demand curves facing individual firms	Totally elastic	Can be either elastic or inelastic	Kinked; inelastic below kink; more elastic above	Can be either elastic or inelastic
Examples	Alberta beef farm	Best Buy stores	Petro-Canada	Liquor Control Board of Ontario

variable costs Costs that change with the level of production (such as labour and raw materials costs).

fixed costs Costs that remain stable at any production level within a certain range (such as lease payments or insurance costs).

average total costs Costs calculated by dividing the sum of the variable and fixed costs by the number of units produced.

marginal cost Change in total cost that results from producing an additional unit of output.

facing the individual firm. Elasticity—the degree of consumer responsiveness to changes in price—is discussed in more detail in a later section.

Cost and Revenue Curves

Marketers must set a price for a product that generates sufficient revenue to cover the costs of producing and marketing it. A product's total cost is composed of total variable costs and total fixed costs. **Variable costs** change with the level of production (such as raw materials and labour costs), and **fixed costs** remain stable at any production level within a certain range (such as lease payments or insurance costs). **Average total costs** are calculated by dividing the sum of the variable and fixed costs by the number of units produced. Finally, **marginal cost** is the change in total cost that results from producing an additional unit of output.

The demand side of the pricing equation focuses on revenue curves. Average revenue is calculated by dividing total revenue by the quantity associated with these revenues. Average revenue is actually the demand curve facing the firm. Marginal revenue is the change in total revenue that results from selling an additional unit of output. Figure 16.1 shows the relationships of various cost and revenue measures; the firm maximizes its profits when marginal costs equal marginal revenues.

Table 16.3 illustrates why the intersection of the marginal cost and marginal revenue curves is the logical point at which to maximize revenue for the organization. Although the firm can earn a profit

figure 16.1

Determining Price by Relating Marginal Revenue to Marginal Cost

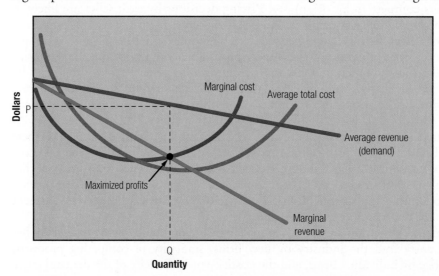

table 16.3 *Price Determination Using Marginal Analysis*

PRICE	NUMBER SOLD	TOTAL REVENUE	MARGINAL REVENUE	TOTAL COSTS	MARGINAL COSTS	PROFITS (TOTAL REVENUE MINUS TOTAL COSTS)
—	—	—	—	—	—	($50)
$34	1	$34	$34	$57	$7	(23)
32	2	64	30	62	5	2
30	3	90	26	66	4	24
28	4	112	22	69	3	43
26	5	130	18	73	4	57
24	6	144	14	78	5	66
22	7	154	10	84	6	70
20	8	160	6	91	7	69
18	9	162	2	100	9	62
16	10	160	(2)	110	11	50

at several different prices, the price at which it earns maximum profits is $22. At a price of $24, $66 in profits are earned—$4 less than the $70 profit at the $22 price. If a price of $20 is set to attract additional sales, the marginal costs of the extra sales ($7) are greater than the marginal revenues received ($6), and total profits decline.

THE CONCEPT OF ELASTICITY IN PRICING STRATEGY

Although the intersection of the marginal cost and marginal revenue curves determines the level of output, the impact of changes in price on sales varies greatly. To understand why it fluctuates, it is necessary to understand the concept of elasticity.

Elasticity is the measure of the responsiveness of purchasers and suppliers to price changes. The price elasticity of demand (or elasticity of demand) is the percentage change in the quantity of a good or service demanded divided by the percentage change in its price. A 10 percent increase in the price of eggs that results in a 5 percent decrease in the quantity of eggs demanded yields a price elasticity of demand for eggs of 0.5. The price elasticity of supply of a product is the percentage change in the quantity of a good or service supplied divided by the percentage change in its price. A 10 percent increase in the price of shampoo that results in a 25 percent increase in the quantity supplied yields a price elasticity of supply for shampoo of 2.5.

Consider a case in which a 1 percent change in price causes more than a 1 percent change in the quantity supplied or demanded. Numerically, that means an elasticity measurement greater than 1.0. When the elasticity of demand or supply is greater than 1.0, that demand or supply is said to be elastic. If a 1 percent change in price results in less than a 1 percent change in quantity, a product's elasticity of demand or supply will be less than 1.0. In that case, the demand or supply is called inelastic. For example, the demand for cigarettes is relatively inelastic; research studies have shown that a 10 percent increase in cigarette prices results in only a 4 percent sales decline.

In some countries whose economies are in shambles, price levels bear little resemblance to the laws of elasticity or supply and demand. Prices in Zimbabwe are rising at unheard-of rates, the result of hyper-inflation that rose to more than 7600 percent in a *month*—estimated to be as high as 12.5 million percent a year. More recently, however, changes in the country's monetary policies, including the abandonment of its local currency, began to bring prices down and it appeared that inflation in Zimbabwe might soon be a thing of the past.[13]

assessment check 2a

2.1 What are the two basic ways in which marketers determine prices?

2.2 What are the four types of market structures?

2.3 Identify the two types of costs that make up a product's total cost.

elasticity Measure of responsiveness of purchasers and suppliers to a change in price.

H. F. (HERB) MACKENZIE

A 10 percent increase in the price of eggs that results in a 5 percent decrease in the quantity of eggs demanded yields a price elasticity of demand for eggs of 0.5.

Determinants of Elasticity

Why is the elasticity of supply or demand high for some products and low for others? What determines demand elasticity? One major factor influencing the elasticity of demand is the availability of substitutes or complements. The "Marketing in a Digital World" feature describes the effect of high airfares from Canadian airports and how travellers are finding less costly alternatives. If consumers can easily find close substitutes for a good or service, the product's demand tends to be elastic. A product's role as a complement to the use of another product also affects its degree of price elasticity. For example, the relatively inelastic demand for motor oil reflects its role as a complement to a more important product, gasoline. High prices of gasoline, in turn, are fuelling the search for alternative fuels.[14]

As increasing numbers of buyers and sellers complete their business transactions online, the elasticity of a product's demand is drastically affected. Take major discounters and other price-competitive box stores, for example. Small businesses and individual do-it-yourselfers shop at Canadian Tire for tools, such as wheelbarrows; parents look for birthday gifts at Walmart; and homeowners go to Future Shop for new refrigerators or stoves. Today, however, the Internet lets consumers contact many more providers directly, often giving them better selections and prices for their efforts with service sites such as Shopbot.ca, PriceGrabber.ca, and Shopzilla.com for consumer goods and electronics; Net-a-Porter.com for high-fashion clothing; and Kayak.com and Expedia.ca for travel bargains. The increased options available to shoppers combine to create a market characterized by demand elasticity.

Marketoid

Cigarettes are price inelastic: in a recent 10-year period in New Brunswick, cigarette prices increased by 113 percent; consumption fell by only 11 percent.

| MARKETING IN A DIGITAL WORLD | **Airfare Prices: High for Canadians and High for Canada** |

WANT to save money on your airfare? Get online and buy your ticket, and then follow millions of your fellow Canadians south of the border where savings are frequently 50 percent or more. But if you really want the best deals, you have to be Internet-savvy; you should do some comparison shopping and, even then, the best fares go quickly. In 2009, 4.6 million Canadians made one-way trips from U.S. airports.

Flyers from British Columbia simply travel south to Washington. Albertans fly from Montana, Manitobans fly from North Dakota, Ontarians fly from Michigan and New York, and Quebecers fly from New York and Vermont. On one afternoon in 2010, 40 percent of the cars at the Buffalo, New York, airport had Ontario licence plates. The cost to Canada: fewer jobs at airports, fewer cab drives taken, fewer hotel rooms booked, fewer restaurant meals served, fewer car rentals made.

In short, according to Toronto-based consultancy AirTrav Inc., air passenger leakage costs Canada in excess of $1.1 billion a year in economic output.

But not only are high prices driving Canadians to fly from U.S. airports, according to Giovanni Bisignani, head of the International Air Transport Association, they are also hobbling efforts to attract visitors to Canada. In less than a decade, he says, Canada has gone from the eighth-most visited country in the world to fifteenth. Canada is certainly paying a high price for its airfare.

Sources: Bernard Marotte, "Canada's 'Excessive' Airport Taxes Driving Tourists Away, IATA Says," *The Globe and Mail*, January 21, 2011, p. B5; Brent Jang, "An Ominous Flight Pattern," *The Globe and Mail*, November 27, 2010, p. B6; Susan Pigg, "Bargains in Buffalo; Toronto Fliers Are Finding the Drive Across the Line Worthwhile in the Search for Low-Cost Air Travel," *Toronto Star* (Ontario Edition), February 16, 2002, p. 01.

Elasticity of demand also depends on whether a product is perceived as a necessity or a luxury. The Four Seasons chain of luxury hotels and resorts enjoys such a strong reputation for service, comfort, and exclusiveness that it has become a favourite among affluent individual travellers and business professionals. In other contexts, specialty shops such as Starbucks are considered necessities by some consumers today.

Most people regard high-fashion clothes, such as a $1500 Escada embroidered silk dress, as luxuries. If prices for designer outfits increase dramatically, people can respond by purchasing lower-priced substitutes instead. In contrast, dental care is considered a necessity, so price changes have little effect on the frequency of visits to the dentist.

Elasticity also depends on the portion of a person's budget that he or she spends on a good or service. For example, people no longer really need matches; they can easily find good substitutes. Nonetheless, the demand for matches remains very inelastic because people spend so little on them that they hardly notice a price change. In contrast, the demand for housing or transportation is not totally inelastic, even though they are necessities, because both consume large parts of a consumer's budget.

Elasticity of demand also responds to consumers' time perspectives. Demand often shows less elasticity in the short run than in the long run. Consider the demand for home air conditioning. In the short run, people pay rising energy prices because they find it difficult to cut back on the quantities they use. Accustomed to living with specific temperature settings and dressing in certain ways, they prefer to pay more during a few months of the year than to explore other possibilities. Over the long term, though, they may consider insulating their homes and planting shade trees to reduce cooling costs.

Elasticity and Revenue

The elasticity of demand exerts an important influence on variations in total revenue as a result of changes in the price of a good or service. Assume, for example, that the Toronto Transit Commission (TTC) officials are considering alternative methods of raising more money for their budget. One possible method for increasing revenues would be to increase fares for commuters. But should the TTC raise or lower the price of a pass? The correct answer depends on the elasticity of demand for its services. A 10 percent decrease in fares should attract more riders, but unless it stimulates more than a 10 percent increase in riders, total revenue will fall. A 10 percent increase in fares will bring in more money per rider, but if more than 10 percent of the riders stop using TTC services, total revenue will fall. A price cut will increase revenue only for a product with elastic demand, and a price increase will raise revenue only for a product with inelastic demand. TTC officials seemed to believe that the demand for its services is inelastic; they recently raised fares as they needed more money to cover operating costs.

assessment check 2b

2.4 What are the determinants of elasticity?

2.5 What is the usual relationship between elasticity and revenue?

PRACTICAL PROBLEMS OF PRICE THEORY

Marketers may thoroughly understand price theory concepts but still encounter difficulty applying them in practice. What practical limitations interfere with setting prices? First, many firms do not attempt to maximize profits. Economic analysis is subject to the same limitations as the assumptions on which it is based—for example, the proposition that all firms attempt to maximize profits. Second, it is difficult to estimate demand curves. Modern accounting procedures provide managers with a clear understanding of cost structures, so managers can readily comprehend the supply side of the pricing equation. But they find it difficult to estimate demand at various price levels. Demand curves must be based on marketing research estimates that may be less exact than cost figures. Although the demand element can be identified, it is often difficult to measure in real-world settings.

assessment check 2c

2.6 List the three reasons why it is difficult to put price theory into practice.

PRICE DETERMINATION IN PRACTICE

cost-plus pricing
Practice of adding a percentage of specified dollar amount—or markup—to the base cost of a product to cover unassigned costs and to provide a profit.

The practical limitations inherent in price theory have forced practitioners to turn to other techniques. **Cost-plus pricing**, the most popular method, uses a base-cost figure per unit and adds a markup to cover unassigned costs and to provide a profit. The only real difference among the multitude of cost-plus techniques is the relative sophistication of the costing procedures employed. For example, a local apparel shop may set prices by adding a 45 percent markup to the invoice price charged by the supplier. The markup is expected to cover all other expenses and permit the owner to earn a reasonable return on the sale of clothes.

In contrast to this rather simple pricing mechanism, a large manufacturer may employ a complex pricing formula requiring computer calculations. However, this method merely adds a more complicated procedure to the simpler, traditional method for calculating costs. In the end, someone still must make a decision about the markup. The apparel shop and the large manufacturer may figure costs differently, but they are remarkably similar in completing the markup side of the equation.

Cost-plus pricing often works well for a business that keeps its costs low, allowing it to set its prices lower than those of competitors and still make a profit. Walmart keeps costs low by buying most of its inventory directly from manufacturers, using a supply chain that slashes inventory costs by quickly replenishing inventory as items are sold, and relying on wholesalers and other intermediaries only in special instances like localized items. This strategy has played a major role in the discounter becoming the world's largest retailer.

Alternative Pricing Procedures

full-cost pricing Pricing method that uses all relevant variable costs in setting a product's price and allocates those fixed costs not directly attributed to the production of the priced item.

The two most common cost-oriented pricing procedures are the full-cost method and the incremental-cost method. **Full-cost pricing** uses all relevant variable costs in setting a product's price. In addition, it allocates those fixed costs that cannot be directly attributed to the production of the specific item being priced. Under the full-cost method, if job order 515 in a printing plant amounts to 0.000127 percent of the plant's total output, then 0.000127 percent of the firm's overhead expenses are charged to that job. This approach allows the marketer to recover all costs plus the amount added as a profit margin.

The full-cost approach has two basic deficiencies. First, there is no consideration of competition or demand for the item. Perhaps no one wants to pay the price the firm has calculated. Second, any method for allocating overhead (fixed expenses) is arbitrary and may be unrealistic. In manufacturing, overhead allocations often are tied to direct labour hours. In retailing, the area of each profit centre is sometimes the factor used in computations. Regardless of the technique employed, it is difficult to show a cause–effect relationship between the allocated cost and most products.

incremental-cost pricing Pricing method that attempts to use only costs directly attributable to a specific output in setting prices.

One way to overcome the arbitrary allocation of fixed expenses is with **incremental-cost pricing**, which attempts to use only those costs directly attributable to a specific output in setting prices. Consider a very small-scale manufacturer with the following income statement:

Sales (10 000 units at $10)		$100 000
Expenses:		
Variable	$50 000	
Fixed	40 000	90 000
Net Profit		$ 10 000

Suppose the firm is offered a contract for an additional 5000 units. Since the peak season is over, these items can be produced at the same average variable cost. Assume that the labour force would otherwise be working on maintenance projects. How low should the firm price its product to get the contract?

Under the full-cost approach, the lowest price would be $9 per unit. This figure is obtained by dividing the $90 000 in expenses by an output of 10 000 units. The incremental approach, on the other hand, could permit any price above $5, which would significantly increase the possibility of securing the additional contract. This price would be composed of the $5 variable cost associated with each unit of production plus some additional per-unit contribution to fixed expenses and overhead.

With a $5.10 proposed price ($.10 over the variable cost), for example, the income statement now looks like this:

Sales (10 000 at $10; 5000 at $5.10)		$125 500
Expenses:		
Variable	$75 000	
Fixed	40 000	115 000
Net Profit		$ 10 500

Profits thus increase under the incremental approach.

Admittedly, the illustration is based on two assumptions: (1) the ability to isolate markets such that selling at the lower price will not affect the price received in other markets, and (2) the absence of legal restrictions on the firm. The example, however, does illustrate that profits can sometimes be enhanced by using the incremental approach.

assessment check 2d

2.7 What is full-cost pricing?

2.8 What is incremental-cost pricing?

Break-Even Analysis

Break-even analysis is a means of determining the number of goods or services that must be sold at a given price to generate sufficient revenue to cover total costs. Figure 16.2 graphically depicts this process. The total cost curve includes both fixed and variable segments, and total fixed cost is represented by a horizontal line. Average variable cost is assumed to be constant per unit as it was in the example for incremental pricing.

The break-even point is the point at which total revenue equals total cost. In the example in Figure 16.2, a selling price of $10 and an average variable cost of $5 result in a per-unit contribution to fixed cost of $5. The break-even point in units is found by using the following formula, where the per-unit contribution equals the product's price less the variable cost per unit:

break-even analysis
Pricing technique used to determine the number of products that must be sold at a specified price to generate enough revenue to cover total cost.

$$\text{Break-Even Point (in units)} = \frac{\text{Total Fixed Cost}}{\text{Per-Unit Contribution to Fixed Cost}}$$

$$\text{Break-Even Point (in units)} = \frac{\$40\ 000}{\$5} = 8000 \text{ units}$$

The break-even point in dollars is found with the following formula:

$$\text{Break-Even Point (in dollars)} = \frac{\text{Total Fixed Cost}}{1 - \text{Variable Cost per Unit Price}}$$

$$\text{Break-Even Point (in dollars)} = \frac{\$40\ 000}{1 - (\$5/\$10)}$$

$$= \frac{\$40\ 000}{0.5} = \$80\ 000$$

figure 16.2
Break-Even Chart

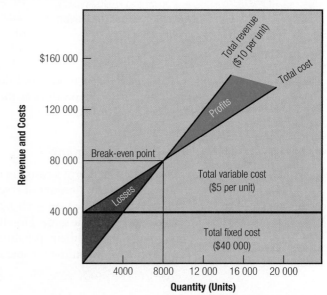

Sometimes break-even is reached by reducing costs. Faced with declining sales and revenues, Ford Motor Co. recently beat its own goals for cost reductions by reducing costs, as well as restructuring debt.[15]

Once the break-even point has been reached, sufficient revenues will have been obtained from sales to cover all fixed costs. Any additional sales will generate per-unit profits equal to the difference between the product's selling price and the variable cost of each unit. As Figure 16.2 reveals, sales of 8001 units (1 unit above the break-even point) will produce net profits of $5 ($10 sales price less per-unit variable cost of $5). Once all fixed costs have been covered, the per-unit contribution will become the per-unit profit.

Target Returns

Although break-even analysis indicates the sales level at which the firm will incur neither profits nor losses, most firms' managers include a targeted profit in their analyses. In some instances, management sets a desired dollar return when considering a proposed new product or other marketing action. A retailer may set a desired profit of $250 000 in considering whether to expand to a second location. In other instances, the target return may be expressed in percentages, such as a 15 percent return on sales. These target returns can be calculated as follows:

$$\text{Break-Even Point (including specific dollar target return)} = \frac{\text{Total Fixed Cost} + \text{Profit Objective}}{\text{Per-Unit Contribution}}$$

$$\text{Break-Even Point (in units)} = \frac{\$40\,000 + \$15\,000}{\$5} = 11\,000 \text{ units}$$

If the target return is expressed as a percentage of sales, it can be included in the break-even formula as a variable cost. Suppose the marketer in the preceding example seeks a 10 percent return on sales. The desired return is $1 for each product sold (the $10 per-unit selling price multiplied by the 10 percent return on sales). In this case, the basic break-even formula will remain unchanged, although the variable cost per unit will be increased to reflect the target return, and the per-unit contribution to fixed cost will be reduced to $4. As a result, the break-even point will increase from 8000 to 10 000 units:

$$\text{Break-Even Point} = \frac{\$40\,000}{\$4} = 10\,000 \text{ units}$$

assessment check 2e

2.9   Give the formula for finding the break-even point, in units and in dollars.

2.10   What adjustments to the basic break-even calculation must be made to include target returns?

2.11   What are the advantages of break-even analysis?

2.12   What are the disadvantages of break-even analysis?

Evaluation of Break-Even Analysis

Break-even analysis is an effective tool for marketers in assessing the sales required for covering costs and achieving specified profit levels. It is easily understood by both marketing and nonmarketing executives and may help them decide whether required sales levels for a certain price are in fact realistic goals. However, it has its shortcomings.

First, the model assumes that costs can be divided into fixed and variable categories. Some costs, such as salaries and advertising outlays, may be either fixed or variable depending on the particular situation. In addition, the model assumes that per-unit variable costs do not change at different levels of operation. However, these may vary because of quantity discounts, more efficient utilization of the workforce, or other economies resulting from increased levels of production and sales. Finally, the basic break-even model does not consider demand. It is a cost-based model and does not directly address the crucial question of whether consumers will purchase the product at the specified price and in the quantities required for breaking even or generating profits.

Yield Management

yield management
Pricing strategy that allows marketers to vary prices based on such factors as demand, even though the cost of providing those goods or services remains the same; designed to maximize revenues in situations such as airfares, lodging, auto rentals, and theatre tickets, where costs are fixed.

When most of a firm's costs are fixed over a wide range of outputs, the primary determinant of profitability will be the amount of revenue generated by sales. **Yield management** strategies allow marketers to vary prices based on such factors as demand, even though the cost of providing those goods or services remains the same. Hotels use software to track customer patterns and help determine attractive discounts that fill their spas during off-peak hours such as weekdays. The lowered prices also reduce unprofitable downtime for specialized spa employees.[16]

Similar yield management strategies typify the marketing of such goods and services as the following:

- *Sports teams*—the Ottawa Senators and Vancouver Canucks charge more for single-game tickets for games featuring high-profile opponents

- *Lodging*—lower prices off season and higher prices during peak season periods; low-priced weekend rates for most hotels, motels, and bed-and-breakfasts across Canada

- *Auto rental*—lower prices on weekends when business demand is low and higher prices during the week when business demand is higher

- *Airfares*—lower prices on nonrefundable tickets with travel restrictions such as advance-purchase and Saturday-night stay requirements and penalties for flight changes and higher prices on refundable tickets that can be changed without penalty

The following example from the airline industry demonstrates how yield management maximizes revenues in situations where costs are fixed.[17] Airlines constantly monitor reservations on every flight. Beginning approximately 330 days before the flight, space is allocated among full-fare, discount-fare, and free tickets for frequent flyers who qualify for complimentary tickets. This allocation is monitored and adjusted at regular intervals until the flight departs.

Assume, for example, that Air Canada has scheduled a 180-seat plane as Flight AC123 with an 8 a.m. departure from St. John's to Calgary on October 23. When Flight AC123 leaves its gate, all costs associated with the flight (fuel, crew, and other operating expenses) are fixed. The pricing that maximizes revenues on this flight will also maximize profits. An examination of past sales indicates that Air Canada could sell 40 to 60 one-way, full-fare tickets at $600 per passenger and 100 to 150 one-way restricted-fare tickets at $200 per passenger. Demand for frequent-flyer space should be at least 10 seats.

If Air Canada reserves 60 seats for full-fare passengers and accepts reservations for 110 restricted-fare tickets but sells only 40 full-fare tickets (leaving 20 vacant seats), total revenues will be

$$\text{Revenues} = (40 \times \$600) + (110 \times \$200) = \$46\ 000$$

However, if Air Canada's pricing decision makers want to reduce vacancies, they might decide to reduce the number of full-fare tickets to 20 and increase the restricted-fare tickets to 150. If the plane leaves the gate at full capacity, the flight will generate the following total revenues:

$$\text{Revenues} = (20 \times \$600) + (150 \times \$200) = \$42\ 000$$

Instead of rigidly maintaining the allocations established nearly a year before the flight, Air Canada will use yield management to maximize the revenue per flight. In this example, the airline initially holds 60 full-fare seats and accepts reservations for up to 110 restricted-fare seats. Thirty days before the October 23 departure, updated computer projections indicate that 40 full-fare seats are likely to be sold. The allocation is now revised to 40 full-fare and 130 restricted-fare tickets. A full flight leaves the gate and revenues are:

$$\text{Revenues} = (40 \times \$600) + (130 \times \$200) = \$50\ 000$$

Applying yield management for the St. John's to Calgary flight increases revenues by at least $4000 over the inflexible approach of making advance allocations and failing to adjust them based on passenger reservations and other data.

Marketoid

In July 2011, the fuel surcharge for an Air Canada flight between Toronto and Paris was $340, approximately 40 percent of the ticket price. In August 2011, Air Canada was fined $50 000 in the United States for deceptive advertising: failing to disclose taxes and fees in addition to its advertised fare.

assessment check 2f

2.13 Explain the goal of yield management.

PRICING STRATEGIES

The specific strategies that firms use to price goods and services grow out of the marketing strategies they formulate to accomplish overall organizational objectives. One firm's marketers may price their products to attract customers across a wide range; another group of marketers may set prices to appeal to a small segment of a larger market; still another group may simply try to match competitors' price tags. In general, firms can choose from three pricing strategies: skimming, penetration, and competitive pricing. The following sections look at these choices in more detail.

SKIMMING PRICING STRATEGY

skimming pricing strategy Pricing strategy involving the use of an initial high price relative to competitive offerings. Price is dropped in incremental steps as supply begins to exceed demand, or when competition catches up.

Derived from the expression "skimming the cream," **skimming pricing strategies** are also known as *market-plus pricing*. They involve the intentional setting of a relatively high price compared with the prices of competing products. Although some firms continue to utilize a skimming strategy throughout most stages of the product life cycle, it is more commonly used as a market entry price for distinctive goods or services with little or no initial competition. As supply begins to exceed demand, or when competition catches up, the initial high price is incrementally dropped.

Such was the case with high-definition televisions (HDTVs), whose average price was approximately $20 000, including installation, when they were introduced. The resulting sticker shock kept them out of the range of most household budgets. But nearly a decade later, price cuts have brought LCD models into the reach of mainstream consumers. At Best Buy, shoppers can pick up a Philips 22-inch flat panel LCD model for $229.99. On the higher end, they can purchase a Sony Bravia 55-inch flat-panel LCD model for $1199.99.[18]

step out Pricing practice in which one firm raises prices and then waits to see if others follow suit.

A company may practise a skimming strategy in setting a market-entry price when it introduces a distinctive good or service with little or no competition. Or it may use this strategy to market higher-end goods. British vacuum cleaner manufacturer Dyson has used this practice. Offering entirely new design and engineering, Dyson sells its vacuum cleaners for between $500 and $700, significantly more than the average vacuum. Even the various models of iRobot's Roomba vacuum sell for $200 and up, and the company claims it does all the work for you.[19]

In some cases, a firm may maintain a skimming strategy throughout most stages of a product's life cycle. The jewellery category is a good example. Although discounters such as Costco and Walmart offer heavier pieces for a few hundred dollars, firms such as Tiffany and Cartier are able to command prices 10 times that amount just for the brand name. Exclusivity justifies the pricing—and the price, once set, rarely falls.

Sometimes maintaining a high price through the product's life cycle works, but sometimes it does not. High prices can drive away otherwise loyal customers. Hockey fans may shift from attending NHL games to junior league hockey games because of ticket, parking, and food prices. Amusement park visitors may shy away from high admission prices and head to the beach instead. If an industry or firm has been known to cut prices at certain points in the past, consumers—and retailers—will expect it. If the price cut doesn't come, consumers must decide whether to pay the higher tab or try a competitor's products.

Significant price changes in the retail gasoline and airline industries occur in the form of a **step out**, in which one firm raises prices and then waits to see if others follow suit. If competitors fail to respond by increasing their prices, the company making the step out usually reduces

British vacuum cleaner company Dyson uses a skimming strategy, pricing its vacuum cleaner models significantly higher than the average vacuum, and even higher than iRobot's Roomba vacuum, which iRobot claims does all of the work for the consumer.

H. F. (HERB) MACKENZIE

prices to the original level. Although companies are prohibited by law from collectively setting prices, they can follow each other's example.

Despite the risk of backlash, a skimming strategy does offer benefits. It allows a manufacturer to quickly recover its research and development (R&D) costs. Pharmaceutical companies, which fiercely protect their patents on new drugs, justify high prices because of astronomical R&D costs—an average of 16 cents of every sales dollar, compared with 8 cents for computer makers and 4 cents in the aerospace industry. To protect their brand names from competition from lower-cost generics, drug makers frequently make small changes to their products—such as combining the original product with a complementary prescription drug that treats different aspects of the ailment.

figure 16.3

Price Reductions to Increase Market Share

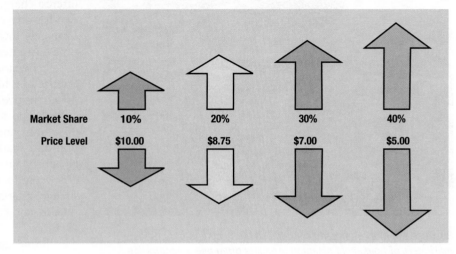

A skimming strategy also permits marketers to control demand in the introductory stages of a product's life cycle and then adjust productive capacity to match changing demand. A low initial price for a new product could lead to fulfillment problems and loss of shopper goodwill if demand outstrips the firm's production capacity. The result is likely to be consumer and retailer complaints and possibly permanent damage to the product's image. Excess demand occasionally leads to quality issues, as the firm strives to satisfy consumer desires for the product with inadequate production facilities.

During the late growth and early maturity stages of its life cycle, a product's price typically falls for two reasons: (1) the pressure of competition and (2) the desire to expand its market. Figure 16.3 shows that 10 percent of the market may buy Product X at $10.00, and another 20 percent could be added to its customer base at a price of $8.75. Successive price declines may expand the firm's market size and meet challenges posed by new competitors.

A skimming strategy has one inherent chief disadvantage: it attracts competition. Potential competitors see innovative firms reaping large financial returns and decide to enter the market. This new supply may force the price of the original product even lower than its eventual level under a sequential skimming procedure. However, if patent protection or some other unique proprietary ability allows a firm to exclude competitors from its market, it may extend a skimming strategy.

PENETRATION PRICING STRATEGY

A **penetration pricing strategy** sets a low price as a major marketing weapon. Marketers often price products noticeably lower than competing offerings when they enter new industries characterized by dozens of competing brands. Once the product achieves some market recognition through consumer trial purchases stimulated by its low price, marketers may increase the price to the level of competing products. Marketers of consumer products such as detergents often use this strategy. A penetration pricing strategy may also extend over several stages of the product life cycle as the firm seeks to maintain a reputation as a low-price competitor.

A penetration pricing strategy is sometimes called *market-minus pricing* when it implements the premise that a lower-than-market price will attract buyers and move a brand from an unknown newcomer to at least the brand-recognition stage or even to the brand-preference stage. Since many firms begin penetration pricing with the intention of increasing prices in the future, success depends on generating many trial purchases. Penetration pricing is common among credit-card firms, which typically offer low or zero interest rates for a specified introductory period, then raise the rates. If competitors view the new product as a threat, marketers attempting to use a penetration strategy often discover that rivals will simply match their prices.

penetration pricing strategy Pricing strategy involving the use of a relatively low entry price compared with competitive offerings, based on the theory that this initial low price will help secure market acceptance.

H. F. (HERB) MACKENZIE

Because the market already contains so many competing brands, marketers of household cleaning products often use a penetration pricing strategy when they enter the market, pricing products noticeably lower than the competition.

Retailers may use penetration pricing to lure shoppers to new stores. Strategies might take such forms as zero interest charges for credit purchases at a new furniture store, two-for-one offers for dinner at a new restaurant, or an extremely low price on a single product purchase for first-time customers to get them to come in and shop.

Penetration pricing works best for goods or services characterized by highly elastic demand. Large numbers of highly price-sensitive consumers pay close attention to this type of appeal. The strategy also suits situations in which large-scale operations and long production runs result in low production and marketing costs. Finally, penetration pricing may be appropriate in market situations in which introduction of a new product will likely attract strong competitors. Such a strategy may allow a new product to reach the mass market quickly and capture a large share prior to entry by competitors.

Some auto manufacturers have been using penetration pricing for some new models to attract customers who might not otherwise consider purchasing a vehicle during a given year or who might be looking at a more expensive competitor. India's Tata Motors launched the world's cheapest car: the Nano, which carries a price tag of $2500 (U.S.) in India. Tata has unveiled plans to sell the Nano in Europe, too, for about $8000 (U.S.), but it has yet to confirm when the Nano will be available in North America. Company spokespersons indicate its price tag would be similar to that of the European model—considerably less than the Hyundai Accent, which, at a sticker price of $13 599, is the lowest-priced car in Canada.[20]

Everyday Low Pricing

everyday low pricing (EDLP) Pricing strategy of continuously offering low prices rather than relying on such short-term price cuts as cents-off coupons, rebates, and special sales.

Closely related to penetration pricing is **everyday low pricing (EDLP)**, a strategy devoted to continuous low prices as opposed to relying on short-term, price-cutting tactics such as cents-off coupons, rebates, and special sales. EDLP can take two forms. In the first, retailers such as Walmart and Canadian Tire compete by consistently offering consumers low prices on a broad range of items. Through its EDLP policy, Lowe's Canada offers not only to match any price the consumer sees elsewhere but also to take off an additional 10 percent. Walmart states that it achieves EDLP by negotiating better prices from suppliers and by cutting its own costs. In addition, Walmart holds suppliers to a strict four-day delivery window. Goods that arrive at the regional distribution centre before or after the window are assessed a 3 percent penalty.[21]

H. F. (HERB) MACKENZIE

Walmart employs everyday low pricing, a strategy devoted to continuous low prices instead of special sales and other short-term pricing tactics.

The second form of the EDLP pricing strategy involves its use by the manufacturer in dealing with channel members. Manufacturers may seek to set stable wholesale prices that undercut offers that competitors make to retailers, offers that typically rise and fall with the latest trade promotion deals. Many marketers reduce the list prices on a number of products while simultaneously reducing promotion allowances to retailers. While reductions in allowances mean that retailers may not fund such in-store promotions as shelf merchandising and end-aisle displays, the manufacturers hope that stable low prices will stimulate sales instead.

Some retailers oppose EDLP strategies. Many grocery stores, for instance, operate on "high-low" strategies that set profitable regular prices to offset losses of frequent specials and promotions. Other retailers believe that EDLP will ultimately benefit both sellers and buyers. Supporters of EDLP in the grocery industry point out that it already succeeds at two of the biggest competitors, Walmart and warehouse clubs such as Costco.

One popular pricing myth is that a low price is a sure sell. Low prices are an easy means of distinguishing the offerings of one marketer from other sellers, but such moves are easy to counter by competitors. Unless overall demand is price elastic, overall price cuts will mean less revenue for all firms in the industry. In addition, low prices may generate an image of questionable quality.

COMPETITIVE PRICING STRATEGY

Although many organizations rely heavily on price as a competitive weapon, even more implement **competitive pricing strategies**. These organizations try to reduce the emphasis on price competition by matching other firms' prices and concentrating their own marketing efforts on the product, distribution, and promotion elements of the marketing mix. As pointed out earlier, while price offers a dramatic means of achieving competitive advantage, it is also the easiest marketing variable for competitors to match. In fact, in industries with relatively homogeneous products, competitors must match each other's price reductions to maintain market share and remain competitive.

Retailers such as Home Depot and Future Shop both use price-matching strategies, assuring consumers they will meet—and beat—competitors' prices. Grocery chains such as Loblaws, Safeway, Provigo, and Sobeys often compete with seasonal items: watermelon, soft drinks, and hot dogs in the summer; apples, hot chocolate, and turkeys in the winter. As soon as one store lowers the price of an item such as turkey, the rest follow suit.

Another form of competitive pricing is setting an **opening price point** within a category. Retailers often achieve this by pricing a quality private-label product below the competition. Many grocery chains have begun actively advertising their private label goods, most of which are priced below those of their manufacturers' brands. In a turbulent economy, more consumers are giving private label products a try, and many say the quality is comparable to that of national brands.[22]

Prices can really drop when companies continually match each other's prices, as has been evident periodically in the airline and computer industries. But competitive pricing can be tricky; a price reduction affects not only the first company but also the entire industry as other firms match the price reduction. Unless the lower prices can attract new customers and expand the overall market enough to offset the loss of per-unit revenue, the price cut will leave all competitors with less revenue. Research shows that nearly two-thirds of all firms set prices using competitive pricing as their primary pricing strategy.

One type of store seems well positioned against the powerful chain, Walmart: the so-called dollar stores. Today's equivalent of the five-and-dime variety stores of the 20th century, dollar stores sell inexpensive items such as cleaning supplies, paper plates, toothpaste, greeting cards, and other household products and compete on price and convenience, especially parking and easy access to the goods. Once competitors are routinely matching each other on price, marketers must turn away from price as a marketing strategy, emphasizing other variables to develop areas of distinctive competence and attract customers. That might mean offering personalized services such as gift wrapping or a sales associate who knows the type of clothing or books you like.

> **competitive pricing strategy** Pricing strategy designed to de-emphasize price as a competitive variable by pricing a good or service at the general level of comparable offerings.

> **opening price point** Setting an opening price below that of the competition, usually on a high-quality private label item.

assessment check 3

3.1 What are the three major pricing strategies?

3.2 What is EDLP?

PRICE QUOTATIONS

④ Describe how prices are quoted.

The choice of the best method for quoting prices depends on many industry conditions, including competitive trends, cost structures, and traditional practices, along with the policies of individual firms. This section examines the reasoning and methodology behind price quotation practices.

Most price structures are built around **list prices**—the rates normally quoted to potential buyers. Marketers usually determine list prices by one or a combination of the methods discussed earlier in this chapter. The sticker price on a new automobile is a good example: it shows the list price for the basic model and then adds the prices of options. The sticker price for a new Kia Forte sedan is $15 995. But you can add such features as keyless entry, front tweeter speakers, heated front seats, and more—all at additional cost. Most car manufacturers bundle features into packages for one price. So if you order trim level EX on the Forte, you automatically get those features, among other add-ons.[23]

> **list price** Established price normally quoted to potential buyers.

figure 16.4

2007 Canadian Average Pump Price

COURTESY PETRO-CANADA. SOURCE: HTTP://RETAIL.PETRO-CANADA.CA/EN/FUELSAVINGS/2132.ASPX

market price
Price a consumer or marketing intermediary actually pays for a product after subtracting any discounts, allowances, or rebates from the list price.

cash discount
Price reduction offered to a consumer, business user, or marketing intermediary in return for prompt payment of a bill.

The price of oil is equally important to consumers—particularly those who drive cars—because it directly affects the list price of gasoline. Factors such as refinery shutdowns, hurricanes, and wars affect the price of oil and ultimately the price that drivers pay at the pump. Prices may also fluctuate seasonally, as demand for gasoline rises and falls. Demand for gasoline is much higher in Canada during the summer when tourists visit and when Canadians travel longer distances for their vacations. Figure 16.4 illustrates where the money from a litre of gas goes on its journey from the oil field to your gas tank.

REDUCTIONS FROM LIST PRICE

The amount that a consumer pays for a product—its **market price**—may or may not equal the list price. Discounts and allowances sometimes reduce list prices. A list price often defines a starting point from which discounts set a lower market price. Marketers offer discounts in several classifications: cash, trade, and quantity discounts.

Cash Discounts

Consumers, industrial purchasers, or channel members sometimes receive reductions in price in exchange for prompt payment of bills; these price cuts are known as **cash discounts**. Discount terms usually specify exact time periods, such as 2/10, net 30. This notation means that the customer must pay within 30 days, but payment within 10 days entitles the customer to subtract 2 percent from the amount due. Consumers may receive a cash discount for immediate payment—say, paying with cash instead of a credit card at the gas pump or paying the full cash amount upfront for elective dental services such as braces for teeth. Cash discounts represent a traditional pricing practice in many industries. They fulfill legal requirements provided that all customers can take the same reductions on the same terms.

In recent years, sellers have increasingly attempted to improve their own liquidity positions, reduce their bad-debt losses, and cut collection expenses by moving to a form of *negative cash discount*. Confronted with purchasers who may defer paying their bills as long as possible, a new notice has begun to appear on customer statements:

> **Due on Receipt.** A FINANCE CHARGE of 1.5%
> per month (18% A.P.R.) is computed on and added
> to the unpaid balance as of the statement date.

Past-due accounts may be turned over to collection agencies.

Trade Discounts

trade discount
Payment to a channel member or buyer for performing marketing functions; also known as a *functional discount*.

Payments to channel members for performing marketing functions are known as **trade discounts**, or functional discounts. Services performed by various channel members and the related costs were discussed in Chapters 12 and 13. A manufacturer's list price must incorporate the costs incurred by channel members in performing required marketing functions and expected profit margins for each member.

Trade discounts initially reflected the operating expenses of each category, but they have become more or less customary practices in some industries. In the United States, the Robinson-Patman Act allows trade discounts as long as all buyers in the same category, such as all wholesalers or all retailers, receive the same discount privileges. In Canada, the Competition Act does not recognize trade discounts. Wholesalers and retailers are considered competitors, and they therefore must be treated equally with respect to pricing and related promotional allowances.

Figure 16.5 shows how a chain of trade discounts works. In the first instance, the trade discount is "40 percent, 10 percent off list price" for wholesalers. In other words, the 40 percent discount on the $40 product is the trade discount the retailer receives to cover operating expenses and earn a profit. The wholesaler receives 10 percent of the $24 price to retailers to cover expenses and earn a profit. The manufacturer receives $21.60 from the wholesaler for each order.

In the second example, the manufacturer and retailer decide to bypass the wholesaler. The producer offers a trade discount of 45 percent to the retailer. In this instance, the retailer receives

$18 for each product sold at its list price, and the manufacturer receives the remaining $22. Either the retailer or the manufacturer must assume responsibility for the services previously performed by the wholesaler, or they can share these duties between them.

Quantity Discounts

Price reductions granted for large-volume purchases are known as **quantity discounts**. Sellers justify these discounts on the grounds that large orders reduce selling expenses and may shift some costs for storage, transportation, and financing to buyers. The law allows quantity discounts provided they are applied on the same basis to all customers.

Quantity discounts may specify either cumulative or noncumulative terms. **Cumulative quantity discounts** reduce prices in amounts determined by purchases over stated time periods. Annual purchases of at least $25 000 might entitle a buyer to a 3 percent rebate, and purchases exceeding $50 000 would increase the refund to 5 percent. These reductions are really patronage discounts because they tend to bind customers to a single supply source.

Noncumulative quantity discounts provide one-time reductions in the list price. For example, a firm might offer the following discount schedule for a product priced at $100 per unit:

1 unit	List: $100
2–5 units	List less 10 percent
6–10 units	List less 20 percent
Over 10 units	List less 25 percent

Many businesses have come to expect quantity discounts from suppliers. For example, Atlantic Inkjet has a corporate discount program that offers a 5 percent discount for orders over $250, a 10 percent discount for orders over $500, and a 15 percent discount for orders over $1000.[24] Marketers typically favour combinations of cash, trade, and quantity discounts.

Allowances

Allowances resemble discounts by specifying deductions from list price. The major categories of allowances are trade-ins and promotional allowances. **Trade-ins** are often used in sales of durable goods such as automobiles. The new product's basic list price remains unchanged, but the seller accepts less money from the customer along with a used product—usually the same kind of product as the buyer purchases.

Promotional allowances reduce prices as part of attempts to integrate promotional strategies within distribution channels. Manufacturers often return part of the prices that buyers pay in the form of advertising and sales-support allowances for channel members. Automobile manufacturers frequently offer allowances to retail dealers to induce them to lower prices and stimulate sales. In an effort to alert consumers to the difference between a car's sticker price and the price the dealer actually pays to the manufacturer, *Consumer Reports* recently began selling car and truck buyers a breakdown on dealers' wholesale costs. The information reveals undisclosed dealer profits such as manufacturers' incentives, rebates from dealer-invoice price, and "holdbacks"—amounts refunded to the dealer after sales are completed.[25] Dealers dislike the move to reveal their markups, arguing that no other retail sector is forced to give consumers details of their promotional allowances.

Minimum advertised pricing (MAP) occurs when a manufacturer pays a retailer not to advertise a product below a certain price. However, some retailers invite shoppers to call or e-mail for lower— unpublished—prices on items as varied as espresso machines and desktop computers.[26]

figure 16.5

Chain of Trade Discounts

"40 PERCENT, 10 PERCENT OFF" TRADE DISCOUNT			
List Price	− Retail Trade Discount	− Wholesale Trade Discount	= Manufacturer Proceeds
$40	− $16 ($40 × 40%)	− $2.40 ($24 × 10%)	= $21.60 ($40 − $16 − $2.40)

"45 PERCENT" TRADE DISCOUNT		
List Price	− Retail Trade Discount =	Manufacturer Proceeds
$40	− $18 ($40 × 45%) =	$22 ($40 − $18)

quantity discount Price reduction granted for a large-volume purchase.

cumulative quantity discount Price discount determined by amounts of purchases over stated time periods.

noncumulative quantity discount Price reduction granted on a one-time-only basis.

allowance Specified deduction from list price, including a trade-in or promotional allowance.

trade-in Credit allowance given for a used item when a customer purchases a new item.

promotional allowance Promotional incentive in which the manufacturer agrees to pay the reseller a certain amount to cover the costs of special promotional displays or extensive advertising.

minimum advertised pricing (MAP) Fees paid to retailers who agree not to advertise products below set prices.

H. F. (HERB) MACKENZIE

Golf Town customers can get discounts on new golf equipment when they trade in used equipment during the company's annual trade-in event.

rebate Refund of a portion of the purchase price, usually granted by the product's manufacturer.

Rebates

In still another way to reduce the price paid by customers, marketers may offer a **rebate**—a refund of a portion of the purchase price. Rebates appear everywhere—on cosmetics packages, appliances, over-the-counter medications, and in automobile promotions—by manufacturers eager to get consumers to try their products or to move products during periods of slow sales. Mattress manufacturer Sealy has successfully used rebates to move consumers up to more expensive models in its product line, offering the biggest rebates for its top-priced mattresses.

Rebates can have their problems. Manufacturers point out that many consumers never apply for their legitimate rebates. Many consumers complain of the amount of paperwork they have to fill out to get a rebate, particularly on larger items such as computers and kitchen appliances. Some say they fill out the paperwork only to be denied the claim on a technicality. Others report never receiving the rebate—or even a response—at all. The Better Business Bureau notes that the number of complaints filed relating to rebates has grown significantly in the past few years.[27]

GEOGRAPHIC CONSIDERATIONS

In industries dominated by catalogue and online marketers, geographic considerations weigh heavily on the firm's ability to deliver orders in a cost-effective manner at the right time and place. In other instances, geographic factors affect the marketer's ability to receive additional inventory quickly in response to demand fluctuations. And although geographic considerations strongly influence prices when costs include shipping heavy, bulky, low-unit-value products, they can also affect lightweight, lower-cost products.

Buyers and sellers can handle transportation expenses in several ways: (1) the buyer pays all transportation charges, (2) the seller pays all transportation charges, or (3) the buyer and the seller share the charges. This decision has major effects on a firm's efforts to expand its geographic coverage to distant markets. How can marketers compete with local suppliers in distant markets who are able to avoid the considerable shipping costs that their firms must pay? Sellers can implement several alternatives for handling transportation costs in their pricing policies.

FOB (free on board) plant (FOB origin) Price quotation that does not include shipping charges.

FOB Pricing

FOB (free on board) plant, or **FOB origin,** prices include no shipping charges. The buyer must pay all freight charges to transport the product from the manufacturer's loading dock. The seller pays only to load the merchandise aboard the carrier selected by the buyer. Legal title and responsibility pass to the buyer after the seller's employees load the purchase and get a receipt from the representative of the common carrier. Firms such as Walmart often handle freight charges over the entire supply chain. Because Walmart sources so many products from China, "FOB China" is now becoming common.

Many marketing intermediaries sell only on FOB plant terms to downstream channel members. These distributors believe that their customers have more clout than they do in negotiating with carriers. They prefer to assign transportation costs to the channel members in the best positions to secure the most cost-effective shipping terms.

Uniform-Delivered Pricing

When a firm quotes the same price, including transportation expenses, to all buyers, it adopts a **uniform-delivered price** policy. This method of handling transportation expenses is the exact opposite of FOB origin pricing. The uniform-delivered system resembles the pricing structure for mail service, so it is sometimes called *postage-stamp pricing*. The price quote includes a transportation charge averaged over all of the firm's customers, meaning that distant customers actually pay a smaller share of shipping costs while nearby customers pay what is known as *phantom freight* (the amount by which the average transportation charge exceeds the actual cost of shipping). Both amazon.ca and chapters.indigo.ca use uniform-delivered pricing for orders over $25.

uniform-delivered price Pricing system for handling transportation costs under which all buyers are quoted the same price, including transportation expenses. Sometimes known as *postage-stamp pricing*.

Zone Pricing

Zone pricing modifies a uniform-delivered pricing system by dividing the overall market into different zones and establishing a single price within each zone. This pricing structure incorporates average transportation costs for shipments within each zone as part of the delivered price of goods sold there; by narrowing distances, it greatly reduces but does not completely eliminate phantom freight. The primary advantage of zone pricing comes from easy administration methods that help a seller to compete in distant markets. Canada Post's parcel rates depend on zone pricing.

zone pricing Pricing system for handling transportation costs under which the market is divided into geographic regions and a different price is set in each region.

Zone pricing helps explain why gasoline can cost more in one suburb than it costs in a neighbourhood just four or five kilometres down the road. One way in which gasoline marketers boost profits is by mapping out areas based on formulas that factor in location, affluence, or simply what the local market will bear. Dealers are then charged different wholesale prices, which are reflected in the prices paid at the pump by customers. Some dealers argue that zone pricing should be prohibited. When drivers shop around for cheaper gas in other zones, stations in high-price zones are unable to compete. Ironically, it is the local dealer, not just the major oil company, which many consumers suspect of price gouging.

Basing-Point Pricing

In **basing-point pricing**, the price of a product includes the list price at the factory plus freight charges from the basing-point city nearest the buyer. The basing point specifies a location from which freight charges are calculated—not necessarily the point from which the goods are actually shipped. In either case, the actual shipping point does not affect the price quotation. For example, a seller might quote a customer a price of $1000 per ton for a shipment of steel from Montreal, but designate the basing point as Hamilton, Ontario. The customer pays for the steel plus a charge equal to the freight that would have resulted had the shipment been made from Hamilton. Such a system seeks to equalize competition— usually for heavy commodity-type items—between distant marketers since all competitors quote identical transportation rates. Few buyers would accept a basing-point system today.

basing-point pricing System used in some industries during the early 20th century in which the buyer paid the factory price plus freight charges from the basing-point city nearest the buyer.

assessment check 4

4.1 What are the three major types of discounts?

4.2 Identify the four alternatives for handling transportation costs in pricing policies.

PRICING POLICIES

⑤ Identify the various pricing policy decisions that marketers must make.

Pricing policies contribute important information to buyers as they assess the firm's total image. A coherent policy provides an overall framework and consistency that guide day-to-day pricing decisions. Formally, a **pricing policy** is a general guideline that reflects marketing objectives and influences specific pricing decisions.

Decisions concerning price structure generally tend to focus on technical, detailed questions, but decisions concerning pricing policies cover broader issues. Price-structure decisions take the firm's pricing policy as a given, from which they specify applicable discounts. Pricing policies have important strategic effects, particularly in guiding competitive efforts. They form the basis for more practical price-structure decisions.

pricing policy General guideline that reflects marketing objectives and influences specific pricing decisions.

Firms implement variations of four basic types of pricing policies: psychological pricing, price flexibility, product-line pricing, and promotional pricing. Specific policies deal effectively with various

Preventing Sales from Going Down When Prices Go Up

NO marketer likes to deliver bad news to a customer, but sometimes—as in the case of a price increase—it's unavoidable. When you find yourself in this situation, here are some tips for softening the blow:

- *Slow down.* When you're delivering bad news, speak slowly and in a lowered tone of voice. You'll sound calm and rational rather than excited and emotional.
- *Explain what the price increase is and why.* Be honest. Tell them which products—if only a few—will increase in price and why. Without revealing every detail of your business, explain which of your costs has increased; perhaps it's the price of lumber or the cost of shipping.
- *Give advance warning.* If possible, notify customers well before the increase takes place so they can make budget adjustments. If a product is being phased out and replaced by a new product at a higher price, notify customers of this as well.
- *Help customers find alternatives.* Perhaps your firm has similar products comparable to the ones a particular customer has been using and will not be increasing in price.

- *Create new pricing packages, bundles, or product groupings.* By regrouping certain products—or separating products if they were previously grouped—you might be able to offer a better price despite the increase.
- *Emphasize value.* If the price increases because of your commitment to quality, say so. Perhaps your firm provides a better value overall. A product might be more concentrated to last longer, or packages might contain more items.
- *Use promotions.* Offer a promotional price, discount coupon, or rebate for a short period of time prior to the increase.

Sources: Devra Gartenstein, "The Best Way to Announce a Price Increase," eHow, http://www.ehow.com, March 22, 2010; Jeff Mowatt, "10 Ways to Break It to Them Gently," Business Know-how, http://www.businessknowhow.com, March 19, 2010; Mark Hunter, "Selling a Price Increase in a Soft Market," *Business Know-how*, http://www.businessknowhow.com, March 18, 2010; Beth Jinks, "Carnival Jumps after Announcing 5% Price Increase," *BusinessWeek*, February 24, 2010, http://www.businessweek.com; Propex Announces Price Increase in Its Furnishing Solutions Business Unit," PR Newswire, February 10, 2010, http://www.prnewswire.com Kevin Daley, "How to Deliver Bad News to a Group," *Harvard Business Review*, October 16, 2009, http://blogs.hbr.org.

competitive situations; the final choice depends on the environment within which marketers must make their pricing decisions. Regardless of the strategy selected, however, marketers sometimes must raise prices. Although it is never easy to deliver this decision to customers, if it is accomplished with honesty and tact, customers are likely to remain loyal. The "Career Readiness" feature provides some pointers on communicating price increases.

PSYCHOLOGICAL PRICING

psychological pricing Pricing policy based on the belief that certain prices or price ranges make a good or service more appealing than others to buyers.

odd pricing Pricing policy based on the belief that a price ending with an odd number just under a round number is more appealing, for instance, $9.97 rather than $10.

unit pricing Pricing policy in which prices are stated in terms of a recognized unit of measurement or a standard numerical count.

Psychological pricing applies the belief that certain prices or price ranges make products more appealing than others to buyers. No research offers a consistent foundation for such thinking, however, and studies often report mixed findings. Nevertheless, marketers practise several forms of psychological pricing. Prestige pricing, discussed in this chapter, sets a relatively high price to convey an image of quality and exclusiveness. Two more psychological pricing techniques are odd pricing and unit pricing.

In **odd pricing**, marketers set prices at odd numbers just under round numbers. Many people assume that a price of $4.95 appeals more strongly to consumers than $5, supposedly because buyers interpret it as $4 plus change. Odd pricing originated as a way to force clerks to make change, thus serving as a cash-control device, and it remains a common feature of contemporary price quotations. Some producers and retailers practise odd pricing but avoid prices ending in 5, 9, or 0. These marketers believe that customers view price tags of $5.95, $5.99, or $6.00 as regular retail prices, but they think of an amount like $5.97 as a discount price. Walmart avoids using 9s at the end of its prices, and even uses numbers such as 3 or 7.

Unit pricing states prices in terms of some recognized unit of measurement (such as grams and litres) or a standard numerical count. Unit pricing began to be widely used during the late 1960s to make price comparisons more convenient following complaints by consumer advocates about the difficulty of comparing the true prices of products packaged in different sizes. These advocates thought that posting prices in terms of standard units would help shoppers make better informed purchases. However, unit pricing has not improved consumers' shopping habits as much as supporters originally envisioned. Instead, research shows that unit pricing most often affects purchases only by relatively well-educated consumers with high earnings.

PRICE FLEXIBILITY

Marketing executives must also set company policies that determine whether their firm will permit **price flexibility**—that is, the decision of whether to set one price that applies to every buyer or to permit variable prices for different customers. Generally, one-price policies suit mass-selling marketing programs, whereas variable pricing is more likely to be applied in marketing programs based on individual bargaining. In a large department store, customers do not expect to haggle over prices with retail salespeople. Instead, they expect to pay the amounts shown on the price tags. Generally, customers pay less only when the retailer replaces regular prices with sale prices or offers discounts on damaged merchandise. Variable pricing usually applies to larger purchases such as automobiles, real estate, and hotel room rates. While variable pricing adds some flexibility to selling situations, it may also lead to retaliatory pricing by competitors, and it may stir complaints among customers who find that they paid higher prices than necessary.

In recent years, Internet service providers such as Bell Canada and Rogers Communications have set usage caps on customer accounts. Both offer a number of Internet plans with prices based on the usage allowance and the connection speed that customers choose to meet their needs.

price flexibility Pricing policy permitting variable prices for goods and services.

PRODUCT-LINE PRICING

Since most firms market several product lines, an effective pricing strategy must consider the relationships among all these items instead of viewing each in isolation. **Product-line pricing** is the practice of setting a limited number of prices for a selection of merchandise. For example, a clothier might offer three lines of men's suits—one priced at $400, a second at $600, and the most expensive at $1200. These price points help the retailer to define important product characteristics that differentiate the three product lines and assist the customer in deciding on whether to trade up or trade down.

Retailers practise extensive product-line pricing. In earlier days, five-and-dime variety stores exemplified this technique. It remains popular, however, because it offers advantages to both retailers and customers. Shoppers can choose desired price ranges and then concentrate on other product variables such as colours, styles, and materials. Retailers can purchase and offer specific lines in limited price categories instead of more general assortments with dozens of different prices.

Sunglasses have become a hot fashion item in recent years, and prices for designer glasses have jumped from an average of approximately $250 per pair to as much as $900 for Thornhill Aviators at Fifth Avenue department store Bergdorf Goodman. While sales of other luxury goods have softened, sunglass sales are getting long looks from retailers. Younger consumers—teens and young women—seem to be snapping up designer shades most often. Bvlgari, Dolce & Gabbana, Prada, Stella McCartney, and Versace all offer high-end glasses carried by luxury retailers.

product-line pricing Practice of setting a limited number of prices for a selection of merchandise and marketing different product lines at each of these price levels.

promotional pricing Pricing policy in which a lower than normal price is used as a temporary ingredient in a firm's marketing strategy.

PROMOTIONAL PRICING

In **promotional pricing**, a lower than normal price is used as a temporary ingredient in a firm's marketing strategy. Some promotional pricing arrangements form part of recurrent marketing initiatives, such as a shoe store's annual "buy one pair, get the second pair for one cent" sale. Another firm may introduce a promotional model or brand with a special price to begin competing in a new market.

Managing promotional pricing efforts requires marketing skill. Customers may get hooked on sales and other promotional pricing events. If they know their favourite department store has a one-day sale every month, they are likely to wait to make their purchases on that day. Car shoppers have been offered so many price incentives that it is becoming harder and harder for manufacturers and dealers to take them away—or to come up with new ones.

In an effort to preserve customer traffic despite a tough economy, fast-food restaurants are trying a variety

Many retailers are known for regularly using promotional pricing to attract consumers to their stores.

Pricing Strategy: The New Battleground for Franchisors and Franchisees

THE rising cost of food and a struggling economy have combined to create the perfect storm in the fast-food industry, causing many companies, including McDonald's, Burger King, KFC, and Taco Bell, to tinker with their pricing strategy. By introducing new menu items and pricing promotions geared to draw consumers back into their restaurants, companies are raising the ire of their franchisees, who find their already slim profit margins shaved to the bone.

Should fast-food companies unilaterally set pricing policies?

PRO

1. Pricing policy cannot be left to the discretion of individual franchisees: uniformity from store to store is an important facet of the company's brand.
2. Fast-food restaurants have to be creative in trying new things to stay competitive. What's more, in devising promotions, marketers must consider every possibility as they attempt to pull customers away from their competition. For example, promoting $1 fountain drinks during the summer months creates an opportunity to woo customers away from minimarts and convenience stores; introducing specialty coffees puts them head to head with coffee houses.

CON

1. Franchise operators are at the mercy of the parent company because they have little say over corporate decisions like pricing policy and must pay a percentage of their sales to the parent. Some recent promotions—such as Burger King's introduction of the $1 double cheeseburger—actually lost money for franchisees because the item cost more than $1 to prepare and serve.
2. Because franchises represent the lifeblood of companies like McDonald's and Burger King, it is important for the parent company to maintain a good relationship with its franchisees. If franchisees perceive they have little power in influencing their store's future, they may decide their investment was a poor one—and the company would be in trouble.

Where do you stand: pro or con?

Sources: "McDonald's Eyeing $1 Drinks for Summer," *Chicago Tribune* Breaking Business, March 17, 2010, http://www.chicagobreakingbusiness.com; Lisa Baertlein, "Burger King Pulling Slice from Double Cheeseburger," Reuters, February 17, 2010, http://www.reuters.com; Dionne Rose, "Fast Food Price Hike—Customers Paying More at KFC, Burger, King, Island Grill," *Jamaica Gleaner Online*, January 10, 2010, http://www.jamaica-gleaner.com; David Sterrett, "Price Hikes on Menu at McD's; Bigger Boosts Would Ease Pressure on Franchisee Profit but Risk Irking Customers," *Crain's Chicago Business*, April 13, 2009, http://www.chicagobusiness.com.

---

loss leader Product offered to consumers at less than cost to attract them to stores in the hope that they will buy other merchandise at regular prices.

leader pricing Variant of loss-leader pricing in which marketers offer prices slightly above cost to avoid violating minimum-markup regulations and earn a minimal return on promotional sales.

of promotions designed to attract business. However, where franchisees operate the fast-food restaurants, they often bear the brunt of those value-priced promotions, as discussed in the "Solving an Ethical Controversy" feature.

Loss Leaders and Leader Pricing

Retailers rely most heavily on promotional pricing. In one type of technique, stores offer loss leaders—goods priced below cost to attract customers who, the retailer hopes, will also buy other, regularly priced merchandise. Loss leaders can form part of an effective marketing program.

Retailers frequently use a variant of loss-leader pricing called leader pricing. To earn some return on promotional sales, they offer so-called leader merchandise at prices slightly above cost. Among the most frequent practitioners of this combination pricing/promotion strategy are mass merchandisers and supermarkets such as Walmart and Sobeys. Retailers sometimes treat private label products (such as George, Equate, and Great Value products at Walmart or Our Compliments products at Sobeys) as leader merchandise because the store brands cost, on average, about 27 percent less than those of comparable national brands. While store brand items generate lower per-unit revenues than national brands would produce, higher sales volume will probably offset some of the difference, as will related sales of high-margin products such as toiletries and cosmetics.

Digital cameras are a good example. Although a digital point-and-shoot camera once ranged from $400 to $600, today, for the same money, shoppers can get a more technologically advanced digital SLR camera. Meanwhile, prices on the point-and-shoot models have dropped. A Vivitar V5028 is now priced under $50, and other brands and models are available for under $200.[28]

assessment check 5a ✓

5.1 Define pricing policy.

5.2 Describe the two types of psychological pricing other than prestige pricing.

5.3 What is promotional pricing?

Marketers should anticipate two potential pitfalls when making a promotional pricing decision:

1. Some buyers are not attracted by promotional pricing.

2. By maintaining an artificially low price for a period of time, marketers may lead customers to expect it as a customary feature of the product. That is the situation currently faced by North American car manufacturers; sales of their models lag when they do not offer price incentives.

PRICE–QUALITY RELATIONSHIPS

One of the most thoroughly researched aspects of pricing is its relationship to consumer perceptions of product quality. In the absence of other cues, price serves as an important indicator of a product's quality to prospective purchasers. Many buyers interpret high prices as signals of high-quality products. Prestige is also often associated with high prices. However, a recent marketing study found that while consumers form more positive impressions about higher-priced products, those perceptions don't translate to heightened demand.[29] A new type of prestige surrounds eco-friendly products. Many consumers are willing to pay more for green goods and services—those made with environmentally friendly materials and processes. These purchases make consumers feel good about themselves and convey status among others.

Despite the appeal of prestige, nearly every consumer loves a good deal. Marketers work hard to convince consumers they are offering high-quality products at the lowest possible price. Motels were once considered both cheap and seedy. The Motel 6 chain, for example, was so named because when it opened in the United States in 1962, a room cost just $6 per night. Today, a night at Motel 6 is still low priced. In 2011, travellers could stay in Canadian Motel 6 locations for as little as $40, and the chain is renovating its properties to convey a chic yet efficient look, with pedestal beds, 32-inch flat-screen TVs, granite countertops, wood-look laminate floors, and more.[30]

Probably the best statement of the price–quality connection is the idea of price limits. Consumers define certain limits within which their product–quality perceptions vary directly with price. A potential buyer regards a price below the lower limit as too cheap, and a price above the higher limit seems too expensive. This perception holds true for both national brands and private-label products.

Marketoid

Grand pianos: approximately $2000 to $4000 from China or Indonesia to as much as $400 000 for a Fazioli.

assessment check 5b

5.4 Describe the price–quality connection.

5.5 What are price limits?

SOME SPECIAL TOPICS IN PRICING

⑥ List and explain a number of special issues in pricing.

A discussion of pricing concepts and strategies would not be complete without considering some of the special topics in pricing that are important to some marketing managers, in particular marketing environments. These include competitive bidding and negotiated prices, pricing in global markets, the dilemma of transfer pricing, online pricing considerations, and bundle pricing.

COMPETITIVE BIDDING AND NEGOTIATED PRICES

Many government and organizational procurement departments do not pay set prices for their purchases, particularly for large purchases. Instead, they determine the lowest prices available for items that meet specifications through **competitive bidding**. This process consists of inviting potential suppliers to quote prices on proposed purchases or contracts. Detailed specifications describe the good or service that the government agency or business organization wishes to acquire. One of the most important procurement tasks is to develop accurate descriptions of products that the organization seeks to buy. This process generally requires the assistance of the firm's technical personnel, such as engineers, designers, and chemists.

In competing for students, colleges and universities across Canada differentiate themselves on many dimensions, including price. In order to keep operating costs down, institutions routinely invite competitive bids in many areas of operation, including building maintenance and janitorial services, landscaping, and food service. With costs soaring for everything related to academic life, schools look for ways to economize without diminishing their appeal in the eyes of prospective students and their parents.

competitive bidding
Inviting potential suppliers to quote prices on proposed purchases or contracts.

H. F. (HERB) MACKENZIE

Goods made with environmentally friendly materials and processes have a new prestige. Many consumers are willing to pay more for these eco-friendly products.

In some cases, business and government purchasers negotiate contracts with favoured suppliers instead of inviting competitive bids from all interested parties. The terms of such a contract emerge through offers and counteroffers between the buyer and the seller. When only one supplier offers a desired product, or when projects require extensive research and development, buyers and sellers often set purchase terms through negotiated contracts. In addition, some government and business customers allow their buyers to skip the formal bid process and negotiate purchases under certain dollar limits—say $500 or $1000. This policy seeks to eliminate economic waste that would result from obtaining and processing bids for relatively minor purchases.

PRICING IN GLOBAL MARKETS

It is equally important for a firm engaging in global marketing to use a pricing strategy that reflects its overall marketing strategy. Prices must support the company's broader goals, including product development, advertising and sales, customer support, competitive plans, and financial objectives.

In addition to the four pricing objectives discussed at the beginning of this chapter—profitability, volume, meeting competition, and prestige—firms involved in global marketing often work to achieve a fifth objective: price stability. Although price stability is desirable in international markets, it is often difficult to achieve. Wars, terrorism, economic downturns, changing governments, and shifting trade policies can alter prices.

Price stability can be especially important for producers of commodities—goods and services that have easily accessible substitutes that other nations can supply quickly. Countries that export international commodities, such as wood, chemicals, and agricultural crops, suffer economically when their prices fluctuate. A nation such as Nicaragua, which exports sugar cane, can find that its balance of payments changes drastically when the international price for sugar shifts. This makes it vulnerable to stiff price competition from other sugar cane producers. In contrast, countries that export value-oriented products, rather than commodities, tend to enjoy more stable prices. Prices of electronic equipment and automobiles tend to fluctuate far less than prices of crops such as sugar cane.

When it comes to global pricing strategies, in general, a company can implement one of three export pricing strategies: a standard worldwide price, dual pricing, or market-differentiated pricing. Exporters often set standard worldwide prices, regardless of their target markets. This strategy can succeed if foreign marketing costs remain low enough that they do not affect overall costs or if their prices reflect average unit costs. A company that implements a standard pricing program must monitor the international marketplace carefully, however, to make sure that domestic competitors do not undercut its prices.

The dual pricing strategy distinguishes prices for domestic and export sales. Some exporters practise cost-plus pricing to establish dual prices that fully allocate their true domestic and foreign costs to product sales in those markets. These prices ensure that an exporter makes a profit on any product it sells, but final prices may exceed those of competitors. Other companies opt for flexible cost-plus pricing schemes that allow marketers to grant discounts or change prices according to shifts in the competitive environment or fluctuations in the international exchange rate.

The third strategy, market-differentiated pricing, makes even more flexible arrangements to set prices according to local marketplace conditions. The dynamic global marketplace often requires frequent price changes by exporters who choose this approach. Effective market-differentiated pricing depends on access to quick, accurate market information.

assessment check 6a

6.1 What is competitive bidding?

6.2 Why is price stability difficult to achieve in global marketing?

6.3 What are the three traditional global pricing strategies?

6.4 Which is the most flexible global pricing strategy?

figure 16.6

Transfer Pricing to Escape Taxation

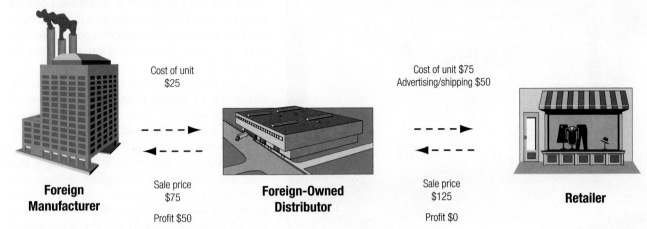

Foreign Manufacturer

Cost of unit $25

Sale price $75
Profit $50

Foreign-Owned Distributor

Cost of unit $75
Advertising/shipping $50

Sale price $125
Profit $0

Retailer

THE TRANSFER PRICING DILEMMA

A pricing problem peculiar to large-scale enterprises is the determination of an internal **transfer price**—the price for moving goods between **profit centres**, which are any part of the organization to which revenue and controllable costs can be assigned, such as a department. As companies expand, they tend to decentralize management and set up profit centres as a control device in the newly decentralized operation.

In a large company, profit centres might secure many needed resources from sellers within their own organization. The pricing problem thus poses several questions: What rate should profit centre A (maintenance department) charge profit centre B (production department) for the cleaning compound used on B's floors? Should the price be the same as it would be if A did the work for an outside party? Should B receive a discount? The answers to these questions depend on the philosophy of the firm involved.

Transfer pricing can be complicated, especially for multinational organizations. The government closely monitors transfer pricing practices because these exchanges offer easy ways for companies to avoid paying taxes on profits. Figure 16.6 shows how this type of pricing manipulation might work. Suppose a South Korean manufacturer of DVD players sells its machines to its Canadian subsidiary for distribution to dealers. Although each unit costs $25 to build, the manufacturer charges its subsidiary $75. In turn, the distributor sells the DVD players to retailers for $125 each. This arrangement gives the South Korean manufacturer a $50 profit on each machine, on which it pays taxes only in South Korea. Meanwhile, the Canadian subsidiary writes off $50 for advertising and shipping costs, leaving it with no profits—and no tax liability.

transfer price
Cost assessed when a product is moved from one profit centre in a firm to another.

profit centre
Any part of an organization to which revenue and controllable costs can be assigned.

assessment check 6b

6.5 Define transfer price.

6.6 What is a profit centre?

ONLINE PRICING CONSIDERATIONS

Throughout this text, we have seen the impact of the Internet on every component of the marketing mix. Many people see the Internet as one big auction site. Whether it's toys, art, or automobiles, there seems to be an online auction site to serve every person's needs—buyer and seller alike. Auctions are the purest form of negotiated pricing.

Ticket sales are an online auction favourite. Consumers can bid on tickets for all sorts of events: Broadway shows, professional sports, and rock concerts. Razor Gator and Ticket Liquidator are two such online ticket sellers. Razor Gator specializes in finding tickets to sold-out events and providing a "VIP experience." Ticket Liquidator offers low prices on tickets for more than 80 000 events daily.[31]

Online auctions also take place at sites such as eBay—which calls itself The World's Online Marketplace—where consumers can buy and sell items that include collectibles, books, electronic products, and cars. Millions of items are listed on eBay on an average day. Recently, eBay reported that more than half of its transactions now take place through its "Buy It Now" option, suggesting that

Marketoid

eBay has extended its brand to cars.ebay.ca, where consumers can buy used cars, boats, and motorcycles, and to stores.ebay.ca/Police-Auctions-Canada, where consumers can enjoy the excitement of an online auction with the thrill of a police auction. Approximately 6 million Canadians are registered on eBay.

H. F. (HERB) MACKENZIE

Many people see the Internet as one big auction site. Auctions can occur at many places, including sites like eBay.

the novelty of online bidding may have worn off or that consumers prefer to secure an item by paying a set price for it. Regardless of how it is purchased, merchandise on eBay continues to move at astonishing speed: a cell phone sells every seven seconds, while a car sells every 56 seconds.[32]

Another characteristic of online pricing is the use of search programs called **bots** or **shopbots**—derived from the word *robots*—that act as comparison shopping agents. Bots, such as shopbot.ca, search the Web for a specific product and print a list of sites that offer the best prices. In online selling, bots force marketers to keep prices low. However, marketing researchers report that almost four of every five online shoppers will check out several sites before buying, and price is not the only variable they consider when making a purchase decision. Service quality and support information are powerful motivators in the decision process. Also, although price is an important factor with products such as books and DVDs,

bot (shopbot) Software program that allows online shoppers to compare the price of a particular product offered by several online retailers.

it is not as important with complex or highly differentiated products, such as real estate or investment banking. Brand image and customer service may outweigh price in these purchase decisions.

To deal with the influences of the Internet on pricing policies and practices, marketers are applying old strategies in new ways and companies are updating operations to compete with new electronic technologies. Some firms offer online specials that do not appear in their stores or mail-order catalogues. These may take such forms as limited-time discounts, free shipping offers, or coupons that are good only online.

THE CANNIBALIZATION DILEMMA

cannibalization Loss of sales of an existing product due to competition from a new product in the same line.

By pricing the same products differently online, companies run the risk of **cannibalization**. The new twist to an old tactic is that companies are self-inflicting price cuts by creating competition among their own products. During the first decade of e-business, marketers debated whether it was worth taking the risk of alienating customers and channel members by offering lower prices for their products online—which then was an unproven retail outlet. But today, marketers are more savvy about integrating marketing channels, including online sites and affiliated stores—different stores owned by the same company. The trend is moving toward standardizing pricing across channels. As consumers become *multi-channel shoppers,* shopping their preferred retailers both online and off, they expect retailers to recognize them as regular shoppers, regardless of the channel they choose. Research shows that multi-channel shoppers are more profitable than those who stick to one channel.[33]

BUNDLE PRICING

bundle pricing Offering two or more complementary products and selling them for a single price.

As marketers have watched e-commerce weaken their control over prices, they have modified their use of the price variable in the marketing mix. Whenever possible, they have moved to an approach called **bundle pricing**, in which customers acquire a host of goods and services in addition to the tangible products they purchase.

Nowhere is bundle pricing more prevalent than in the telecommunications industry. Consumers are bombarded daily by advertisements for all kinds of Internet, cell phone, and cable or satellite TV packages. Telus, Rogers Communications, and Bell Canada all compete with discounted bundles of services. For example, customers who bundle two qualified services from Rogers Communications can save 5 percent, and the saving increases to 10 percent for three qualified services, and 15 percent for four qualified services.

But sometimes consumers resist the practice of bundling, claiming they are forced to pay for services they don't want in order to receive the ones they do. This is particularly the case with cable television. Cable companies insist they have spent billions of dollars to expand their networks and technology and would be left with unused capacity if they sold only a few channels at a time. Consumer advocates argue that customers are not only forced to pay for unwanted services but also wind up paying inflated prices. The solution seems to be à la carte pricing—allowing consumers to pick and choose the shows or channels they want. While in the past some industry observers believed bundling kept prices low, today the market shows signs of change. Some cable companies believe offerings should be required to stand on their own merits. À la carte pricing is growing in popularity in the United States and is available in Quebec, where it was first offered by Vidéotron, a Quebec-based cable service provider. Forced to meet competition, Bell Canada has been offering à la carte pricing in Quebec since 2010, but does not offer it in the rest of Canada. Rogers Communications offers individual channels for $2.79 per channel—once customers subscribe to a basic package—nearly three times what Quebec consumers pay for individual channels. A more competitive landscape throughout Canada would likely see an increased movement to à la carte pricing.

assessment check 6c

6.7 Describe the benefits of an auction—to the buyer and to the seller.

6.8 What is cannibalization?

6.9 What is bundle pricing?

PRICING AND THE LAW

(7) Outline the legal constraints on pricing.

Pricing decisions are influenced by a variety of legal constraints imposed by federal, provincial, and municipal governments. Included in the price of products are not only the cost of the raw materials, processing and packaging, and profit for the business but also the various taxes that governments require providers to charge. For instance, excise taxes are levied on a variety of products—including cigarettes, alcoholic beverages, and motor fuels. Sales taxes are charged on purchases of most products and services in Canada.

In the global marketplace, prices are directly affected by special types of taxes called *tariffs*. These taxes—levied on the sale of imported goods and services—often make it possible for firms to protect their local markets and still set prices on domestically produced goods well above world market levels. The average tariff on fruits and vegetables around the world is more than 50 percent, although it varies considerably from country to country. Canada and the United States have relatively low tariffs on produce and, due to NAFTA (see Chapter 6), trade virtually duty free with each other and with Mexico.

In some instances, punitive tariffs are levied. Canada and the European Union recently levied a 15 percent penalty tariff on imports of a wide range of consumer products such as clothing, paper products, cigarettes, sweet corn, and oysters from the United States in retaliation for American government subsidies to domestic producers that the World Trade Organization ruled illegal.[34] These tariffs will raise prices in Canadian and EU markets, making these U.S. products less competitive. In still other instances, tariffs are levied to prevent foreign producers from engaging in a practice described in Chapter 6: *dumping* foreign-produced products in international markets at prices lower than those set in their domestic market.

Not every "regulatory" price increase is a tax, however. Rate increases to cover costly government regulations imposed on the telecommunications industry have been appearing on cell phone bills as system access fees or similarly named costs. But these charges are not taxes, since the companies keep all the income from the fees and apply only some of it to complying with the regulations. In essence, such fees are a source of additional revenues in an industry so price-sensitive that any announced price increase is likely to send some customers fleeing to competitors.[35] In a recent Saskatchewan court ruling, a decision was made to allow a class-action lawsuit to proceed against cell phone companies to recover these fees on behalf of Canadian customers. The suit claims that customers were misled into thinking these fees were a tax or regulatory levy when, in fact, they were not. If the suit is successful, the refund to cell phone customers could be as large as $20 billion.[36]

Almost every person looking for a ticket to a high-demand sporting or concert event has encountered an expensive—and often illegal—form of pricing called *ticket scalping*. Scalpers camp out in ticket lines (or hire someone else to stand in line) to purchase tickets they expect to resell at a higher price.

H. F. (HERB) MACKENZIE

Canadian consumers have access to quality fruits and vegetables at reasonable prices because Canada has relatively low tariffs on imported produce.

Although some cities have enacted laws prohibiting the practice, it continues to occur in many locations.

But the ticket reselling market is both highly fragmented and susceptible to fraud and distorted pricing. In response, buyers and sellers are finding that the Internet is helping to create a market where both buyers and sellers can compare prices and seat locations. Web firms such as StubHub.com and TicketsNow.com act as ticket clearinghouses for this secondary market and have signed deals with several professional sports teams that allow season ticket holders to sell unwanted tickets and for buyers to purchase them with a guarantee.

Pricing is also regulated by the general constraints of the Competition Act legislation, as outlined in Chapter 3. The following sections review some of the most important pricing laws for contemporary marketers.

COMPETITION ACT

Canada has a long history of competition legislation that goes back to the 1889 act for the prevention and suppression of combines formed in restraint of trade. The Combines Investigation Act was passed in 1923, and the current **Competition Act** has been in effect since 1986. The purpose of the competition act is to

Competition Act
The most comprehensive legislation in Canada, designed to help both consumers and businesses by promoting a healthy competitive environment.

- promote the efficiency and adaptability of the Canadian economy
- expand opportunities for Canadian participation in world markets while at the same time recognizing the role of foreign competition in Canada
- ensure that small and medium-sized enterprises have an equitable opportunity to participate in the Canadian economy
- provide consumers with competitive prices and product choices.[37]

The Competition Act tries to balance the interests of businesses and consumers; it tries to foster a fair competitive environment to protect businesses from each other and to protect consumers from unfair business practices. It focuses on a number of pricing-related practices, including *price discrimination, price fixing (a form of collusion), bid rigging, predatory pricing, false or misleading ordinary selling price representations*, and many others.

price discrimination
Occurs when some customers pay more than others for the same product.

Price discrimination, which occurs when some customers pay more than others for the same product, dates back to the very beginnings of trade and commerce. Today, however, technology has added to the frequency and complexity of price discrimination, as well as the strategies marketers adopt to get around it. For example, marketers may encourage repeat business by inviting purchasers to become preferred customers, entitling them to average discounts of 10 percent. As long as companies can demonstrate that their price discounts and promotional allowances do not restrict competition, they avoid penalties under the Competition Act. Direct mail marketers frequently send out catalogues of identical goods but with different prices in different editions of the catalogues. Postal code areas that traditionally consist of high spenders get the catalogues with the higher prices, while postal code areas where price-sensitive customers live get the catalogues with the lower prices. Victoria's Secret, Staples, and Simon & Schuster are among the hundreds of companies that employ legal price discrimination strategies.

Firms accused of price discrimination often argue that they set price differentials to meet competitors' prices and that cost differences justify variations in prices. When a firm asserts that it maintains price differentials as good-faith methods of competing with rivals, a logical question arises: What constitutes good-faith pricing behaviour? The answer depends on the particular situation.

A defence based on cost differentials works only if the price differences do not exceed the cost differences resulting from selling to various classes of buyers. Marketers must then be prepared to justify the cost differences. Many authorities consider this provision one of the most confusing areas in the

Marketoid

Germany's largest drug maker, Bayer AG, was fined $3.65 million for price fixing involving its rubber and chemicals business in Canada.

Competition Act. Courts handle most charges brought under the act as individual cases. Therefore, domestic marketers must continually evaluate their pricing actions to avoid potential violations. Price discrimination becomes a more important issue when one company charges different prices to two or more companies that are in competition with each other. This clearly interferes with competition in the marketplace. There have been only three convictions for discriminatory pricing under the Competition Act, all since 1984, with fines ranging from $15 000 to $50 000.[38]

Price fixing is a form of collusion in which sellers get together and collude to set prices higher than they would otherwise be in a free market. For the first time in Canadian history, gas companies have been found guilty of price fixing. Fourteen companies and 38 individuals have been charged in four Quebec cities. Fines have ranged from $20 000 for an individual gas station operator to $1.85 million for Ultramar. A total of $2.8 million in fines have been levied, although the investigations continue. Some individuals have received 12-month prison terms, although they were "served in the community."[39] In investigations by the European Union and the U.S. government, a number of the world's largest airlines were investigated for conspiracy to fix prices, some for freight services and some for passenger fares. Included in the investigations were Air Canada, British Airways, Air France, KLM, SAS, Lufthansa, Korean Air, Cathay Pacific, and Qantas Airways. Among those found guilty, fines have ranged from $61 million (U.S.) to $300 million (U.S.) although investigations are not complete and the guilt of several companies has yet to be determined.[40] In one recent year, the EU levied price-fixing fines of approximately $4 billion.[41]

Bid rigging is another form of collusion, similar to price fixing. It occurs when sellers get together and collude to set prices with respect to one or more requests for competitive proposals. The intent is that one of the sellers will provide the lowest price but, unknown to the customer, one that is higher than it would be in a free market. The winner then agrees to let another competitor "win" another bid, again at an inflated price. Four Toronto-based electrical contractors were fined a total of $2.55 million when it was determined they set prices 10 to 15 percent higher than they should have been on several bids.[42] In Japan, a city government cancelled a bid request after one bidding company accidentally faxed information concerning who should win the bid and at what price. The fax asked other bidders to cooperate in the bid rigging.[43]

Predatory pricing occurs when companies set prices below their cost for a sufficiently long period of time to discourage or eliminate competition and then raise their prices or otherwise interfere with competition. Europe's largest drug maker, GlaxoSmithKline, was recently fined $15.5 million for manipulating prices on antibiotics to keep competitors out of the French market.[44]

False or misleading price representations is one form of misleading advertising. A coordinated probe in 16 EU countries found 226 websites that failed to show taxes and fees in published prices, or engaged in other misleading practices. The EU Consumer Protection Commissioner has vowed to shut down or fine those companies that fail to change their ways.[45] Consumer groups have long accused Carrefour, the world's second-largest retailer, of advertising misleading prices. In a recent French court action, it was fined $2.9 million.[46] Misleading price advertising has been common in Canada. Suzy Shier paid a $1-million fine for a second offence, following a previous $300-million fine. Sears Canada was fined $100 000 for misrepresenting savings on tires. Premier Health Club was fined $30 000, and GoodLife Fitness Clubs, which operates more than 90 fitness clubs in Canada, was fined $75 000.[47]

price fixing A form of collusion in which sellers get together and collude to set prices higher than they would otherwise be in a free market.

bid rigging Occurs when sellers get together and collude to set prices with respect to one or more requests for competitive proposals.

predatory pricing Occurs when companies set prices below their cost for a sufficiently long period of time to discourage or eliminate competition and then raise their prices or otherwise interfere with competition.

false or misleading price representations One form of misleading advertising.

assessment check 7 ✓

7.1 What does the Competition Act try to accomplish?

7.2 What is price discrimination? Is it always considered anticompetitive? Explain.

7.3 What is the difference between price fixing and bid rigging?

A number of health clubs in Canada have been charged with violations under the Competition Act.

H. F. (HERB) MACKENZIE

Strategic Implications

This chapter has focused on traditional pricing concepts and methods, and on setting prices as an important part of a firm's marketing program designed to help it achieve its overall business objectives. Technology has forever changed the marketplace, which affects the pricing function. A growing number of products are not made until they are ordered, and increasingly, their prices are no longer fixed; instead, prices can shift up and down in response to changing market conditions.

Customers can now compare prices quickly, heightening competitive intensity. Online price comparison engines, known as *shopping bots*, promise to help customers find the lowest price for any good or service. The Web allows for prices to be negotiated on the spot, and anything can be auctioned. Reverse auctions—gaining in popularity in both consumer and business markets—allow customers to submit the highest price they are willing to pay for an increasing number of products.

The Web connects buyers and sellers from around the globe. A customer in Thunder Bay, Ontario, might want to purchase a wool sweater from Norway. Global transportation systems have lowered delivery costs and increased delivery speeds as volumes have increased, increasing the likelihood of such purchases. Firms today must be concerned with price competition across borders, and not simply across town.

To succeed in today's more competitive pricing environment, marketers must continue to offer value—fair prices for quality goods and services—and superior customer service. These are the critical success factors in marketing today. ◆◆◆

REVIEW OF CHAPTER OBJECTIVES

① Identify the major categories of pricing objectives.

Pricing objectives should be the natural consequence of overall organizational goals and more specific marketing goals. They can be classified into four major groups: (1) profitability objectives, including profit maximization and target returns; (2) volume objectives, including sales maximization and market share; (3) meeting competition objectives; and (4) prestige objectives.

② Explain the methods of determining prices.

Marketers determine prices in two basic ways: by applying the theoretical concepts of supply and demand and by completing cost-oriented analyses. The assumption that firms attempt to maximize profit, the difficulty of estimating demand curves, and inadequate training of managers to use economic theory all present problems with the first approach. Cost-plus pricing is the most commonly used method of setting prices today. There are two primary cost-oriented pricing procedures: full-cost pricing and incremental-cost pricing. Break-even analysis, another cost-based model, can be helpful, but also has some limitations. The basic limitation of all cost-oriented pricing approaches is that they do not adequately account for product demand. When most of a firm's costs are fixed over a wide range of outputs, yield management pricing strategies can help maximize revenues and, hence, maximize profit.

③ Compare the alternative pricing strategies and explain when each is most appropriate.

The alternative pricing strategies are skimming pricing strategy, penetration pricing strategy, and competitive pricing strategy. Skimming pricing is commonly used as a market-entry price for distinctive products with little or no initial competition. Penetration pricing is used when there is a wide array of competing brands. Everyday low pricing (EDLP), a variant of penetration pricing, is used by discounters that attempt to hold the line on prices without having to rely heavily on short-term coupons, rebates, and other price concessions. Competitive pricing is employed when marketers wish to concentrate their competitive efforts on marketing variables other than price.

④ **Describe how prices are quoted.**

Methods for quoting prices depend on such factors as cost structures, traditional practices in the particular industry, and policies of individual firms. Price quotes can involve list prices, market prices, cash discounts, trade discounts, quantity discounts, and allowances such as trade-ins, promotional allowances, and rebates. Shipping costs often figure heavily into the pricing of goods. A number of alternatives for dealing with these costs exist: FOB plant pricing, in which the price includes no shipping charges; FOB origin, freight allowed, or freight absorbed, which allows the buyer to deduct transportation expenses from the bill; uniform-delivered price, in which the same price, including shipping expenses, is charged to all buyers; and zone pricing, in which a set price exists within each region.

⑤ **Identify the various pricing policy decisions that marketers must make.**

A pricing policy is a general guideline based on pricing objectives and is intended for use in specific pricing decisions. Pricing policies include psychological pricing, unit pricing, price flexibility, product-line pricing, and promotional pricing. An important pricing consideration for marketing managers is the price-quality relationship. In the absence of other cues, price is an important influence on how the consumer perceives the product's quality.

⑥ **List and explain a number of special issues in pricing.**

A number of special issues in pricing were discussed. Competitive bidding and negotiated prices are pricing techniques used primarily in the B2B sector and in government and organizational markets. For global marketers, in addition to the traditional four pricing objectives, a fifth objective is often price stability. Global marketers can choose from three export pricing strategies: a standard worldwide price, dual pricing, or market-differentiated pricing. A phenomenon in large corporations—and particularly in global marketing companies—is transfer pricing, in which a company sets prices for transferring goods or services from one company profit centre to another. To deal with the influences of the Internet on pricing policies and practices, marketers are updating operations to compete with new electronic technologies. For customers, bots, also known as shopbots, act as comparison-shopping agents. Cannibalization secures additional sales through lower prices that take sales away from the marketer's other products. It can be an important problem for companies that price their products differently online than through other channels. Bundle pricing is offering two or more complementary products and selling them for a single price.

⑦ **Outline the legal constraints on pricing.**

A variety of laws affect pricing decisions. The Competition Act of 1986 is the major legislation in Canada that governs pricing and other competitive business practices. Among the pricing-related issues covered by this legislation are price discrimination, price fixing, bid rigging, predatory pricing, and false or misleading ordinary selling price representations. The Competition Act tries to balance the interests of businesses and consumers; it tries to foster a fair competitive environment to protect businesses from each other and to protect consumers from unfair business practices.

assessment check answers

1.1 What are target-return objectives?
Target-return objectives are short-run or long-run goals that are usually stated as percentages of sales or investment.

1.2 What is value pricing?
Value pricing emphasizes the benefits a product provides in comparison to the price and quality levels of competing offerings.

1.3 How do prestige objectives affect a seller's pricing strategy?
Prestige pricing establishes a relatively high price to develop and maintain an image of quality that appeals to status-conscious customers. The seller uses price to create an overall image of the firm.

1.4 What goals does pricing strategy help a not-for-profit organization achieve?
Pricing strategy helps not-for-profit organizations achieve a variety of goals: profit maximization, cost recovery, market incentives, and market suppression.

2.1 What are the two basic ways in which marketers determine prices?
Marketers determine prices by applying the theoretical concepts of supply and demand and by completing cost-oriented analysis.

2.2 What are the four types of market structures?

The four types of market structures are pure competition, monopolistic competition, oligopoly, and monopoly.

2.3 Identify the two types of costs that make up a product's total cost.

A product's total cost is composed of total variable costs and total fixed costs.

2.4 What are the determinants of elasticity?

The degree of consumer responsiveness to price changes—elasticity—is affected by such factors as (1) availability of substitute or complementary goods, (2) the classification of a good or service as a luxury or a necessity, (3) the portion of a person's budget spent on an item, and (4) the time perspective.

2.5 What is the usual relationship between elasticity and revenue?

A price cut increases revenue only for a product with elastic demand, and a price increase raises revenue only for a product with inelastic demand.

2.6 List the three reasons why it is difficult to put price theory into practice.

A basic assumption of price theory is that all firms attempt to maximize profits. This does not always happen in practice. A second reason is that demand curves can be extremely difficult to estimate. Finally, managers can be inadequately trained, causing poor communication between economists and managers, which makes it difficult to apply price theory in the real world.

2.7 What is full-cost pricing?

Full-cost pricing uses all relevant variable costs in setting a product's price.

2.8 What is incremental-cost pricing?

Incremental-cost pricing attempts to use only costs directly attributable to a specific output in setting prices to overcome the arbitrary allocation of fixed expenses.

2.9 Give the formula for finding the break-even point, in units and in dollars.

Break-even point (in units) = Total fixed cost/Per-unit contribution to fixed cost. Break-even point (in dollars) = Total fixed cost/(1 − Variable cost per unit price).

2.10 What adjustments to the basic break-even calculation must be made to include target returns?

Break-even point (including specific dollar target return) = (Total fixed cost + Profit objective)/Per-unit contribution.

2.11 What are the advantages of break-even analysis?

Breakeven analysis is easily understood by managers and may help them decide whether required sales levels for a certain price are realistic goals.

2.12 What are the disadvantages of break-even analysis?

First, the model assumes that cost can be divided into fixed and variable categories and ignores the problems of arbitrarily making some allocations. Second, it assumes that per-unit variable costs do not change at different levels of operation, ignoring the possibility of quantity discounts, more efficient use of the workforce, and other possible economies. Third, the basic break-even model does not consider demand.

2.13 Explain the goal of yield management.

Yield management pricing strategies are designed to maximize revenues in situations in which costs are fixed, such as airfares, auto rentals, and theatre tickets.

3.1 What are the three major pricing strategies?

The three major pricing strategies are skimming, penetration, and competitive.

3.2 What is EDLP?

EDLP stands for everyday low pricing. It is a variation of penetration pricing often used by discounters.

4.1 What are the three major types of discounts?

The three major types of discounts are cash discounts, trade discounts, and quantity discounts.

4.2 Identify the four alternatives for handling transportation costs in pricing policies.

The four alternatives for handling transportation costs are FOB pricing, uniform-delivered pricing, zone pricing, and basing-point pricing.

5.1 Define pricing policy.

A pricing policy is a general guideline that reflects marketing objectives and influences specific pricing decisions.

5.2 Describe the two types of psychological pricing other than prestige pricing.

The two additional types of psychological pricing are odd pricing, in which marketers set prices at odd numbers just under round numbers, and unit pricing, which states prices in terms of a recognized unit of measurement.

5.3 What is promotional pricing?

Promotional pricing is a lower-than-normal price for a set period of time.

5.4 Describe the price–quality connection.

Price serves as an important indicator of a product's quality. However, many marketers now work hard to convince consumers that they are offering high-quality products at the lowest possible price.

5.5 What are price limits?

Price limits indicate certain boundaries within which consumers' product-quality perceptions vary directly with price. A price set lower than expected seems too cheap, and one set above the expected limit is seen as too expensive.

6.1 What is competitive bidding?

Competitive bidding consists of inviting potential suppliers to quote prices on proposed purchases or contracts.

6.2 Why is price stability difficult to achieve in global marketing?

Price stability is difficult to achieve because wars, terrorism, economic trends, changing governments, and shifting trade policies can alter prices.

6.3 What are the three traditional global pricing strategies?

The three global pricing strategies are standard worldwide pricing, dual pricing, and market-differentiated pricing.

6.4 Which is the most flexible global pricing strategy?

The most flexible global pricing strategy is market-differentiated pricing, which allows firms to set prices according to actual conditions.

6.5 Define transfer price.

A transfer price is the price for moving goods between profit centres.

6.6 What is a profit centre?

A profit centre is any part of the organization to which revenue and controllable costs can be assigned.

6.7 Describe the benefits of an auction—to the buyer and to the seller.

An auction can provide buyers with opportunities to buy goods and services at very low prices. It can also offer the seller an opportunity to sell to a wider audience (online) perhaps at a higher price than otherwise would be possible, if the item is particularly popular.

6.8 What is cannibalization?

Cannibalization involves cutting prices in one selling channel, which creates direct competition with a firm's own products.

6.9 What is bundle pricing?

Bundle pricing involves combining a number of goods or services together and offering them at a set price.

7.1 What does the Competition Act try to accomplish?

The Competition Act tries to foster a fair competitive environment to protect businesses from each other and to protect consumers from unfair business practices.

7.2 What is price discrimination? Is it always considered anticompetitive? Explain.

Price discrimination occurs when some customers pay more than others for the same product. It is acceptable when discounts are given to meet competition, or can be justified due to cost savings resulting from selling to some customers.

7.3 What is the difference between price fixing and bid rigging?

Both are forms of price collusion and are illegal; however, price fixing occurs when sellers decide to establish prices higher than would exist in a free market whereas bid rigging occurs when the prices relate to one or more competitive bids.

MARKETING TERMS YOU NEED TO KNOW

These terms are printed in red in the text. They are defined in the margins of the chapter and in the Glossary that begins on p. G-1.

price 502
marginal analysis 504
profit maximization 504
target-return objectives 504
market-share objective 505
Profit Impact of Market Strategies (PIMS) project 505
value pricing 506
customary prices 508
demand 508
supply 508
pure competition 508
monopolistic competition 509
oligopoly 509
monopoly 509
variable costs 510
fixed costs 510
average total costs 510
marginal cost 510
elasticity 511
cost-plus pricing 514
full-cost pricing 514
incremental-cost pricing 514

break-even analysis 515
yield management 516
skimming pricing strategy 518
step out 518
penetration pricing strategy 519
everyday low price (EDLP) 520
competitive pricing strategy 521
opening price point 521
list price 521
market price 522
cash discount 522
trade discount 522
quantity discount 523
cumulative quantity discount 523
noncumulative quantity discount 523
allowance 523
trade-in 523
promotional allowance 523
minimum advertised pricing (MAP) 523
rebate 524
FOB (free on board) plant (FOB origin) 524
uniform-delivered pricing 525

zone pricing 525
basing-point pricing 525
pricing policy 525
psychological pricing 526
odd pricing 526
unit pricing 526
price flexibility 527
product-line pricing 527
promotional pricing 527
loss leader 528
leader pricing 528
competitive bidding 529
transfer price 531
profit centre 531
bot (or shopbot) 532
cannibalization 532
bundle pricing 532
Competition Act 534
price discrimination 534
price fixing 535
bid rigging 535
predatory pricing 535
false or misleading representations 535

PROJECTS AND TEAMWORK EXERCISES

1. In small teams, categorize each of the following as a specific type of pricing objective. Suggest a company or product likely to use each pricing objective. Compare your findings.
   a. 5 percent increase in profits over the previous year
   b. prices no more than 6 percent higher than prices quoted by independent dealers
   c. 5 percent increase in market share
   d. 25 percent return on investment (before taxes)
   e. setting the highest prices in the product category to maintain favourable brand image

2. How are the following prices determined, and what do they have in common?
   a. ticket to a local museum
   b. college or university tuition
   c. provincial sales tax
   d. printing of business cards
   e. lawn mowers

3. WebSmart Development of Winnipeg, Manitoba, is considering the introduction of a new product proposed by its research and development staff. The firm's marketing director estimates the product can be marketed at a price of $70. Total fixed cost is $278 000, and average variable cost is calculated at $48.
   a. What is the break-even point in units for the proposed product? In sales dollars?
   b. The firm's CEO has suggested a target return of $214 000 for the proposed product. How many units must be sold to break even and achieve this target return?

4. With a classmate, create two advertisements for the same product. One advertisement should feature a high price, and the other advertisement should feature a low price. Present your advertisements to the students in your class. Record students' perceptions of the price–quality relationship.

5. On your own or with a classmate, visit a local supermarket to find examples of promotional pricing and loss leaders. Note instances of both. Does the promotional pricing make you more apt to purchase a product? Does knowing the store uses loss-leader pricing of bananas or apples make you more inclined to buy them? Present your findings and opinions to the class.

CRITICAL-THINKING EXERCISES

1. Music artists earn only about 9 percent in royalties per CD, using a royalty base of retail price less 25 percent for packaging costs. The rest goes to the producer and to cover recording costs, promotion, copies given away to radio stations and reviewers, and other costs such as videos. What do you think happens to the artist's royalties when a CD is marked down to sell faster? Consider two cases: (a) the marked-down CD sells more copies, and (b) it sells the same number of copies as before.

2. Some finance experts advise consumers not to worry about rising gasoline prices, the cost of which can easily be covered by forgoing one takeout meal a month, but to worry about how high energy prices will affect the rest of the economy. For example, each dollar-a-barrel price increase is equivalent to several millions of dollars a day "tax" on the economy. Explain what this means.

3. When Dell recently launched its Mini3 smartphone, it targeted consumers not in Canada and the United States, but in China and Brazil. Its strategy: to create loyal customers as those markets emerge. A few years ago, when Dell introduced computers into the emerging markets of China and India, it used a penetration pricing strategy. That is, it priced the new computers under $500, significantly less than its computers sold for in its home markets.[48] Why do you think Dell choose that pricing strategy? Do you think it was successful? Do you predict Dell will use the same pricing strategy for its smartphone? Why or why not?

4. As a consumer, would you rather shop at a store that features a sale once a month or a store that practises everyday low pricing (EDLP)? Why?

5. Go online to a shopping site you use regularly and note the prices for different types of products. Does the firm use psychological pricing? Product line pricing? Note any pricing strategies you can identify. Do any of these strategies make you prefer the site over a competitor's site?

ETHICS EXERCISE

You work for a major restaurant in your town. The manager is facing cost pressures from rising food prices and says she needs to raise revenues. She decides to reduce the size of the meal portions and use cheaper cuts of meat and fish in some entrées while holding the menu prices constant. She tells you and other staff members not to mention the changes to customers and to deflect any questions or complaints you hear. The descriptions in the menu will not be changed, she says, "because the printing costs would be too high."

1. You know the restaurant advertises the quality of its ingredients in the local media. But the menu changes are not advertised, and it bothers you. What course of action would you take?
2. A customer mentions the beef in a dish he ordered is "tough and dry" and the order seems smaller than before. What would you do?

INTERNET EXERCISES

1. **Pricing strategies.** Shopbot.ca (www.shopbot.ca) is a so-called shopping bot. Enter a product, and Shopbot.ca searches through online retailers and identifies those that sell that particular product along with the price. Visit Shopbot.ca and go shopping for the following products. Do the prices of these products vary from online retailer to online retailer? Do some products cost the same regardless of where they are purchased? Prepare a brief report on your findings and what they tell you about the pricing strategies used by various companies.
   a. a Canon PowerShot SX30 IS digital camera (or another model)
   b. Bose 251 Environmental Speakers (or another model)
   c. A BlackBerry Torch 9800 smartphone (or another model)

2. **Price markups.** Assume you're in the market for a new car or truck. Visit CarCostCanada (www.carcostcanada .com). Pick two or three makes and models that interest you. View a sample price report. Compare the M.S.R.P. price and the dealer invoice price. Are you surprised by the markup? What do you think is a fair markup? What tips and advice can you find for buying a new car? Summarize your findings and bring your report to class so you can participate in a discussion on pricing.

Note: Internet Web addresses change frequently. If you don't find the exact sites listed, you may need to access the organization's or company's home page and search from there or use a search engine such as Google.

CASE 16.1

Holding the (Price) Line on Luxury Goods

In a tough economy, the market for luxury goods and services faces unique challenges. Many people who at one time might have splurged on a Rolex watch or a Lexus sedan are now unemployed and, possibly, facing foreclosure on their home. Even those with high net worth felt the pinch when their investments—affected by a stock market in free-fall—took a hit, some losing as much as 50 percent of value. Thus even the wealthy had less disposable income for high-priced vacations and weekly spa treatments.

The luxury goods market experienced a several-quarter drought during which sales fell 8 percent—several billion dollars. As the stock market began to stabilize, however, sales in the sector have begun to pick up: high-fashion house Hermès posted a 19 percent spike in sales for a recent quarter, and LVMH Moët Hennessy Louis Vuitton reported an 11 percent increase.

Still, luxury retailers aren't out of the woods yet, and they resist applying the same promotional strategies to bring in business that more mainstream retailers might try. Tiffany's—widely

regarded as one of the world's premier jewellers—would risk damaging its carefully tended image if it were to advertise, for instance, a "buy one, get one free" sale or discounts on its crystal or sterling patterns. Interestingly, these types of promotions by retailers such as Sears Canada or restaurant chains such as Swiss Chalet seemingly have no adverse effect on shoppers' perception of value.

Recently, Tiffany's quietly discounted its prime line, diamond engagement rings, by about 10 percent, but did it without hoopla. Only those shopping for an engagement ring would have known about the reduced prices, having been informed by the salesperson. Discounting merchandise without making it widely known allows retailers like Tiffany's to maintain their traditional pricing policy—outwardly, at least.

But what can a luxury retailer do to increase traffic during a recession if it doesn't advertise a sale? Many retailers choose to be discreet and communicate sales only through emails to regular customers. Others communicate more publicly, positioning the sale as "clearing inventory" while bolstering revenues. During a recent holiday season, another premier retailer, Saks Fifth Avenue, announced savings of as much as 70 percent, through print and Web ads, store signage, and emails. Saks management said the sales didn't hurt the store's image at all.

When spas and beauty salons discount the cost of services to encourage business, they run the risk that customers will think the service was initially overpriced. Instead, spas and salons have found success in bundling services: for example, a customer who gets a manicure can, for a reduced price, get a facial at the same time. For some reason, the notion of bundled services does not diminish their value in the customer's mind. Another tactic that works is the incentive plus special offer: for example, by referring a customer to your spa or salon, you'll receive a coupon good for 10 percent off on your next appointment. Such a promotion can also encourage the purchase of several services.

Questions for Critical Thinking

1. What other pricing promotions could a luxury retailer offer to build sales? Should a retailer use different strategies when targeting existing customers and new customers? Why?
2. How do you think the price–quality relationship affects the marketing of luxury goods?

Sources: David Eisen, "Luxury Good Sales Show Improvement," *Luxury Travel Advisor*, May 7, 2010, http://www.luxuryta.com; Astrid Wendlandt, "Bain Sees 2010 Global Luxury Goods Sales up 4 Percent," Reuters, April 15, 2010, http://www.reuters.com; Vanessa O'Connell, "Luxury-Goods Sales Still Soft, Recovery Unlikely before 2011," *The Wall Street Journal*, October 20, 2009, http://online.wsj.com; Brian Burnsed, "Where Discounting Can Be Dangerous," *Business-Week*, August 3, 2009, http://www.businessweek.com; "Restrained Indulgence: As More Clients Refrain from Spending, Luxury Service Providers Redouble Efforts to Entice Business," *Crain's Cleveland Business*, March 9, 2009, http://www.crainscleveland.com.

CASE 16.2

Electricity: A Changing Price Model

A good piece of advice for any marketer: when you change your price strategy, do a good job of informing your customers in advance of why you are making the change and how it will affect them. If you don't communicate effectively with your customers, they will make assumptions, sometimes erroneously. You stand to lose customers who then look for alternative suppliers, unless, of course, you have a monopoly.

Ontario has led the way in Canada, installing "smart" meters in 2010 to measure electricity use, and having 95 percent of all eligible endpoints (mainly households) using them by the end of that year. There are now 4.5 million smart meters in use in Ontario. British Columbia intends to have 1.9 million smart meters installed by the end of 2012. Quebec announced that it plans to have smart meters installed throughout the province starting in 2012, culminating in 3.8 million installations by 2017. Other provinces will likely follow suit, but not before there is considerable market development in the United States, where, currently, California and Texas are leading the way. Newfoundland Power has decided that it will wait until the industry has matured—when increased manufacturing capacity will drive down the cost of smart meters and when communications protocols that work with the smart meters have been standardized. (The cost of a smart meter in 2010 was $700.54, and the cost of installation was $145.00.)

How will smart meters affect electricity costs for consumers? That's certainly the question everyone has, but there is certainly considerable debate over the answer as more stakeholders get involved in the discussions. Consumers remain skeptical that the new pricing model will benefit them. Too often the reality is that price changes create winners and losers, and almost always more losers than winners. That is, price changes are seldom, if ever, designed to be revenue neutral.

The Government of Ontario website claims the typical residential consumer will save approximately $153.60 annually. Toronto Hydro stated in 2011 that four of five customers had an increase averaging $1.50 per month, and one in five had a decrease averaging $3.70 per month. But every jurisdiction that is planning to adopt smart meters is looking at the long term. B.C. Hydro estimates that installations will cost $1.1 billion but will provide $1.6 billion in benefits over 20 years. Hydro-Québec, which will have twice as many installations as B.C., estimates that smart meters will save almost $300 million over 20 years. However, has the impact of reduced tax revenues been considered? For example, using smart meters in Quebec is estimated to reduce the need for meter readers, resulting in the loss of upwards of 800 jobs. Will the immediate loss of taxes be felt as well as the cost, at least in the short term, of increased social benefits due to increased unemployment? Who knows what's going to happen?

Certainly, there are good reasons to deploy smart meters, regardless of short-term pain and the potential for long-term cost savings. Using less electricity is good for the environment. But so is shifting demand for electricity from peak to nonpeak times. This is a greater concern in Ontario than in many provinces because its electricity system is already strained. Having to meet peak demand adds cost and could require additional infrastructure (power lines, buildings, power plants, etc.) earlier than otherwise needed. The greater availability of information about consumption usage, by hour of day and day of week, will allow better planning by electricity providers. Of course, some people are concerned the information that is used could be abused by possibly being sold to marketers or matched with other government data that it has on consumers.

Some consumers are questioning what was wrong with the old model: simply charging consumers a premium for excessive use. Under the old system, consumers paid $0.068 per kWh for the first 600 kWh used in a month, and $0.079 for each additional kWh. Increasing the price premium for high-demand users could be used to reduce demand. In the new model, which went into effect on May 1, 2011, prices vary depending on time of use (based on summer rates in effect between May 1 and October 31):

Weekdays:	Weekends:
7 a.m. to 11 a.m.	$0.089 per kWh
11 a.m. to 5 p.m.	$0.107 per kWh
5 p.m. to 7 p.m.	$0.089 per kWh
7 p.m. to 7 a.m.	$0.059 per kWh

In theory, this looks good. All consumers need to do is change their demand to off-peak periods and save money. Many chores that are done during the day or early evening could be moved to after 7 p.m. or to weekends. Unfortunately, the burden and ability to shift electricity use does not fall equally on all consumers. Senior citizens, for example, are home during the day and need to have heat or air conditioning throughout the day, and this is particularly true for those who have medical conditions. Larger families that must prepare meals must do so after 7 a.m., before school or work, and can seldom wait until after 7 p.m. to begin preparing the evening meal. Some appliances—especially those electricity hogs, refrigerators and freezers—have to run 24/7. Most small businesses that serve the public must be open and operating during peak times. A restaurant serving lunch, for example, has to operate fully during the peak period. One Chamber of Commerce chairperson suggested that 90 percent of businesses in his area would be hurt by the new pricing model.

Ontario Energy Minister Brad Duguid proudly announced that smart meters have already shifted 4 percent of electricity use from off-peak hours by summer 2011. Concerns about the impact of the price change—which unfortunately also came during the second-hottest summer on record, and closely following Ontario's imposition of the HST—has helped prompt the government to initiate a 10 percent cut to electricity bills as part of the Ontario

Clean Energy Benefit program. This will reduce any sting from the price change for at least the five years it will be in effect (and until after the impending 2011 election).

Questions for Critical Thinking

1. Are you for or against time-of-use pricing for electricity? Be prepared to defend your choice.
2. Why are governments moving to time-of-use models? What alternatives could have been considered?
3. Assume that your household uses 750 kWh of electricity during an average month. How much would you pay under the old pricing model (exclusive of taxes and other add-ons). Now assume that your household uses 10 percent of its electricity during peak times, 20 percent during mid-peak times, and 70 percent during off-peak times. By how much are you better or worse off? What would happen if your consumption changed: 20 percent during peak times, 35 percent during mid-peak times, and 45 percent during off-peak times? Prepare the same calculations for a household that uses 1050 kWh per month of electricity.
4. Visit **www.ieso.ca/house/default.asp**. Calculate what it would cost to wash and dry three loads of laundry on Sunday afternoon, and compare this to the cost had you done the same laundry on Wednesday afternoon. Be sure to check out the dog in the top-floor bedroom.

Sources: Government of Ontario, Ministry of Energy website, "Ontario Clean Energy Benefit," http://www.mei.gov.on.ca/en/energy/index.php?page=oceb, August 7, 2011; Lynn Moore, "Smart Meters Dumb Move: Union," *Gazette* (Montreal), July 20, 2011, p. 3; Elizabeth Denham, "Smart Meters Open Door to Privacy Issues: B.C. Hydro Initiative Must Build Security Into Modernization of Grid," *Times-Colonist* (Victoria, B.C.), June 29, 2011; Brian Cross, "Smart Meter Pricing Comes Under Fire: ERWIN Gets Extension until 2012, but We Pay Now For Units," *Windsor Star*, June 8, 2011, p. 1; Lynn Moore, "Hydro-Quebec To Roll Out 'Smart' Meters," *Gazette* (Montreal), May 26, 2011, http://www.montrealgazette.com; Dean Chuang, "Smart Metering in Canada," Computerworld, March 24, 2011, http://news.idg.no/cw/art.cfm?id=1A796C36-1A64-6A71-CE9E2FB65F221D43, August 7, 2011; John Spears and Robert Benzie, "What's the Return on $1 Billion Smart Meter Investment?" *Toronto Star*, March 4, 2011, p. 1; Tyler Hamilton, "Smart Meters Are Here to Stay. Get Over It," *Toronto Star*, October 8, 2010, p. 2.

Financial Analysis in Marketing

A number of basic concepts from accounting and finance offer invaluable tools to marketers. Understanding the contributions made by these analytic tools can improve the quality of marketing decisions. In addition, marketers are frequently called on to explain and defend their decisions in financial terms. These accounting and financial tools can be used to supply quantitative data to justify decisions made by marketing managers. In this appendix, we describe the major accounting and finance concepts that have marketing implications and explain how they assist in making informed marketing decisions.

FINANCIAL STATEMENTS

All companies prepare a set of financial statements on a regular basis. Two of the most important financial statements are the income statement and balance sheet. The analogy of a motion picture is often used to describe an *income statement*, since it presents a financial record of a company's revenues, expenses, and profits over a period of time, such as a month, quarter, or year. In contrast, the *balance sheet* is a snapshot of what a company owns—called *assets*—and what it owes—called *liabilities*—at a point in time, such as at the end of the month, quarter, or year. The difference between assets and liabilities is referred to as *owner's, partners', or shareholders' equity*—the amount of funds the firm's owners have invested in its formation and continued operations. Of the two financial statements, the income statement contains more marketing-related information.

A sample income statement for Composite Technology is shown in Figure 1. Composite Technology is a B2B producer and marketer. The firm designs and manufactures a variety of composite components for manufacturers of consumer, industrial, and government products. Total sales revenues for 2012 amounted to $675 million. Total expenses, including taxes, for the year were $583.1 million. The year 2012 proved to be profitable for Composite Technology—the firm reported a profit, referred to as net income, of $91.9 million. While total revenue is a fairly straightforward number, several of the expenses shown on the income statement require additional explanation.

For any company that makes its own products (a manufacturer) or simply markets one or more items produced by others (an importer, retailer, or wholesaler), the largest single expense is usually a category called *cost of goods sold*. This reflects the cost, to the firm, of the goods that it markets to its customers. In the case of Composite Technology, the cost of goods sold represents the cost of components and raw materials as well as the cost of designing and manufacturing the composite panels the firm produces and markets to its business customers.

The income statement illustrates how cost of goods sold is calculated. The calculation begins with the value of the firm's inventory at the beginning of 2012. Inventory is the value of raw materials, partially completed products, and finished products held by the firm at the end of a specified time period, say, the end of the year. The cost of materials purchased by Composite Technology buyers during the year and the direct cost of manufacturing the finished products are then added to the beginning inventory figure. The result is cost of goods the firm has available for sale during the year. Once the firm's accountants subtract the value of inventory held by the firm at the end of 2012, they know the cost of goods sold. By simply subtracting cost of goods sold from total sales revenues generated during the year, they determine that Composite achieved gross profits of $270 million in 2012.

figure 1

2012 Income Statement for Composite Technology, Inc.

Composite Technology, Inc.
500 Ridley Road
Somewhere, MB

CT

INCOME STATEMENT
For the Year Ended December 31, 2012
(in $ millions)

Sales	675.0
Cost of Goods Sold	405.0
Gross Income	270.0
Selling, Administrative, and General Expenses	82.1
Research and Development Expenses	25.4
Operating Income	162.5
Depreciation	18.6
Net Interest Expense	2.5
Before Tax Income	141.4
Provision for Income Taxes	49.5
Net Income	91.9

Cost of Goods Sold Calculation	($ millions)
Beginning Inventory	158.0
plus: Raw Materials Purchased	200.7
plus: Direct Manufacturing Expenses	226.3
Total Cost of Goods	585.0
minus: Ending Inventory	(180.0)
Cost of Goods Sold	405.0

Operating expenses are another significant cost for most firms. This broad category includes such marketing outlays as sales compensation and expenses, advertising and other promotions, and other expenses incurred in implementing marketing plans. Accountants typically combine these financial outlays into a single category with the label *Selling, Administrative, and General Expenses.* Other expense items included in the operating expenses section of the income statement are administrative salaries, utilities, and insurance.

Another significant expense for Composite Technology is research and development (R&D). This includes the cost of developing new products and modifying existing ones. Firms such as pharmaceutical, biotechnology, and computer companies spend significant amounts of money each year on R&D. Subtracting selling, administrative, and general expenses and R&D expenses from the gross profit equals the firm's operating income. For 2012, Composite had operating income of $162.5 million.

Depreciation represents the systematic reduction over time in the value of certain company assets, such as production machinery, office furniture, or laptops provided for the firm's sales representatives. Depreciation is an unusual expense in that it does not involve an actual cash expenditure. However, it does reflect the reality that equipment owned by the company is physically wearing out over time from use and/or from technological obsolescence. Also, charging a portion of the total cost of these long-lived items to each of the years in which they are used results in a more accurate determination of the total costs involved in the firm's operation each year.

Net interest expense is the difference between what a firm paid in interest on various loans and what it collected in interest on any investments made during the time period involved. Subtracting depreciation and net interest expense from the firm's operating profit reveals the firm's *before-tax income.* Composite had depreciation of $18.6 million and a net interest expense of $2.5 million for the year, so its 2012 taxable income was $141.4 million.

Profit-seeking firms pay taxes calculated as a percentage of their taxable income. Composite paid $49.5 million in taxes in 2012. Subtracting taxes from taxable income gives us the firm's *net income* of $91.9 million.

PERFORMANCE RATIOS

Managers often compute a variety of financial ratios to assess the performance of their firm. These ratios are calculated using data found on both the income statement and the balance sheet. Ratios are then compared with industry standards and with data from previous years. Several ratios are of particular interest to marketers.

A number of commonly used financial ratios focus on *profitability measures.* They are used to assess the firm's ability to generate revenues in excess of expenses and earn an adequate rate of return. Profitability measures include gross profit margin, net profit margin, and return on assets.

Gross Profit Margin

The gross profit margin equals the firm's gross profit divided by its sales revenues. In 2012, Composite had a gross profit margin of

$$\frac{\text{Gross Profit}}{\text{Sales}} = \frac{\$270 \text{ million}}{\$675 \text{ million}} = 40\%$$

The gross profit margin is the percentage of each sales dollar that can be used to pay other expenses and meet the firm's profit objectives. Ideally, businesses would like to see gross profit margins that are equal to or higher than those of other firms in their industry. A declining gross profit margin may indicate that the firm is under some competitive price pressures or that its prices have not been adjusted to account for increases in raw materials or other product costs.

Net Profit Margin

The net profit margin equals net income divided by sales. For 2012, Composite had a net profit margin of

$$\frac{\text{Net Income}}{\text{Sales}} = \frac{\$91.9 \text{ million}}{\$675 \text{ million}} = 13.6\%$$

The net profit margin is the percentage of each sales dollar that the firm earns in profit or retains after all expenses have been paid. Companies—and their shareholders—generally want to see rising, or at least stable, net profit margins.

Return on Assets (ROA)

A third profitability ratio, return on assets, measures the firm's efficiency in generating sales and profits from the total amount invested in the company. For 2012, Composite's ROA is calculated as follows:

$$\frac{\text{Net Income}}{\text{Average Assets}} = \frac{\text{Sales}}{\text{Average Assets}} \times \frac{\text{Net Income}}{\text{Sales}}$$

$$\frac{\$675 \text{ million}}{\$595 \text{ million}} \times \frac{91.9 \text{ million}}{\$675 \text{ million}} = 1.13 \times 13.6\% = 15.4\%$$

The ROA ratio actually consists of two components. The first component, called *asset turnover,* is the amount of sales generated for each dollar invested. The second component is *net profit margin.* Data for total assets are found on the firm's balance sheet.

Assume that Composite began 2012 with $560 million in assets and ended the year with $630 million in assets. Its average assets for the year would be $595 million. As was the case for the other profitability ratios, Composite's ROA should be compared with that of other firms in the industry and with its own previous performance to be meaningful.

Inventory Turnover

Inventory turnover is typically categorized as an *activity ratio* because it evaluates the effectiveness of the firm's resource use. Specifically, it measures the number of times a firm "turns" its inventory each year. The ratio can help answer the question of whether the firm has the appropriate level of inventory. Inventory turnover equals sales divided by average inventory. From the income statement, we see that Composite Technology began 2012 with $158 million in inventory and ended the year with $180 million in inventory. Therefore, the firm's average inventory was $169 million. The firm's inventory turnover ratio equals

$$\frac{\text{Sales}}{\text{Average Inventory}} = \frac{\$675 \text{ million}}{\$169 \text{ million}} = 3.99$$

For 2012, Composite Technology turned its inventory almost four times a year. While a faster inventory turn is usually a sign of greater efficiency, to be really meaningful the inventory turnover ratio must be compared with historical data and appropriate peer firm averages. Different organizations can have s different inventory turnover ratios depending on the types of products they sell. For instance, a supermarket such as Safeway might turn its inventory every two weeks for an annual rate of 26 times per year. In contrast, a large furniture retailer is likely to average only about two turns per year. Again, the determination of a "good" or "inadequate" inventory turnover rate depends on typical rates in the industry and the firm's performance in previous years.

Accounts Receivable Turnover

Another activity ratio that may be of interest to marketers is accounts receivable turnover. This ratio measures the number of times per year a company "turns" its receivables. Dividing accounts receivable turnover into 365 gives us the average age of the company's receivables.

Companies make sales on either a cash or credit basis. Credit sales allow the buyer to obtain a product now and pay for it at a specified later date. In essence, the seller is providing credit to the buyer. Credit sales are common in B2B transactions. It should be noted that sales to buyers using credit cards such as MasterCard and VISA are included as cash sales since the issuer of the credit card, rather than the seller, is providing credit to the buyer. Consequently, most B2C sales are cash sales.

Receivables are uncollected credit sales. Measuring accounts receivable turnover and the average age of receivables is important for firms where credit sales make up a high proportion of total sales. Accounts receivable turnover is defined as

$$\text{Accounts Receivable Turnover} = \frac{\text{Credit Sales}}{\text{Average Accounts Receivable}}$$

Assume that all of Composite Technology's sales are credit sales. Also assume that the firm began 2012 with $50 million in receivables and ended the year with $60 million in receivables (both numbers can be found on the balance sheet). Therefore, it had an average of $55 million in receivables. The firm's receivables turnover and average age equal

$$\frac{\$675 \text{ million}}{\$55 \text{ million}} = 12.3 \text{ times}$$

$$\frac{365}{12.3} = 29.7 \text{ days}$$

Composite turned its receivables slightly more than 12 times per year. The average age of its receivables was slightly less than 30 days. Since Composite expects its customers to pay outstanding invoices within 30 days, these numbers appear appropriate. As with other ratios, however, receivables turnover and average age of receivables should also be compared with peer firms and historical data.

MARKUPS AND MARKDOWNS

In previous chapters, we discussed the importance of pricing decisions for firms. This section expands on our earlier discussion by introducing two important pricing concepts: markups and markdowns. They can help to establish selling prices and evaluate various pricing strategies and are closely tied to a firm's income statement.

Markups

The amount that a marketer adds to a product's cost to set the final selling price is the markup. The amount of the markup typically results from two marketing decisions:

1. The services performed by the marketer. Other things being equal, retailers who offer more services charge larger markups to cover their costs.

2. The inventory turnover rate. Other things being equal, retailers with a higher turnover rate can cover their costs and earn a profit while charging a smaller markup.

A marketer's markup exerts an important influence on its image among present and potential customers. In addition, it affects the retailer's ability to attract shoppers. An excessive markup may drive away customers; an inadequate markup may fail to generate sufficient revenues needed by the retailer to cover costs and earn a profit.

Markups are typically stated as percentages of either the selling prices or the costs of the products. The formulas for calculating markups are as follows:

$$\text{Markup Percentage on Selling Price} = \frac{\text{Amount Added to Cost (Markup)}}{\text{Selling Price}}$$

$$\text{Markup Percentage on Cost} = \frac{\text{Amount Added to Cost (Markup)}}{\text{Cost}}$$

Consider a product with an invoice of 60 cents and a selling price of $1. The total markup (selling price less cost) is 40 cents. The two markup percentages are calculated as follows:

$$\text{Markup Percentage on Selling Price} = \frac{\$0.40}{\$1.00} = 40\%$$

$$\text{Markup Percentage on Cost} = \frac{\$0.40}{\$0.60} = 66.7\%$$

To determine the selling price knowing only the cost and markup percentage on selling price, a marketer applies the following formula:

$$\text{Price} = \frac{\text{Cost in Dollars}}{(100\% - \text{Markup Percentage on Selling Price})}$$

In the previous example, to determine the correct selling price of $1, the marketer would make the following calculation:

$$\text{Price} = \frac{\$0.60}{(100\% - 40\%)} = \$1.00$$

Similarly, you can convert the markup percentage for a specific item based on the selling price to one based on cost and the reverse using these formulas:

$$\text{Markup Percentage on Selling Price} = \frac{\text{Markup Percentage on Cost}}{(100\% + \text{Markup Percentage on Cost})}$$

$$\text{Markup Percentage on Cost} = \frac{\text{Markup Percentage on Selling Price}}{(100\% - \text{Markup Percentage on Selling Price})}$$

Again, data from the previous example give the following conversions:

$$\text{Markup Percentage on Selling Price} = \frac{66.7\%}{(100\% + 66.7\%)} = 40\%$$

$$\text{Markup Percentage on Cost} = \frac{40\%}{(100\% - 40\%)} = 66.7\%$$

Marketers determine markups based partly on their judgments of the amounts that consumers will pay for a given product. When buyers refuse to pay a product's stated price, however, or when improvements in other products or fashion changes reduce the appeal of the current merchandise, a producer or retailer must take a markdown.

Markdowns

A markdown is a price reduction a firm makes on an item. Reasons for markdowns include sales promotions featuring price reductions or a decision that the initial price was too high. Unlike markups, markdowns cannot be determined from the income statement since the price reduction takes place before the sale occurs. The markdown percentage equals dollar markdowns divided by sales. For example, a retailer decides to reduce the price of an item by $10, from $50 to $40, and sells 1000 units. The markdown percentage equals

$$\frac{(1000 \times \$10)}{(1000 \times \$40)} = \frac{\$10\ 000}{\$40\ 000} = 25\%$$

ASSIGNMENTS

1. Assume that a product has an invoice price of $45 and a selling price of $60. Calculate the markup as a percentage of both the selling price and the cost.

2. A product has an invoice price of $92.50. The seller wants to include a markup on the selling price of 25 percent. Calculate the selling price.

3. Assume a retailer decides to reduce the price of an item by $5, from $15 to $10, and sells 5000 units. Calculate the markdown percentage.

4. Obtain a recent income statement and balance sheet for a business of your choosing whose stock is publicly traded. An easy way to find these is to visit the company's website and click on a link for "Investor Relations." Then look for the company's annual report. Use the relevant data included on the income statement to calculate each of the following ratios:

   a. gross profit margin

   b. net profit margin

   c. inventory turnover

   d. return on assets

   e. price markup

5. This appendix has described how the industry in which a firm operates affects its financial ratios. Solve this critical-thinking exercise by matching the following set of financial ratios to each of the following firms: 3M, Gap, Pfizer, and Walmart. Consider the industry in which each company operates and the way it is likely to affect profits, return on assets, and inventory turnover rates.

For example, which of the four would you expect to have the lowest profit margin and which should have the highest profit margin?

FINANCIAL RATIO	FIRM A	FIRM B	FIRM C	FIRM D
Net profit margin	28.4%	3.5%	13.9%	6.5%
Return on assets	20.6%	8.6%	14.6%	10.0%
Inventory turnover	2.1	7.6	3.4	4.9

Relationship Marketing and Customer Relationship Management (CRM)

Overview

MARKETING revolves around relationships with customers and with all the business processes involved in identifying and satisfying them. The shift from transaction-based marketing, which focuses on short-term, one-time exchanges, to customer-focused relationship marketing is one of the most important trends in marketing today. Companies know that they cannot prosper simply by identifying and attracting new customers; to succeed, they must build loyal, mutually beneficial relationships with both new and existing customers, suppliers, distributors, and employees. This strategy benefits the bottom line because retaining customers costs much less than acquiring new ones. Building and managing long-term relationships between buyers and sellers are the hallmarks of relationship marketing. Relationship marketing is the development, growth, and maintenance of cost-effective, high-value relationships with individual customers, suppliers, distributors, retailers, and other partners for mutual benefit over time.

Relationship marketing is based on promises: the promise of low prices, the promise of high quality, the promise of prompt delivery, the promise of superior service. A network of promises—within the organization, between the organization and its supply chain, and between buyer and seller—determines whether a relationship will grow. A firm is responsible for keeping or exceeding the agreements it makes, with the ultimate goal of achieving customer satisfaction. ◆◆◆

THE SHIFT FROM TRANSACTION-BASED MARKETING TO RELATIONSHIP MARKETING

Since the Industrial Revolution, most manufacturers have run production-oriented operations. They have focused on making products and then promoting them to customers in the hope of selling enough to cover costs and earn profits. The emphasis has been on individual sales or transactions. In transaction-based marketing, buyer and seller exchanges are characterized by limited communications and little or no ongoing relationships. The primary goal is to entice a buyer to make a purchase through such inducements as low price, convenience, or packaging. The goal is simple and short term: sell.

figure 1

Forms of Buyer–Seller Interactions on a Continuum from Conflict to Integration

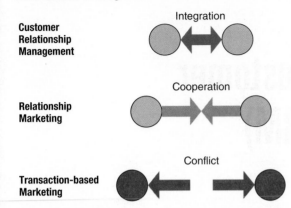

Source: From BOONE/KURTZ. *Contemporary Marketing*, 13E. © 2008 South-Western, a part of Cengage Learning, Inc. Reproduced by permission. **www.cengage.com/permissions**

Today, many organizations have embraced an alternative approach. Relationship marketing views customers as equal partners in buyer–seller transactions. By motivating customers to enter a long-term relationship in which they repeat purchases or buy many brands from the firm, marketers obtain a clearer understanding of customer needs over time. This process leads to improved products or customer service, which pays off through increased sales and lower marketing costs. In addition, marketers have discovered that it is less expensive to retain satisfied customers than it is to attract new ones or to repair damaged relationships.

The move from transactions to relationships is reflected in the changing nature of the interactions between customers and sellers. In transaction-based marketing, exchanges with customers are generally sporadic and in some instances disrupted by conflict. As interactions become relationship oriented, however, conflict changes to cooperation, and infrequent contacts between buyers and sellers become ongoing exchanges.

As Figure 1 illustrates, relationship marketing emphasizes cooperation rather than conflict between all the parties involved. This ongoing collaborative exchange creates value for both parties and builds customer loyalty. Customer relationship management goes a step further and integrates the customer's needs into all aspects of the firm's operations and its relationships with suppliers, distributors, and strategic partners. It combines people, processes, and technology with the long-term goal of maximizing customer value through mutually satisfying interactions and transactions.

Twenty-first-century marketers now understand they must do more than simply create products and then sell them. With so many goods and services to choose from, customers look for added value from their marketing relationships.

In general, the differences between the narrow focus of transaction marketing and the much broader view of relationship marketing can be summarized as follows:

Relationship marketing

- focuses on the long term rather than the short term

- emphasizes retaining customers over making a sale

- ranks customer service as a high priority

- encourages frequent customer contact

- fosters customer commitment with the firm

- bases customer interactions on cooperation and trust

- commits all employees to provide high-quality products

As a result, the buyer–seller bonds developed in a relationship marketing partnership last longer and cover a much wider scope than those developed in transaction marketing.

ELEMENTS OF RELATIONSHIP MARKETING

To build long-term customer relationships, marketers need to place customers at the centre of their efforts. When a company integrates customer service and quality with marketing, the result is a relationship marketing orientation.

But how do firms achieve these long-term relationships? They build them with four basic elements.

1. They gather information about their customers. Database technology, discussed later, helps a company identify current and potential customers with selected demographic, purchase, and lifestyle characteristics.

2. They analyze the data collected and use it to modify their marketing mix to deliver differentiated messages and customized marketing programs to individual consumers.

3. Through relationship marketing, they monitor their interactions with customers. They can assess the customer's level of satisfaction or dissatisfaction with their service. Marketers can also calculate the cost of attracting one new customer and figure out how much profit that customer will generate during the relationship. Information is fed back, and they are then able to seek ways to add value to the buyer–seller transaction so that the relationship will continue.

4. With customer relationship management (CRM) software, they use intimate knowledge of customers and customer preferences to orient every part of the organization, including both its internal and external partners, toward building a unique company differentiation based on strong, unbreakable bonds with customers. Sophisticated technology and the Internet help make that happen.

INTERNAL MARKETING

The concepts of customer satisfaction and relationship marketing are usually discussed in terms of **external customers**—people or organizations that buy or use a firm's goods or services. But marketing in organizations concerned with customer satisfaction and long-term relationships must also address **internal customers**—employees or departments within the organization whose success depends on the work of other employees or departments. A person processing an order for a new piece of equipment is the internal customer of the salesperson who completed the sale, just as the person who bought the product is the salesperson's external customer. Although the order processor might never directly encounter an external customer, his or her performance can have a direct impact on the overall value the firm is able to deliver.

Internal marketing involves managerial actions that enable all members of an organization to understand, accept, and fulfill their respective roles in implementing a marketing strategy. Good internal customer satisfaction helps organizations attract, select, and retain outstanding employees who appreciate and value their role in the delivery of superior service to external customers.

Employee knowledge and involvement are important goals of internal marketing. Companies that excel at satisfying customers typically place a priority on keeping employees informed about corporate goals, strategies, and customer needs. Employees must also have the necessary tools to address

external customer
People or organizations that buy or use another firm's goods or services.

internal customer
Employees or departments within an organization that depend on the work of another employee or department to perform tasks.

internal marketing
Managerial actions that help all members of the organization understand and accept their respective roles in implementing a marketing strategy.

Companies like Boston Pizza often have special programs for their employees.

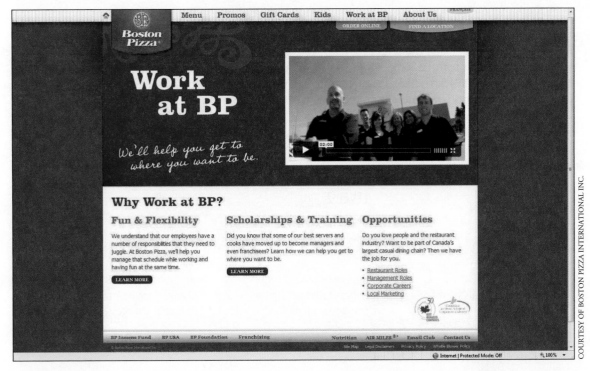

COURTESY OF BOSTON PIZZA INTERNATIONAL INC.

customer requests and problems in a timely manner. Company-wide computer networks aid the flow of communications between departments and functions. Several companies also include key suppliers in their networks to speed and ease communication of all aspects of business from product design to inventory control.

employee satisfaction
Employee's level of satisfaction for his or her company and the extent to which that loyalty or lack of loyalty is communicated to external customers.

Employee satisfaction is another critical objective of internal marketing. Employees seldom, if ever, satisfy customers when they themselves are unhappy. Dissatisfied employees are likely to spread negative word-of-mouth messages to relatives, friends, and acquaintances, and these reports can affect purchasing behaviour. Satisfied employees buy their employer's products, tell friends and families how good the customer service is, and ultimately send a powerful message to customers. One recommended strategy for offering consistently good service is to attract good employees, hire good employees, and retain good employees.

THE RELATIONSHIP MARKETING CONTINUUM

Like all other interpersonal relationships, buyer–seller relationships function at a variety of levels. As an individual or firm progresses from the lowest level to the highest level on the continuum of relationship marketing, as shown in Table 1, the strength of commitment between the parties grows. The likelihood of a continuing, long-term relationship grows as well. Whenever possible, marketers want to move their customers along this continuum, converting them from Level 1 purchasers, who focus mainly on price, to Level 3 customers, who receive specialized services and value-added benefits that may not be available from another firm.

FIRST LEVEL: FOCUS ON PRICE

Interactions at the first level of relationship marketing are the most superficial and the least likely to lead to a long-term relationship. In the most prevalent examples of this first level, relationship marketing efforts rely on pricing and other financial incentives to motivate customers to enter into buying relationships with a seller. Although price-related programs can be attractive to users, they may not create long-term buyer relationships. Because the programs are not customized to the needs of individual buyers, they are easily duplicated by competitors. The lesson is that it takes more than a low price or other financial incentives to create a long-term relationship between buyer and seller.

SECOND LEVEL: SOCIAL INTERACTIONS

As buyers and sellers reach the second level of relationship marketing, their interactions develop on a social level, one that features deeper and less superficial links than the financially motivated first level. Sellers have begun to learn that social relationships with buyers can be very effective marketing tools. Customer service and communication are key factors at this stage.

table 1   *Three Levels of Relationship Marketing*

CHARACTERISTIC	LEVEL 1	LEVEL 2	LEVEL 3
Primary bond	Financial	Social	Structural
Degree of Customization	Low	Medium	Medium to high
Potential for sustained competitive advantage	Low	Moderate	High
Examples	Car dealer's no-interest financial plan	Harley-Davidson's Harley Owners Group (HOG)	Chapters' member program of discounts and special offers

Source: Reprinted with the permission of Free Press, a Division of Simon & Schuster Inc., from *MARKETING SERVICES: Competing Through Quality* by Leonard L. Berry and A. Parasuraman. Copyright © 1991 by The Free Press. All Rights Reserved.

Social interaction can take many forms. The owner of a local shoe store or dry cleaner might chat with customers about local events.

THIRD LEVEL: INTERDEPENDENT PARTNERSHIP

At the third level of relationship marketing, relationships are transformed into structural changes that ensure buyer and seller are true business partners. As buyer and seller work more closely together, they develop a dependence on one another that continues to grow over time. Companies that maintain member programs are examples of third-level relationship marketing.

BRAND X PICTURES/JUPITER IMAGES

The first level of relationship marketing.

ENHANCING CUSTOMER SATISFACTION

Marketers monitor customer satisfaction through various methods of marketing research. As part of an ongoing relationship with customers, marketers must continually measure and improve how well they meet customer needs. As Figure 2 shows, three major steps are involved in this process: understanding customer needs, obtaining customer feedback, and instituting an ongoing program to ensure customer satisfaction. The research methods available to institute an ongoing customer satisfaction program are discussed in Chapter 7.

UNDERSTANDING CUSTOMER NEEDS

Knowledge of what customers need, want, and expect is a central concern of companies focused on building long-term relationships. This information is also a vital first step in setting up a system to measure **customer satisfaction**. Marketers must carefully monitor the characteristics of their product that really matter to customers. They also must remain constantly alert to new elements that might affect satisfaction.

customer satisfaction
Extent to which customers are satisfied with their purchases.

Satisfaction can be measured in terms of the gaps between what customers expect and what they perceive they have received. Such gaps can produce favourable or unfavourable impressions. Goods or services may be better or worse than expected. If they are better, marketers can use the opportunity to create loyal customers. If goods or services are worse than expected, a company may start to lose customers.

To avoid unfavourable service gaps, marketers need to keep in touch with the needs of current and potential customers. They must look beyond traditional performance measures and explore the factors that determine purchasing behaviour to formulate customer-based missions, goals, and performance standards.

OBTAINING CUSTOMER FEEDBACK AND ENSURING CUSTOMER SATISFACTION

The second step in measuring customer satisfaction is to compile feedback from customers regarding current performance. Increasingly, marketers try to improve customers' access to their companies by including toll-free 800 numbers or website addresses in their advertising. Most firms rely on reactive methods of collecting feedback. Rather than solicit complaints, they might, for example, monitor blogs or other online discussion groups to track customers' comments and attitudes about the value received. Some companies hire mystery shoppers, who visit or call businesses posing as customers, to evaluate the service they receive. Their unbiased appraisals are usually conducted semiannually or quarterly to monitor employees, diagnose problem areas in customer service, and measure the impact of employee training. Other companies are using websites to obtain customers' feedback, allowing them to accurately identify and respond to customers' needs.

figure 2

Three Steps to Measure Customer Satisfaction

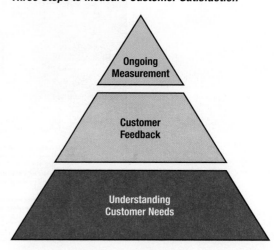

Unhappy customers typically talk about their experience more than happy customers do. The cost of dissatisfaction can be high so it makes sense to try to resolve problems quickly. In addition to training employees to resolve complaints, firms can benefit from providing several different ways for customers to make their dissatisfaction known, including prepaid mail questionnaires, telephone help lines, comment cards, and face-to-face exit surveys as people leave the premises. Any method that makes it easier for customers to complain actually benefits a firm. Customer complaints offer firms the opportunity to overcome problems and prove their commitment to service. People often have greater loyalty to a company after a conflict has been resolved than if they had never complained at all.

Many organizations also use proactive methods to assess customer satisfaction, including visiting, calling, or mailing out surveys to clients to find out their level of satisfaction. Companies are also paying more and more attention to the millions of bloggers on the Internet.

BUILDING BUYER–SELLER RELATIONSHIPS

Marketers of consumer goods and services have discovered that they must do more than simply create products and then sell them. With a dizzying array of products to choose from, many customers are seeking ways to simplify both their business and personal lives, and relationships provide a way to do this.

One reason consumers form continuing relationships is their desire to reduce choices. Through relationships, they can simplify information gathering and the entire buying process as well as decrease the risk of dissatisfaction. They find comfort in brands that have become familiar through their ongoing relationships with companies. Such relationships may lead to more efficient decision making by customers and higher levels of customer satisfaction. A key benefit to consumers in long-term buyer–seller relationships is the perceived positive value they receive. Relationships add value because of increased opportunities for frequent customers to save money through discounts, rebates, and similar offers; via special recognition from the relationship programs; and through convenience in shopping.

Sun Life: Adding value by providing information to help people make financial decisions.

Marketers should also understand why consumers end relationships. Computerized technologies and the Internet have made consumers better informed than ever before by giving them unprecedented abilities to compare prices, merchandise, and customer service. If they perceive that a competitor's product or customer service is better, customers may switch loyalties. Many consumers dislike feeling that they are locked into a relationship with one company, and that is reason enough for them to try a competing item next time they buy. Some customers simply become bored with their current providers and decide to sample the competition.

HOW MARKETERS KEEP CUSTOMERS

One of the major forces driving the push from transaction-based marketing to relationship marketing is the realization that retaining customers is far more profitable than losing them. It costs five times as much to acquire a new customer as it does to keep a loyal one. Customer churn, or turnover, is expensive.

Also, customers usually enable a firm to generate more profits with each additional year of the relationship. Some companies use **frequency marketing**. These programs reward top customers with cash, rebates, merchandise, or other premiums. Buyers who purchase an item more often earn higher rewards. Frequency marketing focuses on a company's best customers with the goal of increasing their motivation to buy even more of the same or other products from the seller. Many different types of companies use frequency programs—such as fast-food restaurants, retail stores, telecommunications companies, and travel firms. Popular programs include airline frequent-flyer programs and retail programs.

In addition to frequency programs, companies use **affinity marketing** to retain customers. Each of us holds certain things dear. Some feel strongly about their college or university, while for others it's a sports team or not-for-profit organization. These examples, along with an almost unending variety of others, are subjects of affinity programs. An affinity program is a marketing effort sponsored by an organization that solicits involvement by individuals who share common interests and activities. With affinity programs, organizations create extra value for members and encourage stronger relationships. Affinity credit cards are a popular form of this marketing technique. The sponsor's name appears prominently in promotional materials, on the card itself, and on monthly statements.

frequency marketing
Frequent buyer or user marketing programs that reward customers with cash, rebates, merchandise, or other premiums.

affinity marketing
Marketing effort sponsored by an organization that solicits responses from individuals who share common interests and activities.

DATABASE MARKETING

The use of information technology to analyze data about customers and their transactions is referred to as **database marketing**. The results form the basis of new advertising or promotions targeted to carefully identified groups of customers. Database marketing is a particularly effective tool for building relationships because it allows sellers to sort through huge quantities of data from many sources on the buying habits or preferences of thousands or even millions of customers. Companies can then track buying patterns, develop customer relationship profiles, customize their offerings and sales promotions, and even personalize customer service to suit the needs of targeted groups of customers. Properly used, databases can help companies in several ways, including these:

database marketing
Use of software to analyze marketing information, identifying and targeting messages toward specific groups of potential customers.

- identifying their most profitable customers

- calculating the lifetime value of each customer's business

- creating a meaningful dialogue that builds relationships and encourages genuine brand loyalty

- improving customer retention and referral rates

- reducing marketing and promotion costs

- boosting sales volume per customer or targeted customer group

Where do organizations find all the data that fill these vast marketing databases? Everywhere! Credit-card applications, software registration, and product warranties all provide vital statistics of individual customers. Point-of-sale register scanners, customer opinion surveys, and sweepstakes entry forms may offer not just details of name and address but information on preferred brands and shopping habits. Websites offer free access in return for personal data, allowing companies to amass increasingly rich marketing information.

Newer technologies such as radio frequency identification (RFID) allow retailers to identify shipping pallets and cargo containers, but most observers anticipate that in the near future RFID will be cost effective enough to permit tagging of individual store items, allowing retailers to gather information about the purchaser as well as managing inventory and deterring theft, but raising privacy concerns.

Interactive television delivers even more valuable data—information on real consumer behaviour and attitudes toward brands. Linked to digital television, sophisticated set-top boxes already collect vast amounts of data on television viewer behaviour, organized in incredible detail. As the technology makes its way into more homes, marketers receive first-hand knowledge of the kind of programming and products their targeted customers want. In addition, rather than using television to advertise to the masses, they can talk directly to the viewers most interested in their products. At a click of a button, viewers can skip ads, but they also can click to a full-length infomercial on any brand that captures their interest.

New technologies like widgets—small software applications, such as games, easily passed from friend to friend on sites like Facebook—are becoming popular marketing tools. Cell phone advertising is increasing, and with it the prospect that it can become highly targeted because telecom companies already have access to users' personal and credit card information, and even their current locations. Discount offers can be sent to users passing a particular store, for instance. Marketers can even build their own social networks rather than relying on Facebook.

As database marketing becomes more complex, a variety of software tools and services enable marketers to target consumers more and more narrowly while enriching their communications to selected groups. After all, a huge collection of data isn't valuable unless it can be turned into information that is useful to a firm's marketers. Application service providers (ASPs) assist marketers by providing software when it is needed to capture, manipulate, and analyze masses of consumer data. One type of software collects data on product specifications and details, which marketers can use to isolate products that best meet a customer's needs. This feature would be particularly important in selling expensive business products that require high involvement in making a purchase decision.

CUSTOMERS AS ADVOCATES

grassroots marketing
Efforts that connect directly with existing and potential customers through non-mainstream channels.

Recent relationship marketing efforts focus on turning customers from passive partners into active proponents of a product. **Grassroots marketing** involves connecting directly with existing and potential customers through non-mainstream channels. The grassroots approach relies on marketing strategies that are unconventional, nontraditional, and extremely flexible. Grassroots marketing is sometimes characterized by a relatively small budget and lots of legwork, but its hallmark is the ability to develop long-lasting, individual relationships with loyal customers. Viral and buzz marketing discussed in Chapter 13, are examples of grassroots marketing.

CUSTOMER RELATIONSHIP MANAGEMENT

Emerging from—and closely linked to—relationship marketing, customer relationship management (CRM) is the combination of strategies and technologies that empowers relationship programs, reorienting the entire organization to a concentrated focus on satisfying customers. Made possible by technological advances, it leverages technology as a means to manage customer relationships and to integrate all stakeholders into a company's product design and development, manufacturing, marketing, sales, and customer service processes.

CRM represents a shift in thinking for everyone involved with a firm—from the CEO down and encompassing all other key stakeholders, including suppliers, dealers, and other partners. All recognize that solid customer relations are fostered by similarly strong relationships with other major stakeholders. Since CRM goes well beyond traditional sales, marketing, or customer service functions, it requires a top-down commitment and must permeate every aspect of a firm's business. Technology makes that possible by allowing firms—regardless of size and no matter how far-flung their operations—to manage activities across functions, from location to location, and among their internal and external partners.

BENEFITS OF CRM

CRM software systems are capable of making sense of the vast amounts of customer data that technology allows firms to collect. B2B firms benefit just as much as retailers. Another key benefit of customer relationship management systems is that they simplify complex business processes while keeping the best interests of customers at heart.

Maximizer Software: simplifying CRM systems.

COURTESY OF MAXIMIZER SOFTWARE INC.

Selecting the right CRM software system is critical to the success of a firm's entire CRM program. CRM can be used at two different levels—on-demand accessed via the Internet as a Web-based service, and on premises, installed on a company's computer system on site. A firm may choose to buy a system from a company or rent hosted CRM applications through websites. Purchasing a customized system can cost millions of dollars and take months to implement, while hosted solutions—rented through a website—are cheaper and quicker to get up and running. But purchasing a system allows a firm to expand and customize, whereas hosted systems are more limited. Experienced marketers also warn that it is easy to get mired in a system that is complicated for staff to use.

Software solutions are just one component of a successful CRM initiative. The most effective companies approach customer relationship management as a complete business strategy, in which people, processes, and technology are organized around delivering superior value to customers. Successful CRM systems share the following qualities:

- They create partnerships with customers in ways that align with the company's mission and goals.

- They reduce costs by empowering customers to find the information they need to manage their own orders.

- They improve customer service by centralizing data and help sales representatives guide customers to information.

- They reduce response time and thus increase customer satisfaction.

- They improve customer retention and loyalty, leading to more repeat business and new business from word of mouth.

- They can provide a complete picture of customers.

- Their results are measurable.[1]

Once the groundwork has been laid, technology solutions drive firms toward a clearer understanding of each customer and his or her needs.

PROBLEMS WITH CRM

CRM is not a magic wand. The strategy needs to be thought out in advance, and everyone in the firm must be committed to it and understand how to use it. If no one can put the system to work, it is an expensive mistake.

Experts explain that failures with CRM often result from failure to organize—or reorganize—the company's people and business processes to take advantage of the benefits the CRM system offers. For instance, it might be important to empower salespeople to negotiate price with their customers to close more sales with CRM, but if a company does not adapt its centralized pricing system, its CRM efforts will be hampered. Second, if sales and service employees do not have input in the CRM process during its design phase, they might be less willing to use its tools—no matter how much training is offered. "It is important to clearly communicate the benefits of the CRM, train employees how to use it, and have an onsite, dedicated 'go-to' person they can call on for help," says one marketing manager who managed four CRM implementations.[2] A third factor is that some CRM "failures" are actually at least partially successful, but companies or their executives have set their expectations too high. Having a realistic idea what CRM can accomplish is as important to success as properly implementing the program. Finally, truly understanding customers, their needs, and the ways they differ from customers of the past is a critical element in any successful CRM project.

RETRIEVING LOST CUSTOMERS

customer winback
Process of rejuvenating lost relationships with customers.

Customers defect from an organization's goods and services for a variety of reasons. They might be bored, they might move away from the region, they might not need the product anymore, or they might have tried—and preferred—competing products. An increasingly important part of an effective CRM strategy is **customer winback**, the process of rejuvenating lost relationships with customers.

In many cases, a relationship gone sour can be sweetened again with the right approach. A good rule for service providers is to anticipate where problems will arise and figure out in advance how to prevent them in the first place. The second part of this strategy is to accept that mistakes will occur in even the best system and to have a high-quality recovery effort in place that employees are empowered to enact. Sometimes, however, the missteps are so great that it is almost impossible for a company to repair the damage until enough time has passed for attention to simply turn elsewhere.

BUYER–SELLER RELATIONSHIPS IN BUSINESS-TO-BUSINESS MARKETS

Customer relationship management and relationship marketing are not limited to consumer goods and services. Building strong buyer–seller relationships is a critical component of business-to-business marketing as well.

Business-to-business marketing involves an organization's purchase of goods and services to support company operations or the production of other products. Buyer–seller relationships between companies involve working together to provide advantages that benefit both parties. These advantages might include lower prices for supplies, quicker delivery of inventory, improved quality and reliability, customized product features, and more favourable financing terms.

partnership
Affiliation of two or more companies that help each other achieve common goals.

A **partnership** is an affiliation of two or more companies that help each other achieve common goals. Partnerships cover a wide spectrum of relationships from informal cooperative purchasing arrangements to formal production and marketing agreements. In business-to-business markets, partnerships form the basis of relationship marketing.

A variety of common goals motivate firms to form partnerships. Companies may want to protect or improve their positions in existing markets, gain access to new domestic or international markets, or quickly enter new markets. Expansion of a product line—to fill in gaps, broaden the product line, or differentiate the product—is another key reason for joining forces. Other motives include sharing resources, reducing costs, warding off threats of future competition, raising or creating barriers to entry, and learning new skills.

CHOOSING BUSINESS PARTNERS

How does an organization decide which companies to select as partners? The first priority is to locate firms that can add value to the relationship—whether through financial resources, contacts, extra manufacturing capacity, technical know-how, or distribution capabilities. The greater the value added, the greater the desirability of the partnership. In many cases, the attributes of each partner complement those of the other; each firm brings something to the relationship that the other party needs but cannot provide on its own. Other partnerships join firms with similar skills and resources to reduce costs. Organizations must share similar values and goals for a partnership to succeed in the long run.

TYPES OF PARTNERSHIPS

Companies form four key types of partnerships in business-to-business markets: buyer, seller, internal, and lateral partnerships. This section briefly examines each category.

In a buyer partnership, a firm purchases goods and services from one or more providers. When a company assumes the buyer position in a relationship, it has a unique set of needs and requirements that vendors must meet to make the relationship successful. While buyers want sellers to provide fair prices, quick delivery, and high quality levels, a lasting relationship often requires more effort. To induce a buyer to form a long-term partnership, a supplier must also be responsive to the purchaser's unique needs.

Seller partnerships set up long-term exchanges of goods and services in return for cash or other consideration. Sellers, too, have specific needs as partners in ongoing relationships. Most prefer to develop long-term.

The importance of internal partnerships is widely recognized in business today. The classic definition of the word *customer* as the buyer of a good or service is now more carefully defined in terms of external customers. However, customers within an organization also have their own needs. Internal partnerships are the foundation of an organization and its ability to meet its commitments to external entities. If the purchasing department selects a parts vendor that fails to ship on the dates required by manufacturing, production will halt, and products will not be delivered to customers as promised. As a result, external customers will likely seek other more reliable suppliers. Without building and maintaining internal partnerships, an organization will have difficulty meeting the needs of its external partnerships.

Lateral partnerships include strategic alliances with other companies or with not-for-profit organizations and research alliances between for-profit firms and colleges and universities. The relationship focuses on external entities—such as customers of the partner firm—and involves no direct buyer–seller interactions. Strategic alliances are discussed in a later section.

CO-BRANDING AND CO-MARKETING

Two other types of business marketing relationships are co-branding and co-marketing. Co-branding joins together two strong brand names, perhaps owned by two different companies, to sell a product.

In a co-marketing effort, two organizations join to sell their products in an allied marketing campaign.

IMPROVING BUYER–SELLER RELATIONSHIPS IN BUSINESS-TO-BUSINESS MARKETS

Organizations that know how to find and nurture partner relationships, whether through informal deals or contracted partnerships, can enhance revenues and increase profits. Partnering often leads to lower prices, better products, and improved distribution, resulting in higher levels of customer satisfaction. Partners who know each other's needs and expectations are more likely to satisfy them and forge stronger long-term bonds. Often, partnerships can be cemented through personal relationships, no matter where firms are located.

In the past, business relationships were conducted primarily in person, over the phone, or by mail. Today, businesses are using the latest electronic, computer, and communications technology to link up. E-mail, the Internet, and other telecommunications services allow businesses to communicate anytime and anyplace.

NATIONAL ACCOUNT SELLING

Some relationships are more important than others due to the large investments at stake. Large manufacturers such as Procter & Gamble and Clorox pay special attention to the needs of major retailers such as Walmart. Manufacturers use a technique called national account selling to serve their largest, most profitable customers. The large collection of supplier offices in northwestern Arkansas—near Walmart's home office—suggests how national account selling might be implemented. These offices are usually called teams or support teams.

The advantages of national account selling are many. By assembling a team of individuals to serve just one account, the seller demonstrates the depth of its commitment to the customer. The buyer–seller relationship is strengthened as both collaborate to find mutually beneficial solutions. Finally, cooperative buyer–seller efforts can bring about dramatic improvements in both efficiency and effectiveness for both partners. These improvements find their way to the bottom line in the form of decreased costs and increased profits.

BUSINESS-TO-BUSINESS DATABASES

As noted earlier, databases are indispensable tools in relationship marketing. They are also essential in building business-to-business relationships. Using information generated from sales reports, scanners, and many other sources, sellers can create databases that help guide their own efforts and those of buyers who resell products to final users.

ELECTRONIC DATA INTERCHANGE AND WEB SERVICES

electronic data interchange (EDI) Computer-to-computer exchanges of invoices, orders, and other business documents.

Technology has transformed the ways in which companies control their inventories and replenish stock. Gone are the days when a retailer would notice stocks were running low, call the vendor, check prices, and reorder. Today's **electronic data interchanges (EDIs)** automate the entire process. EDI involves computer-to-computer exchanges of invoices, orders, and other business documents. It allows firms to reduce costs and improve efficiency and competitiveness. Retailers such as Walmart require vendors to use EDI as a core quick-response merchandising tool. Quick-response merchandising is a just-in-time strategy that reduces the time merchandise is held in inventory, resulting in substantial cost savings. An added advantage of EDI is that it opens new channels for gathering marketing information that is helpful in developing long-term business-to-business relationships.

Web services provide a way for companies to communicate even if they are not running the same or compatible software, hardware, databases, or network platforms. Companies in a customer–supplier relationship, or a partnership such as airlines and car rental firms, may have difficulty getting their computer systems to work together or exchange data easily. Web services are platform-independent information exchange systems that use the Internet to allow interaction between the firms. They are usually simple, self-contained applications that can handle functions from the simple to the complex.

VENDOR-MANAGED INVENTORY

The proliferation of electronic communication technologies and the constant pressure on suppliers to improve response time have led to another way for buyers and sellers to do business. Vendor-managed inventory (VMI) has replaced buyer-managed inventory in many instances. It is an inventory management system in which the seller—based on an existing agreement with the buyer—determines how much of a product a buyer needs and automatically ships new supplies to that buyer.

Some firms have modified VMI to an approach called collaborative planning, forecasting, and replenishment (CPFaR). This approach is a planning and forecasting technique involving collaborative efforts by both purchasers and vendors.

MANAGING THE SUPPLY CHAIN

Good relationships between businesses require careful management of the supply chain, sometimes called the *value chain*, which is the entire sequence of suppliers that contribute to the creation and delivery of a product. This process affects both upstream relationships between the company and its suppliers and downstream relationships with the product's end users.

Effective supply chain management can provide an important competitive advantage for a business marketer that results in

- increased innovation

- decreased costs

- improved conflict resolution within the chain

- improved communication and involvement among members of the chain

By coordinating operations with the other companies in the chain, boosting quality, and improving its operating systems, a firm can improve speed and efficiency. Because companies spend considerable resources on goods and services from outside suppliers, cooperative relationships can pay off in many ways.

BUSINESS-TO-BUSINESS ALLIANCES

Strategic alliances are the ultimate expression of relationship marketing. A strategic alliance is a partnership formed to create a competitive advantage. These more formal long-term partnership arrangements improve each partner's supply chain relationships and enhance flexibility in operating in today's complex and rapidly changing marketplace. The size and location of strategic partners are not important. Strategic alliances include businesses of all sizes, of all kinds, and in many locations; it is what each partner can offer the other that is important.

Effective supply chain management can provide an important competitive advantage for a business marketer.

COLORBLIND IMAGES/BLEND IMAGES/JUPITER IMAGES

Companies can structure strategic alliances in two ways. Alliance partners can establish a new business unit in which each takes an ownership position. In such a joint venture, one partner might own 40 percent, while the other owns 60 percent. Alternatively, the partners may decide to form a less formal cooperative relationship that does not involve ownership—for example, a joint new-product design team. The cooperative alliance can operate more flexibly and can change more easily as market forces or other conditions dictate. In either arrangement, the partners agree in advance on the skills and resources that each will bring into the alliance to achieve their mutual objectives and gain a competitive advantage. Resources typically include patents, product lines, brand equity, product and market knowledge, company and brand image, and reputation for product quality, innovation, or customer service. Relationships with customers and suppliers are also desirable resources, as are a convenient manufacturing facility, economies of scale and scope, information technology, and a large sales force. Alliance partners can contribute marketing skills such as innovation and product development, manufacturing skills including low-cost or flexible manufacturing, and planning and research and development expertise.

Companies form many types of strategic alliances. Some create horizontal alliances between firms at the same level in the supply chain; others define vertical links between firms at adjacent stages. The firms may serve the same or different industries. Alliances can involve cooperation among rivals who are market leaders or between a market leader and a follower.

EVALUATING CUSTOMER RELATIONSHIP PROGRAMS

One of the most important measures of relationship marketing programs, whether in consumer or business-to-business markets, is the lifetime value of a customer. This concept can be defined as the revenues and intangible benefits such as referrals and customer feedback that a customer brings to the seller over an average lifetime of the relationship, less the amount the company must spend to acquire, market to, and service the customer. Long-term customers are usually more valuable assets than new ones because they buy more, cost less to serve, refer other customers, and provide valuable feedback. The "average lifetime" of a customer relationship depends on industry and product characteristics. Customer lifetime for a consumer product such as microwave pizza may be very short, while that for an automobile or computer will last longer.

For a simple example of a lifetime value calculation, assume that a Chinese takeout restaurant determines that its average customer buys dinner twice a month at an average cost of $25 per order over a lifetime of five years. That business translates this calculation to revenues of $600 per year and $3000 for five years. The restaurant can calculate and subtract its average costs for food, labour, and overhead to arrive at the per-customer profit. This figure serves as a baseline against which to measure strategies to increase the restaurant's sales volume, customer retention, or customer referral rate.

Another approach is to calculate the payback from a customer relationship, or the length of time it takes to break even on customer acquisition costs. Assume that an Internet service provider spends $75 per new customer on direct mail and enrolment incentives. Based on average revenues per subscriber, the company takes about three months to recover that $75. If an average customer stays with the service 32 months and generates $800 in revenues, the rate of return is nearly 11 times the original investment. Once the customer stays past the payback period, the provider should make a profit on that business.

In addition to lifetime value analysis and payback, companies use many other techniques to evaluate relationship programs, including the following:

- tracking rebate requests, coupon redemption, credit card purchases, and product registrations

- monitoring complaints and returned merchandise and analyzing why customers leave

- reviewing reply cards, comment forms, and surveys

- monitoring click-through behaviour on websites to identify why customers stay and why they leave

These tools give the organization information about customer priorities so that managers can make changes to their systems, if necessary, and set appropriate, measurable goals for relationship programs.

A hotel chain may set a goal of improving the rate of repeat visits from 44 to 52 percent. A mail-order company may want to reduce time from 48 to 24 hours to process and mail orders. If a customer survey reveals late flight arrivals as the number one complaint of an airline's passengers, the airline might set an objective of increasing the number of on-time arrivals from 87 to 93 percent.

Companies large and small can implement technology to help measure the value of customers and the return on investment from expenditures on developing customer relationships. They can choose from among a growing number of software products, many of which are tailored to specific industries or flexible enough to suit companies of varying sizes.

CHAPTER 1

1. Company website, http://investors.walmartstores.com, accessed February 23, 2010; Barbara Farfan, "U.S. Green Retailing: Will Wal-Mart Profit from Sustainability Labeling," *About.com*, http://retailindustry.about.com, accessed February 10, 2010; Kate Rockwood, "Attention, Walmart Shoppers: Clean-up in Aisle Nine," *Fast Company*, February 2010, pp. 30, 32; Catherine Greener, "Quality Expert Says Walmart's Sustainability Journey Is the Real Deal," *GreenBiz.com*, www.greenbiz.com, July 16, 2009; Marc Gunther, "Wal-Mart to Become Green Umpire," *The Big Money*, www.thebigmoney.com, July 13, 2009.

2. Jamie Sturgeon, "Skype Offers Free Cellphone Service App," *Postmedia News*, September 9, 2009.

3. Vince Knightley, "Electronic Reading Devices Reviews—3 Different Ebook Readers to Compare Before You Buy," *Artipot*, http://artipot.com, January 2, 2010.

4. Golf Without Limits website, www.golfwithoutlimits.com, accessed July 28, 2011.

5. Mark Anderson, "A New Spin on an Old Toy," *IEEE Spectrum*, http://spectrum.ieee.org, November 2009.

6. Joseph P. Guiltinan and Gordon W. Paul, *Marketing Management*, 6th ed. (New York: McGraw-Hill), 1996, pp. 3–4.

7. American Marketing Association, "Resource Library," www.marketingpower.com, accessed February 5, 2010.

8. Air Canada website, www.aircanada.com/en/travelinfo/airport/baggage, accessed July 28, 2011.

9. Karl Gerth, *As China Goes, So Goes the World* (New York: Hill and Wang, 2010), pp. 24, 27.

10. Ibid., p. 35.

11. Emily-Sue Sloane, "U.S. Manufacturing Slides in Cost-Competitiveness Study," *Managing Automation*, www.managingautomation.com, February 3, 2010.

12. Jack Ewing, "Telecom's Last Great Growth Markets," *BusinessWeek*, May 22, 2008, www.businessweek.com.

13. Statistics Canada, "International Merchandise Trade: Annual Review 2010," Catalogue 65-208-X.

14. Steve Lohr, "Steve Jobs and the Economics of Elitism," *New York Times*, www.nytimes.com, January 29, 2010.

15. Gregory Polek, "UAL Finalizes Boeing 787 Order," *AINonline*, www.ainonline.com, February 25, 2010; Boeing website, "Boeing 787 Dreamliner Will Provide New Solutions for Airlines, Passengers," www.boeing.com, accessed March 3, 2010.

16. "Wirefly's Top 10 Best Selling Phones of '09 and Wireless Trends '10," *Wirefly*, www.wirefly.com, January 26, 2010.

17. Brennon Slattery, "Apple's Future Is in Solar-Powered Devices," *PC World*, www.pcworld.com, January 22, 2010.

18. Imagine Canada website, www.imaginecanada.ca/node/32, accessed July 28, 2011.

19. SickKids Foundation news archives, "SickKids Has 10 Million Reasons to Be Thankful," www.sickkidsfoundation.com/news/NewsWalmart.asp, accessed July 28, 2011.

20. Food Banks Canada website, http://foodbankscanada.ca/aboutus.htm and http://foodbankscanada.ca/fooddonors.htm, accessed July 28, 2011.

21. Canadian Red Cross, "Canadian Red Cross Sends $5 Million to Japan Donated by Generous Canadians," news release, available www.redcross.ca/article.asp?id=38530&tid=001, accessed July 28, 2011; Salvation Army, "Helping Hand from Telus," March 31, 2011, www.salvationarmy.ca/?s=Japan&x=9&y=15, accessed July 28, 2011.

22. M&M Meat Shops website, www.mmmeatshops.com/en/aboutmm/donations.asp, accessed July 28, 2011.

23. Rafe Needleman, "Piryz Raises Money for Your Cause," *CNET News*, http://news.cnet.com, September 22, 2009.

24. "Cause Awareness Calls for Promo Products," Virgo Publishing, www.corporatelogo.com, October 13, 2009.

25. Jane Taber, "Why Voters Elected the NDP's 'Vegas Girl' Anyway," *The Globe and Mail*, May 5, 2011, www.theglobeandmail.com/news/politics/ottawa-notebook/why-voters-elected-the-ndps-vegas-girl-anyway/article2010885, accessed July 28, 2011.

26. Kate Lunau, "Marketing: Pretty Valuable Faces: How Spending Millions to Reveal Celebrities' Pimple Problems Has Turned Proactiv into an International Bestseller," *Maclean's*, February 7, 2011, p. 42.

27. "Manning Brothers and 'Double Trump' Face-off for the Future of the Oreo Double Stuf Racing League," *Market Watch*, www.marketwatch.com, January 12, 2010; Barry Janoff, "Eli Manning Already Scoring off MVP Showing," *BrandWeek*, February 6, 2008, www.brandweek.com; Tim Arango, "Top 10 Endorsement Superstars," *Fortune*, November 2007, http://money.cnn.com, accessed September 29, 2008; Tim Arango, "LeBron Inc.," *Fortune*, November 28, 2007, http://money.cnn.com, accessed September 29, 2008.

28. Neal Karlinsky and Eloise Harper, "Law Vegas Gambles on $8.5 Billion CityCenter," *ABC News*, http://abcnews.com, December 16, 2009.

29. Scott Simpson, "Canadian Visitors Feeling Right at Home in U.S. Destinations; On the Flip Side, Tourism Vancouver Officials Are Also Expecting Solid Results for 2011," *Vancouver Sun*, April 26, 2011, p. 1.

30. Brent Jang, "Canada Lagging in Fight for Tourist Dollars," *The Globe and Mail*, November 2, 2010, p. 7.

31. Scott Deveau, "Number of Chinese Tourists Taking Flight; 'Huge Opportunity'; China to Drive Increase in Global Air Travel," *National Post*, February 15, 2011, p. 5.

32. Staples Canada website, www.staples.ca/ENG/Static/static_pages.asp?pagename=soulcommunity, accessed July 28, 2011.

33. Thomas Alan Gray, "Official Suppliers at Vancouver 2010," *Marketing PR*, www.suite101.com, September 30, 2009.

34. Melissa Martin, "New Friends' CEO Says $25-M Goal Attainable," *Winnipeg Free Press*, April 16, 2011, p. 17.

35. John H. Ostdick, "Embracing Social Media," *Success*, March 2010, pp. 65–69.

36. Spencer E. Ante, "The Real Value of Tweets," *Bloomberg Businessweek*, January 18, 2010, p. 31.

37. "Terror Leader's Death Prompts Tweeting Frenzy Says Company," *Calgary Herald*, May 3, 2011, p. 2; Cathal Kelly, "Twitter Confirms You Were Right to Care," *Toronto Star*, July 19, 2011, p. 3.

38. John Moore, "Four Big Ideas Influencing Marketing in 2010," *Promo*, www.promomagazine.com, December 17, 2009.

39. Ostdick, "Embracing Social Media."

40. Emmanuel Samoglou, "His Customers Are All a-Twitter About His Offers: Barbecue Restaurant Boss Uses Twitter, Foursquare App to Build Relationships and Drive His Sales," *Toronto Star*, May 5, 2011, p. 1.

41. Ostdick, "Embracing Social Media."

42. Steve Brearton, "Sounding Out the CEOs," *The Globe and Mail*, February 26, 2011, p. 9.

43. TransForce website, "TransForce Inc. and DHL Express Canada to Offer Fully Integrated Transportation Solutions to Canadian Businesses," available www.transforcecompany.com/pr/20110429E.asp, accessed July 28, 2011.

44. Sobeys website, www.sobeyscorporate.com/en/Social-Responsibility/Community-Involvement.aspx, accessed July 28, 2011.

45. Geoff Colvin, "Interview with Linda Fisher," *Fortune*, November 23, 2009, pp. 45–50.

46. Ibid.

47. Dean Krehmeyer, Michael Lenox, and Brian Moriarty, "Sustainability Strategy and Corporate Strategy," *Ethisphere*, http://ethisphere.com, November 2, 2009.

48. Ibid.

49. Matt Ford, "Green Electronics: The Good, the Bad and the Better," *CNN.com*, http://cnn.com, January 15, 2010.

CHAPTER 1 MARKETOID NOTES

Page 5   Strategic Networks Group, "Economic Impact Study of Golf in Canada," 2009.

Page 7   Canadian Tire website, "Business Overview," available http://corp.canadiantire.ca/EN/AboutUs/Pages/BusinessOverview.aspx, accessed July 28, 2011.

Page 14   Statistics Canada, *Canada Yearbook 2010*, p. 379.

Page 16   Statistics Canada, *Canada Yearbook 2010*, p. 122.

Page 21   Sarah Boesveld, "The Green Building Impact on Employees," *The Globe and Mail*, October 19, 2010, p. 12.

CHAPTER 2

1. Company website, www.afexa.com, accessed August 1, 2011; Company Annual Reports 2004–2011, www.afexa.com/investors/annual_reports.html, accessed August 1, 2011.

2. Alicia Chang, "Virgin Galactic Unveils Commercial Spaceship," *Associated Press*, December 7, 2009, http://news.yahoo.com; "Out of This World," *Calgary Herald*, June 28, 2011, p. 12.

3. "New Solar Panel Conveyor Displayed at Photovoltaic Technology Show," January 7, 2010, www.shuttleworth.com.

4. Procter & Gamble website, www.pg.com, accessed January 12, 2010.

5. "Toyota Canada Recalls Almost 150,000 More Vehicles Over Accelerator Concerns," *Postmedia News*, February 24, 2011.

6. Tanya Irwin, "Study: 2/3 of Marketers Invest in Social Media," *MediaPost Publications*, January 21, 2010, www.mediapost.com.

7. Hollie Shaw, "It's In the Bag; Canada Scores By Sticking With 'Noisy' Chip Bags," *Ottawa Citizen*, January 7, 2011, p. 4.

8. "Microsoft Explores Ad Business," *MediaPost News*, February 2, 2010, www.mediapost.com.

9. Sean Gregory, "Latte with Fries? McDonald's Takes Aim at Starbucks," *Time*, May 7, 2009, www.time.com.

10. Nanette Byrnes, "Why Dr Pepper Is in the Pink of Health," *BusinessWeek*, October 26, 2009, p. 59.

11. Ibid.

12. Derek F. Abell, "Strategic Windows," *Journal of Marketing,* 42, no. 3 (July 1978), pp. 21–26.

13. Mary Teresa Bitti, "Eye on the Long Game Pays Off," *National Post,* June 6, 2011, p. 1.

14. Walmart website, www.walmart.com, accessed February 3, 2010.

15. Sass Consignment website, www.sassconsignment.com, accessed March 12, 2011.

16. Julie Jargon, "Kraft Reformulates Oreo, Scores in China," *Wall Street Journal,* http://wsj.com, accessed February 3, 2010.

17. Maria Ermakova and Duane D. Stanford, "Kraft Beats Russian Recession with Bolshevik Biscuits," *Bloomberg.com,* www.bloomberg.com, accessed February 11, 2010.

18. S. Ramesh Kumar, "Addressing Diversity: The Marketing Challenge in India," *Wall Street Journal,* http://wsj.com, accessed February 3, 2010.

19. "Kindle e-Book Sales Surpass Printed Books," *Winnipeg Free Press,* May 20, 2011, p. 2.

20. Tim Hortons website, www.rolluptherimtowin.com, accessed March 12, 2011.

21. Dave Cooper, "Canada's Sought-After Retail Space Affordable; Downtown Edmonton Comes in At Low End, Report Says," *Edmonton Journal,* June 8, 2011, p. 3.

22. David Booth, "The Race Is on for No. 1," *National Post,* February 4, 2011, p. DT2.

23. Karl Gerth, *As China Goes, So Goes the World* (New York: Hill and Wang, 2010), p. 36.

24. Brian Quinton, "On the Move," *Promo Magazine,* December 1, 2009, http://promomagazine.com.

25. EBay, www.ebay.com, accessed February 4, 2010.

26. "About IBM," www.ibm.com, accessed February 4, 2010.

27. Omar El Akkad, "Feeling Squeezed, RIM Learns to Share," *The Globe and Mail,* May 7, 2011, p. 4; Tom Katsiroubas, "Feature-Packed Android a Good Alternative to Apple's iPhone," *Toronto Star,* June 9, 2011, p. 2; "Can RIM Recover?" *Maclean's,* July 11, 2011, pp. 58–60.

28. Microsoft website, www.microsoft.com, accessed February 4, 2010.

29. Geoffrey York, "McCain Laying Down Its Chips on African Strategy," *The Globe and Mail,* December 22, 2009, p. 3.

30. "Women Are So Generous—Especially With Bacon," *Winnipeg Free Press,* November 22, 2010, p. 2; Julia Johnson, "The Double Down Comeback; KFC Brings Back Its Bunless 'Chickenwich' in Marketing Strategy That Says It Can Be Good to Be Bad," *Ottawa Citizen,* June 11, 2011, p. 1.

31. Debra Black, "Light My Fire: With Fewer of Us Lighting Up, Zippo Smells New Opportunity in the Cologne Business," *Toronto Star,* March 11, 2011, p. 1.

32. Moon Ihlwan, "Sony and Samsung's Strategic Split," *Bloomberg Businessweek,* January 18, 2010, p. 52.

33. Sarah Schmidt, "Food Chains Fail to Meet Self-Declared Fat Content Limits," *Postmedia News,* December 16, 2010.

34. "Diet Shocker: Food Calorie Counts Are Often Off," *Associated Press,* as reported by MSNBC.com, January 7, 2010, www.msnbc.com.

CHAPTER 2 MARKETOID NOTES

Page 33   "Out of This World," *Calgary Herald,* June 28, 2011, p. 12.

Page 37   Tim Hortons website, www.timhortons.com/ca/en/about/index.html, accessed August 2, 2011.

Page 43   Statistics Canada, "2006 Census: Ethnic Origin, Visible Minorities, Place of Work, and Mode of Transportation," *The Daily,* April 2, 2008.

Page 46   Karl Gerth, *As China Goes, So Goes the World* (New York: Hill and Wang, 2010), p. 136.

Page 46   Tom Katsiroubas, "Feature-Packed Android a Good Alternative to Apple's iPhone," *Toronto Star,* June 9, 2011, p. 2.

CHAPTER 3

1. Leora Broydo Vestel, "Nike Makes Environmental Strides and Abandons Carbon Offsets," *New York Times,* February 2, 2010, http://greeninc.blogs.nytimes.com; "Nike Outlines Global Strategy for Creating a More Sustainable Business," company press release, January 22, 2010, www.nikebiz.com/media/pr; company website, "Corporate Responsibility Report," www.nikebiz.com/responsibility/reporting.html, accessed January 13, 2010; Reena Jana, "Nike Goes Green, Very Quietly," *BusinessWeek,* June 22, 2009, p. 56.

2. Terry Maxon, "High Fuel Costs, Recession Prompt U.S. Airlines to Cut Capacity," *Dallas Morning News,* January 19, 2010, www.dallasnews.com.

3. Susanne Baillie, Dee Van Dyk, and Kali Pearson, "Best Businesses to Go Into Now," *Profit,* December 1, 2002, available ProQuest document 631394561.

4. RenewABILITY Energy website, www.renewability.com, accessed July 29, 2011.

5. Vanessa O'Connell, "Why Philip Morris Decided to Make Friends with FDA," *Wall Street Journal,* November 25, 2003, p. 11.

6. Calum MacLeod, "China Wants to Rival Boeing, Airbus with Its C919 'Big Plane,'" *USA Today,* October 12, 2009, www.usatoday.com.

7. Company website, www.costco.com, accessed February 15, 2010.

8. Natural Resources Canada, "Frequently Asked Questions About ENERGY STAR®," available http://oee.nrcan.gc.ca/residential/business/energystar/faq.cfm?attr=0#qa, accessed July 29, 2011.

9. "WiFi Hotspot Market Stages Revival in 2009," *Microwave Journal,* January 1, 2010, www.mwjournal.com.

10. "Accor to Split into 2 Companies," *Hotels,* December 15, 2009, www.hotelsmag.com; Adrian Kerr, "Cable & Wireless Aims to Demerge by March 31, 2010," *Dow Jones Newswires,* November 17, 2009, www.wsj.com.

11. Matthew Herper, "What J&J's Cougar Buy Means," *Forbes,* May 22, 2009, www.forbes.com.

12. Ted Mininni, "What Stonyfield, Method, and Green Mountain Roasters Know (and You Should, Too)," *MarketingProfs,* January 26, 2010, www.marketingprofs.com.

13. Stonyfield Farm website, www.stonyfield.ca, accessed July 29, 2011.

14. Peter Nowak, "PlayBook Could Be a Contender, But Not Yet," www.cbc.ca, April 19, 2011, available www.cbc.ca/news/technology/story/2011/04/18/f-playbook-rim-tablet-review.html, accessed July 29, 2011.

15. Government of Canada, Consumer Measures Committee website, "About the CMC," available www.ic.gc.ca/eic/site/cmc-cmc.nsf/eng/h_fe00013.html, accessed July 29, 2011.

16. National Energy Board, "Our Responsibilities," www.neb.gc.ca/clf-nsi/rthnb/whwrndrgvrnnc/rrspnsblt-eng.html, accessed July 29, 2011.

17. Advertising Standards Canada, "Celebrating 50 Years of Advertising Self-Regulation," *Canadian Business,* Advertising Supplement.

18. "Fourth Quarter GDP Growth Surprises at 5.7%," *InvestorCentric Blog,* February 1, 2010, www.nuwireinvestor.com.

19. J. David Goodman, "An Electric Boost for Bicyclists," *New York Times,* February 1, 2010, www.nytimes.com.

20. Eric Beauchesne, "Canada a Haven from Inflation among Industrial Countries: Annual Rate Fell to 1.4 Percent in March, Report Says," *Vancouver Sun,* April 18, 2008, p. F2.

21. Damien Cave, "In Recession, Americans Doing More, Buying Less," *New York Times,* January 3, 2010, www.nytimes.com.

22. "Food Shortages Coming, Buy Commodities: Jim Rogers," *CNBC.com,* January 15, 2010, www.cnbc.com; "Government Cover-up of Food Shortage Feared," *WorldNetDaily,* January 10, 2010, www.wnd.com.

23. Sam Abuelsamid, "CNG-Fueled Honda Civic GX Ranked #1 on ACEEE Greenest Vehicle List. Again," *Autoblog,* January 22, 2010, http://green.autoblog.com.

24. Tu Thanh Ha, "Montreal Clothing Plant to Shut, 540 to Lose Jobs," www.reporton-business.com, March 3, 2008; "Men's Wearhouse Closing Montreal Plant," The Canadian Press, www.reportonbusiness.com, March 3, 2008.

25. Michael Wines, "As China Rises, Fears Grow on Whether Boom Can Endure," *New York Times,* January 12, 2010, www.nytimes.com.

26. International Monetary Fund website, "Frequently Asked Questions: Greece," available www.imf.org/external/np/exr/faq/greecefaqs.htm, accessed July 29, 2011.

27. Dean A. Ayers, "Implant 'RFID' Chips in Your Dogs, Cats or Pets? No Way!", *Associated Content,* November 12, 2009, www.associatedcontent.com; Mary Catherine O'Connor, "Students to Develop RFID-Enabled Robotic Guide Dog," *RFID Journal,* September 14, 2009, www.rfidjournal.com.

28. David Barker, "MSU Researches Nonfood Biofuel," *State News,* February 2, 2010, www.statenews.com; Jim Lane, "Algae, Algae, Algae," *World Biofuels Markets News,* October 19, 2009, www.worldbiofuelsmarkets.com.

29. "Research Universities Join Effort to Reduce Costs of Drug Development, Manufacturing," Purdue University, November 3, 2005, http://news.uns.purdue.edu.

30. Valerie Marchant, "The New Face of Work," *Canadian Business,* March 29–April 11, 2004, pp. 37–41.

31. Joanna Stern, "Cheap Mobile Calls, Even Overseas," *New York Times,* January 7, 2010, www.nytimes.com.

32. Continuum Crew, "Baby Boomers Emerging as New Social Media Mavens, Continuum Crew Survey Finds," press release, January 20, 2010, www.newsguide.us.

33. Rogers Communications website, "Programming and Channels," available www.rogers.com/web/Rogers.portal?_nfpb=true&_pageLabel=PTV_PROG_LANDING, accessed July 29, 2011.

34. Marke Andrews, "Rogers Buys Channel M; The Company Has Long Sought to Have a Multicultural Station in Vancouver," *Vancouver Sun,* July 7, 2007, p. G1.

35. Ethical Consumer website, www.ethicalconsumer.org/boycotts/boycottsarchive.htm, accessed July 29, 2011.

36. Nortel website, "Code of Business Conduct," www.nortel.com/corporate/community/ethics/collateral/english_code_2007.pdf, accessed June 18, 2008; Steve Maich, "Selling Ethics at Nortel," *Maclean's,* January 24, 2005, p. 32.

37. The Ontario Tobacco Research Unit, "Litigation Against the Tobacco Industry: Monitoring Update," October 27, 2010, available www.otru.org/pdf/16mr/16mr_litigation.pdf, accessed July 29, 2011.

38. Rob Linke, "$10B Up in Smoke; Health Smoking-Related Illnesses Have Cost Province More Than $10B in Last 60 Years, Lawyer Says," *Telegraph-Journal* (Saint John), March 24, 2008, p. A1.

39. "Spain Arrests Anonymous Members in Sony Attack," *Leader Post* (Regina), June 11, 2011, p. 8.

40. Company website, www.kelloggcompany.com, accessed February 21, 2010.

41. Mike Adams, "Food Industry Continues to Market Junk Food to Children," *NaturalNews,* January 27, 2010, www.sott.net; Julie Deardorff, "Pact to Limit Sugary Cereals to Kids Not Worth Its Salt," *Chicago Tribune,* January 20, 2010, www.chicagotribune.com.

42. Bruce Horovitz, "Alcohol Makers on Tricky Path in Marketing to College Crowd," *USA Today,* November 17, 2005, www.usatoday.com; Alan Mozes, "Alcohol Merchandise Encourages Underage Drinking," Yahoo! News, May 17, 2005, http://story.news.yahoo.com.

43. Deborah Mendenhall, "Keep Your Credit under Control," *Family Circle,* March 2006, pp. 42–49.

44. International Labor Rights Forum, "2010 Sweatshop Hall of Shame," November 17, 2009, www.laborrights.org.

45. SWEEP media release, "Sweep Milestone Reached as 20 Millionth Pound Recycled," June 15, 2011, available www.sweepit.ca/images/stories/documents/media_release/SWEEP-MediaRelease-15June2011.pdf, accessed July 29, 2011.

46. inkCanada website, "Statistics | Facts HP Inkjet Printer Cartridge," www.inkcanada.ca/2005_09_01_archive.html, accessed July 29, 2011.

47. Theresa Howard, "Being Eco-Friendly Can Pay Economically," *USA Today,* August 15, 2005, www.usatoday.com.

CHAPTER 3 MARKETOID NOTES

Page 72   Statistics Canada, "Energy Use and Greenhouse Gas Emissions," *The Daily,* March 28, 2011.

Page 74   Loblaw Companies, 2010 Annual Report.

Page 78   Statistics Canada, *Canada Year Book 2010,* p. 252.

Page 79   Advertising Standards Canada website, "Ad Complaints Report 2010," available www.adstandards.com/en/ConsumerComplaints/2010AdComplaintsReport.pdf, accessed July 29, 2011.

Page 82   Statistics Canada, *Canada Year Book 2010,* p. 269.

Page 91   Anonymous, "Xentel fined $500 000," *The Province* (Vancouver, BC), December 19, 2010; Laura Stone, "Bell Slapped With $1.3 Million Penalty," *Leader Post* (Regina), December 21, 2010; "Telemarketing Fraudster Given 14-Year Sentence," *Times–Colonist* (Victoria, BC), November 25, 2010, p. 7.

Page 92   Jessica Leeder, "Campbell's Nourish Brand Aims to Tackle World Hunger," *The Globe and Mail,* February 26, 2011, p. 17.

Page 95   Sarah Schmidt, "Food Chains Fail to Meet Self-Declared Fat Content Limits," *Postmedia News,* December 16, 2010.

CHAPTER 4

1. Envirosell website, www.envirosell.com, accessed February 10, 2010; Gary McCartney, "It's a Woman's World," *Inside Retailing,* February 10, 2010, www.envirosell.com; "RichRelevance and Envirosell's Paco Underhill to Present New Findings on Consumer Retailing at NRF Big Show," *BusinessWire,* January 8, 2010, www.businesswire.com; Damien Cave, "In Recession, Americans Doing More, Buying Less," *New York Times,* January 2, 2010, www.nytimes.com; Paco Underhill, "Drop How You Shop," *Washington Post,* November 29, 2009, www.washingtonpost.com; Chris Powell, "Canadians Making 'Brand Friends' for Free Stuff: TNS Study," *Marketing,* December 13, 2010; Chris Powell, "Social Shoppers Are the Future: Delvinia," *Marketing,* March 4, 2011.

2. Kristin Laird, "The A-List," *Marketing,* www.marketingmag.ca, May 31, 2010.

3. "Canadian Social Values—Dominant Themes in Canadian Culture," Canadian Marketing Association; http://canadianmarketingblog.com, accessed March 25, 2011.

4. Michael Adams website, www.michaeladams.ca, accessed March 25, 2011.

5. "Study, Projections of the Diversity of the Canadian Population," Statistics Canada website, www.statcan.gc.ca, March 9, 2010.

6. "Study, Projections of the Diversity of the Canadian Population," Statistics Canada website, www.statcan.gc.ca, March 9, 2010.

7. Government of Quebec website, www.gouv.qc.ca, accessed March 26, 2011.

8. Government of Quebec website, www.gouv.qc.ca, accessed March 26, 2011.

9. Matt Semansky, "Plus ca change," *Marketing,* www.marketingmag.ca, October 27, 2008; Headspace Marketing website, www.headspacemarketing.com, accessed March 31, 2011.

10. Eric Blais, "The 36 Keys of the Quebecois Revisited," *Marketing,* November 15, 2004, pp. 11–12; Yves Leveille, "What Quebec Wants Now," *Marketing,* June 20, 2005, p. 46; Danny Kucharsky, "Redecorating Quebec's Creative Bedrooms," *Marketing,* February 11, 2002, p. 8.

11. "Indepth: China: Chinese Immigration," www.cbc.ca, accessed July 12, 2005; Statistics Canada, "Study: Projections of the Diversity of the Canadian Population: 2006 to 2031," www.statcan.gc.ca, March 9, 2010.

12. Kristin Laird, "Adams Presents the Stats Behind Canada's Multicultural Makeup," *Marketing,* www.marketingmag.ca, March 23, 2011; Don Miller, "Chinese Challenge," *Marketing,* March 13, 2006, p. 24; Rebecca Harris, "Embrace and Prosper," *Marketing,* January 23, 2006, p. 11.

13. Council of Agencies Serving South Asians, "Constructing a Community in Diversity: The South Asian Experience," www.cassa.on.ca, accessed July 12, 2005.

14. Kristin Laird, "Multicultural Marketing Panel Opens Window on South Asian Pop Culture," *Marketing,* www.marketingmag.ca, March 24, 2011; Chris Daniels, "In-House Champions," *Marketing,* www.marketingmag.ca, April 30, 2010.

15. "Projections of the Diversity of the Canadian Population: 2006 to 2031," Statistics Canada, Catalogue no. 91-551-X, March 2010.

16. "Gap Unveils Premium Denim Line for Babies Zero to 2," *Retailing Today,* February 11, 2010, www.mediapost.com.

17. Amanda Lenhart, Kristen Purcell, Aaron Smith, and Kathryn Zickuhr, "Social Media and Mobile Internet Use Among Teens and Adults," *Pew Research Center Publications,* February 3, 2010, http://pewresearch.org.

18. "Oprah's No Phone Zone Pledge," *The Oprah Winfrey Show,* January 18, 2010, www.oprah.com.

19. "Canadian Social Trends," Statistics Canada Catalogue No. 11-008; www.statcan.gc.ca, accessed April 2, 2011; "2006 Census: Families, Marital Status, Households and Dwelling Characteristics," Statistics Canada, www.statcan.gc.ca, accessed April 2, 2011; CIA-The World Factbook website, www.cia.gov, accessed April 2, 2011.

20. "Hottest Retail Trends in 2010," *Food Product Design,* January 4, 2010, www.foodproductdesign.com.

21. Kevin Davis, "Teens, Parents Face Special Issues When Buying Cars," *Crain's Chicago,* February 8, 2010, www.chicagobusiness.com.

22. "The Internet as an Information and Economic Appliance in the Lives of Teens and Young Adults," Pew Internet and American Life Project, www.pewinternet.org, accessed February 15, 2010.

23. Connie Thompson, "Predicting Consumer Trends for 2010," *KOMO News,* January 14, 2010, www.komonews.com.

24. Gord Hotchkiss, "Decisiveness and Search: Two Different Strategies," *MediaPost Publications,* February 11, 2010, www.mediapost.com.

25. These categories were originally suggested in John A. Howard, *Marketing Management: Analysis and Planning* (Homewood, Ill.: Richard D. Irwin, 1963); Henry Assael, "Consumer Behavior and Marketing Action," Kent Publishing Company, 1987, p. 87.

26. Lee Eisenberg, "The American Shopper: Down but Not Out," *Business Week,* October 26, 2009, www.businessweek.com.

27. Gavin O'Malley, "Nielsen: Consumers Will Spend Money Online on Certain Content, But News Has Become a Commodity," *MediaPost News,* February 17, 2010, www.mediapost.com.

CHAPTER 4 MARKETOID NOTES

All Marketoids: "Projections of the Diversity of the Canadian Population: 2006 to 2031," Statistics Canada, Catalogue no. 91-551-X; "Births," *The Daily,* April 27, 2011, Statistics Canada, www.statcan.gc.ca; "Canada's Population Estimates," *The Daily,* June 22, 2011, Statistics Canada, www.statcan.gc.ca.

CHAPTER 5

1. The Original Maple Bat Corp. website, www.sambat.com, accessed August 2, 2011; Steve Maich, "Big-league Awakening," Macleans.ca, www.macleans.ca/topstories/sports/article.jsp?content=20050701_108717_108717, accessed September 4, 2005.

2. Government of Canada website, http://contractscanada.gc.ca/en/how-e.htm, accessed May 9, 2008.

3. Cassandra Kyle, "Hey Ottawa, Let Us in on the Action," *Star-Phoenix* (Saskatoon), October 26, 2007, p. D1.

4. "E-Stats," U.S. Census Bureau, www.census.gov/econ/estats, May 11, 2005, accessed March 24, 2006.

5. Bell Canada website, www.bell.ca/enterprise/EntPrd_Unified_Communications_Solutions.page, accessed May 23, 2011.

6. Company website, www.jan-pro.com/canada/, accessed August 2, 2011; and www.jan-pro.com, accessed February 17, 2010.

7. "ACCO Brands Corporation—Investing," www.blogged.com, accessed February 17, 2010.

8. "E-Stats," U.S. Census Bureau, May 16, 2008, www.census.gov.

9. "B2B Online Marketing Holds Strong Growth Potential," www.marketingcharts.com, February 4, 2010.

10. Company website, The Seam, www.theseam.com, accessed February 17, 2010.

11. Marcus Gee, "Looking Beyond America to the Riches of India," *The Globe and Mail,* January 16, 2008, p. B10.

12. "Kirtsy.com and Microsoft Office Live Team to Present Free 'Hands On Small Business' Sessions Across the Country," www.marketwire.com, October 2009.

13. Company website, Tetra Tech, www.tetratech.com, accessed February 17, 2010.

14. Statistics Canada website, www.statcan.gc.ca/subjects-sujets/standard-norme/naics-scian/2007/introduction-eng.htm, accessed August 2, 2011.

15. Akuni Adventures website, www.akuni.com/Discounts/discounts.html, accessed August 2, 2011.

16. Government of Canada, "Satyam Opens a New Development Center in Mississauga," http://investincanada.com/english/view.asp?t=&pid=&x=528&id=66, accessed July 10, 2005.

17. Company website, www.cdw.com, accessed February 18, 2010.

18. Walmart website, "Canada Fact Sheet 5-2011," available http://walmartstores.com/Search/?q=Miracle+network&t=a&p=1&s=r&fd=a&fa=p, accessed May 23, 2011.

19. "OPK, Indiana Jones and 4.6 Billion Other People," company blog, http://conversations.nokia.com, January 8, 2010.

20. Ramanathan Nagasamy, "Top Outsourcing Destination—India," www.articlealley.com, February 12, 2010.

21. "Brand Name Companies Go Bankrupt," http://money.cnn.com, September 25, 2009.
22. "Walmart Reports Fourth Quarter and Fiscal Year 2010 Results," www.forbes.com, February 28, 2010.
23. "Xerox at a Glance," company website, www.xerox.com, accessed February 21, 2010.
24. Christine Dobby, "Rebirth of U.S. Industrial Manufacturing Will Benefit Canada," *The Gazette* (Montreal), May 7, 2011, p. 4.
25. "Outsourcing and Offshoring Overview," Plunkett Research Ltd., www.plunkettresearch.com, accessed February 19, 2010.
26. "The Keurig Story," company website, www.keurig.com, accessed March 9, 2010.
27. "Keurig Introduces First Single-Cup Commercial Brewers with Touch Screen User Interface," www.thestreet.com, February 2, 2010.
28. "FedEx Couriers Play Cupid This Valentine's Day," www.businesswire.com, February 11, 2010.
29. "Indiana University," company website, www.hp.com, accessed April 16, 2010.
30. Public Works and Government Services Canada website, www.tpsgc-pwgsc.gc.ca/apropos-about/ctvts-bsnss-eng.html, accessed August 2, 2011.
31. Niagara Public Purchasing Committee website, http://nppc.ca, accessed August 2, 2011.

CHAPTER 5 MARKETOID NOTES

Page 141   Public Works and Government Services Canada, "What Is Crown Assets Distribution?" http://crownassets.pwgsc.gc.ca, accessed August 2, 2011.
Page 144   Statistics Canada website, www.statcan.gc.ca/subjects-sujets/standard-norme/naics-scian/2007/introduction-eng.htm, accessed August 2, 2011.
Page 148   "China Demand Driving World Wine Market Growth: Study," *The Independent,* available www.independent.co.uk/life-style/food-and-drink/china-demand-driving-world-wine-market-growth-study-1915107.html, accessed August 2, 2011.
Page 149   Institute for Manufacturing, University of Cambridge, "JIT Just-in-Time Manufacturing," available www.ifm.eng.cam.ac.uk/dstools/process/jit.html, accessed August 2, 2011.
Page 158   Purchasing Management Association of Canada website, "About PMAC," available www.pmac.ca/en/about-pmac, accessed August 2, 2011.
Page 160   Public Works and Government Services Canada, "What We Do," http://crownassets.pwgsc.gc.ca/mn-eng.cfm?snc=info&sc=acasc, and "Vehicles," http://crownassets.pwgsc.gc.ca/mn-eng.cfm?snc=info&sc=agcs, both accessed August 2, 2011.

CHAPTER 6

1. Company website, www.mcdonalds.com, accessed April 29, 2011; Peter Gumbel, "Big Mac's Local Flavor," *Fortune,* May 5, 2008, pp. 114–121; "McDonald's Now a British Institution," *St Petersburg Times,* January 29, 2008, www.sptimes.com; "McDonald's Closing Down in Iceland," *Marketing,* www.marketingmag.ca, October 26, 2009.
2. Statistics Canada, "Imports, Exports and Trade Balance of Goods on a Balance-of-Payments Basis, By Country or Country Grouping," www40.statcan.gc.ca, accessed April 29, 2011.
3. United Nations Conference on Trade and Development, *World Investment Report 2009,* www.unctad.org, p. xxi.
4. Statistics Canada, "International Merchandise Trade Annual Review: 2010," catalogue no. 65-208-X, www.statcan.ca, accessed April 30, 2011.
5. Statistics Canada, "Imports, Exports and Trade Balance of Goods on a Balance-of-Payments Basis, By Country or Country Grouping."
6. Andrew Clark, "Wal-Mart, the U.S. Retailer Taking over the World by Stealth," *Guardian co.uk,* January 12, 2010, www.guardian.co.uk.
7. Chris Powell, "Gorilla Arrives in Montreal," *Marketing,* www.marketingmag.ca, December 10, 2010; company website, http://gorillanation.com, accessed April 30, 2011.
8. Statistics Canada, "Employment by Industry,"; "Gross Domestic Product at Basic Prices by Industry," www.statcan.ca, accessed April 30, 2011.
9. Christine Roy, "The Service Industries and Trade in Services," Statistics Canada, #63F0002XIB, 2001.
10. Statistics Canada, *Canada Year Book 2010,* Chapter 20, International Trade, Catalogue no. 11-402-X.
11. "Tourism Snapshot: 2009 Year-in-review," Canadian Tourism Commission website, http://en-corporate.canada.travel, accessed May 2, 2011.
12. "Yum Brands Sets Sights on Indian Market," *2point6billion.com,* December 17, 2009, www.2point6billion.com.
13. Chris Kenning and Alex Davis, "Pizza Chain Plans 120 Stores This Year," *Business Opportunities Journal,* www.boj.com, accessed February 19, 2010; company website, "Papa John's Takes the Field as Official Pizza Sponsor of the NFL and Super Bowl XLIV," press release, January 12, 2010, www.papajohns.com.
14. "China GDP Per Capita (PPP), Us Dollars Statistics," *Economy Watch,* February 23, 2010, www.economywatch.com; "India GDP Per (PPP), Us Dollars Statistics," *Economy Watch,* February 23, 2010, www.economywatch.com; "United States GDP Per Capita (PPP), US Dollars Statistics," *Economy Watch,* February 23, 2010, www.economywatch.com.
15. Ibid.
16. "Will India's Population Rise to 2 Billion?" *Earthsky Blogs,* February 7, 2009, www.earthsky.org.
17. Desire Athow, "IBM to Create 5000 New Jobs in India," *ITProlPortal.com,* January 11, 2010, www.itproportal.com.
18. "Internet Usage Statistics," *Internet World Stats,* www.internetworldstats.com, accessed May 3, 2011.
19. "'Frankenstein' –Food Fears Keep GMOs out of Europe," *Global News Journal,* February 5, 2010, http://blogs.reuters.com.
20. Robert J. Rosoff, "Addressing Labor Rights Problems in China," *China Business Review,* www.chinabusinessreview.com, accessed February 22, 2010.
21. "About ISO," *International Organization for Standardization website,* www.iso.org, accessed May 3, 2011.
22. Canadian Trade Commissioner Service website, www.tradecommissioner.gc.ca, accessed May 3, 2011; The Canadian Trade Commissioner Service (TCS) Linkedin site, www.linkedin.com; Canadian Business website, www.canadabusiness.ca, accessed May 3, 2011; Foreign Affairs and International Trade Canada website, http://international.gc.ca, accessed May 3, 2011.
23. Mike Masnick, "How China's Attempts to Censor the Internet Are Failing," *Techdirt,* January 4, 2010, www.techdirt.com; Charles Arthur, "China's Internet Users Surpass US Population," *The Guardian,* July 16, 2009, www.guardian.co.uk.
24. Free Trade of the Americas, www.ftaa-alca.org, accessed May 9, 2011.
25. Foreign Affairs and International Trade Canada website, www.international.gc.ca, accessed May 13, 2011.
26. "Europe Strikes 'Banana War' Deal," *BBC News,* December 15, 2009, www.bbc.co.uk/news.
27. "Canada's International Market Access Report—2008," Foreign Affairs and International Trade Canada website, www.international.gc.ca, March 4, 2011.
28. "Subsidies to Boost China's 3G Handset Market in 2010," *EDN Asia,* February 8, 2010, www.ednasia.com.
29. Elsie Owen, "Standards in China: Behind the Headlines," *China Business Review,* January–February 2010, chinabusinessreview.com.
30. Industry Canada website, www.ic.gc.ca, accessed May 21, 2011.
31. Lucy Hornby and Niu Shuping, "China to Levy Anti-Dumping Duties on U.S. Chicken," *Reuters,* February 5, 2010, www.reuters.com.
32. World Trade Organization website, www.wto.org, accessed May 22, 2011.
33. Ibid.
34. Thomas L. Gallagher, "NAFTA Trade Grew for Fifth Month in October," *Journal of Commerce,* January 6, 2010, www.joc.com.
35. European Union website, http://europa.eu, accessed May 22, 2011.
36. Jason Burke, "Vaclav Klaus Sets Seal on Lisbon Treaty Ratification," *The Guardian,* November 3, 2009, www.guardian.co.uk.
37. "Adida and the Italian Tennis Player Flavia Pennetta Team up until 2012," press release, February 5, 2010, www.press.adidas.com; "Adidas JABULIANI Official Match Ball of the 2010 FIFA World Cup—Grip'n'Groove Profile for Football 'Celebration' in South Africa," press release, December 4, 2009, www.press.adidas.com.
38. Company website, www.ikea.com, accessed March 3, 2010.
39. "EA SPORTS to Expand Brand with Launch of New Peripherals," press release, January 7, 2010, http://investor.ea.com.
40. "Working Conditions in Sports Show Factories in China," *AF1STAR.com,* January 2, 2010. www.af1star.com.
41. Foreign Affairs and International Trade Canada website, www.international.gc.ca, accessed May 23, 2011.
42. Ibid.
43. Christian Fea, "Follow Wal-Mart's Joint Venture Example," *ChristianFea.com,* October 21, 2009, www.christianfea.com.
44. "A. T. Kearney Report Finds Multinational Companies turning to Chile for Global Services," press release, February 2, 2010, www.redorbit.com; "Chile Selected for ABB's First Remote Service Center in Latin America," press release, October 26, 2009, www.prnewswire.com.
45. "Innovating from the Outside In," *P&G Views,* December 16, 2009, www.pg.com.
46. "Is Singapore Ready for a Renewed Domino's Pizza Effect?," *Media,* February 22, 2010, www.media.asia.
47. "UPS Rival FedEx Launches International Ad Campaign," *Business First,* December 22, 2009, www.louisville.bizjournals.com.
48. "Avoiding Culture Clash," *Global Communicator,* December 2009, www.globallanguages.com.
49. Industry Canada website, www.ic.gc.ca, accessed May 23, 2011; "Ontario's Auto Sector Continues to Rev Up," Province of Ontario website, www.sse.gov.on.ca, January 13, 2011.
50. Joe Castaldo, "Is Canada Losing Control?," *Canadian Business,* May 21, 2007, pp. 24–26; "6 Questions: One-on-one with Deniss Hamilton, President & CEO, ERMS Corp," Canadian Business Online, June 6, 2007, www.canadianbusiness.com, accessed September 14, 2007.

CHAPTER 6 MARKETOID NOTES

All Marketoids: "International Merchandise Trade: Annual Review: 2010," Statistics Canada, Catalogue no. 65-208-X.

CHAPTER 7

1. Alicia Androich and Kristin Laird, "Secrets of Canada's Top Loyalty Programs," *Marketing*, April 7, 2011, www.marketingmag.ca; Maritz company website, www.maritizcanada.com, accessed May 31, 2011; Chris Powell, "HAVAS Opens Toronto Office for Euro RSCG Discover," *Marketing*, May 18, 2011, www.marketingmag.ca; David Menzies, "Drink n' Swipe," *Marketing*, September 17, 2007, p. 42; Rebecca Harris, "Kids with Cards," *Marketing*, July 3, 2006, p. 6; Laura Pratt, "Bottom-up Value," *Marketing*, March 7, 2005, p. 17; "Building Loyalty," supplement to *Marketing*, 2006.

2. J. D. Power and Associates website, www.jdpower.com, accessed June 3, 2011.

3. Environics Research Group, http://research-environics-net.sitepreview.ca, accessed June 3, 2011.

4. Nielsen Media company, www.nielsenmedia.ca, accessed June 3, 2011.

5. Company website, BazaarVoice, www.bazaarvoice.com, accessed February 26, 2010.

6. Chris Powell, "Boston Pizza Quits Holiday Meals Cold Turkey," *Marketing*, January 7, 2011, www.marketingmag.ca.

7. Leonor Vivanco, "Mac Snack Wrap, Other Items Dreamed Up in McDonald's Test Kitchen," Chicago Tribune.com, www.chicagotribune.com, February 21, 2010.

8. Statistics Canada, www.statcan.ca, accessed June 4, 2011.

9. Industry Canada, www.ic.gc.ca, accessed June 4, 2011.

10. "Wal-Mart Radio Tags to Track Clothing," *Wall Street Journal*, July 23, 2010, http://online.wsj.com.

11. "Who We Are," company website, Datamonitor Group, www.datamonitor.com, accessed March 1, 2010.

12. Company website, Google Analytics, www.google.com, accessed March 12, 2010; Brian Kraemer, "Facebook Partners with Nielsen on Tracking," *ChannelWeb*, www.crn.com, September 22, 2009; Evan Gerber, "Making Twitter Success Measureable," *MarketingProfs.com*, www.marketingprofs.com, September 8, 2009.

13. Company website, YouTube, www.help.youtube.com, accessed March 1, 2010.

14. David McMillin, "4 Tips to Lowering Survey Abandonment," http://survey.cvent.com, March 1, 2010.

15. Company website, TRU, www.teenresearch.com, accessed March 1, 2010.

16. Peter Sims, "How Google and P&G Approach New Customers, New Markets," *The Conversation*, http://blogs.hbr.org, March 2, 2009.

17. Marc Brenner, "Ethnography App Debuts on iTunes Store," *Research*, www.research-live.com, December 21, 2009.

18. Canadian Radio-television and Telecommunications Commission website, www.crtc.gc.ca, accessed June 13, 2011.

19. Department of Justice Canada website, Personal Information Protection and Electronic Documents Act, http://laws-lois.justice.gc.ca, accessed June 13, 2011.

20. Susan Grindstaff, "How to Hold Focus Groups," eHow website, www.ehow.com, accessed June 13, 2011.

21. "Led by Facebook, Twitter, Global Time Spent on Social Media Sites Up 82% over Year," *NielsenWire*, http://blog.neilsen.com, January 22, 2010.

22. Mary K. Pratt, "What's Your Twitter ROI? How to Measure Social Media Payoff," *Computerworld*, www.computerworld.com, September 21, 2009.

23. Mike Shields, "Coke, P&G Test MySpace 'In-Stream' Ads," *Brandweek*, www.brandweek.com, February 23, 2010.

24. Industry Canada, http://www.ic.gc.ca, accessed June 14, 2011.

25. "Toyota-Led Quality 'Evolution' Inspires Volkswagen, Ford 'Revolution, Says Strategic Vision's Total Value Index ™ Report," press release, November 23, 2009.

CHAPTER 7 MARKETOID NOTES

All Marketoids: "Spending Patterns in Canada: 2009," Statistics Canada, catalogue no. 62-202-X, www.statscan.gc.ca, accessed June 18, 2011.

CHAPTER 8

1. Nicolas Ritoux, "Quebec Milk Bureau," *Marketing*, November 8, 2010, p. 16; Milk Marketing Board of Canada website, www.dairygoodness.ca, accessed April 16, 2011; Aurore Lehmann and Jeromy Lloyd, "Quebec's Milk Producers Put Their Sweaters on Again," *Marketing*, www.marketingmag.ca, February 3, 2011; Eve Lazarus, "BC Dairy Foundation Store Selling Weak Products," *Marketing*, www.marketingmag.ca, October 16, 2009; The Weak Shop website, http://theweakshop.com, accessed April 16, 2011; "Under-Consumption of Milk Products," Milk Marketing Board website, www.dairynutrition.ca, accessed April 15, 2011; Alicia Androich, "Famed Milk Calendar Taking Canadians' Votes for Top Recipes," *Marketing*, www.marketingmag.ca, accessed April 14, 2011.

2. U.S. Census Bureau, "U.S. & World Population Clock," www.census.gov, accessed April 16, 2010; Statistics Canada, www.statcan.gc.ca, accessed April 16, 2011.

3. Statistics Canada, "Projections of the Diversity of the Canadian Population; 2006–2031," www.statcan.gc.ca, Catalogue no. 91-551-X.

4. Kristin Laird, "Hitting the Mark," *Marketing*, www.marketingmag.ca, April 30, 2010.

5. Kristin Laird, "Courting the DIY Crowd," *Marketing*, www.marketingmag.ca, April 16, 2010.

6. Kristin Laird, "Hitting the Mark," *Marketing*, www.marketingmag.ca, April 30, 2010.

7. "H-D and Jillian Michaels Encourage Women to Ride," Harley-Davidson press release, March 5, 2010, www.motorcycle-usa.com; Harley-Davidson of Toronto website, http://hdto.com, accessed April 17, 2011.

8. Statistics Canada "Population of Census Metropolitan Areas," www40.statcan.gc.ca, accessed April 17, 2011.

9. Statistics Canada, "Quarterly Population Estimates, National Perspective," www40.statcan.ca, accessed April 17, 2011; Prince Edward Island, "36th Annual Statistical Review: 2009," p. 36.

10. "Country Comparison: Population," *CIA World FactBook*, www.cia.gov, accessed March 21, 2010.

11. "World: Largest Cities" and "World: Metropolitan Areas," *World Gazetteer*, http://world-gazetteer.com, accessed March 21, 2010.

12. "Population and Dwelling Counts," *The Daily*, March 13, 2007, www.statcan.gc.ca.

13. "Information on Standard Geographical Classification (SGC) 2006," Statistics Canada, www.statcan.gc.ca, accessed April 17, 2011.

14. Laird, "Hitting the Mark."

15. Joanna Pachner and Alicia Androich, "Kids in Play," *Marketing*, www.marketingmag.ca, March 25, 2011.

16. Bea Fields, "Marketing to Gen Y: What You Can't Afford Not to Know," *Startup Nation*, www.startupnation.com, accessed March 22, 2010; Matt Semansky, "Little Kids Have Big Say in Family Shopping," *Marketing*, www.marketingmag.ca, February 22, 2008.

17. "Baby Boomer Statistics," *Business Week*, September 26, 2009.

18. Michael Adams, *Sex in the Snow: Canadian Social Values at the End of the Millennium* (Toronto: Viking, 1997), p. 80.

19. Chris Powell, "Zoomer Teams With Navigate to Better Target N. America's Boomers," *Marketing*, www.marketingmag.ca, October 22, 2010.

20. "Boomer Demographics and Media Usage," *Research and Markets*, www.researchandmarkets.com, accessed March 23, 2010; Mark Briggs, "Targeting Baby Boomer, the 'Forwarding Generation,'" *LostRemote.com*, March 1, 2010, www.lostremote.com; Chris Powell, "Zoomer Teams With Navigate To Better Target N. America's Boomers."

21. Daisy Nguyen, "Beefing Up: Aging Bikers Are Turning to Trikes to Stay on the Road," Associated Press, February 26, 2010, http://blog.marketplace.nwsource.com; "Motorized Trikes Are Great Alternative for Baby Boomers," *TRIKE.US*, February 15, 2010, www.trike.us.

22. Statistics Canada, www.statcan.gc.ca, accessed April 18, 2011.

23. Company website, "Marketing to Seniors," http://comingofage.com, accessed March 23, 2010.

24. Bea Fields, "Marketing to Gen Y: What You Can't Afford Not to Know," *Startup Nation*, www.startupnation.com, accessed March 22, 2010.

25. "Projections of the Diversity of the Canadian Population: 2006 to 2032," Statistics Canada, Catalogue no. 91-551-X.

26. "Projections of the Diversity of the Canadian Population: 2006 to 2032."

27. "The 1940's Landmark Canadian Advertisements," *Marketing*, September 28, 1998.

28. Eric Blais, "The 36 Keys of the Quebecois Revisited," *Marketing*, November 15, 2004, pp. 11–12.

29. Caroline Fortin, "Boston Pizza 'Changes' Its Name," *Marketing*, www.marketingmag.ca, April 14, 2011.

30. Patrick Fong, "Defining the Chinese Market," *Marketing*, June 3, 2002, p. 15; Michael McCullough, "Fireworks Had Died on the Morning of July 1," *Marketing*, September 8, 1997, p. 23.

31. Jeromy Lloyd, David Brown, and Tom Gierasimczuk, "The Incredible Rise of the Ethnic Consumer," *Marketing*, March 28, 2011, pp. 28–33.

32. Lloyd, Brown, and Gierasimczuk, "The Incredible Rise of the Ethnic Consumer."

33. Jeromy Lloyd, "Bet on Black," *Marketing*, March 28, 2011, pp. 34–38.

34. Statistics Canada, *Canada Year Book 2010*, Catalogue no. 11-402-X, p. 173.

35. Jeff Beer, "Retirement Isn't All About Leisure: Consumerology Report," *Marketing*, www.marketingmag.ca, November 5, 2010.

36. Statistic Canada, "2001 Census: Marital Status, Common-law Status, Families, Dwellings and Households," www.statcan.gc.ca, October 22, 2002; "Household Size, by Province and Territory (2006 Census)," www40.statcan.gc.ca, accessed December 19, 2007.

37. "2006 Census: Families, Marital Status, Households and Dwelling Characteristics," *The Daily*, September 12, 2007, www.statcan.gc.ca, accessed December 19, 2007; "Selected Trend Data for Canada, 2006, 2001 and 1996 Censuses," www12.statcan.gc.ca, accessed December 19, 2007.

38. "2006 Census: Families, Marital Status, Households and Dwelling Characteristics."

39. Jo-Ann Heslin, "Grocer Shopping Forecasts 2010—What to Expect," *HealthNewsDigest.com*, January 10, 2010, http://healthnewsdigest.com.

40. U.S. Department of Agriculture, "Food CPI and Expenditure: Table 7," http://ers.usda.gov, accessed March 23, 2010.

41. Company website, "Japan—VALS ™," www.strategicbusinessinsights.com, accessed March 23, 2010.

42. Adams, *Sex in the Snow*.

43. Helen Leggatt, "Experian Segments Mobile Users by Behavior/Attitudes," *BizReport*, March 18, 2010, www.bizreport.com.

44. Ashley M. Heher, "Burger King to Upgrade Its Coffee with Starbucks Line," *Detroit News*, February 17, 2010, http://detnews.com.

45. Philip Elmer-DeWitt, "Day 1 Estimate: 120,000 iPads Sold," *Brainstorm Tech,* March 13, 2010, http://brainstormtech.blogs.fortune.cnn.com.
46. Competition Bureau, www.competitionbureau.gc.ca, accessed April 21, 2011.
47. Cathy Jett, "Extreme Makeover for McDonald's," *AllBusiness,* February 26, 2010, www.allbusiness.com.
48. "Billabong to Keep West 49 Banner After Acquisition," *Marketing,* www.marketingmag.ca, August 25, 2010; Michelle Halpern, "Cute, but Scary," *Marketing,* August 9, 2004, pp. 13–15.
49. Frank Filipponio, "Spyker Releases More Details on Saab Purchase, Promises New 9-3 for 2012," *Autoblog,* February 2, 2010, www.autoblog.com.

CHAPTER 8 MARKETOID NOTES

All Marketoids: Government of Canada, "Consumption of Dairy Products," www.dairyinfo.gc.ca, accessed April 16, 2011.

CHAPTER 9

1. "Clorox Celebrates Successful First Year for Greenworks," *Marketing,* January 13, 2009, www.marketingmag.ca; "Best New Product Awards 2009—Bagging a Winner," *Marketing,* March 31, 2009, www.marketingmag.ca; company website, www.greenworkscleaners.com, accessed May 12, 2009; Elaine Korry, "Clorox Enters Booming Market for 'Green' Cleaners," *National Public Radio,* July 14, 2008, www.npr.org; Felicity Barringer, "Clorox Courts Sierra Club, and a Product Endorsement," *New York Times,* March 26, 2008, www.nyt.com; Siel, "Emerald City," *Los Angeles Times,* January 15, 2008, www.latimes.com/news/blogs/; Ilana Debare, "Clorox Introduces Green Line of Cleaning Products," *San Francisco Chronicle,* January 14, 2008, www.sfgate.com; "Clorox to Launch Green Cleaning Line Across U.S.," *Reuters,* September 6, 2007, www.reuters.com.
2. "Rankings of Canada's top 1000 Public Companies by Profit," *The Globe and Mail,* www.theglobeandmail.com, accessed June 20, 2011.
3. "Trade in Services: Canada and Trade in Services," Foreign Affairs and International Trade Canada, June 8, 2011, http://international.gc.ca.
4. Ibid.
5. Canada Flowers website, www.canadaflowers.ca, accessed June 20, 2011.
6. Concept introduced by Christopher H. Lovelock, "Classifying Services to Gain Strategic Marketing Insights," *Journal of Marketing,* Summer 1983, p. 10.
7. "Car Rankings," *U.S. News & World Report,* March 2010, usnews.rankingsandreviews.com; "Aston Martin Rumored to Launch a One-77 Roadster," *Car Buyers' Notebook,* www.carbuyersnotebook.com, accessed April 5, 2010.
8. Company website, www.bose.com, accessed June 21, 2011 .
9. Company website, www.cargill.com, accessed June 21, 2011.
10. Company website, www.staples.ca, accessed June 21, 2011.
11. Company website, www.regus.ca, accessed June 21, 2011.
12. National Quality Institute website, www.nqi.ca, accessed June 21, 2011.
13. International Organization for Standardization website, "ISO 9001: Frequently Asked Questions," www.praxiom.com, accessed April 30, 2010; "Quality Portal," www.nist.gov, accessed April 30, 2010.
14. "Improving the Quality Function: Driving Organizational Impact & Efficiency," *Research and Markets,* www.researchandmarkets.com, accessed April 5, 2010.
15. "Canadians Forgo Customer Service for Low Prices: Retail Loyalty Report," Colloquy company website, July 26, 2010, www.colloquy.com.
16. Company website, www.roots.com, accessed June 21, 2011.
17. Company website, www.tilley.com, accessed June 21, 2011.
18. Calgary Stampede Park website, http://venues.calgarystampede.com, accessed June 21, 2011.
19. Company website, www.jnjcanda.com, accessed June 26, 2011.
20. Company website, www.geox.ca; Marie-Louise Gumachian and Christina Carlevaro, "Geox's H1 Revenue Up, Sees Year Sales Flat," *Reuters,* July 28, 2009, www.reuters.com.
21. "Canadian Tire to Acquire Sporting Goods Retailer Forzani Group for $771 Million," *Marketing,* May 9, 2011, www.marketingmag.ca.
22. Kristin Laird, "Dinner Time Is Prime Time for Maple Leaf Foods," *Marketing,* June 16, 2011, www.marketingmag.ca.
23. Chris Foresman, "Years Late, Universal Cuts CD Prices to Combat Poor Sales," *Ars Technica,* http://arstechnica.com, accessed April 5, 2010.
24. "GPS Guide," *Consumer Reports,* www.consumerreports.com, accessed April 5, 2010.
25. Company website, www.bestbuy.com, accessed May 1, 2010.
26. Company website, http://nikerunning.nike.com, accessed June 26, 2011; "Nike Launches Mercurial Vapor SuperFly II, Delivering Greater Speed and Exclusive Insider Access to the World's Top Players," press release, February 24, 2010, www.nikebiz.com.
27. Jacqui Cheng, "Digital Albums, Vinyls Made a Comeback in '09 while CDs Slide," *Ars Technica,* January 7, 2010, http://arstechnica.com.
28. Company website, http://armandhammer.ca, accessed June 27, 2011.
29. Kristin Laird, "Cracker Barrel Returns to Wholesome," *Marketing,* June 9, 2011, www.marketingmag.ca.
30. "Holiday Inn Relaunches 1000th Hotel," press release, July 24, 2009, www.ihgplc.com.
31. Deepa Seetharaman, "Spirit Air to Experiment with Carry-On Bag Fee," Reuters, April 6, 2010, www.reuters.com.

CHAPTER 9 MARKETOID NOTES

All Marketoids: *Canada Year Book 2010 Edition,* Statistics Canada, catalogue no. 111-402-X, Chapter 3, "Business, Consumer and Property Services," pp. 29–38.

CHAPTER 10

1. Loblaws company website, www.loblaws.ca, accessed July 7, 2011; "The Price of Oil," *CBC News,* July 18, 2007, www.cbc.ca; "Study: Comparing the 2008–2010 Recession and Recovery with Previous Cycles," Statistics Canada, *The Daily,* January 13, 2011, www.statcan.gc.ca, "Study: The Year in Review: The Revenge of the Old Economy," Statistics Canada, *The Daily,* April 13, 2006, www.statcan.gc.ca, President's Choice website, www.presidentschoice.ca, accessed July 9, 2011; Robert Levy, "Private Label's Big Push," *Marketing,* April 2, 2009, www.marketingmag.ca; Jeromy Lloyd, "A True Trailblazer," *Marketing,* February 26, 2010, www.marketingmag.ca; Marina Strauss, "Memories of Excel," Globeandmail.com, January 26, 2007, https://secure.globeadvisor.com; James Cowan, "The Push on Private-Label Brands," *CanadianBusiness.com,* April 7, 2011, www.canadianbusiness.com.
2. Matt Semansky, "Private Label Shopper Changing With Times: Nielsen," *Marketing,* October 19, 2010, www.marketingmag.ca; Allison Ross, "Private Label Sales Hurting Branded Labels," *Palm Beach Post,* May 11, 2010, www.palmbeachpost.com/blogs/.
3. "Recession Changed Consumers: Rona CEO," *Marketing,* February 2, 2011, www.marketingmag.ca; Staples company website, www.staples.ca, accessed July 11, 2011.
4. Canadian Tire website, www.canadiantire.ca, accessed July 11, 2011.
5. Interbrand, "Best Global Brands of 2010," Interbrand website, www.interbrand.com, accessed July 11, 2011; "Brandz: Top 100 Most Valuable Global Brands," Millward Brown Canada website, www.wpp.com, accessed July 11, 2011.
6. "BrandAsset Valuator," *Consult Brand Strategy,* www.consultbrandstrategy.com, accessed April 9, 2010.
7. Category Management Association website, "What Is Category Management?" www.cpgcatnet.org, accessed May 11, 2010.
8. Ibid.
9. Company website, www.igd.com, accessed April 12, 2010.
10. Company website, www.hersheys.com, accessed April 12, 2010.
11. "Laser Etching Safe Alternative for Labeling Grapefruit," *PhysOrg.com,* November 3, 2009, www.physorg.com.
12. "A Guide to Trade-Marks," Industry Canada website, www.ic.gc.ca, accessed July 11, 2011.
13. Ibid.
14. Linda Lisanti, "Sara Lee Sees Daypart Traffic Shift at C-Stores," *Packaging Digest,* December 6, 2009, www.packagingdigest.com.
15. Mark Vanover, "The Future of Packaging," *Marketing,* October 28, 2008, www.marketingmag.ca.
16. Competition Bureau, Canada, website, www.competitionbureau.gc.ca, accessed July 12, 2011; Health Canada website, www.hc-sc.gc.ca, accessed July 12, 2011.
17. Company website, http://wiifit.com, accessed July 12, 2011.
18. Company website, http://barbieshanghai.com, accessed May 12, 2010; "Thanks to a Big Mattel Move, Toys and Movies Come One Step Closer to Being the Same Exact Thing," *New York Magazine,* March 24, 2010, www.nymag.com.
19. "Licensing Royalty Rates," *InventionStatistics.com,* www.inventionstatistics.com, accessed April 12, 2010.
20. Mario Marsicano, "Cheetos Lip Balm and More Bizarre Brand Extensions," *Wall Street Journal,* July 15, 2009, http://online.wsj.com.
21. Greg Beato, "Starbucks Midlife Crisis," *Reason,* March 2010, http://reason.com; Susan Berfield, "Steaming over Via Instant Coffee at Starbucks," *Business Week,* November 11, 2009, www.businessweek.com; Ted Mininni, "Starbucks: Undercutting Its Own Brand?" *MarketingProfsDailyFix.com,* October 8, 2009, www.mpdailyfix.com; "Starbucks Extension Tempts Failure," *Branding Strategy Insider,* May 7, 2009, www.brandingstrategyinsider.com.
22. Chris Powell, "Energizer Feeling Positive About New Brand Positioning," *Marketing,* May 19, 2011, www.marketingmag.ca.
23. Matt Semansky, "RBC Constructs a Great Wall in Chinatown," *Marketing,* June 8, 2011, www.marketingmag.ca.
24. Erik Gruenwedel, "Panasonic Sells World's First 3D TV System," *Hollywood Reporter,* March 10, 2010, www.hollywoodreporter.com.
25. "Pepsi Gets a Makeover," *Economist.com,* March 25, 2010, www.economist.com.
26. Kristin Laird, "Riceworks' Sampling Program Goes Outside This Summer," *Marketing,* June 24, 2010, www.marketingmag.ca.
27. Company website, www.bose.com, accessed May 12, 2010.
28. Dev Patnaik, "The Fundamentals of Innovation," *Business Week,* February 10, 2010, www.businessweek.com.
29. Company website, www.thescottmiraclegrocompany.com, accessed April 12, 2010.

CHAPTER 10 MARKETOID NOTES

All Marketoids: "Information and Communications Technology," *Canada Year Book 2010,* Statistics Canada, Catalogue no. 11-402-X, pp. 243–54.

CHAPTER 11

1. Tavia Grant, "Panama Canal Gets a Revamp—and So Does Global Trade," *The Globe and Mail*, March 26, 2011, p. 5; "Panama Canal Expansion Will Loosen LNG Trade," *Oil & Gas Journal*, March 15, 2010, www.ogj.com; Rick Jervis, "Ports Get in Shipshape for Wider Panama Canal; More Traffic in 2014 Could Channel Profits," *USA Today*, February 16, 2010, www.usatoday.com; "Panama Canal Expansion Moving Forward as Planned," *BBC*, January 27, 2010, www.news.bbc.co.uk; "A Plan to Unlock Prosperity," *The Economist*, December 5, 2009, www.economist.com; Sean Mattson, "Panama Canal Bulks Up; Mega-Ship Capability Expected to Boost Trade with U.S. and Caribbean," *National Post*, November 19, 2009, www.nationalpost.com; Brad Reagan, "The Panama Canal's Ultimate Upgrade," *Popular Mechanics*, October 1, 2009, www.popularmechanics.com.

2. "Want to Make Money on Twitter? Take a Look at How Dell Does It," *Open Forum*, January 7, 2010, www.openforum.com; Matthew Yeomans, "How Dell Got Out of Hell," *The Big Money*, December 14, 2009, www.thebigmoney.com.

3. Company website, www.stelladot.com, accessed April 18, 2010; Grace L. Williams, "How I . . . Scaled Quickly to Handle Rapid Growth," *Wall Street Journal*, October 30, 2009, http://online.wsj.com.

4. Alexandru Nistor, "Netflix Brings All of Their Movie Content on the Nintendo Wii Console," *Softpedia*, April 12, 2010, http://gadgets.softpedia.com.

5. Company website, "Community Action," www.caasco.com, accessed August 7, 2011.

6. Company website, www.nikereuseashoe.com, accessed May 28, 2010; "Staples Expands Ink Cartridge Recycling Program," *Small Business Trends*, January 27, 2009, www.smallbiztrends.com.

7. Ginny Parker, "Vending the Rules," *Time*, May 10, 2006, www.time.com.

8. Nick Haramis, "Automatic for the People; From China to California, Vending Machines Dispensing the Ordinary and the Exotic Are Supplying a Universal Demand for Fast (and Freaky) Needs," *Wall Street Journal (Online)*, April 29, 2011; Carolyn Jarvis, "Crab Vending Machines," *Global News Transcripts* (Toronto), October 22, 2010.

9. Lana Diaz, StaplesOnline, email correspondence, May 19, 2011.

10. Brian Stelter, "Networks Wary of Apple's Push to Cut Show Prices," *New York Times*, February 22, 2010, www.nytimes.com.

11. "The Changing World of Industrial Distribution," *B2B International*, www.b2binternational.com, accessed April 18, 2010.

12. Bruce Blythe, "Wal-Mart Makes Few Food Price Changes—So Far," *The Packer*, April 16, 2010, www.thepacker.com.

13. Barbara Yaffe, "Landing Rights Dispute With UAE May Force 'Open Skies' Debate," *Vancouver Sun*, October 14, 2010, p. 6; John Hughes, "American, British Airways Accord Accepted by U.S.," *Bloomberg BusinessWeek*, February 13, 2010, www.businessweek.com.

14. Company website, www.tru2way.com, accessed April 18, 2010.

15. Kevin Voigt, "iPad Hits Hong Kong—Before Global Release," *CNN.com*, April 8, 2010, www.cnn.com; Owen Fletcher, "Amazon Kindle Hits China's Grey Market," *Macworld UK*, March 30, 2010, www.macworld.co.uk.

16. Brian Stelter, "Discovery, Imax and Sony Form 3-D Television Channel," *New York Times*, January 5, 2010, http://mediadecoder.blogs.nytimes.com.

17. Company website, "About Roots," www.roots.com, accessed August 7, 2011.

18. Company website, "About True Value," www.truevaluecompany.com, accessed August 7, 2011.

19. Industry Canada, "Stat-USA Market Research Reports," http://strategis.ic.gc.ca/epic/internet/inimr-ri.nsf/fr/gr127348f.html, accessed November 24, 2007.

20. Company website, www.pier1.com, accessed April 18, 2010.

21. Company website, www.jda.com, accessed May 30, 2010.

22. "Boeing RFID Progress," presentation, May 18, 2010, www.ataebiz.org.

23. "2010 Prediction: The Year ERP (SAP, Oracle, and Infor) Get Spend Management Right," *SpendMatters.com*, January 10, 2010, www.spendmatters.com.

24. Philip Quinn, "Export Firms Facing Rising Costs: Companies Spend More to Expedite Border Clearances," *Vancouver Sun*, October 17, 2006, p. F.11.

25. Dick Armstrong, "Third-Party Logistics: Near-Term Clarity," *Journal of Commerce*, January 10, 2011.

26. Company website, "Policies," www.1800flowers.ca, accessed August 7, 2011.

27. "Warren Buffett's $5Billion Railroad Stake … And How to Profit by Following in His 'Tracks,'" *Investment U*, www.investmentu.com, accessed April 18, 2010.

28. FedEx Small Business Center, "Holtkamp Greenhouses," www.fedex.com, accessed April 19, 2010.

29. Personal correspondence with Mike LoVecchio, Senior Manager, Media Relations, Canadian Pacific Railway, July 4, 2008.

30. Statistics Canada, *Canada Year Book 2007*, Table 30.6, p. 476.

31. Brandi Kruse, "Truckers Worries about the Long-Haul," *ABC News*, February 26, 2010, http://abcnews.com.

32. Company website, "Corporate Overview," www.csl.ca, accessed August 7, 2011.

33. Port Metro Vancouver, "Statistics Overview 2010," available www.portmetrovancouver.com/Libraries/ABOUT_Facts_Stats/Port_Metro_Vancouver_2010_Statistics_Overview.sflb.ashx, accessed August 7, 2011.

34. Statistics Canada, *Canada Year Book 2007*, p. 468.

35. Patrick Burnson, "Ocean Cargo/Global Logistics: Carriers Are Now in Position to Make Rate Hikes Stick," *Logistics Management*, February 8, 2010, www.logisticsmgmt.com.

36. Company website, "About Us," www.transcanada.com, accessed August 7, 2011.

37. Company website, "Our Pipelines," www.enbridge.com, accessed August 7, 2011.

38. Company website, www.ups.com, accessed April 19, 2010.

39. Company website, "About Purolator: Facts," www.purolator.com, accessed August 7, 2011.

40. Company website, "About Conestoga," www.coldstorage.com, accessed August 7, 2011.

41. "Clayco to Build $65M Caterpillar Distribution Center," *St. Louis Business Journal*, March 24, 2010, www.bizjournals.com.

42. "New Parts Distribution Centre to Be Opened by Pratt & Whitney Canada in Singapore," *Airline Industry Information*, May 23, 2007, p. 1.

43. "Hubbell Managed Vendor Inventory (VMI) Program Wins Progressive Manufacturing Award," *Marketwire*, April 9, 2010, www.marketwire.com.

44. Company website, "At Port Wentworth, a More Efficient Way to Make a Pallet," www.iscnewsroom.com, accessed April 19, 2010.

45. Jennifer Levitz, "Heists Targeting Truckers on Rise," *Wall Street Journal*, February 1, 2010, http://online.wsj.com.

CHAPTER 11 MARKETOID NOTES

Page 328   "Canadian Online Shopping Tops $15B a Year," www.cbc.ca, September 27, 2010, available www.cbc.ca/news/story/2010/09/27/con-internet-shopping.html, accessed August 7, 2011.

Page 332   Statistics Canada, "Recycling by Canadian Households, 2007," Catalogue no. 16-001-M, no. 13.

Page 346   Statistics Canada, *Canada Year Book 2010*, Table 30.1, p. 396.

Page 348   Statistics Canada, "Aircraft Movement Statistics: NAV CANADA Towers and Flight Service Stations: Annual Report (TP 577) 2010," Catalogue No. 51-209-X.

Page 351   Company website, "About the Port: Facts & Stats," www.portmetrovancouver.com, accessed August 7, 2011.

CHAPTER 12

1. Company website, www.tilley.com, accessed August 7, 2011; Judy Steed, "It Takes Hard Work to Be Endurable; A Childhood Fall Means Alex Tilley Must Rely on Those Around Him to Help When Memory Fails," *Toronto Star*, August 29, 2009; Andy Holloway, "Alex Tilley," *Canadian Business*, January 16–January 29, 2006, p. 66.

2. "The End of the Sam Walton Era," *Wal-Mart Watch*, http://walmartwatch.com, accessed February 25, 2010.

3. Tim Yip, "Kia Brass Celebrate Cutting-Edge Dealerships; Local Dealers Early Adopters of Company's New-Look Facilities," *Edmonton Journal*, November 19, 2010, p. 2.

4. Mario Toneguzzi, "Calgary on Target for Six Stores," *Calgary Herald*, May 27, 2011, p. 1.

5. Company website, "Women, Men Debunk D-I-Y Gender Myths; Survey Shows Both Sexes Envision Level Playing Field in Home Improvement Abilities," press release, August 20, 2009, lowes.mediaroom.com.

6. Hollie Shaw, "Joe Fresh Fashions Low-Cost U.S. Invasion; Loblaw Retailer Opening Flagship in New York City," *National Post*, February 24, 2011, p. 1.

7. Company website, www.callwave.com, accessed February 25, 2010.

8. Michelle Magnan, "As Good As It Gets?" *Profit*, March 2007, pp. 44–49.

9. Company website, www.lapalmera.com, accessed March 7, 2010.

10. Eve Lazarus, "Main Street Malls," *Marketing*, April 3, 2006, pp. 11–12.

11. Company website, "Attractions," www.wem.ca, accessed August 7, 2011.

12. Emma Hall and Normandy Madden, "IKEA Courts Buyers with Offbeat Ideas," *Advertising Age*, April 12, 2002, p. 10.

13. Barney Beal, "Smartphones Changing the Face of Web Analytics," *Enterprise Innovation*, February 1, 2010, www.enterpriseinnovation.net.

14. Janet L. Hoffman and Renee V. Sang, "The 'Me-Tail' Revolution," *Accenture Outlook*, February 2010, www.accenture.com.

15. Kristen Fritz, "The Sephora Experience: Shopping Simplified," *The Next Great Generation*, February 1, 2010, www.thenextgreatgeneration.com.

16. Canadian Tire website, www.canadiantire.ca, accessed October 10, 2007.

17. Retail Council of Canada, "2005/2006 Federal Pre-Budget Submission Profile of the Retail Industry," www.retailcouncil.org/membersonly/submissions/budgets/prebudget_federal05/profile.asp, accessed April 28, 2005.

18. Georgia Flight, "Whole Fuels," *Business 2.0*, December 2005, p. 78.

19. Chris Daniels, "The Dawn of a New Bay," *Marketing*, April 30, 2007, pp. 39–42.

20. Company website, http://sale.vente-privee.com, accessed March 10, 2010.

21. Rich Whittle, "Wal-Mart Tests Drive-Thru Window," *Business Opportunities*, December 21, 2009, www.business-opportunities.com.

22. Nikki Finke, "Wal-Mart Is Buying Digital Entertainment Provider VUDU," *Deadline Hollywood*, February 22, 2010, www.deadline.com.

23. Hollie Shaw, "Camisoles & Cabbages," *National Post*, April 27, 2006, p. FP.1.

24. Company website, www.dominioncitrus.com, accessed August 7, 2011.

25. Company website, www.wfsltd.com, accessed August 7, 2011; Rick Thurston, company president, personal interview, May 25, 2011.

26. "Merchandising Service Companies," *Product Profitability,* www.productprofitability.com, accessed February 25, 2010.
27. Craig Shutko, "Uponor Canada Knows What It Takes to Provide Quality," *Leader Post* (Regina), August 30, 2007, p. E.5.
28. Michelle Warren, "Counting on Catalogues," *Marketing,* March 6, 2006, pp. 11–13.
29. "Milestones," *Time,* July 13, 2009, p. 21; David Hinckley, "Billy Mays: Pitch Perfect," *New York Daily News,* June 29, 2009, www.nydailynews.com.
30. "Vending Machine Operators," *First Research,* www.bvmarketdata.com, accessed March 15, 2010.
31. Monica Hesse, "Vending Machine Food: Just a Touch-Screen Away," *Washington Post,* February 4, 2010, www.washingtonpost.com.

CHAPTER 12 MARKETOID NOTES

Page 360   Statistics Canada, "Annual Retail Trade 2009," Catalogue no. 63-270-X; and "Annual Wholesale trade 2009," Catalogue no. 63-271-X.
Page 362   Company website, "Financial Information," www.dollarama.com, accessed August 7, 2011.
Page 364   Hollie Shaw, "Americans Fed up With Service Quality," *National Post,* June 10, 2011, p. 12.
Page 370   Company website, "About UFA" and "Frequently Asked Questions," www.ufa.com, accessed August 7, 2011.
Page 377   Company website, "About Us," www.acklandsgrainger.com, accessed August 7, 2011.

CHAPTER 13

1. Chris Daniels, "Kitchen Magicians," *Marketing,* May 28, 2007, p. 26; Jeromy Lloyd, "Kraft and CBC to Bring Hockeyville to Little Mosque," *Marketing,* January 8, 2010, www.marketingmag.ca, accessed January 5, 2011; Chris Daniels, "Research: Surfing for Sports," *Marketing,* May 28, 2007; Chris Powell, "Kraft Brings Back Hockeyville to Showcase Canadian Passion for Hockey," *Marketing,* November 9, 2010, www.marketingmag.ca, accessed January 5, 2011; Jeff Beer, "How to Maximize Your Sports Sponsorship Dollars," *Marketing,* May 17, 2010, pp. 35–37; CBC website, www.cbc.ca, accessed January 5, 2011; Jeromy Lloyd, "Kraft Scores With Hockeyville at Sponsorship Marketing Awards," *Marketing,* April 22, 2010, www.marketingmag.ca, accessed January 4, 2010.
2. *Canadian Media Directors' Council Media Digest 10/11,* September 27, 2010, p. 12.
3. Amy Chozick, "NBC Rallies for the Count," *Wall Street Journal,* http://online.wsj.com, February 16, 2010; Chris Powell, "Gold Mettle," *Marketing,* www.marketingmag.ca, January 10, 2011.
4. Organization website, "MoneySmarts," AARP Financial, www.moneysmarts.com, accessed March 31, 2010.
5. Matt Semansky, "Newfoundland Tourism on Target at ICE Awards," *Marketing,* www.marketingmag.ca, accessed January 8, 2011; "PEI Government Says Regis and Kelly Visit Worth Millions," *Marketing,* www.marketingmag.ca, accessed January 8, 2011.
6. "Media Innovation Awards 2010: Television," *Marketing,* p. 5, December 13, 2010.
7. Kristin Laird, "In Fashion," *Marketing,* www.marketingmag.ca, January 10, 2011; Company website, www2.hbc.com, September 30, 2011.
8. "Five Words to Never Use in an Ad," *InternetmarketingMatrix-e.com,* http://internetmarketing.matrix-e.com, accessed March 31, 2010.
9. Tim Hortons website, www.timhortons.com, accessed January 8, 2011.
10. Wayne Friedman, "Nissan Drives 'Parenthood' Premiere," *Media Daily News,* www.mediapost.com, March 2, 2010; Wayne Friedman, "TV Product Placement Delivers for '24'," *Media Daily News,* www.mediapost.com, January 10, 2010.
11. "Product Placement Is Now on Twitter," *Product Placement,* www.productplacement.biz, March 26, 2010; David Castillo, "More Product Placement on YouTube for 2011," *Product Placement,* http://productplacement.Biz, January 4, 2011.
12. "Evian's Skating Babies Go From Viral to TV," *Marketing,* www.marketingmag.ca, April 15, 2010; Michael Learmonth, "Evian Takes Viral Mega-Hit Roller Babies to TV," *Advertising Age,* http://adage.com, April 15, 2010.
13. Jeromy Lloyd, "Grey Gets Salvation Army on the Street, Hires Jocelyn Renaud," *Marketing,* www.marketingmag.ca, January 22, 2010; Kristin Laird, "Salvation Army Puts Its Christmas Kettles Online," *Marketing,* www.marketingmag.ca, December 3, 2010.
14. James Bickford, "Get Verbal, Be Genuine," *NZ Marketing Magazine,* November/December 2010, p. 72.
15. Jeromy Lloyd, "Olympic Marketers Discuss Their War on 'Ambush Marketers,'" *Marketing,* www.marketingmag.ca, May 13, 2010.
16. Lloyd, "Olympic Marketers Discuss Their War on 'Ambush Marketers'"; Kristin Laird, "Scotiabank," *Marketing,* www.marketingmag.ca, August 11, 2010.
17. "Net Advertising Volume by Medium," *Canadian Media Directors' Council: Media Digest 10/11,* p. 12.
18. Eve Lazarus, "Direct Destination," *Marketing,* March 20, 2006, p. 9.
19. "CRTC Hits Bell Canada With $1.3M Penalty for Violating Do Not Call Rules," *Marketing,* www.marketingmag.ca, December 21, 2010.
20. "Net Advertising Volume by Medium."
21. "Kodak Connects Comprehensive Ecosystem to the World's Largest Retail Photo Kiosk Feel to Drive More In-Store Printing," *PR Newswire,* www.prnewswire.com, February 20, 2010.
22. Chris Powell, "Air Canada Evokes a New Golden Age of Air Travel," *Marketing,* www.marketingmag.ca, October 19, 2010.
23. Kristin Laird, "MADD Presents Drunk-Driving Expert," *Marketing,* www.marketingmag.ca, January 7, 2010.
24. Eve Lazarus, "CTC Exploring Marketing on a Budget," *Marketing,* August 30, 2010, p. 7.

CHAPTER 13 MARKETOID NOTES

All Marketoids: "Advertising and Related Services," Statistics Canada, Catalogue no. 63-257-XWE, June 7, 2010.

CHAPTER 14

1. Company website, www.salesforce.com, accessed June 4, 2010; "Betty White's Golden Touch Keeps Her Red-Hot," *Los Angeles Times,* April 12, 2010, www.latimes.com; Emily Bryson York, "Snickers Uses Humor to Satisfy Generations of Hunger," *Advertising Age,* March 29, 2010, http://adage.com; David Gianatasio, "Snickers' 'Celebrity Sack' Tops 'USA Today' Ad Meter," *Adweek.com,* February 8, 2010, www.adweek.com; Bruce Horovitz, "Betty White and Snickers Score Top Ad Honors," *USA Today,* February 8, 2010, www.usatoday.com; Rick Kissell, "Super Bowl Breaks Ratings Records," *Variety,* February 8, 2010, www.variety.com; "Snickers Debuts Campy, Celeb-Filled Ad Campaign during Super Bowl," *Progressive Grocer,* February 7, 2010, www.progressivegrocer.com; "Super Bowl Low on Canadian Advertiser Lists: Poll," *Marketing,* January 28, 2011, www.marketingmag.ca.
2. Sarah LeTrent, "Brand-Placement Marketing Targets Huge Airline Traveler Audience," *CNN.com,* March 26, 2010, www.cnn.com.
3. Rich Thomaselli, "Latest Lincoln Effort Stars 'Mad Man' John Slattery," *Advertising Age* website, http://adage.com, September 30, 2010; Kristin Laird, "Cover Girl Puts Giant Mascara Wands Underground," *Marketing,* www.marketingmag.ca, February 3, 2010.
4. Bradley Johnson, "Ad Spending Is on the Rise, But Growth Rate May Slow," *Advertising Age,* December 20 2010, pp. 8–14.
5. Chris Powell, "Zenithoptimedia Predicts Increase in Overall 2010 Ad Spend," *Marketing,* www.marketingmag.ca, December 4, 2010.
6. Jeff Beer, "Talking Blue Cat Promotes Reintroduction of Blue Smarties," *Marketing,* www.marketingmag.ca, July 23, 2010.
7. Robert Berner, "Detergent Can Be So Much More," *BusinessWeek,* May 1, 2006, p. 66.
8. Chris Powell, "Quaker Unlocks Partnership With Olympian Bilodeau," *Marketing,* www.marketingmag.ca, January 18, 2011.
9. Jeremy Mullman, "Why Market Size Won't Matter for Lebron James' Endorsements," *Advertising Age,* May 24, 2010, http://adage.com.
10. Jonah Freedman, "The 50 Highest-Earning American Athletes," *SportsIllustrated.com,* http://sportsillustrated.cnn.com, accessed June 6, 2010.
11. Lara Mills, "Campaigns With Legs," *Marketing,* May 15, 2000, p. 12; Chris Powell, "Pepsi Brings 70s Joy To Canada," *Marketing,* www.marketingmag.ca, January 28, 2011.
12. Michael McCarthy, "Safe-Bet Winter Olympics Stars Could See Endorsements Spikes," *USA Today,* March 1, 2010, http://usatoday.com.
13. Darren Rowell, "Wanted: Sidney Crosby's Signature," *CNBC,* March 4, 2010, www.cnbc.com.
14. Meghan Keane, "Online Video Ads Are More Effective Than TV—Because Viewers Are Forced to Watch Them," *eConsultancy.com,* April 23, 2010, http://econsultancy.com.
15. "Outsell Forecasts Advertising/Marketing Spending to Grow, But Only 1.2 Percent," *Outsell,* March 8, 2010, www.outsellinc.com.
16. Natalie Zmuda, "Old Navy Retires 'Supermodelquins,'" *Advertising Age,* http://adage.com, February 17, 2011.
17. "The Four Letter Word in Advertising: Fear," *Insite,* January 27, 2010, http://insite.artinstitutes.edu.
18. Laurel Wentz, "Is Paris Hilton Too Sexy for Brazil?," *Advertising Age,* February 25, 2010, http://adage.com.
19. Peter Novak and Jeromy Lloyd, "Press Start," *Marketing,* www.marketingmag.ca, February 8, 2011.
20. "Deliver Your Message with Impactful Banner Ads," *OrgMarketing.com,* April 1, 2010, www.orgmarketing.com.
21. "Facebook to Surpass MySpace in Ad Revenue," *Adweek,* December 23, 2009, www.adweek.com.
22. Rupert Neate, "TV Advertising Growing for the First Time in Five Years," *Telegraph,* April 7, 2010, www.telegraph.co.uk; "U.S. Ad Spend Trends: 2008," *Advertising Age,* June 22, 2009, http://adage.com.
23. James Gallagher, "Duke Study: TiVo Doesn't Hurt TV Advertising," *Triangle Business Journal,* May 3, 2009, http://adage.com.
24. Company website, www.hulu.com, accessed July 19, 2010; company website, www.clicker.com, accessed April 27, 2010; Harry McCracker, "Five Ways to Get More out of Internet TV," *FOXNews.com,* April 6, 2010, www.foxnews.com.

25. Chris Powell, "Zenithoptimedia Predicts Increase in Overall 2010 Ad Spend," *Marketing,* www.marketingmag.ca, December 6, 2010.

26. "XM Canada, Sirius Canada to Merge in $520M Deal," *Marketing,* www.marketingmag.ca, November 25, 2010.

27. *Canadian Media Directors' Council Media Digest 10/11,* published by *Marketing,* September 27, 2010, p. 31.

28. Chris Powell, "Consumer Magazine Circulation Down 4%: ABC," *Marketing,* www.marketingmag .ca, February 7, 2011; *Canadian Media Directors' Council Media Digest 10/11,* p. 12.

29. *Canadian Media Directors' Council Media Digest 10/11,* p. 12.

30. *Canadian Media Directors' Council Media Digest 10/11,* pp. 12 and 31.

31. *Canadian Media Directors' Council Media Digest 10/11,* p. 56.

32. "Outdoor Advertising Extends Reach Beyond Products to out of Home Media," *MB.com,* April 26, 2010, www.mb.com.ph.

33. t-Immersion website, www.t-immersion.com, accessed February 21, 2011.

34. Autowrapped company website, autowrapped.com, accessed February 21, 2011.

35. Interactive Advertising Bureau, "Internet Ad Revenues Reach Record Quarterly High of $6.3 Billion in Q4 '09," www.iav.net, April 7, 2010.

36. "More Than 95 Percent of All Email Is Spam," *Softpedia,* http://news.softpedia.com, accessed February 14, 2010.

37. Zmuda, "Old Navy Retires 'Supermodelquins.'"

38. Jeremiah Owyang, "2010: Marketers Get Serious about Social Media," *Forbes.com,* www .forbes.com, January 22, 2010; "Facebook Deals Free for Canadian Marketers," *Marketing,* www.marketingmag.ca, February 1, 2011.

39. Jeff Beer, "The New Dot-Com Boom," *Canadian Business,* February 14, 2011, p. 31; David Brown, "Google, Facebook Eyeing Twitter, Valued at Up to $10B," *Marketing,* www .marketingmag.ca, February 10, 2011.

40. Beer, "The New Dot-Com Boom."

41. Jeremiah Owyang, "2010: Marketers Get Serious about Social Media," *Forbes.com,* www .forbes.com, January 22, 2010.

42. Ibid.

43. Ibid.

44. "General Motors Case Study," e20portal.com, 20portal.com, accessed February 15, 2010.

45. *Canadian Media Directors' Council Media Digest 10/11,* p. 68; Rimma Kats, "Augmented Reality Is Next Big Thing in Mobile Advertising: CTIA Panel," *Mobile Marketer,* March 26, 2010, www.mobilemarketer.com.

46. Aliza Sherman, "Which Widgets to Use to Enhance Your Site," *The Digital Marketer,* http://digitalmarketer.quickanddirtytips.com, January 14, 2010.

47. Beer, "The New Dot-Com Boom," p. 30.

48. "World's Top 50 Agency Companies," *Advertising Age,* April 26, 2010, http://adage.com.

49. Bruce Rogers, "Advertising Accountability: Every CEO Wants It, But Few Know How to Get It," *iMediaConnection.com,* March 12, 2010, http://ad-tech.blogs.imediaconnection.com.

50. Advertising Standards Canada website, www.adstandards.com, accessed February 24, 2011.

51. Company website, www.telefonica.com, accessed June 10, 2010.

CHAPTER 14 MARKETOID NOTES

All Marketoids: *Canadian Media Directors' Council: Media Digest 10/11,* published by *Marketing,* September 27, 2010.

CHAPTER 15

1. Company website, www.salesforce.com, accessed June 16, 2010; Cliff Saran, "Clovd Infantes Salesforce Revenues," Computerweekly.com, February 25, 2010; Associated Press, "Salesforce.com IQ Profit Soars on Big Sales Jump," *Boston Globe,* www.boston.com, February 24, 2010; Jessica Hodgson, "Selling and Software," *Wall Street Journal,* December 16, 2009, http://online.wsj.com; "Finance Firm Partners with Salesforce.com," *BusinessWorld,* October 5, 2009, www.businessworld.com; Mary Hayes Weier, "Salesforce.com Helps Launch SaaS Company," *InformationWeek,* September 30, 2009, www.informationweek .com; Jack Loo, "Salesforce.com Opens Its First International Data Centre," *Network World,* July 16, 2009, www.networkworld.com.

2. Gerald L. Manning, Barry L. Reece, Michael Ahearne, and H. F. (Herb) MacKenzie, *Selling Today: Creating Customer Value* (Toronto: Pearson Canada, 2010), p. 29.

3. "Popular 'Ladies Night Out' Returns to the Sony Store," Canada News Wire, April 20, 2006; ProQuest document 455321592, downloaded August 6, 2011.

4. Company website, Annual Report, fiscal year end 2011, available http://phx.corporate-ir .net/phoenix.zhtml?c=83192&p=IROL-reportsannual, accessed August 6, 2011.

5. "Annoying Quotes from Sales Clerks Listed," Associated Press, October 25, 2005, http://news.yahoo.com.

6. Eric Lai, "Panasonic's Toughbook Tablet Takes Swing at Rugged Rivals," *PCWorld,* February 10, 2010, www.pcworld.com.

7. Company website, "Company Quick Facts," www.marykay.ca, accessed August 6, 2011.

8. Tenille Bonoguore, "The End of Unwanted Telemarketing… Almost," *The Globe and Mail,* www.theglobeandmail.com, accessed July 3, 2007.

9. "CRTC Announces That Xentel Has Paid a $500 000 Penalty for Misuse of the Charity Exemption to the National Do Not Call List Rules," Canada NewsWire, December 17, 2010.

10. Larry Kusch, "Call Centre Rings Up Jobs," *Winnipeg Free Press,* August 25, 2006, p. B.4; David Shipley, "Ringing in Era of Stability: Employment Province's Call-centre Industry Reaches State of High-tech Maturity," *New Brunswick Telegraph Journal,* June 4, 2007, p. A1.

11. Company website, "About Us," www.discountcar.com, accessed August 6, 2011.

12. Alexandra Lopez-Pacheco, "From Humble Start to National Brand; Discount Car and Truck Rentals," *National Post,* February 7, 2011.

13. Chris Taylor, "Changing Gears," *Sales & Marketing Management,* October 2005, pp. 34–38.

14. David Graham, "Made to Measure Online: The Tradition of Bespoke Suits Cuts a New Figure by Stepping into the Virtual Fast-Fashion World," *Toronto Star,* March 18, 2010, p. 1.

15. "WestJet Wins Airline Staff Service Excellence Award North America," Canada NewsWire, May 20, 2010.

16. "New Interactive Store Kiosk with Microsoft Silverlight Technology at NRF 2010 from Escalate Retail," *TechArena,* January 12, 2010, www.techarena.com.

17. Grant McCracken, "How Ford Got Social Marketing Right," *Harvard Business Review,* January 7, 2010, http://blogs.hbr.org.

18. Canada's Research-Based Pharmaceutical Companies, "Code of Ethical Practices," available www.canadapharma.org, accessed August 6, 2011.

19. "Five Proven Tools and Techniques to Generate Sales Leads," *Cake Marketing,* March 12, 2010, http://cakemarketing.com.

20. Barry Farber, "Break on Through," *Entrepreneur,* March 2006, www.entrepreneur.com; Paul Kaihla, "Firing Up Your Cold Calls," *Business 2.0,* December 2005, pp. 60–65.

21. "SlideShare Goes beyond PowerPoint and Adds Video," *ReadWriteWeb,* May 5, 2010, www .readwriteweb.com.

22. Kristin Zhivago, "The Tools Your Sellers Need from Your Website," *Revenue Journal,* May 25, 2006, www.revenuejournal.com.

23. Steven J. Schwartz, *How to Make Hot Cold Calls,* revised edition (Markham, ON: Fitzhenry and Whiteside, 2005).

24. Company website, www.blackanddecker.com, accessed May 6, 2010.

25. "The Livermore Way at HP," *BusinessWeek,* January 30, 2006, www.businessweek.com.

26. U.S. Department of Labor, "20 Leading Occupations of Employed Women," March 2010, www.dol.gov.

27. Frank Bucaro, "Sales Ethics: Oxymoron or Opportunity?" *Negotiator Magazine,* www .negotiatormagazine.com, accessed June 23, 2006.

28. Tanya Batallas, "Back-to-School Shoppers Get Their Penny's Worth," *Star-Ledger,* August 21, 2009, www.nj.com.

29. "CRM Best Practices," *CRM Trends,* www.crmtrends.com, accessed August 6, 2011.

30. "Coupon Fact Sheet for the Year 2006—Coupon Use in Canada," Coupon Industry Association of Canada, http://couponscanada.org/html/couponing_facts.html, accessed August 6, 2011.

31. "Study: In-Store Sampling Inspires Repeat Purchases," *Sales & Marketing Management,* www.salesandmarketing.com, accessed July 14, 2011.

32. John Molson Undergraduate Case Competition, February 2011, personal experience.

33. Rebecca Harris, "Buzz Boosts Brands," *Marketing,* February 26, 2007, p. 28.

34. Hollie Shaw, "Let the People Decide… the End; Doritos Again Engages Consumers in Super Bowl Chip-Flavour Tests," *National Post,* February 4, 2011, p. 12.

35. Mario Toneguzzi, "Calgary Promo Show Highlights Evolution of Corporate Gifts; Billion-Dollar Industry No Longer Simply Ball Caps, Pens," *Calgary Herald,* September 11, 2007, p. D1.

36. "Why Capitalize on Advertising Specialties," www.marketingmanner.com, accessed July 14, 2011.

37. Carroll Trosclair, "Point-of-Purchase Advertising Trends," *Advertising,* January 21, 2010, www.advertising.suite101.com.

38. Canadian Gift & Tableware Association website, "Gift Show Facts," www.cgta.org, accessed August 6, 2011.

CHAPTER 15 MARKETOID NOTES

Page 465   Paul Waldie, "A House Even Bill Gates Wouldn't Feel Cramped In," *The Globe and Mail,* April 12, 2010, p. 1.

Page 467   Company website, "Global Presence: India," www.sunlife.com, accessed August 6, 2011.

Page 469   Laura Stone, "Bell Fined $1.3M for Violating Do-Not-Call Rules; Penalty Record for List That Started in 2008," *Calgary Herald,* December 21, 2010, p. 1.

Page 474   Joe Girard's website, www.joegirard.com, accessed August 6, 2011.

Page 487   Wallace Kenyon, "Canadian Tire Cash Buys Dream Wheels: It Took 15 Years and $1053 in Colourful Bills to Meet Teenage Goal," *Toronto Star,* July 16, 2011, p. 10.

Page 490   Promotional Product Professionals of Canada website, "Who We Are," www.pppc .ca, accessed August 6, 2011.

CHAPTER 16

1. "Windows 7 Service Pack 1 Beta Leaks Online," *EWeek,* www.pcmag.com, April 8, 2010; Gavin Clarke, "Discounts Damage for Microsoft Windows 7 PC Boost?" *The Register,* www .theregister.co.uk, January 16, 2010; Alex Pham, "Win 7 Beats Vista in Sales; Aggressive Pricing and Positive Reviews Boost Microsoft's New Operating System," *Los Angeles Times,* www.latimes.com, November 7, 2009; Byron Acohido, "PC Prices Should Stay Low with

Windows 7," *USA Today*, www.usatoday.com, October 13, 2009; Peter Burrows, "Microsoft's Aggressive New Pricing Strategy," *BusinessWeek*, July 27, 2009, p. 51.

2. "American Airlines Blankets Will Cost 8 Dollars," *Huffington Post*, www.huffingtonpost.com, February 8, 2010; Charlie Leocha, "American Airlines Institutes a $50 Coach Standby Fee," *ConsumerTraveler.com*, www.comsumertraveler.com, February 11, 2010.

3. Andy Patrizio, "Could a Cheaper iPhone Be on the Way?" *Enterprise Mobile Today*, www.enterprisemobiletoday.com, February 26, 2010.

4. Deena M. Amato-McCoy, "Focus on Loyalty Programs," *Chain Store Age*, www.chainstoreage.com, February 1, 2010.

5. Robert D. Buzzell, Bradley T. Gale, and Ralph G. M. Sultan, "Market Share, A Key to Profitability," *Harvard Business Review*, http://hbr.org, accessed March 3, 2010.

6. Company website, Skype, www.skype.com, accessed March 3, 2010.

7. Karen Paton-Evans, "Palazzi Brothers' Golden Anniversary; Palazzi Celebrating the First 50 Years," *Windsor Star*, September 16, 2010, p. C6.

8. David Coursey, "PC Sales Up, Prices May Follow. Buy Now?" *PC World*, www.pcworld.com, January 14, 2010.

9. Company website, NetJets, www.netjets.com, accessed March 8, 2010; Thomas Flohr, "Luxury Private Jets Taking Off in Asia," *Business Times*, www.businesstimes.com, February 1, 2010.

10. Brad Tuttle, "Your Butt's Not Getting Bigger," *Time*, http://money.blogs.time.com, February 1, 2010.

11. Statistics Canada, *Canada Year Book 2010*, p. 142; Statistics Canada, *Canada Year Book 2007*, p. 170; "Canada Regains No. 2 Spot for Oil to U.S.," *Calgary Herald*, August 25, 2007, p. C4.

12. "Toyota Unveils 2010 Fuel-Sipper Prius in Detroit," *Japan Today*, www.japantoday.com, January 13, 2010; Nick Kurczewski, "World Debut: New Prius Model Line—2011 Detroit Auto Show," www.roadandtrack.com, January 10, 2011.

13. "Zimbabwe Inflation at –4.8% in January," *The Harare Tribune*, www.hararetribune.com, February 18, 2010; "Zimbabwe Inflation Rising as Disinflationary Effect of Hard-Currency Move Fades," *VOANews.com*, www1.voanews.com, February 18, 2010.

14. "Alternative Fuel Sources—Moving Away from Gas," *Clean Diesel*, http://cleandieselgeorgia.org, February 16, 2010.

15. John Neff, "Ford Earned $2.7B Profit in 2009, Predicts Repeat in 2010," *AutoBlog*, www.autoblog.com, January 28, 2010.

16. "Revenue Management Is Coming to the Spa Industry," *SpaFinder*, http://blog.spafinder.com, accessed March 9, 2010.

17. James L. McKenney, "Stouffer Yield Management System," Harvard Business School Case 9-190-193, Boston: Harvard Business School, 1994; Anirudh Dhebar and Adam Brandenburger, "American Airlines, Inc.: Revenue Management," Harvard Business School Case 9-190-029, Boston: Harvard Business School, 1992.

18. Company website, www.bestbuy.ca, accessed August 9, 2011.

19. Ibid.; www.shopbot.ca, accessed August 9, 2011.

20. Company website, www.hyundaicanada.com, accessed August 9, 2011.

21. Steve Painter and Laurie Whalen, "Wal-Mart Sets Late-Delivery Fee," *Arkansas Democrat Gazette*, February 14, 2010, G1.

22. Jenn Abelson, "Seeking Savings, Some Ditch Brand Loyalty," *Boston.com*, January 29, 2010, www.boston.com.

23. Company website, www.kia.ca, accessed August 9, 2011.

24. Company website, "Corporate Sales," www.atlanticinkjet.com, accessed August 9, 2011.

25. Company website, www.consumerreports.com, accessed March 17, 2010.

26. Brad Stone, "The Fight over Who Sets Prices at the Online Mall," *New York Times*, February 8, 2010, www.nytimes.com.

27. Paula Ebben, "Are Rebates Worth Your Time and Effort?" *WBZTV.com*, February 24, 2010, http://wbztv.com; Mark Huffman, "Consumers Continue to Fall into the Rebate Trap," *ConsumerAffairs.com*, January 5, 2010, www.consumeraffairs.com.

28. Company website, www.bestbuy.ca, accessed January 14, 2011.

29. "Consumers Don't Always Equate Higher Prices with Quality," *PhysOrg.com*, October 14, 2009, www.physorg.com.

30. Helen Anders, "Cheap Chic: Motel 6 Steps up Its Style," *Statesman.com*, January 29, 2010, www.statesman.com; company website, www.motel6.com, accessed January 14, 2011.

31. Company website, www.razorgator.com, accessed March 17, 2010; company website, www.ticketliquidator.com, accessed March 17, 2010.

32. Company website, www.pageonce.com, accessed March 18, 2010; company website, www.ubid.com, accessed March 18, 2010; Murad Ahmed, "eBay's Fixed-Price Sales Over-take Profits from Web Auctions," *Times Online*, December 10, 2009, www.technology.timesonline.co.uk.

33. Company website, www.containerstore.com, accessed March 18, 2010; company website, www.lowes.com, accessed March 18, 2010; Steve Banker, "Multichannel Logistics: Walmart.com's Site-to-Store Strategy," *Logistics Viewpoints*, January 27, 2010, http://logisticsviewpoints.com.

34. "Canada and EU Hit U.S. with Retaliatory Tariffs," *International Herald Tribune*, May 2, 2005, www.iht.com.

35. Ben Charny, "Net Telephone Fees Have Users Fuming," CNet News, January 27, 2005, http://news.com.com.

36. Neil Scott, "SaskTel to Fight Class-action Suit over Cell Charges," *Vancouver Sun*, September 21, 2007, p. C2; "Key Developments for Saskatchewan Telecommunications International, Inc.," businessweek.com, December 14, 2010.

37. Competition Bureau Canada, "Law & Litigation—About the Acts," www.competitionbureau.gc.ca, accessed February 17, 2008.

38. *Competition Law* (North York, ON: CCH Canadian Limited, 1995), p. 4202.

39. Lynn Moore, "Magog Gas Station Owner Fined for Retail Price Fixing; 'Small Fish'; Consumers Should Be Repaid," *Gazette* (Montreal), June 1, 2011, p. 3.

40. "British and Korean Airlines Each Fined $300 Million," *Times-Colonist* (Victoria, B.C.), August 24, 2007, p. D7; "Qantas to Plead Guilty to Price Fixing," *National Post*, November 28, 2007, p. FP18; Huw Jones, "Airlines Charged with Price-fixing; Major European Carriers among Those Affected," *The Gazette* (Montreal), December 22, 2007, p. C5; "Air Canada Included in EC Price-fixing Probe," *The Globe and Mail*, December 26, 2007, p. B2.

41. Matthew Newman, "Videotape Makers Fined $110.5 Million for Price-fixing," *Ottawa Citizen*, November 21, 2007, p. D5.

42. Thomas Claridge, "Four Convicted of Rigging Bids," *The Globe and Mail*, December 20, 1997, p. B5.

43. "Japan: Errant Fax Reveals Firms' Price-fixing Scam," *Ottawa Citizen*, November 10, 2007, p. A10.

44. "Drug Maker Hit with 'Predatory' Prices Penalty," *Toronto Star*, March 15, 2007, p. C2.

45. "Airline Ticket Advertisers Targeted over False Claims," *The Globe and Mail*, November 15, 2007, p. B14.

46. "Retailer Carrefour Fined $2.88 Million for False Ads," *Toronto Star*, June 27, 2007, p. B2.

47. Industry Canada, "Premier Health Club Found Guilty of Misleading Advertising under the Competition Act," news release, April 19, 2005, www.ic.gc.ca/, accessed May 27, 2005; Mitch Moxley, "GoodLife to Pay $75,000 for Misleading Advertising," *National Post*, February 10, 2005, p. FP5.

48. Colin Gibbs, "Dell Wisely Chooses Emerging Markets for Smartphone Play," GigaOM, November 13, 2009, http://gigaom.com.

CHAPTER 16 MARKETOID NOTES

Page 506   Dave McGinn, "World's Most Expensive Dog Sold for $1.5 Million," www.theglobeandmail.com, March 16, 2011.

Page 512   John Philippe, "Getting 'Mileage' Out of Tax Hikes," *Telegraph-Journal* (Saint John, N.B.), April 6, 2011, p. 7.

Page 517   Personal air fare for trip to Paris; "Air Canada Fined for Deceptive Ads," *Calgary Herald*, August 5, 2011, p. C3.

Page 529   "Online Piano Guide," www.onlinepianoguide.com, accessed August 9, 2011; alibaba.com, www.alibaba.com/countrysearch/CN/piano.html, accessed August 9, 2011.

Page 531   Company websites, http://cars.ebay.ca and http://stores.ebay.ca/Police-Auctions-Canada, both accessed August 9, 2011.

Page 534   "Bayer Fined $3.65 million for Price-fixing," *The Globe and Mail*, October 31, 2007, p. B8.

APPENDIX B NOTES

1. "Benefits of a CRM System," Customer Service Point, www.customerserve.point.com, accessed March 7, 2010; "Benefits of CRM," Syatems2Business, www.systems2business.com, accessed March 7, 2010; Gene Gander, "10 Ways an Integrated CRM Tool Can Improve the Forwarding Process," *The Journal of Commerce*, www.joc.com, accessed March 7, 2010.

2. "How to Avoid CRM Implementation Failures," Market for Cause, http://marketforcause.com, February 8, 2010.

glossary

A

accessory equipment Capital items like desktop computers and printers that typically cost less and last for shorter periods of time than installations. p. 273

administered marketing system VMS that achieves channel coordination when a dominant channel member exercises its power. p. 338

adoption process Stages that consumers go through in learning about a new product, trying it, and deciding whether to purchase it again. p. 309

advertising Paid, nonpersonal communication through various media about a business, not-for-profit organization, product, or idea by a sponsor identified in a message that is intended to inform, remind or persuade members of a particular audience. p. 403

advertising agency Firm whose marketing specialists assist advertisers in planning and preparing advertisements. p. 447

advertising campaign Series of different but related ads that use a single theme and appear in different media within a specified time period. p. 436

affinity marketing Marketing effort sponsored by an organization that solicits responses from individuals who share common interests and activities. p. App B 14

AIDA concept Steps through which an individual reaches a purchase decision: attention, interest, desire, and action. p. 397

AIO statements Items on lifestyle surveys that describe various activities, interests, and opinions of respondents. p. 249

allowance Specified deduction from list price, including a trade-in or promotional allowance. p. 523

ambush marketing Attempt by a firm that is not an official sponsor of an event or activity to link itself to the event or activity. p. 409

approach Salesperson's initial contact with a prospective customer. p. 476

atmospherics Combination of physical characteristics and amenities that contribute to a store's image. p. 368

attitudes Person's enduring favourable or unfavourable evaluations, emotions, or action tendencies toward some object or idea. p. 120

average total costs Costs calculated by dividing the sum of the variable and fixed costs by the number of units produced. p. 510

B

baby boomers People born between the years of 1947 and 1965. p. 241

backward integration Process through which a manufacturer attempts to gain greater control over inputs in its production process, such as raw materials. p. 338

banners Advertisements on a Web page that link to an advertiser's site. p. 438

basing-point pricing System used in some industries during the early 20th century in which the buyer paid the factory price plus freight charges from the basing-point city nearest the buyer. p. 525

benchmarking Method of measuring quality by comparing performance against industry leaders. p. 278

bid rigging A form of collusion, similar to price fixing, which occurs when sellers get together and collude to set prices with respect to one or more competitive proposals. p. 535

bonus pack Specially packaged item that gives the purchaser a larger quantity at the regular price. p. 490

bots (shopbots) Online search programs that act as comparison shopping agents. p. 532

bottom line Business jargon referring to the overall profitability of an organization. p. 14

brand Name, term, sign, symbol, design, or some combination that identifies the products of one firm while differentiating them from the competition's. p. 296

brand equity Added value that a respected, well-known brand name gives to a product in the marketplace. p. 300

brand extension Strategy of attaching a popular brand name to a new product in an unrelated product category. p. 307

brand insistence Consumer refusals of alternatives, resulting in an extensive search for desired merchandise. p. 297

brand licensing Firm's authorization of other companies to use its brand names. p. 307

brand manager Marketer within an organization who is responsible for a single brand. p. 301

brand mark Symbol or pictorial design that distinguishes a product. p. 303

brand name Part of a brand consisting of words, numbers or letters that can be spoken and that identifies and distinguished a firm's offerings from those of its competitors. p. 303

brand preference Consumer reliance on previous experiences with a product to choose that product again. p. 297

brand recognition Consumer awareness and identification of a brand. p. 297

break-even analysis Pricing technique used to determine the number of products that must be sold at a specified price to generate enough revenue to cover total cost. p. 515

broker Agent wholesaling intermediary who does not take title to or possession of goods in the course of its primary function, which is to bring together buyers and sellers. p. 379

B2C products *See* consumer products.

bundle pricing Offering two or more complementary products and selling them for a single price. p. 532

business cycle Pattern of differing stages in the level of economic activity of a nation or region. Although the traditional cycle includes the four stages of prosperity, recession, depression, and recovery, most economists believe that future depressions can be prevented through effective economic policies. p. 80

business plan Formal document that outlines a company's objectives, how they will be met, how the business will achieve financing, and how much money the firm expects to earn. p. 57

business products Goods and services purchased for use either directly or indirectly in the production of other goods and services for resale. p. 235

business services Intangible products that firms buy to facilitate their production and operating processes. p. 275

business-to-business (B2B) marketing Organizational sales and purchases of goods and services to support production of other products, for daily company operations, or for resale. p. 138

business-to-business (B2B) product Product that contributes directly or indirectly to the output of other products for resale; also called industrial or organizational product. p. 269

buyer Person who has the formal authority to select a supplier and to implement the procedures for securing a good or service. p. 160

buyer concerns Expressions of sales resistance (previously called *objections*). p. 478

buyer's market Market in which there are more goods and services than people willing to buy them. p. 9

buying centre Participants involved in an organizational buying decision. p. 159

buzz marketing Marketing that gathers volunteers to try products and then relies on them to talk about their experiences with their friends and colleagues. p. 19

C

cannibalization Loss of sales of an existing product due to competition from a new product in the same line. pp. 309, 532

captive brand National brands that are sold exclusively by a retail chain. p. 299

cash discount Price reduction offered to a consumer, business user, or marketing intermediary in return for prompt payment of a bill. p. 522

category advisor (category captain) Vendor who is responsible for dealing with all the suppliers for a project and then presenting the entire package to the buyer. p. 154

category killer Store that offers huge selections and low prices in single product lines. p. 371

category management Product management system in which a category manager—with profit and loss responsibility—oversees a product line. p. 301

cause marketing Identification and marketing of a social issue, cause, or idea to selected target markets. p. 16

census agglomeration (CA) Geographic area with a population over 10 000. p. 238

census metropolitan area (CMA) Geographic area surrounding an urban core with a population of at least 100 000. p. 238

channel Medium through which a message is delivered. p. 397

channel captain Dominant and controlling member of a marketing channel. p. 336

click-throughs *See* cost per response.

closed sales territory Exclusive geographic selling region of a distributor. p. 335

closing Stage of the personal selling process where the salesperson asks the customer to make a purchase decision. p. 478

cognitive dissonance Imbalance between knowledge, beliefs and attitudes that occurs after an action or decision is taken, such as a purchase. p. 126

cohort effect Tendency of members of a generation to be influenced and bound together by events occurring during their key formative years—roughly 17 to 22 years of age. p. 242

cold calling Contacting a prospect without a prior appointment. p. 477

commercial market Individuals and firms that acquire products to support, directly or indirectly, production of other goods and services. p. 140

commission Incentive compensation directly related to the sales or profits achieved by a salesperson. p. 483

commission merchant Agent wholesaling intermediary who takes possession of goods shipped to a central market for sale, acts as the producer's agent, and collects an agreed-upon fee at the time of the sale. p. 378

common carriers Businesses that provide transportation services as for-hire carriers to the general public. p. 345

common market Extension of a customs union by seeking to reconcile all government regulations affecting trade. p. 182

comparative advertising Advertising strategy that emphasizes messages with direct or indirect promotional comparisons between competing brands. p. 433

Competition Act The most comprehensive legislation in Canada, designed to help both consumers and businesses by promoting a healthy competitive environment. pp. 76, 534

competitive bidding Inviting potential suppliers to quote prices on proposed purchases or contracts. p. 529

competitive environment Interactive process that occurs in the marketplace among marketers of directly competitive products, marketers of products that can be substituted for one another, and marketers competing for the consumer's purchasing power. p. 73

competitive pricing strategy Pricing strategy designed to de-emphasize price as a competitive variable by pricing a good or service at the general level of comparable offerings. p. 521

competitive strategy Methods through which a firm deals with its competitive environment. p. 75

component parts and materials Finished business products of one producer that become part of the final products of another producer. p. 274

concentrated marketing Focusing marketing efforts on satisfying a single market segment; also called *niche marketing*. p. 254

concept testing Method for subjecting a product idea to additional study before actual development by involving consumers through focus groups, surveys, in-store polling, and the like. p. 314

consultative selling Meeting customer needs by listening to customers, understanding their problems, paying attention to details, and following through after the sale. p. 471

consumer behaviour Process through which buyers make purchase decisions. p. 108

consumer innovators People who purchase new products almost as soon as the products reach the market. p. 309

consumer orientation Business philosophy incorporating the marketing concept that emphasizes first determining unmet consumer needs and then designing a system for satisfying them. p. 9

consumer products Products bought by ultimate consumers for personal use. p. 234

consumer rights In their most basic form, these rights include a person's right to choose goods and services freely, to be informed about these products and services, to be heard, and to be safe. p. 88

consumerism Social force within the environment designed to aid and protect the consumer by exerting legal, moral, and economic pressures on business and government. p. 87

containerization Process of combining several unitized loads into a single, well-protected load for shipment. p. 352

contest Sales promotional technique that requires entrants to complete a task such as solving a puzzle or answering questions on a quiz for the chance to win a prize. p. 490

contract carriers For-hire transporters that do not offer their services to the general public. p. 345

contractual marketing system VMS that coordinates channel activities through formal agreements among participants. p. 338

controlled experiment Scientific investigation in which a researcher manipulates a test group (or groups) and compares the results with those of a control group that did not receive the experimental controls or manipulations. p. 218

convenience products Goods and services that consumers want to purchase frequently, immediately, and with minimal effort. p. 270

convenience retailer Store that appeals to customers on accessible location, long hours, rapid checkout, and adequate parking. p. 370

conversion rate The percentage of visitors to a website who make a purchase. p. 419

cooperative advertising Strategy in which a retailer shares advertising costs with a manufacturer or wholesaler. p. 434

core region Region from which most major brands get 40 to 80 percent of their sales. p. 238

corporate marketing system VMS in which a single owner operates the entire marketing channel. p. 338

cost per impression Measurement technique that relates the cost of an ad to every thousand people who view it. p. 419

cost per response (also called *click-throughs*) Direct marketing technique that relates the cost of an ad to the number of people who click it. p. 419

cost-plus pricing Practice of adding a percentage of specified dollar amount—or markup—to the base cost of a product to cover unassigned costs and to provide a profit. p. 514

countertrade Form of exporting whereby goods and services are bartered rather than sold for cash. p. 192

coupon Sales promotional technique that offers a discount on the purchase price of goods or services. p. 487

creative selling Personal selling that involves situations in which a considerable degree of analytical decision making on the buyer's part results in the need for skillful proposals of solutions for the customer's needs. p. 473

cross promotion Promotional technique in which marketing partners share the cost of a promotional campaign that meets their mutual needs. p. 435

cross-selling Selling of multiple, often unrelated goods and services to the same customer based on knowledge of that customer's needs. p. 471

culture Values, beliefs, preferences, and tastes handed down from one generation to the next in a society. p. 108

cumulative quantity discount Price discount determined by amounts of purchases over stated time periods. p. 523

customary prices Traditional prices that customers expect to pay for certain goods and services. p. 508

customer relationship management (CRM) Combination of strategies and tools that drives relationship programs, reorienting the entire organization to a concentrated focus on satisfying customers. p. 145

customer satisfaction Extent to which customers are satisfied with their purchases. p. App B 12

customer winback Process of rejuvenating lost relationships with customers. p. App B 17

customer-based segmentation Dividing a business-to-business market into homogeneous groups based on buyers' product specifications. p. 143

customs union Establishment of a free trade area plus a uniform tariff for trade with non-member unions. p. 182

D

data mining Process of searching through customer databases to detect patterns that guide marketing decision making. p. 221

database marketing Use of software to analyze marketing information, identifying and targeting messages toward specific groups of potential customers. p. App B 14

decider Person who chooses a good or service, although another person may have the formal authority to do so. p. 159

decline stage Final stage of the product life cycle, in which a decline in total industry sales occurs. p. 285

decoding Receiver's interpretation of a message. p. 397

Delphi technique Qualitative sales forecasting method that gathers and redistributes several rounds of anonymous forecasts until the participants reach a consensus. p. 223

demand Schedule of the amounts of a firm's product that consumers will purchase at different prices during a specified time period. p. 508

demarketing Process of reducing consumer demand for a good or service to a level that the firm can supply. p. 82

demographic segmentation Division of an overall market into homogeneous groups based on variables such as gender, age, income, occupation, education, sexual orientation, household size, and stage in the family life cycle; also called *socioeconomic segmentation*. p. 239

demonstration Stage in the personal selling process in which the customer has the opportunity to try out or otherwise see how a good or service works before purchase. p. 477

department store Large store that handles a variety of merchandise, including clothing, household goods, appliances, and furniture. p. 371

derived demand Demand for a resource that results from demand for the goods and services that are produced by that resource. p. 149

differentiated marketing Market strategy that focuses on producing several products and pricing, promoting, and distributing them with different marketing mixes designed to satisfy smaller segments. p. 254

diffusion process Process by which new goods or services are accepted in the marketplace. p. 310

direct channel Marketing channel that moves goods directly from a producer to the business purchaser or ultimate user. p. 328

direct mail Communications in the form of sales letters, postcards, brochures, catalogues, and the like conveying messages directly from the marketer to the customer. p. 410

direct marketing Direct communications, other than personal sales contacts, between buyer and seller, designed to generate sales, information requests, or store or website visits. p. 380

direct sales results test Method for measuring promotional effectiveness based on the specific impact on sales revenues for each dollar of promotional spending. p. 418

direct selling Strategy designed to establish direct sales contact between producer and final user. p. 328

discount house Store that charges low prices but may not offer services such as credit. p. 372

discretionary income Money people have available to spend after buying necessities such as food, clothing, and housing. p. 82

distribution Movement of goods and services from producers to customers. p. 326

distribution strategy Planning that ensures that consumers find their products in the proper quantities at the right times and places. p. 44

downstream management Controlling part of the supply chain that involves finished product storage, outbound logistics, marketing and sales, and customer service. p. 341

drop shipper Limited-function merchant wholesaler who accepts orders from customers and forwards these orders to producers, which then ship directly to the customers who place the orders. p. 378

dual distribution Network that moves products to a firm's target market through more than one marketing channel. p. 331

dumping Practice of selling a product in a foreign market at a price lower than what it receives in the product's domestic market p. 182

E

80/20 principle Generally accepted rule that 80 percent of a product's revenues come from 20 percent of its total customers. p. 252

economic environment Factors that influence consumer buying power and marketing strategies, including stage of the business cycle, inflation, unemployment, income, and resource availability. p. 80

elasticity Measure of responsiveness of purchasers and suppliers to a change in price. p. 511

electronic data interchange (EDI) Computer-to-computer exchanges of invoices, orders, and other business documents. p. App B 19

embargo A complete ban on the import of a product. p. 181

emergency goods and services Products bought in response to unexpected and urgent needs. p. 270

employee satisfaction Employee's level of satisfaction for his or her company and the extent to which that loyalty or lack of loyalty is communicated to external customers. p. App B 11

encoding Translating a message into understandable terms. p. 397

end-use application segmentation Segmenting a business-to-business market based on how industrial purchasers will use the product. p. 144

enterprise resource planning (ERP) system Software system that consolidates data from among a firm's various business units. p. 342

environmental management Attainment of organizational objectives by predicting and influencing the competitive, political–legal, economic, technological, and social–cultural environments. p. 72

environmental scanning Process of collecting information about the external marketing environment to identify and interpret potential trends. p. 72

ethics Moral standards of behaviour expected by a society. p. 22

European Union (EU) Customs union that is moving in the direction of an economic union by adopting a common currency, removing trade restrictions, and permitting free flow of goods and workers throughout the member nations. p. 185

evaluative criteria Features that a consumer considers in choosing among alternatives. p. 126

event marketing Marketing of sporting, cultural, and charitable activities to selected target markets. p. 16

everyday low pricing (EDLP) Pricing strategy of continuously offering low prices rather than relying on such short-term price cuts as cents-off coupons, rebates, and special sales. p. 520

evoked set Number of alternatives that a consumer actually considers in making a purchase decision. p. 125

exchange control Method used to regulate the privilege of international trade among importing organizations by controlling access to foreign currencies. p. 181

exchange functions Buying and selling functions of marketing. p. 21

exchange process Activity in which two or more parties give something of value to each other to satisfy perceived needs. p. 8

exchange rate Price of one nation's currency in terms of another country's currency. p. 176

exclusive distribution Distribution of a product through a single wholesaler or retailer in a specific geographic region. p. 334

expectancy theory Theory stating that motivation depends on an individual's expectations of his or her ability to perform a job and how that performance relates to attaining a desired reward. p. 482

exploratory research Process of discussing a marketing problem with informed sources both within and outside the firm and examining information from secondary sources. p. 208

exponential smoothing Quantitative forecasting technique that assigns weights to historical sales data, giving the greatest weight to the most recent data. p. 224

exporting Marketing domestically produced goods and services in foreign countries. p. 172

extended problem solving Situation that involves lengthy external searches and long deliberation; results when brands are difficult to categorize or evaluate. p. 128

external customer People or organizations that buy or use another firm's goods or services. p. App B 10

F

false or misleading ordinary selling price representation A form of misleading advertising where consumers are misled with regard to the regular price of a product. p. 535

family brand Single brand name that identifies several related products. p. 299

family life cycle Process of family formation and dissolution. p. 245

feedback Receiver's response to a message. p. 397

field selling Sales presentations made at prospective customers' locations on a face-to-face basis. p. 466

first mover strategy Theory advocating that the company that is first to offer a product in a marketplace will be the long-term market winner. p. 40

fixed costs Costs that remain stable at any production level within a certain range (such as lease payments or insurance costs). p. 510

fixed-sum-per-unit method Method of promotional budgeting in which a predetermined amount is allocated to each sales or production unit. p. 417

FOB (free on board) plant (FOB origin) Price quotation that does not include shipping charges. p. 524

focus group Simultaneous personal interview of a small group of individuals, which relies on group discussion about a certain topic. p. 216

follow-up Post-sales activities that often determine whether an individual who has made a recent purchase will become a repeat customer. p. 479

foreign licensing Agreement that grants foreign marketers the right to distribute a firm's merchandise or to use its trademark, patent, or process in a specified geographic area. p. 188

forward integration Process through which a firm attempts to control downstream distribution. p. 338

franchise Contractual arrangement in which a wholesaler or retailer agrees to meet the operating requirements of a manufacturer or other franchiser. pp. 188, 339

free trade area Region in which participating nations agree to the free trade of goods among themselves, abolishing tariffs and trade restrictions. p. 182

Free Trade Area of the Americas (FTAA) Proposed free trade area stretching the length of the entire Western hemisphere and designed to extend free trade benefits to additional nations in North, Central, and South America. p. 184

frequency marketing Frequent buyer or user marketing programs that reward customers with cash, rebates, merchandise, or other premiums. p. App B 14

full-cost pricing Pricing method that uses all relevant variable costs in setting a product's price and also allocates those fixed costs that cannot be directly attributed to the production of the specific item being priced. p. 514

full-service research supplier Marketing research organization that contracts with clients to conduct complete marketing research project. p. 206

G

gatekeeper Person who controls the information that all buying centre members will review. p. 159

General Agreement on Tariffs and Trade (GATT) International trade accord that has helped reduce world tariffs. p. 184

general merchandise retailer Store that carries a wide variety of product lines, stocking all of them in some depth. p. 371

Generation X The group born between 1966 and 1981—who are now in their early 30s to early 40s. p. 241

generic products Products characterized by plain labels, no advertising, and the absence of brand names. p. 297

geographic segmentation Division of an overall market into homogeneous groups based on their locations. p. 236

global marketing strategy Standardized marketing mix with minimal modifications that a firm uses in all its domestic and foreign markets. p. 190

global sourcing Purchasing goods and services from suppliers worldwide. p. 148

good Tangible product that customers can see, hear, smell, taste, or touch. p. 266

goods–services continuum Spectrum along which goods and services fall according to their attributes, from pure good to pure service. p. 267

grassroots marketing Efforts that connect directly with existing and potential customers through non-mainstream channels. p. App B 15

green marketing Production, promotion, and reclamation of environmentally sensitive products. p. 97

grey goods Products manufactured abroad under licence from a Canadian firm and then sold in the Canadian market in competition with that firm's own domestic output. p. 337

gross domestic product (GDP) Sum of all goods and services produced by a nation in a year. p. 80

growth stage Second stage of the product life cycle, which begins when a firm starts to realize substantial profits from its investment in the product. p. 284

guerrilla marketing Unconventional, innovative, and low-cost marketing techniques designed to get consumers' attention in unusual ways. p. 405

H

high-involvement purchase decision Buying decision that evokes high levels of potential social or economic consequence. p. 124

home shopping channel Television direct marketing in which a variety of products are offered and consumers can order them directly by phone or online. p. 412

hypermarkets Giant one-stop shopping facilities that offer wide selections of grocery and general merchandise products at discount prices typically filling up 200 000 or more square feet of selling space (about a third larger than most supercentres). p. 372

hypothesis Tentative explanation for some specific event. p. 208

I

import quotas Trade restrictions that limit the number of units of certain goods that can enter a country for resale. p. 108

importing Purchasing foreign goods, services, and raw materials. p. 172

impulse goods and services Products purchased on the spur of the moment. p. 270

inbound telemarketing Sales method in which prospects call a toll-free number to obtain information, make reservations, and purchase goods and services. p. 469

incremental-cost pricing Pricing method that attempts to use only costs directly attributable to a specific output in setting prices. p. 514

indirect evaluation Method for measuring promotional effectiveness by concentrating on quantifiable indicators of effectiveness such as recall and readership. p. 418

individual brand Single brand that uniquely identifies a product itself. p. 299

industrial products *See* business-to-business (B2B) product.

inelastic demand Demand that, throughout an industry, will not change significantly due to a price change. p. 149

inflation Rising prices caused by some combination of excess consumer demand and increases in the costs of one or more factors of production. p. 81

influencers Typically, technical staff such as engineers who affect the buying decision by supplying information to guide evaluation of alternatives or by setting buying specifications. p. 159

infomercial Paid 30-minute product commercial that resembles a regular television program. p. 412

informative advertising Promotion that seeks to develop initial demand for a good, service, organization, person, place, idea, or cause. p. 432

inside selling Selling by phone, mail, and electronic commerce. p. 469

installations Business products like factories, assembly lines, and huge machinery that are major capital investments. p. 273

institutional advertising Promotion of a concept, idea, philosophy, or goodwill of an industry, company, organization, person, geographic location, or government agency. p. 431

integrated marketing communications (IMC) Coordination of all promotional activities to produce a unified, customer-focused promotional message. p. 392

intensive distribution Distribution of a product through all available channels. p. 334

interactive advertising Two-way promotional messages transmitted through communication channels that induce message recipients to participate actively in the promotional effort. p. 434

interactive marketing Buyer–seller communications in which the customer controls the amount and type of information received from a marketer through such channels as the Internet, CD-ROMs, interactive toll-free telephone numbers, and virtual reality kiosks. p. 18

intermodal operations Combination of transport modes such as rail and highway carriers (piggyback), air and highway carriers (birdyback), and water and highway carriers (fishyback) to improve customer service and achieve cost advantages. p. 346

internal customer Employees or departments within an organization that depend on the work of another employee or department to perform tasks. p. App B 10

internal marketing Managerial actions that help all members of the organization understand and accept their respective roles in implementing a marketing strategy. p. App B 10

interpretative research Observational research method developed by social anthropologists in which customers are observed in their natural setting and their behaviour is interpreted based on an understanding of social and cultural characteristics; also known as *ethnography*, or going native. p. 214

introductory stage First stage of the product life cycle, in which a firm works to stimulate demand for the new market entry. p. 283

ISO (International Organization for Standardization) certification Internationally recognized standards that ensure a company's goods and services meet established quality levels and that ensure its operations minimize harm to the environment. p. 178

ISO 9001:2000 International quality standards developed by the International Organization for Standardization in Switzerland to ensure consistent quality among products manufactured and sold throughout the European Union (EU). p. 278

J

joint demand Demand for a product that depends on the demand for another product used in combination with it. p. 149

jury of executive opinion Qualitative sales forecasting method that assesses the sales expectations of various executives. p. 222

just-in-time (JIT)/just-in-time II (JIT II) Inventory practices that seek to boost efficiency by cutting inventories to absolute minimum levels. With JIT II, suppliers' representatives work at the customer's facility. p. 150

L

label Branding component that carries an item's brand name or symbol, the name and address of the manufacturer or distributor, information about the product, and recommended uses. p. 306

leader pricing Variant of loss-leader pricing in which marketers offer prices slightly above cost to avoid violating minimum-markup regulations and earn a minimal return on promotional sales. p. 528

learning Knowledge or skill that is acquired as a result of experience, which changes consumer behaviour. p. 122

limited problem solving Situation in which the consumer invests some small amount of time and energy in searching for and evaluating alternatives. p. 128

limited-line store Retailer that offers a large assortment within a single product line or within a few related product lines. p. 371

limited-service research supplier Marketing research firm that specializes in a limited number of research activities, such as conducting field interviews or performing data processing. p. 206

line extension Development of individual offerings that appeal to different market segments while remaining closely related to the existing product line. p. 282

list price Established price normally quoted to potential buyers. p. 521

logistics Process of coordinating the flow of information, goods, and services among members of the distribution channel. p. 326

loss leader Product offered to consumers at less than cost to attract them to stores in the hope that they will buy other merchandise at regular prices. p. 528

low-involvement purchase decision Routine purchase that poses little risk to the consumer, either socially or economically. p. 124

M

mail-order wholesaler Limited-function merchant wholesaler who distributes catalogues instead of sending sales representatives to contact customers. p. 378

mall intercepts Interviews conducted inside retail shopping centres. p. 215

manufacturer's brand Brand name owned by a manufacturer or other producer. p. 298

manufacturers' representative Agent wholesaling intermediary who represents a number of manufacturers of related but noncompeting products and who receives a commission on each sale. pp. 331, 379

marginal analysis Method of analyzing the relationship between costs, sales price, and increased sales volume. p. 504

marginal cost Change in total cost that results from producing an additional unit of output. p. 510

markdown Amount by which a retailer reduces the original selling price of a product. p. 366

market Group of people with sufficient purchasing power, authority, and willingness to buy. p. 234

market development strategy Strategy that concentrates on finding new markets for existing products. p. 308

market penetration strategy Strategy that seeks to increase sales of existing products in existing markets. p. 308

market price Price that a consumer or marketing intermediary actually pays for a product after subtracting any discounts, allowances, or rebates from the list price. p. 522

market segmentation Division of the total market into smaller, relatively homogeneous groups. p. 235

marketing Organizational function and a set of processes for creating, communicating, and delivering value to customers and for managing customer relationships in ways that benefit the organization and its stakeholders. p. 6

marketing (distribution) channel System of marketing institutions that enhances the physical flow of goods and services, along with ownership title, from producer to consumer or business user. p. 326

marketing communications Messages that deal with buyer–seller relationships. p. 392

marketing concept Company-wide consumer orientation with the objective of achieving long-run success. p. 9

marketing decision support system (MDSS) Marketing information system component that links a decision maker with relevant databases and analysis tools. p. 220

marketing ethics Marketers' standards of conduct and moral values. p. 90

marketing information system (MIS) Planned, computer-based system designed to provide managers with a continuous flow of information relevant to their specific decisions and areas of responsibility. p. 220

marketing intermediary (middleman) Wholesaler or retailer that operates between producers and consumers or business users. p. 327

marketing mix Blending of the four strategy elements—product, distribution, promotion, and pricing—to fit the needs and preferences of a specific target market. p. 44

marketing myopia Management's failure to recognize the scope of its business. p. 12

marketing plan Detailed description of the resources and actions needed to achieve stated marketing objectives. p. 57

marketing planning Implementing planning activities devoted to achieving marketing objectives. p. 33

marketing public relations (MPR) Narrowly focused public relations activities that directly support marketing goals. p. 407

marketing research Process of collecting and using information for marketing decision making. p. 204

marketing strategy Overall company-wide program for selecting a particular target market and then satisfying consumers in that market through the marketing mix. p. 37

market-share objective Volume-related pricing objective in which the goal is to achieve control of a portion of the market for a firm's good or service. p. 505

markup Amount that a retailer adds to the cost of a product to determine its selling price. p. 366

mass merchandiser Store that stocks a wider line of goods than a department store, usually without the same depth of assortment within each line. p. 372

materials handling system Set of activities that move production inputs and other goods within plants, warehouses, and transportation terminals. p. 351

maturity stage Third stage of the product life cycle, in which industry sales level out. p. 284

media research Advertising research that assesses how well a particular medium delivers an advertiser's message, where and when to place the advertisement, and the size of the audience. p. 449

media scheduling Setting the timing and sequence for a series of advertisements. p. 446

meeting competition Method of promotional budgeting that simply matches competitors' outlays. p. 417

merchandisers Buyers who are responsible for securing needed business products at the best possible prices. p. 154

merchant wholesaler Independently owned wholesaling intermediary who takes title to the goods that it handles; also known as an industrial distributor in the business-goods market. p. 377

message Communication of information, advice, or a request by the sender to the receiver. p. 396

message research Advertising research that tests consumer reactions to an advertisement's creative message. p. 449

microcultures Smaller groups within a society that have their own distinct characteristics and modes of behaviour. p. 110

micromarketing Targeting potential customers at very narrow, basic levels, such as by postal code, specific occupation, or lifestyle—possibly even individuals themselves. p. 255

middleman *See* marketing intermediary.

minimum advertised pricing (MAP) Fees paid to retailers that agree not to advertise products below set prices. p. 523

mission Essential purpose that differentiates one company from others. p. 37

missionary selling Indirect type of selling in which specialized salespeople promote the firm's goodwill among indirect customers, often by assisting customers in product use. p. 474

mobile marketing Marketing messages transmitted via wireless technology. p. 18

modified rebuy Situation in which a purchaser is willing to re-evaluate available options for repurchasing a good or service. p. 158

monopolistic competition Market structure involving a heterogeneous product and product differentiation among competing suppliers, allowing the marketer some degree of control over prices. p. 509

monopoly Market structure in which a single seller dominates trade in a good or service for which buyers can find no close substitutes. pp. 73, 509

motive Inner state that directs a person toward the goal of satisfying a need. p. 117

MRO items Business supplies that include maintenance items, repair items, and operating supplies. p. 275

multi-domestic marketing strategy Application of market segmentation to foreign markets by tailoring the firm's marketing mix to match specific target markets in each nation. p. 191

multinational corporation Firm with significant operations and marketing activities outside its home country. p. 189

multiple sourcing Purchasing from several vendors. p. 154

N

national accounts organization Organizational arrangement that assigns sales teams to a firm's largest accounts. p. 482

nearshoring Moving jobs to vendors in countries close to the business's home country. p. 152

need Imbalance between a consumer's actual and desired states. p. 117

network marketing Personal selling that relies on lists of family members and friends of the salesperson who organizes a gathering of potential customers for a demonstration of products. p. 467

new-task buying First-time or unique purchase situation that requires considerable effort by decision makers. p. 158

noise Any stimulus that distracts a receiver from receiving a message. p. 397

noncumulative quantity discount Price reduction granted on a one-time-only basis. p. 523

nonmarketing public relations Organizational messages about general management issues. p. 407

nonpersonal selling Promotion that includes advertising, product placement, sales promotion, direct marketing, guerrilla marketing, and public relations—all conducted without being face to face with the buyer. p. 403

nonprobability sample Sample that involves personal judgment somewhere in the selection process. p. 213

North American Free Trade Agreement (NAFTA) Accord removing trade barriers among Canada, Mexico, and the United States. p. 184

North American Industry Classification System (NAICS) Classification used by NAFTA countries to categorize the business marketplace into detailed market segments. p. 144

O

odd pricing Pricing policy based on the belief that a price ending with an odd number just under a round number is more appealing—for instance, $9.97 rather than $10. p. 526

offshoring Movement of high-wage jobs from Canada to lower-cost overseas locations. p. 152

oligopoly Market structure, like those in the steel and telecommunications industries, in which relatively few sellers compete, and where high start-up costs form barriers to keep out new competitors. pp. 74, 509

opening price point Setting an opening price below that of the competition, usually on a high-quality private-label item. p. 521

opinion leaders Trendsetters who purchase new products before others in a group and then influence others in their purchases. p. 115

order processing Selling, mostly at the wholesale and retail levels, that involves identifying customer needs, pointing them out to customers, and completing orders. p. 473

organization marketing Marketing by mutual-benefit organizations, service organizations, and government organizations intended to influence others to accept their goals, receive their services, or contribute to them in some way. p. 17

organizational product *See* business-to-business (B2B) product.

outbound telemarketing Sales method in which sales representatives place phone calls to prospects and try to conclude the sale over the phone. p. 468

outsourcing Using outside vendors to produce goods and services formerly produced in-house. p. 152

over-the-counter selling Personal selling conducted in retail and some wholesale locations in which customers come to the seller's place of business. p. 465

P

partnership Affiliation of two or more companies that assist each other in the achievement of common goals. p. App B 17

penetration pricing strategy Pricing strategy involving the use of a relatively low entry price compared with competitive offerings, based on the theory that this initial low price will help secure market acceptance. p. 519

percentage-of-sales method Method of promotional budgeting in which a dollar amount is based on a percentage of past or projected sales. p. 417

perception Meaning that a person attributes to incoming stimuli gathered through the five senses. p. 119

perceptual screen Mental filter or block through which all inputs must pass to be noticed. p. 119

person marketing Marketing efforts designed to cultivate the attention, interest, and preference of a target market toward a person (typically a political candidate or celebrity). p. 15

personal selling Interpersonal influence process involving a seller's promotional presentation conducted on a person-to-person basis with the buyer. pp. 403, 464

persuasive advertising Promotion that attempts to increase demand for an existing good, service, organization, person, place, idea, or cause. p. 432

physical distribution Broad range of activities aimed at efficient movement of finished goods from the end of the production line to the consumer. p. 326

place marketing Marketing efforts to attract people and organizations to a particular geographic area. p. 15

planned shopping centre Group of retail stores planned, coordinated, and marketed as a unit. p. 366

planning Process of anticipating future events and conditions and of determining the best way to achieve organizational goals. p. 32

point-of-purchase (POP) advertising Display or other promotion placed near the site of the actual buying decision. p. 491

political risk assessment (PRA) Units within a firm that evaluate the political risks of the marketplaces in which they operate as well as proposed new marketplaces. p. 178

political-legal environment Component of the marketing environment consisting of laws and interpretations of laws that require firms to operate under competitive conditions and to protect consumer rights. p. 76

population (universe) Total group that researchers want to study. p. 212

Porter's Five Forces Model developed by strategy expert Michael Porter, which identifies five competitive forces that influence planning strategies: the threat of new entrants, the threat of substitute products, rivalry among competitors, the bargaining power of buyers, and the bargaining power of suppliers. p. 39

positioning Placing a product at a certain point or location within a market in the minds of prospective buyers. p. 255

positioning map A tool that helps marketers place products in a market by graphically illustrating consumers' perceptions of competing products within an industry. p. 256

post-testing Research that assesses advertising effectiveness after it has appeared in a print or broadcast medium. p. 450

precall planning Use of information collected during the prospecting and qualifying stages of the sales process and during previous contacts with the prospect to tailor the approach and presentation to match the customer's needs. p. 476

predatory pricing A pricing practice in which companies set prices below their cost for a sufficiently long period of time to discourage or eliminate competition and then raise their prices or otherwise interfere with competition. p. 535

premium Item given free or at reduced cost with purchases of other products. p. 490

presentation Personal selling function of describing a product's major features and relating them to a customer's problems or needs. p. 476

pretesting Research that evaluates an ad during its development stage. p. 449

price Exchange value of a good or service. p. 502

price discrimination A practice in which some customers pay more than others for the same product. p. 534

price fixing A form of collusion where sellers get together and collude to set prices higher than they would otherwise be in a free market. p. 535

price flexibility Pricing policy permitting variable prices for goods and services. p. 527

pricing policy General guideline that reflects marketing objectives and influences specific pricing decisions. p. 525

pricing strategy Methods of setting profitable and justifiable prices. p. 45

primary data Information collected for a specific investigation. p. 209

primary demand Desire for a general product category. p. 401

private brand Brand offered by a wholesaler or retailer. p. 298

private carriers Transporters that provide service solely for internally generated freight. p. 345

probability sample Sample that gives every member of the population a chance of being selected. p. 212

product Bundle of physical, service, and symbolic attributes designed to satisfy a customer's wants and needs. p. 266

product advertising Nonpersonal selling of a particular good or service. p. 431

product development Introduction of new products into identifiable or established markets. p. 308

product differentiation When consumers regard a firm's products as different in some way from those of competitors. p. 402

product diversification strategy Developing entirely new products for new markets. p. 309

product liability Responsibility of manufacturers and marketers for injuries and damages caused by their products. p. 315

product life cycle Progression of a product through introduction, growth, maturity, and decline stages. p. 282

product line Series of related products offered by one company. p. 280

product manager Marketer within an organization who is responsible for an individual product or product line; also called a brand manager. p. 312

product mix Assortment of product lines and individual product offerings that a company sells. p. 280

product placement Form of promotion in which a marketer pays a motion picture or television program owner a fee to display a product prominently in the film or show. p. 403

product positioning Consumers' perceptions of a product's attributes, uses, quality, and advantages and disadvantages relative to competing brands. p. 308

product strategy Decisions about what goods or services a firm will offer its customers; also includes decisions about customer service, packaging, brand names, and the like. p. 44

production orientation Business philosophy stressing efficiency in producing a quality product, with the attitude toward marketing that "a good product will sell itself." p. 8

product-line pricing Practice of setting a limited number of prices for a selection of merchandise and marketing different product lines in each of these price levels. p. 527

product-related segmentation Division of a population into homogeneous groups based on their relationships to the product. p. 252

profit centre Any part of an organization to which revenue and controllable costs can be assigned. p. 531

Profit Impact of Market Strategies (PIMS) project Research that discovered a strong positive relationship between a firm's market share and product quality and its return on investment. p. 505

profit maximization Point at which the additional revenue gained by increasing the price of a product equals the increase in total costs. p. 504

promotion Communications link between buyers and sellers. Function of informing, persuading, and influencing a consumer's purchase decision. pp. 45, 392

promotional allowance Promotional incentive in which the manufacturer agrees to pay the reseller a certain amount to cover the costs of special promotional displays or extensive advertising. p. 523

promotional mix Subset of the marketing mix in which marketers attempt to achieve the optimal blending of the elements of personal and nonpersonal selling to achieve promotional objectives. p. 402

promotional pricing Pricing policy in which a lower than normal price is used as a temporary ingredient in a firm's marketing strategy. p. 527

prospecting Personal selling function of identifying potential customers. p. 475

protective tariffs Taxes designed to raise the retail price of an imported product to match or exceed that of a similar domestic tariff. p. 180

psychographic segmentation Division of a population into groups that have similar psychological characteristics, attitudes, values, and lifestyles. p. 249

psychological pricing Pricing policy based on the belief that certain prices or price ranges make a good or service more appealing than others to buyers. p. 526

public relations Firm's communications and relationships with its various publics. p. 404

publicity Non-paid—for communication about the company or products, generally in some form of media. p. 405

pulling strategy Promotional effort by the seller to stimulate final-user demand, which then exerts pressure on the distribution channel. p. 416

pure competition Market structure characterized by homogeneous products in which there are so many buyers and sellers that none has a significant influence on price. p. 508

push money Financial incentive that gives retail salespeople cash rewards for every unit of a product they sell. p. 492

pushing strategy Promotional effort by the seller directed to members of the marketing channel rather than final users. p. 416

Q

qualifying Determining that a prospect has the needs, income, and purchase authority necessary for being a potential customer. p. 476

qualitative forecasting Use of subjective techniques to forecast sales, such as the jury of executive opinion, Delphi technique, sales force composite, and surveys of buyer intentions. p. 222

quantitative forecasting Use of statistical forecasting techniques such as trend analysis and exponential smoothing. p. 222

quantity discount Price reduction granted for a large-volume purchase. p. 523

R

rack jobber Full-function merchant wholesaler who markets specialized lines of merchandise to retail stores. p. 377

radio frequency identification (RFID) Technology that uses a tiny chip with identification information that can be read from a distance by a scanner using radio waves. p. 341

raw materials Natural resources such as farm products, coal, copper, or lumber, which become part of a final product. p. 274

rebate Refund of a portion of the purchase price, usually granted by the product's manufacturer. p. 524

reciprocity Policy to extend purchasing preference to suppliers that are also customers. p. 158

reference groups People or institutions whose opinions are valued and to whom a person looks for guidance in his or her own behaviour, values, and conduct, such as family, friends, or celebrities. p. 113

refund Cash given back to consumers who send in proof of purchase for one or more products. p. 489

relationship marketing Development and maintenance of long-term, cost-effective relationships with individual customers, suppliers, employees, and other partners for mutual benefit. p. 11 App B p. 8

relationship selling Regular contacts between sales representatives and customers over an extended period to establish a sustained seller–buyer relationship. p. 470

remanufacturing Production to restore worn-out products to like-new condition. p. 163

reminder advertising Advertising that reinforces previous promotional activity by keeping the name of a good, service, organization, person, place, idea, or cause before the public. p. 432

repositioning Changing the position of a product within the minds of prospective buyers relative to the positions of competing products. p. 256

resellers Marketing intermediaries that operate in the trade sector. p. 140

retail advertising Advertising by stores that sell goods or services directly to the consuming public. p. 434

retail convergence A situation in which similar merchandise is available from multiple retail outlets, resulting in the blurring of distinctions between type of retailer and merchandise offered. p. 373

retail cooperative Group of retailers that establish a shared wholesaling operation to help them compete with chains. p. 339

retailing Activities involved in selling merchandise to ultimate consumers. p. 360

revenue tariffs Taxes designed to raise funds for the importing government. p. 180

reverse channel Channel designed to return goods to their producers. p. 331

routinized response behaviour Rapid consumer problem solving in which no new information is considered; the consumer has already set evaluative criteria and identified available options. p. 128

S

salary Fixed compensation payment made periodically to an employee. p. 483

sales analysis In-depth evaluation of a firm's sales. p. 208

sales force composite Qualitative sales forecasting method based on the combined sales estimates of the firm's salespeople. p. 223

sales forecast Estimate of company revenue for a specified future period. p. 221

sales incentives Programs that reward salespeople for superior performance. p. 474

sales orientation Business assumption that consumers will resist purchasing nonessential goods and services with the attitude toward marketing that only creative advertising and personal selling can overcome consumers' resistance and convince them to buy. p. 9

sales promotion Marketing activities other than personal selling, advertising, guerrilla marketing, and public relations that stimulate consumer purchasing and dealer effectiveness. pp. 403, 486

sales quota Level of expected sales for a territory, product, customer, or salesperson against which actual results are compared. p. 483

sampling In marketing research, the process of selecting survey respondents or research participants; in sales promotion, free distribution of a product in an attempt to obtain future sales. pp. 212, 489

scrambled merchandising Retailing practice of combining dissimilar product lines to boost sales volume. p. 373

secondary data Previously published information. p. 209

second mover strategy Theory that advocates observing closely the innovations of first movers and then introducing new products that improve on the original offering to gain advantage in the marketplace. p. 41

selective demand Desire for a specific brand within a product category. p. 401

selective distribution Distribution of a product through a limited number of channels. p. 334

self-concept Person's multifaceted picture of himself or herself. p. 123

seller's market Market in which there are more buyers for fewer goods and services. p. 9

selling agent Agent wholesaling intermediary responsible for the entire marketing program of a firm's product line. p. 379

sender Source of the message communicated to the receiver. p. 396

service Intangible activity that satisfies the needs of consumer and business users. p. 266

service encounter Point at which the customer and service provider interact. p. 278

service quality Expected and perceived quality of a service offering. p. 278

shaping Process of applying a series of rewards and reinforcements to permit more complex behaviour to evolve over time. p. 122

shopping products Products that consumers purchase after comparing competing offerings. p. 270

skimming pricing strategy Pricing strategy involving the use of an initial high price relative to competitive offerings. Price is dropped in incremental steps as supply begins to exceed demand, or when competition catches up. p. 518

social marketing The use of online social media as a communications channel for marketing messages. p. 19

social responsibility Marketing philosophies, policies, procedures, and actions that have the enhancement of society's welfare as a primary objective. pp. 22, 94

social-cultural environment Component of the marketing environment consisting of the relationship between the marketer and society and its culture. p. 86

sole sourcing Purchasing a firm's entire stock of an item from just one vendor. p. 150

span of control The number of representatives who report to first-level sales managers. p. 482

specialty advertising Sales promotion technique that places the advertiser's name, address, and advertising message on useful articles that are then distributed to target consumers. p. 490

specialty products Products that offer unique characteristics that cause buyers to prize those particular brands. p. 271

specialty retailer Store that combines carefully defined product lines, services, and reputation to convince shoppers to spend considerable shopping effort there. p. 370

split runs Methods of testing alternative ads by dividing a cable TV audience or a publication's subscribers in two, using two different ads, and then evaluating the relative effectiveness of each. p. 450

sponsorship Relationship in which an organization provides funds or in-kind resources to an event or activity in exchange for a direct association with that event or activity. p. 408

spreadsheet analysis Grid that organizes information in a standardized, easily understood format. p. 59

staples Convenience goods and services that consumers constantly replenish to maintain a ready inventory. p. 270

step out Pricing practice in which one firm raises prices and then waits to see if others follow suit. p. 518

stockkeeping unit (SKU) Offering within a product line such as a specific size of liquid detergent. p. 363

straight rebuy Recurring purchase decision in which a customer repurchases a good or service that has performed satisfactorily in the past. p. 157

strategic alliance Partnership in which two or more companies combine resources and capital to create competitive advantages in a new market. pp. 20, 73

strategic business units (SBUs) Key business units within diversified firms. p. 48

strategic planning Process of determining an organization's primary objectives and adopting courses of action that will achieve these objectives. pp. 34, 57

strategic window Limited periods during which the key requirements of a market and the particular competencies of a firm best fit together. p. 42

subcontracting Contractual agreements that assign the production of goods or services to local or smaller firms. p. 188

suboptimization Condition that results when individual operations achieve their objectives but interfere with progress toward broader organizational goals. p. 344

subsidy Government financial support of a private industry. p. 181

supercentre Large store, smaller than a hypermarket, that combines groceries with discount store merchandise. p. 372

supplies Regular expenses that a firm incurs in its daily operations. p. 275

supply Schedule of the amounts of a good or service that firms will offer for sale at different prices during a specified time period. p. 508

supply chain Sequence of suppliers that contribute to the creation and delivery of a good or service. p. 340

supply-chain management Control of the activities of purchasing, processing, and delivery through which raw materials are transformed into products and made available to final consumers. p. 326

survey of buyer intentions Qualitative sales forecasting method that samples opinions among groups of present and potential customers concerning their purchase intentions. p. 223

sustainable products Products that can be produced, used, and disposed of with minimal impact on the environment. p. 22

sweepstakes Sales promotional technique in which prize winners are selected by chance. p. 490

SWOT analysis Analysis that helps planners compare internal organizational strengths and weaknesses with external opportunities and threats. p. 41

syndicated service Organization that provides standardized data to all customers. p. 206

systems integration Centralization of the procurement function within an internal division or as a service of an external supplier. p. 154

T

tactical planning Planning that guides the implementation of activities specified in the strategic plan. p. 34

target market Group of people to whom a firm decides to direct its marketing efforts and ultimately its goods and services. pp. 43, 234

target-return objectives Short-run or long-run pricing objectives of achieving a specified return on either sales or investment. p. 504

tariff Tax levied against imported goods. p. 180

task-objective method Development of a promotional budget based on evaluation of the firm's promotional objectives. p. 418

team selling Selling situation in which several sales associates or other members of the organization are recruited to assist the lead sales representative in reaching all those who influence the purchase decision. p. 471

technological environment Applications to marketing of knowledge based on discoveries in science, inventions, and innovations. p. 84

telemarketing Promotional presentation involving the use of the telephone on an outbound basis by salespeople or on an inbound basis by customers who initiate calls to obtain information and place orders. pp. 411, 468

test-marketing Marketing research technique that involves introducing a new product in a specific area and then measuring its degree of success. p. 218

third-party (contract) logistics firm Company that specializes in handling logistics activities for other firms. p. 343

time-based competition Strategy of developing and distributing goods and services more quickly than competitors. p. 75

total quality management (TQM) Continuous effort to improve products and work processes with the goal of achieving customer satisfaction and world-class performance. p. 276

trade allowance Special financial incentive offered to wholesalers and retailers that purchase or promote specific products. p. 491

trade discount Payment to a channel member or buyer for performing marketing functions; also known as a *functional discount*. p. 522

trade dress Visual components that contribute to the overall look of a brand. p. 304

trade industries Retailers or wholesalers that purchase products for resale to others. p. 140

trade promotion Sales promotion that appeals to marketing intermediaries rather than to consumers. pp. 404, 490

trade show Product exhibition organized by industry trade associations to showcase goods and services. p. 491

trade-in Credit allowance given for a used item when a customer purchases a new item. p. 523

trademark Brand for which the owner claims exclusive legal protection. p. 304

transaction-based marketing Buyer and seller exchanges characterized by limited communications and little or no ongoing relationships between the parties. p. 18 App B p. 8

transfer price Cost assessed when a product is moved from one profit centre in a firm to another. p. 531

trend analysis Quantitative sales forecasting method that estimates future sales through statistical analyses of historical sales patterns. p. 223

truck wholesaler Limited-function merchant wholesaler who markets perishable food items; also called a *truck jobber*. p. 378

tying agreement Arrangement that requires a marketing intermediary to carry items other than those they want to sell. p. 335

U

undifferentiated marketing Market strategy that focuses on producing a single product and marketing it to all customers; also called *mass marketing*. p. 254

unemployment Proportion of people in the economy who are actively seeking work but do not have jobs. p. 82

uniform-delivered pricing Pricing system for handling transportation costs under which all buyers are quoted the same price, including transportation expenses. Sometimes known as *postage-stamp pricing*. p. 525

unit pricing Pricing policy in which prices are stated in terms of a recognized unit of measurement or a standard numerical count. p. 526

Universal Product Code (UPC) Numerical bar code system used to record product and price information. p. 307

unsought products Products marketed to consumers who may not yet recognize a need for them. p. 269

upstream management Controlling part of the supply chain that involves raw materials, inbound logistics, and warehouse and storage facilities. p. 341

user Individual or group that actually uses a business good or service. p. 159

utility Want-satisfying power of a good or service. p. 5

V

VALS™ Segmentation system that divides consumers into eight psychographic categories: actualizers, fulfilleds, believers, achievers, strivers, experiencers, makers, and strugglers. p. 250

value analysis Systematic study of the components of a purchase to determine the most cost-effective approach. p. 159

value pricing Pricing strategy emphasizing benefits derived from a product in comparison to the price and quality levels of competing offerings. p. 506

variable costs Costs that change with the level of production (such as labour and raw materials costs). p. 510

vendor analysis Assessment of supplier performance in areas such as price, back orders, timely delivery, and attention to special requests. p. 159

vendor-managed inventory (VMI) Inventory management system in which the seller—based on an existing agreement with a buyer—determines how much of a product is needed. p. 351

venture team Associates from different areas of an organization who work together in developing new products. p. 312

vertical marketing system (VMS) Planned channel system designed to improve distribution efficiency and cost effectiveness by integrating various functions throughout the distribution chain. p. 338

Video Game Generation A group called by several names: Generation Y, the Millennial Generation, Generation Next, the 9-11 generation, and the Echo Boomers (an echo of baby boomers). p. 243

virtual sales team Network of strategic partners, trade associations, suppliers, and others who recommend a firm's goods or services. p. 472

VoIP A phone connection through a personal computer with any type of broadband Internet connection. p. 85

W

wheel of retailing Hypothesis that each new type of retailer gains a competitive foothold by offering lower prices than current suppliers charge; the result of reducing or eliminating services. p. 360

wholesaler Channel intermediary that takes title to goods it handles and then distributes these goods to retailers, other distributors, or B2B customers. pp. 327, 374

wholesaling intermediary Comprehensive term that describes wholesalers as well as agents and brokers. p. 374

World Trade Organization (WTO) Organization that replaces GATT, overseeing GATT agreements, making binding decisions in mediating disputes, and reducing trade barriers. p. 184

Y

yield management Pricing strategy that allows marketers to vary prices based on such factors as demand, even though the cost of providing those goods or services remains the same; designed to maximize revenues in situations such as airfares, lodging, auto rentals, and theatre tickets, where costs are fixed. p. 516

Z

zone pricing Pricing system for handling transportation costs under which the market is divided into geographic regions and a different price is set in each region. p. 525

name and company index

subject index